THE GUINNESS
WHO'S WHO
— OF —

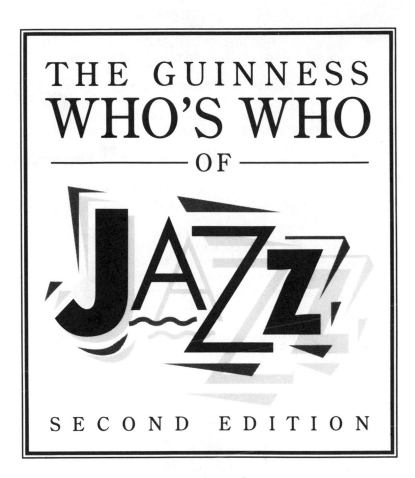

SECOND EDITION

General Editor: Colin Larkin

GUINNESS PUBLISHING

Dedicated to Reid Miles

FIRST EDITION 1992
SECOND EDITION PUBLISHED IN 1995
BY
GUINNESS PUBLISHING LTD
33 LONDON ROAD, ENFIELD, MIDDLESEX EN2 6DJ, ENGLAND

ALL EDITORIAL CORRESPONDENCE TO
THE EDITOR
GUINNESS ENCYCLOPEDIA OF POPULAR MUSIC
IRON BRIDGE HOUSE, 3 BRIDGE APPROACH, CHALK FARM, LONDON NW1 8BD

BRITISH LIBRARY CATALOGUING-IN-PUBLICATION DATA
A CATALOGUE RECORD FOR THIS BOOK IS AVAILABLE FROM THE BRITISH LIBRARY

ISBN 0-85112-674-X

CONCEIVED, DESIGNED, EDITED AND PRODUCED BY COLIN LARKIN FOR
SQUARE ONE BOOKS LTD
IRON BRIDGE HOUSE, 3 BRIDGE APPROACH, CHALK FARM, LONDON NW1 8BD

EDITOR AND DESIGNER: COLIN LARKIN
ASSISTANT EDITOR: ALEX OGG
PICTURE EDITOR: COLIN LARKIN
EDITORIAL AND PRODUCTION ASSISTANT: SUSAN PIPE
SPECIAL THANKS TO DAVID ROBERTS OF GUINNESS PUBLISHING,
SUE STOREY FOR SUPPLYING ALL THE PHOTOGRAPHS,
BRUCE CROWTHER AND LINTON CHISWICK FOR UPDATES AND NEW ENTRIES.

REPRINT 10 9 8 7 6 5 4 3 2 1 0
PRINTED AND BOUND IN GREAT BRITAIN BY THE BATH PRESS

EDITOR'S NOTE

The Second Edition of *The Guinness Who's Who Of Jazz* forms a part of the multi-volume series taken from the *Guinness Encyclopedia Of Popular Music*. 15 specialist single volumes have already been published and new editions and other titles are being planned for the near future.

Already available:
The Guinness Who's Who Of Indie And New Wave Music.
The Guinness Who's Who Of Reggae.
The Guinness Who's Who Of Film Musicals.
The Guinness Who's Who Of Rap, Dance And Techno.
The Guinness Who's Who Of Fifties Music.
The Guinness Who's Who Of Sixties Music.
The Guinness Who's Who Of Seventies Music.
The Guinness Who's Who Of Heavy Metal.
The Guinness Who's Who Of Country Music.
The Guinness Who's Who Of Blues.
The Guinness Who's Who Of Soul.
The Guinness Who's Who Of Folk Music.
The Guinness Who's Who Of Stage Musicals.
The Guinness All Time Top 1000 Albums.

This new edition goes a long way towards placating those readers who were quick to respond with suggestions of missing entries from the first edition. Due to lack of space in that book I had to take the agonizing decision to leave out over 300 entries. This editorial ruling upset a few serious jazz buffs. This time around we have over 500 pages - and even though I am aware that we still cannot fit everybody in, I think we have the perfect balance of traditional, mainstream, avant garde and contemporary artists. What I have learnt from mixing with jazzers over the past few years, is that they are as territorial in their area of jazz as any pop fan. Heavy metal v. ambient pop is equal to an ECM fan v. a GRP fan. Albert Ayler and Kenny G do not mix! We have catered for all tastes and hope to appease readers of the pro-ECM, *Wire* magazine, together with the GRP faction who subscribe to *Jazziz*. Jazz is a very wide area of popular music and one that too often becomes elitist. Tolerence of other people's taste is the key here.

To the many readers who wrote to me with their suggestions (and complaints), I think you will see that I have listened. One popular suggestion was to include record labels in the discography at the end of each entry. About a year ago we started to include all new releases on our database with the record label. This has been carried forward by adding labels to reissued albums. The CD revolution has resulted in a marvellous opportunity for re-packaging and in many cases re-mastering. This has resulted in some spectacular box sets and collected works. We have attempted to list the more recent reissued compilations and the most recent reissue label. For example, Original Jazz Classics in place of Prestige or Riverside. The younger jazz fans I meet are not remotely interested in a two album vinyl set of 1947 recordings deleted in 1956! They want the CD with full and appropriate annotation. The reissue programme is very healthy as I write; may we continue to have the original covers reproduced but not taken to extremes for the back or inside covers. One perfect and irritating example of this sloppy lack of concern for the new student is *Black Saint And The Sinner Lady* by Charles Mingus. The inner sleeve notes, reproduced from the original, appear in minute type - totally unreadable without a magnifying glass. A black mark for MCA/Impulse on an otherwise worthy reissue. Typographical designers please note, CD sleeves should be read.

For those readers who still feel that artists have been missed out may I direct you to the *Guinness Encyclopedia Of Popular Music*, where most will be found.

In addition to the original contributors thanked in the first edition I would like to acknowledge, Bruce Crowther (once again) and Linton Chiswick for their continuing participation as our main contributors. Bruce will have more time when he returns to the UK from non-stop sunshine and red wine after residing in Spain and I promise faithfully to give Linton longer deadlines to fit in with his better paying work, as I realise he will never become rich writing for us. Graham Lock is away at University in Nottingham working on his jazz thesis, and whilst we look forward to its completion (and eventual publication) we have missed his involvement in this edition as well as his delight in commas and sticky buns. Thanks to John Martland and Alex Ogg for their input and Susan Pipe who flowed the text into Quark Express, dropped in the photographs and searched desperately for a typo. Thanks to Bruce for finding Sue Storey who supplied all the photographs inside the book. Kirsten Mackness and Steven Sanderson at New Note and Dorothy Howe at CMP were always helpful with review copies and biogs. And finally, to my partner and jazz lover Diana Luke, who does not like Pat Metheny's ear challenging *Zero Tolerence For Silence* one itty bit.

Colin Larkin, February 1995

A

29th Street Saxophone Quartet

Jim Hartog (baritone saxophone), Ed Jackson (alto saxophone), Rich Rothenburg (tenor saxophone), Bobby Watson (alto saxophone). The 29th Street Saxophone Quartet first came together for a European tour in 1983, though the idea for the group had been mooted by Hartog and Jackson in the late 70s, and partly put into practice in the early 80s, when the pair had jammed with other New York-based saxophonists both in and outside Hartog's 29th Street loft apartment. In 1983 the arrival of Watson, already a player with a growing international reputation and several years' experience of working with Art Blakey, really launched the group on the road to worldwide success. A popular live act, the quartet's core allegiance to hard bop secured them their particular niche among comparable ensembles (such as the World and ROVA Saxophone Quartet's) and also helped to fuel their direct emotional power and danceability. All four are outstanding soloists, but their records are also characterized by what one writer has called 'a state of integrated motion', the horns threading together in quickfire counterpoint or complex rhythmic interweavings. As early as *Watch Your Step*, the group had introduced rap onto one track and their recent *Underground* leavens or dilutes (according to one's point of view) the original saxophone quartet concept with guest appearances by vocalist Pamela Watson, pianist Benny Green and trumpeter Hugh Masekela among others.
Albums: *Pointillistic Groove* (1984), *Watch Your Step* (1985), *Live* (1987), *The Real Deal* (1989), *Underground* (1991), *Your Move* (1992).

AACM (Association for the Advancement of Creative Musicians)

Founded in 1965 in Chicago by Muhal Richard Abrams, Jodie Christian, Steve McCall and Phillip Cohran, this musically, spiritually and socially influential co-operative spawned important bands, including Air and the Art Ensemble Of Chicago, and nurtured musicians such as Anthony Braxton, Phillip Wilson, Leo Smith and Chico Freeman. Abrams was the prime-mover of its extra-musical ethos, encouraging members to study in other disciplines, to see themselves as part of the wider community as well as of the co-operative, and to explore sounds and textures rather than simply pursue proficiency in negotiating fast tempi and complex chord cycles. This interest in sound led to the use of a host of 'little instruments' (from swanee whistles and ocarinas to hose-pipes and kitchen utensils) which became almost a trade-mark of Roscoe Mitchell and the Art Ensemble. The neglect of the competitive 'cutting contest' aspect of jazz was, it has been suggested, a function of the AACM's birth in Chicago rather than hectic New York City. The success of the AACM led to the formation of similar organizations in other cities, the best-known of which was probably the Black Artists Group (BAG) of St. Louis.

Abdul-Malik, Ahmed

b. Sam Gill, 30 January 1927, New York City, New York, USA. Abdul-Malik, who adopted his Muslim name in the 50s, has enjoyed successful careers in two musical areas, sometimes bringing them together. As a jazz bassist, he has played with enough major artists to secure a firm place in the jazz history books. Accompanying Art Blakey and Don Byas in 1948, Randy Weston for three years starting in 1954, Thelonious Monk in 1957/8, Herbie Mann in 1961, Earl Hines in 1964, and Ken McIntyre in 1971, he has appeared at jazz festivals in Montreux, Switzerland, and New York. Abdul-Malik's other area of expertise developed after studying African and Middle-Eastern music at university. Playing the 'ud (similar to a lute), he recorded with John Coltrane in 1961, and undertook a US State Department-sponsored tour of South America the same year. Playing at the historic African Jazz Festival in Tangier in 1972, and recording with Hamiet Bluiett in 1977, Abdul-Malik was a deserving recipient of the BMI's Pioneer in Jazz Award in 1985. Since 1970 he has taught at New York University, and more recently in the Department of African Studies at Brooklyn College.
Albums: *Jazz Sahara* (1958), *The Music Of Ahmed Abdul-Malik* (1961), *Ahmed Abdul-Malik/Sounds Of Africa* (1962).

Abdullah, Ahmed

b. Leroy Bland, 10 May 1946, New York City, USA. Inspired originally by Louis Armstrong, Abdullah has played with mainstream jazzmen such as Calvin Massey, R&B singers including Solomon Burke, Little Johnny Taylor and Joe Simon and with the free jazz Master Brotherhood. In the 70s he worked with the Melodic Art-tet, a co-operative that included bassist William Parker and saxophonist Charles Brackeen, and, after stints with Rashied Ali and Ed Blackwell, led his own group, Abdullah. In 1976 he joined Sun Ra's Arkestra for two years, returning for further spells in the 80s and 90s when not working with one of the three bands he leads himself. His evocative yet immediate trumpet contributed a crucial vibrancy to Billy Bang's masterpiece *The Fire From Within* (1984) and in the late 80s he recorded two albums as leader for the Swedish Silkheart label. Still shamefully under-represented on record, his free, fighting trumpet has the generous vision of the past characteristic of post-Loft creative jazz.
Albums: *Liquid Magic* (1987), *Ahmed Abdullah And The Solomnic Quartet* (1988).

Abercrombie, John

b. 16 December 1944, Portchester, New York, USA. After studying at Berklee College Of Music in Boston, Abercrombie spent four years playing guitar in Johnny 'Hammond' Smith's group. Touring with an established band offered him the kind of practical study which was ideal after the Berklee academic hot-house of the late 60s. Moving back to New York in 1969, his already unusual technical command of the instrument

John Abercrombie

meant he had little difficulty finding opportunities to play with fine musicians. In the ensuing five years he played alongside Randy and Michael Brecker in the group Dreams, and toured with the Chico Hamilton Band, including an appearance at the Montreux Jazz Festival. In demand as a sideman from countless bandleaders, from Gil Evans to Gato Barbieri, it was in Billy Cobham's fusion group Spectrum that Abercrombie's reputation quickly spread. This hard-driving rock-influenced band was the perfect vehicle for his prodigious technique and imagination at this early stage in his career. However, by the mid-70s, Abercrombie was discovering a new and altogether different voice. Treating fusion in a similar manner to which the MJQ had treated bop, he formed his highly regarded trio Timeless, playing in a softer, more delicate style. This band was replaced in 1975 by his Gateway trio, with Dave Holland and Jack DeJohnette, and then by a quartet three years later. Since 1981, Abercrombie has performed and recorded prolifically. As well as continuing to collaborate with DeJohnette, he has produced some highly regarded duet work with Ralph Towner, led a quartet featuring Michael Brecker and was involved in the all-star big band that recently debuted and recorded Charles Mingus' *Epitaph*. Abercrombie remains one of the most versatile and gifted guitarists of post-war jazz and fortunately appears to be hitting a prolific phase during the 90s.
Albums: *Timeless* (ECM 1974), *Gateway* (ECM 1975),
Characters (1977), *Night* (ECM 1984), *Current Events* (ECM 1985), *Getting There* (ECM 1988), *John Abercrombie Trio* (ECM 1989), *Animato* (ECM 1990), *While We're Young* (1993), with Marc Johnson, Peter Erskine, John Surman *November* (ECM 1994), *Speak Of The Devil* (ECM 1994). Compilation: *Works* (ECM 1989).

Abrahams, Brian

b. 26 June 1947, Cape Town, South Africa. Abrahams became known first for his ability as a singer. From the age of 13 he sang with local groups, but by the early 70s was established as a drummer and percussionist, often backing vocal and dance groups. While working with a trio in Swaziland, Abrahams accompanied the American artists Sarah Vaughan and Nancy Wilson. In 1975 Abrahams moved to London where he played with a number of English bands including Ronnie Scott's, and with members of the expatriate South African community, especially Dudu Pukwana and Chris McGregor. In the early 80s, Abrahams formed his own band, District 6, named after a sector of Cape Town, which has successfully worked at fusing African folk themes with European influences. The group's patience and effort paid off, allowing a sophistication and drive rare in a unit that retains its local identity. Abrahams acknowledges the influences of Duke Ellington, Thelonious Monk, and McGregor and admires the drumming of Art Blakey, Max

Roach and Jack DeJohnette. Abrahams is also an educator and runs regular workshops, often in conjunction with District 6. Albums: with Chris McGregor *Yes Please* (1982), with District 6 *Akuzwakale* (1984), *To Be Free* (1987), *Imgoma Yabantwana* (District Six 1989).

Abrams, Muhal Richard

b. 19 September 1930, Chicago, Illinois, USA. Abrams began studying piano at Chicago Music College at the age of 17 and started working professionally a year later. In 1955 he formed Modern Jazz Two + 3 with tenor saxophonist Eddie Harris. After this group folded he kept a low profile until 1961, when he organized the Experimental Band, a contrast to his earlier hard bop venture in its use of free jazz concepts for a fluctuating line-up. The band evolved into the AACM, emerging in 1965 with Abrams as its president. He is an accomplished pianist and composer with a deep sense of tradition, and from the mid-70s has been able to record more frequently with his own groups (including an excellent big band), but it is as the spiritual leader of the AACM that he has probably made his most lasting mark. Despite being remembered by Leroy Jenkins as a thug when he was at school, in maturity Abrams was to be responsible for fostering amongst black musicians in Chicago (and beyond) a sense of their value and dignity as artists and for showing them the importance of the link between artists and the community.
Albums: *Levels And Degrees Of Light* (Delmark 1967), *Young At Heart, Wise In Time* (1969), *Things To Come From Those Now Gone* (1970), *Afrisong* (1975), *Sightsong* (1976), *Lifea Blinec* (1978), *Live At Montreux* (1978), *1-OQA+19* (Black Saint 1978), *Mama And Daddy* (Black Saint 1980), *Spihumonesty* (Black Saint 1980), with Amina Claudine Myers *Duet* (Black Saint 1981), *Blues Forever* (Black Saint 1982), *Rejoicing With The Light* (1983), *View From Within* (Black Saint 1986), *Blues Forever* (Black Saint 1986), *Colors In Thirty-Third* (Black Saint 1987), *The Hearinga Suite* (1989), *Blu Blu Blu* (Black Saint 1992), *Family Talk* (Black Saint 1993).

Acoustic Alchemy

Formed in the mid-80s, Acoustic Alchemy is essentially Greg Carmichael (b. 1953, London, England; nylon string guitar) and Nick Webb (b. 1954, Manchester, England; steel string guitar). Their blend of instrumental music is neither jazz nor pop, but it has elements of both, together with flamenco, reggae and folk. Similar to Sky in sound, their four albums are refreshing and uplifting. Their debut contains one of their finest compositions 'Mr Chow', an example of Chinese Reggae! Nick Webb was originally influenced by John Martyn and Pentangle. He recorded one album with Simon James in the early 80s and linked up with Carmichael in 1986 (released as *Early Alchemy*). Carmichael had studied classical guitar at the London College of Music and gained experience playing with jazz groups. Their break came, when frustrated by the apathy for their music in England, they took a Virgin in-flight gig, and literally played their way to America. They were signed to MCA as part of their Master Series, and debuted with the excellent *Red Dust And Spanish Lace*. Following *Blue Chip* they joined GRP Records, although their debut there, *Reference Point* lacked the life and sparkle of their MCA work. They redressed the balance with *Back On The Case* in 1991.
Albums: *Red Dust And Spanish Lace* (1987), *Natural Elements* (1988), *Blue Chip* (1989), *Reference Point* (1990), *Back On The Case* (1991), *Early Alchemy* (1992), *The New Edge* (1993).

Adams, George Rufus

b. 29 April 1940, Covington, Georgia, USA, d. 14 November 1992. Adams began playing piano at the age of 11, but took up the saxophone (alto first, tenor later) while still at school and was soon gigging with local R&B bands. A scholarship to Clark College, Atlanta, brought him tuition from Wayman Carver (in the 30s a mainstay of the Chick Webb band and perhaps the first man to play jazz flute, an instrument Adams also took up). Adams spent the 60s working with a wide range of musicians and in 1968, in New York, he joined Roy Haynes and subsequently worked with Gil Evans and Art Blakey. Most influential on Adams' later work was a stint with Charles Mingus in the mid-70s. At the end of the decade he was co-leader, with Don Pullen, of a·quartet which also included Dannie Richmond and which stayed in existence, recording prolifically, until Richmond's death in 1988. Initially, Adams was strongly influenced by John Coltrane, but a 1988 album, *Nightingale*, showed him to have a deeply romantic vein. In every aspect of his work, the often overlooked Adams always displayed a marked affinity with the blues. He also sang occasionally, in a hoarse, croaky but very effective blues voice.
Albums: *Jazz Confronto 22* (1975), *Suite For Swingers* (1975), *Paradise Space Shuttle* (Timeless 1979), *Sound Suggestions* (1979), with Dannie Richmond *Hand To Hand* (1980), with Don Pullen *Lifeline* (1981), *Melodic Excursions* (1982), with Pullen *Live At The Village Vanguard Vols 1 & 2* (Soul Note 1983), with Pullen *Decisions* (1984), with Pullen *Live At Montmartre* (Timeless 1985), *More Sightings* (1985), with Pullen *Don't Lose Control* (Soul Note 1987), *Nightingale* (Blue Note 1988), *George Adams And The Don Pullen Quartet* (1988), *America* (Blue Note 1989), with Pullen *Earth Beans* (Timeless 1990), with Pullen *City Gates* (Timeless 1991).

Adams, Pepper

b. Park Adams III, 8 October 1930, Highland Park, Michigan, USA, d. 10 September 1986. While Adams was still a child his family moved to Rochester, New York, where he became involved in the local jazz music scene. Inspired by Coleman Hawkins, Adams decided to become a tenor saxophone player but quickly fell under the spell of Harry Carney, taking up the baritone in the mid-40s. (Somewhat self-depreciatingly, Adams would later insist that the chief reason he took up the baritone was because he was able to pick up an instrument cheap.) A stint with Lionel Hampton allied to freelance work, mostly around Detroit, with Wardell Gray, Barry Harris, Frank Foster, Tommy Flanagan and others gave Adams a broad musical base. For a while he was involved in the big bands of Stan Kenton and Maynard Ferguson, but still found time to work with Chet

Baker, Donald Byrd, Benny Goodman and Thelonious Monk. His robust, big sound and forceful soloing made him an important member of the Thad Jones-Mel Lewis Jazz Orchestra for a dozen years from 1965. In the late 70s and on through the 80s he worked festivals around the world and recorded with Kenny Wheeler, Lionel Hampton, Zoot Sims and Peter Leitch. Adams died of cancer in September 1986.

Albums: *Pepper Adams Quintet* (1957), *Critics' Choice* (1957), *The Cool Sound Of Pepper Adams* (1957), with Donald Byrd *Stardust* (1957), with Jimmy Knepper *Pepper-Knepper Quintet* (1958), *10-4 At The 5-Spot* (1958), *Out Of This World* (1961), *Jammin' With Herbie Hancock/Pepper Adams Quintet* (1961), *Pepper Adams Plays The Compositions Of Charles Mingus* (1963), *Mean What You Say* (1966), with Zoot Sims *Encounter!* (1968), *Ephemera* (1973), *Julian* (1975), *Twelfth And Pingree* (1975), *Live In Europe* (1977), *Reflectory* (1978), *Be-bop* (1979), *The Master* (1980), *Urban Dreams* (1981), with Peter Leitch *Exhilaration* (1984). Compilations: *My One And Only Love* (West Wind 1993), *The Cool Sound Of Pepper Adams* (Savoy 1992).

Adderley, Cannonball

b. Julian Edwin Adderley, 15 September 1928, Tampa, Florida, USA, d. 8 August 1975. Cannonball Adderley was one of the great saxophonists of his generation. His fiery, blues-soaked interpretations of Charlie Parker's alto legacy brought jazz to many people hitherto untouched by it. In the 60s he launched a new genre whose popularity has survived undiminished into the 90s: soul jazz. Cannonball is derived from 'Cannibal', a nickname earned at high school on account of his prodigious appetite. He studied brass and reed instruments there between 1944 and 1948. Until 1956 he was band director at Dillerd High School, Lauderdale, Florida, as well as leader of his own jazz quartet. While serving in the forces he became director of the 36th Army Band, an ensemble that included his younger brother Nat Adderley on trumpet. Persuaded to go to New York by legendary alto saxophonist and R&B singer Eddie 'Cleanhead' Vinson, Cannonball created a sensation at the Cafe Bohemia, playing alongside bassist Oscar Pettiford. In 1958 he signed to Riverside Records and over the next six years released a series of albums, many of them recorded live, that laid the foundations of the soul-jazz genre. As well as his brother Nat, Adderley's first group featured a superb rhythm section in Sam Jones and Louis Hayes, supplemented by pianist Bobby Timmons, who also wrote the group's first hit, 'This Here'. From 1957-59 Adderley was part of the classic Miles Davis Quintet, an astonishing group of individuals which also included John Coltrane (tenor), Bill Evans or Red Garland (piano), Paul Chambers (bass) and Philly Joe Jones (drums). As well as playing on the celebrated *Kind Of Blue*, Cannonball recorded his own album *Somethin' Else* for Blue Note Records - Davis appeared as a sideman, a rare honour.

After leaving Davis, Cannonball re-formed his own outfit, with his brother Nat still on cornet and in 1961 Yusef Lateef joined on tenor saxophone and stayed for two productive years. This band nurtured the talents of electric pianists Joe Zawinul and then George Duke. It was Zawinul's 'Mercy, Mercy, Mercy' - recorded live at the Club Delisa in Chicago - that provided Adderley with his next major hit: it reached number 11 in the US charts, in February 1967. The title indicates the kind of gospel-orientated, black consciousness groove the group was into. Their last hit was 'Country Preacher', again a Zawinul composition, that peaked in early 1970 (29 in the R&B charts). Straight jazz was never to have this mass appeal again. When asked about his inspirations, Cannonball cited the swing alto saxophonist Benny Carter and of course Charlie Parker - but his understanding of blues distortion also enabled him to apply the *avant garde* lessons of John Coltrane and Ornette Coleman. His alto saxophone had a special immediacy, a welcome reminder of the blues at the heart of bebop, an element that jazz rock - the bastard offspring of soul jazz - too often suppressed.

Albums: *Presenting Cannonball* (1955), *Julian 'Cannonball' Adderley And Strings* (1956), *In The Land Of Hi-Fi* (1956), *Sophisticated Swing* (1957), *Cannonball's Sharpshooters* (1958), *Jump For Joy* (1958), *Portrait Of Cannonball* (1958), *Somethin' Else* (Blue Note 1958), *Alabama Concerto* (1958), *The Cannonball Adderley Quintet In San Francisco* (Original Jazz Classics 1959), *Cannonball Adderley Quintet In Chicago* (1959), *Cannonball Takes Charge* (1959), *Cannonball Adderley Quintet At The Lighthouse* (1960), *Them Dirty Blues* (1960), *Them Dirty Blues* (1960), *African Waltz* (1961), *African Waltz* (1961), *Cannonball Enroute* (1961), *Cannonball Adderley And The Poll-Winners* (1961), *Cannonball Adderley Quintet Plus* (1961), with Nancy Wilson *Nancy Wilson/Cannonball Adderley* (1962), with Bill Evans *Know What I Mean* (1962), *The Cannonball Adderley Sextet in New York* (Original Jazz Classics 1962), *Cannonball's Bossa Nova* (1963), *Jazz Workshop Revisited* (1963), *Nippon Soul* (1964), *Cannonball And Coltrane* (Emarcy 1964), *Domination* (1965), *Fiddler On The Roof* (1965), with Ernie Andrews *Live Session* (1965), *Cannonball Adderley Live* (1965), *Great Love Themes* (1966), *Why Am I Treated So Bad* (1966), with Ray Brown *Two For The Blues* (1966), *Mercy Mercy Mercy* (1967), *74 Miles Away - Walk Tall* (1967), *Cannonball In Europe* (1967), *Things Are Getting Better* (1968), with Milt Jackson *Accent On Africa* (1968), *Country Preacher* (1970), *Experience In E, Tensity, Dialogues* (1970), *The Price You Got To Pay To Be Free* (1971), *The Black Messiah* (1972), *Inside Straight* (1973), *Phenix* (1975), *Spontaneous Combustion* (Savoy 1976, rec 1955), *What Is This Thing Called Soul* (1984, rec 1960). *Know What I Mean* (Fantasy 1986), with Wynton Kelly, *Cannonball Takes Charge* (1988), *Cannonball In Europe* (1988, rec 1962), *In Japan* (Blue Note 1990), *Radio Nights* (Virgin 1991), *Dizzy's Business* (Ace 1993), *Inside Straight* (Original Jazz Classics 1993).

Selected compilations: *Cannonball's Greatest Hits* (1962), *Cannonball Adderley Collection Vols 1 to 7* (Landmark 1988), *Best Of Cannonball Adderley The Capitol Years* (Capitol 1991), *Quintet Plus* (Ace 1992), *Portrait Of Cannonball* (Ace 1993).

Adderley, Nat

b. Nathaniel Adderley, 25 November 1931, Tampa, Florida,

Nat Adderley

USA. The younger brother of Cannonball Adderley, Nathaniel was a singer until his voice broke and he took up the trumpet. In the early 50s he served in the army with his brother and played in the 36th Army Band. His professional break came in 1954, when Lionel Hampton asked him to join his riotously swinging, R&B-inflected big band, he stayed for only a year. Later he played with Woody Herman and J.J. Johnson. In 1960 he released *Work Song*, a brilliant amalgam of the soul jazz he is celebrated for and a more 'cool' style, chamber music instrumentation (including cello and guitar, the latter played by Wes Montgomery). Throughout the 60s and early 70s he played in his brother's combo and since the latter's death in 1975 has kept alive that special brand of warm, rootsy bop, both on his own recordings and playing in a variety of contexts, such as Nathan Davis's Paris Reunion Band.

Albums: *That's Nat* (1955), *Introducing Nat Adderley* (1955), *To The Ivy League From Nat* (1956), *Branching Out* (1958), *Much Brass* (1959), *That's Right* (1960), *Work Song* (1960), *Naturally!* (1961), *In The Bag* (1962), *The Adderley Brothers In New Orleans* (1962), *Little Big Horn* (1964), *Autobiography* (1965), *Sayin' Something* (1966), *Live At Memory Lane* (1967), *The Scavenger* (1968), *Comin' Out Of The Shadows* (1968), *You, Baby* (1968), *Calling Out Loud* (1969), *Zodiac Soul* (1970), *Soul Of The Bible* (1972), *Double Exposure* (1974), *Don't Look Back* (1976), *A Little New York Midtown Music* (1978), *On The Move* (1983), *Blue Autumn* (1983), *Thats Nat* (1985), *Blue Autumn* (Theresa 1987), *Work Songs* (Fantasy 1987), *Talkin' About You* (Landmark 1991), *We Remember Cannon* (In & Out 1991), *The Old Country* (Enja 1992), *Working* (1993), *On The Move* (Evidence 1994).

Addison, Bernard

b. 15 April 1905, Annapolis, Maryland, USA. Addison's rhythmic jazz guitar playing made him best known for his section work rather than as a soloist. In his teens he was co-leader with Claude Hopkins of a band in Washington, DC, then moved to New York, where he became a member of the house band at Small's Paradise, remaining there until 1929. Equally at home in big bands and small groups, in the early 30s Addison worked with Louis Armstrong, Fletcher Henderson, Bubber Miley, Jelly Roll Morton, Art Tatum, and Fats Waller. He was also accompanist to the Mills Brothers (later working with the Ink Spots). Spells with Sidney Bechet, Teddy Bunn, Mezz Mezzrow and Stuff Smith led to his appearance on numerous recording dates in the 30s and 40s, including Benny Carter's 1936 London session. In the 50s he worked with musicians as diverse as Eubie Blake and Pete Brown; from the 60s onwards he was concerned with teaching but continued to take an active interest in jazz.

Albums: with Benny Carter *Swingin' At Maida Vale* (1936), with Pete Brown *Pete's Last Date* (1961).

Air

Jazz conglomeration comprising Henry Threadgill (reeds), Fred Hopkins (bass), Steve McCall (drums). Air, originally called Reflection, was formed in Chicago in 1971 when AACM colleagues Threadgill, Hopkins and McCall came together to play for a stageshow about Scott Joplin. Although the trio did later record a set of Joplin and Jelly Roll Morton tunes (*Air Lore*), they are better known for the music that Threadgill wrote for them when they began to tour in 1975. He brought a new angle to jazz ensemble playing by composing 'from the bass . . . from the drums': 'It changes the whole frame of reference in terms of what accompaniment is all about, you know. It kind of kills accompaniment and puts everything on an equal footing, and that's what I'm after.' Threadgill's pieces were steeped in the AACM's structural modernisms: ambitious, democratic, unresolved; filled with space, strength (of mind, feeling, technique) and a rigorous sense of inquiry; spiced with Threadgill's particular sense of the enigmatic; and brought to life by the trio's extraordinary instrumental virtuosity. In the mid-70s Air moved to New York and in 1982, when McCall left (to be replaced by Pheeroan akLaff), they changed their name to New Air. The group's most recent recording, *Air Show No 1*, which features singer Cassandra Wilson, was released in 1986: since which time they have, in Threadgill's words, been 'on the back burner' while he concentrates on various other group projects. In their earlier incarnation, Air was one of the crucial new jazz groups of the 70s and - together with the Art Ensemble Of Chicago and the different groups led by Muhal Richard Abrams and Anthony Braxton - standard-bearers for the AACM's claim to have inspired the most original and exciting jazz music of the post-Coltrane era.

Albums: *Air Song* (1976), *Air Raid* (1977), *Air Time* (1978), *Open Air Suite* (1978), *Montreux Suisse* (1978), *Air Lore* (Bluebird 1979), *Live Air* (1980, rec. 1976/7), *Air Mail* (1980), *80% Below '82* (1982), as New Air *Live At The Montreal International Jazz Festival* (1984), as New Air *Air Show No 1* (1986).

Akiyoshi, Toshiko

b. 12 December 1929, Dairen, Manchuria (of Japanese parents). Akiyoshi went to live in Japan in 1947, by which time she was already an accomplished, classically-trained pianist. Turning to jazz, she soon became one of Japan's highest-paid entertainers. After recording for Norman Granz, Akiyoshi followed the advice of Oscar Peterson and moved to America, where she enrolled at Berklee College Of Music. She worked as a member of various small bop groups, including those led by Charlie Mariano (to whom she was briefly married) and Charles Mingus. Although a fleet and inventive pianist who was much influenced by Bud Powell, Akiyoshi's greatest interest lay in composing, and in particular she wanted to write for big bands. In 1967 a specially-assembled big band played pieces by her at a concert in New York's Town Hall. In the early 70s, now resident in Los Angeles, Akiyoshi worked with, and later married, tenor saxophonist Lew Tabackin. They formed a rehearsal band, which employed many of the best available west-coast session men and which was designed primarily as a showcase for Akiyoshi's talents as a composer and for Tabackin's as a forceful, freewheeling soloist. Based in New York since the mid-80s, Akiyoshi has continued to develop her big band writing and also leads a small group, but - under-represented on records and rarely touring - she remains little known to foreign audiences. An outstanding musician by any standards, she is one of the best two or three living composer-arrangers of big band music in jazz and holds a very high place in the overall history of big band music. A documentary film, *Toshiko Akiyoshi: Jazz Is My Native Language* (1984), traces her life and career.

Albums: *Toshiko's Piano* (1953), *Amazing Toshiko Akiyoshi* i (1954), *The Toshiko Trio* (1954), with others *Jam Session For Musicians III: The Historic Mocambo Session '54* (1954), *Toshiko, Her Trio* (1956), *Toshiko, Her Quartet* (1956), one side only *Amazing Toshiko Akiyoshi* ii (1957), *The Many Sides Of Toshiko* (1957), *United Nations* (1958), *Toshiko Meets Her Old Pals* (1961), with Steve Kuhn *Country And Western Jazz Pianos* (1963), with Charlie Mariano *Mariano-Toshiko Quartet* (1963), *Toshiko Akiyoshi* (1965), *Toshiko At The Top Of The Gate* (Denon 1968), *Toshiko Akiyoshi Quartet* i (1970), *Toshiko Akiyoshi Quartet* ii (1971), *Toshiko Akiyoshi Quartet* iii (1971), *Solo Piano* (1971), with Lew Tabackin *Kogun* (1974), with Tabackin *Long Yellow Road* (1974-75), with Tabackin *Tales Of A Courtesan* (1975), with Tabackin *Road Time* (1976), with Tabackin *Insights* (1976), *Dedications* (1976-77), with Tabackin *March Of The Tadpoles* (1977), with Tabackin *Dedications II* (1977), with Tabackin *Toshiko Akiyoshi-Lew Tabackin Big Band Live At Newport '77* (1977), with Tabackin *Live At Newport II* (1977), *Toshiko Akiyoshi Plays Billy Strayhorn* (1978), *Finesse* (1978), with Tabackin *Salted Ginko Nuts* (1978), *Notorious Tourist From The East* (1978), with Tabackin *Sumi-e* (1979), with Tabackin *Farewell To Mingus* (1980), *Just Be-Bop* (1980), *Tuttie Flutie* (1980), with Tabackin *From Toshiko With Love* (1981), with Tabackin *Tanuki's Night Out* (1981), with Tabackin *European Memoirs* (1982), *Interlude* (Concord Jazz 1987), *Remembering Bud - Cleopatra's Dream* (Evidence 1992), *Desert Lady-Fantasy* (Columbia 1994). Compilation: *Collection* (Novus 1991).

Albam, Manny

b. 24 June 1922, Samana, Dominican Republic. Brought up in New York, Albam became interested in jazz as a child and occasionally sat in at a club in the Village, playing alto saxophone. At the age of 16 he graduated from high school and joined Muggsy Spanier's band, then went with Bob Chester before playing baritone saxophone with Georgie Auld. Albam also played with the bands of Sam Donahue, Charlie Barnet and Charlie Spivak but, encouraged by Budd Johnson, began to make his mark as an arranger. In 1957 he wrote a jazz arrangement of Leonard Bernstein's music from *West Side Story* which met with the composer's approval. That same year he began to experiment with long works which resulted in a succession of fine albums including *The Blues Is Everybody's Business, Soul Of The City* and *The Drum Suite*, with its unusual instrumentation. Rooted in late-swing era big band style, Albam's work exemplifies the best of mainstream writing. However, inspired by Dizzy Gillespie, he absorbed later concepts in jazz to become an accomplished arranger for countless small groups including those led by Stan Getz, Terry Gibbs, Gillespie and Gerry Mulligan. He also devised effective arrangements for major song stylists such as Sarah Vaughan and Carmen McRae. In the 50s Albam briefly studied classical composition under Tibor Serly and his works include 'Concerto For Trombone And Strings'. Always eager to learn and to pass on his knowledge and experience, Albam has been involved in teaching, mostly at Eastman College, since the mid-60s.

Albums: *The Jazz Workshop* (1955), *The Drum Suite* (1956), *West Side Story* (1957), *The Jazz Greats Of Our Time Vols 1 & 2* (1957), *The Blues Is Everybody's Business* (1957), *Sophisticated Lady: Songs Of Duke Ellington* (1958), *Steve Allen's Songs* (1958), *Jazz Goes To The Movies* (1962), *Brass On Fire* (1966), *Soul Of The City* (c.60s), *Manny Albam And His Orchestra* (1966), *The Jazz Workshop* (1983), *Sketches From The Book Of The Life* (1991).

Albany, Joe

b. 24 January 1924, Atlantic City, New Jersey, USA, d. 12 January 1988. After formal studies as a child, Albany began playing piano professionally and formed a friendship with Charlie Parker. By his mid-teens he was working extensively on the west coast, playing with Benny Carter's orchestra in 1943 and appearing with many leading jazzmen. Early in 1946 he took part in club dates with Parker and Miles Davis. Albany missed Parker's important Dial record date on 28 March 1946 when, following a quarrel with the saxophonist, he quit in the middle of the set at a club the previous night. Albany's playing was of such a high standard that, along with other white piano-playing proponents of bop, in particular Al Haig and George Wallington, he helped to establish the genre. He also worked briefly with Georgie Auld and Boyd Raeburn and recorded with Lester Young. Drug dependency severely damaged Albany's career and he did very little during the following decades, making fleeting appearances with Warne Marsh, Charles Mingus and a handful of other jazzmen. For some years he lived in Europe and his seclusion continued into the 70s; then, he returned to the jazz scene, re-establishing a reputation as a formidable bop pianist and allowing latterday audiences to gain some insight into the reason for the high regard in which, despite his erratic career, he had long been held by fellow pianists. A film documentary, *Joe Albany...a Jazz Life* (1980), helped sustain his new stature in jazz.

Albums: with Warne Marsh *The Right Combination* (1957), *At Home Alone* (1971), *The Church Of Truth* (1972), *Birdtown Birds* (1973), one side only *Joe Plus Joe* (1974), *Two's Company* (1974), with Joe Venuti *Joe And Joe* (1974), *The Legendary Joe Albany* (1974), *This Is For My Friends* (1976), *Joe Albany Plays George Gershwin And Burton Lane* (1976), *The Albany Touch* (1977), *Bird Lives* (Storyville 1979), *Portrait Of An Artist* (1982), *At Home* (1983), *Proto-Bopper* (1983), *The Right Combination* (1988).

Alcorn, Alvin

b. 7 September 1912, New Orleans, Louisiana, USA. After studying trumpet as a child, Alcorn began playing professionally in the mid-20s. He played for various bands, occasionally as leader. In the early 30s he joined Don Albert where he remained until 1937. From the mid-40s he worked mostly in New Orleans, then moved to the west coast to join Kid Ory's band in the mid-50s. Later in the decade, he played with George Lewis, Paul Barbarin and other leading New Orleans-style musicians. In the mid-60s and several times in the 70s he toured Europe and the UK. Alcorn continued to play into the 80s. A solid lead trumpeter, Alcorn's playing was ideally suited to the New Orleans tradition of collective improvisation.

Albums: *Kid Ory's Creole Jazz Band* (1954), *Alvin Alcorn* i (1964), *Alvin Alcorn* ii (1967), *Alvin Alcorn* iii (1970), *An Original New Orleans Brunch* (1976).

Alden, Howard

b. 17 October 1958, Newport Beach, California, USA. Alden began playing guitar when he was 10 years old, using recordings by well-known jazzmen as his guide. In his early teens he played professionally in the Los Angeles area and at 16 took formal lessons from Jimmy Wyble, a former member of the Red Norvo Trio. He later met Dan Barrett, with whom he formed a friendship, and continued to find work in and around Los Angeles. In the late 70s Alden joined Norvo for a season in Atlantic City. In 1982 he relocated to New York City and was immediately in demand, working with leading jazz players such as Joe Bushkin, Ruby Braff, Joe Williams and Woody Herman. Throughout the 80s and into the 90s he continued to play in the New York area, with artists such as Warren Vaché Jnr., Kenny Davern, Benny Carter, Monty Alexander, and Flip Phillips, and established a significant musical relationship with Dan Barrett, making records and touring the world for concert and festival appearances. Their group plays mostly in the mainstream and uses a wide range of material, in particular charts especially commissioned from Buck Clayton, several of which are originals. A masterly technician, Alden plays with fluency and wit. As an accompanist he is subtly supportive, while as a soloist he is assured and imaginative. One of the outstanding jazz musicians of his generation, Alden's reputation and his wide repertoire look set to make him one of the future names in jazz.

Albums: with Dan Barrett *Swing Street* (Concord Jazz 1986), with Flip Phillips *A Real Swinger* (1988), *Howard Alden Plays The Music Of Harry Reser* (1988), with Barrett *The A-B-Q Salutes Buck Clayton* (Concord Jazz 1989), *Howard Alden Trio* (Concord Jazz 1989), with Jack Lesberg *No Amps Allowed* (1990), *Snowy Morning Blues* (Concord Jazz 1990), with George Van Eps *13 Strings* (Concord Jazz 1991), *Misterioso*

(Concord Jazz 1991), *Hand Crafted Swing* (Concord Jazz 1992), *A Good Likeness* (1993), with Ken Peplowski *Concord Duo Series Vol. 3* (1993).

Alexander, Monty

b. 6 June 1944, Kingston, Jamaica. Resident in Miami after moving to the USA in 1961, Alexander built a reputation as a dynamic and technically brilliant pianist in the Art Tatum/Oscar Peterson seam without ever extending that virtuoso tradition. In the 60s he worked and recorded with Ray Brown and Milt Jackson before forming his own trio - the format in which he has since preferred to work. Highly popular in live performance, where the sometimes clinical accuracy of his recorded work is pleasantly animated, Alexander occasionally uses his native West Indian musical heritage to impressive effect. Indeed, on two albums of the late 80s, *Ivory And Steel* and *Jamboree,* he successfully, if improbably, incorporated jazz piano with a steel band.

Albums: *Zing* (1967), *Here Comes The Sun* (1971), *We've Only Just Begun* (1971), *Perception!* (1973), *Rass* (1974), *Unlimited Love* (1974), *Live In Germany* (1974), *Monty Strikes Again* (1974), *Love And Sunshine* (1974), *Now's The Time* (1974), *Montreux Alexander* (Pablo Jazz 1976), *Live In Holland* (1977), *Soul Fusion* (1977), *Cobilimbo* (1977), *Jamento* (1978), *Monty Alexander In Tokyo* (1979), *The Way It Is* (1979), *Facets* (Concord Jazz 1979), *So What* (1979), *Ivory And Steel* (Concord Jazz 1980), *Solo* (L&R 1980), *Trio* (1980), *Monty Alexander And Ernest Ranglin* (1980), *Triple Treat* (1982), *Look Up* (1982), *Duke Ellington Songbook* (MPS 1984), *The River* (Concord Jazz 1985), *Threesome* (1985), *Full Steam Ahead* (Concord 1986), *To Nat, With Love* (Master Mix 1986), *Triple Treat ii* (1987), *Triple Treat iii* (1987), *Jamboree* (Concord Picante 1988), *Saturday NIghts* (Timeless 1989), *Caribbean Circle* (Chesky 1992).

Alexandria, Lorez

b. 14 August 1929, Chicago, Illinois, USA. Like so many other young black singers, Alexandria began singing in church and later performed gospel music. Her early professional career was centred in clubs and really took off towards the end of the 50s with a series of well-received albums. After working with Ramsey Lewis she began to concentrate on jazz, recording extensively with Howard McGhee, Wynton Kelly and others during the early 60s. Around this time she relocated to the west coast, singing on television, recording and playing club dates. Alexandria sings with a deep, burnished tone and if her interpretations of a composer's intentions sometimes come second to her exploitation of her wide range of vocal devices, she remains one of the better, if lesser-known, jazz singers. Albums such as *A Woman Knows*, which includes what might well be the definitive version of the much-recorded song 'I Can't Get Started', and *Harlem Butterfly* are musical *tours de force*. These albums enjoyed deserved popularity amongst lovers of jazz singing.

Albums: *This Is Lorez Alexandria With The King Fleming Quartet* (1957), *Lorez Sings Pres* (King 1957), *Standards With A Touch Of Jazz* (1959), *The Band Swings, Lorez Sings* (King 1959), *Deep Roots* (1960), *Alexandria The Great* (Impulse 1964), *From Broadway To Hollywood* (1977), *How Will I Remember You* (1978), *A Woman Knows* (1978), *The Songs Of Johnny Mercer* (1980), *Harlem Butterfly* (1984), *Tangerine* (Trend 1984), *Singing Songs Everyone Knows* (King 1990), *May I Come In* (Muse 1991).

Ali, Rashied

b. Robert Patterson, 1 July 1935, Philadelphia, USA. When his father changed his name to Rashied Ali, Robert Patterson Junior followed suit. Ali's mother sang with the Jimmie Lunceford Orchestra and the entire family sang in their Baptist church. Ali had piano lessons from his grandmother. Saturated with music in his childhood, Ali became a revolutionary jazz drummer who established a new kind of continuity - heated, flickering, responsive, dissolving the explicit beat into the surge required by free jazz players. John Coltrane - with whom he played between 1965 and 1967 - said: 'He allows the soloist maximum freedom, he's laying down multi-directional rhythms all the time. To me, he's definitely one of the great drummers'. Since Coltrane's death Ali has been criminally under-recorded, yet he continues to extend the tradition of radical black music. When the dust settles on the 80s, it may well become apparent that Phalanx, Ali (drums), Sirone (bass), George Adams (tenor saxophone) and James 'Blood' Ulmer (guitar), was one of the decade's crucial bands.

Albums: with John Coltrane *Interstellar Space* (1967), *Original Phalanx* (1987), with Phalanx *In Touch* (1988).

Allen, Annisteen

b. Ernestine Allen, late 20s, Toledo, Ohio, USA, 10 August 1992, New York, USA. An exceptionally soulful big band vocalist who excelled at both ballads and blues, Allen was influenced by Ella Fitzgerald and discovered by Louis Jordan. He recommended her to fellow bandleader Lucky Millinder, with whom she toured from 1945 and recorded for Queen/King, Decca and RCA Victor scoring R&B chart hits such as 'More, More, More', 'Let It Roll', 'Moanin' The Blues' and 'I'll Never Be Free'. In 1951 she went solo and continued her recording career on King/Federal (1951-53), Capitol Records (1954-55) and Decca (1956-57). She finished the decade recording singles for small concerns like Todd, Warwick and Wig Records, before cutting a much acclaimed debut album in 1961 with King Curtis' band on Tru-Sound and retiring from the music business.

Selected albums: *Love For Sale* (1961), *Fujiyama Mama* (1986), *Give It Up 1945-1953* (1989).

Allen, Geri

b. 12 June 1957, Pontiac, Michigan, USA. Pianist Allen grew up in Detroit, steeped in the city's strong bebop and black pop traditions (and one early gig was playing with Mary Wilson and the Supremes) though Eric Dolphy, Herbie Nichols and Thelonious Monk were also major influences. She studied music at Washington's Howard University and at the

University of Pittsburgh (with Nathan Davis) and later with Roscoe Mitchell. Moving to New York in the early 80s she played with numerous contemporary jazz musicians, including James Newton and Lester Bowie, and recorded her debut *The Printmakers* in 1984 with a trio that featured Andrew Cyrille. She also became involved with the M-BASE and Black Rock Coalition organizations and the former's Steve Coleman and Robin Eubanks played on her *Open On All Sides In The Middle*. Later in the 80s she was a regular member of Oliver Lake's groups (*Plug It, Gallery, Impala, Otherside*) and toured and recorded with several leaders, including Dewey Redman (*Living On The Edge*), Frank Lowe (*Decision In Paradise*), Greg Osby (*Mindgames*) and Charlie Haden's Liberation Music Orchestra. With Haden and Paul Motian she formed an acoustic trio that has become celebrated for its intimate versions of modern mainstream jazz; and she also guested on Motian's own *Monk In Motian* and Betty Carter's *Droppin' Things*. An acutely sensitive player with a lovely touch, in the early 90s Allen signed to Blue Note Records.

Albums: *The Printmakers* (1984), *Homegrown* (1985), *Open On All Sides In The Middle* (Impetus 1987), with Charlie Haden, Paul Motian *Etudes* (1988), with Haden, Motian *In The Year Of The Dragon* (JMT 1989), with Haden, Motian *Segments* (1989), *Twylight* (Impetus 1989), *Printmakers* (Impetus 1990), with Haden, Motian *Live At The Village Vanguard* (DIW 1991), *The Nurturer* (Blue Note 1991), *Maroons* (Blue Note 1993).

Allen, Harry

b. 12 October 1966, Washington, D.C., USA. When he was aged one, Allen's parents moved to Los Angeles and it was there that he began playing music but at that time chose the accordion and later the piano. When he was 11 years old the family moved again, this time to Rhode Island and there, at junior high school, he began playing clarinet and finally the tenor saxophone on which instrument he decided to specialize. Encouraged by his father, Morry Allen, a school friend of Paul Gonsalves who had played drums during the swing era with the Boston-based George Johnson band, he listened to jazz records. These were by the likes of Louis Armstrong, Duke Ellington and Benny Goodman, although his musical education on his earlier instruments was classically orientated. Later, at Rutgers University, he was encouraged to develop his jazz playing in the formulaic John Coltrane mode but resisted, preferring instead to follow the path of the tenor players he had listened to on record as a young teenager: Gonsalves, Ben Webster, Coleman Hawkins. By the time his education ended he had already established himself as a jazz musician playing in the New York area where he worked with leading figures such as Ruby Braff, George Masso, Bucky Pizzarelli, Kenny Barron, John Bunch and Oliver Jackson. He recorded extensively during the late 80s, often backing singers and usually on obscure and poorly promoted labels. By the early 90s, however, he was a popular figure on the international scene, playing clubs and festivals throughout Europe, in Canada and the USA. An exceptionally fine interpreter of ballads, Allen belongs firmly in the late mainstream, drawing upon the great traditions of the movement but never sounding dated or lacking in originality.

Albums: *I Know That You Know* (Master Mix 1991), *I'll Never Be The Same* (1992), *Someone To Light Up Your Life* (Master Mix 1992), *How Long Has This Been Going On* (Progressive 1992), with Christian Josi *I Walks With My Feet Off The Ground* (1994).

Allen, Henry 'Red'

b. 7 January 1908, New Orleans, Louisiana, USA, d. 17 April 1967. One of the outstanding trumpeters in jazz, Allen's career found him vacillating between New Orleans' traditionalism, big band jazz, and an early kind of experimentalism that appealed to beboppers and freeform fans. His questing musical nature and deep affinity for the blues ensured his place as a major jazz player, yet, commercially and artistically (and most unfairly), he was obliged to spend much of his career in the shadow of Louis Armstrong. Allen had already worked with George Lewis, Fate Marable, Joe 'King' Oliver and Clarence Williams when, in 1928, he was hired by the Victor label as a rival attraction to Armstrong, then recording for their competitors OKeh. In 1929 Allen joined Luis Russell's New York-based band and for several years was a dominant voice in a number of important big bands of the burgeoning swing era. His musical collaborations with J.C. Higginbotham and Coleman Hawkins, during a stint with the Fletcher Henderson Orchestra, became almost legendary. A 1937 career move took him back to the Russell band, but this proved a detrimental step when the band became little more than an anonymous backing group for Armstrong. Two dominant musical personalities, both of them trumpeters, were too much for one band, so in 1940 Allen forsook big band work to join the New Orleans Revivalist movement. However, his forward-looking nature was such that he refused to stay in a stylistic groove. Over the years, he developed an adventurous and impressive arsenal of sounds with both open horn and mute. His powerful, blues-drenched playing (and occasional singing) was shot through with burning rips and aggressive smears, to the point where he attracted the attention of notable jazz frontiersmen such as Don Ellis, who described Allen in a 1965 *Downbeat* article as 'the most *avant garde* trumpeter in New York'. Throughout the 50s and 60s Allen worked in traditional and mainstream small groups, at home and abroad, as both sideman and leader. He recorded regularly during this period and often to great effect, as on his mid-50s reunion sessions with Coleman Hawkins or the later *Feeling Good*. In an oft-quoted and somewhat inaccurate jazz trumpet lineage, Roy Eldridge is cited as the link between Armstrong and Dizzy Gillespie. In many respects Allen might be the better choice, to connect the New Orleans tradition with both bop and elements of the freer music that followed it. He died in New York in April 1967, shortly after completing his last tour of the UK.

Selected albums: *Red Allen Dixielanders Featuring Big Chief Moore* (1951), *Stuyvesant Casino Nights Vol. 1* (c.1951-52), *The Red Allen-Tony Parenti All Stars* (1955-57), *Red Allen Featuring Kid Ory & Jack Teagarden At Newport* (1957), *Nice* (1957),

World On A String (1957), *Ride, Red, Ride In Hi-Fi* (1957), *Warhorses* (1957), *Stormy Weather* (1957-58), *All Star Jazz Session* (1958-59), *Live At The London House* (1961), *Rare Red Allen Trio Performances* (1962), *Mr Allen* (1962), *Feeling Good* (1965), *Live 1965* (1965), *The College Concert* (1966). Compilations: *Henry Allen 1929 To 1936* (1929-36), *The Chronological Red Allen Vols 1 - 4* (1929-37), *Red Allen And His Friends* (1932-56), with Spike Hughes *Spike Hughes And His All-American Orchestra* (1933), with others *Red Allen And The Blues Singers Vols 1 & 2* (1938-40), *The Very Great Henry 'Red' Allen Vol. 1* (1941-46), *Jazz Classics In Digital Stereo* (BBC 1990), *World On A String* (Bluebird 1991).

Allen, Marshall

b. 25 May 1924, Louisville, Kentucky, USA. At school Allen learned to play clarinet and C-melody saxophone. He studied at the National Conservatory of Music in Paris while playing jazz with pianist Art Simmons. In the early 50s he toured Europe with James Moody. On his return to the States in 1954, Allen joined up with a bandleader whose influences - both musical and philosophical - predated bebop: Sun Ra. He was introduced by King Kolax, a trumpet player who lead one of Chicago's pre-eminent R&B bands. Allen told Nat Hentoff in a 1966 *Downbeat* interview: 'I felt I wanted to play on a broader sound basis rather than on chords: I couldn't play this way until I started playing with Sun Ra.' Allen's alto saxophone has become as central to Sun Ra's sound as Johnny Hodges's was to Duke Ellington's, and his tenure has proved even longer. He also plays flute, oboe, cor anglais, clarinet and the *morrow*, an instrument he invented himself. As with many of Sun Ra's players, Allen's monumental contribution to modern music has frequently eluded the pundits, who too often dismiss the band as Sun Ra's wacko circus. Actually, Sun Ra's monastic discipline and regular tours have honed a technique that has made Marshall Allen a legend among alto saxophone players. The best-known of his rare recordings away from the Arkestra is a 1964 session with the Paul Bley quintet, *Barrage*.

Allen, Pete

b. 23 November 1953, Newbury, Berkshire, England. Although Allen has chosen to follow the well-trodden path of other British jazz traditionalists such as Freddie Randall and Kenny Ball, he has managed to avoid sameness through a combination of musical flair and determination. His fluid, bluesy clarinet style is complemented by his use of alto and soprano saxophones, both of which allow him to augment the traditional dixieland line-up to good effect. Displaying a sound business sense (on a par with that of Chris Barber), Allen has led a succession of enthusiastic young musicians prepared to turn their backs on the new trends followed by their contemporaries. Unlike many latterday British reed players, who have chosen to model themselves upon John Coltrane, Allen himself has followed the lineage exemplified by Edmond Hall. Largely by dint of his expressive playing and total commitment, Allen's decision to follow a traditional style has in no way limited his musical development and he continues to play an interesting

and entertaining brand of jazz.
Selected albums: *Down In Honky-Tonk Town!* (c.70s), *Turkey Trot* (c.70s), *Gonna Build A Mountain* (c.80s), *Jazzin' Around* ii (c.80s), *While We Danced At The Mardi Gras* (c.80s), *One For The Road* (c.80s), *Wild Cat Blues* (c.80s), *Dixie Date* (c.80s), *Martinique* (c.80s), *Jazz You Like It* (PAR 1991), *Beau Sejour* (PAR 1991).

Allison, Mose

b. 11 November 1927, Tippo, Mississippi, USA. Allison began piano lessons at the age of five, and played trumpet in high school, although he has featured the latter instrument less frequently in recent years. His music is a highly individual mix of blues and modern jazz, with influences on his cool, laconic singing and piano playing ranging from Tampa Red and Sonny Boy 'Rice Miller' Williamson to Charlie Parker, Duke Ellington, and Thelonious Monk. He moved to New York in 1956 and worked mainly in jazz settings, playing with Stan Getz and recording for numerous companies. During the 60s Allison's work was much in evidence as he became a major influence on the burgeoning R&B scene. Pete Townshend, one of Mose's greatest fans recorded his 'A Young Man's Blues' for the Who's *Live At Leeds*. Similarly John Mayall was one of dozens who recorded his classic 'Parchman Farm' and Georgie Fame featured many Allison songs in his heyday with the Blueflames. Fame's nasal and understated vocal was similar to Allison's, as is Ben Sidran's style and voice. In the 80s he saw a resurgence in his popularity after becoming a hero to the new, young audience for modern jazz. Ultimately his work is seen as hugely influential; and this has to a degree limited the success of his own considerable recording career.
Selected albums: *Back Country Suite* (1957), *Mose Alive* (1966), *I've Been Doin' Some Thinkin'* (1968), *Hello There* (1969), *Universe* (1969), *Western Man* (1971), *Mose In Your Ear* (1972), *Your Mind's On Vacation* (1976), *Middle Class White Boy* (1982), *Ever Since The World Ended* (Blue Note 1983), *Lessons In Living* (1983), *My Backyard* (Blue Note 1990), *Sings And Plays* (Fantasy 1991). Compilation: *Mose Allison Sings The Seventh Son* (1988).

Allyn, David

b. 19 July 1923, Hartford, Connecticut, USA. From a musical family, his mother was a singer and his father a French horn player, Allyn became a semi-pro vocalist by the time he was 17, before joining Jack Teagarden's short-lived big band of the early 40s. After service in World War II, during which he was awarded the Purple Heart, he worked for leaders such as Van Alexander and Henry Jerome before joining the Boyd Raeburn orchestra where his musical skills were tested by the demanding work of several forward-looking arrangers, including George Handy. In the 40s, apart from his work with Raeburn, Allyn also recorded with such jazzmen as Lucky Thompson. When the Raeburn band split up, Allyn moved to the west coast and became solo act. His Dick Haymes-like vocals gained him regular club work and a recording contract with Discovery, and later, World Pacific. During the 50s he recorded some highly regarded albums with arrangements by Johnny Mandel and Bill Holman and with accompanists of the calibre of Jimmy Rowles, Frank Rosolino and Barry Harris. In the late 60s and early 70s Allyn worked infrequently in music, spending time actively involved in social work including the rehabilitation of drug users. Allyn's good pitch and diction, allied to his intense feeling for jazz and consummate musical skill, made him one of the best male singers of jazz and standard songs of his time, albeit one little known to the popular or even fringe jazz audience. In 1986, on the basis of an 'up-from-the-ashes' life story and generous recommendations from some major singers, Allyn was again receiving favourable reviews for his 'smoky instrument that he uses to glide through songs with effortless power', at clubs such as George's in Chicago. (On some recordings Allyn's name is spelled Allen).

Albums: *Sure Thing* (1957), *Yours Sincerely* (1958), *I Only Have Eyes For You* (1959), with Jimmy Rowles, Frank Rosolino *In The Blue Of The Evening* (1966), with Barry Harris *Don't Look Back* (1975), *Soft As Spring* (1976). Compilations: *Boyd Raeburn On The Air Vol. 2* (1945-48 recordings), *Boyd Raeburn On The Air Vol. 1* (1946), *Boyd Raeburn* (1946-47 recordings).

Almeida, Laurindo

b. 2 September 1917, Sao Paulo, Brazil. A fluent and skilled musician, famous in his native country as a classical Spanish guitar player, Almeida came to the USA in the 40s to work in film and television studios. His jazz work was first widely exposed during a spell with Stan Kenton in the late 40s. Although continuing his studio work, Almeida also took many opportunities to play jazz, joining forces with bassist Harry Babasin, altoist Bud Shank and drummer Roy Harte in 1953. The work of this group anticipated many of the hallmarks of the bossa nova craze which came a few years later. In 1974 Almeida gained further appreciation when he was teamed with bassist Ray Brown, drummer Chuck Flores and Shank to form the LA Four. Records by this group, with Flores replaced successively by Shelly Manne and Jeff Hamilton, and later teamings with Shank in duo performances and with fellow guitarists Larry Coryell and Charlie Byrd, show Almeida to have lost none of the distinctive style that sets his work apart from the mainstream of jazz guitar.

Selected albums: with Stan Kenton *Encores* (1947), with Kenton *A Concert In Progressive Jazz* (1947), with Bud Shank *Braziliance Vol. 1* (1953), *The Laurindo Almeida Quartet Featuring Bud Shank* (1954), with Shank *Braziliance Vol. 2* (1958), *Laurindo Almeida i* (1962), *Laurindo Almeida ii* (1962), *Laurindo Almeida iii* (1963), *Laurindo Almeida iv* (1964), *Suenos (Dreams)* (1965), *Latin Guitar* (1974), with LA Four *The LA Four Scores!* (1975), *Virtuoso Guitar* (1977), with LA Four *Watch What Happens* (1977), with LA Four *Just Friends* (1978), *Chamber Jazz* (Concord 1978), *Concierto De Aranjuez* (1978), *New Directions* (1979), *First Concerto For Guitar And Orchestra* (1979), with Charlie Byrd *Brazilian Soul* (Concord Picante 1980) with Byrd *Latin Odyssey* (Concord Picamte 1982), *The Laurindo Almeida Trio* (1984), *Tango* (Concord Picante 1985), *New Directions Of Virtuoso Guitar*

(Teldec 1987), with Byrd *Music Of The Brazilian Masters* (New Note 1989), *Outra Vez (Once Again)* (Concord Jazz 1992), with Shank *Baa-Too-Kee* (1993).

Almond, Johnny

b. 20 July 1946, Enfield, Middlesex, England. This accomplished saxophonist and flautist rose to prominence during the mid-60s as a member of London R&B group Tony Knight's Chessmen. In 1965 he replaced Clive Burrows in Zoot Money's Big Roll Band and two years later joined the successful Alan Price Set. This group became known as the Paul Williams Set following the original leader's departure and the same unit also formed the basis for a 1969 venture, Johnny Almond's Music Machine. Williams (vocals), Jimmy Crawford (guitar), Geoff Condon (trumpet), John Wiggins (keyboards), Roger Sutton (bass) and Alan White (drums) were featured on *Patent Pending*, a propulsive set drawing inspiration from both jazz and blues, but Almond subsequently disbanded the lineup, and a second album, *Hollywood Blues*, was completed with the aid of American musicians. A session musician on albums by Fleetwood Mac (*Mr. Wonderful*) and John Mayall (*Bluesbreakers With Eric Clapton*), the saxophonist joined the latter in 1970 in a pioneering 'drummer-less' unit captured on *The Turning Point* and *Empty Rooms*. Here Almond forged a partnership with guitarist Jon Mark, which resulted in the formation of a breakaway act, Mark-Almond in 1971. This imaginative ensemble completed a series of albums during the 70s and although less prolific, continued their partnership into the subsequent decade.

Albums: *Patent Pending* (1969), *Hollywood Blues* (1970), *Enchanted* (Parlophone 1970); As Mark-Almond *The Best Of Mark-Almond* (1993).

Altena, Maarten

b. Maarten van Regteren Altena, 1943. When Altena broke his wrist falling downstairs in his Amsterdam home in 1973, he responded by putting his bass in a plaster-cast, too, the results documented on *Handicaps*. On this debut solo recording it seemed safe to place Altena as an archetype of the clownish Dutch 'school' personified by Han Bennink but, before and since, Altena has been a restless explorer rather than an idiomatic musician. In the 60s he came out of the Amsterdam conservatory, then played jazz, backing artists such as Dexter Gordon before joining Misha Mengelberg's band. In the late 70s, he threw himself wholeheartedly into the stylistic conflicts of Company, the pool of musicians headed by Derek Bailey. Within a decade, however, he had exhausted his interests in 'pure' free improvisation and formed his own Maarten Altena Ensemble, comprised of Dutch musicians from jazz, pop and classical backgrounds. In the Ensemble he took his cue from Stravinsky, aiming to make each composition a self-contained sound-world. There is enormous variety in the music, which establishes rigorous structures only to dismantle them with great energy and good humour.

Albums: *Handicaps* (1973), *Tuning The Bass* (1975), with Evan Parker, Derek Bailey, Tristan Honsinger *Company 1* (1977),

Live Performances (1977), *K'Ploeng* (1978), with Steve Lacy *High, Low And Order* (1979), *Op Stap* (1980), with Peter Kowald *Two Making A Triangle* (1982), *Rif* (1988), *Weerwerk* (1988), *Quotl* (1989), *Cities And Streets* (Hat Art 1991), *Code* (Hat Art 1992).

Altschul, Barry

b. 6 January 1943, New York City, New York, USA. Born into a classical music family, drummer Altschul was fascinated by the rhythms of the street. An early school report said 'He isn't doing any work, he's only playing music with Black people.' He sat in with jazz musicians in the neighbourhood - including trumpeter Charles Tolliver and tenor saxophonist Junior Cook - and learned the fundamentals of bebop touring with Johnny Griffin and Sonny Criss. His work (1970-72) with Circle, a free improvising quartet that featured Anthony Braxton (reeds), Chick Corea (piano), and Dave Holland (bass), established him as a pre-eminent *avant garde* player, a reputation he solidified as a member of Braxton's ground-breaking quartet of the mid-70s. His sensitivity to space and timbre means that he truly deserves the description 'percussionist'. He has also played throughout his career with Sam Rivers, Ray Anderson and Anthony Davis.

Albums: with Circle *Paris Concert* (1971), *You Can't Name Your Own Tune* (1977), *Another Time, Another Place* (1978) with Paul Bley, Gary Peacock *Virtuosi* (AI 1992).

AMM

Formed in 1965 by jazz saxophonist Lou Gare, guitarist Keith Rowe and drummer Eddie Prevost with cellist and clarinettist Lawrence Sheaff, AMM is a vehicle for free improvisation that leaves room for the operation of chance: a mid-60s programme note suggested that the noise made by members of the audience leaving could be regarded as part of the performance. Passages of silence have also been an integral part of AMM music, and Gare in particular seems able to give a potent impression of phrases continuing to develop through the gaps he leaves. The structure and personnel of AMM has always fluctuated: at one period it comprised Gare and Prevost only, when the group was perhaps at its most jazz orientated since its inception. The use of chance and other techniques from *avant garde* 'classical' music was imported by composer Cornelius Cardew, initially against opposition from Rowe, and during the 80s other classical musicians (pianist John Tilbury and Arditti Quartet cellist Rohan de Saram) have been members of the band.

Albums: *AMMMusic* (Impetus 1967, re-released as *AMMMusic 1966* in 1989), with MEV *Live Electronic Music Improvised* (1968), *The Crypt* (1968), *To Hear And Back Again* (1974), *It Had Been An Ordinary Enough Day in Pueblo, Colorado* (1979), *Generative Themes* (1983), *The Inexhaustible Document* (1987), *Combine And Laminate* (1991, rec. 1984), *The Nameless Uncarved Block* (1991).

Ammons, Albert

b. 23 September 1907, Chicago, Illinois, USA, d. 2 December 1949. Ammons began playing piano as a small child and worked in Chicago clubs while still a youth. In the late 20s and early 30s he played in a number of small bands but his real forte was as a soloist. After establishing himself as an important blues piano player in Chicago in the mid-30s, a period which saw him leading a small group at many of the city's top nightspots, Ammons moved to New York City. With Pete Johnson he formed a piano duo, playing in the newly popular boogie-woogie style. In New York Ammons and Johnson appeared at the Cafe Society and occasionally added Meade 'Lux' Lewis to their group to form a powerful boogie-woogie trio. By the mid-40s Ammons had returned to playing as a single, touring the USA before settling back in his home town, where he died in December 1949. Although best known for his contribution to the briefly popular craze for boogie-woogie, Ammons was one of the outstanding blues piano players. His son, Gene 'Jug' Ammons, played tenor saxophone.

Compilations: *King Of Boogie And Blues 1939-49* (1988), *Albert Ammons Vol 1 & 2* (1988).

Ammons, Gene 'Jug'

b. 14 April 1925, Chicago, Illinois, USA, d. 6 August 1974. Ammons chose to make the tenor saxophone his instrument in preference to the piano played by his father, the famous boogie-woogie exponent Albert Ammons. Gene left school at the age of 18 and within two years was a member of Billy Eckstine's bebop-orientated big band. Despite working alongside leading lights of the new form such as Fats Navarro, Leo Parker and Art Blakey, Ammons proved to be very much his own man, developing a distinctive, warm sound which nevertheless fitted well into the hard-edged playing of his colleagues. After leaving Eckstine, Ammons worked mainly in small groups, sometimes as leader, but also had a short spell with Woody Herman's big band in 1949. A year later he joined forces with Sonny Stitt to co-lead a small group which played rich, soulful music overlaid with an aggressive attack - a style that moved him towards the outer edges of the bop tradition yet never quite slipped over into fully-fledged soul or R&B. Ammons worked extensively in small group settings for the next dozen years but drug addiction led to prison terms which, altogether, robbed his career of 10 years from the late 50s through to the late 60s. Between his release from prison in 1969 and his death from cancer and pneumonia in August 1974, Ammons enjoyed considerable success thanks in part to his enthusiastic playing and the concurrent popularity of jazz-soul music.

Selected albums: with Sonny Stitt *Woofin' And Tweetin'* (1955), *The Gene Ammons Band* (1955), *The Happy Blues* (1956), *Jammin' With The Gene Ammons All Stars* (1956), *Funky* (1957), *Jammin' In Hi-Fi With Gene Ammons* (1957), *Gene Ammons All Stars* (1958), *Blue Gene* (1958), *Boss Tenor* (1960), *Angel Eyes* (1960), *Nice An' Cool* (1961), *Jug* (1961), *Gene Ammons i* (1961), with Richard 'Groove' Holmes *Groovin' With Jug* (1961), with Stitt *Boss Tenors* (1961), with Stitt *Dig Him* (1961), *Just Jug/Live! In Chicago* (1961), *Twisting The Jug* (1961), *Up Tight* (1961), *Nothing But Soul* (1962), *Soul Summit* (1962), with Stitt *Boss Tenors In Orbit* (1962), *Gene*

Ammons ii (1962), *The Soulful Moods Of Gene Ammons* (1962), *Blue Groove* (1962), *Preachin'* (1962), *Jug And Dodo* (1962), *Gene Ammons* iii (1962), *Bad! Bossa Nova/Jungle Soul* (1962), *Swingin' The Jug* (c.1962), *The Boss Is Back* (1969), *Brother Jug* (1969), *Gene Ammons* iv (1970), *Hooray For John Coltrane* (1970), *The Chase* (1970), *The Black Cat* (1970), *You Talk That Talk* (1971), *My Way* (1971), *Chicago Concert* (1971), *Free Again* (1972), *Big Bad Jug* (1972), *Gene Ammons And Friends At Montreux* (1973), *Gene Ammons In Sweden* (1973), *Together Again For The Last Time* (1973), *Brasswind* (1973-74), *Goodbye* (1974). Compilations: with Billy Eckstine *Blowing The Blues Away* (1944), with Eckstine *Together!* (1945), with Woody Herman *More Moon* (1949), *Boogie Woogie And The Blues* (1987).

Amran, David Werner, III

b. 17 November 1930, Philadelphia, Pennsylvania, USA. After studying classical music, Amran played horn with the National Symphony Orchestra in Washington. During his military service, he was based in Paris with the Seventh Army Symphony Orchestra. On his return to New York he studied at the Manhattan School of Music with Gunter Schuller, recorded with Charles Mingus and played in a band with Oscar Pettiford. In 1956 he began a long association with Joseph Papp and the New York Shakespeare Festival for which he wrote 25 scores over the next 10 years. He has become increasingly well-known as a composer of orchestral and instrumental music including film scores and incidental music for the stage. He won a Pulitzer Prize in 1959 for the music for Archie MacLeish's *JB*. He led a group with George Barrow (tenor saxophone) which played regularly at New York's Five Spot in the mid-60s and was composer in residence with the New York Philharmonic Orchestra (1966-67) with whom he organized concerts for children and workshops on folk music (especially Latin American) and jazz. In 1969 he went on a State Department sponsored tour to Brazil and during the 70s visited Kenya, Cuba, the Middle East and Central America. These tours added to his 'dramatic, colourful scores', which nevertheless retain the rhythmic, improvisatory character of jazz.
Albums: *Jazz Studio Six* (1957), *Triple Concerto For Woodwind, Brass, Jazz Quartet And Orchestra* (1970), *Havana/New York* (1977), *Latin Jazz Celebration* (1982).

Amy, Curtis

b. 11 October 1929, Houston, Texas, USA. Having previously learned to play clarinet while growing up in Texas, Amy took up the tenor saxophone during his army service. Later he became a musical educator in Tennessee, following his graduation from Kentucky State College. He continued to play in nightclubs, however, and in the mid-50s he moved to the west coast, where he became extensively involved in the contemporary music scene. Amy recorded with Dizzy Gillespie, but, eager to experiment, in the early 60s he led several small groups that explored the possibilities of modal jazz. In the mid-60s he recorded with a big band led by Gerald Wilson, a swing era veteran noted for his musically adventurous ideas. Amy's later stu-

dio work has found him backing many pop singers, including Carole King and the Doors.
Albums: *The Blues Message* (1960), *Groovin' Blue* (1961), *Meeting Here* (1961), *Way Down Featuring Victor Feldman* (1962), *Tippin' On Through* (1962), *Katanga!* (1963), *Curtis Amy* (1965), *Mustang* (c.60s).

Andersen, Arild

b. 27 October 1945, Oslo, Norway. His career as a jazz bassist began under the tutelage of Karel Netolicka and the influential American jazz composer and theorist George Russell, who was then resident in Sweden. From 1966-73 Andersen toured throughout Scandinavia, working with Russell's orchestra and sextet, Jan Garbarek's trio and quartet, Karin Krog, Edward Vesala and others. In West Germany he worked with Don Cherry and in France with Stan Getz. Visits to New York brought recordings with Sam Rivers, Paul Bley and Barry Altschul. In 1974 he led his own quartet which recorded the acclaimed bop-influenced *Clouds In My Head* a year later. *Shimri* and *Green Shading Into Blue* followed a more romantic course and divided the critics. The early 80s saw the introduction of non-Norwegian musicians in Andersen-led projects, such as Americans Alphonse Mouzon and Bill Frisell, Canadian Kenny Wheeler and Briton John Taylor. From 1983 he toured and recorded with the Norwegian quintet Masqualero. *Sagn*, a series of compositions based on folk songs from the south of Norway, received its premiere at the Vossajazz festival in Norway in 1990. Andersen has received a number of awards for his bass playing, including the Buddy Award from the Norwegian Jazz Federation in 1969.
Albums: *Clouds In My Head* (1975), *Shimri* (1976), *Green Shading Into Blue* (1978), *Lifelines* (1980), *A Molde Concert* (1981), *Sagn* (1990), with Masqualero *Masqualero* (1983), *Bande A Parte* (1985), with Ralph Towner, Nana Vasconcelos *If You Look Far Enough* (1993).

Anderson, Cat

b. William Alonzo Anderson, 12 September 1916, Greenville, South Carolina, USA, d. 29 April 1981. Learning to play the trumpet while at a South Carolina orphanage, Anderson developed a fearsome technique that earned him jobs with the bands of Lucky Millinder, Lionel Hampton, Erskine Hawkins, Claude Hopkins and Sabby Lewis. In 1944, Anderson joined Duke Ellington where he remained for three years. From 1947 he alternated between leading his own bands and working for others; but he kept returning to Ellington, for whom he played more or less continuously for two long stretches, 1950-59 and 1961-71. When he finally left Ellington, Anderson settled in Los Angeles - which was where Bill Berry reformed his Ellington-inspired big band in 1971 and Anderson became an occasional member. Although noted for his extraordinary five-octave range, Anderson was highly accomplished in all aspects of his instrument and excelled at the colourful use of half-valve and plunger-mute techniques, which made him such an integral part of Ellington's composing palette. Unlike many other high-note specialists, Anderson was able to play melodically in the top registers, not merely make noises. In the late 70s Anderson toured with Hampton's All Star band, playing festivals and making records in the USA and Europe.

Albums: *Cat Anderson Plays At 4 a.m.* (1958), *Cat On A Hot Tin Horn* (1958), *A Flower Is A Lovesome Thing* (1959), *A 'Chat' With Cat* (1964), *Ellingtonians In Paris 1950-1964* (1964), *Cat Anderson/Claude Bolling & Co.* (1965), *Cat Speaks* (1977), *Cat Anderson Plays W.C. Handy* (1977-1978)(Black And Blue re-issue 1991), *Old Folks* (1979), *Cat Anderson Et Les Four Bones* (1979).

Anderson, Ernestine

b. 11 November 1928, Houston, Texas, USA. Raised in Seattle, Anderson has been singing professionally since her mid-teens. She worked extensively with R&B bands in the 40s, including those led by Russell Jacquet and Johnny Otis. A year with Lionel Hampton in the early 50s and a Scandinavian tour with bop trumpeter Rolf Ericson broadened her repertoire, but she remained well-rooted in the blues. In later years Anderson developed her technique and range, her rich, molten sound being especially effective on the better contemporary pop songs. Despite spending long periods overseas (including several years' residence in England from 1965), her international appeal remained limited. Indeed, the spell in Europe adversely affected her career in her homeland; even a national magazine profile, which described her as the 'new Sarah Vaughan and Ella Fitzgerald', did not help. A chance appearance at the 1976 Concord Summer Jazz Festival deservedly brought her to the attention of a new and wider audience, and since then she has performed and recorded extensively, although she is now based chiefly on the west coast.

Albums: *Ernestine Anderson With The Gigi Gryce Orchestra And Quartet* (1955), with Rolf Ericson *Hot Cargo* (1956), *Ernestine Anderson* i (1958), *Ernestine Anderson* ii (1959), *Ernestine Anderson* iii (1960), *Ernestine Anderson* iv (1960), *Moanin', Moanin', Moanin'* (1960), *Ernestine Anderson* v (1963-64), *Hello Like Before* (Concord Jazz 1976), *Live From Concord To London* (1976-77), *Sunshine* (Concord 1979), *Never Make Your Move Too Soon* (c.1980), *Big City* (Concord Jazz 1983), *When The Sun Goes Down* (Concord 1984), *Be Mine Tonight* (Concord Jazz 1986), with Capp-Pierce Juggernaut *Live At The Alleycat* (1987), with George Shearing *A Perfect Match* (1988), *Boogie Down* (Concord 1990), *Live At The Concord Festival: The Third Set* (1990), Late At Night (King 1992), *Now And Then* (1993).

Anderson, Ivie

b. 10 July 1905, Gilroy, California, USA, d. 28 December 1949. Although best known for her work with Duke Ellington in the 30s, Anderson had already worked extensively both in the USA, where she sang at the Cotton Club in the mid-20s, and overseas, touring Australia with Sonny Clay towards the end of the decade. Her light-toned voice and relaxed style were well-suited to the swing era and she was one of the best of her kind. Given Ellington's notoriously eccentric choice of singers for his band, the fact that he hired her at all is surprising, but once there she proved to be an important asset. She was with Ellington from 1931-42, making numerous records, including the first and possibly definitive version of 'It Don't Mean A Thing If It Ain't Got That Swing', and appearing on film. After leaving Ellington, Anderson retired from singing and went into the restaurant business, but she returned to the studios in 1946 for an excellent session on which she was accompanied by Charles Mingus, Willie Smith, Lucky Thompson and others. She died in December 1949.

Compilations: *Duke Ellington Presents Ivie Anderson* (1932-40), *The Indispensable Duke Ellington Vols. 3/4-5/6* (1934-40), *Ivie Anderson And Her All Stars* (1946).

Anderson, Ray

b. 16 October 1952, Chicago, Illinois, USA. Anderson started playing trombone as soon as he was tall enough, at the age of eight. Initially inspired by his father's dixieland record collection, he played in school alongside George Lewis, the other pre-eminent trombonist of his generation. Anderson has always involved himself with a generous spectrum of music, from harmonica-player Jeff Carp's blues band as a teenager to classical orchestras. Concerts by the local black self-help organization, the AACM, were an inspiration. Lewis joined the AACM, Anderson went to Minneapolis and then San Francisco to study music. However, Anderson has always kept in touch with the Chicago players and, like Lewis, has had a fruitful relationship with Anthony Braxton. In California he played with Charles Moffet and David Murray. In 1972 he relocated to New York, where he sat in with Charles Mingus and George Adams. In the late 70s he toured and recorded with Braxton and Barry Altschul. In 1981 he won the *Downbeat* poll as Talent Deserving Wider Recognition and formed an entertaining funk band, Slickaphonics. His 1985 release *Old Bottles - New Wine* on the Enja label had him playing standards in the formidable company of Kenny Barron, Cecil McBee and Dannie Richmond. His trio with Mark Helias and Gerry Hemingway, also known as both Oahspe and BassDrumBone, is an excellent foil for his startlingly fluid, responsive and subversive stylings. Anderson is a convincing representative of a generation of musicians who see no reason not to fuse the furthest outreaches of free improvisation with funk or farce as the fancy takes them. Coupled with the Louis Armstrong-style multiphonics of his singing voice, his excavation of the narrow line between emotional extension and comedy - and his staggering technique - has given him an enthusiastic and loyal following.

Albums: *Oahspe* (1979), *Harrisburg Half Life* (Moers 1981), with Mark Helias, Gerry Hemingway *Right Down Your Alley* (Soul Note 1984), *Old Bottles - New Wine* (Enja 1985), with Helias, Hemingway *You Be* (1986), *It Just So Happens* (Enja 1986), with BassDrumBone *Wooferloo* (1987), *Blues Bred In The Bone* (Enja 1989), *What Because* (Gramavision 1990), *Wishbone* (Gramavision 1991), *Everyone Of Us* (Gramavision 1992), *Don't Mow Your Lawn* (Enja 1994).

Peter Appleyard

Andrews, Ernie

b. USA. A robust and energetic singer of the blues, Andrews remains little known outside the west coast where he can be heard singing in clubs and at festivals, often with the backing of all-star big bands such as the Capp-Pierce Juggernaut. On popular songs of the day, Andrews sometimes displays lack of judgement in his selection of material but frequently makes the poor songs he sings sound better than they should. He is at his best shouting the blues above the roar of a big band.

Albums: *Ernie Andrews* i (1957), *Ernie Andrews* ii (1959), *Soul Proprietor* (c.1965), with Capp-Pierce Juggernaut *Juggernaut* (1976), *Hear Me Now* (1979), *From The Heart* (1980).

Andriessen, Louis

b. 6 June 1939, Utrecht, Holland. Son of composer Hendrik Andriessen, Louis Andriessen writes some of the most forbidding minimalist music, and has inspired some of the most accessible. He studied under his father at Utrecht Conservatory, under Kees van Baaren at the Royal Conservatory in the Hague (where he won the composition prize in 1962) and finally with Luciano Berio in Milan and Berlin during 1964/5. Like many of the American minimalists he revolted against the academic and elitist contemporary classical mainstream, and in 1972 he founded De Volharding, intended to allow composition for individuals rather than instruments. Since 1974 he has taught at the Royal

Conservatory where, in 1976, he began a minimalist music project which developed into the band Hoketus. Later he assembled another unit, Kaalslag, from musicians out of de Volharding and Hoketus. His music, which is usually rhythmic, percussive and frequently very loud, has been a major influence on a generation of Dutch minimalists and inspired the formation of the British band Icebreaker.

Albums: *Symphonies Of The Netherlands* (1974), *de Staat* (The Republic 1976), *De Tijd* (Time 1981), *Mausoleum & De Snelheid* (Velocity 1984), *De Stijl* (included on *Live* by the band Kaalslag) (1985), *Melodie & Symphony For Open Strings* (1986), *Hoketus* (included on *Balans* by the band Hoketus) (1986).

Appleyard, Peter

b. 26 August 1929, Cleethorpes, Lincolnshire, England. His musical career began when he played drums in a Boys' Brigade band in his home town. He graduated to playing drums in local dance bands before joining the popular band led by Felix Mendelssohn. During the mid-40s he played with various bands in the UK and towards the end of the decade worked in Bermuda. In 1951 he moved to Canada. By this time Appleyard had begun to play vibraphone and it was on this instrument that he made his impact on the international jazz scene. He decided to remain in Canada, playing with groups led by Calvin Jackson and others. In the late 50s he also played regularly in New York and during the following decades he toured extensively, working with Benny Goodman and in Peanuts Hucko's Pied Pipers. In Toronto, he regularly hosted a jazz show on television. He has recorded frequently, as leader and sideman, with such jazzmen as Rob McConnell, Ed Bickert, Hucko and others. A dynamic and exciting player, Appleyard's career has been musically successful and financially rewarding. His decision to live in Canada has, however, tended to shield him from view and he is often unfairly overlooked by observers of the international jazz scene.

Albums: *The Peter Appleyard Quartet* (1956-57), *The Vibe Sound* (1958), *Per-cus-sive Jazz* (1960), *Peter Appleyard* i (c.1960), *Peter Appleyard* ii (1962), *Peter Appleyard* iii (1963), *The Many Moods Of Peter Appleyard* (1969), *On Stage With Benny Goodman And His Sextet* (1972), *The Lincolnshire Poacher* (c.1973), *Sophisticated Vibes* (1976), *Peter Appleyard Presents* (1977), *Peter Appleyard* iv (1979), *Peter Appleyard* v (1980), *Peter Appleyard* vi (1980), *Peter Appleyard* vii (1988), *Barbados Heat* (Concord 1990), *Barbados Cool* (Concord 1991).

Archer, Martin

b. 9 March 1957, Sheffield, England. The leading light in the Sheffield free improvisation scene, it is surprising to note that Archer's origins are in rock. In 1972 he was in Blasé, a glam rock outfit that shared the Lou Reed/Roxy Music ethos. When punk hit in 1977 he was in Rissole, a jazz rock group inspired by the Soft Machine and Henry Cow (it broke up due to Archer's habit of involving non-musicians and playing saxophone solos). He was also listening to Evan Parker and Anthony Braxton, and for a few years played nothing but free improvisation. Like contemporaries Rip Rig And Panic, his next group, Bass Tone Trap, fused early 80s post-punk tribalism with free form dazzle. In 1986 he founded the Hornweb Saxophone Quartet, which impressed critics with its innovative use of a difficult format - thanks in no small part to Archer's pithy compositions. Since then, further Hornweb releases and his own *Wild Pathway Favourites* have attracted attention to Archer's specific achievement: compositions that draw on jazz and free form, 12-tone and monody, without a hint of self-consciousness. In the early 90s Archer was improvising with computers in a new version of Hornweb (no longer a quartet and no longer all saxophones). His own soprano saxophone playing - crystalline yet explosive - is also justly celebrated.

Albums: with Bass Tone Trap *Trapping* (1984), with Hornweb *Kinesis* (1986), *Wild Pathway Favourites* (1988), with Hornweb *Universe Works* (1989).

Archey, Jimmy

b. 12 October 1902, Norfolk, Virginia, USA, d. 16 November 1967. A highly accomplished trombone player, Archey held an important place in many of the best big bands of the 30s. Earlier, he had built an enviable reputation working in New York and recording with the bands of Edgar Hayes, Fletcher Henderson, James P. Johnson and Joe 'King' Oliver. For most of the 30s he was with Luis Russell, where he worked alongside

Henry 'Red' Allen. Towards the end of the decade he played in the bands of Willie Bryant, Benny Carter, Ella Fitzgerald and Coleman Hawkins, and later deputized with Cab Calloway and Duke Ellington. In the mid-40s the decline of the big bands pointed Archey towards the New Orleans Revivalist movement, and in 1950 he became leader of Bob Wilber's band. The 50s saw Archey holding long residencies with traditional bands at clubs in Boston, New York and San Francisco (the latter alongside Earl Hines), gigs that placed few demands upon such a technically-gifted player. Serious illness kept him from the scene in the early 60s, but he returned to tour the USA and Europe until his death in November 1967.

Album: with Mutt Carey, Punch Miller *Jazz New Orleans* (1947), with others *Jazz Dance* (1954, film soundtrack).

Ardley, Neil

b. 26 May 1937, Carshalton, Surrey, England. After graduating from Bristol University, Ardley studied composition and arranging under Raymond Premru and Bill Russo. In the mid-to late 60s he led the New Jazz Orchestra and throughout the 70s continued to lead his own orchestra for recording dates, concerts and occasional tours. During this time he was able to infiltrate his Gil Evans and Duke Ellington influences to a more contemporary audience. His groups included important musicians such as Harry Beckett, Ian Carr, Mike Gibbs, Don Rendell and Barbara Thompson. Ardley composed much of the music played by his orchestras but his sidemen were also encouraged to write. He has also written for television and is the author of numerous books on a wide range of subjects including music and several of the sciences. A much lower musical profile in recent years has resulted in his work being neglected, but with Mike Gibbs and Mike Westbrook he still remains an important figure in the development of 'progressive' orchestrated jazz in the 60s.

Albums: *Western Reunion* (1965), *Le Déjeuner Sur L'Herbe* (1968), *The Greek Variations* (1969), *A Symphony Of Amaranths* (1971), *Kaleidoscope Of Rainbows* (1975), *The Harmony Of The Spheres* (1978).

Argüelles, Julian

b. Julian Argüelles Clarke, 28 January 1966, Lichfield, Staffordshire, England. During his teenage, saxophonist and composer Argüelles played with various big bands in and around Birmingham, England. He also played in the National Youth Jazz Orchestra and the European Community Big Band. In 1984 he moved to London to study at Trinity College of Music, then joined Loose Tubes touring with this band throughout Europe. Argüelles also worked with Chris McGregor's Brotherhood Of Breath, touring Americans including Archie Shepp, and with his brother Steve Argüelles. He also formed his own small groups, usually trios and quartets, for UK tours of clubs and other venues. In the early 90s he toured with Kenny Wheeler's big band, the Mike Gibbs orchestra, John Scofield, Steve Swallow, Carla Bley, Tommy Smith, John Taylor and others. During this period he recorded with most of the foregoing artists and also released *Phaedrus*

under his own name. A gifted musician, adept on several members of the saxophone family, Argüelles plays in a distinctive style which is fully attuned to recent developments on jazz but which also displays a thorough understanding of the music's heritage, qualities which also appear in his compositions.
Albums: with Loose Tubes *Delightful Precipice* (1986), with Brotherhood Of Breath *Country Cooking* (1990), *Steve Argüelles* (1990), *Phaedrus* (Ah-Um 1991).

Argüelles, Steve

b. Stephen Argüelles Clarke, 16 November 1963, Crowborough, Sussex, England. Raised in Birmingham, Argüelles began playing drums at school. He soon turned to jazz, playing in a rehearsal band with the Midland Youth Jazz Orchestra and accompanying visiting jazzmen. After leaving school he moved to London where he played with the National Jazz Youth Orchestra. He then became deeply involved in the contemporary jazz scene and was a founder member of Loose Tubes. Continuously active, Argüelles has become one of the most accomplished and in-demand drummers in the UK. He has worked with jazzmen as diverse as George Coleman, Kenny Wheeler, Lee Konitz, Charlie Mariano, John Taylor, Hugh Masakela, Chris McGregor, Dudu Pukwana and Django Bates. With Bates he formed Human Chain and with his brother, Julian Argüelles, he formed a band known as Argüelles. This last named group features music that happily mixes folk, country, a touch of Cajun and other exotica with hard bop. Through his broad repertoire which includes a great many of his own compositions, Argüelles has swiftly developed into one of the most original and inventive drummers in contemporary music.
Albums: *Human Chain* (1986), with Loose Tubes *Open Letter* (1987), with Steve Lacy *Image* (1987), with Human Chain *Cashin' In* (1988), with Dudu Pukwana *Cosmics Chapter 90* (1990), *Steve Argüelles* (Ah-Um 1990), *Blue Moon In A Function Room* (1990), with John Taylor *Blue Grass* (1992), with Jorrit Dykstra, Mischa Kool *Dykstra, Argüelles, Kool* (1992).

Armstrong, Lillian

b. Lillian Hardin, 3 February 1898, Memphis, Tennessee, USA, d. 27 August 1971, Chicago, Illinois, USA. A classically-trained pianist, Hardin worked extensively in Chicago in the 20s, becoming highly popular, both as a solo performer and also playing with the bands of Sugar Johnny, Freddie Keppard and Joe 'King' Oliver. It was while she was with Oliver that she met and married the band's newest recruit, Louis Armstrong. Aware of her new husband's massive talent, and being hugely ambitious for him, she persuaded Louis to start his own band, and was herself a crucial presence in his classic Hot Five and Hot Seven groups. Personality clashes later made their marriage untenable and they were divorced. Lillian Armstrong's subsequent career found her leading bands for club work and on numerous radio and recording dates. From the 50s onwards she worked mostly as a solo pianist and singer, usually in Chicago, although she sometimes played at festivals in the USA and

Europe, where she also appeared in clubs. An occasional composer, one of her songs, 'Just For A Thrill', was recorded in the 50s by Ray Charles. She died in 1971 while taking part in a memorial concert for Louis, who had died a few weeks earlier.
Albums: *Satchmo And Me* (c.1960), *Lil Armstrong* (1961). Compilations: *Louis Armstrong Hot Five/Hot Seven* (1926-27), *Born To Swing* (1936-37) (1989), *Harlem On A Saturday Night* (1936-38), *The Swing Orchestra* (1936-40).

Armstrong, Louis 'Satchmo'

b. 4 August 1901, New Orleans, Louisiana, USA, d. 6 July 1971. It is impossible to overstate Armstrong's importance in jazz. He was one of the most influential artists in the music's history. He was also more than just a jazz musician, he was an enormously popular entertainer (a facet which some critics frowned upon) and although other black jazz men and women would eventually be welcomed in the upper echelons of white society, Armstrong was one of the first. He certainly found his way into millions of hearts otherwise closed to his kind. Had Armstrong been born white and privileged, his achievement would have been extraordinary; that he was born black and in desperately deprived circumstances makes his success almost miraculous. Armstrong achieved this astonishing breakthrough largely by the sheer force of his personality.
Louis Armstrong was born and raised in and around the notorious Storyville district of New Orleans. His exact date of birth is unknown although for many years he claimed it to be 4 July 1900, a date which was both patriotic and easy to remember and, as some chroniclers have suggested, might have exempted him from army service. Run-down apartment buildings, many of them converted to occasional use as brothels, honky-tonks, dance halls and even churches, were his surroundings as he grew up with his mother and younger sister (his father having abandoned the family at the time of Louis' birth). His childhood combined being free to run the streets with obligations towards his family, who needed him to earn money. His formal education was severely restricted but he was a bright child and swiftly accumulated the kind of wisdom needed for survival; long before the term existed, Louis Armstrong was 'streetwise'. From the first he learned how to hustle for money and it was a lesson he never forgot. Even late in life, when he was rich and famous, he would still regard his career as a 'hustle'. As a child, apart from regular work, among the means he had of earning money was singing at street corners in a semi-formal group. Armstrong's life underwent a dramatic change when, still in his early teens, he was sent to the Colored Waifs Home. The popularly supposed reason for this incarceration, encouraged by Armstrong's assisted autobiography, was that, in a fit of youthful exuberance he had celebrated New Year's Eve (either 1912 or 1913) by firing off a borrowed pistol in the street. Whatever the reason, the period he spent in the home changed his life. Given the opportunity to play in the home's band, first as a singer, then as a percussionist, then a bugler and finally as a cornetist, Armstrong found his metier. From the first, he displayed a remarkable affinity for music, and quickly achieved an enviable level of competence not only at playing the cornet but

also in understanding harmony. Released from the home after a couple of years, it was some time before Armstrong could afford to buy an instrument of his own but he continued to advance his playing ability, borrowing a cornet whenever he could and playing with any band that would hire him. He was, of course, some years away from earning his living through music but took playing jobs in order to supplement earnings from manual work, mainly delivering coal with a horse and cart. Through his late teens, Armstrong played in many of the countless bands which made their home in New Orleans (not all of which could be thought of as jazz groups), gradually working his way upwards until he was in demand for engagements with some of the city's best bands. The fact that Armstrong's introduction to music came through the home's band is significant in that he was inducted into a musical tradition different to that which was currently developing into the newly emergent style known as jazz. The Waif's Home band played formal brass band music which placed certain demands upon musicians, not least of which were precision and an ornate bravura style. When Armstrong put this concept of music to work with the ideals of jazz, it resulted in a much more flamboyant and personalized musical form than the ensemble playing of the new New Orleans jazz bands. Not surprisingly, this precocious young cornet player attracted the attention of the city's jazz masters, one of whom, Joe 'King' Oliver, was sufficiently impressed to become his musical coach and occasional employer. By the time that Armstrong came under Oliver's wing, around 1917, the older man was generally regarded as the best cornetist in New Orleans and few challenged his being named the King.

Already displaying signs of great ambition, Armstrong knew that he needed the kind of advancement and kudos King Oliver could offer, even though Oliver's style of playing was rather simplistic and close to that of other early New Orleans cornetists, such as near-contemporaries Freddie Keppard and Buddy Petit. Much more important to Armstrong's career than musical tuition was the fact that his association with Oliver opened many doors that might otherwise have remained closed. Of special importance was the fact that through Oliver the younger man would be given the chance to take his talent out of the constrictions of one city and into the wide world beyond the bayous of Louisiana. In 1919 Oliver had been invited to take a band to Chicago (and before leaving recommended his young protégé as his replacement with Kid Ory), and by 1922 his was the most popular ensemble in the Windy City. Back in New Orleans, Armstrong's star continued to rise even though he declined to stay with Ory when the latter was invited to take his band to Los Angeles. Armstrong, chronically shy, preferred to stay in the place that he knew; but when Oliver sent word for him to come to Chicago, he went. The reason he overcame his earlier reluctance to travel was in part his ambition and also the fact that he trusted Oliver and felt that so long as he was with him Chicago would not be too bad a place to live and work. From the moment of Armstrong's arrival in Chicago the local musical scene was tipped onto its ear; musicians raved about the duets of the King and the young

pretender and if the lay members of the audience did not know what exactly it was that they were hearing they certainly knew that it was something special.

For two years Oliver and Armstrong made musical history and, had it not been for the piano player in the band, they might well have continued doing so for many more years. The piano player was Lillian Hardin, who took a special interest in the young cornetist and became the second major influence in his life. By 1924 Armstrong and Hardin were married and her influence had prompted him to quit Oliver's band and soon afterwards to head for New York. In New York, Armstrong joined Fletcher Henderson's orchestra, bringing to that band a quality of solo playing far exceeding anything the city had heard thus far in jazz. His musical ideas, some of which were harmonies he and Oliver had developed, were also a spur to the writing of Henderson's staff arranger, Don Redman. Armstrong stayed with Henderson for a little over a year, returning to Chicago in 1925 at his wife's behest to star as the World's Greatest Trumpeter with her band. Over the next two or three years he recorded extensively, including the first of the famous Hot Five and Hot Seven sessions and as accompanist to the best of the blues singers, among them Bessie Smith, Clara Smith and Trixie Smith. He worked ceaselessly, in 1926 doubling with the orchestras of Carroll Dickerson and Erskine Tate, and becoming, briefly, a club owner with two of his closest musical companions, Earl Hines and Zutty Singleton. By the end of the decade Armstrong was in demand across the country, playing important engagements in Chicago, New York, Washington DC, Los Angeles (but not New Orleans, a city to which he would hardly ever return).

By the 30s, Armstrong had forsaken the cornet for the trumpet. He frequently worked with name bands yet equally often travelled alone, fronting whichever house band was available at his destination. He worked and recorded in Los Angeles with Les Hite's band (in which the drummer was Lionel Hampton), and in New York with Chick Webb. In 1932, and 1933 he made his first visits to Europe, playing to largely ecstatic audiences, although some, accustomed only to hearing him on record, found his stage mannerisms - the mugging and clowning, to say nothing of the sweating - rather difficult to accommodate. From 1935 onwards Armstrong fronted the Luis Russell orchestra, eclipsing the remarkable talents of the band's leading trumpeter, Henry 'Red' Allen. In 1938 Louis and Lillian were divorced and he married Alpha Smith. However, by 1942 he had married again, to Lucille Wilson, who survived him. In some respects, the swing era passed Louis Armstrong by, leading some observers to suggest that his career was on a downward slide from that point on. Certainly, the big band Armstrong fronted in the 30s was generally inferior to many of its competitors, but his playing was always at least as strong as that of any of the other virtuoso instrumentalist leaders of the era. His musical style, however, was a little out of step with public demand, and by the early 40s he was out of vogue. Since 1935 Armstrong's career had been in the hands of Joe Glaser, a tough-talking, hard-nosed extrovert whom people either loved or hated. Ruthless in his determination to make his clients rich and famous, Glaser promoted Armstrong intensively. When the big band showed signs of flagging, Glaser fired everyone and then hired younger, more aggressive (if not always musically appropriate) people to back his star client. When this failed to work out, Glaser took a cue from an engagement at New York's Town Hall at which Armstrong fronted a small band to great acclaim. Glaser set out to form a new band that would be made up of stars and which he planned to market under the name, Louis Armstrong And His All Stars. It proved to be a perfect format for Armstrong and it remained the setting for his music for the rest of his life - even though changes in personnel gradually made a nonsense of the band's hyperbolic title.

With the All Stars, Armstrong began a relentless succession of world tours with barely a night off, occasionally playing clubs and festivals but most often filling concert halls with adoring crowds. The first All Stars included Jack Teagarden, Barney Bigard, Earl Hines and Big Sid Catlett; replacements in the early years included Trummy Young, Edmond Hall, Billy Kyle and Cozy Cole. Later substitutes, when standards slipped, included Russell Moore, Joe Darensbourg, and Barrett Deems. Regulars for many years were bassist Arvell Shaw and singer Velma Middleton. The format and content of the All Stars shows (copied to dire and detrimental effect by numerous bands in the traditional jazz boom of the 50s and 60s) were predictable, with solos being repeated night after night, often note for note. This helped to fuel the contention that Armstrong was past his best. In fact, some of the All Stars' recordings, even those made with the lesser bands, show that this was not the case. The earliest All Stars are excitingly presented on *Satchmo At Symphony Hall* and *New Orleans Nights*, while the later bands produced some classic performances on *Louis Armstrong Plays W.C. Handy* and *Satch Plays Fats*. On all these recordings Armstrong's own playing is outstanding. But time necessarily took its toll and eventually even Armstrong's powerful lip weakened. It was then that another facet of his great talent came into its own. Apparent to any who cared to hear it since the 20s, Armstrong was a remarkable singer. By almost any standards but those of the jazz world, his voice was beyond redemption, but through jazz it became recognized for what it was: a perfect instrument for jazz singing. Armstrong's throaty voice, his lazy-sounding delivery, his perfect timing and effortlessly immaculate rhythmic presentation, brought to songs of all kinds a remarkable sense of rightness. Perfect examples of this form were the riotous '(I Want) A Butter And Egg Man' through such soulfully moving lyrics as '(What Did I Do To Be So) Black And Blue', 'Do You Know What It Means To Miss New Orleans', and countless superb renditions of the blues. He added comic absurdities to 'Baby, It's Cold Outside' and over-sentimentality to 'It's A Wonderful World', which in 1968 gave him a UK number 1 hit. He added texture and warmth and a rare measure of understanding often far exceeding anything that had been put there by the songs' writers. Additionally, he was one of the first performers to sing scat (the improvisation of wordless vocal sounds in place of the formal lyrics), and certainly the first to do so with skill and intelligence and not through mere chance (although he always claimed that he began scatting when the sheet music for 'Heebie Jeebies' fell on the floor during a 1926 recording session and he had to improvise the words). It was in his late years, as a singer and entertainer rather than as a trumpet star, that Armstrong became a world figure, known by name, sight and sound to tens of millions of people of all nationalities and creeds who also loved him in a way that the urchin kid from the wrong side of the tracks in turn-of-the-century New Orleans could never have imagined.

Armstrong's world status caused him some problems with other black Americans, many of whom believed he should have done more for his fellow blacks. He was openly criticized for the manner in which he behaved, whether on stage or off, some accusing him of being an Uncle Tom and thus pandering to stereotypical expectations of behaviour. Certainly, he was no militant, although he did explode briefly in a fit of anger when interviewed at the time of the Civil Rights protests over events in Little Rock in 1958. What his critics overlooked was that, by the time of Little Rock, Armstrong was already 60 years old, and when the Civil Rights movement hit its full stride he was past the age at which most of his contemporaries were slipping contentedly into retirement. To expect a man of this age to wholeheartedly embrace the Civil Rights movement, having been born and raised in conditions even fellow blacks of one or two generations later could scarcely comprehend, was simply asking too much. For almost 50 years he had been an entertainer - he would probably have preferred and used the term 'hustler' - and he was not about to change. Louis Armstrong toured on until almost the very end, recovering from at least one heart attack (news reports tended to be very cagey about his illnesses - doubtless Joe Glaser saw to that). He died in his sleep at his New York home on 6 July 1971. With only a handful of exceptions, most trumpet players who came after Armstrong owe some debt to his pioneering stylistic developments. By the early 40s, the date chosen by many as marking the first decline in Armstrong's importance and ability, jazz style was undergoing major changes. Brought about largely by the work of Charlie Parker and his musical collaborators, chief among whom was trumpeter Dizzy Gillespie, jazz trumpet style changed and the Armstrong style no longer had immediate currency. But his influence was only sidetracked; it never completely disappeared, and in the post-bop era the qualities of technical proficiency and dazzling technique that he brought to jazz were once again appreciated for the remarkable achievements they were. In the early 20s Louis Armstrong had become a major influence on jazz musicians and jazz music; he altered the way musicians thought about their instruments and the way that they played them. There have been many virtuoso performers in jazz since Armstrong first came onto the scene, but nobody has matched his virtuosity nor displayed a comparable level of commitment to jazz, a feeling for the blues, or such simple and highly communicable *joie de vivre*. Louis Armstrong was unique. The music world is fortunate to have received his outstanding contribution.

Selected albums: *New Orleans* (1946, film soundtrack), *Town*

Hall Concert Plus (1947), *Carnegie Hall Concert With Edmond Hall's Sextet* (1947), *This Is Jazz* (1947), *A Song Is Born* (1947, film soundtrack), *Satchmo At Symphony Hall* (1947), *Louis Armstrong And His All Stars At Nice* (1948), *Louis Armstrong And His All Stars Live At Ciro's, Philadelphia* (1948), *Louis Armstrong And His All Stars Live At The Empire Room, Los Angeles* (1948), *Louis Armstrong And His All Stars Live At The Clique Club Vols 1-5* (1948-49), *Louis Armstrong At The Eddie Condon Floor Show* (1949), *Chicago Concert* (1956), *New Orleans Nights* (1950-54), *Louis Armstrong And His All Stars Live At Pasadena* i (1951), *The Greatest Concert* (1951), *Glory Alley* (1952, film soundtrack), *Louis Armstrong And His All Stars In Concert* (1953), *Louis Armstrong And His All Stars In Yokohama* (1953), *Louis Armstrong And His All Stars Live At The Crescendo Club, Los Angeles* (1955), *Louis Armstrong Plays W.C. Handy* (1954), *Satch Plays Fats* (1955), *Ambassador Satch* (1955), *Satchmo The Great* (1956, film soundtrack), *Louis Armstrong And His All Stars Live At Pasadena* ii (1956), *Satchmo: A Musical Autobiography* (1956-57), with Ella Fitzgerald *Ella And Louis* (1957), with Fitzgerald *Porgy And Bess* (1957), with Fitzgerald *Ella And Louis Again* (1957), *Louis Under The Stars* (1957), *Louis Armstrong Meets Oscar Peterson* (1957), *The Five Pennies* (1958, film soundtrack), *Louis And The Good Book* (1958), *Louis Armstrong And The Dukes Of Dixieland* i (1959), *Louis Armstrong And The Dukes Of Dixieland: The Definitive Album/Sweetheart* (1959), *Snake Rag* (1959), *Louis Armstrong And The Dukes Of Dixieland* ii (1960), with Bing Crosby *Muskrat Ramble* (1960), *The Real Ambassador* (1961), *Louis Armstrong And Duke Ellington: The Great Reunion* (1961), *Louis Armstrong And Duke Ellington: Together Again* (1961), *Satchmo Story* (1962), *Louis Armstrong And His All Stars Live At Juan-Les-Pins* (1967), *What A Wonderful World* (1967), *Disney Songs The Satchmo Way* (1968), *Louis 'Country & Western' Armstrong* (1970). Compilations: *King Oliver's Creole Jazz Band* (1923), *Louis Armstrong & Sidney Bechet* (1924-25), *Louis Armstrong And The Fletcher Henderson Orchestra* (1924-26), *The Hot Fives And Hot Sevens Vols 1-4* (1925-28), *His Greatest Years Vol. 1-4* (1925-28), *Louis Armstrong And The Blues Singers* (1925-29), *The Louis Armstrong Legend Vols 1-4* (1925-29), *Louis Armstrong VSOP Vols 1-8* (1925-32), *Satchmo Style* (1929-30), *Louis In Los Angeles* (1930-31), *Young Louis Armstrong* (1930-33), *Louis Armstrong European Tour* (1933-34), *Louis Sings The Blues* (1933-47), *Louis Armstrong And His Orchestra* (1935-41), *Swing That Music* (1935-44), *The Mills Brothers And Louis Armstrong* (1937-40), *Midnight At V-Disc* (1944), *The California Concerts* (1992, rec 1951 & 1955), with Fletcher Henderson *Complete 1924 - 1925* (1993), *Classics 1940-42* (1993), *Gold Collection* (1993), *The Pure Genius Of* (1994), *The Ultimate Collection* (RCA 1994).

Further reading: *Satchmo: My Life In New Orleans*, Louis Armstrong. *Salute To Satchmo*, Max Jones, John Chilton and Leonard Feather. *Louis Armstrong: An American Genius*, James Lincoln Collier. *Satchmo*, Gary Giddins.

Arodin, Sidney

b. Sidney Arnondrin, 29 March 1901, Westwego, Louisiana, USA, d. 6 February 1948. Arodin began playing clarinet in his early teens and was soon working professionally. In the early 20s he moved to New York and joined the Original New Orleans Jazz Band, then returned to the south to play in Texas and Louisiana. Arodin made records with Johnny Miller, Wingy Manone and the band co-led by Lee Collins and Davey Jones and also played with Louis Prima and other popular bands of the late 20s and 30s. In 1930 Arodin wrote the music for 'Lazy River' which, with verse and lyrics by Hoagy Carmichael, became a staple in the repertoire of Louis Armstrong. From the early 40s Arodin was plagued with poor health. Admired by his fellow musicians, Arodin was a melodic and interesting clarinettist.

Compilations: with Johnny Miller *New Orleans Stomp* (1928), with Louis Prima *Swing Me With Rhythm* (1934/5 recordings), *New Orleans Rhythm Kings Featuring Joe 'Wingy' Manone* (1934/5), *Wingy Manone Vol. 3* (1935).

Art Ensemble Of Chicago

Founded in 1968 by trumpeter Lester Bowie, saxophonists Roscoe Mitchell and Joseph Jarman and bassist Malachi Favors, the AEC grew out of a number of projects connected with the AACM. Most directly it evolved from the Roscoe Mitchell Quartet. Mitchell has said: 'It was my band, but I couldn't afford to pay those guys what they deserved, so everybody was shouldering an equal amount of responsibility. We became a co-operative unit in order to remain committed to one another and in order to survive.' In the early days there was no regular drummer, and all of the members of the AEC would double on percussion. In 1969, after trying out various candidates, including William Howell and Phillip Wilson, the band met Famoudou Don Moye in Paris and he became the permanent occupant of the drum chair, but all five continued to use an array of 'little instruments' such as whistles, bells, cooking utensils or indeed any object that could be shaken, blown, strummed or beaten rhythmically. Mitchell and Jarman between them play the full range of saxophones as well as clarinets, flutes and the oboe, and represent the two poles of the ensemble's craft: Jarman brings the bulk of the theatrical impulse, Mitchell is the musical structuralist. The music is as all-embracing as the instrumentation: basically free-form jazz, a performance will allude to New Orleans, blues, Africa, rock 'n' roll, vaudeville or anything that takes their fancy, and the ensemble is capable of playing bop as hard as you like. Receiving little recognition at home, the band went to Paris in 1969 where they recorded enough material for about 14 albums inside two years, including a couple which featured singer Fontella Bass. The title track of one of their French recordings, 'The Spiritual', not only charts the development of black music from early slavery to the 60s but symbolizes the progress of black people in the USA. This consciousness of social and political issues is typical of the AACM circle, and the AEC adds to it considerable theatricality. Jarman once appeared on stage wearing only his saxophone sling. Bowie, whether with the ensemble or his own group, Brass Fantasy, habitually affects a doctor's white coat, whilst the others paint their faces and bodies and wear African styles. This dramatizing of the spirit of a culture is no less serious because of the strong element of puckish parody in their playing, which the AEC prefers to term Great Black Music rather than jazz. The Paris sessions show the ensemble defining and setting the agenda for their music: that agenda is now well settled - and has been documented on a variety of record labels, including Atlantic, ECM, DIW and the group's own AECO company - but they can still surprise and delight. Recently, however, they have taken to recording with other musicians and ensembles (including Lester Bowie's Brass Fantasy, Cecil Taylor and a South African choir) in an apparent attempt to find a fresh menu. In addition, to flesh out our picture of them, *Eda Wobu*, a Parisian radio session from just before Don Moye joined, was released in 1991, on which Bowie is particularly impressive.

Selected albums: *A Jackson In Your House* (Affinity 1969), *The Spiritual* (1969), *Tutankhamun* (1969), *People In Sorrow* (1969), *Message To Our Folks* (1969), *Rees And The Smooth Ones* (1969), *Certain Blacks* (1970), *Go Home* (1970), *Chi Congo* (1970), *Les Stances A Sophie* (1970), *With Fontella Bass* (1970), *Live Part I* (1970), *Live Part 2* (1970), *Phase One* (1971), *Live At Mandel Hall* (1972), *Bap Tizum* (1973), *Fanfare For The Warriors* (1974), *Kabalaba* (1974), *Nice Guys* (ECM 1978), *Full Force* (ECM 1980), *Live In Berlin* (West Wind 1980), *Urban Bushmen* (ECM 1980), *Among The People* (1981), *The Third Decade* (ECM 1985), *Live In Japan* (1985), *Vol I Ancient To The Future* (DIW 1987), *Complete Live In Japan* (1988, rec. 1984), *The Alternate Express* (DIW 1989), *Naked* (DIW 1989, rec. 1985-6), with Brass Fantasy *Live At The 6th Tokyo Music Joy '90* (DIW 1990), *Amabutho Male Chorus Art Ensemble Of Soweto* (DIW 1990), *Eda Wobu* (JMY 1991, rec. 1969), as Art Ensemble Of Soweto *America/South Africa* (1991, rec. 1989-90), with Cecil Taylor *Vol II Thelonious Sphere Monk* (DIW 1991), *Dreaming Of The Masters Suite* (DIW 1991).

Ashby, Dorothy

b. 6 August 1932, Detroit, Michigan, USA. Born into a musical family (her father played jazz guitar) Ashby studied music at high school, where a fellow student was Donald Byrd. After graduation, she played piano and harp with several small groups, often as leader. She recorded with Richard Davis, Jimmy Cobb, Frank Wess and others in the late 50s and early 60s. Also in the early 60s she had her own radio show in her home town. Her husband, drummer John Ashby, played in her early trios and was founder of a theatre company, the Ashby Players of Detroit, for which his wife wrote scores. After relocating to the west coast she played in studio orchestras, sometimes appearing on albums featuring leading jazz musicians. One of very few harpists to play jazz convincingly, Ashby is perhaps the only such instrumentalist to successfully adapt the instrument to accommodate the language of bop.

Albums: *Jazz Harpist* (1957), *Hip Harp* (1958), *In A Minor Groove* (1958), *Soft Winds: The Swinging Harp Of Dorothy Ashby* (1961), *Dorothy Ashby Plays For The Beautiful People* (1961), *Afro-Harping* (c.1961), *The Fantastic Jazz Harp Of Dorothy Ashby* (1965), *Soul Vibrations* (1968), *The Rubaiyat Of Dorothy Ashby* (1969), *Dorothy's Harp* (1969). Compilations: *The Best Of Dorothy Ashby* (c.60s), *Django - Misty* (Emarcy 1985), *Jazz Harpist* (Savoy 1992).

Ashby, Harold

b. 27 March 1925, Kansas City, Missouri, USA. After taking up the tenor saxophone as a child, Ashby played in territory bands in the mid-west. In the early 50s he settled in Chicago, playing in various bands, often in an R&B or strongly blues-based style. In the late 50s he moved to New York, working with Mercer Ellington and also occasionally with Duke Ellington. Ashby made records during the late 50s and early 60s, often with ex-Ellingtonians such as Lawrence Brown and Johnny Hodges, and in 1968 became a permanent member of the Ellington orchestra. After Ellington's death he played with Mercer Ellington, Benny Goodman and others and also began playing concerts and festivals around the world, usually as a single. A striking player, moulded in the tradition of Ben Webster but with a distinctive hard-edged tone, Ashby's playing deserves the international attention it has begun to attract in the late 80s and early 90s.

Albums: *Born To Swing* (1959), with Lawrence Brown *Inspired Abandon* (1965), *Duke Ellington's 70th Birthday Concert* (1969), with Ellington *Togo Brava Suite* (1971), with Ellington *Eastbourne Performance* (1973), *Scufflin'* (1978), *The Viking* (Gemini 1988), *On The Sunny Side Of The Street* (Timeless 1992), *I'm Old Fashioned* (Stash 1992), *What Am I Here For?* (Criss Cross 1993).

Ashby, Irving

b. 29 December 1920, Somerville, Massachusetts, USA. Ashby first came to prominence in 1947 as a member of Nat 'King' Cole's popular trio. He had previously worked with Lionel Hampton, where his rock-solid rhythmic playing was often overlooked in the excitement that Hampton's band generated. After leaving Cole, Ashby gigged mainly on the west coast, then in the early 50s joined Oscar Peterson's trio. From the 60s onwards he worked mostly outside music, but continued to play occasionally when the opportunity arose.

Album: *Memories* (c.1976). Compilation: with Nat 'King' Cole *Twenty Dynamic Fingers* (1949 recordings).

Ashton, Bill

b. 6 December 1936, Blackpool, Lancashire, England. While studying at Oxford University in the late 50s Ashton played saxophone in jazz bands, some of which he also led. By the early 60s he was teaching in London, playing occasionally at various jazz clubs. In the mid-60s, prompted by the prodigious musical talent of a student, Frank Ricotti, at an ill-equipped London school, Ashton conceived the idea of a schools orchestra. His concept was that the orchestra would allow unfledged musicians to develop their craft playing jazz and other forms of contemporary popular music. His proposals met with general indifference within the education system, and in some instances with downright hostility and sabotage. Ashton persisted, however, and his London Schools Jazz Orchestra survived, becoming the London Youth Jazz Orchestra and, eventually, the National Youth Jazz Orchestra. In 1974 NYJO became a fully professional organization and four years later Ashton was awarded the MBE for his services to youth and music, an award he sees as an honour for the organization rather than his alone. He continues to direct the orchestra, writing arrangements, original music, and song lyrics. Tireless in his promotion of his brainchild, Ashton single-handedly produces and edits NYJO's house magazine, most of which he also writes.

Asmussen, Svend

b. 28 February 1916, Copenhagen, Denmark. Asmussen began playing violin as a small child. A superbly accomplished musician, he first played professionally in 1933. In the mid-30s he played with Kai Ewens and other Danish musicians, recording and broadcasting on the radio. He also played with visiting American stars, including Fats Waller. During World War II he continued to work in show business. In the late 40s and early 50s much of his recorded output was of currently popular American and British songs, although there were always jazz sides interspersed amongst them. In the early 60s he worked with Alice Babs, Ulrik Neumann and Duke Ellington, and also with John Lewis. Despite the earlier interest of Benny Goodman, it was the Lewis recording date that drew widespread attention to his talents and in later years he worked with many other jazz artists, including Stéphane Grappelli, Kenny Drew, Niels-Henning Ørsted Pedersen, Lionel Hampton and Bucky Pizzarelli. Throughout the 70s and 80s he continued to record and appear at international festivals and was still active on the scene into the 90s.

Albums: *Rhythm Is Our Business* (1955), *Danish Imports* (1959), *Svend Asmussen* i (1961), *Svend Asmussen* ii (1961), *European Encounter: John Lewis And Svend Asmussen* (1962), with Duke Ellington *Jazz Violin Session* (1963), with Stéphane Grappelli *Violin Summit* (1966), *Svend Asmussen Sextet* (1966), *Svend Asmussen* iii (1968), *Amazing Strings* (1974), *Prize Winners* (1978), with Lionel Hampton *As Time Goes By* (1978), *June Night* (1983), *String Swing* (1983), *Svend Asmussen Live At Slukafter* (1984), with Grappelli *Two Of A Kind* (Storyville 1989).

Auld, Georgie

b. John Altwerger, 19 May 1919, Toronto, Canada, d. 7 January 1990. Originally an alto saxophonist, Auld found work in the early 30s in New York, where his family had recently moved. In 1936 he switched to tenor saxophone under the influence of Coleman Hawkins and, after leading a small group, joined the big band of Bunny Berigan. In 1939, after two years with Berigan, he was hired by Artie Shaw on the recommendation of Billie Holiday. He persuaded Shaw to recruit Buddy Rich, then, after the Shaw band folded, he worked briefly for Jan Savitt, Benny Goodman and Shaw again, before

forming his own modern-sounding big band in 1943. The latter included Serge Chaloff, Erroll Garner, Dizzy Gillespie and Stan Levey. After 1946 Auld worked mostly as leader of bop-oriented small groups but with occasional stints in big bands, including those of Billy Eckstine and Goodman, and he also worked with Count Basie's 1950 small band. Auld tried his hand at acting (on Broadway), and played in film and television studios, mainly in Los Angeles. Despite suffering from cancer, he toured extensively, and in the 70s proved especially popular in Japan. In 1977 he coached and ghosted for Robert De Niro in the film *New York, New York*, in which he also appeared. In the 80s Auld worked only infrequently, visiting Japan and Europe, where he appeared at the 1984 North Sea Jazz Festival.

Selected albums: *Homage* (1959), *Georgie Auld Plays The Winners* (1963), *One For The Losers* (1965). Compilations: *The Indispensable Artie Shaw Vol. 1/2* (1938), with Benny Goodman *Solo Flight* (1940/1), *Charlie Christian With The Benny Goodman Sextet And Orchestra* (1940/1), *Jump, Georgie, Jump* (1944), *By George* (1949), *Canyon Passage* (Musicraft 1988), *Georgie Porgie* (Musicraft 1988).

Austin, Cuba

b. c.1906, Charleston, West Virginia, USA, d. 60s. Starting out as a dancer, Austin turned to drums and in 1926 joined McKinney's Cotton Pickers when McKinney, himself a drummer, decided to concentrate on the full-time management of the band. In 1931 the band split into several new groups, one of which, billed as 'the Original Cotton Pickers', played under Austin's leadership. In 1934 this band folded and thereafter Austin worked outside music in Baltimore, although he continued to play part-time in local bands.

Compilation: *McKinney's Cotton Pickers* (1928-29).

Austin, Sil

b. Sylvestor Austin, 17 September 1929, Dunnellon, Florida, USA. A quintessential R&B tenor saxophone 'honker', Austin started his career by winning a talent contest at Harlem's Apollo theatre. He learned his craft in the big bands of Roy Eldridge and Cootie Williams. In 1956 he reached the Top 20 with 'Slow Walk' and had later hits with 'Balin' Wire', 'Birthday Party' and 'Shufflin' Home', irresistible slices of high energy R&B. Later on, Austin recorded for Shelby Singleton's SSS label.

Album: *Honey Sax* (1974).

Autrey, Herman

b. 4 December 1904, Evergreen, Alabama, USA, d. 14 June 1980. Born into a musical family (his father and two brothers were musicians) Autrey first played alto horn before switching to trumpet. As a teenager he played in bands in and around Pittsburgh, Pennsylvania, then toured before settling in Florida. After playing in and leading bands he began working his way northwards, first to Washington, D.C., then to Philadelphia and finally to New York, where he arrived in 1933. He played in the band led by Charlie 'Fess' Johnson, then became a regular associate of Fats Waller. He recorded extensively with Waller but found time to gig with many other leading bands of the day, including those led by Fletcher Henderson and Claude Hopkins. In the early and mid-40s he was active as sideman and leader, playing with Stuff Smith and Una Mae Carlisle. In the middle of the decade he returned to Philadelphia where he led a band for several years. In 1954 he sustained serious injuries in a road accident but returned to playing after a layoff lasting about a year. In the 60s he was a member of the popular Saints And Sinners touring band. By the 70s he was playing less but continued to perform as a singer. A robust and energetic trumpeter, Autrey's obvious admiration for Louis Armstrong never resulted in attempts to copy. His playing on the many records he made with Waller demonstrate his youthful ability, while his performances with Saints And Sinners and other late record dates show that in his maturity he was still a capable and dramatic performer.

Albums: *Saints And Sinners In Europe* (1968), *Finger Poppin'* (1971-72). Compilations: *Fats Waller And His Rhythm* (1934-36), *The Indispensable Fats Waller Vols 3/4* (1935-36).

Ayers, Roy

b. 10 September 1940, Los Angeles, California, USA. A popular jazz vibraphonist and vocalist, Ayers reached the peak of his commercial popularity during the mid-70s and early 80s. He played piano as a child and took an interest in the vibes after meeting Lionel Hampton. In high school Ayers formed his first group, the Latin Lyrics, and in the early 60s began working professionally with flautist/saxophonist Curtis Edward Amy. Ayers' first album under his own name was *West Coast Vibes* on United Artists Records in 1964, which featured Amy. He also worked with Chico Hamilton, Hampton Hawes and Herbie Mann, with whom he first gained prominence between 1966 and 1970. He recorded three albums for Atlantic Records in the late 60s. In 1971 Ayers formed Roy Ayers Ubiquity, incorporating funk and R&B styles into his jazz. The group was signed to Polydor Records. Using a number of prominent sidemen such as Herbie Hancock, Ron Carter, Sonny Fortune, George Benson and Billy Cobham, Ubiquity's albums helped popularize the jazz/funk crossover style. The group charted with five albums and three R&B singles between 1974 and 1977, including the Top 20 disco-influenced R&B hit 'Running Away'. Ayers dropped the Ubiquity group name in 1978 and continued to have chart success with both his solo albums and singles through the late 80s The 1978 single 'Heat Of The Beat' was billed as a duet with Wayne Henderson of the Crusaders. After touring Africa, Ayers recorded *Africa, Center Of The World* with Fela Kuti in 1979. He switched to Columbia Records in 1984 but released records less frequently as the 80s came to a close. During the 90s he was under contract with Ronnie Scott's Jazz House label.

Selected albums: *West Coast Vibes* (1964), *Stoned Soul Picnic* (1968), *Daddy Bug And Friends* (1969), *Ubiquity* (1970), *He's Coming* (1971), *Live At Montreux* (1972), *Red, Black And Green* (1973), *Virgo Red* (1974), *Change Up The Groove* (1974), *A Tear To A Smile* (1975), *Mystic Voyage* (1976), *Everybody Loves*

The Sunshine (1976), *Vibrations* (1976), *Lifeline* (1977), *Starbooty* (1978), *Let's Do It* (Urban 1978), *You Send Me* (Urban 1978), *Step Into Our Life* (1978), *Fever* (Urban 1979), *No Stranger To Love* (1979), *Love Fantasy* (1980), *Prime Time* (1980), *Africa, Center Of The World* (Polydor 1981), *Feeling Good* (1982), *In The Dark* (1984), *You Might Be Surprised* (1985), *I'm The One (For Your Love Tonight)* (1987), *Drive* (Ichiban 1988), *Wake Up* (Ichiban 1989), *Easy Money: Live At Ronnie Scott's* (Essential 1990), *Rare* (Polydor 1990), *Rare Vol II* (Polydor 1990), *Vibrant - The Very Best Of* (1993), *A Shining Symbol: The Ultimate Collection* (Polydor 1993), *Searchin'* (Ronnie Scott's Jazz House 1993), *Hot* (Ronnie Scott's Jazz House 1993), *Vibrant* (Connoisseur 1993), *Get On Up, Get On Down: Best Of Vol. 2* (Polydor 1993).

Ayler, Albert

b. 13 July 1936, Cleveland, Ohio, USA, d. 25 November 1970. In common with many of the radical figures of the 60s *avant garde*, tenor and alto saxophonist Ayler paid his dues in R&B bands. He started his musical education on alto, and played in the church attended by his family. At the age of 10 he began studying at the local academy of music, continuing to do so for some seven years. During this time he was section leader in his high school orchestra. In his late teens he got a job with blues legend Little Walter Jacobs. Subsequently he formed his own R&B band but this folded and, after giving up college due to financial difficulties, he joined the army. His national service took him to Europe, where he decided to stay for a while after his discharge. His first few albums were taped either in Europe or for European labels, but his reputation was made with the recordings for the New York label ESP, which was established by Bernard Stollman particularly to promote Ayler's music. In 1966 Ayler signed with Impulse! where he continued to provoke poisonous controversy even among enthusiasts of contemporary jazz. On 25 November 1970 his body was recovered from New York City's East River. One bizarre rumour claimed that there was a bullet hole in the back of the neck. Ayler had not been seen for some 20 days before his body was discovered, and the circumstances of his death remain unclear. The theory that he had been killed by the police has been given much currency. However, he had been very depressed about the breakdown suffered by his brother, Donald Ayler, and close friends have confirmed that he had talked about taking his own life.

Until the late 50s the tendency in the development of jazz had been one of increasing harmonic complexity and sophistication. Ornette Coleman and Ayler created styles which, though neither atonal nor entirely free, re-established the primacy of melody. Ironically, the mass of the jazz public found this music less accessible than the more technically complicated work of figures like John Coltrane, Miles Davis, Gil Evans and Charles Mingus. Although Ayler cited Lester Young and Sidney Bechet as favourites, he seems to have owed something to Sonny Rollins, but one can also hear strong elements taken from New Orleans jazz, from gospel and work songs, and a number of techniques common in traditional African vocal music. It is, however, unwise to try to appreciate his music without having some regard to its spiritual dimension and to the raw emotional components. In an interview with Nat Hentoff for *Downbeat* in November 1966, Ayler and his trumpeter brother Donald advised that the way to listen to their music was 'not to focus on the notes and stuff like that. Instead, try to move your imagination toward the sound . . . you really have to play your instruments to escape from notes to sound.' The Aylers were amongst the first to reject the term jazz as redolent of Jim Crow and Uncle Tom attitudes. Standards and bop classics were still central to his repertoire, at least on record, and his articulation often sounded inadequate for the job. The cynical have suggested that this was the reason behind his predilection for dirge-like tunes, flexible, dream-like tempi and phrases that sprawl carelessly across bar-lines, but his proficiency, though often questioned, can scarcely be in doubt: his apprenticeship in school, church and army bands, and the recollections of those who heard him play in the 50s testify to his technical credentials. In any event, precision and pyrotechnics were not the point of what he was doing.

One important key to his work lies in the album of spirituals recorded for the Debut label in February 1964. Although it features some of his least inventive playing, it does provide a link between his early work with blues and mainstream modern jazz bands and the albums for ESP and Impulse! Set 'Mothers' alongside, say, 'Flee As A Bird' by the Olympia Brass Band or 'Amazing Grace' by Aretha Franklin, and Ayler slots into place in an evolutionary tradition that has its roots in Africa. In the remarkable series of albums made in 1964, with Gary Peacock and Sunny Murray buoying him up on a tide of oblique but potent rhythm, we can hear, not the strongly-pulsed aspects of African music, but rather its melody-stretching and elaborate tonal and timbral play. Ayler's attitude to rhythm made even his early, inadequately-realised recordings seem dangerous. At the time much attention was focused on his sound, a strident braying with an enormously exaggerated vibrato that could make his lines seem deceptively maudlin. Such tonal distortions had always been present in the playing of musicians on the borders of jazz, blues and R&B, such as Arnett Cobb and Jay McNeely, and vibrati as wide as the Mississippi delta were common with New Orleans brass band saxophonists like Emmanuel Paul and, indeed, Bechet. What alarmed people was not the sound itself, but Ayler's cavalier attitude to the beat and the way he used squeals, honks, cries and moans as an integral part of his style instead of reserving them for climactic moments. He was, though, first and foremost a melodist. He told Hentoff 'I like to play something that people can hum . . . songs like I used to sing when I was real small. From simple melody to complicated textures to simplicity again . . .' a process that is clearly at work in all his recordings.

It was not until 1964 that Ayler was able to record with musicians who really understood what was going on. His first recordings were done in Stockholm in October 1962 with a willing but baffled bassist and drummer. With Peacock or Henry Grimes on bass, Murray on drums and Don Cherry's bright and agile pocket-trumpet it was now possible to hear Ayler's music properly realized. Gone were the rather ungainly refashionings of standards, to be replaced by Ayler compositions such as 'Mothers', 'Witches And Devils' and the ubiquitous 'Ghosts'. His broad and incantatory lines have a strange grace. In the second half of the 60s Ayler began using two bassists and, in the group that recorded the definitive *In Greenwich Village*, a violinist and cellist. With brother Donald replacing Cherry, and with one of the bassists concentrating on arco work, the music became a closely-woven pattern of keening lines, developing a harder, shriller feel. These intense sides baptized his contract with Impulse! It was with this label that he made what were paradoxically his least 'way out' but most controversial albums. Even at his most abstract Ayler had been deeply rooted in spirituals and blues, but *Music Is The Healing Force Of The Universe* and *New Grass* found him involved in an uncomfortable species of pedestrian soul/funk/jazz fusion. There is some raunchy and direct sax playing, but these gems are marred by their tacky setting.

Ayler spawned fewer imitators than John Coltrane (who admitted to being influenced by Ayler) or even Coleman, but there are those - notably Matthias Schubert - who overtly base their playing on his style. Tommy Smith's first album leaned intriguingly on his example, David Murray has paid musical tribute to him, and his spirit is often heard in the work of Jan Kopinski in the otherwise harmolodics-based environment of Pinski Zoo. Ayler's ideas have been so thoroughly absorbed into the contemporary mainstream that his own work may no longer seem so startling. His effect at the time may be gauged by the fact that BBC television, after bringing Ayler's quintet to Britain especially to record two programmes, were so alarmed by the music that the tapes were locked away and surreptitiously wiped without ever being shown.

Albums: *Something Different!* (1963, reissued as *The First Recordings*), *My Name Is Albert Ayler* (1963, reissued as *Free Jazz*), *Spirits* (1964, reissued as *Witches And Devils*), *Spiritual Unity* (1964), *Ghosts* (1965, reissued as *Vibrations*), *Bells* (1965), *Spirits Rejoice* (1965), *New York Eye And Ear Control* (1966, rec. 1964), *In Greenwich Village* (Impulse 1967), *Love Cry* (1968), *New Grass* (1969), *Music Is The Healing Force Of The Universe* (1970), *The Last Album* (1971, rec. 1969), *Albert Ayler Vols. 1 &2* (70s, rec. 1970, reissued as *Nuits De La Fondation Maeght*), *Prophecy* (1976, rec. 1964), *The Village Concerts* (1978, rec. 1966), *Swing Low Sweet Spiritual* (80s, rec. 1964), *Jesus* (1981, rec. 1966), *Lörrach/Paris 1966* (1982, rec. 1966), *At Slug's Saloon, Vols 1 &2* (1982, rec. 1966), *The Hilversum Session* (1982, rec. 1964), *The Berlin Concerts - 1966* (1983, rec. 1966), *The First Recordings Volume 2* (1990, rec. 1962), *Albert Ayler* (1991, rec. 1964, 1966).

Ayler, Donald

b. 5 October, 1942, Cleveland, Ohio, USA. The younger brother of Albert Ayler, Donald also began playing alto but, discouraged by his relative lack of facility on the saxophone, he switched to trumpet. When Albert left to work in Europe in 1964 he asked Charles Tyler, a saxophonist with whom Donald was then working, and who was a distant relation of the Aylers, to help Donald bring his playing to a professional level. On returning home Albert formed a band including Tyler and Donald. Donald was first heard on record on 'Holy Ghost' which appeared on an Impulse 'sampler' called *The New Wave In Jazz*. He was also on *Bells*, the controversial single-sided pink vinyl album issued in 1965, and on the classic sides of *In Greenwich Village*. His singing tone and majestic presentation of Albert's arching themes reinforced their hymn-like grace, whilst his improvizations were a scurrying counterpart to the saxophone's lines. As well as his own and his brother's band he played with Paul Bley, Elvin Jones and John Coltrane. However, in 1968, when Albert disbanded the group which included Donald, the trumpeter suffered a breakdown, and his brother seems to have blamed himself. Donald returned to Cleveland, where his health improved, but it was six years before he would pick up his trumpet again. He was deeply affected by Albert's death in 1970, and has only played occasionally since then. He recorded only one album under his own name.

Albums: with Albert Ayler: *The New Wave in Jazz* (1 track only), *Bells* (1965), *Spirits Rejoice* (1965), *At Slug's Saloon Volumes 1 & 2* (1966), *Black Revolt* (1966), *Lorrach/Paris 1966* (1966), *In Greenwich Village* (1967), *The Village Concerts* (1978, rec. 1966/7), *Love Cry* (1967).

B

Babbington, Roy

b. 8 July 1940, Kempston, Bedfordshire, England. Self-taught, Babbington began playing bass professionally in the late 50s. For several years he played in dance bands and jazz groups before moving to London. This was at the end of the 60s and he quickly became sought after for studio work. His jazz playing continued apace, and during the 70s he worked with many leading jazz musicians including Harry Beckett, Graham Collier, Barbara Thompson, Keith Tippett and Mike Westbrook. He also worked with the jazz-rock fusion group, Soft Machine. In the 80s Babbington often played with Stan Tracey and was regularly called upon to accompany visiting American jazz artists. He has also continued to work in the studios with many broadcasting and recording bands. An accomplished technician, Babbington is also a sensitive accompanist and is comfortable backing song stylists and forward-thinking jazz players.

Album: with Stan Tracey *Genesis* (1987).

Babs, Alice

b. Alice Nilson, 26 January 1924, Kalmar, Sweden. Well-versed in popular music and in the folk songs of her native Sweden, Babs first attracted wider attention with an appearance at the 1949 Paris Jazz Fair. Switching back and forth between jazz and popular song, she worked for a few years with fellow Scandinavians Ulrik Neumann and Svend Asmussen. In 1963 she met Duke Ellington, with whom she made concert appearances and records. The same year, her record of 'After You've Gone' reached number 43 in the UK charts. Despite such successes, her pure soprano and crystal-clear diction inclined her towards classical music, which she studied in the 60s. However, she worked again with Ellington on one of his religious concerts, which was performed in Spain. Now retired in Spain, Babs regularly attends the Ellington Conferences (begun in 1983), delighting other delegates with her impromptu vocal interventions, her vibrant enthusiasm and her obvious love for Ellington's music. That Ellington's feelings were reciprocal is apparent from his remark: 'Alice Babs is a composer's dream, for with her he can forget all the limitations and just write his heart out.'

Albums: *Alice And Wonderland* (1959), with Duke Ellington *Serenade To Sweden* (1963), *Music With A Jazz Flavour* (1973), *Far Away Star* (1974-6), *Alice Babs* i (1978), *Alice Babs* ii (1980).

Back Door

This jazz-rock trio from Blakey, Yorkshire, comprised Colin Hodgkinson (bass, vocals), Ron Aspery (saxophone, keyboards, flute, clarinet) and Tony Hicks (drums). This trio attracted much interest due to Hodgkinson's unique, adept full-chording bass technique. Their critically acclaimed first album recorded in 1972 was initially released on the independent Blakey label. The praise and attention generated by the album resulted in the band signing to Warner Brothers which later re-issued the set. Subsequent releases, which included production work from Felix Pappalardi and Carl Palmer of Emerson, Lake And Palmer, failed to capture the spirit of the debut set or the fire of their live performances. By the time of the fourth album, *Activate* in 1976, Hicks had departed to be replaced by Adrian Tilbrook before the group split the following year. Aspery went on to work with the Icelandic jazz rock group Mezzoforte, while Hodgkinson guested with various artists including, Alexis Korner, Jan Hammer and Brian Auger.

Albums: *Back Door* (1972), *8th Street Blues* (1974), *Another Mine Mess* (1975), *Activate* (1976).

Badini, Gerard

b. 16 April 1931, Paris, France. After training as a classical singer, Badini began playing clarinet in 1950. He worked in his native France and in other parts of Europe in various traditional jazz bands, including those led by Michel Attenoux and Claude Bolling. By the end of the 50s he had switched to tenor saxophone. Through the 60s and on into the 70s he worked extensively both as leader of his own small groups, which included Swing Machine, and teamed with visiting Americans, notably Helen Humes and several ex-members of Duke Ellington's band. He lived in New York for several years at the end of the 70s, but returned to France in 1982. Two years later he formed an exciting big band which he named the Super Swing Machine. Badini plays with a gutsy driving style on up-tempo pieces but is at his best playing ballads, where his warm, breathy, emotion-packed tone is reminiscent of Ben Webster.

Albums: *Cat Anderson, Claude Bolling And Co* (1965), with Helen Humes *Sneakin' Around* (1974), *The Swing Machine* (1975), *French Cooking* (1980).

Bailey, Benny

b. 13 August 1925, Cleveland, Ohio, USA. Although he began playing trumpet professionally in R&B bands, including that led by Jay McShann, Bailey's work hit a peak when he began playing bop, joining Dizzy Gillespie's big band in 1947. By this time Bailey had already greatly advanced his knowledge of music through studies with George Russell, and he brought intelligence and great finesse into all the bands with which he worked, whether as section leader or soloist. He spent five years in Lionel Hampton's All-Star Band, which included Clifford Brown, and visited Europe in 1953. Bailey liked Europe and decided to settle there, working in Sweden (with Harry Arnold's Big Band) and elsewhere before joining Quincy Jones, who also worked with Arnold. His time with Jones took Bailey back to the USA, but in 1960 he returned to Europe, where he worked on radio and in recording studios, especially in Germany. He was a founder member of the Clarke-Boland Big Band and remained with the group until 1973. Bailey continued to be much in demand for studio work in the 70s and 80s, though he took time off for jazz festival appearances and, in 1986, a tour as a member the Paris Reunion Band. In 1988, he recorded an excellent album with Tony Coe and Horace Parlan, proving that his many years in radio and studio bands had in no way diminished his fascinating and thoughtful approach to jazz.

Albums: *Benny Bailey In Stockholm* (1959), *Big Brass* (Candid 1960), *Benny Bailey With Strings* (1964), *Soul Eyes* (1968), *The Balkan In My Soul* (1968), *Folklore In Swing* (early 1970), *My Greatest Love* (1975), *How Deep Can You Go?* (1976), *Islands* (1976), *Serenade To A Planet* (1976), *Islands* (Enja 1977), *Grand Slam* (Storyville 1978), *East Of Isar* (1978), *For Heaven's Sake* (Hot House 1988), *While My Lady Sleeps* (Gemini 1990).

Bailey, Buster

b. William C. Bailey, 19 July 1902, Memphis, Tennessee, USA, d. 12 April 1967. Bailey was one of two famous jazzmen to be taught by the Chicago-based classicist Franz Schoepp, the other being Benny Goodman. After working with bands led by W.C. Handy, Erskine Tate and Joe 'King' Oliver, Bailey joined Fletcher Henderson's orchestra in New York in 1924. He remained an important member of the band until 1937, playing alongside outstanding reed players such as Coleman Hawkins, Hilton Jefferson, Russell Procope and Ben Webster. After leaving Henderson, Bailey moved to John Kirby's musically-distinguished sextet. It was in this setting, in association with perfectionists such as Procope, Charlie Shavers and Billy Kyle, that the clarinettist came into his own and the exemplary technique developed during his tuition under Schoepp was allowed to shine. The stylish playing of the Kirby band earned it great and justified popularity, in concert and on record. Apart from minor layoffs, Bailey stayed with Kirby until 1946, whereafter he played in a number of traditional or mainstream bands including those led by Wilbur De Paris and Red Allen. In 1957, he was a member of the Henderson All Star big band assembled for the Great South Bay Jazz Festival. Bailey continued working into the 60s, playing again with Red Allen and with Wild Bill Davison. In 1965, he joined Louis Armstrong's All Stars, with whom he remained until his death in April 1967.

Albums: with the Dixie All Stars *Dixiecats* (1957), *All About Memphis* (London 1958). Compilation: *Complete Recordings 1934-40* (1981).

Bailey, Derek

b. 29 January 1932, Sheffield, Yorkshire, England. Bailey is one of the few jazz guitarists who can accurately be described as unique and entirely original, in that there are no real precedents for his style. His father and grandfather were professional musicians and Bailey studied music and guitar formally from 1941-52. From 1952-65, he undertook all types of commercial work, including as a session man in recording studios and as a member of pit orchestras: one celebrated engagement involved accompanying Gracie Fields. In 1963, he encountered Tony Oxley and Gavin Bryars, and the interplay of ideas within this trio set off a severe evaluation of his direction which resulted in a fearsomely austere and abstract music and a longstanding commitment to *total* improvisation. Bailey's music is difficult to decipher, and listeners lacking a taste for stern rhetoric subverted by unpredictable flashes of mordant humour will get little out of it. Scoffers claim that his playing sounds merely random, but anyone who thinks this should be invited to try to mimic it: his mastery of the guitar involves extreme precision, used to examine material in microscopic detail, and that material never rests on conventional melody, chords or rhythm. He strives to exclude repetition and memory too. He frequently plays solo, but on the occasions when he works with other musicians (he has played with both the Spontaneous Music Ensemble and the Globe Unity Orchestra and as well as in numerous duos with musicians such as Anthony Braxton, Evan Parker and Han Bennink) it is as if he tries to avoid hearing them, playing with his head bent down over the guitar, until he will suddenly produce some sharp and apposite interjection. If he has done little to attract the general jazz public he has earned enormous respect from other musicians in the field of free jazz and improvised music. He has also contributed much to the survival of the genre, co-founding the Incus label in 1970 and running the Company festival which, surviving since 1976 against all the odds, facilitates jam sessions of both obscure toilers in the free and improvised fields and superstars like Parker and Peter Kowald. He has recorded over 60 albums, including several with various Company line-ups, and written an influential book, *Improvisation - Its Nature And Practice In Music* (1980), which was used as the basis for the four-part television series *On The Edge*, filmed in 1990-91 and first transmitted in February 1992.

Albums: *Derek Bailey/Han Bennink* (1969), with others *Instant Composers Pool* (1970), with Instant Composers Pool *Groupcomposing* (1970), *Music Improvisation Company 1968/70* (1970), with Evan Parker, Han Bennink *Topography Of The Lungs* (1970), *The Music Improvisation Company 1968-71* (1971), *Solo Guitar* Vol I (Incus 1971), with Dave Holland *Improvisation For Cello And Guitar* (1971), with Bennink *At Verity's Palace* (1972), *Derek Bailey* (1973), *Concert In Milwaukee* (1973), *One Music Ensemble* (1973), *Lot 74 - Solo Improvisations* (1974), *Improvisation* (1975), with Parker *London Concert* (1975), *Domestic And Public Pieces* (1976), with Tristan Honsinger *Duo* (1976), with Andrea Centazzo *Drops* (1977), with Anthony Braxton *Duo 1 & 2* (1977, rec. 1974 - reissued as *Live At Wigmore*), with others *Company 1* (1977), with Braxton and Parker *Company 2* (1977), with Bennink *Company 3* (1977), with Steve Lacy *Company 4* (1977), *New Sights - Old Sounds* (1978), with others *Duo And Trio Improvisations* (1978), with others *Company, Vols. 5-7* (1978), with Company *Fictions* (1978), with Tony Coe *Time* (Incus 1979), *Aida* (1980), with Company *Fables* (1980), with Christine Jeffrey *Views From Six Windows* (1980), with Jamie Muir *Dart Drug* (Incus 1981), with Company *Epiphany* (1982), with George Lewis, John Zorn *Yankees* (1983), with Braxton *Royal, Volume One* (1984, rec. 1974), *Notes* (1985), with Parker *Compatibles* (Incus 1986), with Company *Trios* (1986, rec. 1983), with Braxton *Moment Précieux* (1987), with Cyro Baptista *Cyro* (Incus 1988, rec. 1982), with Bennink *Han* (Incus 1988, rec. 1986), with Company *Once* (1988), *In Whose Tradition* (1988, rec. 1971-87), with Cecil Taylor *Pleistozaen Mit Wasser* (1989), with Barre Phillips *Figuring* (Incus 1989), with Louis Moholo, Thebe Lipere *Village Life* (1992), *Solo Guitar Volume Two* (Incus 1992).

Further reading: *Improvisation - Its Nature And Practice In Music*, Derek Bailey.

Bailey, Mildred

b. Mildred Rinker, 27 February 1907, Tekoa, Washington, USA, d. 12 December 1951. By the early 20s Bailey was singing and playing piano in silent picture theatres as well as working as a song demonstrator and performing in revues and on the radio. When only 18 years old she was headlining a Hollywood nightclub, singing popular songs, blues and some of the raunchier vaudeville numbers. She regularly worked with jazz musicians, with whom she displayed a remarkable affinity, and made her first records with guitarist Eddie Lang in 1929. That same year she was hired by Paul Whiteman, in whose band she encountered some of the best white jazz musicians of the day (her brother, Al Rinker, with Bing Crosby and Harry Barris, was a member of Whiteman's vocal trio, the Rhythm Boys). Already a well-known radio personality, she was now offered innumerable engagements and in time had her own regular show. In 1932, she had a massive hit with Hoagy

Carmichael's 'Rockin' Chair' and thereafter was known as the 'Rockin' Chair Lady'. Married for a time to xylophonist Red Norvo, Bailey continued to work with jazzmen while retaining a substantial measure of popularity with a wider audience thanks to her radio work. She sang with a fragile sweet-toned voice which belied her exceedingly ample proportions, handling even the banalities of some 30s lyrics with uncloying tenderness. The first white female to deserve fully the term 'jazz singer', Bailey always swung effortlessly and was admired and respected (and, in her stormier moments, rather feared) by the many jazz musicians with whom she worked, among them Bunny Berigan, Buck Clayton, Benny Goodman, Coleman Hawkins, Johnny Hodges and Teddy Wilson. Never in particularly good health, she was only 44 years old and destitute when she died of heart-related problems in 1951. A strong following still exists as the repackaging continues year after year.

Selected compilations: *The Uncollected Mildred Bailey - CBS Radio Show (1944)* (1979), *Mildred Bailey With Paul Barron's Orchestra (1944)* (1979), *All Of Me (1945)* (1979), *Rarest Of All Rare Performances (1944)* (1982), *Mildred Bailey (1938-39)* (1982), *The Mildred Bailey Collection - 20 Golden Hits* (1987), *Harlem Lullaby* (Living Era 1989), *Squeeze Me* (Charly 1991), *Me And The Blues* (Savoy 1992),

Baker, Chet

b. Chesney H. Baker, 23 December 1929, Yale, Oklahoma, USA, d. 13 May 1988. One of the more lyrical of the early post-war trumpeters, Baker's fragile sound epitomized the so-called 'cool' school of west coast musicians who dominated the American jazz scene of the 50s. Baker studied music while in the army and soon after his discharge, in 1951, he was playing with Charlie Parker. He gained international prominence as a member of Gerry Mulligan's pianoless quartet and in late 1953, after another short stint with Parker, formed his own group, which proved to be extremely popular. Baker kept this band together for the next three years, but he was not cut out for the life of a bandleader, nor was he able to withstand the pressures and temptations which fame brought him. He succumbed to drug addiction and the rest of his life was a battle against dependency. Inevitably, his music frequently fell by the wayside. In the 80s, in control of his life, although not fully over his addiction, he was once again a regular visitor to international jazz venues and also made a few incursions into the pop world, guesting, for example, on Elvis Costello's 'Shipbuilding'. Probably his best work from this later period comes on a series of records he made for the Danish Steeplechase label with a trio that comprised Doug Raney and Niels-Henning Ørsted Pedersen. By this time his clean-cut boyish good looks had vanished beneath a mass of lines and wrinkles - fellow trumpeter Jack Sheldon, told by Baker that they were laugh-lines remarked, 'Nothing's that funny!'. In his brief prime, Baker's silvery filigrees of sound, albeit severely restricted in tonal and emotional range, brought an unmistakable touch to many fine records; however, his lack of self-esteem rarely allowed him to assert himself or to break through the stylistic bounds imposed by exemplars such as Miles Davis. A film, *Let's Get Lost* (1989), charts the closing years of the erratic life of this largely unful-filled musician, who died falling, or possibly jumping, from an Amsterdam hotel window.

Selected albums: *Mulligan-Baker* (1952), *The Complete Pacific Jazz Recordings Of The Chet Baker Quartet* (1953-56), *Live At The Trade Winds 1952*(1953), *Witch Doctor* (1953), *Chet Baker Quartet* (1955), *The Newport Years* (1955-56), with Art Pepper *Playboys* (Pacific Jazz 1956), *Exitus: Live In Europe Vol. 1* (1956), *Cool Blues: Live In Europe Vol. 2* (1956), *At The Forum Theater* (Fresh Sound 1957), *Grey December* (Pacific Jazz 1957), *The Route* (Pacific Jazz 1957), *Chet Baker Cools Out* (Boblicity 1957), *It Could Happen To You* (1958), *Italian Movies* (1958-62), *Chet In New York* (1959), *Chet* (1959), *Chet Baker In Milano* (1959), *Chet Baket With Strings* (1959), *Chet Is Back* (1962), *The Italian Sessions* (1962), *Chet Baker Sings & Plays Billie Holiday* (1965), *Boppin' With The Chet Baker Quintet* (1965), *Groovin' With The Chet Baker Quintet* (1965), *Smokin' With The Chet Baker Quintet* (1965), *Comin' On With The Chet Baker Quintet* (1965), *Cool Burnin' With The Chet Baker Quintet* (1965), *Chet Baker With The Carmel Strings* (60s), *In The Mood* (60s), *Blood, Chet And Tears* (70s), *You Can't Go Home Again* (1973), *She Was Too Good To Me* (1974), *Chet Baker In Concert* (1974), *Once Upon A Summer Time* (1977), *Flic Ou Voyou* (1977), *The Incredible Chet Baker Plays And Sings* (1977), *Broken Wing* (1978), *Two A Day* (1978), *Chet Baker In Paris* (1978), *Live At Nick's* (1978), with Wolfgang Lackerschmid *Ballads For Two* (Inak 1979), *The Touch Of Your Lips* (Steeplechase 1979), *Rendez-vous* (1979), *All Blues* (1979), *No Problem* (Steeplechase 1979), *Daybreak* (Steeplechase 1979), *In Paris Vol II* (West Wind 1979), *This Is Always* (Steeplechase 1979), *Chet Baker/Wolfgang Lackerschmid* (1979), *Live In Chateauvallon 1978* (1979), *Someday My Prince Will Come* (1979), *Deep In A Dream Of You* (1980), *Un/Deux* (1980), *In Your Own Sweet Way* (1980), *Tune Up* (1980), *Night Bird* (1980), *Salsamba* (1980), *Soft Journey* (1980), *Leaving* (80s), *Seven Faces Of My Funny Valentine* (1980-87), *My Funny Valentine* (1981), *Chet Baker Live: 'Round Midnight* (1981), *Peace* (Enja 1982), *Studio Trieste* (1982), *Les Landis D'Hortense* (1983), *Chet Baker Live In Sweden* (Dragon 1983), *The Improviser* (1983), *Chet Baker At Capolinea* (1983), *Everything Happens To Me* (Timeless 1984), *Blues For A Reason* (Criss Cross 1984), *Sings Again* (Timeless 1984), *The Chet Baker Trio* (1985), *Chet's Choice* (1985), *My Foolish Heart* (IRD 1985), *Misty* (IRD 1985), *Time After Time* (IRD 1985), *Live From The Moonlight* (1985), *Diane* (Steeplechase 1985), *Strollin'* (Enja 1985), *Candy* (1985), *Naima* (1985-87), *As Time Goes By* (1986), *Night Bird* (1986), *Live At Rosenheimer* (1988), *When Sunny Gets Blue* (Steeplechase 1988), *Little Girl Blue* (Philology 1988), *Straight From The Heart* (Enja 1988), *Let's Get Lost* (1989, film soundtrack), *Live At Fat Tuesday's* (Fresh Sounds 1991), *Live In Brussells 1964* (1993), *Live In Buffalo* (New Note 1993), *The Pacific Years* (Pacific Jazz 1994).

Baker, David Nathaniel, Jnr.

b. 21 December 1931, Indianapolis, Indiana, USA. After win-ning a degree in Music Education at Indiana University Baker played with Stan Kenton (1956) and Maynard Ferguson (1957) before leading his own band in Indianapolis (1958-9) and joining Quincy Jones's Orchestra (1961). He played with George Russell between 1959 and 1962 displaying a first rate technique to which he had added all the *avant garde* effects such as slides and smears. Muscular problems forced him to give up the trombone but he took up the cello and recorded with Charles Tyler in 1967. Baker had become increasingly involved in teaching and in 1966 joined the jazz department of Indiana University. He served as chairman of the jazz, folk and ethnic advisory panel to the NEA and on the jazz panel of the Kennedy Centre. In the late 80s he was President of the National Jazz Service Organization. He was able to return to the trombone in the 70s and again worked with George Russell. He is an interesting composer in many styles whose jazz pieces, such as 'Honesty', have proved popular with other musicians. He has written in excess of 2,000 pieces (many of them commissioned) sometimes applying the techniques of European classical to jazz material. He was nominated for a Pulitzer Prize in 1973 for his *Concerto For Double Bass, Jazz Band, Wind And Strings*.

Selected albums: with George Russell *Jazz In The Space Age* (1960), with Russell *Stratosphunk* (1960), with Russell *Ezz-thetics* (1961), *Dave Baker's Twenty First Century Bebop Band* (1984), *RSVP* (1985).

Baker, Harold 'Shorty'

b. 26 May 1914, St. Louis, Missouri, USA, d. 8 November 1966, New York, USA. An accomplished lead trumpet player and jazz soloist, Baker played in his brother's band, Winfield Baker And His St. Louis Crackerjacks, before moving on to work with riverboat bandleader Fate Marable, Eddie Johnson and Erskine Tate in the early 30s. During the late 30s, he had spells with Don Redman, Duke Ellington and Teddy Wilson's big band. In the early 40s, Baker joined Andy Kirk for about two years before leading his own combo with his wife, pianist-composer-arranger Mary Lou Williams. The 50s and early 60s were spent mostly with Duke Ellington, the Johnny Hodges combo, general freelancing, and leading his own band for a time. He featured on many records, including 'Trumpet No End', 'Beale Street Blues' and 'Jam With Sam' (all with Ellington), 'Baby Dear' and 'Harmony Blues' (with Williams) and 'Sweet As Bear Meat' (with Hodges). He was working until shortly before his death from throat cancer in 1966.

Selected albums: with Bud Freeman *The Bud Freeman All Stars Featuring Shorty Baker* (1960), *Summer Concert* (1960), *Shorty And Doc* (1961), with Duke Ellington *All American In Jazz* (1962).

Baker, Kenny

b. 1 March 1921, Withernsea, Yorkshire, England. After taking up the trumpet and playing in brass bands, Baker moved to London, in the late 30s, to become a professional musician. During the next few years he established himself as an out-standing technician capable of playing in any jazz or dance band. In the early 40s, he played in the bands of Lew Stone and

George Chisholm before joining Ted Heath in 1944. He remained with Heath until 1949, and was featured on many recording sessions and countless concerts. In the early 50s he was regularly on the radio, leading his own band, the Baker's Dozen, on a weekly late-night show which lasted throughout the decade. In the 60s he led his own groups and recorded film soundtracks, all the while building his reputation as one of the best trumpet players in the world even though he played only rarely outside the UK. At the end of the decade he was featured in Benny Goodman's British band. Baker's career continued throughout the 70s, with appearances as co-leader of the Best of British Jazz touring package, and with Ted Heath recreations and the bands led by Don Lusher and other former colleagues. In the early 80s, Baker turned down an invitation to take over leadership of the Harry James band after the latter's death. He could still be regularly heard playing concerts and club dates and was also on television, usually off-camera, playing soundtracks for Alan Plater's popular UK television series *The Beiderbecke Affair* and *The Beiderbecke Tapes*. In 1989, he took part in a major recording undertaking which set out to recreate the classic recordings of Louis Armstrong using modern recording techniques. Baker took the Armstrong role, comfortably confounding the date on his birth certificate with his masterful playing. A fiery soloist with a remarkable technical capacity which he never uses simply for effect, Baker is one of the UK's greatest contributions to the international jazz scene.

Albums: *Kenny Baker's Half-Dozen* (1957), *Date With The Dozen* (1957), *Presents The Half-Dozen* (Dormouse 1958), *Baker Plays McHugh* (1958), *The Phase 4 World Of Kenny Baker* (1977), with Benny Goodman *London Date* (1969), *George Chisholm* (1973), *The Very Best Of British Jazz* (1983), with Don Lusher *The Big Band Sound Of Ted Heath* (1986), *The Louis Armstrong Connection Vols 1-7* (1989), *Tribute To The Great Trumpeters* (1993).

Baldock, Ken

b. 5 April 1932, London, England. Baldock played the piano from the age of six and later studied piano and double bass at the Guildhall School of Music. In 1964 he played bass in the Peter King quartet at Annie's Room in London. He joined John Dankworth's Orchestra (1965-73) and also worked with Oscar Peterson at the 1972 Montreux Jazz Festival and in two television series. He had his own sextet in 1973, which featured Henry Lowther; played in Ronnie Scott's quartet with Louis Stewart; and then in a variety of groups with Phil Lee and John Horler, as well as accompanying musicians as diverse as Milt Jackson, Cleo Laine, Barney Kessel and Jay McShann. In the 80s, he played in Bobby Wellins's quartet and continued to work freelance. He is a reliable bass player with a solid technique who is also an able composer. In 1983, he was awarded an Arts Council grant for his composition *Kosen Rufu*. He also teaches both privately and at the Barry Summer School.

Albums: with Barney Kessel *Summertime In Montreux* (1973), *Jay McShann And Al Casey* (1984).

Ball, Kenny

b. 22 May 1930, Ilford, Essex, England. The most successful survivor of the early-60s 'trad boom', Ball played the harmonica and bugle in a local band before switching to the trumpet. Having previously played alongside Charlie Galbraith for a BBC radio broadcast and deputized for Britain's leading dixieland trumpet player, Freddy Randall, Ball joined clarinettist Sid Phillips' band in 1954 and later formed his own dixieland styled Jazzmen four years later, between which time he had worked with Eric Delaney, George Chisholm, Terry Lightfoot and Al Fairweather. The Jazzmen did not record until the summer of 1959, resulting in the single 'Waterloo'/'Wabash Cannonball'. Signed to Pye Records, his first hit was in 1961 with Cole Porter's 'Samantha' originally from the Bing Crosby/Frank Sinatra movie *High Society*. This was followed by the million-selling 'Midnight In Moscow', number 2 in the UK and US charts, 'March Of The Siamese Children' from *The King And I*, 'The Green Leaves Of Summer', 'Sukiyaki' and several more throughout the 60s. Ball featured alongside Chris Barber and Acker Bilk in the compilation album of the best of British dixieland/trad jazz, *The Best Of Ball, Barber And Bilk*, which reached UK number 1 in 1962. The band made its film debut in 1963 in *Live It Up* with Gene Vincent, and appeared in *It's Trad Dad*. In the same year Ball was made an honorary citizen of New Orleans. For three years, 1962-64, he received the Carl Alan Award for the Most Outstanding Traditional Jazz Band, and in 1968 the band appeared with Louis Armstrong on his last European visit. Throughout the 70s and 80s Ball extensively toured abroad while maintaining his UK popularity with regular concerts, featuring guests from the 'old days' such as Acker Bilk, Kenny Baker, Lonnie Donegan and George Chisholm. Ball claims his career peaked in 1981 when he and the Jazzmen played at the reception following the wedding of Prince Charles and Princess Diana. The early 90s Jazzmen include founder member John Bennett (trombone), Andy Cooper (clarinet, ex-Charlie Galbraith and Alan Elsdon bands), John Benson (bass/vocals, ex-Monty Sunshine Band), John Fenner (guitar/vocals), Hugh Ledigo (piano, ex-Pasadena Roof Orchestra) and Ron Bowden (drums, ex-Ken Colyer, Lonnie Donegan and Chris Barber bands).

Albums: *Kenny Ball And His Jazzmen* (1961), *The Kenny Ball Show* (1962), with Gary Miller *Gary On The Ball* (1962), *Midnight In Moscow* (1962, US only release), *It's Trad* (1962, US only release), *The Big Ones - Kenny Ball Style* (1963), *Jazz Band Ball* (1964), *Colonel Bogey And Eleven Japanese Marches* (1964, Japan only release), *Kenny Ball Plays For The Jet Set* (1964, US only release), *Tribute To Tokyo* (1964), *The Sound Of Kenny Ball* (1968), *Kenny Ball And His Jazzmen Live In Berlin Volume 1/Volume 2* (1968, German releases), *King Of The Swingers* (1969), *At The Jazz Band Ball* (1970), *Fleet Street Lightning* (1970), *Saturday Night With Kenny Ball And His Band* (1970), *Pixie Dust (A Tribute To Walt Disney)* (1971), *My Very Good Friend...Fats Waller* (1972), *Have A Drink On Me* (1972), *Let's All Sing A Happy Song* (1973), with the Johnny Arthey Orchestra and the Eddie Lester Singers *A Friend To You* (1974), *Titillating Tango* (1976), *Saturday Night At The Mill*

(1977), *In Concert* (1978), *Way Down Yonder* (1977), *The Bulldog And Kangaroo* (1977, Australasian only release), *Kenny In Concert In The USA, Volume 1/Volume 2* (1979, US only releases), *Soap* (1981), *Ball, Barber And Bilk Live At The Royal Festival Hall* (1984), *Greensleeves* (1986, Netherlands release), *Kenny Ball And His Jazzmen Play The Movie Greats* (1987), *On Stage* (Start 1988), *Dixie* (Pickwick 1989), *Kenny Ball Plays British* (MFP 1989), *Jazz Classics* (1990), *Steppin' Out* (Castle 1992), *Strictly Jazz* (Kaz 1992), *Kenny Ball Now* (1990), with Chris Barber and Acker Bilk *The Ultimate!* (1991), *Lighting Up The Town* (Intersound 1993). Compilations: *Best Of Ball, Barber And Bilk* (1962), *Kenny Ball's Golden Hits* (1963), *Golden Hour* (1971), *Golden Hour Presents Kenny Ball 'Hello Dolly'* (1973), *Cheers!* (1979), *Golden Hits* (1986), *Kenny Ball's Cotton Club* (1986), *The Singles Collection* (1987), *Images* (Images 1990), *Kenny Ball - The Collection* (Castle 1990).

Ball, Ronnie

b. 22 December 1927, Birmingham, Warwickshire, England. After playing piano as a semi-pro during his teenage years, Ball emerged as a leading light of the British bop scene in the early 50s. No sooner had he made his mark than he decided to move to New York, where, from 1952 onwards, he worked and recorded with bop luminaries such as Lennie Tristano, Dizzy Gillespie, Kenny Clarke, Hank Mobley, Art Pepper and Warne Marsh. The mainstream then beckoned and by the end of the decade he had played with Buddy Rich, Gene Krupa and Roy Eldridge. For a few years in the early 60s he was accompanist to singer Chris Connor and soon after became deeply involved in studio work providing deftly supportive accompaniment for singers and instrumentalists alike. His early bop recordings display a fleet inventive soloist at ease and at one with the most distinguished company.
Album: *All About Ronnie* (1956).

Ballamy, Iain

b. 20 February 1964, Guildford, Surrey, England. Ballamy is largely self-taught, having started to learn piano before taking to reed instruments. He formed his own group, the Iains, in 1983 and in the same year worked with Graham Collier in a band which eventually became Loose Tubes. Among his closest musical associates are Django Bates (a member of the Iains and Loose Tubes) and Bill Bruford, with whose band, Earthworks, Ballamy has played with since 1986. He has also worked with Gil Evans and Billy Jenkins's Voice Of God Collective. Although deriving much inspiration from John Coltrane, Ballamy has not allowed this to lead him into a musical *cul-de-sac*, as has happened to many of his contemporaries. and is rapidly developing into a significant leader of musical fashion. He exhibits not only an impressive technique, whether on alto, tenor or soprano saxophone, but also a glorious heart-on-sleeve romanticism which he displays, for example, on one of his own compositions, 'All I Ask Of You', on his first album as leader.
Albums: with Loose Tubes *Open Letter* (1987), with Earthworks *Dig?* (1988), *Balloon Man* (Editions EG 1988).

Bang, Billy

b. Billy Walker, 20 September 1947, Mobile, Alabama, USA. Growing up in New York's South Bronx, learning violin was the last thing anyone wanted to do. 'It was the most hated instrument for me', Bang told the *LA Times*, 'it's too European and it's never been in my blood. The Temptations never played it and James Brown never sang with one.' Nonetheless, learn it he did at school. In the early 60s he abandoned the violin for percussion, getting into African-Cuban rhythms. Drafted to Vietnam, he had a political awakening and returned to America to throw himself into the anti-war movement. When he began to play music again in 1971 he experimented with saxophones, but came back to the violin, recognizing that this was where his technical facility lay. Bang became known as an associate of Sam Rivers and Frank Lowe, his skidding, diabolically transgressive playing an essential component of the celebrated Loft scene. In the early 70s he formed his own group, the Survival Ensemble, and in 1977 co-founded the String Trio Of New York, which wooed audiences with seductive themes that then opened into state-of-the-art string improvisations. Associations with Sun Ra, Don Cherry, Marilyn Crispell and James 'Blood' Ulmer were also productive. Like other musicians of his generation, Bang refuses categories. *Untitled Gift*, recorded in 1982, was elegant free jazz; *Bangception* and *Outline No 12* were austere art music. In 1987, he guested on Kahil El'Zabar's *Another Kind Of Groove*, and in 1988 on Bootsy Collins's come-back 'What's Bootsy Doin'. His sextet album *The Fire From Within* (1984) launched an exotic front-line of trumpet, guitar and marimba: together with Bang's microtonal panache and his polyrhythmic vamps it made a deliriously pretty platform for some amazing playing. It seemed to have found a way of making freedom accessible without adopting the flash professionalism of fusion. *Live At Carlos 1* delivered more of the same. On other projects, such as the Jazz Doctors quartet, the presence of long-term Cecil Taylor-associate Dennis Charles on drums has assured a precise and understated swing. In 1988 Bang toured Europe and recorded *Value No 10* with a quartet that comprised Charles, Lowe and Sirone. Billy Bang delivers music with infectious energy and an honesty about achievement which is most moving.
Albums: *New York Collage* (1978), *Sweet Space* (1979), *Rainbow Gladiator* (Soul Note 1981), *Untitled Gift* (1982), *Invitation* (Soul Note 1982), *Outline No 12* (1982), *Bangception* (1983), *Distinction Without A Difference* (1983), with the Jazz Doctors *Intensive Care* (1984), *The Fire From Within* (1985), *The Fire From Within* (Soul Note 1986), *Live At Carlos I* (Soul Note 1987), with Kahil El'Zabar *Another Kind Of Groove* (1987), *Valve No 10* (Soul Note 1991, rec. 1988), *A Tribute To Stuff Smith* (Soul Note 1994).

Banks, Billy

b. c.1908, Alton, Illinois, USA, d. 19 October 1967. A mildly engaging, if somewhat eccentric, singer, Banks's chief claim to jazz fame is the set of records he made in 1932, which featured Red Allen, Pee Wee Russell, Tommy Dorsey, Eddie Condon, Jess Stacy, Fats Waller, Zutty Singleton and others. The record companies concerned claimed these as being the 'hottest jazz records ever made', and for once their customary hyperbole is very nearly justified. Banks's high-pitched vocals (he was, at one time, a female impersonator) are the weakest link on these classic sides, but there is so much superb music being played all around him that his peculiarities can be happily overlooked and even enjoyed as the curiosity they really are. Little is known of Banks's career before 1932 and not much happened to him afterwards, although he joined Noble Sissle's band in 1934, in which he remained for four years, before going into a cabaret spot at Billy Rose's Diamond Horseshoe, an engagement which continued unbroken until June 1948. From then onwards he worked in cabaret in New York, touring Europe in the 50s and then Australia and the Far East. In the late 50s he settled in Japan, where he remained until his death in 1967.

Compilation: *Billy Banks And The Rhythmmakers* (1932).

Barbarin, Louis

b. 24 October 1902, New Orleans, Louisiana, USA. Barbarin was born into a musical family, taking up drums as a small child. His father, Isidore, played alto horn, his brother William played cornet and his other brothers, Lucien and Paul Barbarin, were also drummers. After playing in parade and New Orleans-style dance and jazz bands throughout the 20s, Barbarin joined Papa Celestin. This association began in the late 30s and continued until Celestin's death, and thereafter Barbarin stayed with the band when it was led by Albert French. Barbarin belongs in the tradition of unspectacular New Orleans drummers whose role was recognized as being that of timekeeper.

Albums: with Albert French *A Night At Dixieland Hall* (1963).

Barbarin, Paul

b. 5 May 1899, New Orleans, Louisiana, USA, d. 17 February 1969. The best-known member of a respected New Orleans musical family, Barbarin became one of the Crescent City's most famous and best drummers. With his father, Isadore, an established brass player and a member of the Onward Brass Band, and his brothers, Louis (drums), Lucien (drums) and William (cornet) all playing jazz, Paul Barbarin could hardly have done anything but become a jazz musician. While still in his mid-teens, he was a member of Buddy Petit's band, then moved to Chicago, where he worked with the bands of Joe 'King' Oliver and Jimmy Noone. From 1928 Barbarin worked mainly in New York with the Luis Russell band, which in 1935, came under the nominal leadership of Louis Armstrong. In 1939, Barbarin returned home and, apart from occasional trips to Chicago in the 40s and 50s when he worked with Red Allen, Sidney Bechet, Art Hodes, he also led his own band. It was in New Orleans that he stayed, playing long and successful engagements and enjoying life as an elder statesman of jazz. Barbarin played with the simplistic drive of the earliest New Orleans drummers; though he lacked the polish of Baby Dodds and the flair of Zutty Singleton, he always swung any band in which he played. One of his notable compositions is 'Bourbon Street Parade'. In later years he continued family tradition

when, like his father before him, he became leader of the Onward Brass Band. It was while leading this band in a New Orleans street parade in February 1969 that he collapsed and died.

Albums: *The Streets Of The City* (1950), *Paul Barbarin: Recorded In New Orleans* (1956), *Paul Barbarin And His New Orleans Band* (Atlantic 1956), *Barbarin's Best At Dixieland Hall* (1964).

Barber, Chris

b. 17 April 1930, Welwyn Garden City, Hertfordshire, England. In the 40s Barber studied trombone and bass at the Guildhall School of Music, eventually choosing the former as his principal instrument (although he occasionally played bass in later years). In the late 40s he formed his first band which, unusually, was formed as a co-operative. Also in the band were Monty Sunshine, Ron Bowden and Lonnie Donegan. By the early 50s the band had gained a considerable following but it was nevertheless decided to invite Ken Colyer to join. The move was musically promising but proved to be unsuccessful when the personalities involved clashed repeatedly. Eventually, Colyer left and was replaced by Pat Halcox. With a remarkably consistent personnel the Barber band was soon one of the UK's leading traditional groups and well placed to take advantage of the surge of interest in this form of jazz in the late 50s and early 60s. The decline of popularity in 'trad', which came on the heels of the rock explosion, had a dramatic effect on many British jazz bands but Barber's fared much better than most. In part this was due to his astute business sense and in part thanks to his keen awareness of musical trends and a willingness to accommodate other forms without compromising his high musical standards. In the 60s Barber changed the name of the band to the Chris Barber Blues and Jazz Band. Into the traditional elements of the band's book he incorporated ragtime but also worked with such modern musicians as Joe Harriott. Amongst his most important activities at this time was his active promotion of R&B and the blues, which he underlined by bringing major American artists to the UK, often at his own expense. Through such philanthropy he brought to the attention of British audiences the likes of Sister Rosetta Tharpe, Brownie McGhee, Louis Jordan and Muddy Waters. Not content with performing the older blues styles, Barber also acknowledged the contemporary interest in blues evinced by rock musicians and audiences and hired such players as John Slaughter and Pete York (ex-Spencer Davis Group), who worked happily beside long-serving sidemen Halcox, Ian Wheeler, Vic Pitt and others. In the 70s, Barber focused more on mainstream music, showing a special affinity for small Duke Ellington-styled bands, and now toured with visitors like Russell Procope, Wild Bill Davis, Trummy Young and John Lewis. He also maintained his contact with his jazz roots and, simultaneously, the contemporary blues scene by touring widely with his *Take Me Back To New Orleans* show, which featured Dr. John. As a trombone player, Barber's work is enhanced by his rich sound and flowing solo style. It is, however, as bandleader and trendspotter that he has made his greatest contribution to the jazz scene, both internationally and, especially, in the UK. In the early 90s he was happily entering his fifth decade as a bandleader with no discernible flagging of his interest, enthusiasm, skill or, indeed, of his audience. In 1991 he was awarded the OBE, the same year as *Panama!* was released, which features the excellent trumpet playing of Wendell Brunious.

Selected albums: *Live In 1954-55* (London 1955), *Ragtime* (1960), *Chris Barber At The London Palladium* (1961), *Trad Tavern* (Philips 1962), *Getting Around* (1963), *Battersea Rain Dance* (1967-68), *Live In East Berlin* (Black Lion 1968), *Get Rolling!* (1969-71), *Sideways* (1974), *Echoes Of Ellington* (1976), *The Grand Reunion Concert* (Timeless 1976), *Take Me Back To New Orleans* (1980), *Creole Love Call* (Timeless 1981), *Mardi Gras At The Marquee* (1983), *Live In 85* (Timeless 1986), *Concert For The BBC* (1986), *Everybody Knows* (1987), *In Budapest* (1987), *When Its Thursday Night In Egypt* (1988), *Classics Concerts In Berlin* (1988, rec. 1959), *Stardust* (1988), *Mardi Gras At The Marquee* (Timeless 1989), *Get Yourself To Jackson Square* (1990), *Echoes Of Ellington Vol I* (1991), *Echoes Of Ellington Vol II* (1991), *In Concert* (1991), with Wendell Brunious *Panama!* (Timeless 1991), *Who's Blues* (L&R 1991). Compilations: *30 Years, Chris Barber* (Timeless 1985), *Can't We Get It Together? (1954-84)* (1986), *Best Sellers* (1988), *The Best Of Chris Barber (1959-62)* (1988), *The Ultimate* (1989), *The Entertainer* (Polydor 1988), *Essential Chris Barber* (1990).

Barbieri, Gato

b. Leandro J. Barbieri, 28 November 1934, Rosario, Argentina. After studying clarinet while still a child, Barbieri took up alto saxophone when his family moved to Buenos Aires. He joined Lalo Schifrin's band and, despite the early influence of Charlie Parker, soon switched to tenor. He formed his own quartet, often supporting visiting American jazzmen, and his playing began to reveal the influence of John Coltrane. In 1962, Barbieri left South America for Italy, where he worked for a while with a free-form band led by Don Cherry. Although Barbieri had earlier turned his back on the music of his native land, the physical distancing he now experienced gave him more appreciation of its potential in jazz. From the mid-60s onwards, his music took on a steadily more distinctive flavour as he began to incorporate the many dance rhythms of South America into a rich and ever-changing backcloth for his driving tenor playing. Performing the commercial title track to the film *Last Tango In Paris* has since become his Albatross. Since the early 70s Barbieri has spent much time in South America, where by his example and encouragement he has helped to foster both jazz and a deeper understanding of the sub-continent's own musical heritage.

Albums: *In Search Of The Mystery* (1967), *Confluence* (Affinity 1968), *The Third World* (1969), *Under Fire* (c.1970), *Last Tango In Paris* (c.1972), *Chapter One: Latin America* (1973), *Chapter Three: Viva Emiliano Zapata* (Impulse 1974), *Bolivia* (RCA 1974), *Chapter Four: Alive In New York* (1975), *Caliente* (1976), *Obsession* (1978), *Euphoria* (1979), *Under Fire* (1980), *Para Los Amigos* (1983), *Apassionado* (Polydor 1983),

Gato...Para Los Amigos! (Dillion 1983), *Hamba Khale* (1987), *The Third World Revisited* (Bluebird 1988), *Chapter One - Latin America* (1989), *Two Pictures 1965-68* (1990).

Barefield, Eddie

b. 12 December 1909, Scandia, Iowa, USA. After formal studies on piano, Barefield taught himself to play alto (and later tenor and soprano) saxophone. By his late teens he had begun a period of several years' work in territory bands and name bands, including those of Bennie Moten, Zack Whyte, the Cotton Pickers (under Cuba Austin) and Cab Calloway. He stayed with Calloway for three years, leaving in 1936 to settle on the west coast, where he worked with Charlie Echols and also formed a number of bands under his own leadership. Unable to stay out of the big time for long, Barefield was in New York in 1938 as a member of Fletcher Henderson's band. After leaving Henderson, he played again with Calloway, then in the early 40s he drifted in and out of big bands and small groups, working under leaders such as Don Redman, Duke Ellington, Coleman Hawkins, Benny Carter and Ella Fitzgerald, for whom he was musical director. Barefield's all-round competence as both musician and arranger ensured that he was always in demand; he was also frequently called upon by studios and established a reputation for his work in the theatre. In the 50s and 60s, he continued to work in the theatre and also played with Sy Oliver, Redman again (touring Europe with him in 1953), and with Sammy Price, Wilbur De Paris, the Dukes Of Dixieland and the Saints And Sinners band. He also appeared in a number of motion pictures including *Every Day A Holiday* (1937), *The Night They Raided Minsky's* (1968) and *L'Aventure Du Jazz* (1969). In the 70s Barefield showed no signs of slowing down, spending most of that decade in the house band for the Ringling Brothers and Barnum & Bailey Circus. He also remained active in jazz, working on into the late 80s with Dick Vance and Illinois Jacquet, among many others. Barefield's playing style, although initially influenced by Lester Young, carries a distinctive vibrancy and his soprano saxophone work is especially notable for its buzz-saw attack and urgency.

Albums: *Cab Calloway Accompanied By Eddie Barefield's Orchestra* (1958), *Eddie Barefield* i (1962-63), *Eddie Barefield* ii (1964), *Eddie Barefield* iii (1964), *L'Aventure Du Jazz* (1969, film soundtrack), *Eddie Barefield* iv (c.70s), *Eddie Barefield* v (1973), *The Indestructible Eddie Barefield* (1977), *Introducing Eddie Barefield* (1980).

Barker, Danny

b. 13 January 1909, New Orleans, Louisiana, USA, d. 13 March 1994. One of the grand old men of jazz, Barker's career, while rooted in traditionalism, spanned a wide musical range. Before settling on the guitar as his instrument, Barker received tuition on clarinet from Barney Bigard, on drums from his uncle Paul Barbarin and then played ukelele and banjo in the Storyville district of New Orleans (often alongside blues player Cousin Joe, with whom he also recorded for Mezz Mezzrow's King Jazz label). In the early 20s he was accompanying blues

singer Little Brother Montgomery and by the end of the decade was working with Lee Collins and other leading local musicians. In 1930 Barker moved to New York, where he worked clubs and recorded extensively with Red Allen, Sidney Bechet, James P. Johnson, Jelly Roll Morton (who gave him his nickname, 'Hometown', following his move from New Orleans to New York), and with his wife, singer Blue Lu Barker. Barker also worked with several big bands of the mid-and late 30s, including those led by Lucky Millinder, Benny Carter and Cab Calloway (with whom he and Blue Lu spent nine years, whilst also recording for Decca). He was also to be found working on sessions by Billie Holiday, Charlie Parker and others. From the late 40s onwards he was active in the Revivalist movement, playing with Bunk Johnson, Paul Barbarin and Albert Nicholas, and scoring one notable hit alongside his wife with 'Here's A Little Girl From Jacksonville'. In the mid-60s Barker returned to his home town, where his great interest in and knowledge of early jazz history led to his appointment as Curator of the New Orleans Jazz Museum. He also instigated the Fairview Baptist Brass Band to maintain the marching band tradition, and engaged in a round of lectures. He wrote extensively (he was co-author with Jack V. Buerkle of *Bourbon Street Black* and his autobiography, *A Life In Jazz*, was published in 1986), and continued to play whenever the spirit moved him. Selected albums: *Danny Barker* (1958), *Danny Barker's Band* (1986). Compilation: with Bunk Johnson *The Last Testament Of A Great Jazzman* (1947 recordings).
Further reading: *A Life In Jazz*, Danny Barker.

Barker, Guy

b. 26 December 1957, London, England. Barker took up the trumpet as a child and studied formally at the Royal College of Music. One of several brilliant British musicians to come up through the ranks of the National Youth Jazz Orchestra, Barker attracted media attention both then and after his departure into the wider world of the professional jazz musician. Playing with NYJO at the Cleveland Jazz Festival at Middlesbrough, England, in 1978, he was joined unexpectedly on stage by Clark Terry for a duet, a moment he took in his confident stride. At the age of 20 Barker toured the UK with his own quintet, using young American jazzmen he had met during a visit to New York. Also in the late 70s and early 80s, he played with Mike Westbrook, John Dankworth, Chris Hunter and Hubbard's Cubbard, a jazz-rock group. His major breakthrough came with a spell with Gil Evans, touring and recording, and work with Stan Tracey, Clark Tracey, with whom he toured the Far East, Europe and the UK, and Ornette Coleman. Alongside his jazz work, Barker has appeared as soloist with the London Symphony Orchestra and in groups backing Frank Sinatra, Lena Horne, Sammy Davis Jnr., Mel Tormé and Liza Minnelli. Simultaneously, he has been busy in film, television and recording studios, playing with Evans on the soundtrack of *Insignificance* (1985), and on *Absolute Beginners* (1986) and *The Living Daylights* (1987). He has also appeared on many rock albums featuring artists such as Paul McCartney, Grace Jones and Joan Armatrading. Throughout

the 80s he made numerous jazz record dates with Westbrook, Evans, Stan Tracey's Hexad and big band, Clark Tracey, Peter King, Jim Mullen and the Jack Sharpe Big Band. He has continued this high level of activity into the 90s playing on Sinatra's 1991 tour of the UK, and a tour to Hong Kong with Georgie Fame in a package paying tribute to Chet Baker. There have also been club and festival dates, a series of concerts re-creating the music of Bix Beiderbecke and recording sessions with Carla Bley and with his own quintet. Barker's pure-toned melodic playing allied to a crackling, boppish attack makes his solo work particularly attractive and exhilarating. His wide range of musical interests, evident in his concert tours honouring trumpeters as diverse as Baker and Beiderbecke, has not resulted in his becoming a copyist. Indeed, his highly distinctive playing style is already one of the great joys of jazz in the 90s. Barker's sober on-stage demeanour and dress conceal a vibrant musical personality whose future appears to have no bounds. After Barker's outstanding performance at the 1989 South Bank Jazz Festival at Grimsby, Lincolnshire, Lee Konitz remarked, 'One day that guy's gonna be a genius.' That day is already here.
Albums: *Hubbard's Cubbard* (1983), with Hubbard's Cubbard *Nip It In The Bud* (1985), with Clark Tracey *Suddenly Last Tuesday* (1986), with Tracey *Stiperstones* (1987), with Peter King *Brother Bernard* (1988), *Holly J* (Miles Music 1989), *Isn't It?* (Spotlite 1991).

Barker, Thurman

b. 8 January 1948, Chicago, Illinois, USA. Emerging from the Chicago free scene, a founder member of the AACM, percussionist Barker first played and recorded with fellow Chicagoans Kalaparush Maurice McIntyre, Joseph Jarman, Muhal Richard Abrams and Anthony Braxton, in whose quartet he played in the late 70s. Economic survival meant periods of working in musical pit bands, but joining Cecil Taylor's Unit in 1986 brought further exposure. Taylor's dense, polyrhythmic style requires the services of someone with an acute sense of structure and an incisive attack. These Barker has in abundance. At the suggestion of Billy Bang, Barker has added the marimba to his armoury, playing with exquisite grace and fire on Bang's exotic *The Fire From Within*. His drumwork on guitarist Joe Morris's *Human Rites* is equally impressive.
Albums: with Anthony Braxton *Seven Compositions 1978* (1980), with Braxton *Performance 1979* (1981), with Billy Bang *The Fire From Within* (1985), with Joe Morris *Human Rites* (1986), with Cecil Taylor Unit *Live In Bologna* (1987).

Barnes, Alan

b. 23 July 1959, Altrincham, Cheshire, England. Between 1977 and 1980, he studied saxophone and woodwinds at the Leeds College of Music before moving to London. In 1980 he played with the Midnite Follies Orchestra and the following year was with the Pasadena Roof Orchestra, working in London and on a European tour. He stayed with the Pasadena group until 1983 when he joined the hard bop band led by Tommy Chase. The period with Chase attracted considerable

Alan Barnes

attention to Barnes as a rising star of the UK jazz scene. He left Chase in 1986 to join the Jazz Renegades for a three-year stint. With this unit he travelled to Japan and also recorded. While still with the Renegades he began working with Humphrey Lyttelton and in 1989 became leader of the Pizza Express Modern Jazz Sextet. In the early 90s Barnes was still playing with Lyttelton and had also formed his own quartet, which included David Newton, and was co-leader of a quintet with John Barnes (no relation). In addition to the hectic schedule he has set, Barnes has also found time to record with Tommy Whittle, to play with the big bands formed by Bob Wilber for various engagements and with Mike Westbrook's Brass Band and Westbrook Rossini. In addition to his jazz work, Barnes also plays regularly with the BBC Radio Orchestra. An outstanding musician with a distinctive and highly melodic playing style, Barnes is one of the most inventive and original talents to appear in the UK in recent years. His wide-ranging repertoire and his talent for arranging and composing place him in a strong position to be a major voice in the world of jazz in the next century.

Selected albums: *Blues Going Up* (1977), *Plays So Good* (1977), *Affiliation* (1987).

Barnes, George

b. 17 July 1921, Chicago Heights, Illinois, USA, d. 5 September 1977. Although first achieving a measure of national prominence by winning a Tommy Dorsey Amateur Swing Contest in 1937 when he was only 16 years old, Barnes was already a seasoned guitarist. He had previously worked extensively in the mid-west as leader of his own small group. He followed his contest success with a string of recording dates in which he accompanied leading blues singers, among them Big Bill Broonzy, Blind John Davis, Jazz Gillum and Washboard Sam. Interestingly enough, given such classical country blues associations, Barnes had been an early exponent of the electric guitar, which he had taken up in 1931. Apart from his army service, Barnes spent most of the 40s in staff jobs with NBC and ABC in Chicago and with Decca in New York. In the 60s, Barnes worked with fellow guitarists Carl Kress and Bucky Pizzarelli. Known as a decidedly prickly individual, Barnes broke up publicly with Pizzarelli before beginning an equally antagonistic - but musically profound - partnership with cornetist Ruby Braff. Barnes's blues playing was always superb, as was his melodic interpretation of the best standards. He played and recorded many fine examples of his brilliant single-line solos. His duets, especially with Braff and Joe Venuti, reveal an almost supernatural understanding of his fellow musicians. His death, in September 1977, while still very much in his prime, was a great loss to jazz guitar playing.

Albums: *Two Guitars And A Horn* (1962), with Carl Kress *Something Tender* (1963), *Guitars Pure And Honest* (early 70s), *Swing Guitar* (1972), *The Braff-Barnes Quartet Plays Gershwin* (1974), *The Best I've Heard: The Braff-Barnes Quartet* (1976), with Joe Venuti *Live At The Concord Summer Jazz Festival*

(1976). Compilation: *The Uncollected George Barnes* (1946 recordings).

Barnes, John

b. 15 May 1932, Manchester, Lancashire, England. Unusually, Barnes began his musical career as both a brass and reed player, but quickly abandoned the flügelhorn in favour of the clarinet. At first he played traditional jazz with the Zenith Six, Mike Daniels's Delta Jazzmen and Alan Elsdon. By the mid-60s, however, when he was with Alex Welsh, Barnes had extended his stylistic range and had also started to play alto, soprano, baritone saxophones and flute. Barnes spent a decade with Welsh, and by the time he left, in 1977, he was widely regarded as the best baritone saxophonist in Europe and one of the best in the world. Since leaving Welsh he has worked with the Midnite Follies Orchestra, Humphrey Lyttelton, as co-leader of a small group with Roy Williams and with numerous visiting American jazz musicians.
Albums: *The John Barnes-Roy Williams Jazzband* (1975), with Alex Welsh *In Concert In Dresden* (1977), *Fancy Our Meeting* (Calligraph 1988).

Barnet, Charlie

b. 26 October 1913, New York City, New York, USA, d. 4 September 1991. Of all the swing era bandleaders, Barnet was the one most able to do as he pleased. Born into a rich New York family, he played piano and reed instruments while still at school and by his teens had decided that he wanted to play jazz. For a number of years he played on ocean-going liners, often as leader, and also paid his dues in numerous bands across the USA. He formed his first mainland big band in 1933 and, on and off, continued to lead a band throughout the swing era. Barnet could afford to indulge his whims and his musical preferences and did so. Although he lived riotously, marrying six times, to his credit he adopted high musical standards and refused to compromise on commercial matters. Also, Barnet was a leading figure in breaking racial taboos in the hiring of black musicians and as early as 1935 he had a mixed-race band. Over the years, the roster of black artists hired by Barnet includes such distinguished names as Frankie Newton, Peanuts Holland, Clark Terry, Charlie Shavers, Lena Horne, Dizzy Gillespie and Trummy Young. Although he never matched the huge popular success of Benny Goodman, Shaw and Tommy Dorsey, Barnet had some hit records including 'Cherokee', 'Things Ain't What They Used to Be' and 'That Old Black Magic'. By the 40s Barnet's was one of the best big bands and he had several more popular records, such as 'Skyliner'. Adept on several saxophones, Barnet favoured the alto although it was his use of the soprano that helped to give his band its distinctive sound. His arrangers, notably Billy May and Bill Holman, were particularly gifted, but while Barnet's devotion to the music of Duke Ellington ensured that he constantly strove for the highest qualities, he rarely attained the Duke's degree of perfection. By the end of the 40s, Barnet had done all that he wanted in the big band business. He folded his band and became a hotelier. In later years, he periodically formed small groups and big bands for special engagements, usually hiring top-flight musicians, like Conte Candoli, Willie Smith, Nat Pierce, Don Lamond and Al Porcino, all of whom were given free rein to play hard-swinging big band jazz. Barnet's autobiography is a no-stone-unturned account of his wild life.
Albums: *Charlie Barnet Jubilee* (1945), *On The Air In The Fifties* (1955), *Live At Basin Street East* (1966), *Charlie Barnet Big Band - 1967* (1967). Compilations: *The Indispensable Charlie Barnet Vols 1/2* (1939-40), *The Indispensable Charlie Barnet Vols 3/4* (1940-41), *Down Beat With Charlie Barnet* (1940), *Skyliner* (1942-46), *Clap Hands Here Comes Charlie* (Bluebird 1988), *Cherokee* (1939-41) (Bluebird 1992), *Drop Me Off In Harlem* (1942-46) (GRP 1992).
Further reading: *Those Swinging Years: The Autobiography Of Charlie Barnet*, Charlie Barnet with Stanley Dance.

Barrett, Dan

b. 14 December 1955, Pasadena, California, USA. He first took up the trombone as a young teenager, encouraged by a teacher named Ken Owen. He began playing professionally while still at high school, sitting in with a traditional band at a local restaurant. In 1977, by now at college, he visited Europe to take part in the Breda Jazz festival in Holland. Barrett continued to play in various parts of California, usually in a traditional jazz setting but with occasional excursions into the mainstream. A meeting with Howard Alden led to thoughts of a group of their own but the time was not yet right for either man. In 1983, he moved to New York City and was soon a member of the Widespread Depression Orchestra, often sitting-in at clubs like Eddie Condon's and Jimmy Ryan's. By this time Alden was also in New York and they formed their quintet, a mainstream group with a wide swing-based repertoire with several of the band's arrangements being supplied by Buck Clayton. The band also uses material originally written for the John Kirby band in the 30s and which was handed on from Kirby's wife, Maxine Sullivan, to Benny Carter and then, via Bill Berry, to Barrett and Alden. Barrett continued to play clubs in New York, working with Ed Polcer, Billy Butterfield, Doc Cheatham, Scott Hamilton, Warren Vaché, Benny Goodman and others. With Alden he has also played in an orchestra formed by Clayton. In the late 80s and early 90s he made several overseas tours, visiting Europe and Japan for festival and club dates sometimes as a single, with Alden, and also with Dick Hyman, Flip Phillips, Kenny Davern, Jake Hanna and others. A highly accomplished technician, Barrett's love for and dedication to music of an earlier age in no way diminishes his status in the contemporary jazz scene; indeed, in many respects his position is enhanced by his eclecticism. A major new voice in jazz, with an engagingly melodic approach, Barrett is very much a musician for the 90s.
Albums: with Howard Alden *Swing Street* (1986), *Strictly Instrumental* (Concord 1987), with Alden *The A-B-Q Salutes Buck Clayton* (1989), *Jubilesta!* (1993).

Barrett, Sweet Emma

b. 25 March 1897, New Orleans, Louisiana, USA. d. 28

January 1983. After deciding upon a musical career, Barrett played piano in a number of New Orleans bands during the 20s including that led by Papa Celestin. She continued working in New Orleans bands during the 30s and 40s, with bands such as those led by Sidney Desvigne and John Robichaux. In the 50s she worked with Percy Humphrey and Israel Gorman and also led her own band of New Orleans veterans, sometimes touring. In the 60s she suffered periods of ill-health but even a stroke did not stop her. Somewhat flamboyant in her younger days, she was known as the Bell Gal because of her habit of wearing bells on her garters, in her later years she developed rather grandiose ideas about her abilities. She took it as a sign of her due that during one tour her musicians clustered at one side of the stage, leaving her in isolated splendour at the other, oblivious to the fact that they were eager to stay as far away as possible from the odour of an unclean dressing on her injured foot. For all her eccentricities, however, Barrett helped perpetuate the music of her home town with unending enthusiasm.
Albums: *The Bell Gal And Her Dixieland Boys* (1961), *Sweet Emma Barrett And Her New Orleans Music* (1963), *Sweet Emma Barrett At Disneyland* (1964), *Sweet Emma Barrett And Her Preservation Hall Jazz Band* (1964), *Sweet Emma, The Bell Gal And Her New Orleans Jazz Band* (1966), *Sweet Emma Barrett And Her Original Tuxedo Jass Band At Dixieland Hall* (1968).

Barron, Kenny

b. 9 June 1943, Philadelphia, Pennsylvania, USA. After studying piano as a child, Barron began playing professionally when still in his early teens. Performing first in R&B bands, he began to concentrate on jazz and in the late 50s and early 60s played briefly with Philly Joe Jones and Yusef Lateef. From 1961, he was resident in New York, playing with James Moody, Lee Morgan, his brother Bill Barron, a saxophonist, and then joined Dizzy Gillespie for an association which lasted until 1966. During his sojourn with Gillespie he toured extensively. In the late 60s he was briefly with Stanley Turrentine and then spent two years with Freddie Hubbard, following this engagement with a long stint with Lateef. By this time Barron had become established as a composer and teacher and in 1973 was appointed to a senior post at Rutgers University. During this same period he also worked with Ron Carter. In the 80s he continued teaching, writing and playing, co-leading the group Sphere, which featured Charlie Rouse, Buster Williams and Ben Riley, and recording with Frank Wess and others. He then enjoyed a long and deeply satisfying musical relationship with Stan Getz, playing on several notable albums. He has also proved to be a sensitive accompanist for singers including Judy Niemack, Sathima Bea Benjamin and Teresa Brewer. Although he has enjoyed a high profile amongst musicians, appearing in the rhythm sections of many bands on numerous albums, Barron's main contribution to jazz might well prove to be his teaching and composing.
Albums: with Bill Barron *The Tenor Stylings Of Bill Barron* (1961), with Dizzy Gillespie *Charlie Parker Memorial Concert* (1965), with Stanley Turrentine *New Time Shuffle* (1967), with Freddie Hubbard, *High Blues Pressure* (1967-68), with Yusef

Lateef *The Gentle Giant* (1971), *Sunset To Dawn* (Muse 1973), *Peruvian Blue* (Muse 1974), *Lucifer* (Muse 1975), with Ron Carter *Piccolo* (1977), *Golden Lotus* (1980), *At The Piano* (1981), with Sphere *Four In One* (1982), *Green Chimneys* (Criss Cross 1983), with Sphere *Flight Path* (1983), with Frank Wess *Two At The Top* (1983), *1+1+1* (Black Hawk 1984), *Landscape* (Limetree 1984), *Scratch* (Enja 1985), *What If* (Enja 1986), *Live At Fat Tuesday's* (Enja 1988), *Rhythm-A-Ning* (Candid 1989), *Quickstep* (Enja 1991), *Invitation* (Criss Cross 1991), *The Only One* (1993), *Other Places* (Verve 1994), *Wanton Spirit* (1994).

Bartz, Gary

b. 26 September 1940, Baltimore, Maryland, USA. Bartz, whose father ran a jazz club, began playing alto saxophone at the age of 11. He played in the Alabama State Teachers College band, at his father's club, and studied at the Juilliard School, New York and the Peabody Conservatory in Baltimore. He worked with Lee Morgan and Grachan Moncur III, but his first regular professional engagement was with the Max Roach/Abbey Lincoln band in 1964. From 1965-66 he was one of Art Blakey's Jazz Messengers, then had a second stint with Roach and periods with Charles Tolliver, Blue Mitchell and McCoy Tyner (in what Tyner once described as the happiest and most integrated band he had ever led). For 18 months beginning in August 1970 he was with Miles Davis (*Live - Evil*), in 1972 formed Ntu Troop, and during the 70s moved further into the funk fusion field. In recent years he has returned to the hard bop fold, a genre which shows off his assertive and agile improvising to best advantage. Originally inspired to take up the saxophone by hearing Charlie Parker, he has helped to keep the succession alive, and his playing is in the tradition of Phil Woods and, especially, Jackie McLean, with whom he has made some fine music (*Ode To Super*). *There Goes The Neighborhood* is an exceptional album. Recorded live at New York's famous Birdland Club in November 1990, it is a vivid record from one of modern jazz's most intense and exciting living saxophonists, playing at his peak. Pianist Kenny Barron, bassist Ray Drummond and drummer Ben Riley offer firm support for Bartz's powerful plaintive alto, as he powers his way through a well-chosen programme of standards and original tunes. Bartz by this time had got over his bland jazz/pop flirtation, and was playing a strong combination of neo-bop and heavy, John Coltrane-influenced shapes. The inspired version of 'Impressions' is not to be missed.
Albums: *Libra* (1967), *Another Earth* (1968), *Home!* (1969), *Harlem Bush Music - Taifa* (1970), with Miles Davis *Live - Evil* (1970), *Harlem Bush Music - Uhuru* (1971), *Follow The Medicine Man* (1972), *Ju-Ju Street Songs* (1972), *I've Known Rivers* (1973), with Jackie McLean *Ode To Super* (1973), *Singarella - A Ghetto Fairytale* (1974), *The Shadow Do* (1975), *Music Is My Sanctuary* (1975), *Ju-Ju Man* (1976), , with McCoy Tyner *Focal Point* (1976), *Love Affair* (1978), *Bartz* (1980), Monsoon (Steeplechase 1988), *Reflections Of Monk* (Steeplechase 1989), *West 42nd Street* (Candid 1990), with Cosmo Intini *My Favourite Roots* (1990), *There Goes The*

Neighborhood (Candid 1991), *Shadows* (JSP 1992).

Basie, Count

b. William Basie, 21 August 1904, Red Bank, New Jersey, USA, d. 26 April 1984. Bandleader and pianist Basie grew up in Red Bank, just across the Hudson River from New York City. His mother gave him his first lessons at the piano, and he used every opportunity to hear the celebrated kings of New York keyboard - James P. Johnson, Willie 'The Lion' Smith and especially Fats Waller. Ragtime was all the rage, and these keyboard professors ransacked the European tradition to achieve ever more spectacular improvisations. The young Basie listened to Fats Waller playing the organ in Harlem's Lincoln Theater and received tuition from him. Pianists were in demand to accompany vaudeville acts, and Waller recommended Basie as his successor in the Katie Crippen And Her Kids troupe, and with them he toured black venues throughout America (often referred to as the 'chitlin' circuit'). Stranded in Kansas City after the Gonzel White tour collapsed, Basie found it 'wide-open'. Owing to the *laissez-faire* administration of Democrat leader Tom Pendergast, musicians could easily find work, and jazz blossomed alongside gambling and prostitution (many people trace the origins of modern jazz to these circumstances - see Kansas City Jazz). Basie played to silent movies for a while, then in 1928 joined Walter Page's Blue Devils, starting a 20-year-long association with the bassist. When the Blue Devils broke up, Basie joined Bennie Moten, then, in 1935 started his own band at the Reno Club and quickly lured Moten's best musicians into its ranks. Unfettered drinking hours, regular broadcasts on local radio and Basie's feel for swing honed the band into quite simply the most classy and propulsive unit in the history of music. Duke Ellington's band may have been more ambitious, but for sheer unstoppable *swing* Basie could not be beaten. Impresario John Hammond recognised as much when he heard them on their local broadcast. In January 1937 an augmented Basie band made its recording debut for Decca. By this time the classic rhythm section - Freddie Green (guitar), Walter Page (bass) and Jo Jones (drums) - had been established. The horns - which included Lester Young (tenor saxophone) and Buck Clayton (trumpet) - sounded magnificent buoyed by this team and the goadings of Basie's deceptively simple piano. Basie frequently called himself a 'non-pianist'; actually, his incisive minimalism had great power and influence - not least on Thelonious Monk, one of bebop's principal architects.

In 1938, the band recorded the classic track 'Jumpin' At The Woodside', a Basie composition featuring solos by Earle Warren (alto saxophone) and Herschel Evans (clarinet), as well as Young and Clayton. The track could be taken as a definition of swing. Basie's residency at the Famous Door club on New York's West 52nd Street from July 1938 to January 1939 was a great success, CBS broadcasting the band over its radio network (transcriptions of these broadcasts have recently been made available - although hardly hi-fi, they are fascinating documents, with Lester Young playing clarinet as well as tenor). This booking was followed by a six-month residency in Chicago. It is this kind of regular work - spontaneity balanced with regular application - that explains why the recorded sides of the period are some of the great music of the century. In 1939 Basie left Decca for Columbia, with whom he stayed until 1946. Throughout the 40s the Count Basie band provided dancers with conducive rhythms and jazz fans with astonishing solos: both appreciated his characteristic contrast of brass and reeds. Outstanding tenors emerged: Don Byas, Buddy Tate, Lucky Thompson, Illinois Jacquet, Paul Gonsalves, as well as trumpeters (Al Killian and Joe Newman) and trombonists (Vic Dickenson and J.J. Johnson). On vocals Basie used Jimmy Rushing for the blues material and Helen Humes for pop and novelty numbers. Economic necessity pared down the Basie band to seven members at the start of the 50s, but otherwise Basie maintained a big band right through to his death in 1984. In 1954 he made his first tour of Europe, using arrangements by Ernie Wilkins and Neal Hefti. In June 1957 Basie broke the colour bar at New York's Waldorf-Astoria Hotel; his was the first black band to play there, and they stayed for a four month engagement. The 1957 *The Atomic Mr Basie* set Hefti's arrangements in glorious stereo sound and was acknowledged as a classic. Even the cover made its mark: in the 70s Blondie adapted its period nuclear-chic to frame singer Debbie Harry.

In 1960, Jimmy Rushing left the band, depriving it of a popular frontman, but the European tours continued - a groundbreaking tour of Japan in 1963 was also a great success. Count Basie was embraced by the American entertainment industry and appeared in the films *Sex And The Single Girl* and *Made In Paris*. He became a regular television guest alongside the likes of Frank Sinatra, Fred Astaire, Sammy Davis Jnr. and Tony Bennett. Arranging for Basie was a significant step in the career of Quincy Jones (now famous as Michael Jackson's producer). The onslaught of the Beatles and rock music in the 60s was giving jazz a hard time; Basie responded by giving current pop tunes the big band treatment. Jones arranged *Hits Of The 50s And 60s*. Its resounding commercial success led to a string of similar albums arranged by Bill Byers; the brass adopted the stridency of John Barry's James Bond scores and, unlike the work of the previous decades, these records now sound dated. In 1965, Basie signed to Sinatra's Reprise label, and made several recordings and appearances with him.

By 1969 most of Basie's original sidemen had left the band, though Freddie Green was still with him. Eddie 'Lockjaw' Davis (tenor) was now his most distinguished soloist. The arranger Sammy Nestico provided some interesting compositions, and 1979 saw the release of *Afrique*, an intriguing and unconventional album arranged by Oliver Nelson with tunes by *avant garde* saxophonists such as Albert Ayler and Pharoah Sanders. In 1975, after recording for a slew of different labels, Basie found a home on Pablo Records (owned by Norman Granz, organizer of the Jazz At The Philharmonic showcases). This produced a late flowering, as, unlike previous producers, Granz let Basie do what he does best - swing the blues - rather than collaborate with popular singers. In 1983, the death of his wife Catherine, whom he had married 40 years before while he was with the Bennie Moten band, struck a heavy blow and he himself died the following year. The later compromises should not cloud Basie's achievements: during the 30s he integrated the bounce of the blues into sophisticated ensemble playing. His piano work showed that rhythm and space were more important than technical virtuosity: his composing gave many eminent soloists their finest moments. Without the Count Basie Orchestra's sublimely aerated versions of 'Cherokee' it is unlikely that Charlie Parker could have ever created 'Koko'. Modern jazz stands indubitably in Basie's debt. For newcomers to the work of Basie the *Original American Decca Recordings* is an unbeatable starting point.

Selected albums: *Jumpin' At The Woodside* (1938 recordings), *Count Basie And His Orchestra* (1944 recordings), *At The Blue Note* (1955-56 recordings), *April In Paris* (Verve 1956), *Basie In London* (Verve 1957), *At Newport* (Verve 1957), *The Atomic Mr Basie* (Roulette 1957), *Sing Along With Basie* (Roulette 1958), *One More Time* (Roulette 1959), with Tony Bennett *Basie Swings, Bennett Sings* (Roulette 1959), *Count Basie and the Kansas City Seven* (1962), *Lil' Ol' Groovemaker. . . Basie* (Verve 1963), *Basie's Bounce* (Affinity 1965), *Our Shining Hour* (Verve 1965), *Live At Antibes 1968* (1968), *The Bosses* (Pablo 1973), *Basie Jam* (Pablo 1973), *For The First Time* (Pablo 1974), *For The Second Time* (Original Jazz Classics 1974), *Satch And Josh* (Pablo 1975), *Jam Session At The Montreux Jazz Festival* (Pablo 1975), *Basie Big Band* (Pablo 1975), *I Told You So* (Pablo 1976), with Dizzy Gillespie *The Gifted Ones* (1977), *Prime Time* (Pablo 1977), *Satch And Josh . . . Again* (Pablo 1977), *Live In Japan* (Pablo 1978), *The Timekeepers* (Pablo 1978), *Afrique* (1979), *Basic Basie* (1974), *On The Road* (Pablo 1980), *Get Together* (Pablo 1980), *Kansas City 7* (Original Jazz Classics 1980), *Kansas City Shout* (Pablo 1980), *Warm Breeze* (Pablo 1981), *Basie And Friends* (Pablo 1982), *Farmers Market Barbecue* (Pablo 1982), *Me And You* (Pablo 1983), *88 Basie Street* (Pablo 1983), *Fancy Pants* (Pablo 1984), *Live In Japan '78* (1985), *Birdland Era, Vols. 1 & 2* (1986), *Complete American Decca Recordings 1937-39* (Decca 1992), *The Swing Machine* (Giants Of Jazz 1992, CD box set), *The Complete Atomic Basie* (1994).

Bass, Ralph

b. 1 May 1911, New York, USA. A pivotal figure in the history of R&B, Bass began his career during the 40s, promoting live jazz shows in Los Angeles. He subsequently worked for Black And White Records, producing 'Open The Door, Richard' for Jack McVea, but later left to found several small-scale outlets with releases by Errol Garner and Dexter Gordon. Bass also recorded (Little) Esther Phillips, the Robins and Johnny Otis for the Savoy label, and in 1951 became one of the era's first independent producers through the aegis of the Cincinnati-based King company. Armed with his own outlet, Federal, and its Armo publishing wing, he built an impressive roster of acts around Hank Ballard And The Midnighters, the Dominoes and James Brown, whom Bass signed in 1955 on hearing a demo disc at an Atlanta radio station. Although initially unimpressed by the singer's untutored delivery, King

managing director Syd Nathan changed his mind when 'Please Please Please' became a best-seller. Brown remained a Federal artist until 1960 but was switched to the parent outlet when Bass departed for Chess. The producer brought Etta James and Pigmeat Markham to his new employers, and in turn worked with several established acts, including Muddy Waters, Howlin' Wolf and Ramsey Lewis. Bass remained with the label until the mid-70s when its Chicago office was closed. He continued to record R&B acts, the masters from which were latterly compiled on a series of albums under the generic title, *I Didn't Give A Damn If Whites Bought It.*

Basso, Gianni

b. 24 May 1931, Asti, Italy. Basso studied clarinet at the Conservatorio di Asti before playing with various American groups in Belgium and Germany in the late 40s. When he returned to Italy he played in dance orchestras before joining the radio orchestra of Armando Trovajoli in 1956. He co-led one of Italy's best bands with trumpeter Oscar Valdambrini (1955-60) and worked with a succession of touring American musicians including Chet Baker, Buddy Collette, Slide Hampton, Maynard Ferguson, Phil Woods and Gerry Mulligan. In the late 70s he founded the band Saxes Machine. His first influence as a tenor saxophone player was Stan Getz but he was later influenced by Sonny Rollins. His playing is characterized by the impetuosity associated with free jazz. Though he still plays club dates he now works mostly as a studio musician in Rome.

Albums: *The Best Modern Jazz In Italy* (1959), *Lunet* (Splasc 1982), *Maestro + Maestro = Exciting Duo* (Splasc 1983), *Gianni Basso Quartet* (Pentaflowers 1992).

Batchelor, Wayne

Batchelor, a skilled and stylish bass player, is one of several excellent black British jazz players who have been building a reputation for years and who have come to notice in the slipstream of Courtney Pine's celebrity. In common with others of the Jazz Warriors circle he exhibits a highly serious and dedicated attitude to his music. For a while he led a fine quartet, comprising saxophonist Brian Edwards, pianist Jonathan Gee and drummer Winston Clifford. He also played as a member of the Ed Jones Quartet and the Shelly Ambury Quartet. He has played with Steve Williamson and Williamson, in turn, has played in Batchelor's band, producing some of his finest work on a 1989 demo-disc which, sadly, is not publicly available.

Bates, Django

b. Leon Bates, 2 October 1960, Beckenham, Kent, England. A self-taught pianist, Bates formally studied the instrument, together with trumpet and violin, at London's Centre for Young Musicians in the 70s and later attended the young musicians course at Morley College. In 1978, he dropped out from the Royal College of Music (after two weeks). Bates began a series of important associations with many of the leading young musicians who graced the burgeoning British jazz scene of the 80s and several of the concurrently popular African jazz musicians. In 1983, by which time he had already experienced stints with Tim Whitehead, Steve Argüelles (with whom he formed the trio Human Chain), Bill Bruford, Harry Beckett and Dudu Pukwana's Zila, he became a founder member of Loose Tubes. In 1986, Bates guested with the George Russell Orchestra on their UK tour, and by this time was also playing in the quartet First House, with alto saxophonist Ken Stubbs, and in Bruford's jazz rock group, Earthworks. Bates's eclectic musical tastes are evidenced by his playing and composing, neither of which can be readily pigeon-holed. Whether on keyboards or on tenor horn (an unusual instrument in jazz circles and one on which Bates is particularly effective) he is a distinctive and adventurous musician and one who seems incapable of a bad or uninteresting performance. In 1990, Bates's suite *Music For The Third Policeman* (based on the novel by Flann O'Brien) was recorded by his specially-formed Powder Room Collapse Orchestra, and in the summer of 1991 he assembled another big band, Delightful Precipice (named after a Loose Tubes' album), for a show which also featured a circus! Earlier that year he toured the UK in a group led by Norwegian singer Sidsel Endresen.

Albums: *First House* (1985), with Human Chain *Cashin' In* (1988), with First House *Cantilena* (1989), *Music For The Third Policeman* (Ah-Um 1990), *Summer Fruits (And Unrest)* (PolyGram 1993), as Doran, Studer, Minton, Bates, Ali *Play The Music Of Jimi Hendrix* (Call It Anything 1994).

Batiste, Alvin

b. 1937, New Orleans, Louisiana, USA. Batiste played jazz clarinet with Ed Blackwell in high school, which led to a long association with Ornette Coleman, with whom he jammed in Los Angeles in the mid-50s. After a spell freelancing in New Orleans, Batiste toured with the Ray Charles band in 1958. From the late 60s to the mid-80s he devoted much of his time to teaching at Southern University in Baton Rouge, although he did record with Cannonball Adderley on the saxophonist's last album, *Lovers*, in 1975. In 1981 he joined John Carter, David Murray and Jimmy Hamilton in the group Clarinet Summit and in 1984 released his first album as leader, *Musique D'Afrique Nouvelle Orleans*, which comprised a suite celebrating Crescent City Culture (originally written for the New Orleans Philharmonic Orchestra) plus two pieces that revealed Batiste's deep interest in mysticism: in the sleeve-notes he also mentions that he has studied music with the Rosicrucian Order, AMORC. An eclectic player, as happy to work in classical modes as in jazz, Batiste's recent *Bayou Magic* is a more conventional set of post-bebop tunes but still provides an exhilarating showcase for his brilliant technique and astonishing invention on clarinet. In 1987, for a festival dedicated to Blackwell, he was reunited with various 50s' associates (such as Ellis Marsalis and Blackwell himself) in the American Jazz Quintet, whose *From Bad To Badder* documented their first concert together for some 30 years.

Albums: *Musique D'Afrique Nouvelle Orleans* (1984), *Clarinet Summit* (1984, rec. 1982), *Clarinet Summit Volume 2* (1985, rec. 1982), with Clarinet Summit *Southern Belles* (1988), *Bayou Magic* (India Navigation 1991), with American Jazz Quintet *From Bad To Badder* (1992, rec. 1987).

Battle, Edgar 'Puddenhead'

b. 3 October 1907, Atlanta, Georgia, USA, d. 6 February 1977. Trumpet, trombone, saxophones, piano, arranger, composer. Thanks to his vast instrumental versatility, Battle played in the trumpet, trombone and reed sections of several 30s' big bands including those led by Andy Kirk, Blanche Calloway, Benny Carter and Willie Bryant. In 1937 he briefly led his own band (and in the late 40s co-led a band with Shirley Clay) before deciding to concentrate on arranging. His charts were played by the bands of Count Basie, Cab Calloway, Earl Hines, Jack Teagarden, Fats Waller and others. Battle's best-known composition is 'Topsy' which has been recorded many times and was a 50s' hit for Cozy Cole.

Bauduc, Ray

b. 18 June 1909, New Orleans, Louisiana, USA, d. 8 January 1988. Bauduc's New Orleans origins instilled in him a love for two-beat drumming, which he retained even when he played with Bob Crosby's swing era big band. Before the popularity and prominence of his Crosby days, Bauduc had worked with Johnny Bayersdorffer, Eddie Lang, Joe Venuti and Freddie Rich, in whose band he was also featured as a dancer. In 1928, he joined the Ben Pollack band when Pollack decided to give up drumming and simply lead. When the Pollack band dissolved and became one of the few co-operative bands in jazz, under the nominal leadership of Bob Crosby, Bauduc was among its most important members. Unlike the majority of bands of the era, which usually played in 4/4 time, the Crosby band was spurred on by Bauduc's lively 2/4 drumming. Extensively featured with the band (and in the spin-off small groups, the Bob Cats and Four Of The Bob Cats), Bauduc's most memorable moment of glory came when an encore at the Blackhawk Ballroom found just him and bassist Bob Haggart improvising a tune during which Haggart whistled and Bauduc drummed on the strings of the bass. The result, 'Big Noise From Winnetka', was one of the band's biggest hits. Another popular success, 'South Rampart Street Parade', was also a co-composition by Bauduc and Haggart (written on a tablecloth at the New Yorker Hotel). Bauduc's regular feature with the band, 'The Big Crash From China', provided an excellent example of his intelligent soloing and superb cymbal work. After leaving Crosby when the band broke up in 1942, Bauduc worked with Jimmy Dorsey, Jack Teagarden and others and in the 50s became co-leader, with former Crosby-colleague Nappy Lamare, of a popular west coast-based band. From 1960, Bauduc lived in Texas in semi-retirement, but visited New Orleans in 1983 where he was greeted effusively. In 1985 he showed that he had lost none of his enthusiasm and little of his skill in a reunion of the Crosby band at the Mid-America Jazz Festival in St Louis. Bauduc's snappy, clean exuberant drumming gave any band in which he worked an exciting, happy sound.

Albums: with Pete Fountain *New Orleans In LA* (1954-56

recordings), with Nappy Lamare *Riverboat Dandies* (1957). Compilations: with Bob Crosby *South Rampart Street Parade* (1937-42 recordings), with Crosby *Big Noise From Winnetka* (1935-42 recordings).

Bauer, Billy

b. 14 November 1915, New York City, New York, USA. One of the few jazz guitarists of his generation to avoid the influence of Charlie Christian, Bauer's most famous associations were with Woody Herman and Lennie Tristano. During his time with Herman (the 1944-46 First Herd), Bauer also recorded extensively with small spin-off groups, including those led by Bill Harris, Chubby Jackson and Flip Phillips. One of Bauer's improvised solo features with the Herd, 'Billy Bauer's Tune', was later formalized under the title, 'Pam'. When the First Herd folded, Bauer played with bands led by Tommy Dorsey, Benny Goodman and Jack Teagarden; he was also with Charlie Ventura's interesting if short-lived big band. This same period, the late 40s, saw him entering a somewhat different musical world as a member of Lennie Tristano's trio (later sextet). By 1949, Tristano had started to experiment with a form of jazz in which musicians improvised in unison without predetermined key signatures or orthodox structures. Bauer's precise, metallic playing fitted well into these surroundings, which proved to be of only limited appeal to fans. Bauer continued to work in jazz from the 50s onwards, recording with the band of J.J. Johnson-Kai Winding and with Tristano, Lee Konitz and others, but most of his time was spent in studio work and in operating his own music publishing company.

Albums: *Billy Bauer* (1953), *Plectrist* (1956). Compilations: with Lennie Tristano *The Rarest Trio/Quartet Sessions* (1946-47 recordings).

Bauza, Mario

b. 28 April 1911, Havana, Cuba, d. 11 July 1993. One of the outstanding if unsung section men of the swing era, often cited as the man who invented 'latin jazz'. Bauza's trumpet playing was only one facet of his broad talent. Until 1932 Bauza had played clarinet, oboe and other reeds and woodwinds with various bands both in Cuba, where he graduated at the Havana Municipal Conservatory of Music, and New York, where he worked for Noble Sissle's society band and Sam Wooding. It was while he was there that Bauza learned to play trumpet in just two weeks, in order to make a record date with the Cuban singer Cuarteto Machin. Bauza began to concentrate on trumpet and it was on this instrument that he joined the Missourians and later became a mainstay of the Chick Webb band. In 1938, after five years with Webb during which he mostly played lead and also acted as musical director, he moved to the Don Redman band. He also played with Fletcher Henderson and Cab Calloway and is credited with persuading Calloway to hire Dizzy Gillespie (having previously failed to convince Webb to hire him). In 1941, Bauza joined the strongly jazz-orientated Latin American band led by his brother-in-law, Frank 'Machito' Grillo. Bauza stayed with Machito for 35 years during which time the band enjoyed the company of many guesting jazz stars including Charlie Parker, Cannonball Adderley, Joe Newman, Doc Cheatham, Howard McGhee and Buddy Rich. Machito credited Bauza as the architect behind his sound. As musical director and principal arranger for the Machito band, Bauza was responsible for overseeing numerous shifts in taste culminating in the 70s with the widespread popularity of salsa. After leaving Machito in 1976 Bauza continued to work, leading his own band the African-Cuban Jazz Orchestra for recording dates and appearing regularly in New York. His two albums in the 90s for the Messidor label are worthy of investigation.

Albums: with Machito *The Definitive Charlie Parker* (1948-50 recordings), with Machito *Kenya* (1957), *Afro-Cuban Jazz* (1986), *Tanga* (Messidor 1992), *My Time Is Now* (Messidor 1993). Compilation: with Chick Webb *The King Of Swing* (1937-39 recordings).

Bechet, Sidney

b. 14 May 1897, New Orleans, Louisiana, USA, d. 14 May 1959. A major figure in early jazz, an outstanding clarinettist, and for decades the only performer of consequence on soprano saxophone, Sidney Bechet's career began in 1909. During the next few years he played clarinet in bands led by legendary musicians such as Buddy Petit, John Robichaux and Bunk Johnson. By 1917 Bechet had left New Orleans behind, both literally and musically, visiting Europe in 1919 as a member of Will Marion Cook's orchestra. Whilst in London during this tour, Bechet purchased a straight soprano saxophone and eventually achieved mastery over this notoriously difficult instrument, thus becoming the first real jazz saxophonist. Bechet's European trip was a mixed affair: he received rave reviews, including one, (much-quoted), from the Swiss conductor Ernest Ansermet, and was briefly imprisoned in London after a fracas with a lady of doubtful virtue. Back in the USA, Bechet worked with James P. Johnson and Duke Ellington before returning to Europe for an extended visit. This time Bechet encountered problems with the law in Paris. His stay being forcibly extended by almost a year after he was involved in a shooting incident with pianist Mike McKendrick. Out of prison and back once more in the USA, Bechet settled into a long association with Noble Sissle, which lasted throughout the 30s. During this period he worked and recorded with numerous jazzmen of note, including Louis Armstrong, Tommy Ladnier and Eddie Condon. In 1938 Bechet temporarily retired from the music business and began business as a tailor in New York. However, the following year he recorded 'Summertime' for the fledgling Blue Note label and scored both a popular hit and one of his greatest performances. In the 40s Bechet continued much as before but was now teaching, (he had earlier briefly schooled Johnny Hodges), and one of his pupils was Bob Wilber, who not only studied but also worked with the master. The end of the 40s saw Bechet risking Europe again and this time there was none of the trouble that had overshadowed his previous visits. His 1949 appearance at the Salle Pleyel Jazz Festival in Paris was a massive success. Later that same year he made another trip to France and this time he stayed. Throughout the 50s Bechet was a king in his new-found homeland, experiencing a freedom and a measure of appreciation and adulation that had always escaped him in the USA. He continued to play and record extensively, visiting the USA but always thinking of France as home. Right until the end, his powerful playing, for example at the 1958 Brussels Exhibition, gave no indication of his approaching death from cancer, which came on 14 May 1959, his 62nd birthday. In Antibes, where he had made his home, they erected a statue of him and also named a square after him.

A lyrical heart-on-sleeve player with a wide vibrato, Bechet was also one of the most passionate of performers, on either of his instruments. On soprano he could hold his own with anyone, even trumpeters as powerful as Louis Armstrong. Although his recorded legacy is melodically rich and immensely satisfying in its emotional intensity, only a handful of players, of whom Wilber is the outstanding example, have noticeably followed the path he signposted. Bechet's autobiography *Treat It Gentle* is a romantic, highly-readable but not always accurate account of his life.

Selected albums: *Deux Heures Du Matin Au Vieux Colombier* (1952), *Olympia Concert* (1954), *Refreshing Tracks* (1958) with Teddy Buckner *Parisian Encounter* (1958), *Concert At The World's Fair, Brussells* (1958). Compilations: *Sidney Bechet* i (1923-38 recordings), with Noble Sissle, Tommy Ladnier *Sidney Bechet In Digital Stereo* (1924-38 recordings), *The Complete Sidney Bechet Vols 1-4* (1932-41 recordings), *Bechet Of New Orleans* (1932-42 recordings), *The Bluebird Sessions* (Bluebird 1989, 1932-43 recordings), *The Panassie Sessions* (1938-39 recordings), *Jazz Classics Volumes 1 And 2* (RCA 1983, 1939-51 recordings), *The Sidney Bechet-Muggsy Spanier Big Four: A Jam Session* (1940 recordings), with Louis Armstrong *New Orleans Days* (1940 recordings), *Sidney Bechet And His New Orleans Feetwarmers Vols 1-3* (1940-41 recordings), *Sidney Bechet* ii (1945-51 recordings), with Bob Wilber *Sidney Bechet* iii (1949 recordings), *In New York* (1937-40 recordings).

Further reading: *Treat It Gentle*, Sidney Bechet. *Sidney Bechet: The Wizard Of Jazz*, John Chilton.

Beck, Gordon

b. 16 September 1936, London, England. Beck, unlike many of his contemporaries, did not 'pay his dues' with the show and dance bands of the era. He studied piano at school but opted for a career as a draughtsman. It was exposure in Canada to the popular playing of George Shearing and Dave Brubeck that persuaded Beck to return to music and back in England he progressed rapidly, working with Bobby Wellins, Tony Crombie and others. In 1962, Beck joined the Tubby Hayes Quintet with whom he recorded. In 1965 he formed a trio with Tony Oxley and Jeff Clyne, and then spent a number of years as house pianist at Ronnie Scott's club where he played behind Joe Henderson, Lee Konitz, Helen Merrill and others. During this period Beck played with Phil Woods and when George Gruntz left Woods's band in 1969, Beck was asked to join. Tours of Europe and the USA followed exposing the pianist to

universal accolade: the critic, Jean-Louis Ginibre said at the time 'Phil called in the only other pianist in Europe who could fill the chair'. Beck developed as a composer with Woods, his compositions have been recorded by Cleo Laine and Gary Burton. After 1972, Beck worked with his trio, his larger group, Gyroscope, with Don Sebesky and with Piano Conclave, the six keyboard group led by Gruntz. During the 80s he has toured regularly in Europe, and most successfully in France, where he has also recorded solo projects and albums with Allan Holdsworth and Helen Merrill. Beck is one of the few English jazz musicians whose work bears comparison with his influences, of whom he has named particularly Bud Powell, Bill Evans and Herbie Hancock.

Selected albums: with Ronnie Scott *Live At Ronnie Scotts* (1968), with Phil Woods *Live At Frankfurt* (1971), trio *Experiments With Pops* (1967), *Gyroscope* (1968), *Sunbird* (1979), *The Things You See* (1980), *Dreams* (JMS 1989), *For Evans Sake* (JMS 1993).

Beckett, Harry

b. 30 May 1935, St Michael Parish, Barbados. Resident in the UK since 1954, trumpeter Beckett has associated with many leading post-boppers and fusionists, including Graham Collier, in whose band he worked for about 15 years, beginning in the early 60s. In 1961 Beckett worked with Charles Mingus in London, appearing in the film, *All Through The Night*. Throughout the 60s and 70s, he led his own small groups, notably Joy Unlimited, and also played with John Surman, Mike Westbrook, Mike Gibbs, Stan Tracey, Dudu Pukwana and Chris MacGregor's Brotherhood Of Breath. He also touched the mainstream during engagements with Ronnie Scott and John Dankworth and made occasional forays into jazz-rock with Keef Hartley. In the 80s he worked extensively with students and on his own compositions, touring world-wide. Beckett's playing on both trumpet and flügelhorn is characterized by a fluid lyricism shot through with dazzling and sometimes fierce bursts of free inventiveness. His 1985 *Pictures Of You* was one of the first albums on the short-lived Paladin label and in the same year he recorded *Angolan Quartet* as a member of the Johnny Dyani Quartet. In the late 80s Beckett was for a while *eminence grise* with the young Jazz Warriors and also played frequently with Courtney Pine. In the early 90s a longtime association with Elton Dean took a new twist as the pair joined up with Enrico Fazio (bass) and Fiorenzi Sardini (drums) to form the Anglo-Italian Quartet, which made its first UK tour in 1991 and released its debut album (on the Italian Splasch label) in the same year.

Albums: with Graham Collier *Deep Dark Blue Centre* (1967), *Flare Up* (1970), *Warm Smiles* (1971), *Themes For Fega* (1972), *Joy Unlimited* (1974), *Memoirs Of Bacares* (1976), *Got It Made* (1977), *Pictures Of You* (Paladin 1984), *The Bremen Concert* (West Wind 1987), with the Anglo-Italian Quartet *Put It Right Mr. Smoothie* (1991), *All Four One* (Spotlite 1992), with Courtney Pine *Live Vol II* (West Wind 1992), *Images Of Clarity* (Evidence 1994).

Beiderbecke, Bix

b. Leon Bix Beiderbecke, 10 March 1903, Davenport, Iowa, USA, d. 6 August 1931, New York, USA. One of the legends of jazz, a role he would doubtless have found wryly amusing had he lived to know of it, Bix Beiderbecke entered music when he began picking out tunes on piano and cornet at the age of 15. Inspired by records of the Original Dixieland Jazz Band and by hearing bands on the Mississippi riverboats, Beiderbecke broke away from his middle-class, middle-American family background (an act for which his family appeared never to forgive him) and by 1923 was already achieving fame with the Wolverines. In New York and Chicago, Beiderbecke played with dancebands but spent his free time listening to the leading black musicians of the day, notably Louis Armstrong and Joe 'King' Oliver. In 1926 he worked with Frankie Trumbauer, both men moving on to the bands of Jean Goldkette and Paul Whiteman, whom they joined in 1928. Throughout his time with these two jazz-age showbands, Beiderbecke was the featured jazz soloist and was very well paid. These two facts go some way to countering the accepted wisdom that such jobs, especially that with Whiteman, destroyed his creative impulse and accelerated his decline. In fact, these same years saw Beiderbecke freelancing with numerous jazz groups, many of which included other fine jazz artists whom Goldkette and Whiteman hired. The problems which assailed Beiderbecke seem to have been largely generated by his desire to 'dignify' his work with classical overtones, his rejection by his family (his film biographer, Brigitte Berman reveals how, on a visit to his home, he found all his records which he had proudly mailed to his parents lying unopened in a cupboard) and a general weakness of character. These troubles led him to take refuge in drink and this swiftly degenerated into chronic alcoholism. This, and allied ill-health, kept Beiderbecke out of the Whiteman band for long periods, although Whiteman kept his chair empty for him and paid all his bills. By the end of 1929 he was back home in Davenport trying, vainly, to restore himself to fitness. During his last year, Beiderbecke tried out for the Casa Loma Orchestra and played with pick-up groups in New York including sessions with Benny Goodman, Red Nichols and others.

When he died in August 1931, Beiderbecke was still only 28-years-old. Set against the bold and barrier-breaking glories of Armstrong's playing, Beiderbecke's technique was limited, but within it he played with great panache. The sound of his cornet had a fragile, crystalline quality which suited his detached, introspective formalism (not surprisingly, he admired Debussy). He wrote a few pieces for piano, one of which, 'In A Mist', strongly indicates the would-be classicist buried inside him. His recorded work, whether in small groups ('Singin' The Blues' with Trumbauer) or in big bands ('San' and 'Dardanella' with Whiteman), continually demonstrated his fertile imagination. Beiderbecke's early death and the manner of his passing helped to make him a legend, and a novel based on his life, Dorothy Baker's Young Man With A Horn romanticized his life. As often happens in such cases, there was a long period when the legend substantially outweighed reality. More recently,

thanks in part to extensive reissues of his recorded legacy and accurate portrayals of his life in the Richard Sudhalter-Philip Evans biography and Berman's excellent filmed documentary, a more balanced view of Beiderbecke's work has been made possible. Although his contribution to jazz falls well short of the concurrent advances being made by Armstrong, he frequently displayed a measure of sensitivity and introspection that foreshadowed the cooler approach to jazz trumpet of a later generation.

Selected albums: The Complete Bix Beiderbecke In Chronological Order Vols 1-9 (1924-30 recordings), At The Jazz Band Ball (1924-28 recordings), Bixology Vols 1-14 (1924-30 recordings), The Studio Groups (1927 recordings), Bix Beiderbecke And The Wolverines (1993, rec. 1924), Bix Beiderbecke And The Chicage Cornets (Milestine 1980), Bix Beiderbecke Vols 1-14 (Joker 1981), Bix Beiderbecke Collection (Deja Vu 1985), The Bix Beiderbecke Story (CBS 1986),

Further reading: Remembering Bix, Ralph Berton. Bix: Man And Legend, Richard M. Sudhalter and Philip R. Evans.

Bell, Graeme

b. 7 September 1914, Melbourne, Victoria, Australia. Early in the 40s, Bell played piano in local jazz groups with his trumpet-playing brother, Roger. In addition to playing jazz, he was one of the leading promoters of the music in Australia. He was greatly responsible for building a jazz following in the country and by the late 40s his reputation was such that he brought his band to the UK, where he delighted the local scene thanks in part to his policy of encouraging young people to dance to his music. At the end of the 40s he formed his own recording company, Swaggie, and both then and during the 50s he toured internationally. Bell also brought American jazz stars to Australia, among them Rex Stewart with whom he broadcast (a 1949 show being captured on record). He continued his tireless promotion of jazz by performing and by various other activities throughout the 70s and into the early 80s. Direct and uncomplicated, the bands Bell led were filled with energetic and cheerful musicians, among them Ade Monsborough, John Sangster and Dave Dallwitz. Bell's musical policy was such that, in common with England's Chris Barber, he was never content merely to rehash material from original sources. Instead, he stamped it with his own style, writing and arranging with skill and integrity within the format of a traditional band.

Albums: Graeme Bell And His Australian Jazz Band (Swaggie 1983, 1949-52 recordings), Top Of The Town (1950), Cakewalkin' Babies Back Home (1951), Hernando's Hideaway (1962), Czechoslovak Journey (Swaggie 1983), Paris 1948 (Swaggie 1983).

Bell, Jimmy

b. 29 August 1910, Peoria, Illinois, USA. d. 31 December 1987, Chicago, Illinois, USA. In high school, Bell learned guitar and piano, and boxed semi-professionally, before becoming a full-time musician in 1930. He worked as a jazz and swing band pianist in the midwest, picking up repertoire and stylistic influences from Roosevelt Sykes, Albert Ammons, Pete Johnson, Art Tatum and Earl Hines. After the war, Bell played sophisticated jump blues, influenced by the Nat 'King' Cole Trio, and made a few recordings. Gambling led to financial problems, and thence to crime, including dealing in heroin, for which he served prison terms in the 50s and 60s. In 1979 he received a six-year sentence for possession of forged food stamps. If not as original as he claimed, Bell remained a forceful and versatile musician in the 70s, playing cocktail music for a living, but still well in command of an eclectic blues, boogie and swing repertoire.

Album: *Stranger In Your Town* (1979).

Bellson, Louie

b. 26 July 1924, Rock Falls, Illinois, USA. Drummer Bellson first gained public attention by winning a Gene Krupa talent contest in 1940 and one of his early professional jobs was with Krupa's old boss, Benny Goodman. Bellson also worked with the big bands of Tommy Dorsey, Harry James and in 1951 joined Duke Ellington where his dynamic and aggressive style was startlingly different to that of his sometimes lackadaisical predecessor, Sonny Greer. Ellington used a number of Bellson's compositions including 'The Hawk Talks' (written for James) and 'Skin Deep', a marathon drum feature. After leaving Ellington, Bellson recorded and toured with small groups and occasionally-assembled big bands. In the mid-50s he returned briefly to Tommy Dorsey and also recorded for Norman Granz accompanying Louis Armstrong, Benny Carter, Ella Fitzgerald, Oscar Peterson, Art Tatum and others. In these settings he proved to be a restrained accompanist thus confounding those who had thought him merely a thunderer. From the early 60s until her death he was musical director/accompanist to his wife, singer Pearl Bailey, but continued to record and tour with small and large bands both under his own name and (in the mid-60s) made brief return visits to Ellington and James. Apart from his jazz compositions, Bellson has also written for the ballet and for jazz and symphony orchestra combinations. He is wholly ambidextrous, displays remarkable finger control, and is one of the most technically accomplished drummers jazz has known. A sought-after teacher and clinician, he is greatly admired by fellow musicians. When on tour Bellson frequently searches out orphanages and the like, putting on free shows. Onstage, he is a spectacular and exciting performer. He popularized a kit with twin-bass drums but unlike most of his imitators uses this set up in a logical and gimmick-free fashion. Offstage, he is quiet, sincere and shy, and is one of the best-liked musicians of his era of jazz.

Albums: *Duke Ellington's Coronets* (1951), *Ellington Uptown* (1952), *Louie Bellson Quintet* (1954), *Big Band Jazz From The Summit* (1962), *With Bells On* (Vogue 1962), with Gene Krupa *The Mighty Two* (1963), *Thunderbird* (1963), *The Dynamic Drums Of Louie Bellson* (1968), *Louie In London* (1970), with Duke Ellington *Duke's Big 4* (1973), *150 MPH* (1974), *The Louie Bellson Explosion* (1975), *Louie Bellson's 7* (1976), *Ecué - Ritmos Cubanos* (1977), *Prime Time* (1977), *Sunshine Rock* (Pablo 1977), *Note Smoking* (1978), *Raincheck* (1978),

Intensive Care (1978), *Louie Bellson Jam* (1978), *Matterhorn* (Pablo 1978), *Side Track* (1979), *Dynamite!* (1979), *Originals* (1979), *Louie Bellson's Big Band Explosion Live* (PRT 1979), *London Scene* (1980), *The London Concert* (1981), *Cool Cool Blue* (Pablo 1982), *The London Gig* (Pablo 1982), *Louis Bellson Jam* (Pablo 1982), *East Side Suite* (Music Masters 1987), *Live At Jazz Showcase* (Concord 1987), *Hot* (Music Masters 1987), *Jazz Giants* (1989), *1959 At The Flamingo Hotel* (Jazz Hour 1993)

Beneke, Tex

b. Gordon Beneke, 12 February 1914, Fort Worth, Texas, USA. Starting out on soprano saxophone, Beneke switched to tenor, working with various bands in the southwest. In 1938 he joined Glenn Miller where, in addition to featured tenor, he was also a regular vocalist. Tex sang with engaging charm if limited ability on such classic hits as 'I Gotta Gal In Kalamazoo' and 'Chattanooga Choo Choo'. Strongly influenced by the driving, big-toned tradition of Texas tenors, Beneke's playing added a jazz flavour to many Miller dance hits, including 'In The Mood' and 'String Of Pearls', on which he duetted with fellow tenor Al Klink. At the outbreak of World War II, Beneke worked with Miller's singing group, the Modernaires, then joined the US Navy where he played in a navy band. After the war, following Miller's death, Beneke was invited by Miller's executors to direct the Miller orchestra. In 1950 he relinquished this role but continued to lead his own band which, not surprisingly, played Miller-style music. He continued playing and leading bands into the late 80s, bringing unfailing good humour and enthusiasm to a somewhat overexposed corner of popular music.

Selected albums: *Beneke On Broadway* (70s). Compilations: *Loose Like* (1946), *Moonlight Serenade* (1946-47), *Tex Beneke's Jubilee* (1948), *Shooting Star* (1948 recordings), *Memories* (1949), *Tex Beneke Salutes Glenn Miller* (40s recordings), *With No Strings* (Hep Jazz 1981, 1949-51 recordings).

Benjamin, Sathima Bea

b. 17 October 1936, Cape Town, South Africa. Benjamin began singing in the 50s, and towards the end of the decade met pianist Abdullah Ibrahim, (formerly Dollar Brand), whom she later married. In 1962 Benjamin and Ibrahim visited Switzerland where they met Duke Ellington, who invited them to Paris for a recording date. Ibrahim's records were released, hers were not. Three years later, Benjamin sang with Ellington at the Newport Jazz Festival. For the next decade Benjamin worked mostly with her husband, but in 1976 their declaration of membership of the outlawed African National Congress forced the couple into exile. Living in New York since then, Benjamin has continued to work mostly on the east coast although her regular recording sessions, on which she is often accompanied by such leading contemporary musicians as Billy Higgins and Buster Williams, helped bring her unusual talents to the attention of a worldwide audience. Her background gives her material, some of which she writes herself, an angle unusual among artists of her generation. This and her distinctive singing style, filled with nuances of meaning which show a deep appreciation of the lyrics she sings, help make Benjamin's work particularly rewarding. Like so many other fine contemporary singers, Benjamin's repertoire extends far beyond the limitations implied by the term 'jazz singer', incorporating as it does popular standards and songs from musical comedies and Broadway shows.

Albums: *African Songbird* (1976), *Sathima Sings Ellington* (1979), *Dedications* (1982), *Memories And Dreams* (Ekapa 1983), *Wind Song* (1985), *Lovelight* (1987), *Sothern Touch* (Enja 1992).

Bennett, Betty

b. 23 October 1921, Lincoln, Nebraska, USA. Bennett studied piano and singing, with the intention of becoming an opera singer. She was attracted to jazz when her mother introduced her to the music of Ellington and Basie. She joined Georgie Auld's band, then worked with big bands led by Claude Thornhill, Alvino Rey, Charlie Ventura, where she replaced Jackie Cain and Roy Kral, and was also briefly with Stan Kenton and Woody Herman. In the 50s, she played and recorded with her then husband, André Previn, and also appeared at the Monterey Jazz Festival. In 1975 she married Mundell Lowe at a ceremony held at the Monterey festival. Later, although semi-retired for some years, she returned to singing in the USA and UK. Initially concerned with singing jazz, during her time with Ventura Bennett took an increasing interest in the lyrics of the songs she sang, eventually developing into a very good, all-round and musically intelligent song stylist.

Albums: *Betty Bennett* (1953), with André Previn *Nobody Else But Me* (1955).

Bennett, Cuban

b. Theodore Bennett, c.1902, USA, d. 28 November 1965, Pittsburgh, Pennsylvania, USA. Although he never recorded, Bennett is frequently cited by other trumpeters as an outstanding talent with ideas well ahead of his time. His cousin, Benny Carter, considered him to be so harmonically advanced that in the 20s he was playing in a way others would not emulate for another two decades. Bennett worked for many bands in and around New York but was footloose and showed little interest in a steady job, preferring instead to hang out and play the way he wanted. Bennett eventually disappeared from the scene.

Bennink, Han

b. 17 April 1942, Zaandam, Netherlands. Bennink is an intense, energetic percussionist with a strong streak of anarchic, deadpan mockery that seems to be common among Dutch jazz musicians. He tends not to confine his playing to the kit, frequently venturing away from the stool to play on the floor, walls or anything else within reach that he considers will make the sound he wants: the personnel details on the sleeve of *Outspan No 2* lists him as using 'dr, perc, everything, anything' and those of *Schwardzwaldfahrt*, recorded in the open air, credit him with playing 'wood, trees, sand, land, water, air'. He is notoriously hard on sticks, habitually breaking several per gig, often to the peril of members of the audience. While he is primarily associated with the European free improvisation scene he has worked with a wide variety of players, including Ben Webster, Dexter Gordon, Don Byas and Johnny Griffin from the jazz mainstream, musicians like Sonny Rollins and Lee Konitz who have at least flirted with the *avant garde*, as well as free players such as Derek Bailey, Evan Parker and Peter Brötzmann. He also played with Eric Dolphy on one of the saxophonists final recordings (*Last Date*, 1964). In the late 80s he toured with Steve Lacy and his longtime associate Misha Mengelberg as part of the Monk Project, and for many years he has been involved with the Instant Composers Pool, which he founded in 1967 with Mengelberg and Willem Breuker. His favourite drummers include Chick Webb, Big Sid Catlett, Jo Jones and Philly Joe Jones. Bennink also learned from his father, who was in a radio orchestra and did many commercial engagements in bands accompanying dancers and singers. Han's first instrument was clarinet, and he will still sometimes break off from drumming in mid-gig to play a tune on it, or on banjo, viola or saxophone. He has appeared on many records, mostly for musician-run labels such as FMP, ICP and Incus, and in the early 90s featured with Andy Sheppard's *Soft On The Inside* big band.

Albums: with Willem Breuker *New Acoustic Swing Duo* (1967), with Misha Mengelberg, John Tchicai *Instant Composers Pool* (1968), *Derek Bailey And Han Bennink* (1969), with others *Instant Composers Pool* (1970), with Instant Composers Pool *Groupcomposing* (1970), with Bailey, Evan Parker *The Topography Of The Lungs* (1970), with Peter Brötzmann, Fred Van Hove *Balls* (1970), with Mengelberg *Instant Composers Pool* (1971), *Han Bennink Solo* (1972), with others *Elements* (1972), with others *Couscouss De La Mauresque* (1972), with others *The End* (1972), with Bailey *At Verity's Place* (1972), with Brötzmann, Van Hove *Free Jazz Und Kinder* (1972), *Brötzmann, Van Hove, Bennick* (1973), with Brötzmann, Van Hove *Einheitsfrontlied* (1973), with Mengelberg *Eine Partie Tischtennis* (1974), with others *Outspan* i (1974), with others *Outspan* ii (1974), with Mengelberg *Coincidents* (1975, rec 1973-75), with Mengelberg (untitled album) (1975), with Brötzmann, Van Hove *Tscüs* (1975), with Bailey *Company 3* (1975), with Brötzmann *Ein Halber Hund Kann Nicht Pinkeln* (1977), with Brötzmann *Schwarzwaldfahrt* (1977), with Mengelberg *Midwoud 77* (1977), with others *Company 6* (1978), with others *Company 7* (1978), with Mengelberg, Dudu Pukwana *Yi Yole* (1978), with Mengelberg *A European Proposal* (1978), with Kees Hazevoet *Calling Down The Flevo Spirit* (1978), *Solo West Ost* (1978), with Brötzmann, Mengelberg *Three Points And A Mountain* (1979), *Mengelberg-Bennink* (1980), with Brötzmann *Atsugi Concert* (1980), *Tempo Comodo* (1982), with others *Regeneration* (1983), with Breuker *Sendai Sjors/Sendai Sjimmie* (1984), with Bailey *Han* (1988, rec 1986), with Steve Beresford *Directly To Pyjamas* (1988), with Cecil Taylor *Spots, Circles, And Fantasy* (1989).

Benoit, David

b. 1953, Bakersfield, California, USA. Benoit gained an early appreciation of music from his parents who played guitar and piano. He began piano lessons at the age of 14 by which time he was steeped in the influences of both Ramsey Lewis and Henry Mancini. Following his musical studies at El Camino College he met with composer Richard Baskin and played piano on the movie soundtrack *Nashville* in 1975. He gained valuable experience playing in clubs and bars and became Gloria Lynne's pianist. He toured with the Duke Ellington Orchestra in 1976 as Lainie Kazan's arranger and accompanist. His debut recording was with drummer Alphonse Mouzon and it was during these sessions he met with Dave Grusin, who became an important figure in his future career. He recorded a number of albums on a small label which demonstrated his fluid and skilful playing, although these recordings suffered from an overall blandness which resulted in their disappointing sales. *This Side Up* in 1985 changed everything. It contained the stunning 'Beach Trails', put Benoit in the USA jazz best-sellers and led to a call from Larry Rosen, Dave Grusin's partner at GRP Records. Benoit has now become one of their leading artists with a series of best-selling albums of easy yet beautifully constructed music, forging a similar path to that of Grusin and bridging the gap between jazz and pop. Each album contains a balanced mixture but it is Benoit's delicate rippling style on some of the quieter numbers that best demonstrate his dexterity. 'Kei's Song' from *Freedom At Midnight* and 'The Key To You' from *Every Step Of the Way* are outstanding compositions. His pure acoustic style was highlighted on *Waiting For Spring*, a concept album featuring Emily Remler and Peter Erskine. Imaginative readings of 'Cast Your Fate To the Wind', 'Secret Love' and 'My Romance' were mixed with Benoit originals. He maintained this high standard with *Inner Motion* in 1990, which opened with the Grusin styled 'M.W.A.' and peaked with the sublime tribute to the late Remler, 'Six String Poet'. His *Letter To Evan* was another acoustic excursion enlisting the talent of Larry Carlton. The collaboration with guitarist Russ Freeman in 1994 was a wholehearted success and stayed in the *Billboard* jazz chart for many weeks. That same year Benoit attempted another theme album, this time echoing his remembrances of the 60s, as good as *Shaken Not Stirred* was, it sounded just like another David Benoit album, clean, accessible and easy. Benoit is now a star, having refined his brand of music to perfection. In his own words 'I didn't want instant stardom like those artists whose fall is as quick as their rise'.

Albums: *Can You Imagine* (1980), *Stages* (Bluemoon 1981), *Waves Of Raves* (1982), *Digits* (Bluemoon 1983), *Heavier Than Yesterday* (1983), *Christmastime* (1984), *This Side Up* (GRP 1985), *Freedom At Midnight* (GRP 1987), *Every Step Of The Way* (GRP 1988), *Urban Daydreams* (GRP 1989), *Waiting For Spring* (GRP 1989), *Inner Motion* (GRP 1990), *Shadows* (GRP 1991), *Letter To Evan* (GRP 1993), with Russ Freeman *The Benoit/Freeman Project* (GRP 1994), *Shaken Not Stirred* (GRP 1994).

Benson, George

b. 22 March 1943, Pittsburgh, Pennsylvania, USA. This guitarist and singer successfully planted his feet in both the modern jazz and easy-listening pop camps in the mid-70s when jazz-pop as well as jazz-rock became a most lucrative proposition. Before a move to New York in 1963, he had played in various R&B outfits local to Pittsburgh, and recorded a single, 'It Should Have Been Me', in 1954. By 1965, Benson was an established jazz guitarist, having worked with Brother Jack McDuff, Herbie Hancock - and, crucially, Wes Montgomery, whose repertoire was drawn largely from pop, light classical and other non-jazz sources. When Montgomery died in 1969, critics predicted that Benson - contracted to Columbia in 1966 - would be his stylistic successor. Further testament to Benson's prestige was the presence of Hancock, Earl Klugh, Miles Davis, Joe Farrell and other jazz musicians on his early albums. Four of these were produced by Montgomery's Creed Taylor who signed Benson to his own CTI label in 1971. Benson was impressing audiences in concert with extrapolations of such as 'California Dreamin'', 'Come Together' and, digging deeper into mainstream pop, 'Cry Me A River' and 'Unchained Melody'. From *Beyond The Blue Horizon*, an arrangement of Jefferson Airplane's 'White Rabbit' was a turntable hit, and chart success seemed inevitable - especially as he was now recording a majority of vocal items. After *Bad Benson* reached the USA album lists and, via disco floors, the title song of *Supership* cracked European charts, he was well-placed to negotiate a favourable deal with Warner Brothers who reaped an immediate Grammy-winning harvest with 1976's *Breezin'* (and its memorable 'This Masquerade'). Then companies with rights to the prolific Benson's earlier product cashed in, with reissues such as *The Other Side Of Abbey Road*, a track-for-track interpretation of an entire Beatles' album. Profit from film themes like 'The Greatest Love Of All' (from the Muhammed Ali bio-pic *The Greatest*), million-selling *Give Me The Night* and the television-advertised *The Love Songs* have allowed him to indulge artistic whims such as a nod to jazz roots via 1987's excellent *Collaboration* with Earl Klugh, and a more commercial merger with Aretha Franklin on 'Love All The Hurt Away'. Moreover, a fondness for pop standards has proved marketable too; epitomized by revivals of 'On Broadway' - a US Top 10 single from 1978's *Weekend In LA* - and Bobby Darin's 'Beyond The Sea (La Mer)'. Like Darin, Benson also found success with Nat 'King' Cole's 'Nature Boy' (a single from *In Flight*) - and a lesser hit with Cole's 'Tenderly' in 1989, another balance of sophistication, hard-bought professionalism and intelligent response to chart climate. 1990 brought a full-length collaboration with the Count Basie Orchestra, accompanied by a sell-out UK tour. Benson is one of a handful of artists who have achieved major critical and commercial success in different genres - soul, jazz and pop, this pedigree makes him one of the most respected performers of the past 30 years.

Albums: *The New Boss Guitar* (OJC 1964), *It's Uptown* (1966), *Benson Burner* (1966), *Giblet Gravy* (1967), *The Other Side Of Abbey Road* (1970), *Beyond The Blue Horizon* (CTI 1973), *White Rabbit* (CTI 1973), *Body Talk* (CTI 1973), *Good King*

Bad (1973), *Bad Benson* (CTI 1974), *In Concert At Carnegie Hall* (CTI 1975), *Supership* (1975), *Breezin'* (WEA 1976), with Joe Farrell *Benson And Farrell* (CTI 1976), *In Flight* (WEA 1977), with Jack McDuff *George Benson And Jack McDuff* (Prestige 1977), *Weekend In LA* (WEA 1978), *Living Inside Your Love* (WEA 1979), *Give Me The Night* (WEA 1980), *Blue Benson* (Polydor 1983), *In Your Eyes* (WEA 1983), *Stormy Weather* (CBS 1984), *20/20* (WEA 1985), *The Electrifying George Benson* (Affinity 1985), *In Concert* (Premier 1985), *Love Walked In* (Platinum 1985), *Its Uptown/George Benson Cookbook* (CBS 1985), *While The City Sleeps* (WEA 1986), *Shape Of Things To Come* (A&M 1986), with Earl Klugh *Collaboration* (1987), *Exclusive Benson* (Connoisseur Collection 1987), *Love For Sale* (Masters 1988), *Twice The Love* (WEA 1988), *Detroit's George Benson* (Parkwood 1988), *Tenderly* (WEA 1989), *Big Boss Band* (WEA 1990), *Lil' Darlin'* (Thunderbolt 1990), *Live At The Casa Caribe Vols 1-3* (Jazz View 1992), *Love Remembers* (Warners 1993). Selected compilations: *The George Benson Collection* (1981), *Early Years* (CTI 1982), *Best Of George Benson* (A&M 1982), *The Wonderful Years* (Proton 1984), *The Love Songs* (K-Tel 1985), *The Silver Collection* (Verve 1985), *Compact Jazz* (Verve 1988), *Best Of* (Epic 1992), *Guitar Giants* (Pickwick 1992).

Bent, Phillip

b. London, England. Bent played the recorder at school then went on to study flute because he wanted a bigger sound. Sound itself, the exploration of textures, is important to him, but there is nothing academic or abstract about his music. He uses amplified flute - essential when there are electric instruments in his band - and rhythms from rock, funk and reggae. Like many of his generation of black British players he grew up on reggae, funk and soul and was attracted to jazz by hearing Louis Armstrong, Harold McNair and Miles Davis. Davis is clearly the most important influence in his work, but Bent is dedicated to developing his own voice on his own terms. He was a member of the Jazz Warriors, appearing on their live debut, *Out Of Many One People* (1987).
Albums: *Get Wise* (1986, one track only), *Mellow Mayhem* (1989, one track only), with the Jazz Warriors *Out Of Many One People* (1987), *The Pressure* (1993).

Berg, Bob

b. 7 April 1951, Brooklyn, New York, USA. Studying for a short time at the New York School of Performing Arts, before leaving prematurely to take a year's practical course at the Juilliard School of Music, as a young tenor saxophonist, Berg's interests were very much in the free jazz scene and the later work of John Coltrane. He involved himself in this area of jazz from 1966 onwards. In 1969 he became tired of its uncertainties and, deciding to study bop's solid harmonic schemes, joined Brother Jack McDuff's band. The next 15 years were spent in traditional hard-bop environments, where Berg could practice and expand his harmonic knowledge. Between 1973 and 1976 he worked in Horace Silver's band, and then followed this with seven years in Cedar Walton's group, touring

regularly and recording. However, Berg's present musical identity was really formed after Miles Davis invited him to join his fusion band in 1984. After a series of worldwide tours, he left with a reputation as one of the more interesting Michael Brecker-influenced saxophonists in the New York studio style. His solo career has produced some undulating albums with Denon, with *In The Shadows* so far the most satisfying.
Albums: with Horace Silver *Silver 'n' Brass* (1975), with Sam Jones *Visitation* (1978), with Cedar Walton *Eastern Rebellion Vols 1-2* (1983), with Miles Davis *You're Under Arrest* (CBS 1985), with Mike Stern *Upside Downside* (1986), *Steppin' - Live In Europe* (Red 1987), *Short Stories* (Denon 1988), *In The Shadows* (Denon), *Back Roads* (Denon 1991), *Enter The Spirit* (1993), *Virtual Reality* (Denon 1993).

Berger, Karl

b. 30 March 1935, Heidelberg, Germany. Berger studied piano, musicology and philosophy at his hometown university. In 1960, he took up vibes in order to play jazz. After gaining his PhD in 1963 he left for Paris, where he joined Don Cherry's quintet, with whom he worked for a year and a half. In 1966 he relocated to New York, finding a ready welcome in the free scene. His recording debut, *Tune In*, featured drummer Ed Blackwell, bassist Dave Holland and alto saxophonist Carlos Ward. An energetic educationalist, he established a music school in Woodstock where students were taught by *avant garde* luminaries, including George Russell, Roscoe Mitchell, John Cage and Sam Rivers, until its closure in the early 80s. Berger continues to record, often in collaboration with his wife, Ingrid, who is a singer.
Albums: *Tune In* (1969), *With Silence* (1972), *Changing the Time* (1977), with the Woodstock Workshop Orchestra *New Moon* (1980), *All Kinds Of Time* (Sackville 1981), *Around* (Black Saint 1991), *With Silence* (Enja 1992), *Crystal Fire* (Enja 1992).

Bergonzi, Jerry

b. 1947, Boston, Massachusetts, USA. Of all the legions of John Coltrane-inspired saxophonists to have emerged in the 80s in the USA, Jerry Bergonzi has been one of the most distinctive, and yet has had to wait the longest for his personal break. He played clarinet and alto saxophone from the age of eight, and took up the tenor at 12, being taught by instructors from the nearby Berklee College Of Music while still at high school. Bergonzi graduated from Lowell State University in 1972 and went to New York that year, soon beginning what was to be a 10-year association with Dave Brubeck, first in the Two Generations band, then as the featured horn in Brubeck's quartet. Bergonzi returned to Boston in 1987, and began a series of recording projects under his own name for his own label, and also for Italy's Red Records. He ran his own bands, the quartet Con Brio and the Trio Gonz, and when Mike Brecker's young pianist Joey Calderazzo got his recording debut for Blue Note Records in 1990, he called on Brecker, Branford Marsalis and Bergonzi to be the horns. Bergonzi's spirited performance convinced Blue Note that his big-time debut was overdue.

Albums: with Dave Brubeck *Back Home* (1979), *Con Brio* (1985), *Jerry On Red* (Red 1989), *Lineage* (1989), with Joey Calderazzo *In The Door* (1990), with Calderazzo *To Know One* (1991), *Standard Gonz* (Blue Note 1991), *Lieage* (Red 1991), *Tilt* (Red 1992), With Trio Idea *Napoli Connection* (1994).

Berigan, Bunny

b. Rowland Bernart Berigan, 2 November 1908, Hilbert, Calumet, Wisconsin, USA, d. 2 June 1942. One of the outstanding trumpeters of the swing era, Berigan was heavily influenced by Louis Armstrong and at his best played with much of his idol's attack and zest. In the early 30s he worked with numerous bands, including those of Paul Whiteman, Fred Rich, Tommy Dorsey and Benny Goodman (with whom he was playing when the band made its popular breakthrough at the Palomar Ballroom in Los Angeles in August 1936, the gig that launched the swing era). Berigan also worked in the studios, playing in house bands, and in 1937 formed his own big band. The band was very popular and had several hits, including a version of 'I Can't Get Started' on which the leader sings engagingly and plays one of the most celebrated jazz solos of the era. Berigan played with a full and gorgeous sound, his open horn having a burnished quality that brought added texture to his interpretation of the more melodic yet soulful tunes he loved to play. Unfortunately, he lacked discipline in his playing, which could spiral out of control, in much the same way that it was absent from his personal life. Berigan's big band folded in 1940, by which time the leader's drinking was severely damaging his health. He rejoined Dorsey for a while, then reformed his own band in mid-1941. Early the following year he was taken ill with pneumonia but continued working - and drinking cheap liquor - until he collapsed at the end of May and died in June 1942.

Compilations: *Bunny Berigan With Hal Kemp And His Orchestra* (1930), *Bunny Berigan* (1931), *Saturday Night Swing Club* (1936), *The Indispensable Benny Goodman* (1936), *The Indispensable Tommy Dorsey* (1937), *Down By The Old Mill Stream* (1936-39), *The Indispensable Bunny Berigan* (1937-39 recordings, RCA 1983), *Bunny Berigan* (Charly 1986), *Portrait Of Bunny Berigan* (Living Era 1989), *1938 Broadcasts, Paradise Restaurant* (Jazz Hour 1993)

Further reading: *Bunny Berigan: Elusive Legend Of Jazz*, Robert Dupuis.

Berman, Sonny

b. Saul Berman, 21 April 1925, New Haven, Connecticut, USA, d. 16 January 1947. A child prodigy, Berman was playing trumpet in Louis Prima's band by his early teens. He followed this early induction into the big time with a rapid swing through the bands of Georgie Auld, Tommy Dorsey, Sonny Dunham, Benny Goodman and Harry James, before settling into Woody Herman's First Herd at the beginning of 1945. He remained with Herman until the band folded at the end of the following year. A musician of immense if undeveloped talent, Berman's solo playing ranged over intensely-felt dramatic

works, like 'Nocturne', '125th Street Prophet' and 'Sidewalks Of Cuba' to the raw excitement of 'Apple Honey'. Influenced by the early bebop playing of Dizzy Gillespie, Berman's career ended abruptly when he suffered heart failure, apparently as a result of a drugs overdose, and died in January 1947 when still only 21 years old.

Compilations: with Woody Herman *The V-Disc Years Vol. 1* (1945), *Beautiful Jewish Music* (1946), *Jazz Immortal* (1946).

Berne, Tim

b. 16 October 1954, Syracuse, New York, USA. One of the outstanding young members of New York's *avant garde* jazz scene, alto saxophonist Berne did not begin to play the instrument until he was 19 years old. After studying with both Anthony Braxton and, especially, Julius Hemphill, he set up his own record label, Empire Productions, and in 1979 travelled to the west coast to record his debut album because he found New York musicians 'too aggressive'. His second album, *7X*, also features west coast players (Vinny Golia, Alex Cline and Roberto Miranda are on both records), but subsequent releases *Spectres* and *Songs And Rituals In Real Time . . .* were recorded in New York and included appearances by Olu Dara, Ed Schuller and Paul Motian. The latter pair also formed the rhythm section on Berne's following two albums, *The Ancestors* and *Mutant Variations*, both released on the Italian Soul Note label. His final album on his own Empire Productions was *Theoretically*, a 1984 duo with upcoming guitarist Bill Frisell (and later reissued on the German Minor Music label with an extra track). With his career at a temporary standstill, Berne took a job serving behind the counter at New York's Tower Records shop, where a chance meeting turned his luck around: a childhood friend Gary Lucas (ex-Captain Beefheart guitarist and then working as an advertising executive for Columbia Records) spotted Berne in Tower and persuaded CBS to sign him up. His two records for the label, *Fulton Street Maul* and *Sanctified Dreams*, won huge critical acclaim and, although the company refused to renew his contract ('The people in the higher echelon positions didn't like the music, they had a real negative attitude to it.'), Berne was now established as a major voice in contemporary jazz. He formed the co-operative trio Miniature, with Hank Roberts and Joey Baron; guested on John Zorn's Ornette Coleman tribute, *Spy Vs Spy*; and in 1991 toured Europe in a duo with pianist Marilyn Crispell. However, his own group remains his top priority: usually a five or six-piece that often includes longtime associates Baron, Roberts, Mark Dresser and Herb Robertson, Berne describes their music as 'about rhythms, textures, harmonic ideas, tonal things, nontonal things, moods, shapes . . . (I use) little motifs and fragments . . . to set up a context for spontaneity'. The result is a striking, fresh-sounding small-group jazz that looks set to lead the field well into the 90s.

Albums: *The Five-Year Plan* (1979), *7X* (1980), *Spectres* (1981), *Songs And Rituals In Real Time...* (1982), *The Ancestors* (Soul Note 1983), *Mutant Variations* (Soul Note 1984), with Bill Frisell *Theoretically* (Minor 1984), *Fulton Street Maul* (1987), *Sanctified Dreams* (CBS 1987), with Hank Roberts,

Joey Baron *Miniature* (1988), *Fractured Fairy Tales* (JMT 1989), *Pace Yourself* (JMT 1991), with Miniature *I Can't Put My Finger On It* (1991), with Michael Formanek, Jeff Hirshfield *Loose Cannon* (1993).

Bernhardt, Clyde

b. 11 July 1905, Gold Hill, North Carolina, USA, d. 20 May 1986, Newark, New Jersey, USA. Trombonist Bernhardt, aka Ed Barron, paid the usual dues of the jazzman by playing in myriad small territory bands in the mid-west, before moving to New York City in 1928. In 1930, he hit the big time when he was hired by Joe 'King' Oliver to play and sing with his Harlem Syncopators; later with Vernon Andrade, Edgar Hayes (with whom he made his recording debut for Decca), Horace Henderson, Oran 'Hot Lips' Page, Stuff Smith, Fats Waller, Jay McShann, Cecil Scott, Luis Russell, Claude Hopkins and Dud Bascomb. After World War II, Bernhardt formed his own R&B jump combo. Bernhardt's strong feeling for the blues made him a natural for the R&B scene and he led his own band the Blue Blazers, with whom he recorded in his own right for several small specialist labels between 1946 and 1953, and also backed Wynonie Harris on his debut session for King Records. On these recordings, Bernhardt proved himself to be a talented blues singer in the Jimmy Rushing/Big Joe Turner mould (he once claimed he had been shouting the blues in this style since playing with King Oliver in 1930). From the mid-50s, apart from the occasional gig, Bernhardt worked mainly outside music but was rediscovered in 1968 when he was brought out of retirement to record for Saydisc Matchbox's Blues Series. He formed his own label in 1975 and began touring with his Harlem Blues & Jazz Band which remained hugely popular in Europe, even after Bernhardt's death.
Albums: *Blowin' My Top* (1968), *Blues And Jazz From Harlem* (1972), *More Blues And Jazz From Harlem, Sittin' On Top Of The World!* (1975), *Clyde Bernhardt And The Harlem Blues And Jazz Band* (1975), *Clyde Bernhardt And The Harlem Blues And Jazz Band At The 7th International Jazz Festival, Breda* (1977), *Clyde Bernhardt & The Harlem Blues Jazz Band* (1978), *More Blues & Jazz From Harlem* (1979).
Further reading: *I Remember: Eighty Years Of Black Entertainment, Big Bands And Blues*, Clyde E. B. Bernhardt, Sheldon Harris.

Berry, Bill

b. 14 September 1930, Benton Harbor, Michigan, USA. A largely self-taught cornetist, Berry's first job was with Don Strickland, who led a mid-west territory band. In the mid-50s Berry worked with Herb Pomeroy's Boston-based band and from there went into one of Woody Herman's lesser-known bands ('We called it the un-Herd'). After leaving Herman he joined Maynard Ferguson and in 1961 was invited to join Duke Ellington, an experience which he readily admits changed his whole life. After two years with Ellington Berry worked extensively in New York studios, but also played and recorded with jazz artists such as Coleman Hawkins and Jimmy Rushing. He played with the Thad Jones-Mel Lewis band in

New York in the mid-60s and also formed a rehearsal band which met with local success. When the television show on which he worked every week was abruptly relocated to Los Angeles, Berry took up the offer of continued employment and has been based on the west coast ever since. In 1971 he reformed his rehearsal band, through whose ranks have passed a remarkable group of players, including Cat Anderson, Conte and Pete Candoli, Blue Mitchell, Jimmy Cleveland, Buster Cooper, Richie Kamuca, Bob Cooper, Jake Hanna, Dave Frishberg and Teddy Edwards. Although he still worked extensively in film and television studios (including ghosting for Frank Sinatra Jnr. in *A Man Called Adam* and for Bruce Willis in an episode of *Moonlighting*), Berry gradually concentrated more and more on jazz until by the 80s he was fully engaged in tours of Europe and Japan. He is especially popular in Japan, appearing there as a single, with fellow visitors such as Benny Carter, and as musical director of both the Monterey Jazz Festival All Stars and the same festival's annual all-star university students' band.
In 1989 and 1990 Berry played several UK concerts as a guest artist with the Brian Priestley Special Septet and recorded with them on a limited-edition cassette release, *Bilberry Jam*. He also performs regularly with small groups and his own big band in and around Los Angeles. Preferring cornet to trumpet, Berry plays ballads with considerable melodic grace and charm, while on up-tempo tunes his playing crackles with boppish phrases. He also favours playing tightly muted, working close to the microphone to create an exhilarating sound. In 1991 he broke new ground with an appearance in an acting role, as an American trumpeter, in Alan Plater's *Misterioso*, a film made for British television. His LA big band was host to the 1991 Ellington Conference in Los Angeles, receiving rave press notices. The same year his big band accompanied Mel Tormé in concert at the Hollywood Bowl. Held in great respect by his peers, both for his musical abilities and for his personal warmth and enthusiasm, Berry is also a skilled arranger and composer. Amongst his compositions are 'Bloose' and 'Betty', the latter a delightful ballad written for his wife, a former singer.
Albums: with Duke Ellington *All American* (1962), with Ellington *My People* (1963), *The Bill Berry Quartet* (1963), with Coleman Hawkins *Wrapped Tight* (1965), *Hot And Happy* (1974), *Hello Rev* (Concord 1976), *A Tribute To Duke* (1977), *Shortcake* (Concord 1978), *For Duke* (1978), with Brian Priestley *Bilberry Jam* (1990).

Berry, Chu

b Leon Berry, 13 September 1910, Wheeling, West Virginia, USA, d. 30 October 1941. In the early 30s Berry played tenor saxophone with a number of New York bands, including sessions for Spike Hughes and spells with the bands of Benny Carter and Fletcher Henderson. He was in great demand among leaders who were setting up recording and club sessions and played on memorable dates with Roy Eldridge and Lionel Hampton. In 1937, he was added to the star-studded Cab Calloway band, where his musical influence helped build the band's reputation as a fine jazz outfit (despite the leader's exhibitionism). A superbly eloquent soloist, Berry's playing was in the mould of Coleman Hawkins, with a rich and emotional sound. However, before he was able to forge a completely distinctive style, he received severe head injuries in a car crash while touring with Calloway and died a few days later.

Selected albums: *The Calloway Years* (1937-41), *A Giant Of The Tenor Sax* (1938-41), *The Complete Lionel Hampton* (1939), *Chu Berry And His Jazz Ensemble* (1941), *The Rarest 1937-40* (Everybody's 1982), *The Indispensible* (RCA 1985), *Giant Of The Tenor Sax* (Commodore Class 1986), *The Calloway Years (1937)* (Meritt 1988), *Chu Berry Story* (Zeta 1991).

Berry, Emmett

b. 23 July 1915, Macon, Georgia, USA. In 1933, within a year of his first professional job, Berry was in New York and playing trumpet with leading bands of the day. In 1936 he joined Fletcher Henderson's band, replacing Roy Eldridge. He remained with Henderson for three years, moving on to the band led by Fletcher's brother, Horace. In the early 40s Berry was with Teddy Wilson's elegant sextet and also worked with Lionel Hampton, Benny Carter, John Kirby and Roy Eldridge's Little Jazz Trumpet Ensemble. The second half of the decade was spent almost continuously with Count Basie. In the 50s Berry played with Jimmy Rushing, Johnny Hodges, Cootie Williams and Sammy Price, recording extensively. In the 60s he settled in Los Angeles but was soon back on the road again with Peanuts Hucko and Wilbur De Paris. A masterly player, Berry's solos were always immaculately conceived and executed with fire and passion. Retired since 1970, Berry left his distinctive mark on countless records.

Selected albums: *Sam Price And His Bluesicians* (1955), with Jimmy Rushing *Listen To The Blues* (1955).

Bert, Eddie

b. 16 May 1922, Yonkers, New York, USA. After studying trombone with Benny Powell, Bert's first name-band job was with Sam Donahue in 1940. Army service interrupted his career, but three years later he continued his apprenticeship with bands led by Red Norvo, Charlie Barnet and Woody Herman. In 1946, Bert began a period of sustained big band work which lasted eight years, during which time he had two important spells with Stan Kenton. Throughout the 50s Bert worked mostly in small groups (sometimes as leader), including Charles Mingus's Jazz Workshop and a regular Monday night gig at Birdland. Towards the end of the decade and throughout most of the 60s, he worked in the theatre in New York and also advanced his musical education with formal studies. Whenever possible he played jazz, working for leaders such as Mingus, Benny Goodman (with whose band he had briefly played in the late 40s) and Thelonious Monk. Although a flexible player, capable of blending into small bebop groups and mainstream bands, Bert's power and attack lend themselves best to a big band setting, as he proved when with the Thad Jones-Mel Lewis band and on the festival circuit with Lionel Hampton's all-star orchestra in 1978.

Selected albums: *Eddie Bert Quintet* (1953), *Let's Dig Bert* (1955), *Eddie Bert With The Hank Jones Trio* (1955), *Encore* (1955), *Kaleidoscope* (1955), *The Thelonious Monk Orchestra At Town Hall* (1959), *Westchester Workshop* (60s), *Skeleton Of The Band* (1976), with J.R. Monterose *Live At Birdland* (1993).

Best, Denzil De Costa

b. 27 April 1917, USA, d. 24 May 1965, New York, USA. A multi-instrumentalist, playing trumpet, piano and bass, Best did not begin playing drums until he was in his mid-twenties. Despite this late start, he was almost instantly in demand as a session musician, playing and recording with such leading 40s jazz artists as Coleman Hawkins, Illinois Jacquet, Lee Konitz, Thelonious Monk (with whom he wrote 'Bemsha Swing') and Ben Webster. In 1949 he was a member of George Shearing's original quintet, and in the 50s worked extensively with Erroll Garner. A subtle and discreet player, especially effective on brushes, Best suffered from a progressive disease in which calcium deposits on the bones in his wrists gradually made it impossible for him to play. Best composed several bop standards including 'Move' and 'Wee'. He died in 1965 from injuries sustained from a fall on a New York subway staircase.

Album: with Erroll Garner *Concert By The Sea* (1955). Compilations: with Coleman Hawkins *Hollywood Stampede* (1945), *The Best Of George Shearing* (1949-51).

Bickert, Ed

b. 29 November 1932, Hochfeld, Manitoba, Canada. A highly gifted guitarist, Bickert was active in Toronto in the 50s, playing with several leading musicians including Ron Collier, Paul Desmond and Rob McConnell. He attracted wider attention thanks in part to his regularly accompanying of visiting American jazz musicians, including Dave McKenna, and by his contributions to Desmond's last recordings in the mid-70s. It was not until the late 70s, however, that Bickert took full advantage of the manner in which fellow musicians accepted his gently understated skills. He toured overseas with Milt Jackson, recorded with Oscar Peterson, Scott Hamilton, Benny Carter and Rosemary Clooney, and also made records under his own name. In the 80s he visited the UK with Peter Appleyard and also appeared there with George Shearing. He continued to make records, including *Mutual Street*, an interesting duo set with McConnell. In 1990 he appeared at the Concord Summer Jazz Festival in California, playing with Marshal Royal, Ernestine Anderson and others. A highly musical player, interestingly combining introspection with a curiously unassertive authority, Bickert is clearly a major if still widely unrecognized talent.

Albums: *Ed Bickert* (1975), *I Like To Recognize The Tune* (1977), *The Ed Bickert-Don Thompson Duo* (1978), *From Canada With Love* (PM 1979), *In Concert At The Garden Party* (Sackville 1981), *The Ed Bickert 5 At Toronto's Bourbon Street* (Concord 1983), *Bye Bye Baby* (Concord 1983), *Border Crossing* (Concord 1983), with Don Thompson *Dance To The Lady* (Sackville 1983), *Mutual Street* (1984), *Ed Bickert/Lorne Lofsky Quartet* (1985), *I Wished On The Moon* (Concord

1985), *Third Floor Richard* (Concord 1989), *Ed Bickert/Lorne Lofsky: This Is New* (Concord 1989), *Mutual Street* (Jazz Alliance 1991).

Bigard, Barney

b. Albany Leon Bigard, 3 March 1906, New Orleans, Louisiana, USA, d. 27 June 1980. Born into a highly musical family, Bigard began studying clarinet at the age of seven, taking lessons from the noted teacher, Lorenzo Tio Jnr. He worked in street parades but then switched to tenor saxophone in 1922 to join the band led by Albert Nicholas. During the next two years, Bigard played in several bands in New Orleans before going to Chicago to join Joe 'King' Oliver. While with Oliver he reverted to clarinet. In the mid-20s he played in Chicago and New York in the bands of Charlie Elgar and Luis Russell before joining Duke Ellington in December 1927. In common with so many Ellingtonians, he remained a member of the band for many years, but eventually left in mid-summer 1942 and for the next few years he led his own small bands, worked in the film studios of Hollywood and was also briefly with Freddy Slack. In 1947 he joined Louis Armstrong's newly formed All Stars. He was with Armstrong for five years and then, after a period leading his own band, returned for a further two years in the mid-50s. After working with several bands in the late 50s he rejoined Armstrong for another stint in the early 60s and then played in various bands, including those led by Johnny St Cyr, Muggsy Spanier, Rex Stewart and Art Hodes. In the 70s he toured with Hodes, Eddie Condon and many others, including the Legends Of Jazz. In his later years he worked in many places, appeared on television and radio, thoroughly enjoying his role as an elder statesman of jazz. Bigard's was one of the most distinctive jazz voices, his playing characterized by a rich, flowing sound and his habitual use of the lower, chalumeau, register of the clarinet. After joining Ellington, Bigard lost his previous close affinity with the musical forms traditionally associated with his birthplace. Nevertheless, there were always echoes of his origins in his best work, which came mostly during his years with Ellington.

Among his classic recordings from this period of his career are 'Clarinet Lament' ('Barney's Concerto'), 'Mood Indigo', 'Saturday Night Function', 'Barney Goin' Easy' and 'C Jam Blues'. Some of these tunes originated in ideas and fragments Bigard created and which were fashioned by Ellington into minor masterpieces. Although this was Ellington's common practice, in later years Bigard would occasionally disconcert interviewers by ferociously declaring, 'I wrote that!' whenever almost any Ellington composition was mentioned. Although Bigard was a pleasure to hear in later years, there was a great deal of repetition in his work. Indeed, some of his solos, especially on such famous features as 'C Jam Blues', 'Rose Room' and 'Tea For Two', were repeated night after night, year upon year regardless of the company he was keeping. In fairness, it might be added that, having achieved a kind of perfection, he may well have thought there was little point in tampering with what he knew was his best.

Selected albums: with Louis Armstrong *Satchmo At Symphony Hall* (1947), *Bucket's Got A Hole In It* (1968), *Easy On The Ears* (1973), *Clarinet Gumbo* (1973), *Barney Bigard And The Legends Of Jazz* (1974), *Jazz Giants In Nice* (1974), *From Rag To Swing* (1975), *Barney Bigard And The Pelican Trio* (1976). Compilations: *The Indispensable Duke Ellington Vols 1/2-5/6* (1927-40), with Ellington *The Blanton-Webster Years* (1940-42), *Barney Goin' Easy* (1937-40), *Fantasy For Clarinet And Strings* (1944), with Claude Luter *Paris December 1960* (Vogue 1990).

Bilk, Acker

b. Bernard Stanley Bilk, 28 January 1929, Pensford, Somerset, England. After playing as a semi-professional in Bristol, Bilk received his big break in the jazz world when he joined Ken Colyer as a clarinettist in 1954. Four years later, under the self-referential title 'Mr.' Acker Bilk, he enjoyed his first UK Top 10 hit with 'Summer Set'. Backed by the Paramount Jazz Band, Bilk was at the forefront of the British trad jazz boom of the early 60s. With their distinctive uniform of bowler hats and striped waistcoats, Bilk and company enjoyed a number of UK hits including 'Buona Sera' and 'That's My Home'. It was with the Leon Young String Chorale, however, that Bilk achieved his most remarkable hit. 'Stranger On The Shore' was a US number 1 in May 1962 and peaking at number 2 in the UK it achieved an endurance record for its 55 weeks on the best-sellers list. Although the beat boom all but ended the careers of many trad jazzers, Bilk continued to enjoy a successful career in cabaret and even returned to the Top 10 as late as 1976 with 'Aria'. He continues to perform alongside contemporaries Kenny Ball and Chris Barber, recreating the UK number 1 album, *The Best Of Ball, Barber And Bilk* in 1962. Bilk remains a major figure in traditional jazz.

Albums: *Mr. Acker Requests* (1958), *Mr. Acker Marches On* (1958), *Mr. Acker Bilk Sings* (1959), *Mr. Acker Bilk Requests (Part One)* (1959), *Mr. Acker Bilk Requests (Part Two)* (1959), *The Noble Art Of Mr. Acker Bilk* (1959), *Seven Ages Of Acker* (1960), *Mr. Acker Bilk's Omnibus* (Pye 1960), *Acker* (Columbia EMI 1960), *A Golden Treasury Of Bilk* (Columbia EMI 1961), *Mr. Acker Bilk's Lansdowne Folio* (1961), *Stranger On The Shore* (Columbia EMI 1961), *Above The Stars And Other Romantic Fancies* (1962), *A Taste Of Honey* (Columbia EMI 1963), *Great Themes From Great European Movies* (1965), *Acker In Paris* (1966), *Blue Acker* (1968), *Some Of My Favourite Things* (PRT 1973), *That's My Desire* (1974), *Serenade* (1975), *The One For Me* (PRT 1976), *Invitation* (PRT 1977), *Meanwhile* (1977), *Sheer Magic* (Warwick 1977), *Extremely Live In Studio 1* (1978), *Free* (1978), *When The Lights Are Low* (1978), with Max Bygraves *Twogether* (1980), *Unissued Acker* (1980), *Made In Hungary* (PRT 1980), *The Moment I'm With You* (1980), *Mama Told Me So* (PRT 1980), *The Moment I'm With You* (PRT 1981), *Relaxin'* (PRT 1981), *Wereldsuccessen* (Philips 1982), *I Think The Best Thing About This Record Is The Music* (Bell 1982), *Acker Bilk In Holland* (Timeless 1985), *Nature Boy* (PRT 1985), *Unissued Acker* (Harlequin 1985), *Acker's Choice* (Teldec 1985), *John, Paul And Acker* (1986) *Love Songs My Way* (Topline 1987), reissued as *Acker Bilk Plays Lennon And*

McCartney (GNP 1988), *On Stage* (Start 1988), with Ken Colyer *It Looks* (Stomp Off 1988), *That's My Home* (1988), *The Love Album* (Pickwick 1989), with Chris Barber, Kenny Ball *Trad Days 1959/60* (1990), *Imagine* (Pulse 1991), *Blaze Away* (Timeless 1990), *The Ultimate!* (1991). *Heartbeats* (Pickwick 1991), with Humphrey Lyttelton *At Sundown* (Calligraph 1992) Compilations: *The Best Of Ball, Barber And Bilk* (1962), *Golden Hour Of Acker Bilk* (Knight 1974) *Very Best Of Acker Bilk* (1978), *Evergreen* (Warwick 1978), *The Acker Bilk Saga* (Polydor 1979), *Sheer Magic* (1979), *The Best Of Acker Bilk, Volume Two* (1979), *Mellow Music* (1980), *Spotlight On Acker Bilk* (PRT 1980), *100 Minutes Of Bilk* (PRT 1982), *Spotlight On Acker Bilk Vol 2* (PRT 1982), *I'm In The Mood For Love* (Philips 1983), *Finest Moments* (Castle 1986), *Magic Clarinet Of Acker Bilk* (K-Tel 1986), *16 Golden Memories* (Spectrum 1988), *Best Of Acker Bilk His Clarinet And Strings* (PRT 1988), *Hits Blues And Classics* (Kaz 1988), *The Collection* (Castle 1989), *Images* (Knight 1989), *After Midnight* (Pickwick 1990), *In A Mellow Mood* (Castle 1992), *Reflections* (Spectrum 1993). *Acker Bilk Songbook* (Tring 1993).

Biscoe, Chris

b. 5 February 1947, East Barnet, Hertfordshire, England. Biscoe taught himself to play alto saxophone in 1963, later adding tenor, soprano and baritone saxophones and the comparatively rare alto clarinet. From 1970-73 he played with the National Youth Jazz Orchestra, then worked with various groups in London, including Redbrass. In 1979, he began a long (and continuing) association with Mike Westbrook, making outstanding contributions to many Westbrook projects, notably the brass band (*Bright As Fire*), the orchestra (*The Cortege* and *On Duke's Birthday*) and the trio (*A Little Westbrook Music* and *Love For Sale*). From 1983 he also worked with Chris McGregor's Brotherhood Of Breath (*Country Cooking*) and in 1985 he released a cassette of his own music, *Quintet And Duo*, followed the next year by a sextet album, on his own Walking Wig label, which featured Italian trombonist Danilo Terenzi. In the late 80s and 90s Biscoe toured and recorded with both George Russell (*The London Concert*) and Andy Sheppard (*Soft On The Inside*), as well as playing in France with Didier Levallet's groups and in the collective band Zhivaro, which includes Levallet and Henri Texier. He continues to lead his own quartet and also plays with improvisers Full Monte (Brian Godding, Tony Marsh, Marcio Mattos): in 1991 he released a second cassette of his own music, *Modern Alarms*, and recorded in the Dedication Orchestra on the *Spirits Rejoice* project. An exciting modern stylist, especially inventive on baritone saxophone, Biscoe has yet to receive the attention and the recording opportunities as leader that his creativity warrants.
Albums: *Quintet And Duo* (1985), *The Chris Biscoe Sextet* (1986), with Full Monte *Life In The Grand Hotel* (1991), *Modern Alarms* (1991).

Bishop, Walter, Jnr.

b. 10 April 1927, New York City, New York, USA. Bishop began playing piano as a child, encouraged by his father, a Jamaican songwriter whose 'Swing, Brother, Swing' was recorded by, among others, Billie Holiday with Count Basie. During the 40s Bishop's musical direction was dictated by his interest in the work of Bud Powell and he played with numerous small groups, including those led by Charlie Parker, Miles Davis and Oscar Pettiford. A period of drug addiction interrupted Bishop's career in the 50s, but the following decade proved successful both musically and in terms of conquering his habit. He worked with Curtis Fuller and also led his own small groups, with which he recorded. He resumed his musical studies too, and after relocating in Los Angeles at the end of the 60s he took up teaching. In the late 70s he was back on the east coast, playing and teaching. Rarely performing outside the New York area, and with only a few recordings that fully demonstrate his skills, Bishop remains largely unknown to the wider jazz audience, despite being held in high regard by his fellow musicians. He is the author of a book on jazz theory.
Albums: *Speak Low* (Muse 1961), *Bish Bash* (1964), *Walter Bishop Trio: 1965* (1965, rec. 1962-63), *Summertime* (Fresh Sound 1964), *Coral Keys* (1971), *Keeper Of My Soul* (1973), *Valley Land* (Muse 1974), *Old Folks* (1976), *Soliloquy* (1976), *Soul Village* (Muse 1977), with others *I Remember Bebop* (1977), *Hot House* (Muse 1978), *Cubicle* (Muse 1978), *Just In Time* (Interplay 1988), *Milestones* (Black Lion 1989), *What's New* (DIW 1990), *Midnight Blue* (Red 1993). Compilation: with Miles Davis *Collector's Items* (1953-56).

Black, James

b. 1 February 1940, New Orleans, Louisiana, USA, d. 30 August 1988. Born into a musical family, Black studied music at Southern University, Baton Rouge, and also drummed in the quintessential training ground for New Orleans rhythm, a marching band. His first professional break came with an R&B outfit in 1958. He replaced Ed Blackwell in Ellis Marsalis's band when Blackwell left to join Ornette Coleman in California. In the early 60s he relocated to New York with R&B singer Joe Jones and toured with Lionel Hampton. It is Black playing drums on the Dixie Cups' 'Chapel Of Love'. He played and recorded with Cannonball Adderley, Yusef Lateef and Horace Silver. If Black had not subsequently returned to New Orleans (working with artists including Professor Longhair, the Meters, Fats Domino and Lee Dorsey) his unerring beat - funky but free - would have made him a big name in jazz.
Albums: *The Adderley Brothers In New Orleans* (1962), with Yusef Lateef *Live At Pep's* (1964).

Blackman, Cindy

b. 18 November 1959, Yellow Springs, Ohio, USA. One of a growing number of female drummers, she is a powerful but unbombastic player, part of the tradition which includes Max Roach and one of her main influences, Tony Williams. Her mother and grandmother were classical musicians and an uncle was a vibes player. She decided to specialize in percussion at such an early age she cannot remember exactly when it was, but she worked hard at learning her craft in her spare time and at school. She studied classical percussion at the University of Hartford, then went on to the Berklee College Of Music, where she was taught by Alan Dawson and Lennie Nelson. In 1982 she moved to New York and played with Freddie Hubbard, Sam Rivers and Jackie McLean, whose regular drummer she became in 1987. By then she had served a tough apprenticeship, as house-drummer in Ted Curson's all-night jam sessions at the Blue Note Club, and playing for several hours at a time in a band that performed on the corner of 42nd Street and 6th Avenue. Her recording debut with an all-star band displayed her skills as leader, composer and percussionist. In 1990, she joined Don Pullen's trio for some festival appearances and since then she has concentrated on her solo career. Albums: *Arcane* (Muse 1987), *Autumn Leaves* (1989), *Code Red* (Muse 1992), *Trio + Two* (Freelance 1992), *Telepathy* (Muse 1994).

Blackwell, Ed

b. 10 October 1929, New Orleans, Louisiana, USA, d. 7 October 1992. Blackwell began playing drums in his home town, where he took careful notice of the rudiments of jazz-playing as demonstrated by local past-masters of the trade, such as Baby Dodds and Zutty Singleton. Despite these traditional affiliations, Blackwell's first jobs were with mainstream bands and he also played R&B. Meeting Ornette Coleman changed his musical ideas and he played with Coleman on the west coast in the early 50s. However, he returned to New Orleans, and resumed playing mainstream and R&B music, including a spell with Ray Charles. At the start of the 60s he was back with Coleman, this time in New York. It was here that he also began a long-lasting association with Don Cherry. In the mid-60s he played in bands led by Cherry, Coleman and Randy Weston. He and Weston lived for a while in Morocco, where Blackwell extended his knowledge of percussion, later incorporating several additional instruments into his kit to increase his tonal palette. In the early 70s he was again with Coleman and also played with Thelonious Monk. This period also saw him cutting back on playing through a combination of poor health and a teaching engagement. Later in the 70s he resumed his association with Cherry when he joined the quartet, Old And New Dreams, to pursue further Coleman's music. The other members of the band were Charlie Haden and Dewey Redman. In 1981 he joined fellow drummers Sonny Murray, Dennis Charles and Steve McCall to form Drums Inter-Actuel, and also recorded with Anthony Braxton and others. A vigorous player with a brilliant sound and subtle beat, he had a sharp awareness of the needs of his front line comrades. Blackwell was one of the outstanding free jazz drummers and his fast-thinking polyphonic interplay with Coleman was frequently awesome in its complexity. His work with Cherry was also remarkable for the manner in which he stayed abreast of the trumpeter's quicksilver thinking and playing. Albums: with Ornette Coleman *This Is Our Music* (1960), with Coleman *To Whom He Keeps A Record* (1960), with Coleman *Free Jazz* (1961), with Don Cherry *Mu* (1969), with Old And New Dreams *Old And New Dreams* i (Black Saint 1976), *Old And New Dreams* ii (1979), *Playtime* (1981), with Anthony Braxton *SK Compositions: Quartet* (1982), *El Corazón* (1982), with Cherry *El Corazon* (ECM 1986), with Cherry *A Tribute To Ed Blackwell* (1987), with Cherry *Multikulti* (1990), *What It Is?* (Enja 1993), *What It Be Like?* (Enja 1994).

Blake, Eubie

b. James Hubert Blake, 7 February 1883, Baltimore, Maryland, USA, d. 12 February 1983. Eubie Blake grew up to the sounds of ragtime music, and before the turn of the century was playing piano in sporting houses and other similar establishments. Blake was a composer too, and in 1915 joined forces with Noble Sissle; they played in vaudeville as a double act and also wrote together extensively. In 1921 Sissle and Blake wrote the score for a Broadway show - a remarkable accomplishment for blacks at that time. *Shuffle Along*, which starred Flournoy Miller, Aubrey Lyles, Gertrude Saunders, and Sissle himself (with Blake on the piano), included several admirable songs, including 'Bandana Days', 'Gypsy Blues', 'Love Will Find A Way', 'Everything Reminds Me Of You', 'Shuffle Along', and 'If You've Never Been Vamped By A Brown Skin (You've Never Been Vamped At All)'. There was also one enormous hit, 'I'm Just Wild About Harry', which became popular at the time for artists such as Marion Harris, Ray Miller, and Paul Whiteman, amongst others, and gave a boost to Harry S. Truman's election campaign in 1948. Blake contributed to other Broadway musicals and revues such as *Elsie*, *Andre Charlot's Revue Of 1924*, and Lew Leslie's *Blackbird's Of 1930*. For the latter he and Razaf wrote 'Baby Mine', 'That Lindy Hop', 'My Handy Man Ain't Handy No More', and another substantial hit, the lovely reflective ballad 'Memories Of You'. After one more Broadway musical *Swing It* (1937), Blake reunited with Sissle for a while, and then spent much of World War II entertaining troops with the USO.

In the 50s Blake demonstrated and lectured on ragtime but his day seemed to be past. Then, in 1969, at the age of 86, Blake's fortunes were revived when John Hammond Jnr. recorded the old man playing piano and talking about his life. The concurrent vogue for ragtime helped his comeback and the next years were filled with honours, recordings, concerts, festivals and television appearances; in 1978, his life and music were celebrated in a Broadway show, *Eubie*, which was also televised in the USA and later staged in London. In 1983 Blake contributed to the lists of favourite quotations when, on the occasion of his 100th birthday, he said: 'If I'd known I was going to live this long, I would've taken better care of myself.' He died five days later.

Selected albums: *The Wizard Of Ragtime* (1959), *The Eighty-six Years Of Eubie Blake* (1969), *At The Piano* (1974), *Eubie Blake In Concert* (1987). Compilations: *Eubie Blake, Blues And Rags: His Earliest Piano Rolls* (1917-21 recordings), *Rags To Riches* (Stash 1988), *The Eighty Six Years* (CBS 1988), *Memories Of You* (Biograph 1991).

Further reading: *Reminiscing With Sissle And Blake*, Robert Kimball and William Bolcom.

Blake, Ran

b. 20 April 1935, Springfield, Massachusetts, USA. Growing up in Springfield and later in Suffield, Connecticut, Blake began piano lessons at the age of four but was largely self-taught. A film buff from childhood, his interest in soundtracks led him to an appreciation of 20th-century European composers such as Bartok, Debussy and Prokofiev. A simultaneous love of gospel music was sparked by the records of Mahalia Jackson and, particularly, by his exposure to the choir at the local Church of God in Christ in Hartford, Connecticut. Blake studied at Bard College from 1956-60, devising his own jazz course there, and also began to work with singer Jeanne Lee - they recorded together in 1961 and toured Europe in 1963. Studies with Gunther Schuller, then a leading proponent of Third Stream Music, gave Blake the confidence to pursue his personal synthesis of African-American, European classical and various ethnic folk musics. When Schuller became President of Boston's New England Conservatory of Music in 1967, Blake went to work there too and in 1973 was made Chairperson of the Third Stream Department, where he has since remained. Although many of his recordings are solo, he has also worked with singers such as Lee, Chris Connor and Eleni Odoni, and saxophonists Anthony Braxton, Steve Lacy, Houston Person and Ricky Ford, whom Blake 'discovered' playing in Boston at the age of 16. Other notable projects include his work with the New England Conservatory Symphony Orchestra (on *Portfolio Of Doktor Mabuse*) and his appearance as featured guest artist on Franz Koglmann's 1989 *Orte Der Geometrie*. Typical Blakean characteristics, usually evident in his music in some guise, include his anti-racism and radical social perspectives, his abiding love of spirituals and his continuing fascination with film and its relationship to music (*Film Noir* and *Vertigo*). His utterly individual piano style is like a distillation of Thelonious Monk and Erik Satie: very terse, very quiet and capable of both acute dissonance and delicate romanticism - his phrases often resemble shards or beads of sound that float and trickle across great chasms of silence. A recent release, *That Certain Feeling*, features the tunes of George Gershwin and is the second of a planned series of homages that also includes *Duke Dreams* (dedicated to Duke Ellington and Billy Strayhorn) and projected tributes to Monk and Charles Mingus.

Albums: with Jeanne Lee *The Newest Sound Around* (1961), *Plays Solo Piano* (1965), *The Blue Potato* (1969), *Breakthru* (1976), *Wende* (1977), *Crystal Trip* (1977), *Open City* (1977), *Take One* (1977), *Take Two* (1977), *Realization Of A Dream* (1978), *Rapport* (1978), *Third Stream Recompositions* (1980, rec. 1977), *Film Noir* (1980), with Jaki Byard *Improvisations* (Soul Note 1981), *Duke Dreams* (1981), *Portfolio Of Doktor Mabuse* (1983, rec. 1979, 1977), with Houston Person *Suffield Gothic* (Soul Note 1984), *Painted Rhythms Volume I* (GM 1986), *Vertigo* (1987, rec. 1984), *Short Life Of Barbara Monk* (Soul Note 1987), *Painted Rhythms Volume II* (GM 1988, rec. 1985), with Lee *You Stepped Out Of A Cloud* (Owl 1990), with Ricky Ford, Steve Lacy *That Certain Feeling* (1991), *Epistrophy* (Soul Note 1991).

Blakey, Art

b. Arthur Blakey, 11 October 1919, Pittsburgh, Pennsylvania, USA, d. 16 October 1990. Blakey was a pianist first; the move to drums has been variously attributed to Erroll Garner appearing on the scene, the regular drummer being off sick and (Blakey's favourite) a gangster's unarguable directive. Whatever, Art Blakey drummed for Mary Lou Williams on her New York debut in 1942, Fletcher Henderson's mighty swing orchestra (1943/4) and the legendary Billy Eckstine band that included Charlie Parker, Dexter Gordon, Dizzy Gillespie, Miles Davis and Thelonious Monk (1944-47). The classic bebop sessions tended to have Max Roach or Kenny Clarke behind the drums, but Blakey had the last laugh, becoming the pre-eminent leader of the hard bop movement. In contrast to the baroque orchestrations of the West Coast Jazz 'cool' school, hard bop combined bebop's instrumental freedoms with a surging backbeat out of gospel. Ideally suited to the new long-playing record, tunes lengthened into rhythmic epics that featured contrasting solos. The pressure of Blakey's hi-hat and snare became legendary, as did the musicians who passed through the ranks of the Jazz Messengers. Blakey never tired of telling his sidemen (and sidewomen - pianist JoAnne Brackeen was one of his discoveries) to go off and form their own bands: his band became an on-the-road college. His insistence on complete musicianship was complemented by an understanding that without risk jazz is dead. Impatient with timidity and safeness, his drumming encouraged daring and brilliance. He would lean with his elbow on the surface of the drum to change its intonation: such 'press rolls' became a musical trademark. That his power was not from want of subtlety was illustrated by his uncanny sympathy for Thelonious Monk's sense of rhythm: his contribution to Monk's historic 1957 group that included both Coleman Hawkins and John Coltrane was devastating, and the London trio recordings he made with Monk in 1971 (*Something In Blue* and *The Man I Love*) are perhaps his most impressive achievements as a player. Blakey was a beacon for the creativity and drive of acoustic jazz through the electric 70s. Miles Davis once remarked 'If Art Blakey's old-fashioned, I'm white': this was borne out in the 80s when hard bop became all the rage. Ex-Jazz Messengers Wynton Marsalis and Terence Blanchard became the apostles of a return to jazz values. In England, a televised encounter in 1986 with the young turks of black British jazz - including Courtney Pine and Steve Williamson - showed how Blakey's hipness transcended generations, as he taught the IDJ Dancers (ex-break dancers who decided 'I Dance Jazz') the complexities of 'A Night In Tunisia'. Until his death in 1990, Art Blakey continually found new musicians and put them through his special discipline of heat and precision. When he played, Blakey invariably had his mouth open in a grimace of pleasure and concentration: memories of his drumming still makes the jaw drop today. For a period following his conversion to Islam, Blakey changed his name to Abdullah Ibn Buhaina, which led to his nickname 'Bu'. As a drummer Blakey will not be forgotten, but as a catalyst for hundreds of past messengers he will be forever praised.

Selected albums: *A Night At Birdland Vol 1* (Blue Note 1954),

A Night At The Birdland Vol 2 (Blue Note 1954), *At The Cafe Bohemia Vol 1* (Blue Note 1956), *At The Cafe Bohemia Vol 2* (Blue Note 1956), *Hard Bop* (1956), *The Hard Bop Academy* (Affinity 1958), *Art Blakey's Jazz Messengers With Thelonius Monk* (Atlantic 1958), *Ritual* (Blue Note 1958), *Moanin'* (Blue Note 1958), *At The Jazz Corner Of The World* (Blue Note), *A Night In Tunisia* (Blue Note 1960), *The Big Beat* (Blue Note 1960), *Like Someone In Love* (1960), *Roots & Herbs* (1961), *Jazz Messengers* (Impulse 1961), *Mosaic* (Blue Note 1962), *A Jazz Message* (Impulse 1964), *Buhaina's Delight* (Blue Note 1962), *Free For All* (Blue Note 1965), *Kyoto* (1968), *Mellow Blues* (Moon 1969), with Thelonious Monk *Something In Blue* (1971), *Gypsy Folk Tales* (1977), *In This Corner* (Concord 1979), *Messages* (Vogue 1979), *Straight Ahead* (1981), *Album Of the Year* (Timeless 1981), *In My Prime Vol 1* (Timeless 1981), *Straight Ahead* (Concord 1981), *Blues Bag* (Affinity 1981), *Keystone 3* (Concord 1982), *In Sweden* (Amigo 1982), *Oh, By The Way* (Timeless 1982), *New York Scene* (Concord 1984), *Blue Night* (Timeless 1985), *Big Beat* (Blue Note 1985), *Dr Jeckyl* (Paddle Wheel 1985), *Blues March* (Vogue 1985), *Farewell* (Paddle Wheel 1985), *In My Prime Vol 2* (Timeless 1986), *Live At Ronnie Scott's* (Hendring 1987), *Not Yet* (Soul Note 1988), *Feeling Good* (Delos 1988), *Hard Champion* (Electric Bird 1988), *Like Someone In Love* (Blue Note 1989), *I Get A Kick Out Of Bu* (Soul Note 1989), *Live In Berlin 1959-62* (Jazzup 1989), *One For All* (A&M 1990), *Live In Europe 1959* (Creole 1992). Selected compilations: *The Best Of Art Blakey* (Emarcy 1980), *Art Collection* (Concord 1986), *The Best Of Art Blakey And The Jazz Messengers* (Blue Note 1989), *Compact Jazz* (Verve 1992), *The History Of Art Blakey & The Jazz Messengers* (Blue Note 1992, 3-CD set).

Blanchard, Terence

b. 13 March 1962, New Orleans, Louisiana, USA. One of several brilliant young musicians emerging from New Orleans in the 80s, Blanchard began playing piano at the age of five and sang with a vocal group, the Harlem Harmony Kings. He too up the trumpet at the age of eight and began lessons in his early teens while studying at the New Orleans Center for Creative Arts under Ellis Marsalis, father of Blanchard's contemporaries and fellow New Orleanians, Branford and Wynton Marsalis. A year later, Blanchard was studying composition and in 1980 went to Rutgers University. That same year he joined Lionel Hampton with whom he played for two years before replacing Wynton Marsalis in Art Blakey's Jazz Messengers. At the same time, Donald Harrison, a fellow student from his days in New Orleans, replaced Branford in the Messengers. Blanchard stayed with Blakey until 1986 when he formed his own band with Harrison. In the 90s he became involved with films, writing scores for Spike Lee's *Jungle Fever* and *Malcolm X* and for the BBC Television documentary about black migration, *The Promised Land*. A technically-gifted musician, Blanchard's play-

Carla Bley

ing displays a marked awareness of the lyricism of some of the early bop trumpeters, like Clifford Brown. Although much less well known than Marsalis, Blanchard's work displays a similar restraint but stronger jazz feeling.

Albums: with Donald Harrison *New York Second Line* (George Wein Collection 1983), with Art Blakey *New York Scene* (1984), with Harrison *Discernment* (Concord 1986), with Harrison *Nascence* (1986), *Terence Blanchard* (Columbia 1991), *Simply Stated* (Columbia 1992), *X* (Columbia 1994), *The Billie Holiday Songbook* (Columbia 1994).

Blanton, Jimmy

b. October 1918, Chatanooga, Tennessee, USA, d. 30 July 1942. Starting out as a violinist, Blanton studied musical theory before switching to bass while still at school. He played in several local bands and during 1936/7 worked with the Jeter-Pillars Orchestra in St. Louis and Fate Marable's Cotton Pickers. In October 1939 he was hired by Duke Ellington and celebrated this event by changing from three-string to four-string bass. For a few months he shared the spot with Billy Taylor, but from early 1940 he was on his own. A remarkably dextrous player, Blanton's technique, his range, harmonic sense and unfailing swing gave the Ellington band enormous lift. His work attracted the attention of countless other bass players whose own work subsequently bore echoes of his innovations. Off-duty from the Ellington band, Blanton also played with early bop musicians at Minton's Playhouse where he was a major contributor to the changes taking place in jazz. While with Ellington Blanton recorded extensively, not only with the band but also in ducts with the leader. Blanton's death, when only 23 years old, was an exceptional loss but his influence on jazz bass playing remains profound.

Compilations: *The Indispensable Duke Ellington Vols 5/6* (1940), with Duke Ellington *The Blanton-Webster Band* (1940-42).

Bley, Carla

b. Carla Borg, 11 May 1938, Oakland, California, USA. Bley began to learn piano from her father, who was a piano teacher and church organist, at an early age, but discontinued the formal lessons when she was five years old. Her main musical experience was in church choirs and as a church organist until she became interested in jazz at the age of 17. On moving to New York City she had to work as a waitress, unable to earn a living either as a pianist or composer. In 1957 she married Paul Bley and from 1959 began writing many fine compositions, still using her maiden name initially: thus, the composer credit was to 'Borg' when George Russell first recorded one of her pieces ('Dance Class') in 1960. Russell used several of her tunes, as did husband Paul. As her reputation grew, her compositions were sought by the likes of Jimmy Giuffre, Art Farmer, Gary Burton and Charlie Haden (with whom she would work on his various Liberation Music Orchestra projects). In 1964 Bill Dixon invited her to be a charter member of the Jazz Composers' Guild, and at the end of the year she and Michael Mantler, who was later to become her second hus-

band, led the Jazz Composers' Guild Orchestra in a series of concerts at Judson Hall. Her critical standing really began to blossom after she joined the Jazz Composers' Orchestra Association, founded by Mantler in 1966 on the model of the defunct Guild. The Association and its associated Orchestra (JCO) gave writers the opportunity to write works of an epic scale for large forces, and Carla grasped the opportunity. Two of her works, *A Genuine Tong Funeral* (Dark Opera Without Words) (recorded by a band centred on the Gary Burton Quartet) and the massive *Escalator Over The Hill* (taking up six album sides) were conceived as a kind of music theatre, and were widely acclaimed: *Escalator* in particular remains a genre in itself. Many of her small-scale pieces have also achieved standard status, including 'Mother Of The Dead Man' (originally part of *Tong Funeral*), 'Closer', 'Ida Lupino' and 'Sing Me Softly Of The Blues'. She became a full-time musician in 1964, working with Pharoah Sanders and Charles Moffett at the beginning of that year. From December she co-led the JCO with Mantler. Her first orchestral piece, 'Roast', dates from this time, but she was also heavily committed to free jazz at this point. After the JCO appeared at the 1965 Newport Jazz Festival, Bley organized the Jazz Realities Quintet, which also included Mantler and Steve Lacy, to tour Europe. It was during another tour of Europe, this time with Peter Brötzmann and Peter Kowald in 1966, that she became disillusioned with free jazz, a change of heart that led ultimately to the production of *Funeral*. For some years she concentrated on writing, though there was a spell with Jack Bruce's band in 1974, but from 1976 she again began leading a band on a regular basis. Throughout the 80s she continued to play keyboards and to lead medium to small-sized bands but, as she pointed out herself on a visit to London in 1990, although she is not among the great pianists she is a unique writer. Her association with composer and former Gary Burton bassist Steve Swallow contributed to the flavour of her successful and accessible Sextet, which toured regularly in the late 80s. While the critics (though not the jazz public) began to grow cool towards the Sextet by the end of the decade, her tour with the Very Big Carla Bley Band at the end of 1990 confirmed that she had not lost her individual writing voice, nor her ability to deal convincingly with orchestral forces. Bley's contribution on the 'administrative' side of music deserves recognition too. She has been part of the movement to give musicians a degree of control, self-determination and independence from the industry's establishment. With Paul Bley she was a member of the Jazz Composers' Guild, a co-operative formed in autumn 1964, and subsequently helped establish the JCOA. She and Mantler also set up two record labels, Watt for their own recordings and JCOA Records to promote the work of others. Her compositions have been recorded by a number of musicians.

Selected albums: with others *Jazz Realities* (1966), *A Genuine Tong Funeral* (1968), with Charlie Haden *Liberation Music* (1969), *Escalator Over The Hill* (ECM 1971), *Tropic Appetites* (1974), *Dinner Music* (Watt 1977), with Michael Mantler *The Hapless Child* (1976), *Carla Bley Band European Tour 1977* (Watt 1978), *Musique Mecanique* (Watt 1979), with Steve

Swallow *Afterglow* (c.80s), *Social Studies* (Watt 1981), *Carla Bley Live!* (Watt 1982), *Ballad Of The Fallen* (1983), *Mortelle Randonnee* (IMS 1983), *I Hate To Sing* (ECM 1984), *Heavy Heart* (Watt 1984), *Night-Glo* (Watt 1985), *Sextet* (Watt 1987), *European Tour 1977* (ECM 1987), with Swallow *Duets* (Watt 1988), *Fleur Carnivore* (Watt 1990), *The Very Little Big Carla Bley Band* (Watt 1991), with Swallow *Go Together* (Watt 1992), *Big Band Theory* (ECM 1993).

Bley, Paul

b. 10 November 1932, Montreal, Canada. Pianist Bley would merit a place in jazz history on the strength of his instincts as a talent scout alone. The legendary Ornette Coleman Quartet (with Don Cherry, Charlie Haden and Billy Higgins) made its earliest impact as four-fifths of Bley's quintet. He encouraged the coming-out of wife Carla Bley and Annette Peacock as composers, building his repertoire in the 60s and 70s around their tunes. He had Pat Metheny and Jaco Pastorius in his band when both were callow youths, and was the first to record them. All of this, however, is of less significance than his own music, the earliest examples of which still seem entirely 'modern'. For 40 years Bley has remained on the cutting edge of creative music, from bebop to free jazz and beyond. At the age of 20, he befriended and played with Charlie Parker. On New York's 52nd Street, Jackie McLean and Donald Byrd regularly augmented Bley's trio. Charles Mingus was responsible for initiating Bley's recording career, and played bass on *Introducing Paul Bley*, Art Blakey was the drummer. Bley has always been drawn to the most creative players, and they to him. In the 60s, he put his stamp on every area of the new music. He played piano duets with Bill Evans inside George Russell's orchestra, helped set in motion an introspective, intellectual improvisatory music in the trios of Don Ellis and Jimmy Giuffre, and recorded the classic *Footloose* - these endeavours setting the scene for, for example, ECM's development of a 'chamber jazz'. *Footloose*'s concentrated, quiet improvisation was counterbalanced by Bley's ferocious quintet on *Barrage*, featuring Sun Ra saxophonist Marshall Allen. Albert Ayler and John Gilmore also played with Bley in 1964. At the decade's end, Bley was playing Arp synthesizer and utilizing all the noise potential of electronics, and the drummers who passed through his group included Han Bennink (see *Improvisie* and *Dual Unity*) and Soft Machine's Robert Wyatt. The common denominator through all these activities is Bley's sense of form; his improvisations have the rightness and logic of composition. Bley returned to acoustic music in the 70s - his bleak, haunting *Open, To Love* setting the direction for future work - and formed his own label, IAI, donning the producer's hat to record Sun Ra, Ran Blake, Marion Brown, Sam Rivers and others. Through the 80s, Bley issued a steady stream of albums, of consistently high quality, which proved that emotional expressiveness is not the exclusive preserve of the shouters and screamers. 'Music', Bley once said, 'is the business of pain', and he can wound the heart with his carefully chosen notes.
Selected albums: *Introducing Paul Bley* (Original Jazz Classics 1954), *Paul Bley* (1955), *Solemn Meditation* (GNP Crescendo

1958), *Footloose* (Savoy 1963), *Barrage* (ESP 1965), *Closer* (ESP 1966), *Touching* (Black Lion 1966), *Ramblin'* (1967), *Blood* (1967), *Paul Bley In Haarlem* (1967), *Mr Joy* (1968), *The Fabulous Paul Bley Quintet* (Musidisc 1969, rec. 1958), *Paul Bley Trio In Canada* (1969), *Paul Bley With Gary Peacock* (ECM 1970, rec. 1963 and 1968), *Ballads* (1970, rec 1967), *The Paul Bley Synthesizer Show* (1971), *Improvisie* (1971), with Annette Peacock *Dual Unity* (1972), with Peacock *Revenge - The Bigger The Love The Greater The Hate* (1972, rec. 1969), *Paul Bley And Scorpio* (1973), *Open To Love* (ECM 1973), *Paul Bley/NHOP* (1974), with Jimmy Giuffre, Bill Connors *Quiet Song* (Improvising Artists 1974), *Alone Again* (DIW 1975), *Copenhagen And Haarlem* (1975, rec. 1965, 1966), *Turning Point* (Improvising Artists 1975, rec. 1964, 1968), *Virtuosi* (1975, rec. 1967), *Bley/Metheny/Pastorius/Ditmas* (1975, re-released as *Jaco* 1978), *Japan Suite* (Improvising Artists 1976), *Axis* (Improvising Artists 1978), *Sonor* (1983), *Tango Palace* (Soul Note 1983), *Tears* (Owl 1984), with Chet Baker *Diane* (1985) *Questions* (1985), *Hot* (1986), *My Standard* (1986), *Paul Bley & Jesper Lundgaard Live* (1986), *Fragments* (ECM 1986), with Jesper Lundgaard *Live Again* (1987), with Peacock, Barry Altschul *Ballads* (ECM 1987), *The Paul Bley Quartet* (ECM 1988), with Paul Motian *Notes* (Soul Note 1988), *Solo* (Justin Time 1988), *Solo Piano* (Steeplechase 1988), *Floater Syndrome* (1989, rec. 1962, 1963), *The Nearness Of You* (Steeplechase 1990), with Gary Peacock *Partners* (Owl 1990), *Bebopbebopbebopbebop* (Steeplechase 1990), *Rejoicing* (Steeplechase 1990), with Giuffre, Steve Swallow *The Life Of A Trio - Saturday* and *The Life Of A Trio - Sunday* (1990), *12 + 6 (In A Row)* (Hat Art 1991), *Blues For Red* (Red 1991), *Live At Sweet Basil* (Soul Note 1991, rec. 1988), *Memoirs* (Soul Note 1991), *Lyrics* (Splasc 1991), *Indian Summer* (Steeplechase 1991, rec. 1987), with Gary Burton *Right Time, Right Place* (1991), with John Ballentyne *A Musing* (1991), with Gary Peacock, Altschul *Japan Suite* (1992), *Changing Hands* (Justin Time 1992), *Paul Plays Carla* (Steeplechase 1992), *Caravan Suite* (Steeplechase 1993), with Franz Koglmann, Gary Peacock *Annette* (Hat Art 1993), *In The Evenings Out There* (ECM 1993), with Keshavan Maslak *Not To Be A Star* (1993), with Maslak *Romance In The City* (Leo 1993).

Bloom, Jane Ira

b. 1955, Newtown, Massachusetts, USA. Bloom studied music as a child and mastered the saxophone in her teens. She turned down an opportunity to tour with the Duke Ellington orchestra in favour of taking BA and MA degrees at Yale University. In 1977, she studied under George Coleman in New York and in 1979 formed her own record label, Outline. She recorded two albums, the second with Marimba and vibes player David Friedman, who introduced her to a wider public through his contact with the German label, Enja. In 1982 Bloom recorded with Charlie Haden and Ed Blackwell, establishing herself as one of the most prominent players and composers to emerge from the 70s. She recorded two more albums during the late 80s, and continues to play in a variety of settings (she has appeared solo in the Houston baseball Astrodome). Bloom recently declared that her aim is '. . . to bring more *avant garde* improvising to people who don't usually listen to it'.

Albums: *Mighty Lights* (Enja 1983), *Modern Drama* (1987), *Shalom* (1988), *Art & Aviation* (Arabesque 1993).

Bluiett, Hamiet

b. 16 September 1940, Lovejoy, Illinois, USA. Bluiett was taught music by his aunt, who directed a choir, and began to play the clarinet at the age of nine. He later studied flute and baritone saxophone at Southern Illinois University, then spent several years in the navy. In the mid-60s he moved to St. Louis, where he studied with George Hudson and became part of a collective of black musicians, later to be called BAG (Black Artists Group). In 1969 he relocated to New York, where he worked with the Sam Rivers Large Ensemble, the Thad Jones/Mel Lewis Big Band, Abdullah Ibrahim, Julius Hemphill, Charles Mingus and Don Pullen as well as soul artists Aretha Franklin and Stevie Wonder. In December 1976 he helped to form the World Saxophone Quartet for a concert in New Orleans, and this has since become the most visible showcase for his arrangements and sterling baritone saxophone. In 1981, he recorded with Lester Bowie on the trumpeter's *The Great Pretender*, adding hilarious, growling saxophone to the title track. Bluiett has also recorded an impressive series of albums as leader (featuring musicians such as Pullen, Fred Hopkins, Don Moye, John Hicks and Marvin 'Smitty' Smith), including a concert with his clarinet group, the Clarinet Family.

Selected albums: *Endangered Species* (1976), *Bars* (1977), *Birthright* (1977), *Orchestra, Duo & Septet* (1977), *Resolution* (Black Saint 1978), *S.O.S.* (1979), *Dangerously Suite* (Soul Note 1981), *Ebu* (Soul Note 1984), *The Clarinet Family* (Black Saint 1987, rec. 1984), *Nali Kola* (Soul Note 1989), *You Don't Need To Know . . . If You Have To Ask* (Tutu 1991), *Sankofa/Rear Garde* (Soul Note 1993)

Blythe, Arthur

b. 5 July 1940, Los Angeles, California, USA. From infancy Blythe lived in San Diego, returning to Los Angeles when he was 19 years old. He had taken up alto saxophone at the age of nine playing R&B until his mid-teens when he discovered jazz. He studied with David Jackson and ex-Jimmie Lunceford altoist Kirtland (Kirk) Bradford. In the mid-60s he was part of UGMAA (The Underground Musicians and Artists Association), a west coast counterpart to Chicago's AACM founded by Horace Tapscott, on whose 1969 *The Giant Is Awakened* he made his recording debut. Blythe, aka Black Arthur, began leading his own group in 1970, often using unusual instrumentation, including tuba and cello, as well as James 'Blood' Ulmer's remarkable guitar, and during the early 70s he did some rock session work. Although he first went to New York City in 1968 he did not settle there until 1974. He was soon able to give up his job as security man at a pornography cinema when he was invited to join Chico Hamilton's group. Amongst other bands he has played with are those of Ray Charles, Tapscott (1963-73), Owen Marshall, Stanley

Crouch (1967-73), Black Music Infinity, Leon Thomas, Julius Hemphill, Chico Hamilton, Ted Daniel, Lester Bowie (1978-80), Gil Evans (1976-80), Jack DeJohnette and all-star band the Leaders (with Bowie, Chico Freeman, Kirk Lightsey, Cecil McBee and Don Moye). He has also guested with Craig Harris's homage-to-James Brown-band, Cold Sweat. At the end of the 70s he added a conventional saxophone and rhythm quartet, In The Tradition, to his ventures, running this alongside the guitar and cello group into the 80s. In 1990 he replaced founder member Hemphill as the alto voice in the World Saxophone Quartet. A distinctive alto and soprano saxophonist, Blythe appears to be in the Albert Ayler tradition, though he cites Eric Dolphy, Thelonious Monk and John Coltrane as his major influences: basically a melodist, with clear gospel influences, he often uses a pronounced vibrato, though he has a generally lighter, more translucent sound than Ayler's. He has explained that his wide vibrato stems from using reeds that were too hard for him to control as a youth rather than a desire to emulate Ayler. Not a free player, Blythe nevertheless ranges far and wide in his improvisations, though an attempt at disco music with 1985's *Put Sunshine In It* (reputedly at the behest of his record label, Columbia) was neither a critical nor a commercial success. Despite living in New York for many years he still considers himself a Californian player: he once told writer Francis Davis that a musician's style was affected by his/her accent and dialect 'because your music is a direct reflection of your speech'.

Albums: *The Grip* (India Navigation 1977), *Metamorphosis* (1977), *Bush Baby* (Echo 1977), *In Concert* (India Navigation 1978), *Lenox Avenue Breakdown* (CBS 1979), *In The Tradition* (CBS 1979), with In The Tradition *Illusions* (1980), *Blythe Spirit* (CBS 1981), *Elaboration* (CBS 1982), *Light Blue* (CBS 1983), *Put Sunshine In It* (CBS 1985), *Da-Da* (CBS 1986), *Basic Blythe* (CBS 1988), with the Leaders *Mudfoot* (1986), with the Leaders *Unforeseen Blessings* (1990), with the World Saxophone Quartet *Metamorphosis* (1991), *Hipmotism* (Enja 1991), *Retroflection* (Enja 1994).

Blythe, Jimmy

b. c.1901, Louisville, Kentucky, USA, d. 21 June 1931. Growing up in Chicago, Blythe was taught to play piano and made his first records in 1924. He recorded extensively, if often anonymously, being first-call accompanist for numerous record dates by singers. He also formed and led many pick-up bands for record dates, using such names as the State Street Ramblers, the Chicago Footwarmers and the Washboard Ragamuffins. Along the way Blythe worked with many fine jazzmen of the 20s, amongst them Johnny Dodds and Freddie Keppard. By the end of the 20s he was in less demand and he died in 1931.

Compilations: *Cutting The Boogie: Piano Blues And Boogie Woogie* (1924-41 recordings), *Stomp Your Stuff* (Swaggie 1983, 1927-31 recordings).

Bocage, Peter

b. 31 July 1887, New Orleans, Louisiana, USA. d. 3 December 1967. A gifted multi-instrumentalist, Bocage came from a musical family. In the early years of the century he played violin in several dance bands in New Orleans. Later, he began playing cornet in bands including that led by Papa Celestin before joining Armand J. Piron for a lengthy spell. He stayed with Piron until the end of the 20s, becoming a member of the Creole Serenaders, a band led by Louis Warneke. Resident in the north-east, by the beginning of the 40s Bocage was playing only part-time but gigged and recorded with Sidney Bechet and others. In the mid-40s he returned to New Orleans where he remained for the rest of his life, playing with Emile Barnes, the Eureka Brass Band and other local groups. Bocage's instrumental versatility, he also played guitar, xylophone, baritone horn, trombone, trumpet and banjo, allied to a inherent good taste made him a popular figure with audiences and his colleagues.

Albums: *The Barnes-Bocage Big Five* (1954), *Peter Bocage And His Creole Serenaders* (1961), *Peter Bocage And His Creole Serenaders* (1962), *Peter Bocage Quartet* (1963), *Peter Bocage At The San Jacinto Hall* (Jazzology 1964), *New Orleans - The Legends Live* (Jazzology 1986).

Bofill, Angela

b. 1954, West Bronx, New York City, USA, Bofill began writing songs at the age of 12. She formed her first group whilst still at high school, the Puerto Rican Supremes, which performed in church and local school dances. Her father, another Latin music singer, had once sung with Cuban band leader Machito. After graduating from the Manhattan School of Music she toured with Ricardo Morrero and recorded her first single, 'My Friend', which earned her a nomination as best Latin female vocalist from *Latin New York* magazine. Encouraged by this success, she embarked on a solo career, writing and performing the jazz suite, 'Under The Moon And Over The Sky', in conjunction with the Brooklyn Academy of Music. She then became lead vocalist with the Dance Theater of Harlem Chorus and performed alongside Stan Getz and Benny Goodman at Madison Square Garden. Following an introduction by Dave Valentin, she was signed as a soloist with Dave Grusin's GRP record label. The debut *Angie* set included a reworking of 'Under The Moon', as well as 'Baby, I Need Your Love' and 'The Only Thing I Would Wish For'. Straying from jazz, Bofill worked in more conventional soul and R&B territory on her albums for Arista, where she teamed with producer Narada Michael Waldren before the System production team helmed her final three efforts for the label. She moved to Capitol later in the decade, where producers including Norman Connors were invited to assist. Bofill continued to tour widely between recording sessions, often with the New York Jazz Explosion, and also guested on Stanley Clarke's 'Where Do We Go' cut (from his *Hideaway* album). Although she has yet to chart a hit single, she has recorded increasingly impressive albums within the jazz-soul style and established herself as an accomplished vocalist.

Albums: *Angie* (GRP 1978), *Angel Of The Night* (GRP 1979), *Something About You* (Arista 1982), *Too Tough* (Arista 1983), *Teaser* (Arista 1983), *Let Me Be The One* (Arista 1984), *Tell Me Tomorrow* (Arista 1985), *Intuition* (Capitol 1988). Compilations: *Best Of Angela Bofill* (Arista 1986), *Best Of Angie (Next Time I'll Be Sweeter)* (Arista 1991).

Boland, Francy

b. François Boland, 6 November 1929, Namur, Belgium. A classically trained musician, Boland's first exposure to jazz came through concerts and records which he heard during World War II. His first contributions to the music were arrangements written for the bands of Bobby Jaspar, Henri Renaud and others. In the early 50s he spent much time in Paris, arranging and playing piano, and worked with visiting Americans such as Chet Baker and Nat Peck. In the late 50s he was writing for Kurt Edelhagen's German-based, multi-national big band. In 1958 he visited New York, writing charts for Count Basie. At the same time, Boland met drummer Kenny Clarke and with the financial backing of entrepreneur Gigi Campi they formed the Clarke-Boland Big Band. This, too, was a multi-national band and featured players such as Peck, Derek Humble, Benny Bailey, Jimmy Deuchar, Aake Persson, Sahib Shihab, Ronnie Scott and Johnny Griffin. Boland played piano in the band and also composed for it, but his principal contribution was his arranging, which magnificently combined the band's members into a powerful collective whole without ever subduing their potential for inventive soloing. The band was on the brink of folding in the early 70s, but stayed together thanks to the desire of the musicians to continue playing even when the financial burden was almost intolerable. Since 1976 Boland has lived and worked in Europe (mostly based in Switzerland), writing and arranging for artists such as Sarah Vaughan.

Albums: *Jazz Is Universal* (1961), *The Francy Boland Big Band* (1963), *Now Hear Our Meaning* (1963), *Karl Drewo Und Die Clarke-Boland Big Band* (1966), *Out Of The Background* (1967), with C-BBB *Flirt And Dream* (1967), *Music For The Small Hours* (1967); the following with C-BBB unless stated *Out Of The Folk Bag* (1967), *Open Door* (Muse 1967), *17 Men And Their Music* (1967), *Let's Face The Music/Smile* (1968), *Faces* (1968), *More* (1968), *Latin Kaleidoscope* (1968), *Fellini 712* (1968), *Volcano/Live At Ronnie Scott's* (1969), *Rue Chaptal* (1969), *All Blues* (1969), *More Smiles* (1969), *Francy Boland And His Orchestra In Warsaw* (1969), *At Her Majesty's Pleasure* (1969), *The Francy Boland-Kenny Clarke Trio* (1970), *Boland Piano And Strings* (1970), *Off Limmits* (1970), *Our Kind Of Sabi* (1970), *Change Of Scenes* (1971); as Francy Boland Orchestra *Blue Flame* (1976), *Red Hot* (1976), *White Heat* (1976), *Live TNP Paris 1969* (1993).

Bolden, Buddy

b. Charles Joseph Bolden, 6 September 1877, New Orleans, Louisiana, USA, d. 4 November 1931. The first great jazz legend, Bolden's reputation depends largely upon the reminiscences of the next generation of cornet and trumpet players of early jazz. They recalled him as being an inspiration, a driving, rhythmic and emotional player, and the 'first jazz trumpeter'. Research by writer Don Marquis, suggests that Bolden was merely an adequate musician who became immensely popular

in turn-of-the-century New Orleans, thanks mainly to his powerful playing of the kind of music the crowds wanted to hear allied to enormous personal magnetism. In the early 1900s Bolden began to drink heavily and six years later was showing signs of mental disorder. In 1907 he was incarcerated in the Jackson Mental Institution, where he remained until his death in the 30s. Bolden never recorded, although rumours persist that he made some cylinder recordings in the 1890s, but his stylistic influence was ostensibly apparent in the work of many early New Orleans cornetists, including Bunk Johnson. A fictional account of Bolden's life was the basis for Michael Ondaatje's brilliantly inventive 1976 novel, *Coming Through Slaughter*.
Further reading: *In Search Of Buddy Bolden, First Man Of Jazz*, Don Marquis.

Bolling, Claude

b. 10 April 1930, Cannes, France. After showing prodigious talent as a child pianist, Bolling began playing professionally while still in his early teens. Strongly influenced by ragtime and early jazz pianists and by other figures as diverse as Duke Ellington and Art Tatum, Bolling swiftly became recognized in France as a major pianist. He played at concerts, festivals and on record with many visiting jazzmen including Paul Gonsalves, Lionel Hampton and Rex Stewart. He also led his own small groups from the late 40s onwards, forming bigger bands in the 50s including the Show Biz Band which remained in intermittent existence for the next three decades. In addition to playing jazz, Bolling has also written for films. He has composed and recorded music which mixes jazz and the classical form although he has done so in a manner which remains closer to the mainstream than the so-called third stream. Bolling makes infrequent appearances outside his homeland but has played in the UK, leading his powerful big band from the piano.
Albums: with Lionel Hampton *The Complete 1953 Paris Session* (1953), *Claude Bolling Plays Duke Ellington* (1959), *Cat Anderson, Claude Bolling And Co.* (1965), *Original Ragtime* (1966), *Original Boogie Woogie* (1968), *Original Piano Blues* (1969), *Original Jazz Classics* (c.1970), *Original Piano Greats* (1972), *Swing Session* (1973), *Jazz Party* (1974), *Suite For Violin And Jazz Piano* (c.1975), *With The Help Of My Friends* (c.1975), *Keep Swingin' Vol. 4* (c.1975), *Suite For Flute And Jazz Piano* (1975), *Hot Sounds* (c.1976), *Concerto For Classic Guitar And Jazz Piano* (HMV 1975), *California Suite* (1977-78), *Suite For Chamber Orchestra And Jazz Piano Trio* (c.1978), *Jazz Gala 79* (1979), *Just For Fun* (c.1980), *Toot Suite* (1981), *Claude Bolling* (RCA 1981), *Suite For Cello And Jazz Piano Trio* (c.1982), *Claude Bolling Live At The Méridien* (1984), *Jazz À La Françcaise* (CBS 1984), *Live At The Meridien* (CBS 1985), *Nuances* (DRG 1988).

Bonano, Joseph 'Sharkey'

b. 9 April c.1902, Milneburg, Louisiana, USA, d. 27 March 1972. A powerful, hot trumpeter, Bonano played in and around his home town as a teenager. In 1920 he went to New

York to work with Eddie Edwards but was soon back home playing with various lesser-known New Orleans bands, including Norman Brownlee's with whom he made his first recordings in 1925. During this same period he made sporadic attempts to enter the big time, auditioning for the Wolverines and working with the band led by Jimmy Durante (before the pianist turned comic). In 1927, Bonano was briefly with Jean Goldkette and also worked with Larry Shields in Los Angeles. In the late 20s Bonano temporarily stopped striving for the national big time and settled instead for being a popular figure in New Orleans where he led his own band. He also worked in harness with Louis Prima's brother, Leon. In 1936 he tried New York again, this time with much more success, working with Ben Pollack and also leading his own band. The Revival movement helped Bonano retain his popularity and he worked throughout the 40s and into the 50s sometimes leading a band, often appearing as a solo act, singing and playing trumpet. Bonano's playing was variable but on a good day he was an exciting, aggressive and thoroughly entertaining player. Fortunately, some of his best work was captured on recording dates especially those of the early 50s. Bonano played into the 60s, but ill health gradually curtailed his activity and he died in 1972.
Selected albums: *Midnight On Bourbon Street* (1951-52), *Dixieland At The Roundtable* (1960). Compilations: *Sharkey Bonano And His New Orleans Boys And Sharks Of Rhythm* (Holmia 1986, 1936 recordings), *Sharkey And His Kings Of Dixieland* (GHB 1986), *Sharkey Bonano 1928-1937* (Timeless 1992).

Bostic, Earl

b. Eugene Earl Bostic, 25 April 1913, Tulsa, Oklahoma, USA, d. 28 October 1965. The romantic and smooth sound of Bostic's band, usually featuring the vibes of Gene Redd, piano of Fletcher Smith, bass of Margo Gibson, drums of Charles Walton, guitar of Alan Seltzer, and the marvellous alto saxophone of Bostic was one of the great and distinctive sounds of both R&B and pop music, and his records became perennials on the juke boxes during the 50s. Bostic was best known for his alto saxophone sound but he also played tenor saxophone, flute and clarinet on his records. Bostic was formally trained in music, having received a degree in music theory at Xavier University. He moved to New York City and formed a jazz combo in 1938. In the early 40s he was playing in the Lionel Hampton band. He left Hampton in 1945 to form a combo, recording tracks for Majestic, but did not make much of an impression until he signed with New York-based Gotham in 1948. He immediately hit with 'Temptation' (US R&B number 10). During the 50s he recorded prolifically for Cincinnati-based King Records, and had two big singles, 'Sleep' (US R&B number 6) and 'Flamingo' (US R&B number 1) in 1951. The smooth but perky performance on the latter became his signature tune and made him something of a Beach Music artist in the Carolinas.
Selected albums: *The Best of Bostic* (1956), *For You* (1956), *Alto-Tude* (1957), *Dancetime* (1957), *Let's Dance* (1957),

Invitation To Dance (1957), *C'mon & Dance* (1957), *Bostic Rocks-Hits From The Swing Age* (1958), *Bostic Showcase Of Swinging Dance Hits* (1958), *Alto Magic In Hi-Fi* (King 1958), *Sweet Tunes Of The Fantastic 50's* (1958), *Sweet Tunes Of The Roaring 20's* (1959), *Sweet Tunes Of the Swinging 30's* (1959), *Sweet Tunes Of The Sentimental 40's* (1959), *Musical Pearls* (1960), *Hit Tunes Of The Big Broadway Shows* (1961), *By Popular Demand* (1962), *Bossa Nova* (1963), *Jazz I Feel It* (1963), *The Best Of Earl Bostic Vol. 2* (1964), *The Great Hits Of 1964* (1964), *Harlem Nocturne* (1969), *Sax'O Woogie* (1984), *Blows A Fuse* (1985), *That's Earl, Brother* (1985), *Bostic Rocks* (Swingtime 1987), *Dance Time* (Sing 1988), *Bostic For You* (Sing 1988), *Let's Dance* (Charly 1987). *Dance Music From The Bostic Workshop* (Charly 1988).

Boutté, Lillian

b. 6 August 1949, New Orleans, Louisiana, USA. After singing in a church choir and studying music, Boutté became a professional singer in her early 20s. Initially, she sang R&B but her striking personality and wide-ranging musical knowledge brought her a key role in the show *One Mo' Time*. Her first European tour began in 1980 and she created a substantial following, particularly in France and the UK. In 1983 she collaborated with saxophonist Thomas l'Etienne, whom she married, to form the group Music Friends and, later, the Boutté-l'Etienne Jazz Ensemble. Her touring schedule was stepped up with important appearances at many festivals around the world, including Ascona where she headlined for several years from 1985, Brecon, the 1988 Ellington Convention, and other prestigious engagements. Also in the late 80s she performed with Humphrey Lyttelton. A vibrant and exceptionally talented singer, Boutté's predilection for the traditional end of the jazz song spectrum may have shielded her from the attention of the fans of contemporary music. This is unfortunate because her powerful, imaginative blues-based style makes her one of the few singers of her generation who can evoke with ease the important place held by the blues in the art of jazz song.
Selected albums: *Music Is My Life* (Timeless 1984), *A Fine Romance* (1985), *New Orleans Gospel* (Herman 1986), *Let Them Talk* (Storyville 1988), *Lillian Boutté With Humphrey Lyttelton And Band* (Calligraph 1988) *I Sing Because I'm Happy* (Timeless 1988), *Having A Good Time!* (Calligraph 1989), *Birthday Party* (Music Mecca 1989), *Lipstick Traces* (Blues Beacon 1991), *Live In Tivoli* (Music Mecca 1993).

Bowie, Joe

b. 1958, St. Louis, Missouri, USA. Younger brother of trumpeter Lester Bowie, Joseph learned piano and congas but finally settled with trombone. At the age of 15 he played with bluesmen Albert King and Little Milton and soul saxophonist Oliver Sain. He spent two years in Paris with other members of BAG (Black Artists Group), then in the late 70s recorded with Charles 'Bobo' Shaw in the Human Arts Ensemble and the St. Louis Creative Ensemble before returning to New York to work with the Contortions, James Chance's harmolodic/punk No Wave group. The horn section became an opening act and then

a band in its own right: Defunkt. This unit combined jazz chops and *nouveau*-funk cheer: they toured with the Clash and Talking Heads. After a heroin-induced layoff Bowie returned in 1985 with an amazing physique and an excellent album, *In America*, which featured Kim Annette Clarke's bass guitar (described by one reviewer as 'funky as the chain on Judge Dredd's motorbike'). Since then, Bowie has steered between dance music and *avant garde* jazz with a verve that ridicules the usual pigeon-holes.
Albums: *Joseph Bowie - Oliver Lake* (1976), with St. Louis Creative Ensemble *I Can't Figure Out* (1979), *Defunkt* (1980), *Thermonuclear Sweat* (1982), *In America* (1988), with Michael Marcus *Under The Wire* (1991).

Bowie, Lester

b. 11 October 1941, Frederick, Maryland, USA. After taking up the trumpet as a child Bowie played in several R&B bands in and around St. Louis, Missouri. He led his own R&B bands and married singer Fontella Bass, accompanying her as musical director. Despite this and earlier connections with the R&B scene, Bowie's chief musical interests lay elsewhere. Based in Chicago from the mid-60s, he was actively involved with the Association for the Advancement of Creative Musicians and was co-founder of the Art Ensemble Of Chicago. From its inception in 1969 into the 80s he remained closely linked with AEC, touring and recording extensively, especially in France. Always eager to experiment with fusions of seemingly differing aspects of the jazz tradition, he has constantly brought traditional blues roots into his work with such forward-thinking musicians as Archie Shepp, Roscoe Mitchell and David Murray. Bowie is also involved with the groups Brass Fantasy, Leaders and From The Root To The Source, and has played with reggae groups in Jamaica and spent time in Nigeria playing in Fela Kuti's Egypt 80 band. Bowie composed many numbers recorded by AEC and by other groups with which he has been associated. Amongst his extended works are 'Gittin' To Know Y'All', originally performed by the Baden-Baden Free Jazz Orchestra. Bowie happily works with groups of all sizes, from the smallest to a 60-piece orchestra assembled for some of his concerts. Bowie appeared on David Bowie's (no relation) *Black Tie White Noise* in 1993. A remarkably gifted trumpeter, with a full, rich tone and a comprehensive range of effects, Bowie's work frequently contains welcome elements of self-parodying humour and witty inventiveness.
Album: with AEC *Numbers 1 & 2* (1967), with Roscoe Mitchell *Congliptious* (1968), *Gittin' To Know Y'All* (1969), *Fast Last!* (1974), *Rope A Dope* (1976), *The Fifth Power* (Black Saint 1978), *African Children* (1978), *Works* (1980-82), *The Great Pretender* (ECM 1982), *All The Magic* (ECM 1983), *I Only Have Eyes For You* (ECM 1985), *Avant Pop* (ECM 1986), *Twilight Dreams* (1987), *Serious Fun* (DIW 1989), *My Way* (DIW 1990), *The Organizer* (DIW 1991), *The Fire This Time* (In And Out 1993), with Phillip Wilson *Duet* (1993). Compilation: *Works* (ECM 1989).

Bowman, Dave

b. 8 September 1914, Buffalo, New York, USA, d. 28 December 1964. Bowman began playing piano as a child, and later went on to study formally. He was in the UK in the mid-30s, playing in Jack Hylton's band in London. At the end of the 30s he was resident in New York, working in small traditional bands with such leading jazzmen as Sidney Bechet and Bud Freeman. During the early 40s he was with Jack Teagarden, Muggsy Spanier and others. He drifted into radio work, becoming adept at accompanying singers both in the jazz field, with Lee Wiley, and elsewhere, with Perry Como. In the 50s he was again with Freeman and also played as a single. He continued playing jazz into the early 60s but was rarely in the big time. A competent pianist, he was at his best as a relatively anonymous member of the rhythm section of several solid traditional bands. He died in a car accident in December 1964.
Compilation: with Bud Freeman *Chicagoans In New York* (1935-40 recordings).

Brackeen, Charles

b. 13 March 1940, White's Chapel (renamed Eufaula), Oklahoma, USA. As a child Brackeen studied piano and violin before taking up saxophone at the age of 10. After living briefly in Texas and New York, he moved to Los Angeles in 1956, where he met musicians such as Don Cherry, Ornette Coleman, Charlie Haden, Billy Higgins and Paul Bley, so furthering an interest in new jazz already sparked by his love for the records of John Coltrane and Sonny Rollins. In 1960 he married pianist JoAnne Brackeen (they later divorced) and in 1965 moved back to New York. After playing 'all types of music', including gigs with West Indian musicians, Brackeen recorded *Rhythm X* in 1969; with Haden, Cherry and Ed Blackwell as his associates, the record was virtually a homage to Coleman. From 1970-72, he played in the Melodic Art-tet (with Ahmed Abdullah, bassist Ronnie Boykins and drummer Roger Blank), performing regularly on New York's *avant garde* loft scene. Brackeen next worked with Blackwell again, with Ronald Shannon Jackson and with Paul Motian, playing on the latter's *Dance* (1977) and *Le Voyage* (1979). After recording with Blackwell's quartet in 1982 (the album remains unreleased), Brackeen returned to Los Angeles the following year and is still living there. In 1987 he was invited by Dennis Gonzalez to record for the Silkheart label and has so far issued three albums as leader as well as appearing on records by Abdullah (*Liquid Magic*) and Gonzalez (*Namesake, Debenge-Debenge*). A compelling tenor saxophonist, with echoes of Rollins and Albert Ayler in his playing style and the influence of Ornette Coleman discernible in his writing, Brackeen plays a disciplined post-free jazz that is shot through with a broad streak of lyricism. He is also a persuasive, if rare, performer on soprano saxophone.
Albums: *Rhythm X* (Strata East 1970), *Bannar* (Silkheart 1987), *Attainment* (Silkheart 1988), *Worshippers Come Nigh* (Silkheart 1988).

Brackeen, JoAnne

b. Joanne Grogan, 26 July 1938, Ventura, California, USA. Brackeen was self-taught, academic tuition did not suit: she left the Los Angeles Conservatory of Music after three days. Despite this, her piano playing became much in demand among the most exacting jazz leaders on the west coast: Harold Land, Teddy Edwards and Charles Lloyd. Unimpeded by marriage (to saxophonist Charles Brackeen) and four children, she relocated to New York in 1965, playing with Woody Shaw and David Liebman. Between 1969 and 1971 she worked with Art Blakey's Jazz Messengers: that a woman (and a white woman at that) could hold down such a position says much about her abilities. Like all the essential pianists in jazz, Brackeen has a touch with a ballad that is utterly unique yet reverberates with the whole tradition. The high quality of her accompanists - Cecil McBee (bass), Al Foster (drums), Branford Marsalis (saxophone) - is another demonstration of her achievements.
Albums: *New True Illusion* (Timeless 1976), *Invitation* (1978), *Trinkets And Things* (1981), with Clint Houston *New True Illusion* (Timeless 1981), with Ryo Kawaski *Trinkets And Things* (Timeless 1981), *Special Identity* (Antilles 1982), *Havin' Fun* (Concord 1985), *AFT* (Timeless 1986), *Fi-fi Goes To Heaven* (Concord 1987), *Live At Maybeck Recital Hall, Vol 1* (Concord 1990), *Where Legends Dwell* (Ken 1992), *Breath Of Brazil* (Concord 1992).

Bradford, Bobby

b. 19 July 1934, Cleveland, Mississippi, USA. Bradford's family moved to Dallas in 1946 and he took up the cornet in 1949. He was at high school with James Clay, Cedar Walton and David Newman and played in a dance band with Leo Wright. He also worked around Dallas with Buster Smith and John Hardee. He moved to Los Angeles in 1953 and, although he had known and played with Ornette Coleman since their teens in Dallas-Fort Worth, it was not until the move to Los Angeles that their musical collaboration really began, and Bradford did not record with Coleman until the early 70s, when he appeared on some of the tracks on *Science Fiction* and *Broken Shadows*. In California he had worked with Wardell Gray, Gerald Wilson and Eric Dolphy. In 1961, after completing his military service, he went to New York to rejoin Coleman for two years, replacing Don Cherry in Coleman's quartet. He then returned to Los Angeles and co-led the New Art Jazz Ensemble with John Carter from 1965-74. When the Ensemble split up Carter and Bradford continued to work together in a workshop, the Little Big Horn. For a short while Bradford also led a group that comprised Stanley Crouch, Mark Dresser and then-teenagers David Murray and James Newton. In the meantime Bradford had been to Europe in 1971, where he recorded with John Stevens's Spontaneous Music Ensemble (SME) in London and Paris. After the *Science Fiction* date he returned to Europe for an extended stay (1972-74), during which he recorded with the SME again, as he did on a further visit in 1986. In 1974, he returned to California to teach. In 1980 Bradford was featured in Peter Bull's documentary *The New Music*. In 1986 he was re-united with Stevens in the trio Detail, which also included bassist Johnny Dyani (*Way It Goes/ Dance Of The Soul*). He had also resumed his partnership with Carter, playing on the clarinettist's five-album suite, *Roots And Folklore* (1982-89) and on the co-led *Comin' On* (1989). A melodic and rhythmically subtle player, Bradford has been a vital catalyst of Californian new jazz for more than 25 years.

Albums: with New Art Jazz Ensemble *Seeking* (1969), with NAJE *Flight For Four* (1970, reissued as part of *West Coast Hot*), with NAJE *Self-Determination Music* (1971), with Ornette Coleman *Science Fiction* (1971), *Bobby Bradford With The Spontaneous Music Ensemble* (1971), with NAJE, John Carter *Secrets* (1973), with SME *Love Dreams* (1973), with Carter *Variations On Selected Themes For Jazz Quintet* (1978), with Carter *A Suite Of American Folk Pieces For Solo Clarinet* (1979), with Carter *Dauwhe* (1982), with David Murray *Murray's Steps* (1982), *Lost In LA* (Soul Note 1983), with Carter *Castles Of Ghana* (1985), with Carter *Fields* (1988), with Carter *Shadows On A Wall* (1989), *One Night Stand* (Soul Note 1989), with Carter *Comin' On* (Hat Art 1989).

Bradshaw, Tiny

b. Myron Bradshaw, 23 September 1905, Youngstown, Ohio, USA, d. 26 November 1958. While studying psychology at the Wilberforce University, Ohio, Bradshaw became involved in the campus's flourishing musical sub-culture. He joined Horace Henderson's Collegians as the band's singer. In 1932 he came to New York where he played drums with several bands including the Savoy Bearcats and the Mills Blue Rhythm Band. In the same year he sang with Luis Russell and then formed his own band which toured extensively, playing several long engagements at hotels and dance halls. During this period, Bradshaw modelled his style on that of Cab Calloway, both men having spent time in Marion Hardy's Alabamians. He had some success on record in the 30s, notably with 'Shout, Sister, Shout' and 'The Darktown Strutters' Ball'. During World War II Bradshaw led a US Army big band. After the war he kept a band together by adapting to the popularity of R&B, attracting the attention of several young white performers amongst whom was Buddy Holly. In the mid-50s poor health forced Bradshaw to fold his band and he died in November 1958. A lively entertainer, Bradshaw never quite made the big time. Indeed, at one time he suffered the mild indignity of being billed as the 'super Cab Calloway'. Bradshaw often hired first-rate musicians and arrangers for his bands, amongst them Shad Collins, Russell Procope, Happy Caldwell, Charlie Shavers, Billy Kyle, Charlie Fowlkes, Bobby Plater, Shadow Wilson, Fred Radcliffe, Sonny Stitt, Gil Fuller, Big Nick Nicholas, Gigi Gryce and Red Prysock.

Compilations: *Tiny Bradshaw 1934* (1934), *Stomping Room Only* (Krazy Kat 1984), *Breaking Up The House (50s)* (Charly 1985), *A Tribute To The Late Tiny Bradshaw* (Charly 1987), *The Great Composer (1950-58)* (King 1988), *I'm A High Ballin' Daddy* (Jukebox Lil 1988).

Braff, Ruby

b. Reuben Braff, 16 March 1927, Boston, Massachusetts, USA.

Although Braff did not make a notable impact on the jazz scene until the mid-50s, he was already an accomplished and experienced cornet player. He had worked extensively in the Boston area from the late 40s, playing with Pee Wee Russell and Edmond Hall, recording with the latter in 1949. It was, however, Braff's 1953 recordings with Vic Dickenson that drew the attention of jazz fans. Between the boppers and the Revivalist movement lay the mainstream jazzmen of which Braff was a singularly attractive example. His lyrical and expressive style, shot through with bursts of white-hot excitement, lent itself especially well to ballads and during the rest of the 50s he made several excellent records in distinguished company such as Buck Clayton, Mel Powell, Bud Freeman and Benny Goodman. Despite this period of remarkable creativity, Braff's career then stalled, thanks in part to his determination to play the way he wanted, rather than as the public or club owners might demand. A second factor which hindered his progress was his habitual bluntness in manner and speech; Braff said what he thought, regardless of the effect his statements might have on his chances of a return engagement. His circumstances improved in the 60s, although there were no signs that he was any easier to get on with; perhaps people had simply grown accustomed to his manner. In a succession of concert and festival appearances, and in numerous recordings, Braff proved his continuing excellence both in taste and performance. His musical partnerships included one with George Barnes, which resulted in superb music and countless arguments. He also worked with Dick Hyman and Scott Hamilton. In the 80s Braff continued to work, displaying his elegant, melodic and full-toned playing all around the world, and still possessing enough of the old prickliness to frighten off all but the most determined interviewers.

Albums: *Hustlin' And Bustlin'* (Black Lion 1951-54), with Pee Wee Russell *Jazz At Storyville* (1952), *The Vic Dickenson Septet* (1953), *Mel Powell And His All Stars At Carnegie Hall* (1954), with Buck Clayton *Buck Meets Ruby* (1954), *Holiday In Braff* (1954-55), *Adoration Of The Melody* (1955), *The Mighty Braff* (Affinity 1955), *Braff!* (1956), *Hear Me Talkin'* (Black Lion 1967), *On Sunnie's Side Of The Street* (1968), *Ruby Braff Plays Louis Armstrong* (1969), *Swing That Music* (Affinity 1970), with Ellis Larkins *The Grand Reunion* (1972), *The Music Of Ruby Braff And His International Jazz Quartet* (1972), with George Barnes *Live At The New School* (1974), *The Ruby Braff/George Barnes Quartet Plays Gershwin* (Concord 1974), *The Ruby Braff/George Barnes Quartet Salutes Rodgers And Hart* (Concord 1974), with Barnes *To Fred Astaire With Love* (1975), with Dick Hyman *Fats Waller's Heavenly Jive* (1976), *Them There Eyes* (1976), *Pretties* (1978), *Swinging On A Star: Braff Plays Bing Vol. 1* (1978), *Ruby Braff With The Ed Bickert Trio* (1979), *Braff Plays Bing* (Pizza Express 1979), *Very Sinatra* (1981), with Hyman *A Pipe Organ Recital Plus One* (Concord 1982), with Scott Hamilton *Mr Braff To You* (Phontastic 1983), *Easy Now* (RCA 1983), *Best I've Heard* (Vogue 1983), with Hyman *America The Beautiful* (George Wein Collection 1984), with Hyman *Manhattan Jazz* (1985), with Scott Hamilton *A Fine Match* (Concord 1985), *A First* (Concord

1985), with Hamilton *A Sailboat In The Moonlight* (Concord 1986), *Bravura Eloquence* (Concord 1988), *Me, Myself And I* (Concord 1988), with Hyman *Younger Than Swingtime* (Concord 1990), *Music From MY Fair Lady* (Concord 1990), with Dick Hyman *Music From South Pacific* (Concord 1991), *And His New England Songhounds: Vol 1 and 2* (Concord 1991, *Cornet Chop Suey* (1991).

Braxton, Anthony

b. 4 June 1945, Chicago, Illinois, USA. Braxton began playing clarinet in high school, studied music for one semester at Wilson Junior College, then joined the US Army, where he played clarinet and alto saxophone. In 1966 he joined Chicago's Association for the Advancement of Creative Musicians (the AACM), a newly-formed musicians' co-operative whose leading members included Muhal Richard Abrams and Roscoe Mitchell. Braxton formed his own group (later called the Creative Construction Company) with Leroy Jenkins and Leo Smith and their first release, *Three Compositions Of New Jazz*, was recorded in 1968. Their music typified the Chicagoans' new experimentalism, with its emphasis on sound, space, texture - as opposed to the Coltrane-led energy music prevalent in New York. Braxton also followed the AACM trend towards multi-instrumentalism, becoming an accomplished master on most members of the saxophone, clarinet and flute families. However, alto sax had become his main instrument and in late 1968 he recorded his epochal double-album, *For Alto*, the first ever full-length recording of solo saxophone music. In 1969 the Creative Construction Company moved to Paris, only to disband within a year. Braxton returned to the USA, lodged with Ornette Coleman and for several months earned a living as a professional chess player. In 1970 he joined Chick Corea, Dave Holland and Barry Altschul to form the group Circle, but disagreements with Corea over their involvement with the Scientology movement broke up the band and Braxton returned to Paris, where he began to play with various European improvisers, leading to later appearances with Alex Von Schlippenbach's Globe Unity Orchestra and at Derek Bailey's Company festivals. In 1974 producer Michael Cuscuna offered him a contract with Arista Records and he returned to the USA, recording and performing with a regular quartet that now comprised Holland, Altschul and Kenny Wheeler (the latter replaced briefly by George Lewis). For the next six years, the Arista contract meant Braxton's music had a relatively high profile.

Already regarded as eccentric because he titled his compositions with enigmatic diagrams, Braxton quickly became a controversial figure in jazz circles as releases such as *For Trio* (1978), *For Four Orchestras* (1978) and *For Two Pianos* (1982), inspired in part by the work of Schoenberg, Stockhausen and Cage, revealed his growing interest in contemporary composition. However, Braxton never denied his love for jazz, constantly citing John Coltrane, Paul Desmond and Warne Marsh as major influences on his saxophone playing; and in 1974 he had anticipated the 80s' obsession with traditional jazz repertoire by recording the two *In The Tradition* sessions (later followed by others, including outstanding tribute records to Thelonious Monk and Lennie Tristano). Also in the 70s he recorded two sets of improvised duos with the great bebop drummer Max Roach, a superb live quartet concert in Dortmund (not released until 1991) and a collection of *avant garde* big band pieces, the prize-winning *Creative Orchestra Music 1976*, which many people still regard as one of his finest releases. In the 80s Braxton's music showed a growing concern with mysticism, theatre and collage-structures. He developed a series of 'ritual and ceremonial' works, which incorporated elements of astrology, numerology, costume and dance, and which culminated in his latest, ongoing project - a series of 12 operas, entitled *Trillium*. (The visual basis of much of this music is perhaps attributable to his chromesthetic vision; that is, like the composer Scriabin, he literally *sees* sounds as colours and shapes.) His quartet music, often the chief focus of his jazz-related experimentalism, has also became increasingly complex. *On Four Compositions (Quartet) 1983* he introduced the concept of 'pulse track structures' as an alternative to chord changes and modal music.

A little later he began playing 'multiple logics music', in which members of the quartet (for the last six years a regular line-up of Marilyn Crispell, Mark Dresser and Gerry Hemingway) might be playing two, three or four compositions simultaneously *Quartet (London) 1985*, *Quartet (Birmingham) 1985*, *Quartet (Willisau) 1991*). Now teaching at Wesleyan College, Connecticut, Braxton remains formidably prolific: he has written nearly 400 compositions, made over 70 records as leader and appeared on at least 50 others. In 1985 he published his three-volume, philosophical *Tri-axium Writings* and in 1988 the first five volumes of his *Composition Notes*. His latest recordings include further sets of solo, duo, trio, quartet and large ensemble works, plus collaborations with the ROVA Saxophone Quartet and the London Jazz Composers Orchestra. His most recent visit to the UK was in April 1991, with his quartet; their three London concerts showed that his music is now reaching new levels of intensity, abstraction and gracefulness while continuing to explore fresh concepts of form. Though still regarded with suspicion by some hardline traditionalists (and black nationalists), Braxton's importance as an innovator is increasingly evident in the jazz world, his influence proclaimed by upcoming players such as Tim Berne and John Zorn. 'The challenge of creativity,' he has said, 'is to move towards the highest thought that you can think of '; and in pursuit of that goal he has played at the extremes of register and tempo, dreamed of a music played by orchestras on different planets and forged a unique musical synthesis of new and old, Africa and Europe, structure and freedom.

Selected albums: *Three Compositions Of New Jazz* (1968), *B-X°-NO/47A* (1970), *This Time* (1970), *For Alto* (1971, rec. 1968), *Recital Paris '71* (1971), *Steps Out* (1971), *Donna Lee* (1972), *Saxophone Improvisations Series F* (1972), *Town Hall 1972* (1972), with Gunter Hampel and Jeanne Lee *Familie* (1972), *Four Compositions (1973)* (1973), *Silence* (1974, rec. 1969), with Joseph Jarman *Together Alone* (1974, rec. 1972), *In The Tradition Volume One* (1974), *Solo: Live At Moers Festival*

(1974), *Live At Moers Festival* (1974), *Trio & Duet* (1974), *New York Fall 1974* (1975), with Creative Construction Company *CCC Volume One* (1975, rec 1970), *Creative Music Orchestra: RBN - 3°/K12* (1975, rec. 1972, three-album box-set), *Five Pieces 1975* (1975), with CCC *CCC Volume Two* (1976, rec. 1970), *In The Tradition Volume Two* (1976, rec. 1974), *Creative Orchestra Music 1976* (1976), with George Lewis *Elements Of Surprise* (1976), with Muhal Richard Abrams *Duets 1976* (1976), *The Complete Braxton* (1977, rec. 1971), with Derek Bailey *Duo* (1977, rec. 1974), *The Montreux/Berlin Concerts* (1977, rec. 1975-6), with Richard Teitelbaum *Time Zones* (1977), with Bailey, Evan Parker *Company 2* (1977), *For Trio* (1978, rec. 1977), with Roscoe Mitchell *Duets* (1978, rec. 1977), *For Four Orchestras* (1978, three-album box-set), with Max Roach *Birth/Rebirth* (1978), *Alto Saxophone Improvisations 1979* (1979), with Roach *One In Two - Two In One* (1980), *Seven Compositions 1978* (1980), *Performance 9/1/79* (1981, reissued as *Performance (Quartet)*), *Composition 98* (1981), *For Two Pianos* (1982, rec. 1980), with Giorgio Gaslini *Four Pieces* (1982), *Six Compositions: Quartet* (1982), with Teitelbaum *Open Aspects '82* (1982), with John Lindberg *Six Duets 1982* (1982), *Four Compositions (Quartet) 1983* (1983), with Bailey *Royal Volume One* (1984, rec. 1974), with Neighbours *With Anthony Braxton* (1984, rec. 1980), *Composition 113* (1984), with Gyorgy Szabados *Szabraxtondos* (1985), *Six Compositions (Quartet) 1984* (1985), *Seven Standards 1985 Volume One* (1985), *Seven Standards 1985 Volume Two* (1986), *Anthony Braxton/Robert Schumann String Quartet* (1986, rec 1979), *Five Compositions (Quartet) 1986* (Black Saint 1986), with Bailey *Moment Precieux* (1987), with Gino Robair *Duets 1987* (1987), *Six Monk's Compositions, 1987* (Black Saint 1988), with the London Jazz Composers Orchestra *Zurich Concerts* (1988), *Composition 96* (1989, rec. 1981), *Quartet (London) 1985* (1989, rec. 1985, three-album box-set), with ROVA Saxophone Quartet *The Aggregate* (1989, rec. 1986-88), *Ensemble (Victoriaville) 1988* (1989), *19 (Solo) Compositions, 1988* (1989), *Compositions 99, 101, 107 & 139* (Hat Art 1989, rec. 1982-88 reissued as *Four Compositions (Solo, Duo & Trio) 1982/1988*), *Seven Compositions (Trio) 1989* (1989), with Andrew Voigt *Kol Nidre* (1990, rec. 1988), with Marilyn Crispell *Duets Vancouver 1989* (1990), *Eight (+3) Tristano Compositions 1989 For Warne Marsh* (1990), *Prag 1984 (Quartet Performance)* (1991, rec. 1984), *Dortmund (Quartet) 1976* (1991, rec. 1976), *Solo (London) 1988* (1991, rec. 1988), *Eugene (1989)* (1991, rec. 1989), *Quartet (Birmingham) 1985* (1992, rec. 1985), with Peter Niklas Wilson *Eight Duets (Hamburg) 1991* (1992, rec 1991), *Composition No. 165* (New Albion 1992), *Two Compositions (Ensemble) 1989-91* (1992, rec. 1989, 1991), *Quartet (Willisau) 1991* (Hat Art 1992, rec. 1991, four-CD box-set), *Quartet (Coventry) 1985* (1993, rec. 1985), *Wesleyan (12 Altosolos)* (Hat Art 1993), *Duo (London) 1993* (Leo 1993).

Further reading: *Tri-axium Writings, Vols 1-3*, Anthony Braxton. *Composition Notes, Books A-E*, Anthony Braxton. *Forces In Motion: Anthony Braxton & The Meta-reality Of Creative Music*, Graham Lock.

Brecker, Michael

b. 29 March 1949, Philadelphia, Pennsylvania, USA. Like many musicians of his generation, saxophonist Brecker was attracted in equal measure to R&B and the music of John Coltrane. In 1970 he left home for New York and joined a band led by drummer Billy Cobham. Subsequent gigs included work with the jazz rock group Dreams, Horace Silver, James Taylor and Yoko Ono. With his brother, Randy Brecker, he formed the Brecker Brothers, which became one of the pre-eminent fusion units. In the early 80s he toured and recorded with David Sancious and recorded as Steps Ahead, for many the definitive jazz rock group. A very in-demand player, Brecker also freelanced with a wide variety of jazz and pop artists, including Charles Mingus, John Lennon, Pat Metheny, Eric Clapton, Herbie Hancock and John Abercrombie. In 1987, at the prompting of Impulse! Records, he started recording as a leader. Brecker's smooth, strong version of Coltrane's middle-period playing has been much imitated by mainstream and session players. In 1991 he was a featured soloist on Paul Simon's Rhythm Of The Saints tour.

Michael Brecker solo: *Michael Brecker* (MCA 1987), *Don't Try This At Home* (MCA 1989), *Now You See It...Now You Don't* (GRP 1990),

For Brecker Brothers' recordings see Randy Brecker entry.

Brecker, Randy

b. 27 November 1945, Philadelphia, Pennsylvania, USA. Brecker studied classical trumpet at school, meanwhile playing in local R&B bands. He turned to jazz when at Indiana University and was a member of a student band which visited Europe. He quit the band and the university, remaining in Europe for a while before returning to the USA to take up a career in music. In 1967 he was with Blood, Sweat And Tears and thereafter played with various jazz groups including those led by Horace Silver, Art Blakey and Clark Terry. He also accompanied performers from the worlds of rock and pop, including Janis Joplin, Stevie Wonder and James Brown. In 1969 he became co-leader with his brother, Michael Brecker, of the band, Dreams. In the early 70s he worked in the studios, playing jazz gigs with Larry Coryell, Billy Cobham, Hal Galper and others. He also formed another band with his brother, this time simply named the Brecker Brothers, which made some enormously successful albums and became one of the most popular and musically skilled and influential jazz-rock bands. In the late 70s he played with Charles Mingus and in the early 80s Brecker led his own groups and also worked with his wife, Eliane Elias, and with various jazzmen including Lew Tabackin. An exceptionally talented musician with great technical facility and flair, Brecker has become one of the major figures in jazz-rock, lending fluency and inventiveness to this area of popular music.

Albums: with Horace Silver *You Gotta Take A Little Love* (1969), with Dreams *Imagine My Surprise* (70s), with Billy Cobham *Crosswinds* (1974), with Charles Mingus *Me, Myself An Eye* (1978), Lew Tabackin Quartet (1983), *Amanda* (Sonet 1986), *Live At Sweet Basil* (1988), *Toe To Toe* (1989), *Score*

Michael Brecker

(1993); as the Brecker Brothers *The Brecker Brothers* (1975), *Back To Back* (1976), *Don't Stop The Music* (1977), *Heavy Metal Bebop* (1978), *Return Of The Brecker Brothers* (1992), *Out Of The Loop* (GRP 1994).

Breuker, Willem

b. 4 November 1944, Amsterdam, Holland. At school Breuker wanted to play piano but economic circumstances in post-war Holland made that impossible. He learned to read music and play the recorder at the Labour Music school, and later took up the clarinet, still one of his main instruments, alongside various saxophones. He began improvising when, as he tells it, he was too lazy to turn the pages of his music exercises. At the start of his teens he discovered the *avant garde* classical music of Arnold Schoenberg and Edgard Varèse, and was prompted to compose. He joined a marching band and, during the 50s, worked his way through the evolution of jazz. In the early 60s he met Misha Mengelberg, who was outraging musicians and audiences with his piano-playing, and recognised a kindred spirit. In 1966 he organized a 23-piece orchestra to play his composition 'Litany', which was so controversial it made the front pages of the national newspapers. He was involved in setting up De Volharding with Louis Andriessen, and in 1967 he, Han Bennink and Mengelberg founded the Instant Composers Pool, which is still flourishing. The Dadaist, Absurdist approach of those days (for radio broadcasts Mengelberg might not play a note, but would, for example, read a newspaper) is still very much a part of Breuker's act. In 1974 he left the ICP to found the BVHaast label and also initiated the Willem Breuker Kollektief, a remarkable band which mixes various schools of jazz (from New Orleans to the *avant garde*), marching band music, film and theatre scores, cabaret, Latin, and classical (light and heavy) with hilarious, deadpan clowning. Their live performances are an experience which it is difficult to compare or describe, the audience simultaneously rocking with laughter whilst appreciating formidable precision routines interspersed with virtuoso improvisation. Breuker writes most of the music but also arranges composers as varied as Prokofiev, Ennio Morricone, Kurt Weill, Reginald Foresythe and Duke Ellington or audacious parodies of, for example, Ravel's 'Bolero' which somehow incorporates fragments of songs like 'Little Drummer Boy' and 'Never On A Sunday'. The overall effect is like a hybrid of Spike Jones, the Bonzo Dog Doo-Dah Band, Gerard Hoffnung, Archie Shepp and Ellington. One of the most disconcerting aspects of the Kollektief's performances is Breuker's lampooning of the corrosive, all-stops out free jazz that he plays for real in other bands - for example, his appearance on the still-notorious *Machine Gun* with Peter Brötzmann's octet.

Selected albums: with Han Bennink *New Acoustic Swing Duo* (1967), *Instant Composers Pool* (1970), *Renais Sense* (1972), *Bertolt Brecht/Herman Heijermans* (BVHAAST 1974), *Baal-Brecht-Breuker-Handke* (BVHAAST 1974), *Live In Berlin* (1976), *The European Scene* (1976), with Leo Cuypers *Superstars* (1978), *Doodzonde* (1979), *In Holland* (1981), *Rhapsody In Blue* (1982), *Driebergen-Zeist* (1984), *Willem*

Breuker Kollektief/Willem Breuker Collective (1984), with Bennink *Sendai Sjors/Sendai Sjimmie* (1984), *De Illusionist*, *Kkkomediant* (BVHAAST 1986), *Klap Op De Vuurpijl 1985* (1986), *Bob's Gallery* (BVHAAST 1988), *George Gershwin* (1988), *George Gershwin-Willem Breuker-Ennio Morricone-Alex Von Schlippenbach* (1988), *Metropolis* (BVHAAST 1989), *Parade* (BVHAAST 1990), *To Remain* (BVHAAST 1990), *Heijermans/Brecht* (1990, rec. 1983,1989), *Heibel* (1991), *De Onderste Steen* (Entr'acte 1992), *Summer Music A Paris* (1993), *Deze Kant Op, Dames/This Way, Ladies* (BVHAAST 1993).

Bridgewater, Dee Dee

b. Denise Garrett, 27 May 1950, Memphis, Tennessee, USA. After making her first public performances singing in the American north-west, she was featured vocalist with a university big band. In 1970 she married trumpeter Cecil Bridgewater, thereafter using her new surname even after their divorce. The couple recorded together, including the well-received *Afro-Blue*, which also featured tenor saxophonist Ron Bridgewater. In New York during the early 70s she sang regularly with the Thad Jones-Mel Lewis Jazz Orchestra. She also began her parallel career as a performer in stage musicals including *The Wiz* for which she won a Tony award in 1975. By the late 70s she had opted to work outside jazz, singing pop music on the west coast of America. A long sojourn in Europe found her working more in the jazz field and further stage appearances, this time in London in the leading role in *Lady Day*. At the end of the decade she was back in the USA and a frequent visitor to jazz festivals in various parts of the world. A powerful singer, with a style well-rooted in gospel to which she brings a fresh and contemporary feeling, Bridgewater has all the qualities needed to make a lasting mark as a jazz singer. However, her successes in other fields may well persuade her to broaden her repertoire still further which might tend to dilute her jazz core. *Precious Things* featured an excellent duet with Ray Charles on 'Til The Next Somewhere'.

Albums: *Brains On Fire Vols 1 & 2* (1966-67), *Afro-Blue* (1974), with Thad Jones-Mel Lewis *Suite For Pops* (1972), *Just Family* (1978), *Dee Dee Bridgewater* (Elektra 1980), *Live In Paris* (Affinity 1986), *Precious Thing s* (Prestige 1992).

Brignola, Nick

b. 17 July 1936, Troy, New York, USA. A largely self-taught baritone saxophonist, Brignola played professionally for some years before learning to read music. Later, he studied at Berklee College Of Music where he worked and recorded with Herb Pomeroy. In 1957 he was a member of the band voted best college jazz group in *Downbeat* magazine. After briefly leading his own band in the late 50s, he played for various leaders, including Woody Herman and Ted Curson. From the mid-60s he led a jazz-rock group before reuniting with Curson. Brignola also taught, both privately and in college. In the 70s, he played with Dave Holland, Bill Watrous and Pepper Adams and also recorded with Sal Nistico and Sal Salvador. In the 80s Brignola recorded with Kenny Barron and others and he played in the Mingus Superband at the Nice Jazz Festival. In the early 90s he played with Phil Woods. A gifted player, adept also on most members of the saxophone family, Brignola has a distinctive veiled sound. An admirer of many kinds of music and different schools of jazz, Brignola brings to his work a delightful fluency which suits admirably the post-bop urgency of his modern-mainstream playing. (This artist is unrelated to the baritone saxophonist Mike Brignola who played with Herman in the 80s.)

Albums: *This Is It!* (1967), with Ted Curson *Jubilant Power* (1976), *Baritone Madness* (1977), *New York Bound* (Interplay 1979), *LA Bound* (Night Life 1979), *Burn Brigade* (1979), *Triste* (1981-84 recordings), *Signals...In From Somewhere* (Discovery 1983), *Northern Lights* (Discovery c.1984), *Raincheck* (Reservoir 1988), *On A Different Level* (Reservoir 1989), *What It Takes* (Reservoir 1990), *It's Time* (Reservoir 1992), *Live At Sweet Basil* First Set (Reservoir 1993).

Brisker, Gordon

b. 6 November 1937, Cincinnati, Ohio, USA. Educated at the Cincinnati Conservatory of Music, Brisker began playing professionally while still at high school. He played tenor saxophone in jazz and dance bands and once played piano in a Las Vegas rock 'n' roll show. He later studied at Berklee College Of Music, where he also wrote arrangements for the Herb Pomeroy band. In 1960 he joined Woody Herman's big band and by the time he left, in 1963, had attracted attention in the jazz world. Since then Brisker has written for, and played with several leaders, including Louie Bellson, Freddie Hubbard, Stanley Clarke, Jack DeJohnette, Airto, Pat Longo and Bobby Shew. Brisker's musical tastes are wide: in addition to recording with numerous jazz musicians he has worked with the Los Angeles Philharmonic and the Cincinnati and Boston Symphony Orchestras, and has written for both James Brown and Rosemary Clooney. In the mid-80s he was back at Berklee, this time teaching and once again writing charts for the Pomeroy band. He has also taught at universities in Oregon, Hawaii and California. In 1987 he recorded an album of his arrangements for his own big band. Two years later he was touring as musical director and accompanist to singer Anita O'Day. A robust, bop-orientated player, it is as a writer that Brisker seems destined to make his biggest mark on jazz in general and on big band music in particular.

Albums: *Woody Herman: 1963* (1963), with Pat Longo *Billy May For President* (1982), *About Charlie* (80s), *New Beginning* (Discovery 1987), with Anita O'Day *In A Mello Tone* (1989).

Broadbent, Alan

b. 23 April 1947, Auckland, New Zealand. After studying piano and musical theory in his homeland, in the mid-60s Broadbent moved to the USA to study at the Berklee College Of Music. After studying with Lennie Tristano he began arranging for Woody Herman, his work appearing on the 1973 album, *Giant Steps*. In the 70s, Broadbent composed music in the classical form while simultaneously playing with jazz groups including those led by John Klemmer, Bill Berry and Bud Shank. In the 80s Broadbent played with Warne Marsh,

Charlie Haden and others. Having previously shown himself to be adept at accompanying singers, he recorded with Irene Kral in the early 70s, in the 90s Broadbent arranged for and accompanied Sue Raney. A fleet and inventive soloist with imaginative gifts, Broadbent is also an ideal section player, effectively accompanying soloists and lending authority to ensembles. Nevertheless, his writing, especially his jazz arranging, may well prove to be his most important contribution to music.

Albums: with Irene Kral *Where Is Love?* (1974), with Bill Berry *Shortcake* (1977), with Bud Shank *Crystal Moments* (1979), *Warne Marsh Meets Gary Foster* (1982), *Everything I Love* (Discovery 1986), *Another Time* (1987), *Away From You* (1989), with Sue Raney *In Good Company* (1991), *Live At Maybeck Concert Hall Vol. 14* (Concord 1991), with Gary Foster *Concord Duo Series Vol. 4* (Concord 1993).

Brookmeyer, Bob

b. 19 December 1929, Kansas City, Missouri, USA. Although he began his career as a pianist, it was when he took up the valve trombone in the early 50s that Brookmeyer began attracting serious attention. In 1953 he joined Gerry Mulligan, making numerous concert appearances and recordings, all of which demonstrated his considerable technical ability. His precise playing fitted well into Mulligan's rather thoughtful approach. He worked with Clark Terry in the early 60s and also played in the Thad Jones-Mel Lewis big band. A gifted arranger for both small and big bands, Brookmeyer also composes but it is as a player that he has made his chief contribution.

Albums: *The Fabulous Gerry Mulligan Quartet: Paris Concert* (1954), *The Dual Role Of Bob Brookmeyer* (1955), with Zoot Sims *Tonite's Music Today* (1956), *Quintets* (Vogue 1956), *Traditionalism Revisted* (1957), *Street Swingers* (1957), with Sims *Stretching Out* (1958), *Kansas City Revisited* (1958), with Bill Evans *The Ivory Hunters* (1959), *Jazz Is A Kick* (1960), *Gloomy Sunday And Other Bright Moments* (1961), *Stan Getz/Bobby Brookmeyer* (1961), *Bob Brookmeyer And Friends* (1964), with Clark Terry *Tonight* (1964), *The Power Of Positive Swinging* (1964), *Suitably Zoot* (1965), *Gingerbread Men* (1966), *Back Again* (Sonet 1978), *The Bob Brookmeyer Small Band* (1978), with Mel Lewis *Live At The Village Vanguard* (Rhapsody 1980), *Through A Looking Glass* (1982), *Bobby Brookmeyer And His Orchestra* (RCA 1983), *Traditionalism Revistited* (Affinity 1984), *Blues Hot And Cold* (Verve 1984), *Oslo* (Concord 1987), *Kansas City Revisited* (Fresh Sounds 1988), *Dreams* (Dragon 1989), *Bob Brookmeyer With The Stockholm Jazz Orchestra* (Dragon 1989), *Bob Brookmeyer And Friends* (Columbia 1993).

Brötzmann, Peter

b. 6 March 1941, Remscheid, Germany. Once the holder of the dubious title of loudest saxophonist in the world, Brötzmann plays several varieties of saxophone and clarinet (including the Hungarian taragato) with awesome skill, power and intensity. He started playing dixieland at school but was more interested in art than music. Whilst at art college he played in a semi-pro swing band. During this time music

Bob Brookmeyer

became more important to him, and he began to explore new areas of free improvised music. In 1966, he toured with Jazz Realities, including Carla Bley, Michael Mantler and Steve Lacy, and made his record debut in 1967 with Peter Kowald and Sven-Ake Johannsen. In 1969 he, Kowald, Hans Reichel and several other musicians set up the FMP label as a co-operative, and ever since he has recorded a stream of outstanding albums for the label in various contexts from solo to big bands, though few have surpassed the ferocity of his octet's 1968 recording, *Machine Gun*, now regarded as one of the early classics of European free jazz. In 1986, he formed Last Exit with Bill Laswell, Sonny Sharrock and Ronald Shannon Jackson. In 1990 he toured and recorded with B-Shops For The Poor in Britain and Nicky Skopelitis, Sharrock and Ginger Baker in the US, but at the time of writing the albums had not been released. He has also worked with Don Cherry, Albert Mangelsdorff, the Globe Unity Orchestra and his guitarist son, Casper, who leads the rock trio Massaker.

Albums: *For Adolphe Saxe* (1967), *Machine Gun* (FMP 1968), *Nipples* (1969), with Fred Van Hove, Han Bennink *Balls* (1970), with others *Elements* (1971), with others *Couscouss De La Mauresque* (1971), *The Berlin Concert* (1972), with others *The End* (1971), with Van Hove, Bennink *Free Jazz Und Kinder* (1972), *Brötzmann, Van Hove, Bennink* (1973), *Einheitsfrontlied* (1973), with others *Hot Lotta* (1973), with others *Outspan 1* (1974), with others *Outspan 2* (1974), with Van Hove, Bennink *Tschüs* (1975), *Solo* (1976), with Bennink *Ein Halber Hund Kann Nicht Pinkeln* (1977), with Bennink, Misha Mengelberg *Three Points And A Mountain* (1979), with Harry Miller, Louis Moholo *The Nearer The Bone The Sweeter The Meat* (1979), with Bennink *Atsugi Concert* (1980), with Miller, Moholo *Opened, But Hardly Touched* (1980), with Willi Kellers *Edelgard-Maar-Helaas* (1980), *Alarm* (1981), *Andrew Cyrille Meets Peter Brötzmann In Berlin* (1982), with Albert Mangelsdorff, Günter Sommer *Pica Pica* (1982), *14 Love Poems - Solo* (1984), *Berlin Djungle* (1984), with Company *Trios* (1986, rec 1983), with Bill Laswell *Low Life* (1987), with Alfred 23 Harth *Go-No-Go* (1987), with others *No Material* (1987), with others *In A State Of Undress* (1989), *Reserve* (FMP 1989), *Wie Das Leben So Spielt* (FMP 1990), *Last Home* (Pathological 1990), *No Nothing* (FMP 1991), *Dare Devil* (DIW 1992), *The Marz Combo* (FMP 1992).

Brown, Clifford

b. 30 October 1930, Wilmington, Delaware, USA, d. 26 June 1956. As a young high school student Brown began playing trumpet and within a very short time was active in college and other youth bands. By his late teens he had attracted the favourable attention of leading jazzmen, including fellow trumpeters Dizzy Gillespie, Miles Davis and Fats Navarro. At the end of the 40s he was studying music at Maryland University and in 1952, following recovery from a serious road accident, he made his first records with Chris Powell and Tadd Dameron. In the autumn of 1953 he was a member of the big band Lionel Hampton took to Europe. Liberally filled with precocious talent, this band attracted considerable attention during its tour. Contrary to contractual stipulations, many of the young musicians moonlighted on various recordings and Brown in particular was singled out for such sessions.

Back in the USA, Brown was fired along with most of the rest of the band when Hampton learned of the records they had made. Brown then joined Art Blakey and in mid-1954 teamed up with Max Roach to form the Clifford Brown-Max Roach Quintet. The quintet was quickly recognised as one of the outstanding groups in contemporary jazz and Brown as a major trumpeter and composer. In June 1956, while driving between engagements during a nationwide tour, Brown and another quintet member, pianist Richie Powell, were killed in a road accident.

The early death of musicians in jazz, and of talented artists in other fields, has often led to the creation of legends. Inevitably, in many cases the legend greatly exceeds the reality and speculation on what might have been relies more upon the imagination of the recounter than upon any hard evidence. In the case of Clifford Brown, the reality of the legend is impossible to refute. At a time when many modern jazz trumpeters sought technical expertise at the expense of tone, Brown, in common with his friend and paradigm, Navarro, had technique to spare but also developed a rich, full and frequently beautiful tone. At the same time, whether playing at scorching tempos or on languorous ballads, his range was exhaustive. He was enormously and brilliantly inventive but his search for original ideas was never executed at the expense of taste. In all his work, Brown displayed the rare combination of supreme intelligence and great emotional depths. His playing was only one aspect of his talent; he was also a fine composer, creating many works which have become modern jazz standards. Although his career was brief, Brown's influence persisted for a while in the work of Lee Morgan and throughout succeeding decades in that of Freddie Hubbard. Fortunately for jazz fans, Brown's own work persists in the form of his recordings almost any of which can be safely recommended as outstanding examples of the very best of jazz. Indeed, all of his recordings with Roach are classics.

Albums: *The Clifford Brown Memorial Album* (Blue Note 1953), *Clifford Brown In Paris* (Original Jazz Classics 1953), *Stockholm Sweetenin'* (1953), with Art Blakey *A Night At Birdland, Vols 1 & 2* (1954), *Clifford Brown & Max Roach Inc.* (1954), with Max Roach *Clifford Brown Jam Session* (1954), with Roach *Jordu* (1954-55), with Roach *Study In Brown* (1955), *Clifford Brown With Strings* (1955), *Raw Genius: Live At The Bee Hive In Chicago, Vols 1 & 2* (1955), *Pure Genius, Vol. 1* (1956), *Clifford Brown And Max Roach At Basin Street* (1956), *With Strings* (Emarcy 1983), *Memorial Album* (Blue Note 1984). Compilations: *Clifford Brown Vols 1-4* (Jazz Reactivations 1983), *Compact Jazz* (Emarcy 1990), *The Complete Paris Sessions Vols. 1 - 3* (Vogue 1994).

Brown, Gerry

b. 9 November 1951, Philadelphia, Pennsylvania, USA. After training in a conservatory in the early 70s, Brown came to Europe in 1972 playing drums for John Lee. He stayed and recorded with Chris Hinze, Joachim Kuhn, Toots Thielemans and Charlie Mariano. On his return to New York in 1976 he played with Stanley Clarke before joining Chick Corea's Return To Forever. He is a deft musician, able to provide a firm rhythmic bass for any band. In 1979 he returned to Europe to play the Montreux International Jazz Festival with Didier Lockwood. He remained in France and Germany for a while, but by 1984 was back in New York recording with Arthur Blythe.

Selected album: *Return To Forever Live* (1977).

Brown, Lawrence

b. 3 August 1907, Lawrence, Kansas, USA, d. 5 September 1988. Having previously mastered piano, violin and tuba, Brown settled with the trombone while studying medicine in California. At this time he was moonlighting with school and local bands and by 1926 he had abandoned his academic studies in favour of a career in music. After first working with Charlie Echols, he played with several popular west coast-based bands, including those of Paul Howard (where one of his fellow sidemen was Lionel Hampton), Curtis Mosby and Les Hite. In 1932 Brown joined Duke Ellington, with whom he remained for the greater part of the next two decades. After leaving Ellington in 1951, Brown worked with another ex-Ellingtonian, Johnny Hodges, until 1955. After studio work in New York, Brown rejoined Ellington in 1960 and stayed with the band for another decade. One of the most musicianly trombonists in jazz, Brown's first appearance with Ellington shocked some fans accustomed to the more aggressive playing of his predecessors and contemporaries. His melodic and gently lyrical playing seemed at first to be at odds with the music that was happening around him; his early feature number with the band, the ballad 'Trees', with its echoes of Victorian parlours, only added to the impression. Brown also kept apart from the general drinking and good-timing that the rest of the band enjoyed, thus earning the nickname, the Deacon. In time both the fans and his fellow musicians began to recognize him for what he was - a remarkably gifted player with a beautiful tone and the ability to immerse himself totally in the needs of the Ellington orchestra. Indeed, Brown was so ready to commit himself to Ellington's music that, during his second spell with the band, he acquired the arsenal of effects which had been perfected in the 30s by fellow Ellington trombonist Joe 'Tricky Sam' Nanton, even though he felt that excessive use of the plunger mute risked damaging his lip and was detrimental to his own legato style. Brown retired from music in 1970 and lived in California, where he worked as a business and political consultant until his death.

Albums: *Lawrence Brown* (1956), with Duke Ellington *Piano In The Background* (1960), *Inspired Abandon* (Jasmine 1965).

Brown, Marion

b. 8 September 1935, Atlanta, Georgia, USA. Brown made his name as an alto saxophonist after mastering clarinet and oboe. In the 50s he studied music at Clark College, Atlanta and law at Howard University, Washington, DC - an experience that contrasted sharply with his poor southern background. He spent 18 months playing the clarinet in an army band on the Japanese island of Hokkaido. In 1962 he moved to New York and was helped by Ornette Coleman. His first musical exposure came with Archie Shepp and he played on John Coltrane's historic *Ascension*. Sun Ra also recruited him: Brown commented 'it was all rehearsing and no jobs' but treasured the experience. He toured Europe with vibes player Gunter Hampel in the early 70s, made a series of extremely individual records with *avant gardists* such as Leo Smith, Muhal Richard Abrams and Steve McCall, and led his own groups into the 90s. He has continued to investigate the ethnomusicology of African-America both musically and academically, and recent recordings have included the solo *Recollections* and two duos with pianist Mal Waldron, *Songs Of Love And Regret* and *Much More*. He has written a book of essays on his life and music, also titled *Recollections*, which was published in Germany in 1985. Brown's dry, breathy alto sound and the tenacious logic of his improvisations mark him as a great player.

Albums: *Porto Novo* (1967), *In Sommerhausen* (1969), *Afternoon Of A Georgia Faun* (1970), *Duets* (1973), *Geecheee Recollections* (1973), *Sweet Earth Flying* (1974), *Vista* (1975), *Solo Saxophone* (1977), with Gunter Hampel *Reeds 'N' Vibes* (1978), *La Placita - Live In Willisau* (Timeless 1979), *Gemini* (Birth 1983), *Recollections* (1985), *Marion Brown Quartet* (ESP 1988), *Back To Paris* (Freelance 1989), with Mal Waldron *Songs Of Love And Regret* (1985), with Waldron *Much More* (1988), *Native Land* (ITM 1991), *Why Not* (ESP 1993, 1966 recordings).

Further reading: *Recollections*, Marion Brown.

Brown, Pete

b. 9 November 1906, Baltimore, Maryland, USA, d. 20 September 1963. Although adept on trumpet, piano, violin and tenor saxophone, it was on alto that Brown made his mark on jazz. After working extensively in his home town and in Atlantic City in the mid-20s, Brown moved to New York in 1927 and remained there, more or less continuously, for the rest of his life. Brown sometimes led his own groups and also played with a wide range of bands, including those led by John Kirby and Frankie Newton. A quirkily distinctive player, Brown's style was rooted in the blues and he was at his best playing in the hard-swinging jump bands popular along New York's 52nd Street during the 30s. When bop began to make its appearance in the early 40s, Brown was one of the few swing era musicians who made a serious attempt to come to terms with it. To some extent his clipped, aggressive yet witty sound suited certain elements of the new music, but he never wholly assimilated its implications into his style. In many respects his playing was better suited to the concurrent rhythm and blues explosion and his tough, rasping sound was aped with varying degrees of success by many saxophonists working in that field. Brown was one of several musicians whose divergences from the norm attracted the attention of Charlie Parker during his formative years, and he has also been cited by Paul Desmond

as an influence. In his later years Brown was frequently in poor health, but, continued to work and teach. Numbered among his pupils are Cecil Payne and Joe 'Flip' Phillips.

Albums: *Peter The Great* (1954), with Joe Turner *Boss Of The Blues* (1956), with Coleman Hawkins, Roy Eldridge *The Newport Years, Vol.4* (1957), *Pete Brown* (1959). Compilation: *Jump, Blues & Swing* (1944 recordings).

Brown, Ray

b. 13 October 1926, Pittsburgh, Pennsylvania, USA. One of the outstanding bass players in jazz history, Brown's top-league experience began when, in 1945, at the age of 19, he joined Dizzy Gillespie. Two years later he was leading a trio accompanying Ella Fitzgerald, to whom he was married from 1948-52. In 1951 Brown joined the Oscar Peterson trio and stayed for most of the next 15 years. In 1966 he left Peterson and settled in Los Angeles, which has remained his base ever since. Dividing his time between teaching, working in film and television studios, personal management and playing jazz clubs and festivals, Brown is in constant demand. A founder member of the LA Four, he has also recorded with Duke Ellington. In 1989-90 he was a member of the Philip Morris Superband (led by Gene Harris). Although essentially a mainstream musician, Brown is thoroughly at home in bop, and plays with a great blues feeling. Remarkable for the accuracy of his playing and his lovely tone, Brown's work is a constant lesson to all other bass players regardless of the field of music in which they perform.

Selected albums: with Oscar Peterson *One O'Clock Jump* (1953), *The Oscar Peterson Trio At The Stratford Shakespearean Festival* (1956), *Jazz Cello* (1960), *Ray Brown And His Orchestra i* (1960), *Ray Brown And His Orchestra ii* (1962), *Ella Fitzgerald At The Opera House* (1963), *Ray Brown And His Orchestra iii* (1964), *The Ray Brown Big Band* (1969), with Duke Ellington *This One's For Blanton* (1972), *Brown's Bag* (Concord 1975), *Something For Lester* (Original Jazz Classics 1977), *The Most Special Joint* (1977), *As Good As It Gets* (Concord 1977), with Jimmy Rowles *Tasty!* (1979), *Live At The Concord Festival* (Concord 1979), *Summerwind* (Bell 1980), with Laurindo Almeida *Moonlight Serenade* (Bell 1981), with LA Four *Montage* (1981), *A Ray Brown Three* (1983), with LA Four *Soular Energy* (Concord 1984), with LA Four *Don't Forget The Blues* (Concord 1985), *The Red Hot* (Concord 1986), *The Gene Harris Trio Plus One* (1986), *Gene Harris And The Philip Morris Superband* (1989), *Bam Bam Bam* (Concord 1989), *Summer Wind* (Concord 1989), with John Clayton *Super Bass* (late 80s), *Black Orpheus* (Paddle Wheel 1992), *3 Dimensional* (Concord 1992), *Moore Makes 4* (Concord 1992), *Bass Face* (Telarc 1993). Compilation: *Dizzy Gillespie 1946-49* (1946-49 recordings).

Brown, Rob

b. 27 February 1962, Hampton, Virginia, USA. A striking new voice on alto saxophone, Brown began on piano as a child but switched to saxophone at the age of 13. He studied briefly at James Madison University, Berklee College Of Music and New

York University but credits the celebrated Philadelphia teacher Dennis Sandole (whose students have included John Coltrane, Art Farmer and Tommy Flanagan) as his major influence - together with recordings by Sonny Rollins, Ornette Coleman, Albert Ayler and Roscoe Mitchell. While based in Boston in the early 80s, Brown met pianist Matthew Shipp, with whom he has continued to work in New York (where both men relocated in 1985). They co-lead a trio, Right Hemisphere, and their debut recording was the duo *Sonic Explorations*. Brown also leads his own trio, with William Parker and Dennis Charles; their *Breath Rhyme* was one of the outstanding new jazz releases of 1990. Brown plays essentially a fiery free jazz, but with superb control and self-discipline.

Albums: with Matthew Shipp *Sonic Explorations* (1988), *Breath Rhyme* (1990), *Youniverse* (Riti 1993).

Brown, Ruth

b. 30 January 1928, Portsmouth, Virginia, USA. Brown started her musical career singing gospel at an early age in the church choir led by her father. In 1948 she was singing with a band led by her husband Jimmy in Washington, DC, when Willis Conover (from the radio show *Voice Of America*) recommended her to Ahmet Ertegun of the newly-formed Atlantic Records. Ertegun signed her, despite competition from Capitol, but on the way up to New York for an appearance at the Apollo Theatre, she was involved in a car crash. Hospitalized for nine months, her medical bills were paid by Atlantic and she rewarded them handsomely with her first big hit, 'Teardrops From My Eyes', in 1950. More hits followed with '5-10-15 Hours' (1952) and 'Mama, He Treats Your Daughter Mean' (1953). Atlantic's first real star, Brown became a major figure in 50s R&B, forming a strong link between that music and early rock 'n' roll. Her records were characterized by her rich and expressive singing voice (not unlike that of Dinah Washington) and accompaniment by breathy saxophone solos (initially by Budd Johnson, later by Willie Jackson). Between 1949 and 1955 her songs were on the charts 129 weeks, including five number 1s. Brown's concentration upon R&B has not kept her from associations with the jazz world; very early in her career she sang briefly with the Lucky Millinder band, and has recorded with Jerome Richardson and the Thad Jones-Mel Lewis big band. She also brought a distinctively soulful treatment to varied material such as 'Yes, Sir, That's My Baby', 'Sonny Boy', 'Black Coffee' and 'I Can Dream, Can't I?'. In 1989 she won a Tony Award for her performance in the Broadway show, *Black And Blue*, and was receiving enthusiastic reviews for her nightclub act in New York, at Michael's Pub and the Blue Note, into the 90s. In 1993 Brown was to be heard broadcasting on a New York radio station. In 1994 she undertook a European tour much to the delight to her small but loyal group of fans.

Albums: *Ruth Brown Sings* (1956), *Ruth Brown* (1957), *Late Date With Ruth Brown* (1959), *Miss Rhythm* (1959), *Along Comes Ruth* (1962), *Gospel Time* (1962), *Ruth Brown '65* (1964), *Black Is Brown And Brown Is Beautiful* (Rhapsody 1969), *The Real Ruth Brown* (70s), *You Don't Know Me* (70s),

Touch Me In The Morning (70s), *Sugar Babe* (President 1977), *Takin' Care Of Business* (1980), *The Soul Survives* (1982), *Brown Sugar* (Topline 1986), *Sweet Baby Of Mine* (Route 66 1987), *I'll Wait For You* (Official 1988), *Blues On Broadway* (1989), with Linda Hopkins, Carrie Smith *Black And Blue* (1989), *Fine And Mellow* (1992), *The Songs Of My Life* (Fantasy 1993). Compilations: *The Best Of Ruth Brown* (1963), *Rockin' With Ruth* (Charly 1984, 1950-60 recordings), *Brown Black And Beautiful* (SDEG 1990), *Miss Rhythm, Greatest Hits And More* (Atlantic 1983), *Blues On Broadway* (Ace 1994).

Brown, Sandy

b. Alexander Brown, 25 February 1929, Izatnagar, Bareilly, India, d. 15 March 1975. Raised in Edinburgh from the age of six, Brown began playing clarinet with Al Fairweather and Stan Greig, fellow-students at the Royal High School. He made his first important impression on the UK jazz scene in the mid-50s, when the Fairweather-Brown All Stars were formed. This was the period of the trad jazz boom, and Brown's skilful yet impassioned clarinet playing was one of that era's highlights. Unlike many of his fellow trad bandleaders, Brown's interests were ever-expanding, and any bands under his leadership were home to adventurous musical souls, such as Brian Lemon and Tony Coe. Through the 50s and 60s Brown pursued musical excellence, making a string of classic albums, including *McJazz* and *The Incredible McJazz*, and working with such diverse jazz personalities as George Chisholm and Kenny Wheeler. In addition to his playing activity, he was a perceptive and witty writer (*The McJazz Manuscripts*), and was heavily involved in running an architectural practice that specialized in building acoustic recording studios. His health began to fail in the 70s, although he was able to visit the USA where he recorded with Earle Warren. His death in 1975, came at a time when he still had much to offer the jazz world.

Albums: *Fifty-Fifty Blues* (1956), *Sandy's Sidemen* (1956), *McJazz* (1957), *Doctor McJazz* (1960), *The Incredible McJazz* (1962), *Hair At Its Hairiest* (1968), *Barrelhouse And Blues* (1969), with the Brian Lemon Trio *In The Evening* (Hep Jazz 1971), with Earle Warren *Everybody Loves Saturday Night* (1974), *Splanky* (Spotlite 1983), *Clarinet Opening* (CSA 1988), *McJazz* (Dormouse 1988).

Further reading: *The McJazz Manuscripts*, Sandy Brown.

Brubeck, Dave

b. David Warren Brubeck, 6 December 1920, Concord, California, USA. Initially taught piano by his mother, Brubeck showed an immediate flair for the instrument, and was performing with professional jazz groups at the age of 13. Enrolling at the College of the Pacific in Stockton, California, he continued his involvement in jazz by establishing a 12-piece band, but most of his time was spent in the study of theory and composition under Darius Milhaud. After he graduated from Pacific, Brubeck decided to continue his formal classical training. However, his time at Mills College, studying under Schoenberg, was interrupted by military service in World War II. Returning from Europe in 1946, he went back to Milhaud, and about this time formed his first serious jazz group - the Jazz Workshop Ensemble, an eight-piece unit which recorded three years later as the Dave Brubeck Octet. He began a more consistent professional involvement in the jazz scene in 1949, with the creation of his first trio, with Cal Tjader and Norman Bates (who was soon replaced by Ron Crotty), but it was with the addition of alto saxophonist Paul Desmond in 1951, that Brubeck's group achieved major critical acclaim. Replacing Tjader and Crotty with Gene Wright and Joe Morello towards the end of the 50s, Brubeck led this celebrated and prolific quartet as a unit until 1967, when Desmond left the group. After replacing him for a short time with Gerry Mulligan, Brubeck began using a new group in 1972 involving his three sons and, apart from a brief classic quartet reunion in 1976, most of his now rare concert appearances have since been in this setting. Brubeck's musical relationship with Desmond was central to his success. The group's 1959 classic 'Take Five' was composed by Desmond, and it was the saxophonist's extraordinary gift for melodic improvisation that gave the group much of its musical strength. Always seeing himself primarily as a composer rather than a pianist, Brubeck, in his own solos, tended to rely too much on his ability to work in complex time-signatures (often two at once). His work in the field of composition has produced, several jazz standards, two ballets, a musical, a mass, works for television and film, an oratorio and two cantatas. However Brubeck will always be primarily associated with his quartet recordings with Paul Desmond, and 'Take Five' in particular. Throughout the 60s when jazz was able to cross over into other territories it was primarily Miles Davis, John Coltrane and Brubeck that were quoted, cited and applauded. Brubeck (even the name) was so incredibly hip! His band has been a central attraction at almost all the major international jazz festivals, and during the 50s and 60s, frequently won both *Downbeat* and *Metronome* polls. As early as 1954, Brubeck appeared on the cover of *Time* magazine, and 10 years later was invited to play at the White House (which he repeated in 1981). Brubeck made the pop charts all over the world and in doing so, bought jazz to unsuspecting ears. He remains a household name in modern jazz, and was still working on projects such as the Take Five UK Jazz Tour, in the early 90s. Those students wishing to understand how important and how very good this man is should invest in the superb box set released in 1993. This covers the widest possible selection of a career that fortunately still continues.

Selected albums: *Dave Brubeck Octet* (1949), *Jazz At Oberlin* (Original Jazz Classics 1953), *In Concert* (1953), *Dave Brubeck At Storyville: 1954* (1955), *Interchange '54* (Columbia 1955), *Brubeck Time* (1955), *Jazz: Red Hot And Cool* (1955), *Jazz Impressions Of The USA* (1957), *Jazz Goes To Junior College* (1957), *Reunion* (Original Jazz Classics 1957), *Solo Piano* (1957), *Time Out Featuring 'Take Five'* (Columbia 1959), with the New York Philharmonic Orchestra *Bernstein Plays Brubeck Plays Bernstein* (1960), *Gone With The Wind* (Columbia 1960), *Brubeck A La Mode* (Original Jazz Classics 1960), *Jazz Impressions Of Eurasia* (Columbia 1960), *Time Further Out* (1961), *Countdown - Time In Outer Space* (1962), *Bossa Nova*

USA (1963), *At Carnegie Hall* (1963), *The Great Concerts* (Columbia 1963), *Brandenburg Gate: Revisited* (1963), *Time Changes* (1964), *Jazz Impressions Of Japan* (1964), *Jazz Impressions Of New York* (1965), *Angel Eyes* (1965), *My Favorite Things* (1966), *Brubeck Plays Music From West Side Story And ...* (Columbia 1966), with Gerry Mulligan *Compadres* (1968), *Adventures In Time* (1972), *The Last Set At Newport* (Atlantic 1972), *We're All Together Again For The First Time* (Atlantic), with Paul Desmond *Duets* (1975), *All The Things We Are* (Atlantic 1975), *The Dave Brubeck Quartet 25th Anniversary Reunion* (1976), *Live At Montreaux* (Tomato 1978), *Paper Moon* (Concord 1982), *Concord On A Summer Night* (Concord 1982), *For Iola* (Concord 1985), *Reflections* (Concord 1986), *Blue Rondo* (Concord 1987), *Moscow Night* (Concord 1987), *New Wine* (Limelight 1988), *Trio Brubeck* (Limelight 1988), *Quiet As The Moon* (Limelight 1992), *Once When I Was Very Young* (Limelight 1992). Compilations: *Dave Brubeck's Greatest Hits* (Columbia 1966), *Collection* (1985), *The Essential Dave Brubeck* (1992), *Time Signatures; A Career Retrospective* (Columbia/Legacy 1993, 4CD box set).

Bruford, Bill

b. 17 May 1949, Sevenoaks, Kent, England. A founder member of Yes in 1968, Bruford left the group four years later at the height of its popularity. An accomplished drummer, he opted to join King Crimson, where his skills were put to even greater test, and remained there until leader Robert Fripp dissolved the line-up in 1974. Bruford subsequently worked with Pavlov's Dog, before forming the jazz-rock ensemble, UK. The initial line-up also featured guitarist Allan Holdsworth, who joined the drummer for his solo debut *Feels Good To Me*. The two musicians then broke away to found Bruford, which was completed by Dave Stewart (keyboards) and Jeff Berlin (bass). However the artist's independent career was sidelined in 1981 when Fripp invited him to join the reconstituted King Crimson. Following the second collapse of King Crimson, Bruford toured with Al DiMeola and David Torn. Bruford subsequently formed his own jazz-based group, Bill Bruford's Earthworks, which included keyboardist Django Bates and saxophonist Iain Ballamy. He became involved with the re-union of Yes in the late 80s, touring and recording under the banner of Anderson, Bruford, Wakeman And Howe until such legal matters as to the ownership of the Yes name had been resolved, becoming once more the Yes drummer in 1990. One of the finest drummers in British rock, Bruford continues his desire to progress, rather than rest on his laurels.

Albums: *Feels Good To Me* (Polydor 1978), *One Of A Kind* (Polydor 1979), *The Bruford Tapes* (Editions EG 1980), *Gradually Going Tornado* (Editions EG 1980), *Earthworks* (Editions EG 1987), *Dig* (1989), *All Heaven Broke Loose* (1991), *Earthworks Live* (Virgin 1994). Compilation: *Master Strokes 1978-1985* (Editions EG 1986).

Bruninghaus, Rainer

b. 21 November 1949, Bad Pyrmont, Germany. Bruninghaus studied piano and music at Cologne Conservatory (1973-6).

After graduation he joined Volker Kriegel's group Spectrum before moving on to Eberhard Weber's influential band Colours (1975-80). Though it infuriated Weber when critics sometimes spoke of the band as a European counterpart to Weather Report, there were times when Bruninghaus's compositions leaned very close to the Americans' style, particularly on Colour's later albums. He made a crucial contribution to the success of the band both in composition and in his keyboard playing which demonstrated great technical facility and a keen sensitivity. When he left Colours he worked with Manfred Schoof's quintet then in 1981 formed his own trio with Markus Stockhausen (trumpet) and Fredy Studer (drums). Their *Continuum* won the German Record Critics' Prize in 1984. Throughout his career Bruninghaus has worked with a wide range of musicians including Kenny Wheeler, Albert Mangelsdorff, Toots Thielemans, Archie Shepp, Carla Bley and Bobby McFerrin. He composes and arranges for big bands and has continued with classical composition. When there is opportunity, he also teaches at a music college in Cologne.

Albums: with Colours *Yellow Fields* (1977), *Silent Feet* (1979), *Little Movements* (1980), *Freigeweht* (1980), *Continuum* (1983).

Brunis, Georg

b. George Clarence Brunies, 6 February 1900, New Orleans, Louisiana, USA, d. 19 November 1974. The best-known member of a distinguished musical family, Brunis (who changed the spelling of his first and last names on the advice of a numerologist) had played trombone from his pre-teen years. In New Orleans he worked with Leon Roppolo and Elmer Schoebel; by 1920 he was working in Chicago with Paul Mares's Friars Society Orchestra. The band later became known as the New Orleans Rhythm Kings but Brunis moved on, joining Ted Lewis in 1924, with whom he remained for a decade. From 1934 he worked extensively in New York, recording and playing in numerous bands and playing at clubs, especially Nick's, where he was a semi-permanent fixture through the late 30s and into the 40s. From then until the end of the 60s he worked steadily, partnering Art Hodes, Wild Bill Davison, Muggsy Spanier and others, making some classic recordings. A tough, gutsy player, not above playing to the audience, Brunis was a skilful trombonist who preferred to stay within a framework that was far more limited than his technical ability warranted.

Albums: *Georg Brunis* i (1964), *Georg Brunis* ii (1965), with Wild Bill Davison *Reunion In Brass* (1973). Compilations: with Muggsy Spanier *The Great Sixteen* (1939), with the All Star Stompers *This Is Jazz* (1947), with Davison *Tin Roof Blues* (1943-46), with Davison *Davison-Brunis Sessions Vol 1* (Decca 1980), *Davison-Brunis Sessions Vol 2* (Decca 1980), *Friars Inn Revisited* (Delmark 1990).

Bryant, Ray

b. 24 December 1931, Philadelphia, Pennsylvania, USA. Coming from a musical family gave Bryant an advantage - his mother played piano and his sister sang in a gospel choir. He started on bass, but left it to his older brother Tom, in order to play piano. The Bryant Brothers became the house band for Philadelphia's Blue Note Club, where they played with Charlie Parker and Miles Davis. It was these contacts that led to recordings with Davis, Sonny Rollins and Carmen McRae. He led a trio at New York's Village Vanguard in 1959. In 1960 he had a surprise hit with the infectious and memorable 'Little Susie', named for his daughter, and 'Cubano Chant' and 'Slow Freight'. Initially inspired by the style of Teddy Wilson, Bryant's gospel inflections give his playing a modern, rootsy edge, his left hand bass chords can rumble like thunder. For a number of years much of his work was unavailable, fortunately in recent years, notably with the advent of the compact disc, Bryant's highly underrated work has been reissued. He continues to perform and record prolifically as both a soloist and leader of a trio. *Through The Years* Volumes 1 and 2 was an excellent recording, covering Bryant's entire career this newly recorded collection demonstrated, if anything, that Bryant's technique is more fluid and has improved with age.

Selected albums: *Gotta Travel On* (1966), *Slow Feight* (1967), *Alone At Montreaux* (Atlantic 1973), *Hot Turkey* (Black And Blue 1975), *Montreaux 77* (Original Jazz Classics 1978), *Here's Ray Bryant* (Pablo 1982), *Ray Bryant* (1982), *Solo Flight* (Pablo 1982), *Potpourri* (Pablo 1982), *All Blues* (Pablo 1982), *Ray Bryant Trio* (JVC 1987), *Alone With The Blues* (Original Jazz Classics 1987), *Trio* (1987), *Con Alma* (CBS 1988), *Plays Basie And Ellington* (Emarcy 1988), *Blue Moods* (Emarcy 1989), *All Mine All Yours* (Emarcy 1990), Compilations: *Best Of Ray Bryant* (Pablo 1982), *Through The Years (Vols. 1&2) - The 60th Birthday Recordings* (Emarcy 1992).

Bryden, Beryl

b. 11 May 1926, Norwich, Norfolk, England. In the mid-40s Bryden was active in local jazz circles, organizing concerts and club dates and singing with various bands. In London in the late 40s she sang and played washboard with many of the important bands of the British trad-jazz explosion, including those of George Webb, Freddy Randall, Alex Welsh, Humphrey Lyttelton and Chris Barber. Despite all this activity and a growing following, singing was only a part-time occupation for her, and it was not until the early 50s that she became a full-time performer. In the 50s and 60s her career was perhaps stronger in Europe than the UK and she waited until the early 70s before visiting the USA. In the 70s she toured extensively, sometimes as a solo artist, other times in company with jazz musicians such as Pete Allen. A robust performer of songs from the classic period of the blues and vaudeville, Bryden's popularity with audiences is matched by the fellow-feeling she induces in her musical companions (a quality singers often fail to achieve). Apart from performing, Bryden has also developed a second-string career as a good jazz photographer. Her retirement in the 80s was not taken too seriously, either by her fellow artists or by Bryden herself. In the early 90s she was still on the road and delighting her many fans and friends.

Selected albums: *Way Down Yonder In New Orleans* (1975), *Basin Street Blues* (CBS 1991), *Big Daddy* (CBS 1991).

Buckner, Milt

b. 10 July 1915, St. Louis, Missouri, USA, d. 27 July 1977. Orphaned as a child, Buckner was taught music by an uncle in Detroit. Playing piano and arranging for local bands, he attracted the attention of McKinney's Cotton Pickers, for whom he wrote arrangements. In November 1941 he joined Lionel Hampton's newly-formed big band, acting as pianist and staff arranger, and he remained there for seven years. For the next two years he led his own short-lived big band, and then rejoined Hampton. It was at this time that Buckner began to concentrate on playing organ, and he worked as a solo or in harness with Jo Jones, Sam Woodyard and Illinois Jacquet, frequently returning to Hampton for record and concert dates. From the early 30s Buckner had experimented with a technique of piano playing which became known as the 'locked hands' style and which was later developed by George Shearing and Buckner himself. Buckner's playing was always strongly rhythmic and any band of which he was a member was guaranteed to swing, but his solos, especially on organ, were often little more than technical exercises.

Selected albums: *Rockin' With Milt* (1955), *Rockin' Hammond* (1956), *Mighty High* (1959), *Please, Mr. Organ Player* (1960), *Mighty Mood* (1961), *The New World Of Milt Buckner* (1962), *Milt Buckner Plays Chords* (1966), *Play, Milt, Play* (1966-71), with Buddy Tate *Midnight Slows, Vol. 1* (Black And Blue 1967), with Tate *Crazy Rhythm* (1968), *Locked Hands* (1968), *Them There Eyes* (Black And Blue 1968), *More Chords* (1969), *Birthday Party For H.G.B.S.* (1970), with Jay McShann *Kansas City Memories* (1970-73), *Milt Buckner And Jo Jones* (1971), with Illinois Jacquet *Genius At Work* (1971), *Boogie Woogie* (70s), *Rockin' Again* (1972), *Black And Blue Stomp* (1973), *Requiem Pour Un Chat* (1973), with Arnett Cobb, Clarence 'Gatemouth' Brown *Midnight Slows, Vol. 3* (1973), with Tate *Midnight Slows, Vol. 5* (1974), *Blues For Diane* (1974), *Green Onions* (1975), *A Night At The Popcorn* (1975), *Pianistically Yours* (1975), with Cobb *Midnight Slows, Vol. 6* (1976), *The Gruntin' Genius* (1976), *Green Onions* (Black And Blue 1977), *Boogie Woogie USA* (1977), with Guy Lafitte *Midnight Slows Vol. 7* (1977), with Lionel Hampton *Blues In Toulouse* (1977), with Tate *Midnight Slows, Vol. 7* (1977), *Unforgettable* (MPS 1979), *Rockin' Hammond* (Capitol 1983), *Please Mr Organ Player* (1992). Compilation: *The Early Years, 1947-53* (Official 80s).

Buckner, Teddy

b. 16 July 1909, Sherman, Texas, USA, d. 25 September 1994, Los Angeles, California, USA. A fervent disciple of Louis Armstrong from his youth, Buckner remained so all his life. Although his technique was strong enough for him to have worked in whatever style he chose, he deliberately modelled his trumpet playing upon that of his idol, even when it became unfashionable. During the 20s and early 30s Buckner worked mostly in California with bands such as those led by Sonny Clay, Curtis Mosby, Buck Clayton (with whom he visited China in 1934) and Lionel Hampton. When Hampton left California, in order to take up an offer to join Benny Goodman, Buckner took over the band. In the 40s he worked with several stylistically disparate bands, among them Benny Carter, Gerald Wilson and Johnny Otis, although he always stuck to his favoured style. In the early 50s he was with Kid Ory's band and was playing as well as ever. In the mid-60s Buckner became a popular attraction at Disneyland, California, playing old favourites and popular songs of the day in the manner of his stylistic mentor, and continued to work there for many years.

Selected albums: *Teddy Buckner* (1955), with Sidney Bechet *Parisian Encounter* (1958), *Kid Ory Plays W.C. Handy* (1959), *An Evening With Teddy Buckner* (1978), *La Grand Parade De La Nouvelle Orleans* (Vogue 1988), *Teddy Buckner At The Cresendo* (Dixieland Jubilee 1988), *Teddy Buckner In Concert* (Dixieland Jubilee 1988), (*Martinique* (Vogue 1989).

Budd, Roy

b. 14 March 1947, Mitcham, Surrey, England, d. 7 August 1993. A self-taught pianist, Budd appeared on television and in London's theatreland when only 12 years old. In his teenage he formed a trio, which at one time included bassist Dave Holland, and was for a while house pianist at one of London's leading jazz venues, the Bull's Head at Barnes. He continued to appear on television and on stage and was soon lured to write music for films, first in the UK and, later, in Hollywood. In addition to writing film scores, Budd also composed classical music. His scores include *Soldier Blue* (1970), *Get Carter* (1971), *Fear Is The Key* (1972) and in the 90s he scored for the re-release of the silent classic, *Phantom Of The Opera*. In the 70s he married singer Caterina Valente but they were later divorced. His sudden death, from a brain haemorrhage, came while he was still at work on a symphony. Stylistically, Budd's jazz playing owed a considerable debt to Oscar Peterson yet while he may have started out as a copyist, his maturity brought an individual stamp beautifully exemplified on seemingly unpromising material such as that displayed on a 1989 set of Christmas songs.

Albums: *Budd 'N' Bossa Nova* (60s), *Roy Budd Plays And Conducts Great Themes* (60s) *Fear Is The Key* (70s), *Have A Jazzy Christmas* (Master Mix 1989).

Budwig, Monty

b. 26 December 1929, Pender, Nebraska, USA, d. 9 March 1992. Budwig began playing bass while still at high school and turned professional soon after graduating. His first name-band engagement was a brief spell with Vido Musso in 1951, after which he served in the armed forces where he played in an air force band. On his discharge Budwig moved to California where he remained based, playing with bands led by Barney Kessel, Zoot Sims, Red Norvo and Woody Herman. He also worked frequently with Shelly Manne and made occasional tours with Benny Goodman, but concentrated on studio work and played jazz whenever the opportunity presented itself. Either as a member of Bill Berry's LA band, or as house musician for Concord Records, Budwig made his mark on the west coast scene of the 70s and 80s. A fluid, strong and rhythmic player, his presence in any rhythm section was a guarantee of impeccable timekeeping and solid swing.

Albums: with Shelly Manne *At The Blackhawk* (1959), with Barney Kessel *Soaring* (1976), *Dig* (1978), with Stan Getz *The Dolphin* (1981).

Bugger All Stars

The Bugger All Stars were formed in London in 1980. It was one of the few bands keeping the faith of free improvisation at a time when this uncommercial genre was probably at its most unsaleable. Mike Hames (alto saxophone/bass clarinet) invited Hugh Metcalfe, (guitar/electronics) to form a band with him. Metcalfe suggested Jim Lebaigue (drums) and Lebaigue recommended Phil Wachsmann, (violin/electronics/miscellaneous instruments). Originally inspired by Eric Dolphy (hence his choice of instruments) and an authority on Albert Ayler, Hames is not an obvious follower of either, and the band has more in common with the abstract Improvised Music tradition of Europe (and, perhaps, with the AACM school of Chicago in its concern for exploring sounds and textures rather than melody, harmony and rhythms) than with the fiery, headlong music of the 60s New Thing. The other three remain active on the improvised music scene but Hames retired from playing in 1986 when he began a degree course.

Albums: *Bugger All Stars* (1981), *Bonzo Bites Back* (1983).

Bunch, John

b. 1 December 1921, Tipton, Indiana, USA. After studying piano as a child, Bunch began playing semi-professionally while barely in his teenage years. Through listening to records he learned to appreciate the work of musicians such as Fats Waller, Count Basie and Duke Ellington. As he later recalled for interviewer Martin Richards, while still a child he was taken to hear the Basie band, which then included Lester Young, Jo Jones and Jimmy Rushing. Despite this early start, Bunch remained on the fringes of the jazz scene until he was well into his 30s. Part of the problem lay in the effects of the Depression on his family and his need to try to earn a living. With America's entry into World War II, Bunch enlisted in the air force, was shot down and served out the war in a prison camp. In the post-war years Bunch's early tuition was shown to be inadequate and his poor reading ability meant that he was unable to gain a place in a music college. However, he persisted in his ambition to become a professional musician and endured several years scuffling for low pay until he began to make an impact on the Los Angeles jazz scene, where he worked with Georgie Auld. In the mid- to late 50s he became well-known through his work with the bands of Woody Herman, Benny Goodman, Maynard Ferguson and Buddy Rich. In the 60s and 70s he recorded and sometimes played club and festival dates with several leading jazzmen, including Goodman, Zoot Sims and Gene Krupa and also led his own group. From the mid-60s into the early 70s he was also active outside jazz, serving for more than seven years as Tony Bennett's musical director. In the 80s he continued his round of recording sessions and live performances, usually in compa-

ny with important mainstream artists, among them Joe 'Flip' Phillips and Scott Hamilton. Highly regarded by his fellow musicians, Bunch is one of an unfortunately long list of jazzmen whose work is not as well-known to audiences as his talent deserves. Festival appearances in many parts of the world in the late 80s and early 90s, and some excellent records, may help to improve his profile in the jazz market.

Albums: *John Bunch Plays Kurt Weill* (Chiaroscuro 1975), *John's Bunch* (1975), *John's Other Bunch* (1977), *Slick Funk* (1977), *It's Love In The Spring* (1977), *The Swinging Young Scott Hamilton* (1977), with Joe 'Flip' Phillips *A Sound Investment* (1987), *Jubilee* (Audiophole 1988), *The Best Thing For You* (Concord 1988), with Bucky Pizzarelli *NY Swing* (LRC 1992).

Bunker, Larry

b. 4 November 1928, Long Beach, California, USA. A gifted percussionist, Bunker's career has ably straddled the worlds of jazz and classical music together with the commercial demands of film and television studios. On the west coast in the early 50s, he played drums with Gerry Mulligan, Stan Getz, Warne Marsh and others. From 1963, he spent almost two years as a member of the Bill Evans trio. Subtle and always listening, Bunker has worked effectively behind singers. He occasionally plays vibraphone and his classical and studio work has also made him a master of a wide range of percussion instruments.

Albums: *Bill Evans At Shelly's Manne-Hole* (1963), with Clare Fischer *Extension* (1963), with Gary Burton *The Time Machine* (1966), with Fischer *T'Da-a-a!* (1972), with Pat Williams *Threshold* (1973), with Dave Grusin *Discovered Again!* (1976), with Lew Tabackin, Warne Marsh *Tenor Gladness* (1976).

Bunn, Teddy

b. c.1909, Freeport, Long Island, New York, USA, d. 20 July 1978. A remarkably gifted self-taught guitarist, Bunn freelanced for most of his life. Perhaps as a result of his never being long in one place, his achievements are often overlooked. He was an inventive soloist, skilfully weaving intriguing patterns from deceptively simple single lines. In this respect, he predated Charlie Christian, whose arrival on the jazz scene effectively obliterated the efforts of every other guitarist. In Bunn's case this was unfortunate and his subsequent neglect is unfair. He switched from acoustic to electric guitar around 1940. Bunn was also a vocalist (he started out as a calypso singer) and this led him into an important musical collaboration with Leo Watson. Their group, the Spirits Of Rhythm, were one of the most original vocal outfits of the 30s and 40s. During this same period, Bunn played guitar with several leading blues and jazzmen, including Duke Ellington, John Kirby, Jimmy Noone, Bob Howard, Johnny Dodds, Oran 'Hot Lips' Page, Peetie Wheatstraw, Mezz Mezzrow, Sidney Bechet and Lionel Hampton. Bunn was able to move comfortably into R&B in the 50s, working with Jack McVea and Louis Jordan. By the end of the decade he had taken the extra step into rock 'n' roll. During the last decade of his life Bunn was in very poor health and worked only rarely.

Compilations: *Teddy Bunn 1930-39* (Blues Document 1989),

The Spirits Of Rhythm (JSP 1989, 1932-34 recordings), with Mezz Mezzrow, Tommy Ladnier *The Panassie Sessions* (1938-39).

Burbank, Albert

b. 25 March 1902, New Orleans, Louisiana, USA, d. 15 August 1976. One of the great classical New Orleans clarinettists, Burbank rarely worked outside his home town. In his youth he worked with the bands of Buddie Petit, Chris Kelly and Punch Miller, but his best period was the decade following his discharge from the armed forces in 1945. Working and recording with 'Wooden' Joe Nicholas, Paul Barbarin, Herb Morand, Kid Howard, Kid Ory and others, he gave consistent demonstrations of his powerful, sobbing vibrato. Perhaps the most distinctive feature of Burbank's playing was the rich sonority of his lower register. From the mid-50s onwards, Burbank worked continuously in New Orleans, mostly with lesser musicians. However, he did record with Kid Thomas in the 60s, and in the 70s worked with Percy Humphrey and the Preservation Hall Jazz Band.
Albums: *Albert Burbank With Kid Ory And His Creole Jazzband* (Storyville, 1954 recordings), *Kid Thomas And His Algiers Stompers* (1961), *Kid Howard's Olympia Band Featuring Albert Burbank The Clarinet Wizard* (1962), *Albert Burbank* (1969). Compilations: *Wooden Joe Nicholas* (1945-49), *Creole Clarinet* (Smokey 1979).

Burchell, Chas

b. Charles Burchell, 30 October 1925, London, England, d. 3 June 1986. Originally a George Formby fan, Burchell began to learn the ukelele, then guitar, before hearing an Artie Shaw record which inspired him to take up the clarinet and play jazz. Switching to alto saxophone, he started his own quintet in 1943, then tried tenor sax before he was drafted into the Royal Air Force. Transferred to the army in 1944, he played in Greece with the British Divisional Band and, following his discharge in 1947, worked in London with the Toni Antone big band. In 1949 he gave up full-time musicianship and worked in a factory so that he would not have to perform music he did not like in order to make a living: 'All my playing is playing for love,' he told writer Victor Schonfield in 1978. A disciple of Lennie Tristano and a devoted admirer of Warne Marsh, Burchell continued to play part-time, leading his own quintet for more than 20 years, guesting with distinguished visitors such as Clark Terry, Emily Remler and Nathan Davis, and recording for Peter Ind's Wave label, as well as playing with Ind in the group that supported Tristano on his only UK concert, at Harrogate in 1968. A wonderfully supple, lyrical tenor saxophonist whose unpredictable twists and turns of phrase recall the style of his idol Marsh, Burchell died of a heart attack in 1986. He remains, in the words of his friend and musical associate, journalist Mike Hennessey, 'one of the great unsung heroes of British jazz'.
Albums: *Jazz At The 1969 Richmond Festival* (1969), *No Kidding* (1974), *Peter Ind Sextet* (1975). Compilations: *Unsung Hero* (1994).

Burke, Ray

b. Raymond Barrois, 6 June 1904, New Orleans, Louisiana, USA, d. 21 March 1986. A self-taught clarinettist, Burke played in several New Orleans bands in his teens. He recorded in 1927 but the results were not released. Throughout the 20s and 30s Burke played in bands, mostly in New Orleans. In the 40s he led his own band but also recorded with 'Wooden' Joe Nicholas. Burke continued to play in New Orleans during the 50s and 60s, content to stay in his home town. He was still playing in the late 70s and early 80s, lending to several bands his discreet and elegant sound.
Album: with Wendell Eugen *West India Blues* (1978). Compilations: *Ray Burke's Speakeasy Boys* i (New Orleans 1989, 1937-45 recordings), *Ray Burke's Speakeasy Boys* ii (American Music 1994, 1937-1949 recordings).

Burnap, Campbell

b. 10 September 1939, Derby, England. Burnap caught the New Orleans jazz bug in his school days, playing washboard with a group of like-minded fellow pupils. His switch to trombone happened in the late 50s, when he emigrated to New Zealand, joining the Omega Jazz Band in 1958 and recording with them in 1961. Four years later, after gigging around and recording in Australia, he returned to England playing regularly with Terry Lightfoot. Another four years on, after visiting both Australia and New Orleans he joined Ian Armit. This time his wanderlust seems to have abated - his subsequent freelance career has included two long spells with regular bands Alan Elsdon (1970-75) and Acker Bilk (1980-87). As well as playing with virtually every well-known New Orleans/mainstream band in England, Burnap has appeared with visiting American jazz musicians including Billy Butterfield, Bud Freeman, Bob Haggart, and Kenny Davern. Burnap also broadcast regularly as a jazz presenter with London's JFM and BBC Radio 2, where he was also heard as a panellist on the quiz-show *Jazz Score*. He also writes on jazz topics - his short story *A Bit Of A Scrape* appeared in Quartet Books' 1986 collection *B-Flat, Bebop, Scat*. With a playing and singing style much indebted to that of Jack Teagarden, possessing great warmth and a strong personal touch, Burnap deserves his reputation as 'one of Britain's most stylish trombonists'.
Albums: *Alan Elsdon & His Jazzband* (1973), with Pat Halcox *Seventh Avenue* (1978), with Wally Fawkes *The Neo-Troglodytes* (1978), with Acker Bilk *Live In Holland* (1983), with Bilk *On Stage* (1987), with the Legends Of British Trad *Legends Of British Trad* (1991).

Burns, Ralph

b. 29 June 1922, Newton, Massachusetts, USA. After studying music at the New England Conservatory in Boston, Burns worked with several late swing era bands, including Charlie Barnet's, as both pianist and arranger. His best-known period was as a member of Woody Herman's First Herd, during which time he was not only one-fourth of a great rhythm section (the others being Billy Bauer, Chubby Jackson and Dave Tough), but also arranged some of the band's most successful numbers

(in some cases formalizing classic head arrangements, like that of 'Apple Honey'). In 1945 Burns decided to concentrate on writing and arranging, and contributed some exciting charts for Herman's Four Brothers band. He also composed some longer works, amongst which are 'Lady McGowan's Dream' and 'Summer Sequence', both recorded by Herman. When the record company decided to reissue 'Summer Sequence', they requested that a further section be added to the original three-part suite to fill the fourth side of a pair of 78 rpm releases. Burns obliged, and although some years had elapsed since the recording of the first three parts and the Herman band's personnel and style had substantially altered, he was able to recapture the mood successfully. The new piece, entitled 'Early Autumn', became a favourite of many jazz players, including Stan Getz. Freelancing in the 50s and 60s, Burns gradually moved away from jazz and into the film studios, although even here, as in *New York, New York* (1977), he was sometimes able to make use of his extensive knowledge of the jazz world. He won Academy Awards for his work on *Cabaret* (1972) and *All That Jazz* (1979), and continued to score for a mixture of feature and television movies such as *Lenny*, *Piaf*, *Lucky Lady*, *Movie Movie*, *Make Me An Offer*, *Urban Cowboy*, *Golden Gate*, *Pennies From Heaven*, (with Marvin Hamlisch), *Annie*, *Kiss Me Goodbye*, *My Favourite Year*, *Star 80*, *Ernie Kovacs-Between The Laughter*, *A Chorus Line*, *Moving Violations*, *The Christmas Star*, *In The Mood*, *Bert Rigby, You're A Fool*, *Sweet Bird Of Youth*, *All Dogs Go To Heaven*, and *The Joséphine Baker Story* (1991).
Selected albums: with Woody Herman *Summer Sequence* (1945-47), *Piaf* (1974, film soundtrack), *Ralph Burns Conducts* (Raretone 1988, rec. 1951-54), *Bijou* (Fresh Sounds 1988, rec. 1955).

Burrell, Dave

b. Herman Davis Burrell, 10 September 1940, Middleton, Ohio, USA. Burrell's mother was a singer, organist and choir director. Dave Burrell studied music (Berklee College Of Music for four years, Hawaii University for nine) and composed filmscores (*Crucifado*). This strong foundation serves to remind those who dismiss late 60s jazz freedom as improvised excess that its protagonists were sophisticated musical organisers. He went straight from his academic studies into the maelstrom of the black *avant garde*, playing with Archie Shepp, Marion Brown and Grachan Moncur III. He played at the 1969 Pan-African Music Festival in Algiers, the historic encounter of the New Thing with ethnic Africa. Shortly afterwards he recorded *Echo* for the Parisian BYG label, a towering blast of revolutionary energy. Since then Burrell has actively involved himself with both Rastafarian and Haitian off-shoots of African music/ritual and composed a version of Puccini's *La Boheme*. In 1988 he participated in the series of classic recordings David Murray made for the Japanese DIW label, his deep grasp of gospel particularly arresting on *Spirituals*. Burrell's feel for untempered intensity interacts with his academic sophistication in a complex yet exciting dialectic: like the better known Andrew Hill he demonstrates how jazz can be the real confrontation of the street and the academy.

Albums: *Echo* (Affinity 1969), *La Vie De Bohème* (1969), *After Love* (1971), *Dreams* (1973), *Only Me* (1973), *Black Spring* (1977), *Teardrops For Jimmy* (1977), *Lush Life* (Denon 1978), *Round Midnight* (1978), *Windward Passages* (Hat Art 1979), *Dave Burrell Plays Ellington And Monk* (Denon 1979), *Round Midnight* (Denon 1982), with others *Lucky Four* (1989), *Daybreak* (Gazell 1990), *In Concert* (Victo 1992).

Burrell, Kenny

b. 31 July 1931, Detroit, Michigan, USA. Coming from a family that encouraged music (all his three brothers were musicians), Burrell studied classical guitar for a mere 18 months (1952-53). In 1955 he received a Bachelor of Music degree from Detroit's Wayne University. He played guitar with the Candy Johnson Sextet in 1948, with Count Belcher in 1949 and Tommy Barnett in 1950. In 1951 Dizzy Gillespie visited Detroit and they recorded together. In March 1955 he stood in for Herb Ellis in the Oscar Peterson trio and in 1957 saw work with Benny Goodman. Discovered by the prestigious Blue Note label, he formed an association with organist Jimmy Smith and recorded with John Coltrane under the name The Cats. Like all jazz guitarists of his generation Burrell was primarily influenced by Charlie Christian, but developed a clear, warm set of licks that belonged to him entirely. Burrell has the special ability to play easily without resorting to clichés or sentimentality: his authoritative yet sensual guitar notes are some of the crucial sounds of jazz. His series of 60s albums for Blue Note and Verve contain his classic work. Arguably *Midnight Blue* featuring Stanley Turrentine (with its famous Reid Miles typography and inspiration behind Elvis Costello's *Almost Blue* sleeve) is his best album. The track 'Midnight Blue' has been cited as the influence for Van Morrison's 'Moondance'. The excellent *Guitar Forms* with Gil Evans in 1964 is another important work, this ambitious suite demonstrated wide influences. Along with Grant Green, nobody plays 'smokey guitar jazz' better than Burrell. In the late 80s his encouragement of young black talent - especially the drummer Kenny Washington - gave his trio an edge that belied his reputation for classy easy listening. In 1994 he was touring the world with the Jimmy Smith Trio once again.
Selected albums: All Night Long (Original Jazz Classics 1957), *All Day Long* (Original Jazz Classics 1957), *Blue Moods* (Original Jazz Classics 1957), *The Cats* (Original Jazz Classics 1957), *Kenny Burrell - John Coltrane* (Original Jazz Classics 1958), *On View At The Five Spot Cafe, Vol. 1* (Blue Note 1959), *Blue Lights, Vols. 1 and 2* (Blue Note 1959), *Midnight Blue* (Blue Note 1963), *Live At The Village Vanguard* (60s), *Guitar Forms* (Verve 1965), *For Charlie Christian And Benny Goodman* (Verve 1967), *Ellington Is Forever Vol 1* (Fantasy 1975), *Handcrafted* (1978), *Kenny Burrell In New York* (Muse 1981), *Night Song* (1982), *Listen To The Dawn* (Muse 1983), *Bluesin' Around* (CBS 1984), *Al La Carte* (Muse 1986), *Generations* (Blue Note 1987), *Togethering* (1989), *Recapitulation* (Charly 1989), *Guiding Spirit* (Contemporary 1990), *Sunnup To Sundown* (Contemporary 1992), with Jimmy Smith Trio *The Master* (Blue Note 1994).

Burton, Gary

b. 23 January 1943, Anderson, Indiana, USA. After teaching himself to play piano Burton studied music formally before switching to vibraphone. In 1960 he recorded with Hank Garland, a country guitarist, but then moved solidly into jazz with a two-year stint at Berklee College Of Music where he began an important musical association with Mike Gibbs. In 1963 he became a member of George Shearing's group, following this with two years in company with Stan Getz. Later in the 60s, Burton formed his own small band, playing jazz-rock. Throughout the decade and on into the 70s, Burton led a succession of fine bands which included such musicians as Larry Coryell, Steve Swallow, Roy Haynes, Pat Metheny and Eberhard Weber. He was also teamed on record with Stéphane Grappelli, Carla Bley, Keith Jarrett, Chick Corea, Michael Brecker, Peter Erskine and others. From 1971 Burton taught at Berklee, often finding empathetic musicians amongst his students. In the 80s his musical associates included Tommy Smith. Although he followed many more famous vibraphonists, not least Lionel Hampton and Milt Jackson, Burton was the first player of this instrument to create a new and wholly original musical style. His extensive simultaneous use of four mallets gave him a less percussive sound, allowing him to develop more complex ideas in a manner usually available only to pianists and especially players of wind instruments. Burton's Six Pack in 1993 was a refreshing excursion featuring six guitar players; B.B. King, John Scofield, Jim Hall, Kurt Rosenwinkel Kevin Eubanks and familiar partner Ralph Towner. His early musical experience of country and rock have all been thoroughly absorbed into a strongly jazz-orientated concept. Burton's interests and enthusiasms, allied as they are to a virtuoso technique, have made him a leading exemplar of contemporary music. However, although others have followed his example, he remains the only vibraphonist of his generation to be measured alongside major interpreters and innovators in jazz.

Albums: *Duster* (1967), *Lofty Fake Anagram* (1967), *Country Roads And Other Places* (1968), with Carla Bley *A Genuine Tong Funeral* (1968), with Stéphane Grappelli *Paris Encounter* (1969), *Green Apple* (1969), *Gary Burton And Keith Jarrett* (1970), *Alone At Last* (Atlantic 1972), with Chick Corea *Crystal Silence* (1972), *The New Quartet* (ECM 1973), with Steve Swallow *Hotel Hello* (ECM 1974), *Matchbook* (ECM 1974), *Dreams So Real* (ECM 1975), with Eberhard Weber *Ring* (ECM 1974), with Weber *Passengers* (ECM 1976), with Chick Corea *Duet* (ECM 1978), *Easy As Pie* (ECM 1980), *Picture This* (ECM 1983), *Somethings Coming* (RCA 1984), *Real Life Hits* (ECM 1984), with Ralph Towner *Slide Show* (ECM 1986), *Whiz Kids* (ECM 1986), *Times Like These* (GRP 1988), with Pat Metheny *Reunion* (ECM 1989), *Cool Nights* (GRP 1990), with Paul Bley *Right Time Right Place* (Sonet 1991), *Six Pack* (GRP 1993). Compilations: *Artists Choice* (Bluebird 1988), *Works* (ECM 1989).

Bushkin, Joe

b. 7 November 1916, New York City, New York, USA. While still in his early teens Bushkin played piano (and trumpet) with New York dance bands, and by the mid-30s was a regular sitter-in along 52nd Street, playing and recording with Eddie Condon, Muggsy Spanier and Billie Holiday. He joined Bunny Berigan's big band in 1935 and spent several years with Joe Marsala before taking up an offer from Tommy Dorsey in 1940. One of Bushkin's songs, 'Oh Look At Me Now', was recorded by Dorsey and the band's singer, Frank Sinatra, and became a success. After war service Bushkin worked with Benny Goodman and Louis Armstrong and accommodated changes in musical taste by easily shifting into a more commercial mode during the 60s and 70s. Although semi-retired, in the mid-70s Bushkin was tempted back into the spotlight by an invitation to accompany Bing Crosby on a tour of the USA and Europe. In the mid-80s Bushkin was still hard at work, effortlessly blending with latter-day mainstream jazzmen such as Warren Vaché Jnr.

Albums: *Joe Bushkin* i (1950), *Joe Bushkin* ii (1951), *Live At The Embers* (1951-53), *Joe Bushkin* iii (1955), *Joe Bushkin* iv (1955), *Joe Bushkin* v (1955), *Joe Bushkin With Strings* i (1957), *Joe Bushkin With Strings* ii (1957), *Joe Bushkin Live At The Town Hall* (1964), *Joe Bushkin Celebrates 100 Years Of Recorded Sound* (1977). Compilation: *World Is Waiting* (Commodore 1982, 1942-46 recordings).

Butler, Frank

b. 18 February 1928, Kansas City, Missouri, USA, d. 24 July 1984. Learning to play drums in school, Butler played in his home town where he took tuition from the city's finest drummer, Jo Jones. Despite such swing era roots, however, and notwithstanding a brief stint depping with Duke Ellington, Butler's interest lay in modern developments. From the late 50s onwards he worked with Curtis Counce, Art Pepper, Harold Land and other west coast luminaries and also played in groups led by Miles Davis and John Coltrane. His career faltered in the mid-60s but he returned a decade later, playing with great drive and flair and was at ease in the milieu of the hard-bop resurgence.

Albums: with Curtis Counce *Landslide* (1956), with Harold Land *The Fox* (1959), with John Coltrane *Kulu Se Mama* (1965), with Dolo Coker *Dolo!* (1977), with Xanadu All Stars *Xanadu At Montreux* (1978), *Wheelin' And Dealin'* (1978), with Art Pepper *Among Friends* (1978), *The Stepper* (Xanadu 1979).

Butterfield, Billy

b. 14 January 1917, Middleton, Ohio, USA, d. 18 March 1988. As a child Butterfield was taught by cornetist Frank Simons, but as a teenager he began to study medicine. He continued playing music to such good effect that he was soon working regularly with the bands of Austin Wylie and Andy Anderson and eventually quit his medical studies. Although adept on several instruments he concentrated on trumpet, later adding flügelhorn, and in 1937 was hired by the Bob Crosby band. Butterfield's gorgeous, fat-toned sound was particularly suited to ballads and his recording of Bob Haggart's 'What's New?', originally entitled 'I'm Free', was a hit. In 1940 he joined Artie Shaw, then worked with Benny Goodman and Les Brown, but soon entered the more reliable area of studio work. After the war Butterfield indulged himself with every sideman's dream and formed his own big band, in collaboration with former Crosby colleague Bill Stegmeyer. Butterfield took the enterprise seriously, commissioning arrangements from Ralph Burns, Bob Haggart, Bob Peck and Neal Hefti. For all his good intentions, however, the band proved to be a financial disaster. For a while he returned to studio work but then began freelancing, working with old comrades such as Eddie Condon, recording with Louis Armstrong (playing the trumpet obbligato to Satchmo's vocal on the 1949 recording of 'Blueberry Hill') and leading small groups. In the late 60s he became a member of the World's Greatest Jazz Band alongside former Crosby sidemen Bob Haggart and Yank Lawson. In the 70s he worked with Joe 'Flip' Phillips and toured extensively, usually as a solo. Much admired by fellow musicians, and eventually attracting the kind of attention from fans he had always deserved, Butterfield enjoyed a late flowering of his career even though suffering from emphysema.

Selected albums: *Jammin' At Condon's* (1954), *Billy Butterfield And His Orchestra* (1954), *Billy Butterfield At NYU* (1955), *Billy Butterfield Quintet* (1959), with WGJB *Live At The Roosevelt Grill* (1970), with WGJB *Century Plaza* (1972), *In A Mellow Tone* (1975), *For Better Blues And Ballads* (1975), *International Session* (1975), *Billy Butterfield Plays George Gershwin* (1977), *Watch What Happens* (Flyright 1977), *The Incomparable Butterfield Horn* (1977), *Swinging At The Elks* (1978), *Rapport* (1979), *Just Friends* (Jazzology 70s), *You Can Depend On Me* (1980). Compilations: with Bob Crosby *South Rampart Street Parade* (1937-38), *The Uncollected Billy Butterfield Orchestra* (1946), *Billy Butterfield 1946* (Hindsight 1989).

Byard, Jaki

b. John Byard, 15 June 1922, Worcester, Massachusetts, USA. A gifted multi-instrumentalist, Byard learned trumpet and piano as a child and later took up guitar, drums, trombone and tenor saxophone too. In 1949 he played piano in Earl Bostic's R&B band, and followed that with a spell as a solo pianist and then joined Herb Pomeroy's big band on tenor. After the Pomeroy stint he returned to playing piano, this time with the Maynard Ferguson band. Throughout the 60s Byard was deeply involved in what was often a very adventurous musical scene, working with Eric Dolphy, Don Ellis, Booker Ervin, Charles Mingus, Rahsaan Roland Kirk and others. In the 70s Byard worked mostly solo, but found time to experiment with his own big band, the Apollo Stompers, and to teach at Boston's New England Conservatory. Byard's wide-ranging musical interests make his work particularly interesting as he effectively incorporates ideas and styles from different periods of jazz and the classical repertoire: just one indication of his range is the series of piano duo albums he has made with players as diverse as Earl Hines, Ran Blake and Howard Riley.

Albums: with Herb Pomeroy *Life Is A Many Splendoured Gig* (1957), *Blues For Smoke* (Candid 1961), *Here's Jaki* (1961), *Hi-*

Fly (1962), with Charles Mingus *The Black Saint And The Sinner Lady* (1963), *Out Front* (1964), *Live At Lennie's On The Turnpike* (Prestige 1965), *Freedom Together* (1966), *On The Spot!* (1967), *The Sunshine Of My Soul* (1967), *Jaki Byard With Strings!* (1968), *The Jaki Byard Experience* (1968), *Solo* (1969), *Parisian Solos* (1971), *Live At The Jazz Inn* (1971), *Duet* (1972), *The Entertainer* (1972), *There'll Be Some Changes Made* (1972), *Empirical* (Muse 1973), *Flight Of The Fly* (c.1976), *Family Man* (Muse 1978), *Amarcord Nino Rota* (80s), *To Them - To Us* (Soul Note 1981), *There'll Be Some Changes Made* (Muse 1981), *Phantasies* (Soul Note 1984), *Foolin' Myself* (Soul Note 1988), *Phantasies II* (Soul Note 1988), with Howard Riley *Live At The Royal Festival Hall* (Leo 1988).

Byas, Don

b. 21 October 1912, Muskogee, Oklahoma, USA, d. 24 August 1972. In his teens, Byas played alto saxophone with the mid-west bands of Bennie Moten, Terrence Holder and Walter Page, but switched to tenor in the early 30s while working on the west coast. He played in Lionel Hampton's band at the Paradise Club in Los Angeles and, when Hampton joined Benny Goodman, Byas moved restlessly through the bands of Eddie Barefield, Buck Clayton, Don Redman, Benny Carter, Lucky Millinder and many others. In 1941 he succeeded Lester Young in the Count Basie band. In 1943 Byas quit Basie and began playing with small groups in clubs, mostly in New York, where his musical associates were emergent beboppers such as Dizzy Gillespie and Charlie Parker. Byas had known Parker as a young teenager and the two friends would jam together, with Byas claiming later that Parker had been his pupil. (Parker always denied this and the two men almost came to blows after a row in Paris.) Despite his bebop associations, however, Byas remained deeply rooted in the swinging sounds of the southwest. Given the period in which he worked, it was inevitable that he would start out by emulating the tenor saxophone style of Coleman Hawkins, but Byas always cited Art Tatum as his greatest influence, declaring: 'I haven't got any style. I just blow, like Art.' He took up residence in Paris in the late 40s, followed by long periods living in Amsterdam and in Copenhagen, and became enormously popular as a balladeer. His full, rich sound, allied to his harmonically complex playing, made him an instantly identifiable soloist. Byas was a significant player in the history of the development of the tenor saxophone and one whose contribution should not be, but (despite the exaggerated claims of his own importance) often is, overlooked.

Selected albums: *Don Byas And His Rhythm* (1951), *Don Byas Meets The Girls* (1953-5), with Brew Moore *Danish Brew* (1959), with Bud Powell *A Tribute To Cannonball* (1961), *Don Byas With Strings* (1962), *All The Things You Are* (Jazz Hour 1963), *A Night In Tunisia* (Black Lion 1963), *Walkin'* (Black Lion 1963), *Anthropology* (1963), *Don Byas Meets Ben Webster* (1968), *Don Byas In Japan* (1971), *Ambiences Et Slows* (Barclay 1979), Compilations: with various artists *Midnight At Minton's* (1941), with others *Savoy Jam Party* (1944-46), *Don Byas - 1945* (1945).

Byrd, Charlie

b. 16 September 1925, Chuckatuck, Virginia, USA. Byrd began playing guitar while still a small child and by the start of World War II was already highly proficient. During the war he met and played with Django Reinhardt and soon after the end of the war he became a full-time professional musician. He played in a number of popular dance bands but at the end of the 40s abandoned ambitions to play jazz and turned instead to the study of classical guitar. After studying under several leading tutors, including Andrès Segovia, he returned to the USA where he formed his own band in Washington, DC. With this group he played jazz but brought to his interpretations many of the techniques and some of the forms of the classical repertoire. In the late 50s he was with Woody Herman and in the early 60s played with Stan Getz, with whom he developed his interest in Latin American music thus helping to generate the jazz-bossa nova craze. In 1973 he became co-founder, with Barney Kessel and Herb Ellis, of Great Guitars. During the rest of the 70s and on through the 80s he performed regularly on the international club and festival circuit, sometimes as a single, sometimes in duo and often with Great Guitars. Byrd's jazz work is distinguished by his classical training and his interest in other musical forms. As a jazz soloist he sometimes lacks the fluid swing of such contemporaries as Kessel and Ellis but he is a masterly technician.

Selected albums: *Jazz Recital/The Spanish Guitar Of Charlie Byrd* (Savoy 1957), *Midnight Guitar* (1957), *First Flight* (1957), *Jazz At The Showboat/Byrd's Word* (1958), *Byrd In The Wind* (1959), *Jazz At The Showboat, Vol. 3* (1959), *The Guitar Artistry Of Charlie Byrd* (1960), *Charlie Byrd At The Village Vanguard* (1961), *Blues Sonata* (1961), *Latin Impressions* (1962), with Stan Getz *Jazz Samba* (1962), *Bossa Nova Pelos Passaros* (1962), *Byrd At The Gate* (1963), *Byrd Sony* (60s), *Solo Flight* (1965), *Charlie Byrd Plays Villa-Lobos* (60s), *Crystal Silence* (1973), *Byrd By The Sea* (1974), *Tambu* (Fantasy 1974) *Top Hat* (1975), *Three Guitars* (Concord 1975), *Great Guitars* (1976), *Triste* (1976), *Great Guitars: Straight Tracks* (70s), *Blue Byrd* (Concord 1978), *Sugarloaf Suite* (1979), *Latin Byrd* (Milestone 1980), *Great Guitars At The Winery* (1980), *Brazilville* (Concord 1981), *Christmas Album* (Concord 1982), *Great Guitars At Charlie's, Georgetown* (1982), *Latin Odyssey* (1983), *Isn't It Romantic* (Concord 1984), *Byrd & Brass* (Concord 1986), *Byrd At The Gate* (Original Jazz Classics 1987), with Scott Hamilton *It's A Wonderful World* (Concord 1988), *The Bossa Nova Years* (Concord 1991), *Charlie Byrd/The Washington Guitar Quintet* (Concord 1992), *Jazz Recital* (Savoy 1992).

Byrd, Donald

b. 9 December 1932, Detroit, Michigan, USA. In the early 50s Byrd studied trumpet and composition and also played in bands during his military service. Later in the decade he was frequently called upon to record with leading bop musicians including John Coltrane, Jackie McLean, Phil Woods, Sonny Rollins, Art Blakey and Kenny Clarke. At the end of the 50s he was in a partnership with Pepper Adams, which lasted until

1961. Shortly thereafter Byrd resumed his studies, this time in Europe. In the mid-60s he began a long and parallel career as a jazz educator, teaching at some of the USA's most important seats of learning including Rutgers and Howard universities. He continued to record, playing with musicians including Dexter Gordon. During the 70s, Byrd experimented with jazz-rock and achieved some commercial success with his records. Much of this work was soul and funk inspired and he founded the Blackbyrds with this in mind. Their series of albums are pure funk and the jazz hardliners were often critical of this musical heresy. He continued his teaching, however, and retained his strong links with the hard bop movement in jazz. A leading bop trumpet stylist, Byrd's striking technique is associated with a rich and beautiful tone which helps make him one of the most lyrical of his generation of jazzmen.

Selected albums: with Kenny Clarke *Bohemia After Dark* (1955), *First Flight* (Delmark 1955), *Long Green* (1955), with Art Blakey *The Jazz Messengers* (1956), *Byrd's Word* (Savoy 1956), *Two Trumpets* (1956), *The Young Bloods* (1956), *September Afternoon* (1957), *At Newport* (1957), *X-tacy* (1957), *Jazz Eyes* (1957), with John Coltrane *Lush Life* (1958), *Byrd In Paris, Vols. 1 & 2* (1958), with Pepper Adams *10 To 4 at The 5 Spot* (1958), *Off To The Races* (1958), *Byrd In Flight* (1960), *Fuego* (Blue Note 1960), *At The Half Note Vol 1* (Blue Note 1961), *Royal Flush* (1961), *Chant* (1961), *Groovin' For Nat* (Black Lion 1962), *Free Form* (Blue Note 1962), with Dexter Gordon *One Flight Up* (1964), with Kenny Burrell, Herbie Hancock *A New Perspective* (Blue Note 1964), *Mustang* (1966), *The Creeper* (1967), *Electric Byrd* (1970), *Blackbyrd* (Blue Note 1973), *Street Lady* (1974), *Steppin' Into Tomorrow* (1975), *Places And Spaces* (1975), *Caricatures* (1977), *Thank You...For F.U.M.L. (Funking Up My Life)* (1978), *Love Byrd* (1981), *Words, Sounds, Colors And Shapes* (1982), *Harlem Blues* (Landmark 1987), *And 125th Street* NYC (Elektra 1988), *Getting Down To Business* (Landmark 1989), *A City Called Heaven* (Landmark 1993). Compilations: *Donald Byrd's Best* (1976), *Early Byrd - The Best Of* (Blue Note 1993), *The Best Of Donald Byrd* (Blue Note).

Byron, Don

b. 8 November 1958, New York City, New York, USA. A single-minded individualist and eclectic, Byron has performed in classical, klezmer, salsa, classic jazz and free-music contexts, earning a reputation for an intense artistic curiosity, and helping to re-establish credibility for the clarinet as a contemporary jazz instrument. Growing up in the Bronx, he was constantly exposed to music by his parents (who played piano and bass in amateur bands) and was inevitably influenced by the thriving local Hispanic music, its daring and exuberant improvisations over swinging rhythms. Byron would pay regular visits to the nearby Garden Of Roses, where he could hear Machito's awesome group, and would use his classical clarinet training to transcribe salsa music by Ray Barretto and Luis 'Perico' Ortiz for local bands. Continuing his studies at the New England Conservatory of Music, the proximity of Berklee College Of Music's prestigious jazz hot-house led to a greater degree of interest in the jazz tradition, and some creative exchanges with jazz students Donald 'Duck' Harrison, Jean Toussaint and Greg Osby. But it was the Klezmer Conservatory Band and its clarinet-led Jewish folk music that really captured Byron's imagination, sowing the seeds for his highly acclaimed klezmer project 'Don Byron Plays The Music Of Mickey Katz'. Katz was a Jewish bandleader, composer and paradist who embodied the 'mischief' in the music that Byron says first attracted him, and his work provided Byron with exactly the right mix of music and narrative to deal with an ever-present political content. Since leaving college, Byron's jazz credits have included tours with the David Murray Big Band, Bobby Previte, the Mercer Ellington Orchestra (in which he played Harry Carney's lines on the baritone saxophone), Bill Frisell and Ralph Peterson, and appeared in a free, *avant garde* context in the 1993 Company line-up. His debut album *Tuskegee Experiments* addressed an American racist outrage, in which a large number of black syphilis patients were left untreated in a 'medical experiment', and features contributions from Bill Frisell, Ralph Peterson Jnr., Reggie Workman and a powerful poem by Sadiq. He recently followed this up with an album by the Katz project.

Selected albums: *Tuskegee Experiments* (Elektra Nonesuch 1992), *David Murray Big Band Conducted By Butch Morris* (1992), with Bobby Previte *Track Fast* (1992), with Ralph Peterson *Presents The Fo'tet* (1990), *Ornettology* (1992), *Don Byron Plays The Music Of Mickey Katz* (Elektra Nonesuch 1993), with Bill Frisell *Have A Little Faith* (1993). Compilation: *Live At The Knitting Factory Vol. 3* (1991).

C

Caceres, Ernie
b. 22 November 1911, Rockport, Texas, USA, d. 10 January 1971. A highly-skilled musician, Caceres played guitar early in his career before turning to reed instruments. His first professional engagements took him from Texas to Detroit and New York, often playing in small groups organized and led by his brother, violinist Emilio. In 1938 Caceres joined Bobby Hackett, then played briefly with big bands led by Jack Teagarden, Bob Zurke, Glenn Miller, Tommy Dorsey, Benny Goodman, Woody Herman, Billy Butterfield and Hackett again. With these bands he mostly played clarinet and alto and baritone saxophones, but occasionally doubled on tenor. His recording career also included sessions with Sidney Bechet and Eddie Condon. For many years Caceres was one of the two most highly-regarded baritone players in jazz and if he never

attained the sonority of Harry Carney, he was a forceful and flexible player. Although his roots were in big bands and dixieland, he ventured successfully into more modern company when he played on Metronome All Stars recordings in 1949, including musicians such as Dizzy Gillespie, Miles Davis, Fats Navarro, Charlie Parker. In the 60s Caceres returned to Texas and played with various bands, including Jim Cullum's San Antonio-based outfit. His great-nephew, David Caceres, is a fine bop alto saxophonist.

Selected albums: with Emilio Caceres *No More Blues* (1937), with Louis Armstrong *Midnight At V-Disc* (1944), with Bobby Hackett *Jazz Ultimate* (1957), *Ernie And Emilio Caceres* (Audiophile 1969), with Hackett, Eddie Condon *Jam Session (1948)* (1986), with Metronome All Stars *Victory Ball (1949)* (1988).

Caldwell, Happy
b. Albert W. Caldwell, 25 July 1903, Chicago, Illinois, USA, d. 29 December 1978. After starting out on clarinet, Caldwell switched to tenor saxophone. He became one of the earliest jazzmen to adopt this instrument and in the 20s and 30s worked with several bands including those led by Bernie Young, Tiny Bradshaw, Fletcher Henderson and Elmer Snowden. He also accompanied singer Mamie Smith. He appeared on many recording dates, including some with Louis Armstrong and Jelly Roll Morton. Mostly based in New York, Caldwell played many club engagements through the 40s and into the 50s and 60s. In the 70s he joined Clyde Bernhardt's band with which he recorded and toured. A sound craftsman, he was related to and took lessons from Buster Bailey. Despite his early ground-breaking use of the tenor saxophone, Caldwell chose not to move with the musical times; this has rather unfairly led to his neglect.

Album: with Clyde Bernhardt *More Blues And Jazz from Harlem* (1973). Compilation: with Billy Banks *The Rhythmakers* (1932).

Callender, Red
b. George Sylvester Callender, 6 March 1916, Haynesville, Virginia, USA, d. 8 March 1992, Los Angeles, California, USA. Callender began performing in jazz groups, playing bass, while still in his teens. By the mid-30s he had settled in California and during the next few years worked with a succession of bands, including those led by Buck Clayton, Louis Armstrong, Erroll Garner and Lester Young. From the early 40s Callender was deeply involved in bebop, adapting comfortably to the new concept. He recorded extensively with prominent beboppers such as Charlie Parker, Wardell Gray and Dexter Gordon. As well as appearing in the Nat 'King' Cole trio during this period, Callender also led his own small groups, usually a trio, one of which included Lester Young. In the 50s Callender's skilled musicianship led to his becoming a sought-after studio player; he subsequently worked on record dates with artists as diverse as Frank Sinatra and Stevie Wonder but also continued to work with jazzmen. A particularly noteworthy set of recordings came in the mid-50s when he was

signed by Norman Granz to accompany Art Tatum. In later years Callender frequently turned to playing tuba, an instrument on which he proved to have remarkable dexterity. In addition to his playing, Callender has also composed and arranged and in 1985 published his autobiography, *Unfinished Dream*.

Selected albums: *Swinging Suite* (1956), *Red Callender Speaks Low* (1957), *Basin Street Blues* (1973), with Gerry Wiggins *Night Mist Blues* (1983), with Jeannie and Jimmy Cheatham *Homeward Bound* (1987).

Further reading: *Unfinished Dream*, Red Callender with Elaine Cohen.

Calloway, Cab

b. Cabell Calloway, 25 December 1907, Rochester, New York, USA, d. 18 November 1994, Cokebury Village, Delaware, USA. Involved in show business from an early age, vocalist Calloway was an occasional drummer and MC, working mostly in Baltimore, where he was raised, and Chicago, where he relocated in the late 20s. He worked with his sister Blanche, and then, in 1929, he became frontman for the Alabamians. Engagements with this band took him to New York; in the same year he fronted the Missourians, a band for which he had briefly worked a year earlier. The Missourians were hired for New York's Savoy Ballroom; although the band consisted of proficient musicians, there is no doubt that it was Calloway's flamboyant leadership that attracted most attention. Dressing

outlandishly in an eye-catching 'Zoot Suit' - knee-length drape jacket, voluminous trousers, huge wide-brimmed hat and a floor-trailing watch chain - he was the centre of attraction. His speech was peppered with hip phraseology and his catch-phrase 'Hi-De-Hi', echoed by the fans, became a permanent part of the language. The popularity of the band and of its leader led to changes. Renamed as Cab Calloway And His Orchestra, the band moved into the Cotton Club in 1931 as replacement for Duke Ellington, allegedly at the insistence of the club's Mafia-connected owners. The radio exposure this brought helped to establish Calloway as a national figure. As a singer Calloway proved difficult for jazz fans to swallow. His eccentricities of dress extended into his vocal style, which carried echoes of the blues, crass sentimentality and cantorial religiosity. At his best, however, as on 'Geechy Joe' and 'Sunday In Savannah', which he sang in the 1943 film *Stormy Weather*, he could be highly effective. His greatest popular hits were a succession of songs, the lyrics of which were replete with veiled references to drugs that, presumably, the record company executives failed to recognize. 'Minnie The Moocher' was the first of these, recorded in March 1931 with 'Kicking The Gong Around', an expression which means smoking opium, released in October the same year. Other hits, about sexual prowess, were Fats Waller's 'Six Or Seven Times' and the Harold Arlen-Ted Koehler song 'Triggeration'. For the more perceptive jazz fans who were patient enough to sit through the razzmatazz, and what one of his sidemen referred to as 'all that hooping and hollering',

Cab Calloway

Calloway's chief contribution to the music came through the extraordinary calibre of the musicians he hired. In the earlier band he had the remarkable cornetist Reuben Reeves, trombonist Ed Swayzee, Doc Cheatham and Bennie Payne. As his popularity increased, Calloway began hiring the best men he could find, paying excellent salaries and allowing plenty of solo space, even if the records were usually heavily-orientated towards his singing. By the early 40s the band included outstanding players such as Chu Berry featured on 'Ghost Of A Chance' and 'Tappin' Off', Hilton Jefferson ('Willow Weep For Me'), Milt Hinton ('Pluckin' The Bass'), Cozy Cole ('Ratamacue' and 'Crescendo In Drums') and Jonah Jones ('Jonah Joins The Cab').

With such outstanding musicians including Ben Webster, Shad Collins, Garvin Bushell, Mario Bauza, Walter 'Foots' Thomas, Tyree Glenn, J.C. Heard and Dizzy Gillespie, the Calloway band was a force to be reckoned with and was one of the outstanding big bands of the swing era. In later years Cab worked on the stage in *Porgy And Bess* and *Hello, Dolly!*, and took acting roles in films such as *The Blues Brothers* (1980). His other films, over the years, included *The Big Broadcast* (1932), *International House*, *The Singing Kid*, *Manhattan Merry Go Round*, *Sensations Of 1945*, *St. Louis Blues*, *The Cincinnati Kid*, and *A Man Called Adam* (1966). Calloway enjoyed a resurgence of popularity in the 70s with a Broadway appearance in *Bubbling Brown Sugar*. In the 80s he was seen and heard on stages and television screens in the USA and UK, sometimes as star, sometimes as support but always as the centre of attraction. In 1993 he appeared at London' Barbican Centre, and in the same year celebrated his honorary doctorate in fine arts at the University of Rochester in New York State by leading the 9,000 graduates and guests in a singalong to 'Minnie The Moocher'.

Selected compilations: *Club Zanzibar Broadcasts* (1981), *Kicking The Gong Around* (1982), *Minnie The Moocher* (RCA 1982), *Cab & Co.* (1985), *Cab Calloway Collection - 20 Greatest Hits* (Deja Vu 1986), *Missourians* (1986), *The Cab Calloway Story* (Deja Vu 1989), *Hi-De-Hi* (1991), *Classics 1941-42* (1993), *Cruisin With Cab* (Submarine Records 1993).

Further reading: *Of Minnie The Moocher And Me* (his autobiography).

Candido

b. Candido Camero de Guerra, 22 April 1921, Havana, Cuba. Turning to percussion in his early teenage, after a brief flirtation with bass and guitar, Candido became an important member of the Cuban musical hierarchy. Despite his popularity in Cuba, in 1952 he was tempted to the USA by Dizzy Gillespie with whom he played and, later, recorded. During the mid-50s, he played with Billy Taylor, Stan Kenton and others, usually performing on conga and bongo drums. Eclectic in taste and style, Candido was able to blend his urgent, exhilarating Latin roots with the demands of bop and mainstream artists alike. A list of his musical associates from the late 50s through to the late 70s rings with important names such as Erroll Garner, Al Cohn, Art Blakey, Phil Woods, Sonny Rollins, Wes Montgomery, Elvin Jones and Lionel Hampton. In the 80s, Candido was still active in the USA but by now was heard less in jazz circles, more often playing in studio orchestras. A seminal figure in the growth of popularity of Latin rhythms in jazz in the third quarter of the century, Candido's skill, dexterity and propulsive swing has set standards achieved only by a few of his successors.

Albums: *Candido In Indigo* (1958), *Latin Fire* (1959), *Conga Soul* (1962), *Candido's Comparsa* (1963), *Candido, Featuring Al Cohn* (1965), *Thousand Finger Man* (1970), *Candido The Beautiful* (1970), *Drum Fever* (1973).

Candoli, Conte

b. Secondo Candoli, 12 July 1927, Mishawaka, Indiana, USA. At the age of 13 Candoli was already showing a prodigious talent playing the trumpet, and studying alongside his older brother, Pete Candoli, with whom he performed briefly in the Woody Herman band at the early age of 16. He went back home to finish school, then rejoined Herman but was drafted into the army. After leaving the services he joined a small group led by ex-Herman bassist Chubby Jackson, with whom he toured Scandinavia in 1947. During the next few years Candoli worked with several bands, including Charlie Ventura's, but spent most of the early 50s, very successfully, with Stan Kenton. Candoli worked with numerous small groups, sometimes as leader, and was an important contributor to the development of west coast jazz, the so-called 'cool school'. In the 60s he played with Terry Gibbs, was with Herman again, worked extensively with Shelly Manne, and returned to Kenton as a member of the LA Neophonic Orchestra. From time to time he has also worked in a small group as co-leader with his brother and through the 70s and 80s continued to perform in clubs and at festivals, making regular recordings with a wide range of musical associates, and was a member of Supersax. Candoli's playing is characterized by a fluid, reflective approach while his warm and full sound adds immeasurably to his inventive solos.

Selected albums: with Howard Rumsey *In The Solo Spotlight* (1954), *Sincerely Conte: Conte Candoli* (1954), *West Coast Wailers* (1955), *Mucho Calor* (1957), *The Brothers Candoli* (1958), *Sessions, Live* (1958), *The Brothers Candoli Sextet* (1959), *Conte Candoli All-Stars* (1960), with Stan Kenton *Wagner* (1964), with Shelly Manne *Boss Sounds* (1967), *Conversation* (1973), with Louie Bellson *150 mph* (1974), *Echo* (1982).

Candoli, Pete

b. Walter J. Candoli, 23 June 1923, Mishawaka, Indiana, USA. Despite having learnt to play the bass and French horn by the time he was 12 years old, Candoli was by his mid-teens making his name as a trumpeter, working in swing era big bands his musicianship made him a valuable sideman. At first he worked in the more commercial end of the music scene, playing in the bands of Sonny Dunham and Will Bradley/Ray McKinley. In 1942 Candoli was briefly with Benny Goodman and then worked with Tommy Dorsey, Freddie Slack, Teddy Powell, Alvino Rey and Charlie Barnet. Candoli's precocity and startling technique (as a high-note man he was second only to Cat Anderson) first attracted the attention of jazz fans when he joined Woody Herman's First Herd. His playing on hits such as 'Caldonia', 'Apple Honey' and 'Northwest Passage' was forceful and exciting and he lived up to his 'Superman' nickname by wearing a Superman suit for his featured solos. He also worked with Boyd Raeburn's musically-adventurous band, but later in the 40s returned to rather more prosaic territory with Tex Beneke, Jerry Grey and Les Brown, eventually settling on the west coast where he became a studio musician, working in films such as *The Man With The Golden Arm* (1956). The call of jazz was too strong to ignore altogether, and Candoli worked with Milt Bernhart's Brass Ensemble and joined Stan Kenton's New Concepts and LA Neophonic bands. In the early 70s he also worked as a double act with his then wife, singer Edie Adams, and has periodically worked in tandem with his brother, Conte Candoli. A bold, fiercely attacking player, Candoli's tone is warm and his solos are filled with rhythmically dramatic lines and great flair.

Selected albums: *Bell, Book And Candoli* (1958), *The Brothers Candoli* (1958).

Capp, Frank

b. 20 August 1931, Worcester, Massachusetts, USA. In his late teens, while studying music at the Berklee College Of Music in Boston, Massachusetts, Capp was invited to join Stan Kenton's Orchestra as replacement drummer for Shelly Manne. This was in early 1952; by the end of the year Capp had left to join Neal Hefti's band. As he later admitted, this was the wrong way round; the Hefti band, a commercially-orientated dance band, was a better training ground than the powerhouse Kenton band. Capp then became accompanist to Peggy Lee before joining the big bands of Billy May and Harry James and small groups led by Charlie Barnet and Shorty Rogers. Through the 50s and into the 60s, Capp spent much of his working life in television and film studios but also made numerous albums with Benny Goodman, Terry Gibbs, Barney Kessel, and several with André Previn. In the mid-70s Capp formed a big band with Nat Pierce, which became known as the Capp-Pierce Juggernaut. In the 80s Capp continued to play in small and big bands, using his extensive technical proficiency and bringing enthusiasm and hard-swinging excitement to any performance.

Selected albums: *Frank Capp And His Orchestra* (50s/60s), *A Tribute To Harry James* (50s/60s), *Percussion In A Tribute To Artie Shaw* (50s/60s), *Percussion In A Tribute To Benny Goodman* (50s/60s), *Percussion In A Tribute To Duke Ellington* (50s/60s), *Percussion In A Tribute To Glenn Miller* (50s/60s), *Percussion In A Tribute To Perez Prado* (50s/60s), *Percussion In A Tribute To The Dorsey Brothers* (50s/60s), *Percussion In A Tribute To Henry Mancini* (50s/60s), *Percussion In A Tribute To Les Brown* (50s/60s), *Juggernaut* (Concord 1979), *Juggernaut Strikes Again* (Concord 1981), *Live At The Alley Cat* (Concord 1988). *The Frankie Capp Trio Introduces Rickey Woodard* (Concord 1991).

Capp-Pierce Juggernaut

In 1975 American big band drummer Frank Capp temporarily took over Nat Pierce's duties as contractor for the Neal Hefti Orchestra. When the band abruptly folded, Capp was left with an engagement, for which the club owner asked him to provide an alternative band. Capp formed the group from leading west coast session men and decided to use the occasion as a tribute to Hefti's great arranging skills. A disagreement with Hefti led to Capp contacting Pierce, whose own arranging talents had graced the bandbooks of both Woody Herman and Count Basie. Using Pierce's Basie-style charts and with the pianist as his co-leader, the band was a great success; they began to make more dates and eventually were heard by writer Leonard Feather, who headlined his newspaper article: 'A Juggernaut On Basie Street'. Renaming their band accordingly, Capp and Pierce made records, the first of which sold well, and continued to work whenever and wherever they could, concentrating on Basie-ish material played with enormous zest and enthusiasm but also displaying great versatility when the occasion demanded. Unfortunately, the collective personnel make it a band far too expensive ever to tour. Among the personnel have been Bill Berry, Bobby Shew, Marshal Royal, Blue Mitchell, Herb Ellis, Chuck Berghofer and Richie Kamuca, while the singers who have worked and sometimes recorded with the band have been Ernie Andrews, Joe Williams, Ernestine Anderson and Nancy Wilson.

Albums: *Juggernaut* (Concord 1976), *Juggernaut Live At Century Plaza* (1978), *The Capp-Pierce Juggernaut* (1979), *Juggernaut Strikes Again!* (Concord 1981), *Juggernaut Live At The Alleycat* (1987).

Carey, 'Papa' Mutt

b. Thomas Carey, 1891, Hahnville, Louisiana, USA, d. 3 September 1948. Born into a musical family, Carey played drums and guitar throughout his early years before taking up the cornet, and later the trumpet, when in his early twenties. He worked in New Orleans with several bands, many of them marching bands, before teaming up with Kid Ory in 1914. After touring in a show with Johnny Dodds, Carey returned to New Orleans where he played alongside Chris Kelly, Wade Whalley and others, then rejoined Ory who was by this time working in California. From 1919 the two remained together until 1925 when Carey took over as leader, gradually increasing the size of the band throughout the late 20s and into the early swing era. Despite the revival of interest in New Orleans music, the early 40s found Carey no longer able to sustain a living as a full-time musician but he continued to play whenever possible. In 1944 he once more plunged into full-time playing and a renewed association with Ory, a partnership which lasted until 1947. A gifted trumpeter with unusual sensitivity and great melodic gifts, Carey's playing was characterized by a wide vibrato and he brought to the traditional trumpet playing of New Orleans music a distinction rarely equalled.

Selected album: *Kid Ory's Creole Jazz Band (1944-45)* (1986).

Carlisle, Una Mae

b. 26 December 1915, Xenia, Ohio, USA, d. 7 November 1956. Playing piano and singing professionally while still in her teens, Carlisle was heard by Fats Waller, in 1932. Hired by Waller with whom she established a close relationship, Carlisle made several records in the late 30s. Waller joined her on some of these, notably a delightful version of 'I Can't Give You Anything But Love', but she also established a name for herself in her own right. Shortly before the outbreak of World War II she became highly successful in England, Germany and France, where she worked at the Boeuf sur le Toit in Paris. She then returned to New York where she undertook several successful engagements and record dates. In 1941 she recorded with John Kirby and was nominal leader of several small bands, which featured such leading jazzmen as Russell Procope, Charlie Shavers, Ray Nance, Lester Young and Benny Carter. Also in the early 40s she became popular on radio and, before the decade was out, she had successfully transferred to television. In the early 50s she was still popular, playing with artists such as Don Redman, but her health was failing and she retired in 1954. A competent pianist with a stylistic debt to Waller, Carlisle sang in a huskily intimate manner, her warm sensual voice proving especially effective on ballads. Her use of delayed phrasing gave her jazz performances a highly effective lazy swing.

Compilation: *Una Mae Carlisle & Savannah Churchill 1944* (Harlequin 1982).

Carlton, Larry

b. 2 March 1948, Torrance, California, USA. Often cited as the guitarist's guitarist Carlton has successfully courted rock, jazz and acoustic 'new age' with considerable success. The former member of the Crusaders carved a career during the 70s as a sought after session musician. His profile improved following some outstanding fluid playing over a number of years with Steely Dan. His distinctive 'creamy' Gibson 335 guitar sound was heard on countless records and his work on numerous Joni Mitchell albums arguably contributed to their success. Two notable examples are *Court And Spark* and *Hejira*. His solo debut appeared in 1978. It was not until *Sleepwalk*, including its title track (formerly a hit for Santo And Johnny), that Carlton was fully accepted as a solo artist in his own right. *Alone But Never Alone* found Larry playing acoustic guitar and the record proved a critical and commercial success. Both that album and *Discovery* broadened Carlton's following. The live *Last Night* however saw a return to his jazz roots, and contains moments of breathtaking virtuosity. His version of Miles Davis' 'So What' is one of the finest ever interpretations. With *On Solid Ground* Carlton demonstrated a stronger rock influence and produced a credible cover of Clapton's 'Layla' and Steely Dan's 'Josie'. He was awarded a Grammy in 1981 and again in 1987 for his version of 'Minute By Minute'. In 1988 Carlton was shot in the neck by an intruder at his studio. After an emergency operation and many months of physio-therapy he made a full recovery. Carlton remains a master musician with an almost flawless catalogue.

Albums: *Larry Carlton* (WEA 1978), *Live In Japan* (Flyover 1979), *Mr 335* (1979), *Sleepwalk* (WEA 1982), *Strikes Twice* (1980), *Friends* (WEA 1983), *Alone But Never Alone* (MCA 1986), *Discovery* (MCA 1987), *Last Nite* (MCA 1987), *One Night Of Sin* (1989), *Christmas At My House* (1989), *On Solid Ground* (MCA 1989), *Kid Gloves* (GRP 1992), *Renegade Gentleman* (GRP 1993). Compilation: *The Collection* (GRP 1990).

Carney, Harry

b. 1 April 1910, Boston, Massachusetts, USA, d. 8 October 1974. Carney began his professional musical career at the age of 13, playing clarinet and later the alto and baritone saxophone in Boston bands. Among his childhood friends were Johnny Hodges and Charlie Holmes, with whom he visited New York in 1927. Carney played at the Savoy Ballroom with Charlie 'Fess' Williams before joining Duke Ellington, who was about to play in the young musician's home town. When this engagement was over Carney left for a tour with Ellington, who had taken on the role of guardian. The job with Ellington lasted until Duke's death 47 years later. Shortly after joining Ellington, Carney was persuaded to play alto saxophone but soon gravitated to the baritone, an instrument he proceeded to make his own. Carney's rich sonority became an essential element in Ellington's tonal palette and for decades listeners gloried in the full-throated lower register which, in a band brimming with individualists, had a character all its own. Nevertheless, despite his virtuosity on the baritone, Carney would take up the clarinet on frequent occasions to show he was truly a master of the reed instruments. Carney's relationship with Ellington transcended that of musician and leader; he was Ellington's confidante and for decades he drove the Duke from gig to gig. The closeness of their relationship was underlined by Carney when he said: 'It's not only been an education being with him but also a great pleasure. At times I've been ashamed to take the money.' After Ellington's death, at the end of May 1974, Carney said, 'Without Duke I have nothing to live for.' He died a little over four months later.

Selected albums: *The Indispensable Duke Ellington, Volumes 1-6 (1927-40)*, with Duke Ellington *Togo Brava Suite* (1971).

Carr, Ian

b. 21 April 1933, Dumfries, Scotland. Carr taught himself trumpet from the age of 17. Between 1952 and 1956 he studied English literature at Newcastle University, and has had a career as writer, broadcaster, teacher and musician, all furthering the cause of jazz. Between 1960 and 1962 he played with the EmCee Five, the Newcastle bop quintet, before moving to London to work with tenor saxophonist Don Rendell. The Rendell-Carr group lasted until 1969, recording five albums and making international tours. Carr left to form Nucleus, which followed Miles Davis into the world of amplified jazz rock. *Elastic Rock*, their debut, was released in 1970. Tours followed, including Europe and the USA. Leonard Feather wrote, 'Many listeners and critics have agreed that Nucleus has been a seminal influence on jazz-rock groups in Europe and else-

Ian Carr

where'. In 1973 his book on contemporary UK jazz, *Music Outside*, was published. Carr's sometimes academic approach to music has resulted in long compositions, including *Solar Plexus* (1971) and *Labyrinth* (1974). In 1982 he became an associate professor at the Guildhall School of Music in London and was given the Calabria award for 'outstanding contribution in the field of jazz'. The same year saw the publication of his acclaimed biography of Miles Davis. In 1986 he composed *Spirit Of Place* for Tony Coe and Eberhard Weber. His *Jazz: The Essential Companion* (1987) (co-written with Digby Fairweather and Brian Priestley) was for some time the most in-depth jazz encyclopedia available in the UK, although some registered disquiet at Carr's apparent lack of sympathy for free improvisation, harmolodics and the black *avant garde*. 1987 also saw Carr working with the Mike Gibbs Orchestra and was the featured soloist with the Hamburg Radio Orchestra under Gibbs' direction.

Carr's recent projects include a trilogy of jazz compositions inspired by his years in Newcastle Upon Tyne. The first piece, *Old Heartland*, inspired by the highly underrated novelist Sid Chaplin, was recorded in 1988; the second part is called *Going Home* which was performed alongside Alan Plater's play of the same name; and the third, a suite entitled *North Eastern Song Lives*, was commissioned by Jazz North East to mark their 25th anniversary and first performed in Newcastle in October 1991. Since then, Carr has had a further jazz biography published; *Keith Jarrett: The Man And His Music*, and has performed with

the United Jazz And Rock Ensemble. Carr is one the most literate and emotional artists to come out of the fertile 60s UK jazz scene.

Albums: with Don Rendell *Shades Of Blue* (1965), with Rendell *Phase III* (1968), with Rendell, Neil Ardley *Greek Variations* (1970), *Belladonna* (Core 1972), *Old Heartland* (MMC 1988). see also Nucleus discography.

Further reading: *Music Outside*, Ian Carr. *Miles Davis*, Ian Carr.

Carr, Mike

b. Michael Anthony Carr, 7 December 1937, South Shields, Co. Durham, England. The brother of trumpet-player Ian Carr, Mike taught himself the organ, piano, and vibes, and gained a reputation in the Newcastle based EmCee Five. By the late 60s, he was running a trio which included John McLaughlin and accompanying distinguished visiting musicians. He toured with Ronnie Scott's group between 1971 and 1975, appearing with them at Carnegie Hall in 1974. Since then his own quartet have toured Europe, and he has established Cargo - a jazz-rock group which recorded a successful album in 1985. The Mike Carr Trio continues to appear around the country, playing a hard-swinging, dynamic music rooted in bebop.

Selected albums: with the Emcee Five *Let's Take Five* (1961), with Tony Crombie *Hammond Under Pressure* (1968), with Ronnie Scott *Scott At Ronnie's* (1973), *Live At Ronnie Scott's* (1979), *Good Times & The Blues* (Cargogold 1993).

Carroll, Baikida

b. 15 January 1947, St Louis, Missouri, USA. Caroll studied trumpet and flügelhorn at Southern Illinois University and the Armed Forces School of Music, directing the Third Infantry Division Ensemble. He also studied music in Germany. Like many other black musicians of his generation in St Louis, Carroll gained exposure to the world of creative music via BAG (the Black Artists Group). Although associated with the *avant garde*, Carroll has an impressive resume, including work with blues singers Albert King and Little Milton, soul saxophonist Oliver Sain, Fontella Bass and Sam And Dave. In 1973 he left the USA to live in Europe. In 1974 he issued *Orange Fish Tears*, a deft combination of world music evocation and free jazz. Back in the USA he has worked with Oliver Lake, guitarist Michael Gregory Jackson, Muhal Richard Abrams, Jack DeJohnette, Anthony Braxton, Michele Rosewoman and David Murray, playing in the latter's octet and big band. His long association with Julius Hemphill has been particularly productive; Carroll plays on several of Hemphill's albums who returns the favour on *Shadows And Reflections*. Since 1985 he has been a regular member of Charlie Haden's Liberation Music Orchestra. Baikida's vocalized playing is supported by an unerring grasp of thematic continuity, admirably demonstrated by *The Spoken Word*, a two record set of unaccompanied trumpet. He has also composed scores for films.

Albums: *Orange Fish Tears* (1974), *The Spoken Word* (1978), *Shadows And Reflections* (1982).

Carroll, Joe

b. 25 November 1919, Philadelphia, Pennsylvania, USA, d. 1 February 1981. Rooted in Louis Armstrong's singing style, but shaped by that of Leo Watson and the musical thought of Lester Young, Carroll was one of the first singers in jazz to fully assimilate bebop. He worked with Dizzy Gillespie from 1949-53, writing with him one of the bop vocal anthems, 'Oo-Shoo-Be-Do-Be'. He made a number of recordings in the 50s and early 60s under his own name and in 1964 toured with Woody Herman. Carroll's hard-edged, rough-toned voice had a limited range but he compensated with his exuberant swing and inventive lines.

Selected albums: *Joe Carroll: Man With A Happy Sound* (1962). Compilations: *Dee Gee Days (1951-52)* (1978), *Dizzy Gillespie 1946-1949* (1983).

Carter, Benny

b. Bennett Lester Carter, 8 August 1907, New York City, New York, USA. Carter was born and raised in the area of New York known as San Juan Hill, a tough neighbourhood. His working-class parents encouraged their children to take up music and Carter and his two sisters received piano tuition from their mother, Sadie Bennett Carter. A cousin, Theodore 'Cuban' Bennett was a well-known trumpeter in New York jazz clubs in the 20s, while another cousin, Darnell Howard, played clarinet with the bands of W.C. Handy, Joe 'King' Oliver and Carroll Dickerson in the 20s. Apart from his mother's tuition, Carter took early lessons on the C-melody saxophone from a succession of teachers, among them Harold Proctor and Lt. Eugene Mickell Snr. Musician neighbours of Carter, in his youth, included Bubber Miley, Freddy Johnson, Rudy Powell, Russell Procope and Bobby Stark. Carter was already familiar with the Harlem jazz scene when, in 1923, his family settled there. By the late 20s, Carter, who had by then switched to the alto saxophone, was becoming known as a reliable and dedicated young musician who had gained valuable experience in bands led by Billy Fowler, Duke Ellington and Fletcher Henderson. In 1928 he was working in the band led by Fletcher's brother, Horace Henderson. When Horace left, Carter took over as leader. Despite engagements at top dance halls, the band proved short-lived due, in part, to Carter's personal manner and attitude towards music. A naturally elegant man and musically a perfectionist and utter professional, Carter refused to resort to the kind of flash and showmanship audiences expected. After the band folded, Carter worked as musical director of McKinney's Cotton Pickers, a period during which he began to develop his interest in arranging. During the early 30s Carter also played trumpet, surprising fellow musicians with the ease at which he switched from reeds to brass and back again. By this time he was also adept on clarinet, tenor saxophone, trombone and piano. He pursued his interest in writing, providing arrangements for many leading bands of the day, including those of Chick Webb, for whom he also played alto, and Benny Goodman. In 1933 he formed a new big band, which featured Chu Berry and Dicky Wells. In this same year he also played on recording dates organized by British composer-bass player Spike Hughes. In 1935 Carter joined Willie Lewis's band, with which he visited Europe. In all, Carter was away for three years, working in several countries including France, Holland and Denmark. At the urging of writer Leonard Feather, Carter was hired by Henry Hall as staff arranger for the BBC Dance Orchestra in London. In 1938, aware of the commercial successes of the swing era back in the USA, he returned home and formed a new big band. Once again, his refusal to compromise his standards meant that the band enjoyed little commercial success. He also recorded extensively on small group sessions, such as Lionel Hampton's RCA recordings, for some of which he wrote arrangements. Other bands included the Chocolate Dandies, in which he played alongside Coleman Hawkins and Roy Eldridge, and the Varsity Seven. In 1942 Carter settled in California, formed a new big band and signed with agent Carlos Gastel, who also handled Nat 'King' Cole, Sonny Dunham and Stan Kenton. Employed to write for films, Carter proved a fast learner and, although he was sometimes uncredited, because blacks had yet to achieve full status in Hollywood, he worked on numerous scores for 20th Century-Fox, Warner Brothers and MGM. In the winter of 1946/7 Carter folded his big band for the last time but continued to reform for special recording dates. In the early 50s he began touring with Jazz At The Philharmonic and made numerous records for Norman Granz. He also arranged and provided orchestral backing for a host of singers, notably Peggy Lee, Ella Fitzgerald and Mel Tormé. A heart attack in January 1956 barely slowed him down and he remained active in his writing and playing; the same year he married for the fourth time. The late 50s and early 60s were especially fruitful times and he composed, arranged and played on a succession of important albums, including *Aspects*, *Further Definitions* and *Additions To Further Definitions*. He also wrote a major work for Count Basie, the *Kansas City Suite*. By now he was also working in television and touring the international festival circuit. In the early 70s Carter began a continuing association with Princeton University, where he became Visiting Lecturer in the Council of Humanities and the African-American Studies Programme. His personal contact with Morroe Berger at Princeton led to the appearance of Berger's major biography, *Benny Carter: A Life In American Music* (1982). During the 70s Carter began a regular string of visits to Japan, where he became extremely popular, and also continued to record, again for Norman Granz. In the 80s Carter toured and recorded, on many occasions scoring and composing extensively. As a player, on any of his many instruments, Carter is skilled and always inventive and delightful to hear. It is on alto saxophone, however, that he has made his greatest contribution. A liquid player in the tradition of Johnny Hodges and Willie Smith, the two contemporary giants with whom he is usually grouped, Carter displays a striking pungency and an effortless capacity for creating solos of interest and fascination. As a composer of tunes such as 'Doozy' and 'When Lights Are Low' he has contributed greatly to the jazz catalogue. As an arranger in the 30s he was a major force in shaping big band music and has continued to demonstrate his skills in this area and in small group settings to lasting effect. His longevity and the fact that neither his playing nor writing skills have shown any signs of diminishing are truly remarkable. In 1987 he joined forces with John Lewis and the All-American Jazz Orchestra, an occasionally-assembled repertory band dedicated to the performance of music especially written for big bands. For a concert and subsequent recording date, Carter composed and arranged a new major work, *Central City Sketches*. Additionally, Carter rehearsed the orchestra, conducted, played solo alto and drew from the musicians taking part admiration, enthusiasm and a sparkling performance. In the late summer of 1989 the Classical Jazz series of concerts at New York's Lincoln Center celebrated Carter's 82nd birthday with a set of his songs, sung by Ernestine Anderson and Sylvia Syms. In the same week, at the Chicago Jazz Festival, he presented a recreation of his *Further Definitions* album, using some of the original musicians. In February 1990, Carter led an all-star big band at the Lincoln Center in a concert tribute to Ella Fitzgerald. Events such as these added to the endless and imperishable catalogue of achievements of this remarkable man. It was probably Ben Webster who first dubbed Carter 'The King', a name which stuck because, unlike titles bestowed by outsiders, this one was offered in tribute to qualities that jazz musicians themselves esteemed.

Selected albums: *Jazz Off The Air* (1944), *Alone Together*

Betty Carter

(1952), *Cosmopolite* (1952), *Sessions, Live* (1957), *Jazz Giant* (Original Jazz Classics 1957), *Swingin' The Twenties* (Original Jazz Classics 1958), *Aspects* (1959), *Further Definitions* (1961), *B.B.B. & Co.* (1962), *The World Of Sight And Sounds* (1963), *Additions To Further Definitions* (1966), *The King* (Pablo 1976), *Carter, Gillespie Inc.* (1976), *Wonderland* (Pablo 1976), *Benny Carter At Montreux '77* (Original Jazz Classics 1977), *Live And Well In Japan* (Original Jazz Classics 1977), *Jazz Allstar Orchestra Live In Japan '79* (1979), *Summer Serenade* (Storyville 1980), *Gentlemen Of Swing* (1980), *Skyline Drive* (1982), *The Benny Carter All Stars Featuring Nat Adderley And Red Norvo* (1985), *Benny Carter Meets Oscar Peterson* (Pablo 1986), *A Gentleman And His Music* (Concord 1986), with the All-American Jazz Orchestra *Central City Sketches* (Limelight 1987), *In The Mood For Swing* (Limelight 1987), *My Kind Of Trouble* (Pablo 1988), *Cooking At Carlos 1* (Limelight 1989), *My Man Benny, My Man Phil* (Limelight 1990), *All That Jazz Live At Princeton* (Limelight 1991), *Harlem Renaissance* (1993). Compilations: *The Best Of Benny Carter* (Pablo 1982), *Benny Carter 1928-52* (1983), *The Benny Carter Collection - 16 Golden Greats* (1987), *When Lights Are Low* (1987), *3,4,5 - The Verve Small Group Sessions* (1991, 50s sessions), *The Complete Recordings* (Affinity/Charly 1992), *These Foolish Things* (Tring 1993).

Carter, Betty

b. Lillie Mae Jones, 16 May 1930, Flint, Michigan, USA. Growing up in Detroit, Carter sang with touring jazzmen, including Charlie Parker and Dizzy Gillespie. In her late teens, she joined Lionel Hampton, using the stage name Lorraine Carter. With Hampton she enjoyed a love-hate relationship; he would regularly fire her only to have his wife and business manager, Gladys Hampton, re-hire her immediately. Carter's predilection for bop earned from Hampton the mildly disparaging nickname of 'Bebop Betty', by which name she became known thereafter. In the early 50s she worked on the edge of the R&B scene, sharing stages with blues artists of the calibre of Muddy Waters. Throughout the remainder of the 50s and into the 60s she worked mostly in and around New York City, establishing a reputation as a fiercely independent and dedicated jazz singer. She took time out for tours with packages headlined by Ray Charles (with whom she recorded a highly-regarded album of duets), but preferred to concentrate on her own shows and club performances. She also found time for marriage and a family. Her insistence upon certain standards in her recording sessions led eventually to the formation of her own record company, Bet-Car. During the 80s, Carter continued to perform in clubs in New York and London, occasionally working with large orchestras but customarily with a regular trio of piano, bass and drums, the ideal setting for her spectacular improvisations. Taking her inspiration from instrumentalists like Parker and Sonny Rollins rather than from other singers, Carter's technique draws little from the vocal tradition in jazz. Her kinship with the blues is never far from the surface, however complex and contemporary that surface might be. In performance, Carter tends to employ the lower register of her wide range. Always aurally witty and frequently displaying scant regard for the lyrics of the songs she sings, Carter's inventiveness is ably displayed on such performances as 'Sounds', a vocalese excursion which, in one recorded form, lasts for more than 25 minutes. Despite such extraordinary performances and the breakneck tempos she employs on 'The Trolley Song' and 'My Favourite Things', she can sing ballads with uncloying tenderness. In concert, Carter dominates the stage, pacing like a tigress from side to side and delivering her material with devastating attack. The authority with which she stamps her performances, especially in vocalese and the boppish side of her repertoire, helps make unchallengable her position as the major jazz singer of the 80s and early 90s.

Selected albums: *Meet Betty Carter And Ray Bryant* (1955), *The Bebop Girl* (1955-56), *Social Call* (1956), *Out There* (1958), *Finally* i (1959), *The Modern Sound Of Betty Carter* (1960), *I Can't Help It* (Impulse 1961), with Ray Charles *Ray Charles And Betty Carter* (ABC 1961), *'Round Midnight* (1963), *Inside Betty Carter* (1963), *Finally* ii (Roulette 1969), *Live At The Village Vanguard* (Verve 1970), *The Betty Carter Album* (1972), *Now It's My Turn* (1976), *What A Little Moonlight Can Do* (1977), *I Didn't Know What Time It Was* (Verve 1979), *The Audience With Betty Carter* (Verve 1979), *Whatever Happened To Love?* (Bet-Car 1982), *Look What I Got* (Verve 1988), *Droppin' Things* (Verve 1990), *It's Not About The Melody* (Verve 1992).*Feed The Fire* (1993). Compilation: *Compact Jazz* (Philips 1990).

Carter, Ron

b. 4 May 1937, Ferndale, Michigan, USA. As a child Carter played cello, hoping for a career in classical music. Adept on several instruments, including violin, clarinet and trombone, he eventually settled on bass. He also opted for a career in jazz when he became aware of the difficulties confronting any black youth with musical ambitions centred upon the concert platform. He was in his early 20s before he began to perform regularly in jazz, securing a place in Chico Hamilton's quintet. In the early 60s he worked with Eric Dolphy, Don Ellis, Cannonball Adderley, Mal Waldron and Thelonious Monk amongst many leading modern jazzmen. In 1963 he joined Miles Davis, remaining in the group until 1968, where his rhythm section partners were Herbie Hancock and Tony Williams. In addition to his work with Davis, Carter was in constant demand for studio sessions, recording many hundreds of albums. He continued this double life, playing on studio dates with, amongst others, George Benson and Stanley Turrentine. He also played concerts with the New York Jazz Sextet/Quartet, Sonny Rollins, V.S.O.P. (a band which featured Hancock, Williams, Freddie Hubbard and Wayne Shorter), McCoy Tyner and the Milestone All Stars. Also, he occasionally led bands for record and club and concert dates. In the 80s he continued his tireless round of concerts, festivals and recording sessions, always in company with leading artists like Hubbard, Cedar Walton, Jim Hall and George Duke. He was also once again reunited with Hancock and Williams for a USA tour with Wynton Marsalis. As one of the greatest bass players jazz has ever known, Carter's impeccable technique and the powerful propulsive swing of his playing enhance any rhythm section in which he appears. As an accompanist for singers he is beyond praise, regularly working with Lena Horne, recording with Aretha Franklin and others, while his solo accompaniment to Helen Merrill's 1968 recording of 'My Funny Valentine' is an object lesson in bass playing. His soloing on such of his compositions as 'The Third Plane' is similarly immaculate. Nevertheless, his greatest strength lies in his section playing and within that context his period with Hancock and Williams in the Davis band stand as eloquent testimonial to a master of his craft caught at a peak from which, a quarter of a century on, he has yet to descend.

Selected albums: with Eric Dolphy *Out There* (1960), with Don Ellis *How Time Passes* (1960), with Miles Davis *Seven Steps To Heaven* (1963), with Herbie Hancock *Maiden Voyage* (1965), with Davis *Miles In The Sky* (1968), with Helen Merrill *A Shade Of Difference* (1968), *All Blues* (1973), *Blues Farm* (1973), *Spanish Blue* (CTI 1975), *VSOP - Live Under The Sky* (1977), *Pastels* (Original Jazz Classics 1977), *Peg Leg* (Original Jazz Classics 1978), *Third Plane* (Original Jazz Classics 1979), *Parade* (Milestone 1980), *Pick Em* (Milestone 1980), *Patrao* (Original Jazz Classics 1980), *Wynton Marsalis* (1981), with Cedar Walton *Heart And Soul* (Timeless 1981), *Etudes* (1983), with Jim Hall *Telephone* (Concord 1984), *Ron Carter Plays Bach* (1988), *Panamanhatten* (Fnac 1991), with Hall *Live At Village West* (1993, reissue), with Hancock, Wayne Shorter, Wallace Roney, Tony Williams *A Tribute To Miles* (QWest/Reprise 1994).

Cary, Dick

b. 10 July 1916, Hartford, Connecticut, USA, d. 6 April 1994, Glendale, California, USA. A formally-trained violinist, Cary played with a local symphony orchestra while still in his teens but by the early 40s was regularly playing piano in various dixieland bands, notably those led by Joe Marsala and Wild Bill Davison. Around this time Cary also arranged music for Benny Goodman and other big bands of the day, playing briefly with the Casa Loma Orchestra, but his heart was in the more traditional areas of jazz. Throughout the 40s he worked extensively, sometimes as a soloist, occasionally with Muggsy Spanier, Eddie Condon and Davison. In 1947 he became a founder member of Louis Armstrong's All Stars but left, ostensibly pleading boredom, to advance his musical studies. From the 50s Cary worked as a freelance, arranged and played with a wide range of artists, always exhibiting considerable skill and refusing to compromise his exacting standards. In addition to his keyboard skills he also practised trumpet, trombone and alto horn. He relocated from New York to Los Angeles in 1959, where he also arranged as well as playing with top-flight dixieland teams. His scores, often accentuated by oboes and bassoons, included a transcription of Bix Beiderbecke's 'In A Mist' for Jimmy McPartland.

Selected albums: with Louis Armstrong *Town Hall Concert* (1947), with Eddie Condon *Jammin' At Condon's* (1954), *Dick Cary* (1957), *Hot And Cool* (1958), *Dick Cary And His*

Dixieland Doodlers (1959), *The Amazing Dick Cary* (1975), *California Doings* (1980), *Dick Cary With Ted Easton's Jazzband* (Southland 1988).

Casa Loma Orchestra

Canadian tycoon Sir Henry Pellatt had delusions of grandeur similar to those exhibited by William Randolph Hearst. Pellatt's equivalent to Hearst's castle at San Simeon was Casa Loma, a house he built near Toronto. In 1929 a group of musicians, originally controlled by contractor Jean Goldkette and working as the Orange Blossoms, mainly in Canada, decided to strike out on their own. Forming a co-operative band under the nominal leadership of alto saxophonist Glen Gray, the musicians decided to adopt the name of Pellatt's folly and soon showed the musical world that their venture was based upon firm foundations. In its hey-days the band was regarded by black and other white musicians as one of the hottest around. The Casa Lomans featured several good musicians, including Sonny Dunham and Clarence Hutchenrider, and also a very popular singer, Kenny Sargent. Musically, the band's key-man was guitarist Gene Gifford, whose excellent arrangements provided a distinctive sound. Precision playing and a smooth, subtly dynamic swing brought the band widespread popularity during the early 30s. Although often overlooked in swing era surveys, the band continued to play prestigious residencies into the 40s, when musicians of the calibre of Herb Ellis and Bobby Hackett were in its ranks. Later, the band continued to record, although Gray died in 1963, and still attracted attention thanks to an impressive array of sidemen, including Jonah Jones and Nick Fatool.

Compilations: *The Casa Loma Band* (1930-36), *Glen Gray And The Casa Loma Orchestra 1943-46* (1979), *Solo Spotlight* (1986), *Casa Loma Stomp 1929-30* (Hep Jazz 1986), *Glen Gray And The Casa Loma Orchestra 1939-40* (1988), *White Jazz (1931-34)* (Old Bean 1988).

Casey, Al

b. 15 September 1915, Louisville, Kentucky, USA. Casey's first professional job as a guitarist was with Fats Waller, with whom he recorded extensively from 1934 until Waller's death in 1943. Also in the 30s, Casey worked with Teddy Wilson in his small groups, sometimes accompanying Billie Holiday, and big band. After switching from acoustic to electric guitar, on which instrument he proved to be an able disciple of Charlie Christian, Casey extended his range into R&B, recording with King Curtis. In demand for recording dates with artists such as Helen Humes, Casey was briefly confined to the studio, but in the 80s was back in full flow, touring extensively and delighting international audiences with his vigour and inventiveness.

Selected albums: with Fletcher Henderson All Stars *Big Reunion* (1957), *Buck Jumpin'* (1960), *The Al Casey Quartet* (1960), *Jumpin' With Al* (Black And Blue 1973), *Six Swinging Strings* (JSP 1981), *Best Of Friends* (JSP 1981), *Genius Of The Jazz Guitar* (JSP 1981), *Al Casey And George Kelly With Fessor's Session Boys* (1983), *Al Casey Remembers King Curtis* (1985). Compilation: *Fats Waller And His Rhythm* (1934-36).

Cash, Bernie

b. 18 January 1935, Scarborough, Yorkshire, England, d. 7 October 1988. Cash began performing as a trumpet player and during the traditional jazz boom of the 50s worked with Bruce Turner among others. In the 60s he switched to bass and although adept enough to teach the flute, piccolo and most of the saxophone family, it was on bass that he established his musical reputation. Also in the 60s he began a long musical partnership with fellow bass player Peter Ind, with whom he played and recorded. In the late 70s Cash formed his Great Jazz Solos Revisited Orchestra, designed to feature his arrangements of transcribed classic solos by past masters such as Charlie Parker and Louis Armstrong. Among the musicians Cash admired was Lester Young; in 1982 he obtained his MA degree at the University of Hull with a thesis on his idol. Four years later, Cash wrote the score for the jazz opera *Prez*, with book and lyrics by Alan Plater. Apart from his jazz work Cash also played regularly with the BBC Northern Symphony Orchestra, Yorkshire Opera and the Royal Philharmonic Orchestra. It was during a European tour with the RPO that he collapsed and died on 7 October 1988.

Albums: with Peter Ind *Jazz At The 1969 Richmond Festival* (1969), with Ind *Contra Bach* (Wave 1975), *Great Jazz Solos Revisited* (1978).

Cathcart, Dick

b. 6 November 1924, Michigan City, Indiana, USA, d. 8 November 1993, Woodland Hills, California, USA. A fine trumpeter, his first major band appearance was with Ray McKinley. He later played in bands in the US Army during World War II and after the war was with Bob Crosby before a spell in the Hollywood studios. Among the film soundtracks on which he can be heard are *Dragnet* (1954), *Battle Stations* (1955), *Nightmare* (1956), in which he dubbed for the on-screen Billy May who was more than capable of blowing his own trumpet, and *The Five Pennies* (1959). Cathcart played in other name bands in the late 40s and 50s but became best known, by sound if not by name, when he played trumpet for the leading character in a 1952 USA radio series entitled *Pete Kelly's Blues*. When the programme also became a feature film in 1955 and transferred to television later in the decade, Cathcart again ghosted for the star (Jack Webb in the film, William Reynolds on television), although he also appeared on-camera in the small screen version. Cathcart made a series of successful small group jazz albums, not surprisingly taking the sound marketing step of naming his band Pete Kelly's Big Seven. Apart from playing trumpet with a bell-like tone, Cathcart also sang; it was in this capacity that he was most active in the 60s and 70s. By the 80s he was back on jazz stages, playing trumpet as well as ever.

Selected albums: *Pete Kelly At Home* (1956), *Bix MCMLIX* (1959).

Catherine, Philip

b. 27 October 1942, London, England. Born of a Belgian father, Philip Catherine came to notice in 1969 as the guitarist on Scott Bradford's *Rock Slide*, thereby initiating an extremely busy period of session work. During this time Catherine contributed to the works of musicians such as Jean-Luc Ponty, Larry Coryell, Alphonse Mouzon and Zbigniew Seifert. When not doing sessions, Catherine found time to record a series of solo albums on which he also played bass and keyboards. However, in 1976 when Jan Akkerman suddenly left the Scandinavian rock band Focus, Catherine replaced him, winning considerable praise for his lyrical playing. Prior to joining Focus, Catherine had played with the Chris Hinze Combination during 1974. His solo career blossomed in the 90s, and in keeping with John Scofield, in recent years, he has developed in leaps and bounds and has hit a particularly prolific period.

Albums: with Scott Bradford *Rock Slide* (1969), with Jean-Luc Ponty *Open Strings* (1972), *Stream* (1972), with Ponty *Ponty Grappelli* (1973), *September Man* (1974), with Passport *Doldinger Jubilee 75* (1975), *Guitars* (Atlantic 1975), with Larry Coryell *Twin House* (1976), with Joachim Kuhn *Spring Fever* (1977), *Zbigniew Seifert* (1977), with Coryell *Splendid* (1978), with Coryell, Alphonse Mouzon *Back Together Again* (1978), with Focus *Focus Con Proby* (1978), *Sleep My Love* (CMP 1979), with Seifert *We'll Remember Zbiggy* (1980), *Babel* (Elektra 1980), *End Of August* (1982), *Transparence* (Inak 1987), *September Sky* (September 1989), *I Remember You* (Criss Cross 1991), *Moods Vol. 1* (Criss Cross 1992), *Spanish Nights* (Enja 1992), *Oscar* (Igloo 1992), *Moods Vol. 2* (Criss Cross 1993).

Catingub, Matt

b. 25 March 1961, North Hollywood, California, USA. Born into a musical family (his mother is singer Mavis Rivers), Catingub taught himself to play the piano at the age of seven and four years later was also proficient on the clarinet. At 16 he began arranging and composing and additionally took up formal music studies. The following year he switched to alto saxophone. In 1978 he was a member of the California All-Star High School big band which annually appears at the Monterey Jazz Festival. His composition 'Monterey I' was played at the festival and helped him to win a festival scholarship. That same year he visited Japan as a member of the Monterey All-Stars in company with artists such as Thad Jones, Mel Lewis and Dizzy Gillespie. In 1979 (and again in 1981), he joined Louie Bellson's big band, for which he also composed and arranged. In 1980 Catingub formed his own big band, filling it with fellow prodigies; the group played festivals and made its first record in 1983. In the early 80s he regularly accompanied his mother in concert appearances, on recordings and foreign tours. In 1982 he took the lead alto position in the big band led by Toshiko Akiyoshi and Lew Tabackin and toured with it extensively. By the mid-80s he was an established touring and recording artist and had formed the Woodshed Music School. A forceful soloist with an edgy tone, Catingub is an outstanding contemporary talent with an abiding interest in big band music which he finds challenging and a continuing inspiration. Catingub demonstrated his remarkable versatility with an album, *Hi-Tech Big Band*, on which, aided by multi-tracking techniques, he played every instrument.

Albums: *My Mommy And Me* (1983), *Your Friendly Neighborhood Big Band* (1984), *Hi-Tech Big Band* (Sea Breeze 1985), *Land Of The Long White Cloud* (Sea Breeze 1988), *Matt Catingub Big Band With Mavis Rivers* (Sea Breeze 1990).

Catlett, 'Big' Sid

b. 17 January 1910, Evansville, Indiana, USA, d. 25 March 1951. After briefly trying piano, Catlett switched to drums and received formal tuition when his family settled in Chicago. After working with Darnell Howard, Catlett moved to New York where he played with Elmer Snowden and Benny Carter, following these sessions by drumming with McKinney's Cotton Pickers, Fletcher Henderson and Don Redman. Catlett happily switched from big bands to small groups, such as those led by Eddie Condon and Lionel Hampton, without any discernible difficulty. In 1941 he joined Benny Goodman, giving that band an overwhelming plangency it never received from any other drummer. In the late 30s and early 40s Catlett worked and played endlessly, appearing on countless recording sessions with a staggeringly wide variety of musicians. The advent of bebop appeared not to trouble him and if he never fully adapted his style he certainly gave his front-line colleagues few problems. In the early 40s Catlett was a member of the superb Teddy Wilson Sextet; when this engagement ended he led his own bands until he joined Louis Armstrong's All Stars in 1947. He remained with Armstrong until 1949 when the years of all-night jam sessions began to catch up with him. Ill or not, Catlett continued to work, but on 25 March 1951 he collapsed and died while visiting friends backstage at a Oran 'Hot Lips' Page benefit concert at the Chicago Opera House. Although a brilliant technician, Catlett chose to play in a deceptively simple style. With the fleet, smoothly-swinging Wilson sextet he was discreet and self-effacing; with Goodman he rolled the band remorselessly onward, with Armstrong he gave each of his fellow musicians an individualized accompaniment that defied them not to swing. Instantly identifiable, especially through his thundercrack rimshots, Catlett always swung mightily. On stage, he was a spectacular showman, clothing his massive frame in green plaid suits, tossing his sticks high in the air during solos and generally enjoying himself.

Album: with Louis Armstrong *Satchmo At Symphony Hall* (1947). Compilations: with Lionel Hampton *Historical Recording Sessions* (1939), with Benny Goodman *Benny And Sid 'Roll 'Em'* (1941), with Teddy Wilson *B Flat Swing* (1944).

Celestin, Oscar 'Papa'

b. 1 January 1884, Napoleonville, Louisiana, USA, d. 15 December 1954. When he was 20-years-old Celestin relocated to New Orleans and having previously dabbled in music on a variety of instruments, he finally chose the trumpet. Working first in marching bands, including the Indiana Brass Band, Celestin soon attracted a good deal of attention and in 1910 formed the first of several bands he would lead. In 1917 his band, the Original Tuxedo Brass Band, featured many leading musicians of the formative years of jazz. Although he recorded in the early 20s, Celestin stayed close to his origins, mostly restricting his tours to the southern states. In the 30s he worked outside music but continued to play part-time. After a street accident in the mid-40s, he began playing more and recorded again. Celestin benefited from the resurgence of interest in early jazz during the New Orleans Revival movement and, apart from recording, also appeared on radio and television. Although his technique was rather limited, as was his inventiveness, Celestin was a good ensemble player and the sidemen in his bands responded to his cheerful and encouraging leadership.

Selected compilations: *Papa Celestin And His New Orleans Ragtime Band* (Jazzology 1986), *Papa Celestin And His New Orleans Jazz Band* (Folklyric 1986), *Celestin's Original Tuxedo Jazz Band (1926-28)* (VJM 1988), with Sam Morgan *New Orleans Classics* (Azure 1992).

Ceroli, Nick

b. 22 December 1939, Warren, Ohio, USA, d. 11 August 1985. Although adept in all settings, Ceroli's early career marked him out as a big band drummer. In the early 60s he worked with Ray Anthony and Gerald Wilson before joining Stan Kenton's LA Neophonic Orchestra in 1965. For the next four years he was with Herb Alpert's Tijuana Brass but then settled in Los Angeles, where he was soon in demand as a studio musician and also in a wide range of jazz groups for club and recording dates. Among the musicians eager to hire him for small group work were Zoot Sims, Richie Kamuca, Warne Marsh, Pete Christlieb (with whom he recorded a sizzling performance at a Los Angeles club, Dino's, in 1983) and Bill Berry. But his experience and skill in big band music drew him inevitably into that area of performing, and his association with Bob Florence produced some of the finest big band jazz of the late 70s and early 80s. His playing on 'Party Hearty' on Florence's *Concerts By The Sea* album is an object lesson for all aspiring big band drummers. Ceroli's interest in all kinds of music was comprehensive; he owned a huge record collection of music by Beethoven and Duke Ellington, and he communicated his enthusiasm through his playing. A fluid, supple drummer, Ceroli gave a tremendous lift to any band he worked with. His death in 1985 came when he was still very much in his prime.

Selected albums: with Bill Berry *Shortcake* (1978), with Pete Christlieb, Warne Marsh *Apogee* (1978), with Bob Florence *Concerts By The Sea* (1979), with Christlieb *Dino's '83* (1983).

Chaloff, Serge

b. 24 November 1923, Boston, Massachusetts, USA, d. 16 July 1957. Coming from a musical family, Chaloff studied formally on piano and clarinet but, entranced by the playing of Harry Carney, he taught himself to play baritone saxophone. In the early 40s he worked with a number of swing era big bands; however, his interest in the musical developments of the beboppers drew him to Boyd Raeburn's adventurous band, which he joined in 1945. Thereafter he played with Georgie Auld and

Jimmy Dorsey, extending the appeal of his instrument through his ability to play complex material without losing either his feeling for swing or the sonority that Carney achieved on baritone. In 1947 Chaloff became a member of Woody Herman's Four Brothers band and for the next two years he was the most talked-about baritone player in jazz. Later he worked with Count Basie, but Chaloff had fallen victim to drug addiction and the remainder of his career was blighted. He taught for a while, continued to record, mostly with small groups, and proved on these recordings that his talent was undiminished, indeed, it was continuing to develop. Partially paralysed, Chaloff appeared at a Four Brothers reunion date in February 1957 but on 16 July that year he died.

Selected albums: *Pumpernickel* (1947), *Gabardine And Serge* (1947), *The Most* (1949), *The Fable Of Mabel* (Black Lion 1954), *Boston Blow-Up* (1955), *Blue Serge* (1956).

Chambers, Henderson

b. 1 May 1908, Alexandria, Louisiana, USA, d. 19 October 1967. After gaining experience, playing the trombone with a number of territory bands, including those of Zack Whyte, Speed Webb and Tiny Bradshaw, Chambers settled in New York in 1939. During the next few years he worked with a number of bands, notably Louis Armstrong's. During the 40s and 50s he worked with small and big bands led by men such as Edmond Hall, Don Redman, Sy Oliver, Lucky Millinder, Count Basie and Cab Calloway. Additionally, he played for short spells, sometimes as substitute, with Duke Ellington and in the 60s with Ray Charles and Basie again. He appeared on numerous recording sessions, including some outstanding ones with Buck Clayton. A powerful player and a valued member of the brass section of any band with which he played, Chambers was less well-known as a soloist, although when given the opportunity he showed that he could shine as well as most of his contemporaries.

Selected albums: *Buck Clayton Jam Session* (1953), with Ray Charles *Ingredients In A Recipe For Soul* (1963).

Chambers, Joe

b. 25 June 1942, Stoneacre, Virginia, USA. Joseph Arthur Chambers studied music theory at the Philadelphia Conservatory and the American University in Washington while drumming with the JFK Quintet. In 1964 he moved to New York to play with Eric Dolphy, Freddie Hubbard and Andrew Hill, doyens of the Blue Note label, while also attending Hall Overton's composition classes. Chambers shone on vibist Bobby Hutcherson's records as both drummer and composer, contributing the title tracks to *Dialogue* and *Oblique* and a masterful, side-long suite to *Components* that pursued Hall Overton's Third Stream inclinations between Thelonious Monk and Igor Stravinsky. Since the early 70s he has also appeared with and composed for Max Roach's percussion ensemble M'Boom. In 1974 his 'The Almoravid' was played at Carnegie Hall. A ferociously accurate drummer with a feel both for swing and space, his compositional imagination informs every nuance.

Albums: with Bobby Hutcherson *Dialogue* (1965), with Hutcherson *Components* (1966), with Hutcherson *Oblique* (1967), *The Almoravid* (1973), *Double Exposure* (1978), with M'Boom *Collage* (1984), *Phantom Of The City* (Candid 1991).

Chambers, Paul

b. Paul Laurence Dunbar Chambers Jnr., 22 April 1935, Pittsburgh, Pennsylvania, USA, d. 4 January 1969, New York City, New York, USA. Chambers' early death deprived jazz of one of its most influential, creative and lyrical bassists who had been present on several of the most important and enduring recordings of the 50s and early 60s. He grew up in Detroit, where he studied tuba before taking up the string bass. He worked with Paul Quinichette (1954), Bennie Green (1955), Jay and Kai (J.J. Johnson and Kai Winding) (1955), George Wallington (1955), and was with Miles Davis from 1955-63. He then joined Wynton Kelly, another Davis alumnus, until 1966. The Miles Davis Quintet of which Chambers was a member was then nicknamed 'The D & D Band' (drink and drugs), but despite his heroin habit Chambers was a fine, dependable bass player. Whilst with Davis he popularised the use of arco (bowed) solos. His light, agile phrasing was coupled with a firm tone which provided strong, telling accompaniment, a sturdy foundation for the explorations of soloists such as Davis and John Coltrane, who wrote the tune 'Mr P.C.' in his honour. During his short but prolific and brilliant career he also worked with, amongst many others, Art Pepper, Sonny Rollins, Bill Evans, Sonny Clark and Johnny Griffin.

Selected albums: *Whims Of Chambers* (1956), *The East West Controversy* (Xanadu 1957), *Paul Chambers Quartet* (1957), *Bass On Top* (Blue Note 1957), with Cannonball Adderley *Ease It* (Affinity 1959), with John Coltrane *High Step* (1975, rec 1955-56).

Charles, Dennis

b. 4 December 1933, St. Croix, Virgin Islands. Charles moved to New York in 1945 but his roots are nevertheless Caribbean: he began by playing congas in calypso and mambo bands. He taught himself on the drumkit and a year later (1955) was playing in Harlem with Cecil Taylor and recorded on the pianist's first album. In 1957 he played at the Newport Jazz Festival with Taylor, Steve Lacy and Buell Neidlinger and in 1961 performed with Taylor and Archie Shepp in the Living Theatre production of *The Connection*. In 1962 he supplied calypso beats for Sonny Rollins. Unfortunately the theme of *The Connection* (heroin addiction) proved a little too close to home and Charles dropped out of the music scene for over a decade. He re-emerged as one of the Jazz Doctors, an ensemble that included Billy Bang and Frank Lowe, in the early 80s. In 1982 he recorded *Bangception*, a delightful duet album, with Bang on violin. Charles's incisive, regular time is a perfect foil to wildmen like Taylor and Bang, having the imagination and suppleness to both answer and contain them. Later recordings with Bang's quartet (*Valve No. 10*) and new alto saxophonist Rob Brown (*Breath Rhyme*) were capped by his own debut as leader on 1991's *Queen Mary*.

Albums: with Cecil Taylor *Looking Ahead!* (1959), with Taylor *The World of Cecil Taylor* (1960), with Billy Bang *Rainbow Gladiator* (1981), with Bang *Bangception* (1982), with the Jazz Doctors *Intensive Care* (1983), *Queen Mary* (1991).

Charles, Teddy

b. Theodore Charles Cohen, 13 April 1928, Chicopee Falls, Massachusetts, USA. After studying percussion at the New York Juilliard School of Music, Charles worked in a number of late-swing era big bands, including those led by Benny Goodman and Artie Shaw. From the late 40s onwards he performed with numerous small groups, some of which were still dedicated to swing, but his interest lay in more progressive musical styles. Although he worked with many beboppers, Charles was attracted to the possibilities of extending the range of jazz through advanced composing techniques. Apart from experimenting with modality himself he encouraged others, such as George Russell, in similar areas. The complexities of such music made Charles appear inaccessible to many jazz fans and his reputation as a composer and arranger is valued more within the profession than with the general public. Conversely, his driving vibes playing has strong audience appeal even if he gives it rather less of his time. From the mid-50s onwards Charles became involved in record production, working with leading modern jazz artists such as Herbie Hancock and John Coltrane.

Albums: *Teddy Cohen/Charles And His Trio* (1951), *The Teddy Charles Quartet* (1952), *The Teddy Charles Trio* (1953), *Teddy Charles' West Coasters* (1953), *New Directions* (1953), *Collaboration: West* (Original Jazz Classics 1953), *The Dual Role Of Bob Brookmeyer* (1954), *Evolution* (Original Jazz Classics 1955), *The Teddy Charles Tentet* (Atlantic 1956), *A Word From Bird* (1956), *Teddy Charles' Vibe-rant Quintet* (1957), *Salute To Hamp: Flyin' Home* (1958), with Booker Little, Booker Ervin *Sounds Of Inner City* (1960), *On Campus!: Ivy League Concert* (1960), *Live At The Verona Jazz Festival 1988* (Soul Note 1988).

Chase, Bill

b. 1935, Boston, Massachusetts, USA, d. 9 August 1974, Jackson, Minnesota, USA. In the mid-50s Chase studied trumpet at Berklee College Of Music under Herb Pomeroy. Towards the end of the decade he played with Maynard Ferguson, Stan Kenton and Woody Herman. Throughout the 60s he frequently returned to the Herman band but turned increasingly to jazz-rock, later forming his own band Chase in 1971; three years later he toured with a reformed version of the band. It was while on tour that, on 9 August 1974, he and other members of the band - John Emma (guitar), Walter Clark (drums) and Wally York (keyboards) - were killed in an airplane crash.

Selected albums: with Maynard Ferguson *A Message From Newport* (1958), with Woody Herman *Woody's Winners* (1965); as Chase *Chase* (1971), *Ennea* (1972), *Pure Music* (1974).

Chase, Tommy

b. 22 March 1947, Manchester, England. Largely self-taught at the drums, Chase had to wait for a jazz revival pioneered by the next generation to bring his chosen genre - steaming soul jazz - into favour. Professional since the mid-60s he began playing pure jazz in London from the early 70s, with tenor saxophonist Art Themen and trumpeter Harry Beckett. The jazz dancers of the mid-80s responded to a band of young-bloods (including tenor saxophonist Alan Barnes, 1983-86), bringing out the lindy-hop basis of break-dancing to tunes like 'Night In Tunisia'. Later on, his use of a Hammond organ featuring the excellent Gary Baldwin, confirmed what many people had suspected: boasting that he was the Art Blakey of British jazz, in actual fact he is its Dr Feelgood - playing unpretentious, driving music with a great feel for stage dynamics. His quartet in 1992 is arguably his finest, featuring the inspired driving string bass of Australian Les Miller, Chris Watson (guitar) and Dave Lewis (tenor saxophone/saxello). Chase is in complete control of his drumkit, he can change pace in breathtaking fashion, willing his musicians on to follow his extraordinary timing.

Albums: with Ray Warleigh *One Way* (Spotlite 1983), *Hard* (Boplicity 1984), *Drive!* (Paladin 1985), *Groove Merchant* (Stiff 1987), *Rebel Fire* (Moles 1990).

Cheatham, Doc

b. Adolphus Anthony Cheatham, 13 June 1905, Nashville, Tennessee, USA. Cheatham's remarkably long career began in the early 20s when he worked in vaudeville theatre pit bands, often accompanying important blues singers of the era. In the middle of the decade he worked in Chicago where he encountered the main influence on his life, Louis Armstrong. Until this point Cheatham had dabbled with the saxophone, playing soprano with Ma Rainey, but now he concentrated on trumpet, developing a striking technique but never sacrificing his lovely tone. During the second half of the 20s and on into the early 30s, Cheatham played with many bands, including those of Wilbur De Paris, Chick Webb, Sam Wooding (who took him a tour of Europe in 1928-29), and Cab Calloway, with whom he remained for six years, during which time he again toured Europe. In 1939 Cheatham became a member of Teddy Wilson's big band and followed this with a spell in the equally elegant orchestra of Benny Carter. Through the 40s he worked in big and small bands, bringing to each job the graceful presence that was echoed in his playing. In New York in the 60s he led his own band for several years and also played often with Benny Goodman. Contrary to the limitations age usually imposes on brass players, his public performances and numerous recording sessions proved that he was, in fact, playing even better than before. In the 70s and on into the 80s he defied age and changing tastes in music, visiting Europe for festival and club dates and playing with his still-faultless technique and magnificent sound.

Selected albums: *Doc Cheatham* (1950), *Adolphus 'Doc' Cheatham* (1973), *Hey Doc!* (Black And Blue 1975), with Sammy Price *Doc And Sammy* (1976), *Black Beauty* (Sackville 1979), *John, Doc And Herb* (1979), *It's A Good Life* (1982), *Too Marvellous For Words* (1982), *I've Got A Crush On You* (1982), *The Fabulous Doc Cheatham* (Parkwood 1983), with George

Kelly *Highlights In Jazz* (1985), *Art Hodes, Carrie Smith And Doc Cheatham* (1985), *A Tribute To Billie Holiday* (1987), with Price *In New Orleans* (1988), *Dear Doc* (Orange Blue 1989), *I've Got A Crush On You Vol. 2* (New York 1989), with Jim Galloway *At The Bern Jazz Festival* (Sackville 1992, rec 1983-85), *The Eighty Seven Years Of Doc Cheatham* (Columbia 1993), *Doc Cheatham Live* (Natasha 1993).

Cherry, Don

b. 18 November 1936, Oklahoma City, Oklahoma, USA. Cherry began playing trumpet while still attending high school in Los Angeles, where he was raised. He also played piano and some of his first public performances were on this instrument when he worked in R&B bands. An early musical associate was Billy Higgins and in the mid-50s the two men, by then playing bebop, joined Ornette Coleman and began to adapt their musical thought to the new concept of free jazz. Cherry and Higgins played on Coleman's 1958 quintet album, *Something Else!!!!*, an album which represents an early and important flowering of the freedom principle. Coleman's group became a quartet, the fourth member being Charlie Haden. The quartet's success was recognized by an extended engagement at New York's Five Spot Cafe which began in November 1959 and continued into the following spring when Higgins was replaced by Ed Blackwell. Later, Haden too was succeeded by Scott La Faro and then Jimmy Garrison. The group made several important albums, which established the concept of free jazz as a major 60s movement in jazz and also demonstrated the qualities of the individual musicians. During this same period, Cherry recorded with John Coltrane and with Archie Shepp, in whose group he played alongside John Tchicai and Bill Dixon. In 1964 Cherry and Tchicai joined Albert Ayler's group for a recording session which was later used as soundtrack for the film, *New York Eye And Ear Control*. Later that year Cherry visited Europe with Ayler and also recorded *Vibrations* with him. Cherry's next association was with Gato Barbieri, with whom he led a small band which toured and recorded in Europe and the USA. While in Europe, he also worked with George Russell. Towards the end of the decade, Cherry began touring Europe, Africa and Asia, absorbing ethnic musical concepts and learning to play a variety of instruments including wooden flutes from northern Europe and the doussn'gouni (a kind of guitar). He was also using a Pakistani pocket trumpet with a distorted mouthpiece, an instrument which he favoured in much of his subsequent work. He began to adapt Asian ideas and sounds into his own music, becoming one of the few jazz musicians to do so successfully. By the early 70s, Cherry, who was then living in Sweden with his wife, Moki, was the most authoritative voice in the development of a musical style which was eventually established as 'world music'. Together with his wife, he created performances which depended almost as much upon visual and other senses as upon sounds. In the mid-70s Cherry again teamed up with Haden and Blackwell and, with Dewey Redman, formed a quartet which created new concepts of Coleman's music alongside original material. This group, which took its name, Old And New Dreams, from the title of

its first album, was only one of Cherry's musical ventures of the late 70s and early 80s. He also played with rock bands, guested with Abdullah Ibrahim and formed a trio, Codona, with Collin Walcott and Nana Vasconcelos. His continuing association with Blackwell, himself a gatherer of musical concepts and instruments, added to Cherry's status as a major figure in world music in the late 80s and early 90s. In his trumpet playing, especially on the pocket trumpet, Cherry might not dazzle in the manner of many of his contemporaries who remained more closely linked to bop but he nevertheless achieves a bright, incisive sound. As a composer, both in the formal sense of that term and in the manner in which he creates musical happenings, Cherry is one of the most distinctive contributors to contemporary music.

Albums: *Something Else!!!! The Music Of Ornette Coleman* (1958), with Coleman *Change Of The Century* (1959), with Coleman *Free Jazz* (1960), with John Coltrane *The Avant Garde* (1960), *Future I* (1963), with Albert Ayler *New York Ear And Eye Control* (1964), *Complete Communion* (1965), *Where Is Brooklyn?* (1966), *Live At The Montmartre Vols 1 and 2* (Magnetic 1966), *Eternal Rhythm* (1968), with Charlie Haden *Liberation Music Orchestra* (1969), *Human Music* (1969-70), *Mu* (Affinity 1970), *Orient* (Affinity 1973), *Eternal Now* (1973), *Hear And Now* (1976), *Brown Rice* (1976), *Live In Anhara* (1978, recorded 1969), as Codona *Codona i* (1980), with Ed Blackwell *El Corazón* (ECM 1982), *Codona ii* (1982), *Codona iii* (1983), *Home Boy* (1985), *A Tribute To Blackwell* (1987), *Art Deco* (A&M 1988), *Multikulti* (A&M 1990), *Dona Nostra* (ECM 1994).

Childers, Buddy

b. Marion Childers, 12 February 1926, St. Louis, Missouri, USA. He began playing trumpet as a small child and was soon performing in bands in Belleville, Illinois, just across the Mississippi River from his home town. In 1942, at the age of 16, Childers was hired by Stan Kenton. Although he would later wryly suggest that this was because all the other trumpeters were being drafted into the armed forces, his new boss thought enough of him to make him lead trumpet in his powerful band. On and off, Childers played with Kenton until the mid-50s but during this same period also worked in bands led by Woody Herman, Tommy Dorsey and others. Settling in Los Angeles, he began working in film and television studios but found time for occasional jazz gigs and recording dates. The role of the lead trumpet is such that his importance is often more apparent to fellow musicians than to audiences. For this reason, Childers is one of several unsung heroes of big band jazz.

Albums: with Stan Kenton *Portraits On Standards* (1953), *Music Of Bill Holman* (1953-54), *Buddy Childers Quintet* (1955), with Toshiko Akiyoshi, Lew Tabackin *Tanuki's Night Out* (1981).

Chilton, John

b. 16 July 1932, London, England. A sound trumpeter and skilful arranger, Chilton led his own band in the mid-50s before joining the Bruce Turner Jump Band in 1958. He remained with Turner for five years, playing and writing arrangements. In the early 60s he was with Alex Welsh and Mike Daniels before forming another band of his own. At the end of the 60s he became co-leader with Wally Fawkes of a band they named the Feetwarmers, taking over as leader in 1974. Almost at once, Chilton became musical director for George Melly and ever since has toured, recorded and broadcast with the singer. So far as the wider public is concerned, Chilton's place in British jazz may rest on his relationship with Melly but for the *cogniscenti* it is his role as a writer and tireless researcher into jazz history that makes him a figure of considerable importance. Amongst his many publications are *Who's Who Of Jazz: Storyville To Swing Street*, a work which ably demonstrates the awe-inspiring meticulousness of his research; *Louis: The Louis Armstrong Story*, a biography written in collaboration with Max Jones; *Jazz*, a history written for the 'Teach Yourself' series of publications; *Billie's Blues,* a partial biography of Billie Holiday, plus historical accounts of the Jenkins Orphanage bands, McKinney's Cotton Pickers, the Bob Crosby Bobcats, and definitive biographies of Sidney Bechet and Coleman Hawkins. In the early 90s Chilton was still on the road with Melly and still writing about his branch of jazz, on which he is an acknowledged expert.

Chisholm, George

b. 29 March 1915, Glasgow, Scotland. In his early 20s Chisholm arrived in London, where he played trombone in the popular dance bands led by Teddy Joyce and Bert Ambrose. Inspired originally by recordings of Jack Teagarden, Chisholm naturally gravitated towards the contemporary jazz scene and was thus on hand for informal sessions and even the occasional recording date with visiting American stars such as Benny Carter, Coleman Hawkins and Fats Waller. During World War II he played with the Royal Air Force's dance band, the Squadronaires, with whom he remained in the post-war years. Later he became a regular studio and session musician, playing with several of the BBC's house bands. In the late 50s and on through the 60s Chisholm's exuberant sense of humour led to a succession of television appearances, both as musician and comic, and if his eccentric dress, black tights and George Robey-style bowler hat caused jazz fans some displeasure, the music he played was always excellent. During this period he made many records with leading British and American jazz artists including Sandy Brown and Wild Bill Davison. In the 80s, despite having had heart surgery, Chisholm played on, often working with Keith Smith's Hefty Jazz or his own band, the Gentlemen of Jazz. He continued to delight audiences with his fluid technique and his ability to blend an urgent attack with a smooth style of playing and endless touches of irreverent humour. He was awarded an OBE in 1984. In 1990 he was still on the road, touring with visiting Americans, such as Spike Robinson. Soon afterwards, however, his state of health forced him to retire from active playing but did nothing to damage his high spirits and sense of humour.
Selected albums: *George Chisholm And His Band* (1956), *Stars Play Jazz* (1961), *George Chisholm* (1967), with Sandy Brown *Hair At Its Hairiest* (1968), *Along The Chisholm Trail* (1971), *In A Mellow Mood* (1973), *Trombone Showcase* (1976), *The Swingin' Mr C* (Zodiac 1986), *That's A-Plenty!* (Zodiac 1987), with John Petters *Swinging Down Memory Lane* (CMJ 1989). Compilations: with Benny Carter *Swingin' At Maida Vale* (1937), *Fats Waller In London* (1938), with Squadronaires *There's Something In The Air* (1941-50).

Chittison, Herman

b. 15 October 1908, Flemingsburg, Kentucky, USA, d. 8 March 1967. After studying piano formally at school and college, Chittison joined Zack Whyte's Chocolate Beau Brummels in 1928. He stayed with Whyte for three years and then freelanced as an accompanying pianist to singers Adelaide Hall and Ethel Waters, and also made recordings with Clarence Williams. In 1934 he joined the Willie Lewis band, which was bound for Europe. Although he remained associated with Lewis for the next few years Chittison continued to work with other jazzmen, including Louis Armstrong, and also began a career as a solo recording artist. A band he co-led with Bill Coleman, the Harlem Rhythm Makers, worked extensively in Egypt, but with the outbreak of World War II he returned to the USA. From this point onwards, Chittison rarely left the east coast, leading his own small group, working as a solo, occasionally accompanying visiting singers, and appearing on a weekly radio show. He was a deft and often exciting soloist.
Selected albums: *The Herman Chittison Trio* (1944), *Keyboard Capers* (1950), *The Elegant Piano Styling Of Herman Chittison, Volumes 1 & 2* (both 1962), *The Elegant Piano Styling Of Herman Chittison, Volume 3* (1964). Compilations: At The Piano (Holmia Classics 1986), with Zack Whyte *Jammin' For The Jackpot (1929)*, *In Paris 1925-37* (1988), *Piano Genius* (Misicraft 1988), *The Master Of Stride Piano* (Meritt 1988), *Cocktail Piano Favourites* (CBS 1989), *Herman Chittison 1933-41* (Classic Jazz Masters 1993).

Christenson, Jon

b. 20 March 1943, Oslo, Norway. Christenson won the Norwegian Jazz Amateur Competition at the age of 17 and soon became the regular drummer behind visiting American musicians. For the last two decades he has pursued two concurrent musical careers. On the international jazz festival circuit he has played with artists as varied as Dexter Gordon, Gary Burton, Sonny Rollins, Terje Rypdal and Stan Getz. But perhaps more importantly he has become the central drummer in the impressionist European style characterized by the ECM label, drumming for Keith Jarrett's European Quartet, Eberhard Weber's Colours, and Jan Garbarek's Quartet. Voted number 1 drummer by the Polish magazine *Jazz Forum* from 1973-84, Christenson remains one of the most versatile jazz drummers around.
Selected albums: *Masqualero* (1983), *Bande A Part* (1985), with Keith Jarrett *Personal Mountains* (1989).

Christian, Charlie

b. 29 July 1916, Bonham, Texas, USA, d. 2 March 1942. Much of Christian's early life is shadowy but he grew up in Oklahoma City where, thanks to the research of eminent writer Ralph Ellison, something of his deprived background has emerged. His father, who was blind, was an itinerant guitarist-singer and Christian's two brothers were also musically-inclined. Too poor to buy an instrument of his own, Christian made a guitar out of cigar boxes and soon developed an impressive if localized reputation amongst musicians. In the early 30s he worked professionally with territory bands led by Anna Mae Winburn, who later led the International Sweethearts Of Rhythm, Nat Towles, Alphonso Trent, with whom he played bass, and others. As early as 1937 he was experimenting with electrical amplification and had built upon his early reputation. In 1939, at the urging of Mildred Bailey, he was heard at the Ritz Cafe in Oklahoma City by entrepreneur and jazz enthusiast John Hammond, who tried to persuade Benny Goodman to hire him for a Los Angeles recording date. Goodman wasn't interested, disliking both the concept of an electric guitar and Christian's appearance - he favoured vividly-coloured clothes. Hammond persisted and that evening he helped Christian haul his cumbersome amplifiers onto the stage at the Victor Hugo Restaurant in Beverly Hills, where Goodman was appearing. When Goodman returned to the stand after the interval he was dismayed and angry but was too professional to create a scene and instead counted off 'Rose Room', a tune he expected the newcomer not to know. When it was Christian's turn to solo, he played 25 brilliant choruses that had the audience, the other musicians, and Goodman, yelling for more. This performance of 'Rose Room', unfortunately not recorded that night, lasted 45 minutes and, not surprisingly, Christian was thereafter a member of the Goodman entourage. Goodman's small groups had been steadily increasing in size and Christian was featured in the Sextet. Being with Goodman gave him maximum exposure to the public and enormous fame. However, Christian was more interested in new musical developments and became an important member of the underground movement which eventually flowered into bebop. Sadly, Christian was unable to adjust to the fame and fortune that had come his way. Apart from playing music whenever and wherever he could, he indulged in alcohol and promiscuous behaviour, rarely slept and by the middle of 1941 was seriously ill with tuberculosis. In hospital his friends decided to continue their numerous parties at his bedside. It was all too much for Christian's wasted constitution and he died on 2 March 1942. It is difficult to overstate the importance of Charlie Christian in the history of jazz and popular music. His after-hours sessions at Minton's Playhouse in New York, some of which were recorded by a fan, show him to have been an important fellow-architect of bebop with Charlie Parker and Dizzy Gillespie. A brilliantly inventive soloist, his deceptively simple, single-line solos radicalized thinking not only amongst fellow guitarists but also among front-line soloists. Although he was not the first guitarist to electrically amplify his instrument, he was one of a tiny number to achieve widespread attention and, thanks to his record-ings with Goodman, this concept attained a level of popularity which it has never lost. Any of his records stands as an example of a genius of jazz sadly cut off before his full potential had been realized.

Selected albums: *Lester Young And Charlie Christian (1939-40)*, with Benny Goodman *Live (1939-41)*, with Goodman *Charlie Christian (1939-41)* (Giants Of Jazz 1987), with Goodman *Solo Flight (1939-41)*, with others *Swing To Bop (c.1941)*, (NB: those with Benny Goodman are often reissued under Christian's name), *Live Sessions, Mintons* (1974), *1941 Historical Performances* (Vogue 1988), *1941 Live Sessions* (Vogue 1988), *Live At Minton's 1941* (Jazz Anthology 1989), *Genius Of The Electric Guitar* (CBS 1988), with Lester Young *Together* (Jazz Archives 1992), *Airchecks And Private Recordings* (Recording Arts 1993), *Guitar Wizard* (Le Jazz 1993), *Swing To The Bop* (Natasha 1993).

Christlieb, Pete

b. 16 February 1945, Los Angeles, California, USA. Formally educated in music as a violinist, Christlieb then began playing tenor saxophone in his early teenage years. In his late teens he became a professional musician working with big bands and small groups under the leadership of Si Zentner, Jerry Grey, Woody Herman and others. In 1967 he became a regular member of Louie Bellson's big band, an association which lasted for the next two decades. During this period Christlieb worked with many other leaders, among them Doc Severinsen, whose *Tonight Show* band included many of the best musicians on the west coast, Count Basie, Benny Goodman, Bill Berry, Mel Lewis and Bob Florence. He also played in small groups at clubs and for record dates, most notably a band he co-led with Warne Marsh whose *Apogee* was well received. He regularly led his own quartet, which included Mike Melvoin, Jim Hughart and Nick Ceroli. A technically proficient player, Christlieb has a zestful, attacking style which makes his playing on up-tempo numbers particularly exciting, whilst his ballads always have an undercurrent of urgency.

Selected albums: *Jazz City: A Quartet With Pete Christlieb* (1971), with Warne Marsh *Apogee* (1978), with Marsh *Conversations With Warne, Volume 1* (Criss Cross 1978), with Bob Florence *Concerts By The Sea* (1979), with Florence *Westlake* (1981), *Going My Way* (1982), *Live At Dino's '83* (1983), *Live* (Capri 1991).

Christmann, Günter

b. 1942, Srem, Poland. Trombonist and bassist Christmann, although influenced by the new jazz of John Coltrane, Ornette Coleman, and Cecil Taylor, was amongst the first European improvisers to reject the idea of free music as pure emotional catharsis. Though still committed to spontaneous creation he aims for the clarity and concentrated expression of such 20th-century composers as Anton Webern and Arnold Schoenberg and has worked as much on the *avant garde* 'straight music' circuit as in the jazz clubs. He has made new developments in trombone playing by doctoring his sound with electronics. His group Vario, whose line-up fluctuates constantly, aims to move between the arts, and often features the interaction of musicians and dancers. Christmann resides in Germany and has been a member of Alexander Von Schlippenbach's Globe Unity Orchestra since 1973.

Albums: with Detlef Schönenberg *We Play* (1973), with Schönenberg and Harald Bojé *Remarks* (1975), with Schönenberg *Topic* (1976), with Schönenberg *Live At Moers Festival '76* (1977), *Solomusik Für Posaune Und Kontrabass* (1977), with Tristan Honsinger *Earmeals* (1978), with Gerd Dudek, Albert Mangelsdorff, Kenny Wheeler, Paul Rutherford and Manfred Schoof *Horns* (1979), *Off* (1980), with Maarten Altena and Paul Lovens *Weavers* (1980), *Vario II* (1981), *Vario* (1986, recorded 1983-85), with Torsten Müller *Carte Blanche* (1986).

Christy, June

b. Shirley Luster, 20 November 1925, Springfield, Illinois, USA, d. 21 June 1990. Christy first came to prominence with the bands of Boyd Raeburn and Stan Kenton, although her chirpy singing style sometimes sat oddly with the earnestly progressive experiments of her employers. Her bright, bubbling personality glowed through her performances and she was especially effective on up-tempo swingers. Yet she was also adept on reflective ballads and was never afraid to have fun with a song. With Kenton she had successes in all of these areas. One of her first recordings with the band was 'Tampico', which became a million-seller; another was 'How High The Moon'. During the late 40s she was one of the band's main attractions. Kenton and his chief arranger, Pete Rugolo, responded by providing effective settings for her voice which, while of limited range, was engaging and her performances were always highly professional. In January 1947 she married Kenton tenor saxophonist Bob Cooper, with whom she made some fine recordings backed by his small group. After leaving Kenton in 1948 Christy worked as a solo artist, making many successful recordings for Capitol Records, including three US Top 20 albums, *Something Cool* (imaginatively arranged for her by Rugolo), *The Misty Miss Christy* and *June - Fair And Warmer!*. After many years in retirement, she died in June 1990.

Albums: *Shorty Rogers Plus Kenton And Christy* (1950), *Something Cool* (Capitol 1955), with Stan Kenton *Duet* (1955), *The Misty Miss Christy* (Capitol 1956), *June - Fair And Warmer!* (1957), *Gone For The Day* (1957), *June's Got Rhythm* (1958), *The Song Is June!* (1959), with Kenton *The Road Show, Volumes 1 & 2* (1959), *June Christy Recalls Those Kenton Days* (Capitol 1959), *Ballads For Night People* (1959), *The Cool School* (1960), *Off Beat* (1961), *Do-Re-Mi* (1961, film soundtrack), *That Time Of Year* (1961), *Big Band Specials* (1962), *The Intimate June Christy* (1962), *Something Broadway, Something Latin* (1965), *Impromptu* (Discovery 1977), *Willow Weep For Me* (c.1979), *Interlude* (Discovery 1985). Compilations: *This Is June Christy* (Capitol 1956), *The Best Of June Christy* (Capitol 1962), *The Capitol Years* (Capitol 1989), *A Lovely Way To Spend An Evening* (Jasmine 1989), *Something Cool* (Capitol 1991).

Clare, Alan

b. 31 May 1921, London, England, d. 29 November 1993. A self-taught pianist, Clare became a professional musician at the age of 15 and during the next few years became a familiar figure on the London jazz scene. He played with Carlo Krahmer, Sid Phillips and others in the early 40s before military service intervened. Wounded soon after D-Day, he returned to civilian life, playing in the comedy band led by Sid Milward and also began a long sporadic association with Stéphane Grappelli. From the 50s onwards, Clare was busy playing jazz in small groups, some of which he led, mostly in nightclubs but also appearing occasionally on television. An exceptionally gifted pianist with a light, subtle touch, he had a seemingly endless knowledge of tunes and chord progressions. Allied to a gift for accompaniment and the ability to play with unflagging swing, Clare was an outstanding figure of British jazz. His chosen milieu, however, and the relatively few recordings he made, often deleted with indecent haste, conspired to keep his gleaming talent from the widespread audience he so richly deserved. Albums: *Jazz Around The Clock* (1958), with Stéphane Grappelli *Stardust* (1973), *Midnight Moods* (Ditto 1988).

Clare, Kenny

b. 8 June 1929, London, England, d. 21 December 1984. Clare played drums as a teenager and in 1949 joined the popular broadcasting danceband led by Oscar Rabin. In 1954 he moved over to the Jack Parnell band for a while before settling into the John Dankworth orchestra. He was with Dankworth until the early 60s, when he joined Ted Heath. During this period he also recorded with a band he co-led with fellow drummer Ronnie Stephenson. Later in the decade, he became a member of the Clarke-Boland Big Band. From 1972 he worked with many bands, large and small, played in studio orchestras for recording sessions, television and radio programmes, and on film soundtracks. He also toured extensively as accompanist to Tom Jones. Amongst his recording dates are sessions with Ella Fitzgerald, Joe Pass and Stéphane Grappelli. Clare was a gifted all-round percussionist, filled with enormous enthusiasm.

Selected albums: with Ronnie Stephenson *Drum Spectacular* (1966), with the Clarke-Boland Big Band *Off Limits* (1970), with Colin Busby *Big Swing Favourites* (1984).

Clark, Sonny

b. Conrad Yeatis, 21 July 1931, Herminie, nr Elizabeth, Pennsylvania, USA, d. 13 January 1963. An underrated piano genius of the hard-bop era, Clark cast a glorious ray of sunshine over some of the Blue Note label's most memorable sessions. Art Tatum, one of his childhood heroes, and Count Basie, whose big band radio broadcasts were a popular feature of his youth, are two pianists whose influence *can* be heard in his minimal and understated style. But his succinct and melodic approach took as much from wind players as other pianists, his left hand providing the barest of occasional accompaniments, while he stressed instead an elegant and sophisticated single note approach. He moved to the west coast in the early 50s, and soon began working with saxophonist Vido Musso and bassist Oscar Pettiford. Throughout the mid-50s, he was an active element of the west coast scene, touring with clarinettist Buddy De Franco, saxophonist Sonny Criss and others. In 1957 he moved to New York, working first with vocalist Dinah Washington, and enjoying a new boom of attention, leading various small groups (his *Sonny's Crib* features John Coltrane) and working as a sideman with saxophonists Sonny Rollins, Clifford Jordan, and Hank Mobley and trombonist Curtis Fuller, before the combined ravishes of alcohol and hard-drugs took their toll. Recommended listening are *Leapin' And Lopin'* on Blue Note – an inspired 1961 date with saxophonists Ike Quebec and Charlie Rouse – the popular *Cool Struttin'* and baritone saxophone genius Serge Chaloff's classic *Blue Serge*.

Albums: with Teddy Charles *Teddy Charles With Wardell Gray* (1953), with Buddy De Franco *The Complete Verve Buddy De Franco/Sonny Clark* (1954), with Serge Chaloff *Blue Serge* (1956), with Sonny Rollins *The Sound Of Sonny* (1957), *Sonny Clark Trio* (Blue Note 1957), *Sonny's Crib* (1957), *Dial S For Sonny* (1957), *Cool Struttin'* (1958), *The Sonny Clark Memorial Album* (1959), *Sonny Clark* (Bainbridge Time 1960), *Leapin' And Lopin'* (1961), with Dexter Gordon *Go!* (1962), *A Swinging Affair* (1962), with Grant Green *Born To Be Blue* (1962).

Clarke, Kenny 'Klook'

b. 9 January 1914, Pittsburgh, Pennsylvania, USA, d. 26 January 1985. Clarke began playing drums as a child and while in his teens played in several bands in his home town. He later joined Roy Eldridge and also played in the Jeter-Pillars Orchestra and in those led by Edgar Hayes, Claude Hopkins and Teddy Hill. In Hill's band at the time (1939) was Dizzy Gillespie, in whom Clarke found a kindred revolutionary spirit. Both in the band and at after-hours sessions at Minton's Playhouse, Clarke began to develop new concepts of jazz drumming. His seemingly eccentric playing, 'dropping bombs' (see below), confused many musicians but was greeted with enthusiasm by the more radical newcomers. During this period, Clarke worked with leading jazzmen such as Charlie Parker, Thelonious Monk, Bud Powell and Charlie Christian. After a mid-40s hiatus for military service, Clarke was soon active in recording studios with Gillespie and other modernists, but his skills were also in demand for other, more orthodox sessions and he recorded with stalwarts of the traditional scene such as Sidney Bechet. In 1951 he was a member of Milt Jackson's quartet, a group which later evolved into the Modern Jazz Quartet. In the mid-50s he appeared on scores of albums, playing in different contexts and styles but usually favouring contemporary sounds. In 1956 Clarke relocated to Paris, France, where he worked with Powell and other visiting Americans, including Miles Davis and Dexter Gordon. From 1961 he co-led the impressive Clarke-Boland Big Band with Francy Boland. This band stayed in existence for over a decade, playing as often as was possible given its international personnel. In the 70s and early 80s he continued to live and work in Europe, in demand for concerts, recording dates, as a writer for

films and as a tutor. The founding father of bop drumming, Clarke was almost single-handedly responsible for the shift away from strict-tempoed drumming which harnessed the 4/4 beat to the bass drum. Clarke maintained the pulse on the ride cymbal, using bass and snare drums for explosive bursts of sound, as effective punctuation for the soloists. This style established the pattern and set the standards for all other bop drummers. His technique was comprehensive and he seldom allowed his enthusiasm for his work to run away with what he saw as an essentially supportive role. Despite his importance in establishing bop drumming, by the late 50s and especially during his period with the big band he co-led in Europe, Clarke had abandoned that style to concentrate upon hard-swinging drumming which reflected his admiration for the earlier work of Jo Jones. Clarke was a major contributor to jazz and one of the few jazz innovators on his chosen instrument.

Albums: *The Kenny Clarke All Stars* (1954), with Milt Jackson *Opus De Jazz* (1955), *Bohemia After Dark* (Savoy 1955), *Klook's Clique* (1956), *Kenny Clarke Meets The Detroit Jazzmen* (1956), with Dexter Gordon *Our Man In Paris* (1963), all following with Clarke-Boland Big Band unless stated *Karl Drewo Und Die Clarke-Boland Big Band* (1966), *Flirt And Dream* (1967), *Music For The Small Hours* (1967), *Out Of The Folk Bag* (1967), *Open Door* (1967), *17 Men And Their Music* (1967), *Let's Face The Music/Smile* (1968), *Faces* (1968), *More* (1968), *Latin Kaleidoscope* (1968), *Fellini 712* (1968), *Volcano/Live At Ronnie Scott's* (1969), *Rue Chaptal* (1969), *All Blues* (1969), *More Smiles* (1969), *At Her Majesty's Pleasure* (1969), *The Francy Boland-Kenny Clarke Trio* (1970), *Off Limits* (1970), *Our Kind Of Sahi* (1970), *Change Of Scenes* (1971), *Live TNP Paris 1969* (1993), small group *Jazz A Confronto* (1974), small group *Kenny Today* (1980), *Pieces Of Time* (Soul Note 1984). Compilations: with Charlie Christian *Jazz Immortal* (1941), *Sidney Bechet 1949* (1949), *Paris Bebop Sessions* (1950).

Further Reading: *Klook: The Story Of Kenny Clarke*, Mike Hennessy.

Clarke, Stanley

b. 21 July 1951, Philadelphia, Pennsylvania, USA. Clarke started on violin, then transferred to cello, double bass and finally the bass guitar. After formal training at school and at the Philadelphia Musical Academy, his first experience was in funk outfits; he then got a taste for playing jazz working with Horace Silver for six months in 1970. He played with tenor saxophonist Joe Henderson and with Pharoah Sanders on the latter's *Black Unity*. A spell with Chick Corea and his Return For Forever band reminded Clarke of his aptitude for the electric bass, and he became a pioneer of fusion as 'cosmic' as it was commercial: *Journey To Love* (1975) had glossy production a million miles from Sanders's abrasive poly-rhythms. A partnership with George Duke, also a fugitive from acoustic jazz, provided audiences with spectacular virtuoso work-outs. Gifted with jaw-dropping technique, Clarke's rise to fame coincided with a period when demonstrating chops was considered to be at the cutting edge of the music. His slapping style has produced a host of imitators, though none can quite match his speed and confidence.

Albums: with Pharoah Sanders *Black Unity* (1972), with Return To Forever *Return To Forever* (1972), *Stanley Clarke* (Epic 1974), *Journey To Love* (1975), *School Days* (Atlantic 1976), *Modern Man* (CBS 1978), *I Wanna Play For You* (1979), *Rocks, Pebbles And Sand* (Epic 1980), You/Me Together (Epic 1980), with George Duke *The Clarke/Duke Project* (1981), *Let Me Know You* (Epic 1982), with George Duke *The Clarke/Duke Project II* (1983), *Time Exposure* (Epic 1984), *Find Out* (1985), *Hideaway* (Epic 1986), *Shieldstone* (Optimism 1987), *If This Bass Could Only Talk* (1988), with George Duke 3 (Epic 1990), *East River Drive* (1993). Compilation: *The Collection* (Castle 1990).

Clayton, Buck

b. Wilbur Dorsey Clayton, 12 November 1911, Parsons, Kansas, USA, d. 8 December 1991. By his late teens Clayton was already an accomplished trumpeter, having worked locally in Kansas and briefly in California. He returned to the west coast, playing in several Los Angeles-based bands including that led by Charlie Echols. He also formed his own unit, which he took to China for two years. Back in California he found that his reputation had spread and in 1936 he was invited to join Count Basie. He remained with Basie until drafted for military service in 1943, by which time his fame was guaranteed thanks to a succession of fine solos on many of the Basie band's best recordings. After the war he worked mostly with small bands and also appeared as a member of Jazz At The Philharmonic. He worked, too, with a former Basie colleague Jimmy Rushing and occasionally formed bands, big and small, under his own leadership. He toured extensively and made numerous records, including a series of very highly-regarded jam sessions in the early and mid-50s which brought together several major mainstream musicians. These sessions used Clayton's marvellously loose arrangements and became exemplars of their kind. He had begun arranging with Basie, and other bandleaders who used his charts included Benny Goodman and Harry James. In the 50s he toured with Mezz Mezzrow, Eddie Condon and Sidney Bechet. A gifted soloist with a clean, mellow tone, his arranging skills stood him in good stead when, in the late 60s, he began to suffer from severe lip problems. Extensive surgery failed to improve matters and he eventually abandoned playing in favour of arranging. In the late 70s he led a number of bands on international tours under the auspices of the US State Department and occasionally played a little. His activities as bandleader, lecturer and, especially, arranger continued into the late 80s. A major figure in the establishment of mainstream jazz, Clayton became one of the most respected musicians in jazz.

Selected albums: *Buck Clayton Jam Sessions* (1953), *Buck Clayton In Paris* (1953), *Buck 'N' The Blues* (1957), with Sidney Bechet *Concert At The World's Fair, Brussels* (1958), *Little Jimmy Rushing And The Big Brass* (1958), *Tenderly* (1959), *Copenhagen Concert* (1959), with Buddy Tate *Buck And Buddy* (1960), *Olympia Concert/Live In Paris* (1961), *Passport To Paradise* (1961), *A La Buck* (1961), with Tate, Buck And

Buddy *Blow The Blues* (1961), *Le Vrai Buck Clayton* (1964), *Feel So Fine* (1965), *Swingin' The Blues* (1966), *Le Vrai Buck Clayton, Volume 2* (1966), *Trumpet Summi* (1967); all following as arranger only *A Buck Clayton Jam Session* (1974), *Jay Hawk* (1974), *Jam Session* (1975), *Jam Session Volume 3* (1976), *Live In Paris* (Vogue 1977), *1966 Buck Clayton And Humphrey Lyttelton* (Harlequin 1985), *Baden Switzerland 1966* (1993), *Buck Special* (1993). Compilations: *Rarities Vol 1* (Swingtime 1988), *A Swingin' Dream* (Stash 1990), *Buck Special* (Vogue 1993).

Further reading: *Buck Clayton's Jazz World*, Buck Clayton with Nancy Miller Elliott.

Clayton, Jeff

b. 16 February 1955, Venice, California, USA. Clayton's musical education began at a local Baptist church, where his mother was pianist and conductor of the choir. He began playing various reed instruments, including clarinet, but concentrated on alto saxophone. He later added soprano saxophone and flute, extending his studies during high school and university where his principal instrument was the oboe. He dropped out of university before graduating in order to go on the road with Stevie Wonder. Later, he mixed studio work with touring, playing with artists as diverse as Gladys Knight and Kenny Rogers, Patti Labelle and Michael Jackson. He gradually shifted towards a more jazz-orientated repertoire and although he continued to work in orchestras backing popular singers such as Frank Sinatra, Mel Tormé, Lena Horne and Sammy Davis Jnr., it was in the jazz world that he established his reputation during the 80s. He played in the Tommy Dorsey Orchestra under the direction of Murray McEachern, with Count Basie, the continuing Basie band under Thad Jones, Alphonse Mouzon, Juggernaut, Woody Herman, Lionel Hampton, Ella Fitzgerald, the Phillip Morris Superband led by Gene Harris, Monty Alexander, Ray Brown and many others. Clayton continued to work with pop stars, playing saxophone solos on an album by Madonna and on the soundtrack of the film *Dick Tracy* (1990), in which she starred. Clayton has worked extensively in partnership with his brother, John Clayton; and the Claytons are also active in the big band they co-lead with Jeff Hamilton. A hugely talented musician, Clayton's playing of the alto saxophone is especially distinguished. Although he has developed a distinctive style of his own, his playing reveals his respect and admiration for the sensitive manner in which Johnny Hodges richly interpreted ballads and the harder-edged drive and phrasing of Cannonball Adderley. In addition to his performing, which has recently included playing classical music with the Icelandic Philharmonic Orchestra, Clayton also teaches, conducts clinics, and writes. In his capacity as a writer he has composed songs for Jon Hendricks. In the early 90s Clayton continued to play numerous festivals, concerts and make records either under his own name or with major stars of jazz and popular music. Clearly a leading figure in contemporary music, his continuing career is one to watch.

Albums: with Clayton-Hamilton Big Band *Groove Shop* (1989), *Gene Harris And The Phillip Morris Superband* (1990), with Ray Brown *Evergreen* (1990), with Clayton-Hamilton Big Band *Heart And Soul* (1991), with John Clayton *The Sweet Man* (1991), as the Clayton Brothers *The Music* (1993).

Clayton, John

b. 1952, Los Angeles, California, USA. Born into a musical family, Clayton took up the bass and at the age of 16 was studying with Ray Brown. Three years later he was in the orchestra for the US television series *The Mancini Generation,* but left to resume his studies. His playing career continued via stints with Monty Alexander and the Count Basie band and he also served for five years as principal bass with the Amsterdam Philharmonic Orchestra. Aside from playing, Clayton teaches bass and has appeared on a number of instructional videos with Brown and Milt Hinton. He is also an accomplished composer, drawing inspiration from Henry Mancini and especially Johnny Mandel. In 1989 he spent time in Germany, writing for the Cologne Radio Orchestra. He has appeared regularly in the Doc Severinson Orchestra on the *Tonight* television show and was a member of the Gene Harris/Philip Morris Superband for its 1989 world tour. He has recorded with Ernestine Anderson, the Cunninghams, Brown, Mancini, Rosemary Clooney and with the big band he has co-led with his brother, Jeff Clayton, and Jeff Hamilton since 1985. Many of the charts played by the Clayton-Hamilton band are written by him and he has deliberately set out to emulate Duke Ellington in seeking to create formats which effectively draw upon the abilities of individual musicians within the orchestra. An outstanding technician, Clayton is one of the most respected and sought-after bassists working in jazz in the 90s.
Selected albums: with Jeff Clayton *Jeff & John* (1978), with Jeff Clayton *It's All In The Family* (1980), with Ray Brown *Super Bass* (early 80s), with Clayton-Hamilton *Groove Shop* (Capri 1989), with Jeff Clayton *The Sweet Man* (1991), as the Clayton Brothers *The Music* (1993), with Clayton Hamilton *Heart And Soul* (Capri 1993).

Cless, Rod

b. 20 May 1907, Lennox, Iowa, USA, d. 8 December 1944. After playing clarinet in local bands while still a schoolboy, Cless met Frank Teschemacher, then a member of the Wolverines, in 1925 and in two years later played with him in Chicago. Influenced by Teschemacher and his brother-in-law Bud Freeman, the next few years found Cless playing with numerous bands in the mid-western and southern states and establishing a sound reputation. In 1939 he joined Muggsy Spanier, then worked around New York and up into Canada with musicians including Art Hodes, Wild Bill Davison and Bobby Hackett. In 1944, by now drinking heavily, he worked regularly with Max Kaminsky at New York's Pied Piper Club. Walking home from the club one night he fell, was severely injured, and died four days later. In his short career Cless won the respect of musicians for his skilled, inventive playing which was, fortunately, captured on his recordings with Spanier.
Selected album: with Muggsy Spanier *The Great Sixteen* (1939).

Cleveland, Jimmy

b. 3 May 1926, Wartrace, Tennessee, USA. By the time he joined Lionel Hampton in 1950 Cleveland was already a highly-experienced trombonist, having worked with a band formed by his musical family and in the orchestra of Tennessee State University. With Hampton he played with surging power, a wonderfully rich and warm tone and great blues feeling. A brilliant technician, his playing always has great authority and his prowess makes him a much sought-after studio and session musician. After his time with Hampton he played with numerous other big bands, mostly those gathered for one-off recording dates or club and concert engagements. Among the leaders with whom he has performed are Gerry Mulligan, Quincy Jones, Dizzy Gillespie, Miles Davis, Gil Evans, Oliver Nelson, Bill Berry and Gerald Wilson.
Selected albums: *Introducing Jimmy Cleveland And His All Stars* (1955), *Gil Evans Plus Ten* (1957), *The Great Wide World Of Quincy Jones* (1959), with Bill Berry *Hello Rev* (1976), with Urbie Green, Frank Rehak *Trombone Scene* (1988).

Cleyndert, Andy

b. 8 January 1963, Birmingham, West Midlands, England. Cleyndert began playing bass while still at school and, on completing his studies in 1981, immediately became a professional musician. His first engagements were at a Manchester club where he was a member of the Tony Mann Trio, which backed visiting jazzmen such as Peter King and Art Farmer. He moved to London where he played with Bobby Wellins, Don Weller and other leading figures on the British jazz scene. Naturally associating with other rising young stars, he worked with Clark Tracey and Iain Ballamy and was briefly with the National Youth Jazz Orchestra. In 1983 he recorded with Tommy Chase and the following year toured with Ted Curson. In 1985 he toured with Bobby Watson and broadcast with the Kenny Wheeler big band. In 1986 he began teaching at music summer schools. In the late 80s he was a member of the Bryan Spring Trio and was regularly called upon to accompany visiting American jazzmen, including Bud Shank, Red Rodney, Charlie Rouse and Spike Robinson. He also toured overseas with Slim Gaillard, Spirit Level, Louis Stewart and Martin Taylor. In 1990 Cleyndert was a member of the Anglo-American band led by George Coleman Jnr. Despite the intense level of work he has sustained throughout his career, Cleyndert found time to study, and in 1990 gained a degree in mathematics and psychology. One of the best of the new generation of jazz musicians to emerge on the UK scene, Cleyndert's broad musical base allied to his already wide experience assures him of an important place in the future of jazz.

Clyne, Jeff

b. 29 January 1937, London, England. An admirer of Scott La Faro, Eddie Gomez, Jaco Pastorius and Stanley Clarke, Clyne is a versatile performer on the electric and conventional basses and was in heavy demand throughout the 60s and 70s for his ability to contribute convincingly to a wide range of styles. He fitted in equally comfortably with the fusion of Turning Point

Jeff Clyne

or the free experimentalism of the Spontaneous Music Ensemble (SME). He is primarily self-taught, although he did spend some time studying with orchestral players and, like the majority of British players of this vintage, gained valuable experience during his National Service with the 3rd Hussars in the mid-50s. After spells with Tony Crombie's Rockets and Stan Tracey he joined the Jazz Couriers, co-led by tenorists Ronnie Scott and Tubby Hayes, in 1958. His association with Hayes continued for the next 10 years or so, but he also worked with a whole string of influential and acclaimed bands during the following two decades. He was an original member of the SME and was also a partner in its sister band, Trevor Watts's Amalgam. In the mid-60s he worked with Tracey again, his warm sound contributing much to the acclaimed *Under Milk Wood.* After taking up the bass guitar he became a founder member of Ian Carr's Nucleus, where he stayed from 1969 to 1971. Turning Point was founded with Pepi Lemer in 1976. He has also worked with (among many others) Gary Boyle's Isotope, John McLaughlin, Tony Oxley, Keith Tippett's Centipede, Dudley Moore, Blossom Dearie, Norma Winstone, 'Lucky' Thompson, Zoot Sims, Phil Woods, Phil Lee and Eddie 'Lockjaw' Davis and the London Jazz Composers' Orchestra.

Selected albums: with Tubby Hayes *Tubby's Groove* (1959), with Stan Tracey *Under Milk Wood* (1965), with John Stevens (including SME) *Challenge* (1965), with Stevens *Springboard* (1966), with Hayes *100% Proof* (1966), with Gordon Beck *Experiments With Pops* (1967), *Gyroscope* (1968), with Michael Gibbs *Tanglewood '63* (1970), with Nucleus *Elastic Rock* (1970), with Nucleus *We'll Talk About It Later* (1970), with Turning Point *Creatures Of The Night* (1977), with Turning Point *Silent Promise* (1978), with Stevens *Freebop* (1982), with Phil Lee *Twice Upon A Time* (Cadillac 1987).

Cobb, Arnett

b. 10 August 1918, Houston, Texas, USA, d. 24 March 1989. Cobb began playing the tenor saxophone professionally in 1933. He spent several of his early years in the fine territory band led by Milt Larkins, a unit which numerous musicians of the older generation still hold in awe. Approached in 1941 by Lionel Hampton, who was then in the process of forming a new band after deciding to leave Benny Goodman, Cobb chose to stay with Larkins and Hampton took on Larkins's altoist, Illinois Jacquet instead, persuading him to switch to tenor and try to imitate Cobb. In 1942 Hampton proffered a second invitation and this time Cobb joined him. In 1947 he briefly fronted his own band, through to the early 50s, interrupted briefly by an illness. In 1956 he was seriously injured in a road accident while driving his band's bus and spent the rest of his life on crutches and in considerable pain. None of this stopped him from playing and he worked extensively, often back in Texas, where he raised a daughter after the death of his wife. In later years he became a familiar and popular figure on the international festival circuit, playing in small groups, then in big bands, and occasionally working with his old boss, Hampton. A powerful, gritty player, drenched in the blues,

Cobb is an outstanding member of the distinguished school of 'Texas tenors'. His sound, shifting constantly between breathy confidentiality and eruptive, emotion-packed roars, brought pleasure to many who could never imagine from his playing the grave physical discomfort which he courageously disguised for more than 30 years.

Selected albums: *Arnett Cobb And His Mob* (1952), *Blow, Arnett, Blow* (1959), *Smooth Sailing* (1959), *Party Time* (1959), *More Party Time* (1960), *Blow Arnett Blow* (Original Jazz Classics (1960), *Movin' Right Along* (1960), *Sizzlin'* (1960), *Ballads By Cobb* (1960), *Blue And Sentimental* (Prestige 1961), *Again With Milt Buckner* (1973), *Jumping At The Woodside* (1974), *Live In Paris* (1974), with Milt Buckner *Again With Milt Buckner* (Black And Blue 1974), *Midnight Show Vol. 2* (Black And Blue 1974), *The Wild Man From Texas* (Black And Blue 1974), *Arnett Cobb Is Back!* (Progressive 1978), *Live At Sandy's!* (Muse 1978), *Live At Sandy's! More* (1978), *Funky Butt* (Progressive 1980), *Live* (Timeless 1982), *Keep On Pushin'* (1984), *Show Time* (Fantasy 1988). Compilations: with Lionel Hampton *Leapin' With Lionel (1942-46)* (1983), *The Complete Apollo Sessions* (Vogue 1984).

Cobb, Jimmy

b. 20 January 1929, Washington DC, USA. A self-taught drummer, Cobb gained a great deal of experience working in his home town behind such visiting jazz artists as Charlie Rouse, Leo Parker and Billie Holiday. In 1951 he joined Earl Bostic and later that year married and became musical director for Dinah Washington. In the mid-50s, now located in New York, Cobb worked with many leading jazz players including Dizzy Gillespie, John Coltrane and Stan Getz and in 1958 he began a five-year period with Miles Davis. During a large part of the 60s Cobb was with Wynton Kelly after whose death he began a long association as Sarah Vaughan's regular drummer. A dynamic, aggressive player in the mould of such leading hard bop drummers as Kenny Clarke and Art Blakey, Cobb is a welcome member of any band in which he plays and a constant encouragement to his front line.

Selected albums: with Miles Davis *Kind Of Blue* (1959), *Coltrane Jazz* (1959-60), with Davis *Friday Night And Saturday Night At The Blackhawk* (1961), with Wynton Kelly *Walkin' At The Half Note* (1965), with Sarah Vaughan *More For Live* (1973).

Cobham, Billy

b. 16 May 1944, Panama. Cobham began playing drums while growing up in New York City, to where his family had moved while he was still a small child. He studied at the city's High School of Music before entering military service. In the army he played in a band and by the time of his discharge had achieved a high level of proficiency. In the late 60s he played in the New York Jazz Sextet and with Horace Silver. In 1969 he formed a jazz-rock band, Dreams, with Michael and Randy Brecker. The growing popularity of jazz-rock kept Cobham busy with recording dates, including some with Miles Davis, and he then joined John McLaughlin's Mahavishnu Orchestra, one of the most influential and highly regarded jazz-rock bands. In 1973 Cobham capitalized upon his international fame by forming his own band and continued to lead fusion bands for the next several years. He played all around the world, at festivals and in concert, teaching and presenting drum clinics. In 1984 he and McLaughlin were reunited in a new version of the Mahavishnu Orchestra. Perhaps the best and most technically accomplished of all the jazz-rock drummers, Cobham's rhythmic dexterity, all-round ability and his dedication to musical excellence has resulted in many copyists. For all his spectacular pyrotechnics, however, Cobham's talent runs deep and his abilities as a teacher and clinician ensure that his methods are being handed on to future generations of drummers.

Albums: with Horace Silver *Serenade To A Soul Sister* (1968), with Miles Davis *A Tribute To Jack Johnson* (1970), *Dreams* (1970), with the Mahavishnu Orchestra *The Inner Mounting Flame* (1971), with the Mahavishnu Orchestra *Between Nothingness And Eternity* (1972), *Spectrum* (Atlantic 1973), *Total Eclipse* (Atlantic 1974), *Crosswinds* (Atlantic 1974), *Life And Times* (Atlantic 1976), *B.C.* (CBS 1979), *Flight Time* (Inak 1981), *Stratus* (Inak 1981), *Smokin'* (Elektra 1983), *Warning* (GRP 1985), *Power Play* (GRP 1986), *Picture This* (GRP 1987), *Same Ol Love* (GRP 1987), *Live On Tour In Europe* (Atlantic 1988), *By Design* (1992). Compilations: *Best Of Billy Cobham* (CBS 1980), *Billy's Best Hits* (GRP 1987), *Best Of Billy Cobham* (Atlantic 1988).

Codona

This jazz group was formed in 1977 by Collin Walcott (sitar, tabla, sanza, dulcimer, timpani, voice), Don Cherry (trumpet, flutes, doussn'gouni, melodica, organ, voice) and Nana Vasconcelos (berimbau, talking drum, cuica, percussion, voice). Codona's three members came together at the instigation of ECM producer Manfred Eicher, Cherry and Walcott playing on the latter's *Grazing Dreams* and Nana encountering Walcott at the session for Egberto Gismonti's *Sol Do Meio Dia*. At the first trio recording the following year the players revelled in a shared enthusiasm for what Cherry called 'Universal World Folklore', this being defined by Walcott as an attempt to merge the most divergent musical forms 'without turning the whole world into milktoast'. 'Love and respect for the traditions was vital,' he said. Ten years ahead of the 'world music' boom, Codona would playfully mix ragas with Japanese music, write a piece dedicated to both Stevie Wonder and Ornette Coleman, or showcase the sitar on a standard blues. The group's potential was cut short by the death of Walcott in a tour bus crash in East Germany in 1984.

Albums: *Codona* (ECM 1978), *Codona 2* (ECM 1981), *Codona 3* (ECM 1983).

Coe, Tony

b. 29 November 1934, Canterbury, Kent, England. A formally-trained musician proficient on clarinet, bass clarinet and tenor saxophone, Coe's early jazz experience was as a member of Humphrey Lyttelton's band (1957-62). Later he led his own group for a while, then worked with John Dankworth's Orchestra in the late 60s, as well as playing with the Kenny Clarke-Francy Boland big band (1967-73) and beginning a long association with Stan Tracey on 1969's *We Love You Madly*. During the 70s and 80s, Coe extended his horizons dramatically, moving away from the more traditional areas of jazz to explore a variety of musics, including total improvisation with Derek Bailey, classical music with Alan Hacker's Matrix ensemble and film music - he plays on the soundtracks of *The Devils*, *The Boy Friend* and the *Pink Panther* films. He also continued to lead his own modern jazz groups, with line-ups that featured Kenny Wheeler and Tony Oxley; wrote an extended piece, *Zeitgeist*, which mixed elements of jazz, rock and classical music; and toured with both the United Jazz And Rock Ensemble and the Mike Gibbs band. In the 80s, he recorded a wide range of material for the French Nato and Chabada labels, sometimes with the comedy-vocal group Melody Four (actually a trio, with Lol Coxhill and Steve Beresford). His 1988 *Canterbury Song* is a beautiful example of modern mainstream jazz, while a continuing association with Franz Koglmann has recently been taking him back into more abstract areas (*L'Heure Bleue*). A versatile and gifted player, Coe is one of the UK's most celebrated instrumentalists, an outstanding performer in all forms of jazz and classical music.

Selected albums: *Swingin' Til The Girls Come Home* (1962), *Zeitgeist* (1976), *Coe-Existence* (Lee Lambert 1978), with Derek Bailey *Time* (1979), with Al Grey *Get It Together* (1979), *Tournée Du Chat* (Nato 1982), *Nutty On Willisau* (Hat Art 1983, remixed as *Nutty*), *Le Chat Se Retourne* (Nato 1984), *Mainly Mancini* (Nato 1986), *Canterbury Song* (Hot House 1988), *Tony Coe* (Hep Jazz 1988), *Les Voix D'Itxassou* (Nato 1991), *Some Other Autumn* (Hep Jazz 1993).

Cohn, Al

b. 24 November 1925, New York City, New York, USA, d. 15 February 1988. As a teenager Cohn gained experience playing the tenor saxophone with Joe Marsala and Georgie Auld, for whom he also arranged. A forward-thinking musician, Cohn worked extensively in big bands during the mid-late 40s, most famously as a member of Woody Herman's Four Brothers band. He continued to perform, and write for, big bands, including those of Artie Shaw and Elliot Lawrence, with whom he was associated for a substantial part of the 50s. In 1957 Cohn teamed up with Zoot Sims, a partnership that lasted into the 80s. During this period he also worked as leader of small groups and as a touring soloist. Cohn's writing continued throughout this time and he was responsible for scoring a number of stage musicals. A warm-toned melodic player, Cohn was stylistically in the mould of Lester Young but incorporated into his music many elements that were his own. Respected in jazz circles for his playing, he was also very popular with musicians for his ready wit. Towards the end of his life he sometimes worked with his guitarist son, Joe.

Selected albums: *Cohn's Tones/Brothers And Other Mothers* (Savoy 1950), *The Progressive Al Cohn* (1953), *Al Cohn Quintet* (1953), *Broadway - 1954* (Original Jazz Classics 1954), *Mr*

Music (1954), *Natural Seven* (1955), *Al Cohn* i (1955), *Al Cohn* ii (1955), *The Brothers!* (1955), with Zoot Sims *From A To Z And Beyond* (Bluebird 1956), *Be Loose* (1956), *Al Cohn And Bob Brookmeyer* (1956), *Al And Zoot* (1957), with Sims *Happy Over Hoagy* (1958), *The Vibes Are On* (1960), *You 'N' Me* (1960), *Either Way* (Evidence 1961), *Body And Soul* (1973), *Motoring Along* (1974), *Play It Now* (1975), *Motoring Along* (1976), *Silver Blue* (Xanadu 1976), *True Blue* (Xanadu 1976), *Al Cohn's America* (Xanadu 1976), *Heavy Love* (Xanadu 1977), *No Problem* (Xanadu 1979), *Non-Pareil* (1981), with Scott Hamilton, Buddy Tate *Tour De Force* (Concord 1981), *Overtones* (1982), *Standards Of Excellence* (Concord 1983), with Totti Bergh *I Hear A Rhapsody* (1985), with Bergh *Tenor Gladness* (1986), with Laila Dalseth *Travelling Light* (1986), *Keeper Of The Flame* (Jazz House 1987), *Al Cohn Meets Al Porcino* (Red Baron), *The Final Performance* (1987), Rifftide (Timeless 1987).

Coker, Henry

b. 24 December 1919, Dallas, Texas, USA, d. 23 November 1979. Coker's first professional engagement, in 1935, playing the trombone, was with a band led by John White and two years later, his reputation was such that he was hired by Nat Towles, one of the most esteemed territory bands. After leaving Towles he worked in the Hawaiian Islands, returning home after the bombing of Pearl Harbor. On the west coast in the mid-40s, he mixed studio work with jobs in bands led by Benny Carter and Eddie Heywood, then joined Illinois Jacquet. Starting in 1952 he enjoyed a decade as a member of Count Basie's band, contributing powerful solos. After Basie he returned to studio work, this time in New York, and then, in 1966, joined Ray Charles with whom he remained until 1971. In the 70s he was mostly engaged in film and television work in Los Angeles but played brief return engagements with both Basie and Charles.
Selected albums: *Count Basie Big Band* (1952), *The Count Basie Story* (1960).

Cole, Nat 'King'

b. Nathaniel Adams Coles, 17 March 1916, Montgomery, Alabama, USA, d. 15 February 1965. Cole was born into a family that held a key position in the black community: his father was pastor of the First Baptist Church. In 1921 the family migrated to Chicago, part of the mass exodus of black people seeking a better life in the booming industrial towns of the north. He learned piano by ear from his mother, who was choir director in the church, from the age of four. When he was 12 years old he took lessons in classical piano, 'everything from Bach to Rachmaninoff'. Jazz was everywhere in Chicago, and Cole's school was a musical hotbed, producing musicians of the stature of Ray Nance, Eddie South and Milt Hinton. Cole's first professional break came touring with the show *Shuffle Along*, a revival of the first all-black show to make it to Broadway, which he joined with his bass-playing brother, Eddie. Stranded in Los Angeles when the show folded, Cole looked for club work and found it at the Century Club on Santa Monica Boulevard. It was a hangout for musicians and the young pianist made a splash: 'All the musicians dug him,' said Robert 'Bumps' Blackwell, 'that cat could play! He was unique.' In 1939 Cole formed an innovative trio with Oscar Moore on guitar and Wesley Prince on bass, eschewing the noise of drums. Like Fats Waller in the previous generation, Cole managed to combine pleasing and humorous ditties with piano stylings that were state-of-the-art. Times had moved on, and Cole had a suave sophistication that expressed the new aspirations of the black community. In 1943 he cut his 'Straighten Up And Fly Right' for Capitol - it was an instant hit. Cole's future as a pop success was assured. In 1946 'The Christmas Song' added strings, starting a process that would lead to Nat Cole emerging as a middle-of-the-road singer, accompanied by leading arrangers and conductors including Nelson Riddle, Gordon Jenkins, Ralph Carmichael, Pete Rugolo, and Billy May. Before that happened, in the 40s Cole made several memorable sides with the Trio, including 'Sweet Lorraine', 'It's Only A Paper Moon', '(Get Your Kicks) On Route 66' and '(I Love You) For Sentimental Reasons'. By 1948, and 'Nature Boy' (a US number 1), on which Cole was accompanied by Frank DeVol's Orchestra, the move away from small group jazz, towards his eventual position as one of the most popular vocalists of the day, was well under way. Absolute confirmation came in 1950, when Cole, with Les Baxter conducting Nelson Riddle's lush arrangement of 'Mona Lisa', spent eight weeks at the top of the US chart with what was to become one of his most celebrated recordings. Throughout the 50s the singles hits continued to flow, mostly with ballads such as 'Too Young', 'Faith Can Move Mountains', 'Because You're Mine', 'Unforgettable', 'Somewhere Along The Way', 'Funny (Not Much)', 'Pretend', 'Can't I?', 'Answer Me, My Love', 'Smile', 'Darling Je Vous Aime Beaucoup', 'The Sand And The Sea', 'A Blossom Fell', 'When I Fall In Love' and 'Stardust' (said to be composer Hoagy Carmichael's favourite version of his song). No doubt because of his jazz grounding, Cole was equally at home with the more up-tempo 'Orange Coloured Sky', backed by Stan Kenton And His Orchestra, 'Walkin' My Baby Back Home', 'Night Lights' and 'Ballerina'. In the same period, his best-selling albums included *After Midnight* (with the Trio), *Love Is The Thing*, which was at the top of the US chart for eight weeks, *Just One Of Those Things*, *Cole Espanol* and *The Very Thought Of You*. During the 50s he was urged to make films, but his appearances were few and far between - character parts in such as *Blue Gardenia*, *China Gate* and *Night Of The Quarter Moon*. Cole's most effective movie role came in 1958 when he played W.C. Handy in *St. Louis Blues*. He also appeared on screen with Stubby Kaye, singing the linking ballads in the spoof western, *Cat Ballou* (1965), but it was clear that his enormous appeal lay in concerts and records. One of his lesser-known albums, *Welcome To The Club*, featured the Basie Orchestra, without Count Basie himself (for contractual reasons), and included Cole's superior readings of 'She's Funny That Way', 'Avalon' and 'Look Out For Love'. The title track was composed by Noel Sherman, who, with his brother Joe, wrote 'Mr Cole Won't Rock And Roll', an amusing piece performed by the singer in his concert show, 'Sights And Sounds', which played over 100 cities in the early 60s. It was not so much rock 'n' roll that concerned Cole's purist fans around that time: they had acute reservations about another of the Sherman Brothers' numbers, 'Ramblin' Rose' (1962), the singer's first big hit in four years, which came complete with a 'twangy C&W feeling'. They also objected to 'Those Lazy Hazy Crazy Days Of Summer' ('unabashed corn'), which also made the Top 10 in the following year. Cole himself felt that he was 'just adjusting to the market: as soon as you start to make money in the popular field, they scream about how good you were in the old days, and what a bum you are now'. As part of his most agreeable musical association during the early 60s, *Nat King Cole Sings/George Shearing Plays*, Cole went back to 1940 for Ian Grant and Lionel Rand's 'Let There Be Love'. His version became a hit single in many parts of the world, and remains a particularly fondly remembered performance. In a way, he was back to where he started out at around the time the song was written: singing with a small jazz group - albeit this time with George Shearing's polite piano and the inevitable 'String Choir'. During the years of Cole's enormous popularity in the 'easy listening' field, jazz fans had to turn out to see him in the clubs to hear his glorious piano - an extension of the Earl Hines style that had many features of the new, hip sounds of bebop. If Cole had not had such an effective singing voice he might have well been one of bebop's leaders. Bebop was an expression of black pride, but so was Cole's career, creating opportunities for all kinds of 'sepia Sinatras' (Charles Brown, Sammy Davis Jnr., etc) who proved that whites had no monopoly on sophistication. Cole bore the brunt of racism, meeting objections when he bought a house in fashionable Beverly Hills, being the first black television presenter (he abandoned the role in 1957, protesting that the agencies would not find him a national sponsor). Though his position entailed compromises that gained him the hostility of civil rights activists in the early 60s, he was a brave and decent figure in a period when race prejudice was at its most demeaning. Before his death from lung cancer in 1965, he was planning a production of James Baldwin's play *Amen Corner*, showing an interest in radical black literature at odds with his image as a sentimental crooner. Nat Cole's voice, which floats butter-won't-melt vowel sounds in an easy, dark drawl, is one of the great moments of black music, and no matter how sugary the arrangements he always managed to sing as if it mattered. In 1991 his daughter Natalie Cole revived his 'Unforgettable', singing a duet with his recorded vocal. Despite the questionable taste of duets-beyond-the-grave, Cole's piano intro was a startling reminder of the extraordinary harmonic creativity he brought to the pop music of his time. Perhaps, like Louis Armstrong, the most moving aspect of his legacy is the way his music cuts across the usual boundaries - chart watchers and jazz heads, rock 'n' rollers and MOR fans can all have a good time with his music. The amount of Nat Cole albums available is overwhelming, those considering a serious collection should invest (and indeed try to find a second-hand copy) in the 18 CD box set of his Capitol years, it is a spectacular collection that will see you through a lifetime.

Selected albums: *The King Cole Trio* (1950), *Penthouse Serenade* (1953), *Unforgettable* (1953), *Nat 'King' Cole Sings For Two In Love* (1954), *Tenth Anniversary Album* (1954), *Vocal Classics* (1955), *Instrumental Classics* (1955), *The Piano Style of Nat King Cole* (1956), *Ballads Of The Day* (1956), *After Midnight* (1957), *Love Is The Thing* (1957), *This Is Nat 'King' Cole* (1957), *Just One Of Those Things* (1957), *St. Louis Blues* (1958, film soundtrack), *Cole Espanol* (1958), *The Very Thought Of You* (1958), *Welcome To The Club* (1959), *To Whom It May Concern* (1959), *Tell Me All About Yourself* (1960), *Wild Is Love* (1960), *The Touch Of Your Lips* (1961), *String Along With Nat 'King' Cole* (1961), *Nat 'King' Cole Sings/George Shearing Plays* (1962), *Ramblin' Rose* (1962), *Dear Lonely Hearts* (1962), *Where Did Everyone Go?* (1963), *Those Lazy-Hazy-Crazy Days Of Summer* (1963), *The Christmas Song* (1963), *I Don't Want To Be Hurt Anymore* (1964), *My Fair Lady* (1964), *L-O-V-E* (1965), *Songs From 'Cat Ballou' And Other Motion Pictures* (1965), *Looking Back* (1965), *Nat 'King' Cole At The Sands* (1966), *The Great Songs!* (1966, recorded in 1957), *Close-Up* (1969), with Dean Martin *White Christmas* (1971), *Christmas With Nat 'King' Cole* (1988). Selected compilations: *20 Golden Greats* (1978), *Greatest Love Songs* (1982), *Trio Days* (1984), *The Capitol Years* (Capitol 1990, 18CD boxed set), *The Unforgettable Nat 'King' Cole* (1991), *The Nat King Cole Gold Collection* (1993), *Lush Life* (Capitol 1993), *World War II Transcriptions* (1994).

Further reading: *Nat King Cole, The Man And His Music*, James Haskins with Kathleen Benson. *Unforgettable - The Life And Mystique Of Nat King Cole*, Leslie Gourse.

Cole, Richie

b. 29 February 1948, Trenton, New Jersey, USA. Cole took up the guitar as a small child, having heard jazz at two clubs, the Harlem and Hubby's Inn, owned by his father. Before reaching his teens he had switched to alto saxophone on which instrument he studied with Phil Woods. Later, he attended Berklee College Of Music and then, in 1969, he joined Buddy Rich. In the early 70s he played in several bands, including Lionel Hampton's, led his own small bands and worked with Eddie Jefferson. On and off, Cole was with Jefferson from 1973 until the singer's murder in 1979. Next to Woods, Jefferson was the major influence on Cole's musical life and in a 1987 interview, he indicated that he was writing a symphony dedicated to Jefferson. Throughout the 80s and into the 90s Cole has led his own band, Alto Madness, with considerable success. His open musical mind is evident from the eagerness with which he has absorbed the techniques of artists as diverse as Jefferson and country music's Boots Randolph, with whom he recorded *Yakety Madness*. A saxophonist in the tradition of Charlie Parker and his mentor, Woods, Cole's playing is filled with a burning urgency. His performances are always exciting, but only as he matures is he starting to underpin the surface with greater emotional depths.

Selected albums: with Buddy Rich *Keep The Customers Satisfied* (1970), *Trenton Makes - The World Takes* (1975), *Starburst*

(1976), with Eddie Jefferson *The Live-liest* (1976), *New York Afternoon* (Muse 1977), *Still On The Planet* (Muse 1977), *Alto Madness* (Muse 1977), *Keeper of The Flame* (1978), *Hollywood Madness* (Muse 1979), *Side By Side* (Muse 1980), *Some Things Speak For Themselves* (1981), *Cool 'C'* (Muse 1981), *Richie Cole...Alive! At The Village Vanguard* (Muse 1981), *Return To Alto Acres* (Palo Alto 1982), *Yakety Madness* (1982), *Popbop* (Milestone 1987), *Pure Imagination* (Concord 1987), *Signature* (Milestone 1988), *Bossa Nova International* (Milestone 1988).

Cole, William 'Cozy'

b. 17 October 1909, East Orange, New Jersey, USA, d. 29 January 1981. Cole took up drumming as a child and by his early teens was studying and developing his craft. His first professional engagement was with clarinet virtuoso Wilbur Sweatman who led bands in several New York clubs and theatres. By the end of the 20s Cole had already briefly led his own band and in 1930 he recorded with Jelly Roll Morton. During the early 30s he worked successively with Blanche Calloway, Benny Carter and Willie Bryant and then, in 1936, joined the Onyx Club band co-led by Stuff Smith and Jonah Jones. In 1938 he began a four-year tenure with Cab Calloway during which he was given solo space in shows and on record. He also made many records with the small groups led by Lionel Hampton for his classic RCA sessions. Following his departure from Calloway, Cole returned to his studies, this time at Juilliard, and did theatrical work which included a featured spot in *Carmen Jones*. He led his own groups in the mid-40s and all-star 'pick-up' bands for record dates which are today usually issued under the names of one or another of his more illustrious sidemen, Coleman Hawkins and Earl Hines. In the late 40s he led various small groups and then joined Louis Armstrong's All Stars where he remained for a little over three years. During this period he was extensively featured on the soundtrack of a film, *The Strip* (1951), which starred Mickey Rooney as a drummer with Armstrong's band. In the early and mid-50s Cole was active in New York where he ran a drum school in partnership with Gene Krupa. He appeared in a number of films including *The Glenn Miller Story* (1953) in which he duetted with Krupa. In the late 50s he became a member of the all-star band co-led by Jack Teagarden and Earl 'Fatha' Hines which toured Europe and in 1958 had a surprising double-sided US hit single with 'Topsy I'/'Topsy II' - 'Turvy' reached the Top 40 later that same year. In 1961 appeared in an excellent television pilot, *After Hours*, with Coleman Hawkins and Roy Eldridge, the soundtrack of which was later bootlegged on an obscure Dutch label. Throughout the 60s and 70s Cole worked in a variety of settings, notably in a group which reunited him with Jonah Jones, touring internationally and appearing at numerous festivals. A brilliant technician with a meticulous sense of time, Cole could sometimes sound a little stiff. He dramatically altered the sound of the Armstrong All Stars to that which his more loosely swinging predecessor, 'Big' Sid Catlett, had created but he could be relied upon to push front-line soloists along with an urgency they rarely received from other, more famous drummers. Cole

died of cancer in January 1981.

Albums: with Louis Armstrong *New Orleans Nights* (1950), with Armstrong *Satchmo At Pasadena* (1951), with Armstrong *Rare Films: The Strip* (1951, film soundtrack), *The Jack Teagarden-Earl Hines All Stars In England* (1957), *Topsy* (1958), *Earl's Backroom And Cozy's Caravan* (1958), *Music For The Whole Crowd* (1959), *Carmen* (1961), *The Netherlands Salute Coleman Hawkins/Roy Eldridge* (1961, television soundtrack), *A Cozy Beat* (early 60s), *It's A Rocking Thing* (1966), *Lionel Hampton Presents Cozy Cole And Marty Napoleon* (1977). Compilations: *Stuff Smith And His Onyx Club Orchestra (1936)* (1988), with Lionel Hampton *Historical Recording Sessions (1937-39)*, *The Best Of Cab Calloway (1938-42)* (1988), *Hawkins And Hines* (1944).

Coleman, Bill

b. 4 August 1904, Centreville, Kentucky, USA, d. 24 August 1981. Despite trying various reed instruments, Coleman switched to trumpet after hearing records by Louis Armstrong and served his apprenticeship during the late 20s and early 30s in a string of amateur, semi-pro and professional bands, including those led by J.C. Higginbotham, Edgar Hayes, Lloyd and Cecil Scott, Luis Russell, Charlie 'Fess' Johnson, Lucky Millinder, Benny Carter, Teddy Hill and Fats Waller. By the mid-30s Coleman's wide experience meant that he was in great demand, but wanderlust led him to join all-round entertainer Freddy Taylor, whom Coleman had taught to play trumpet while in the Millinder band. The Taylor band spent time in Paris and then Coleman headed for Bombay, India, with Leon Abbey, returning to Paris for an engagement with Willie Lewis. In 1938 he co-led a band with Herman Chittison, which worked in Egypt until shortly after the outbreak of World War II. Back in the USA in 1940 he worked again with Benny Carter and Fats Waller and thereafter with the bands of Andy Kirk, Noble Sissle, Mary Lou Williams and John Kirby. After World War II he returned to Paris, where he resided for the rest of his life, touring other European countries and making only rare trips back to his homeland. A fluid, inventive player, Coleman was an elegant trumpeter with a full, rich sound which echoed his childhood idolization of Armstrong, but which he cloaked in his own, unmistakable style. He died in 1981.

Albums: *Town Hall Concert* (1945), *At The Salle Pleyel* (1952), *Eartha Kitt, Doc Cheatham, Bill Coleman In Paris* (1956), *Reunion In Paris* (1956), *Album Of Cities* (1956), *Swingin' In Switzerland* (1957), *The Great Parisian Session* (1960), *From Boogie To Funk* (1960), *Swing Low, Sweet Chariot/Bill Coleman Sings And Plays Spirituals* (1967), *Swingin' In London* (1967), *Together At Last* (1968), *Bill And The Boys* (1968), *Three Generations Jam* (1969), *Bill Coleman With The Original Jazz Band Of Raymond Fonsèque* (1971), *Bill Coleman In Milan With Lino Patruno & Friends* (1972), *Mainstream At Montreux* (1973), *Paris 1973* (1973), *Hommage A Duke Ellington* (1974), *Meeting The New Ragtime Band* (1976), *Cave's Blues* (1979), *Really I Do* (1980). Compilations: *Bill Coleman In Paris Volume 1 (1935-8)* (1983), *1935-37* (1984), *Bill Coleman In Paris*

Volume 2 (1936-8) (1988), *1929-40* (1993).

Coleman, George

b. 8 March 1935, Memphis, Tennessee, USA. A self-taught musician, Coleman began playing alto saxophone and worked in the early 50s with B.B. King. While with King he switched to tenor and began to shift his musical base until, in 1958, he joined Max Roach. During the 60s Coleman worked mostly in small post-bebop bands, including those led by Slide Hampton, Wild Bill Davis, Miles Davis, becoming the first permanent replacement for John Coltrane and featuring on Davis' brilliant *My Funny Valentine* live album, and Lee Morgan. He also worked in Lionel Hampton's big band but it was as a small group player that Coleman excelled. From the early 70s he worked mostly as leader of such groups, which varied from quartet to octet in size, and which regularly included Frank Strozier and Harold Mabern. A gifted and highly-accomplished technician, Coleman's playing is often more attractive than that of many of his better-known contemporaries who have attained more popular success.

Selected albums: with Max Roach *Deeds, Not Words* (1958), with Elvin Jones *Live At The Village Vanguard* (1962), *Miles Davis In Europe* (1963), *Cote Blues* (1963), with Davis Miles *In Antibes* (1963), with Davis *Seven Steps To Heaven* (1963), with Davis *My Funny Valentine* (1964), with Herbie Hancock *Maiden Voyage* (1964), *Revival!* (1976), with Tete Montoliu *Meditation* (1977), *Big George* (Charly 1977), with Montoliu *Duo* (1979, rec. 1977), *Live At Ronnie Scott's* (1978), *Playing Changes* (1979), *Amsterdam After Dark* (Timeless 1980), *Bongo Joe* (Arhoolie 1981), *Manhatten Panorama* (Evidence 1983), *At Yoshi's* (Evidence 1987), *Playing Changes* (Ronnie Scott's Jazz House 1994).

Coleman, Ornette

b. 19 March 1930, Fort Worth, Texas, USA. The evolution of any art form is a complex process and it is always an over-simplification to attribute a development to a single person. If there is anyone apart from Louis Armstrong for whom that claim could be made, however, Ornette Coleman would be a tenable candidate. Charlie Parker and John Coltrane were great forces for progress, but they focused and made viable certain concepts that were already in the air and which only awaited some exceptionally talented artist to give them concrete shape. They accelerated evolution, but did not change the direction of jazz in the way that Armstrong and Coleman seem to have done. Of course, certain elements of Coleman's music, including free improvisation, had been tried before and he certainly did not reject what had gone before: his playing is well-rooted in the soil of Parker's bop tradition, and in R&B - Coleman's playing is a logical development from both - but he set the melody free and jolted jazz out of its 30-year obsession with chords. His role is somewhat analogous to that of Arnold Schoenberg in European classical music, although, unlike Schoenberg, Coleman did not forge a second set of shackles to replace the ones he burst. Those who do not recognise Coleman's contribution to music select two sticks from his early career with which to beat him. The first is that, when he acquired his first saxophone at the age of 14, he thought the low C on the alto was the A in his instruction book. Of course, he discovered his mistake after a while, but the realisation of his error caused him to look at pitch and harmony in a fresh way, and this started the process which led to a style based on freely moving melody unhindered by a repetitive harmonic substructure and, eventually, to the theory of harmolodics. The second was that, when in Pee Wee Crayton's band, he was playing so badly that he was paid to keep silent. Crayton remembered it slightly differently: he said that Coleman was quite capable of playing the blues convincingly, but chose not to, so Crayton told him forcefully that that's what he was paid to do. In 1946 Coleman had taken up the tenor saxophone and joined the 'Red' Connors band. He played in blues and R&B bands for some while, sat in with Stan Kenton on one occasion, and in 1949 took the tenor chair in a touring minstrel show. He recorded several of his own tunes in Natchez, Mississippi, in the same year, but these have never resurfaced. He was stranded in New Orleans, where he found it hard to get anyone to play with him, and eventually hooked up with Crayton's band, which took him to Los Angeles in 1950. He took a number of jobs unconnected with music, but continued his study of theory when he could. In the early and mid-50s he began to establish contact with musicians who were in sympathy with his ideas, such as Bobby Bradford, Ed Blackwell and Don Cherry, and in 1958 he recorded for Contemporary in Los Angeles. He met John Lewis, who arranged for the Coleman quartet - then comprising Cherry, Charlie Haden and Billy Higgins - to play a two-week engagement at New York's Five Spot Cafe; this turned into a legendary 54-month stay during which Coleman was physically assaulted by an irate bebop drummer, described as 'psychotic' by Miles Davis, and hailed as the saviour of jazz by others. Lewis also secured Coleman a recording contract with Atlantic Records, where he made a series of influential but controversial albums, most notably *Free Jazz*, a collective improvisation for double quartet. After signing him, Atlantic sponsored Coleman and Don Cherry at the Lennox School of Jazz. At this time he earned the admiration of classical composer/academics like Gunther Schuller, who involved him in a number of Third Stream works (eg on the John Lewis album *Jazz Abstractions*). During 1963/4 he went into retirement, learning trumpet and violin, before appearing again in 1965 with the highly influential trio with David Izenzon and Charles Moffett that he had introduced on the 1962 *Town Hall* album. It was during the currency of this trio that Coleman began to promote his 'classical' writing (*Saints And Soldiers*). Also in the mid-60s, Coleman turned his attention to writing film-scores, the best-known of which is *Chappaque Suite*, which features Pharoah Sanders. He also made a guest appearance - on trumpet! on Jackie MacLean's *Old And New Gospel*. In 1968 a second saxophonist, Dewey Redman, was added to the group, and Izenzon and Moffett were replaced by Jimmy Garrison and Elvin Jones, John Coltrane's former bassist and drummer.

By the end of the 60s, Coleman was again playing with his

early associates, such as Haden, Cherry, Bradford, Higgins and Blackwell, various combinations of which can be heard on *Crisis, Paris Concert, Science Fiction* and *Broken Shadows*. In the mid-70s Coleman began using electric guitars and basses and some rock rhythms with a band that eventually evolved into Prime Time, which continues to this day. The theory of harmolodics has underpinned his music for the last 20 years in particular. Even musicians who have worked with Coleman extensively confess that they do not understand what the theory is about, but there are some threads which can be discerned: two of the most readily understood are that all instruments have their own peculiar, natural voice and should play in the appropriate range, regardless of conventional notions of key, and, secondly, that there is a sort of democracy of instruments, whereby the distinction between soloist and accompanist, leader and sidemen, front-line instruments and rhythm section, is broken down. Coleman is such a powerful improviser that in performance the soloist-accompanist division often remains, but the concept of harmolodics has been quite influential, and is evident in the music of James 'Blood' Ulmer, Ronald Shannon Jackson and the Decoding Society (Ulmer and Jackson were both members of the proto-Prime Time and Coleman guests on the former's 1978 *Tales Of Captain Black*) and Pinski Zoo. While Coleman is seen by many as the father of free jazz his music has never been as abstract, as centred on pure sound, as that of the Chicago AACM circle or of many European exponents of improvised music. His playing is always intensely personal, with a 'human vocalised' sound especially notable on alto, and there is usually a strong, if fluid, rhythmic feel which has become increasingly obvious with Prime Time. There is often a sense of a tonal centre, albeit not one related to the European tempered system, and melodically, both as a writer and improviser, he evinces an acute talent for pleasing design. This he manages without the safety-net of a chord-cycle: instead of the more traditional method of creating symmetrical shapes within a pre-existing structure, his improvisations are based on linear, thematic development, spinning out open-ended, spontaneous compositions which have their own rigorous and indisputable internal logic. Since the mid-70s, with Prime Time and its immediate predecessors, this method began to give way to a more fragmented style, the edgy but elegant depth of emotion being replaced by an intensely agitated feel which sometimes seems to cloak an element of desperation. His 1987 double album, *In All Languages*, featured one disc by a reformed version of the classic late 50s/early 60s quartet, and one by Prime Time, with most themes common to both records, and is an ideal crash-course in Coleman's evolution. As a composer he has written a number of durable themes, such as 'Beauty Is A Rare Thing', 'Focus On Sanity', 'Ramblin'', 'Sadness', 'When Will The Blues Leave', 'Tears Inside' and the ravishing 'Lonely Woman' as well as the massive and rather baffling suite *Skies Of America* written for his group and a symphony orchestra. In the 80s and early 90s he turned increasingly to his notated musics, writing a series of chamber and solo pieces that, excepting *Prime Time/Time Design* (for string quartet and percussion), remain unrecorded.

Selected albums: *Something Else!* (Original Jazz Classics 1958), *Tomorrow Is The Question* (Original Jazz Classics 1959), *The Shape Of Jazz To Come* (Atlantic 1959), *Change Of The Century* (Atlantic 1960), *This Is Our Music* (Atlantic 1961), *Free Jazz* (Atlantic 1961), *Ornette!* (Atlantic 1962), *Ornette On Tenor* (Atlantic 1962), *The Town Hall Concert 1962* (1963), *Chappaque Suite* (1965), *The Great London Concert* aka *An Evening With Ornette Coleman* (1966), *At The Golden Circle, Volumes 1 & 2* (Blue Note 1966), *The Empty Foxhole* (1966), *Music Of Ornette Coleman* aka *Saints And Soldiers* (1967), *The Unprecedented Music Of Ornette Coleman* (1967), *New York Is Now!* (Blue Note 1968), *Love Call* (Blue Note 1968), *Ornette At 12* (1969), *Crisis* (1969), *Friends And Neighbours* (1970), *The Art Of Improvisers* (Atlantic 1970, rec 1959-61), *Twins* (Atlantic 1972, rec 1959-61), *Science Fiction* (1972), *Skies Of America* (1972), *To Whom Who Keeps A Record* (Atlantic 1975), *Dancing In Your Head* (1976), *Body Meta* (1976), *Paris Concert* (1977, rec 1971), *Coleman Classics Volume One* (1977, rec 1958), with Charlie Haden *Soapsuds, Soapsuds* (1977), *Broken Shadows* (Moon 1982, rec 1971-72), *Of Human Feelings* (1982, rec 1979), *Who's Crazy* (Affinity 1983), *Opening The Caravan Of Dreams* (1985), *Prime Time/Time Design* (1985), with Pat Metheny *Song X* (Geffen 1986), *In All Languages* (1987), *Virgin Beauty* (1988), *Live In Milano 1968* (1989, rec 1968), *Jazzbuhne Berlin 88* (1990, rec 1988), *Naked Lunch* (1992), *Languages* (1993), *The Empty Foxhole* (Connoisseur 1994). Compilation: *Beauty Is A Rare Thing: The Complete Atlantic Recordings* (Rhino/Atlantic 1993, 6-CD box set).
Further reading: *Ornette Coleman*, Barry McCrae. *Four Lives In The Bebop Business*, A.B. Spellman.

Coleman, Steve

b. 20 September 1956, Chicago, Illinois, USA. Growing up surrounded by dance music - funk, rock, soul and blues - in Chicago's south side gave Coleman a taste for rhythm he never lost. He learned violin in school, but abandoned it for the alto saxophone at the age of 15, playing in James Brown cover bands. At Illinois Wesleyan University he was the only black person in the music department, quite a shock for someone who says he 'did not know any white people until he was 17 or something'. Told to improvise in his jazz band, he checked out his record collection to find that his father - a 'Bird' fanatic - had slipped in a Charlie Parker album. He learned the solos, just as he had Maceo Parker's. Returning to Chicago he hooked up with Von Freeman, the legendary tenor player and pedagogue, learning the rudiments of bebop on the bandstand. He moved to New York in 1978 to join the Mel Lewis-Thad Jones Big Band, later playing in the Cecil Taylor Orchestra and Sam Rivers' Winds Of Manhattan group. Active and articulate, he and kindred spirits - including singer Cassandra Wilson - formed M-Base, a self-help organization for black musicians, seeking to integrate all forms of black music into a new ecumenical style. Refreshingly, they by-passed the John Coltrane/Michael Brecker style of the Berklee College mainstream for a quirky, electric jazz/funk with a dash of Thelonious Monk and harmolodics too. Coleman has been hailed as the successor to Charlie Parker and attacked as a self-hyped mediocrity. Critics have favoured his work with Dave Holland's group, playing relatively straight ahead bop, but Coleman claims to play the same style in his group Five Elements. Certainly Coleman and M-Base are important movers for black music in the 90s.

Albums: *Motherland Pulse* (1985), *On The Edge of Tomorrow* (1986), *World Expansion* (JMT 1987), *Sine Die* (Pangaea 1988), *Rhythm People* (Novus 1990), *Black Science* (Novus 1991), *Drop Kick* (Novus 1992), *Rhythm In Mind* (Novus 1992), with Dave Holland *Phase = Space* (DIW 1993, rec. 1991), *The Tao Of Mad Phat* (Novus 1993).

Coles, Johnny

b. 3 July 1926, Trenton, New Jersey, USA. A self-taught trumpet and flugelhorn player, Coles joined John Coltrane and Red Garland in Eddie 'Cleanhead' Vinson's band in 1949, and then went on to work with Philly Joe Jones, Bullmoose Jackson, and James Moody in the 50s. After performing and recording with the Gil Evans Orchestra (1958-64), he toured with the Charles Mingus Workshop, recorded with Duke Pearson and Astrud Gilberto, and joined Herbie Hancock in 1968. Since then Coles has graced the big bands of Ray Charles (1969-84), Duke Ellington (1971-74), and Count Basie (1984-86) with his warm and lyrical style. He now lives in San Francisco.

Selected albums: with Charles Mingus *The Great Concert Of Charles Mingus* (1964), with Gil Evans *Out Of The Cool* (1966), *Katumbo Dance* (1971), *New Morning* (Criss Cross 1992).

Collie, Max

b. 21 February 1931, Melbourne, Victoria, Australia. After achieving some success as a semi-pro trombonist in his homeland, Collie visited the UK in 1962 with the Melbourne New Orleans Jazz Band. He stayed behind when the band returned home and joined the London City Stompers. He spent the rest of the 60s building a reputation for the band, now renamed Max Collie's Rhythm Aces. Their success exceeded Collie's expectations thanks to their hard work, unbridled enthusiasm and the application of marketing expertise learnt at university. Tours of the USA established the Aces as one of the top post-Revival bands in the world and they won the so-called World Championship of Jazz in 1975. Collie soldiered on into the 80s playing his fiery brand of rough-hewn traditional jazz and unmoved by the commercial success achieved by other British traditionalists who had long since shifted their ground. In 1984 he co-led the *New Orleans Mardi Gras* road show alongside fellow veterans Ken Colyer and Cy Laurie.

Selected albums: *At The Beiderbecke Festival* (1975), *World Champions Of Jazz* (1976), *Ten Years Together* (1976), *Gospel Train* (Black Lion 1977), *Max Collie Rhythm Aces* (1977), *Jazz Rools OK* (1978), *By Popular Demand* (Black Lion 1979), *Live In Sweden* (Sweet Folk All 1981), *Ten Years Together* (Sweet Folk All 1981), *Live: Max Collie* (1983), *20 Years Jubilee* (Timeless 1986), *Battle Of Trafalgar* (1987), *Sensation* (Timeless 1988), *The Thrill Of Jazz* (1989). Compilations *Max*

Collie's Rhythm Aces, Volume 1 and *2* (both 1987), *The High Society Show* (Reality 1992).

Collier, Graham

b. 21 February 1937, Tynemouth, Northumberland, England. Collier began his musical career playing trumpet in bands in the north of England before entering the British Army as a bandsman. He was in the army, playing dance music and jazz as well as military music, for six years and then won a scholarship to Berklee College Of Music. He worked for a while in the USA, playing bass in the Jimmy Dorsey Orchestra. From 1964 he led his own band in the UK, largely performing his own music. Amongst Collier's sidemen have been many outstanding British musicians of his generation including Harry Beckett, Mike Gibbs, John Surman and Kenny Wheeler. Varying the size and format of his bands, Collier encouraged new concepts and young musicians, establishing the orchestral base from which Loose Tubes sprang. In addition to his career as a performer, Collier has also formed his own recording company, Mosaic, teaches jazz at London's Royal Academy of Music, has composed music for films and television, and has written a number of books on jazz. In 1987 his considerable services to jazz were recognized with an OBE. His compositions are inventive, thoroughly modern and carefully structured, while allowing full and free rein to the improvisational abilities of his soloists.

Albums: *Down Another Road* (1969), *Songs For My Father* (1970), *Mosaics* (1971), *Darius* (1974), *Midnight Blue* (Mosaic 1975), *New Conditions* (Mosaic 1976), *Symphony Of Scorpions* (Mosaic 1976), *Darius* (Mosaic 1977), *Day Of The Dead* (Mosaic 1978), *Something British* (1985).

Collins, Cal

b. Calvin Collins, 5 May 1933, Medora, Indiana, USA. Collins was born and raised in an atmosphere of bluegrass and country music. Although he had taken up the guitar, he began listening to jazz piano players, particularly Art Tatum, Fats Waller, George Shearing and Nat 'King' Cole. In the 50s he settled in Cincinnati, Ohio, playing guitar in local clubs where he sometimes accompanied visiting jazzmen including Andy Simpkins and Harold Jones. It was not until the mid-70s that he achieved wider recognition when he joined Benny Goodman, an engagement that lasted almost four years. This exposure led to a recording contract with Carl Jefferson's Concord Records where he has been teamed with Warren Vaché Jnr., Buddy Tate, Al Cohn, Marshal Royal and Scott Hamilton. Collins has also been recorded by Helen Morr of Mopro Records, who allied him with John Von Ohlen and the rest of the excellent house band's rhythm section at Cincinnati's Blue Wisp Club. During the 80s and early 90s Collins has worked regularly with all-star groups, as a solo and also as accompanist to jazz-orientated singers, notably Rosemary Clooney, playing numerous club, college and festival engagements across the USA and in other countries. Collins is also in demand as a teacher and clinician. In 1991 he was a member of the Woody Herman All Stars led by Terry Gibbs on a tour of Germany and was featured at a series of concerts in California under the generic title, 'Masters of the String Guitar'. Although he drew his early inspiration from jazz pianists Collins was also influenced by country music's Merle Travis. His jazz guitar mentors were Django Reinhardt and Charlie Christian and some of the latter's flowing single-line artistry is echoed in Collins's best work, especially when he plays the blues. His interest in pianists led to his developing an unconventional style of playing in which he uses his left thumb to create a walking bass line while playing intricate patterns with all five fingers of his right hand.

Selected albums: *Benny Goodman: Live At Carnegie Hall, 40th Anniversary Concert* (1978), *Cincinnati To LA* (1978), with Warren Vaché *Cal Collins* (Concord 1979), *Ohio Boss Guitar* (Famous Door 1979), *Polished Brass* (1979), with Scott Hamilton, Buddy Tate *Scott's Buddy* (1980), *Cross Country* (Concord 1981), *Crack'd Rib* (1984), *Ohio Style* (Concord 1990).

Collins, Joyce

b. 5 May 1930, Battle Mountain, Nevada, USA. Collins began playing piano professionally at the age of 15 while still attending Reno High School in Nevada. Later, while studying music and teaching at San Francisco State College, she played in groups and solo at various jazz clubs, eventually going on tour with the Frankie Carle band. In the late 50s Collins settled in Los Angeles, working there and also in Reno and Las Vegas, where she became the first women to conduct one of the resort's show bands. During this time Collins worked in film and television studios, spending 10 years in the band on the *Mary Tyler Moore Show* and also on comedian Bob Newhart's shows. In 1975 she recorded with Bill Henderson and their subsequent *Street Of Dreams* and *Tribute To Johnny Mercer* were Grammy nominees. Collins continued to work in films, coaching actors Jeff and Beau Bridges for their roles in *The Fabulous Baker Boys* (1989). Since 1975 Collins has been associated with the Dick Grove Music School where she teaches jazz piano. Collins has also written and arranged extensively, including a programme, performed live and on radio, tracing the involvement of women in jazz as composers and lyricists. Although she performs mostly in solo, duo and trio work, Collins occasionally sits in with big bands, such as that led by Bill Berry. She has also recorded with Paul Horn and under her own name. Her first album appeared in 1961, her next, *Sweet Madness*, after an inappropriately long gap. Centred mainly upon Los Angeles, Collins has worked farther afield in places such as Mexico City, Paris and, in recent years, New York and Brazil. A gifted, fluent pianist with a strong sense of time and the historical role of the piano in jazz, Collins makes a considerable impression as a performer. Her composing and arranging talents are also worthy of mention and she also sings pleasantly and with a delicate understanding of the lyricists intentions.

Albums: *Girl Here Plays Mean Piano* (1961), with Gene Estes *Westville* (1968), *The Paul Horn Concert Ensemble* (1969), with Bill Henderson *Live At The Times* (1975), with Henderson *Street Of Dreams* (1981), with Henderson *Tribute To Johnny Mercer* (1984), *Moment To Moment* (Discovery 1988), *Sweet Madness* (Audiophile 1990).

Collins, Lee

b. 17 October 1901, New Orleans, Louisiana, USA, d. 3 July 1960. As a youth, Collins gained valuable experience playing trumpet in several marching bands in his home town and also worked with George 'Pops' Foster, Oscar 'Papa' Celestin and Zutty Singleton. By the early 20s his reputation was such, that when Louis Armstrong left the King Oliver band Collins was called to Chicago as his replacement. He later toured extensively, often leading his own bands but failed to achieve widespread recognition. He worked steadily throughout the 30s and 40s but by the early 50s he was in failing health. He suffered from emphysema which inevitably limited his career but he toured Europe with a Franco-American band in 1951, which included Mezz Mezzrow and Zutty Singleton, and returned for a second tour in 1954. This time the strain was too much and he ceased playing, living on for another six years. Despite such moments of glory as when he replaced Armstrong with Oliver and also when he took Red Allen's place in the Luis Russell band in 1930, Collins however was not in their class. He was a gifted player with a rich tone and, on occasions, an exhilarating and inventive soloist.

Selected albums: with Mezz Mezzrow *Clarinet Marmalade* (1951), *A Night At The Victory Club* (New Orleans 1979), with Ralph Sutton *Ralph Sutton's Jazzola Six, Volumes 1* and *2* (Rarities both 1981), *Lee Collins In The 30s* (1986).

Further reading: *Oh, Didn't He Ramble: The Life Story Of Lee Collins*, Lee Collins and Mary Collins, F.J. Gillis and J.W. Miner (Eds).

Collins, Shad

b. Lester R. Collins, 27 June 1910, Elizabeth, New Jersey, USA, d. June 1978. The early years of Collins's career were spent playing trumpet in a succession of top-flight New York-based jazz bands, including those led by Chick Webb, Benny Carter and Tiny Bradshaw. In 1936 he toured Europe with Teddy Hill, remained in Paris for a while, and then returned to the USA to join Count Basie in 1939 when the Basie band was then in full and glorious flight. Collins worked in a trumpet section which also included Buck Clayton and Harry Edison and he was thus somewhat overshadowed as a soloist. In the early 40s Collins played in small groups in New York and then returned to big band music by replacing Dizzy Gillespie in the Cab Calloway orchestra. He stayed with Calloway until 1946 and thereafter worked in various small groups. One of these, led by Sam 'The Man' Taylor, were involved in the R&B boom of the early and mid-50s. However, Collins occasionally recorded with outstanding mainstream groups, including one which featured trombonist Vic Dickenson and rising cornet star, Ruby Braff. Collins retired from active participation in music during the 60s and died in June 1978.

Selected album: with Vic Dickenson *Vic Dickenson Showcase* (1954).

Coltrane, Alice

b. Alice McLeod, 27 August 1937, Detroit, Michigan, USA. Alice came from a musical family (bassist Ernie Farrow is her brother), and studied piano in Detroit, where she worked in a trio and with vibes-player Terry Pollard, before going to Europe and coming under the influence of Bud Powell's playing. She worked with Terry Gibbs on her return to the USA and it was during her stint with Gibbs (1962-63) that she first met John Coltrane. After his divorce from Naima, Alice married him in 1966 and they had three children together. At the end of 1965 she had replaced McCoy Tyner in Coltrane's band, and while she is not the pianist Tyner was, her tentative, gently probing style fitted the requirements of Trane's music at that point. After Coltrane's death in 1967 she carried on promoting his music, issuing through Impulse! Records a number of sessions which might not otherwise have seen the light of day. On some sessions she added her own harp playing and strings arranged by Ornette Coleman, an extremely controversial move. In an interview with writer Pauline Rivelli, she said 'I am really not concerned with results, my only concern is the work, the effort put forth . . . if I give you a leaf or a pearl that you trample in the dust I'm sorry. It's my gift, or offering to you. You do with it as you wish'. Playing mostly piano and organ, she subsequently led her own groups which have featured Frank Lowe, Archie Shepp, Jimmy Garrison, Clifford Jarvis and Jack DeJohnette. From the mid-70s she was less active in music, instead pursuing the spiritual and mystical interests that had already led to her adopting the name Turiya Aparana. But in 1987, to mark the 20th anniversary of her husband's death, she toured with the Coltrane Legacy band, featuring sons Oran and Ravi on saxophones, Reggie Workman on bass and Rashied Ali on drums.

Albums: *A Monastic Trio* (1968), *Universal Consciousness* (1971), *Lord Of Lords* (1972), *Journey In Satchidanada* (MCA 1974), with Carlos Santana *Iluminations* (1974), *Eternity* (1976), *Cosmic Music* (1977), *Reflection On Creation And Space* (1977).

Coltrane, John

b. John William Coltrane, 23 September 1926, Hamlet, North Carolina, USA, d. 17 July 1967. Coltrane grew up in the house of his maternal grandfather, Rev. William Blair (who gave him his middle name), a preacher and community spokesman. While he was taking clarinet lessons at school, his school band leader suggested his mother buy him an alto saxophone. In 1939 his grandfather and then his father died. After finishing high school he joined his mother in Philadelphia. He spent a short period at the Ornstein School of Music and the Granoff Studios, where he won scholarships for both performance and composition, but his real education began as he started gigging. Two years' military service was spent in a navy band (1945-46), after which he toured in the King Kolax and Eddie 'Cleanhead' Vinson bands, playing goodtime, rhythmic big band music. It was while playing in the Dizzy Gillespie Big Band (1949-51) that he switched to tenor saxophone. Coltrane's musical roots were in acoustic black music that combined swing and instru-

mental prowess in solos, the forerunner of R&B. He toured with Earl Bostic (1952), Johnny Hodges (1953-54) and Jimmy Smith (1955). However, it was his induction into Miles Davis's band of 1955 - rightly termed the Classic Quintet - that he was noticed. Next to Miles's filigree sensitivity, Trane sounds awkward and crude, and Miles received criticism for his choice of sideman. However, even in these early gropings you can hear a new seriousness. The only precedent for such modernist interrogation of tenor harmony was John Gilmore's playing with Sun Ra. Critics found Coltrane's tone raw and shocking after years in which the cool school of Lester Young and Stan Getz had held sway. It was generally acknowledged, though, that his ideas were first rate. Along with Sonny Rollins, he became New York's most in-demand hard bop tenor player: 1957 saw him appearing on 21 important recordings, and enjoying a brief but fruitful association with Thelonious Monk. That same year he returned to Philadelphia and kicked his longtime heroin habit and started to develop his own music (Coltrane's notes to the later *A Love Supreme* refer to a 'spiritual awakening'). He also found half of his 'classic' quartet: at the Red Rooster (a nightclub he was taken to by trumpeter Calvin Massey, an old friend from the 40s) he discovered pianist McCoy Tyner and bassist Jimmy Garrison.

After recording numerous albums for the Prestige label, Coltrane signed to Atlantic Records and, on 15 August 1959, he recorded *Giant Steps*. Although it did not use the talents of his new friends from Philadelphia, it featured a dizzying torrent of tenor solos that harked back to the pressure-cooker creativity of bebop, whilst incorporating the muscular gospel attack of hard bop. Pianist Tommy Flanagan (later celebrated for his sensitive backings for singers like Ella Fitzgerald and Tony Bennett) and drummer Art Taylor provided the best performances of their lives. Although this record is rightly hailed as a masterpiece, it encapsulated a problem: where could hard bop go from here? Luckily, Trane knew the answer. After a second spell with Miles (1958-60), Coltrane formed his best-known quartet, with Tyner, Garrison and the amazing polyrhythmic drummer Elvin Jones. Jazz has been recovering ever since.

The social situation of the 60s meant that Coltrane's innovations were simultaneously applauded as *avant garde* statements of black revolution and efficiently recorded and marketed. The Impulse! label, to which he switched from Atlantic in 1961, has a staggering catalogue that includes most of Coltrane's landmark records plus several experimental sessions from the mid-60s which still remain unreleased (though they missed *My Favourite Things*, recorded in 1960 for Atlantic, in which Trane established the soprano saxophone as an important instrument). Between 1961 and his death in 1967, Coltrane made music that has become the groundbase of modern jazz. For commercial reasons Impulse! Records had a habit of delaying the release of his music: fans came out of the live performances in shock at the pace of his evolution. A record of *Ballads* and an encounter with Duke Ellington in 1962 seemed designed to deflect criticisms of coarseness although Coltrane later attributed their relatively temperate ambience to persistent problems with his mouthpiece. *A Love Supreme* was more hypnotic and lulling on record than in live performance, but nevertheless a classic. After that the records became wilder and wilder. The unstinting commitment to new horizons led to ruptures within the group. Elvin Jones left after Trane incorporated a second drummer (Rashied Ali). McCoy Tyner was replaced by Alice McLeod (who married Coltrane in 1966). Coltrane was especially interested in new saxophone players and *Ascension* (1965) made space for Archie Shepp, Pharoah Sanders, Marion Brown and John Tchicai. Eric Dolphy, although he represented a different tradition of playing from Coltrane (a modernist projection of Charlie Parker), had also been frequent guest player with the quartet in the early 60s, touring Europe with them in 1961. *Interstellar Space* (1967), a duet record pitched Coltrane's tenor against Ali's drums, is a fascinating hint of new directions. Coltrane's death in 1967 robbed *avant garde* jazz of its father figure. The commercial ubiquity of fusion in the 70s obscured his music and the 80s jazz revival concentrated on his hard bop period. Only Reggie Workman's Ensemble and Ali's Phalanx carried the huge ambition of Trane's later music into the 90s. As soloists, though, few tenor players have remained untouched by his example. It is interesting that the saxophonists Coltrane encouraged did not sound like him: since his death his 'sound' has become a mainstream commodity, from the Berklee College Of Music-style of Michael Brecker to the 'European' variant of Jan Garbarek. New stars like Andy Sheppard have established new audiences for jazz without finding new ways of playing. Coltrane's music - like that of Jimi Hendrix - ran parallel with a tide of mass political action and consciousness. Perhaps those conditions are required for the creation of such innovative and intense music. Nevertheless, Coltrane's music reached a wide audience, and was particularly popular with the younger generation of listeners who were also big fans of rock music. *A Love Supreme* sold sufficient copies to win a gold disc, while the Byrds used the theme of Coltrane's tune 'India' as the basis of their hit single 'Eight Miles High'. Perhaps by alerting the rock audience to the presence of jazz, Coltrane can be said to have - inadvertently - prepared the way for fusion.

Selected albums: with Hank Mobley *Two Tenors* (1956), with various artists *Tenor Conclave* (1957), *Thelonious Monk With John Coltrane* (1957), *Dakar* (Original Jazz Classics 1957), *John Coltrane - Paul Quinichette Quintet* (1957), *Cattin' With Coltrane And Quinichette* (Original Jazz Classics 1957), *Wheelin' And Dealing* (Original Jazz Classics 1957), *The First Trane* (1957), *Miles Davis And John Coltrane Play Richard Rodgers* (1958), *Lush Life* (Original Jazz Classics 1958), *Traneing In* (Original Jazz Classics 1958), *Tenor Conclave* (Original Jazz Classics 1958), *Blue Train* (Blue Note 1958), *Trane's Reign* (1958), *Soultrane* (Original Jazz Classics 1958), *Kenny Burrell - John Coltrane* (1958), *Settin The Pace* (Original Jazz Classics 1958), *Coltrane Plays For Lovers* (1959), *The Believer* (1959), *The Last Trane* (Original Jazz Classics 1959), *Black Pearls* (Original Jazz Classics 1959), *Stardust* (1959), *The Standard Coltrane* (Prestige 1959), *Bahia* (Original Jazz Classics 1959), John Coltrane And The Jazz Giants (Prestige 1959), *Coltrane Time* (1959), with Milt Jackson *Bags And Trane*

(1959), *Giant Steps* (Atlantic 1960), *Coltrane Jazz* (Atlantic 1961), with Don Cherry *The Avant-Garde* (Atlantic 1961), *My Favourite Things* (Atlantic 1961), *Coltrane Plays The Blues* (Atlantic 1961), *Coltrane's Sound* (Atlantic 1961), *Africa/Brass* (MCA 1961), *Live At The Village Vanguard* (MCA 1961), *Olé Coltrane* (Atlantic 1962), *John Coltrane Quartet* (1962), *Coltrane* (MCA 1962), *Ballads* (Impulse 1963), *Duke Ellington And John Coltrane* (1963), *...And Johnny Hartman* (Impulse 1963), *Impressions* (MCA 1963), *Live At Birdland* (Charly 1964), *Crescent* (Impulse 1964), *A Love Supreme* (MCA 1965), *The John Coltrane Quartet Plays* (Impulse 1965), *Kule Se Mama* (1965), *Ascension* (1965), *Transition* (Impulse 1965), *Selflessness* (1966, rec. 1963, 1965), *Meditations* (Impulse 1966), with Archie Shepp *New Thing At Newport* (Impulse 1966), *Om* (Impulse 1966), *Live At The Village Vanguard Again!* (Impulse 1966), *Expression* (Impulse 1967), *Sun Ship* (1971, rec. 1965), *Dear Old Stockholm* (Impulse 1965), *Live In Seattle* (Impulse 1971, rec. 1965), *Africa Brass, Volume Two* (1974, rec. 1961), *Interstellar Space* (Impulse 1974, rec. 1967), *First Meditations - For Quartet* (Impulse 1977, rec. 1965), *The Other Village Vanguard Tapes* (1977, rec. 1961), *Afro-Blue Impressions* (Pablo 1977, rec. 1962), *The Paris Concert* (1979, rec. 1962), *The European Tour* (1980, rec. 1962), *Bye Bye Blackbird* (1981, rec. 1962), *Live At Birdland - Featuring Eric Dolphy* (1982, rec. 1962). Compilations: *The Art Of John Coltrane - The Atlantic Years* (1973), *The Mastery Of John Coltrane, Vols 1-4* (1978), *The Gentle Side Of John Coltrane* (Impulse 1992), *The Major Works Of John Coltrane* (Impulse 1992), *The Impulse! Years* (Impulse 1993).

Further reading: *Chasin' The Trane*, J.C. Thomas, *John Coltrane*, Bill Cole.

Colyer, Ken

b. 18 April 1928, Great Yarmouth, Norfolk, England, d. 8 March 1988, south of France. Of all the musicians involved in the British Revivalist movement of the late 40s and early 50s, trumpeter Colyer was the only one to achieve the status of a jazz legend. He achieved this through a gritty determination to stick to what he believed to be the true spirit of jazz. Colyer first demonstrated his obsession with the great traditions of New Orleans jazz in the early 50s. He joined the Merchant Navy in order to visit the USA, where he promptly jumped ship and headed for the Crescent City. In New Orleans he sat in with local grand masters, including George Lewis and Emile Barnes, before the authorities caught up with him and he was deported. Before his visit to the USA Colyer had already worked with the Crane River Jazz Band and the Christie Brothers Stompers, but his American exploits had made him a big name in the UK and he was invited to front the co-operative band formed a little earlier by Chris Barber and Monty Sunshine. Although this unit was working regularly and building a reputation, Barber and Sunshine felt that Colyer's fame would be an asset. For a while this assumption proved correct but personality clashes developed, particularly when Colyer appeared to lose sight of the fact that the band he was leading was not his own but was a collective venture. In 1954 Barber took over the reins and Colyer formed his own band, which, with various personnel changes, he continued to lead for the next 30 years. Among the many musicians who worked under Colyer's leadership were Acker Bilk, Diz Disley, Ian Wheeler and Sammy Rimington. Conceding that his technique was limited, Colyer overcame any deficiencies in style through an unflinching determination not to be swayed by changing public tastes or commercial considerations, although he did play guitar and sing in a skiffle group in the mid-50s. In 1957 he returned to the US and joined the George Lewis band, and arranged their trips to Europe. His last significant work was as part of the touring jazz show *New Orleans Mardi Gras*. Colyer defeated cancer, and the temporary retirement this necessitated, playing on into the 80s. A year after he died a commemorative blue plaque was placed on the wall of the 100 Club in London, and many of his former colleagues took part in a concert organized by the Ken Colyer Trust.

Selected albums: *Ken Colyer In New Orleans* (1953), *New Orleans To London* (1953), *In The Beginning...* (1954), *A Very Good Year* (1957), Sensation (Lake 1960), *When I Leave The World Behind* (Lake 1963), *Out Of Nowhere* (1965), *Live At The Dancing Slipper* (1969), *Ken Colyer And His Handpicked Jazzmen* (1972), *Spirituals, Vols. 1* and *2* (Joy both 1974), *Swinging And Singing* (1975), *Painting The Clouds With Sunshine* (1979), *Ken Colyer With John Petters' New Orleans Allstars* (1985), with Max Collie, Cy Laurie *New Orleans Mardi Gras* (1985), with Acker Bilk *It Looks Like A Big Time Tonight* (1985), *Too Busy* (CMJ 1985). Selected compilations: *The Decca Years, Vol. 1 (1955-1959)* (Lake 1985), *The Decca Years, Vol. 2 (1955-1959)* (1986), *The Decca Skiffle Sessions (1954-7)* (1987), *The Decca Years, Vol. 3 (1955-1959)* (1987), *The Guv'nor (1959-61)* (1989).

Further Reading: *When Dreams Are In The Dust (The Path Of A Jazzman)*, Ken Colyer (1989).

Condon, Eddie

b. 16 November 1905, Goodland, Indiana, USA, d. 4 July 1973. After working in local bands, guitar and banjoist Condon moved to Chicago in the early 20s. He quickly associated himself with the very finest young white musicians based there: Bix Beiderbecke, Frank Teschemacher, Jimmy McPartland, Bud Freeman, Dave Tough and other members of the Austin High School Gang. In 1928, soon after making his first record, he tried his brand of music in New York, happily starving in between recording dates with, among others, Fats Waller and Louis Armstrong. Despite some indifference amongst audiences, local musicians were impressed both with Condon and some of the friends he had brought along, including Gene Krupa and, later, Jack Teagarden. Condon stayed on in New York, building a reputation as an organizer of concerts and recording dates. A regular at several clubs, notably Nick's, he eventually opened his own which became synonymous with the best of Chicago-style jazz as played by such long-time friends and musical partners as Wild Bill Davison and Pee Wee Russell. A tough-talking, hard-drinking, wisecracking entrepreneur, Condon never lost his abiding love for the music of his youth, dismissing bebop with a joke 'They play their flatted fifths, we drink ours', just as he did to outside criticism 'Do we tell those Frogs how to jump on a grape?'. Unlike many wits, Condon was able to retain his humour in print and his three books provide fascinating and funny insights into the world in which he lived and worked. In his later years he made occasional overseas tours and continued to make record dates. Although a good rhythm player, Condon was often disinclined to perform, leaving his instrument, nicknamed 'Porkchop', in its case while he got on with the serious business of talking to customers and drinking. His reluctance to play often infiltrated record dates and on many he either laid out or contented himself with providing a discreet pulse which only the other musicians could hear. Consequently, he is not necessarily always audible on the records which bear his name. His influence, however, is always apparent.

Selected albums: *Jam Session Coast To Coast* (1953), *Bixieland* (1955), *Live In Tokyo* (1964), with Wild Bill Davison, Gene Krupa *Jazz At The New School* (1972). Compilations: *The Spirit Of Condon* (1979), *Intoxicating Dixieland (1944-45)* (1981), *The Eddie Condon Band (1945)* (1981), *The Eddie Condon Floorshow, Volumes 1* and *2 (1949)* (Queendisc 1981), *His Windy City 7 Jam Sessions At Commodore (1935)* (1985), *Chicago Style (1927-33)* (VJM 1985), *The Town Hall Broadcasts (1944-45)* (1986), *The Town Hall Concerts, Volumes 1-6 (1944-45)* (Jazzology 1988), *At The Jazz Band Ball (1944-50)* (1986), *The Liederkranz Sessions* (1987), *Jazz On The Air - Eddie Condon Floorshow* (Delta 1988), *Dixieland Jam* (CBS 1991), *We Dig Dixieland Jazz* (Savoy 1993).

Further Reading: *We Called It Music*, Eddie Condon with Thomas Sugrue. *Eddie Condon's Treasury Of Jazz. Eddie Condon's Scrapbook Of Jazz*, Eddie Condon and Hank O'Neal.

Connor, Chris

b. 8 November 1927, Kansas City, Missouri, USA. After singing publicly while still at school, Connor worked with the bands of Claude Thornhill, where she was a member of the vocal group, the Snowflakes, and Herbie Fields in the late 40s and early 50s. Audibly influenced by Anita O'Day, Connor quickly developed her own recognizable style and built a localized reputation. Having sung in high school with a Kenton-style band it was especially appropriate when June Christy, in 1953, recommended Chris to Stan Kenton as her replacement, after this period her career was much enhanced. She continued singing for the next 30-plus years, working mostly as a soloist and usually with jazz musicians in her backing group. In the late 80s she was to be heard singing in Europe showing a few signs of deterioration in her voice while, stylistically, she was as good as ever. In 1990 she was a featured artist at London's Soho Jazz Festival.

Selected albums: with Stan Kenton *Some Women I've Known* (1953), *Chris Connor With Ellis Larkins/Lullabies Of Birdland* (1954), *Chris Connor Sings Lullabies For Lovers* (1954), *This Is Chris* (1955), *Chris* (1955), *Cocktails At Dusk* (1955), *Out Of This World* (Affinity 1956), *Songs* (1956), *A Jazz Date With Chris Connor* (1956), *Chris Connor i* (1957), *Chris Craft*

(1958), *Ballads Of The Sad Cafe* (1959), *Chris In Person* (1959), *Witchcraft* (1959), *Chris Connor* ii (1959), *Portrait Of Chris* (1960), *Double Exposure* (1960), *Chris Connor* iii (1962), *Live At The Village Gate* (1963), *Chris Connor* iv (c.60s), *Chris Connor* v (1965), *Chris Connor* vi (c.60s), *Sketches* (1972), *Chris Moves* (1976), *Sweet And Swinging* (Progressive 1978), *Alone Together* (1978), *Chris Connor Live* (1981), *I Hear Music* (Affinity 1983), *Love Being Here With You* (1983), *Cool Chris* (Charly 1988), *As Time Goes By* (1992), *London Connection* (Audiophile 1993).

Connors, Bill

b. 24 September 1949, Los Angeles, California, USA. Like so many young men of his generation, Connors was attracted to rock music and the electric guitar. His interest underwent a slight shift of direction and he became a leading figure of the jazz/rock scene of the early 70s. He toured with Chick Corea's then current Return To Forever band and also played with fellow jazz/rock bass guitarist Stanley Clarke. By the late 70s, Connors, ever searching, had also moved into free jazz and during these years he worked with Lee Konitz, Gary Peacock, Jan Garbarek and others. In addition to playing electric guitar, Connors also occasionally plays the acoustic instrument, for example on his solo album, *Theme To The Guardian*. His first love, however, remained the electric guitar and stylistically he has always been most at home playing jazz/rock.

Albums: *Theme To The Guardian* (ECM 1974), *Step It* (Core 1985), *Double Up* (Core 1985), *Assembler* (Line 1989), *Swimming With A Hole In My Body* (ECM 1992), *Of Mist And Melting* (ECM 1993).

Cook, Junior

b. Herman Cook, 22 July 1934, Pensacola, Florida, USA, d. 3 February 1992. Raised in a musical family, Cook began playing alto saxophone, then later switched to tenor. He joined Dizzy Gillespie in the late 50s and also played with Horace Silver. He remained with Silver for about five years, after which he teamed up with Blue Mitchell for another long stint. In the early 70s he taught at Berklee College Of Music. During the early and mid-70s he played with Freddie Hubbard, then with Louis Hayes. During the late 70s and early 80s Cook recorded with several artists, including Mickey Tucker, Clifford Jordan and Eddie Jefferson and led his own small group for club and festival dates. A highly talented post-bop saxophonist, Cook's abilities, while well-served on record, have yet to be fully recognized by the international jazz world.

Albums: with Horace Silver *Horace-scope* (1960), *Junior's Cookin'* (1961), with Blue Mitchell *Head's Up!* (1967), with Freddie Hubbard *Keep Your Soul Together* (1973), *Pressure Cooker* (1977), *Good Cookin'* (Muse 1979), *Something's Cookin'* (Muse 1981), *The Place To Be* (1988), *On A Misty Night* (1989), with George Coleman *Stablemates* (Affinity 1990).

Cooke, Micky

b. 6 August 1945, Hyde, Cheshire, England. Trombonist Cooke began his career as a semi-pro player with Manchester band the Blue Lotus Jazzmen in the early 60s, and also played with many other local outfits including the Smoky City Jazzband, Johnny Tippet's Jazzmen, and the Red River Jazzmen. In 1967 he left Manchester for Birmingham, before moving further south to join Terry Lightfoot in 1968. Following spells with bandleaders Alan Elsdon and Alex Welsh, Cooke worked as a freelance with Digby Fairweather, Lennie Hastings and Dave Shepherd, before beginning a seven-year association with Keith Smith, with whose 'Hefty Jazz' he recorded and toured extensively, visiting the US in 1985. He has a justified reputation as one of Britain's most technically-gifted trombonists, and plays in a hot, shouting style, strongly influenced by Abe Lincoln. In mid-1987 Cooke replaced Campbell Burnap in the Acker Bilk band.

Selected albums: with Alan Elsdon *Jazz Journeymen* (1977), with Acker Bilk *Hits, Blues And Classics* (1988).

Cooper, Bob

b. 6 December 1925, Pittsburgh, Pennsylvania, USA, d. 5 August 1993, Los Angeles, California, USA. After studying music at high school, Cooper showed early prowess on tenor saxophone and by the age of 20 was hired by Stan Kenton, with whom he remained for the next six years. During this period Cooper made numerous records with the band and also led a small group largely drawn from fellow sidemen. On some engagements he accompanied Kenton's singer, June Christy, whom he married in 1947. After Kenton, Cooper stayed on the west coast working in the studios and playing jazz with like-minded musicians, especially Shelly Manne and Shorty Rogers. Throughout the 60s, 70s and 80s, Cooper continued working, mainly on the coast, dividing his time between the studios and jazz groups including those led by Terry Gibbs and his old stablemate Rogers. He was also called upon by several of the big bands formed in California, including those led by Bob Florence, Frank Capp-Nat Pierce and Bill Berry. A fluent and inventive soloist, Cooper's bop and post-bop leanings were often submerged in his freewheeling, swing-orientated playing.

Selected albums: *The Travelling Mr Cooper* (1957), *Coop!* (1957), *Tenor Sax Jazz Impressions* (Trend 1979), *Bob Cooper Plays The Music Of Michel Legrand* (Discovery 1980), *Group Activity (1954-55)* (Affinity 1981), *Shifting Winds (1954-55)* (Affinity 1981), *In A Mellotone* (1985), with Bob Florence *Trash Can City* (1986), *For All We Know* (Fresh Sound 1991), *Mosaic* (Capri 1993).

Cooper, Buster

b. George Cooper, 4 April 1929, St. Petersburg, Florida, USA. Coming from a musical family - his brother Steve plays bass-trombonist Cooper worked briefly in a band led by a cousin, then joined Nat Towles's famous Texas-based band. He later advanced his musical knowledge studying in New York before joining Lionel Hampton in 1953. He spent the rest of the 50s working with various bands including those led by Benny Goodman and Lucky Millinder and also co-leading a band with his brother. In 1962 he joined Duke Ellington, who would sometimes dryly introduce him as 'Trombonio-Bustosoissimo', where he remained for seven years before returning to his home state and another joint band with his brother. In the early 70s he decided to relocate to the west coast and since then has worked with several big bands, notably those led by Frank Capp-Nat Pierce and Bill Berry. He has also toured both as a soloist and with Berry and Marshal Royal as an Ellington alumni group. A powerful player with a searing attack and brilliant technique, Cooper's solos are frequently characterized by humour and by extraordinary cadenzas which leave audiences and fellow musicians, but not him, breathless. In a more mellow mood, when he performs ballads, he brings to his playing an attractive and delicately-romantic touch.

Selected albums: with Duke Ellington *Will The Big Bands Ever Come Back? (1962-3)* (1976), with Capp-Pierce *Juggernaut Strikes Again* (1981).

Cooper, Jerome

b. George Cooper, 14 December 1946, Chicago, Illinois, USA. Cooper came up drumming with blues bands on Chicago's south side and stormed awhile with Rahsaan Roland Kirk. In Paris, he worked with Steve Lacy and the Art Ensemble Of Chicago, then quit the freelancing life to commit his energies to the influential Revolutionary Ensemble (1970-1977), which he co-founded. Despite surfacing briefly as Cecil Taylor's drummer, Cooper has, since 1978, concentrated primarily on solo performances in which he augments his drum kit with African talking drum and balafon and also plays chirimia (a high-pitched oboe of Spanish origin) and synthesizer. He cites shamanism as an important influence on his work and collaborates periodically with the similarly-inspired English performance artist Colin Gilder, Cooper providing the live soundtrack - both improvised and composed - to Gilder's plays and happenings.

Albums: *Positions 369* (1977), *Root Assumptions* (1978), *For The People* (1979), *The Unpredictability Of Predictability* (1980), *Outer And Interactions* (1988).

Cooper, Lindsay

b. March 1951, London, England. Multi-instrumentalist Cooper studied at Dartington College and the Royal Academy Of Music, becoming proficient on bassoon, sopranino and alto saxophones, oboe, flute, piano and accordion, though in recent years she concentrated almost exclusively on the first three of these instruments. After working briefly as a classical bassoonist, she turned her attention to theatre, pop and improvised musics. From 1974-78 she was a member of experimental rock group Henry Cow; in 1977 she co-founded the Feminist Improvising Group, its name indicating the primary concern of much of her subsequent work, notably in projects with other FIG and EWIG (European Women's Improvising Group) artists such as Maggie Nicols, Anna Marie Roelofs, Joëlle Léandre and Irène Schweizer. In the early 80s she was a regular performer on the European jazz scene, playing on various Mike Westbrook projects (*The Cortege, Westbrook-Rossini*) and joining the Maarten Altena Octet (*Tel*). She also kept a foot in the rock camp, recording with David Thomas's Pedestrians (*Winter*

Comes Home, More Places For Ever) and as part of the group News From Babel (with Chris Cutler), Dagmar Krause and Zeena Parkins). A talented composer, her own *Rags, The Gold Diggers* and *Music For Other Occasions* comprised pieces she had written for various film, television and theatre projects, often in association with singer/director Sally Potter. In 1989 Cooper's song-cycle *Oh Moscow* was recorded live at Canada's Victoriaville Festival; 1991 saw the release of both the classically-oriented *An Angel On The Bridge* and a collection of contemporary dance pieces, *Schrodinger's Cat*. In 1992 her 'Concerto For Sopranino Saxophone And Strings' was premiered in London by the European Women's Orchestra, and her new 'Songs For Bassoon And Orchestra' was presented in Bologna. The same year, her chamber pieces 'The Road Is Wider Than Long' was included on Lontrano's *British Women Composers Volume 1,* and the long jazz vocal composition *Sahara Dust* (lyrics by Robyn Archer) was released, reaffirming her rare gift of versatility across so many musical genres.

Albums: *Feminist Improvising Group* (1979), *Rags,* (1980), *The Gold Diggers* (1983), with Maggie Nicols, Joëlle Léandre *Live At The Bastille* (1984, rec 1982), with News From Babel *Work Resumed On The Tower* (1984), with News From Babel *Letters Home* (1986), *Music For Other Occasions* (1986), *An Angel On The Bridge* (1991), *Schrodinger's Cat* (Femme 1991), with others *British Women Composers Volume 1* (1992), *Sahara Dust* (1992), *Oh Moscow* (Victo 1993).

Corea, Chick

b. Armando Anthony Corea, 12 June 1941, Chelsea, Massachusetts, USA. After a very musical home environment, pianist Corea's first notable professional engagements were in the Latin bands of Mongo Santamaría and Willie Bobo (1962-63), playing a style of music which continues to influence him today. Joining Blue Mitchell's band in 1964, he spent two years with the trumpeter, and got a chance to record some of his own compositions on Blue Note Records. Corea's first recordings appeared in 1966 with *Tones For Joan's Bones*, and show a pianist influenced mainly by hard-bop. In 1968, he joined Miles Davis for the trumpeter's first real experiments with fusion. Playing on some of Davis's most important albums, Corea's electric piano became integral to the new sound. Leaving Davis in 1970 to explore free music within an acoustic setting, he formed Circle with Dave Holland, Barry Altschul, and later Anthony Braxton. Although Circle lasted only a year, it managed to make some important recordings before Corea, now involved in Scientology, became interested in a style with more widespread appeal. Forming the first of three bands called Return To Forever in 1971, he played a Latin-influenced fusion featuring the vocalist Flora Purim and percussionist Airto Moreiro, before he changed the band's line-up to produce a more rock-orientated sound in the mid-70s. The final Return To Forever hinted at classical music with string and brass groups, but disbanded in 1980 after only moderate success. After playing with numerous top musicians in the early 80s (including Herbie Hancock and Michael Brecker), since 1985 he has concentrated on his Akoustic and Elektric Bands and now records for GRP Records. Joined by John Patitucci (bass) and Dave Weckl (drums), he is presently involved in a music which challenges the extremes of virtuosity; mixing passages of complex arrangement with solos in the fusion style.

Selected albums: *Tones For Joan's Bones* (1966), *Bliss* (1967), with Roy Haynes, Miroslav Vitous *Now He Sings, Now He Sobs* (Blue Note 1968), with Haynes, Vitous *Circling In* (1968), *Is 69* (1969), *Sun Dance* (1969), *The Song Of Singing* (Blue Note 1970), with Circle *Circulus* (1970), with Circle *Paris Concert* (1971), *A.R.C.* (ECM 1971), *Early Circle* (Blue Note 1971), *Piano Improvisations Vols. 1 & 2* (ECM 1971), *Inner Space* (1972), *Return To Forever* (ECM 1972), with Gary Burton *Crystal Silence* (1973), *Light As A Feather* (Polydor 1973), *Hymn Of The Seventh Galaxy* (Polydor 1973), *Where Have I Known You Before* (Polydor 1974), *Chick Corea* (1975), *Chick Corea Quartet: Live In New York City, 1974* (1976), *The Leprechaun* (1976), *My Spanish Heart* (Polydor 1976), *Before Forever* (1977), *The Mad Hatter* (Verve 1978), *Friends* (Polydor 1978), *Secret Agent* (1978), with Burton *Duet* (1979), *An Evening With Herbie Hancock And Chick Corea* (1979, live 1978 recordings), *Corea/Hancock* (Polydor 1979), *Delphi 1: Solo Piano Improvisations* (1979), *Crystal Silence* (ECM 1979), *In Concert, Zurich, October 28, 1978* (ECM 1980), *Delphi 2 & 3* (1980), *Tap Step* (1980), *Three Quartets* (Stretch 1981), *Trio Music* (ECM 1981), *Touchstone* (Streych 1982), with Nicolas Economou *On Two Pianos* (1982), with Friedrich Gulda *The Meeting* (1982), *Again And Again (The Joburg Sessions)* (1983), *Children's Songs* (ECM 1983), with Burton *Lyric Suite For Sextet* (ECM 1983), *Voyage* (ECM 1984), *Trio Music, Live In Europe* (ECM 1984), *Septet* (ECM 1985), with Steve Kujala *Voyage* (1985), *Early Days* (LRC 1986, 1969 recordings), *Elektric Band* (GRP 1986), *Light Years* (GRP 1987), *Eye Of The Beholder* (GRP 1988), *Chick Corea Akoustic Band* (GRP 1989), *Inside Out* (GRP 1990), *Beneath The Mask* (GRP 1991), *Alive* (GRP 1991), with Bobby McFerrin *Play* (1992), *Inner Space* (Atlantic 1993), *Paint The World* (GRP 1993), *Expressions* (GRP 1994). Compilations: *Verve Jazz Masters* (Verve 1979), *Chick Corea Works* (ECM 1985).

Coryell, Larry

b. 2 April 1943, Galveston, Texas, USA. Coryell grew up in the state of Washington. He first worked as a guitarist in 1958 when he formed a rock 'n' roll band with keyboard player Michael Mandel. In 1965 he relocated to New York and joined Chico Hamilton's band, overlapping with the legendary guitarist Gabor Szabo, whom he eventually replaced. In 1966 he formed Free Spirits with American Indian tenor player Jim Pepper. He toured with Gary Burton (1967-68) and played on Herbie Mann's *Memphis Underground* (1968). Coryell was impressed with the exploits of Jimi Hendrix and Eric Clapton with Cream, and his performance on Michael Mantler's *Jazz Composers Orchestra* project in 1968 was scarifying electric guitar at its best. Coryell's early solo albums featured strong support from Elvin Jones and Jim Garrison (*Lady Coryell*), and John McLaughlin and Billy Cobham (*Spaces*). *Fairyland*, recorded live at Montreux in 1971 with soul veterans Chuck

Rainey (bass) and Bernard 'Pretty' Purdie (drums), a power trio format, was packed with sublime solos. *Barefoot Boy*, recorded the same year at Electric Lady Studios (built by Hendrix), was notable for its simultaneous use of non-pareil jazz drummer Roy Haynes and electric feedback and distortion. Coryell formed Eleventh House with Mandel, honing his experimental music into a dependable showcase for his virtuosity. Coryell, seeming to have sensed that a spark had gone, broke up the band and gave up electricity for a while. He began playing with other guitarists - Philip Catherine, McLaughlin, Paco De Lucia and John Scofield. He played on Charles Mingus's *Three Or Four Shades Of Blue* in 1977 and recorded arrangements of Stravinsky for Nippon Phonogram. In the mid-80s Coryell started playing electric again, with Bunny Brunel (bass) and Alphonse Mouzon (drums). In 1990 he recorded with Don Lanphere, using his considerable name to spotlight an old friend's rekindled career: easy, unassuming acoustic jazz. Despite his extraordinary technique and his early promise, Coryell has never really created his own music, instead playing with undeniable finesse in a variety of contexts.

Selected albums: with Herbie Mann *Memphis Underground* (1968), with Michael Mantler *Jazz Composers Orchestra* (1968), *Lady Coryell* (1969), *Coryell* (1969), *Spaces* (Vanguard 1970), *Fairyland* (1971), *Larry Coryell At The Village Gate* (1971), *Barefoot Boy* (1971), *Offering* (1972), *The Real Great Escape* (1973), *Introducing The Eleventh House* (1974), *The Restful Mind* (1975), *Planet End* (1976), *Level One* (1976), *Basics* (1976, recordings from 1968), *Aspects* (1976), *Lion And The Ram* (1976), with Steve Kahn *Two For The Road* (1976), with Philip Catherine *Twin House* (Act 1976), *Back Together* (1977), *Splendid* (1978), *European Impressions* (1978), *Standing Ovation* (1978), *Return* (1979), with John Scofield, Joe Beck *Tributaries* (Novus 1979), *Bolero* (String 1981), *'Round Midnight* (1983), *Scheherazade* (1984), *The Firebird And Petrouchka* (1984), *Together* (Concord 1986), *Coming Home* (Muse 1986), *Equipoise* (Muse 1987), *Toku Du* (Muse 1988), *A Quiet Day In Spring* (Steeplechase 1988), *Just Like Being Born* (1989), *Don Lanphere/Larry Coryell* (1990), *Shining Hour* (Muse 1991), *Twelve Frets To One Octave* (Koch 1992), *Live From Bahia* (CTI 1992), *Fallen Angel* (CTI 1994).

Cottrell, Louis, Jnr.

b. 7 March 1911, New Orleans, Louisiana, USA. d. 21 March 1978. Born into a musical family, Cottrell studied clarinet with Lorenzo Tio. After playing with local bands he spent the 30s touring with Don Albert with whom he also played tenor saxophone. At the end of the decade he returned to New Orleans where he played with bands such as those led by Paul Barbarin and Sidney Desvigne. He continued to play through the 50s and 60s with the bands of Barbarin and others, then formed his own band which he led for the remainder of his life. A sound and professional player, Cottrell's spell with Albert displayed his ability to work effectively in surroundings other than the New Orleans style he favoured. His father was Louis Cottrell Snr. (1878-1927), an influential New Orleans drummer.

Albums: *Bourbon Street Parade* (1961), *Louis Cottrell And His*

New Orleans Jazz Band (1964).

Counce, Curtis

b. 23 January 1926, Kansas City, Missouri, USA, d. 31 July 1963. After studying various instruments, bassist Counce gained early professional experience playing with Nat Towles's territory band. This was in the early 40s and he subsequently worked for three years with Edgar Hayes. By the end of the decade Counce had begun a period of intensive association with many of the leading west coast beboppers currently engaged in creating the 'cool school' of jazz. In 1953 he record-ed with Teddy Charles and was on the Shorty Rogers *Cool And Crazy* album. The powerful swing engendered by Rogers' big band, made up almost entirely of Stan Kenton sidemen, was due in no small part to the rhythm section of Marty Paich, Shelly Manne and Counce. That same year, Counce recorded with small groups led by Manne. In 1954 Counce was available for a record date with an expanded version of the Max Roach-Clifford Brown quintet, the surging powerhouse playing of one breakneck-tempoed tune, 'Coronado', effectively demolishing charges of effeteness frequently levelled at the west coast school. The following year he was again with Rogers, this time for a record date as a member of the Giants, which resulted in two extremely well-received albums, *The Swinging Mr Rogers* and *Martians Come Back*. By now, Counce was an established figure and one of few black musicians to be working extensive-ly in the studios. In 1956 he joined Stan Kenton with whom he toured Europe. On his return he formed his own band which, musically, was in tune with the east coast-based Jazz Messengers of Horace Silver. Counce's group featured Harold Land, Jack Sheldon, Carl Perkins and Frank Butler and was musically successful. The band's records sold well although it failed to garner the critical or popular credit of the Messengers. They stayed together until 1958, making their last recording shortly before Perkins's death. Restructured and renamed as the Curtis Counce Quintet, the unit made another album later in 1958, but did not quite measure up to the remarkable earlier standards. The Curtis Counce Group was one of the most exciting of the many 50s Los Angeles-based bands and while the individual members can all be credited for their part in its success, the leader in particular must be singled out for the care with which he selected his sidemen. Counce's premature death was a great loss for the jazz world.

Selected albums: *The Curtis Counce Group/Landslide* (1956), *You Get More Bounce With Curtis Counce* (Original Jazz Classics 1957), *Landslide* (Original Jazz Classics 1958), *Carl's Blues* (1958), *Exploring The Future* (Boblicity 1958), *Sonority* (Contemporary 1959), Compilations: *Counceltation* (1981), *Carl's Blues* (Contemporary 1987).

Coursil, Jacques

b. 1939, Paris, France. Coursil's parents were immigrants from Martinique and he grew up listening to Creole songs, the beguins. After a false start trying to play the violin at the age of nine, he attended the local conservatory, ostensibly to learn clarinet - his idol was Sidney Bechet, then living in Paris - but took up a cornet when it was handed him. Arriving in New York in the early 60s he studied with Jaki Byard for two years and involved himself in the burgeoning black *avant garde*, play-ing with tenor saxophonist Frank Wright. In 1966 he recorded with Sunny Murray for ESP-Disk. He also played lead trumpet in the Sun Ra Arkestra. However, although he loved the music he could not swallow Sun Ra's philosophy and left to play with Rashied Ali and Marion Brown. Interested in serial procedures, Coursil wrote *Black Suite* in 1967. This was released by BYG Records of Paris in 1969 and features Anthony Braxton. It is a powerful and highly original piece, making one regret Coursil's subsequent neglect by the record labels. He has, though, made another contribution to modern music: it was while teaching John Zorn French that he introduced the young composer to jazz.

Albums: *Sunny Murray Quintet* (1966), *Black Suite* (1969).

Coxhill, Lol

b. Lowen Coxhill, 19 September 1932, Portsmouth, Hampshire, England. Coxhill first attracted attention in the early 60s playing soprano saxophone with a startlingly wide variety of bands. In his early career, he was at home playing with R&B singers, rock groups, free jazz ensembles and was especially adept playing unaccompanied solos. On occasion, he would also happily sit in with traditional bands, making no attempt to adapt his forthright and contemporary style and yet improbably making the results work. In the 70s and 80s Coxhill was involved with such musicians as Chris McGregor's Brotherhood Of Breath, Bobby Wellins, Evan Parker, Derek Bailey and Tony Coe; he worked frequently with pianist Steve Miller, was co-leader of the now-defunct Johnny Rondo Trio, and is now a member of two regular groups - the Recedents (with Mike Cooper and Roger Turner) and the Melody Four (actually a trio, with Tony Coe and Steve Beresford). For a while in the early 80s, he was a guest member of the punk group, the Damned. In the 70s he also began to develop a side-line career as an actor, and has appeared in a number of plays in the theatre and on television: he was also the subject of the documentary film, *Frog Dance*. A strikingly original player, Coxhill's fiercely independent approach to his music has always been leavened by his droll sense of humour and a broad-mind-ed eclecticism - in the early 90s he was playing early jazz with bassist Dave Green, singing Marx Brothers songs with the Melody Four and continuing his total improvisations both solo and with the Recedents.

Albums: *Ear Of The Beholder* (1971), *Toverbal Sweet* (1971), with Steve Miller *Coxhill/Miller* (1973), *The Story So Far...Oh Really, One Side?* (Caroline 1974), *Lol Coxhill And The Welfare State* (1975), *Fleas In The Custard* (Caroline 1975), *Diverse* (1977), *Lid* (1978), *The Joy Of Paranoia* (Ogun 1978), *Moot* (1978), with Morgan Fisher *Slow Music* (1978), *Chantenay '80* (1980), *The Dunois Solos* (Nato 1981), *Instant Replay* (1982), with Eyeless In Gaza *Home Produce* (1982), *Cou$ Cou$* (Nato 1983), with Fred Frith *French Gigs* (AAA 1983), *Frog Dance* (1986), with Daniel Deshays *10:02* (Nato 1986), *Instant Replay* (Nato 1986), *The Inimitable* (Chabada 1986), *Café De*

La Place (1986), *Before My Time* (1987), *Looking Back Forwards* (1990), *Lol Coxhill* (1990), *The Bald Soprano Companion* (Tak 1990), *Hollywood Concert* (Slam 1990).
Further reading: *The Bald Soprano*, Jeff Nuttall.

Crawford, Hank

b. Bennie Crawford, 21 December 1934, Memphis, Tennessee, USA. One of the most prolific jazz/blues saxophonists, Crawford came to prominence as a member of the Ray Charles band in the late 50s. After studying at the University of Tennessee, he joined Charles in 1958, playing baritone saxophone and working closely with the leader on arrangements and new material. Eventually he was given the title musical director. Crawford later switched to alto-saxophone and while still a member of the Charles band, he was signed in 1961 to a solo recording contract with Atlantic Records. His earliest recordings included fellow Charles sideman David 'Fathead' Newman on tenor saxophone and reproduced the funky feel of Charles' own work. Crawford left Ray Charles and formed his own group in 1964, the year after Hollywood arranger Marty Paich had worked with him on an album of standards such as 'Stardust' and 'Stormy Weather', but the bulk of Crawford's Atlantic output consisted of booting soul-blues material. From 1972, he recorded for Kudu, an easy-listening jazz label set up by Creed Taylor. His repertoire was now drawn from current hits (Kris Kristofferson's 'Help Me Make It Through The Night') and Ray Charles standards ('I Can't Stop Loving You') as well as original compositions. On several of the albums he was accompanied by members of the New York session mafia, notably Richard Tee (keyboards), Eric Gale and Hugh McCracken (guitars), Randy Brecker (trumpet) and Bernard Purdie (drums). After Kudu closed down, Crawford recorded for Milestone. *Soul Survivors* was made with master organist Jimmy McGriff and produced by Rudy van Gelder. It included a new version of the Charles classic 'One Mint Julep'. The same year, Dr. John played and sang in a strong Crawford band that included Purdie, Brecker and 'Fathead' Newman. His albums during the late 80s were very much a formula, albeit a good formula - featuring the likes of McGriff, Billy Preston, George Benson and Mel Lewis.
Albums: *More Soul* (1961), *Soul Clinic* (1961), *From The Heart* (1962), *Soul From The Ballad* (1963), *True Blue* (1964), *Dig These Blues* (1965), *After Hours* (1967), *Mr Blues* (1967), *Double Cross* (1968), *Mr Blues Plays Lady Soul* (1969), *Help Me Make It Through The Night* (1972), *Wildflower* (CBS 1973), *Don't You Worry 'Bout A Thing* (1974), *I Hear A Symphony* (1975), *Hank Crawford's Back* (Kudu 1976), *Tico Rico* (Kudu 1977), *Cajun Sunrise* (Polydor 1979), *Midnight Ramble* (Milestone 1983), *Indigo Blue* (Milestone 1983), *Roadhouse Symphony* (Milestone 1986), *Mr Chips* (Milestone 1986), *Soul Survivors* (1986), *Steppin' Up* (Milestone 1988), *Night Beat* (Milestone 1989), with McGriff *Soul Brothers* (Milestone 1989), *On The Blue Side* (Milestone 1990), *Groove Master* (Milestone 1991), *Portrait* (Milestone 1991), *South-Central* (Milestone 1993).

Crawford, Jimmy

b. 14 January 1910, Memphis, Tennessee, USA, d. 28 January 1980. Crawford began his musical career in good company when, at Manassas County High School in the late 20s, he met Jimmie Lunceford, Moses Allen and other young musicians who played together in the Lunceford-led Chickasaw Syncopators. When Lunceford took the band on tour, Crawford went along as the drummer, contributing greatly to the band's gradual progress until, in 1933, they made their breakthrough into the big-time at New York's Lafayette Theater. In 1934 they were booked into the Savoy, a severe test for any band - and especially its drummer, as this was where Chick Webb dominated. The success of the Lunceford band was built largely upon the extraordinary talents of its arrangers, Ed Wilcox, Eddie Durham and especially Sy Oliver, also the playing and the exacting standards set by lead alto saxophonist Willie Smith, and the urgent, exuberant drumming of Crawford was a permanent encouragement to the band, helping it gain both the admiration of other musicians and enthusiasm of the fans. Unusually among big band drummers of the swing era, Crawford favoured a two-beat style which gave the silky-smooth ensemble playing of this extremely well-rehearsed and talented band an enormous lift. After leaving Lunceford in 1943 Crawford worked mostly with small groups, including those of Ben Webster, Harry James, Edmond Hall and Benny Goodman. In the 50s he was extensively involved in the theatre, playing in the pit bands of many Broadway shows (including *Pal Joey*) and also performed with Ella Fitzgerald, Dizzy Gillespie and Count Basie. At heart, Crawford was a big band drummer and he proved his worth in the 1957 Henderson All Stars recording date, on which his playing and shouts of encouragement helped make this one of the best of big band albums.
Selected album: with Henderson All Stars *Big Reunion* (1957).
Compilations: with Jimmie Lunceford *The Jimmie Lunceford And His Orchestra (1935-41)* (1982), *The Complete Set* (1986, a four album set).

Crawford, Ray

b. 7 February 1924, Pittsburgh, Pennsylvania, USA. A much underrated musician throughout his career, Crawford played clarinet and saxophone with Fletcher Henderson in the early 40s before tuberculosis forced a change to guitar. He established his reputation playing with the influential first Ahmed Jamal trio in Pittsburgh and Chicago (1951-56), and later played with organist Jimmy Smith and with Gil Evans. Crawford was a principal soloist on Evans' seminal *Out Of The Cool*, and his individual approach and percussive effects on his instrument can be heard on the track 'La Nevada'. A move to Los Angeles led to the formation, in 1961, of a sextet with Johnny Coles and Cecil Payne. During the 60s and 70s he played as an accompanist with Sonny Stitt and Sonny Criss; his association with Jimmy Smith has continued into the 80s.
Selected albums: with Gil Evans *Old Wine, New Bottles* (1959), with Evans *Out Of The Cool* (1960), as leader *Smooth Groove* (Candid 1961).

Crimmins, Roy

b. 2 August 1929, Perth, Scotland. A self-taught musician, trombonist Crimmins began his professional career during the early 50s traditional jazz boom. He worked with various bands, including the Galleon Jazz Band and those led by Mick Mulligan and Freddy Randall before becoming a founder member of Alex Welsh's highly popular outfit in 1954. It was more than a decade before he decided to move on. After forming his own band in 1965, Crimmins toured Germany, remaining there for the next 13 years, though he worked too in Austria, where he appeared frequently on television, and in Switzerland. In 1978 he returned to the UK and rejoined Welsh, staying with the band until the leader's death in 1982. Since then Crimmins has worked in various bands, including those of Harry Gold and Bob Wilber and the popular trombone-dominated group, Five-a-Slide. A powerful player with excellent technique, Crimmins's long association with the more traditional forms of jazz conceal the fact that his is a wide-ranging talent.

Selected albums: with Alex Welsh *Echoes Of Chicago* (1962), with Fatty George *Chicagoan All Stars* (1973).

Crispell, Marilyn

b. Marilyn Braune, 30 March 1947, Philadelphia, Pennsylvania, USA. Crispell began piano lessons at the age of seven, later studying classical piano at the Peabody Music School in Baltimore, where she spent her later childhood, and piano and composition at the New England Conservatory of Music in Boston. After graduating in 1969, she gave up music for marriage and medical work. Six years later she divorced and moved to Cape Cod, where a local pianist, George Kahn, introduced her to modern jazz on record. One night, listening to John Coltrane's *A Love Supreme*, 'something in the music - its feeling, its energy - caught me: I became incredibly moved. I said to myself, I have to learn to play this music. I loved it so much.' She studied jazz harmony with teacher Charlie Banacos in Boston, then attended Karl Berger's Creative Music Studio in Woodstock, later staying on to work as a teacher. At the studio, she met Anthony Braxton and toured Europe in his Creative Music Orchestra in 1978, later recording on his *Composition 98* in 1981. By the early 80s she had started to develop her own music, both solo (*Rhythms Hung In Undrawn Sky*, *Concert In Berlin*) and in a group that featured Billy Bang and drummer John Betsch (*Spirit Music*, *Live In Berlin*). This sudden flurry of releases was followed by a series of albums on the UK Leo Records label: *And Your Ivory Voice Sings* (a duo with drummer Doug James), *Quartet Improvisations - Paris 1986* and *Gaia*, a trio with James and Reggie Workman that *Wire* magazine later voted one of the top 50 albums of the 80s. Crispell continued to work with Braxton, becoming a regular member of his quartet in 1983, and also joined Workman's Ensemble (*Synthesis, Images*), as well as playing occasional concerts with a wide range of artists: Andrew Cyrille (one duo track on the compilation *Live At The Knitting Factory Volume Three*), Leo Smith, Anthony Davis (in his opera, *X*), Pauline Oliveros, Tim Berne Marcio Mattos and Eddie Prevost, with

whom she toured in the UK as a duo in 1991. Recent recordings of her own music have included the solos *Labyrinths* and *Live In San Francisco*, duos with Braxton and Irène Schweizer, two trio sets - *The Kitchen Concert*, with her Braxton Quartet colleagues Mark Dresser and Gerry Hemingway; *Live In Zurich*, with Workman and Paul Motian - and an electrifying ensemble session, *Circles*, with Workman, Hemingway and saxophonists Peter Buettner and Oliver Lake, which had writer Ben Watson enthusing that she had 'tapped into the physical assault of late Trane'. In fact, while Coltrane remains an idol - and her versions of his 'Dear Lord' and 'After The Rain' show an astonishing power and beauty - it is Cecil Taylor, with his phenomenal force, speed and intensity, who is her primary musical influence; and she also cites Thelonious Monk, Paul Bley, Leo Smith, African pop music (for its rhythmic qualities) and Braxton (for his use of space and structure) as important models. Taylor has lauded her work as spearheading 'a new lyricism', but - although recent albums have explored more reflective modes - the essential components of her music are, as she stated in 1988, counterpoint, pointillism and, especially, energy: 'I think of energy as carrying itself forward (in the music), being directed but not decided . . . When you're really hooked into the music, you can reach another level of energy that goes beyond the mechanics of it; a feeling of going higher, to a non-mundane state.' One of the most exciting improvisers to have appeared in the last 20 years, Crispell is the first and perhaps to date the only genuine member of a post-Taylor era of jazz pianism: she has not merely accommodated elements of his style into her playing, but has used his language as the launching-pad from which she has developed her own, entirely personal and utterly distinctive music. To quote Braxton, 'she has the kind of facility that is awesome'.

Albums: *Spirit Music* (1983, rec. 1981-82), *Rhythms Hung In Undrawn Sky* (Leo 1983), *Concert In Berlin* (1983), *Live In Berlin* (Black Saint 1984, rec. 1982), with Doug James *And Your Ivory Voice Sings* (Leo 1985), *Quartet Improvisations - Paris 1986* (Leo 1987), *Gaia* (Leo 1988), *Labyrinths* (1988), *Live In San Francisco* (Music And Arts 1990), *For Coltrane* (Leo 1990), *Live In Zurich* (Leo 1990), with Anthony Braxton *Duets Vancouver 1989* (1990), *The Kitchen Concert* (Leo 1991, rec. 1989), with Irène Schweizer *Overlapping Hands: Eight Segments* (FMP 1991), *Circles* (1991), *Highlights From The 1992 American Tour* (1993), with Georg Graewe *Piano Duets (Tuned & Detuned Pianos)* (Leo 1993), *Santuerio* (Leo 1993), *Duo* (Knitting Factory 1993), *Stellar Pulsations/ Three Composers* (Leo 1993).

Criss, Sonny

b. William Criss, 23 October 1923, Memphis, Tennessee, USA, d. 19 November 1977. Criss first came to prominence in Los Angeles in the mid-late 40s, playing with Howard McGhee, Billy Eckstine, Gerald Wilson and Jazz At The Philharmonic. One of the first alto saxophonists to absorb the lessons of Charlie Parker, Criss developed into a fluent, intense bebopper whom Ornette Coleman later described as 'the fastest man alive'. In the mid-50s he worked with Buddy Rich's quintet and also led his own groups, including line-ups with Sonny Clark and Wynton Kelly. In 1961 he settled in Paris for a number of years, then returned to Los Angeles and recorded a series of mostly excellent albums for Prestige (1966-69). Perhaps most outstanding was the big band *Sonny's Dream (Birth Of The New Cool)*, which featured the compositions and arrangements of Criss's west coast colleague Horace Tapscott. Following a breakdown, Criss became involved in social work, chiefly with alcoholics but also playing and teaching in schools. In 1974 he revisited Europe and a little later began recording again, making a trio of superb small-group albums that displayed as well as ever the uniquely affecting alto tone which writer Mark Gardner called 'a piercing, passionate sound from the heart'. Two later albums that laden Criss with strings and a supposedly funky beat were less successful artistically. In November 1977, shortly before a scheduled tour of Japan, Criss died at home from gunshot wounds that were possibly the result of an accident but, it is generally believed, were more probably self-inflicted.

Albums: *Jazz USA* (1955), *Go Man* (1956), *Blues Pour Flirters* (1963), *This Is Criss!* (Original Jazz Classics 1966), *Portrait Of Sonny Criss* (Original Jazz Classics 1967), *Up, Up And Away* (1968), *Rockin' In Rhythm* (1968), *Sonny's Dream* (Original Jazz Classics 1968), *I'll Catch The Sun* (Prestige 1969), *Crisscraft* (Muse 1975), *Saturday Morning* (Xanadu 1975), *Out Of Nowhere* (Muse 1976), *Warm And Sunny* (1976), *The Joy Of Sax* (1977), *Live In Italy* (Fresh Sounds 1988), *Sonny Criss In Paris* (Fresh Sounds 1988). Compilation: with Kenny Dorham *The Bopmasters* (1978, rec 1959).

Critchenson, John

b. 24 December 1934, London, England. Pianist Critchenson seemed to spring from nowhere in 1979 when he joined Ronnie Scott's Quintet. In fact he had played semi-professionally for many years while retaining his non-musical 'day job'. He had taken piano lessons early on, but he was a good player 'by ear' and was thus effectively self-taught. From 1980-83 he was with the highly successful Morrissey-Mullen band and continued with Scott: indeed he once toured with both bands simultaneously. He is still with Scott's house band and also works with Scott drummer Martin Drew's own group.

Albums: *Summer Afternoon* (1982), *New Night* (1984)

Crombie, Tony

b. 27 August 1925, London, England. Active among the eager young British beboppers of the early 40s, Crombie, a self-taught drummer, broadened his musical knowledge by securing work on post-war transatlantic liners. The main objective of many British musicians, like Crombie, who obtained such employment, was not to play dance music for the passengers but to get to New York to hear American bebop artists in person. In the late 40s and early 50s he was still playing in London clubs and also working as an accompanist to visiting American stars, including singers Lena Horne and Carmen McRae. In the 50s he worked regularly with Ronnie Scott and Victor Feldman and was much in demand to accompany jazz solo

musicians touring the UK. Anything but narrow in his musical tastes, in 1956 Crombie formed a rock 'n' roll band, the Rockets (a name he also used, confusingly, for a 1958 band which featured many of the outstanding British jazzmen of the period, including Scott and Tubby Hayes). Crombie's roots were in jazz, however, and he was a member of the resident rhythm section at Ronnie Scott's club. In the late 50s and throughout the 60s, he turned more and more to writing: he wrote scores for films and television and also composed tunes recorded by a wide range of artists including Miles Davis, who featured 'So Near, So Far' on *Seven Steps To Heaven*. A duo he formed with organist Alan Haven had considerable popular success. In the 70s and 80s he continued to write but also played frequently at clubs and in concert, often with Scott but also with the popular jazz-loving singer/organist Georgie Fame. A highly versatile musician, Crombie also plays piano and vibraphone. His piano playing, especially on his own compositions, has a sombre beauty which reflects his love and admiration for the music of Duke Ellington.

Selected albums: *At The Royal Festival Hall With The Ronnie Scott Orchestra And Tony Crombie* (1956), *Atmosphere* (1958), *Relaunch* (1958), *Man From Interpol* (1960), *Tony Crombie (i)* (1960), *Tony Crombie (ii)* (1960), *Sweet, Wild And Blue* (1960), with Alan Haven *Through Till Two* (1966), with Mike Carr *Hammond Under Pressure* (1968), *Tony Crombie And Friends* (Renaissance 1989).

Crosby, Bob

b. George Robert Crosby, 25 August 1913, Spokane, Washington, USA, d. 9 March 1993, La Jolla, California, USA. For most of his early career, Crosby was inevitably overshadowed by his older brother, Bing Crosby. Nevertheless, he made a modest success thanks to a pleasant voice and a matching personality. In the immediate pre-swing era years he sang with Anson Weeks and then joined the band co-led by brothers Jimmy and Tommy Dorsey. In 1935 the disaffected musicians who had left the Ben Pollack band decided to form a co-operative group but wanted a frontman. They approached Crosby who accepted the job, bringing a casual relaxed air to one of the swing era's liveliest bands. Unusually, the band favoured an energetic two-beat dixieland style which became extremely popular. The leading musicians in the band were trumpeters Billy Butterfield and Yank Lawson, saxophonists Eddie Miller, Irving Fazola and Matty Matlock and rhythm players Bob Zurke, Hilton 'Nappy' Lamare, Bob Haggart and Ray Bauduc. After the band folded in 1942 Crosby continued to make films and personal appearances, sometimes as leader of reconstituted dixieland-style bands, sometimes of more contemporary-sounding bands. Generally, by the 70s and 80s, these groups bore little resemblance to the original Bob Crosby band, but the fans loved it all. Crosby died of cancer at Scripps Memorial Torrey Pines Convalescent Hospital in 1993.

Selected albums: *One Night Stand* (1946), *The Uncollected Bob Crosby Volume 2* (1952), *The Golden Days Of Jazz* (1954), *Bob Crosby* i (1957), *Bob Crosby* ii (1958), *Bob Crosby* iii (1959), *The Sounds Of The Swing Years* (1960), *Live At The Rainbow*

Grill (1960), *Mardi Gras Parade* (1960), *Bob Crosby* iv (1961). Selected compilations: *Bob Crosby On The Air, 1940* (1979), *Bob Crosby And His Orchestra, 1935-36* (1981), *That Da Da Strain* (Joker 1981), *20 Golden Pieces* (1981), *Camel Caravans - The Summer Of '39* (1985), *Mourning' Blues* (Affinity 1985), *Suddenly It's 1939* (Giants Of Jazz 1985), *The Big Apple, 1936-40* (1988), *Sugar Foot Strut (1936-42)* (1988), *Bob Crosby - Jazz Classics In Digital Stereo* (BBC 1988, 1937-1938 recordings), *South Rampart Street Parade* (GRP 1992).
Further reading: *Stomp Off, Let's Go!: The Story Of Bob Crosby's Bob Cats & Big Band*, John Chilton.

Crosby, Gary

b. 26 January 1955, London, England. Born in London of Jamaican parents, and nephew of the unjustly-neglected guitarist Ernest Ranglin, Crosby was (along with a few others, like the fine tenor saxophonist Ray Carless) one of the pioneer black British jazz talents, making his reputation before the scene blossomed so dramatically in the mid-80s. He began to study trumpet at the age of 13, although he had played around on various other instruments at home. He took trumpet lessons at a community centre in Fulham for a couple of years, but subsequently switched to bass, studying with Peter Ind between the ages of 19 and 23. His first gig was with Ed Bentley alongside Carless. Later on, he was an original member of the Jazz Warriors. He has established a group of his own which is designed to give young musicians space for a year or two so they can develop themselves, strike out on their own and be replaced by other young musicians, generally from the Warriors circle. The band played regular sessions at London's Jazz Café. Like most bassists he gets far less of the limelight than the saxophonists, pianists and drummers, and certainly far less than his talent deserves. An excellent, thoroughly dependable bass player, he has worked with, amongst many others, Steve Williamson and John Stevens.
Albums: with Courtney Pine *Journey To The Urge Within* (1986), with Jazz Warriors *Out Of Many One People* (1987), with Pine *Destiny's Song And The Image Of Pursuance* (1988), with Bukky Leo *River Nile* (1990), with Steve Williamson *Waltz For Grace* (1990), with Cleveland Watkiss *Blessing In Disguise* (1991), with Williamson *Rhyme Time* (1991).

Crosby, Israel

b. 19 January 1919, Chicago, Illinois, USA, d. 11 August 1962. A musical prodigy, Crosby had mastered several instruments before taking up the bass in 1934. Within a year he was noticed by John Hammond and had made his first recordings with Gene Krupa and Jess Stacy and among the results was 'Blues For Israel' which attained classic status. On this track he demonstrated a new style of bass-playing in jazz which was to blossom more fully a little later with the emergence of the better-known Jimmy Blanton. Crosby went on to work with Fletcher Henderson and made records with several small groups including those of Teddy Wilson, Roy Eldridge and Coleman Hawkins. A master musician with a virtuoso technique, Crosby was mostly engaged in studio work throughout

the 40s and 50s but also struck up an musical partnership with Ahmad Jamal, and he also played jazz with Benny Goodman and George Shearing. He died in August 1962.
Album: *Ahmad Jamal At The Pershing* (1958). Compilations: *Gene Krupa, Volume 1 (1935-38)* (1979), *The Indispensable Benny Goodman, Volumes 1 & 2 (1935-39)* (1986).

Cullum, Jim

b. 20 September 1941, San Antonio, Texas, USA. Although little known outside his home state for many years, cornetist Cullum has played an important part in preserving interest in traditional jazz in America. He first played in a band led by his namesake father, later taking over leadership and running both the family recording company and a jazz room at San Antonio's Landing Hotel. Visiting guest musicians or resident old-timers like Ernie Caceres always fitted in well with the band's style. Cullum's records show his band to be a lively, entertaining group with good solos and a tight ensemble sound - what they lack in profundity they certainly make up in spirit. In 1991, his band was one of the musical attractions of the San Antonio Centennial Fiesta.
Selected albums: *'Tis The Season To Be Jamming* (1985), *Super Satch* (Stomp Off 1986), *Hooray For Hoagy* (Audiophile 1990), *Music Of Jelly Roll Morton* (Stomp Off 1993).

Curson, Ted

b. Theodore Curson, 3 June 1935, Philadelphia, Pennsylvania, USA. Trumpeter Curson played carnival gigs at the age of 12 and studied with tenor player Jimmy Heath. In the mid-50s he relocated to New York and worked with top pianists Mal Waldron, Red Garland and Cecil Taylor. He made his name with Charles Mingus, playing alongside Eric Dolphy and Booker Ervin in the 1959-60 band. Next he co-led a band with Philadelphian tenor saxophonist Bill Barron, recording the moving *Tears For Dolphy* in 1964; but then left for Europe 1965. In 1973 he played in Zurich's Playhouse orchestra and in the 70s freelanced in Paris and New York, playing with pianists Andrew Hill and Kenny Barron among others. Keen to spread jazz interest he has frequently played and lectured at UCLA, the University of Vermont and at Denmark's Vallekilde Music School. In the 80s he ran a New York City jazz radio show. He brings a special, fervent tone to everything he plays, combining it with an assured grasp of the history of the music.
Albums: with Charles Mingus *Mingus Revisited* (1960), *Plays Fire Down Below* (Original Jazz Classics 1963), *Tears For Dolphy* (Black Lion 1964), *Jubilant Power* (1976), *The Trio* (Interplay 1979), *I Heard Mingus* (Interplay 1980), *Ted Curson And Co* (India Navigation 1984), *Canadian Concert Of Ted Curson* (Can-Am 1987).

Cuscuna, Michael

b. 20 September 1948, Stamford, Connecticut, USA. Cuscuna developed an interest in jazz and began to learn drums at the age of 12, also exploring saxophone and flute. Realizing he would not make it as a professional player, he enrolled at the University of Pennsylvania Wharton School of Business in

1966 with the idea of creating his own record label. Business studies were not congenial and he switched to English literature. Later he began a nightly jazz radio show (WXPN), which led to part-time work for ESP-Disk, the legendary New York free music label of the 60s. He started writing about jazz (*Jazz And Pop, Downbeat*) and promoting in Philadelphia (Joe Henderson, Paul Bley). Producing a session for guitarist George Freeman (subsequently released on Delmark Records), Cuscuna became interested in the blues, recording Buddy Guy and Junior Wells. He pioneered underground rock radio at WMMR (Philadelphia), then WABC FM (New York), but left due to the imposition of formats and playlists in 1971. Next he recorded singer-songwriter Bonnie Raitt, started to produce for Atlantic Records (Dave Brubeck, Art Ensemble Of Chicago) then went freelance, producing for Atlantic, Motown, ABC (where he initiated a famous reissue series of 60s jazz from the Impulse! label), Muse and Arista. In 1977 he worked with Alan Douglas on the *Wildflower* series, the famous document of the black *avant garde* loft scene. Jazz editor of the trade magazine *Record World* (1971-76) he was also producer of a magnificent set of Anthony Braxton recordings for Arista (1974-82), where he helped to set up the Freedom and Novus labels as outlets for new jazz. Artists who recorded for him included Oliver Lake, Julius Hemphill, Henry Threadgill, Leo Smith, Cecil Taylor, Andrew Hill and Marion Brown. After five years of trying, he finally gained access to the vaults of Blue Note Records and began releasing unissued material (100 albums came out between 1975 and 1981). In 1983 he set up Mosaic Records to release limited-edition box-sets, mostly of bebop-related music from the 40s, 50s and 60s: music issued to date includes complete sessions by Thelonious Monk, Clifford Brown, Ike Quebec, Charles Mingus, Herbie Nichols, Tina Brooks, Nat 'King' Cole and many others, much of the material culled from the vaults of the Blue Note and Pacific Jazz labels and often including previously unreleased material. In 1984 he was involved with the reactivation of Blue Note, producing new sessions by McCoy Tyner, Tony Williams and Don Pullen among others as well as overseeing the label's latest reissue programme. In 1979 he was voted *Downbeat*'s 'Producer Of The Year' and has been voted number one or two ever since. Michael Cuscuna is a prime example of those enthusiasts who fight within the industry to give jazz more space on the record shelves.

Cyrille, Andrew

b. 10 November 1939, Brooklyn, New York, USA. Cyrille graduated from the Juilliard School in 1958 and studied drums with Philly Joe Jones in the same year. In the early 60s he worked with the *risqué* nightclub singer Nellie Lutcher and tenor saxophonists Coleman Hawkins and Illinois Jacquet. In 1965 he started a 15-year association with Cecil Taylor, also working with musicians in the soul jazz camp such as Stanley Turrentine and Junior Mance. In 1969 he recorded *What About?* in Paris for BYG, one of the few completely successful solo drum records. In 1971 he formed Dialogue Of The Drums with Milford Graves and Rashied Ali. In the 70s he was

artist-in-residence at Antioch College, Ohio. Cyrille is capable of playing time, free and everything in between, contributing rhythmic clarity to Taylor's music and supplying a flexible rhythmic base to the compositions of Muhal Richard Abrams and John Carter. In 1977 he toured Europe with Carla Bley and in the 80s he recorded several albums with his group Manao, which often featured trumpeter Ted Daniel, saxophonist David S. Ware and bassist Nick de Geronimo. He also recorded two duo albums with his Cecil Taylor Unit colleague, Jimmy Lyons and a trio album with Lyons and Jeanne Lee. In recent years, Cyrille has worked with the Reggie Workman Ensemble, played live duets with Marilyn Crispell and recorded with a wide range of artists, from Horace Tapscott and Geri Allen to Anthony Braxton and Billy Bang. In 1990 he toured the UK with a trio that featured free improviser Paul Rogers on bass and ex-Lou Reed guitarist Mark Hewins playing everything from John Coltrane to power psychedelia. Cyrille's open-minded attitude complements his consummate musicality.

Albums: *What About?* (Affinity 1969), with Milford Graves *Dialogue Of The Drums* (1974), *Metamusicians' Stomp* (Black Saint 1978), with Jeanne Lee, Jimmy Lyons *Nuba* (Black Saint 1979), *Junction* (IPS 1980), *Celebration* (IPS 1980), *Special People* (1981), with Lyons *Something In Return* (1988, rec. 1981), *The Navigator* (1984), with Lyons *Burnt Offering* (1991, rec. 1982), *Galaxies* (Music And Arts 1991), *My Friend Louis* (DIW 1992).

D

D'Andrea, Franco

b. 8 March 1941, Merano, Italy. D'Andrea developed his piano playing style during the 60s in the bands of Ninzio Rotondo, Gato Barbieri and Franco Ambrosetti. From 1968 he led the Modern Art Trio. In 1972 he formed the jazz rock band Perigeo and started to use synthesizers as well as the piano. His playing is technically adept and reflects an interest in pianists as diverse as James P. Johnson and Martial Solal. From the 60s onwards he accompanied and recorded with visiting Americans like Dexter Gordon (tenor saxophone), Slide Hampton (trombone), Max Roach (drums), Lee Konitz (alto saxophone), Johnny Griffin (tenor saxophone) and Lucky Thompson (tenor saxophone). D'Andrea played with the Rava Quartet in 1979 before forming his own quartet in 1981. His work has won many prizes in Italy and he was twice voted Italian Jazz Musician of the Year (1982 and 1984) in the magazine *Musica Jazz*.

Albums: *Modern Art Trio* (1971), *Nuvolao* (1978), *From East

To West (1979), *My One And Only Love* (1983), *No Idea Of Time* (1984), with Giovanni Tommaso, Roberto Gatto *Airegin* (1993).

Dailey, Pete

b. 5 May 1911, Portland, Indiana, USA, d. 23 August 1986. A dixieland cornetist, with his own popular combos in the USA in the 40s and 50s, Dailey initially played the tuba before switching to cornet. He first played professionally in Chicago, working with Bud Freeman, Art Van Damme and Frank Melrose. After forming his own band in the early 40s, he moved to California and worked with Mike Riley and Ozzie Nelson. After military service in World War II he rejoined Nelson in 1945, before forming his own dixieland outfit, Pete Dailey's Chicagoans, in 1946, based in California. The group was popular there for several years and their records for Capitol Records included, 'Johnson Rag', 'Take Me Out To The Ball Game', 'Dixieland Shuffle', 'Walkin' The Dog', and many more. Later in his career he took up valve trombone, but poor health caused him to work only spasmodically during the 60s and early 70s.

Dallwitz, Dave

b. 25 October 1914, Freeling, Australia. Dallwitz led a Dixieland jazz band called the Southern Jazz Group in the late 40s before turning to write and perform classical music. He returned to jazz in 1972 and has led a variety of bands including a scholarly ragtime ensemble which plays the classic rags as well as his own compositions in that style. He more often writes in a mainstream style which reflects his classical background. Among the musicians with whom he has worked is John Sangster (vibraphone).
Albums: *Melbourne Suite* (1973), *Ern Malley Suite* (1975).

Dameron, Tadd

b. Tadley E. Dameron, 21 February 1917, Cleveland, Ohio, USA, d. 8 March 1965. Dameron's early career found him working in several territory bands including those of Freddie Webster, Zack Whyte and Blanche Calloway, for whom he played piano and wrote arrangements. His first major impact on jazz came in 1939 when he joined Harlan Leonard's Kansas City-based band, the Rockets. One of the best of the lesser-known KC bands, the Rockets achieved considerable success in the mid-west and Dameron's charts for his own tunes 'A La Bridges' and 'Dameron Stomp' were outstanding, the first featuring Hank Bridges with both numbers giving solo space to the magnificent trombonist Fred Beckett. Dameron's arrangements subtly combined the loping swing which characterized KC bands, and the new ideas entering jazz from the bebop movement. During the early 40s, Dameron often sat in on New York after-hours sessions with Dizzy Gillespie and Charlie Parker but simultaneously worked on arrangements for some of the big swing bands, including those of Jimmie Lunceford and Count Basie, and more appropriately, the forward-thinking bands led by Georgie Auld and Billy Eckstine. In the late 40s Dameron wrote for Gillespie's big band and his composition

'Good Bait' became a bop standard. He also formed his own small (rising to 10-piece) groups which featured Fats Navarro and, later, Miles Davis. At the end of the 40s he spent some time in Europe working with Kenny Clarke and writing for the Ted Heath band. In the early 50s Dameron worked briefly with Clifford Brown but the mid-50s found him wrestling with drug addiction problems. He wrote for such diverse musicians as Artie Shaw and Carmen McRae, but his addiction led to periods of inactivity in music and eventually a spell in prison commencing in 1958. Released in 1960, he wrote for artists including Sonny Stitt and Milt Jackson and also recorded again. He died in March 1965. Throughout his troubled career, Dameron wrote with skill and finesse, displaying a marked appreciation of the more melodic aspects of bebop which he integrated into medium and big band formats with more success than most of his contemporaries or successors were able to achieve. In the early 80s, Philly Joe Jones, who had played in a 1953 Dameron band, formed a group, Dameronia, which recreated his music.
Albums: *Clifford Brown Memorial* (1953), with John Coltrane *Mating Call* (1956) *Fontainebleau* (1956), *The Magic Touch* (Original Jazz Classics 1962). Compilations: *Harlan Leonard Vol. 2* (1940), *The Fabulous Fats Navarro Vols 1 & 2* (1947-8), with Dodo Marmarosa *Keybop* (Jazz Live 1981).

Daniels, Eddie

b. 19 October 1941, New York City, New York, USA. Before choosing the clarinet as his principal instrument, Daniels played both alto and tenor saxophones. A graduate of the New York High School of the Performing Arts, Brooklyn College and the Juilliard School of Music, he worked as a teenager with Marshall Brown's Youth Band and Tony Scott. In the mid-60s, he began a six-year association with the Thad Jones-Mel Lewis big band and also played and recorded with leading jazz figures such as Freddie Hubbard, Sonny Rollins and Richard Davis. Gifted with a phenomenal technique, Daniels has been tempted into third-stream music, recording with Friedrich Gulda and has performed several works in a classical vein. His bright, clearly articulated playing has attracted a considerable following. As always with technically proficient musicians in jazz, there are some who question the depths of his jazz feeling. Clarinettist predecessors who also attracted criticism of this kind include Benny Goodman and Buddy De Franco, so if this is a flaw then Daniels is certainly in good company. In a period when the clarinet has been in the shadows of jazz, Daniels' work has been one of the few bright lights that have helped maintain the instrument's role. His work in the 80s and 90s has produced a steady flow of technically perfect albums for GRP Records, which for some are too 'digital' to fully appreciate this instrument.
Albums: *First Prize!* (Original Jazz Classics 1966), with Thad Jones-Mel Lewis *Monday Night* (1968), *Muses For Richard Davis* (1969), *The Hub Of Hubbard* (1969), with Bucky Pizzarelli *A Flower For All Seasons* (1973), *Brief Encounter* (Muse 1977), *Breakthrough* (GRP 1985), *To Bird With Love* (GRP 1987), *Memo's From Paradise* (GRP 1988), *Blackwood*

(GRP 1989), *Nepenthe (No Sorrow)* (GRP 1990), *This Is Now* (GRP 1991), *Benny Rides Again* (GRP 1992), *Under The Influence* (GRP 1993).

Daniels, Joe

b. 9 March 1908, Zeerust, Transvaal, South Africa, d. 2 July 1993. This bandleader/drummer moved to London when he was two years old. By the age of 10 he was a confident drummer. Four years later Daniels was working in London, playing in various bands at clubs and restaurants including that led by Harry and Burton Lester (the Cowboy Syncopaters). Among the other units in which he played were those led by Al Kaplan, Billy Mason, Fred Elizalde, and Sid Roy brother of Harry Roy. In the mid-20s Daniels formed his own group, which featured trumpeter Max Goldberg. For most of the 30s Daniels was with Harry Roy, and also made many records under his own name as leader of the hugely successful Hotshots. After World War II Daniels continued his bandleading career, playing mostly an engaging if not very profound brand of dixieland. He regularly filled the Slough Palais where he was resident for many years, in addition to playing at numerous holiday camps. When the Big Band boom had subsided in the late 50s he also ran his own Wimpy Bar. During this musically barren time he recorded as Washboard Joe And The Scrubbers. His regular band was an early home for the excellent clarinettist Dave Shepherd and trumpeter Alan Wickham.
Compilations: *Swing High, Swing Low* (Harlequin 1988, 1935-37 recs.), *Steppin' Out To Swing* (Saville 1984, 1940-45 recs).

Daniels, Mike

b. 13 April 1939, Stanmore, Middlesex, England. One of many bands which took advantage of the UK's early 50s traditional jazz boom, Mike Daniels and his Delta Jazz Band were much more credible than all but a handful of other groups. Adhering closely to, but not directly imitating the music of Jelly Roll Morton, Joe 'King' Oliver and early Louis Armstrong, Daniels built a reputation for the high quality of his band's performances and won an enthusiastic following. As the trad scene faded, Daniels formed a big band, but eventually retired from the UK jazz scene and emigrated. In 1985 a return trip to the UK and the reformation of his old band attracted enormous attention from an army of devoted fans. Daniels' trumpet playing, while never spectacular, always offered a cogent reminder of the fire and sensitivity of his idol, King Oliver.
Albums: *Mike Daniels And His Delta Jazzmen* (Harlequin 1986, 1957-59 recordings), *Together Again - Thirty Years On* (1988-89), *Mike Daniels* (Stomp Off 1991).
Further reading: *The Mike Daniels Delta Jazz Band*, Mike Bowen.

Dankworth, John

b. 20 September 1927, London, England. Dankworth started playing clarinet as a child and in the early 40s was a member of a traditional jazz band. In the mid-40s he studied at the Royal Academy of Music and extended his knowledge of jazz by taking work on transatlantic liners, so that he could hear leading jazzmen in New York. Among his influences at this time was Charlie Parker and Dankworth now concentrated on alto saxophone. He was an active participant in the London bebop scene of the late 40s and early 50s, often playing at the Club 11. In 1950 he formed his own band, the Johnny Dankworth Seven, which included Jimmy Deuchar and Don Rendell. Three years later he formed a big band, playing his own, sometimes innovative, arrangements. The band's singer was Cleo Laine whom Dankworth married in 1958. For his big band Dankworth drew upon the best available modern jazzmen; at one time or another artists such as Dick Hawdon, Kenny Wheeler, Rendell, Danny Moss, Peter King, Dudley Moore and Kenny Clare were in its ranks. Dankworth's writing, especially for the big band, demonstrated his considerable arranging skills, although for many fans it is performances by the Seven that linger longest in fond memory. In the 60s Dankworth was in demand for film work, which together with the growing popularity of Laine led to a shift in policy. In the early 70s Dankworth became Laine's musical director, touring extensively with her and making many records. Dankworth's musical interests extend beyond jazz and he has composed in the classical form, including a nine-movement work, 'Fair Oak Fusions', written for cellist Julian Lloyd Webber. He has also experimented with third-stream music. His deep interest in music education led in 1969 to the founding of the Wavendon Allmusic Plan, which has continued to attract performers, students and audiences from around the world to concerts, classes, courses and lectures. Although a reliable performer on alto, it is as an arranger and tireless promoter of music that Dankworth has made his greatest contributions to the international jazz scene. In 1974, in recognition of his work, he became a Companion of the British Empire.
Selected albums: *What The Dickens!* (1963), *Zodiac Variations* (1964), *Shakespeare - And All That Jazz* (1964), *The $1,000,000 Collection* (1970), *Full Circle* (1972), *Lifeline* (1973), *Movies 'N' Me* (1974), with Cleo Laine *Lover And His Lass* (Esquire 1976), *Sepia* (c.1979), *Fair Oak Fusions* (c.1982), *Metro* (Repertoire 1983), *Zodiac Variations* (Sepia 1983), *Gone Hitchin'* (Sepia 1983), *What The Dickens?* (Sepia 1983), *Octavius* (Sepia 1983), *Symphonic Fusions* (Pickwick 1985), *Innovations* (Pickwick 1987), *Live At Ronnie Scott's* (Total 1992), *Generation Big Band* (Jazz House 1994). Compilations: with others *Bop At Club 11* (1949 recordings), *Johnny Dankworth Seven And Orchestra* (1953-57 recordings), *Featuring Cleo Laine* (Retrospect 1984, 1953-58 recordings), *The John Dankworth Big Band, Vintage Years 1953-1959* (Sepia 1990).

Dardanelle

b. Dardanelle Breckenridge, 27 December 1917, Avalon, Mississippi, USA. Playing piano and singing from childhood, Dardanelle developed her skills throughout high school and university. In the late 30s and early 40s she worked with several bands along the east coast and in Washington, DC, and Philadelphia. Eventually she decided to form her own group with Paul Edenfield and Tal Farlow. The trio became successful and in 1945 started a year-long residency at the Copacabana club in New York. During the rest of the decade the trio played in several top New York hotels, made records and toured the USA. In addition to playing piano and singing, Dardanelle also played vibraphone. In 1949 Dardanelle married Walter Hadley and gave up her New York-based career. During the next few years she devoted her time to raising a family, but in 1956, now resident in Chicago, she became staff organist at a local radio and television station and appeared for four years on a childrens' show. In the early 60s she freelanced in Chicago, was active in church work, including conducting choirs, and began broadcasting a regular family show from home. In 1966 her husband's business effected another move, this time to New Jersey, where she formed a new trio with her son, Skip Hadley, on drums. The trio played largely for private functions and in local clubs for several years. In the mid-70s Dardanelle again began performing with leading jazz artists including Bucky Pizzarelli and George Duvivier. In 1978 she returned to the recording studios for an album with Duvivier, Pizzarelli and Grady Tate. In the late 70s Dardanelle survived a divorce and the tragic death of her son, Skip, and by the early 80s was a popular figure at jazz clubs, festivals and concerts, appearing at the Cookery, Carnegie Hall and many other prestigious venues. She continued to record, most commonly in good jazz company. She also appeared on television as performer and host of the *Music In Our Lives* show and on cruise ships, including the *QE II*. Although victim of a brutal assault, Dardanelle made many club and record dates during the next few years, including a long residency in Tokyo. Since 1984 Dardanelle has made her home in Oxford, Mississippi, but still plays concerts, festivals, radio and television and makes records. In many performances she is joined by her second son, Brian Hadley, on bass. For a period in the late 80s she was artist-in-residence at the University of Mississippi. At the end of the decade she began writing her autobiography, reading extracts of work in progress on radio in Mississippi and Tennessee. A distinctive song stylist with a penchant for reflective ballads which speak of love for people and places, especially the deep south, Dardanelle has made an important contribution to popular music, not only through her singing and playing but also through the enthusiastic manner in which she has transmitted her love of music to audiences and students.

Selected albums: *Songs For New Lovers* (1978), *New York, New York: Sounds Of The Apple* (WEA 1980-91), *Colors Of My Life* (Stash 1982), *The Two Of Us* (1983), *Dardanelle Down Home* (Audiophile 1986), *Dardanelle Echoes Singing Ladies* (Audiophile 1986), *Gold Braid* (Audiophile 1986), *Woman's Intuition* (Audiophile 1988), *That's My Style* (1989), *Swingin' In London* (Audiophile 1994). Compilations: *Gold Braid* (1945), *Piano Moods* (1950-51).

Darensbourg, Joe

b. 9 July 1906, Baton Rouge, Louisiana, USA, d. 24 May 1985. After trying various other instruments, Darensbourg chose the clarinet, receiving tuition from noted masters such as Alphonse Picou. His progress was such that before the end of the 20s he had played in New Orleans bands led by eminent figures such as Buddy Petit, Fate Marable, Charlie Creath and Mutt Carey. Starting in 1929, Darensbourg spent 15 profitable, but somewhat obscure, years playing mostly in the Seattle area and also in western Canada. In the mid to late 40s he played briefly with Kid Ory and Wingy Manone but it was not until the 50s that he began to make an impact on the jazz world with his recordings of his own compositions, 'Yellow Dog Blues' and 'Lou-easy-an-ia', and a period with Teddy Buckner's popular band. In the early 60s he joined Louis Armstrong's All Stars, touring extensively and playing to a wider audience than ever before. Although his was, in some respects, a dated style of playing, Darensbourg was a capable musician and brought to his work a dedication to the old traditions of New Orleans music that was never conventional. His autobiography was published in 1987.

Albums: with Teddy Buckner *Salute To Armstrong* (1956), *On A Lark In Dixieland* (1957), *Joe Darensbourg And His Dixie Flyers* (1958). Compilations: *Barrelhousin' With Joe* (GHB 1988), *Petite Fleur* (Dixieland Jubilee 1988), *Yellow Dog Blues* (Dixieland Jubilee 1988).

Further reading: *Telling It Like It Is*, Joe Darensbourg with Peter Vacher.

Darling, David

b. 4 March 1941, Elkhart, Indiana, USA. Darling studied the piano and cello as well as playing the double bass and alto saxophone in the school dance band of which he eventually became the leader. He studied the cello and music education at Indiana University from where he graduated in 1965. After teaching for four years he played with the Paul Winter Consort throughout the 70s and then formed the band Radiance with other Winter alumni. Getting acquainted with ethnic music with the Consort and trying to play it on the cello 'was mind-blowing'. He was able to develop his particular style as he turned to the use of a solid bodied eight-string electric cello and was able to introduce electronic effects into his playing through the use of an echoplex and other devices. Although he turned increasingly to classical composition after 1978, he played with Spiro Gyra in 1980. The following year he formed the band Gallery, and recorded with Glen Moore and Ralph Towner. He later worked in a duo with Terje Rypdal. Darling does not see his music as new age but as music 'that doesn't have the busyness of progressive jazz, that has a meditative quality'.

Albums: with Winter *Icarus* (1971), with Radiance *Inverness, Lake Unto The Clouds* (70s), *A Song For The Earth* (70s), with Towner *Trios/Solos* (1973), with Terje Rypdal *Journal October* (ECM 1979), with Gallery *Gallery* (1981), with Rypdal *Cycles* (ECM 1981), with Rypdal *Eos* (1983), *Cello* (ECM 1992).

Dauner, Wolfgang

b. 30 December 1935, Stuttgart, Germany. Brought up by his aunt, a piano teacher, Dauner has been playing piano since the age of five. He turned professional at the age of 22, then studied piano and trumpet at Stuttgart College of Music. In 1963 he formed a trio with bassist Eberhard Weber and forceful American drummer Fred Braceful. On-stage destruction of instruments and stunts like presenting a choir in stocking masks ran a musical parallel to the neo-dada of artists like Joseph Beauys. In 1967 he recorded *Free Action* and *Sunday Walk*, both with violinist Jean-Luc Ponty: the first is free jazz, the second dense, John Coltrane-ish bop. Since 1969 Dauner has led the Stuttgart Radio jazz group, backing guests on a monthly basis. ECM Records released a trio recording called *Output* in 1970: Dauner's use of ringmodulator and clavinet was extravagantly creative, a combination of chaos and funk reminiscent of the Mothers Of Invention. Dauner founded the United Jazz And Rock Ensemble in 1975 and also started a record company, Mood. In 1983 he recorded a duet album with Albert Mangelsdorff and two years later wrote a concerto for him. Dauner combines superb pianistic ability with an interest in electronics and modern painting that keeps his projects fresh and lively.

Albums: *Dream Talk* (1964), *Free Action* (1967), with Jean-Luc Ponty *Sunday Walk* (1967), *Output* (1970), *Changes* (Mood 1979), *Dauner-Mangelsdorff* (1982), *Dauner Solo Piano* (Mood 1983), *Two Is Company* (Mood 1983), *One Night In '88* (Mood 1989), *Pas De Trois* (Mood 1989).

Davenport, Charles Edward 'Cow Cow'

b. 23 April 1894, Anniston, Alabama, USA, d. 3 December 1955, Chicago, Illinois, USA. One of the most distinctive themes utilized in boogie-woogie is the train imitation 'Cow Cow Blues' from which this consummate performer derived his nickname. Charles Davenport's father, a preacher, wanted to see his son follow him to a career in the church but it was not to be. Instead the piano laid claim to Charles at an early age and he took up the insecure life of the medicine show musician. He joined Barhoot's Travelling Carnival working the backwaters of Alabama. Here his basically rag-time piano style was subjected to the influence of Bob Davis and the lusty, rolling result was to be the basis of Charles' success on record throughout the 20s. He moved into vaudeville with blues singer Dora Carr as 'Davenport And Co'. Davenport made his first recordings for Gennett (unissued) and Paramount in 1927. Thereafter he linked up with Vocalion both as performer and talent scout. As well as recording under his own name (and as George Hamilton, the Georgia Grinder and Bat The Hummingbird) he supported many other artists, forming a particularly successful liaison with singer Ivy Smith. During this period he tried several ventures outside music, failing as a record shop owner and opening his own café. He also fell foul of southern law and spent six months in jail. In 1938 he suffered an attack of apoplexy which left him deficient in his right hand. He continued to perform as a singer but a move to New York found him eventually washing dishes in the Onyx Club, from where he was rescued by pianist Art Hodes. He recovered sufficiently to record again as a pianist, for the Comet and Circle labels, in 1945 and 1946. Davenport worked towns as far apart as Atlanta, Cleveland and Nashville. He has composer credit for two much-played standbys of the traditional jazz scene, 'Mama Don't Allow' and '(I'll Be Glad When You're Dead) You Rascal You' and was sole composer of the 40s hit, 'Cow Cow Boogie'.

Selected albums: *Cow Cow Blues* (Oldie Blues 1978), *Alabama Strut* (Magpie 1979), *Cow Cow Davenport 1926-38* (Best Of Blues 1988), *Cow Cow Davenport 1927-29* (Document 1989), *The Accompanist 1924-29* (Blues Document 1993).

Davern, Kenny

b. 7 January 1935, Huntington, New York, USA. A professional musician at the age of 16, Davern worked with Jack Teagarden and Phil Napoleon in the mid-50s, moving on to play with Red Allen and Buck Clayton. In the early 60s he led his own small group and also played with the Dukes Of Dixieland. Later in the decade he worked with Ruby Braff. In the early 70s, he teamed up with Bob Wilber to form Soprano Summit. This band featured Davern and Wilber on clarinets, occasionally altos, but, as the name implies, mostly soprano saxophones. Backed by a variety of rhythm sections, Soprano Summit made a string of enormously successful concert and festival dates and numerous record albums which enjoyed good sales. In 1979 the partnership ended and Davern thereafter concentrated more on clarinet. Throughout the 80s and into the 90s, Davern led several small groups, played briefly in the World's Greatest Jazz Band, co-led the Blue Three, with Bobby Rosengarden and Dick Wellstood, and toured and recorded extensively. Although best-remembered by many fans for his work with Wilber, all of which displayed staggering technical dexterity and magnificent musicianship, Davern is a fully-rounded artist whose latterday clarinet-playing shows him to be one of the hottest players on this instrument. Although his early work was in the traditional area of jazz, and most of his later work is in the mainstream, Davern has shown himself to be attuned to new musical developments and his enormous technical proficiency allows him to play confidently in any style he chooses. Very much his own man, and with a devastatingly accurate and pungent wit, Davern is one of the latest in a short but important line in dynamic, contemporary clarinettists whose strong feeling for the past does not deter them from experimenting with new ideas.

Selected albums: with Jack Teagarden *Original Dixieland* (1954), with Bob Wilber *Soprano Summit* (1973), with Wilber *Soprano Summit II* (1974-77), with Wilber *Chalumeau Blue* (1976), with Wilber *Soprano Summit In Concert* (1976), *The Hot Three* (Jazzology 1979), with the Blue Three *The Blue Three At Hanratty's* (1981), *Stretchin' Out* (Jazzology 1984), *Live Hot Jazz* (1984), *The Very Thought Of You* (1984), *Live And Swinging* (1985), *This Old Gang Of Ours* (1985), *Playing For Kicks* (Jazzology 1985), *I'll See You In My Dreams* (Music Masters 1988), *One Hour Tonight* (Musicmasters 1988), with Wilber *Summit Reunion* (1990), *My Inspiration* (Limelight 1991).

Davis, Anthony

b. 20 February 1951, Paterson, New Jersey, USA. Coming from an academic background (his father was the first black faculty member at Princeton University and, as chairman of African-American Studies at Yale, devised one of the first and best black studies programmes in the USA), Davis grew up in Princeton and State College in Pennsylvania. He began to take classical piano lessons at the age of seven. He studied music at Yale University and played in nearby New Haven with trombonist George Lewis and drummer Gerry Hemingway in a group called Advent. He graduated with a BA in 1975, forming a quartet which featured the master drummer Ed Blackwell in the same year. From 1974-77 he was a member of Leo Smith's New Dalta Ahkri. In 1977 he moved to New York and became involved with the burgeoning Loft scene (documented in the *Wildflowers* series), later recording with Oliver Lake (*Shine*), Anthony Braxton (*Six Compositions: Quartet*) and Leroy Jenkins (*The Legend of A. Glatson, Space Minds, New Worlds, Survival Of America*). In 1978 he formed a long-standing partnership with flautist James Newton: they co-lead the group which plays on *Hidden Volices*, work together in a trio with Abdul Wadud and Davis has recorded on Newton's *Paseo Del Mar* and *James Newton*. In 1981 Davis said 'I don't see the need to be self-consciously *avant garde*', proving as much with the octet Episteme, which, whilst recognising Ornette Coleman's innovations, represented a return to tonality. In 1982 he started teaching at Yale. In 1985 he wrote *X*, an opera about Malcolm X and his politics. Davis lists Messiaen and Stravinsky alongside the great jazz pianists as influences, and a 'composer's' approach characterizes his work. Sometimes criticized for his supposedly 'European' leanings, Davis's riposte was 'If somebody uses tradition as a way of limiting your choices, in a way that's as racist as saying you have to sit at the back of the bus.'

Albums: *Song For The Old World* (India Navigation 1978), *Past Lives* (Red Rhino 1979), *Of Blues And Dreams* (Sackville 1979), with James Newton *Hidden Voices* (1979), *Lady Of The Mirrors* (India Navigation 1980), *Under The Double Moon* (1980), *Episterie* (Gramavision 1981), with Newton, Abdul Wadud *I've Known Rivers* (Gramavision 1982), *Hemispheres* (Gramavision 1983), *Middle Passage* (Gramavision 1984), *Undine* (1987), *The Ghost Factory* (1989, rec.1987-8), with Newton, Wadud *Trio 2* (Gramavision 1990), *X: The Life And Times Of Malcolm X* (1993).

Davis, Eddie 'Lockjaw'

b. 2 March 1922, New York City, New York, USA, d. 3 November 1986. Davis began to make his mark on the jazz scene in his home town when he worked at Clark Monroe's Uptown House in the late 30s. Despite this establishment's close ties with the emergence of bebop a few years later, Davis's tenor saxophone playing was rooted in swing and the blues, and early in his career he displayed a marked affinity with the tough school of Texas tenors. In the early 40s he worked with a number of big bands, including those of Cootie Williams, Lucky Millinder and Andy Kirk. He also led his own small group for club and record dates. In 1952 he made the first of several appearances with the Count Basie band which extended through the 60s and into the 70s. It was with Basie that he

made his greatest impact, although in between these stints he continued to lead his own small groups, notably with fellow-tenorist Johnny Griffin in the early 60s, Roy Eldridge in the mid-70s and Harry Edison in the late 70s and early 80s. Davis' playing style showed him to be at ease on both gutsy, hard-driving swingers and slow, tender ballads. The former are most evident in his partnership with Griffin and his showstoppers with Basie, such as 'Whirlybird' on *The Atomic Mr Basie*, while the latter facet of his musical character came to the fore on a fine album of ballads he made with Paul Gonsalves.

Selected albums: with Sonny Stitt *At Birdland* (1954), *Modern Jazz Expressions* (1955), *Uptown* (1955-58), *Eddie's Function* (1956-57), *Jazz With A Beat* (1956-57), *Count Basie Presents Eddie Davis* (1957), with Count Basie *The Atomic Mr Basie* (1957), *Eddie 'Lockjaw' Davis Cookbook Vols 1-3* (Original Jazz Classics 1958), *Smokin'* (Original Jazz Classics 1959), *Jaws In Orbit* (1959), *Bacalao* (1959), *At Ease* (1960), *Misty* (1960), *Battle Stations* (1960), *Very Saxy* (Original Jazz Classics 1960), *Trane Whistle* (1960), with Johnny Griffin *Tough Tenors* (1960), with Griffin *Hey Lock!/Griff And Lock* (1960), *Trane Whistle* (Original Jazz Classics 1961), *Live At Minton's* (1961), *Lookin' At Monk* (1961), *Blues Up And Down* (1961), *Afro Jaws* (1961), with Griffin *Tough Tenor Favorites* (1962), *Goin' To The Meeting* (1962), *I Only Have Eyes For You/Trackin'* (1962), *The Fox And The Hounds* (1966), *Lock The Fox* (1966), *In London* (1967), with Paul Gonsalves *Love Calls* (1967), *Tough Tenors Again 'N' Again* (1970), *Leapin' On Lenox* (1974), *Chewin' The Fat* (1974), *What's New?* (1975), *Light And Lovely* (1975), *Jaws Strikes Again* (Black And Blue 1976), *Swingin' Till The Girls Come Home* (1976), *Straight Ahead* (Original Jazz Classics 1976), *Eddie 'Lockjaw' Davis And Harry 'Sweets' Edison With The John Darville Quartet Featuring Kenny Drew* (1976), *Opus De Funk* (1976), *Eddie 'Lockjaw' Davis 4/Montreux '77 Collection* (Original Jazz classics 1977), with Michel Attenoux *Eddie 'Lockjaw' Davis With Michel Attenoux* (Storyville 1976), *All Of Me* i (1978), *Sweets And Jaws* (1978), *The Heavy Hitter* (1979), *Jaw's Blues* (1981), *Land Of Dreams* (1982), *Live At The Widder, Vols. 1 & 2* (Enja 1982), *That's All* (1983), *All Of Me* ii (1983), *Save Your Love For Me* (Bluebird 1989).

Davis, Miles

b. 26 May 1926, Alton, Illinois, USA, d. 28 September 1991. Miles was born into a comparatively wealthy middle-class family and both his mother and sister were capable musicians. Davis was given a trumpet for his 13th birthday by his dentist father, who could not have conceived that his gift would set his son on the road to becoming one of the giant figures in the development of jazz. Notwithstanding his outstanding talent as master of the trumpet, Davis' versatility encompassed flügel-horn and keyboards together with a considerable gift as a composer. This extraordinary list of talents earned Davis an unassailable reputation as the greatest leader/catalyst in the history of jazz. Such accolades were not used lightly, and Davis can justifiably be termed a 'musical genius'. Davis quickly progressed from his high school band into Eddie Randall's band in 1941, after his family had moved to St. Louis. He studied at the

Juilliard School of Music in New York in 1945 before joining Charlie Parker, with whom he had previously played in the Billy Eckstine band.

By 1948 Miles had played or recorded with many jazz giants, most notably Coleman Hawkins, Dizzy Gillespie, Benny Carter, John Lewis, Illinois Jacquet and Gerry Mulligan. That year was to be a landmark for jazz and Davis, in collaboration with Gil Evans, made a series of 78s which were eventually released in 1957 as the highly influential album *The Birth Of The Cool*. Miles had now refined his innovative style of playing, which was based upon understatement rather than the hurried action of the great bebop players.

During the early 50s Davis became dependant on heroin and his career was put on hold for a lengthy period. This spell of inactivity lasted until as late as 1954. The following year his seminal quintet included variously Red Garland, John Coltrane, Charles Mingus, Paul Chambers, Philly Joe Jones, Bill Evans and Sonny Rollins. Among their output were the acclaimed series of collections *Cookin'*, *Relaxin'*, *Workin'* and *Steamin'*. During this time Miles was consistently voted the number 1 artist in all the major jazz polls. Now no longer dependant on drugs, he set about collaborating with Gil Evans once again. The series of orchestral albums made with Evans between 1957 and 1959 have all become classics; *Miles Ahead*, *Porgy And Bess* and the sparsely beautiful *Sketches Of Spain* (influenced by composer Joaquin Rodrigo). Evans was able to blend lush and full orchestration with Miles' trumpet - allowing it the space and clarity it richly deserved. Miles went on further, assembling a sextet featuring a spectacular line-up including Coltrane, Chambers, Evans, Jimmy Cobb and Cannonball Adderley. Two further landmark albums during this fertile period were the aptly titled *Milestones* followed by *Kind Of Blue*. The latter album is cited by many critics as the finest in jazz history. More than 30 years later his albums are still available. They form an essential part of any jazz record collection, with *Kind Of Blue* at the top of the list. 'So What', the opening track, has been covered by dozens of artists, the most recent offerings have been from guitarist Ronnie Jordan, Larry Carlton, saxophonist Candy Dulfer and reggae star Smiley Culture who added his own lyrics and performed it in the film *Absolute Beginners*. Ian Carr, Davis' leading biographer, perceptively stated of *Kind Of Blue* in 1982: 'The more it is listened to, the more it reveals new delights and fresh depths'.

In 1959, following the bizarre arrest and beating he received from the New York Police, Davis took out a lawsuit, which he subsequently and wisely dropped. Davis entered the 60s comfortably, still the leading innovator in jazz, and shrugged off attempts from John Coltrane to dethrone him in the jazz polls. Miles chose to keep to his sparse style, allowing his musicians air and range. In 1964 while the world experienced Beatlemania, Miles created another musical landmark when he assembled arguably his finest line-up. The combination of Herbie Hancock, Wayne Shorter, Ron Carter and Tony Williams delivered the monumental *E.S.P.* in 1965. He continued with this acoustic line-up through another three recordings; including *Miles Smiles* and ending with *Nefertiti*. By the time of *Filles De Kilimanjaro* Miles had gradually electrified his various groups and took bold steps towards rock music integrating multiple electric keyboards and utilizing a wah-wah pedal connected to his electrified trumpet, additionally his own fascination with the possibilities of electric guitar, as demonstrated by Jimi Hendrix, took an increasing position in his bands. Young American west coast rock musicians had begun to produce a form of music based upon improvisation (mostly through the use of hallucinogenics). This clearly interested Miles who saw the potential of blending traditional rock rhythms with jazz, although he was often contemptuous of some white rock musicians at this time. The decade closed with his band being accepted by rock fans. Miles appeared at major festivals with deliriously stoned audiences appreciating his line-up which now featured the brilliant electric guitarist John McLaughlin, of whom Miles stated in deference to black musicians. 'Show me a black who can play like him, and I'd have him instead'. Other outstanding musicians Davis employed included Keith Jarrett, Airto, Chick Corea, Dave Holland, Joe Zawinul, Billy Cobham and Jack DeJohnette. Two major albums from this period were *In A Silent Way* and *Bitches Brew*, which unconsciously invented jazz-rock and what was later to be called fusion. These records were marketed as rock albums, and consequently appeared in the regular charts. By the early 70s Miles had alienated himself from the mainstream jazz purists by continuing to flirt with rock music. In 1975, after a succession of personal upheavals including a car crash, further drug problems, a shooting incident, more police harassment and eventual arrest, Miles, not surprisingly, retired. During this time he became seriously ill, and it was generally felt that he would never play again.

As unpredictable as ever, Davis returned six years later healthy and fit with the comeback album, *The Man With The Horn*. He assembled a new band and received favourable reviews for live performances. Among the personnel were guitarist John Scofield and saxophonist Bill Evans. On the predominantly funk-based *You're Under Arrest*, he tackled pure pop songs, and although unambitious by jazz standards, tracks like Cyndi Lauper's 'Time After Time' and Michael Jackson's 'Human Nature' were given Miles' brilliant master touch. The aggressive disco album *Tutu* followed with his trumpet played through a synthesizer. A recent soundtrack recording for the Dennis Hopper film, *The Hot Spot*, found Davis playing the blues alongside Taj Mahal, John Lee Hooker, Tim Drummond and Roy Rogers.

During his last years Davis settled into a comfortable pattern of touring the world and recording, able to dictate the pace of his life with the knowledge that ecstatic audiences were waiting for him everywhere. Following further bouts of ill health during which times he took to painting, Miles was admitted to hospital in California and died in September 1991. Miles was a 'genius' and a 'cool dude' and he was totally uncompromising. The worldwide obituaries were neither sycophantic nor morose. All the great things had already been said about Miles for many years. Django Bates stated that his personal favourite Davis recordings were those between 1926 and mid-1991. Ian

Carr added, in his impressive obituary, with regard to Miles' music; 'unflagging intelligence, great courage, integrity, honesty and a sustained spirit of enquiry always in the pursuit of art - never mere experimentation for its own sake'. Miles Davis' influence on rock music is considerable; his influence on jazz is inestimable.

Selected albums: *Bopping The Blues* (Black Lion, 1946 recordings), *Cool Boppin'* (Fresh Sounds, 1948-49 recordings), *Miles Davis With Horns* (Original Jazz Classics, 1951, 1953 recordings), *Dig* (Original Jazz Classics, 1951 recordings), *Collector's Items* (Original Jazz Classics, 1953, 1956 recordings), *Miles Davis Vols 1 & 2* (Blue Note 1954), *Walkin,* (Prestige 1955), *Blue Haze* (Original Jazz Classics, 1953, 1954 recordings), *Miles Davis And The Modern Jazz Giants* (Original Jazz Classics (50s), *Workin'* (Prestige 1956), *Steamin'* (Prestige 1956), *Cookin'* (Prestige 1956), *Relaxin'* (Prestige 1956), *The Birth Of The Cool* (Capitol 1957, 1949-50 recordings), *Blue Moods* (Original Jazz Classics, 1955 recordings), *Miles* (Original Jazz Classics (1956), *Quintet/Sextet* (Original Jazz Classics 1956), *Round About Midnight* (Columbia 1957), *Miles Ahead* (Columbia 1957), *'58 Miles* (Columbia 1958), with John Coltrane *Miles And Coltrane* (Columbia 1958), *Milestones* (Columbia 1958), *Porgy And Bess* (Columbia 1959), *Kind Of Blue* (Columbia 1959), *Sketches Of Spain* (Columbia 1960), *On Green Dolphin Street* (Jazz Door, 1960 recordings), *Live In Zurich* 1960 (Jazz Unlimited 1960 recordings), *Live In Stockholm* 1960 (Royal Jazz, 1960 recordings), *Miles Davis In Person (Friday And Saturday Nights At The Blackhawk)* (Columbia 1961), *Someday My Prince Will Come* (Columbia 1961), *At Carnegie Hall* (Columbia 1962), *Seven Steps To Heaven* (Columbia 1963), *Quiet Nights* (Columbia 1963), *Miles In Antibes* (Columbia 1964), *Miles Davis In Europe* (1964), *My Funny Valentine* (1964), *'Four' And More* (1964), *ESP* (Columbia 1965), *Miles Smiles* (Columbia 1966), *Sorcerer* (Columbia 1967), *Nefertiti* (Columbia 1967), *Miles In The Sky* (Columbia 1968), *Filles De Kilimanjaro* (Columbia 1968), *In A Silent Way* (Columbia 1969), *Double Image* (Moon, 1969 recordings), *Paraphernalia* (JMY, 1969 recording), *Bitches Brew* (Columbia 1970), *At The Fillmore* (Columbia 1970), *A Tribute To Jack Johnson* (Columbia 1971), *What I Say? Vols 1 and 2* (JMY, 1971 recording), *Live-Evil* (Columbia 1972), *On The Corner* (Columbia 1972), *Tallest Trees* (1973), *In Concert* (1973), *Black Beauty* (1974), *Big Fun* (Columbia 1974), *Get Up With It* (1974), *Jazz At The Plaza Vol 1* (1974), *Agharta* (1976), *Pangaea* (Columbia 1976), *Live At The Plugged Nickel* (Columbia 1976), *Water Babies* (1977), *Circle In The Round* (Columbia 1979, 1955 - 1970 recordings), *Directions* (1981), *Man With The Horn* (1981), *A Night In Tunisia* (1981), *We Want Miles* (1982), *Star People* (1983), *Blue Christmas* (1983), *Heard 'Round the World* (1983), *Blue Haze* (1984/6), *At Last* (1985), *Decoy* (Columbia 1984), *Your Under Arrest* (Columbia 1985), *Tutu* (Warner 1986), *Music From Siesta '88* (Warner 1988), *Amandla* (Warner 1989), *Aura* (Columbia 1989), *Mellow Miles* (Columbia 1989, 1961-63 recordings), *Ballads* (Columbia 1989, 1961-63 recordings), *The Hot Spot* (1990), *Dingo* (Warners 1991), *Doo-Bop* (1993), *Live In Europe 1988* (1993), with Quincy Jones *Miles and Quincy Jones Live At Montreux* (Warners 1993, rec. 1991). Selected compilations: *The CBS Years 1955-1985* (1989, box set), *The Collection* (1990), *Gold Collection* (1993).

Video: *Miles Davis And Quincy Jones: Live At Montreux* (1993).

Further reading: *Miles Davis,* Ian Carr. *From Satchmo To Miles,* Leonard Feather. *Miles; The Autobiography. The Art Of Miles Davis,* Miles Davis.

Davis, Nathan

b. 15 February 1937, Kansas City, Kansas, USA. Davis began to play trombone at the age of 17, but soon switched to reeds and is now an accomplished player on flute, bass clarinet, tenor and soprano saxophones. His first noteworthy job was with the Jay McShann band, and a little later he became one of the few males who has ever played with the usually all-female International Sweethearts Of Rhythm. While studying at Kansas University, Davis lead a group with Carmell Jones; then army service in 1960 took him to Berlin. On leaving the army in 1963 he remained in Europe and was invited to Paris by Kenny Clarke, with whom he played for most of the next six years. In 1964 Davis joined Eric Dolphy for a brief residency at the Chat Qui Peche club and also played on the revolutionary reedsman's last recordings, made for the French radio station ORTF. The next year Davis toured Europe with Art Blakey's Jazz Messengers and was asked to join the band on a permanent basis; however, he declined, feeling that the touring life was too precarious. After making a series of excellent (but long-deleted) albums for small European labels - featuring players such as Jones, Clarke, Woody Shaw, Larry Young, Mal Waldron and Hampton Hawes - Davis returned to the USA in 1969 to teach jazz at Pittsburgh University, where he has since remained. He continued to record sporadically, making two albums for the small Pittsburgh company Segue followed by three more for his own Tomorrow International label, on which he tried his hand at fusion: but, as with his European releases, these were never widely distributed. Davis has had bad luck with recordings: not only are most of his own albums unavailable, but his work with Blakey, Clarke and Dolphy remains largely unreleased. The situation began to change in the 80s: the London-based Hot House label reissued his 1967 John Coltrane homage, *Rules Of Freedom,* and later released the new *London By Night.* Davis also formed the neo-bebop Paris Reunion Band, comprising various USA musicians who had lived in Paris in the 60s, recording and touring with them in the late 80s: personnel, at different times, has included Johnny Griffin, Joe Henderson, Shaw, Nat Adderley, Dizzy Reece, Slide Hampton, Kenny Drew, Jimmy Woode and Idris Muhammad. Nevertheless, it is early albums such as *Hip Walk* and *Sixth Sense* that represent Davis' finest work. In particular, his superb tenor on the former's 'While Children Sleep' and his glorious bass clarinet on the latter's 'The Shadow Of Your Smile' suggest he is one of the great balladeers of modern jazz.

Albums: *Happy Girl* (1965), *Hip Walk* (1966), *Rules Of Freedom* (Hot House 1968), *Live At Schola Cantorum* (1969), *Makatuka* (1970), *Sixth Sense Of The 11th House* (1972), *If*

(1976), *A Tribute To Dr. Martin Luther King* (1976), *Faces Of Love* (1982), *London By Night* (DIW 1987), *Nathan Davis Sextet* (1990, rec. 1965), with Arthur Blythe, Chico Freeman, Sam Rivers *Roots* (1992).

Davis, Richard

b. 15 April 1930, Chicago, Illinois, USA. A superbly accomplished jazz bass player, Davis worked in and around his home town during the late 40s and early 50s while continuing his musical studies. Between 1953 and 1955 he worked with Sun Ra, Ahmad Jamal and Don Shirley and later in the decade began a long association with Sarah Vaughan. In the 60s Davis worked with a number of musicians associated with the more forward-thinking areas of jazz. Notable among these was Eric Dolphy and also Jaki Byard. Davis' eclecticism was such that he was called upon for recording dates and public appearances with musicians as diverse as Earl Hines, Ben Webster, Stan Getz, Billy Cobham and Igor Stravinsky. For a long period at the end of the 60s he was also first-call bass player for the Thad Jones-Mel Lewis Jazz Orchestra. In 1977 Davis began teaching at the University of Wisconsin. A masterly technician, Davis plays with a full sound and his accompaniment is a great benefit to soloists. His own solos are conceived with intelligence and a powerful yet always tuneful plangency.

Albums: with Eric Dolphy *Out To Lunch* (1964), with Ben Webster *See You At The Fair* (1964), with Thad Jones-Mel Lewis *Live At The Village Vanguard* (1967), *Muses For Richard Davis* (1969), *Epistrophy And Now's The Time* (Muse 1972), with Jill McManus *As One* (1975), with Walt Dickerson *Divine Gemini* (1977), *Fancy Free* (Galaxy 1977), *Way Out West* (Muse 1981), *Harvest* (Muse 1988), *Persia My Dear* (DIW 1988), *One For Frederick* (Hep 1989), *Dealin'* (Sweet Basil 1991).

Davis, Wild Bill

b. 24 November 1918, Glasgow, Missouri, USA. Davis' early career found him playing piano, guitar, or simply writing arrangements for the bands of Milt Larkin, Earl Hines and Louis Jordan. At the end of the 40s he began concentrating on playing the Hammond organ. His organ-led trio was very successful and he also worked with Duke Ellington, Lionel Hampton and Count Basie. He was due to record his arrangement of 'April In Paris' with Basie but arrived late at the studio so Basie proceeded without him and as a result had one of his best-selling hits. Davis worked extensively in Europe, recording with a succession of visiting Americans including Buddy Tate and Al Grey. In the late 70s and early 80s he once again worked with Hampton but was mostly engaged in leading his own small groups and appearing solo at concerts and festivals around the world.

Albums: *At Birdland* (1956), *Wild Bill Davis* i (1956-57), *Wild Bill Davis* ii (1956-57), *Wild Bill Davis* iii (1958), *Organ 1959* (1959), *Wild Bill Davis* iv (1960), *Wild Bill Davis* v (1960), *One More Time* (1962), *Con Soul & Sax* (1965), *Live At Count Basie's* (1966), *Wild Bill Davis In Atlantic City* (1966), *Wild Bill Davis* vi (1967), *Impulsions* (1972), *Live* (1976), *All Right, Okay, You Win* (1976), *With Lionel Hampton Live In Emmen,* *Holland* (1978), *Swing System 'D'* (1978).

Davison, Wild Bill

b. 5 January 1906, Defiance, Ohio, USA, d. 14 November 1989. As a youth Davison played with local bands, making occasional trips to Cincinnati and even New York in the mid-20s. While playing with the Seattle Harmony Kings, Davison made his first visit to Chicago, the city where he was to remain stylistically linked for the rest of his long life. This first visit to Chicago lasted five years; then, after a spell of bandleading with Frank Teschemacher, he worked in Milwaukee for several years, and, from 1941, played mostly in New York. For the next few years, broken only by military service during World War II, he was a regular at the city's popular Dixieland clubs, including Nick's, Ryan's and Condon's. With Eddie Condon, Davison made numerous recordings and also toured Europe. In the 60s he divided his time between jobs on the east and west coasts, recording and touring, often as a single, but sometimes in harness with some of his old musical comrades. A tough-talking, hard-drinking in his younger days, and driving cornetist, Davison's aggressive playing won him a host of admirers and was viewed by many as the epitome of Chicago style. In fact, as can be seen from his career summary, Davison's connection with Chicago was assumed rather than real. Although his rasping, forceful sound, replete with searing rips and flares, was most readily appropriate to the traditional repertoire, he had a fine way with ballads, and an album he recorded with strings late in his career showed him to have a warm-hearted, almost rhapsodic side to his personality. Remarkably, Davison retained his playing ability into old age and still practised daily when in his 80s.

Selected albums: with Eddie Condon *Jam Session Coast To Coast* (1953), with Condon *Dixieland* (1955), *After Hours* (Jazzology 1966), *Surfside Jazz* (Jazzology 1966), *Live In New York* (c.1969), *Jazz On A Saturday Afternoon Vols 1 - 2* (Jazzology 1971), with Condon, Gene Krupa *Jazz At The New School* (1972), *S'Wonderful* (Jazzology 1972), *Just A Gig* (Jazzology 1973), *Sweet And Lovely* (1976), *All American Band* (1981), *Solo Flight* (Jazzology 1981), *Lady Of The Evening* (Jazzology 1982), *Running Wild* (1981), *Wild Bill Davison All Stars* (1986), *But Beautiful* (Storyville 1986), *Showcase* (Jazzology 1992),

Dawson, Alan

b. 14 July 1929, Marietta, Pennsylvania, USA. After studying extensively in Boston, where he also worked with the Sabby Lewis band, drummer Dawson joined Lionel Hampton. In 1953 he travelled to Europe with the band. This put Dawson in company with many outstanding young musicians, including Gigi Gryce and Clifford Brown. They made some excellent recordings although this went expressly against Hampton's orders, and when the band returned home most were dismissed. Dawson returned to Boston where he rejoined the Lewis band and later in the 50s began teaching at Berklee College Of Music. A regular in Boston clubs, he played with a wide range of visiting jazz artists and also recorded occasional-

Buddy De Franco

ly with artists such as Dave Brubeck, Tal Farlow, Dexter Gordon and Phil Woods. In 1965 he appeared at the Berlin Jazz Festival with Sonny Rollins and Bill Evans. Gifted as a performer, Dawson also has the rare ability to fully communicate his skills; and among his pupils are Tony Williams and Pat La Barbera.

Albums: with Gigi Gryce, Clifford Brown *The Paris Collection* (1953), *Tal Farlow Returns* (1969), with Dexter Gordon *The Panther!* (1970), with Dave Brubeck *We're All Together Again For The First Time* (1972), with Phil Woods *Musique Du Bois* (1974).

De Franco, Buddy

b. Boniface F. De Franco, 17 February 1923, Camden, New Jersey, USA. A child prodigy, De Franco won an amateur contest playing the clarinet while still only 14 years old. Four years later he was in Gene Krupa's band, then joined Charlie Barnet; and in 1944 became a featured player with Tommy Dorsey, who had been sponsor of the amateur contest that launched De Franco's career. After abortive attempts to establish his own big band, De Franco worked mostly with small groups, including those of Count Basie and Art Blakey and in 1954 toured Europe with Billie Holiday. In the 60s, he continued playing in small groups, sometimes under his own leadership, and also taught. In 1966 he became leader of the Glenn Miller Orchestra, a job which lasted until 1974. Since then he has mixed teaching with playing, touring extensively, recording and developing a long-standing musical relationship with Terry Gibbs. A marvellously accomplished player, De Franco has been criticized for sacrificing emotional depth for the sake of technique. While to some extent justifiable, this censure unfairly condemns a gifted musician who has consistently set for himself, and attained, the highest standards of performance. Selected albums: *Gene Norman Presents Buddy De Franco* (1953), *Buddy De Franco Quartet* I (1953), *Buddy De Franco* i (1954), *Buddy De Franco* ii (1954), *Buddy De Franco* iii (1954), *The Complete Verve Recordings With Sonny Clark* (1954-55), *Cooking The Blues* (1955-56), *Art Tatum-Buddy De Franco Quartet* (1956), *Harry 'Sweets' Edison-Buddy De Franco Sextet* (1956), *Buddy De Franco With The Oscar Peterson Quartet* (1956-57), *Buddy De Franco Quintet* (1956-57), *Buddy De Franco* iv (1957), *Sessions, Live* (1957), *Harry 'Sweets' Edison-Buddy De Franco Septet* i (1957), *Harry 'Sweets' Edison-Buddy De Franco Septet* ii (1957), *Buddy De Franco* v (1957), *Buddy De Franco Plays Benny Goodman* (1957), *Buddy De Franco* vi (1957), *Cross-country Suite* (1959), *Buddy De Franco* vii (1959), *Buddy De Franco And Tommy Gumina* i (1960), *Buddy De Franco And Tommy Gumina* ii (1961), *Buddy De Franco And Tommy Gumina* iii (1962), *Buddy De Franco And Tommy Gumina* iv (1963), *Buddy De Franco And Tommy Gumina* v (1964), *Blues Bag* (1964), *Buddy De Franco And His Orchestra At The Glen Island Casino* (1967), *Free Sail* (1974), *Boronquin* (Sonet 1975), *Like Someone In Love* (Progressive 1977), *Waterbed* (1977), *Love Affair With A Clarinet* (1977), *Listen And Sit-In* (1978), *Buddy de Franco In Argentina* (1980), *The Liveliest* (Hep jazz 1980), with Terry Gibbs *Jazz Party: First Time Together* (1981), *On Tour: UK* (1983), *Buddy De Franco Presents John Denman* (c.1984), *Garden Of Dreams* (Hep jazz 1984), *Mr Lucky* (Pablo 1984), *Groovin'* (1984), *'Hark': Buddy De Franco Meets The Oscar Peterson Quartet* (Pablo 1985), with Gibbs *Chicago Fire* (1987), with Al Raymond *Born To Swing!* (1988), *Mood Indigo* (Hep Jazz 1988), *Like Someone In Love* (1989), *A Chip Off The Old Bop* (1992), *Five Notes Of Blues* (Musidisc 1993). Compilations: with Tommy Dorsey *The All Time Hit Parade Rehearsals* (1944), *Radio Discs Of Tommy Dorsey* (1944).

De Paris, Sidney

b. 30 May 1905, Crawfordsville, Indiana, USA, d. 13 September 1967. In the early 20s De Paris played trumpet in bands in Washington, DC, before moving to New York where he joined Andy Preer's band. In the late 20s he worked in units led by Charlie 'Fess' Johnson, by his brother, Wilbur De Paris, and then into the 30s with a succession of bands with which he briefly worked: Benny Carter, McKinney's Cotton Pickers, Don Redman, Noble Sissle, Willie Bryant and Mezz Mezzrow. At the end of the 30s, despite the all-pervading swing era, De Paris began to move towards an association with traditional jazz which was to continue for the rest of his life. In 1939 and 1940 he worked with Zutty Singleton, Jelly Roll Morton and Sidney Bechet. He later played with Art Hodes and had brief spells deputizing in the big bands of Benny Carter, Charlie Barnet and Roy Eldridge; but from 1947 he was principally in permanent collaboration with his brother. Their band offered a high standard of traditional jazz performances, always played with reverence for the past but with a sprightly sense of the present. Albums: *Sidney De Paris And His Blue Note Stompers* (1951), *The Fabulous Sidney Bechet And His Hot Six With Sidney De Paris* (1951), *Wilbur De Paris And His Rampart Street Ramblers* (1952), *Wilbur De Paris At Symphony Hall* (1956). Compilations: *De Paris Dixie* (1944-51 recordings).

De Paris, Wilbur

b. 11 January 1900, Crawfordsville, Indiana, USA, d. 3 January 1973. After working in tent shows and carnivals, trombonist De Paris appeared in New Orleans in the early 20s where he played with Louis Armstrong and other young musicians. Throughout the 20s he toured extensively, working with a wide range of small groups and big bands. He continued this pattern into the 30s where his jobs included playing in the band Teddy Hill brought to Europe and another spell with Armstrong. In 1940 he joined the old Chick Webb band which was continuing under Ella Fitzgerald's leadership. During the early and mid-40s he also played with Roy Eldridge and Duke Ellington but in 1947 formed his own band which featured his brother, Sidney De Paris, and stayed in existence for the next two decades. The De Paris brothers' band employed the music and inspiration of the New Orleans masters of an earlier generation but it was overlaid with a skilful blend of contemporary stylization and up-to-the-minute projection. Enormously popular in concert and on records, the band was one of the most successful of its kind.

Albums: *Wilbur De Paris And His Rampart Street Ramblers* (1952), *Wilbur De Paris At Symphony Hall* (1956), *Wilbur De Paris Plays Cole Porter* (1957-58), *That's A-Plenty* (1958-59), *The Wild Jazz Age* (1960), *Wilbur De Paris On The Riviera* (1960).

Dean, Elton

b. 28 October 1945, Nottingham, England. Dean is a fiery, self-taught saxophonist, who mainly features alto but sometimes uses saxello. He had lessons on piano from four years old and on violin from the age of 11. He hated these and took up clarinet and tenor saxophone, picking up the techniques himself and playing in various trad bands as a semi-professional. He went to Germany with a soul band, Lester Square and the GTs, and then joined the Irish Crickets, a showband. Regular work and wages enabled him to return to England, where he formed his own group, the Soul Pushers. In 1967 he joined Bluesology, who were at the start of their association with Long John Baldry. It was here that he first played with Marc Charig, later a front-line partner in the Keith Tippett Sextet. (For collectors of trivia, when Bluesology split up, the organist, Reg Dwight, took his stage name from colleagues Elton Dean and John Baldry to become Elton John.) Dean first met Tippett at the 1967 Barry (Wales) Summer School. He was a member of the Tippett Sextet which, in 1968, was the first beneficiary of the London Jazz Centre Society's scheme to give six-week residencies to new bands at its Monday sessions at London's 100 Club. As a result of these exciting gigs the reputation of the band and its individual members spread rapidly. From 1969-72 Dean was with Soft Machine at a time when the group's evolution from art rock to jazz-rock was becoming settled. Dean was with the edition of the Softs which was invited to play at the Proms, and it was usually his acerbic sax which would pull the band's fascinating but often diffuse improvisations into focus. After leaving Soft Machine, he led or co-led a series of bands, including Just Us, EDQ, Ninesense, and El Skid (co-led with Alan Skidmore.) More recently he has toured Europe and South America with his own bands of various line-ups, and has started his own label to issue new recordings of his group. Since 1990 he has had a powerful trio with Paul Rogers and Mark Sanders featuring Dean's long, a stringently lyrical improvisations. He has also worked with the London Jazz Composers Orchestra, Georgie Fame, Carla Bley and with Dutch rock band Supersister.

Selected albums: *Elton Dean* (1971), *Oh For The Edge* (1976), *They All Be On This Old Road* (1976), *The Cheque Is In The Mail* (Ogun 1977), *Happy Daze* (Ogun 1977), *El Skid* (1977), *Boundaries* (1981), *Welcomet* (Impetus 1987), *The Bologna Tape* (Ogun 1988), *Oh For The Edge* (Ogun 1988), *Duos* (ED 1989), *Trios* (ED 1989), *Unlimited Saxophone Company* (Ogun 1989), *Elton Dean Quartet Live* (ED 1989), *Two's And Three's* (ED 1989), with Howard Riley *All The Tradition* (Slam 1991), *The Vortex Tapes* (Slam 1992).

Dearie, Blossom

b. 28 April 1928, East Durham, New York, USA. A singer, pianist and songwriter, with a 'wispy, little-girlish' voice, Dearie is regarded as one of the great supper club singers. Her father was of Scottish and Irish descent; her mother emigrated from Oslo, Norway. Dearie is said to have been given her unusual first name after a neighbour brought peach blossoms to her house on the day she was born. She began taking piano lessons when she was five, and studied classical music until she was in her teens, when she played in her high school dance band and began to listen to jazz. Early influences included Art Tatum, Count Basie, Duke Ellington and Martha Tilton, who sang with the Benny Goodman Band. Dearie graduated from high school in the mid-40s and moved to New York City to pursue a music career. She joined the Blue Flames, a vocal group within the Woody Herman Big Band, and then sang with the Blue Reys, a similar formation in the Alvino Rey Band. In 1952, while working at the Chantilly Club in Greenwich Village, Dearie met Nicole Barclay who, with her husband, owned Barclay Records. At her suggestion she went to Paris and formed a vocal group, the Blue Stars. The group consisted of four male singers/instrumentalists, and four female singers; Dearie contributed many of the arrangements. They had a hit in France and the USA with one of their first recordings, a French version of 'Lullaby Of Birdland'. While in Paris, Dearie met impresario and record producer Norman Granz, who signed her for Verve Records, for whom she eventually made six solo albums, including the highly regarded *My Gentleman Friend*. Unable to take the Blue Stars to the USA because of passport problems (they later evolved into the Swingle Singers), she returned to New York and resumed her solo career, singing to her own piano accompaniment at New York nightclubs, such as the Versailles, the Blue Angel and the Village Vanguard. She also appeared on US television with Jack Paar, Merv Griffin and Johnny Carson. In 1966 she made the first of what were to become annual appearances at Ronnie Scott's Club in London, receiving excellent reviews as 'a singer's singer', whose most important asset is her power to bring a personal interpretation to a song, while showing the utmost respect for a composer's intentions'. In the 60s she also made some albums for Capitol Records, including *May I Come In?*, a set of standards arranged and conducted by Jack Marshall. In the early 70s, disillusioned by the major record companies' lack of interest in her kind of music, she started her own company, Daffodil Records in 1974. Her first album for the label, *Blossom Dearie Sings*, was followed by a two-record set entitled *My New Celebrity Is You*, which contained eight of her own compositions. The album's title song was written especially for her by Johnny Mercer, and is said to be the last piece he wrote before his death in 1976. During the 70s Dearie performed at Carnegie Hall with former Count Basie blues singer Joe Williams, and jazz vocalist Anita O'Day in a show called *The Jazz Singers*. In 1981 she appeared with Dave Frishberg for three weeks at Michael's Pub in Manhattan. Frishberg, besides being a songwriter, also sings and plays the piano, and Dearie frequently performed several of his songs, such as 'Peel Me A Grape', 'I'm Hip' and 'My Attorney Bernie'. Her own compositions include 'I Like You, You're Nice', 'I'm Shadowing You' and 'Hey John'. From 1983, she performed regularly for six months a year at the Ballroom, a nightclub in Manhattan, and in 1985 was the first recipient of the Mabel Mercer Foundation Award, which is presented annually to an outstanding supper-club performer. Appreciated mostly in New York and London, where she appeared several times in the late 80s/early 90s at the Pizza On The Park, Dearie, with her intimate style and unique voice remains one of the few survivors of a specialized art.

Selected albums: *My Gentleman Friend* (1961), *May I Come In?* (1966), *My New Celebrity Is You* (1979), *Blossom Dearie Sings 1973* (Daffodil 1979), *Blossom Dearie Sings 1975* (Daffodil 1979), *Winchester In Apple Blossom Time* (Master Mix 1979), *May I Come In* (Capitol 1981), *Blossom Dearie* (Verve 1983), *Needlepoint Magic* (Master Mix 1988), *Featuring Bobby Jasper* (1988), *Songs Of Chelsea* (Master Mix 1988), *Et Tu Bruce* (1989), *Christmas Spice, It's So Nice* (Master Mix 1991), *Once Upon A Summertime* (1993). Compilation: *The Special Magic Of Blossom Dearie* (1975).

Deems, Barrett

b. 1 March 1914, Springfield, Illinois, USA. Throughout the 30s Deems worked with Paul Ash and led his own small bands. Towards the end of the decade he worked extensively with Joe Venuti, an association which took him to the mid-40s. Thereafter, Deems played in bands led by Red Norvo, Charlie Barnet and Muggsy Spanier. Billed as the 'World's Fastest Drummer', Deems had an eccentric on-stage personality which was captured on film during a solo-feature in *Rhythm Inn* (1951). In 1954 he joined Louis Armstrong's All Stars, touring several countries and again appearing on film, this time in a feature, *High Society*, and the Ed Morrow television documentary *Satchmo The Great* (both 1956). In the 60s he worked with Jack Teagarden and the Dukes Of Dixieland before settling in Chicago where he played in clubs, often backing visiting jazzmen. In 1976 he toured with Benny Goodman, and in the 80s worked with Wild Bill Davison and as a member of Keith Smith's package celebrating the music of Louis Armstrong. At this time Deems' eccentricity was enhanced by his wild, beard-ed appearance and his off-stage volubility. He referred to himself as the oldest teenager in the business and ruined countless recorded interviews with his irreverent and frequently unbroadcastable wit. Despite the flamboyance of his appearance and self-billing, Deems played with a powerful attack and his spell with Armstrong included the album of W.C. Handy tunes, which proved to be a classic of the leader's later work.

Albums: *Louis Armstrong Plays W.C. Handy* (1954), *Louis Armstrong At The Pasadena Civic Auditoreum* (1956), with the Dukes Of Dixieland *World's Fair* (1964), *Deemus* (1979).

DeFaut, Volly

b. Voltaire De Faut, 14 March 1904, Little Rock, Arkansas, USA, d. 29 May 1973. After studying violin, De Faut switched to clarinet in his early teens. By this time he was living with his family in Chicago; and when aged 19 replaced Leon Roppolo, whose style he emulated, in the New Orleans Rhythm Kings. Later in the 20s he worked with Merrit Brunies, Muggsy

Spanier and Jelly Roll Morton. In the pre-swing years he played with some of the best dance bands, including that led by Isham Jones and one of contractor Jean Goldkette's bands. A highly-gifted musician, Benny Goodman always spoke well of him, as one who could have commanded a high salary during the swing era, De Faut nevertheless chose to have a succession of jobs in radio orchestras throughout the 30s. From the 50s onwards De Faut worked mostly outside music but made occasional appearances with small bands, some of which, like that led by Art Hodes, made records.

Selected albums: with Art Hodes *The Trios* (1953), *Friar's Inn Revisited* (1968), with Hodes *Up In Volly's Room* (1993, rec. 50s).

Defries, David

b. 24 May 1952, London, England. A multi-instrumentalist specializing in the trumpet, Defries stayed for just two terms of his course at Leeds College of Music, gaining experience in the Surrey County Youth Orchestra instead. During his twenties he played in Don Weller's Major Surgery, Julian Bahula's Jabula, and Dudu Pukwana's Zila. In the early 80s, as well as playing with Chris MacGregor's Brotherhood Of Breath, he co-led Sunwind with guitarist Mark Wood, which won the 1982 Greater London Arts Council Jazz Competition. He has more recently worked with the Breakfast Band and Loose Tubes.

Album: with Loose Tubes *Open Letter* (1988).

Dejan, Harold

b. 4 February 1909, New Orleans, Louisiana, USA. After studying clarinet with Lorenzo Tio Jnr., Dejan began playing professionally while still in his early teenage. He played in several New Orleans-style bands in the 20s and 30s. After military service Dejan took up the alto saxophone, playing with various bands into the 50s. In 1958 he formed his Olympia Brass Band, inspired by the brass bands he saw and heard during his childhood. A vigorous and enthusiastic performer, Dejan communicated his love of jazz through a wide-ranging repertoire. For all his love for the traditions, he did not hesitate to incorporate currently popular styles, including R&B and even bop-inflected numbers. Dejan continued to lead his band into the late 80s.

Albums: *Harold Dejan's Olympia Brass Band* (1962), *The Mighty Four* (1963), *Dejan's Olympia Brass Band In Europe* (1968), *Harold Dejan's Olympia Brass Band In London* (1968), *Harold Dejan's Olympia Brass Band In Berlin* (1968), *The Olympia Brass Band Of New Orleans* (1971).

DeJohnette, Jack

b. 9 August 1942, Chicago, Illinois, USA. DeJohnette studied piano for 10 years, graduating from the American Conservatory of Music in Chicago. He also played saxophone, but was inspired by the example of Max Roach to take up drums, which he played with the high school band. He would practise for four hours on drums and four on piano, and played in all sorts of situations, from free jazz to R&B. Finally settling

Jack DeJohnette

on drums, in 1963 he became a member of Richard Muhal Abrams' Experimental Band and was later involved with the AACM. In 1966 he played with John Coltrane during the interregnum between the departure of Elvin Jones and the final choice of Rashied Ali as his replacement. In the same year he settled in New York, playing with Big John Patton, Jackie McLean, Betty Carter and Abbey Lincoln. At the end of the year he joined the Charles Lloyd Quartet, where he stayed until 1969, but during that time he also gigged with Thelonious Monk, Freddie Hubbard, Bill Evans, Keith Jarrett, Chick Corea and Stan Getz. In August 1969 he took part in sessions for Miles Davis's *Bitches Brew*, and in April 1970 he formally joined Davis. After departing in mid-1971 he set up his own band, Compost.

During the 70s he became virtually a session drummer for the ECM label, recording with Jan Garbarek, Kenny Wheeler and John Abercrombie among others. With Abercrombie and Dave Holland, he played in the occasional trio Gateway. In 1978 he formed and recorded with his New Directions band, which involved Abercrombie and Lester Bowie, and in 1980 formed the acclaimed Special Edition, whose varying personnel has featured David Murray, Chico Freeman and Arthur Blythe. In 1985, reverting temporarily to his earlier talent, he released a solo piano album. During the late 80s and early 90s DeJohnette has been part of Keith Jarrett's Standards Trio with Gary Peacock and has toured as a duo with John Surman, both of them doubling on keyboards and electronics. (He had earli-

er featured on Surman's 1981 *The Amazing Adventures Of Simon Simon.*) He has also worked with Michael Brecker, Tommy Smith and with Ornette Coleman and Pat Metheny on their *Song X* collaboration. His further collaborations with Metheny in 1990 with *Parallel Realities* and with Lyle Mays and Marc Johnson in 1993 were both inspiring excursions. In some contexts, DeJohnette's approach to the rhythm can be so oblique that his grip on time can seem precarious, but this is deceptive. He is a powerfully propulsive percussionist with an exceptional sense of structure and texture, perhaps heard at its most exotic in his vivid splashes of colour with the Lloyd Quartet.

Albums: *The Jack DeJohnette Complex* (Original Jazz Classics 1968), *Have You Heard?* (1970), with Compost *Take Off Your Body* (1972), with Keith Jarrett *Ruta And Daitya* (1973), *Sorcery* (1974), *Cosmic Chicken* (1975), *Gateway* (1975), *Untitled* (1976), *New Rags* (1977), *New Directions* (ECM 1977), *Gateway 2* (1978), *Special Edition* (ECM 1980), *New Directions In Europe* (ECM 1980), *Tin Can Alley* (ECM 1981), *Inflation Blues* (ECM 1982), *Album Album* (ECM 1984), *The Piano Album* (Landmark 1985), with Lester Bowie *Zebra* (Pan 1985), with David Murray *In Our Style* (1986), *Irresistible Force* (1987), *Audio Visualscapes* (Impulse 1988), *Parallel Realities* (MCA 1990), *Earth Walk* (Blue Note 1991), with Lyle Mays, Marc Johnson *Fictionary* (1993), *Music For The Fifth World* (1993), *Pictures* (1993). Compilation: *Works* (ECM 1985).

Delmar, Elaine

b. 13 September 1939, Harpenden, Hertfordshire, England. Delmar was a popular singer in the UK, whose style was doubtless influenced by her Jamaican-born father, the jazz trumpeter, Leslie 'Jiver' Hutchinson. After studying music from the age of six, she made her first broadcast, as a pianist, seven years later on *Children's Hour*. While still at school, she sang with her father's band at US Air Force bases in Britain, and was on tour with him at the time of his fatal accident in 1959. In 1952 she appeared in a revival of *Finian's Rainbow* in Liverpool. For a while she was a member of the Dominoes group, before going solo and playing the club circuit and touring overseas. From the early 60s, she made several appearances on the London stage in shows such as *No Strings, Cowardy Custard, Bubbling Brown Sugar* (with Billy Daniels), *The Wiz* and *Jerome Kern Goes To Hollywood* (1985), which marked the centenary of the composer's birth. After the latter show's brief Broadway run, Delmar made her New York cabaret debut at the Ballroom in New York. In 1991, she co-starred with actor and singer, Paul Jones, in the concert tour of *Let's Do It*, another centenary celebration of the great American songwriter, Cole Porter. In the following year, Delmar teamed with Jones again for a series of concerts entitled *Hooray For Hollywood*, which featured songs from movies such as *Porgy And Bess, Annie Get Your Gun* and *Top Hat*. Amongst her albums, which contained popular standards, she has also released the highly acclaimed *Elaine Sings Wilder*, a tribute to one of America's lesser known composers, Alec Wilder. The pianist and musical director on the record was Colin Beaton, one of Delmar's mentors and early influences. The antithesis of Wilder would be Gustav Mahler, and Delmar played the part of the Princess in Ken Russell's 1974 film biography of the famous composer. In 1983, she appeared at London's National Theatre in the straight play, *Map Of The World*. A popular regular at Ronnie Scott's club, she has appeared in concert with jazz giants such as Benny Carter, Herb Ellis and Stéphane Grappelli. A polished performer whose execution is faultless, jazz remains her first love; her accompanists are always impeccable improvisers and have included Eddie Thompson, Brian Dee and Jeff Clyne.

Albums: *Elaine Sings Wilder* (1966), *Sneaking Up On You* (1968), *La Belle Elaine* (1968), *I've Got The World On A String* (1976), *Elaine Delmar And Friends* (1980), *Yours Sincerely* (1985), *In Town* (1987), *Spirit Of The Song* (1990), *S'Wonderful* (1992).

Dennerlein, Barbara

b. 25 September 1965, Munich, Germany. Dennerlein started to learn organ when she was 11-years-old and soon acquired a Hammond B3, the classic instrument; she was performing in Munich jazz clubs by the age of 15. She played alongside Jimmy Smith on his German tour and with altoist Sonny Fortune. Her self-produced albums *Jazz Live At The Munich Domicile* and *Bebop* both won German Record Critics awards. Her trio with Christopher Widmoser (guitar) and Andreas

Elaine Delmare

Witte (drums) toured, played festivals and made radio and television appearances in the mid-80s. Playing foot-pedal bass in the authentic manner, Dennerlein's combination of down-home groove and modernist freakishness was well documented on *Straight Ahead* (1988), for which drummer Ronnie Burrage supplied his fantastic swirling drum textures, and Ray Anderson bravura trombone. After enthusiastic critical reception in England, Dennerlein recorded *Hot Stuff* in 1990 with drummer Mark Mondesir and saxophonist Andy Sheppard, prominent figures in the English jazz revival of the 1980s. In 1991 she played London's Jazz Cafe and toured Europe with Widmoser and drummer Stephan Eppinger. Altoist Bobby Watson also sat in with her. She has customised her Hammond with a Midi interface so that she can unleash synthesizer sounds, but it is her understanding of classic black organ music - blues and bebop - that makes her playing so forceful.

Albums: *Jazz Live At The Munich Domicile* (80s), Orgelspiele (Bebab 1985), *Bebab* (Bebab 1986), *Straight Ahead* (Enja 1988), with Andreas Witte *Duo* (1990, rec. 1988), *Live On Tour* (Bebab 1989), *Hot Stuff* (Enja 1990), *Plays Classics* (Bebab 1991), *That's Me* (Enja 1992), *Solo* (1993).

Desmond, Paul

b. Paul Breitenfeld, 25 November 1924, San Francisco, California, USA, d. 30 May 1977. Alto saxophonist Desmond is best-known as a member of the Dave Brubeck quartet, in which he played from 1951-67 and to whose popular success he greatly contributed by writing the hit 'Take Five'. However, aficionados and critics alike agree that much of his best work was done away from Brubeck's often stiff improvisations and tricky time signatures; in particular, on two albums with Gerry Mulligan (*Blues In Time, Two Of A Mind*) and five with Jim Hall (*East Of The Sun, Bossa Antigua, Glad To Be Unhappy, Take Ten, Easy Living*), which Mosaic Records later reissued in one of their splendidly-packaged box-sets. Influenced by Lee Konitz, but very much his own man, Desmond's pure tone and fluid, inventive solos - into which he often wove witty quotes from other songs - marked him out as one of modern jazz's most original and distinctive voices. A noted humorist too, he once declared his aim was to make his saxophone 'sound like a dry martini' and also claimed to have won prizes as 'the world's slowest alto player'. In fact, Desmond's pellucid tone and relaxed, floating style required an architect's sense of structure and the lightning reflexes of a master improviser. In the late 60s/early 70s he sometimes sounded out of place on the CTI label, amid fusion, strings, Simon And Garfunkel songs and the other accoutrements of Creed Taylor's production; but a 1971 date with the Modern Jazz Quartet, and two albums from a 1975 concert with his own quartet, catch him back at his best. In 1975 he also recorded a set of duets with Brubeck and rejoined the pianist's quartet for a reunion tour. In 1976 his doctor diagnosed lung cancer - 'I only went with swollen feet,' Desmond wryly remarked - and he died the following May. Desmond is remembered as one of the most literate, amusing and reflective of jazzmen.

Selected albums : *The Paul Desmond Quintet* (1954), *The Paul Desmond Quartet* (Original Jazz Classics 1956), with Gerry Mulligan *Blues In Time* (1957), *First Place Again!* (1959, reissued as *Paul Desmond With Friends* and as *East Of The Sun*), *Desmond Blue* (1961), with Mulligan *Two Of A Mind* (1962), *Take Ten* (1963), *Bossa Antigua* (1965), *Glad To Be Unhappy* (1965), *Easy Living* (Bluebird 1966), *Polka Dots And Moonbeams* (Bluebird 1966), *Summertime* (1969), *From The Hot Afternoon* (1969), *Crystal Illusions* (1969), *Bridge Over Troubled Water* (1970), *Skylark* (CBS 1974), *Pure Desmond* (CTI 1975), with Dave Brubeck *1975: The Duets* (1975), *The Paul Desmond Quartet Live* (1976), *Like Someone In Love* (Telarc 1976), *Paul Desmond* (1978, rec 1975), with the MJQ *The Only Recorded Performance* (1984, rec 1971). Compilations: *Greatest Hits* (RCA 1986), *The Complete Recordings Of The Paul Desmond Quartet With Jim Hall* (1987, rec 1959-65, six-album box-set), *Late Lament* (1987, rec 1961-62).

Deuchar, Jimmy

b. 26 June 1930, Dundee, Scotland, d. 9 September 1993. Like so many of the young British musicians entering jazz in the immediate post-World War II years, trumpeter Deuchar was involved in regular bebop sessions at a handful of London clubs. Arising from this came his first important professional engagement, with the John Dankworth Seven. In the early 50s he worked with a number of popular dancebands, playing jazz with artists including Ronnie Scott and Tony Crombie. In the mid-50s he worked with Lionel Hampton, then became a member of Kurt Edelhagen's radio big band alongside musicians such as Derek Humble and Dusko Goykovich. During his association with Edelhagen, Deuchar turned more to arranging, although he found time to perform with Scott and Tubby Hayes. In the second half of the 60s, still based in Europe, Deuchar became a member of the multi-national big band co-led by Kenny Clarke and Francy Boland. In the 70s Deuchar relocated to his native Scotland, concentrating upon arranging with only occasional recording dates as a performer, showing that he had lost none of his considerable ability. His arranging continued into the 80s despite ill-health, and included a fine album by Spike Robinson, *The Gershwin Collection*, on which Deuchar showed a clear grasp of how an arranger should overcome the problems associated with blending strings into a jazz performance.

Albums: *Jimmy Deuchar Sextet* (1953), *Thou Swell* (1954-5), *Pub Crawling* (1955), *Jimmy Deuchar Quartet* (1955), *Presenting The Ronnie Scott Sextet* (1957), *Kurt Edelhagen Presents* (1957), *Pal Jimmy* (1958), with Tubby Hayes *Late Spot At Scott's* (1962), *The Scots Connection* (1979).

Dickenson, Vic

b. 6 August 1906, Xenia, Ohio, USA, d. 16 November 1984. A self-taught musician, Dickenson's early experience came playing trombone in the territory bands of Speed Webb and Zack Whyte. By the 30s he was ready for the big time and worked with bands led by Luis Russell, Claude Hopkins, Benny Carter and Count Basie. Throughout the 40s he was active mostly with small groups, including those of Sidney Bechet, Frankie Newton, Eddie Heywood (for a long spell), and as leader of his own groups. This pattern continued into the 50s and 60s when he worked with Bobby Hackett, Red Allen and others. Although rooted in the more traditional jazz style, Dickenson's big band experience, allied to his instinctive melodic grace, made him an ideal musician to enter the mainstream. Indeed, his record albums of the early and mid-50s, especially dates with Ruby Braff, were important milestones in the emergence of this strand of jazz. In addition to his mastery of his instrument, Dickenson brought a refreshing sense of humour to his playing, inserting little musical asides that help to make his work readily identifiable.

Albums: *The Vic Dickenson Septet* i (1953), with Ruby Braff *Vic Dickenson Showcase Vol. 1* (1953), *The Vic Dickenson Septet* ii (Vanguard 1954), *The Vic Dickenson Showcase Vol. 2/The Essential Vic Dickenson* (Vogue 1954), *The Vic Dickenson Quartet* (1956-57), *Jive At Five* (1975), *Gentleman Of The Trombone* (Storyville 1975), *Vic Dickenson In Holland* (1975), *Plays Bessie Smith - Trombone Cholly* (Sonet 1976), *The Vic Dickenson Quintet* (1976), *Vic Dickenson In Sessions* (c.1978), *Yacht Club Swing* (Harlequin 1986, 1964-65 recordings).

Dickerson, Carroll

b. 1895, USA, d. October 1957. Although little is known of his early life, Dickerson became highly popular in Chicago in the 20s. His own violin playing was inadequate, but he had a keen ear for good jazz musicians and employed a succession of leading players in his band, among them Johnny Dunn, Tommy Ladnier, Buster Bailey and Earl Hines (who had recalled that Dickerson would get so drunk he would sometimes try to play his violin with the back of the bow or continue to conduct the band long after the tune was over). Dickerson's most important acquisition arrived in 1926 when Louis Armstrong joined the band. After a second spell in the band, in 1927/8, Armstrong became the leader and Dickerson formed a rival band. In early 1929, once again with Armstrong, Dickerson took his band to New York where they enjoyed great success in clubs and theatres. During his time with Dickerson, Armstrong made some of his classic Hot Five recordings using sidemen from the band, among them Hines and Zutty Singleton. In 1930 Dickerson's band folded and he worked briefly with Joe 'King' Oliver and the Mills Blue Rhythm Band before returning to Chicago and reforming his own band. He continued to lead bands in Chicago through the 30s and into the 40s, but never attained the prominence he had enjoyed when Armstrong was with him.

Compilations: *The Louis Armstrong Legend Vol. 4* (1925-29), included on *Chicago In The Twenties Vol. 1* (c.20s).

DiMeola, Al

b. 22 July 1954, Jersey City, New Jersey, USA. After learning the drums at a very early age, DiMeola was inspired by the Beatles to take up the guitar, at the age of nine. Private lessons continued until, at the age of 15, he was performing in a C&W context. A growing interest in jazz led DiMeola to enter Berklee College Of Music in 1971, but he soon left to join Barry Miles' fusion group, returning in 1974 to study arranging. He was invited by Chick Corea to join his popular and influential Return To Forever. During this time DiMeola made a name for himself with his furious and sometimes spellbinding playing. It was 1976 before DiMeola began working as a leader and recording for Columbia, mostly in a jazz-rock style. In 1982 and 1983 he recorded two flamenco-influenced albums with John McLaughlin and Paco de Lucia, as part of an acoustic trio. The Al DiMeola Project was born in 1985 and remains his most celebrated venture. Recording on Manhattan and touring internationally, this group mixed his delicate, classical-influenced acoustic guitar with the futuristic synthesizer work of Phil Markowitz and ethnic percussion of Airto Moreiro to form a new and influential sound. Al DiMeola remains one of the most accessible and respected guitarists in jazz.

Albums: *Land Of The Midnight Sun* (CBS 1976), *Elegant Gypsy* (CBS 1977), *Casino* (CBS 1978), *Splendido Hotel* (1979), Roller *Jubilee* (CBS 1980), *Electric Rendevous* (CBS 1982), *Tour De Force Live* (CBS 1982), *Scenario* (1983), *Cielo e Terra* (EMI 1983), *Soaring Through A Dream* (EMI 1985), *Tiramu Su* (EMI 1987), *Heart Of The Immigrants* (Tomato 1993), *Kiss My Axe* (Tomato 1993), *World Sinfonia* (Tomato 1993), *Orange And Blue* (1994). Compilation: *The Best Of Al DiMeola* (Manhattan 1993).

Disley, Diz

b. William C. Disley, 27 May 1931, Winnipeg, Manitoba, Canada. Disley grew up in Wales and the north of England, where he learned to play banjo, switching to guitar at the age of 14 when he heard Django Reinhardt. Among his earliest jazz gigs was a period with the Yorkshire Jazz Band. In the 50s he lived in London, working as a newspaper cartoonist and playing in a variety of bands. Although many of Disley's engagements in the 50s and 60s were with traditional bands, he also played skiffle and folk music. Eager to restore the place of the acoustic guitar in the face of the pop-scene successes of its electric counterpart, he gradually developed a substantial reputation as a leading mainstream guitarist. In the early 70s he began a fruitful association with Stéphane Grappelli, persuading the organizers of the Cambridge Folk Festival to book the violinist. With the group rounded out by guitarist Denny Wright, who had worked with Grappelli in 1944, they were a huge success and Grappelli's resurgence was assured. Later, Disley added Len Skeat and continued to accompany the violinist on some of the most memorable moments of his career comeback. On and off, Disley was with Grappelli for about a decade, a period which also saw record dates with Teresa Brewer and others, and tours of Australia, Europe and the USA. Undoubtedly, Disley's acute business sense, allied to his impeccable musical taste and dedication to Reinhardt was a significant factor in the renewal of Grappelli's career. Subsequently, Disley formed his own group which worked mostly in London through the 80s. He continues to play, bringing wit and invention, allied to an urgent unflagging swing to all his sessions.

Albums: with Stéphane Grappelli *I Got Rhythm* (1973), with Grappelli *Violinspiration* (1975), *Zing Went The Strings* (Waterfront 1986).

Dixon, Bill

b. 5 October 1925, Nantucket Island, Massachusetts, USA. Though born of the generation that brought bebop to fruition, Dixon did not rise to prominence until the early 60s, when he emerged as one of the leading pioneers of the New Music. He grew up in New York, started on trumpet at the age of 18, studied painting at Boston University and then attended the Hartnott School of Music (1946-51). In the 50s he freelanced in the New York area as a trumpeter and arranger, and struck up friendships with Cecil Taylor and, later, Archie Shepp, with whom he co-lead a quartet and helped to found the New York Contemporary Five (which also featured Don Cherry, John Tchicai and J.C. Moses: Dixon himself never actually played with the group). In 1964 he organized the October Revolution - six nights of concerts by young *avant gardists* such as Taylor, Shepp, Roswell Rudd, Paul Bley, Milford Graves and the not-so-young Sun Ra - which is generally acknowledged as the event which gave the New Thing its identity as a movement. Its success led him to form the short-lived Jazz Composers Guild, one of the first musicians' self-help organizations (its history is recounted in Valerie Wilmer's *As Serious As Your Life*). In 1965 Dixon met dancer/choreographer Judith Dunn, with whom he worked for many years, their first notable collaboration being at the Newport Jazz Festival in 1966. That same year Dixon played on Taylor's *Conquistador*, his tersely lyrical style a rare counterweight to the pianist's volcanic energy, and also recorded his own *Intents And Purposes*, with tracks by a 10-piece orchestra, a quintet and two brief, overdubbed solo pieces. Dixon's insistence on total artistic control over his music and its presentation has meant that *Intents And Purposes* (on RCA) remains the only recording he has been able to release on a major USA label. Already known as a teacher of art history, he became involved in music education, helping to initiate New York's University of the Streets community programme and, in 1968, taking up a teaching post at Bennington College in Vermont, where he set up a Black Music department (and where he continues to work). In 1976 he was invited to perform at the Paris Autumn Festival, where he premiered his 'Autumn Sequences From A Paris Diary' over five days with regular associates Stephen Horenstein (saxophones) and bassist Alan Silva. Throughout the 70s and 80s, Dixon has been recording his music himself, a little of which has appeared on European labels such as Soul Note and Fore, while a limited-edition two-album box-set of his solo music was released by the independent USA Cadence label in 1985. A painter too, who has exhibited widely in Europe and the USA, Dixon's music could be described as painterly, though its attention to form, line, texture and colour is as much the mark of a composer (and of a superb instrumental technique). His musical evocations of times, seasons, moods etc. are more abstract than representational and record titles such as *Considerations* and *Thoughts* indicate the essentially reflective quality of his music.

In his small-group recordings he has often shown a preference for darker sonorities, sometimes using two or three bassists, and the results are remarkable for their balance of intellectual freight, sensitivity to nuance and implicit structural coherence. One of America's most original, and neglected, instrumentalist/composers, Dixon is currently working on an autobiography, *The Fifth Of October*. In 1986 he published *L'Opera*, a collection of letters, writings, musical scores and drawings.

Albums: with Archie Shepp *Peace* (1962), *Archie Shepp/Bill Dixon* (1965), *Intents And Purposes* (1967), *For Franz* (1977), *Bill Dixon In Italy - Volume One* (1980), *Bill Dixon In Italy - Volume Two* (Soul Note 1981), *Considerations 1* (1981, rec. 1972-76), *Considerations 2* (1981, rec. 1972-76), *November 1981* (1982), *Bill Dixon 1970-73* (1983), *Collection* (1985), *Thoughts* (Soul Note 1987, rec. 1985), *Son Of Sisyphus* (Soul Note 1990, rec. 1988).

Dixon, Charlie

b. c.1898, Jersey City, New Jersey, USA, d. 6 December 1940. In 1922, banjo player, Dixon joined the orchestra of Sam Wooding before moving on to play with Fletcher Henderson. Although often overlooked in potted accounts of the development of big band music, Dixon was a skilled arranger and provided many musical scores for the Henderson band, which helped establish it as the forerunner of the commercial successes of the swing era. After leaving the band he continued in music mostly as an arranger. During the next few years he wrote for Henderson and, notably, Chick Webb, for whom he arranged 'That Naughty Waltz' and 'Harlem Congo'.

Compilations: as arranger *The Chronological Chick Webb 1935-1938* (1935-38).

Dodds, Baby

b. Warren Dodds, 24 December 1898, New Orleans, Louisiana, USA, d. 14 February 1959. Dodds began taking drum lessons in his early teens and made appearances in street parades. Among his first professional engagements were stints in the bands of Bunk Johnson, Willie Hightower, Papa Celestin and Fate Marable, with whom he stayed for three years until 1921. He then joined King Oliver, who was working in San Francisco, and travelled with the band to Chicago the following year. From 1924 he played in a succession of leading bands, mostly in Chicago, among them those of Honore Dutrey, Freddie Keppard and his older brother, Johnny Dodds. Throughout the 30s Dodds was still based in Chicago, playing with his brother, and recorded with many leading traditionalists. In the early 40s Dodds again worked with Bunk Johnson, now a rediscovered trumpet legend. He also played with Mezz Mezzrow, Art Hodes and Miff Mole. In 1950 he suffered a stroke but was soon back, playing with Natty Dominique and also performing in pick-up groups at various clubs in New York and Chicago. Persistent ill-health eventually resulted in partial paralysis. and he died in 1959. Generally held to be the master of New Orleans drumming, Dodds's style was based upon immaculate timekeeping and faultless technique. Eagerly studied by young drummers in Chicago during his many years there, he was a formative influence upon Dave Tough, who urged his slightly younger colleague Gene Krupa to listen to the same source. In practice, few of his devotees ever played like him, mainly because, in performance, Dodds did much more than merely keep time. His accompaniment, especially for soloists, was usually a display of all of his many skills and was, consequently, much fussier than many front-line players liked. Although he adhered closely to the New Orleans tradition, Dodd used his drum patterns in a manner that was in advance of his time and which was not fully exploited until the advent of bebop. In 1946 he recorded a session for Circle Records, during which he explained his technique and played several demonstration solos.

Selected albums: with Johnny Dodds *Blue Clarinet Stomp* (1926-28), *Talking And Drum Solos* (1945-46), *The Baby Dodds Trio* (1946), *Jazz A La Creole* (GHB c.1946), *Footnotes To Jazz* (1946-51).

Further reading: *The Baby Dodds Story*, Warren 'Baby' Dodds and Larry Gara.

Dodds, Johnny

b. 12 April 1892, New Orleans, Louisiana, USA, d. 8 August 1940. Dodds did not begin playing clarinet until he was aged 17, but in taking lessons from Lorenzo Tio ensured that his late start did not hamper his career. In the years before World War I he played with Kid Ory and Fate Marable, mostly in his home town, and also worked with a minstrel show where he met Mutt Carey. In 1920 he joined King Oliver in Chicago. After leaving Oliver at the end of 1923 he worked with among others Honore Dutrey and Freddie Keppard. During this period he appeared on the classic Hot Five and Hot Seven records with Louis Armstrong. In the 30s he worked mostly in Chicago, leading bands at various clubs. A heart attack in 1939 withdrew him from music for a few months. However, he returned in early 1940 but ill-health persisted and he died in August that year. A striking performer with a fluent style, Dodds made an important contribution to jazz, and to clarinet-playing in particular. His death occurred when clarinettists were in the ascendancy. Not only were big band leaders Benny Goodman and Artie Shaw enjoying great commercial success, but also more traditionally inclined players such as Sidney Bechet, Jimmy Noone and George Lewis were benefiting from a resurgence of interest in early forms of jazz. Despite the passage of time and the wide-ranging developments in jazz, not least the decline in popularity of the clarinet as a front-line instrument, Dodds' recordings of the 20s and 30s are still high-points in the history of jazz recording and are rarely out of print.

Selected albums: *Johnny Dodds Vols 1 & 2* (1926-40), *Johnny Dodds* (Swaggie 1989, 1928-29 recordings), *Blue Clarinet Stomp* (Bluebird 1990,1926-28 recordings), *King Of The New Orleans Clarinet 1926-1938* (Black And Blue 1992), *Johnny Dodds Vol 1-2* (Village Jazz 1992).

Doldinger, Klaus

b. 12 May 1936, Berlin, Germany. Doldinger studied classical piano and clarinet at the Robert Scumann Institut der Musichochshule Rheinland, Dusseldorf. He played traditional jazz as an amateur in the early 50s before turning to the tenor saxophone and developing a more modern style. In the 60s he toured extensively in a quintet with Ingfried Hoffman: Europe, Africa, South America and Asia. Then he formed a jazz-rock group Passport, with which he found success in the 70s. He also began to write film scores, the best known of which are the music for *Das Boot* and *The Eternal Story*.

Albums: *Live At The Blue Note, Berlin* (1963), *The Ambassador* (1969), with Passport *Lookin Thru* (1973), *Cross Collateral* (1974), *Infinity Machine* (1976).

Dolphy, Eric

b. 20 June 1928, Los Angeles, California, USA, d. 29 June 1964. A fluent performer on several reed instruments, Dolphy began to play clarinet while still at school. On the west coast of America in the second half of the 40s he worked with Roy Porter's band, before spending a couple of years in the US army. After his discharge, he played with several leading musicians, including Gerald Wilson, before becoming a member of the popular Chico Hamilton quintet. The stint with Hamilton brought Dolphy to the attention of a wide audience and many other young musicians. In New York in 1959 Dolphy joined Charles Mingus, all the time freelancing at clubs and on recording dates with such influential musicians as George Russell and John Coltrane. In the early 60s, Dolphy began a hugely prolific and arduous period of touring and recording throughout the USA and Europe. He played in bands led by Ornette Coleman (on the seminal *Free Jazz* sessions), John Lewis, Ron Carter, Mal Waldron, Oliver Nelson, Max Roach, Gil Evans, Andrew Hill, Booker Little, Abbey Lincoln, Mingus and Coltrane, with whose quartet he toured Europe in 1961. He also recorded a series of albums as leader, perhaps most notably the *At The Five Spot* sessions, with the brilliant young trumpeter Booker Little (later reissued as *The Great Concert Of Eric Dolphy*), and his Blue Note debut *Out To Lunch*. The latter, with its dislocated rhythms and unusual instrumental textures (Bobby Hutcherson's vibes sharing front line duties with Freddie Hubbard's trumpet and Dolphy's reeds), is a landmark of modern music, and was voted best post-war jazz LP in a 1984 poll of *Wire* magazine critics. Shortly after recording *Out To Lunch* Dolphy left the USA to live in Europe because, as he told writer A.B. Spellman, 'if you try to do anything different in this country, people put you down for it'. He was working in Germany when he suffered a complete circulatory collapse caused by too much sugar in the bloodstream (he was diabetic), and died suddenly on 29 June 1964.

A major influence on jazz, and especially on alto saxophone players, Dolphy was a remarkably gifted musician. During his short career he established himself as a significant force, playing alto, flute and bass clarinet, an instrument before and since unusual in jazz. He was comfortable in the varied idioms of the bands in which he played, from the relatively orthodox Hamilton to the forward-thinking Coltrane and the third-stream innovations of Gunther Schuller. He was, however, very much his own man, creating strikingly original solo lines, frequently dashed off at breakneck tempos and encompassing wide intervallic leaps. Although he is rightly associated with the concept of free jazz, Dolphy brought to this area of music his own carefully reasoned attitude, and he is perhaps better thought of as someone who stretched bebop to its very limits. Thirty years after his death, the importance of Dolphy's contribution to jazz is still being explored by musicians.

Selected albums: with Chico Hamilton *Goings East* (1958), with Ornette Coleman *Free Jazz* (1960), *Charles Mingus Presents Charles Mingus* (1960), with Gunther Schuller *Jazz Abstractions* (1960), *Out There* (Original Jazz Classics 1960), *Outward Bound* (Original Jazz Classics 1960), *Candid Dolphy* (Candid 1960-61), *Great Concert Of Eric Dolphy* (1961), *Eric Dolphy At The Five Spot* (1961), *Stockholm Sessions* (1961), with John Coltrane *Live At The Village Vanguard* (1961), with Coltrane *European Impressions* (1961), with Mingus *Town Hall Concert* (1962), *The Great Concert Of Charles Mingus* (1962), *Eric Dolphy Quartet* (Tempo 1962), *In Europe; Vol 1-3* (Original Jazz Classics 1962), *Music Matador* (1963), *Conversations* (1963), *Unrealized Tapes* (1964), *Naima* (West Wind 1964), *Last Date* (Emarcy 1964). *Out To Lunch* (Blue Note 1964), *Other Aspects* (Blue Note 1982, 1960, 1962 recordings).

Further reading: *Like A Human Voice - The Eric Dolphy Discography*, Uwe Reichardt. *Eric Dolphy: A Musical Biography And Discography*, Vladimir Simosko and Barry Tepperman.

Dominique, Natty

b. 2 August 1896, New Orleans, Louisiana, USA, d. 30 August 1982. Born into a musical environment with Barney Bigard as a cousin, Dominique studied trumpet with Manuel Perez before heading north in 1913 to play in Chicago. In the early 20s he joined Carroll Dickerson's band. Later that decade he played with Johnny Dodds, with whom he remained substantially throughout the 30s. In the early 40s ill health forced him to leave music, but he reappeared in 1949 and began leading his own band in the 50s, employing such kindred spirits as Baby Dodds and Volly De Faut. He continued playing into the mid-60s but then faded from sight. He died in August 1982.
Album: *Natty Dominique And His New Orleans Hot Six* (1954).
Compilation: *Johnny Dodds* (1926-28).

Donald, Peter

b. 15 May 1945, San Francisco, California, USA. In his late teens, Donald studied at Berklee College Of Music, Boston and received drum tuition from Alan Dawson. In the early 70s he returned to California, this time taking up residence in Los Angeles, where he became noted for his sensitive accompaniment to singers who included Carmen McRae. He achieved notable success, however, as a member of the powerful big band co-led by Toshiko Akiyoshi and Lew Tabackin. When Akiyoshi decided to return to New York, Donald remained in Los Angeles, working in films and television studios and playing with musicians including John Abercrombie and Warne Marsh. In 1985, following the death of Nick Ceroli, he took

his place in Bob Florence's Limited Edition big band. An all-round percussionist equally at home in jazz, pop and rock, Donald is very much a part of the new generation of jazz artists, but partly through his early tutelage under Dawson retains strong links with earlier strands of jazz.
Albums: with Akiyoshi-Tabackin *Road Time* (1976), with Bob Florence *Trash Can City* (1986).

Donaldson, Lou

b. 1 November 1926, Badin, North Carolina, USA. Donaldson started out on clarinet but, while playing in a band in the US Navy alongside Willie Smith and Clark Terry, he switched to alto saxophone. In the early 50s he was in New York, playing with Thelonious Monk, Horace Silver, Blue Mitchell, Art Blakey and other leading jazzmen. In 1954 he and Clifford Brown joined Blakey's Jazz Messengers. During the 60s and 70s he toured extensively, usually as leader of a small band, playing concerts and festivals in the USA and Europe. He recorded prolifically for Blue Note, producing a number of excellent soul-jazz albums, including *Alligator Boogaloo*. During this period, Donaldson made some stylistic changes, experimenting with an R&B-inflected style and playing jazz-funk; but by the 80s he was back in a hard bop groove, where his striking technique and inventiveness assured him of a welcome place on the international circuit.
Albums: *New Faces, New Sounds* i (1952), *New Faces, New Sounds* ii (1953), *Lou Donaldson With Clifford Brown* (1953), with Art Blakey *A Night At Birdland* (1954), *Wailing With Lou* (1955), *Swing And Soul* (1957), *Blues Walk* (Blue Note 1958), *The Time Is Right* (1959), *Here 'Tis* (Blue Note 1961), *The Natural Soul* (Blue Note 1962), *Good Gracious* (Blue Note 1963), *Cole Slaw* (1964), *At His Best* (1966), *Lush Life* (Blue Note 1967), *Alligator Boogaloo* (Blue Note 1967), *Mr Shing-a-ling* (Blue Note 1967), *Hot Dog* (Blue Note 1969), *Pretty Things* (Blue Note 1970), *Sophisticated Lou* (1972), *Back Street* (Muse 1972), *A Different Scene* (1976), *Sweet Poppa Lou* (1981), *Forgotten Man* (Timeless 1981), *Life In Bologna* (Timeless 1984), *Play the Right Thing* (Milestone 1990), *Birdseed* (Milestone 1992), *Caracas* (Milestone 1992).

Dorham, Kenny

b. McKinley Howard Dorham, 30 August 1924, Fairfield, Texas, USA, d. 5 December 1972. After learning to play trumpet while at high school, Dorham played in several late 40s big bands, including Lionel Hampton's and, more significantly given his musical leanings, the bop-orientated outfits of Dizzy Gillespie and Billy Eckstine. In 1948 he succeeded Miles Davis as trumpeter with Charlie Parker's quintet, and in 1954 joined Horace Silver in the first edition of what became Art Blakey's long-running Jazz Messengers. He also worked with Max Roach (stepping in when Roach's co-leader, Clifford Brown, was killed), Sonny Rollins and Charles Mingus. From the mid-50s onwards Dorham mostly led his own groups, which included the excellent Jazz Prophets, modelled as the name suggests, upon the Messengers, and made many fine recordings notably both as leader and with artists Joe Henderson, Herb

Geller and Jackie McLean - making several outstanding performances for the Blue Note label. Although rightly viewed as one of the outstanding bebop trumpeters, stylistically Dorham's playing reflected his awareness of the roots of jazz and the blues. Universally admired among his contemporaries, Dorham's death led unfairly to a decline in awareness of his stature as a fine modern musician.

Selected albums: *The Be Bop Boys* (1946), *Kenny Dorham Quintet* (Original Jazz Classics 1953), *Horace Silver And The Jazz Messengers* (1954), *Sonny Rollins Quintet* (1954), *Afro Cuban* (Blue Note 1955), *Kenny Dorham's Jazz Prophets Vols 1 & 2* (1956), *'Round About Midnight At The Café Bohemia* (Blue Note 1956), *Jazz Contrast* (Original Jazz Classics 1957), *Two Horns, Two Rhythm* (Original Jazz Classics 1957), with Herb Geller *Fire In The West* (1957), *Max Roach 4 Plays Charlie Parker* (1957-8), *This Is The Moment* (1958), *Blue Spring* (Original Jazz Classics 1959), *Quiet Kenny* (Original Jazz Classics 1959), *The Kenny Dorham Memorial Album* (1960), *Jazz Contemporary* (1960), *Showboat* (1960), *The Arrival Of Kenny Dorham* (Fresh Sound 1960), *Osmosis* (Black Lion 1961), *Ease It* (Muse 1961), *Whistle Stop* (1961), *West 42nd Street* (Black Lion 1961), *Hot Stuff From Brazil* (West Wind 1961), *Inta Something* (1961), *Matador* (Blue Note 1962), *Una Mas* (Blue Note 1963), *Scandia Skies* (Steeplechase 1963), *Short Story* (1963), *Trumpet Toccata* (Blue Note 1964), *New York 1953-56* (Landscape 1993).

Dorsey, Jimmy

b. 29 February 1904, Shenandoah, Pennsylvania, USA, d. 12 June 1957. Musically active as a small child under the tutelage of his father, who was a coal miner turned music teacher, Dorsey switched from brass to reed instruments while still in his early teens. Concentrating on clarinet and alto saxophone, he played in various bands, mostly with his brother, Tommy Dorsey. Their co-led group, Dorseys Novelty Six, later renamed Dorseys Wild Canaries, was one of the first jazz bands to broadcast on the radio. Dorsey later joined the California Ramblers. Sometimes with his brother, sometimes alone, Dorsey played in a number of leading bands, including those led by Jean Goldkette, Paul Whiteman, Red Nichols and Ted Lewis. He also recorded frequently, often in company with Nichols and his Goldkette/Whiteman colleague, Bix Beiderbecke. He continued to associate with his brother, and in 1934 they formed the Dorsey Brothers Orchestra, which became extremely popular. Unfortunately for the band, the brothers frequently disagreed, sometimes violently, and after one such argument, on the stand at the Glen Island Casino in May 1935, Tommy walked out leaving Jimmy to run the band on his own. One of the most accomplished of the white bands of the swing era, Jimmy Dorsey's band retained a strong jazz element but also catered to popular demands. Particularly successful in this respect was a series of hit records devised by arranger Tutti Camarata. In an attempt to present all aspects of the band's work in one three-minute radio spot, Camarata made an arrangement of a song which featured first the band's male singer, Bob Eberly, in ballad mood, then the leader with

an up-tempo jazz solo on alto, and finally, a wailing sensual vocal chorus by the band's other singer, Helen O'Connell (b. 23 May 1920, Lima, Ohio, USA, d. 9 September 1993, San Diego, California, USA). The first song treated in this manner was 'Amapola', followed by 'Yours' and then 'Green Eyes', which was a runaway hit, as was the later 'Tangerine'. Records like these ensured Dorsey's success and, by the mid-40s, his was one of the most popular of the big bands. This ensured Dorsey's survival over the hard winter of 1946/7, a time which saw many big bands fold, but the 50s proved difficult too, and in 1953 he was reunited with his brother who promptly renamed his own still-successful band as the Dorsey Brothers Orchestra. Jimmy remained with the band until Tommy's death, by which time he too was terminally ill. An outstanding technician, Jimmy Dorsey was one of the finest jazz saxophonists of his era and a major influence on many of his contemporaries and successors.

Selected albums: *The Fabulous Dorseys In Hi-Fi Vols 1 & 2* (1954-55), with Dorsey Brothers *Live In Hi-Fi* (1955-56), *The Fabulous Dorseys Vols 2 & 3* (1956), with Dorsey Brothers *Live In New York* (1955-56). Compilations: *The Dorsey Brothers Orchestra* (1932-34), *The Radio Years* (1935), *Don't Be That Way* (1935-40), *The Early Years* (1936-41), *Mostly 1940* (1939-40), *The Uncollected Jimmy Dorsey Vols 1-5* (1939-50), *Film Tracks 1941-1948* (1941-48), *Spotlighting The Fabulous Dorseys* (1942-45), part only *The Essential V-Discs* (1943-46), *Contrasts* (1945), *One Night Stand With Jimmy Dorsey And His Orchestra* (1949), *Jimmy Dorsey Collection* (Deja Vu 1988), *Pennies From Heaven* (Living Era 1988), *Shine On Harvest Moon* (Tring 1993).

Further Reading: *Tommy And Jimmy: The Dorsey Years*, Herb Sanford.

Dorsey, Tommy

b. 19 November 1905, Shenandoah, Pennsylvania, USA, d. 26 November 1956. Like his older brother, Jimmy Dorsey, Tommy was taught as a small child by his father, a music teacher. He first learned to play trumpet, but switched to trombone while still very young. He played in various bands, often with his brother, their co-led group known first as Dorseys Novelty Six, later renamed Dorseys Wild Canaries. With his brother, Dorsey later played in a number of leading bands, including those led by Jean Goldkette and Paul Whiteman. He also recorded frequently, often in the company of leading jazzmen of the day. In 1934 he and Jimmy formed the Dorsey Brothers Orchestra, which became extremely popular. Despite, or perhaps because of, their close relationship, the brothers frequently argued, sometimes violently, and after one such disagreement in May 1935, Tommy walked out leaving Jimmy to take over leadership of the orchestra. Tommy then took over the excellent danceband led by Joe Haymes. Highly ambitious, Dorsey set about turning the band, which was already a sound and well-disciplined unit, into the finest dance orchestra of the era. Over the years he employed first rate arrangers, including Axel Stordahl, Carmen Mastren, Paul Weston and, most influential of all in ensuring the band's success and musical stature,

Sy Oliver. Dorsey also engaged the services of several strong jazz players, including Bunny Berigan, Buddy Rich, Johnny Mince, Yank Lawson, Pee Wee Erwin, Buddy De Franco, Gene Krupa, Charlie Shavers and Bud Freeman. Alert to the demands of audiences, Dorsey also employed some of the finest singers ever to work with the big bands. An early find was Jack Leonard, who sang on one of the band's big hits, 'Marie', and others included Edythe Wright, Jo Stafford, Connie Haines and Dick Haymes. The latter was the able replacement for the best singer Dorsey hired, Frank Sinatra. Although Sinatra had already begun to establish a reputation with Harry James, it was his stint with Dorsey that made him into an international singing star and helped to make the Dorsey band one of the most popular of the swing era - in many ways the band and musical sound which most aptly epitomizes this period in American popular music. Dorsey's popularity was enough to ensure his band's survival after the great days of the 40s were over, and he was one of the few to move into television. Nevertheless, the 50s were difficult times and in 1953, he was happy to be reunited with his brother, whose own outfit had folded. Tommy Dorsey gave Jimmy a featured spot and renamed his band as the Dorsey Brothers Orchestra. Despite his popularity, to say nothing of his determination to succeed and sometimes arrogant self-confidence, Dorsey was always reticent about his ability as a jazz player, although some of his early recordings display a gifted musician with a strong sense of style. Like his brother, Tommy Dorsey was an outstanding technician and brought trombone playing to new heights of perfection. His smooth playing was ideally suited to ballads and his solos on countless records were often exemplary. Even with the advent of later generations of outstanding trombone technicians, few have matched his skill and none have surpassed him in his own particular area of expertise. A heavy eater, Tommy Dorsey choked to death in his sleep.

Albums: *Tommy Dorsey Broadcasts For The American National Guard* (1953), *The Fabulous Dorseys In Hi-Fi Vols 1 & 2* (1954-55), with Dorsey Brothers *Live In Hi-Fi* (1955-56), with Dorsey Brothers *Live In New York* (1955-56), *Tommy Dorsey At The Statler Hotel* (1956), *The Fabulous Dorseys Vols 2 & 3* (1956). Compilations: *The Dorsey Brothers Orchestra, The Indispensable Tommy Dorsey Vols 1/2* (RCA 1935-37), *The Clambake Seven: The Music Goes Round And Round* (1935-47), *The Indispensable Tommy Dorsey Vols 3/4* (RCA 1937-38), *The Indispensable Tommy Dorsey Vols 5/6* (RCA 1938-39), *The Dorsey-Sinatra Sessions* (1940-42), *Spotlighting The Fabulous Dorseys* (1942-45), *One Night Stand With Tommy Dorsey Vol. 2* (1944), *Carnegie Hall V-Disc Session, April 1944* (1944), part only *The Essential V-Discs* (1944-45), *At The Fat Man's* (1946-48), *Solid Swing* (First Heard 1949-50), *Sentimental And Swinging* (1954-55), The Legend Volumes 1-3 (RCA 1987). Further reading: *Tommy And Jimmy: The Dorsey Years*, Herb Sanford.

Dresser, Mark

b. 26 September 1952, Los Angeles, California, USA. Dresser started on bass at the age of 10, played in rock groups in his early teens then studied music at Indiana University for one year, leaving because 'it was too straight for me, like a music factory'. Moving to San Diego, he studied with classical maestro Bertram Turetzky and also played at weekly jam sessions in LA, led by Bobby Bradford - other participants were Stanley Crouch, David Murray and James Newton. Unable to make a living playing new jazz, Dresser moved to the east coast, settling in New Haven, Connecticut, where Leo Smith, Pheeroan akLaff, Gerry Hemingway, Anthony Davis and Jay Hoggard were among his neighbours. Although he played occasional concerts in New York, often with trombonist Ray Anderson, when Dresser followed many of his New Haven colleagues and went to live in the city, he found work increasingly scarce and, disheartened, returned to California. He resumed his LA connection with Bradford and Newton, formed a trio that included Diamanda Galas (then a jazz pianist), and in 1980 toured Europe as part of the Ray Anderson Quartet (*Harrisburg Half Life*). With work still hard to find, Dresser went back to college to study music, meanwhile playing with Charles McPherson, recording with Bradford (*Lost In LA*) and Newton (*Binu*), and releasing his own solo cassette, *Bass Excursions*, in 1983. Later that year he moved to Italy to study, staying for two years, and in 1985 joined the Anthony Braxton Quartet for tours of Europe and the UK. Back in the States, he again moved to New York and has now made his mark on the city's contemporary jazz scene. He remains a member of Braxton's quartet and plays regularly too with Anderson, Tim Berne, the string trio Arcado, which he formed with Hank Roberts and violinist Mark Feldman, and the quartet Tambastics (with Robert Dick, Gerry Hemingway and Denman Maroney). He has also recorded with John Zorn (*Spy Vs Spy*) and Marilyn Crispell (*The Kitchen Concert*). A composer too, his orchestra piece *Castles For Carter* (dedicated to John Carter) was premiered at Amsterdam's October Meeting in 1991.

Albums: *Bass Excursions* (1983), with Hank Roberts, Mark Feldman *Arcado* (1989), with Arcado *Behind The Myth* (1990), with Arcado *For Three Strings And Orchestra* (1992), *Tambastics* (1992).

Drew, Kenny

b. 28 August 1928, New York City, New York, USA, d. 4 August 1993. A child prodigy, Drew studied piano and music, making his first records in 1949 with Howard McGhee. In the 50s, he was much in demand for recording and club dates by mainstream and modern musicians such as Coleman Hawkins, Lester Young and Charlie Parker. He worked regularly with Buddy De Franco and appeared on John Coltrane's seminal *Blue Train*. Towards the end of the 50s he worked with Buddy Rich, but by 1961 Drew was resident in Paris relocating in 1964 to Copenhagen, where he lived until his death. In his adopted city, Drew worked mainly at composing and arranging and also ran successful companies engaged in music publishing and recording. He still found time to record his own playing and regularly accompanied local luminaries, such as Niels-Henning Ørsted Pedersen, and visiting American jazz artists. In performance Drew's playing was exhilaratingly complex, but

he periodically exhibited his love for the dazzling simplicity of Bud Powell's best work. His son, Kenny Drew Jnr., is a gifted pianist who plays in a style reminiscent of his father's.
Selected albums: *Sonny Rollins Quartet* (1951), *New Faces, New Sounds: Introducing The Kenny Drew Trio* (1953), *The Kenny Drew Trio* i (1953), *Kenny Drew Quartet* (1955) *The Kenny Drew Trio* ii (Original Jazz Classics 1956), with John Coltrane *Blue Train* (1957), *This Is New* (Original Jazz Classics 1957), *A Harry Warren Showcase* (1957), *A Harold Arlen Showcase* (1957), *I Love Jerome Kern* (1957), *Jazz Impressions Of Pal Joey* (Original Jazz Classics 1957), *Undercurrent* (1960), with Neils-Henning Ørsted Pedersen *Duo* (Steeplechase 1973), *Everything I Love* (Steeplechase 1973), with Pederson *Duo 2* (Steeplechase 1974), *If You Could See Me Now* (1974), with Pederson Duo *Live In Concert* (Steeplechase 1974), *Morning* (Steeplechase 1975), *The Kenny Drew Trio In Concert* (Steeplechase 1977), *Lite Flite* (Steeplechase 1977), *Ruby My Dear* (1977), *Kenny Drew* (1978), *Home Is Where The Soul Is* (Xanadu 1978), *For Sure!* (Xanadu 1978), *Afternoon In Europe* (RCA 1980), *All The Things You Are* (1981), *It Might As Well Be Spring* (1981), *Your Soft Eyes* (1981), *The Lullaby* (1982), *Moonlit Desert* (1982), *Swingin' Love* (1983), *And Far Away* (Soul Note 1983), *Fantasia* (1983), *By Request* (RCA 1986), *Recollections* (Timeless 1989).

Drew, Martin

b. 11 February 1944, Northampton, Northamptonshire, England. Drew began playing drums as a child, studying under the well-known danceband drummer George Fierstone. Despite this early start, it was some time before he became a full-time professional musician; however, once his career was under way, he was soon one of the busiest drummers in the UK. He played on numerous club and recording dates, accompanying many British and American musicians during tours of the UK: these include Ronnie Scott, Oscar Peterson, Buddy Tate, Dizzy Gillespie, Gil Evans and Freddie Hubbard. He has also worked effectively with singers Ella Fitzgerald, Jimmy Witherspoon, Anita O'Day and Nina Simone. An outstanding mainstream drummer who is also comfortable playing bop, Drew is one of the most sought-after session drummers playing in the UK today, and his subtly swinging skills have enhanced numerous recording sessions.
Albums: *Red Rodney And The Bebop Preservation Society* (1975), *The Martin Drew Band* (1977), *British Jazz Artists Vol 3* (Lee Lambert 1980), *The Oscar Peterson Big Four In Japan* (1982).

Dudek, Gerd

b. Gerhard Rochus Dudek, 28 September 1938, Gross Dober, Germany. Dudek emerged as a key jazz figure in the 60s with Manfred Schoof and Alexander Von Schlippenbach. He played with them over the years, as well as others, including Joachim Kuhn and Albert Mangelsdorff. In Dudek, Europe possesses arguably its most convincing exponent of mid-to-late-period John Coltrane. Dudek has been a key partner in Schlippenbach's projects - in Globe Unity, on their Jelly Roll Morton tribute, and as one of the outstanding soloists on the

Berlin Contemporary Jazz Orchestra session. The co-operative groups the Quartet, the European Jazz Quartet, and the European Jazz Ensemble have all benefited from his hard-driving but lyrical tenor, soprano, clarinet and flute.
Albums: *Open* (1977), with RAI Big Band *Jelly Roll* (1980), with EJQ and Ernst-Ludwig Petrowsky *Interchange* (1987), with EJE *Live* (1988), with BCJO *Berlin Contemporary Jazz Orchestra* (1990).

Dudziak, Urszula

b. 22 October 1943, Straconka, Poland. Although Dudziak studied piano formally for some years, she began to sing in the late 50s after hearing records by Ella Fitzgerald. Within a few years she was one of the most popular jazz artists in her native country. She met and later married Michal Urbaniak, recording with him during the 60s. In the late 60s they began to travel overseas and in the 70s settled in New York. Language barriers hold no problems for her, as she customarily eschews words in favour of a wordless vocalizing that is far more adventurous than scat. Already gifted with a remarkable five-octave range, Dudziak employs electronic devices to extend still further the possibilities of her voice. She has frequently worked with leading contemporary musicians, including Archie Shepp and Lester Bowie, and was a member of the Vocal Summit group, with Jay Clayton, Jeanne Lee, Bobby McFerrin and Lauren Newton. Although her remarkable talent is worthy of greater exposure, Dudziak's chosen style has meant that she has remained relatively unknown except to the *cogniscenti*.
Albums: *Newborn Light* (1972), with Michal Urbaniak *Super Constellation* (c.1973), *Urszula* (1976), *Midnight Train* (1977), with Urbaniak *Urbaniak* (1977), *Future Talk* (1979), *Magic Lady* (In And Out 1980), *Ulla* (1982), with Vocal Summit *Sorrow Is Not Forever...But Love Is* (1983), *Warsaw Jazz Festival 1991* (Jazzmen 1993).

Duke, George

b. 12 January 1946, San Rafael, California, USA. Duke studied the piano at school (where he ran a Les McCann-inspired Latin band) and emerged from the San Francisco Conservatory as a Bachelor of Music in 1967. From 1965-67 he was resident pianist at the Half Note, accompanying musicians such as Dizzy Gillespie and Kenny Dorham. This grounding served as a musical education for the rest of his life. He arranged for a vocal group, the Third Wave, and toured Mexico in 1968. In 1969 he began playing with French violinist Jean-Luc Ponty, using electric piano to accompany Ponty's plugged-in violin. He played on *King Kong*, an album of music Frank Zappa composed for Ponty. He then joined Zappa's group in 1970, an experience that transformed his music. As he put it, previously he had been too 'musically advanced' to play rock 'n' roll piano triplets. Zappa encouraged him to sing and joke and use electronics. Together they wrote 'Uncle Remus' for *Apostrophe* (1972), a song about black attitudes to oppression. His keyboards contributed to a great edition of the Mothers Of Invention - captured on the outstanding *Roxy & Elsewhere* (1975) - which combined fluid jazz playing with rock and *avant garde* sonorities. In 1972 he toured with Cannonball Adderley (replacing Joe Zawinul). Duke had always had a leaning towards soul jazz and after he left Zappa, he went for full-frontal funk. *I Love The Blues She Heard My Cry* (1975) combined a retrospective look at black musical forms with warm good humour and freaky musical ideas: a duet with Johnny Guitar Watson was particularly successful. Duke started duos with fusion power-drummer Billy Cobham, and virtuoso bassist Stanley Clarke, playing quintessential 70s jazz rock: amplification and much attention to 'chops' being the order of the day. Duke always had a sense of humour: 1978's 'Dukey Stick' sounded like a Funkadelic record. The middle of the road beckoned, however, and by *Brazilian Love Affair* (1979) he was providing high class background music. In 1982 *Dream On* showed him happily embracing west coast hip easy listening. However, there has always been an unpredictable edge to Duke. The band he put together for the Wembley Nelson Mandela concert in London backed a stream of soul singers, and his arrangement of 'Backyard Ritual' on Miles Davis's *Tutu* (1986) was excellent. He collaborated with Clark again for the funk-styled *3* and in 1992 he bounced back with the jazz fusion *Snapshot*.

Selected albums: *Jazz Workshop of San Francisco* (1966), with Jean-Luc Ponty *Live In Los Angeles* (1969), *The Inner Source* (1971), *I Love The Blues She Heard My Cry* (MPS 1975), *Reach For It* (1977), *A Brazilian Love Affair* (Epic 1979), *Primal* (MPS 1979), *Secret Rendevous* (Epic 1979), *Follow The Rainbow* (Epic !979), *Master Of The Game* (Epic 1980), *Dream On* (1982), *George Duke* (Epic 1983), *Guardian Of The Light* (Epic 1983), *1976 Solo Keyboard Album* (Epic 1983), *Thief In The Night* (Elektra 1985), *Night After Night* (Elektra 1989), *Reach For It* (Sony 1991), *Snapshot* (Warners 1992). Compilation: *The Collection* (Castle 1991).

Durham, Eddie

b. 19 August 1906, San Marcos, Texas, USA. As a child Durham worked in travelling shows with other musical members of his large family. In the mid-20s he worked in a number of southwest territory bands including Walter Page's Blue Devils from where he, and several others, moved to the Bennie Moten band. Up to this point Durham had been playing both guitar and trombone and now added arranging to his arsenal of skills. During the 30s he played in, and arranged for, the bands of Willie Bryant, Jimmie Lunceford and Count Basie. In the following decade he arranged for several noted swing bands including Artie Shaw's, and also worked closely with the one of the outstanding but neglected bands of the late 40s, the International Sweethearts Of Rhythm. Later in his career Durham arranged more and played less, but did return to the stage in the 70s and 80s with Eddie Barefield, Buddy Tate and other comrades from his Basie days. Durham's contributions to jazz are extensive and include helping develop and refine the electrically amplified guitar. More important still were his loosely swinging arrangements exemplified by such Basie classics as 'Moten Swing' and the popular 'In The Mood' for Glenn Miller. He was also co-composer of 'Topsy' which

became an unexpected hit for Cozy Cole in 1958.

Selected albums: *Eddie Durham* I (1973), *Eddie Barefield* (1973), *Eddie Durham* II (1974), *Blue Bone* (1981). Compilations: *The Complete Bennie Moten Vols 3 & 4* (1928-30), with Count Basie *Swinging The Blues* (1937-9).

Dutch Swing College Band

This outfit's polished, cleverly arranged repertoire was still heard in concert 40 years after its formation by Peter Schilperoort (clarinet/saxophones) in 1945. Among musicians that have passed through its ranks are Wout Steenhuis (guitar), the late Jan Morks (clarinet), Kees Van Dorser (trumpet), UK's Rod Mason (cornet) and the Louis Armstrong-influenced trombonist Oscar Klein. Famous US musicians visiting Europe proudly 'sat in' with the band. Schilperoort became established as the Netherlands' foremost ambassador of trad jazz, following the foundation of his long-standing partnership with Arie Ligthart (banjo/guitar) in 1952. Yet, after embracing saxophonists and even amplification, the combo were to deviate further from the prescribed New Orleans precedent via adaptations of rock 'n' roll, country and military marches, to achieve acceptance in the generalized pop field. By the 70s, Schilperoort started his own DSC Productions record company, and was knighted by Queen Juliana of the Netherlands.

Selected albums: *On Tour* (Philips 1981), *Digital Dixie* (Philips 1982), *Music For The Millions* (Philips 1983), *The Bands Best* (Verve 1984), *Swing Studio Sessions* (Philips 1985), *When The Swing Comes Marching In* (Philips 1985), *40 years 1945-1985, At Its Best* (Timeless 1986), *Digital Anniversary* (Philips 1986), *With Guests Vol 1* (Polydor 1987), *Digital Date* (Philips 1988), *Dutch Samba* (Timeless 1989), *1960* (Philips 1990), *Jubilee Concert* (Philips 1991), *The Old Fashioned Way* (Jazz Hour 1993).

Dutrey, Honore

b. 1894, New Orleans, Louisiana, USA, d. 21 July 1935. In the years preceding World War I, trombonist Dutrey worked in several New Orleans bands but during military service suffered lung damage in a shipboard accident. In the early 20s he worked with Joe 'King' Oliver in Chicago then joined Carroll Dickerson's band. During the mid-20s he led his own unit and also worked in the bands of Louis Armstrong and Johnny Dodds, but his career was truncated and he retired from active playing at the end of the decade. A sound ensemble player, Dutrey appeared on many records by his exceptional contemporaries, always lending solid support to their performances. Compilation: *King Oliver And His Creole Jazz Band: The OKeh Sessions* (1923).

Duvivier, George

b. 17 August 1920, New York City, New York, USA, d. 11 July 1985. After formal musical education, mostly on violin, Duvivier worked with a New York symphony orchestra but soon entered the jazz world where, having recognized the limitations of the violin in that area, he switched to bass. In the early 40s he worked with several leading artists in small and large group settings, among them Coleman Hawkins and Lucky Millinder. He also began arranging and contributing many musical scores for the later Jimmie Lunceford band and the elegant but short-lived Sy Oliver big band. In the 50s he worked extensively in the studios, often accompanying singers on record, with some of whom he also collaborated on tours at home and overseas. Among these were demanding performers such as Lena Horne and Pearl Bailey. He also played with small groups, an activity he continued alongside his writing into the 60s. During this period he was with bands led by Terry Gibbs, Bud Powell, Shelly Manne, Eric Dolphy, Benny Goodman and Ben Webster. A dominant force in any rhythm section, Duvivier played with great precision and attack. He continued to play jazz dates around the world through the 70s and into the 80s, working with musicians such as Zoot Sims, Joe Venuti, Hank Jones and Warren Vaché Jnr.

Albums: *The Amazing Bud Powell* (1953), *Strictly Powell* (1956), *George Duvivier In Paris* (1956), *Joe And Zoot* (1974), with Hank Jones *Bop Redux* (1977), with Warren Vaché *Iridescence* (1981).

Dyani, Johnny Mbizo

b. 30 November 1945, East London, South Africa, d. 25 October 1986. Dyani was a vital, emotional bass player who earned immense respect from musicians everywhere yet, not unusually for such artists, never achieved the recognition he deserved. At the 1962 Johannesburg Jazz Festival Chris McGregor invited him and four more of the best players at the Festival to form a band, and the legendary Blue Notes were created. As a mixed-race band it was impossible for them to work under apartheid and so, in 1964, while touring Europe, they decided to settle in London, where, evolving into the Chris McGregor Group, they made a huge impact on the UK jazz scene. As well as playing in the six-piece McGregor Group and the Brotherhood Of Breath (the big band which McGregor set up after disbanding the sextet), Dyani toured South America in 1966 with Steve Lacy, Enrico Rava and Louis Moholo (the quartet recording *The Forest And The Zoo* under Lacy's name in 1967), and he then worked with the Spontaneous Music Ensemble (1969) and the Musicians Co-Operative (1971). In 1969, at the Actuel Festival organized by the French record company BYG, he took part in a jam which included Frank Zappa, Archie Shepp and Philly Joe Jones. Dyani had been growing unhappy with the direction that McGregor's band was taking, feeling that it was moving too close to free jazz and away from its African roots so, in the early 70s, he moved to Denmark, where he worked with John Tchicai, Don Cherry and Abdullah Ibrahim. He also worked with David Murray, Joseph Jarman and in the trio Detail with John Stevens and saxophonist Frode Gjerstad (they became Detail Plus when Bobby Bradford and others guested with them). After Dyani's death in 1986 several albums were dedicated to his memory including Tchicai's *Put Up The Fight*, Stevens and Dudu Pukwana's *Radebe (They Shoot To Kill)* and *Blue Notes For Johnny*, a searingly emotional tribute by McGregor, Pukwana and Maholo. His son, Thomas, is currently establishing a rep-

utation as a percussionist with his own band.

Albums: with others *Music For Xaba* (1972), with Abdullah Ibrahim *Good News From Africa* (1973), *Blues Notes For Mongezi* (1976), *Blue Notes In Concert* (1978), *Witchdoctor's Son* (1978), *Song For Biko* (1978), with Ibrahim *Echoes From Africa* (1980), *Mbizo* (1981), with Detail *Backwards And Forwards* (1983), *Angolian Cry* (1985), with Detail Plus *Ness* (1987, rec. 1986), with Detail Plus *Way It Goes/Dance Of The Soul* (1989, rec. 1985).

E

Eager, Allen

b. 10 January 1927, New York City, New York, USA. Eager had formal tuition on clarinet but in 1943 received lessons on tenor saxophone from Ben Webster, a switch that marked the start of his professional career. His early experience was gained in big bands on the more lightweight side of the swing era, including those led by Bobby Sherwood and Hal McIntyre. Towards the end of 1943 he joined Woody Herman and later worked with Tommy Dorsey. In Los Angeles he played in Vine Street clubs with Barney Kessel and Zoot Sims, whom he followed into the small group led by Big Sid Catlett. Around this time he heard Lester Young on records by the Count Basie band and thereafter remodelled his playing in the style of the 'Pres'. In the mid-40s Eager was mostly to be found at 52nd Street clubs, playing with Coleman Hawkins, Pete Brown and many beboppers, including Red Rodney, Stan Levey, Max Roach, Al Haig and Serge Chaloff, and sometimes leading his own small groups. He also met Charlie Parker and, although initially unimpressed, he soon became a devotee and they often worked together. In 1948 he recorded with Fats Navarro, Wardell Gray and Ernie Henry as a member of Tadd Dameron's band, taking part in the important sessions that produced 'Our Delight', 'Dameronia' and 'Early Bird'. Eager continued playing into the 50s, recording with Tony Fruscella and Danny Bank, and touring with Oscar Pettiford. In the mid-50s he spent some time living in Paris but gradually drifted out of music preferring to spend his time pursuing other, mainly sporting, activities. In 1982 he returned to music, recording and touring both at home and overseas.

Albums: *Swingin' With Allen Eager* (1953), *Renaissance* (1982). Compilation: with Tadd Dameron *Anthropology* (1948).

ECM Records

ECM Records - the letters stand for Edition for Contemporary Music - was launched in Munich in 1969 with Mal Waldron's

Free At Last and, some 500 recording sessions later, is secure in its status as Europe's pre-eminent independent jazz label, despite a sometimes troubled relationship with the jazz mainstream and an open contempt for the music business. The company's musical direction reflects the taste and personality of its founder, producer Manfred Eicher (b. 1943, Lindau, Germany), who has said, 'I regard the music industry, including concert life, as a kind of environmental pollution'. Formerly a bassist, Eicher was a member of the Berlin Philharmonic Orchestra, but also played free music with Marion Brown and Leo Smith (both of whom later recorded for ECM). Experiences as a production assistant at Deutsche Grammophon prompted him to ask if it were possible to approach jazz recording with the care that the classical companies expended. Norwegian engineer Jan Erik Kongshaug, a partner now for two decades, became an important ally. Eicher's meticulous recordings of solo piano albums by Paul Bley, Keith Jarrett, and Chick Corea were hailed by critic Allan Offstein as 'the most beautiful sound next to silence' - and a trading slogan and *leit-motif* was born. Though the audio quality of the recordings has endeared the label to two generations of hi-fi enthusiasts (and helped to sell more than two million copies of Jarrett's *The Köln Concert*), Eicher feels that technical excellence ought to be given, and is much more interested in the music. Detractors who rail against the 'ECM sound' conveniently overlook the range of the label's catalogue, which has embraced the burning, outgoing energy music of the Art Ensemble Of Chicago, Sam Rivers, and Hal Russell, the rock-influenced guitars of Terje Rypdal, Steve Tibbetts, and Pat Metheny, the straighter jazz of John Abercrombie, Kenny Wheeler, and Dave Holland, the eclectic and folklore-rooted improvisations of Egberto Gismonti, Jan Garbarek, and Collin Walcott. A classical line, the ECM New Series, provides access to the entire art music tradition from Gesualdo to Stockhausen and has introduced Estonian composer Arvo Pärt, whose pure, concentrated music at the edge of silence has proved a major influence in new composition. A New Series anthology in 1989 bore the inscription 'You wish to see; Listen. Hearing is a step towards vision', and the formula works in reverse as well. ECM album sleeve photography - landscapes, seascapes, cloudscapes, mountainscapes - has provided a powerful visual corollary for the music and gives evidence of Eicher's abiding passion for film. He has released two volumes of Eleni Karaindrou's music for the films of Theo Angelopoulos, and in 1992 issued Jean-Luc Godard's *Nouvelle Vague* on laser disc. In 1991, Eicher scripted and co-directed his first film, *Holocene*, based on a Max Frisch novel. An interest in theatre is evidenced in albums of Heiner Goebbels's music for the plays of Heiner Müller, and David Byrne's music for Robert Wilson's *Civil Wars*. ECM has also issued recordings of actor Bruno Ganz reading German poetry, and of Peter Rühmkorf's jazz and poetry fusions. It seems likely that the label will continue to move further away from 'jazz' in the years to come. Having now passed its quarter century the label has avoided ever forsaking itself for commercialism, and those artists such as Metheny who moved on to bigger sales with Geffen Records can never dispute the faith the label had in him as he developed. ECM's honesty and uncompromising route makes it one of the truly great record labels.

Edison, Harry 'Sweets'

b. 10 October 1915, Columbus, Ohio, USA. A trumpeter who was inspired by Louis Armstrong, Edison gained valuable early experience with a number of territory bands, including the excellent Jeter-Pillars orchestra. After a short spell with Lucky Millinder, Edison joined the Count Basie band in 1938, where he remained until Basie folded his big band in 1950. Edison then began a long career as leader of small groups, a solo artist, and studio musician; he also worked occasionally with bandleaders such as Buddy Rich. He toured with Jazz At The Philharmonic and in the 50s his work came to the attention of millions who never knew his name when he performed exquisite trumpet obligati with the Nelson Riddle orchestra behind the vocals of Frank Sinatra. In the 60s he worked occasionally with Basie again but was mostly heard as a soloist touring extensively on the international club and festival circuit. In performance Edison often favours playing with a Harmon mute and, while he has many imitators, few have matched his laconic wit and inventiveness. Indeed, his trademark of repeated single notes is something no other trumpeter has been able to use to such good effect. On his numerous recording dates he has been teamed with most of the big names in jazz and continually defies his advancing years. In November 1989 he appeared as featured soloist with the Frank Wess-Harry Edison Orchestra at the Fujitsu-Concord Jazz Festival in Japan.
Albums: *The Inventive Mr Edison* (1953), *Sweets At The Haig* (1953), *Harry 'Sweets' Edison* i (1956), *Blues For Basie* (Verve 1957), *Harry Edison Swings Buck Clayton And Vice Versa* (1958), *The Swinger* (1958), *Harry 'Sweets' Edison* ii (1960). Selected compilations: *Best Of Harry Edison* (Pablo 1982), *Edison's Lights* (Pablo 1982), *Inventive Mr Edison* (Fresh Sounds 1988), *Swingin' Sweets* (L&R 1993).

Edwards, Teddy

b. 26 April 1924, Jackson, Mississippi, USA. As a child he played alto saxophone with local bands and continued playing this instrument when he moved to Detroit in 1940. He toured with territory bands in Michigan and Florida including those led by Ernie Fields and Stack Walton. In the Walton band he played alongside several proto-boppers including Howard McGhee, Wardell Gray and Al McKibbon. In 1944 Edwards settled in California and after playing with an R&B band led by Roy Milton he joined McGhee, switching to tenor saxophone. The McGhee band worked sporadically over the next couple of years, recording for Ross Russell's Dial Records. The resulting four sides, 'Dilated Pupils', 'Midnight At Minton's', '52nd Street Theme' and 'Up In Dodo's Room' achieved the status of minor classics and the final title alerted fans and musicians to the possibility that the tenor saxophone could go down pathways other than those previously trod by Coleman Hawkins and Lester Young. In part, Edwards's original concept arose from his youthful experience on alto and his interest at the time in the music of Charlie Parker. This was his first recording session but he quickly made up for his late start and during the next months was regularly featured on many of the best west coast record dates. In December 1947 he appeared on a Dexter Gordon date where the two tenor players duetted on 'The Duel', a fairly successful attempt to repeat the earlier success of Gordon's and Gray's 'The Chase'. In the early 50s Edwards became a weekend regular at the Lighthouse, playing with Shorty Rogers, Shelly Manne, Hampton Hawes and others. In 1954 he joined the quintet co-led by Max Roach and Clifford Brown, replacing Sonny Stitt only to be replaced himself soon afterwards by Harold Land. He also worked in San Francisco during this period but periodic bouts of ill health, mostly related to dental problems, kept him out of the spotlight and also away from the recording studios. In 1960 he recorded for Contemporary Records as nominal leader of a co-operative quartet comprising pianist Joe Castro, Leroy Vinnegar and Billy Higgins. Their album, *Teddy's Ready*, proved popular and the following year Edwards was reunited at Contemporary with McGhee, then recovering from a bout of drug addiction. This album, *Together Again!*, was similarly successful and helped the re-establishment of Edwards as a potent voice in jazz. In the 60s he played with Benny Goodman and Milt Jackson and in the 70s worked with Jimmy Smith and singers Sarah Vaughan and Tom Waits. He also began touring internationally and continued doing so throughout the 80s. In 1991, he worked with Bill Berry and his LA Big Band for concerts at the Hollywood Bowl, having played in the band intermittently since the early 70s. In between jazz dates, Edwards has worked extensively in the studios, playing and writing for radio and television. He is the composer of many songs, including 'Sunset Eyes'. In the post-bop era, Edwards has consistently proved to be a fluent and creative performer, bringing his wide experience and imaginative mainstream concepts to bear upon music that is thoroughly contemporary while remaining deeply rooted in the great blues-influenced traditions of jazz.

Selected albums: with Dexter Gordon *The Duel* (1947), *Teddy's Ready* (Comtemporary 1960), *Together Again!* (Original Jazz Classics 1961), *Good Gravy* (Timeless 1961), *Heart And Soul* (1962), *It's Alright* (1967), *Feelin's* (1974), with Bill Berry *Hot And Happy* (1974), *The Inimitable* (1976), *Out Of This World* (Steeplechase 1980). Compilation: with Howard McGhee *Trumpet At Tempo* (1946), *Mississippi Lad* (Antilles 1991), *Tenor Conclave* (Timeless 1992).

Efford, Bob

b. London, England. Before becoming a highly accomplished reed player, especially on tenor saxophone, Efford played piano and trumpet. Drifting seemingly without design into a career in music, he played in some minor British provincial dance bands in the 40s. When one of the bands, Les Ayling's, became resident at the Lyceum Ballroom in London, Efford found his way into the local jazz scene and in 1949 joined Vic Lewis's Kenton-styled band. In the early 50s, he joined Ted Heath, touring the USA and receiving personal acclaim at the band's tour-opening concert at Carnegie Hall. He left Heath in the early 60s, thereafter mostly doing studio work which included sessions under the leadership of visiting American stars such as Benny Goodman and Harry James. In 1976 he moved to Los Angeles where he played in bands led by Dave Pell, Bob Florence, Bill Holman and the Capp-Pierce Juggernaut. In 1980 he made his debut as leader at Carmelo's, playing a bewilderingly huge range of instruments including pretty nearly the entire saxophone family as well as oboe, bassoon, flute, clarinet and cor anglais. Efford's forte remains the tenor saxophone and he is also especially adept as a baritone saxophonist which he plays with an engagingly light tone.

Albums: *Focus On Ted Heath* (c.1959), with Bob Florence *Trash Can City* (1986).

Egan, Mark

b. 14 January 1951, Brockton, Massachusetts, USA. Egan started playing the trumpet at the age of 10 and only turned to the double bass when he was 15. He studied at the University of Miami in the mid-70s and took lessons from Jaco Pastorius, Dave Holland and Andy Laverne (piano). Meanwhile he was working with Ira Sullivan, the Pointer Sisters, Deodato and David Sanborn. In 1977 he started working with Pat Metheny's group with whom he stayed for three years. Egan has since worked with a variety of musicians, including Stan Getz, Gil Evans, Randy Brecker, John McLaughlin, Airto Moreira and Flora Purim. In 1982 he formed Elements with drummer Danny Gottlieb with whom he has spent some time studying ethnic music. He is an educated musician who varies the sound of his playing through his fascination and skill in the use of electronic devices.

Selected albums: *Elements* (1982), *Forward Motion* (1984), *Mosaic* (1984), *A Touch Of Light* (GRP 1988), *Beyond Words* (Blue Beacon 1992).

Eldridge, Roy

b. 30 January 1911, Pittsburgh, Pennsylvania, USA, d. 26 February 1989. One of the chief figures in the established lineage of jazz trumpet playing, Eldridge paid his dues with territory bands in the mid-west, such as those of Speed Webb and Horace Henderson, before moving to New York in 1930. He then played with a number of bands, including that of Teddy Hill and one which he co-led with his brother, Joe Eldridge. In 1935 he joined Fletcher Henderson's orchestra, then formed his own group, which was reasonably successful but not so much so that he could afford to refuse an offer to join Gene Krupa in 1941. The engagement brought Eldridge to great prominence thanks to extensive tours of the USA and numerous recordings, notably solo features on 'Rockin' Chair', 'After You've Gone' and 'Let Me Off Uptown' (on which he partnered Anita O'Day). Despite the enormous boost to his popularity that resulted from the exposure he gained with Krupa, this was a very trying time for Eldridge who, as the only black member of the band, suffered racial harassment which brought him to the brink of a nervous breakdown. When Krupa was jailed in 1943, Eldridge briefly fronted the band before it broke up. He then formed his own band before giving a second chance to the white big band scene with Artie Shaw and once again he encountered discrimination and abuse. After briefly trying another big band of his own, Eldridge settled on leading a small group. In the late 40s he worked again with Krupa and also joined Jazz At The Philharmonic. In the 50s he played with Benny Goodman, spent some time in Europe and continued his association with JATP. This period coincided with a personal crisis during which Eldridge began to doubt his place in jazz as the new generation of trumpeters, led by Dizzy Gillespie, forged new ideas. The stay in Europe convinced him that his place was in the mainstream of jazz, and that it was a place in which he was respected by musicians and admired by fans. In the 60s, Eldridge played with Ella Fitzgerald, Coleman Hawkins and Count Basie and co-led a band with Richie Kamuca. In 1970 he began a residency at Ryans in New York City which lasted into the second half of the decade.

A fiery, combative player, Eldridge is often cited as a link between trumpeters Louis Armstrong and Dizzy Gillespie. Although there is an element of logic in this assessment, it overlooks the important role in jazz trumpet history of Henry 'Red' Allen; and it implies that Eldridge was a proto-bop trumpeter, which is far from being the truth. He was the outstanding trumpet stylist of the 40s, performing with daring aggression, his high register playing achieved with apparent ease and his verve and enthusiasm were such that he invariably brought out the best in his fellow musicians. His suggested link to bebop stems largely from a tiny handful of records which show that he was aware of the changes taking place around him and was unafraid to dabble even if he chose never to take the plunge. He was, however, undoubtedly a goad to Gillespie, with whom he played in many after-hours sessions at Minton's and other New York clubs where bebop was nurtured. In the late 50s and afterwards, having settled back into a swing-based groove, Eldridge showed his mastery of the form and of his instrument. Nicknamed 'Little Jazz', Eldridge was a giant who became an elder statesman of jazz without ever losing the fire and aggression that had always marked his playing. Sadly, his career came to an end when he suffered a stroke in 1980, after which he never played again.

Selected albums: *Heckler's Hop* (1935-40), *The Early Years* (1935-49), *At The Three Deuces Club 1937* (1937), *Roy Eldridge At The Arcadia Ballroom* (1939), *At Jerry Newman's* (1940), with Gene Krupa *Drummin' Man* (1941-42), *The Little Jazz Trumpet Ensemble* (CBS, 1935-1940 recordings), *Rare Broadcasts* (1953), *Roy Eldridge With The Oscar Peterson Quartet* i (1953), *Roy Eldridge With The Oscar Peterson Quartet* ii (1954), with Dizzy Gillespie *Roy And Diz* (Verve 1954), *Trumpet Kings* (1954-55), *Tour De Force* (1955), *Swing Goes Dixie* (1956), *Americans In Sweden* (1957), *That Warm Feeling* (1957), with Coleman Hawkins *At The Opera House* (1957), *Little Jazz Live In 1957* (1957), with Hawkins *The Newport Years Vol. 4* (1957), *The Great English Concert* (1958), *Just You And Me - Live In 59'* (Stash), *Art Ford's Jazz Party* (1958), *Roy Eldridge Sextet* (1962), with Richie Kamuca *Comin' Home Baby* (1965), *The Nifty Cat Strikes West* (1966), *The Nifty Cat* (1970), *Little Jazz And The Jimmy Ryan All-Stars* (1975), *Jazz*

Maturity...Where It's Coming From (1975), *Happy Time* (1975), *The Trumpet Kings At The Montreux Festival, 1975* (1975), *What It's All About* (1976), *Roy Eldridge 4: Montreux '77* (1977), *Dale's Wail* (Verve 1979), with Tiny Grimes *One Is Never Too Old To Swing* (Sonet 1979), *Roy Eldridge At Jerry Newman's* (Xanadu 1983), *Roy Eldridge Vol 1 Nuts* (Vogue 1993, 1950 recordings), *Roy Eldridge Vol 2 French Cooking* (Vogue 1993, 1950-51 recordings).

Elias, Eliane

b. 19 March 1960, São Paulo, Brazil. Before she reached the age of 21, Elias has attracted considerable attention, not only for her keyboard playing but also as a teacher of jazz music. In the early 80s she moved to New York, joined the Brecker brothers jazz/rock group, Steps Ahead, with whom she remained until 1984 and thereafter recorded and toured extensively. She continued to play and record with Randy Brecker, whom she married, and has also recorded with Jack DeJohnette, Nana Vasconcelos and Eddie Gomez (upon whose advice she first tried her luck in the USA). Although a gifted and interesting pianist, Elias has not completely fulfilled her early promise to become a major figure on the contemporary jazz scene.

Albums: *Steps Ahead* (1983), *Illusions* (Denon 1987), *Crosscurrents* (Denon 1988), *So Far So Close* (Blue Note 1990), *Plays Jobim* (Blue Note 1990), *A Long Story* (Manhattan 1990), *Fantasia* (Blue Note 1992), *Paulistana* (Blue Note 1993).

Ellington, Duke

b. Edward Kennedy Ellington, 29 April 1899, Washington, DC, USA, d. 24 May 1974. Ellington began playing piano as a child but, despite some local success, took up a career as a signpainter. In his teens he continued to play piano, studied harmony, composed his first tunes and was generally active in music in Washington. Among his childhood friends were Sonny Greer, Artie Whetsol and Otto Hardwicke; from 1919 he played with them in various bands, sometimes working outside the city. In 1923 he ventured to New York to work with Elmer Snowden, and the following year formed his own band, the Washingtonians. Also in 1924, in collaboration with lyricist Joe Trent, he composed the *Chocolate Kiddies* revue. By 1927, Ellington's band had become established in east coast states and at several New York nightclubs. At the end of the year he successfully auditioned for a residency at Harlem's Cotton Club. The benefits arising from this engagement were immeasurable: regular radio broadcasts from the club ensured a widespread audience and Ellington's tours and recording sessions during the period of the residency, which ended early in 1931, built upon the band's popularity. In the early 30s the band consolidated its reputation with extended tours of the USA, appearances in films and visits to Europe, which included performances in London in 1933. Towards the end of the decade the band returned for further seasons at the Cotton Club. Throughout the 30s and early 40s the band recorded extensively and to great acclaim; they continued to tour and record with little interruption during the rest of the 40s and into the early 50s but, although the quality of the music remained high, the band became significantly less popular than had once been the case. An appearance at the 1956 Newport Jazz Festival revived their popularity, and during the rest of the 50s and the following decade Ellington toured ceaselessly, playing concerts around the world. Ellington had always been a prolific writer, composing thousands of tunes including 'It Don't Mean A Thing (If It Ain't Got That Swing)', 'Sophisticated Lady', 'In A Sentimental Mood', 'Prelude To A Kiss', 'Concert For Cootie (Do Nothin' Till You Hear From Me)', 'Cotton Tail', 'In A Mellotone', 'I Got It Bad And That Ain't Good', 'Don't Get Around Much Anymore', 'I'm Beginning To See The Light' and 'Satin Doll'. In later years he also composed film scores, among them *The Asphalt Jungle* (1950), *Anatomy Of A Murder* (1959), *Paris Blues* (1960) and *Assault On A Queen* (1966). More importantly, he began to concentrate upon extended works, composing several suites and a series of sacred music concerts, the latter mostly performed in churches and cathedrals. Over the years the personnel of Ellington's orchestra proved remarkably stable; several of his sidemen remaining with him for decades. The ceaseless touring continued into the early 70s, with Ellington making few concessions to the advancing years. After his death in 1974 the orchestra continued for a while under the direction of his son, Mercer Ellington, but despite the continuing presence of a handful of survivors, such as Harry Carney who had been in the band virtually without a break for 47 years, the spirit and guiding light was gone. From this moment, Ellington lived on through an immense recorded legacy and in the memories of musicians and an army of fans.

Duke Ellington was elegantly dismissive of analysis; too much talk, he said, stinks up the place. Yet he could talk a good tune. Of the haunting and plaintive 'Mood Indigo' he said: 'Just a story about a little girl and a little boy. They are about eight and the girl loves the boy. They never speak of it, of course, but she just likes the way he wears his hat. Every day he comes to her house at a certain time and she sits in her window and waits. Then one day he doesn't come. "Mood Indigo" just tells how she feels.' The story, and the tune it describes, are characteristically Ellingtonian: they bear the hallmark of true sophistication, which is audacious simplicity. His music is never cluttered. It travels lightly and politely. Every note works its passage. But what notes! And what a journey! Ellington was born into relatively comfortable circumstances. His father had been a butler, including a stint at the White House. The family was deeply religious and musical. Parents and son adored each other. Ellington reports he was 'pampered and spoiled rotten', and of his parents he wrote: 'My mother was beautiful but my father was only handsome.' Years later, when his band was in its majestic prime, he would yell from the piano: 'Everybody look handsome'. And they did. His mother was a piano player; under her influence, Ellington had music lessons from a teacher called Mrs Clinkscales. In later life he whimsically reported that one of the first things she taught him was never to share the stage with Oscar Peterson. But probably more influential than Mrs Clinkscales were the piano players he heard in the pool-rooms where, like any self-respecting, underage, sharp-suited adolescent-about-town, he found his supplementary education, among a diversity of gamblers, lawyers, pickpockets, doctors and hustlers. 'At heart,' he said, 'they were all great artists.' He paid special tribute to Oliver 'Doc' Perry, a pianist who gave him lessons of a less formal but more practical nature than those of Mrs Clinkscales - 'reading the leads and recognizing the chords'. Ellington became a professional musician in his teens. One of his first engagements was playing 'mood' music for a travelling magician and fortune teller, improvising to suit the moment, whether serious or mystical. In 1914 he wrote his first compositions: 'Soda Fountain Rag' and 'What You Gonna Do When The Bed Breaks Down?' By the age of 18 he was leading bands in the Washington area, having quickly learned that the bandleader, as Mr Fixit, generally left the gig with more dollars than the other guys in the band. Thus, by the age of 20, he was pianist, composer and bandleader: the essential Duke Ellington was formed, ready to blossom into one of the most influential musicians in jazz, though, again with characteristic perversity, he insisted that he wrote folk music, not jazz.

By the time of the band's opening at the Cotton Club, in addition to Greer and Hardwicke, Ellington had recruited key players such as James 'Bubber' Miley, his first great 'growling' trumpet player; the trombonist Joe 'Tricky Sam' Nanton; the bassist Wellman Braud and Carney, whose baritone saxophone formed the rich and sturdy foundation of the band's reed section for its entire history. Perhaps as crucial was Ellington's meeting with Irving Mills, who became his manager. For a black musician to survive, let alone prosper, in the America of the 20s and 30s, a tough white manager was an essential safeguard. In 1927 came the first classic recordings of 'Black And Tan Fantasy' and 'Creole Love Call', the latter with the legendary vocal line by Adelaide Hall. In these, and in up-tempo numbers such as 'Hot And Bothered', the Ellington method was fully formed. The conventional way to praise a big band was to say that they played like one man. The quality of the Ellington bands was that they always played like a bunch of highly talented and wildly disparate individuals, recalling the 'great artists' of the pool-room. The Cotton Club provided an ideal workshop and laboratory for Ellington. Situated in Harlem, its performers were exclusively black, its clientele exclusively white and in pursuit of dusky exotic pleasures. Ellington, who enjoyed being a showman, gave the audience what it wanted: music for showgirls and boys to dance to, in every tempo from the slow and sultry to the hot and hectic, coloured with so-called 'jungle sounds' - a notion that these days would be called a marketing concept. It was also a racial slur, but Ellington had the skill and wit to transcend it, creating music that met the specification but disarmingly turned it inside out. The music winked at the audience. Moving into the 30s, the band's repertoire was enriched by pieces such as 'Rocking' In Rhythm', 'Old Man Blues', 'The Mooche' and, of course, 'Mood Indigo'. Its personnel now included Juan Tizol on trombone, Cootie Williams, de facto successor to Miley on trumpet, and the sublime Johnny Hodges on alto saxophone, whose lyricism, tempered with melancholy, became a crucial element in the Ellington palette. Hodges became the most striking example of the truism: once an Ellingtonian, always an Ellingtonian. Like Williams and Tizol, he would leave the band to become a leader in his own right or briefly a sideman in another band, only to return. You could take the man out of the Ellington band, but you couldn't take the Ellington out of the man. The 30s saw the first attempts at compositions longer than the conventional three minutes (the length of a gramophone record), starting with 'Creole Rhapsody' in 1931. The period also saw, to over-simplify the situation, a move into respectability. Critics and musicians from the serious side of the tracks had begun to take notice. People as diverse as Constant Lambert, Percy Grainger, Leopold Stokowski and Igor Stravinsky recognized the extraordinary and unique gifts of Ellington. Phrases like 'America's greatest living composer' crept into print. Ellington continued to refer to himself, gracefully and demurely, as 'our piano player'. To be sure, his composing methods, from all accounts, were radically different from those of other title contenders. He would scribble a few notes on the back of an envelope, or in the back of his head, and develop the piece in rehearsal. The initial themes were often created by musicians in the band - hence the frequent shared composer credits: 'The Blues I Love To Sing' with Miley, 'Caravan' with Tizol, 'Jeep's Blues' with Hodges. 'Bluebird Of Delhi', from the 1966 'Far East Suite', was based on a phrase sung by a bird outside Billy Strayhorn's room. Strayhorn joined the band in 1939, as arranger, composer, occasional piano player, best friend and musical alter ego. A small, quiet and gentle man, he became a vital element in the Ellington success story. His arrival coincided with that of the tenor saxophone player, Ben Webster, and the brilliant young bass player, Jimmy Blanton, who died in 1943, aged 23. By common consent, the Webster/Blanton band produced some of the finest music in the Ellington canon, exemplified by 'Jack The Bear', with Blanton's innovative bass solo, and 'Just A-Settin' And A-Rockin', where Webster demonstrates that the quality of jazz playing lies in discretion and timing rather than vast numbers of notes to the square inch.

Ellington's output as a composer was immense. The late Derek Jewell, in his indispensable biography of the man, estimated that he wrote at least 2000 pieces but, because of his cavalier way with pieces of paper, it may have been as many as 5000. Among them were many tunes that have become popular standards - 'Sophisticated Lady', 'In A Sentimental Mood', 'Don't Get Around Much Anymore' and 'I'm Beginning To See The Light' are just a selected handful. Their significance, aside from the musical, was that their royalty income effectively subsidized the band, particularly during the post-war period when the big bands virtually disappeared under successive onslaughts from inflation, the growth of television, the decline of the dancehalls and, most significantly, the arrival of rock 'n' roll. Even Ellington was not immune to these pressures and in the early 50s looking handsome suddenly became hard work. The turning-point came at the Newport Jazz Festival on 7 July 1956. Morale was low. The previous year had seen embarrassing attempts at cashing in on commercial trends with recordings of 'Twelfth Street Rag Mambo' and 'Bunny Hop Mambo', plus a summer season at an aquashow, with a string section and two harpists. The first set at Newport was equally embarrassing. Ellington arrived onstage to find four of his musicians missing. The band played a few numbers, then departed. They returned around midnight, at full strength, to play the 'Newport Jazz Festival Suite', composed with Strayhorn for the occasion. Then Ellington, possibly still rankled by the earlier behaviour of the band, called 'Diminuendo And Crescendo In Blue', a piece written almost 20 years earlier and by no means a regular item on their usual concert programme. It is in two sections, linked by a bridge passage from, on this occasion, the tenor saxophone player, Paul Gonsalves. Something happened. It cannot be explained, except to say that it only happens if you start living dangerously with a disparate group of dangerous people who also happen to be great artists: the pool-room syndrome. Gonsalves blew 27 choruses, the crowd went wild, the band played four encores, the news travelled around the world on the jazz grapevine and was also reported in detail in *Time* magazine, with a picture of the piano player on the cover. After Newport and until his death, Ellington's life and career became a triumphal and global procession, garlanded with awards, honorary degrees, close encounters with world leaders and, more important, major compositions. 'Such Sweet Thunder', his Shakespearean suite written with Strayhorn, contains gems such as 'Lady Mac' - 'Though she was a lady of noble birth,' said The Duke, 'we suspect there was a little ragtime in her soul' - and 'Madness In Great Ones', dedicated to Hamlet with the laconic remark 'in those days crazy didn't mean the same thing it means now'. Further collaborations with Strayhorn included an enchanting re-working of Tchaikovsky's 'Nutcracker Suite' and 'The Far East Suite' - still adorned with dazzling contributions from various of the now-elder statesmen in the band: Hodges, Gonsalves and Carney in the reeds, Lawrence Brown, Britt Woodman and Tizol among the trombones, Ray Nance and Cat Anderson in the trumpet section. Astonishingly, the band that recorded the *70th Birthday Concert* in England in 1969 included Carney, Hodges and Williams 40 years after they first joined Ellington; and on the record they still sound like a bunch of kids having a good night on the town. The freshness and energy of the band as it tackles material played hundreds of times before are extraordinary.

There was another side to the story. Ellington had always been a religious man. In his later years he turned increasingly to the writing and performance of sacred music. The origins of this can be traced back to 'Come Sunday', from the 1945 suite, 'Black, Brown And Beige', and beyond that to 'Reminiscing In Tempo', written 10 years earlier, following the death of his mother, of which he said: 'My mother's death was the greatest shock. I didn't do anything but brood. The music is representative of all that. It begins with pleasant thoughts. Then something awful gets you down. Then you snap out of it and it ends affirmatively.' From a man who was dismissive of analysis, that is a very shrewd assessment not only of the piece in question, but of his entire output. Working within the framework of the conventional big band line-up - five reeds, four trumpets, three trombones, bass, drums and a remarkable piano player, he produced music of extraordinary diversity. His themes were startling in their simplicity, as if he had picked them off trees, and in a way he did. The tonal qualities of the band - the unique Ellington sound - were based on celebration of its individuals. The music might be lyrical or triumphant, elegiac or celebratory and the blues were never far away. But it always ended affirmatively. To borrow a phrase from Philip Larkin, writing about Sidney Bechet, Duke Ellington's life and music added up to A Resounding Yes.

Selected albums: *Carnegie Hall Concert* (1943), *The Hollywood Bowl Concert Vols. 1 & 2* (1947), *The Duke Is On The Air - From The Blue Note* (1952), *Ellington Plays Ellington* (1953), *Ellington At Newport* (Columbia 1956), *A Drum Is A Woman* (1956), *Such Sweet Thunder* (1957), *Back To Back* (Verve 1959), *Side By Side* (Verve 1959), *Newport '58* (Columbia 1958), *Festival Session* (1959), *Anatomy Of A Murder* (1959), *The Ellington Suites: The Queen's Suite* (1959), *The Goutelas Suite* (1971), *The Uwis Suite* (1972); *Swinging Suites By Edward E. And Edward G. (Suite Thursday/Peer Gynt)* (1960), *Nutcracker Suite* (1960), *Piano In The Background* (1960), *Paris Blues* (1961), *Duke Ellington And His Orchestra Featuring Paul Gonsalves* (1962), with Charles Mingus, Max Roach *Money Jungle* (Blue Note 1962), *Duke Ellington With John Coltrane* (1962), *Duke Ellington Meets Coleman Hawkins* (1963), *Piano In The Foreground* (Columbia 1963), *Symphonic Ellington* (1963), *The Great Paris Concert* (Atlantic 1963), *My People* (1963), *Duke Ellington's Concert Of Sacred Music* (First Sacred Concert) (1964), *The Far East Suite* (1964), with Boston Pops Orchestra *The Duke At Tanglewood* (1965), *Yale Concert* (Original Jazz Classics 1965), with Ella Fitzgerald *Ella And Duke At The Côte D'Azure* (1966), *Far East Suite* (1966), *And His Mother Called Him Bill* (1967), *Second Sacred Concert* (1968), *70th Birthday Concert* (1969), *The Latin American Suite* (1969), *The New Orleans Suite* (Atlantic 1970), *The English Concert/Togo Brava Suite* (1971), with Ray Brown *This One's For Blanton* (1972), *Third Sacred Concert* (1973), *Eastbourne Performance* (1973), *The Unknown Session* (1979, rec. 1960), *In Concert At The Pleyel Pans* (1990, rec. 1958). Selected compilations: *The Indispensable Duke Ellington Vols 1/2* (1927-29 recordings), *The Complete Duke Ellington Vol. 3* (1930-32 recordings), *The Indispensable Duke Ellington Vols 3/4* (1930-34 recordings), *The Complete Duke Ellington Vol. 7* (1936-37 recordings), *The Indispensable Duke Ellington Vols 5/6* (1940 recordings), *The Blanton-Webster Years* (RCA 1987, rec 1940-42), *Johnny Come Lately* (1942-45 recordings), *Black, Brown And Beige: The 1944-46 Band Recordings* (RCA 1988, 3 LP/CD box-set), *Duke Ellington - The Pianist* (1966-74 recordings), *The Intimacy Of The Blues* (1986, rec. 1967, 1970), *Blues In Orbit* (1988, rec. 1958-59), with Blanton and others *Soles, Duets And Trios* (1990, rec. 1932-67).

Further reading: *The World Of Duke Ellington*, Stanley Dance. *Music Is My Mistress*, Duke Ellington. *Duke Ellington In Person*, Mercer Ellington with Stanley Dance. *Duke: A Portrait Of Duke Ellington*, Derek Jewell. *Duke Ellington*, James Lincoln Collier. *Ellington: The Early Years*, Mark Tucker. *Duke Ellington: Jazz Composer*, Ken Rattenbury.

Ellington, Mercer

b. 11 March 1919, Washington, DC, USA. Any son following the same career as a famous father is bound to encounter problems of recognition. For Mercer Ellington the problem was magnified through the fact that his father was Duke Ellington, who was not only one of the two or three greatest figures in jazz history but was also an acknowledged master of 20th-century music. For all the disadvantages of having such a parent, Mercer was determined to have a career in music. He studied formally in Washington and New York in the 20s and formed his own band playing trumpet in the late 30s. He sometimes used musicians more usually associated with his father, among them Cat Anderson and Billy Strayhorn, but also worked with men who only later joined Duke. In addition, he used musicians who were engaged in the emerging bebop movement, including Dizzy Gillespie and Charles Mingus. In the early 40s Ellington was manager of the Cootie Williams band and also played briefly in Duke's band. He composed several tunes taken up by his father, of which the best known are 'Things Ain't What They Used To Be', 'Jumpin' Punkins' and 'Blue Serge'. Ellington spent the second half of the 50s with his father's band, mostly in an administrative capacity. He returned to the band in the mid-60s, remaining until Duke's death in 1974. Thereafter, he took over as leader of the Ellington orchestra and conducted the pit band for the Broadway show *Sophisticated Ladies* in the early 80s. His autobiography (written in collaboration with Stanley Dance) was published in 1978. Ellington has continued to lead an orchestra into the 90s and, while still rooted in Duke's music, as time has passed it can be seen to be developing a creditable musical personality of its own.

Albums: *Steppin' Into Swing Society* (1958), *Continuum* (1975), *Remembering Duke's World* (1977), *Take The Holiday Train* (1980), *Duke Ellington's Sophisticated Ladies* (1981), *Digital Duke* (GRP 1987), *Music Is My Mistress* (Limelight 1989).

Ellis, Don

b. 25 July 1934, Los Angeles, California, USA, d. 17 December 1978. Appreciation of Ellis's work has increased since his death and he is now regarded by many as an important figure in jazz. From childhood he was fascinated with brass instruments and received a trumpet at the age of two. At junior high school he had his own quartet and at Boston university he was a member of the band. His first professional work was as a member of Ray McKinley's Glenn Miller Orchestra. After his national service, Don formed a small group playing coffee houses in New York's Greenwich Village. By the late 50s he was playing with many name bands including those of Woody Herman, Lionel Hampton, Charles Mingus and Maynard Ferguson. Ellis also worked in small groups, enjoying the greater freedom of expression this allowed. In 1961-2 he was a member of George Russell's sextet. In Atlantic City, Ellis took up a teaching fellowship and it was there he developed and explored his interest in the complexities of Indian rhythm patterns. Ellis made a triumphant appearance at the 1966 Monterey Jazz festival with his 23-piece band. His totally original themes were scored using unbelievably complex notation. Customarily, most big band music was played at four beats to the bar but Ellis confidently and successfully experimented with 5-beat bars, then 9-, 11-, 14-, 17-, 19- and even 27- beat bars. Mixing metres created difficulties for his rhythm sections so he taught himself to play drums in order that he might properly instruct his drummers. He also experimented with brass instruments, introducing the four-valve flügelhorn and superbone. During the late 60s the Don Ellis Orchestra was promoted as part of the great CBS progressive music campaign and he found himself performing at rock festivals and concerts. His music found favour with the Woodstock generation, who could also recognize him as an exciting pioneer. His CBS albums were all successful, his work being produced by both John Hammond and Al Kooper. Dubbed the 'Father of the Time Revolution' in jazz, Ellis's music was much more than complex. It was also undeniably joyous. Tunes like the 7/4 romp 'Pussy Wiggle Stomp', 'Barnum's Revenge' (a reworking of 'Bill Bailey') and 'Scratt And Fluggs' (a passing nod to country music's Lester Flatt and Earl Scruggs), are played with zesty enthusiasm, extraordinary skill and enormous good humour. Ellis's trumpet playing was remarkable, combining dazzling technique with a hot jazz feeling that reflected his admiration for Henry 'Red' Allen. He also experimented with electronic devices, such as a Ring Modulator, which transformed his trumpet into a generator of atavistic moans and shouts. Conversely, as he showed on *Haiku*, he could play with delicate charm and often deeply moving emotion. Ellis scored the music for 10 films, including *The French Connection* (1971), for which he won a Grammy. It is, however, his brilliantly ambitious and innovative 'eastern' music, notably 'Indian Lady' and 'Turkish Bath' that makes his work as important as John Coltrane's flirtation with the music of the mystic east. He is indubitably an outstanding figure destined for future reappraisal. Ellis stated 'I am not concerned whether my music is jazz, third stream, classical or anything else, or whether it is even called music. Let it be judged as Don Ellis noise'.

Albums: *How Time Passes* (Candid 1960), *New Ideas* (Original Jazz Classics 1961), *Essence* (1962), *Jazz Jamboree No 1* (1962), *Live At Monterey* (1966), *Live In 3/2/3/4 Time* (1967), *Electric Bath* (CBS 1968), *Shock Treatment* (CBS 1968), *Autumn* (CBS 1969), *The New Don Ellis Band Goes Underground* (CBS 1969), *Don Ellis At Fillmore* (CBS 1970), *Tears Of Joy* (1971), *Connection* (1972), *Soaring* (1973), *Haiku* (1974), *Star Wars* (1977), *Live At Montreux* (Atlantic 1978), *Out Of Nowhere* (Candid 1989, recorded 1961).

Ellis, Herb

b. 4 August 1921, Farmersville, Texas, USA. In 1941 Ellis attended North Texas State College, where his fellow students included Jimmy Giuffre. After graduation, he played guitar in a number of big bands, including the Casa Loma Orchestra and the Jimmy Dorsey outfit. He was next with Soft Winds, a trio formed from the Dorsey rhythm section with John Frigo and Lou Carter, and in 1953 took Barney Kessel's place in the Oscar Peterson trio, where he remained for five years alongside Ray Brown. After leaving Peterson he accompanied Ella Fitzgerald for four years and also worked with Julie London, then spent a decade in the Los Angeles film and television studios. In the early 70s he began a succession of marvellous associations with other guitarists, including Joe Pass, Charlie Byrd and Kessel. In his playing, Ellis constantly reveals a deep affinity for the blues and reflects a thorough awareness of the work of Charlie Christian. As a section player he brings an earthy quality few of his peers can match, and his time with Peterson was of such a high standard that thereafter the pianist rarely used another guitarist. As a soloist his command is outstanding and the bluesy muscularity of his playing is a constant source of delight.

Albums: *The Oscar Peterson Trio At The Stratford Shakespearean Festival* (1956), *Ellis In Wonderland* (1956), *Nothing But The Blues* (1957), *Herb Ellis Meets Jimmy Giuffre* (1959), *Thank You, Charlie Christian* (1960), *Herb Ellis Quartet* (1961), *The Midnight Roll* (1962), *Three Guitars In Bossa Nova Time* (1963), *Herb Ellis & Stuff Smith Together* (1963), *Herb Ellis & Charlie Byrd* (1963), *Herb Ellis Quintet* (1965), *Hello, Herbie* (1969), with Joe Pass *Jazz/Concord* (Concord 1973), with Pass *Seven Come Eleven* (Concord 1973), with Ray Brown *Soft Shoe* (Concord 1974), with Pass *Two For The Road* (1974), *After You've Gone* (1974), *Hot Tracks* (Concord 1975), with Freddie Green *Rhythm Willie* (Concord 1975), with Ross Tompkins *A Pair To Draw To* (1976), *Windflower* (1977), *Soft & Mellow* (Concord 1978), *Great Guitars: Straight Tracks* (c.1978), *Herb Ellis At Montreux* (1979), *Great Guitars At The Winery* (1980), *Herb Mix* (Concord 1981), *Sweet And Lovely* (1983), *When You're Smiling* (1983), with Red Mitchell *Doggin' Around* (Concord 1988), *Roll Call* (Justice 1992).

Elsdon, Alan

b. 15 October 1934, London, England. Elsdon studied trumpet before turning to jazz and working with a succession of British traditional bands in the 50s. His reputation established, in the early 60s he decided to form his own band, but the musical times were changing and he failed to gain the same level of success achieved by many other traditional bands. Nevertheless, Elsdon succeeded in keeping his band afloat, working regularly at clubs and pubs and occasionally at more prestigious venues. He toured the UK with visiting American jazz and blues artists during the 60s and 70s. In the 80s, with his band still around, he also began playing with the Midnite Follies Orchestra and with other groups led by Keith Nichols. Despite his long association with the traditional jazz scene, Elsdon's virile playing style fits comfortably into the mainstream.

Album: *Jazz Journeymen* (Black Lion 1977).

Ericson, Rolf

b. 29 August 1922, Stockholm, Sweden. Ericson had already been playing trumpet for more than two years when, in 1933, he was taken to hear Louis Armstrong during his European tour and was suitably inspired. As a young teenager Ericson was playing professionally and during the late 40s he made a number of recordings. In 1947 he moved to New York and played in several big bands, including those of Charlie Barnet, Woody Herman and Elliot Lawrence. Ericson was attracted by bebop and also played with Wardell Gray. In the early 50s he toured his homeland in company with Charlie Parker and also spent time in numerous big bands, often those assembled for one-off recording and television dates. Later in the decade and on into the 60s he divided his time between the USA and Scandinavia, playing with a wide range of musicians such as Bud Powell, Brew Moore, Kenny Dorham, Stan Kenton, Benny Goodman, Gerry Mulligan, Ernestine Anderson and Duke Ellington. During the second half of the 60s he became deeply involved in studio work, both in the USA and Germany, but found time to play with visiting American musicians. In 1990 he was in Los Angeles, playing as well as ever, and was added to the Ellingtonian small band led by Bill Berry which featured Marshal Royal and Buster Cooper.

Selected albums: with Duke Ellington *The 70th Birthday Concert* (1969), *Oh Pretty Little Neida* (Four Leaf Clover 1971), *Sincerely Ours* (1978), *Stockholm Sweetenin'* (Dragon 1984).

Erskine, Peter

b. 5 June 1954, Somers Point, New Jersey, USA. Erskine began playing drums while still a toddler, and at the age of six was attending the Stan Kenton Stage Band Camps. He studied advanced drum techniques under Alan Dawson and then, at the age of 18, joined Kenton. He played with Kenton for three years, touring internationally and establishing a formidable reputation as a player and teacher. In 1976 he joined Maynard Ferguson, then in a jazz-rock phase, and two years later became a member of Weather Report where he remained into the early 80s. After leaving Weather Report, Erskine worked in the studios and also made records and toured with Michael Brecker and David Sancious in the band known as Steps Ahead and with John Abercrombie. A dazzling technician, Erskine is one of the outstanding jazz-rock drummers, bringing inventiveness and rhythmic clarity to the form and playing with subtlety and swing. In the late 80s he was active as leader of his own group, a band which included Brecker and Abercrombie, playing in the tradition in which Erskine is an established master.

Albums: with Weather Report *8:30* (1979), with Weather Report *Night Passage* (1980), *Weather Report* (1982), *Peter Erskine* (Original Jazz Classics 1982), *Steps Ahead* (1983), with John Abercrombie *Current Events* (1985), *Transition* (Denon 1986), *Motion Poet* (Denon 1988), *Big Theatre* (Ah Um 1989), *Sweet Soul* (RCA 1991), *You Never Know* (ECM 1993), with Abercrombie, Marc Johnson, John Surman *November* (1994).

Ervin, Booker

b. 31 October 1930, Denison, Texas, USA, d. 31 August 1970. As a child, Ervin played trombone but switched to tenor saxophone in the early 50s during his military service. (He led his own small group when he was stationed on Okinawa.) After returning to civilian life, Ervin studied at Berklee College Of Music under Joe Viola, then worked with Ernie Fields's R&B band and several jazz groups in the southwest. A move to New York in 1958 brought him into a long-standing if irregular association with Charles Mingus which continued into the mid-60s. He recorded extensively with Mingus and Randy Weston and also with his own groups. A powerful player, Ervin's style demonstrates his awareness of such diverse tenor saxophonists as the Texas tenor school (his father played trombone with Buddy Tate's band), Lester Young, Dexter Gordon, Sonny Rollins and John Coltrane, but he chose to follow a different star and remained very much his own man. His warm approach to ballads and searing attack on uptempo numbers showed him to be a much hotter player than most of his contemporaries. His death in 1970 came while he was still very much in his prime.

Selected albums: with Charles Mingus *Jazz Portraits* (1959), *The Book Cooks* (1960), with Roland Kirk *Soulful Saxes* (Affinity 1960), *Cookin'* (Savoy 1960), *That's It!* (Candid 1961), *Exultation!* (1963), *The Freedom Book* (1963), *The Song Book* (Original Jazz Classics 1964), *The Blues Book* (Original Jazz Classics 1964), *The Space Book* (1964), with Dexter Gordon *Setting The Pace* (Prestige 1965), *The Trance* (1965), *Lament For Booker Ervin* (1965), *Structurally Sound* (1966), *Heavy!* (1966), *Booker And Brass* (1967), *The 'In' Between* (1967), *Booker Ervin* (1968), *Lament For Booker Ervin* (Enja 1993).

Erwin, George 'Pee Wee'

b. 30 May 1913, Falls City, Nebraska, USA, d. 20 June 1981. A child prodigy, Erwin first attracted attention playing trumpet on the radio with the Coon-Sanders Nighthawks when he was only eight years old. After playing trumpet in local bands, including John Whetstine, with whom he toured when he was just 15, Roland Evans, Eddie Kuhn and Erwin joined the nationally-popular Joe Haymes band in 1931. He followed this with a spell in the Isham Jones orchestra, the outstanding dance band of the day, was briefly with Freddy Martin, and then joined Benny Goodman at the end of 1934. After a short stay with Ray Noble (in a band formed by Glenn Miller which previewed the Miller 'sound') Erwin returned to Goodman for most of 1936 and then flitted through various bands, including Noble's again, Tommy Dorsey's, Raymond Scott's and then took temporary control of the Bunny Berigan band. From the mid-40s Erwin was often in the studios, but at the end of the decade he had become a regular at Nick's in New York. This engagement lasted through the 50s with other regular gigs at the Metropole and on numerous radio and television shows. An enormously popular man and a gifted musician, Erwin began teaching in the 60s and his qualities were imparted to many newcomers to the jazz scene, most notably Warren Vaché Jnr. In the 70s Erwin was constantly in demand for club and festival dates and in 1979 he rejoined Benny Goodman for the Playboy Jazz Festival in Hollywood. That same year his home town of Falls City nominated a 'Pee Wee Erwin Day' and presented him with the keys to the city. He worked almost until the end of his life, playing the Breda Jazz Festival in Holland in May 1981, just a few weeks before his death.

Albums: *Oh Play That Thing!* (1958), with Dick Hyman *Some Rags, Some Stomps, And A Little Blues, Pee Wee In New York* (1980), *Pee Wee In Hollywood* (1980), *Pee Wee Erwin Memorial* (1981).

Etheridge, John

b. 12 January 1948, London, England. Etheridge is a self-taught guitarist who started playing while he was at school. He went on to Essex University and then played with jazz-rock groups in London in the early 70s before joining Soft Machine (1975-78). He is a technically gifted guitarist able to use all the effects available to an electric guitarist in his solos. He has worked with Stéphane Grappelli (1978-81) showing as much facility playing the acoustic guitar with him as he had previously done on the electric. At the same time, he formed his own group Second Vision (1980-81) and then undertook solo concerts in Australia and toured the USA with bassist Brian Torff (1982). In 1983 he toured England in a trio with Paul Rogers (bass) and Nigel Morris (drums). After spells with rock groups like Global Village Trucking Company and Darryl Way's Wolf, Etheridge played some concerts and recorded with the reformed Soft Machine. In the mid-80s he worked with Gary Boyle (guitar) and with a quartet. In recent years he has played with Danny Thompson. He regularly teaches on guitar courses.

Albums: *First Steps* (1980), with Stéphane Grappelli *Live at Carnegie Hall* (1983), with Soft Machine *Softs* (1986), *Ash* (The Jazz Label 1993), with Andy Summers *Invisible Threads* (Mesa 1994).

Eubanks, Kevin

b. 15 November 1957, Philadelphia, Pennsylvania, USA. Eubanks comes from a very musical family: brother Robin Eubanks is a fine trombone player, Ray Bryant is his uncle and his mother, Vera, is a Doctor of Music. Kevin studied guitar at Berklee College Of Music and with Ted Dunbar. Throughout his teens he modelled his style largely on the fiery playing of John McLaughlin, but from the age of 22 he was more influenced by the gentler approach of Wes Montgomery. The Montgomery pedigree is evident in his work, but he also admires Segovia, George Benson and Oscar Peterson. From 1980-81 he was with Art Blakey's Jazz Messengers. He has also worked with Roy Haynes, Slide Hampton, Sam Rivers, Gary Thomas (*While The Gate Is Open*) and Mike Gibbs (*Big Music*). He has made a reputation and a living from smooth, well-produced contemporary fusion, but is quite capable of more challenging playing, as shown by his work on Dave Holland's highly-acclaimed 1990 *Extensions*. Eubanks found his perfect niche as part of the GRP stable of artists where his accessible jazz has found a wide market, although he left the label in 1991 and signed with the illustrious Blue Note Records.

Albums: *Kevin Eubanks - Guitarist* (Discovery 1982), Sundance (GRP 1984), *Opening Night* (GRP 1985), *Face To Face* (GRP 1986), *The Heat Of Heat* (GRP 1988), *Shadow*

Prophets (GRP 1988), *The Searcher* (GRP 1989), *Promise Of Tomorrow* (GRP 1990), *Turning Point* (GRP 1992), *Spirit Talk* (Blue Note 1993).

Evans, Bill (pianist)

b. 16 August 1929, Plainfield, New Jersey, USA, d. 15 September 1980. One of the most important and influential of modern jazz pianists, Evans studied at Southeastern Louisiana University, while summer jobs with Mundell Lowe and Red Mitchell introduced him to the jazz scene. He was in the army from 1951-54; played with Jerry Wald in 1954-55; studied at the Mannes School of Music, New York 1955-56; then began a full-time jazz career with clarinettist Tony Scott. Through Lowe he was introduced to Riverside Records, and made his recording debut as leader (of a trio) in 1956. Evans then recorded with Charles Mingus and George Russell. In 1958 he joined Miles Davis, playing a central role on the album *Kind Of Blue* which was so influential in the development of modal jazz. Evans left Davis after less than a year to form his own trio, and favoured that format thereafter. His recordings with Scott La Faro and Paul Motian (1959-61) are a summit of the genre (*Portrait In Jazz, Explorations*, live sessions at the Village Vanguard). The tragic loss of La Faro in a car accident deprived Evans of his most sympathetic partner, and the later recordings do not quite approach the level of those on Riverside; Eddie Gomez was the most compatible of later bassists. Evans recorded solo, most interestingly on the double-tracked *Conversations With Myself*; in duo with Jim Hall, Bob Brookmeyer and Tony Bennett; and in larger groups with such players as Lee Konitz, Zoot Sims and Freddie Hubbard. Towards the end of his life Evans was building a new trio with Marc Johnson and Joe LaBarbera, and playing with new-found freedom. Although he eventually kicked his heroin habit, he had continuing drug problems and these contributed to his early death from a stomach ulcer and other complications.

Evans's background is significant; he matured away from the bebop scene in New York. Although his earlier playing was indebted to bopper Bud Powell and more strikingly to hardbop pianist Horace Silver, as well as to Lennie Tristano, he gradually developed a more lyrical, 'impressionistic' approach with an understated strength far removed from the aggression of bebop. His ideas were influential in the development of modal jazz and hence of the John Coltrane school, whose major pianistic voice was McCoy Tyner; however, he did not pursue that direction himself, finding it insufficiently lyrical and melodic for his needs. The softer, understated, less obviously dissonant idiom of the great trio with La Faro and Motian embodies the rival pianistic tradition to that of the eventually overbearing Tyner. Contemporary jazz piano tends towards a synthesis of the Evans and Tyner styles, but the Evans legacy is with hindsight the richer one. Technically, Evans led the way in the development of a genuinely pianistic modern jazz style. Most important was his much-imitated but totally distinctive approach to harmony, in particular to the way the notes of the chord are arranged or 'voiced'. Red Garland, who preceded Evans in the Miles Davis group, had moved away from Bud Powell's functional 'shell voicings', but it was Evans (and to a lesser extent Wynton Kelly) who first fully defined the new style of 'rootless voicings'. These retain only the essential tones of the chord (dispensing with the root itself, often played by the bassist), and form the grammatical basis of contemporary jazz piano. Evans employed a wider variety of tone-colour than is usual in jazz piano, with subtle use of the sustaining pedal and varying emphasis of notes in the chord voicing. He improvises thematically, 'rationally'; as he said, 'the science of building a line, if you can call it a science, is enough to occupy somebody for 12 lifetimes'. His influence on pianists is as considerable as that of John Coltrane on saxophonists; most notable on several known to a wider public than he was, such as Herbie Hancock, Keith Jarrett and Chick Corea, but also on Hampton Hawes, Paul Bley and more recently Michel Petrucciani. Legions of imitators have tended to conceal from listeners the complete originality of his style as it developed in the late 50s and early 60s; and Evans's music still continues to yield up secrets.

A trio setting was Evans's ideal format, and his solo piano style is (with the exception of the double-tracked *Conversations With Myself*) less compelling. The trio with La Faro and Motian is surely one of the great combinations in jazz history. The 'collective improvisation' of this group involved rhythmic innovation, with the bass in particular getting away from its standard timekeeping role. Evans commented that 'at that time nobody else was opening trio music in quite that way, letting the music move from an internalized beat, instead of laying it down all the time explicitly'. But the apparent lassitude of Evans's mature style has led to much misunderstanding and criticism. Archie Shepp commented (incorrectly) that 'Debussy and Satie have already done those things'; Cecil Taylor found Evans 'so uninteresting, so predictable and so lacking in vitality'. As James Collier wrote, 'If Milton can write "Il Pensero", surely Bill Evans can produce a "Turn Out The Stars". But Milton also wrote "L'Allegro", and Evans is not often seen dancing in the chequer'd shade'. Melancholy is Evans's natural mood, and rhythm his greatest weakness; he does not swing powerfully, and is not interested enough in the 'groove'. Cannonball Adderley commented that when the pianist joined Davis, 'Miles changed his style from very hard to a softer approach. Bill was brilliant in other areas, but he couldn't make the real hard things come off . . . ' When Evans plays in a determined uptempo (as on *Montreux 1968*) the result can sound merely forced and frantic; and unlike Wynton Kelly or Tommy Flanagan, he is not a first-choice accompanist. Nonetheless, he swings effectively when pushed by a drummer such as Philly Joe Jones on *Everybody Digs Bill Evans* (listen to 'Minority'); and many are the powerful swinging musicians whose music has a fraction of the interest of Evans's. In common with an unusual handful of great jazz musicians, Bill Evans was not a master of the blues. He rapidly learned to avoid straight-ahead blues settings, though his grasp of minor blues (eg John Carisi's wonderful 'Israel') was assured; partly because melodic minor harmony is the basis of the modern jazz sound that he helped to develop. Evans increasingly played his own compositions, which are unfailingly fine and inventive, often involving irreg-

ular phrase lengths and shifting metres, and many, incidentally, named after female friends ('Waltz For Debby', 'One for Helen', 'Show-Type Tune', 'Peri's Scope', 'Laurie', 'Turn Out The Stars', 'Blue In Green'). But his originality was equally apparent in his transformations of standard songs ('Beautiful Love', 'Polka Dots And Moonbeams', 'Someday My Prince Will Come', 'My Romance', 'My Foolish Heart'). His recorded legacy is extensive.

Selected albums: *New Jazz Conceptions* (Original Jazz Classics 1956), *Everybody Digs Bill Evans* (Original Jazz Classics 1958), *Portrait In Jazz* (Original Jazz Classics 1959), with Jim Hall *Undercurrent* (1959), *Explorations* (Original Jazz Classics 1961), *Sunday At The Village Vanguard* (Original Jazz Classics 1961), *Waltz For Debby* (Riverside 1961), *More From The Vanguard* (1961), *Empathy* (1962), *Moonbeams* (Original Jazz Classics 1962), *How My Heart Sings* (Original Jazz Classics 1962), with Freddie Hubbard *Interplay* (Original Jazz Classics 1962), *Conversations With Myself* (Verve 1963), *Undercurrent* (Blue Note 1963), *Trio* (1964), *The Bill Evans Trio Live* (1964), *At Shelly's Manne Hole* (Original Jazz Classics (1964), *Trio 65* (Verve 1965), *Bill Evans At Town Hall* (Verve 1966), with Hall *Intermodulation* (1966), *A Simple Matter Of Conviction* (1966), *Further Conversations With Myself* (Verve 1967), *California Here I Come* (1967), *Alone* (Verve 1968), *Bill Evans At The Montreux Jazz Festival* (Verve 1968), *Jazzhouse* (1969), *Montreux ii* (1970), *You're Gonna Hear From Me* (Milestone 1970), *The Bill Evans Album* (Columbia 1971), with George Russell *Living Time* (1972), *Live In Tokyo* (Original Jazz Classics 1972), *Yesterday I Heard The Rain* (Bandstand 1973), *Since We Met* (Original Jazz Classics 1974), *Re: Person I Knew* (Original Jazz Classics 1974), *Intuition* (1974), *Blue Is Green* (Milestone 1974), *Jazzhouse* (Milestone 1974), *Montreux iii* (Original Jazz Classics 1975), *The Tony Bennett/Bill Evans Album* (Original Jazz Classics 1975), with Tony Bennett *Together Again* (1976), *Alone (Again)* (Original Jazz Classics 1976), *Eloquence* (1976), with Harold Land *Quintessence* (Original Jazz Classics 1976), with Lee Konitz, Warne Marsh *Crosscurrents* (Original Jazz Classics 1977), *From The 70's* (1977), *You Must Believe In Spring* (1977), *New Conversations* (1978), with Toots Thielemans *Affinity* (1978), *I Will Say Goodbye* (Original Jazz Classics 1979), *We Will Meet Again* (1979), *The Complete Fantasy Recordings* (Fantasy 1980), *The Paris Concert: Edition One* (1983, rec 1979), *The Paris Concert: Edition Two* (1984, rec 1979), *Consecration* i and ii (Timeless 1990, rec 1980), *The Brilliant* (Timeless 1990, rec 1980), *Letter To Evan* (Dreyfus 1993).

Evans, Bill (saxophonist)

b. 9 February 1958, Clarendon Hills, nr Chicago, Illinois, USA. Jazz's third famous Bill Evans (the others being the splendid modern jazz pianist and the gifted reedsman who changed his name to Yusef Lateef) this Evans is the fusion tenor and soprano saxophonist. A student of Dave Liebman, it was on Liebman's recommendation that he joined the great trumpeter Miles Davis' jazz/rock band, and was thus catapulted into the spotlight. By 1983 he was recording as a leader, and when he left Davis' band a year later, he was quickly snapped up by guitarist John McLaughlin for his revived Mahavishnu Orchestra, and also began working with Herbie Hancock. A lyrical, gentler voice than is common in the action packed world of fusion, he has a soft tone, and a penchant for fast, precise tonguing in place of the more common headlong, legato style. His own recordings include *Moods Unlimited*, a fine trio session, with the veteran piano and bass team of pianist Hank Jones and bassist Red Mitchell; *The Alternative Man*, a star-studded Blue Note Records session that should appeal to fusion enthusiasts for the presence of guitarist John McLaughlin, keyboardist Mitch Forman, bassist Marcus Miller and drummers Al Foster and Danny Gottlieb; and the more recent *Push*, a funky, breakbeat-orientated session with contributions by Marcus Miller, keyboardist Bob James, pianist Bruce Hornsby and assorted rappers.

Albums: with Miles Davis *The Man With The Horn* (1981), *Moods Unlimited* (1982), with Davis *Star People* (1983), *Living In The Crest Of A Wave* (1983), with Davis *Decoy* (1984), with Mahavishnu Orchestra *Mahavishnu* (1984), *The Alternative Man* (1985), with Gil Evans *Farewell* (1986), with Gil Evans *Bud And Bird* (1986), with Tony Reedus *The Far Side* (1988), with Mark Egan *A Touch Of Light* (1988), with Niels Lan Doky *Friendship* (1989), with Danny Gottlieb *Whirlwind* (1989), *Summertime* (1989), *Let The Juice Loose* (1989), *The Gambler* (1990), with Christian Minh Doky *The Sequel* (1990), *Push* (1993).

Evans, Gil

b. Ian Ernest Gilmore Green, 13 May 1912, Toronto, Canada, d. 20 March 1988. Although self-taught, Evans became extraordinarily proficient as a pianist and composer, though his greatest talent lay in his abilities as an arranger. He formed his first band in 1933 in California, where he was raised. He wrote most of the arrangements, a duty he retained when the band was later fronted by popular singer Skinnay Ennis. Up to this point Evans's work had followed the orthodox line demanded of commercial dancebands, but his musical ambitions lay in other areas. A long stint as chief arranger for Claude Thornhill during the 40s gave him the opportunity he needed to explore different sounds and unusual textures. Thornhill's predilection for soft and slowly shifting pastel patterns as a background for his delicate piano proved to be an interesting workshop for Evans, who would always remark on this experience as being influential upon his later work. Towards the end of his stay with Thornhill, Evans was writing for very large ensembles, creating intense moody music. However, by this time, he was eager to try something new, feeling that the music he was required to write for the band was becoming too static and sombre. During this same period, Gerry Mulligan was a member of the Thornhill band and was also writing arrangements. Both he and Evans had become fascinated by the developments of the radical new beboppers such as Charlie Parker and Miles Davis, and in 1948 the two men embarked upon a series of arrangements for Davis's nine-piece band. These records, subsequently released under the generic title *Birth Of The Cool*,

proved very influential in the 50s. Despite the quality of the material Evans was creating at this point in his career, he did not meet with much commercial or critical success. Towards the end of the 50s Evans again worked with Davis, helping to create landmark albums such as *Miles Ahead* and *Sketches Of Spain*. His writing for Davis was a highly effective amalgam of the concepts developed during his Thornhill period and the needs of the increasingly restrained trumpet style Davis was adopting. Evans's use in these and later arrangements for his own band of such instruments as tubas and bass trombones broadened the range of orchestral colours at his disposal and helped him to create a highly distinctive sound and style. As with many other gifted arrangers and composers, Evans's real need was for a permanent band for the expression of his ideas, but this proved difficult to achieve. Such groups as he did form were in existence for only short periods, although some, fortunately, made records of his seminal works. He continued to write, composing many extended works, often uncertain if they would ever be performed. However, in the early 70s he was able to form a band which played regularly and the music showed his ready absorption of ideas and devices from the current pop music scene.

After a number of international tours during the 70s, his work became more widely known and his stature rose accordingly. So too did his popularity when it became apparent to audiences that his was not esoteric music but was readily accessible and showed a marked respect for the great traditions of earlier jazz. By the late 70s, the music Evans was writing had developed a harder edge than hitherto; he was making extensive use of electronics and once again was happily absorbing aspects of pop. In particular, he arranged and recorded several Jimi Hendrix compositions. His creativity showed no signs of diminishing as the 80s dawned and he continued a punishing round of concert tours, record dates, radio and television appearances, all the while writing more new material for his band. One of his final commissions was with Sting, arranging a fine version of Hendrix's 'Little Wing'.

One of the outstanding arrangers and composers in jazz, Evans was particularly adept at creating complex scores which held at their core a simple and readily understandable concept. Throughout his career, his writing showed his profound respect for the needs of jazz musicians to make their own musical statements within an otherwise formally conceived and structured work. Perhaps this is why so many notable musicians - including Steve Lacy, Elvin Jones, Lew Soloff, George Adams, Ron Carter and David Sanborn - were happy to play in his bands over the years. As a result Evans's work, even at its most sophisticated, maintained an enviable feeling of freedom and spontaneity which few other arrangers of his calibre were able to achieve.

Selected albums: with Miles Davis *Birth Of The Cool* (1948-50), with Davis *Miles Ahead* (1957), *New Bottles Old Wine* (Pacific Jazz 1958), *Gil Evans And Ten* (Prestige 1957), with Davis *Porgy And Bess* (1959), *Great Jazz Standards* (Pacific Jazz 1959), with Davis *Sketches Of Spain* (1960), *Out Of The Cool* (Impulse 1960), *Into The Hot* (Impulse 1961), with Davis

Quiet Nights (1962), *The Individualism Of Gil Evans* (Verve 1964), *Blues In Orbit* (Enja 1971), *Where Flamingos Fly* (1972), *Svengali* (1973), *The Gil Evans Orchestra Plays The Music Of Jimi Hendrix* (1974), *Montreux Jazz Festival '74* (1974), *There Comes A Time* (RCA 1975), *Synthetic Evans* (1976), *Live 76* (Zeta 1976), *Priestess* (Antilles 1977), *Tokyo Concert* (West Wind 1977), *Gil Evans At The Royal Festival Hall* (1978), *The Rest Of Gil Evans At The Royal Festival Hall* (1978), *Little Wing* (1978), *Parabola* (1978), *Live At New York Public Theatre Vol 1* and *2* (Blackhawk 1980), *Lunar Eclypse* (New Tone 1981), *The British Orchestra* (1983), *Live At Sweet Basil Vols 1* and *2* (Electric Bird 1984), *Farewell* (Electric Bird 1987), *Sting And Bill Evans/ Last Session* (Jazz Door 1988). Compilation: *The Thornhill Sound* (1947).

Evans, Herschel

b. 1909, Denton, Texas, USA, d. 9 February 1939. Tenor saxophonist Evans's early career was centred in the southwest where he worked with many of the best territory bands of the 20s and early 30s. Among the bands in which he advanced his considerable skills were those of Edgar Battle, Terrence Holder and Troy Floyd. In 1933 he joined Bennie Moten's outstanding Kansas City-based band, remaining there until 1935. He also worked with Oran 'Hot Lips' Page before deciding on stretching his geographic boundaries. After playing briefly in Chicago he wound up in Los Angeles where he became involved in the bustling Central Avenue club scene, working with the bands of Charlie Echols, Lionel Hampton and Buck Clayton. In 1936 he joined Count Basie where his robust, Coleman Hawkins-influenced style of playing formed a dramatic contrast with the light acerbic sound of his section-mate, Lester Young. Evans's career ended abruptly when he became seriously ill towards the end of 1938 while still playing with the Basie band.
Compilations: with Count Basie *Swingin' The Blues* (1937-39), with Lionel Hampton *Historical Recording Sessions* (1938).

Ewart, Douglas

b. 13 September 1946, Kingston, Jamaica. Ewart moved to Chicago in 1963 and later studied music at the AACM. His early influences included Charles Mingus, Clifford Brown and Eric Dolphy, the latter's example persuading Ewart to learn bassoon and bass clarinet in addition to alto and other saxophones and flute. He has played with many of his AACM colleagues, recording with (for example) Roscoe Mitchell (*Sketches From Bamboo*), Muhal Richard Abrams (*Lifea Blinec*), Anthony Braxton (*For Trio*), Leo Smith (*Budding Of A Rose*) and Henry Threadgill, in the X-75 group. In particular, Ewart formed an association with trombonist George Lewis in 1971 that has continued through to the present: he plays on several of Lewis's projects (*Chicago Slow Dance, Shadowgraph, Homage To Charles Parker*) and has recorded a duo album with him. Leader of a clarinet quartet (Red Hills), Ewart is also an accomplished instrument-maker, particularly renowned for his beautifully-crafted Ewart flutes.
Albums: *George Lewis - Douglas Ewart* (1979), *Red Hills* (1981).

Ewell, Don

b. 14 November 1916, Baltimore, Maryland, USA, d. 9 August 1983. Although classically trained on piano, Ewell was drawn to jazz and in particular to the music of the early jazz masters of New Orleans. This was despite the fact that by the mid-30s, which was when his career got under way, such forms were suffering a decline in popularity under the commercial pressures of the swing era. Undeterred, Ewell followed his bent, working with Bunk Johnson in the mid-40s and later in the decade with Muggsy Spanier and Sidney Bechet. Stylistically, he was influenced by pianists as different as Jelly Roll Morton, Fats Waller and Jimmy Yancey. In the mid-50s Ewell began a particularly rewarding association with Jack Teagarden, which lasted until the trombonist's death in 1964. Thereafter, Ewell toured extensively, sometimes in bands, sometimes in harness with Willie 'The Lion' Smith, but mostly as a soloist, until his death in 1983. Although capable of playing rousing barrelhouse style, he was also able to produce exceptionally fine and intricate playing.
Albums: *Don Ewell Plays King Oliver Creole Band Tunes* (1952), *Music To Listen To Don Ewell By* (1956), *Chicago '57* (1957), with Willie 'The Lion' Smith *Grand Piano* (1967), *Jazz On A Sunday Afternoon* (1969), *Live At The 100 Club* (Solo Arts 1971), *Take It In Stride* (1974), *Don Ewell In Japan* (Jazzology 1975), *Don Ewell Quintet* (Jazzology 1986), *In New Orleans* (GHB 1986), *Piano Solos (Eighty Eighty Upright* 1988), *Yellow Dog Blues* (Jazzology 1988), *Don Ewell And His All Stars* (Jazzology 1988), *Don Ewell's Hot Four* (Center 1992).

Faddis, Jon

b. 24 July 1953, Oakland, California, USA. Faddis began playing trumpet while still a small child and at the age of 11 was introduced by his trumpet teacher, Bill Catalano, to the music of Dizzy Gillespie. At 13 years old Faddis was playing with R&B bands and in mainstream rehearsal big bands and two years later he met Gillespie, sitting in with him at a San Francisco workshop. In 1971 Faddis joined Lionel Hampton, then moved into the Thad Jones-Mel Lewis Jazz Orchestra. He was with this band on and off for the next few years, between times playing with Gil Evans, Oscar Peterson, Charles Mingus and Gillespie. It was while he was with Gillespie that Faddis first attracted widespread attention. Although he had set out deliberately to build his own playing ability through adherence to Gillespie's style, Faddis had succeeded in creating a style of his own. Nevertheless, he was deeply rooted in bebop and helped give the older man a boost at a time when he was under pressure to adapt to the current popularity of jazz-rock. The concerts and recording dates of the two trumpeters were hugely successful, both musically and commercially, and established a working pattern for Faddis for the next few years. In the early 80s Faddis was heavily committed with studio work but found time for recording sessions and tours with Jimmy Smith, Jackie McLean and McCoy Tyner. In the late 80s he joined Gillespie in a big band for a world tour but was mostly active as leader of his own bands. One of the most striking of post-bop trumpeters, Faddis blends a dazzling technique with a thorough understanding of jazz tradition. His clear, bell-like tone, is well-suited to his richly emotional playing and he has earned his place as one of the most gifted and important musicians in jazz. Albums: *Oscar Peterson And Jon Faddis* (1975), *Youngblood* (1976), with Dizzy Gillespie *Dizzy Gillespie Jam, Montreux '77* (1977), *Good And Plenty* (Dunhill 1978), *Young Blood* (Pablo 1982), *Legacy* (Concord 1985), with Clark Terry *Take Double* (1986), with Billy Harper *Jon And Billy* (Blackhawk 1987),

Fagerquist, Don

b. 6 February 1927, Worcester, Massachusetts, USA, d. 24 January 1974. After working with the Mal Hallett band in the early 40s, Fagerquist joined Gene Krupa in 1944. He stayed with Krupa for several years, comfortably adjusting his trumpet playing to the boppish style the band adopted towards the end of the decade. After Krupa's band folded Fagerquist spent a little time with Artie Shaw before becoming a member of Woody Herman's Third Herd. He later worked with Les Brown and the Dave Pell Octet, the Brown band's small-group offshoot. A striking soloist, Fagerquist's thoughtful playing style admirably suited the west coast scene and in the 50s he played extensively and sometimes recorded with Shelly Manne, Pete Rugolo, Art Pepper and others, including the popular big band assembled for record dates by Si Zentner in the mid-60s. Albums: with Gene Krupa *Drummin' Man* (1945-47), with Dave Pell *The Irving Berlin Gallery* (1953) one side only *The Don Fagerquist Nonet* (1955), *Art Pepper Plays Shorty Rogers And Others* (1957), *8 By 8* (1957), with Si Zentner *My Cup Of Tea* (1964).

Fairweather, Al

b. Alastair Fairweather, 12 June 1927, Edinburgh, Scotland, d. 21 June 1993. After a brief flirtation with the trombone, Fairweather settled on the trumpet and while still at school began playing jazz. Amongst his companions at Edinburgh Royal High School were pianist Stan Greig and clarinettist Sandy Brown, both of whom were to be important collaborators in later years. In 1953 Fairweather moved to London where he joined Cy Laurie's band and in 1954 when Brown also came to London they resumed their musical partnership. Over the next few years the Brown-Fairweather band gained in quality and strength and some of their recordings, especially *McJazz*, were widely regarded at the time to be the best to have come from a British band. Leadership of the band was at first nominally with Brown but as his non-musical interests developed Fairweather took charge. Later Brown returned, but in the mid-60s Fairweather joined Acker Bilk and in the mid-70s he began a long association with Greig's London Jazz Big Band. In 1983 he suffered a severe heart attack, thereafter played a little and also painted, eventually retiring to Edinburgh in 1987. Although his early playing recognised his admiration for Louis Armstrong, Fairweather's subtle, fluid and understated style suggested to the less discerning listener that he was the junior in his partnerships with the more forthright Brown. In fact, Fairweather's playing was deliberately couched as a perfect foil for his exuberant partner. His arrangements for their band, and for Greig's big band, reveal his deep understanding of the diverse forms of jazz. As Greig remarked, 'People didn't understand how good he was'.
Albums: with Sandy Brown unless stated *B+B+B* (1953), *Sandy's Sidemen* (1956), *McJazz* (1957), *Fairweather Friends* (1957), *Al And Sandy* (1959), *Al's Pals* (1959), *Doctor McJazz* (1960), *The Incredible McJazz* (60s), *McJazz Lives On!* (60s).

Fairweather, Digby

b. 25 April 1946, Rochford, Essex, England. Fairweather first played trumpet semi-professionally in and around his home town. In 1971 he formed his own small band, later playing with numerous leaders, including Eggy Ley, Dave Shepherd and Alex Welsh. His reputation established, at the beginning of 1977 Fairweather took the plunge and became a full-time musician. Subsequently, he led his own bands and played in the Midnite Follies Orchestra. He also worked in small bands including Velvet, a co-operative band with Len Skeat, Ike Isaacs and Denny Wright, a trumpet-piano duo with Stan Barker, with whom Fairweather was also involved in educational work, the Pizza Express All Stars and Brian Priestley's septet. An excellent mainstream trumpeter with a full, rich tone, Fairweather's graceful playing style is particularly well-suited to ballads. In addition to his playing, Fairweather has also turned to writing and broadcasting; his published works include some jazz-inspired short stories, a trumpet tutor, and, with Priestley and Ian Carr, a biographical directory *Jazz: The Essential Companion*.
Albums: *Dig & De Swarte* (1977), *Havin' Fun* (Black Lion 1978), *Going Out Steppin'* (Black Lion 1979), *Velvet* (Black Lion 1979), *Songs For Sandy* (Hep Jazz 1983), with Stan Barker *Let's Duet* (1984). Compilation: *A Portrait Of Digby Fairweather* (Black Lion 1994, rec 1979, 1984).

Fallon, Jack

b. 13 October 1915, London, Canada. Fallon went to Britain with the Canadian Airforce and settled there in 1946. He established a professional career playing bass in the bands of Ted Heath and Jack Jackson and played with George Shearing in 1948 with whom he accompanied Duke Ellington. Fallon became the staff bassist for Lansdowne Records where he recorded with a wide variety of musicians - from Josh White (vocal/guitar) through Alex Welsh and Humphrey Lyttelton to Joe Harriott. In the mid-50s he had a successful sextet called In Town Tonight. It was during this period that he started his

Cana Agency which later represented Kenny Ball. Fallon played regularly with light orchestral bandleaders like Frank Chacksfield and Ron Goodwin, worked as a violinist with country musicians and even recorded with the Beatles in 1968. Since then he has concentrated on his agency but he did play with Lennie Felix (piano) in the 70s and later with Stan Greig (piano) and Digby Fairweather.

Album: *The In Town Jazz Group* (1955).

Farlow, Tal

b. Talmage Holt Farlow, 7 June 1921, Greensboro, North Carolina, USA. Farlow did not begin playing guitar until 1942 but before the decade was out he had achieved a sufficiently high standard to be hired by cabaret singer Dardanelle, vibraphonist Marjorie Hyams and clarinettist Buddy De Franco. In 1950, by now a fleet and inventive guitarist, he joined forces with another vibes player, Red Norvo, thus beginning a long-running and fruitful, if intermittent, musical partnership. The third member of this group was Charles Mingus. Also in the 50s Farlow led his own trio, but he later drifted into retirement from music and concentrated on his career as a sign-painter. In the late 60s he made a handful of festival appearances, returning to fairly consistent public performances in the late 70s. In the 80s he resumed his working relationship with Red Norvo, touring the USA, UK and Europe and delighting audiences, many of whom had been alerted to this fine musician's talents through a 1981 television documentary, *Talmage Farlow*.

Albums: *Early Tal* (1953), *Tal Farlow Quartet* (1953), *The Tal Farlow Album* (1954), *Autumn In New York* (1954), *The Artistry Of Tal Farlow* (1954), *The Interpretations Of Tal Farlow* (1955), *A Recital By Tal Farlow* (1955), with Red Norvo *The Guitar Player* (1955), *Tal* (1956), *The Swinging Guitar Of Tal Farlow* (1956), *First Set* (Xanadu 1956), *Second Set* (Xanadu 1956), *This Is Tal Farlow* (1958), *The Guitar Artistry Of Tal Farlow* (1959), *The Return Of Tal Farlow* (Original Jazz Classics 1969), *On Stage* (1976), *A Sign Of The Times* (Concord 1976), *Trilogy* (1976), *Tal Farlow 78* (1978), *Chromatic Palette* (Concord 1981), *Cookin' On All Burners* (Concord 1982), *The Legendary Tal Farlow* (Concord 1984), *Standard Recital* (FD Music 1992).

Farmer, Art

b. 21 August 1928, Council Bluffs, Iowa, USA. Farmer began playing early in life, as did his twin brother, bassist Addison Farmer. By the mid-40s Farmer, then playing trumpet, was working in California. He worked in bands led by Jay McShann, Gerald Wilson, Benny Carter and others and in 1952 joined Lionel Hampton, with whom Farmer toured Europe in 1953, attracting considerable attention even in a remarkably star-studded band that included Clifford Brown, Gigi Gryce, Jimmy Cleveland and Quincy Jones. In the mid-to-late 50s, Farmer settled in New York, worked and recorded with artists including Gryce, Jones, Horace Silver, Gerry Mulligan and George Russell, was co-leader, with Benny Golson, of the acclaimed Jazztet and later led a quartet with Jim Hall. In the 60s Farmer began touring extensively as a sin-

gle, playing clubs and festivals around the world, an activity that continued into the 70s. In 1976 he recorded with Art Pepper (*On The Road*). In the 80s he formed an occasional partnership with Clifford Jordan including recording dates such as *Mirage, You Make Me Smile* and the highly-acclaimed *Blame It On My Youth*, and was also reunited with Golson on several albums. In Europe, where he was resident for several years, his lyrical playing became especially popular with audiences. Having changed almost exclusively to flugelhorn in the 60s, Farmer's sound and style proved particularly well-suited to ballads, to which he brings a warm, sometimes plaintive, feel and an ability to reshape the melody with seemingly endless inventiveness.

Albums: with Clifford Brown, Quincy Jones *'Scuse These Bloos* (1953), *The Art Farmer Quintet* (Original Jazz Classics 1954), *Art Farmer Septet* (Original Jazz Classics 1954), *Early Art* (1954), *When Farmer Met Gryce* (Original Jazz Classics 1955), *Evening In Casablanca* (1955), *Farmer's Market* (Original Jazz Classics 1956), with Donald Byrd *Two Trumpets* (Original Jazz Classics 1957), *Portrait Of Art Farmer* (1958), *Modern Art* (Blue Note 1958), *Brass Shout* (1959), *The Aztec Suite* (1959), *Nature Boy* (1960), *Meet The Jazztet* (1960), *Big City Sounds* (1960), *Art* (1960), *The Jazztet & John Lewis* (1961), *The Jazztet At Birdhouse* (1961), *Perception* (1961), *Here And Now* (1962), *Listen To Art Farmer* (1962), *Interaction* (1963), *Live At The Half Note* (Atlantic 1963), *To Sweden With Love* (1964), *The Many Faces Of Art Farmer* (1964), *Sing Me Softly Of The Blues* (1965), *Baroque Sketches* (1966), *The Time And The Place* (1967), *Art Farmer Quintet Plays Great Jazz Hits* (1967), *Art Worker* (1968), *Art Farmer & Phil Woods* (1968), *From Vienna With Art* (1970), *Homecoming* (1971), *Gentle Eyes* (1974), *A Sleeping Bee* (Sonet 1974), *Talk To Me* (1974), *To Duke With Love* (1975), *Yesterday's Thoughts* (1975), *The Summer Knows* (1976), *At Boomers* (1976), *On The Road* (1976), *Crawl Space* (1977), *Art Farmer Live In Tokyo/Art Farmer Meets Jackie McLean* (1977), *Something You Got* (1977), *Big Blues* (1978), *Something Tasty* (1979), *Yama* (1979), *Isis* (1980), *A Work Of Art* (1981), *Manhattan* (Soul Note 1981), *Warm Valley* (Concord 1982), *Mirage* (Soul Note 1982), *Maiden Voyage* (Denon 1983), *Ambrosia* (1983), *You Make Me Smile* (Soul Note 1984), *In Concert* (Enja 1984 *The Jazztet: Moment To Moment* (Soul Note 1984), *Real Time* (Contemporary 1986), *Azure* (Soul Note 1988), *Something To Live For* (Contemporary 1988), *Blame It On My Youth* (1988), *Ph, D* (Contemporary 1990), *Central Avenue Reunion* (Contemporary 1990), *Soul Eyes* (Enja 1993).

Farrell, Joe

b. Joseph Carl Firrantello, 16 December 1937, Chicago Heights, Illinois, USA, d. 10 January 1986. After studying several reed instruments, Farrell concentrated on tenor saxophone from the mid-50s. At the end of the decade he joined Maynard Ferguson in New York, also playing and recording with Slide Hampton, George Russell, Charles Mingus and Jaki Byard. In the mid-60s he became a long-serving member of the Thad Jones-Mel Lewis Jazz Orchestra and also worked with Elvin

Jones. Having been likened to major and various tenor stylists, such as Stan Getz, Sonny Rollins and John Coltrane, it is not surprising that Farrell's musical tastes drew him into many varied byways of jazz. He played on the Bands *Rock Of Ages*, was a member of Chick Corea's Return To Forever (Corea also played on several of Farrell's own albums). Later he was associated with Woody Shaw, Paul Horn, George Benson and JoAnne Brackeen. While still concentrating on his main instrument, Farrell also played effectively on soprano saxophone and flute. He died of bone cancer in January 1986.

Albums: *Joe Farrell Quartet* (1970), *Moon Germs* (1972), *Penny Arcade* (1973), with Chick Corea *Return To Forever* (1973), *Benson And Farrell* (1976), *Skateboard Park* (1979), *Sonic Text* (Original Jazz Classics 1979), *Joe Farrell And Paul Horn* (c.1980), *Vim 'n' Vigour* (Timeless 1984).

Fatool, Nick

b. 2 January 1915, Milbury, Massachusetts, USA. After starting out with the fine 30s dance band of Joe Haymes, drummer Fatool swung through a succession of top-flight big bands, notably those of Benny Goodman (appearing on the excellent Sextet sides of the late 30s and early 40s), and Artie Shaw, being unusually prominent on the original recording of 'Concerto For Clarinet'. In the early 40s Fatool settled in California, where for the next two decades he worked in the film studios but found time to play his drums in numerous bands, including those led by Les Brown, Billy Butterfield and Harry James. He also played and sometimes recorded with Bob Crosby, Louis Armstrong, Tommy Dorsey and many others, gradually moving into the field of latter-day dixieland jazz to which he brought a deftly-swinging lightness that few of his contemporaries could match. Apart from Crosby the dixieland-style bands with whom he has played include those of Charles LaVere, Matty Matlock, Pete Fountain, the Dukes Of Dixieland, Barney Bigard and the World's Greatest Jazz Band. His career continued into the 80s, with tours of the USA and Europe with the Yank Lawson-Bob Haggart band. One of the unsung heroes of jazz drumming, Fatool's self-effacing style meant that he was often overlooked by audiences accustomed to the somewhat more bombastic playing of many of his contemporaries. Conversely, his subtlety and skill were always appreciated by musicians.

Album: with Barney Bigard *Clarinet Gumbo* (1973). Compilations: with Benny Goodman *Solo Flight* (1939-40 recordings), *The Indispensable Artie Shaw Vols 3/4* (1940-42 recordings), with Shaw *The Complete Gramercy Five Sessions* (1940-44 recordings), *LaVere's Chicago Loopers* (1944-50 recordings), *Spring Of '87* (Jazzology 1989).

Favors, Malachi

b. 27 August 1937, Lexington, Mississippi, USA. Favors came from a religious family (his father preached as a pastor) who disapproved of secular music. He took up the bass at the age of 15, initially inspired by Wilbur Ware. He started playing professionally when he left school, accompanying Freddie Hubbard and Dizzy Gillespie. Moving to Chicago, he record-

ed with Andrew Hill in 1955 and in 1961 he played with Muhal Richard Abrams in the Experimental Band, becoming a member of the AACM at its inception in 1965. He played in groups led by Roscoe Mitchell and Lester Bowie and in 1969 joined with them and Joseph Jarman to found the Art Ensemble Of Chicago, who triumphantly carried the banner of 'Great Black Music: Ancient to the Future' into the 90s. Outside of the Art Ensemble, he has recorded on Mitchell's and Bowie's own albums, as well as with fellow AACM member Kalaparusha Maurice McIntyre, drummer Sunny Murray and gospel group From The Root To The Source. *Sightsong*, an album of duos with Abrams, was released in 1976 and two years later the solo *Natural And The Spiritual* appeared on the Art Ensemble's own AECO label. Favors, who has taken to appending Maghostut (in various spellings) to his name, typifies the AACM's interest in mysticism and once gave his biography as 'into being in this universe some 43,000 years ago. Moved around and then was ordered to this Planet Earth by the higher forces, Allah De Lawd Thank You Jesus Good God A Mighty, through the precious channels of Brother Isaac and Sister Maggie Mayfield Favors; of ten. Landed in Chicago by way of Lexington, Mississippi, for the purpose of serving my duty as a Music Messenger.' Perhaps more plausibly he has also claimed that his decision to play freely is a statement that has cost him financial rewards. As well as being a foremost exponent of free jazz upright playing, Favors is also adept at the electric bass, the African *balafon*, the zither and banjo.

Albums: with Muhal Richard Abrams *Sightsong* (1976), *Natural And The Spiritual* (1978).

Favre, Pierre

b. 2 June 1937, Le Locle, nr. Neuchatel, Switzerland. The self-taught Favre spent his formative years drumming with Philly Joe Jones, Bud Powell and Benny Bailey as well as working in a cymbal factory before developing his own style in one of the key 60s free jazz trios with Irène Schweizer on piano and, initially, George Mraz on bass. The latter was replaced by Peter Kowald who came over from Germany. The addition of Evan Parker on saxophones took the group in further new directions. Favre appeared with the other three on *European Echoes* by Manfred Schoof, but tended afterwards to avoid the more explosive areas of European new jazz. Favre's search for new voices led to his involvement with Indian and other percussionists, with the singer Tamia, and with the formation of his Drum Orchestra. A variety of bells, gongs and cymbals contribute to his percussive armoury, which has been heard to great effect in recent years on the ECM label. Favre also played with musicians such as Peter Brötzmann, John Tchicai, Don Cherry and Eje Thelin. A lasting collaboration with the French reed-player Michel Portal began in 1972. With his emphasis on the development of the sound aspects, Favre is an important innovator on his instrument.

Albums: *Santana* (1968), *Pierre Favre Quartet* (1969), with Manfred Schoof *European Echoes* (1969), Michel Portal *à Chateauvallon* (1972), with Gunter Hampel, Joachim Kuhn, Albert Mangelsdorff *Solo Now* (1976), with John Surman, Mal

Waldron *Mal Waldron Plays The Blues* (1976), *Drum Converstaion* (Calligraph 1979), *Arrivederci/Le Chouartse* (1981), with Joe McPhee *Topology* (1981), with Barre Phillips *Music By...* (1981), with Tamia *De La Nuit... Le Jour* (ECM 1982), *Such Winters Of Memory* (1983), *Singing Drums* (ECM 1984).

Fawkes, Wally

b. 21 June 1924, Vancouver, British Columbia, Canada. Fawkes moved to the UK while still very young and in the mid-40s was recruited by George Webb, leader of one of the first bands to attract popular attention during the trad-jazz boom. In 1947 he left Webb along with fellow sideman Humphrey Lyttelton to become a founder-member of the latter's new band. This musical relationship lasted until 1956 and was rewarding for musicians and fans alike. After leaving Lyttelton, Fawkes played with several other leaders, including Bruce Turner and Sandy Brown with whom he recorded in 1954 and 1956 respectively (both sessions being reissued on a single 1989 album) and he also led his own semi-professional band, the Troglodytes, a more loosely-swinging band than many of his contemporaries in the sometimes staid UK trad scene. Later, Fawkes, a gifted, Sidney Bechet-influenced clarinettist whose musical abilities have made him a major name on the trad circuit, chose to play freelance, usually showing a marked preference for out-of-the-way pubs in the London area. For several decades Fawkes, using the byline 'Trog', drew the strip-cartoon 'Flook' in the *Daily Mail*, the script for which was written by singer George Melly. Fawkes continued his occasional jazz career into the 80s with several excellent records, including reunions with Lyttelton and Ian Christie, another sparring partner from the hey-days of British trad jazz.
Albums: with Bruce Turner, Sandy Brown *Juicy And Full Toned* (Lake 1989, 1954-56 recordings), *Wally Fawkes And The Neo-Troglodytes* (c.1978), with Humphrey Lyttelton *It Seems Like Yesterday* (1984), with Ian Christie *That's The Blues Old Man* (1984), *Wally Fawkes And The Rhythm Kings* (Stomp Off 1985), *Whatever Next!* (Stomp Off 1986), *October Song* (Calligraph 1986), *Fidgety Feet* (Stomp Off 1993). Compilation: with Lyttelton *A Tribute To Humph, Vol. 1* (1949-50).

Fazola, Irving

b. Irving H. Prestopnik, 10 December 1910, New Orleans, Louisiana, USA, d. 29 March 1949. In his teens and early 20s Fazola played clarinet with several noted New Orleans-based bandleaders, including Louis Prima and Joseph 'Sharkey' Bonano. Although he played frequently with dixieland-style bands, Fazola's classical training made him eligible for many of the more chart-bound big bands of the swing era. In the 30s his pugilistic nature took him on a headlong dash through numerous jobs, including work with Ben Pollack, Glenn Miller, Jimmy McPartland, Claude Thornhill, Muggsy Spanier and the band with which he attracted most attention, Bob Crosby's. His fiery, ill-tempered nature led him into several violent fights and he was also a heavy drinker and a womanizer. Despite his erratic private life, Fazola was a distinguished and polished performer and with a different nature might well have made the big time as a featured artist. But then, had his nature been different he might well have been a lesser musician. His wild lifestyle finally took its toll and he died still some way short of his 40th birthday.
Album: with Bob Crosby *South Rampart Street Parade* (1938-39 recordings).

Feather, Leonard

b. 13 September 1914, London, England, d. 22 September 1994, Los Angeles, California, USA. After studying piano, Feather advanced his musical interests by teaching himself arranging and in the early 30s produced a number of record sessions, contributing charts and scores. Among the musicians for whom he worked in such capacities was Benny Carter and he was instrumental in persuading Henry Hall to hire Carter for the BBC Dance Orchestra. In the mid-30s Feather went to the USA and during the next decade he continued to work in record production sometimes supplying original material for artists such as Louis Armstrong, Lionel Hampton ('Blowtop Blues') and Dinah Washington ('Evil Gal Blues'). Feather also branched into concert promotion and produced numerous recording sessions. Additionally, he continued to compose songs for such as Sarah Vaughan, Ella Fitzgerald, Cannonball Adderley and Sonny Stitt. Despite all these endeavours, most of his considerable efforts in the cause of jazz were gradually concentrated into writing on the subject for several magazines, including *Esquire* and *Downbeat*, and he also wrote a jazz column for the *Los Angeles Times*. He was the author of several jazz books; notably *Encyclopedia Of Jazz*, *The Jazz Years* and his autobiography, *Ear Witness To An Era*. He was also a frequent broadcaster on jazz on radio and television. His daughter, Lorraine, is an accomplished singer.
Albums: all as producer *Leonard Feather's Swinging Swedes* (1951-54), *Swingin On The Vibories* (1956), *Seven Ages Of Jazz* (1958), *Swedish Punch* (1959), *Leonard Feather's Encyclopedia Of Jazz All Stars* (1967), *Leonard Feather Presents* (VSOP 1988), *Night Blooming* (Mainstream 1991).
Further reading: *The Jazz Years: Ear Witness To A Jazz Era*, Leonard Feather. *The Encyclopedia Of Jazz* (various editions), Leonard Feather.

Feldman, Victor

b. 7 April 1934, London, England, d. 12 May 1987. A remarkable child prodigy, Feldman was encouraged into his professional career by his uncle, drummer Max Bacon, and was playing drums in a family trio at the age of seven, alongside his brothers Robert and Monty. When he was 10 years old he was featured at a concert with Glenn Miller's AAAF band and in his teens he worked with the bands of Ralph Sharon, Roy Fox and Ronnie Scott and like-minded spirits such as John Dankworth, Stan Tracey, Tubby Hayes and Tony Crombie. Feldman also played piano and, at the urging of Carlo Krahmer of Esquire Records, soon added the vibraphone to his armoury of instruments, gradually dropping drumming except for special features. By the mid-50s, when he emigrated to the USA, he was regarded primarily as a vibraphonist, nevertheless, he continued to play piano displaying an especially original and delicate touch. Feldman's first transatlantic job was with Woody Herman and he later became associated with the west coast scene, recording with Shelly Manne. In the late 50s Feldman extended his versatility by studying arranging with Marty Paich. In the 60s he played with diverse jazzmen such as Benny Goodman, with whom he toured Russia in 1962, and Miles Davis, for whom he wrote 'Seven Steps To Heaven'. Before hiring Feldman, Cannonball Adderley took the precaution of playing some of his records to his existing sidemen; only after they had acknowledged that here was an outstanding musical personality they would be happy to work with, did he tell them that their new companion was British, Jewish and white. Always open to new concepts, Feldman ventured into jazz-rock fusion in the 70s and 80s, working with Steely Dan and Tom Scott among many others. He continued to play in the mainstream of jazz, however, and in the 80s recorded with Spike Robinson, with whom he had played in London three decades earlier. He died suddenly, following an asthma attack.

Selected albums: *Victor Feldman With Kenny Graham's Afro-Cubists* (1955), *Vic Feldman's Modern Jazz Quartet* (1955), *Vic Feldman Big Band* (1955), *Victor Feldman In London* (1956), *Suite Sixteen* (Original Jazz Classics 1956), *With Mallets a Fore Thought* (1957), *The Arrival Of Victor Feldman* (1958), *Latinville* (1959), *Shelly Manne And His Men At The Blackhawk* (1959), *Merry Olde Soul* (1960-61), *Stop The World I Want To Get Off* (1962), *Soviet Jazz Themes* (1962), *Love Me With Your Heart* (1964), *It's A Wonderful World* (1964), *Everything In Sight* (1966-67), *The Venezuela Joropo* (1967), *Your Smile* (1973), *Artful Dodger* (Concord 1977), *Rockavibabe* (DJM 1977), *In My Pocket* (1977), *Secret Of The Andes* (Palo Alto 1982), *Transatlantic Alliance* (Jasmine 1983), *In London* (Jasmine 1983), *To Chopin With Love* (1983), *High Visibility* (1985), *To Chopin With Love* (Palo Alto 1984). Compilation: *The Young Vic Vol. 1* (Esquire 1987, 1948-54 recordings).

Ferguson, Maynard

b. 4 May 1928, Montreal, Quebec, Canada. Already a bandleader in his native land by his early teenage years, trumpeter Ferguson played in the bands of Boyd Raeburn, Jimmy Dorsey and Charlie Barnet in the 40s. His breakthrough into public consciousness came in 1950 when he joined Stan Kenton, electrifying audiences with his high-note playing. Unlike many other high-note trumpeters, Ferguson proved that it was possible to actually play music up there rather than simply make noises. However, it is possible that not all his fans appreciated the skills he was demonstrating. After leaving Kenton in 1953 Ferguson worked at Paramount studios in Los Angeles before turning to bandleading, sometimes with a big band, at other times with a small group. Skilful use of arrangements often allowed the Ferguson bands to create an impression of size; the 12-piece band he led at the 1958 Newport Jazz Festival had all the power and impact of many groups twice its size. Among the many fine musicians who worked with Ferguson in the 50s and

60s were Slide Hampton, Don Sebesky, Bill Chase, Don Ellis and Bill Berry. In the late 60s Ferguson moved to the UK, where he formed a big band with which he toured extensively. In the USA again during the 70s, he moved into jazz-rock and reached a new audience who found the music and the flamboyance with which it was presented extremely attractive. Ferguson also plays several other brass instruments with considerable skill, but it is as a trumpeter that he has made his greatest impact. His technical expertise on the instrument has made him a model for many of the up-and-coming young musicians.

Albums: with Stan Kenton *Sketches On Standards* (1953-55), *Dimensions* (1954), *Maynard Ferguson Octet* (1955), *Around The Horn With Maynard Ferguson* (1955), *Maynard Ferguson Conducts The Birdland Dream Band* (Bluebird 1956), *Boy With A Lot Of Brass* (1957), *A Message From Newport* (Roulette 1958), *Swingin' My Way Through College* (Fresh Sounds 1958), *A Message From Birdland* (1959), *Maynard Ferguson Plays Jazz For Dancing* (1959), *Newport Suite* (1960), *Let's Face The Music And Dance* (1960), *Maynard '61* (Roulette 1960-61), *Maynard Ferguson And Chris Connor* (1961), *Straightaway Jazz Themes* (Fresh Sounds 1961), *Maynard '62* (Fresh Sounds 1962), *Si! Si! M. F.* (Roulette 1962), *Maynard '63* (1963), *Message from Maynard* (1963), *Maynard '64* (1964), *The New Sound Of Maynard Ferguson* (1964), *Come, Blow Your Horn* (1964), *Color Him Wild* (1964), *The Blues Roar* (Mobile Fidelity 1964), *Six By Six* (1965), *Ridin' High* (c.1966), one side only *Hooray For The Maynard Ferguson Sextet* (1966), *Maynard Ferguson Live At Expo '67, Montreal* (1967), *Trumpet Rhapsody* (1967), *The Ballad Style Of Maynard Ferguson* (1968), *M.F. Horn* (1970), *Alive And Well In London* (1971), *Magnitude* (c.1971), *M.F. Horn 2* (1972), *M.F. Horn 3* (1973), *M.F. Horn 4 + 5, Live At Jimmy's* (1973), *Chameleon* (1974), *Primal Scream* (1975), *New Vintage* (1977), *Hot* (1977), *Carnival* (1978), *Uncle Joe Shannon* (1978), *Conquistador* (1978), *It's My Time* (1980), *Hollywood* (1982), *Storm* (1982), *Live From San Francisco* (1983), *High Voltage* (Enigma 1988), *Live In Italy Vols 1 and 2* (Jazz Up 1989), *Big Bop Nouveau* (Intima 1989), *Footpath Cafe* (Hot Shot 1993).

Feza, Mongezi

b. 1945, Queenstown, South Africa, d. 14 December 1975, London, England. Feza, nicknamed 'Mongs', began playing trumpet at the age of eight and was gigging regularly by the time he was 16. He took part in the 1962 Johannesburg Jazz Festival, where Chris McGregor invited him and four more of the best players at the Festival to form a band, the legendary Blue Notes. As a mixed race band it was impossible for them to work under apartheid and, in 1964, whilst touring Europe, they decided to settle there. After a year in Switzerland they went to London, where, evolving into the Chris McGregor Group, they made a huge impact in the UK Jazz scene. As well as McGregor's Group and the big band Brotherhood Of Breath, Feza gigged and recorded with Dudu Pukwana and Johnny Mbizo Dyani (who were both colleagues in the McGregor group), Robert Wyatt (who, like Pukwana, had

Mongezi's marvellous composition 'Sonia' in his repertoire), Keith Tippett's Centipede, and Julian Sebothane Bahula. Feza's stinging, restless trumpet contributed hugely to the special edge of the McGregor Group and was a kwela-inspired counterpart to Don Cherry's folk-like melodies in the Ornette Coleman Quartet. Feza was very much affected by the lack of recognition that he and his colleagues had to contend with but, whatever his personal problems, he transformed them into an exhilarating blend of South African and free jazz traditions. His death in 1975 was a shock to his colleagues, dispiriting some of them, such as Dyani, far beyond the musical loss. The official cause of death was pneumonia, but it has been claimed that this was aggravated because Feza was left sick and unattended in a police cell after an arrest for disorderly behaviour. Shortly after his death, the remaining Blue Notes recorded the tribute *Blue Notes For Mongezi*, released in 1976.

Albums: with Chris McGregor *Very Urgent* (1968), *Brotherhood Of Breath* (1971), with others *Music For Xaba* (1972), with Brotherhood of Breath *Brotherhood* (1972), with Dudu Pukwana *In The Townships* (1972), with Brotherhood of Breath *Live At Willisau* (1974), with Pukwana *Flute Music* (1975), with Pukwana *Diamond Express* (1977).

Field, Gregg

b. 21 February 1956, Oakland, California, USA. Field began playing drums as a child, studying and working with local bands in California. Although he first attracted widespread attention after joining Count Basie's band in the early 80s, he had already built a formidable reputation amongst fellow musicians. In addition to appearing on television in shows such as *Saturday Night Live*, *The Merv Griffin Show* and *Frank Sinatra: A Man And His Music*, he has written many arrangements for the *Tonight Show* orchestra. He has toured or recorded with Donald Byrd, Quincy Jones, George Benson, Harry James, Herbie Hancock and Wayne Shorter and an impressive roster of singers, including Frank Sinatra, Ella Fitzgerald, Ray Charles, Sarah Vaughan, Mel Tormé, Dianne Schuur, Tony Bennett and Joe Williams. In addition to performing, Field is also a member of the faculty of the University of Southern California and is active as a record producer. His records with Basie included Grammy-award-winning albums and, following the leader's death, he has worked with all-star alumni bands, including the Frank Wess-Harry Edison all-star band which recorded at the 1989 and 1990 Fujitsu-Concord Jazz Festivals in Tokyo. In 1990 he was a member of an all-star band led by Ray Anthony for a recording session which Field also produced. In 1991, he worked with Bill Berry and his LA Big Band for concerts at the Hollywood Bowl. A superbly accomplished drummer, equipped to play in almost any setting, Field is at his considerable best playing in a mainstream big band. The enthusiastic swing of his performances ensures that a great tradition on jazz drumming continues into the closing years of the century.

Albums: with Count Basie *Warm Breeze* (1981), with Basie *Fancy Pants* (1983), with Basie *Farmer's Market Barbeque* (1985), with Frank Wess-Harry Edison *Dear Mr Basie* (1989), with Ray Anthony *Swing Back To The Forties* (1990).

Fields, 'Kansas'

b. Carl Donnell Fields, 5 December 1915, Chapman, Kansas, USA. As a young teenager Fields moved to Chicago where, a few years later, he began playing drums at various clubs. Among the musicians for whom he worked during the 30s were Jimmie Noone and Horace Henderson. In 1940 he joined Roy Eldridge and then flitted through the bands of Benny Carter, Charlie Barnet, Mel Powell and others, until war service interrupted his career. After the war he was with Cab Calloway, Sidney Bechet, Eldridge again, and also ventured into modern waters with Dizzy Gillespie. Fields was, however, a mainstream drummer and was at his best in such surroundings. In the 50s and early 60s he spent much of his time in Europe working and recording with Mezz Mezzrow, Lionel Hampton and Buck Clayton. He continued working into the 80s.

Albums: with Dizzy Gillespie *Dee Gee Days* (1951), with Lionel Hampton *The Hamp In Paris* (1953), with Sidney Bechet *Concert At The World's Fair, Brussells* (1958).

Finckel, Eddie

b. 23 December 1917, Washington, DC, USA. After studying formally with classicist Otto Leuning, Finckel turned to jazz. In the early and mid-40s he worked as staff arranger for the bands of Boyd Raeburn and Gene Krupa. With Raeburn he helped create the distinctive qualities of this fine, progressive orchestra. Disagreements broke up the association with Raeburn, Finckel claiming sole authorship of several of the band's important numbers including 'Two Spoos In An Igloo', 'Boyd Meets Stravinsky' and 'March Of The Boyds', the last two having been credited to Raeburn and George Handy. Finckel, along with Tadd Dameron, also wrote modern, boppish arrangements for the first Buddy Rich band. In writing charts for Krupa he was faced with the unenviable task of making true the claim that the drummer's 1944 band really was 'the Band that Swings with Strings'. From this period Finckel created hits for Krupa with 'Leave Us Leap', 'Gypsy Mood', 'Starburst' and the breakneck tempoed 'Lover'. He wrote original music for the Ann Arbor Drama Festival and was founder and director of the Young Artists Chamber Orchestra of New Jersey. Finckel also wrote for the Broadway stage. In the classical field he composed a cello concerto, a clarinet concerto and a suite for cello and string orchestra. He also composed music for the ballet *Of Human Kindness*.

Finegan, Bill

b. 3 April 1917, Newark, New Jersey, USA. Pianist Finegan's first successes were the arrangements he wrote for the Tommy Dorsey band, but his real breakthrough came in 1938 when he became a staff arranger for Glenn Miller. Throughout the late 30s and early 40s Finegan wrote extensively for films, but continued to provide charts for Miller, Dorsey, Horace Heidt and others. At the start of the 50s Finegan was studying at the Paris Conservatoire and began corresponding with fellow-arranger Eddie Sauter, who was then hospitalized with tuberculosis. Out of this correspondence emerged a decision to form an orchestra of their own which would play music other leaders might well regard as uncommercial. In 1952 the 21-piece Sauter-Finegan Orchestra made its appearance. With so many musicians, several of whom doubled and even trebled on other instruments, the tonal palette was huge and the two arrangers took full advantage of this. The band was hugely successful with memorable records such as 'The Doodletown Fifers' and 'Sleigh Ride' (based upon music by Prokofiev). On this latter title the sound effect of horses hooves on hard-packed snow was created by Finegan beating his chest. Later, he wryly remarked, 'this is probably my finest effort on wax - or snow'. In the late 50s Finegan worked mostly in radio and television, but in the 70s returned to big band arranging with charts for the Glenn Miller reunion orchestra and for Mel Lewis, who continued to use his work into the 80s.

Albums: all by Sauter-Finegan Orchestra *The Sauter-Finegan Orchestra* i (1952), *The Sauter-Finegan Orchestra* ii (1953), *The Sauter-Finegan Orchestra* iii (1953), *New Directions In Music* (1953-56), *The Sauter-Finegan Orchestra* iv (1954), *The Sons Of Sauter-Finegan* (1955), *Adventure In Time* (1956), *One Night Stand With The Sauter-Finegan Orchestra* (1957), *The Sauter-Finegan Orchestra* v (c.1957), *Return Of The Doodletown Fifers* (c.1961), *Sleigh Ride* (c.1961).

Fischer, Clare

b. 22 October 1926, Durand, Michigan, USA. After formal studies at Michigan State University, Fischer became arranger and accompanist to the popular singing group, the Hi-Lo's. His arrangements, which are often in the more elaborate, left field tradition of Gil Evans and Lennie Tristano, were also used by Donald Byrd and Dizzy Gillespie, with whom he worked on the album, *A Portrait Of Duke Ellington*. In the 60s Fischer formed an occasional big band, an activity that he continued in later decades. Among the musicians attracted into his bands by his forward-thinking, swinging charts, which always leave space for soloists, were Warne Marsh, Bill Perkins, Conte Candoli and Steve Hufstetter. In recent years Fischer has worked more as a pianist, although he continues to write extensively, especially in the Latin idiom which has long been one of his chief musical interests.

Albums: *First Time Out* (1962), *Surging Ahead* (1962), *Easy Living* (1963), *Extensions* (Discovery 1963), *One To Get Ready, Four to Go* (1963), *Fusion 2* (1964), *So Danso Samba* (1964), *Manteca!* (1966), *Easy Livin'* (Revalation 1966), *Songs For Rainy Day Lovers* (1966-67), *Thesaurus* (1968), *Duality* (Discovery 1969), *Great White Hope!* (Revelation 1970), *The Reclamation Act Of 1972* (Revelation 1970-71), *Head, Heart And Hands* (1970-71), *Soon/T' DA-A-A-A-A* (1972), *Clare Fischer And EX-42* (1972-79), *The State Of His Art* (Revelation 1973), *Jazz Song* (Revelation 1973), *Alone Together* (Discovery 1975), *Clare Declares* (1975), *Salsa Picante* (Discovery 1978), *Machacha* (Discovery 1979), *Music Inspired By The Kinetic Sculpture Of Don Conrad Mobiles* (1980), *And Sometimes Voices* (Discovery 1981), *Starbright* (Discovery 1982), *Blues Trilogy* (Discovery 1982), *Whose Woods Are These* (Discovery 1984), *Clare Fischer Plays By And With Himself* (Discovery 1985-86), *Crazy Bird* (Discovery 1985), *Tjaderama* (1987), *Free Fall* (Discovery 1987), *2 + 2* (Discovery 1988), *By And With Myself* (c.1987), *Waltz (Thesaurus/Duality)* (Discovery 1989), *Lembrancas* (Concord 1989).

Fitzgerald, Ella

b. 25 April 1917, Newport News, Virginia, USA. Following the death of her father, Fitzgerald was taken to New York City by her mother. At school she sang with a glee club and showed early promise, but preferred dancing to singing. Even so, chronic shyness militated against her chances of succeeding as an entertainer. Nevertheless, she entered a talent contest as a dancer, but last minute nerves forced her to either just stand there or sing. She sang. Her unexpected success prompted her to try other talent contests and she began to win often enough to keep trying. Eventually, she reached the top end of the talent show circuit, singing at the Harlem Opera House where she was heard by several important people. In later years many claimed to have 'discovered' her, but among those most likely to have had a hand in trying to establish her as a professional singer with the Fletcher Henderson band were Benny Carter and Charles Linton. These early efforts were unsuccessful, however, and she continued her round of the talent shows. An appearance at Harlem's Apollo Theatre, where she won, was the most important stepping stone in her life. She was heard by Linton, who sang with the Chick Webb band at the Savoy Ballroom. Webb took her on, at first paying her out of his own pocket, and for the fringe audience she quickly became the band's main attraction. She recorded extensively with Webb, with a small group led by Teddy Wilson, with the Ink Spots and others, and even recorded with Benny Goodman. Her hits with Webb included 'Sing Me A Swing Song', 'Oh, Yes, Take Another Guess', 'The Dipsy Doodle', 'If Dreams Come True', 'A-Tisket, A-Tasket', (a song on which she collaborated on the lyric), 'F.D.R. Jones' and 'Undecided'. After Webb's death in 1939 she became the nominal leader of the band, a position she retained until 1942. Fitzgerald then began her solo career, recording numerous popular songs, sometimes teaming up with other artists, and in the late 40s signing with Norman Granz. It was Granz's masterly and astute control of her career that helped to establish her as one of America's leading jazz singers. She was certainly the most popular jazz singer with non-jazz audiences, and through judicious choice of repertoire, became the foremost female interpreter of the Great American Popular Song Book. With Granz she worked on the 'songbook' series, placing on record definitive performances of the work of America's leading songwriters, and she also toured extensively as part of his Jazz At The Philharmonic package.

Ella has a wide vocal range, but her voice retained a youthful, light vibrancy throughout the greater part of her career, bringing a fresh and appealing quality to most of her material especially 'scat' singing. However, it proved less suited to the blues, a genre which, for the most part, she wisely avoided. Indeed, in her early work the most apparent musical influence is Connee Boswell. As a jazz singer, Fitzgerald performed with elegantly swinging virtuosity and her work with accompanists such as Ray Brown, to whom she was married for a while (they have an adopted son, Ray Brown Jnr, a drummer), Joe Pass and Tommy Flanagan was always immaculately conceived. However, her recordings with Louis Armstrong reveal the marked difference between her conception and that of a singer for whom the material was always of secondary importance to the improvisation he could weave upon it. For all the enviably high quality of her jazz work, it is as a singer of superior popular songs that Fitzgerald's importance and influence is most profound. Her respect for her material, beautifully displayed in the 'songbook' series, helped her to establish and retain her place as the finest vocalist of her chosen area of music. Owing largely to deteriorating health, by the mid-80s Fitzgerald's career was at a virtual standstill, although her appearances were well-received by an ecstatic audience. In the 90s it was rumoured that she had severe heart trouble and, being confined to a wheelchair for this time it was finally reported that she had undergone surgery for the removal of her legs.

Her most obvious counterpart among male singers is Frank Sinatra and, as the careers of both these artists draw to a close, questions inevitably arise about the fate of the great popular songs of the 30s and 40s. While there are numerous excellent interpreters still around in the early 90s, and many whose work has been strongly influenced by Fitzgerald, it is hard to see any single singer who can take her place emerging in the foreseeable future. This is not a view conceived out of blinkered nostalgia but rather an acute awareness that the conditions which helped to create America's First Lady of Song no longer exist. It seems highly unlikely, therefore, that we shall ever see or hear her like again.

Selected albums: *The Chronological Ella Fitzgerald Vols 1-3* (1935-39), *Webb On The Air* (1940), *Live From The Roseland Ballroom* (1940), *Ella And Ray* (1948), *The Ella Fitzgerald Set* (1949), *Ella Sings Gershwin* (1950), *Ella Fitzgerald Sings The Cole Porter Songbook* (Verve 1956), *Ella Fitzgerald Sings The Rodgers And Hart Songbook* (Verve 1956), with Louis Armstrong *Ella And Louis* (1956), with Armstrong *Porgy And Bess* (1956), *Ella Fitzgerald Sings The Duke Ellington Songbook* (Verve 1957), *Ella Fitzgerald At Newport* (1957), *Ella And Louis Again Vols 1 & 2* (1957), *Ella Fitzgerald At The Opera House* (1957), *Ella Fitzgerald Sings The Irving Berlin Songbook* (Verve 1958), *Ella Sings Sweet Songs For Swingers* (1958), *Ella Swings Lightly* (1958), *Ella Fitzgerald Sings The George And Ira Gershwin Songbook* (Verve 1959), *Mack The Knife - Ella In Berlin* (1960), *Ella Wishes You A Swinging Christmas* (1960), *The Intimate Ella* (1960), *Ella Fitzgerald Sings The Harold Arlen Songbook* (Verve 1961), *Ella Swings Gently With Nelson* (1962), *Ella Fitzgerald Sings The Jerome Kern Songbook* (V Verve 1963), *These Are The Blues* (1963), *Ella At Juan-Les-Pins* (1964), *Hello, Dolly!* (1964), *Ella Fitzgerald Sings The Johnny Mercer Songbook* (Verve 1964), *Ella At Duke's Place* (1965), *Ella In Hamburg* (1965), with Ellington *The Stockholm Concert* (1966), *Ella And Duke At The Côte D'Azure* (1966), *Whisper Not* (1966), *Brighten The Corner* (1967), *Misty Blue* (1967), *30 By Ella* (1968), *Sunshine Of Your Love/Watch What Happens* (1969),

Things Ain't What They Used To Be (1970), *Ella A Nice* (1971), *Ella Fitzgerald And Cole Porter* (1972), *Ella Fitzgerald At Carnegie Hall* (1973), *Take Love Easy* (1974), *Ella In London* (1974), *Fine And Mellow* (1974), *Ella - At The Montreux Jazz Festival 1975* (1975), with Oscar Peterson *Ella And Oscar* (1975), with Joe Pass *Again* (1976), *Montreux '77* (1977), *Lady Time* (1978), with Count Basie *A Classy Pair* (1979), *A Perfect Match - Basie And Ella* (1979), *Ella Fitzgerald Sings The Antonio Carlos Jobim Songbook* (1981), *The Best Is Yet To Come* (1982), *Easy Living* (1983), *Speak Love* (1983), *Nice Work If You Can Get It* (1983), *A 75th Birthday Tribute* (1993), *The Pablo Years* (1993), with Bing Crosby *My Happiness* (1993). Selected compilations: *Best Of Ella Fitzgerald* (MCA 1981), *Compact Jazz* (Verve 1987), *Compact Jazz Ella Fitzgerald & Louis Armstrong* (Verve 1988), *The Complete Songbooks* (18 CD box set) (Verve 1993), *The Complete Recordings 1933-40* (Affinity 1993).

Further reading: *Ella Fitzgerald - A Life Through Jazz*, Jim Haskins. *Ella Fitzgerald*, Stuart Nicholson.

Flanagan, Tommy

b. 16 March 1930, Detroit, Michigan, USA. In his youth Flanagan's piano playing was influenced by Teddy Wilson, Art Tatum and the new bebop voicings of Bud Powell. For much of his solo career Flanagan's work was overshadowed by his careful self-effacement as a remarkably skilful and sensitive accompanist to singers Tony Bennett and Ella Fitzgerald. Despite this deliberate seclusion, however, Flanagan's talents were appreciated by fellow musicians and he worked and sometimes recorded with a long list of major names, including Miles Davis, Coleman Hawkins and Sonny Rollins. In the late 70s Flanagan began playing more as featured soloist and this revealed to a wider audience the talent that had long been kept from view. In the 80s he became a very popular performer at festivals and clubs.

Selected albums: *The Cats* (1957), *Trio Overseas/Tommy Flanagan In Stockholm* (1957), *Jazz...It's Magic* (1957), with Wilbur Haden *The Music Of Rodgers And Hammerstein* (1958), *Lonely Town* (1959), *The Tommy Flanagan Trio* (Bellaphon 1960), with Ella Fitzgerald *Ella At Juan-Les-Pins* (1964), *The Tommy Flanagan Tokyo Recital* (1975), *Positive Intensity* (1976), *Eclypso* (1977), *Montreux '77* (1977), *I Remember Bebop* (1977), *They All Played Bebop* (1977), *Alone Too Long* (1977), with Kenny Barron *Together* (1978), *Our Delights* (1978), *Something Borrowed, Something Blue* (1978), *Ballads And Blues* (1978), *The Super Jazz Trio* (1978), *Communication* (1979), *Tommy Flanagan Plays The Music Of Harold Arlen* (c.1980), *Super-session* (1980), *You're Me* (1980), with Red Mitchell and Phil Woods *Free For All* (1981), *The Magnificent Tommy Flanagan* (1981), *Giant Steps, Thelonica* (1982), *The Master Trio* (1983), *Blues In The Closet* (1983), *Nights At The Vanguard* (1986), *Jazz Poet* (Timeless 1989), *Beyond The Bluebird* (Timeless 1990), *Communication Live At Fat Tuesday's* (Paddlewheel 1993), *Let's* (Enja 1993), *Lady Be Good* (Groovin High 1994).

Florence, Bob

b. 20 May 1932, Los Angeles, California, USA. Florence first attracted widespread attention amongst big band fans when he wrote elegantly-crafted arrangements for Si Zentner's popular recording band in the early 60s. After leaving Zentner, with whom he sometimes played piano too, he wrote for several west coast-based musicians, including Bud Shank and Frank Capp but also varied his technique happily to accommodate blues singers Jimmy Witherspoon and Big Miller, Joanie Summers, Sue Raney and Sergio Mendes. Although an accomplished pianist, Florence's chief talents are his arranging skills and especially his ability to write for big bands. Like other arrangers he eventually realized that the only way to hear his charts (many of which were for his own compositions) played the way he wanted them to was to have his own big band. First formed in the late 50s, the Florence bands continued through succeeding decades, providing object lessons in big band writing and playing. In the late 70s and 80s he was calling upon outstanding musicians such as Bob Cooper, Nick Ceroli, Bob Efford, Steve Hufstetter, Bill Perkins, Kim Richmond, Buddy Childers, Pete Christlieb and Warren Leuning. Although his roots are clearly in the post-swing era style of big band writing, Florence comfortably accommodates bebop and many latter-day fusions. In a *tour de force* on 'The Bebop Treasure Chest' (on *Trash Can City*) he demonstrated his skills by seamlessly blending phrases and quotations from 16 tunes. Florence's big band remains one of the most distinctive of the many based on the west coast.

Albums: *Meet The Bob Florence Trio* (1957), *Bongos, Reeds And Brass* (1958), *Name Band 1959* (1959), with Si Zentner *Up A Lazy River* (1961), *Big Miller With Bob Florence And His Orchestra* (1961), with Zentner *Desafinado* (1962) with Zentner *Waltz In Jazz Time* (1962), *Here And Now* (1965), *Pet Project* (c.1968), *Live At Concerts By The Sea* (Trend 1979), with Joanie Summers *Dream* (1980), *Westlake* (Discovery 1981), *Soaring* (1982), with Sue Raney *The Music Of Johnny Mandel* (1982), *Magic Time* (Trend 1983), with Raney *Ridin' High* (1984), with Raney *Flight Of Fancy - A Journey Of Alan And Marilyn Bergman* (1986), *Norwegian Radio Big Band Meets Bob Florence* (1986), *Trash Can City* (Trend 1986), *State Of The Art* (1988), *State Of The Art* (C5 1989). *Funupsmanship* (1993).

Flory, Chris

b. 13 November 1953, New York City, New York, USA. Flory first played guitar as a child. Strongly influenced by such major guitarists as Charlie Christian and Django Reinhardt, he began playing professionally in 1974. Within a few years he had become a regular associate of Scott Hamilton, touring internationally and making records. Although he continued his links with Hamilton throughout the 80s he also played with other jazzmen including Hank Jones, Bob Wilber and Ruby Braff and for four years from 1979 was a regular member of the occasionally reformed Benny Goodman Sextet. He also played with the Goodman big band in 1985 at what proved to be the leader's final public performance. In the late 80s and early 90s Flory appeared on numerous record dates with artists such as Hamilton, Braff, Wilber, Maxine Sullivan and Rosemary

Clooney. He also became a familiar and popular figure on the international circuit, sometimes in company and other times as a single. A fluent improvisor and gifted accompanist, Flory's solo work bears traces of his idols but he has steadily become a distinctive and distinguished guitarist in his own right.

Album: *For All We Know* (Concord 1988), *City Life* (Concord 1993).

Fontana, Carl

b. 18 July 1928, Monroe, Louisiana, USA. As a teenager Fontana played trombone in a band led by his father, then joined Woody Herman in 1952. Subsequent big band stints came with Lionel Hampton and Stan Kenton. In the late 50s he worked with Kai Winding's four-trombone band. He spent most of the 60s working in house bands in Las Vegas but returned briefly to Herman for a world tour. In the early and mid-70s he was in Supersax and was co-leader with Jake Hanna of the Hanna-Fontana Band. An enormously resourceful and inventive soloist, Fontana combines a phenomenal technique with a beautiful tone that he ably demonstrates on 'A Beautiful Friendship', recorded with Hanna at the 1975 Concord Jazz Festival. He is equally at home in a roaring big band and small groups with bebop or dixieland orientation, but is at his rhapsodic best in mainstream bands where he is given plenty of solo space.

Albums: with Woody Herman *The Third Herd* (1952), *Stan Kenton In Hi Fi* (1956), with Kenton *Cuban Fire* (1956), with others *Unit From The Stan Kenton Band* (1956), with others *Colorado Jazz Party* (1971), *Supersax: Salt Peanuts* (1973), with Jake Hanna *Live At Concord* (1975), *The Great Fontana* (1985).

Ford, Ricky

b. 4 March 1954, Boston, Massachusetts, USA. Ford started to play drums, then changed to tenor saxophone at the age of 15, inspired by Rahaaan Roland Kirk. Ran Blake heard him playing in a Boston Club and persuaded him to study music at the New England Conservatory. (Blake later invited him to play on several albums too, including *Rapport, Short Life Of Barbara Monk* and *That Certain Feeling*). In 1974 Ford joined the Duke Ellington Orchestra under the leadership of Mercer Ellington and in 1976 he replaced George Adams in the Charles Mingus group, recording on *Three Or Four Shades of Blue* and *Me Myself An Eye*. In the late 70s and early 80s he played with Dannie Richmond, Mingus Dynasty, George Russell, Beaver Harris, Lionel Hampton and Adbullah Ibrahim's Ekaya group. However, following the release of his debut album in 1977 he has worked increasingly as a leader, often recording with Jimmy Cobb and ex-Ellington colleague James Spaulding. His latest releases also feature one of his New England Conservatory teachers, Jaki Byard. A strong, authoritative tenor player, Ford's fluency in most idioms of modern jazz has perhaps hindered the development of an individual voice, but he looks set to become a major saxophone presence in the 90s.

Albums: *Loxodonta Africana* (New World 1977), *Manhattan Plaza* (Muse 1978), *Flying Colours* (Muse 1981), *Interpretations* (Muse 1982), *Future's Gold* (Muse 1984), *Shorter Ideas* (Muse

1986), *Looking Ahead* (Muse 1987), *Saxotic Stomp* (Muse 1988) *Hard Groovin* (Muse 1989), *Manhattan Blues* (Candid 1990), *Ebony Rhapsody* (Candid 1991), *Hot Brass* (Candid 1992), *Tenor For The Times* (Muse 1992), *American-African Blues* (Candid 1993).

Forrest, Jimmy

b. 24 January 1920, St. Louis, Missouri, USA, d. 26 August 1980. Forrest's early experience on tenor saxophone came in territory bands, including the Jeter-Pillars Orchestra, Don Albert's San Antonio-based band and the group led by Fate Marable. In 1940 he joined Jay McShann in Kansas City, where one of his section-mates was Charlie Parker. This was followed by a long period in New York with Andy Kirk, but by the end of the 40s he was back home in St. Louis. He had a huge R&B hit with 'Night Train', which actually owed more than was usually credited to a Duke Ellington composition, 'Happy-Go-Lucky Local'. At the end of the 50s he was back in New York, this time with Harry Edison, after which he led his own bands for records and club dates that lasted into the early 70s. He was then with Count Basie for a number of years and also played with the Clarke-Boland Big Band before forming a partnership with Al Grey. Together, Forrest and Grey toured the USA and Europe, playing hard-driving mainstream jazz with contrasting overtones of both R&B and bebop. Forrest's robust style echoed the Texas tenors and he proved enormously popular with audiences wherever he played.
Albums: *Night Train* (1951), with Harry Edison *The Swinger* (1958), *All The Gin Is Gone* (1959), *Black Forrest* (1959), *Forrest Fire* (Original Jazz Classics 1960), *Out Of The Forrest* (1961), *Sit Down And Relax With Jimmy Forrest* (1961), *Most Much* (Original Jazz Classics 1961), with Count Basie *I Told You So* (1976), *Heart Of The Forrest* (1978), with Al Grey *Out Dere* (1980).

Foster, Frank

b. 23 September 1928, Cincinnati, Ohio, USA. Although he began his musical career playing alto saxophone, Foster showed commendable foresight in deciding to change to tenor saxophone and flute, declaring his intention of following his own path and not the one sign-posted by Charlie Parker. In the late 40s he played with several like-minded spirits in the Detroit area, among them Wardell Gray and Snooky Young, before serving in the armed forces. In 1953 he joined Count Basie and became a significant member of the band as soloist, arranger and composer ('Shiny Stockings'). After 11 years with Basie he joined Elvin Jones, another of the musicians with whom he had played in Detroit early in his career. In the mid-60s he formed a big band which continued to play intermittently over the next decade. He also played with the Thad Jones-Mel Lewis Jazz Orchestra and co-led a small group with former Basie section-mate Frank Wess. In the mid-80s Foster fronted the reactivated Basie band, with which he toured the USA and Europe. Foster's arrangements have always shown his affinity with post-war big-band writing and his work for Basie was an important factor in the success of that particular edition of the band. As a soloist, Foster's early decision to go his own way paid dividends as he developed a distinctively acerbic tone which, while reflecting an awareness of his contemporaries, was very much his own.
Albums: *Frank Foster Quartet* (1954), *New Faces, New Sounds* (1954), with Count Basie *Blues Backstage* (1954), *No Count* (Savoy 1956), *Jazz Is Bursting Out All Over* (1957), with Basie *Chairman Of The Board* (1959), *Basie Is Our Boss* (1963), *Fearless Frank Foster* (1965), *Soul Outing* (1966), *Manhattan Fever* i (1968), with Elvin Jones *Coalition* (1970), *The Loud Minority* (Mainstream 1974), *Giants Steps* (1975), *Here And Now* (1976), *Manhattan Fever* ii (Denon 1977), *12 Shades Of Black* (1978), *Shiny Stockings* (Denon 1978), *Roots, Branches And Dances* (1978), *Ciquito Loco: Live At The HNITA Jazz Club* (1979), *A Blues Ain't Nothing But A Trip* (1979), *The House That Love Built* (Steeplechase 1982), with Frank Wess *Two For The Blues* (Pablo 1983), with Wess *Frankly Speaking* (Concord 1984), with James Moody *Sax Talk* (1993).

Foster, George 'Pops'

b. 18 May 1892, McCall, Louisiana, USA, d. 30 October 1969. One of the pioneers of string bass playing, Foster began his musical career as a cellist and also occasionally played brass bass. After performing in New Orleans in the early years of the century with Kid Ory, Joe 'King' Oliver and others, he joined Fate Marable's riverboat band in 1917. He was also with the unit Ory led in California in the early 20s. Foster spent the mid-20s in the St. Louis area and by the end of the decade he was in New York working with Luis Russell. He stayed with Russell for several years, during which time the band became, in effect, the Louis Armstrong orchestra. In 1940, as the revival movement got under way, Foster was in great demand and moved on to freelance work, playing with many bands, including those led by Sidney Bechet and Jimmy Archey. He played on through the 50s and early 60s, touring the USA and Europe with Sammy Price and he also spent time in bands led by Earl Hines, at San Francisco's Hangover Club, and Elmer Snowden. Although deeply-rooted in the traditional forms of New Orleans jazz, Foster's early preference for string bass, which he played in the traditional 'slapping' manner, stood him in good stead when the inevitable musical changes occurred.
Albums: *Luis Russell And His Orchestra Vols 1 & 2* (1926-34), with Jimmy Archey *Jazz Dance* (1954, film soundtrack), with Earl Hines *At The Crescendo* (1956).
Further reading: *Pops Foster: The Autobiography Of A New Orleans Jazzman*, Pops Foster with Tom Stoddard and Ross Russell.

Fountain, Pete

b. 3 July 1930, New Orleans, Louisiana, USA. Taking up the clarinet as a small boy, Fountain was sufficiently adept to play and record before he was out of his teens. In the early 50s he worked with various bands in his home town, including the Basin Street Six. In 1954 he formed his own small band and for the next couple of years played with this group and with the Dukes Of Dixieland. In the later years of the decade he appeared as featured soloist on Lawrence Welk's networked show. Regular performances with Al Hirt ensured that he remained in demand, both in New Orleans and in the vastly different atmosphere of Las Vegas. Fountain's ability transcends the formulaic limitations of some post-revival dixieland. Although he has long been musically associated with this area of jazz, his consummate skills might more accurately place him in the mainstream. Nevertheless, he has chosen to remain in a field which has proved to be enormously popular and commercially successful and has thus, inevitably, met with critical displeasure and disregard.

Albums: with Basin Street Six *Dixieland Jazz Concert* (1951), with Dukes Of Dixieland *At The Jazz Band Ball* (1955), *Lawrence Welk Presents Pete Fountain* (1957), *Music From Dixie* (1961), *South Rampart Street Parade* (1963), with Al Hirt *Super Jazz 1* (Monument 1976), *Alive In New Orleans* (First American 1978), *Live At The Ryman* (1988), *High Society* (Bluebird 1992), *Swingin' Blues* (Start 1992), *At Piper's Opera House* (Jazzology 1993).

Fowlkes, Charlie

b. 16 February 1916, New York City, New York, USA, d. 9 February 1980. Although able to play a variety of instruments, Fowlkes appeared to recognize early on in life that he was destined to be an unsung section musician. He adopted the baritone saxophone as his chosen instrument and spells with Tiny Bradshaw and Lionel Hampton beginning in 1938 kept him busy for a decade. In the late 40s he was in Arnett Cobb's small band and then, in 1951, he became one of the most reliable members of the Count Basie band, remaining there until 1969. Six years later he was back in the band, which was where he remained until his death in 1980.

Albums: *Buck Clayton Jam Session* (1953), *Dance Along With Basie* (1959).

Francis, David 'Panama'

b. 21 December 1918, Miami, Florida, USA. Francis began to play drums at the age of eight, and made his first professional club appearance when he was 13 years old. Twelve months later he was on tour and in 1934 became a member of George Kelly's band. By the time he was in his late teens he was resident in New York, where he quickly found work with Tab Smith and Roy Eldridge. In 1940 he joined Lucky Millinder's big band, remaining there until 1945. Millinder's band was very popular at Harlem's Savoy Ballroom and Francis was a significant factor in that popularity. He then briefly led his own band which toured the south but met with only limited success. In 1947 he was hired by Cab Calloway for a five-year stint. Subsequently Francis worked in radio and was regularly on call as a recording session musician, backing artists such as John Lee Hooker, Eubie Blake, Ella Fitzgerald, Ray Charles and Mahalia Jackson. Francis's long absence from the jazz scene ended in the late 70s, when he returned to play with Lionel Hampton's all-star big band and, most importantly, to lead his own nine-piece band, the Savoy Sultans (named after the Al Cooper band he had played opposite at the Savoy three decades

earlier). The new Sultans included Francis Williams, Norris Turney and Francis's old boss, George Kelly. A highly-accomplished drummer with an exemplary technique, Francis plays with a loosely-flowing swing that benefits any band of which he is a member.

Album: *Panama Francis And The Dixieland Don Juans* (c.1959), *Panama Francis And His Orchestra* (1960), *The Battle Of Jericho* (1962), *Tough Talk* (1963), *Panama Story* (1975), with Lionel Hampton *All Star Band At Newport '78* (1978), *Gettin' In The Groove* (Black And Blue 1979), *Jimmy Witherspoon With Panama Francis' Savoy Sultans* (1979), *Grooving* (Stash 1982), *Everything Swings* (Stash 1984). Compilations: *Lucky Millinder And His Orchestra* (1941-43), *Get Up And Dance* (Stash 1988).

Freeman, Bud

b. Lawrence Freeman, 1 April 1906, Chicago, Illinois, USA; d. 15 March 1991. Freeman's early career found him in company with Jimmy McPartland, Frank Teschemacher and other members of the Austin High School Gang. Having set out playing the 'C' melody saxophone, Freeman switched to tenor in 1925 and quickly established a reputation on that instrument as one of the few genuine rivals to Coleman Hawkins. Through the late 20s and early 30s he worked in numerous bands, recording extensively and consolidating his reputation. He gravitated into big bands, playing with Joe Haymes, Ray Noble, Paul Whiteman, Tommy Dorsey, Benny Goodman and others, but he preferred a different kind of jazz and in 1939 formed his own Summa Cum Laude Orchestra which delighted audiences in New York during its brief life. From 1940 Freeman played in various bands, led his own short-lived big band, and by the middle of the decade had settled into leading a small group at Eddie Condon's New York club. For the rest of his career Freeman played as a freelance, sometimes leading, sometimes as sideman, touring the USA and Europe. A confirmed Anglophile, he lived in London in the 70s and even managed to 'look' British. In 1980 Freeman returned to live in his native Chicago but by the end of the decade his health had failed. In mid-1990 he was almost blind, hospitalized and frail, and he died early in 1991. Freeman's masterly solo on his 1933 recording of 'The Eel' displayed his qualities to the full. In later years some detractors remarked that he spent the rest of his career repeating that solo. While it is true that his playing style did not subsequently alter very much, such adverse criticism failed to recognize that like his great but very different contemporary, Coleman Hawkins, Freeman had achieved such a pinnacle of excellence that wholesale change was pointless. In fact, Freeman's later recordings show him to have an inventive mind which, allied to a fluent delivery, make all his work a delight to the ear. The titles of two memoirs give an indication of his wry humour: *You Don't Look Like A Musician* and *If You Know Of A Better Life, Please Tell Me*.

Selected albums: *The Bud Freeman All-Stars Featuring Shorty Baker* (1960), *Live 1960* (1960), *Chicago* (1962), *Something To Remember You By* (Black Lion 1962), with the World's Greatest Jazz Band *Century Plaza* (1972), with Bucky Pizzarelli *Bucky*

And Bud (c.1975). *Last Night When We Were Young* (Black And Blue 1978), *Chicago* (Black Lion 1985), *Keep Smilin' At Trouble* (Affinity 1987). Compilations: *Chicago-Styled* (1935-40), *The Commodore Years* (1938-39), *See What The Boys In The Backroom Will Have* (1940).

Further reading: *Crazeology: The Autobiography Of A Chicago Jazzman*, Bud Freeman with Robert Wolf. *You Don't Look Like A Musician*, Bud Freeman. *If You Know Of A Better Life, Please Tell Me*, Bud Freeman.

Freeman, Chico

b. Earl Freeman Jnr., 17 July 1949, Chicago, Illinois, USA. Freeman started out playing trumpet but while at university switched to tenor saxophone, the instrument played by his father Von Freeman. After university, where he studied music education, he played in R&B bands, before changing direction and working with Muhal Richard Abrams and the Association for the Advancement of Creative Musicians (AACM). In the mid-to late 70s he continued his studies, meanwhile working with many leading contemporary jazz artists, including Elvin Jones, Sun Ra and Don Pullen. In the early 80s he recorded two albums, *Fathers And Sons* and *Freeman And Freeman*, with his father, toured as leader of his own small group, and also appeared with Wynton Marsalis, Cecil McBee, Jack DeJohnette and others. Interestingly, Freeman's striking playing style blends the post-Coltrane tradition of long angular lines with the rougher-toned urgency of his R&B schooling into a sound which is identifiably his own. The 1979 *Spirit Sensitive* is one of the finest collections of ballads by a modern tenor player, but by the late 80s Freeman was devoting most of his time to his fusion band Brainstorm. He is also a member of the occasional super-group, the Leaders.

Albums: *Morning Prayer* (India Navigation 1976), *Chico* (India Navigation 1977), *Kings Of Mali* (1978), *Beyond The Rain* (Original Jazz Classics 1978), *Spirit Sensitive* (India Navigation 1979), *No Time Left* (Black Saint 1979), *Peaceful Heart, Gentle Spirit* (1980), *Fathers And Sons* (1981), *Freeman And Freeman* (India Navigation 1981), *The Outside Within* (1981), *Destiny's Dance* (Original Jazz Classics 1981), *Tradition In Transition* (Elektra 1982), *Tangents* (c.1984), *The Search* (India Navigation 1984), *Groovin' Late* (1986), *The Pied Piper* (Blackhawk 1986), *Live At Ronnie Scott's* (Hendring 1987), *You'll Know When You Get There* (Black Saint 1988), *Tales Of Ellington* (Blackhawk 1988), *Brainstorm* (1989), *Luminous* (Jazz House 1989), Up And Down (Black Saint 1990), *The Mystical Dreamer* (In And Out 1990), *Sweet Explosion* (In And Out 1990), with Mal Waldron *Up And Down* (1992), *Threshold* (In And Out 1993)

Freeman, Russ

b. Russell Donald Freeman, 28 May 1926, Chicago, Illinois, USA. Emerging onto the west coast jazz scene in the late 40s, Freeman's piano style was typically bop-orientated. He played with many important west coast musicians during the next few years including Art Pepper, Shorty Rogers and Shelly Manne. He collaborated extensively with Manne during the second half

of the 50s but also accompanied important figures from other areas of jazz, amongst them Benny Goodman. As a child Freeman had studied classical music and his range and technical accomplishment allowed him to work in diverse fields of music such as film and television. In common with a growing number of musicians he also formed his own music publishing company thus giving him greater control over his own compositions. Within the jazz world Freeman's bop credentials were overlaid with an ability to accommodate other concepts. His work outside jazz has somewhat overshadowed his reputation with the wider audience but his early recordings, especially those with Manne, reveal him to have been an important contributor to a particularly creative period in the modern jazz movement.

Albums: *Russ Freeman Trio* (1953), with Shelly Manne *New Works* (1954), *Shelly Manne With Russ Freeman* (1954), with Maynard Ferguson *Dimensions* (1954), with Cy Touff *Having A Ball* (1955), *Russ Freeman/Chet Baker Quartet* (1956), *Double Play* (1957), with Manne *Boss Sounds!* (1966), *Trio* (Pacific Jazz 1990).

Freeman, Von

b. Earl Lavon Freeman, 3 October 1922, Chicago, Illinois, USA. Freeman played 'C' melody saxophone as a child, later switching to tenor. In the early 40s he played with several bands including, most notably, that of Horace Henderson. Late in the decade he was briefly with Sun Ra, and then settled into a residency at a Chicago hotel in a band which included his brothers Buzz on drums and George on guitar. Other members of the band included at different times Ahmad Jamal and Muhal Richard Abrams. The band accompanied many visiting jazzmen, notably Charlie Parker and Lester Young. In the 60s Freeman toured with a variety of artists, including several blues singers. From the 70s onwards he was again leading a jazz group, sometimes in harness with his son, Chico Freeman, with whom he recorded the albums, *Freeman And Freeman* and *Fathers And Sons*. Freeman's playing style combines the toughness of the Chicago blues scene with a plangent swing and fluent improvisation; his ballad playing is especially engaging.

Albums: *Doin' It Right Now* (c.1972), *Have No Fear* (Nessa 1975), *Serenade And Blues* (Nessa 1975), *Young And Foolish* (1977), *Von Freeman* (Daybreak 1981), *Young And Foolish* (Affinity 1988), *Walkin' Tuff* (Southport 1989), *Never Let Me Go* (Steeplechase 1992), *Lester Leaps In* (Steeplechase 1992).

Frisell, Bill

b. 18 March 1951, Baltimore, Maryland, USA. Frisell, whose father was a tuba and string-bass player, was raised in Denver, Colorado. He began playing clarinet, then saxophone, finally settling on guitar. He also plays banjo, ukulele and bass. He majored in music at North Colorado University (1969-71) and in 1977 was awarded a diploma in arranging and composition from Berklee College Of Music, as well as winning the Harris Stanton guitar award. He took lessons from Jim Hall, Johnny Smith and Dale Bruning, and his favourite players are Hall, Wes Montgomery and Jimi Hendrix. He has played with many major contemporary figures, including Eberhard Weber, Mike Gibbs, Jan Garbarek, Charlie Haden, Carla Bley, Julius Hemphill, Gunter Hampel, and John Scofield. Since the late 80s he has appeared with Ronald Shannon Jackson and Melvin Gibbs (as Power Tools), John Zorn's harmolodic hardcore indulgence Naked City, the *News For Lulu* bebop trio with Zorn and George Lewis, the Paul Bley Quartet featuring John Surman and Paul Motian, Motian's trio with Frisell and Joe Lovano and his own band, which features the members of Naked City minus Zorn. Frisell's style makes use of electronics to produce long sustained notes with lots of vibrato and legato lines, possibly a legacy of his training as a reed player. He is equally convincing whether stitching feedback howls into the midst of violent Naked City melees or playing gentle country-influenced solo tunes, post-modern bottleneck blues or lop-sided melancholic ballads. Frisell's solo work found a wider audience with the release of *Have A Little Faith* together with a lengthy (by his standards) tour.

Albums: *In Line* (ECM 1983), with Tim Berne *Theoretically* (1984), *Rambler* (ECM 1985), with John Zorn, George Lewis *News For Lulu* (1987), with Power Tools *Strange Meeting* (1987), *Lookout For Hope* (ECM 1988), *Before We Were Born* (Elektra 1989), *Is That You?* (Elektra 1990), *Where In The World?* (Elektra Nonesuch 1991), with Zorn, Lewis *More News For Lulu* (1992, rec. 1989), with John Scofield *Grace Under Pressure* (1992), *This Land* (Elektra Nonesuch 1993), *Have A Little Faith* (1993), with Ginger Baker *Going Back Home* (Atlantic 1994). Compilation *Works* (ECM 1989).

Frishberg, Dave

b. 23 March 1933, St Paul, Minnesota, USA. Frishberg learned to play piano as a child, at one point horrifying his teacher by arranging a Mozart test-piece as a conga. After studying journalism at the University of Minnesota, he spent two years in the US Air Force before he decided to take the plunge and try to earn his living playing piano in New York City. During the 60s, musically his formative decade, he played in bands led by jazz musicians such as Bobby Hackett, Al Cohn, Zoot Sims, Ben Webster, Roy Eldridge and Gene Krupa. He also accompanied many singers, including Carmen McRae, Dick Haymes, Susannah McCorkle, Anita O'Day, Irene Kral and Jimmy Rushing, often creating stylish arrangements which presented the singer in a new light (see for example, the Rushing album, *The You And Me That Used To Be*). During this period, Frishberg was busily writing songs, which were performed by O'Day, Blossom Dearie, Al Jarreau, Cleo Laine and others, while he was gradually summoning up the nerve to perform them himself in public. In 1971 he moved to Los Angeles, where he worked in film and television studios, spent a long stint with Herb Alpert, played occasionally in the big band of Bill Berry and began performing a cabaret-style act that combined superb jazz piano playing with highly sophisticated, witty songs. Although his piano playing is of a very high order, ranging from bebop through mainstream and back to romping stride, it is as a composer and lyricist that Frishberg has made his greatest and probably most lasting mark on music. His

songs, which tell contemporary tales and fables, concern themselves with seemingly mundane topics, such as lawyers, ('My Attorney Bernie'), long-forgotten brands of beer ('White Castle'), love's deceits ('Blizzard Of Lies') and heroes of baseball and jazz ('Van Lingle Mungo') and ('Dear Bix'). His wittily ironic lyric writing, which Daniel Okrent in *Esquire* suggests is how 'Noël Coward would have written had he been born Jewish in St. Paul', combines devilish ingenuity with a childlike innocence and an appreciation of life's better but fleeting moments, as in the song 'Here's To Yesterday', which contains the line, ' . . . tomorrow wasn't built to last.'

In the 80s, Frishberg, now resident in Portland, Oregon, continued to play on the west coast but also regularly appeared in clubs and at festivals across the USA and in the UK. In the early 90s he was still touring, playing the piano and still writing songs which eloquently prove that, for all fears to the contrary, they still *do* write songs like that anymore.

Albums: *Oklahoma Toad* (1968), with Bill Berry *Hot And Happy* (1974), *Getting Some Fun Out Of Life* (1977), *You're A Lucky Guy* (1978), *The Dave Frishberg Songbook, Vols. 1 & 2/Classics* (Fantasy 1981-82), *Live At Vine Street* (1984), *Can't Take You Nowhere* (Fantasy 1985), *Let's Eat Home* (Concord 1989), *Where You At* (Bloomdido 1993).

Frith, Fred

b. 17 February 1949, Heathfield, East Sussex, England. Frith played violin and piano as a child, then fell in love with the guitar. In 1968 he co-founded the left-field rock group Henry Cow and in 1974 recorded an innovative album of electric guitar improvisations, *Guitar Solos*. After Henry Cow's demise in the late 70s, he worked with ex-Cow colleague Chris Cutler in the Art Bears (releasing *Hopes And Fears*, *Winter Songs* and *The World As It Is Today*), but during the 80s was based mostly in New York. There he guested with Material (*Memory Serves*) and played in the groups Skeleton Crew (*The Country Of Blinds* and *Learn To Talk*) and Massacre (*Killing Time*). His own albums showed a quirky blend of guitar experimentation, hard rock, fold music and improvisation. Frith has worked as a session guitarist on records by innumerable artists (including Brian Eno, Robert Wyatt, Gavin Bryars and the Residents); has played total improvisation with Lol Coxhill, Phil Minton, Hans Reichel and many others; has written music for films and dance projects; and has had several of the compositions recorded by the ROVA Saxophone Quartet (*Long On Logic*). In 1989 he formed a new group Keep The Dog. He also plays bass in John Zorn's Naked City and continues to work with long-time collaborators such as Tim Curran, Henry Kaiser, Bill Laswell, Rene Lussier and Tenko. He has also recorded in an occasional group with fellow guitarists Kaiser, Jim French and Richard Thompson (*Live, Love, Larf And Loaf* and *Invisible Means*).

Albums: *Guitar Solos* (Rer Megacorp 1974), *Gravity* (Rer Megacorp 1980), *Speechless* (1981), *Cheap At Half The Price* (1983), with Lol Coxhill *French Gigs* (1983), with Chris Cutler *Live In Prague And Washington* (1983), with Rene Lussier *Nous Autres* (Recommended 1988), with others *The Technology Of Tears* (Recrec 1988), *The Top Of His Head* (1990), *Step Across*

The Border (Rer Megacorp 1991), *Helter Skelter* (1993), *With Enemies Like These Who Needs Friends* (SST 1993).

Fuller, Curtis

b. 15 December 1934, Detroit, Michigan, USA. Fuller began studying trombone in his teens, eventually playing in a band during his military service in the early 50s. As the leader of the band was Cannonball Adderley, it was not surprising that, following his discharge, Fuller quickly turned to jazz. At first he worked in his home town, playing with Kenny Burrell, Yusef Lateef and others, but then moved to New York, where he worked with Dizzy Gillespie, Hampton Hawes, John Coltrane and Miles Davis, led his own small bands and was a founder-member of the Jazztet with Art Farmer and Benny Golson. In the early 60s he was a member of Art Blakey's Jazz Messengers, touring extensively with this band and also with Gillespie. In the 70s Fuller gradually incorporated jazz-rock concepts into his repertoire and worked with musicians such as Stanley Clarke. In the mid-to late 70s he was with Count Basie, Kai Winding, Lionel Hampton, Cedar Walton, Red Garland and Sal Nistico and also continued to lead his own groups. In the 80s his musical associates included Golson again and he also played in a reformed Jazztet and in the Timeless All Stars band. A major post-bop stylist on trombone, Fuller's technical facility on the instrument allows him great freedom to develop his inventive lines.

Albums: with John Coltrane *Blue Train* (1957), *New Trombone* (Original Jazz Classics 1957), *Curtis Fuller With Red Garland* (1957), *Curtis Fuller And Hampton Hawes With French Horns* (1957), *Bone And Bari* (1957), *Arabia* (1959), *Imagination* (Savoy 1959), *Curtis Fuller's Jazztet* (Savoy 1959), *Images* (Savoy 1960), *Blues-ette* (Savoy 1960), *Meet The Jazztet* (1960), *The Jazz Ambassador* (1961), with Art Blakey *Caravan* (1962), *Crankin'* (c.1973), *Smokin'* (c.1974), *Fire And Filigree* (Beehive 1978), with Kai Winding *Giant Bones 80* (1979), with Timeless All Stars *It's Timeless* (1982), *New Trombone* (Prestige 1984), *Four On The Outside* (Timeless 1986), *Curtis Fuller Meets Roma Jazz Trio* (Timeless 1988), *Bluesette Part 2* (Savoy 1993).

Fuller, Gil

b. Walter Gilbert Fuller, 14 April 1920, Los Angeles, California, USA. Although he started out in the early 40s writing for orthodox swing-era big bands such as Charlie Barnet's, Fuller's true *metier* was revealed in 1942 when he began an association with Dizzy Gillespie. In 1944 they were together in the Billy Eckstine band and continued their working relationship when Gillespie formed his 1946 bebop big band. Gillespie's interest in Latin American music was complemented by Fuller, who had previously written for Tito Puente, and his arrangements included 'Manteca'. Despite the importance of his work with Gillespie, Fuller's interest had waned by the end of the 40s. Although he wrote occasionally for Gillespie and Stan Kenton in the 50s and 60s, a new career, in engineering, occupied his time.

G

G., Kenny

b. Kenneth Gorelick, 1959, Seattle, Washington, USA. Gorelick learned saxophone as a child and toured Europe in 1974 with the Franklin High School band. Two years later he played with Barry White's Love Unlimited Orchestra in Seattle before entering the University of Washington to study accounting. Gorelick first recorded with local funk band Cold, Bold & Together and also backed many leading artists on their Seattle shows. After graduation, he joined the Jeff Lorber Fusion, recording with the jazz-rock band for Arista Records, the label which in 1981 signed him to a solo contract. Produced by Preston Glass and Narada Michael Walden, *Duotones* was his biggest success and it included 'Songbird', a Top 10 hit in 1987. Like much of his other work, it featured a flawless, melodic alto saxophone solo. By now, Kenny G was in demand to play solos on albums by such singers as Whitney Houston, Natalie Cole and Aretha Franklin. Among the guest artists on *Silhouette* was Smokey Robinson who sang 'We've Saved The Best Till Last'. Like its predecessor, the album sold over three million copies worldwide. G's extraordinary success has continued into the 90s with the multi-platinum *Breathless*, and he has been acknowledged as fellow musician President Clinton's favourite saxophonist. The crossover into pop is felt to be too strong, as the type of music he plays is very structured and contrived. Popular music has at least given rise to the 'great crossover debate'. Arguments aside; Kenny G. is a phenomenon, he sells albums in rock group proportions and his popularity is consistent. His *Miracles: The Holiday Album* rocketed to the top of the US pop chart, re-igniting interest in *Breathless* which, by the mid-90s had sold over seven million copies in the USA alone.

Albums: *Kenny G* (1982), *G Force* (1983), *Gravity* (1985), *Duotones* (1986), *Silhouette* (1988), *Kenny G Live* (1989), *Breathless* (1992), *Miracles: The Holiday Album.* (1994).

Gabler, Milt

b. 20 May 1911, New York City, New York, USA. In 1926 Gabler's father opened a store, the Commodore Music Shop, at 144 East 42nd Street in New York City. When Gabler took over its operation he sold sporting goods and novelties as sidelines to the main trade, which was in sheet music, records and radio. To buy anything there, however, a customer had to like jazz: all day long Gabler played jazz records on a wind-up phonograph and soon the shop became the in-place for jazz fans to gather. In the late 30s and early 40s the habituees included several noted journalists and academics who wrote on jazz, among them Marshall Stearns, Wilder Hobson and John Hammond Jnr. Gabler's first big steps in serving the needs of jazz fans came when he persuaded several major record companies to reissue sought-after but out-of-print records even though he had to guarantee orders far in excess of likely sales. The next logical step was to make his own records, for which he hired the services of another Commodore regular, Eddie Condon. Additionally, Gabler and Condon launched weekly jam sessions at Jimmy Ryan's, a leading 52nd Street nightspot, and Gabler later opened a branch of his store across the street from Ryan's. Among the many artists recorded by Gabler for his Commodore label was Billie Holiday, who in 1939 made four sides which became classics: 'Yesterdays', 'I Gotta Right To Sing The Blues', 'Fine And Mellow' and the sombre 'Strange Fruit'.

Gadd, Steve

b. 4 September 1945, Rochester, New York, USA. Gadd was taught the drums by an uncle from the age of three: he enjoyed Sousa marches and worked with a drum corps. He spent two years at Manhattan's School of Music before going on to Eastman College in Rochester after which he was drafted into the army and spent three years in an army band. His first professional work was with Chuck Mangione before he joined Chick Corea's Return To Forever in 1975. Corea described him as bringing 'orchestral and compositional thinking to the drum kit while at the same time having a great imagination and a great ability to swing'. Gadd worked extensively in the New York studios from the early 70s onwards and was able to provide the perfect accompaniment for a diverse series of sessions. He developed his own style of linear drumming in which no two drums are sounded at the same time. He played for many artists from Charles Mingus via George Benson to Paul Simon with whom he toured in 1991, directing the large group of percussionists on the *Rhythm Of The Saints* tour. So ubiquitous did he become that it was his sound that was sampled for the earlier drum machines. In 1976 he played in the influential funk band Stuff along with other session musicians like Eric Gale and Richard Tee. Throughout the 80s Gadd continued with a busy studio schedule but also played in the straight jazz Manhattan Jazz Quintet.

Selected albums: with George Benson *In Concert* (1975), *My Spanish Heart* (1976), with Carla Bley *Dinner Music* (1976), with Stuff *Stuff* (1977), *Friends* (1978), *The Mad Hatter* (1978), with Chick Corea *Three Quartets* (1981), with Al DiMeola *Electric Rendezvous* (1982), with Manhattan Jazz Quintet *Manhattan Jazz Quintet* (1986), *Gaddabout* (King 1986), *Autumn Leaves* (1986), with Paul Simon *Rhythm Of The Saints* (1989).

Gaillard, Slim

b. Bulee Gaillard, 4 January 1916, Santa Clara, Cuba, d. 26 February 1991. Gaillard led an adventurous childhood. On one occasion, while travelling on board a ship on which his father was steward, he was left behind in Crete when the ship sailed. His adventures became more exciting every time he recounted his tales and include activities such as professional boxer, mortician and truck driver for bootleggers. Originally based in Detroit, Gaillard entered vaudeville in the early 30s with an act during which he played the guitar while tap-danc-

ing. Later in the decade he moved to New York and formed a duo with bassist Slam Stewart in which Gaillard mostly played guitar and sang. Much of their repertoire was original material with lyrics conceived in Gaillard's personal version of the currently popular 'jive talk', which on his lips developed extraordinary surrealist overtones. Gaillard's language, which he named 'Vout' or 'Vout Oreenie', helped the duo achieve a number of hit records, including 'Flat Foot Floogie'. Their success led to a long-running radio series and an appearance in the film *Hellzapoppin*. In 1943 Stewart was inducted for military service and was replaced by Bam Brown. Now based in Los Angeles, Gaillard continued to write songs, often in collaboration with Brown, and had another big hit with 'Cement Mixer (Put-ti Put-ti)'. With Brown he co-authored a remarkable extended work, 'Opera in Vout', which premiered in Los Angeles in 1946. (In fact, it was not an opera and not much of it was in vout!) Another huge hit was 'Down By The Station', a song which, uniquely for a jazz artist, entered the catalogue of classic children's nursery rhymes. Contrastingly, he also recorded with bebop musicians, including Charlie Parker and Dizzy Gillespie (*Slim's Jam*). In the late 40s he continued his eccentric entertaining, which included such intriguing routines as playing piano with his hands upside-down. Not surprisingly, given his manner of performance and his private language, some people never quite understood Gaillard and one radio station banned his record 'Yep Roc Heresy', declaring it to be degenerate; in fact, the lyric was merely a recitation of the menu from an Armenian restaurant. In the late 50s and for several years thereafter, Gaillard worked mostly outside music but gradually returned to prominence by way of acting roles, (including a part in the USA television series *Roots*), festival appearances with Stewart and, in the 80s, numerous television and stage shows in the UK where he became resident in 1983. His tall, loping figure, invariably topped by a big grin and a rakish white beret, became a familiar sight in London's jazzland. In 1989 he starred in a four-part UK BBC television series, *The World Of Slim Gaillard*. In addition to his singing and guitar playing, Gaillard also played piano, vibraphone and tenor saxophone.

Albums: *Vout, Jam And Jive On The Rudy Vallee Radio Show* (1938), *Jazz At The Philharmonic: Opera In Vout* (1946), *Slim Gaillard Rides Again: Dot Sessions* (1958), *Anytime, Anyplace, Anywhere* (1982), *Live At Billy Berg's: The Voutest!* (1983, rec. 1946). Compilations: *Slim And Slam* (1938-39), *Son Of McVoutie* (1941-46), *The Legendary McVoutie* (1941-46), *McVoutie* (1945), *Slim's Jam* (1945-46), *Laughing In Rhythm* (1945-51), *Tutti Frutti* (1987, rec. 1945), tribute album *The Legendary McVouty* ii (Hep 1993, recorded 1992).

Gale, Eric

b. 20 September 1938, Brooklyn, New York, USA, d. 25 May 1994, Baja California, Mexico. Gale studied chemistry at Niagara University. He took up the double bass when he was 12 years old and also played tenor saxophone, trombone and tuba before he chose the guitar. The basis of his style was formed on the 50s and 60s R&B circuit. He was with the

Drifters, Jackie Wilson, the Flamingos and Maxine Brown, before playing in the 60s with King Curtis, Jimmy Smith, David 'Fathead' Newman, Mongo Santamaría and Aretha Franklin. In the early 70s Gale became the house guitarist with Creed Taylor's new CTI label and worked with Stanley Turrentine's band. He took four years off on his Ohio farm and went to Jamaica where he assimilated the reggae style. On his return to New York in 1976 he was a founder of the influential funk band Stuff along with artists including Steve Gadd, Cornell Dupree and Richard Tee. They played regularly at Mikell's in Manhattan with only minimal rehearsal. In the early 90s he performed as a regular band member in several US television shows. Gale thought like a front line musician and played like a saxophonist.

Albums: *Stuff* (1977), *Ginseng Woman* (1977), *Multiplication* (1979), *Forecast* (1979), *Part Of You* (1979), *Touch Of Silk* (1980), *Blue Horizon* (1982), *Island Breeze* (1984). Compilation: *The Best Of Eric Gale* (1980).

Galloway, Jim

b. 28 July 1936, Kilwinning, Scotland. After working in Glasgow while still a teenager, Galloway, a clarinettist and saxophonist, emigrated to Canada in the mid-60s where he became well known as a sideman, leader of the Metro Stompers, accompanist to visiting American jazz stars, and radio personality. Success at the 1976 Montreux Jazz Festival with a band that included Jay McShann and Buddy Tate led to worldwide recognition for this dedicated musician. Rooted in the mainstream, Galloway's playing of the many instruments on which he performs betrays his admiration for Sidney Bechet, Edmond Hall and Coleman Hawkins among others. A major work, 'Hot And Suite', was given its first performance at the 1985 Edinburgh Arts Festival.

Albums: *Metro Stompers* (Sackville 1973), *Three's Company* (Sackville 1973), *Bojangles* (Hep Jazz 1978), *Featuring Jay McShann* (1981), *Thou Swell* (Sackville 1981).

Gambale, Frank

b. 1959, Australia. A virtuoso guitarist nicknamed 'The Thunder From Down Under', Gambale has lived in Los Angeles for more than a decade and, after making his name with fusion keyboard legend Chick Corea's popular Elektric Band, is most commonly associated with America's west coast fusion/studio scene. In Australia he began his career concentrating on the pop field, singing and playing guitar in vocal-orientated bands. He became involved in Hollywood's celebrated Guitar Institute of Technology in 1982, when he moved to the US, first enrolling as a student and finally staying on as a teacher, before joining Chick Corea's group in 1986. He stayed with the outfit for seven years, soloing seldomly but blinding other guitarists with his advanced technical facility during the band's stunningly fast and intricate ensemble passages. When Corea formed his concurrent Akoustic Band, Gambale had more time on his hands to pursue his solo career, and work with other projects, including drummer Steve Smith's highly-regarded fusion quartet Vital Information. Gambale (and the

virtuoso rhythm section of bassist John Pattitucci and drummer Dave Weckl) left the Elektric Band in 1993, and has since concentrated on his own series of albums on the JVC label. A guitarist with perhaps more technique than he knows what to do with, Gambale plays with a rock sensibility, firing blistering, aggressive lines and more recently reverting to his old interests in singing.

Albums: *Brave New Guitar* (1985), with Chick Corea *Light Years* (1987), with Corea *Eye Of The Beholder* (1988), with Corea *Inside Out* (1990), *Note Worker* (1991), with Corea *Beneath The Mask* (1992), *The Great Explorers* (1993), *Thunder From Down Under* (1993), *Passages* (1994).

Ganelin Trio

When originally formed in 1971 this Soviet trio consisted of Vyacheslav Ganelin (b. 1944, Kraskov, USSR; keyboards, flute, percussion, guitar), Vladimir Chekasin (reeds, trombone, violin, percussion, voice), and Vladimir Tarasov (b. 1947, Archangelsk, USSR; drums, percussion). Although firmly based on composition, a recording or concert performance by the trio is a rich mix of slavonic folk, free jazz, contemporary classical music and parodies of all three traditions. Their first album, *Con Anima*, was recorded in the USSR in 1976, but the Soviet state record label, Melodiya, was highly dilatory about issuing their recordings. Leo Feigin's London-based Leo Records took on the task, though his first releases, of tapes smuggled out of the USSR, were issued with a disclaimer that the musicians bore no responsibility for their music's appearance on record. In the 80s the trio began to play outside the Soviet Union and Eastern bloc, scoring a great success at the 1980 West Berlin Jazz Festival, then visiting Italy in 1981, and the UK on a Contemporary Music Network tour in 1984, where they met with a mixed reception from jazz critics and musicians. Ganelin emigrated to Israel in 1987, where he formed a new trio, exhibiting a more severe style of music on two albums, with Victor Fonarev (bass, percussion) and Mika Markovich (drums, percussion). Tarasov and Chekasin have continued to work together.

Albums: *Con Anima* (Leo 1980, rec. 1976), *Live In East Germany* (Leo 1980, rec. 1978, reissued as *Catalogue*), *Con Fuoco* (Leo 1981, rec. 1978, 1980), *Concerto Grosso* (1982, rec. 1978), *Poi Segue* (1982, rec. 1981), *Ancora Da Capo Part I* (Leo 1982, rec. 1980), *Ancora Da Capo Part 2* (Leo 1982, rec. 1980), *New Wine* (Leo 1983, rec. 1982), *Non Troppo* (1983, rec. 1982), *Vide* (1983, rec. 1981), *Strictly For Our Friends* (1984, rec. 1978), *Vide* (Leo 1984), *Baltic Triangle* (1985, rec. 1981), *Con Affetto* (Leo 1985), *Non Troppo* (Hat Art 1985, rec. 1980, 1983), *Itaango...In Nickelsdorf* (1986, rec. 1985), *Great Concerts Of New Jazz Vol 1* (Leo 1987), *Poco A Poco* (Leo 1988, rec. 1978), *Jerusalem February Cantabile* (1989), with others *Document* (1990, rec. 1980-89, eight-CD box-set), *Opuses* (Leo 1990). Duo albums: Ganelin/Tarasov *Opus AZ* (1983); Ganelin/Chekasin, Ganelin/Tarasov *3-1=3* (1988, rec. 1980-85); Chekasin/Tarasov *1-11=3* (1989). *Great Concerts Of New Jazz Vol 2* (Leo 1988). Solo albums: Vyacheslav Ganelin *Con Amore* (Leo 1987, rec. 1985), with Pyatras Vysniauskas,

Grigory Talas *Inverso* (Leo 1987, rec. 1984), with others *Conspiracy* (Leo 1991, rec. 1989, four-CD box-set); Vladimir Tarasov *Atto, Vols 1-4* (late 80s), with Andrew Cyrille *Galaxies* (1991).

Further reading: *Russian Jazz New Identity*, Leo Feigin (Ed.).

Ganley, Allan

b. 11 March 1931, Tolworth, Surrey, England. A self-taught drummer, in the early 50s Ganley played in the dance band led by Bert Ambrose. In 1953 he came to prominence as a member of John Dankworth's band, then the most popular modern jazz group in the UK. Also in the 50s, he worked with pianist Derek Smith, Dizzy Reece, clarinettist Vic Ash, Ronnie Scott and several visiting American musicians. Towards the end of the decade he was co-leader with Ronnie Ross of a small group known as the Jazzmakers. In the early 60s Ganley was often with Tubby Hayes, playing with his small groups and the occasionally assembled big band. As house drummer at Scott's club he played with numerous leading American jazzmen, including Dizzy Gillespie, Stan Getz, Jim Hall, Freddie Hubbard and Raahsan Roland Kirk. In the early 70s he took time out to study at Berklee College Of Music, then returned to the UK to form and lead a big band, which he maintained sporadically for the next 10 years. Throughout the 70s and 80s Ganley could be seen and heard on countless broadcasts and recording dates, playing with jazz musicians of all styles, effortlessly slipping from traditional to post-bop to big band to mainstream, all the while swinging with great subtlety. In the 90s Ganley was as active as ever, playing club and festival dates throughout the UK with occasional overseas trips. The self-effacing nature of his playing has made him a perfect accompanist for pianists as different as Teddy Wilson and Al Haig and for singers from Carol Kidd to Blossom Dearie. Although less well known for his work as an arranger, Ganley has provided charts for many leading British jazzmen as well as for the BBC Radio Big Band, thus enhancing the enormous yet understated contribution he has made to the British jazz scene over the years.

Albums: with Tubby Hayes *Down At The Village* (1962), with Hayes *Late Spot At Scott's* (1962), with Jim Hall *Commitment* (1976), with Al Haig *Stablemates* (1977), with Carol Kidd *The Night We Called It A Day* (1990).

Garbarek, Jan

b. 4 March 1947, Norway. Inspired by hearing John Coltrane on the radio in 1961, Garbarek taught himself to play tenor saxophone (subsequently adding soprano and bass sax). In 1962 he won an amateur competition, which resulted in his first professional work, and he was soon leading a group with Jon Christensen, Terje Rypdal and Arild Andersen. In 1968 he was the Norwegian representative at the European Broadcasting Union festival, and the recordings of this (notably an impressive version of Coltrane's 'Naima') brought him to wider notice when they were transmitted throughout Europe. Subsequently his style has become more severe, sometimes almost bleak, although there is a restrained warmth to his sound. Garbarek's playing is representative of the kind of music associated with Manfred Eicher's ECM label and of a characteristically Scandinavian strand of jazz, melodic and atmospheric, which has little overt emotionalism but does not lack intensity. His writing and playing display considerable concern with tone and texture and appear to have exerted some influence on Tommy Smith and post-sabbatical Charles Lloyd (with whom he has shared colleagues Christensen, Keith Jarrett and Palle Danielsson) as well as a variety of European players such as Joakim Milder and Alberto Nacci. In the mid-70s he worked in Jarrett's 'Belonging' band with Christensen and Danielsson, recording the much-praised *Belonging* and *My Song*, and also played with Ralph Towner on *Solstice* and *Sounds And Shadows*. In the 80s his own groups have featured Eberhard Weber, Bill Frisell and John Abercrombie among others. His tours in the late 80s with a band including the remarkable percussionist Nana Vasconcelos were highly acclaimed and inspired many other musicians and bands to essay the juxtaposition of glacially imposing saxophone lines with exotic, tropical rhythm. Garbarek has also worked with Don Cherry, Chick Corea, David Torn and with George Russell during Russell's residency in Scandinavia in the late 60s - an association which resulted in a fine series of recordings that featured the young Garbarek, notably *Othello Ballet Suite*, *Trip To Prillarguri* and *Electronic Sonata For Souls Loved By Nature* (though none was released until the 80s). Garbarek has also shown an increasing interest in folk and ethnic musics that has not only coloured his own playing but led to him recording with Ravi Shankar on the 1984 *Song For Everyone* and producing an ECM album for the Norwegian folk singer Agnes Buen Gårnas, 1991's *Rosensfole*. For *Ragas & Sagas* (1993), Garbarek collaborated with the Pakistani classical singer, Usted Fateh Ali Khan and trio of musicians playing tabla and sarangi, a 39-string violin. Garbarek's melodic solos effectively complemented the traditional Pakistani instrumental sounds. In the same year, Garbarek's *Twelve Moons* concentrated once again on the Scandinavian-folk melodies he is continually exploring. The album's emphatic rhythmic 'feel' was due in no small part to the presence of drummer Manu Katche and bassist Eberhard Weber. Rather surprisingly, given his avoidance of gallery-pleasing pyrotechnics, Garbarek has steadily acquired a public following equal to his huge critical reputation.

Albums: *Esoteric Circle* (1969), *Afric Pepperbird* (ECM 1971), *Sart* (ECM 1972), *Triptykon* (ECM 1973), with Art Lande *Red Lanta* (ECM 1974), with Babo Stenson *Witchi-Tai-To* (ECM 1974), with Stenson *Dansere* (ECM 1976), *Dis* (ECM 1977), *Places* (ECM 1978), *Photo With Blue Sky* (ECM 1979), with Charlie Haden, Egberto Gismonti *Magico* (1980), with Kjell Johnsen *Aftenland* (ECM 1980), with Haden, Gismonti *Folksongs* (ECM 1981), *Eventyr* (ECM 1981), *Paths, Prints* (ECM 1982), *Wayfarer* (1983), *It's OK To Listen To The Gray Voice* (ECM 1985), *All Those Born With Wings* (ECM 1986), *Legend Of The Seven Dreams* (ECM 1988), *I Took Up The Runes* (ECM 1990), *Star* (ECM 1991), with Agnes Buen Gårnas *Rosensfole* (ECM 1991), with Usted Fateh Ali Khan and Musicians From Pakistan *Ragas & Sagas* (ECM 1992), *Twelve Moons* (ECM 1993), with Miroslav Vitous *Atmos* (1993),

Madar (ECM 1993), with the Hilliard Ensemble *Officium* (ECM New Series 1994). Compilation: *Works* (ECM 1984).

Garland, Ed 'Montudie'

b. 9 January 1885, New Orleans, Louisiana, USA, d. 22 January 1980. As a child, Garland played drums and brass bass, often working in marching bands in his home town. Among the early jazz stars with whom he claims to have played were Buddy Bolden (1904), Freddie Keppard (1906), and Kid Ory (1910). By 1914 he was based in Chicago, from where he toured the black vaudeville circuit, but was on hand in 1921 to help form a band, led by Joe 'King' Oliver, to play a residency at the city's newly-opened Royal Garden. When the Oliver band toured California, Garland, by now playing string bass, stayed behind in Los Angeles, working frequently with Ory. In 1927 he formed his own group in Los Angeles which lasted for a number of years. Late in 1940 he assembled a band to be led by Jelly Roll Morton for a recording date, but Morton was gravely ill and died before the session could take place. In 1944 Garland was a member of a band assembled by Orson Welles for a series of radio programmes. The 'Mercury Theatre All Stars' included Jimmy Noone, who died on the morning of the third broadcast and an impromptu performance of 'Blues For Jimmy' featured a bowed bass solo by Garland which thereafter became a permanent part of his repertoire. In 1944 he was reunited with Ory and remained with him for the next decade, their relationship ending when a misunderstanding led to a fist-fight at the Hangover club in San Francisco. From 1955 Garland freelanced with Andrew Blakeney, Earl 'Fatha' Hines, Turk Murphy and others. In 1971 he returned to his birthplace for the first time in over half a century to play at the 4th New Orleans Jazz Festival. From 1973 Garland played at several festivals and toured the USA and Europe with Barry Martyn's Legends Of Jazz band. Despite failing sight and hearing, and general frailty, Garland toured until September 1977, when he was hospitalized in Germany. Back home in Los Angeles he retired, at the age of 92, but still played with the Legends Of Jazz whenever they came to town. Although he often played his instrument in the traditional 'slapping' manner, Garland had a notably light touch but he favoured using the bow, thus adding variety to his always rhythmic support.
Albums: *Kid Ory Live At The Club Hangover* (1953-54), *Kid Ory's Creole Jazz Band* (1954).

Garland, Red

b. William M. Garland, 13 May 1923, Dallas, Texas, USA, d. 23 April 1984. Garland turned to the piano in his late teens, having earlier studied and played reed instruments. Although initially inspired by mainstream artists, he moved into bebop in the late 40s, accompanying Charlie Parker, Fats Navarro and others while still playing regularly with musicians such as Coleman Hawkins and Ben Webster. In 1955 he joined Miles Davis, remaining a member of the quintet until 1958. For the next 10 years he led his own trio, which recorded extensively, but drifted into obscurity after 1968 when he settled in Texas. Towards the end of the following decade he returned to the national and international jazz scene. As a soloist Garland was often lyrical if not especially commanding; but he made an important contribution to the powerful rhythm section (with Paul Chambers and Philly Joe Jones) of one of Davis's best bands, where his sophisticated technique, use of harmonic substitutions and block-chording set standards for many contemporary and later bop bands.
Selected albums: *A Garland Of Red* (Original Jazz Classics 1956), *The Red Garland Trio* i (1956), *Red Garland's Piano/The P.C. Blues* (1957), *Groovy/Red Garland Revisited* (Original Jazz Classics 1957), *Saying Something* (1957), *All Mornin' Long* (Original Jazz Classics 1957), *Soul Junction* (Original Jazz Classics 1957), *High Pressure* (Original Jazz Classics 1957), *Dig It* (Original Jazz Classics 1957), *It's A Blue World* (1958), *Manteca* (1958), *Rediscovered Masters* (Original Jazz Classics 1958), *Rojo* (Original Jazz Classics 1958), *The Red Garland Trio* ii (Original Jazz Classics 1958), with Miles Davis *Milestones* (1958), *All Kinds Of Weather* (Original Jazz Classics 1958), *Red In Bluesville* (Original Jazz Classics 1959), *The Red Garland Trio* iii (1959), *The Red Garland Trio With Eddie 'Lockjaw' Davis* (Original Jazz Classics 1959), *Red Alone* (1960), *Alone With The Blues* (1960), *Hallello-y'all* (1960), *Bright And Breezy* (1961), *The Nearness Of You* (1961), *Solar* (Original Jazz Classics 1962), *Red's Good Groove* (1962), *When There Are Grey Skies* (Original Jazz Classics 1962), *Auf Wiedersehen* (1971), *The Quota* (1971), *Crossings* (Original Jazz Classics 1977), *Red Alert* (Original Jazz Classics 1977), *Feelin' Red* (Muse 1978), *I Left My Heart* (1978), *Equinox* (1978), *Stepping Out* (Galaxy 1979), *Strike Up The Band* (1979), *Wee Small Hours* (1980), *Misty Red* (Timeless 1982).

Garner, Erroll

b. 15 June 1921, Pittsburgh, Pennsylvania, USA, d. 2 January 1977. A self-taught pianist, Garner played on the radio at the age of 10 and within a few more years was playing professionally in his home town. Among the bands he played with during this period were those led by Leroy Brown and, reputedly, Fate Marable. In 1944 Garner moved to New York and began working in nightclubs, including the Rendezvous and the Melody Bar. He became a popular and successful performer in such establishments, but also enjoyed playing at the more jazz-orientated joints along 52nd Street, such as Tondelayo's and the Three Deuces. For a short while he worked in a trio led by Slam Stewart, but soon formed his own trio. For the rest of his life, with only occasional exceptions, Garner worked as leader of a trio or as soloist. Throughout the 50s, 60s and early 70s, he toured the USA, playing prestigious club and hotel engagements, appearing at festivals and on radio and television. He also visited Europe and the UK, where he also appeared on television and in 1962 had an album in the UK charts. During these years Garner recorded numerous albums, some of them, such as the classic *Concert By The Sea*, becoming virtual fixtures in the catalogue. Although Garner taught himself to play, he never troubled to learn to read music yet he contrived to create several jazz tunes including one, 'Misty', which became a standard when Johnny Burke added a lyric. Occasionally in

Garner's playing slight echoes of the full sound of Earl 'Fatha' Hines appear, as do touches that suggest he had absorbed the work of the stride piano players, but throughout the bulk of his vast output Garner is uniquely himself. Playing consistently to a very high standard, he developed certain characteristics which bear few resemblances to other pianists. Notably, these include a plangent left-hand, block-chorded pulse, a dancing pattern of seemingly random ideas played with the right hand in chords or single notes, and playful introductions, which appear as independent miniature compositions only to sweep suddenly, with total surprise and complete logic, into an entirely different song. Sumptuously romantic on ballads, fleet and daring on up-tempo swingers, Garner's range was wide. Nicknamed 'The Elf', more perhaps for his diminutive size than the impish good humour of those introductions, Garner was the first jazz pianist since Fats Waller to appeal to the non-jazz audience and the first jazzman ever to achieve popular acclaim by this audience without recourse to singing or clowning. Stylistically, Garner is in a category of which he is, so far, the only member. He came from nowhere, and since his death in 1977, there has been no sign that any other pianist is following his independent path in jazz.

Selected albums: *Serenade To Laura* (Savoy c.50s), *Separate Keyboards* (Savoy c.50s), *Penthouse Serenade* (Savoy c.50s), *Long Ago And Far Away* (Columbia c.50s), *Body And Soul* (Columbia 1953), *Afternoon Of An Elf* (1955), *Concert By The Sea* (CBS 1955), *Dreamstreet* (1959), *Close Up In Swing* (1961), *The Concert Garner In England* (1963), *A Night At The Movies* (1965), *That's My Kick* (1966-67), *Up In Erroll's Room* (c.1968). Selected compilations: *Historical First Recordings* (1944), *Overture To Dawn* (1944), *Passport To Fame* (1944), *Early Erroll: 1945 Stride Vols 1 & 2* (1945), *Gemini* (Decca 1978), *The Great Garner* (Atlantic 1979), *Complete Savoy Sessions Vol. 1* (RCA 1986, 1945-49 recordings), *Yesterdays* (1945-49), *The Elf* (1945-49), *Cocktail Time* (1947), *Body & Soul* (1951-52), *Misty* (CBS, 1951-57 recording), *Erroll Garner Plays Gershwin And Kern* (1958-65), *Complete Savoy Sessions Vol. 2* (RCA 1986, 1949 recording), *Long Ago And Far Away* (CBS 1988), *Jazz Portraits* (Jazz Portraits 1993).

Further reading: *Erroll Garner: The Most Happy Piano*, James M. Doran.

Garrick, Michael

b. 30 May 1933, Enfield, Middlesex, England. Largely self-taught as a pianist and composer, Garrick led bands during the 50s and was active in the 'jazz and poetry' movement. In the mid-60s he worked with the band co-led by Don Rendell and Ian Carr and also fronted his own small group, which often featured the outstanding saxophonist Joe Harriott. A prolific composer, in the late 60s Garrick's writing reflected his beliefs and 'Jazz Praises' was performed at St Paul's Cathedral in London. In keeping with the mood of works such as this, Garrick also played the pipe organ. In the 70s he advanced his own musical knowledge by studying at Berklee College Of Music in the USA and subsequently taught extensively in the UK. In the late 70s he formed a trio with Phil Lee and Norma

Winstone. The 80s saw him active with small and large bands, sometimes under his own leadership, and continuing his interest in jazz education.

Albums: *Michael Garrick* i (1963), *Michael Garrick* ii (1963), *Michael Garrick* iii (1964), *Michael Garrick* iv (1965), *Michael Garrick* v (1965), *Black Marigolds* (1966), *Jazz Praises At St Paul's* (1968), *Poetry And Jazz In Concert 250* (1969), *Michael Garrick* (1970), *Mr Smith's Apocalypse* (1971), *Cold Mountain* (1972), *Home Stretch Blues* (1972), *Troppo* (1973), *You've Changed* (Hep Jazz 1978).

Garrison, Jimmy

b. 3 March 1934, Miami, Florida, USA, d. 7 April 1976. Garrison began playing bass in Philadelphia, where he grew up, moving to New York in the late 50s with Philly Joe Jones. By 1961 he was deeply involved with the free jazz movement, and played with Ornette Coleman at New York's Five Spot. John Coltrane sitting in with the group, was so impressed by Garrison that he invited the bassist to join his own quartet, so beginning a five-year association in which Garrison proved 'the pivot' (to quote McCoy Tyner) of the pre-eminent modern jazz group of the era, thanks to his dynamic and forceful musical personality. In 1963 he took time out to co-lead a sextet session, *Illumination*, with his Coltrane rhythm-section partner, Elvin Jones. After leaving Coltrane in 1966 he led his own group, played with the bands of Hampton Hawes, Archie Shepp and Elvin Jones and recorded again with Ornette Coleman, 1968's *New York Is Now!* and *Love Call* supplementing a previous vinyl meeting on *Ornette On Tenor* (1961). Despite his career-long involvement with the *avant garde*, Garrison retained a traditional view of the role the bass should have in jazz; and although a gifted soloist, he chose to concentrate upon his instrument's rhythmic function, seeing that as the foundation of good group jazz. In the 70s Garrison taught, played with Alice Coltrane and also returned for a further spell with Elvin Jones but was troubled with ill-health. He died of lung cancer in April 1976.

Albums: *Ornette On Tenor* (1961), *Coltrane* (1962), with Elvin Jones *Illumination* (1963), with John Coltrane *A Love Supreme* (1964), with Ornette Coleman *New York Is Now!* (1968), with Jones *The Ultimate* (1968), with Jones *Puttin' It Together* (1968).

Gaskin, Leonard

b. 25 August 1920, New York City, New York, USA. Gaskin first entered jazz at the deep end, playing bass in the regular rhythm section at Clark Monroe's Uptown House where bebop was forged in the early 40s. Among the musicians Gaskin backed there were Charlie Parker and Dizzy Gillespie. Despite his involvement with bebop, Gaskin was also in demand by mainstream jazz artists and played with such diverse groups as those led by Eddie South and Erroll Garner. In 1953 he recorded with Miles Davis and in 1956 joined the traditional line-up led by Eddie Condon. Throughout the 60s and beyond, Gaskin's versatility ensured him a successful career in the studios, from where he regularly emerged to play with many musicians including David 'Panama' Francis and Oliver Jackson. He also became a sought-after teacher.

Albums: *Miles Davis Plays Al Cohn Compositions* (1953), with Eddie Condon *The Roaring 20s* (1957), *A Dixieland Sound Spectacular/At The Jazz Band Ball* (1961), *At The Darktown Strutters Ball* (1962), *Dixieland Hits* (1962), *Oliver Jackson Presents 'Le Quartet'* (1982).

Gaslini, Giorgio

b. 22 October 1929, Milan, Italy. Gaslini learnt the piano as a child and started performing when he was 13 years old, appearing with his own trio at the Florence Jazz Festival in 1947. He studied at the Milan Conservatory before a career in which he has been equally at home in jazz and classical music. He would like to bring these various skills together in what he describes as 'total music'. He composed and played the music for Antonioni's film *La Notte* (1960) and wrote a jazz opera *Colloquio Con Malcolm X* (1970). He was friends with Eric Dolphy and worked with artists including Don Cherry, Gato Barbieri, Max Roach and Roswell Rudd as well as performing as a solo pianist and with his own groups. He has been involved in music education both directly as a teacher and by taking his quartet into less usual venues like factories and hospitals.

Albums: *Africa* (1969), *Colloquio Con Malcolm X* (1970), *Gaslini Plays Monk* (Soul Note 1980), Anthony Braxton *Four Pieces* (1981), *Schumann Reflections* (Soul Note 1984), *Ayler's Wings* (Soul Note 1991).

Gee, Jonathan

b. London, England. After an early classical training between the ages of five and nine, Gee lost interest in the piano during his teens. But it was during his time at Sheffield University that he developed his love of modern jazz, and began to practise the piano again. On his return to London he attended the jazz course at the Guildhall School of Music for a short time, but soon left, disenchanted with the system of jazz education. Since then Gee has quickly earned himself a reputation on the British jazz scene. Leading a trio with Wayne Batchelor and Winston Clifford, he won the 1991 Wire Best Newcomer Award.

Albums: *Blah, Blah, Blah, Etc., Etc.* (1989).

Geller, Herb

b. 2 November 1928, Los Angeles, California, USA. Geller's first major engagement on alto saxophone was with Joe Venuti in the mid-40s. By the end of the decade he was in New York, playing in Claude Thornhill's big band and early in the 50s he was performing with Billy May. In the mid-50s Geller worked with several leading west coast musicians, including Chet Baker, Shelly Manne, Maynard Ferguson, Shorty Rogers and Bill Holman. He was also co-leader of a small group with his wife, pianist Lorraine Walsh. After her sudden death in 1958 Geller worked with Benny Goodman and Louie Bellson, spent some time in South America and toured Europe, where he decided to settle. In 1962 he was in Berlin, playing in radio orchestras and running a nightclub. He later moved to Hamburg, where he again worked in radio and in several big bands, in between times playing and recording with his own small groups. A striking bebop player in the Charlie Parker mould, Geller's chosen pattern of work has limited his exposure to international audiences. However, the early 90s saw his return to touring with visits to the UK and elsewhere.

Selected albums: *Herb Geller Sextet* (1954), *The Gellers* (1955), *Fire In The West* (1957), *Shorty Rogers Plays Richard Rodgers* (1957), *Shelly Manne And His Men Play Peter Gunn* (1959), *Gypsy* (1959), *An American In Hamburg* (1975), *Rhyme To Reason* (Discovery 1978), *Hot House* (1984), *Birdland Stomp* (Enja 1986), *Fire In The West* (Fresh Sounds 1988), *Stax Of Sax* (Fresh Sounds 1988), *A Jazz Songbook Meeting* (Enja 1989), *West Coast Scene* (Vogue 1989).

Gentry, Chuck

b. Charles T. Gentry, 14 December 1911, Belgrade, Nebraska, USA, d. 1988. Starting out on clarinet, Gentry later mastered most of the saxophone family, specializing on the baritone. He began playing professionally in his mid-20s and in 1939 joined Vido Musso's big band, which soon folded; by the following year both Gentry and his former boss were working for Harry James. A year later the two men were still together, but this time with Benny Goodman. After a spell with Jimmy Dorsey, Gentry was drafted into the army and, following basic training, was transferred to the unit of musicians being assembled by Glenn Miller, where he remained until 1944. Once discharged, Gentry joined Artie Shaw and then returned for a second period with Goodman. By the late 40s, with most of the name big bands folding, Gentry was turning to studio work in Hollywood, which is where he spent most of the remainder of his career. He made numerous recordings in orchestras, backing artists such as June Christy and Nancy Wilson and performing with various leaders, including Louis Armstrong, Pete Rugolo, Woody Herman and Benny Carter. Occasionally he emerged from the studios to play dates with, for example, Stan Kenton's Los Angeles Neophonic Orchestra and with Bob Crosby at Disneyland.

Albums: with Pete Rugolo *Reeds In Hi-Fi* (1956), with Stan Kenton *Wagner* (1964).

Getz, Stan

b. 2 February 1927, Philadelphia, Pennsylvania, USA, d. 6 June 1991. Getz played several reed instruments as a child, especially the alto saxophone, but he finally choosing the tenor saxophone and by the age of 15 was playing professionally. Within a year he had made his first records, playing with Jack Teagarden, who became, technically at least, Getz's guardian so that the youngster could go on the road with the band. The following year Getz worked with Stan Kenton, then with the bands of Jimmy Dorsey and Benny Goodman. Although he had already attracted attention in jazz circles during these tenures and through record dates under his own name, it was as a member of Woody Herman's 'Four Brothers' band in 1947 that he became an internationally recognized name. He was with Herman for about two years and then, during the 50s, he began leading a small group on a semi-regular basis. Spells with

Kenton and Jazz At The Philharmonic were followed by an uncertain period as he sought, successfully, to throw off drug addiction. In the late 50s and early 60s he spent some time in Europe, being resident for a while in Copenhagen. Back in the USA in the early 60s he made a milestone album, *Focus*, and worked with Charlie Byrd, developing an interest in Brazilian and other Latin American musical forms. As a result Getz made a number of Latin records that proved to be very popular, amongst them 'The Girl From Ipanema', featuring singer Astrud Gilberto, which helped to launch the bossa nova craze. Throughout the 60s and 70s Getz led small groups, whose line-ups often featured up-and-coming musicians such as Gary Burton, Chick Corea, Jimmy Raney, Al Haig, Steve Swallow, Airto Moreira and JoAnne Brackeen. Nevertheless his activity in these years was sporadic. His earlier popular success and the control he exercised over his career, including production of his own recording sessions, allowed him to work as and when he wanted. In the 80s he became more active again; in addition to playing clubs, concerts and festivals around the world he was also artist-in-residence at Stanford University. He recorded with among others Everything But The Girl. This late period saw a new surge in popularity which sadly coincided with gradual awareness that he was suffering a terminal illness: he died of cancer in June 1991.

One of the most highly-regarded tenor saxophonists in jazz history, Getz's early recording career was highlighted by his work with Herman. His playing on several records, notably 'Early Autumn', a part of Ralph Burns's 'Summer Sequence' suite, displays to great effect the featherweight and almost vibrato-free tone which hints at the admiration he had for the work of Lester Young. Getz followed the success of this recording with a string of fine albums with his own small groups, notably those he made with Haig and Raney, in the process influencing a generation of tenor saxophonists who aspired to his coolly elegant style. The remarkable *Focus* album, a suite composed and arranged by Eddie Sauter for jazz players and a string quartet, and the bossa nova recordings, which included the single, 'Desafinado', were other features of his first period. The smoothness of Getz's sound, the delicate floating effect he created, proved immensely popular with the fringe audience and led some observers to conclude that his was a detached and introspective style. In fact, during this period he had made a conscious attempt to subdue the emotional content of his playing, in order to fit in with current commercial vogues. Beneath the surface calm there was a burning, emotional quality which flared only occasionally. By the mid-60s Getz had become bored with the style he had adopted and entered a new period of brief experimentation with electronics, followed by the gradual development of a new and deeply soulful ballad style. Although he was still playing with a delicately floating sound, his rich melodic sense was given much freer rein. Towards the end of his life, when he knew he was slowly dying of cancer, Getz entered a third and in some respects even more fulfilling phase of his career. Despite, or perhaps because of, the state of his health, the emotional content of his work began to burn with a romantic fire, a glorious outpouring of which is heard on his *Anniversary* and *Serenity* albums. In retrospect it was possible to see that this romanticism had always been there, even if, at various times, it had been deliberately suppressed to accord with the musical spirit of the times. No one could doubt the emotional thrust of his late work. His sound was still smooth but now that quality was more obviously a surface patina beneath which surged a fierce desire to communicate with his audience. He succeeded in doing so, and thus helped to make those years when his life waned as his music waxed a period not of sadness but one of grateful joy for his many admirers .

Selected albums: *Stan Plays Getz* (Verve 1954), *Stan Getz At The Shrine Auditorium* (1954), *At The Shrine* (Verve 1955), *West Coast Jazz* (1955), with Dizzy Gillespie *Diz And Getz* (Verve 1955), *The Steamer* (1956), *Stan Getz And J.J. Johnson At The Philharmonic Hall* (1957), with Gerry Mulligan *Getz Meets Mulligan In Hi-Fi* (Verve 1958), *Stan Getz And The Oscar Peterson Trio* (Verve 1958), *At The Opera House* (Verve 1958), *Stan Getz In Denmark* (1959), *The Early Days* (1959), *Stan Getz In Europe* (1959), *Stan Getz In Poland* (1960), *Focus* (1961), *Brazilian Mood* (1962), *Jazz Samba* (Verve 1962), *Jazz Samba Encore* (Verve 1963), *Getz/Gilberto* (Verve 1963), *Big Band Bossa Nova* (Verve 1963), *The Girl From Ipanema: The Bossa Nova Years* (1964), *Getz Au Go Go* (Verve 1964), *Stan Getz With Strings* (1964), *Stan Getz And Bill Evans* (Verve 1965), *A Song After Sundown* (1966), *Focus* (Verve 1966), *Sweet Rain* (Verve 1967), *The Stan Getz Quartet* (1969), *Didn't We* (1969), *Dynasty* (Verve 1971), *Portrait* (1972), *Captain Marvel* (Columbia 1972), *The Peacocks* (1975), *Best Of Two Worlds* (Columbia 1975), *The Master* (Columbia 1976), *Live At Montmartre* (Steeplechase 1977), *Another World* (Columbia 1978), *In Concert* (1980), *Children Of The World* (Columbia 1980), *The Dolphin* (Concord 1981), *Billy Highstreet Samba* (1981), *Spring Is Here* (Concord 1982), *Pure Getz* (Concord 1982), *Poetry* (1983), *Line For Lyons* (Sonet 1983), *The Stockholm Concert* (Sonet 1983), *The Voyage* (1986), *Anniversary* (Emarcy 1987), *Serenity* (Emarcy 1987), *Apasionado* (A&M 1989), with Kenny Barron *People Time* (Phonogram 1992), *Nobody Else But Me* (Verve 1994). Selected compilations: *The Best Of Woody Herman* (1945-47), *Opus De Bop* (1945-49), *Five Brothers* (1949), *The Stan Getz Quartet & Quintet* (1950-51), *The Roost Quartets* (1950-51), *Tenor Contrasts* (1951), *Stan Getz At Storyville Vols 1 & 2* (1951), *The Complete Recordings Of The Stan Getz 4 With Jimmy Raney* (1951-53), *Stan Getz With European Friends* (1958-71), *'Round Midnight In Paris* (1958-59), *The Best Of The Verve Years* (c.1972), *You The Night And Music* (Jazz Door 1991), *The Roost Years* (Roulette 1991), *New Collection* (Sony 1993), *Early Stan* (Original Jazz Classics 1993).

Gibbs, Mike

b. Michael Clement Irving, 25 September 1937, Harare, Zimbabwe. One of the most individual and original composers and arrangers, Gibbs has said that he began to concentrate on writing because performing solos terrified him. He studied piano between the ages of seven and 13, then took up trombone when he was 17. He moved to Boston, Massachusetts, in 1959 to study at the Berklee College Of Music (where he played and recorded with the college band organized by Herb Pomeroy) and Boston Conservatory. He also took up a scholarship at the Lennox School of Jazz in 1961, where he studied with Gunther Schuller, George Russell and J.J. Johnson. He graduated from Berklee in 1962 and the conservatory in 1963. That same year he obtained another scholarship, this time at Tanglewood, where he studied with classical composers Xenakis, Copland, Foss and Schuller again. After this he returned to Southern Rhodesia (Zimbabwe), then in 1965 he settled in England, playing trombone for Graham Collier and John Dankworth, working in pit orchestras for pantomimes and musicals, and subsequently recording a series of highly acclaimed and influential albums featuring many of the most prominent British-based players. His concert at London's Rainbow Theatre in 1974 was significant in that it was the first time for some decades that the Musicians Union permitted Americans to play with British musicians other than as featured soloists with local rhythm sections. This came about through Gibbs's long association with Gary Burton, whose quartet integrated with Gibbs's big band for this gig. Gibbs and Burton had studied and worked together at Berklee, and Burton had been the first to record Gibbs arrangements in 1963. He returned to Berklee as a tutor and composer-in-residence from 1974-83. In 1983 he resigned from the school to freelance as an arranger and producer, and worked with Michael Mantler,

Joni Mitchell, Pat Metheny, John McLaughlin, Whitney Houston, Peter Gabriel, and Sister Sledge among many others. In 1988 he made an own-name comeback with *Big Music* (composing and arranging all tracks as well as playing piano and trombone), and in 1991 toured with featured guitarist John Scofield, and appeared on Scofield's *Grace Under Pressure* in 1992. He was among the first writers to convincingly incorporate rock elements into orchestral jazz, and shared with one of his major influences, Gil Evans, the ability to organically integrate carefully arranged and scored frameworks with the most 'outside' improvisations. In the early days his writing also bore evidence of an enthusiasm for French contemporary master Olivier Messien. The list of albums below excludes those on which he only arranged or scored other people's music.

Selected albums: *Michael Gibbs* (1969), *Tanglewood '63* (1970), *Just Ahead* (1972), with Gary Burton *In The Public Interest* (1974), *Will Power* (1974), *The Only Chrome Waterfall Orchestra* (Ah-Um 1976), *Big Music* (Virgin 1988), *By The Way* (Ah-Um 1993).

\

Gibbs, Terry

b. Julius Gubenko, 13 October 1924, New York City, New York, USA. After all-round study of percussion, Gibbs briefly played drums professionally before and during military service. After discharge he concentrated on vibraphone, working with leaders such as Tommy Dorsey, Chubby Jackson and Buddy Rich. At the end of the 40s he achieved international promi-

Terry Gibbs

nence thanks to a two-year spell with Woody Herman followed by a brief period as a member of Benny Goodman's sextet. In the early 50s he also formed a big band and worked on television with Mel Tormé. Towards the end of the decade, by then based in California, he reformed a big band, which he led at the prestigious Monterey Jazz Festival in 1961. Gibbs's big bands became a notable annual event in Los Angeles, featuring many well-known players who clearly enjoyed taking time out from the studios to play jazz. In the early 80s Gibbs teamed up with Buddy De Franco for a highly acclaimed album. Gibbs's vibraphone style reflects the hard-driving Lionel Hampton tradition, but with slightly boppish overtones. His playing always swings and with a big band in full cry behind him, he creates some of the most exciting sounds in jazz.

Selected albums: *Terry Gibbs Sextet* i (1951), *Terry Gibbs At The Pythian Temple* (1952), *Terry Gibbs All Stars* (1953), *Terry Gibbs And His Orchestra* i (1953), *Terry Gibbs Quintet* i (1953), *Terry Gibbs Quartet* i (1953), *Terry* (1954), *Terry Gibbs Quartet* ii (1955), *Vibes On Velvet* (1955), *Terry Gibbs Quartet* iii (1956), *Swingin' With Terry Gibbs* (1956), *Jazzband Ball* (1957), *Terry Gibbs Quartet* iv (1957), *Terry Gibbs Quartet* v (1958), *Terry Gibbs And His Orchestra* ii (1958), *Terry Gibbs Big Band At The Versailles Room, Hollywood* (c.1959), *Launching A New Band* (1959), *Dream Band* (1959), *Terry Gibbs And His Big Band* (1960), *Terry Gibbs Quintet* ii (1960), *The Exciting Big Band Of Terry Gibbs* (1961), *The Exciting Terry Gibbs Big Band Recorded Live At The Summit In Hollywood* i (1961), *Main Stem* (Contemporary 1961), *Terry Gibbs Quartet* vi (1961), *The Exciting Terry Gibbs Big Band Recorded Live At The Summit In Hollywood* ii (1962), *Terry Gibbs Sextet* ii (1963), *The Family Album* (1963), *Terry Gibbs Quartet* vii (1963), *Terry Gibbs Sextet* iii (1963), *Terry Gibbs Sextet* iv (1963), *Take It From Me* (Jasmine 1964), *Terry Gibbs Sextet* v (1964), *Terry Gibbs Septet* (1966), *Terry Gibbs Plays Arrangements By Shorty Rogers* (1966), *Bobstacle Course* (Xanadu 1974), *Live At The Lord* (1978), *Smoke 'Em Up* (1978), with Buddy De Franco *Jazz Party: First Time Together* (1981), with De Franco *My Buddy* (1982), *The Latin Connection* (1986), with De Franco *Chicago Fire* (Contemporary 1987), *Holiday For Swing* (Contemporary 1988), *Volume 5: The Big Cat* (Contemporary 1993).

Gibson, Harry 'The Hipster'

b. Harry Raab, 1914, New York City, New York, USA, d. May 1991. Gibson's first job was playing piano in a band which included future jazz musicians such as Joe 'Flip' Phillips and Billy Bauer. At this time he was working under his real name, but later changed it when he formed a double act with singer Ruth Gibson. In the 40s he enjoyed a brief period of fame when he caught to perfection the attitudes, language and mannerisms of a generation of zoot-suited, streetwise hipsters. Much of Gibson's nightclub act was built around his own compositions, which included gems such as 'Who Put the Benzedrine In Mrs Murphy's Ovaltine?' and 'Zoot Gibson Rides Again'. Gibson's lyrics, and the patter with which he surrounded his songs, made a marked impression upon a succeed-

ing generation of stand-up comedians; his peers included Lord Buckley and Lenny Bruce. Gibson's troubled lifestyle was akin to that of Bruce and another friend and musical associate, Charlie Parker. Gibson was reputed to be instrumental in persuading Billy Berg to bring Parker and Dizzy Gillespie to Los Angeles for their ground-breaking engagement in 1945. Despite a frenetic life, which included periods of incarceration for drug offences, several marriages, and a great deal of wildly irreverent humour and much engaging music, Gibson managed to avoid the limelight. Indeed, few jazz reference books mention him and perhaps the longest magazine article on him came in the form of Mark Gardner's obituary in *Jazz Journal International* soon after Gibson's death in May 1991. For all his other-worldliness, Gibson's anarchic humour had much to say that was relevant. His music, especially his piano playing, despite its boppish overtones, was firmly rooted in the older traditions of his early idols such as Fats Waller and Erroll Garner. During his later years Gibson worked sporadically, fronting a band in the 70s that included his sons in its ranks.
Album: *Harry The Hipster Digs Christmas* (1974). Compilations: *Boogie Woogie In Blue* (Musicraft 1988, 40s recordings), *Everybody's Crazy But Me* (Progressive 1988, 40s recordings), under Slim Gaillard *McVouty* (1945-46). Video: *Boogie In Blue* (1992).

Gillespie, Dizzy

b. John Birks Gillespie, 21 October 1917, Cheraw, South Carolina, USA, d. 6 January 1993. Born into a large family, Gillespie began playing trombone at the age of 12 and a year or so later took up the trumpet. Largely self-taught, he won a musical scholarship but preferred playing music to formal study. In 1935 he quit university and went to live in Philadelphia, where he began playing in local bands. It was during this period that he acquired the nickname by which he was to become universally known. The name Dizzy resulted from his zestful behaviour and was actually bestowed by a fellow trumpeter, Fats Palmer, whose life Gillespie saved when Palmer was overcome by fumes in a gas-filled room during a tour with the Frankie Fairfax band. Gillespie's startling technical facility attracted a great deal of attention and in 1937 he went to New York to try out for the Lucky Millinder band. He did not get the job but stayed in town and soon afterwards was hired for a European tour by Teddy Hill, in whose band he succeeded his idol, Roy Eldridge. Back in the USA in 1939, Gillespie played in various New York bands before returning to Hill, where he was joined by drummer Kenny Clarke, in whom he found a kindred spirit, who was similarly tired of big band conventions. When Hill folded his band to become booking manager for Minton's Playhouse in New York, he gave free rein to young musicians eager to experiment and among the regulars were Clarke, Thelonious Monk, Joe Guy and, a little later, Gillespie. In the meantime, Gillespie had joined the Cab Calloway Band, which was then riding high in popular esteem. While with Calloway, Gillespie began to experiment with phrasing that was out of character with what was until this time accepted jazz trumpet parlance. He also appeared on a Lionel

Hampton record date, playing a solo on a tune entitled 'Hot Mallets' which many observers believe to be the first recorded example of what would later be called bebop. The following year, 1940, Gillespie met Charlie Parker in Kansas City, during a tour with the Calloway band, and established musical rapport with the man with whom he was to change the face and sound of jazz. In 1941 Gillespie was fired by Calloway following some on-stage high jinks which ended with Gillespie and his boss embroiled in a minor fracas. Gillespie returned to New York where he worked with numerous musicians, including Benny Carter, Millinder, Charlie Barnet and Earl Hines, in whose band he again met Parker and also singer Billy Eckstine.

Gillespie had begun to hang out, after hours, at Minton's and also at Clark Monroe's Uptown House. He led his own small band for club and record dates, both appealing to a small, specialized, but growing, audience. Amongst his influential recordings of the period were 'Salt Peanuts' and 'Hot House'. In 1944 Gillespie joined the big band Eckstine had just formed: originally intended as a backing group for Eckstine's new career as a solo singer, the outfit quickly became a forcing house for big band bebop. Apart from Gillespie, the sidemen Eckstine hired at various times included Gene Ammons, Sonny Stitt, Wardell Gray, Dexter Gordon, Fats Navarro, Howard McGhee and Miles Davis. Subsequently, Gillespie formed his own big band, which enjoyed only limited commercial success but which was, musically, an early peaking of the concept of big band bebop. He also began playing regularly with Parker in a quintet that the two men co-led. During this period Gillespie was constantly in excellent musical company, playing with most of the major voices in bop and many of those swing era veterans who tried, with varying levels of success, to adapt to the new music. In the big band, Gillespie had employed at one time or another during its two separate periods of existence James Moody, Cecil Payne, Benny Bailey, Al McKibbon, Willie Cook, Big Nick Nicholas, John Lewis, Milt Jackson, Ray Brown and Clarke. In his small groups he recorded with Don Byas, Al Haig and others, but it was in the band he co-led with Parker that Gillespie did his most influential work. The other members of the quintet varied, but initially included Haig, Curley Russell and 'Big' Sid Catlett and, later, Haig, Jackson, Brown and Stan Levey. These small bands brought Gillespie to the fascinated attention of countless musicians; from their performances evolved the establishment of bop as a valid form of jazz, with its necessary renewal of a music which had begun to fall prey to the inroads of blandness, sanitization and formulaic repetitiveness that accompanied the commercial successes of the swing era.

Gillespie was feverishly active as a composer too. And, despite his youth he was fast becoming an *eminence grise* to beboppers. Aided by his stable private life and a disdain for the addictive stimulants increasingly favoured by a small but well-publicized coterie of bebop musicians, he was the epitome of the successful businessman. That he combined such qualities with those of musical explorer and adventurer made him one of the more dominant figures in jazz. Moreover, in his work with Chano Pozo and later Machito he was one of the pioneers of US-based Latin jazz. Most important of all, his personal demeanour helped bop rise above the prevailing tide of contemptuous ignorance which, in those days, often passed for critical comment.

Gillespie's busy career continued into the 50s; he recorded with J.J. Johnson, John Coltrane, Jackson, Art Blakey, Wynton Kelly and others. Many of his record dates of this period were on his own label, Dee Gee Records. With his big band folded, Gillespie toured Europe, returning to New York in 1952 to find that his record company was on the skids. He was already undergoing some difficulties as he adjusted his playing style to accommodate new ideas and the shift from large to small band. In 1953, during a party for his wife, the members of a two-man knockabout act fell on his trumpet. The instrument was badly bent but when Gillespie tried to play it he found that, miraculously, he preferred it that way. The upward 45-degree angle of the bell allowed him to hear the notes he was playing sooner than before. In addition he found that when he was playing from a chart, and therefore was looking down, the horn was pointing outwards towards microphone or audience. He liked all these unexpected benefits and within a few weeks had arranged to have a trumpet especially constructed to incorporate them. By the end of 1953 the temporary hiatus in Gillespie's career was over. A concert in Toronto in this year featured Gillespie and Parker with Bud Powell, Charles Mingus and Max Roach in a group which was billed, and in some quarters received, as *The Quintet Of The Year*. Although all five musicians did better things at other times, collectively it was an exciting and frequently excellent session. Significantly, it was an occasion which displayed the virility of bop at a time when, elsewhere, its fire was being gently doused into something more palatable for the masses. Gillespie then began working with Norman Granz's Jazz At The Philharmonic and he also began a long series of recording dates for Granz, in which he was teamed with a rich and frequently rewarding mixture of musicians. In 1956 Gillespie's standing in jazz circles was such that Adam Clayton Powell Jnr. recommended him to President Dwight D. Eisenhower as the ideal man to lead an orchestra on a State Department-sponsored goodwill tour of Africa, the Middle East and Asia. The tour was a great success, even if Gillespie proved unwilling to play up its propagandist element, and soon after his return to the USA he was invited to make another tour, this time to South America. The all-star band assembled for these tours was maintained for a while and was also recorded by Granz. By the end of the 50s Gillespie was again leading a small group and had embarked upon a ceaseless round of club, concert, festival and recording dates that continued for the next three decades. He continued to work on prestigious projects, which included, in the early 70s, a tour with an all-star group featuring Blakey, Monk, Stitt, McKibbon and Kai Winding. Throughout the 70s and 80s he was the recipient of many awards, and his earlier status as an absurdly young *eminence grise* was succeeded by his later role as an elder statesman of jazz even though when the 70s began, he was still only in his early 50s

By the middle of the 70s Gillespie was once again at a point in his career where a downturn seemed rather more likely than a further climb. In the event, it was another trumpet player who gave him the nudge he needed: Jon Faddis had come into Gillespie's life as an eager fan, but in 1977 was teamed with his idol on a record date at the Montreux festival where their planned performance was abruptly altered when the scheduled rhythm section ended up in the wrong country. Hastily assembling a substitute team of Milt Jackson, Ray Brown, Monty Alexander and drummer Jimmie Smith, the two trumpeters played a highly successful set which was recorded by Norman Granz. Subsequently, Gillespie and Faddis often played together, making a great deal of memorable music, with the veteran seemingly sparked into new life. In the early 80s Gillespie recorded for television in the USA as part of the *Jazz America* project, appeared in London with a new quintet featuring Paquito Rivera, and played at the Nice, Knebworth and Kool festivals in duets with, respectively, such varied artists as Art Farmer, Chico Freeman and Art Blakey. He showed himself eager to experiment although sometimes, as with his less-than-wonderful teaming with Stevie Wonder, his judgement was somewhat awry. In 1987 he celebrated his 70th birthday and found himself again leading a big band, which had no shortage of engagements and some excellent players, including Faddis and Sam Rivers. He was also fêted during the JVC Festival at the Saratoga Springs Performing Arts Center, where he brilliantly matched horns with Faddis and new pretender, Wynton Marsalis. He was not always in the spotlight, however. One night in Los Angeles he went into a club where Bill Berry's LA Big Band was working and sat in, happily playing fourth trumpet. As the 90s began Gillespie was still performing, usually occupying centre stage, but also happy to sit and reminisce with old friends and new, to sit in with other musicians, and to live life pretty much the way he had done for more than half a century. It was a shock to the music world on 6 January 1993 when it was announced that Dizzy was no longer with us, perhaps we had selfishly thought that he was immortal.

In the history of the development of jazz trumpet, Gillespie's place ranked second only to that of Louis Armstrong. In the history of jazz as a whole he was firmly in the small group of major innovators who reshaped the music in a manner so profound that everything that follows has to be measured by reference, conscious or not, to their achievements. Just as Armstrong had created a new trumpet style which affected players of all instruments in the two decades following his emergence in Chicago in 1922, so did Gillespie, in 1940, redirect trumpet players and all other jazz musicians along new and undefined paths. He also reaffirmed the trumpet's vital role in jazz after a decade (the 30s) in which the saxophone had begun its inexorable rise to prominence as the instrument for change. In a wider context Gillespie's steadying hand did much to ensure that bop would survive beyond the impractical, errant genius of Parker.

In much of Gillespie's earlier playing the dazzling speed of his execution frequently gave an impression of a purely technical bravura, but as time passed it became clear that there was no lack of ideas or real emotion in his playing. Throughout his career, Gillespie rarely failed to find fresh thoughts; and, beneath the spectacular high note flourishes, the raw excitement and the exuberant vitality, there was a depth of feeling akin to that of the most romantic balladeers. He earned and will forever retain his place as one of the true giants of jazz. Without his presence, the music would have been not only different but much less than it had become.

Selected albums: *Dizzy Gillespie Live At The Downbeat Club* (1947), *A Nite At Carnegie Hall* (1947), *Paris 1948* (1948), *Dee Gee Days* (1952), *Dizzy Great* (1952), *Pleyel Concert 1953* (Vogue 1953), *The Quintet Of The Year: Jazz At Massey Hall* (1953), *Diz And Getz* (Verve 1955), *Tour De Force* i (1955), *One Night In Washington* (1955), *Live In Hi-Fi From Birdland* (1956), *For Musicians Only* (Verve 1956), with Sonny Stitt, Sonny Rollins *Sonny Side Up* (Verve 1958), *At Newport* (Verve 1958), *Gillespiana; The Carnegie Hall Concert* (Verve 1961), *An Electrifying Evening* (1961), *A Musical Safari* (1961), *The New Continent* (1962), *Dizzy Gillespie And The Double Six Of Paris* (Philips 1964), *Angel City* (Moon 1965), *The Monterey Festival Jazz Orchestra* (Blue Note 1965), *Swing Low, Sweet Cadillac* (1967), *Giants* (1967), *Jazz For A Sunday Afternoon* (1967), *Reunion Big Band* (1968), *Live At The Village Vanguard* (Blue Note 1968), *Portrait Of Jenny* (c.1970), with Bobby Hackett *Giants* (1971), *Dizzy Gillespie And Mitchell-Ruff* (1971), *Tour De Force* ii (c.1971), *Dizzy Gillespie's Big Four* (1974), *The Bop Session* (1975), *The Trumpet Kings At Montreaux '75* (Original Jazz Classics 1975), with Machito *Afro-Cuban Jazz Moods* (1975), with Roy Eldridge *Jazz Maturity* (1975), *Free Ride* (Original Jazz Classics 1977), *Dizzy Gillespie Jam* (1977), *Summertime* (1980), *Alternate Blues* (Original Jazz Classics 1980), *To A Finland Station* (1982), New Faces (GRP 1984), *Closer To The Source* (Atlantic 1984). *Dizzy Gillespie Meets Phil Woods Quintet* (Timeless 1987), with Max Roach *Max And Dizzy, Paris 1989* (A&M 1989), *The Winter In Lisbon* (Milan 1990), *Live At The Royal Festival Hall* (Enja 1990). *To Diz With Love* (Telarc 1992), *To Bird With Love* (Telarc 1992), *Live At Chester* (Jazz Hour 1993). Selected compilations: *Shaw 'Nuff* (1945-46), *Bebop's Heartbeat* (1945-47), *Live At The Spotlite* (1946), *Big Band Live, 1946* (1946), *Dizzy Gillespie 1946-1949* (RCA 1983, rec. 1946-49), *Deegee Days* (Savoy 1985), *The Bebop Revolution* (1946-49), *Dizzy's Diamonds: The Best Of The Verve Years* (Verve 1993), *Birk's Works: Blue Note Plays The Music Of...* (1993), *Legendary Dizzy Gillespie Big Band, Live 1946* (Bandstand 1991), *Memorial Album* (1993, rec. 1953), *Dizzy Songs* (Vogue 1993).

Further reading: *Dizzy: To Be Or Not To Bop*, Dizzy Gillespie and Al Fraser. *Dizzy Gillespie: His Life And Times*, Barry McRae.

Gilmore, John

b. 28 September 1931, Summit, Mississippi, USA. Gilmore moved to Chicago at the age of three, and later studied clarinet at Du Sable High School. Between 1948 and 1952 he was in the air force, and played clarinet and started on tenor saxophone while stationed in San Antonio, Texas. When the Harlem Globetrotters toured America in 1952, music was supplied by pianist Earl 'Fatha' Hines with John Gilmore in the band, playing tenor saxophone. In 1953 he joined Sun Ra, then leading a trio, an association that was to last many decades, interrupted only by a short spell in Art Blakey's Jazz Messengers (1964-65), when he replaced Wayne Shorter. Outside of his work with Sun Ra, Gilmore has recorded with McCoy Tyner, Dizzy Reece, Pete LaRoca, Elmo Hope, Paul Bley (on *Turns*) and with his old Chicago school-friend, pianist Andrew Hill, on two superb mid-60s Blue Note sessions, *Andrew* and *Compulsion*. Nevertheless the vast bulk of his music over the last 35 years has been with Sun Ra. When asked by Graham Lock in *The Wire* what he liked about Sun Ra's music he replied: 'the music is *hard*. He's got some stuff so hard it's unbelievable, it'll blow your mind!'. Gilmore's big-sounding tenor is unique in sounding like John Coltrane *before* Coltrane had established his style (Coltrane is said to have begged him for lessons). If Gilmore had not devoted his playing career to Sun Ra's music he would probably be listed as one of four or five most important tenor players in jazz. His solo on 'Neverness' from 1989's *Purple Night* shows his uncanny ability to combine freeform sonic experimentation with an emotive grandeur, though it is perhaps on Sun Ra's rare small group recordings, such as *New Steps*, that Gilmore is given the space he needs to really stretch out. In addition to tenor saxophone and bass clarinet, he sometimes plays percussion with the Arkestra (and is featured as a percussionist on *My Brother The Wind*) and also sings in an enthusiastic, gravelly voice - his speciality being 'East Of The Sun, West Of The Moon'.

Girard, Adele

b. 1913, USA, d. 7 September 1993. By choosing the harp as her instrument, Girard severely damaged her chances of being taking seriously when she began playing jazz. Nevertheless, she persevered, working in bands such as Harry Sosnick's before coming to wider attention as a member of Joe Marsala's band at 52nd Street's Hickory House in 1938. That same year Girard and Marsala married and continued to play together during the next decade. After Marsala retired from regular performing, Girard continued her career, now as a solo act, also singing and playing piano. She worked in clubs, hotels and casinos in Los Angeles and surrounding areas, especially the popular resorts, and in the 70s appeared briefly in London with the Festival Theatre USC. By dint of her delightful melodic approach, a subtle sense of swing, allied to her perfect pitch, she became an able member of some good small jazz groups and qualified as one of the two or three - of an admittedly small number - best harpists in jazz.
Compilation: *The Chronological Joe Marsala (1936-1942)*.

Gismonti, Egberto

b. 5 December 1947, Carmo, Rio de Janeiro, Brazil. Gismonti had a classical musical education starting to play the piano when he was six years old. He went to Paris in the 60s to study orchestration and analysis with Nadia Boulanger and composition with the *avant garde* composer Barraque. On his return to Brazil in 1966 he became interested in choro, which he has

described as a kind of popular Brazilian funk. Gismonti successfully blends African -Brazilian forms with jazz in his compositions. He taught himself the guitar and was at first influenced by Baden Powell and Deno. His influences during the early 70s were as wide ranging as Django Reinhardt and Jimi Hendrix. In 1973 he changed to the 8-string guitar which allowed him a greater variety of chord voicings, more flexible bass lines and drones: in 1981 he moved on to the 10-string guitar on which the extra strings extended the bass. His performances on either piano or guitar are always exhilarating and tuneful. He toured the USA in 1976 with Airto Moreira and Flora Purim and in 1978/9 with Nana Vasconcelos. Gismonti's compositional and playing styles were influenced by his study in 1976 of the music of Xingu Indians. He described the resulting album as 'a walk through the jungle'. His evocative writing and playing has been used in at least 11 film scores. He has recorded regularly with members of the ECM label, Jan Garbarek, Collin Walcott, Ralph Towner, Charlie Haden, and was the orchestrator on Vasconcelos's *Suadedos* with the Stuttgart RSO.
Selected albums: *Danca Das Cabecas* (ECM 1973), *Sol Do Meia Dia* (ECM 1977), *Magico* (1979), with Jan Garbarek *Folk Songs* (ECM 1979), *Circense* (Cameo 1980), with Nana Vasconcelos *Suadedas* (1980), *Sanfona* (ECM), *Duas Vozes* (1984), *Solo* (ECM 1985), *Danca Dos Escarvos* (ECM 1989), *Arvore* (Cameo 1991), *Kuarup* (Cameo 1991), *Infancia* (ECM 1991). *Academia De Dancas* (Cameo 1992), *Trem Caipira* (Cameo 1992), *Amazonia* (Cameo 1993), *No Caipira* (Cameo 1993). Compilation: *Works* (ECM 1983).

Giuffre, Jimmy

b. 26 April 1921, Dallas, Texas, USA. A graduate of the North Texas College in 1942, Giuffre entered the US Army where he gained professional band experience playing saxophones and clarinet. On his discharge he played in a succession of big bands, including those led by Buddy Rich, Jimmy Dorsey, Boyd Raeburn and Woody Herman. It was with Herman that he gained most attention, both as a member of the saxophone section and as the composer of 'Four Brothers', which gave that particular Herman band its tag. After leaving Herman he worked on the west coast, playing mostly in small groups, and also began to teach. He formed a trio that included Jim Hall and, later, Bob Brookmeyer plus various bassists. He appeared at the 1958 Newport Jazz Festival and in the filmed record of the event, *Jazz On A Summer's Day* (1960), playing his own composition 'The Train And The River'. He made numerous records, including dates with Lee Konitz, for which he wrote beautiful and inventive arrangements, the Modern Jazz Quartet (*At Music Inn*) and Anita O'Day, for whom he devised elegant and deceptively simple charts (*Cool Heat*). Giuffre also began to explore the world of composition, writing both film scores (*The Music Man*) and neo-classical third stream pieces, such as 'Pharoah' and 'Suspensions', both recorded by Gunther Schuller. In the 60s Giuffre became involved in free jazz, leading a trio in which he was accompanied by Paul Bley and Steve Swallow. The trio's recordings became increasingly abstract, culminating in *Free Fall*, a collection of duos and trios interspersed by totally improvised tracks on solo clarinet. *Free Fall* was deleted within a few months of release and then, in Giuffre's words, 'the doors closed' - his unique mixture of quiet, free and drummerless music proved so threatening to 'jazz' prejudices, it was nearly a decade before he was able to record again. In the 70s he was still moving with the times, introducing eastern and African sounds into his work. Later, inspired by Weather Report, he introduced electric bass and keyboards into his quartet, recording three albums for Italy's Black Saint label (*Dragonfly, Quasar, Liquid Dancers*). He also recorded a duo album with André Jaume, *Eiffel* (one of the quietest records ever made!) and in 1989 was reunited with Bley and Swallow for two sessions released by the French Owl label. Giuffre's playing of many of the lesser-known members of the saxophone family, and especially the bass clarinet (*The Jimmy Giuffre Clarinet*), have helped to give his work unusual and frequently sombre shadings. Throughout his career, Giuffre has been an important and visionary member of the *avant garde*, yet his playing was always filled with coolly reflective tonal qualities which prove most attractive. In 1990 Giuffre, his frail appearance proving deceptive, was in fine musical form at the South Bank Jazz Festival in Grimsby, South Humberside, where he premiered a new work, 'Timeless', commissioned by the festival organizers.

Selected albums: *The Music Man* (50s), *Trav'lin' Light* (50s), *Tangents In Jazz* (1955), *World Of Jazz* (1955), *The Jimmy Giuffre Clarinet* (1956), *The Jimmy Giuffre 3* (Atlantic 1956), with others *Historic Jazz Concert At Music Inn* (1957), *Jimmy Giuffre Trios Live 1957-1958* (1958), *Jimmy Giuffre Orchestra* (1958), *Jimmy Giuffre Trio* i (1958), *Jimmy Giuffre Trio* ii (1958), *Jimmy Giuffre Trio* iii (1958), *Western Suite* (1958), *Princess* (1959), *Seven Pieces* (1959), *Ad Lib* (1959), *The Easy Way* (1959), *Lee Konitz Meets Jimmy Giuffre* (1959), with Anita O'Day *Cool Heat* (1959), *Jimmy Giuffre With Strings* (1960), *In Person* (Verve 1960), *Four Brothers* (Verve 1960), *Seven Pieces* (1960), *The Easy Way* (Verve 1960), *Fusion* (Verve 1961), *Thesis* (Verve 1961), *Jimmy Giuffre With Strings* (1961), *Jimmy Giuffre Trio In Concert* (c.1961), *Free Fall* (1962), *Music For People, Birds, Butterflies And Mosquitos* (1972), *Quiet Song* (1974), *River Chant/Mosquito Dance* (1975), with Paul Bley, Bill Connors *Quiet Song* (1975), *IAI Festival* (1978), *Giuffre, Konitz, Connors, Bley* (Improvising Artists 1978), *Tangents In Jazz* (Affinity 1981), *Dragonfly* (1983), *Quasar* (Soul Note 1985), *Liquid Dancers* (Soul Note 1989), with André Jaume *Eiffel* (1989), with Bley, Steve Swallow *The Diary Of A Trio: Saturday* (Owl 1990), with Bley, Swallow *The Diary Of A Trio: Sunday* (Owl 1990), *Fly Away Little Bird* (Owl 1992), *River Station* (1992), *Emphasis, Stuttgart 1961* (1993).

Glenn, Tyree

b. 23 November 1912, Corsicana, Texas, USA, d. 18 May 1974. After working in his home state on vibraphone and principally trombone, Glenn moved to the Washington DC area in the early 30s and by 1936 was in Los Angeles playing with the Charlie Echols band. He also worked with Eddie Barefield,

Benny Carter, Lionel Hampton and in the band Eddie Mallory directed to accompany his wife, Ethel Waters. In 1939 Glenn was briefly with Carter again before joining Cab Calloway, with whom he remained until 1946. He next played with Don Redman and Duke Ellington, where he skilfully essayed the Joe 'Tricky Sam' Nanton trombone role, but by 1952 had turned his attention to studio work. During the next decade he occasionally acted and periodically led his own small groups, sometimes with Shorty Baker, and in 1965 joined Louis Armstrong's All Stars. After three years he again formed his own small band, but later made short return visits to Armstrong and, in the summer of 1971, to Ellington. From then until shortly before his death, in May 1974, he led his own band. A gifted musician, Glenn was an important member of any band in which he played, especially the fine big band of Cab Calloway. Too often for a man with his talent, he appeared content to take a back seat as, for example, when he was in company with Armstrong. When he did solo (other than on the Tricky Sam repertoire) he showed himself to be a robust and inventive player. His vibraphone work, while undistinguished in jazz terms, was always sound. An occasional composer, he wrote 'Sultry Serenade' which was recorded by Ellington and Erroll Garner (under the title 'How Could You Do A Thing Like That to Me'). Glenn's two sons are musicians, Tyree Jnr. plays tenor saxophone, Roger plays vibraphone and flute.

Albums: with Duke Ellington *The Liberian Suite* (1947), *Masterpieces By Ellington* (1950), *Tyree Glenn And His Embers All Stars And Orchestra* (1957), *Tyree Glenn At The Roundhouse* (1958), *Tyree Glenn With Strings* i (1960), *Tyree Glenn With Strings* ii (1960), *Tyree Glenn At The London House* (c.1961), *Tyree Glenn With Sy Oliver And His Orchestra* (1962), with Louis Armstrong *Louis* (1964-66).

Globe Unity Orchestra

This important European orchestra was formed in 1966 by the German free jazz pianist Alexander Von Schlippenbach, initially to perform his composition 'Globe Unity' in Berlin. Until the mid-70s the orchestra worked principally in West Germany, performing at the key festivals of improvised music, such as the Total Music Meeting, the Workshop Freie Musik in Berlin and the Free Jazz Workshop in Wuppertal. Since then it has toured worldwide, playing festivals throughout Europe, the Far East and India. Alongside Schlippenbach, regulars in its distinguished line-up include Germans Peter Brötzmann, Gerd Dudek, Paul Lovens, Albert Mangelsdorff and Manfred Schoof; Britons Derek Bailey, Evan Parker and Paul Rutherford; Canadian Kenny Wheeler and Luxembourgian Michel Pilz. Although the orchestra has its roots in the 60s free jazz tradition, its improvisations sometimes echo earlier styles of jazz as well as contemporary classical music.

Albums: *Globe Unity* (1966), *Live In Wuppertal* (1973), *Hamburg '74* (1974), *Evidence* (1975), *Rumbling* (FMP 1975), *Into The Valley* (1975), *Pearls* (1975), *Local Fair* (1975/6), *Improvisations* (1977), *Compositions* (1979), *20th Anniversary* (FMP 1987).

Golia, Vinny

b. 1946, New York City, New York, USA. Vinny Golia has the unique distinction of having appeared on Blue Note and ECM albums before he'd learned to play an instrument! He did it as an artist: it's his painting on the cover of Chick Corea's *Song Of Singing*, his drawing that adorns the sleeve of Dave Holland's *Music For Two Basses*. Golia graduated with a degree in fine art in 1969 and moved, by chance, into the apartment block where Corea, Holland and Dave Liebman were all living. He began to attend their concerts, drawing the musicians as they played and later turning the sketches into large, abstract canvasses. With the money he received for the *Song Of Singing* sleeve he bought a soprano saxophone and, after taking lessons from Liebman and Anthony Braxton (also an influence on his later composing), spent the next few years teaching himself to play. Then, rather than invite musicians to 'play' his paintings (as happened at one event he staged with Circle), Golia started to play them himself, before deciding he could cut out the painting and simply play. In 1973 he moved to Los Angeles and in 1977 started his own label, Nine Winds, which provided an outlet for a new generation of west coast musicians, including pianist Wayne Peet, bassist Ken Filiano, percussionist Alex Cline, guitarist Nels Cline and trombonist John Rapson. Golia's own recordings include solo, duo, trio and small-group albums (*No Reverse* and *Goin' Ahead* are outstanding) as well as three big band releases - *Compositions For Large Ensemble*, *Facts Of Their Own Lives* and *Pilgrimage To Obscurity* - which feature guests such as Bobby Bradford, John Carter and Tim Berne. Golia also kept practising: he now plays over 20 instruments, all self-taught - they include nearly all of the saxophone, clarinet and flute families plus piccolo, bassoon and various non-Western pieces such as conch, sho, hotchiku, shakuhachi and khee. Though he mostly leads his own groups, he has toured and/or recorded as a sideman with Berne, Braxton, George Gruntz and several of his west coast colleagues. In addition to his jazz activities, Golia's love of chamber music has prompted him to work with various classical players and to record a set of improvised duets with bass maestro Bertram Turetzky.

Albums: *Spirits In Fellowship* (1978), *Openhearted* (1979), *In The Right Order* (1980), *Solo* (1980), *The Gift Of Fury* (1981), *Slice Of Life* (1983), with Wayne Peet *No Reverse* (1984), *Goin' Ahead* (1985), *Compositions For Large Ensemble* (1986, rec. 1982), *Facts Of Their Own Lives* (1987, rec. 1984), *Out For Blood* (1989), *Pilgrimage To Obscurity* (1990, rec. 1985), *Worldwide And Portable* (1990, rec. 1986), with Bertram Turetzky *Intersections* (1991, rec. 1986).

Golson, Benny

b. 25 January 1929, Philadelphia, Pennsylvania, USA. After receiving extensive tuition on a variety of instruments as a child, Golson began playing tenor saxophone professionally in 1951 in Bullmoose Jackson's R&B band. It was here that he first met Tadd Dameron, who had a great influence upon his writing. In the early and mid-50s he played in bands led by Dameron, Lionel Hampton and Earl Bostic, then worked for Dizzy Gillespie, playing in and arranging for the 1956-8 big band. Next, Golson became a member of Art Blakey's Jazz Messengers, for whom he composed several tunes. He later formed bands with Curtis Fuller and Art Farmer (the Jazztet), then went into the studios, writing for films and television but making occasional appearances on record dates and on jazz stages around the world. In the late 70s he returned to regular live work and toured Europe with a reunited Jazztet in 1982. The following year he recorded an acclaimed tribute album to his old Philadelphia jamming partner, John Coltrane. Golson's playing, which followed the melodic progression of late swing era stylists such as Lucky Thompson and Don Byas, was always effective. He remains best-known, however, for his writing and some of his compositions have become latterday jazz standards: 'Blues March', 'Killer Joe', 'Whisper Not' and 'I Remember Clifford'.

Selected albums: *Benny Golson's New York Scene* (1957), *The Modern Touch* (1957), *The Other Side Of Benny Golson* (1958), *Benny Golson's Philadelphians* (1958), *Art Blakey With The Jazz Messengers* (1958), *Benny Golson In Paris* (1958), *Gone With Golson* (1959), *Groovin' With Golson* (1959), *Gettin' With It* (1959), *Take A Number From 1 To 10* (1960), *Meet The Jazztet* (1960), *Just Jazz!* (1962), *Turning Point* (1962), *Free* (1962), *Stockholm Sojourn* (1964), *Are You Real* (1977), *Killer Joe* (1977), *California Message* (1980), *One More Mem'ry* (1981), *Time Speaks* (1982), *This Is For You, John* (1983), *The Jazztet: Moment To Moment* (1983), *In Paris And New York 1958* (1987), *Stardust* (1988), *Benny Golson Quartet* (1990), *Domingo* (1993).

Gomez, Eddie

b. 4 November 1944, San Juan, Texas, USA. Gomez moved to New York as a child and took up the bass when he was 12 years old. He was at the High School of Music and Art before going on to the Juilliard School where he studied with Fred Zimmerman. He played with Marshall Brown's International Youth Band and then in the early 60s with Gary McFarland, Jim Hall, Paul Bley, Jeremy Steig (flute) and Gerry Mulligan before joining Bill Evans with whom he stayed for 10 years (1966-77). He needed his musically agile mind and technical dexterity in that trio with which he often played melodically in the upper register of the bass. During the early 80s he played in the band Steps Ahead which Mike Mainieri (vibes) kept together after a group of New York session musicians made an acclaimed tour of Japan. He has successfully played this fusion music on the amplified double bass rather than moving to bass guitar. Gomez has continued as a very much in-demand musician through the 80s playing and recording with Jack DeJohnette, Hank Jones and JoAnne Brackeen among others. In the 90s he recorded with Chick Corea.

Albums: with Paul Bley *Barrage* (1964), with Bill Evans *A Simple Matter of Conviction* (1966), *What's New* (1969), *Live At Tokyo* (1973), with Bob Moses *Bittersweet In The Ozone* (1975), *Crosscurrent* (1977), with Jack DeJohnette *New Direction* (1978), with JoAnne Brackeen *Special Identity* (1981), *Gomez* (Denon 1985), *Mezgo* (Epic 1986), *Down*

Stretch (Blackhawk 1987), *Power Play* (Epic 1988), with Jeff Gardner *Continuum* (1990), *Streetsmart* (Epic 1990), *Live In Moscow* (B&W 1992), *Next Future* (GRP 1993).

Gonella, Nat

b. 7 March 1908, London, England. This great pioneer of British jazz began playing trumpet as a child and toured music halls in a youth band. At the age of 20, Gonella began a seven-year period during which he played in several leading dance-bands, including those of Billy Cotton, Roy Fox, Ray Noble and Lew Stone. His 1932 recording of 'Georgia On My Mind' proved immensely popular and later became his theme tune, providing the name for his own band, the Georgians. Heavily influenced by Louis Armstrong, Gonella modelled his playing and singing style on that of the master. In the post-war years, Gonella led his own big and small bands, benefiting from the trad-jazz boom of the early 50s but finally losing out to the later rise of pop music. After several years in obscurity, In the 70s Gonella reappeared on the music scene with a hit record in Holland and, in the 80s, with club and concert engagements, record dates, television appearances and a biography.

Albums: *Runnin' Wild* (1958), *The Nat Gonella Story* (1961), *Nat Gonella And His Trumpet* (Ace Of Clubs 1967), *When You're Smiling* (1970), *The Music Goes 'Round And 'Round* (1975), *My Favourite Things* (1975), *Wishing You A Swinging Christmas* (1975). Compilations: *Georgia On My Mind* (Retrospect 1980, 1931-46 recordings), *Mister Rhythm Man* (Retrospect 1984, 1934-35 recordings), *Nat Gonella Story* (1985), *Nat Gonella Scrapbook* (Joy 1985), *Naturally Gonella* (Happy Days 1986, 1935 recordings), *How'm I Doin'* (Old Bean 1987), *Yeah Man* (Harlequin 1988, 1935-37 recordings), *Running Wild* (Harlequin 1988), *Crazy Valves* (Living ERA 1988, 1934-37 recordings), *Nat Gonella Vol 1 1934-35* (Neovox 1990), *Nat Gonella Vol 2 1932-35* (Neovox 1990), *The Cream Of Nat Gonella* (Flapper 1991), *Hold Tight* (Memoir 1991).

Gonsalves, Paul

b. 12 July 1920, Boston, Massachusetts, USA, d. 14 May 1974. Gonsalves's first professional engagement in Boston was on tenor saxophone with the Sabby Lewis band, in which he played both before and after his military service during World War II. On leaving Lewis he played with Count Basie from 1946 until 1949, was briefly with Dizzy Gillespie, and then joined Duke Ellington in 1950. Gonsalves remained with Ellington for the rest of his life, his occasional absences from the band resulting from his addiction to alcohol and narcotics. Like many other would-be Ellingtonian tenor players, Gonsalves began by learning Ben Webster's 'Cottontail' solo note for note, but quickly established his own distinctive style. The circumstance which made Gonsalves's reputation was his appearance with Ellington at the 1956 Newport Jazz Festival, when his storming, 27-chorus bridge between the opening and closing sections of 'Diminuendo In Blue' and 'Crescendo In Blue' helped to focus media attention on the band and provided the basis of Ellington's 'comeback'. Thereafter, Gonsalves

was obliged to play extended gallery-pleasing, up-tempo solos every night, a fact which overshadowed his enormous affinity with ballads. Gonsalves's relaxed and thoughtful approach to tunes displayed a love for melody and an ability to develop long, clean and logical solo lines. His rhapsodic playing on Ellington performances such as 'Happy Reunion', 'Chelsea Bridge', 'Solitude' and 'Mount Harissa' from the *Far East Suite* all testify to his vulnerable, often tender sound. His playing on records made outside the Ellington aegis is usually of a similarly reflective nature. A 1970 album with Ray Nance, *Just A-Sittin' And A-Rockin'*, is a good example, including a marvellous performance of 'Don't Blame Me'. Gonsalves surpassed even this on *Love Calls*, his 1967 album of duets with Eddie 'Lockjaw' Davis, where he delivers what might well be the definitive version of this song. In such performances, the quality of the playing perhaps reflect the man himself: Gonsalves was a sensitive yet fragile human being. He succumbed to drug addiction and alcohol dependence early in life and his career was afterwards dogged by these twin perils. When he died in London, in May 1974, his employer for close on a quarter of a century was himself too ill to be told. Ellington died a few days later and the bodies of both men, and that of Tyree Glenn, lay together in the same New York funeral home.

Albums: *Ellington At Newport* (1956), *Cookin'* (1957), *Ellingtonia Moods And Blues* (1960), *Gettin' Together* (Original Jazz Classics 1960), *Duke Ellington Presents Paul Gonsalves* (1962), *Paul Gonsalves In London I* (1963), *Rare Paul Gonsalves Sextet In Europe* (Jazz Connoisseur 1963), *Tell It The Way It Is!* (Jasmine 1963), *Cleopatra Feelin' Jazzy* (Jasmine 1963), *Paul Gonsalves In London II* (1964), *Paul Gonsalves In London III* (1965), with Ellington *Far East Suite* (1966), with Eddie 'Lockjaw' Davis *Love Calls* (1967), *Encuentro* (1968), *Humming Bird* (1969), *Paul Gonsalves With The Four Bones* (1969), *Paul Gonsalves And His All Stars* (1970), with Ray Nance *Just A-Sittin' And A-Rockin'* (Black Lion 1970), with Earl Hines *It Don't Mean A Thing* (1970-72), *Meets Earl Hines* (Black Lion 1973), with Roy Eldridge *The Mexican Bandit Meets The Pittsburgh Pirate* (Fantasy 1973), *Paul Gonsalves And Paul Quinichette* (1974).

Gonzalez, Dennis

b. 15 August 1954, Abilene, Texas, USA. Born into a Mexican-American family, Gonzalez grew up in Mercedes, Texas, studied French, journalism and music at various institutions and is an accomplished visual artist, linguist, teacher, writer and disc jockey as well as an internationally-acclaimed trumpeter, composer and record-producer. In 1976 he settled in Dallas and two years later founded DAAGNIM (the Dallas Association for Avant Garde and Neo Impressionistic Music), setting up the similarly titled record label in 1979. His first album, *Air Light (Sleep Sailor)*, was recorded in his living room and had him playing a dozen or so instruments - at the time there were few local musicians sympathetic to his music! Later, with the help of reedsman John Purcell, he began to establish an impressive catalogue of work on Daagnim and in 1986 also started to record for the Swedish label Silkheart, releasing three albums of his own music and playing on three more by Charles Brackeen. Of these, it was his own *Stefan* and *Namesake* that really established his talent internationally. Gonzalez has worked hard to link the Dallas new music scene with like-minded communities in other areas of the USA: in particular, he has contacts with Austin, New Orleans, Los Angeles and Jackson, Mississippi, as well as with some of Chicago's AACM members - as a result his recordings feature a wide array of musicians (including Brackeen, Alvin Fielder, Ahmed Abdullah, Douglas Ewart, Malachi Favors and Kidd Jordan) in exotically-named ensembles such as New Dallasorleanssippi. He has also worked in the UK, playing and recording with Keith Tippett, Elton Dean, Louis Moholo and Marcio Mattos (*Catechism*), while two new albums from Berlin's Konnex label have him in the company of Andrew Cyrille, Alex Cline, Carlos Ward and Paul Rogers among others. A flowing, lyrical trumpeter, fond of wide intervals, Gonzalez's music sometimes shows Latin and South African influences but more often draws on the hymns of his Baptist Church upbringing: one hymn in particular, 'Holy Manna', has appeared in different guises on several of his albums. 'I found it to be a perfect link between heaven and earth, a tribute to spiritual strength,' Gonzalez has said, explaining his belief in the spiritual roots of all art. 'We are a creation, and in order to stay alive you must keep creating'. In the early 90s he worked on his first book of poems and stories, as well as recording with Fielder and Cecil Taylor.

Albums: *Air Light (Sleep Sailor)* (1979), *Music From Ancient Texts* (1981), *Kukkia* (1981), *Stars/Air/Stripes* (1982), *Witness* (1983), with John Purcell *Anthem Suite* (1984), with Purcell *Little Toot* (1985), *Stefan* (Silkheart 1986), *Pelin Zena* (1986), *Namesake* (Silkheart 1987), *Catechism* (Silkheart 1988), *Debenge-Debenge* (Silkheart 1989), *Ya Yo Me Cure* (American Clave 1990), *The Earth And The Heart* (Konnex 1991, rec. 1989), *Hymn For The Perfect Heart Of A Pearl* (Konnex 1991), *The River Is Deep* (Enja 1991), *Earth Dance* (Sunnyside 1991), *Obatala* (Enja 1992), *The Desert Wind* (Silkheart 1992), *Welcome To Us* (GOWI 1993).

Goodman, Benny

b. 30 May 1909, Chicago, Illinois, USA, d. 20 June 1986. Born into a large, impoverished family of immigrants, Goodman experienced hard times whilst growing up. Encouraged by his father to learn a musical instrument, Goodman and two of his brothers took lessons; as the youngest and smallest he learned to play the clarinet. These early studies took place at the Kehelah Jacob Synagogue and later at Hull House, a settlement house founded by reformer Jane Addams. From the start, Goodman displayed an exceptional talent and he received personal tuition from James Sylvester and then the renowned classicist Franz Schoepp (who also taught Buster Bailey around the same time). Before he was in his teens, Goodman had begun performing in public and was soon playing in bands with such emerging jazz artists as Jimmy McPartland, Frank Teschemacher and Dave Tough. Goodman's precocious talent allowed him to become a member of the American Federation of Musicians at the age of 14

and that same year he played with Bix Beiderbecke. By his mid-teens Goodman was already established as a leading musician, working on numerous engagements with many bands to the detriment of his formal education. In 1925 he was heard by Gil Rodin, who was then with the popular band led by Ben Pollack. Goodman was hired by Pollack, then working in California, and the following year made a triumphal return to Chicago as featured soloist with the band. Goodman remained with Pollack until 1929, when he became a much in-demand session musician in New York, making many hundreds of record and radio dates. Keenly ambitious and already a determined perfectionist, Goodman continued to develop his craft until he was perhaps the most skilled clarinet player in the country, even if he was virtually unknown to the general public.

During the late 20s and early 30s Goodman played in bands led by Red Nichols, Ben Selvin, Ted Lewis, Sam Lanin and others, sometimes for club, dance hall and theatre engagements and often on record sessions. In 1934 his ambitions led him to form a large dance band, which was successful in being hired for a residency at Billy Rose's Music Hall. After a few months, this date collapsed when Rose was replaced by someone who did not like the band but Goodman persisted and late that same year was successful in gaining one of three places for dance bands on a regular radio show broadcast by NBC. The show, entitled *Let's Dance*, ran for about six months. By this time Goodman was using arrangements by leading writers of the day such as Fletcher Henderson and Lyle 'Spud' Murphy, and including in his band musicians such as Bunny Berigan, trombonists Red Ballard and Jack Lacey, saxophonists Toots Mondello and Hymie Schertzer, and in the rhythm section George Van Eps and Frank Froeba, who were quickly replaced by Allen Reuss and Jess Stacy. Goodman's brother, Harry, was on bass, and the drummer was Stan King, who was soon replaced by the more urgent and exciting Gene Krupa. The band's singer was Helen Ward, one of the most popular band singers of the day. When the *Let's Dance* show ended, Goodman took the band on a nation-wide tour. Prompted in part by producer John Hammond Jnr. and also by his desire for the band to develop, Goodman made many changes to the personnel, something he would continue to do throughout his career as a big band leader, and by the time the tour reached Los Angeles, in August 1935, the band was in extremely good form. Despite the success of the radio show and the band's records, the tour had met with mixed fortunes and some outright failures. However, business picked up on the west coast and on 21 August 1935 the band played a dance at the Palomar Ballroom in Los Angeles. They created a sensation and the massive success that night at the Palomar is generally credited as the time and place where the show business phenomenon which became known as the 'swing era' was born.

After an extended engagement at the Palomar the band headed back east, stopping over in Chicago for another extended run, this time at the Joseph Urban Room at the Congress Hotel. Earlier, Goodman had made some trio recordings using Krupa and pianist Teddy Wilson. The records sold well and he was encouraged by Helen Oakley, later Helen Oakley Dance, to feature Wilson in the trio at the hotel. Goodman eventually was persuaded that featuring a racially mixed group in this manner was not a recipe for disaster and when the occasion passed unremarked, except for musical plaudits, he soon afterwards employed Wilson as a regular member of the featured trio. In 1936 he added Lionel Hampton to form the Benny Goodman Quartet and while this was not the first integrated group in jazz it was by far the one with the highest profile. Goodman's big band continued to attract huge and enthusiastic audiences. In the band now were leading swing era players such as Harry James, Ziggy Elman, Chris Griffin, Vernon Brown, Babe Russin and Arthur Rollini. Goodman had an especially successful date at the Paramount Theatre in New York, beginning on 3 March 1937, and his records continued to sell very well. On 16 January 1938 the band played a concert at Carnegie Hall, sealing its success and Goodman's reputation as the 'King of Swing.' Soon after the Carnegie Hall date the band's personnel underwent significant changes. Krupa left to form his own band, soon followed by Wilson and James. Goodman found replacements and carried on as before although, inevitably, the band sounded different. In the early 40s he had a particularly interesting personnel, which included Cootie Williams, 'Big' Sid Catlett, Georgie Auld and, in the small group (which was now a septet although labelled as the Benny Goodman Sextet), Charlie Christian. Other Goodman musicians of this period included Jimmy Maxwell and Mel Powell, while his singer, who had followed Ward, Martha Tilton and Helen Forrest, was Peggy Lee. With occasional fallow periods, which usually coincided with the persistent back trouble with which he was plagued, Goodman continued to the end of the 40s, dabbling with bop by way of a small group which featured musicians such as Doug Mettome, Stan Hasselgård, Wardell Gray and, fleetingly, Fats Navarro and with big bands which included Mettome, Gray, Stan Getz, Don Lamond and Jimmy Rowles.

Goodman soon ended his flirtation with bop, but the release, in 1953, of a long-playing album made from acetates cut during the 1938 Carnegie Hall concert and forgotten during the intervening years revitalized interest in him and his career. He reformed a band for a concert tour which brought together many of the old gang; but a decision to enhance the tour's chances of success by also featuring Louis Armstrong and his All Stars was an error. The two stars clashed at rehearsals and during the out-of-town warm up concert. By the time the package was ready for its opening at Carnegie Hall, Goodman was in hospital, whether for a genuine illness, or because of a sudden attack of diplomacy, no one is quite sure. In 1955 he recorded the soundtrack for a feature film, *The Benny Goodman Story*, and a soundtrack album was also released which featured Wilson, Hampton, Krupa, James, Getz and other former sidemen. During the rest of the 50s and in succeeding decades, Goodman made many appearances with small groups and with occasional big bands, but his days as a leader of a regular big band were over. Even as a small group leader, his bands tended to be one-off only affairs, although he did regularly associate with musicians for whom he had high regard, amongst them Ruby Braff and Urbie Green. In Europe he led a big band for an appearance at the 1958 World's Fair in Brussells and in 1962 took a band to the USSR for a visit sponsored by the US State Department. Later, he fronted other big bands, including two formed from British musicians for concert tours in 1969 and again in 1970. From the late 60s he began appearing at regular reunions of the quartet with Wilson, Hampton and Krupa. These reunions, along with club and television dates, occasional tours to Europe and the Far East, occupied the 70s. This decade also saw, on 16 January 1978, a Carnegie Hall date which attempted to recreate the magic of his first appearance there, 30 years before. Goodman continued to record and play concert and other dates into the early 80s. In the last few years of his life and ensconced in his apartment on west 44th, Manhattan he lived quietly and is well-remembered with great affection by the local community.

From the earliest days of his career Goodman was marked out as a hot clarinettist. Although he had an early regard for Ted Lewis, it was the playing of such musicians as Teschemacher and Jimmy Noone that most influenced him. By the start of the 30s, however, Goodman was very much his own man, playing in a highly distinctive style and beginning to influence other clarinettists. His dazzling technique, allied to his delight in playing hot jazz, made him one of the most exciting players of his day. Without question, he was the most technically proficient of all musicians regularly playing jazz clarinet. On the many records he made during this period Goodman almost always soloed, yet he rarely made an error, even on unused takes. During the swing era, despite the rising popularity of Artie Shaw and a handful of others, Goodman retained his popularity, even though his jazz style became noticeably less hot as the decade progressed. His dabblings with bop were never fully convincing, although in his playing of the 40s and later there are signs that he was aware of the changes being wrought in jazz. There are also fleeting stylistic nods towards Lester Young, whose playing he clearly admired. From the late 30s Goodman had become steadily more interested in classical music and periodically appeared and recorded in this context, often performing pieces which he had specially commissioned. The classical pursuits led him to adopt a different embouchure thus altering the sound of all his playing, and further attenuating the gap some felt had arisen between the current Goodman style and the hot jazz playing of his youth. As a musician Goodman was a perfectionist, practising every day until the end of his life (in his biography of Goodman, James Lincoln Collier reports that, at the time of his death, the clarinettist, alone at home, appeared to have been playing a Brahms Sonata). As with so many perfectionists, Goodman expected his employees to adhere to his own high standards. Many were similarly dedicated musicians, but they were also individualistic, and in some cases had egos which matched his own. Inevitably, there were many clashes; over the years a succession of Goodman stories have emerged which suggest that he was a man who was totally preoccupied with his music to the exclusion of almost everything else including social niceties.

Goodman's achievements in this particular field of American popular music are virtually matchless. He rose from poverty to become a millionaire before he was 30 years old, a real rags to riches story. He was, for a while, the best-known and most popular musician in the USA. And if the title King of Swing rankled with many musicians and was clearly inappropriate when his work is compared with that of such peers as Armstrong and Duke Ellington, Goodman's band of the late 30s was hard-driving outfit which contrasted sharply with many other white bands of the period and at its best was usually their superior. The trio and quartet brought to small group jazz a sophistication rarely heard before, and seldom matched since; but which nevertheless included much hot music, especially from the leader. It was, perhaps, in the sextet, with Christian, Williams, Auld and others that Goodman made his greatest contribution to jazz. All the tracks recorded by this group before Christian's untimely death are classics of the form. His encouragement of musicians like Christian, Wilson and Hampton not only helped Goodman to promote important careers in jazz but also did much to break down racial taboos in show business and American society. The fact that he was never an innovator means Goodman was not a great jazzman in the sense that Armstrong, Ellington, Charlie Parker and others were. Nevertheless, he was a major figure in jazz and played an important role in the history of 20th century popular music. Selected albums: *Benny Goodman At Carnegie Hall* (1938), *The Benny Goodman Story* (1955), *The Benny Goodman Tentet And Sextet* (1959), *Together Again!* (1963), *Live In Las Vegas* (1967), *London Date* (1969), *Benny Goodman Today* (1970), *Live In Stockholm* (1970), *On Stage With Benny Goodman And His Sextet* (1972), *Seven Come Eleven* (1975), *The King* (1978), *Carnegie Hall Reunion Concert* (1978), *King Of Swing* (1980). Compilations: *BG With Ben Pollack* (1926-31), *The Rare BG* (1927-29), *The Formative Years* (1927-34), *Benny Goodman's Boys* (1928-29), *The Hotsy Totsy Gang With Benny Goodman* (1928-30), *Benny Goodman On The Side* (1929-31), *Red Nichols Featuring Benny Goodman* (1929-31), *Ben Selvin And His Orchestra Featuring Benny Goodman Vols 1, 2, 3* (1929-33), *Benny Goodman In A Melotone Manner* (1930-31), *Ted Lewis And His Band Featuring Benny Goodman* (1931-32), *Benny Goodman Accompanies The Girls* (1931-33), *Benny Goodman: The Early Years* (1931-35), *BG With Chick Bullock And Steve Washington* (1933), *Breakfast Ball* (1934), *BG With Adrian Rollini And His Orchestra* (1933-34), *The 'Let's Dance' Broadcasts Vols 1-3* (1934-35), *The Rhythm Makers Vols 1, 2, 3* (1935), *The Indispensable Benny Goodman Vols 1/2* (1935-36), *The Complete Small Combinations Vols 1/2* (1935-37), *This Is Benny Goodman* (1935-39), *Benny Goodman From The Congress Hotel Vols 1-4* (1936), *The Indispensable Benny Goodman Vols 1/2* (1936-37), *BG -The Camel Caravan Vols 1 & 2* (1937), *Benny Goodman At The Madhattan Room Vols 1-11* (1937), *Benny Goodman Trio And Quartet Live* (1937-38), *The Complete Small Combinations Vols 3/4* (1937-39), *Swingtime* (1938), *Solo Flight: Charlie Christian With The Benny Goodman Sextet And Orchestra* (1939-41), *Charlie Christian With The Benny Goodman Sextet And Orchestra* (1939-41), *Benny And Sid*

'*Roll 'Em*' (1941), *Benny Goodman On V-Disc* (1941-46), *The Forgotten Year* (1943), *Benny Goodman On The Fitch Bandwagon* (1944-45), *Benny Goodman Featuring Jess Stacy* (1944-47), *Live 1945 Broadcasts* (1945), *Benny Goodman In Sweden* (1950), *The Benny Goodman Yale Archives Vols-1-3* (1955-86). Classical recordings include Mozart's *Clarinet Concerto KV 622*, Mozart's *Clarinet Quintet KV 581*, Weber's *Clarinet Concerto No 1 in F Minor, Op 73*, Weber's *Clarinet Concerto No 2 in E Flat, Op 74*. Selected compilations: *The Alternate Goodman Vols 1-9* (Nostalgia 1982), *Benny Goodman* (Flapper 1991), *The Birth Of Swing 1935-36* (Bluebird 1992), *King Of Swing (1935-5)* (Giants Of Jazz 1992), *Air Checks 1937-1938* (Sony 1993).

Further reading: *The Kingdom Of Swing*, Benny Goodman and Irving Kolodin. *Benny Goodman: Listen To His Legacy*, D. Russell Connor. *Benny Goodman And The Swing Era*, James Lincoln Collier. *Swing, Swing, Swing: The Life And Times Of Benny Goodman*, Ross Firestone.

Gordon, Dexter

b. 27 February 1923, Los Angeles, California, USA, d. 1990. Gordon began his musical career studying clarinet; by his mid-teens he had switched to tenor saxophone, on which instrument he played with Lionel Hampton in 1940. He stayed with Hampton for a little over two years, recording with the band and gaining in stature so that no less an artist than Coleman Hawkins could nominate him, in 1941, as one of his favourite tenor players. Gordon then worked with Lee Young, his own small group, Fletcher Henderson, Louis Armstrong and Billy Eckstine. By late 1944 Gordon had absorbed many of the new developments in jazz and his exposure to numerous eager beboppers in the Eckstine band soon won him over completely. In the next few years he played frequently on both the east and west coasts, comfortably ignoring the artificial but effective dividing line in the bop of the early 50s. Amongst his playing partners of this period was Wardell Gray, with whom he made several important and much-imitated records. During the rest of the 50s Gordon's career was disrupted by his addiction to narcotics, but by the 60s he was off drugs and playing better than ever. Throughout the 60s and into the 70s he toured extensively, becoming especially popular in Europe where he mostly resided. He returned to the USA in 1976 and continued to record, attracting considerable attention with his mature yet evolving style. His personal life was then in some disarray due to a second broken marriage and a drink problem. He reached a turning point in 1986 when he secured an acting role in a feature film. He had previously dabbled with acting in the early 60s, but the leading role in a major film was a very different matter. He rose to the challenge and the film, '*Round Midnight*, was widely considered an artistic and commercial success with Gordon being nominated for an Academy Award for his portrayal of an alcoholic saxophonist.

One of the outstanding tenor saxophonists in jazz, Gordon's early influences gave him a deeply felt appreciation of swing. Although he was rightly regarded as a major figure in bop, his playing always displayed his awareness of the swing era cadences. In his uptempo performances, especially in his duets and duels with Gray, there is a thrusting aggression to his playing. On ballads he could be tough or tender, able to enhance any tune through his unique combination of experience and inspiration. His recordings stand as eloquent testimony to a man who influenced many musicians. Perhaps because he was not at his best in his later years (one drummer who worked with him then described the experience as 'a crash course in playing slow'), Gordon was largely ignored by record companies during the 80s, recording only the soundtrack album for 'Round Midnight between 1982 and his death in 1990. However, in 1985 Blue Note Records, for whom he had made many of his finest records in the 60s, did release the double Nights At The Keystone, comprising live recordings from 1978-79, and later added more material from the same sessions to make up a three-volume CD set with the same title, which was reissued in 1990.

Selected albums: with Wardell Gray The Chase (1947), with Gray The Hunt (1947), Daddy Plays The Horn (1955), Dexter Plays Hot And Cool (1955), Doin' Alright (Blue Note 1961), Dexter Calling (Blue Note 1961), Go (Blue Note 1962), A Swingin' Affair (Blue Note 1962), Cry Me A River (Steeplechase 1962), Our Man In Paris (Blue Note 1963), One Flight Up (Blue Note 1964), Cheese Cake (Steeplechase 1964), King Neptune (Steeplechase 1964), I Want More (Steeplechase 1964), It's You Or No One (Steeplechase 1964), Billie's Bounce (Steeplechase 1964), Love For Sale (Steeplechase 1964), Clubhouse (Blue Note 1965), Gettin' Around (Blue Note 1965), The Montmartre Collection (1967), Take The 'A' Train (Black Lion 1967), Both Sides Of Midnight (Black Lion 1967), Body And Soul (Black Lion 1967), Live At The Amsterdam Paradiso (1969), The Tower Of Power/More Power (Original Jazz Classics 1969), with Karin Krog Some Other Spring (1970), At Monteaux (Prestige 1970), The Panther (1970), The Apartment (Steeplechase 1974), Bouncin' With Dex (Steeplechase 1975), Stable Mable (Steeplechase 1975), Homecoming (1976), Lullaby For A Monster (Steeplechase 1977), Biting The Apple (Steeplechase 1977), Sophisticated Giant (1977), More Tha You Know (Steeplechase 1977), Something Different (Steeplechase 1977), Midnight Dream (West Wind 1977), Nights At The Keystone Vol 1-3 (Blue Note 1979), Gotham City (1981), American Classic (1982), 'Round Midnight: Soundtrack (1986), A Gordon Cantata (West Wind 1993, rec. 1978). Selected compilations: Long Tall Dexter (1945-47), Best Of Dexter Gordon, The Blue Note Years (Blue Note 1988), Ballads (Blue Note 1992).

Further reading: Long Tall Dexter, Stan Britt.

Goykovich, Dusko

b. 14 October 1931, Jajce, Yugoslavia. After completing his formal studies at the Academy of Music in Belgrade, Goykovich played trumpet and flügelhorn in various dance-bands and radio orchestras in Europe, including those of Max Greger and Kurt Edelhagen. In the late 50s he travelled to the USA, played at the Newport Jazz Festival and then pursued his studies at Berklee College Of Music. Thereafter, like many

Berklee alumni, he entered the bands of Maynard Ferguson and Woody Herman. Back in Europe he played in the small group led by Sal Nistico and then joined the Clarke-Boland Big Band, where he remained for five years until 1973. In the 70s Goykovich's associates included Slide Hampton and Alvin Queen. He also worked extensively in radio and education in Europe. A fine post-bop trumpeter, Goykovich's style derives from early Miles Davis, but the inclusion of traditional melodies from his homeland in his playing makes him a distinctive soloist. In the 90s Goykovich toured European venues, both as a soloist and in tandem with Italian alto saxophonist Gianni Basso.

Albums: Swinging Macedonia (Enja 1965), After Hours (1971), A Day In Holland (1983), Celebration (DIW 1987).

Graham, Kenny

b. 19 July 1924, London, England. Graham first played professionally at the age of 15, making his debut on alto saxophone with the Nottingham-based Rube Sunshine band. He later moved to London to join Billy Smith at the Cricklewood Palais but used his spare time to good effect, by touring London clubs where he met and played with well-known British jazzmen such as Jack Parnell and Nat Gonella. He spent some time with Johnny Claes's Claepigeons, a band which included drummer Carlo Krahmer (later to found Esquire Records). After military service during World War II he worked with a variety of bands, including Ambrose and Macari and his Dutch Serenaders and was by now usually heard on tenor saxophone. In April 1950 Graham introduced his own band, the Afro-Cubists, which successfully fused bebop with Latin and Caribbean rhythms. The band was home to pianist Ralph Dollimore, Phil Seamen and at one time, a five-man saxophone section that included Derek Humble and Joe Temperley. The band folded in 1958 and thereafter Graham concentrated on arranging, his charts being played and recorded by jazz artists as diverse as Ted Heath and Humphrey Lyttelton. Graham proved especially adept at building interesting arrangements upon unusual tonal effects, a good example being his 'Moondog Suite', which developed the ethereal sounds of Louis Hardin the legendary blind street musician who was recorded on the streets of New York in the early 50s. In the 80s Graham was still writing, and the incorporation of synthesizers and other electronic instruments into his work showed that he had lost none of the enthusiasm for new sounds that had marked his early career.

Albums: Mango Walk (Esquire 1953), Caribbean Suite/Afro Kadabra (Esquire 1953), Moondog And Suncat Suites (1956), Kenny Graham And His Orchestra (1957).

Grappelli, Stéphane

b. 26 January 1908, Paris, France. After learning to play keyboard instruments, Grappelli took up the violin, later studying it formally. In the mid-20s he played in dance bands in Paris, gradually turning more to jazz. In the early 30s he met Django Reinhardt and with him formed the Quintette du Hot Club de France. Until this point in his career Grappelli had been playing piano and violin, but now concentrated on the latter instrument. Performances and especially records by the QHCF alerted the jazz world to the arrival of both an intriguing new sound and, in Reinhardt, the first authentic non-American genius of jazz. In these years Grappelli was still learning, and his early popularity was largely as a result of that of his collaborator. Shortly before the outbreak of World War II Grappelli settled in London, where he played with George Shearing. In the post-war years he worked briefly with Reinhardt again but spent the late 40s and 50s playing to diminishing audiences across Europe. In the 60s he enjoyed a revival of popularity, making records with other violinists such as Stuff Smith and Joe Venuti. In the early 70s he appeared on UK television performing duets with classical violinist Yehudi Menuhin, and the records they made together sold well. However, Grappelli's real breakthrough to the big time had come when, at the urging of Diz Disley, he made appearances at the 1973 UK Cambridge Folk Festival (accompanied by Disley and Denny Wright). Grappelli was a sensation. For the rest of the decade, throughout the 80s and into the early 90s he was on a non-stop tour of the world, playing the most prestigious venues in the UK, Europe, the USA and the Far East. He made records with several backing groups, played duets with Gary Burton, Earl Hines, Martial Solal, Jean-Luc Ponty and many other leading jazzmen. He has also ventured into other areas of music and, in addition to the duets with Menuhin, he has recorded with the western swing fiddler, Vassar Clements. At ease with a repertoire based upon his early career successes, Grappelli's flowing style has steadily matured over the years and the occasional uncertainties of his early work with Reinhardt are long forgotten. Perhaps at odd moments in his later years he seemed to be coasting, yet some of his recorded performances are very good while several of those from the mid- and late 70s are amongst the most distinguished in the history of jazz violin. Of particular merit are *Parisian Thoroughfare*, recorded with the rhythm section of Roland Hanna, George Mraz and Mel Lewis, and a set recorded at the Queen Elizabeth Hall in London in 1973 when he was backed by Disley and Len Skeat. Grappelli's late flowering has done much to prompt appreciation of the old tradition of jazz violin playing, of which he is perhaps the last representative.

Selected albums: *Django* (1962), with Svend Asmussen *Two Of A Kind* (1965), *I Remember Django* (1969), with Joe Venuti *Venupelli Blues* (1969), *Stéphane Grappelli Meets Barney Kessel* (1969), *I Hear Music* (1970), *Satin Doll* (1972), with Yehudi Menuhin *Jealousy* (1972-73), *Just One Of Those Things* (1973), *Parisian Thoroughfare* (1973), *I Got Rhythm* (1973), *Live At The Queen Elizabeth Hall* (1973), *Stéphane Grappelli & Jean-Luc Ponty* (1973), *Live In London* (1973), with Earl 'Fatha' Hines *Giants* (1974), with Slam Stewart *Steff And Slam* (1975), with George Shearing *The Reunion* (1976), *Live At Carnegie Hall* (1978), *Young Django* (1979), with Bucky Pizzarelli *Duet* (1979), *London Meeting* (String 1979), *Tivoli Gardens, Copenhahen, Denmark* (Original Jazz Classics 1980), *Strictly For The Birds* (1980), *At The Winery* (1980), with Martin Taylor *We've Got The World On A String* (1980), *Happy Reunion*

(Owl 1980), *Vintage 1981* (Concord 1981), *At The Winery* (Concord 1981), *Stephanova* (Concord 1983), with Vassar Clements *Together At Last* (1985), *Satin Doll* (Musidisc 1987), *Stéphane Grappelli Plays Jerome Kern* (GRP 1987), *Stéphane Grappelli In Tokyo* (Denon 1990), *Piano My Other Love* (1990), *One On One* (Milestone 1990), *Live At Warsaw Jazz Festival 1991* (1993), *Live 1992* (Birdology 1992), with Joe Venuti *Venupelli Blues* (1993), with Marc Fosset *Looking At You* (1993), with Taylor *Reunion* (1993). Selected compilations: with QHCF *Swing From Paris* (1935-39), *Django Reinhardt And Stéphane Grappelli With The Quintet Of The Hot Club Of France* (1935-46), with QHFC *Stéphane Grappelli 1947-1961* (1947-61), with QHFC *Djangology* (1949), *Grappelli Story* (Verve 1992).

Further reading: *Stéphane Grappelli*, Geoffrey Smith.

Gray, Wardell

b. 13 February 1921, Oklahoma City, Oklahoma, USA, d. 25 May 1955. Growing up in Detroit, Gray first played clarinet before switching to tenor saxophone and joining the Earl 'Fatha' Hines band in 1943. After two years he relocated on the west coast, where he became prominent among local beboppers, notably Dexter Gordon, with whom he played at Central Avenue clubs such as The Bird In The Basket. Gray made some successful recordings with Gordon, among them 'The Chase' and 'The Hunt', and also composed a number of tunes himself, including 'Twisted', which, with lyrics added, became popular with scat singers. In the late 40s and early 50s Gray worked with Benny Carter, Billy Eckstine and Count Basie, and was a member of Benny Goodman's short-lived bebop big band where he elicited a rare compliment from Goodman, who never really liked bebop: 'If Wardell Gray plays bop then it's great because he's wonderful.' He also played in a Goodman small group alongside Stan Hasselgård. Gray's tone was soft and he played light, flowing lines that reflected the influence Lester Young had upon him. Gray died on 25 May 1955 in circumstances that have never been fully resolved: his body was found in the Nevada Desert, his neck broken. The official report gave the cause of death as a drug overdose, though there was no autopsy, and rumours persisted that Gray had been murdered - either for failing to pay gambling debts or simply as a random victim of racial violence.

Albums: *Way Out Wardell* (Boplicity 1947), with Don Lanphere *Thin Man Meets Fat Boy, Vols. 1 & 2* (c.1949-50), with Leo Parker *Thin Man Meets Mad Lad* (c.1949-50), *Live In Hollywood* (1952), *Out Of Nowhere* (1952), *Live At The Haig 1952* (Fresh Sound 1952). Compilations: *Wardell Gray And The Big Bands* (1945-53), *One For Prez* (Black Lion 1946), *Easy Swing* (Swingtime 1946-55), *The Hunt* (1947), with Benny Goodman, Stan Hasselgård *Swedish Pastry/Benny's Bop* (1948), *Light Gray Vol. 1* (1948-50), *Central Avenue* (1949-50), *Memorial* (1949-53), *The Hunt* (Savoy 1979), *Central Avenue* (RCA 1979), *1947-52* (Giants Of Jazz 1987).

Green, Bennie

b. 16 April 1923, Chicago, Illinois, USA, d. 23 March 1977.

After playing locally for a while during his teenage years, trombonist Green joined the bebop-orientated Earl 'Fatha' Hines band in 1942. He continued to be associated with Hines until the early 50s, his spells with the band being interrupted by military service and periods working with Charlie Ventura, the band co-led by Gene Ammons and Sonny Stitt and the small groups he led himself. In the late 60s he was briefly with Duke Ellington, then settled in Las Vegas, where he worked in various hotel and casino house bands. Green's playing ranged widely, encompassing the swing-era style prominent during his formative years; he was one of only a few trombonists to adapt comfortably to bebop, and he also played R&B.

Albums: *Bennie Green* i (1951), *Bennie Green With Strings* (1952), *Bennie Green Blows His Horn* (1955), *Bennie Green & Art Farmer* (1956), *Walking Down* (1956), *Back On The Scene* (1958), *Soul Stirrin'/Juggin' Around* (1958), *Bennie Green Quintet* (1958), *Walkin' And Talkin'* (1959), *Bennie Green Swings The Blues* (c.1960), *Bennie Green* ii (1960), *Gliding Along* (1961), *Bennie Green* iii (1964), with Newport All Stars *Newport In New York '72: The Jam Sessions* (1972).

Green, Benny

b. 4 April 1963, New York City, New York, USA. An exciting and hard-swinging pianist in the Bud Powell mould, Benny Green ranks alongside Mulgrew Miller and Donald Brown, as one of a number of talented hard-bop keyboard stars to have graduate from Art Blakey's Jazz Messengers training ground during America's hard-bop revival of the 80s, leading bands and beginning to establish his own voice towards the end of the decade. A student of classical piano from the age of seven, Green developed a taste for jazz through the influence of his tenor saxophone playing father, and was keen enough as a child to start borrowing records and imitating the bebop sounds of the 40s and 50s. He played in school bands, until his keen ear and obvious commitment brought him to the attention of singer Fay Carroll, with whom he got his first real taste of a working jazz band - learning invaluable lessons about accompaniment and the blues, and gaining his first chance to play in a trio context as a way of opening the set. Still in his teens, he filled the piano chair in a quintet co-led by trumpeter Eddie Henderson and saxophonist Hadley Caliman, and a 12-piece led by bassist Chuck Israels. On finishing high-school, Green moved to the west coast and freelanced around the San Francisco Bay area, gaining experience working as a sideman. But it was with his return to New York in the Spring of 1982 that Green's career took a swift upward turn, benefiting from studies with Walter Bishop Jnr. and joining Betty Carter's band in April 1983 - the beginning of a four year stint of performing, recording and learning with jazz's most respected vocalist. The piano chair in Art Blakey's prestigious Jazz Messengers followed, and then, in 1989, a year with the Freddie Hubbard Quintet. By 1990, Green had already led a couple of blowing dates on the Criss Cross label, but it was with his Blue Note Records debut (*Lineage*) that Green really came of age, earning international respect and a reputation as one of the label's most exciting new stars. Since 1991 he has been touring with a his

regular, finely tuned trio comprising bassist Christian McBride and drummer Carl Allen.

Albums: with Betty Carter *Jazzbuhne '85* (1985), with Ralph Moore *Round Trip* (1985), with Art Blakey *Hard Champion* (1987), with Blakey *Blue Moon* (1987), with Jim Snidero *Mixed Bag* (1987), *Not Yet* (1988), with Freddie Hubbard *Feel The Wind* (1988), with Bob Mover *You Go To My Head* (1988), with Blakey *Standards* (1988), with Blakey *I Get A Kick Out Of Bu* (1988), *Prelude* (Criss Cross 1988), *In This Direction* (Criss Cross 1989), *Lineage* (Blue Note 1990), *Furthermore* (1990), with Larry Gales *A Message From Monk* (1990), *Greens* (Blue Note 1991), with Steve Turre *Right There* (1991), with Bob Belden *Straight To My Heart* (1991), with 29th Street Saxophone Quartet *Underground* (1991), *Testifyin' ! At The Village Vanguard* (Blue Note 1992), *That's Right* (Blue Note 1993), *The Place To Be* (1994).

Green, Dave

b. 5 March 1942, London, England. Surprisingly for a bass player of such skill and prestige, Green is self-taught. His first important engagement as a professional musician was with the Don Rendell-Ian Carr band which he joined in the early 60s. By the end of the decade he had established himself as a major figure, having worked with musicians as diverse as Stan Tracey and Humphrey Lyttelton. He also played and recorded with many front-rank visiting Americans who counted themselves fortunate in having his solidity and flair behind them. For a while in the early 80s he led his own group, Fingers, which featured Lol Coxhill, Bruce Turner and Michael Garrick. Throughout the 80s and on into the early 90s, Green has remained at the forefront of British jazz, working with Peter King, Didier Lockwood, Spike Robinson and a host of other British and visiting jazzmen. A superb timekeeper and exceptional soloist, Green is the essence of the international jazz musician.

Albums: with Don Rendell-Ian Carr *Shades Of Blue* (1964), *Fingers Remembers Mingus* (1980), *Spike Robinson-George Masso Play Arlen* (1991).

Green, Freddie

b. 31 March 1911, Charleston, South Carolina, USA, d. 1 March 1987. A self-taught musician who began on banjo, Green became known around New York jazz clubs in the early 30s. By 1936 he had switched to guitar and was recommended by John Hammond to Count Basie, who was looking for a replacement guitarist in his band. Green was hired in 1937 and became a member of the famous 'All-American Rhythm Section' (with Basie, Walter Page and Jo Jones). He remained there until 1950 when the big band folded and Basie organized a sextet. Unwilling to be left out of the band Green returned, uninvited. He was thus on hand when Basie reformed his big band and was still resident when Basie died in 1984. A meticulous timekeeper, Green's presence helped ensure the superb swing of the Basie band from its freewheeling Kansas City sound of the late 30s and 40s through to the metronomic accuracy of the 50s and after. On some recordings by the band,

Dave Green

Green's contribution is virtually inaudible, but everyone who played with him insisted that his discreet beat was one of the principal factors in ensuring the band's propulsive swing. After Jones's departure Green was seldom happy with his replacements and reputedly kept a long stick by his chair with which to poke any drummer (especially Sonny Payne) who strayed off the beat. After Basie's death Green continued to work, making records with, among others, Manhattan Transfer.

Albums: *Brother John Sellers Sings Blues And Folk Songs* (1954), *Mr Rhythm* (1955), with Count Basie *On My Way And Shouting Again* (1962), with Herb Ellis *Rhythm Willie* (c.1975), with Basie *On The Road* (1979). Compilation: with Basie *The Complete Recorded Works In Chronological Order* (1937-39 recordings).

Green, Grant

b. 6 June 1931, St Louis, Missouri, USA, d. 31 January 1979. Heavily influenced by Charlie Christian, guitarist Green first played professionally with Jimmy Forrest. Although noted particularly for his work in organ-guitar-drum trios in the 50s, throughout his career Green was associated with post-bop musicians and in the 60s he recorded for the Blue Note label with Stanley Turrentine, Hank Mobley, McCoy Tyner, Herbie Hancock and others. The flowing, single-line solos characteristic of Christian's early experiments in bebop were evident in much of Green's work. At home in several areas of jazz, he had a particularly strong affinity with the blues, while one album, *Feelin' The Spirit*, features gospel music. Nevertheless, he was essentially modern in his approach to music. Drug addiction severely limited his career in the 70s and he died in 1979.

Selected albums: *Grant's First Stand* (1961), *Reaching Out* (Black Lion 1961), *Green Street* (1961), *Sunday Mornin'* (1961), *Grantstand* (Blue Note 1961), *Gooden's Corner* (1961), *Nigeria* (1962), *Remembering* (c.1962), *The Latin Bit* (1962), *Goin' West* (Blue Note 1962), *Feelin' The Spirit* (Blue Note 1962), *Born To Be Blue* (Blue Note 1962), *Am I Blue* (Blue Note 1963), *Idle Moments* (Blue Note 1963), *Matador* (Blue Note 1964), *Solid* (1964), *Talkin' About* (1964), *Street Of Dreams* (1964), *I Want To Hold Your Hand* (1965), *His Majesty King Funk* (1965), *Iron City* (1967), *Carryin' On* (Blue Note 1969), *Grant Green Alive!* (Blue Note 1970), *Visions* (1971), *Shades Of Green* (1971), *The Final Comedown* (1972, film soundtrack), *Live At The Lighthouse* (1972), *The Main Attraction* (1976), *Easy/Last Session* (1978), *Iron City* (Black Lion 1981), *Last Session* (Atlantis 1987). Compilation: *Best Of* (Blue Note 1993).

Green, Urbie

b. Urban Clifford Green, 8 August 1926, Mobile, Alabama, USA. Trombonist Green's first major engagement was with Gene Krupa in the late 40s; from there he joined the Woody Herman band. In the early 50s he appeared on Buck Clayton's celebrated Jam Session recordings. He then joined Benny Goodman, occasionally leading the band when Goodman was unwell. In the 60s and thereafter, Green freelanced, played in the studios, made numerous records, some of which were under his own name, gigged with Count Basie and led the reconstituted Tommy Dorsey orchestra. A masterly performer, especially in the upper register, Green has throughout his career consistently demonstrated that it is possible to blend deep jazz feeling with a seemingly perfect technique.

Albums: with Buck Clayton *Jam Session* (1953), *Urbie Green Septet* i (1953), *Buck Clayton Jams Benny Goodman* (1953-54), *Urbie Green And His Orchestra* i (1954), *Urbie Green Septet* ii (1955), *Blues And Other Shades Of Green* (Fresh Sounds 1955), *Urbie Green And His Orchestra* ii (1956), *Urbie Green And His Orchestra* iii (1957), *Urbie Green, His Trombone And Rhythm* (1959), *Urbie Green And His Orchestra* iv (1960-61), *Urbie Green And His Orchestra And Septet* (1961), *Urbie Green Septet* iii (1963), *Urbie Green And Twenty-one Trombones* i (1968), *Urbie Green And Twenty-one Trombones* ii (1968), *The Fox* (1976), *Senor Blues* (1977), *Live At Rick's Café Americain* (1978), *The Message* (Fresh Sounds 1988).

Greer, Sonny

b. William Alexander Greer, 13 December c.1895, Long Branch, New Jersey, USA, d. 23 March 1982. After playing in New Jersey, drummer Greer appeared in Washington in 1919 where he encountered a local musician named Duke Ellington. In the early 20s the two men worked together in New York where Greer became a permanent member of the Ellington entourage. One of Duke's closest acquaintances, Greer was a subtle player who occasionally erred on the side of casualness. His timekeeping was supported initially by guitarist Freddie Guy and later by bassist Jimmy Blanton. Visually, Greer was spectacular, surrounding himself with an astonishing array of percussion instruments, including bells, gongs, timpani and xylophone. During his time with Ellington, Greer rarely went outside the band, although he did play on Lionel Hampton's famous Victor recording sessions. A smooth-talking, sharp-dressing, pool-hustler, Greer's on-stage behaviour gradually deteriorated through his inability to control his drinking. In 1951 Ellington finally asked him to leave and thereafter Greer freelanced, recording with other ex-Ellingtonians such as Johnny Hodges and Tyree Glenn and with Red Allen and J.C. Higginbotham. Despite his failings as a drummer, in retrospect it is possible to see and hear that Greer was the ideal Ellington drummer for the 30s and 40s. In the late 60s and 70s Greer led his own groups, usually a trio, appearing in concerts celebrating Ellington and proving that he was never more at ease than when playing his old boss's music.

Compilation albums: with Duke Ellington *The Blanton-Webster Years* (1940-42), *Sonny Greer And The Duke's Men* (1944-45).

Greig, Stan

b. 12 August 1930, Edinburgh, Scotland. A gifted pianist and competent drummer, Greig began playing in his home town where his school friends and fellow musicians included Al Fairweather and Sandy Brown. He played both piano and drums with Brown in the mid-to late 40s and by the mid-50s was established on the London jazz scene, working mostly in traditional jazz groups. Until the late 60s he primarily played drums but thereafter was heard more often on piano, the instrument with which he found his true, distinctive voice. Once again he stayed mostly in the traditional repertoire but also formed and led the London Jazz Big Band, in which Fairweather also played. In the late 80s he was with Humphrey Lyttelton with whom he had first played in the mid-50s. A solid, blues-based pianist, Greig is an exceptionally interesting soloist and as a band member knows few equals in his field. Rhythmically forceful, perhaps as a result of his drumming, he enhances every rhythm section in which he works.

Albums: with Sandy Brown, Al Fairweather *Fairweather Friends* (1957), *Blues Every Time* (1985).

Grey, Al

b. 6 June 1925, Aldie, Virginia, USA. Early in his career Grey played trombone in bands in the US Navy but soon after World War II he joined Benny Carter, whom he always credited with extending his musical knowledge. After leaving Carter, Grey played in the bands of Jimmie Lunceford and Lucky Millinder. In 1948 he joined Lionel Hampton with whom he remained for five years. Briefly with Dizzy Gillespie, he then played with Count Basie for four years - a spell that gave Grey maximum exposure worldwide. When he later began touring as a single, and in a long and musically rewarding partnership with Jimmy Forrest, his success was assured. Very popular on the international club and festival circuit, Grey is an exciting and adventurous soloist, specializing in the use of the plunger mute. After Forrest's death Grey teamed up with Buddy Tate and continued touring until Tate's string of accidents and illnesses forced Grey back into solo appearances.

Albums: *The Last Of The Big Plungers* (1959), *The Thinking Man's Trombone* (1960), *Al Grey-Billy Mitchell Sextet* (1961), *Snap Your Fingers* (1962), *Night Song* (1962), *Having A Ball* (1963), *Boss-bone* (1964), *Al Grey And His Orchestra* (1965), *The Great Concert Of Count Basie And His Orchestra* (1966), *Al Grey And Wild Bill Davis* (1972), *Grey's Mood* (1973), *Struttin' And Shoutin'* (1976), *Al Grey All Stars Live At Travelers Lounge* (1977), *Al Grey Featuring Arnett Cobb* (Black And Blue 1977), with Basie *Prime Time* (1977), *Trombone By Five* (1977), *Al Grey-Jimmy Forrest Quintet Live At Rick's* (1978), *Get It Together: Live At The Pizza Express* (Pizza Express 1979), *Truly Wonderful* (Stash 1979), *O. D.* (1980), with J.J. Johnson *Things Are Getting Better All The Time* (1983), *Al Grey And The Jesper Thilo Quintet* (Storyville 1986), *The New Al Grey Quintet* (Chiarascuro 1988), *Al Meets Bjarne* (Gemini 1989), *Fab* (Capri 1993), *Christmas Stockin' Stuffer* (Capri 1993). Compilation: *Basic Grey* (Chess 1988).

Griffin, Johnny

b. 24 April 1928, Chicago, Illinois, USA. Griffin studied tenor saxophone at Du Sable High School where his tutor was Walter Dyatt, who also taught Gene Ammons and Von Freeman. In his mid-teens, Griffin joined the Lionel Hampton R&B-based big band and followed this with a spell in a similarly-oriented band led by Joe Morris. During the late 40s and early 50s he worked with numerous mainstream and bebop musicians, including Philly Joe Jones, Thelonious Monk, Bud Powell and Arnett Cobb. After military service, Griffin joined Art Blakey's Jazz Messengers in 1957, worked again with Monk, and co-led a band with Eddie 'Lockjaw' Davis - they dubbed themselves 'tough tenors', a sobriquet which has since been applied to an entire sub-genre of tenor playing. In the early 60s Griffin lived in Europe, where he often accompanied visiting American jazzmen and in 1967-68 was a member of the multi-national Clarke-Boland Big Band. In the 70s Griffin toured extensively, usually as a solo but sometimes in harness with Davis and Cobb; in the 80s he occasionally appeared with the Paris Reunion Band. A remarkably gifted and fiercely combative player, Griffin displays a seemingly endless stream of ideas, often at rapid-fire speeds. His style owes much to his bebop associates and predecessors and he was one of the best hard bop musicians of the 70s and 80s. His 90s recorded work on the Antilles label with Kenny Washington (drums) is particularly fresh and rewarding

Albums: *Johnny Griffin Quartet* i (c.1956), *Introducing Johnny Griffin* (Blue Note 1956), *A Blowing Session* (Blue Note 1957), *The Congregation* (Blue Note 1957), *Johnny Griffin Sextet* (Original Jazz Classics 1958), *Way Out!* (1958), *The Little Giant* (Original jazz Classics 1959), *The Big Soul Band* (Original Jazz Classics 1960), with Eddie 'Lockjaw' Davis *Tough Tenors* (1960), *Studio Jazz Party* (1960), *Change Of Pace* (1961), *Blues Up And Down* (1961), *White Gardenia* (1961), *The Kerry Dancers* (1961), *Grab This* (1962), *Do Nothin' Till You Hear From Me* (1963), *Johnny Griffin Quartet* ii (1964), *Salt Peanuts* (Black Lion 1964), *The Man I Love* (Black Lion 1967), *Hush-A-Bye* (1967), *A Night In Tunisia* (1967), *You Leave Me Breathless* (1967), *Johnny Griffin Quartet* iii (1968), *Johnny Griffin Band* (1968), with Clarke-Boland *All Smiles* (1968), *Jazz Undulation* (1970), *Live At Music Inn* (1974), *The Jamfs Are Coming* (Timeless, 1975-77), *Live In Tokyo* (West Wind 1976), *Return Of The Griffin* (1978), *Bush Dance* (1978), *NYC Underground* (1979), *To The Ladies* (1979), *The Little Giant* (Milestone 1980), *Johnny Griffin Quartet* iv (1980), *Meeting* (c.1981), *Call It Whachawana* (1983), *Blues For Harvey* (Steeplechase 1986, rec. 1973), *The Cat* (Antilles 1991), *Dance Of Passion* (Antilles 1993).

Grimes, Tiny

b. Lloyd Grimes, 7 July 1916, Newport News, Virginia, USA. After playing drums and piano, Grimes turned to the guitar. Unusual among guitarists, he played a four-string instrument and was also an early experimenter with electrical amplification. In the late 30s and early 40s he worked in New York, attracting great attention when he joined Slam Stewart, succeeding Slim Gaillard. Grimes and Stewart then became accompanists to Art Tatum. In the mid-40s Grimes led several small groups, some of which dabbled in early bebop and featured artists such as Charlie Parker. In striking contrast, Grimes also played rock 'n' roll and cocktail lounge jazz to make ends meet. In the 70s and 80s he played clubs and festivals around the world.

Johnny Griffin

Albums: *Blues Groove* (1958), *Callin' The Blues* (1958), *Tiny In Swingville* (Original Jazz Classics 1959), *Tiny Grimes* i (1962), *Chasin' With Milt* (1968), *Tiny Grimes* ii (1970), *Profoundly Blue* (1973), *Some Groovy Fours* (1970-74), *One Is Never Too Old To Swing* (1977), *Profoundly Blue* (Muse 1981). Compilations: *The Art Tatum Trio* (1944), *Loch Lomond* (Whiskey Women & Song 1987, c.1947-50 recordings), *Tiny Grimes And His Rockin' Highlanders* (c.1949-50), *Tiny Grimes Vols 1 & 2* (Krazy Kat 1986, 1949-55 recordings)., *Rock The House* (Swingtime 1987), *Tiny's Boogie* (Oldie Blues 1988, 1948-50 recordings).

Grosz, Marty

b. Martin O. Grosz, 28 February 1930, Berlin, Germany. Resident in the USA since the age of three, Grosz began playing banjo and guitar in and around New York while still attending university. His musical inclinations were towards dixieland jazz, which he played with artists such as Dick Wellstood. After military service he settled in Chicago and played there for several years in local clubs, making a few records but making little impression on the national jazz scene. In the mid-70s he moved back to New York and joined Soprano Summit, the excellent small band co-led by Bob Wilber and Kenny Davern. His compositions 'Let Your Fingers Do The Walking' and 'Goody Goody' were acoustic guitar duets with Wayne Wright. In the late 70s he resumed his working relationship with Wellstood and established a new and musically-rewarding partnership with Dick Sudhalter that continued into the 80s. He also formed his own band, the Blue Angels, and, in addition to his talent for arranging and singing, proved himself to be an able writer on jazz topics.

Albums: *Hooray For Bix* (1957), *Marty Grosz And His Honoris Causa Band* (1957), *Marty Grosz And His Gaslighters* i (1959), *Marty Grosz And His Gaslighters* ii (1959), *Soprano Summit In Concert* (1976), *Let Your Fingers Do The Walking* (1977), with Dick Wellstood *Take Me To The Land Of Jazz* (1978), *Goody Goody* (1978-79), *I Hope Gabriel Likes My Music* (1981), *Marty Grosz Sings Of Love And Other Matters* (1986), *Keepers Of The Flame* (1987), *Swing It!* (Jazzology 1988), *Extra! The Orphan Newsboys* (Jazzology 1989), *Laughing At Life* (1990), *Unsaturated Fats* (Stomp Off 1990), *Songs I Learned At My Mother's Knee And Other Low Joints* (Jazzology 1992), *Live At The L.A. Classic* (Jazzology 1992), *Thanks* (1993).

Gruntz, George

b. 24 June 1932, Basle, Switzerland. Gruntz first attracted attention at the 1958 Newport Jazz Festival, where he appeared as a pianist with the Marshall Brown International Youth Band (which also included Dusko Goykovich). In the early 60s he worked with several leading American jazzmen, including Dexter Gordon; later in the decade he was with Phil Woods in the latter's European Rhythm Machine. In 1970 Gruntz was appointed musical director of the Zurich Schauspielhaus and since 1972 he has been artistic director of the Berlin Jazz Festival. In the early 70s he was co-founder and leader of a multi-national all-star big band, which he later led under the name of the George Gruntz Concert Jazz Band; he experimented with groups comprising multiple keyboard instruments (Piano Conclave), and played with forward-thinking jazz artists such as Don Cherry and Rahsaan Roland Kirk. More than most who have tried, Gruntz has been successful in crossing and recrossing the line between jazz and other musical forms. His compositions include symphonies, ballets and operas which stand alongside music written for all sizes of jazz groups. He has also written film scores and a jazz oratorio, 'The Holy Grail Of Jazz And Joy' (which appears on the album *Theatre*). His work always displays an inquiring and adventurous approach to jazz and has consistently chosen to push against accepted boundaries.

Albums: *Jazz Sound Track* (1962), *Jazz Goes Baroque* (1964), *George Gruntz Et Les Swiss All Stars* (1964), *George Gruntz Ensemble* (1965), *George Gruntz With The International Peter Stuyvesant Orchestra* (1965), *Noon In Tunisia* (1967), *From Sticksland With Love: Drums And Folklore* (1967), *St. Peter Power* (1968), *The Band* (1972), *Monster Sticksland Meeting Two* (1974), *Eternal Baroque* (1974), *Piano Conclave* (1975), *The Band: Recorded Live At The Schauspielhaus* (1976), *Trumpet Machine For Flying Out Proud* (1977), *Percussion Profiles* (1977), *Concert Jazz Band* (1978), *Live At The Quartier Latin, Berlin* (1980), *Live '82* (1982), *Theatre* (ECM 1983), *Happening Now* (Hat Art 1988), *First Prize* (1989).

Grusin, Dave

b. 26 June 1934, Littleton, Colorado, USA. He played piano semi-professionally while studying at the University of Colorado, and almost abandoned music to become a veterinary surgeon. Grusin stated 'I'm still not sure I made the right decision, a lot of dead cows might still be alive today if I hadn't gone to music school.' His musical associates at the time included Art Pepper, Terry Gibbs and Spike Robinson, with whom he worked extensively in the early 50s. In 1959 Grusin was hired as musical director by singer Andy Williams, a role he maintained into the mid-60s. An eclectic musician, Grusin worked with mainstream artists such as Benny Goodman and Thad Jones and also worked with hard bop players. He made many recording dates, including several in the early 70s, accompanying singers amongst whom were Sarah Vaughan and Carmen McRae. Around this same time Grusin began to concentrate more and more on electric piano and keyboards, recording with Gerry Mulligan, Lee Ritenour in the jazz world and with Paul Simon and Billy Joel in pop. He has arranged and produced for the Byrds, Peggy Lee, Grover Washington Jnr., Donna Summer, Barbra Streisand, Al Jarreau, Phoebe Snow and Patti Austin. He is also co-founder and owner, with Larry Rosen, of GRP Records, a label which they founded in 1976 and has an impressive catalogue of singers, jazz and jazz-rock artists including Diane Schuur, Lee Ritenour, David Benoit, his brother Don Grusin, Michael Brecker, Chick Corea, Steve Gadd, Dave Valentin, Special EFX and Gary Burton. The success of GRP has much to do with Grusin's refusal to compromise on quality. With Rosen he pioneered an all digital recording policy, and using 'state of the art' technology their productions reach a pinnacle of recorded quality. In addition to his activities as a player and producer, Grusin has written extensively for films and television. His portfolio is most impressive; in addition to winning a Grammy in 1984 his film scores have received several Academy Award nominations, and include *Divorce Italian Style, The Graduate, The Heart Is A Lonely Hunter, Three Days Of The Condor, Heaven Can Wait, Reds, On Golden Pond, The Champ, Tootsie, Racing With The Moon, The Milagro Beanfield War, Clara's Heart, Tequila Sunrise, A Dry White Season, The Fabulous Baker Boys, Bonfire Of The Vanities, Havana, For The Boys,* and *The Firm* (1993). Additionally one of his most evocative songs 'Mountain Dance' was the title song to *Falling In Love*. His American television credits include *St. Elsewhere, Maude, Roots, It Takes A Thief* and *Baretta*. Grusin is a master musical chemist - able to blend many elements of pop and jazz into uplifting intelligent and accessible music. In 1993 he appeared one again as a performer on the international jazz circuit, away from the day to day running of GRP.

Albums: *Candy* (1961), *The Many Moods Of Dave Grusin* (1962), *Kaleidoscope* (1964), *Don't Touch* (c.1964), *Discovered Again* (1976), *One Of A Kind* (1977), *Dave Grusin And The GRP All Stars Live In Japan Featuring Sadao Watanabe* (GRP 1980), *Out Of The Shadows* (GRP 1982), *Mountain Dance* (GRP 1983), *Night Lines* (GRP 1984), with Lee Ritenour *Harlequin* (GRP 1984), *The NYLA Dream Band* (GRP 1988), with Don Grusin *Sticks And Stones* (GRP 1988), *Migration* (GRP 1989), *The Fabulous Baker Boys* (GRP 1989, film soundtrack), *Havana* (GRP 1990), *The Gershwin Collection* (GRP 1992), *Homage To Duke* (GRP 1993), *Orchestral Album* (GRP 1993). Compilations: *Cinemagic* (GRP 1987), *Dave Grusin Collection* (GRP 1991).

Gryce, Gigi

b. 28 November 1927, Pensacola, Florida, USA, d. 17 March 1983. Alto saxophonist Gryce studied composition at Boston Conservatory and in Paris (with classicist Arthur Honegger) but then turned to jazz with spells in various bands, including that led by Tadd Dameron. In 1953 he was a member of the remarkable band with which Lionel Hampton toured Europe and which featured many other fine young musicians, notably Clifford Brown, Art Farmer, Quincy Jones and Alan Dawson. Although contractually barred from recording while on tour, most of the band were too eager to be bound by contracts and made several big band and small group records, some of which were released under Gryce's name. On their return to the USA the culprits of this breach of contract were fired by Hampton. In the mid- to late 50s Gryce worked with Lee Morgan, Oscar Pettiford, Donald Byrd (co-leading the Jazz Lab quintet with him) and also led his own small group. Gryce's playing was heavily influenced by Charlie Parker, but his writing showed great flair and inventiveness and was eagerly used by many leading post-bop artists. In the 60s Gryce began to concentrate on teaching and also extended his composing into the classical field: he is credited with three symphonies.

Albums: *Gigi Gryce And His Orchestra In Paris* (1953), *Gigi Gryce-Clifford Brown Sextet* (1953), *Jordu* (1954), *Gigi Gryce And His Orchestra* (1955), *Do It Yourself* (Savoy 1955), *Nica's Tempo* (Savoy 1956), *Gigi Gryce And The Jazz Lab Quintet* (1957), *Gigi Gryce* (1958), *Sayin' Something* (1960), *The Hap'nin's* (1960), *The Rat Race Blues* (Original Jazz Classics 1960), *Reminiscin'* (1961).

Guarnieri, Johnny

b. 23 March 1917, New York City, New York, USA, d. 7 January 1985. Although he studied piano formally, Guarnieri's musical future was determined through meeting Fats Waller, Willie 'The Lion' Smith, James P. Johnson and Art Tatum. Johnson told him, 'After me and Fats, you're number three.' Although adept at playing stride piano, despite having remarkably small hands, Guarnieri's breakthrough into the bigtime came when he played with the swing era big bands of Benny Goodman, Artie Shaw and Tommy Dorsey. With Shaw, he played harpsichord in the band-within-the-band, the Gramercy Five. During the early 40s Guarnieri also worked extensively in the studios, making countless broadcasts, many with the Raymond Scott orchestra at CBS, and appearing on numerous record dates including sessions with Lester Young, Coleman Hawkins, Roy Eldridge, Don Byas and Louis Armstrong. Resident on the west coast from the early 60s, he occasionally toured and recorded but spent many years as the house pianist, first at the Hollywood Plaza Hotel and then at The Tail Of The Cock, a restaurant on Ventura Boulevard, Los Angeles. Night after night he played at a Hollywood-style piano-bar, tailoring his playing to suit the needs of the clientele who, too often, were there to be seen and heard rather than to listen. (Guarnieri needed the job to help pay extensive family hospital bills.) Guarnieri's solo recordings display his prodigious technique, his love of old songs, his stride beginnings and a predilection for tunes in 5/4 time.

Albums: *Songs Of Hudson And De Lange* (1956), *Johnny Guarnieri Quartet* i (1956), *Johnny Guarnieri Quartet* ii (1956), *Johnny Guarnieri Quartet* iii (1957), *Johnny Guarnieri* (c.1967), *Johnny Guarnieri Plays Harry Warren* (1973), *Walla Walla* (1975), *Johnny Guarnieri Plays The Music Of Walter Donaldson* (c.1975), *Breakthrough* (1976), *Superstride* (1976), *Stealin' Apples* (1978), *Johnny Garnieri Plays Fats Waller* (Taz Jazz 1979), *Keep On Dreaming* (1979), *Originals* (1979), *Superstride* (Taz Jazz 1979), *Echoes Of Ellington* (c.1984). Compilation: with Artie Shaw *The Complete Gramercy Five Sessions* (1940).

Gullin, Lars

b. 4 May 1928, Visby, Sweden, d. 17 May 1976. After playing clarinet and alto saxophone, Gullin took up the baritone at the age of 21. From 1951-53 he worked with Arne Domnerus and Rolf Ericson, then formed his own quintet. An ardent bebopper, and influenced by Lennie Tristano, Gullin was a radical among Swedish musicians of the time; he also made an impact on the USA jazz scene, winning a *Downbeat* poll as best newcomer in 1954 (a notable achievement for a European musician). Gullin later worked chiefly as a single, playing with local rhythm sections, and recorded regularly with visiting American artists. In 1959 he toured Italy with Chet Baker. Unfortunately, his career was marred by drug addiction and he was inactive for long periods. One of the first European jazz artists to build an international reputation, Gullin's baritone playing was distinguished by his remarkable facility and by a lightness of tone that made it sound at times almost like an alto saxophone. He also wrote several distinctive jazz compositions, which reveal the influence of Swedish classical and folk musics: the tribute set *Dedicated To Lee*, has his admirer Lee Konitz playing on a selection of Gullin's tunes. The outstanding film, *Sven Klang's Kvintett* (1976), is a fictionalized account of his early career.

Selected albums: *Lars Gullin With The Morotone Singers* (1954), *The Great Lars Gullin, Vols. 1 & 2* (1955-56), *The Artistry Of Lars Gullin* (1958), *Portrait Of My Pals* (1964), *Jazz Amour Affair* (1970), *Like Grass* (1973), *Aeros Aromatica Atomica Suite* (1976), *Lars Gullin Vols 1-5 1954-60* (Dragon 1986), *In Concert* (Storyville 1990), *1955/56 Vol. 1 With Chet Baker* (1992).

Gurtu, Trilok

b. 30 October 1951, Bombay, India. Coming from a musical family, Gurtu played tablas from the age of six and studied with Ahmed Jan Thirakwa. In 1965 he formed a percussion group with his brother. He credits John Coltrane's *Plays The Blues* (1960) with inspiring him for jazz. In 1973 he toured Europe with an Indian crossover group and stayed in Italy until 1976, when he relocated to New York and started a longterm association with alto saxophonist Charles Mariano. He also played with trumpeter Don Cherry and bassist Barre Philips. Teamed with Brazilian percussionist Nana Vasconcelos he toured Europe and recorded for the German ECM label, becoming part of a select set of musicians who fuse global music into a tastefully understated whole. After Collin Walcott's death in 1984, Gurtu took his place in Oregon. In 1988 he toured with John McLaughlin. Seated on the floor to play (ie evidently part of the Indian tradition of percussion), he has incorporated devices such as dipping resonating gongs in water (a technique invented by John Cage), always with an immaculate sense of timing and sonority. In 1989 he toured in a band that featured his mother on vocals.

Albums: with Barre Philips *Three Day Moon* (1978), with Shankar *Song For Everyone* (1984), *Living Music* (1993), *Crazy Saints* (CMP 1993).

Guy, Barry

b. 22 April 1947, London, England. Even before he had completed his double-bass and composition studies at the Guildhall School of Music, Guy had earned a formidable reputation as a performer in jazz, improvised music and classical music. He was a member of the Howard Riley trio from 1967-70 and, also in the mid-60s, spent some time with John Stevens's Spontaneous Music Ensemble. He was a founder member of the Musicians' Co-Operative, for which he composed *Ode* for a 21-piece orchestra, that, as the London Jazz Composers' Orchestra, became a long-term project. It is still in existence today, although working more in continental Europe

than in the UK. As well as being an accomplished composer, Guy is a virtuoso performer, with a stunning command of the bass through the whole range of conventional and unorthodox techniques. He is as much in demand for classical and contemporary orchestral work as for jazz gigs, and has worked in many contexts, including with Tony Oxley, Evan Parker, Mike Westbrook, Peter Kowald, Trevor Watts, Bob Downes, Dave Holdsworth, Chris McGregor and, outside jazz, with the BBC Symphony Orchestra, the London Sinfonietta, the Monteverdi Orchestra, the Academy of Ancient Music, Capricorn, the Richard Hickox Orchestra (later renamed the City of London Sinfonia) and in a duo with soprano Jane Manning. He has also been a member of the Michael Nyman Band, appearing on the soundtrack of *The Draughtsman's Contract* (1982). The selection of albums listed below omits Guy's classical work.

Selected albums: with London Jazz Composers Orchestra *Ode For Jazz Orchestra* (Incus 1972), with Paul Rutherford *ISKRA 1903* (1972), *Solo Bass Improvisations* (Incus 1976), *Statements V-XI* (1976), *Improvisations Are Forever Now* (1977), *Endgame* (ECM 1979), with LJCO *Stringer* (1983, rec. 1980), with Evan Parker, Paul Lytton *Tracks* (1983), with Parker, Lytton, George Lewis *Hook, Drift & Shuffle* (1985, rec. 1983), with Peter Kowald *Paintings* (1988), with Parker, Eddie Prevost, Keith Rowe *Supersession* (1988), with Parker *Tai Kyoku* (1988, rec. 1985), *Assist* (1988), with LJCO *Harmos* (1989), with LJCO *Double Trouble* (1990).

Guy, Joe

b. 20 September 1920, Birmingham, Alabama, USA, d. early 60s. After playing trumpet in the big bands led by Teddy Hill and Coleman Hawkins in the late 30s, Guy became deeply involved in the development of bebop. He was a regular performer at Minton's Playhouse, where he often played with Thelonious Monk and Charlie Christian. In 1942 he joined the Cootie Williams big band, a group which had boppish undertones thanks to the presence at one time or another of Guy, Charlie Parker and Bud Powell. In 1944 Guy took part in the first Jazz At The Philharmonic concert staged by Norman Granz. The following year Guy began a brief personal and professional relationship with Billie Holiday, but soon afterwards drifted onto the edges of the jazz scene.

Compilations: with Oran 'Hot Lips' Page *Trumpet Battle At Minton's* (1941), with Charlie Christian *The Origins Of Modern Jazz* (1941), with others *Harlem Odyssey* (1941), *Jazz At The Philharmonic* (1944).

Gwaltney, Tommy

b. 28 February 1921, Norfolk, Virginia, USA. Although he played clarinet as a teenager and during military service, Gwaltney briefly turned to the vibraphone when he suffered lung damage. After the war he started to play the clarinet again, performing in and around Washington, DC, often in name bands passing through the region, including those led by Benny Goodman, Bobby Hackett and Billy Butterfield. Gwaltney was also active in concert and festival promotion and in the mid-60s opened a club in Washington, Blues Alley, at which he assisted in re-launching the career of Maxine Sullivan. In the late 60s he began a long association with the Manassas Jazz Festival, recording for impresario Fat Cat McRee's Fat Cat's Jazz label with several veteran performers, notably Wild Bill Davison, Zutty Singleton and Willie 'The Lion' Smith. Despite a sound playing technique and a deep and abiding interest in the development of early jazz, Gwaltney's work is largely unknown by the wider jazz public. Although few in number, his albums blend differing jazz talents with great skill thanks to his own intelligent arrangements.

Albums: with Bobby Hackett *Gotham Jazz Scene* (1957), with Buck Clayton *Goin' To Kansas City* (1960), *Tommy Gwaltney Trio* (c.1962-63), with Zutty Singleton *Zutty And The Clarinet Kings* (1967), with Wild Bill Davison *I'll Be A Friend With Pleasure* (1967), *Maxine Sullivan - Queen Of Song* (c.1970), with Wally Garner *Clarinets In Tandem* (1972-76 recordings), *Singin' The Blues* (1975).

Hackett, Bobby

b. 31 January 1915, Providence, Rhode Island, USA, d. 7 June 1976. After learning to play a number of instruments while still at school, including cornet and guitar, Hackett became a professional musician when barely into his teens. For the first few years he played violin and guitar but by 1934 he was concentrating on cornet. In 1936 he briefly led his own band, then moved to New York where he played in the society dance bands of Meyer Davis and the Lanin brothers. In 1937 he moved towards the more jazz-oriented currently-popular big bands, working with Joe Marsala and Red McKenzie. In 1938 he was one of the guest musicians at Benny Goodman's prestigious Carnegie Hall concert. At this time Hackett was leading a band at Nick's, a prominent New York nightclub. The last few years of the 30s found him working in radio in New York, on motion pictures in Hollywood, making records and leading his own bands, big and small. In mid-summer 1941 he joined Glenn Miller, playing mostly guitar (though he was featured on cornet on the hit record 'String Of Pearls'), and then spent more time with the Marsala band, the Casa Loma Orchestra, and in staff work at NBC. He played on numerous jazz record and concert dates, including the Town Hall concert in New York that established the Louis Armstrong All Stars. At the end of the 40s and throughout the 50s he worked steadily along the east coast and in Canada and continued to make records. Many of his recordings were classics of their kind, especially his 1955 dates with Jack Teagarden and a series of mood-music albums

he made for comedian Jackie Gleason. A splendid band he led at the Henry Hudson Hotel in New York during 1956/7 featured at different times Tommy Gwaltney and Bob Wilber. In the early 60s Hackett rejoined Goodman, played with Ray McKinley and then became a regular accompanist, on stage and on record, to Tony Bennett. In the late 60s and early 70s he toured the USA and Europe, playing club and festival dates often in company with Vic Dickenson. A superb cornetist with faultless taste, his delightful obligati behind singers as diverse as Bennett, Armstrong, Lee Wiley and Teresa Brewer are ample testimony to his unobtrusive skills. The mood-music albums he made for Gleason similarly demonstrate his extraordinarily graceful playing. He was equally at home both in dixieland and mainstream groups, where his straight jazz work was fiery and inventive but always elegant. Although no one could ever guess it from his cornet playing, ill health, brought on by heavy drinking, plagued Hackett for most of his life.

Selected albums: *Bobby Hackett With Strings* i (1953-54), *In A Mellow Mood* (c.1954), with Jack Teagarden *Coast Concert* (Dormouse 1955), *Rendezvous* (c.1956), *Live From The Voyager Room Vol. 1* (Shoestring 1956-57), *Bobby Hackett At The Voyager Room, Henry Hudson Hotel* (1957), *Bobby Hackett And His Orchestra* i (1957), with Teagarden *Jazz Ultimate* (1957), *Gotham Jazz Scene* (1957), *Don't Take Your Love From Me* (c.1957), *Bobby Hackett Quartet* i (1957), *Bobby Hackett And His Jazz Band* (1957), *Live From The Voyager Room Vol. 2* (Shoestring 1958), *Thanks, Bobby* (1958), *Blues With A Kick* (c.1959), *Bobby Hackett Quartet* ii (1959), *Hawaii Swings* (c.1959-60), *Bobby Hackett Quartet* iii (1960), *Music For Lovers Only* (c.1960), *Bobby Hackett With Johnny Seng And Glenn Osser At The Wurlitzer Pipe Organ* (1960), *Bobby Hackett Quartet!* (1960), *Bobby Hackett With Strings* ii (1960-61), *Bobby Hackett With Strings* iii (1960-61), *Bobby Hackett Quintet* (1961), *Bobby Hackett Sextet* (1962), *Bobby Hackett And His Orchestra* ii (1963), *Bobby Hackett With Strings* iv (1963), *Bobby Hackett And His Orchestra* iii (1963), *Bobby Hackett And His Orchestra* iv (1964), *Bobby Hackett With Strings* v (1965), *Bobby Hackett With Strings* vi (1965), *Bobby Hackett With Strings* vii (1966), *Bobby Hackett With Jim Cullum's Happy Jazz Band* (1966), *Bobby Hackett And His Orchestra* v (1967), *That Midnight Touch* (1967), *A Time For Love* (1967), *Bobby Hackett And Billy Butterfield* (1968), with Vic Dickenson *This Is My Bag* (1968), *Bobby Hackett, Vic Dickenson, Maxine Sullivan At The Fourth Manassas Jazz Festival* (Jazzology 1969), *Bobby Hackett's Sextet* (1970), *Live At The Roosevelt Grill Vols 1-4* (1970), *Rare Italian Dates/Live At Louisiana Dates* (1971), with Teresa Brewer *What A Wonderful World* (1973), *Bobby Hackett-Vic Dickenson Septet* (1973), *Bobby Hackett...Live With Ted Easton's Jazzband* (1973), *Strike Up The Band* (1974), *Butterfly Airs Vols 1 & 2* (c.1975), *Tin Roof Blues* (c.1976). Compilations: *At Nick's* (1944), *That Da Da Strain* (1988, rec late 30s).

Haden, Charlie

b. 6 August 1937, Shenandoah, Iowa, USA. Haden began his musical career when still a child, broadcasting daily on local country music radio. After formal music study he moved to Los Angeles, playing bass with Hampton Hawes, Art Pepper, Red Norvo and Paul Bley. While with Bley's trio he met Ornette Coleman and began rehearsing with him in 1958. By the following year he had moved to New York and become Coleman's regular bassist, exhibiting an exceptional understanding of the saxophonist's music. Haden stayed with Coleman until 1960, but has played with him since on several occasions, including some gigs in 1968 and 1972, where he played in tandem with one of his successors, David Izenzon. Because of drug problems, which he subsequently defeated, he was out of circulation for a while, but returned to the scene in 1964 to play with Danny Zeitlin and Tony Scott. He returned to Coleman's group in 1966 and then joined the Jazz Composers' Orchestra Association. In 1969 he established the Liberation Music Orchestra with Carla Bley. The orchestra's first two albums, *Liberation Music Orchetsra* and *Ballad Of The Fallen*, used themes from the Spanish Civil War and from Latin American resistance movements as the raw material for intense arrangements by Haden and Bley. Along with *Crisis*, a recording of a concert from a tour which Haden made with Ornette Coleman in 1969, *Liberation Music Orchestra* has the distinction of being the object of an attempt by the record companies' shareholders to withdraw it from the catalogue because of its 'anti-American' content. Both albums featured Haden's 'Song For Che' and *Crisis* also contained tunes inspired by the Vietnam conflict. Haden continued his interest in politically-motivated music in 1991 when he issued an album with Carlos Paredes, a Portuguese fado musician who had been an active anti-Fascist and also released a third Liberation Music Orchestra album, *Dream Keeper*, the title track a suite based on a poem by the African American writer Langston Hughes. During the 80s Haden widened his composing horizons, writing for a variety of instrumental combinations, collaborating with other composer-musicians such as Gavin Bryars and leading his own relatively mainstream group, Quartet West. He has also worked with Pat Metheny on a number of his albums, as well as Alice Coltrane (1968-72), Keith Jarrett (1967-75), in Old And New Dreams, virtually a reconstruction of the Ornette Coleman quartet but with Dewey Redman (an associate of Coleman during his later Blue Note period) on saxophone, in *Magico* (a trio with Jan Garbarek and Egberto Gismonti) and Geri Allen and Paul Motian. He also played with Chet Baker, on one of the trumpeter's last recording sessions (*Silence*), and was instrumental in introducing Cuban pianist Gonzalo Rubalcaba to a wider audience, producing and playing on his Blue Note debut, *Discovery*. In 1994 he worked with Ginger Baker on his well-received album *Going Back Home*. Through his own ventures and his contribution to the crucially important Ornette Coleman quartet, Haden carved out his place as one of the most skilful and adventurous bass-players at a time when several exponents of the instrument (including Charles Mingus and two other Coleman bassists, Scott La Faro and Izenzon) were building on the achievements of the likes of Paul Chambers, Ray Brown and Percy Heath, pushing the instrument into the spotlight with their virtuosity and range.

Selected albums: *Liberation Music Orchestra* (1969), *Closeness* (Closeness 1976), *The Golden Number* (1977), with Don Cherry, Dewey Redman, Ed Blackwell *Old And New Dreams* i (1977), with Hampton Hawes *As Long As There's Music* (Verve 1978, rec. 1976), with Ornette Coleman *Soapsuds, Soapsuds* (1979, rec. 1977), with Christian Escoude *Gitane* (1979), *Duo* (Dreyfus Jazz 1979), *Old And New Dreams* ii (1979), with Jan Garbarek, Egberto Gismonti *Magico* (1980), with Garbarek, Gismonti *Folk Songs* (ECM 1981), with Old And New Dreams *Playing* (1981), with Denny Zeitlin *Time Remembers One Time Once* (1983), with Liberation Music Orchestra *The Ballad Of The Fallen* (ECM 1983), *Quartet West* (Verve 1987), with Geri Allen, Paul Motian *Etudes* (1988), *Silence* (Soul Note 1989, rec. 1987), with Allen, Motian *In The Year Of The Dragon* (1989), *In Angel City* (Verve 1989), with Allen, Motian *Segments* (1989), with Allen, Motian *Live At The Village Vanguard* (1991), with Liberation Music Orchestra *Dream Keeper* (Verve 1991), *Haunted Heart* (Verve 1991), *Dream Keeper* (Blue Note 1991), with Carlos Paredes *Dialogues* (Polydor 1991), *First Song* (Soul Note 1991), as Quartet West *Always Say Goodbye* (Verve 1994), *The Montreal Tapes* (Verve 1994), with Ginger Baker, Bill Frisell *Going Back Home* (Atlantic 1994).

Hagans, Tim

b. 19 August 1954, Dayton, Ohio, USA. After completing extensive formal studies at Bowling Green State University, Ohio, Hagans secured his first important professional engagement in 1974 when he joined the trumpet section of Stan Kenton's band. He remained with Kenton for a little over two years, touring, recording and teaching at the Kenton Summer Clinics. He then had a brief spell with Woody Herman before settling in Sweden. During the next few years he worked with other expatriates, including Thad Jones, Ernie Wilkins and Sahib Shihab, played in the Swedish and Danish Radio big bands, and also led his own small group which appeared at clubs and festivals. While in Sweden he continued to teach, working at various establishments including the University of Lund and the Jazz Institute of Malmö where he taught trumpet, improvisation and ensemble playing. In 1981 he returned to the USA, settling in Cincinnati, where he played in the Blue Wisp Big Band led by John Von Ohlen. He made a number of record dates with the band, on some of which his own compositions were played. He was again active in music education, teaching trumpet, improvisation and jazz history at the University of Cincinnati. In 1984 he moved to Boston, Massachusetts, taking up a teaching post at Berklee College Of Music and also playing in various groups, notably his own quintet. Three years later he moved to New York City, teaching privately and playing in various bands, including those led by Bob Belden, Bob Mintzer, Marc Copland, Vic Juris, Fred Hersch, Joe Lovano, Gary Peacock and George Russell. He made a brief return visit to Scandinavia to conduct the UMO (New Music Ensemble) in Helsinki, Finland. In 1986 and again the following year he received a grant from the National Endowment for the Arts to record and to compose a suite for a big band. In the early 90s Hagans was still deeply involved in teaching and playing in the New York area, recording with Copland, Andy LaVerne and others. Hagans' trumpet style is rooted in bop and he plays with great drive and crackling attack on uptempo pieces. On slower tunes he develops long, logical solo lines, using his full tone to great advantage. His inherently lyrical conception is especially suited to ballads and when playing flügelhorn he creates richly atmospheric solos. Although little known outside the immediate areas in which he has played and taught, Hagans is fast developing into a major jazz voice.

Albums: with Stan Kenton *Fire, Fury And Fun* (1974), with Kenton *Journey To Capricorn* (1976), with Thad Jones *Thad Jones' Eclipse* (1980), with Ernie Wilkins *Almost Big Band* (1980), with Blue Wisp *Butterfly* (1982) *From The Neck Down* (1983), with Blue Wisp *Live At Carmelo's* (1984), with Blue Wisp *Rollin' With Von Ohlen* (1984), with Bob Belden *Treasure Island* (1989), with Andy LaVerne *Severe Clear* (1990), with Marc Copland *All Blues At Night* (1990).

Haggart, Bob

b. 13 March 1914, New York City, New York, USA. After formal tuition on guitar and informal playing of trumpet and piano, Haggart switched to bass, on which he is self-taught. After playing with various small-time dance bands, he came to national prominence when he joined the former members of the Ben Pollack unit who were planning their own co-operative band. This new outfit, under the nominal leadership of Bob Crosby, became one of the great successes of the swing era, combining as it did the currently popular dance band music with an exhilarating two-beat dixieland style. Haggart's contribution to the band's success extended far beyond his pivotal role as a member of the sprightly rhythm section. He arranged several of the band's most popular numbers, including 'South Rampart Street Parade' and 'Dogtown Blues'. Haggart was co-creator, with drummer Ray Bauduc, of a tune on which he whistled sibilantly through his front teeth, and pressed the strings of his bass while Bauduc played on them with his sticks. The unusual effect this produced created a massive hit for the duo and 'Big Noise From Winnetka' remains one of the best-known tunes from the swing era. In 1942 Haggart left the Crosby band, turning to studio work and arranging for many artists, including Louis Armstrong, but he retained his playing connections with former Crosby-band colleague Yank Lawson. In the early 50s the Lawson-Haggart Jazz band became very popular; at the end of the 60s the two men again teamed up to create the World's Greatest Jazz Band. Haggart remains a popular figure at festivals and at reunions of the Crosby band, touring the USA and Europe as bandleader and sideman and making records, including some more with Lawson. He is also responsible for at least one other jazz standard, the ballad 'What's New?'.

Albums: with Yank Lawson *Jelly Roll's Jazz* (1951), *The Legendary Lawson-Haggart Jazz Band* (1952-53), *Big Noise From Winnetka* (c.1963), *Sentimental Journey* (1980), with Lawson *Go To New Orleans* (1987). Compilations: with Bob Crosby *South Rampart Street Parade* (1935-42), with Crosby

Big Noise From Winnetka (1937-42), *A Portrait Of Bix* (Jazzology 1987).

Haig, Al

b. 22 July 1924, Newark, New Jersey, USA, d. 16 November 1982. One of the first bop pianists, and for a time among the very best of them, Haig spent the second half of the 40s in excellent musical company. Active in the clubs of New York, he played with Charlie Parker and Dizzy Gillespie and proved to be an outstanding accompanist. After a spell with Stan Getz, which ended in 1951, Haig drifted from the centre of the bebop stage, rarely recording and often accepting engagements which demanded little jazz playing. In the 70s he returned to the jazz scene, demonstrating on record that he had lost none of his understated skills and was also well aware of the musical developments of the intervening years. Despite his piecemeal career, Haig remains an important figure in the development of modern jazz piano playing.

Albums: *Al Haig Trio* (1954), *The Al Haig Trio And Quintet* (1954), *Four!* (1954), *Invitation* (Spotlite 1974), *Special Brew* (1974), *Strings Attached* (1975), *Chelsea Bridge* (1975), *Solitaire* (Spotlite 1976), *Piano Interpretations* (1976), *Duke 'N' Bird* (1976), *Interplay* (1976), *Serendipity* (1977), *A Portrait Of Bud Powell* (1977), *Manhattan Memories* (1977), *Ornithology* (1977), *Reminiscence* (1977), *Jon Eardley-Al Haig Quartet/Quintet* (1977), *Al Haig In Paris* (1977), *Parisian Thoroughfare* (1977), *Al Haig Plays Dizzy Gillespie* (1977), *They All Played Bebop* (1977), *Al Haig Plays The Music Of Jerome Kern* (1978), *Expressly Ellington* (Spotlite 1978), *Jazz Will O' The Wisp* (Fresh Sounds 1988). Compilation: with Dizzy Gillespie *In The Beginning* (1945-6).

Hakim, Omar

b. c.1959, New York City, New York, USA. A graduate of the New York School of Music and Art, Hakim began his career recording with various pop and soul units. When he did play with jazz musicians, his prodigious talent meant that they were artists of the calibre of Gil Evans, George Benson, and David Sanborn. In 1982 he joined Wayne Shorter and Joe Zawinul's Weather Report, in which he impressed with his ability to add complex beat divisions to funk rhythms without losing impetus. During his three years with Weather Report Hakim managed to continue recording, including a 1984 session with John Scofield, and an appearance with pop-star Sting on *Dream Of The Blue Turtles*. Playing at the major 1991 jazz festivals in a quartet completed by Shorter, Herbie Hancock, and Stanley Clarke, Hakim has already established his reputation as a major jazz artist.

Album: *Rhythm Deep* (GRP 1989).

Halcox, Pat

b. 17 March, 1930, London, England. Playing part-time in the early 50s, trumpeter Halcox quickly established himself as a leading figure in the British trad-jazz scene. He teamed up with Chris Barber and Monty Sunshine in their co-operative band, but then decided to pursue the career of research chemist for which he had trained. The Barber band continued trumpetless for a while before engaging Ken Colyer. In 1954 a rift developed in the Barber-Colyer relationship, and Halcox was persuaded to return and become a full-time musician. He has been a member of the band ever since. The eclectic musical personality of the Barber band is an ideal setting for Halcox's wide-ranging style; he remains one of the band's greatest assets and is also one of the UK's leading traditional and mainstream trumpeters.

Albums: *Chris Barber Jubilee Album Vols 1-3* (1958-74 recordings), *7th Avenue* (c.1980), *There's Yes, Yes, In Your Eyes* (Jazzology 1989), *Songs From Tin Pan Alley* (Jazzology 1991).

Hall, Edmond

b. 15 May 1901, New Orleans, Louisiana, USA, d. 11 February 1967. Hall was born into a highly musical family: his father played clarinet and four of his brothers became professional musicians, mostly on reed instruments, the best known of these being clarinettist Herbie Hall. After playing clarinet in his home town with Buddy Petit, Lee Collins, Kid Thomas Valentine and others in the early 20s, Hall headed for the north and a marked change of musical scene. From 1929 and throughout the 30s he became one of the most respected and sought-after clarinettists in jazz, playing in a manner which, while never losing the intrinsic qualities of New Orleans jazz, allowed him to play an important role in the swing era. Among the musicians with whom he worked during these years were Claude Hopkins, Lucky Millinder, Zutty Singleton and Joe Sullivan. In the early 40s Hall played in Red Allen's band, made some excellent quartet records with Charlie Christian, Israel Crosby and Meade 'Lux' Lewis (who played celeste), recorded with the De Paris Brothers Orchestra and turned down an offer to join Duke Ellington. Instead he became a member of Teddy Wilson's marvellous sextet, and after leaving Wilson in 1944, he led his own band in New York and Boston and was then a member of the house band at Eddie Condon's club. In 1955 he joined Louis Armstrong's All Stars, bringing to the band a much-needed fire and excitement at a time when it was beginning to sound a little jaded. He left Armstrong in 1958 and two years later, after living briefly in Ghana, began a sustained period of international touring which ended with his death in February 1967. A fluid and inventive soloist, Hall's playing exhibited a marvellous blend of New Orleans earthiness and Goodman-esque polish. He was one of the outstanding clarinettists of the swing era, as his recordings with his own groups testify. And those he made with the Wilson sextet, are arguably among the best ever by a small mainstream jazz combo.

Albums: *The Edmond Hall All Stars Live From The Savoy Cafe, Boston* (1949), *Edmond Hall At Club Hangover* (Storyville 1954), with Eddie Condon *Bixieland* (1955), with Louis Armstrong *Ambassador Satch* (1956/7 recordings), with Armstrong *A Musical Autobiography* (1956/7 recordings), *Edmond Hall Quartet In Argentina* (1958), *Edmond Hall All Stars* (1958), *Edmond Hall And His Orchestra* (1959), *Edmond Hall With The Gustav Brom Orchestra* (1960), *Edmond Hall Quartet* (1966), *Edmond Hall With Papa Bue's Viking Jazzband*

(1966), *Edmond Hall In Copenhagen* (Storyville 1967), *Edmond Hall's Quartet & Quintet* (1966). Compilations: with others *The Complete Blue Note Sessions* (1941-52 recordings), with Teddy Wilson *B Flat Swing* (1944 recordings), *Rompin' In '44* (1944 recordings), *Compilation Edmond Hall 1941-57* (Giants Of Jazz 1987).

Hall, Jim

b. 4 December 1930, Buffalo, New York, USA. While studying at the Cleveland Institute of Music, Hall made his first professional appearances playing guitar in local bands. In the mid-50s he settled on the west coast, where he continued his studies and also played with Chico Hamilton's quintet. In 1956 he became a member of Jimmy Giuffre's trio, thereafter working with Ella Fitzgerald, Bill Evans, Paul Desmond and in duo with Lee Konitz. In the early 60s he was briefly with Sonny Rollins, a stint which included two important albums, *The Bridge* and *What's New*, then teamed up with Art Farmer to co-lead a small group. In the mid-60s his career was affected by personal problems; but he soon returned to tour internationally and to make records with Evans and in duo with Ron Carter, with whom he recorded *Alone Together*. In the early 70s, he was working again with Desmond, on *Concierto*, and in duo with Red Mitchell. In the early 80s he played once more with Carter, recording *Telephone*, performed with classical violinist Itzhak Perlman and recorded *First Edition* with George Shearing. Throughout his career Hall has displayed a marked preference for working solo or in duos, and his playing is distinguished by self-effacing good taste and a clear understanding of the sensitive role demanded by partnerships such as those with Konitz, Rollins, Evans, Carter and Mitchell. Although less well known to audiences than many other guitarists of his generation, Hall's outstanding improvisational gifts and his abilities as collaborator and composer contribute towards his status as a widely respected figure within the jazz world.

Albums: *Jazz Guitar* (Manhattan 1957), *Good Friday* (1960), with Bill Evans *Undercurrent* (1962), with Evans *Intermodulation* (1966), *It's Nice To Be With You* (1969), *Where Would I Be?* (Original Jazz Classics 1971), with Ron Carter *Alone Together* (Original Jazz Classics 1972), with Paul Desmond *Concierto* (CTI 1975), *Jim Hall Live!* (1975), *Commitment* (1975), *Jim Hall Live In Tokyo* (1976), *Jim Hall And Red Mitchell* (Artists House 1978), *Circles* (Concord 1981), *First Edition* (1982), with Carter *Telephone* (1984), *Jim Hall's Three* (Concord 1986), with Michel Petrucciani, Wayne Shorter *Power Of Three* (1987), with Tom Harrell *These Roots* (Denon 1988), *All Across The City* (Concord 1989), *Live At Town Hall* (Limelight 1991), *Youkali* (CTI 1992), *Subsequently* (Limelight 1992), with Carter *Live At Village West* (1993). *Something Special* (Limelight 1993).

Hallberg, Bengt

b. 13 September 1932, Gothenberg, Sweden. Hallberg was something of a child prodigy at the piano. He made his first recording at the age of 15 and, in 1950, recorded an album with Arne Domnerus which was released in the USA. During

Jim Hall

the early 50s he would travel by train to Stockholm to play with the best Swedish musicians and was often in demand by visiting Americans of the stature of Lee Konitz, Stan Getz and Quincy Jones. In 1954 Hallberg moved to Stockholm to further his study of classical music at the Royal Academy of Music. Throughout the 50s and 60s, while establishing himself as one of Sweden's leading jazz musicians, Hallberg composed for string quartets and chamber groups and found himself much in demand as a session musician and composer of film and radio scores. Today he maintains this diverse output, refusing the restrictions of genre or idiom; his recent work as musical director of the Swedish Radio Jazz Group declare Hallberg's continuing fascination with composition.

Selected albums: *Stan Getz Stockholm Sessions* (1958), *Kiddin' On The Keys* (1959), *At Gyllene Cirklen* (1962), *On His Own* (Phontastic 1976), *Hallberg's Happiness* (Phontastic 1977), *The Hallberg Treasure Chest, A Bouquet From '78* (Phontastic 1979), *The Hallberg Touch* (Phontastic 1980), with Ove Lind *Dialogue In Swing* (Phontastic 1982), with Karen Krog *Two Of A Kind* (Four Leaf Clover 1982), *Egenhandigt* (Phontastic 1982), *Hallberg's Surprise* (Phontastic 1988), *Bo Ohlgren* (Phontastic 1988), *Spring On The Air* (Phono Suecia 1988), with Kjell Baeklelund *Contrasts* (Sonet 1991), *The Tapdancing Butterfly* (Aquila 1992).

Hamilton, Chico

b. Foreststorn Hamilton, 21 September 1921, Los Angeles, California, USA. Hamilton's future career as a drummer was well established even before he left school. By that time he had played with many other young fledgling jazz artists, including Dexter Gordon, Ernie Royal, Charles Mingus and Buddy Collette (who would later become his musical partner). In 1940 he performed briefly with Lionel Hampton and Slim Gaillard, but military service interrupted his career. In the late 40s he worked with Jimmy Mundy, Count Basie and Lester Young; between 1948 and 1955 he was regular accompanist to Lena Horne. In 1952 he recorded with Gerry Mulligan's revolutionary pianoless quartet and in 1955 formed his own quartet which, with shifting personnel, remained in existence for several years. Hamilton's groups of the 50s featured several outstanding musicians - among them Collette, Fred Katz, Eric Dolphy, Ralph Pena, Dennis Budimir and Ron Carter - and experimented with unusual instrumental combinations, notably cello and flute. Their relaxed, mellow sound attracted the attention of fringe jazz audiences and their popularity was enhanced by the film, *Jazz On A Summer's Day* (1960), which showed the group in rehearsal for their appearance at the 1958 Newport Jazz Festival. In the 60s Hamilton's group continued to perform, but changes in instrumentation and style saw the cello replaced by the trombone. In the mid-60s Hamilton was invited to write and perform advertising jingles; this proved so successful that he formed a production company, the running of which kept him from active participation in jazz for several years. In the mid-80s, however, he was back with a new band, Euphoria, which he described as 'heavy metal jazz' and had started to record again.

Selected albums: *The Chico Hamilton Trio* i (1953), *Spectacular* (1955), *The Chico Hamilton Quartet With Buddy Collette* (1955), *Chico Hamilton At Strollers* (1956), *The Chico Hamilton Quintet* i (1956), *The Chico Hamilton Quintet* ii (1956), *The Sweet Smell Of Success* (1957), *The Chico Hamilton Quintet* iii (1958), *The Chico Hamilton Trio* ii (1958), *Chico Hamilton Quintet With Strings* (1958), *The Chico Hamilton Quintet* iv (1958), *Newport Jazz 1958-59* (1958-59), *The Chico Hamilton Sextet* (1959), *Three Faces Of Chico* (1959), *That Hamilton Man* (1959), *The Chico Hamilton Quintet* v (1960), *The Chico Hamilton Quintet* vi (1962), *Passin' Thru* (1962), *The Chico Hamilton Quintet* vii (1962), *Man From Two Worlds* (1963), *The Chico Hamilton Octet* (1965), *Chic, Chic, Chico* (1965), *The Chico Hamilton Group* (1965), *The Further Adventures Of El Chico* (1966), *The Dealer* (MCA 1966), *The Gamut* (1967), *El Exigente* (1970), *Chico The Master* (Ace 1974), *Head Hunters* (c.1974), *Peregrinations* (c.1975), *Chico Hamilton And The Players* (1976), *Reaching For The Top* (1978), *Nomad* (c.1979), *Euphoria* (Discovery 1986), *Reunion* (Soul Note 1989), *Arroyo* (Soul Note 1991), *Trio!* (Soul Note 1992), *Man From Two Worlds* (GRP 1993), *Goings East* (Discovery 1993), *My Panamanian Friend* (Soul Note 1993).

Hamilton, Jeff

b. 4 August 1953, Richmond, Indiana, USA. Hamilton began playing drums as a child and while in his early teens was a member of a trio playing at local clubs. He later studied percussion at Indiana University, where his fellow students included Peter Erskine and John Clayton. Hamilton's interest in jazz developed and he extended his studies to take tuition from John Von Ohlen. In 1974, on Clayton's recommendation, Hamilton was hired to play in the Tommy Dorsey Orchestra under the leadership of Murray McEachern. His next job was a brief stint with Lionel Hampton during 1975 and he then worked with Clayton as a member of the Monty Alexander trio. Two years later he left to play with Woody Herman. In 1978 he joined the LA Four with Ray Brown, Laurindo Almeida and Bud Shank. In the mid-80s Hamilton formed a big band in collaboration with John Clayton and his brother Jeff Clayton. He has also worked with the Philip Morris Superband. An outstanding drummer with the finesse and subtlety demanded of a small group player and the powerful swing needed for a big band, Hamilton is one of the most gifted of the younger generation of American mainstream jazz drummers.

Albums: with Monty Alexander *Live At Montreux* (c.1975), with Woody Herman *Road Father* (1978), with Herman *Chick, Donald, Walter And Woodrow* (1978), with LA Four *Watch What Happens* (1978), with Clayton-Hamilton *Groove Shop* (1989), with Clayton-Hamilton *Heart And Soul* (1991).

Hamilton, Jimmy

b. 25 May 1917, Dillon, South Carolina, USA, d. 20 September 1994, St. Croix, Virgin Islands. A talented multi-instrumentalist as a child, Hamilton played baritone horn, trumpet, trombone and piano. He worked professionally in and around Philadelphia in the 30s, and after taking up tenor saxophone and clarinet, played with several name bands, including those led by Lucky Millinder, Jimmy Mundy and Teddy Wilson. In 1943 he joined Duke Ellington, playing in the saxophone section and as featured clarinet soloist. He remained with Ellington for a quarter of a century, leaving in 1968 to lead his own band briefly before going to live in the Virgin Islands. Since then Hamilton has worked as a teacher, but has also made occasional returns to the jazz scene, playing in the band for the Broadway show, *Sophisticated Ladies*, and as one of the guest soloists at the annual Ellington reunion conventions. He was also a member of the highly-regarded Clarinet Summit (with Alvin Batiste, John Carter and David Murray).Throughout his long stay with Ellington, Hamilton consolidated his position as one of the most fluid and controlled of clarinettists. In contrast, his infrequent tenor solos displayed earthy vitality.

Albums: with Duke Ellington *The Cosmic Scene* (1959), with Ellington *The Nutcracker Suite* (1960), *It's About Time* (Fantasy 1961), *Can't Help Swingin'* (1961), with John Carter *Clarinet Summit Vol. 1* (1981), with Carter *Clarinet Summit Vol. 2* (1985), with Clarinet Summit *Southern Belles* (1988), *Swing Low, Sweet Clarinet* (Fresh Sounds 1988).

Hamilton, Scott

b. 12 September 1954, Providence, Rhode Island, USA. As a child, Hamilton began playing clarinet, on which he had a few lessons, and piano. He then briefly played blues harmonica in a rock 'n' roll band. He took up tenor saxophone as a young teenager, teaching himself largely by listening to records in his father's collection. These records were by jazzmen of the 30s and 40s, and Hamilton thus appeared on the scene as an apparent throwback to those times, recreating the tenor styling of the likes of Ben Webster. As such he was received rapturously by audiences who thought players in this style were long defunct. He worked extensively in and around New York, often teaming up with Warren Vaché, similarly regarded as an important addition to the fading jazz mainstream. Hamilton's success in the late 70s led to his appearing with many leading jazzmen and performing at prestigious venues and major festivals in the USA and overseas. His ready success brought with it some personal problems and to some extent inhibited his growth as a stylist in his own right. By the early 80s, however, he had overcome all such problems and, although he retained his stylistic preferences and occasionally reverted to his early habit of playing in the manner of Webster, he was clearly his own man. He had also become a major figure on the international jazz stage. Most of his numerous concert and record album appearances are under his own name, but he has also appeared as a sideman in bands led by Benny Goodman, Woody Herman, Vaché, John Bunch and Bill Berry. In addition, he has been teamed with Ruby Braff, recording *A First*, with Charlie Byrd, and on *Back To Back* and *Scott's Buddy* he duetted with veteran tenor saxophonist Buddy Tate. In the late 80s and early 90s Hamilton was still hugely popular on the festival circuit, appearing as leader or as principal soloist with all-star groups

such as the Newport Jazz Festival All-Stars and the Concord Superband.

Albums: *The Swinging Young Scott Hamilton* (1977), *Scott Hamilton Is A Good Wind Who Is Blowing Us No Ill* (Concord 1977), *Live At Concord 1977* (Concord 1977), *Scott Hamilton 2* (1978), *Body And Soul* (1978), *Scott's New Band In New York City* (1978), with Buddy Tate *Back To Back* (1978), with Bill Berry *For Duke* (1978), *The Grand Appearance* (1978), *Skyscrapers* (Concord 1979), *Tenorshoes* (Concord 1979), with Tate *Scott's Buddy* (1980), *Apples And Oranges* (1981), with Tate, Al Cohn *Tour De Force* (1981), *Close Up* (Concord 1982), *In Concert* (Concord 1983), *The Second Set* (Concord 1983), *The Right Time* (Concord 1984), *The Newport Jazz Festival All-Stars* (1984), *A First* (1985), *Major League* (Concord 1986), with Charlie Byrd *It's A Wonderful World* (1988), *Scott Hamilton Plays Ballads* (Concord 1989), with Gene Harris *At Last* (1990), *Radio City* (Concord 1990), *Race Point* (Concord 1991), *Groovin' High* (Concord 1992), *With Strings* (1993), *East Of The Sun* (Concord 1994).

Hammond, John, Jnr.

b. John Henry Hammond, 15 December 1910, New York City, USA, d. July 1987. Hammond became a jazz fan as a child and in the early 30s was a record reviewer for *Melody Maker*. Hammond also used his inherited wealth to finance recordings at a time when economic depression had made record companies unwilling to invest in jazz. He produced Billie Holiday's first session as well as tracks by Teddy Wilson, Bessie Smith, Mildred Bailey and Artie Shaw. In 1936 a chance hearing of a broadcast by Count Basie from Kansas City (Hammond was listening on his car radio outside a Chicago hotel where Benny Goodman was appearing) led him to actively promote Basie's career. In 1938/9, Hammond conceived the *Spirituals To Swing* concerts at New York's Carnegie Hall. These were designed to show the full breadth of black American music and featured gospel (Rosetta Tharpe), blues (Big Bill Broonzy), New Orleans jazz (Sidney Bechet) and contemporary dance music (Benny Goodman, who married Hammond's sister, Alice). In the early 40s, he worked for Columbia Records and after army service moved to Keynote, Mercury and Vanguard as a staff producer. Hammond returned to Columbia in 1958 and was chiefly responsible for signing such folk revival artists as Pete Seeger and Bob Dylan, who was known at the company as 'Hammond's folly' in the early years of his contract. Hammond was the producer of Dylan's first two albums. While chiefly involved with jazz and blues - he supervised reissues of Bessie Smith and Robert Johnson and was a founder of the Newport Jazz Festival - Hammond continued to bring new artists to Columbia during the 60s and 70s, most notably Leonard Cohen, George Benson and Bruce Springsteen. His son, John Hammond III (often confusingly titled John Hammond Jnr. himself, which leads to his father being mistakenly identified as Hammond Snr.) is a noted white blues singer whose recording career began in the mid-60s.

Hampton, Lionel

b. 20 April 1908, Louisville, Kentucky, USA. After living briefly in Louisville and Birmingham, Alabama, Hampton was taken to Chicago where he lived with his grandparents. They sent him to Holy Rosary Academy at Collins, Wisconsin, where he was taught the rudiments of military band drumming by a Dominican nun. Following the death of his grandmother, Hampton, now in his early teens, went to live with his uncle, Richard Morgan. A bootlegger and friend to many showbusiness stars, Morgan encouraged his nephew in his ambition to become a musician. (Morgan later became an intimate friend of Bessie Smith and was driving the car in which she had her fatal accident.) Morgan bought Hampton his first drum kit, modelled on that of the boy's idol, Jimmy Bertrand, who played in the Erskine Tate band at the Vendome Theatre. Hampton played in the boys band organized by the *Defender*, Chicago's leading black newspaper, and by the end of the 20s had become a professional musician. He played drums in various territory bands, including those led by Curtis Mosby, Reb Spikes and Paul Howard. On the west coast in the early 30s he was drummer with Vernon Wilkins, Charlie Echols and Les Hite, who led the house band at the Los Angeles Cotton Club. When Louis Armstrong played at the club, Hite's band accompanied him in concert and also on recording sessions. On some of these dates Hampton played vibraphone, an instrument similar to the marimba on which he had become proficient.

By this time Hampton was also occasionally playing piano and singing and soon became sufficiently popular to form his own big band and small groups. In 1936, while leading his band at the Paradise Club on Central Avenue, he was joined one evening by Benny Goodman, Teddy Wilson and Gene Krupa who were passing through LA on a nationwide tour. Goodman was persuaded to visit the club by John Hammond Jnr. and was so impressed, and so much enjoyed their impromptu jam session, that he invited Hampton to attend a recording date already scheduled the following day for the Benny Goodman Trio. The resulting records, by the Benny Goodman Quartet, were so successful that a few months later Goodman asked Hampton to join his entourage. For the next few years Hampton became an integral part of Goodman's success story, recording extensively with the Quartet and, after the arrival of Charlie Christian, with the Sextet. He also occasionally played with the big band, taking over the drums after Krupa's abrupt departure in 1938. While with Goodman, Hampton was asked by Eli Oberstein of RCA Victor to make a series of small group records. The resulting dates, on which Hampton used musicians from whichever big bands happened to be in town, proved to be amongst the best small group recordings in jazz history and are classics of their kind. By the early 40s Hampton was keen to become a leader again and encouraged by his wife, Gladys, and with Goodman's approval (and financial aid), he formed his own big band in 1941. Straw boss of the first band was Marshal Royal and among his sidemen, all relatively unknown at the time, were Ernie Royal, Illinois Jacquet, Jack McVea, Irving Ashby and Milt Buckner. The band proved to be hugely successful, offering a blend of soulful ballads and all-out stomping excitement.

Building on the burgeoning popularity of R&B, Hampton developed a musical style - gutsy, riffing saxophones, powerhouse brass, a slogging back beat and raw, energetic solos - that he retained for the next half century. In the 40s and early 50s Hampton hired (and, when his patience with their antics ran out, regularly fired) outstanding artists such as Jimmy Cleveland, Al Grey, Earl Bostic, Gigi Gryce, Dexter Gordon, Arnett Cobb, Charles Mingus, Clifford Brown, Art Farmer, Fats Navarro, Quincy Jones, Joe Newman and Clark Terry. He also had an ear for singers and gave early breaks to Dinah Washington, Joe Williams and Betty Carter. From the early 50s Hampton regularly toured Europe and became very popular at international festivals, especially in France. In the mid- and late 50s Hampton recorded extensively for Norman Granz, who teamed him with jazzmen such as Stan Getz, Buddy De Franco, Oscar Peterson and Art Tatum. From the mid-60s onwards, Hampton attended many reunions of the original Benny Goodman Quartet, several of which were recorded and a few televised. Also in the 60s Lionel and Gladys Hampton became involved in urban renewal in Harlem, where they had made their home for many years. Gladys' death in 1971 was a severe blow to Hampton, who had relied upon her astute business sense and organizational ability. By the end of the 70s the first of the multi-million-dollar projects that the Hamptons had initiated was opened: eventually two apartment buildings, the Lionel Hampton Houses and the Gladys Hampton Houses, were providing accommodation for over 700 families in the middle and lower income groups, and plans were in hand to build a university.

During this time Hampton never stopped playing; both touring with his own big band and, from the late 70s, fronting all-star orchestras specifically assembled for festivals. The 80s saw Hampton still hard at work - touring, recording only a little less frequently and, despite arthritis, playing, singing and dancing in front of his bands as if time had stood still since 1941. In 1992 he was still active, celebrating 60-plus years in the business, and showing few signs of slowing up until he suffered a 'light brain haemorrhage' during a performance in Paris. In the following year, 'fully recovered', he played UK concerts with his Golden Men Of Jazz, a group which included such luminaries as Junior Mance, Harry Edison, Benny Golson, and Al Grey. Hampton's musical personality is best, if a little superficially, described as that of a Jekyll and Hyde. He switched from introspective balladeer to outrageous swinger at the flick of a vibraphone mallet. As a drummer he was originally a solid player, as his first records with Paul Howard's Quality Serenaders testify. Later he became a flamboyant, spectacular and sometimes tasteless showman. As a pianist he perfected a percussive, two-fingered attacking style which concealed the fact that he could also play in a modern and unusually clipped manner. As a singer he had a limited range but a pleasantly ingratiating voice. It is as a vibraphone player, however, that he made his greatest mark on jazz. Although not the first to use the instrument in jazz, he was the first to use it as anything other than a novelty and once he had mastered it he quickly became an outstanding performer (indeed, for many years he was virtually the only player of the vibraphone in jazz). After the emergence of other virtuosos, such as Milt Jackson and Gary Burton, Hampton retained his pre-eminence simply by ignoring changes in musical styles and continuing to do what he had done so successfully since the early 30s. An astonishingly long-lived and vibrant individual, Hampton's extrovert personality assured him of a prominent place in jazz. Although he was never an innovative musician, and in one sense cannot therefore be accorded a place alongside Louis Armstrong or Duke Ellington, he did become a giant of the music. One thing is certain - if Lionel Hampton had never come along with his electrifying solos, unstoppable dynamism, astonishing enthusiasm and sheer love of life and music, the world of jazz would have been a sadder, greyer place.

Selected albums: *Gene Norman Presents: Stardust* (1947), *European Concert 1953* (1953), *Complete Paris Sessions* (1953), *The Hamp In Paris* (1953), *The Lionel Hampton Quartet* i (1954), *Lionel Hampton Quartet With Buddy De Franco* (1954), *Lionel Hampton At The Trianon Ballroom, Chicago* (1954), *The Lionel Hampton Quartet* ii (1954), *The Lionel Hampton Quintet* i (1954), *The Lionel Hampton Sextet At Jazz At The Philharmonic* (1954), *Lionel Hampton And His Orchestra: Apollo Hall Concert* (1954), *Lionel Hampton And His Orchestra: Live In Graz* (1954), *Lionel Hampton And His French Sound* (1955), *Lionel Hampton And Stan Getz* (1955), *The Hampton-Tatum-Rich Trio* (1955), *The Lionel Hampton Big Band* (1955), *The Lionel Hampton Sextet* (1955), *Lionel Hampton And His Orchestra: Live At The Olympia, Paris* (1956), *Lionel Hampton Meets Fatty George* (1956), *Lionel Hampton And His Rhythm* (1956), *Paris Session* (1956), *Lionel Hampton And His Orchestra: In Madrid* (1956), *Lionel Hampton Concert Hall All Stars* (1956), *Lionel Hampton And His Orchestra* i (1957), *Lionel Hampton And His Orchestra: In Stuttgart* (1958), *Lionel Hampton And His Orchestra: Live In Concert* (c.1958), *Lionel Hampton And His Orchestra* ii (1958), *Lionel Hampton And His Orchestra* iii (1959), *Lionel Hampton And His Orchestra* iv (1960), *Lionel Hampton All Stars* i (1960), *Lionel Hampton And His Orchestra* v (1960), *Lionel Hampton And His Orchestra* vi (1961), *Lionel Hampton And His Orchestra At The Metropole* (1961), *Lionel Hampton And His Orchestra* vii (1962), *Lionel Hampton And Charlie Teagarden* (1963), *Lionel Hampton All Stars* ii (1963), *Lionel Hampton And His Orchestra: Live In Tokyo* (1963), *Lionel Hampton And His Orchestra* vii (1964), *Lionel Hampton And His Jazz Inner Circle* i (1964), *Hamp's Portrait Of A Woman* (c.1964), *You Better Know It* (1964), *Hamp's Big Band Live At Newport* (1965), *Newport Uproar* (1967), *The Works* (1967), *Lionel Hampton And His Jazz Inner Circle* ii (1967), *The Lionel Hampton Quintet* ii (1968), *Lionel Hampton And His Orchestra* ix (c.1970), *Lionel Hampton And His Orchestra* x (c.1970), *Transition* (c.1974), *Chameleon* (1976), *Alive And Jumping* (1977), *Lionel Hampton And His Jazz Giants* (1977), *New York Blackout* (1977), *Giants Of Jazz Vols 1 & 2* (1977), *Jazz Showcase* (1977), *Saturday Night Jazz Fever* (1978), *Live At The Muzeval* (1978), *50th Anniversary Album: Live At Carnegie Hall* (1978), with Svend Asmussen *As*

Time Goes By (1978), *All-Star Band At Newport* (1978), *Hamp In Haarlem* (1979), *Ambassador At Large* (1979), *Outrageous* (1980), *Lionel Hampton And His Orchestra At The Stadt-Casino, Basel* (1980), *Lionel Hampton And His Orchestra At The Aurex Jazz Festival '81, Tokyo* (1981), *The Boogie Woogie Album* (1982), *The Lionel Hampton Quintet* iii (1982), *Lionel Hampton Big Band In Doorwerth, Holland* (1982), *Made In Japan* (Timeless 1982), *Lionel Hampton With Orchestra Directed By Teo Macero* (c.1984-85), *Lionel Hampton And His Orchestra Featuring Sylvia Bennett* (1985), *Mostly Blues* (Limelight 1985), *Mostly Ballads* (Limelight 1990), with others *Live At The Blue Note* (1991), *Two Generations* (Phontastic 1991), *Just Jazz* (Telarc 1993), *Live At The Blue Note* (Telarc 1993). Selected compilations: *Paul Howard's Quality Serenaders* (1929), with Louis Armstrong, Les Hite *Louis In Los Angeles* (1930-31), with Benny Goodman *The Complete Small Combinations* (1936-41), *Historic Recording Sessions* (1937-41), *Leapin' With Lionel* (1941-49).

Further Reading: *Hamp: An Autobiography*, Lionel Hampton with James Haskins.

Hampton, Slide

b. Locksley W. Hampton, 21 April 1932, Jeannette, Pennsylvania, USA. Born into a musical family, several members of which played together for a while, trombonist Hampton joined Buddy Johnson's R&B band in the mid-50s. This engagement brought him to New York where he attracted attention not only for his playing but also for his arranging. After a brief spell with Lionel Hampton he became a member of Maynard Ferguson's band ,where he played and arranged, providing exciting charts on such popular tunes as 'The Fugue', 'Three Little Foxes' and 'Slide's Derangement'. After leaving Ferguson, Hampton led his own eight-piece band, continued arranging for others, and was musical director for singer Lloyd Price. In 1968 he toured with Woody Herman, settling in Europe where he remained until the late 70s. Subsequently he worked with various jazz co-operatives including Continuum, taught, and led his own nine-trombone, three-rhythm band, World of Trombones. A masterly arranger and gifted (left-handed) trombone player, Hampton's career is among the most distinguished in jazz.

Albums: with Maynard Ferguson *A Message From Newport* (1958), *Sister Salvation* (1960), *The Slide Hampton Octet* (1960), with Ferguson *Maynard '61* (1960-61), *Slide Hampton And His Orchestra* i (1961), *Slide Hampton And His Orchestra* ii (1962), *Slide Hampton And Sacha Distel* (1968), *The Fabulous Slide Hampton Quartet* (1969), *Slide Hampton With The Vaclav Zahradnik Big Band* (1971), *Life Music* (1972), *Interjazz 2* (1972), *Give Me A Double* (1974), *World Of Trombones* (Black Lion 1978), with Continuum *Mad About Tadd* (1982), *Roots* (Criss Cross 1985), *Mellow-dy* (LRC 1992), *Dedicated To Diz* (Telard 1993).

Hancock, Herbie

b. 12 April 1940, Chicago, Illinois, USA. Growing up in a musical household, Hancock studied piano from the age of seven and gave his first public performance just two years later. Although he played classical music at his debut Hancock's interest lay mostly in jazz. During high school and college he played in semi-professional bands and on occasion accompanied visiting jazzmen, including Donald Byrd. It was with Byrd that Hancock first played in New York, in 1961, recording with him and as leader of his own small group. Among the tunes on this later album was 'Watermelon Man', a Hancock original that appealed to more than the usual jazz audience. A version of the song, by Mongo Santamaría, reached the US Top 10. During the early and mid-60s Hancock led bands for club engagements and record dates but the move which really boosted his career and international recognition was joining the quintet led by Miles Davis, with whom he stayed for more than five years. Towards the end of the stint with Davis, the band began its move into jazz-rock. Hancock felt comfortable in this style and in 1968 formed a sextet to pursue his own concepts. With musicians such as Julian Priester, Buster Williams and Eddie Henderson, and playing much original material composed by Hancock, the band became one of the most popular and influential of the jazz-rock movement in the early 70s. From 1969 Hancock made extensive use of electronic piano and other electronic keyboard instruments, including synthesizers. In 1973 economic pressures compelled Hancock to cut the band to a quartet, which featured Bennie Maupin, who had also been in the bigger group. The new group's music was again fusion, but this time leaned more towards jazz-funk. Whether by good fortune or through astute observation of the music scene, Hancock's first album with the quartet, *Headhunters*, was widely accepted in the burgeoning disco scene and achieved substantial sales. Throughout the rest of the 70s Hancock's music was concentrated in this area with occasional returns to jazz for record dates. By the end of the decade, however, his popularity in the disco market was such that he cut down still further on straight jazz performances. Certain albums he made, with Chick Corea and with his own band, V.S.O.P (a re-creation of the Davis quintet except with Freddie Hubbard in place of Miles), suggested that he retained an interest, however peripheral, in jazz. His numerous disco successes included 'You Bet Your Love', a UK Top 20 hit in 1979, and in collaboration with the group Material he recorded *Future Shock*, one track from which 'Rockit', reached the UK Top 10 in 1983 and made the top spot in the USA. In 1986 Hancock played and acted in the film *'Round Midnight*; he also wrote the score, for which he won an Academy Award. Subsequently, he became more active in jazz, touring with Williams, Ron Carter, Michael Brecker and others. Although the career moves made by Hancock over the years have tended to alienate the hardcore jazz fans who applauded his earlier work with Davis, his popularity with the disco and related audiences has not been achieved at the expense of quality. All of his successes in this area have been executed to the highest musical and other professional standards; the pop video accompanying 'Rockit' was an award winner. In his use of synthesizers, voice-box and other state-of-the-art electronic devices, Hancock has displayed far-reaching inventiveness, setting standards for the pop industry.

Where his jazz work is concerned, he has displayed an intelligent approach to his material. If the music is often cerebral, it is rarely without heart; indeed, the V.S.O.P. band's re-creations have been notable for their integrity and a measure of passionate intensity that at times matches that of the original.

Selected albums: *Takin' Off* (1962), *My Point Of View* (1963), *Empyrean Isles* (Blue Note 1964), *Maiden Voyage* (Blue Note 1964), *Speak Like A Child* (Blue Note 1968), *The Prisoner* (1969), *Mwandishi* (1971), *Sextant* (1973), *Headhunters* (Columbia 1973), *Mr Hands* (Columbia 1974), *V.S.O.P.* (1976), *V.S.O.P: The Quintet* (1977), *Monster* (CBS 1978), *Feets, Don't Fail Me Now* (CBS 1978), *An Evening With Herbie Hancock And Chick Corea* (Columbia 1978), *Hancock Alley* (Manhattan 1980), *Quartet* (Columbia 1982), *Future Shock* (CBS 1983), *Hot And Heavy* (Premier 1984), *Herbie Hancock And The Rockit Band* (CBS 1984), with Dexter Gordon *'Round Midnight* (1986), *Best Of Vol. 2* (1992), with Wayne Shorter, Ron Carter, Wallace Roney, Tony Williams *A Tribute To Miles* (QWest/Reprise 1994). Compilations: *Greatest Hits* (CBS 1980), *A Jazz Collection* (Sony 1991).

Handy, 'Captain' John

b. 24 June 1900, Pass Christian, Mississippi, USA, d. 12 January 1971. As a child, Handy played various instruments with members of his musical family and sat in, usually on clarinet, with noted musicians such as Kid Howard, Kid Rena and Punch Miller. By his late teens Handy was resident in New Orleans and worked there and in surroundings areas. In the late 20s Handy began playing alto saxophone, an instrument which at that time was unpopular in jazz circles, especially those in which New Orleans-style music was played. However, during the 30s he played regularly with various jazzmen, including Lee Collins and Jim Robinson. Handy's career was centred in New Orleans for many years, but in the early 60s he began to venture further afield, sometimes in company with Kid Sheik Cola and Kid Thomas Valentine. Handy's playing style was decidedly varied, ranging between hard-edged grittiness and smooth romanticism. In the late 60s, touring Europe with Barry Martyn and Sammy Rimington, and at the 1970 Newport Jazz Festival, Handy regularly confounded those who regarded the alto saxophone as an unsuitable instrument on which to play early jazz. On uptempo numbers, Handy's clipped, aggressive tone resembled that of Pete Brown and is also reflected in Rimington's playing.

Albums: *Kid Howard's Band* (1962), with Kid Thomas Valentine *The December Band* (1965), *Capt. John Handy With Geoff Bull And Barry Martyn's Band* (1966), *Handyman* (1966), *Introducing Cap'n John Handy* (1967), *With The Claude Hopkins Band* (RCA 1985), *All Aboard* (GHB 1986), *All Aboard With Jim Robinson* (GHB 1988), *All Aboard With Rimmington* (GHB 1988).

Handy, George

b. 17 January 1920, New York City, New York, USA. After studying piano and composing at both Juilliard and New York University, Handy was tutored by Aaron Copland, the renowned American classical composer. In the early 40s he worked with Raymond Scott's orchestra at CBS studios in New York, but then turned his attention to arranging for the more progressively-minded big band leaders. Among the bands for which he wrote were those led by Alvino Rey, a popular guitarist who led an advanced and often overlooked big band in the mid-40s, and Boyd Raeburn, for whom he made his most notable contributions to jazz. It is difficult to be too precise about which of Raeburn's successes were actually written by Handy as a dispute arose between Handy and Raeburn on the one hand, and Eddie Finckel on the other over authorship of several of the band's best charts. At times Handy played piano with Raeburn, but proved an eccentric personality who was also somewhat unreliable (drummer Irving Kluger recalled that at one time Handy dyed his hair green and would occasionally lapse into unconsciousness over the keyboard). Handy made a few records of his own compositions under his own name, but by the late 40s had left the jazz scene. He reappeared briefly in the mid-50s recording and working with Zoot Sims, but drifted out of sight again. In 1964 he was writing for the New York Saxophone Quartet but this too proved to be only a temporary creative burst from an erratic individual, whose greatest failing might be that he came onto the jazz scene several years before it was ready for him.

Albums: *Boyd Raeburn On The Air Vol. 2* (1945), *George Handy And His Orchestra* (1954), *By George!* (1955). Compilations: with others *Central Avenue Breakdown Vol. 1* (1945).

Handy, John, II

b. 3 February 1933, Dallas, Texas, USA. When Handy's magnificent 1965 recording *Live At The Monterey Jazz Festival* hit the shops, many of the reviewers got carried away. Handy had been around for years, working with Charles Mingus from 1958-59 and again in 1964, appearing with the bassist's band at Monterey as it happened. He had also had his own band from 1959-61, but it was with the creation of the 1965 band, comprising the leader's alto, violin (Michael White), piano (Freddie Redd, replaced by the guitar of Jerry Hahn by the time of the Monterey concert), bass (Don Thompson) and drums (Terry Clarke) that the critics fastened on to him as the new Charlie Parker we had supposedly all been waiting for. Handy's music was exciting, musicianly and well-crafted but it was what it was *not* that caused the excitement. Here was an outstanding alto player who was not threatening in the way that Ornette Coleman was felt to be. He deserved to be valued on more positive virtues, though. Self-taught on clarinet at the age of 13, he took up the alto saxophone at 16, finding time to win an amateur featherweight boxing title in between. He studied music formally at college, then moved to New York in 1958. After the spell with Mingus and his own group he worked in Scandinavia as a soloist, then returned to the USA as soloist with the Santa Clara Symphony Orchestra and the San Francisco State College Symphonic Band. In 1966-67 he toured with the Monterey All-Stars and performed in Gunther Schuller's opera *The Visitation*. In 1968 he began teaching jazz and black history at various colleges and conservatories on the west coast and set up a new band with Mike Nock, Ron McClure and Michael White. In 1970 he completed a *Concerto For Jazz Soloist And Orchestra*, and in 1971 began a collaboration with Ali Akbar Khan, a sarod player, in the band Rainbow. His 1976 album *Hard Work* gave his career its third wind, although this time the critics were less well-disposed, often deploring his funk/rock leanings; 1988's *Excursion In Blue* showed a return to more mainstream jazz settings. Handy also sings and plays tenor, flute and piano.

Albums: *Recorded Live At The Monterey Jazz Festival* (1966), *Dancy Dancy* (1966), *New View* (1967), with Rainbow *Karuna Supreme* (1975), *Hard Work* (Impulse 1976), *Carnival* (1977), *Rainbow* (1980), *Right There* (Gull 1984), with Lee Ritenour *Where Go The Boats* (Inak 1988), *Handy Dandy Man* (Inak 80s), *Musical Dreamland* (Boulevard 80s), *Excursion In Blue* (1988).

Hanna, Jake

b. John Hanna, 4 April 1931, Roxbury, Massachusetts, USA. Hanna began playing drums in a marching band at the age of five in Dorchester, Massachusetts. In his youth he played in and around the Boston area, a territory where many fine jazz musicians were to be found. During the late 40s and early 50s he played in bands led by Tommy Reed and Ted Weems; in the late 50s he worked with pianists Marian McPartland and Toshiko Akiyoshi, and in the big bands of Maynard Ferguson and Woody Herman. He rejoined Herman in 1962, staying for two years in the band the musicians wryly described as the 'un-Herd' and then subbed or otherwise flitted briefly through the bands of Duke Ellington, Harry James and Boston-based teacher and rehearsal band pioneer Herb Pomeroy. What Hanna has described as the best time in his life came when he played with George Wein's band at the impresario's Storyville Club in Boston. In the band were Buck Clayton, Bud Freeman, Pee Wee Russell and Vic Dickenson, with Jimmy Rushing on vocals. In 1964 Hanna became a member of the studio band for the Merv Griffin television show, then based in New York. When the show moved to California, Hanna was one of several musicians who were given the opportunity of moving with it, provided they made their minds up fast. Along with Bill Berry, Richie Kamuca and others, Hanna made the snap decision and ever since has been located on the west coast, even though the Griffin job ended in 1975. Since then he has worked with numerous bands, including Supersax, Count Basie, Herman, Berry, and co-led an occasional small group with Carl Fontana. Although highly skilled in all aspects of his work, Hanna is one of the most self-effacing drummers in jazz, happy to urge a band along with subtlety and discreet dynamics. Any band with which he plays is guaranteed to swing and to have a good time because, apart from his superb musicianship, Hanna is also a witty and gifted raconteur.

Albums: with Carl Fontana *Live At Concord* (Concord 1975), *Kansas City Express* (1976), *Jake Takes Manhattan* (1976).

Hanna, Roland, Sir

b. 10 February 1932, Detroit, Michigan, USA. Having first

played informally with his father, Hanna then studied classical piano while still a child. After military service, and by now deeply interested in jazz, he continued his studies at Juilliard and Eastman College in the 50s, worked briefly with Benny Goodman, Charles Mingus and Sarah Vaughan and also led his own small groups. In 1967 he joined the Thad Jones-Mel Lewis Orchestra, remaining a regular until 1974. In the 70s Hanna was a member of the co-operative New York Jazz Sextet and Quartet. A marvellously inventive pianist, his work reflects his thorough understanding of the roots of jazz. Although eclectic, his playing vividly demonstrates his own powerful personality. He is a masterly accompanist and an excellent big band player, while his solo work is filled with clear, logical ideas delivered with considerable vitality. In the early 80s, concerned that he was getting into a rut, Hanna absented himself from the music scene in order to develop new ideas. A European tour in the late 80s, in company with Al Grey, Clark Terry and Buddy Tate, showed him to have all the fire of old and he had clearly shaken off any tendency, real or imagined, to drift into routine. His title denotes an honorary knighthood bestowed upon him by the Republic of Liberia.

Albums: *Roland Hanna Plays Harold Rome's Destry Rides Again* (1959), *The Roland Hanna Trio* i (1959), with Charles Mingus *Mingus Dynasty* (1959), with Thad Jones-Mel Lewis *Consummation* (1970), *Child Of Gemini* (1971), *Sir Elf* (1973), *Perugia: Live At Montreux* (1974), *The Roland Hanna Trio* ii (1975), *The New York Jazz Quartet In Concert In Japan* (1975), *At Home With Friends/Time For The Dancers* (1977), *Sir Elf Plus One* (1977), *Glove* (1977), *Roland Hanna Plays The Music Of Alec Wilder* (c.1978), *Orange Funk* (1978), *Bird Tracks: Remembering Charlie Parker* (Progressive 1978), *A Gift From The Magi* (1978), *Swing Me No Waltzes* (1979), *Trinity* (1979), *Piano Soliloquy* (1979), *Impressions* (Black And Blue 1979), *Roland Hanna* (1979), *Sunrise, Sunset* (1979), *A Keyboard Event* (1981), *Romanesque* (1982), *Gershwin Carmichael Cats* (CTI 1983), *This Time It's Real* (Storyville 1987), *Glove* (Blackhawk 1988), *Time For The Dancer* (Progressive 1988), *Persia My Dear* (DIW 1988), *Double Exposure* (LRC 1992).

Hardee, John

b. 20 December 1918, Corsicana County, Texas, USA. A tenor saxophone with a tone reminiscent of Chu Berry. Following his demobilization in 1945 he played in and around New York with numerous small bands. He recorded with Tiny Grimes 'Tiny's Boogie Woogie' (1946); and under his own name 'Hardee's Partee', 'Tired', 'Idaho' and 'River Edge Rock' (1946).

Hardwicke, Otto 'Toby'

b. 31 May 1904, Washington, DC, USA, d. 5 August 1970. After playing the bass and C melody saxophones, Hardwicke switched to alto and began working with Duke Ellington, first in his home town and later in New York. He was with Ellington from 1923-28, then spent some time in Europe. Back in the USA, he played in the bands of Chick Webb and Elmer Snowden (with whom he had previously played in

Washington in 1922) and then returned to Ellington in 1932. He stayed with the band until 1946, when he retired from music. A solid section player, Hardwicke was an undistinguished soloist. He did, however, have an ear for a melody and is accorded co-composer credit with Ellington on one of the maestro's loveliest tunes, 'Sophisticated Lady'.

Compilation: *The Indispensable Duke Ellington Vol. 1/2* (1927-29).

Hargrove, Roy

b. 1970, Waco, Texas, USA. His father was in the US Air Force which meant that in his early years, growing up in Mart, a small town just outside Waco, he lived with his grandparents. He started playing trumpet at the age of nine and when his father settled in Dallas, Texas, he began playing music in school thanks to the school band. At home, on records, he mostly heard R&B and soul but he had begun to hear jazz and this is what he played when he auditioned for the Dallas Arts Magnate (a school for the performing arts). At this time, despite formal tuition, he was often playing jazz by ear. The school principal played him some Clifford Brown records, broadly hinting that the rest was up to him. Later, he heard records by Lee Morgan and Freddie Hubbard and when he attended Berklee College Of Music he also heard Fats Navarro records. As he matured into his early twenties, Hargrove developed a distinctive playing style. In his own playing and in that of a band he formed, he sought to extend his jazz lines from a base in classic bop. He works mostly in a quartet setting, with regular accompaniment from alto saxophonist Antonio Hart, bassist Rodney Thomas Whitaker and drummer Greg Hutchinson. An exceptionally gifted musician, with a rich tone and inventive mind, Hargrove is one of the outstanding jazz trumpeters of the 90s.

Albums: *Diamond In The Rough* (Novus 1990), *Public Eye* (Novus 1991), *The Vibe* (Novus 1992), *Of Kindred Souls* (Novus 1993).

Harrell, Tom

b. 16 June 1946, Urbana, Illinois, USA. Harrell's family moved to San Francisco when he was five and he started playing the trumpet when he was 13. During the 70s he worked with the bands of Stan Kenton, Woody Herman and Horace Silver and, after moving to New York, with Chuck Israels' National Jazz Ensemble, Azteca and Arnie Lawrence's Treasure Island. He is an incisive and precise trumpeter with a clear, even tone who has been much in demand for studio work. During the 80s Phil Woods expanded his quartet to a quintet by adding Harrell. He has played with Gerry Mulligan's Orchestra and has led his own bands for which he has composed much of the music.

Albums: with Mulligan *Walk On The Water* (1980), *Play Of Light* (Blackhawk 1984), *Moon Alley* (Criss Cross 1985), *Open Air* (Contemporary 1987), *Visions* (Contemporary 1991), *Passages* (Chesky 1992), *Form* (Contemporary 1993), *Sail Away* (Musidisc 1993), *Stories* (Contemporary 1993), *Upswing* (Chesky 1993).

Harriott, Joe

b. Arthurlin Harriott, 15 July 1928, Jamaica, West Indies, d. 2 January 1973. After performing in dance bands in the West Indies, Harriott emigrated to the UK in 1951 and quickly established himself as a formidable bebop player on alto and baritone saxophones. After working with Tony Kinsey, Ronnie Scott and other leading British players, Harriott formed his own group, believing that his career needed to go in a less orthodox direction than the one most beboppers were following. In the late 50s, after a protracted spell in hospital recovering from tuberculosis, a period he used to develop his musical thoughts, he formed a band with Coleridge Goode, Phil Seamen, Ellsworth 'Shake' Keane and Pat Smythe which explored Harriott's notions of 'abstract music' on three groundbreaking albums, *Free Form*, *Abstract* and *Movement*. Coincidentally, this music appeared at the same time as the free jazz of Ornette Coleman but differed markedly in its concept and realization 'of the various components comprising jazz today,' Harriott explained in his notes to *Abstract*, 'constant time signatures, a steady four-four tempo, themes and predictable harmonic variations, fixed division of the chorus by bar lines, and so on - we aim to retain at least one in each piece. But we may well - if the mood seems to us to demand it - dispense with all the others . . . (our music) is best listened to as a series of different pictures- for it is after all by definition an attempt in free improvisation to paint, as it were, freely in sound.' Ever open to the prospect of new departures, Harriott turned in the mid-60s to jazz fusion, blending his playing with that of Indian musicians in a double quintet that he co-led with violinist John Mayer. In his later years he often worked with Michael Garrick, but was obliged to abandon most of his own musical experiments in the face of uncomprehending UK audiences. Unable to finance a group, he spent his last few years touring the UK as a solo, playing bebop and standards with local rhythm sections, often living in poverty. He died of cancer in 1973. One of the most inventive and original of jazz musicians, Harriott's music was rarely fully appreciated during his lifetime, although in retrospect he can be seen as a major figure in the development of both a European Free Jazz tradition and a jazz-based fusion that incorporated elements of ethnic music. He was invariably a fine improviser too, but it is his experiments with form that have guaranteed Harriott his place in jazz history.

Albums: *Southern Horizons* (1959-60), *Free Form* (1960), *Abstract* (1961-62), *Movement* (1964), with John Mayer *Indo-Jazz Suite* (1965), with Michael Garrick *Black Marigolds* (1966), with Mayer *Indo-Jazz Fusions* (1967), *Swings High* (Cadillac 1967), *Personal Portrait* (1967), with Mayer *Indo-Jazz Fusions II* (1968), with Amancio D'Silva *Hum Dono* (1969). Compilation: with Tony Kinsey *Jump For Me* (Esquire 1987, rec. 1954).

Further reading: *Joe Harriott Memorial - A Bio-Discography*, Roger Cotterrell and Barry Tepperman.

Harris, Barry

b. 15 December 1929, Detroit, Michigan, USA. Harris started to play piano at a very early age and by his teens was well established in his home town, where he performed with Miles Davis, Sonny Stitt, Max Roach and other leading jazzmen. Strongly influenced by Bud Powell and Thelonious Monk, Harris in his turn made an impact upon bebop pianists through his work in Detroit and in New York, where he relocated in the early 60s. Apart from stints with Cannonball Adderley, Dexter Gordon and other leading bebop artists, Harris was also a regular accompanist to Coleman Hawkins and established a reputation as a teacher. He has recorded extensively, both under his own name and with musicians such as Al Cohn, Sonny Criss, Sam Noto, Charles McPherson and Jimmy Heath. Since the early 80s he has been deeply involved in jazz education, running the Jazz Cultural Centre in New York, and is regarded as one of the finest teachers of bebop piano.

Selected albums: *Breakin' It Up* (1958), *At The Jazz Workshop* (Original Jazz Classics 1960), *Preminado* (Original Jazz Classics 1961), *Listen To Barry Harris* (1961), *Newer Than New* (1961), *Chasin' The Bird* (1962), *Luminescence* (1967), *Bull's Eye* (1968), *Magnificent!* (1969), *Vicissitudes* (1973), with Sam Noto *Entrance!* (1975), with Sonny Criss *Saturday Morning* (1975), with Al Cohn *Play It Now* (1975), *Barry Harris Plays Tadd Dameron* (Xanadu 1975), *Live In Tokyo* (Xanadu 1976), *The Detroit Four - Cadillac And Mack* (c.1977), *I Remember Bebop* (1977), *Barry Harris Plays Barry Harris* (Xanadu 1978), *For The Moment* (1984), *At The Jazz Workshop* (JVC 1986), *For The Moment* (Uptown 1988), *Passing It On* (Kay Jazz 1988), *The Bird Of Red And Gold* (Xanadu 1990), *Live At Maybeck Recital Hall Vol 12* (Concord 1991).

Harris, Bill

b. Willard Palmer Harris, 28 October 1916, Philadelphia, Pennsylvania, USA, d. 19 September 1973. Harris first played trombone in name bands when he was in his early twenties, having previously performed mostly in and around his home town. After deputizing with Gene Krupa and Ray McKinley he was hired by Benny Goodman, Charlie Barnet and other well-known band leaders, then in 1944 joined Woody Herman, with whom he worked intermittently for 15 years. It was while he was with Herman that his rumbustious, attacking solo style became known to big band fans. Instantly identifiable from his ripe tone and the broad humour with which he laced his solos, Harris was slightly influenced by bebop but maintained strong links with his swing era roots. Among the bands with which he worked in between his appearances with Herman were those of Boyd Raeburn, Benny Carter, Charlie Ventura, the Sauter-Finegan orchestra, and he also toured with Jazz At The Philharmonic, where his rip-roaring style fitted in well with the wilder side of these concert jam sessions. In the early 60s Harris became resident in Florida, playing with local bands and visiting jazzmen; he also worked for a spell with Charlie Teagarden and occasionally led his own groups.

Albums: *Bill Harris-Charlie Ventura Live At The Three Deuces* (1947), with Ventura *Aces At The Deuces* (Phoenix 1947), *A Knight In The Village* (1947), *Bill Harris And His Orchestra*

(1952), with Benny Carter *New Jazz Sounds* (1954), *Bill Harris And Friends* (Original Jazz Classics 1957), *Bill Harris And The Ex-Hermanites/Bill Harris Memorial Album* (1957), *Woody Herman Live 1957 Featuring Bill Harris Vols 1 & 2* (1957). Compilation: *The Best Of Woody Herman* (1945).

Harris, Craig

b. 10 September 1953, Hempstead, Long Island, USA. Harris emerged as a trombone player with the AACM in Chicago in the late 70s. He played for a year in the Lena Horne orchestra on Broadway and then with the Beaver Harris-Don Pullen 360 Degree Musical Experience. Having been educated at SUNY at Old Westbury (where saxophonist Pat Patrick made a great impression as a teacher) he moved to New York in 1978 and joined Sun Ra's Arkestra, the band in which Patrick played, staying for two years. In 1981 he went on a world tour with pianist Abdullah Ibrahim: Australia made a particular impression on him. He met and played with Aborigine musicians and acquired a dijeridoo, which he now plays to great effect. He later played in David Murray's first octet, participating in one of the great consolidating bands of black music in the 80s. His debut as a leader was *Aboriginal Affairs* in 1983. *Black Bone*, from the same year, had a track 'inspired by the spirit of Jimi Hendrix', while 1985's *Tributes* was dedicated to Trummy Young. *Shelter* (1987), with his new group Tailgaters Tales, was a brilliant exposition of Harris's talents as a composer and band-leader, but the follow-up *Black Out In The Square Root Of Soul* (1988) was less impressive and almost swamped by synthesizers. In 1988 he formed Cold Sweat, a band that reasserts the black tradition of funk from a non-commercial viewpoint. 1990 saw him touring with a new edition of David Murray's Octet. Craig Harris has a dark, brooding, violent trombone sound that is brightened by the warmth and directness of his musical concepts. He looks set to be one of the prime movers for jazz in the 90s.

Albums: *Aboriginal Affairs* (1983), *Black Bone* (Soul Note 1983), *Tributes* (1985), *Shelter* (JMT 1987), *Black Out In The Square Root Of Soul* (JMT 1988), with Cold Sweat *Plays JB* (1989), with Cold Sweat *Foreplay* (JMT 1991).

Harris, Gene

b. 1 September 1933, Benton Harbour, Michigan, USA. A self-taught pianist, Harris extended his playing ability from its original boogie-woogie base while on military service. Later, he formed a trio, The Three Sounds, which played the blues. After moving to New York, the band, which also included Andy Simpkins and Bill Dowdy, made numerous records. After his colleagues moved on, Harris turned towards jazz-rock but returned to the mainstream in the late 70s. In the 80s and early 90s he worked with Ernestine Anderson, Benny Carter, Scott Hamilton, Stanley Turrentine and others, and was leader of the all-star Philip Morris Super Band which toured extensively, was recorded, and appeared at New York's Apollo backing B.B. King. A solid accompanist, for many years Harris was at his exuberant best playing in the blues idiom. More recently, he has broadened his repertoire and plays swinging, muscular

mainstream to bop piano, although the blues are happily never far away.

Albums: *Introducing The Three Sounds* (1958), *The Three Sounds Vol. 2* (1958), *Bottoms Up* (1959), *Good Deal* (1959), *Moods* (1960), *Feelin' Good* (1960), *Here We Come* (1960), *It Just Got To Be* (1960), *Hey There* (1961), *Out Of This World* (1962), *Black Orchid* (1962), *Blue Genes* (1962), *The Three Sounds* i (1962), *Anita O'Day And The Three Sounds* (1962), *The Three Sounds* ii (1963), *The Three Sounds Live At The Living Room* (c.1964), *The Three Sounds* iii (c.1964), *The Three Sounds* iv (1965), *The Three Sounds* v (1966), *Vibrations* (c.1966), *The Three Sounds Live At The Lighthouse* (1967), *Coldwater Flat* (1968), *Elegant Soul* (1968), *Soul Symphony* (1969), *The Three Sounds* (1971), *Astral Signal* (1974), *Gene Harris: The Three Sounds* (1974), with Ernestine Anderson *When The Sun Goes Down* (1984), *Gene Harris Trio Plus One* (1985), *Tribute To Count Basie* (Concord 1987), *Gene Harris And The Philip Morris Super Band: Live At Town Hall, New York City* (Concord 1989), *Listen Here!* (1989), with Anderson *Live At The 1990 Concord Jazz Festival: Third Set* (1990), *Gene Harris And The Philip Morris Super Band: World Tour* (Concord 1990), with Scott Hamilton *At Last* (Concord 1990), *Black And Blue* (Concord 1991), *Like A Lover* (Concord 1992), *At The Maybeck Recital Hall* (Concord 1993), *A Little Piece Of Heaven* (Concord 1994).

Harrison, Donald 'Duck'

b. 23 June 1960, New Orleans, Louisiana, USA. Alto and soprano saxophonist Harrison is part of a wave of young virtuoso musicians (such as Wynton and Branford Marsalis) who emerged from the Crescent City, original home of jazz, in the 80s. While he was at school he studied under Marsalis Senior (the pianist Ellis Marsalis) and Alvin Batiste at the New Orleans Center for the Arts, Southern University. He played with the New Orleans Pops in 1979 after winning an audition, then moved to Boston later in the year to study at the Berklee College Of Music. He worked with Roy Haynes (1980-81), Jack McDuff (1981) and Art Blakey (1982-86). It was in Blakey's Jazz Messengers, alongside trumpeter Terence Blanchard and tenor saxophonist Jean Toussaint, that Harrison caused a stir with his fiery, chromatic playing, providing a relatively radical element in the band. He has since co-led a quintet with Blanchard, and, as player, composer and arranger, has shown the awareness of jazz roots and history which might be expected from a New Orleans musician.

Albums: *New York Second Line* (1984), *Discernment* (1986), *Nascence* (1986), *Crystal Stair* (1987), *Full Circle* (Sweet Basil 1991), *For Art's Sake* (Candid 1991), *Indian Blues* (Candid 1992).

Hart, Clyde

b. 1910, Baltimore, Maryland, USA, d. 19 March 1945. After working as pianist and arranger with the Jap Allen outfit, a leading territory band of the early 30s, Hart spent the second half of the decade in numerous ensembles. A solid performer with particular ability as an accompanist, Hart was in great demand and played with many of the outstanding jazz artists of the period. Among them were McKinney's Cotton Pickers, Andy Kirk, Red Allen, Billy Holiday, Stuff Smith, Roy Eldridge, Lester Young, Lionel Hampton and Frankie Newton. In the early 40s Hart was with various bandleaders, including John Kirby and Wilber De Paris but had begun to take an interest in the new developments in jazz. He adjusted his style to accommodate the needs of bebop soloists, one of the first of the swing era pianists to do so, and subsequently played with Charlie Parker and Dizzy Gillespie, whose first studio session together was under Hart's leadership. One of the usually unsung stalwarts of jazz, whose musical personality kept him very much in the background, Hart played an important part in the transition from swing to bop. However, he was unable to build upon his important early work in this area as he fell victim to tuberculosis and died.

Compilations: with Charlie Parker *Complete Savoy Sessions* (1944-45), *Dizzy Gillespie With Clyde Hart's All Stars* (1945).

Hashim, Michael

b. 1956, Geneva, New York, USA. While attending school at Geneva in upstate New York, Hashim joined the school band programme. His first choices, drums and trombone, were ruled out and he settled instead on alto saxophone. His interest in music had been sparked when he met a fellow student, Phil Flanigan, whose father had an extensive jazz record collection. They listened to a wide range of musicians, from Sidney Bechet to Frank Zappa, by way of Lester Young and Charlie Parker. By chance, he and Flanigan met guitarist Chris Flory and with drummer Johnny Ellis they formed a quartet. By the mid-70s Hashim was working regularly, often with Flanigan and Flory. He played mostly in the New York/Rhode Island area and when Flory went into Scott Hamilton's band (where he was later joined by Flanigan), Hashim joined the Widespread Depression Orchestra of South Vermont. Later, when Widespread moved to New York, Hashim went along too, eventually taking over leadership of the band which continued to perform into the mid-90s. He has played with Muddy Waters, Benny Carter, studied with altoist Jimmy Lyons, and worked for a while in a band led by Jo Jones. He continued to work with Flory, in a trio completed by the excellent young stride pianist Judy Carmichael. He tours extensively throughout the USA and Europe and he also played in China on a US Information Service-backed tour. Although his musical interests lie in post-bop jazz, Hashim's feeling for the tradition is never far from the surface. He continues to attract attention and admiration for his warm-toned, dynamic and always inventive playing on alto and soprano saxophones.

Albums: *Lotus Blossom* (Stash 1990), *The Billy Strayhorn Project* (1990), *Guys And Dolls* (Stash 1992), *A Blue Streak* (Stash 1992).

Hasselgård, 'Stan' Ake

b. Ake Hasselgård, 4 October 1922, Sundsvall, Sweden, d. 23 November 1948. During the 40s Hasselgård played clarinet with several dance bands in his homeland, then moved to the USA in the mid-summer of 1947. Here he attracted considerable attention as not many American clarinettists had adapted to bebop as well as he had done. He played with a number of jazzmen, including Count Basie, Red Norvo and Barney Kessel before he came to the notice of Benny Goodman. Despite his reputation for not sharing the spotlight with any other clarinettist and also for not liking bebop, Goodman delighted in Hasselgård's playing and recorded with him and Wardell Gray, another of the tiny coterie of beboppers of whom Goodman approved. Just how far into bebop Hasselgård might have taken the clarinet can only be a matter for speculation; he died as a result of a road accident in November 1948.

Selected compilations: with Benny Goodman, Wardell Gray *Swedish Pastry* (1948), with Goodman, Gray, others *Jammin' At Jubilee* (1948), *At Click 1948* (Dragon, 1948 recording), *Jammin' At Jubilee* (Dragon 1986), *Young Clarinet* (Dragon 1988, 1940-48 recordings).

Hassell, Jon

b. 1937, Memphis, Tennessee, USA. Hassell acquired several university degrees including a PhD in musicology, before travelling to Cologne, Germany in 1965 to study with Karlheinz Stockhausen. While in Cologne he met and played with Irmin Schmidt and Holgar Czukay, who later went on to form Can. The trumpeter and keyboard player returned to the USA in 1967 and began to play with leading minimalist composers La Monte Young and Terry Riley. As a performer Hassell appeared on Riley's seminal minimalist piece *In C*, released in 1968 and La Monte Young's extended drone cycle *Dreamhouse*. With Young's influence Hassell became interested in Indian classical music and in 1972 he travelled to northern Indian to study Kirana tradition with master vocalist Pandit Pran Nath. From his studies Hassell created a new vocal style which he described as Fourth World - a unified primitive/futuristic sound combining features of world ethnic style with advanced electronic techniques. In 1976 he returned to the USA and recorded *Vernal Equinox*, his first attempt to integrate expand raga studies with technological vocabulary. The record features Brazilian percussionist Nana Vasconcelos. In 1979 *Earthquake Island* was released and continued the highly influential genre of ethnic-inspired music and again featured Vasconcelos, along with Badal Roy and ex-Weather Report bassist Miroslav Vitous. In 1980 Brian Eno arrived in New York, and heard *Vernal Equinox*, and contacted Hassell about the possibility of a collaboration. The highly acclaimed *Fourth World Volume One: Possible Musics* released the same year pushed Hassell into the limelight and he was invited to play on the Eno-produced Talking Heads album *Remain In Light*.

Fourth World Volume Two: Dreamy Theory In Malaya was released in 1981. The recording contained playing by Eno, and engineering by Daniel Lanois' and was again received with critical acclaim. In 1982, Hassell was invited to perform at the Womad festival in Bath, England, and to participate in the prestigious Rencontres Nord-Sud Conference on World Culture in Paris. *AKA/Darbari/Java (Magic Realism)* produced by Lanois in 1983 marked a new high point for Hassell in 'techno-magic' that permit actual sound of music of various epochs and geographies to come together on the same canvas through the use of sampling and computer hardware. With the addition of percussionist J.A. Deane and keyboard player Jean-Philippe Rykiel, Hassell toured Europe and the USA. Eno produced *Powerspot*, in 1986, which contained recordings made by this group in 1983-84 and further Hassells' reputation at the forefront of burgeoning interest in hybrid and world music. In 1984, David Sylvian invited Hassell to play on his first solo album, *Brilliant Trees* and the following year to collaborate on *Alchemy - An Index Of Possibilities*. *The Surgeon Of The Night Sky Restores Dead Things By The Power Of Sound*, again was produced by Eno, released in 1987, documented the concert chemistry of the group that toured Europe in 1986. That same year, Kronos Quartet commissioned string quartet Pano De Costa from Hassell. It appears on their *White Man Sleeps* album. In 1987, Burkino Faso percussion ensemble Farafina invited Hassell to collaborate with them. The group played various festivals around the world, including Womad. The Eno/Lanois produced *Flash On The Spirit* documented this highly original unique blend of styles and cultures. In 1989. Hassell relocated to Los Angeles, where he formed a new group to perform live, and recorded self-produced *City: Works Of Fiction* released to critical acclaim in 1990. Despite continuous problems in locating a label for his recorded work Hassell remains an entirely unique performer with a visionary and highly original sound and style.

Albums: *Vernal Equinox* (Lovely 1977), *Earthquake Island* (Tomato 1979), with Brian Eno *Fourth World Volume One: Possible Musics* (Editions EG 1980), *Dream Theory In Malaya/Fourth World Volume Two* (Editions EG 1981), *Aka/Darbari/Java (Magic Realism)* (Editions EG 1983), *Powerspot* (ECM 1986), *The Surgeon Of The Night Sky Restores Dead Things By The Power Of Sound* (Intuition 1987), with Farafina *Flash Of The Spirit* (Intuition 1988), *City: Works Of Fiction* (Land 1990).

Hastings, Lennie

b. 5 January 1927, London, England, d. 14 July 1978. Although best known for his dixieland-style drumming, Hastings was well-versed in other areas of jazz. He was first noticed playing modern jazz in the late 40s, but by 1949 had joined Freddy Randall's traditional band. After five years with Randall he moved to Alex Welsh, with whom he remained until 1973. Both during and after his time with Welsh, Hastings played in rhythm sections accompanying visiting American artists such as Rex Stewart, Bill Coleman, Bob Wilber and Kenny Davern. An exuberant personality with an outrageous sense of fun, Hastings was given to wearing fright wigs in shades of vitriolic orange. His death in July 1978 left a gap in the UK jazz scene.

Albums: with Alex Welsh *Melody Maker Tribute To Louis Armstrong* (1970), *Always The Best* (Dawn Clun 1978).

Havens, Bob

b. 3 May 1930, Quincy, Illinois, USA. Havens came from a musical family and was learning violin and piano before he took up the trombone when he was aged eight. In the mid-50s he played a month's residency in New Orleans with Ralph Flanagan's orchestra and decided to settle there. He played with George Girard before joining Al Hirt in 1957 for three successful years. He followed Pete Fountain from Hirt to Lawrence Welk's band and stayed with him for 20 years. Since then he has led a band at Disneyland and continued to work in studios, always able to provide the kind of classic dixieland typified by Bob Crosby with whom he worked in 1985. He acknowledges Jack Teagarden as his principal influence. He is involved in teaching and plays with college bands.

Albums: *Bob Havens And His New Orleans All Stars* (Southland 1964), with Pete Fountain *Standing Room Only* (1965).

Hawes, Hampton

b. 13 November 1928, Los Angeles, California, USA, d. 22 May 1977. Born into a musical family (his mother played piano for the church run by his Presbyterian minister father), Hawes taught himself to play piano by listening to records of 30s jazz piano giants, among them Earl 'Fatha' Hines and Fats Waller. He began to play professionally while still attending the Polytechnic High School. In his autobiography, *Raise Up Off Me*, he recalled leaving his graduation ceremony and heading straight for a gig with the Jay McNeely band. Hawes was briefly in New York but soon returned to Los Angeles, where he became an important participant in the burgeoning 'west coast' school of jazz. He was a member of Howard McGhee's band when the trumpeter hired Charlie Parker for a gig at the Hi-De-Ho Club in Los Angeles, shortly after Parker's release from Camarillo. Hawes's first recording date was with Dexter Gordon and Wardell Gray in 1947. He was with Shorty Rogers on his 1951 *Modern Sounds* recording session, which also featured Art Pepper. Hawes was occasionally at the Lighthouse Club during these years, working in the house rhythm section that backed all the major figures of the movement of which he had become an important part. Unfortunately, Hawes had developed a drug habit and his induction into the US Army did little to help his condition. Apart from time spent in military prison for drugs-related offences, Hawes also visited Japan where he became an early admirer and lifelong friend of Toshiko Akiyoshi. Released from the service in 1955, Hawes was recorded by Lester Koenig for his new Contemporary Records. At the same time Hawes formed a trio, with Red Mitchell and Chuck Thompson. The trio's first album was successful but not so much as subsequent albums, which included the enormously influential *All Night Session*. Recorded by a quartet, with the addition of guitarist Jim Hall, this set established Hawes as a major figure; the music on the albums, to which buzz words like 'funky' and 'soul' were applied, was suddenly the in-thing. In the mid-50s Hawes recorded with artists including Art Pepper, Bill Perkins and Charles Mingus, but an excellent 1958 record date, *For Real!*, with Harold Land, was the last for some time. Despite the urgings and advice of the late Wardell Gray, Hawes had sunk into acute drug dependency. He was imprisoned for heroin possession at a time when his musical importance and influence were at their height. Released in 1963 by order of President John F. Kennedy, Hawes returned to recording for Contemporary and other labels in the USA, Europe and Japan. In the 70s, Hawes recorded studio and festival sessions, sometimes using electric piano. A major figure in the development of modern jazz piano playing, Hawes's less successful later work has tended to overshadow the tremendously important contribution he made in his earlier years.

Selected albums: *The Hampton Hawes Trio* (1951), *The Hampton Hawes Memorial Album* (1952), *The Hampton Hawes Quartet* (1952), *Piano East/West* (Original Jazz Classics 1953), *Shorty Rogers And His Giants* (1953), *Volume 1: The Trio* (Original Jazz Classics 1955), *This Is Hampton Hawes, Vol. 2* (1955), *Everybody Likes Hampton Hawes* (1956), *All Night Session Vols 1, 2, 3* (Original Jazz Classics 1956), *Four!* (Original Jazz Classics 1958), *For Real* (1958), *The Green Leaves Of Summer* (Original Jazz Classics 1964), *Here And Now* (Original Jazz Classics 1965), *The Seance* (Original Jazz Classics 1966), *I'm All Smiles* (1966), *Hampton Hawes In Europe* (1967), *Piano Improvisations* (1967-68), *Spanish Steps* (Black Lion 1968), *The Challenge* (Storyville 1968), *Hampton Hawes In Tokyo* (1968), *Hamp's Piano* (1968), with Martial Solal *Key For Two* (Affinity 1969), *Memory Lane* (1970), *The Two Sides Of Hampton Hawes* (c.1970), *The Hampton Hawes Trio At Montreux* (Fresh Sounds 1971), *Anglo-American Jazz Phase O* (1971), *A Little Copenhagen Night Music* (Freedom 1971), *Universe* (1972), *Blues For Walls* (1973), *Live At The Jazz Showcase In Chicago Vol. 1* (1973), *Playin' By The Yard* (1973), *Northern Windows* (1974), *This Guy's In Love With You* (1975 rec. 1971, reissued as *Live At The Montmartre*), *Hampton Hawes Recorded Live At The Great American Music Hall* (1975), *Killing Me Softly With His Song/Hampton Hawes At The Piano* (1976), *Music* (1978, rec. 1971).

Further reading: *Raise Up Off Me*, Hampton Hawes.

Hawkins, Coleman

b. Coleman Randolph Hawkins, 21 November c.1901, St. Joseph, Missouri, USA, d. 19 May 1969. Coleman Hawkins (aka 'Bean' and 'Hawk') is the colossus of the tenor saxophone, and hence of modern jazz. He invented the instrument as a serious means of expression and continued to be alive to new developments for 40 years. Starting piano lessons at the age of five, he later learned cello and took up tenor saxophone when he was nine years old. Within a few years he was playing dances and appearing in Kansas and Chicago. He attended Washburn College in Topeka and toured as a member of Mamie Smith's Jazz Hounds in 1921. He joined Fletcher Henderson's Orchestra in 1924, a sophisticated New York dance band then coming to terms with the new jazz music - hot and improvised - that Louis Armstrong, who had also joined Henderson in 1924, had brought from New Orleans by way of Chicago. Released in 1926, 'The Stampede' featured Hawkins's first notable solo. In his ten years with the band he transformed the tenor sax - previously a novelty instrument for blues and hokum records - from rather quaint imitations of Armstrong's staccato style into a vehicle for the powerful and suave solos that are the essence of swing. 'St Louis Shuffle' (1927), 'Sugar Foot Stomp' (1931) and 'Hocus Pocus' (1934) are three brilliant sides that trace this evolution. By 1934 jazz had become a global music. Coleman Hawkins left Fletcher Henderson and travelled to Europe, where he was welcomed by the local players. He recorded with Jack Hylton in England. Excluded from a Hylton tour of Germany in 1935 by the Nazis' new racial laws, he joined Theo Masman's Ramblers Dance Orchestra and recorded with them for Decca. In 1937 he met up with Django Reinhardt and recorded some memorable music (Stéphane Grappelli was relegated to piano) and he also played with fellow exile Benny Carter. When war broke out in 1939 Hawkins returned to the USA. There his supremacy on tenor sax had been challenged by the languid yet harmonically sophisticated playing of Lester Young, but his recording of 'Body & Soul' (on 11 October 1939) was a massive hit and established him as a national figure, his confessional tender-but-tough tenor the epitome of jazz. In 1940 he toured with his own 16-piece, appearing at premier New York jazz spots the Arcadia and the Savoy Ballroom, but the days of the big band were numbered. In December 1943 his small combo recordings - 'How Deep Is The Ocean', 'Stumpy' and an irresistible swinger called 'Voodte' - are the apex of swing, though the sense of headlong abandon is akin to the new music of bebop. Bebop was black America's first *avant garde* art form, featuring innovations many established musicians felt moved to denounce. Hawkins loved it. He led an early bebop recording session in February 1944 - featuring Don Byas, Dizzy Gillespie and Max Roach. In 1943 he had formed a sextet with Thelonious Monk, Don Byas and trumpeter Benny Harris and a year later gave Monk his recording debut. Most of 1944 and 1945 were spent on the west coast with a band that included Sir Charles Thompson and Howard McGhee. As featured soloist on Norman Granz's *Jazz At The Philharmonic* tours, trips to Europe for him followed in 1950 and 1954.

The popularity of Stan Getz's interpretation of Lester Young made Hawkins and his ripe sound unfashionable in the 50s, but his strength as a player - and his openness of mind - never left him. In 1957 Thelonious Monk repaid the compliment by inviting him to join his septet, and the application of Hawkins' big, swinging tenor to Monk's paradoxical compositions yielded wonderful results on tunes such as 'Off Minor'. Playing next to young turks such as John Coltrane, Hawkins showed that he still had something to contribute. The classic *The Hawk Flies High* (1957) showed what Hawkins could accomplish in a mainstream setting, while a reunion with his ex-Henderson colleague Henry 'Red' Allen in the same year showed he could also shine in a more traditional context. In the 60s Hawkins kept playing, recording with new tenor star Sonny Rollins. The list of his engagements in that decade records the catholic taste an established elder statesman can afford: Pee Wee Russell, Duke Ellington, Bud Powell, Tommy Flanagan, Eric Dolphy, even an appearance on Max Roach's inflammatory *We Insist! Freedom Now* suite and at a 1966 'Tenors Titan' concert that also featured Rollins, Coltrane, Zoot Sims and Yusef Lateef. He played on the last JATP tour (1967) and toured with Oscar Peterson in 1968, though by now he was increasingly prone to bouts of depression and drinking, exacerbated by a refusal to eat. His death from pneumonia in 1969 marked the end of an era; he was a jazz master whose life-work stretched across six decades of the music's history.

Selected albums: *The Hawk In Paris* (Bluebird 1957), *The Hawk Flies High* (Original Jazz Classics 1957), *Soul* (Prestige 1959), *Hawk Eyes* (Original Jazz Classics 1960), *Encounters Ben Webster* (Verve 1960), *At Ease With Colman Hawkins* (Original Jazz Classics 1961), *Night Hawk* (Original Jazz Classics 1961), *The Hawk Swings* (1962), *The Hawk Relaxes* (Original Jazz Classics 1962), *In A Mellow Tone* (Original Jazz Classics 1962), *Desafinado* (MCA 1963), Septet *Today And Now* (1963), Quartet, with Sonny Rollins *Sonny Meets Hawk* (1963), *Meets The Sax Section* (1964), *Wrapped Tight* (Impulse 1965), *Sirius* (1966). Selected compilations: *The Indispensable Coleman Hawkins: Body & Soul* i (rec. 1927-1956), with the Ramblers *The Hawk In Holland* (1935), one side only *Classic Tenors* (1943), *Body And Soul* ii (Bluebird 1988), *1927-39* (1990), *The Complete Recordings 1929 -31* (1992), *The Bean 1929-49* (Giants Of Jazz 1987), *Body And Soul* iii (1993, rec. 1961), *Rainbow Mist* (1993), *April In Paris* (Bluebird 1992, 1939-56 recordings), *Lady Be Good* (Tring 1993), *The Complete Recordings 1929-1940* (Charly 1993).

Further reading: *Coleman Hawkins Vol 1 1922-44, Vol 2 1945-57*, Jean François Villetard. *The Song Of The Hawk*, John Chilton.

Hawkins, Erskine

b. 26 July 1914, Birmingham, Alabama, USA, d. 12 November 1993, New York, USA. By the time he began playing trumpet at the age of 13, Hawkins had already mastered drums and trombone. It was on trumpet, however, that he established his name as a flamboyant player with an astonishing range. Initially an imitator of Louis Armstrong, Hawkins became leader of the 'Bama State Collegians, an orchestra that he built up into an excellent big band. In the 30s, Hawkins rivalled much bigger names in engagements all across the USA, and in particular at prestigious New York venues such as Roseland and the Savoy. He hired good section men and front-rank soloists, not least trumpeters with whom he happily shared the spotlight. Billed as The Twentieth Century Gabriel, Hawkins made a number of very successful records, including 'After Hours' and 'Tuxedo Junction', the latter a composition by Hawkins and several members of the band which became their theme tune. Hawkins continued to lead his big band throughout the 40s, surviving the winter of 1946/7 which saw the end of many name bands. In the 50s he compromised under financial pressure and reduced the band in size, but regularly reassembled the larger unit for special events. In the 60s and 70s he led small groups at New York hotels and clubs and also made occasional appearances at festivals, including a visit to Europe in 1979. In 1986 he was on board the SS *Norway* for the Fifth Annual Floating Jazz Festival. In much the same manner as his white contemporary Harry James, Hawkins succeeded in com-

bining a spectacular technique and an acute awareness of commercial demands with an innate feeling for good jazz.

Selected albums: *Erskine Hawkins Live At The Savoy Ballroom* (1940), *Sneakin' Out* (1942), *Erskine Hawkins At The Hotel Lincoln, New York* (1946), *Live At The Apollo* (1946-47), *25 Golden Years Of Jazz Vols 1 & 2* (1962), *Erskine Hawkins Reunion Party* (1971). Selected compilations: *Complete Erskine Hawkins Vols 1/2* (RCA 1983, 1938-39 recordings), *Original Tuxedo Junction* (Bluebird 1989).

Hawthorne, Vaughan

One of the less-furiously hyped young alto and soprano saxophonists to emerge in the UK in the late 80s, Hawthorne's playing initially lacked the confidence of some of his better-known contemporaries. While drawing extensively upon the musical heritage of the likes of Charlie Parker and Wayne Shorter, Hawthorne regularly introduces his own compositions into his work and in some respects he is happier, certainly more forthrightly original, in such circumstances. Similarly, he displays more confidence on soprano, which he plays with a full rich and commanding tone, than on the thinner-sounding alto. Albums: *Emanon* (1986-87), *The Path* (1988).

Hayes, Edgar

b. 23 May 1904, Lexington, Kentucky, USA, d. 28 June 1979, San Bernadino, California, USA. Hayes's name will always be associated with his tinkling, cocktail-lounge interpretation of Hoagy Carmichael's 'Stardust', which came backed with a version of 'In The Mood', the coupling provided the piano-playing Hayes with a 1938 hit. After studying at Fisk and Wilberforce Universities, he made his debut with Fess Williams, then formed his own Blue Grass Buddies in Ohio in 1924. Throughout the 20s he worked with various bands eventually becoming pianist-arranger with Mills Blue Rhythm Band in 1931 and retaining his place with the unit after Lucky Millinder assumed leadership three years later. Leaving Millinder in mid-1936, he formed his own band, which debuted in early 1937, recording tracks for Varsity and Decca Records. A healthy-sounding 14-piece band, it initially featured Shelton Hemphill (trumpet), Joe Garland (tenor saxophone), Elmer James (bass) and Crawford Wetherington (alto saxophone), all of whom had partnered Hayes in the Millinder line-up. Also, in the rhythm section, was a 22-year-old drummer named Kenny Clarke, later to become one of the kingpins of bebop. Hayes toured Scandinavia in 1938, recording some tracks for the Swedish Odeon label, but neither these nor the rest of the band's Decca titles produced another 'Stardust' and the band folded in 1941. By 1942 Hayes could be found in California where he played a residency at the Somerset House, Riverside up to 1946, after which he led a combo called the Stardusters, playing at various west coast venues through to the early 50s. During the 60s and 70s Hayes opted for a solo career, performing mainly lounge duties and frequently reprising 'Stardust' for anyone who remembered his bandleading days. Compilation: *Edgar Hayes And His Orchestra 1937-1938* (Original Jazz Classics 1986).

Hayes, Louis

b. 31 May 1937, Detroit, Michigan, USA. Hayes began playing drums at an early age and was leading his own band in Detroit when he was in his mid-teenage years. Still in his teens, he moved to New York where he joined the Horace Silver Quintet. He was with Silver for over two years, finding time to record with John Coltrane and other leading jazz artists. Towards the end of the 50s he joined Cannonball Adderley, with whom he remained until the middle of the next decade when he became a member of Oscar Peterson's trio. After leaving Peterson, Hayes led his own bands, usually sextets, during the late 60s and early 70s, working with artists such as Freddie Hubbard, Kenny Barron, Junior Cook and Woody Shaw. With these bands Hayes toured the USA and Europe and made records. Later, he brought Joe Farrell into his band, by this time a quartet, for more successful tours and records. In the mid-80s Hayes was occasionally a member of the McCoy Tyner trio. An exceptionally gifted bop drummer, Hayes has developed a playing style which is simultaneously subtle and hard driving. His sizzling accompaniment has enhanced some fine hard bop albums and his enthusiasm regularly brings out the best in his front line companions.

Albums: with Horace Silver *Finger Poppin'* (1959), *The Cannonball Adderley Quintet At The Lighthouse* (1960), *Louis Hayes* (1960), with Oscar Peterson *Blues Etude* (1965-66), with Freddie Hubbard *The Hub Of Hubbard* (1969), *Breath Of Life* (1974), *Itchi-Ban* (Timeless 1976), *The Real Thing* (Muse 1977), *Variety Is The Spice* (1979), *Light And Lively* (1989), *Una Max* (1989), *The Crawl* (Candid 1991).

Hayes, Tubby

b. Edward Brian Hayes, 30 January 1935, London, England, d. 8 June 1973. Born into a musical family, Hayes studied violin as a child but took up the tenor saxophone before reaching his teens. He matured rapidly and at the age of 15 became a professional musician. In the early 50s he played with several leading jazzmen, including Kenny Baker, Vic Lewis and Jack Parnell. In the mid-50s he formed his own bop-orientated group and later in the decade was co-leader with Ronnie Scott of the Jazz Couriers. In the early 60s he continued to lead small groups for clubs, concerts, record dates and tours of the UK and USA. By this time Hayes had become adept on other instruments, including the vibraphone, flute and most of the saxophone family. He occasionally formed a big band for concerts and television dates and was active as arranger and composer. Towards the end of the 60s Hayes's health was poor and he underwent a heart operation. He returned to playing, but early in the 70s a second heart operation was deemed necessary and he died on the operating table. A virtuoso performer on tenor saxophone, Hayes was a fluent improviser and through his energy, enthusiasm and encouragement he created a new respect for British musicians, especially in the USA. Hayes was world class almost from the outset of his career, and his death in 1973, while he was still very much in his prime, was a grievous loss to jazz.

Albums: *After Lights Out* (Jasmine 1956), *Tubby Hayes With The Jazz Couriers* (1958), *Message From Britain* (1959), *Tubby's Groove* (Jasmine 1959), *Tubbs In NY* (1961), *Palladium Jazz Date* (1961), *Tubby The Tenor* (1961), *Almost Forgotten* (1961), *Tubby Hayes And The All Stars: Return Visit* (1962), *Tubby's Back In Town* (1962), *A Tribute: Tubbs* (Spotlite 1963), *Tubb's Tours* (Mole 1963), *100% Proof* (1966), *Mexican Green* (1967), *The Tubby Hayes Orchestra* (1969), *Where Am I Going To Live* (Harlequin 1986), *New York Sessions* (CBS 1989), *For Members Only* (Miles Music 1990, rec 1967), *Live 1969* (Harlequin 1991), *200% Proof* (Mastermix 1992), *Jazz Tete A Tete* (Progressive 1994).

Haynes, Roy

13 March 1926, Roxbury, Massachusetts, USA. Haynes began his career in his home town where he played drums with Sabby Lewis's big band. In the early 40s he joined Pete Brown's jump band and later in the decade was on the road with the Luis Russell big band and also played in a small group led by Lester Young. In New York in the late 40s and early 50s, Haynes adapted readily to the demands of bebop and became a valued club gig and record session drummer for Charlie Parker, Bud Powell, Stan Getz, Wardell Gray, Miles Davis, Thelonious Monk, John Coltrane and many other important artists. Haynes's career continued through the 60s and into the 70s with many fruitful collaborations with jazzmen such as George Shearing, Art Farmer, Kenny Burrell and Gary Burton, and in several interesting groups under his own leadership. In the early 80s Haynes recorded with Pat Metheny, Freddie Hubbard, joined Chick Corea for worldwide tours and continued to lead his own bands in New York. A major figure in the development of bop drumming, Haynes's relaxed and retiring personality is reflected in his playing style. Perhaps as a result of such diffidence, he is rather less well-known than many other more aggressive but frequently less accomplished drummers on the modern jazz scene.

Selected albums: *We Three* (Original Jazz Classics 1958), with Thelonious Monk *In Action* (1958), *Portrait Of Art Farmer* (1958), *Just Us* (1960), *Out Of The Afternoon* (Jasmine 1962), with John Coltrane *Selflessness* (1963), *Cracklin'* (1963), *Cymbalism* (1963), *People* (1964), *Hip Ensemble* (c.1971), *Senyah* (c.1973), *Togyu* (1973), *Booty* (c.1974), *Jazz A Confronto 29* (1975), *Thank You, Thank You* (Galaxy 1977), *Vistalite* (1977), *Live At The Riverbop* (1979), with Chick Corea *Trio Music* (1981), with Freddie Hubbard *Sweet Return* (1983), *Equipoise* (Mainstream 1991), *True Or False* (Freelance 1992), *When It Haynes It Roars* (Dreyfus 1993), with Kenny Clarke *Transatlantic Meetings* (Vogue 1993), *Homecoming* (Evidence 1994).

Heard, J.C.

b. James Charles Heard, 8 October 1917, Dayton, Ohio, USA, d. 28 September 1988. Heard grew up in Detroit where he began his professional career at an early age, playing drums in pit bands and on the road with vaudeville shows. Encouraged by Butterbeans And Susie, two of the leading entertainers of the day, at the age of 10 Heard was drumming and dancing as

'The Child Wonder'. Influenced by drummers such as Baby Dodds, Walter Johnson, Jimmy Crawford and Chick Webb, Heard gradually turned to jazz, playing with the bands of Bill Johnson and Sammy Price. He then joined the noted territory band of Milt Larkin. In 1939 he was with Teddy Wilson's musically excellent but commercially ill-fated big band, and remained with Wilson in a small group in the early 40s. Briefly with Benny Carter and Louis Jordan, in 1942 Heard succeeded Cozy Cole in the Cab Calloway orchestra, and later deputized with Count Basie. By this time his style had moved more in line with that of Jo Jones, who became one of his closest friends. Heard also led his own small group and in the late 40s and early 50s worked as a member of Jazz At The Philharmonic with whom he travelled around the world, playing concerts in the UK and Japan. He settled for a while in Japan, where he led big and small bands made up of local musicians, and also played in Hong Kong and the Philippines. In the late 50s and early 60s he performed in many parts of the world with leaders such as Coleman Hawkins, Claude Hopkins and Red Norvo and was reunited with Price and Wilson. In the mid- to late 60s he led his own groups which, by the 70s, had developed into an excellent all-star band. He continued playing throughout the 80s, presenting a big band in a 1985 Tribute to Duke Ellington show in Detroit.

Albums: *JATP: Live At The Nichigeki Theatre, Tokyo* (1953), *J.C. Heard With The Calypso Seven* (1956), *This Is Me, J.C. Heard* (1958), with Claude Hopkins *Let's Jam* (1961), *Alive And Well* (1983). Compilation: *Jazz Off The Air Vol. 4: Cab Calloway And His Orchestra* (1943-46).

Heard, John

b. 3 July 1938, Pittsburgh, Pennsylvania, USA. After starting out on saxophones, Heard taught himself to play bass while a teenager. He first attracted serious attention in the early and mid-60s, working with artists such as Tommy Turrentine and Al Jarreau. Towards the end of the decade he was with Sonny Rollins, then settled on the west coast where he became a long-serving member of several bands, including the Ahmad Jamal trio, Count Basie's big band and small recording groups, and Toshiko Akiyoshi's group. He was also first call bass player for the big bands occasionally assembled by Louie Bellson, with whom he visited the UK in the late 70s and early 80s. He then spent time with Oscar Peterson, Cal Tjader, George Duke, Joe Williams, Nancy Wilson, Tal Farlow and many other leading singers and jazz musicians. The quality of the company he keeps is eloquent testimony to Heard's considerable skills. Whether playing in a big band, where his powerful pulse urges along the ensemble, or subtly providing accompaniment to pianists, guitarists or singers, Heard has established an enviable reputation amongst his peers in the jazz world, although he remains relatively little known to audiences.

Albums: with Cal Tjader *Live At The Funky Quarters* (1972), with George Duke *Faces In Reflections* (1974), with Count Basie *Basie & Zoot* (1975), with Oscar Peterson *The Silent Partner* (1979), with Peterson *The London Concert* (1982).

Heath Brothers

James Edward (Jimmy) (b. 25 October 1926, Philadelphia, Pennsylvania, USA; composer, arranger, tenor and soprano saxophones, flute), Percy (b. 30 April 1923, Wilmington, North Carolina, USA; bass) and Albert, 'Tootie' (b. 31 May 1935, Philadelphia, Pennsylvania, USA; drums). They all have had distinguished and prolific careers individually. They worked together as an 'official' Heath Brothers band in the late 50s and produced *Triple Threat*. The concept was revived after Jimmy and Percy appeared on Albert's debut album under his own name in 1973. When the Modern Jazz Quartet, Percy's regular band for 22 years, was disbanded in 1974 the idea seemed more practicable, and in 1975 the brothers reformed with pianist Stanley Cowell. As the band moved into the 80s it expanded the line-up to include guitar and extra percussion. Albert left in 1978 because of a disagreement over musical direction with Jimmy and Percy.

Albums: *Marchin' On* (Strata East 1975), *Passing Thru* (c.1978), *In Motion* (1979), *Live At The Public Theatre* (1979), *Expressions Of Life* (1980), *Brotherly Love* (Antilles 1981), *Brothers And Others* (1983).

Heckstall-Smith, Dick

b. 26 September 1934, Ludlow, Shropshire, England. After first playing soprano saxophone, Heckstall-Smith turned to the tenor saxophone. While studying at Cambridge in the early 50s he began leading the university's jazz band. Towards the end of the decade he worked in London, playing with various bands including that led by Sandy Brown. In addition to playing in jazz bands, in the late 50s and throughout the 60s he also played in bands led by blues and rock artists including the seminal R&B Organisation led by Graham Bond. He was with John Mayall on his pioneering *Bare Wires* and was a founder member of the influential Jon Hiseman's Colosseum. In the early 70s Heckstall-Smith led his own band, DHS1/Manchild, and later in the decade formed Big Chief. In the early 80s he played with Bo Diddley and thereafter freelanced extensively with jazz, jazz-rock, blues and blues-rock bands, in particular developing an interesting working relationship with John Etheridge. Unlike some musicians who have tried, Heckstall-Smith has successfully managed the interchanges necessitated by his eclectic musical tastes without any discernible loss of authenticity and commitment. In performance, his playing readily accommodates the needs of the prevailing musical format, ranging as it does from post-bop jazz to the robustness of the contemporary blues scene. In recent years Heckstall-Smith has constantly toured in Europe where his blistering and sometimes exhilarating playing is appreciated more than at home. A critical re-appraisal is long-overdue for one of Britain's leading saxophonists.

Albums: with Jon Hiseman *Collector's Colosseum* (1968-71), *Woza Nasu* (Interoceter 1990), *Live 1990* (L&R 1990), *Dick Heckstall-Smith Quartet* (L&R 1991), *Obsession Free* (R&M 1992), *A Story Ended* (reissued Sequel 1993).

Further reading: *The Smallest Place In The World*, Dick Heckstall-Smith.

Hefti, Neal

b. 29 October 1922, Hastings, Nebraska, USA. One of the most influential big band arrangers of the 40s and 50s, Hefti's early charts were played by the Nat Towles band in the late 30s. His material was also used by Earl Hines; however, his first real taste of the big time came when he joined Charlie Barnet in 1942 and then moved into the Woody Herman band in 1944. Both engagements were as a member of the trumpet section, but his writing became steadily more important than his playing. For Herman he arranged many of the band's most popular recordings, including 'The Good Earth' and 'Wild Root', and was co-arranger with Ralph Burns of 'Caldonia'. In 1946 Hefti's charts were among those used by the ill-fated Billy Butterfield big band and by Charlie Ventura's equally short-lived band. In the late 40s he wrote for what was one of the best of Harry James's bands; in the mid-50s, along with Ernie Wilkins and Nat Pierce, he helped to give the Count Basie band the new distinctive, tighter style which led to a wholesale re-evaluation of big band music, especially in the UK. Throughout the 50s and 60s Hefti was deeply involved in composing for films and television (including the theme for the US *Batman* television series) and, while much of his work in these quarters was geared to the demands of the medium, there were many moments when he was able to infuse his work with echoes of his jazz heritage. Throughout those years and into the 70s Hefti periodically formed big bands either for club, concert or record dates. The tradition of precise, disciplined arranging, of which Hefti was one of the more important exponents, continues to make itself heard in the work of Sam Nestico, which has proved immensely popular with college and university bands on both sides of the Atlantic.

Albums: *Coral Reef* (1951-52), *Pardon My Doo-wah* (1954), *Light And Right* (c.1954), *Hot 'N' Hearty* (1955), with Count Basie *Basie* (1957), *Basie Plays Hefti* (1958). Compilations: *The Best Of Woody Herman* (1944-48 recordings), *The Band With Young Ideas* (Jasmine 1893).

Hemingway, Gerry

b. 23 March 1955, New Haven, Connecticut, USA. Hemingway comes from a musical family - his grandmother was a concert pianist, his father studied composition with Paul Hindemith - and he was attracted to the drums 'from the first'. A rock fan as a teenager, he was later seduced by the jazz heard in New York's nightclubs and, back in New Haven, began to play with Anthony Davis and George Lewis, both studying at nearby Yale, and Leo Smith, who had recently settled in the area. Hemingway attended the Berklee College Of Music but hated it, dropping out after one semester. Returning to New Haven, he formed a group, Advent, which later turned into the Anthony Davis Quartet (with Davis, Hemingway, Mark Helias and Jay Hoggard). He studied privately with Alan Dawson, attended classes in Indian and West African drumming at Yale and Wesleyan universities, played a series of solo percussion concerts and also began a long working relationship with Ray Anderson. In the late 70s Hemingway set up his own label, Auricle, released his debut *Kwambe* and then *Oahspe*, the latter also the name of the trio he formed with Anderson and Helias. In 1980 he toured Europe with Anderson's quartet, recording *Harrisburg Half Life*, and in 1981 - by now living in New York - released *Solo Works*, inspired in part by his collaborations with composer/electronic music expert/saxophonist Earl Howard. In 1983 he joined the Anthony Braxton Quartet, of which he remains a member, and has toured and recorded with the group many times, thereby establishing himself on the international stage. Oahspe, renamed on occasion the Ray Anderson Trio and BassDrumBone, continued to perform sporadically and Hemingway has also played with Davis's group Episteme (*Undine*), with Marilyn Crispell (*Circles, The Kitchen Concert*) and in Reggie Workman's ensemble. By the late 80s he had become well-known in Europe, following a 1985 UK tour with Derek Bailey, frequent concerts in Holland, often with cellist Ernst Reijseger (currently a member of Hemingway's own quintet) and, most recently, his work as a member of German pianist Georg Gräwe's trio (*Sonic Fiction*). He has also released three albums of his own music on European labels: one is the solo *Tubworks*, the others quintet sessions (*Outerbridge Crossing, Special Detail*) which reveal his love of darker sonorities. Back in New York, he works with the recently-formed quartet Tambastics (with Robert Dick, Mark Dresser and Denman Maroney), whose debut recording was released in 1992. Hemingway is expert at coaxing an incredible range of timbrel colours from his kit, even if it means using unorthodox means such as flicking the cymbals with a towel or rolling coins across his snare drum.

Albums: *Kwambe* (1979), *Oahspe* (1979), *Solo Works* (1981), with Ray Anderson, Mark Helias *Right Down Your Alley* (1984), with Anderson, Helias *You Be* (1986), *Outerbridge Crossing* (Sound Aspects 1987, rec 1985), with BassDrumBone *Woofesloo* (1987), *Tubworks* (1988, rec 1983-87), *Special Detail* (Hat Art 1991), *Tambastics* (1992), *Down To The Wire* (Hat Art 1993), *Demon Chaser* (Hat Art 1994).

Hemphill, Julius

b. 24 January 1938, Fort Worth, Texas, USA. Growing up in the early 40s meant that Hemphill was surrounded by many kinds of music - swing, rural blues, R&B, gospel. He was also aware of modern jazz and was drawn towards 'cool' players like Lee Konitz. He studied harmony, clarinet and saxophone with John Carter in high school, played with a band in the US army (1964) and accompanied Ike Turner. He also attended classes at the Northern Texas State University. In 1968 he moved to St. Louis where he became a founder of BAG, the Black Artists Group, and concentrated on the alto saxophone. In 1971 he formed a group with pianist John Hicks and toured the college circuit. *Kawaida*, a multimedia event comprising music, dance and Hemphill's own lyrics, was presented at St Louis's Washington University in 1972. The same year he formed his own Mbari Records label and recorded *Dogon A.D.* (later reissued on Arista Freedom), played in the film *The Orientation Of Sweet Willie Rollbar* and made a guest appearance on Kool And The Gang's *Hustler's Convention*. He played with Anthony Braxton in Chicago (later guesting on his debut album for

Arista) and made appearances in Stockholm and Paris in 1973. The next year he played on Lester Bowie's *Fast Last*. In the mid-70s Hemphill recorded two solo double-album sets of multi-tracked alto and soprano saxophones and flute, *Blue Boyé* and the 'audiodrama' *Roi Boyé & The Gotham Minstrels*. In 1977 he became a founder member (and principal composer) of the World Saxophone Quartet, a title that was no idle boast, and they became probably his most visible showcase. A string of highly acclaimed albums and festival appearances continued until his departure from the group in 1990. His intense, earthy, nasal sound and flaring ideas mark him as one of the foremost players of his generation. He frequently appears in duets with altoist Oliver Lake and in 1980 led a big band at the Newport Festival.

His small-group album *Flat-Out Jump Suite*, also from 1980, showed how he could maintain his personality on the tenor saxophone. In the next two years he recorded with old friends Baikidaa Carroll and Kalaparush Maurice McIntyre, while an appearance on Jean-Paul Bourelly's *Jungle Cowboy* (1986) showed how well his deep understanding of blues enabled him to relate to the new post-harmolodic concepts of the M-Base generation. However, his own attempts to create a populist musical fusion with his JAH Band proved less successful. In 1989 he premiered the latest version of his 'saxophone opera', *Long Tongue*, an epic combination of big band arrangements, free playing and colloquial black speech rhythms, on which he'd been working since the early 80s. Though serious injuries from a car crash in 1982 have restricted his activities a little, Hemphill remains at the forefront of creative music, his long-standing interest in multi-media events still fuelling one of the most inventive and original composing/arranging brains in contemporary jazz.

Albums: *Dogon A.D.* (1972), *Blue Boyé* (c.70s), *Roi Boyé & The Gotham Minstrels* (1977), *Raw Materials And Residuals* (Sackville 1978), with Oliver Lake *Buster Bee* (Sackville 1978), *Coon Bid'ness* (Freedom 1979), with Abdul Wadud *Live In New York* (Red Pepper 1979), *Flat-Out Jump Suite* (Black Saint 1980), *Big Band* (Elektra 1988), *Georgie Blue* (Minor 1990), *Fat Man And The Hard Blues* (Black Saint 1992), *Live From The New Music Cafe* (Music And Arts 1992).

Henderson, Bill

b. William Randall Henderson, 19 March 1930, Chicago, Illinois, USA. He began singing as a toddler but delayed full entry into show business until he was in his early twenties. In the early 50s he sang in and around Chicago, often with Ramsey Lewis. At the end of the decade he visited New York, playing and recording with a number of leading bop musicians including Horace Silver, before returning to Chicago and Lewis. In the early 60s he had stints with Oscar Peterson and Count Basie, then relocated to Los Angeles where he began a new career as an actor. He did not abandon singing and continued to perform whenever opportunities arose, including work on television and recording. Two of his albums, *Street Of Dreams* and *Tribute To Johnny Mercer* were nominated for Grammy awards. A vibrant, blues-influenced singer with great

rhythmic drive, Henderson's preference for an acting career has kept him from establishing the wide international reputation his talent deserves.

Albums: *Bill Henderson Sings* (1958), *Bill Henderson With The Oscar Peterson Trio* (1963), *Live At The Times* (Discovery 1975), *Street Of Dreams* (Discovery 1979), *Tribute To Johnny Mercer* (Discovery 1984).

Henderson, Eddie

b. 26 October 1940, New York, USA. Henderson learned the trumpet at school and studied music at the San Francisco Conservatory of Music (1954-57). There followed three years in the Air Force. He was already playing enough music to be encouraged by Miles Davis to develop his jazz. He returned to academic study, graduating in zoology (1964) and then in medicine (1968) and has continued to work as a general practitioner and psychiatrist alongside his musical career. During summer holidays he played with John Handy and then with Handy and Philly Joe Jones when he graduated. He played with Herbie Hancock's sextet (1970-73) before spending six months with Art Blakey's Jazz Messengers. Since then he has led his own jazz-rock groups and even achieved chart success with a track from *Comin' Through* (1977).

Albums: with Herbie Hancock *Crossings* (1973), *Realisation* (1973), *Inside Out* (1973), *Sunburst* (1975), *Heritage* (1976), *Comin' Through* (1977), *Mahal* (1978), *Running To Your Love* (Capitol 1979), *Think Of Me* (Steeplechase 1990)

Henderson, Fletcher

b. 18 December 1897, Cuthbert, Georgia, USA, d. 28 December 1952. One of the most important figures in the development of big band music, in the early 30s Henderson set the standards by which early big band jazz was measured. He did this through a combination of selecting leading jazz players for his band and, together with Don Redman, creating a format for big band arrangements that was taken up by all but a handful of arrangers in the next 30 years. Yet, curiously enough, Henderson became a bandleader almost by accident, and an arranger through force of circumstance, rather than by deliberate intent. After gaining a degree in chemistry at Atlanta State University, he travelled to New York in 1920 to continue his studies. As a means of supporting himself he drifted into working as a song-plugger for the Pace-Handy Music Company. Then he became manager of Harry Pace's Black Swan Record Company, playing piano on many of the company's record dates. He next put together a band with which to accompany Ethel Waters on tour. Soon he was leading a band at the Little Club near Broadway, a popular nightspot known by its frequenters as the 'Club Alabam'. The band was really a loose-knit collection of like-minded musicians who elected Henderson as leader because, as Redman put it, 'He made a nice appearance and was well-educated and we figured all that would help in furthering our success'. This was the start of Henderson's ascendancy. Later that same year, 1924, he took his band into Roseland, one of New York's most famous ballrooms. The contract was for four years, but Henderson's connection with Roseland continued intermittently for 10 years. In those days the route to success lay along the path charted by Paul Whiteman, offering the public a selection of tangoes, waltzes and other popular dance tunes. Billed as 'the coloured Paul Whiteman', Henderson's was barely recognizable as a jazz group, despite the presence of outstanding jazzmen such as Coleman Hawkins. The band's musical policy underwent a marked change, however, with the arrival in its ranks of Louis Armstrong. He was there for about a year, leaving towards the end of 1925, but that brief stay forced Don Redman into completely revising the way he wrote his arrangements for the band. Redman's charts simulated the polyphonic New Orleans style of ensemble playing, pitting one section against another and giving full rein to the solo talents of the individual musicians.

By 1927 the band was the most talked-about in New York and, apart from Hawkins, included Tommy Ladnier, Jimmy Harrison, Charlie Green and Buster Bailey. Henderson was ambitious for success, even though he was not an especially astute businessman and had a pleasant unaggressive manner. However, his circumstances were about to alter in a way no one could have forecast. In mid-summer 1927 Redman left to become musical director of McKinney's Cotton Pickers. His departure meant that Henderson had to take up the bulk of the arranging duties for the band, a task he performed admirably. Unfortunately, in 1928 he was involved in a road accident and while his physical injuries were slight he underwent a change of personality. As his wife later said, 'He never had much business qualities anyhow, but after that accident, he had even less'. The most obvious effect of the change was that all ambition deserted him, leaving just an easygoing, casual individual. In the brashly commercial world of early 30s big band music this was not the way for a bandleader to achieve success.

In 1929 Henderson's lackadaisical attitude caused a mass walkout by his star performers, but the following year he re-formed and tried again. Despite the departure of Redman, Henderson had continued to write skilful arrangements, developing ideas for saxophone voicings which, given the fact that he mostly used only a three-piece section, were remarkably intricate. The 1931 Henderson band was an astonishing array of top-flight jazzmen. The trumpets included Rex Stewart and Bobby Stark, Benny Morton was in the trombone section while the saxophones were Hawkins, Russell Procope and Edgar Sampson, himself a leading big-band arranger. The remaining years of the decade saw Henderson leading star-studded bands. In 1934 he had Red Allen and Joe Thomas in the trumpet section, while the 1936 edition included Roy Eldridge, Omer Simeon, Chu Berry, Israel Crosby and 'Big' Sid Catlett. In addition to his arrangements being played by his own band, they were also providing the basis for the successes enjoyed by others, notably Benny Goodman. However, despite the quality of the charts and the stature of the men in his band, Henderson's star was fast-waning. His indifference to commercial considerations rubbed off on his musicians and led in turn to disaffected and diminishing audiences. By 1939 Henderson had had enough of falling attendances, hassles with promoters, unrest in his own

ranks and all the many pressures that came the way of big band leaders during the swing era. He folded his band and joined Goodman as staff arranger and pianist. During the 40s he continued to write for Goodman and others, and once in a while formed a band for special dates. Late in the decade he returned to his earlier role as accompanist to Ethel Waters. In 1950 he fell in the street, apparently as the result of a stroke. Partially incapacitated, he lived for a further year or so, dying on 28 December 1952.

Henderson was one of the most important figures in the development of big band music, although in abbreviated jazz history he is sometimes elevated to a degree that underplays the immense contributions made by others. Of those connected at one time or another with the Henderson band, Redman was an innovator, Sampson was a major contributor and a very talented composer and Horace Henderson, Fletcher's younger brother, was busy writing in the same vein. In other bands, the work of Charlie Dixon and Benny Carter also advanced along similar lines. Later, there would be refinements on the work of Redman and Henderson by gifted musicians such as Sy Oliver, Quincy Jones, Buster Harding, Neal Hefti and others; but until major shifts of style occurred later, the course Henderson had established remained the most significant in big band music. Even today, many big bands - including even some *avant gardists* such as the Sun Ra Arkestra - still trace the paths charted by a man who became a band leader by chance, whose career was blighted by an accident, and whose death came in much the same way at a time when he was all but forgotten.

Selected albums: *The Fletcher Henderson Septet Live In Concert* (1947), *The Fletcher Henderson Sextet* (1950). Compilations: *Fletcher Henderson Vols. 1 & 2* (1923-25), *A Study In Frustration* (1923-38), *The Indispensable Fletcher Henderson Vols 1/2* (Jazz Tribute 1986, 1927-36 recordings), *Under The Harlem Moon* (Living Era 1990), *Hocus Pocus* (RCA 1990), *Fletcher Henderson And His Orchestra 1927* (Original Jazz Classics 1991), with Louis Armstrong *Complete 1924 - 1925* (1993), *Fletcher Henderson & His Orchestra* (Tring 1993).

Henderson, Horace

b. 22 November 1904, Cuthbert, Georgia, USA, d. 29 August 1988. After studying music formally, Henderson led a college band in semi-professional engagements and this eventually became a full-time occupation. The band met with variable success and from time to time Henderson gave up and played piano in other bands, sometimes handing over the leadership. Among the beneficiaries of his changing fortunes were Don Redman and Benny Carter. In 1933 he joined the band led by his elder brother, Fletcher Henderson, for whom he wrote many arrangements although credit sometimes went astray through confusion over names. He also wrote extensively for other big bands of the swing era. In the late 30s Henderson was again active as a bandleader and resumed once more after military service in World War II. He spent some time as accompanist to Lena Horne, and in the 50s continued to lead a big band, avoiding the decline in business by working in theatrical shows and casinos. Inevitably overshadowed by his brother,

Horace Henderson was an effective, if less innovative arranger and a better pianist than Fletcher. He continued to lead a band, mostly in Colorado, throughout the 60s and into the 70s.

Albums: *Horace Henderson 1950* (1950), *Horace Henderson And His Orchestra* (1954). Compilation: *Horace Henderson 1940* (1940).

Henderson, Joe

b. 24 April 1937, Lima, Ohio, USA. Tenor saxophonist Henderson studied in Detroit and after army service, he moved to New York in 1962. He first made his mark on the Blue Note label, recording with Kenny Dorham (*Una Mas*), Lee Morgan (*The Sidewinder*) and Andrew Hill (*Black Fire, Point Of Departure*), as well as leading several sessions of his own. He later worked with Horace Silver (*Song For My Father*) and, towards the end of the 60s, co-led the Jazz Communicators with Freddie Hubbard before joining the Herbie Hancock sextet. In 1970 he played briefly with Blood, Sweat And Tears. In the early 70s he led his own groups, recording a rather erratic series of albums for Milestone, then moved to California, where he became involved in teaching. In the 80s he led an otherwise all-women quartet (which included drummer Cindy Blackman) and recorded for the Italian Red label. His most acclaimed album of recent times, though, was the two-volume *The State Of The Tenor*, a trio set (with Ron Carter and Al Foster) recorded live in 1985 at the Village Vanguard for Blue Note, whose co-founder Alfred Lion declared it 'one of the best ever made' for the label. An acknowledged master of modern tenor craft, Henderson's chief influences were John Coltrane and Sonny Rollins, but he has fashioned a personal style that blends a finespun melodicism with logic, ingenuity and a dab of terse abstraction.

Selected albums: *Page One* (Blue Note 1963), *Our Thing* (1964), *In 'N' Out* (Blue Note 1964), *Inner Urge* (Blue Note 1965), *Mode For Joe* (Blue Note 1966), *The Kicker* (Original Jazz Classics 1967), *Tetragon* (BGP 1971), *Black Is The Colour* (1972), with Alice Coltrane *Elements* (1973), *Multiple* (Original Jazz Classics 1973), *In Japan* (1974), *Black Narcissus* (Milestone 1976), with others *Mirror Mirror* (MPS 1980), *The State Of The Tenor, Volumes 1 & 2* (Blue Note 1987, rec. 1985), *An Evening With Henderson, Haden & Foster* (Red 1989), *Lush Life* (Verve 1992), *The Standard Joe* (Red 1992), *So Near, So Far (Musings For Miles)* (1993), *Barcelona* (Enja 1993). Compilations: *The Best Of Joe Henderson* (Blue Note 1985), *The Blue Note Years* (Blue Note 1994, 4 CD set), *The Milestone Years* (1994).

Henry, Ernie

b. 3 September 1926, New York City, New York, USA, d. 29 December 1957. Henry began playing alto saxophone at the age of 12. Although he was never a brilliant technician, his enthusiasm and the depth of emotion in his playing brought him to the attention of Tadd Dameron, with whom he worked in 1947. This association led to his playing with many leading bebop artists of the day, notably Max Roach and Dizzy Gillespie. In the early and mid-50s Henry was with the bands of Illinois Jacquet and Thelonious Monk and also recorded for Riverside under his own name. However, his career was increasingly interrupted because of drug addiction problems. Later in the decade he joined Gillespie's big band; but after a long period of abstinence, he resumed drug-taking and died from a heroin overdose in December 1957. Although a disciple of Charlie Parker, Henry's playing denotes the presence of a strong musical personality, and many of his recordings, particularly those made with Monk, show a major talent in embryo.

Albums: with Thelonious Monk *Brilliant Corners* (1956), *Presenting Ernie Henry* (1956), *Seven Standards And A Blues* (1957), *Last Chorus* (1956-57 recordings).

Herman, Woody

b. Woodrow Charles Herman, 16 May 1913, Milwaukee, Wisconsin, USA, d. 29 October 1987. A child prodigy, Herman sang and tap-danced in local clubs before touring as a singer in vaudeville. To improve his act he took up the saxophone and later the clarinet, all by the age of 12. By his mid-teens he was sufficiently accomplished to play in a band, and he went on to work in a string of dance bands during the late 20s and early 30s. Last in this line was Isham Jones, Herman first being in Isham Jones's Juniors, with whom he recorded early in 1936. When Jones folded the band later that year, Herman was elected leader by a nucleus of musicians who wanted to continue. Initially a co-operative group, the band included flügelhorn player Joe Bishop, bassist Walt Yoder, drummer Frank Carlson and trombonist Neil Reid. With a positive if uncommercial view of what they wanted to achieve, they were billed as 'The Band That Plays The Blues' and gradually built a following during the swing era. The success of their recordings of 'Golden Wedding', a Jiggs Noble re-working of 'La Cinquantaine', and especially Bishop's 'At The Woodchoppers' Ball' helped the band's fortunes. During the early 40s numerous personnel changes took place, some dictated by the draft, others by a gradual shift in style. By 1944 Herman was leading the band which eventually became labelled as the First Herd. Included in this powerhouse were trumpeters Ray Wetzel, Neal Hefti and Pete Candoli, trombonist Bill Harris, tenor saxophonist Joe 'Flip' Phillips and the remarkable rhythm section of Ralph Burns, Billy Bauer, Chubby Jackson and Dave Tough, to which was added vibraphonist Marjorie Hyams. This band made several records which were not only musically excellent but were also big sellers, amongst them 'Apple Honey', 'Caldonia', 'Northwest Passage' and 'Goosey Gander'. During the next year or so the band's personnel remained fairly stable, although the brilliant if unreliable Tough was replaced in late 1945 by Don Lamond, and they continued to make good records, including 'Bijou', 'Your Father's Mustache', 'Wild Root' and 'Blowin' Up A Storm'. In 1946 the band still included Candoli, Harris, Phillips, Bauer, Jackson and Lamond and amongst the newcomers were trumpeters Sonny Berman, Shorty Rogers and Conrad Gozzo and vibraphonist Red Norvo. The First Herd played a concert at Carnegie Hall to great acclaim but, despite the band's continuing popularity, at the end of this same year,

1946, Herman temporarily disbanded because of economic difficulties. The following year he was back with his Second Herd, known to posterity as the 'Four Brothers' band. This band represented a particularly modern approach to big band music, playing bop-influenced charts by Jimmy Giuffre and others. Most striking, however, and the source of the band's name, was the saxophone section. With Sam Marowitz and Herbie Steward on altos, Stan Getz and Zoot Sims, tenors, and Serge Chaloff, baritone, the section was thrustingly modern; and when Steward doubled on tenor, they created a deeper-toned sound that was utterly different to any other band of the time.

The concept of the reed section had originated with Gene Roland, whose rehearsal band had included Getz, Sims, Steward and Giuffre. Heard by Burns and hired by Herman, these musicians helped create a new excitement and this band was another enormously successful group. Although the modern concepts took precedence, there was still room for straight ahead swingers. The brass section at this time included Rogers, Marky Markowitz and Ernie Royal and trombonist Earl Swope. The rhythm section included Lamond and vibraphonist Terry Gibbs. The reed section was dominant, however, and when Steward was replaced by Al Cohn, it was by far the best in the land. Apart from 'Four Brothers' the band had other successful records, including 'Keen And Peachy', 'The Goof And I' and 'Early Autumn'. This last piece was written by Burns to round out a three-part suite, 'Summer Sequence', he had composed earlier and which had already been recorded. The extra part allowed the record company to release a four-sided set, and Getz's solo on 'Early Autumn' was the first example of the saxophonist's lyrical depths to make an impression upon the jazz world. Unfortunately, despite its successes, the band wasn't quite popular enough, perhaps being a little ahead of its time. Once again Herman folded, only to re-form almost at once. Numbering the Herman Herds was never easy but the leader himself named his early 50s group as the Third Herd. Although lacking the precision of the Four Brothers band and the raw excitement of the First Herd, the new band was capable of swinging superbly. As before, Herman had no difficulty in attracting top-flight musicians, including Red Rodney, Urbie Green, Kai Winding, Richie Kamuca, Bill Perkins, Monty Budwig and Jake Hanna. Of particular importance to the band at this time (and for the next few years) was Nat Pierce, who not only played piano but also wrote many fine arrangements and acted as straw boss. The times were hostile to big bands, however, and by the mid-50s Herman was working in comparative obscurity. Members of the band, who then included Bill Berry, Bobby Lamb, Kamuca, Budwig and Harris, wryly described this particular Herman group as the 'un-Herd'. Towards the end of the decade Herman was still fighting against the tide, but was doing it with some of the best available musicians: Cohn, Sims, Don Lanphere, Bob Brookmeyer, Pierce, Kamuca, Perkins and Med Flory. During the 60s and 70s Herman's bands were given various informal tags; the Swinging Herd, the Thundering Herd. Mostly they did as these names suggested, thundering and swinging through some excellent charts and with many fine sidemen many of whom were culled from the universities. Other leaders did this, of course, but Herman always ensured that he was far from being the solitary veteran on a bandstand full of beginners. He kept many older hands on board to ensure the youngsters had experienced models from whom they could draw inspiration.

Among the sidemen during these years were Pierce, Hanna, Bill Chase, baritone saxophonist Nick Brignola, Sal Nistico, tenor saxophonist Carmen Leggio, John Von Ohlen, Cecil Payne, Carl Fontana, Dusko Goykovich and trombonists Henry Southall and Phil Wilson. In the late 60s Herman dabbled with jazz-rock but, although he subsequently kept a few such numbers in the band's book, it was not an area in which he was comfortable. In 1976 Herman played a major concert at Carnegie Hall, celebrating the 40th anniversary of his first appearance there. As the 80s began, Herman's health was poor and he might have had thoughts of retirement; he had, after all, been performing for a little over 60 years. Unfortunately, this was the time he discovered that his manager for many years had systematically embezzled funds set aside for taxes. Now Herman was not only flat broke and in danger of eviction from his home in the Hollywood Hills, but he also owed the IRS millions of dollars. Forced to play on, he continued to lead bands on punishing tours around the world, tours which were hugely successful but were simultaneously exacerbating his poor physical condition. In 1986 he celebrated 50 years as a bandleader with a tour that featured long-standing sideman Frank Tiberi, baritone saxophonist Mike Brignola, trumpeter Bill Byrne and bassist Lynn Seaton. The following year he was still on the road - and also on the sidewalk, when a gold star in his name was laid along Hollywood Boulevard's Walk of Fame. In March of that same year the Herman Herd, whatever number this one might be, was still thundering away at concerts, some of which fortunately, were recorded. But it could not, of course, go on forever, and Herman died in October 1987. As a clarinettist and saxophonist, sometimes playing alto, latterly soprano, Herman was never a virtuoso player in the manner of swing era contemporaries such as Benny Goodman or Artie Shaw. Unlike theirs, his playing was deeply rooted in the blues, and he brought to his music an unshakeable commitment to jazz. Despite the inevitable ups and downs of his career as a big band leader, he stuck to his principles and if he ever compromised it was always, somehow, on his own terms. He composed little, although many of the First Herd's greatest successes were head arrangements conceived and developed on the bandstand or in rehearsal. Herman's real skills lay in his ability to pick the right people for his band, to enthuse them, and to ensure that they never lost that enthusiasm. In selecting for his band he had patience and an excellent ear. He knew what he wanted and he nearly always got it. Over the many years he led a band, scores of musicians passed through the ranks, many of them amongst the finest in jazz. No one ever had a bad word to say about him. He was admired, respected and loved; even more by his musicians than by his adoring audiences.

Selected albums: *Live At The Hollywood Palladium* (1951),

with Charlie Parker *Bird With The Herd* (1951), *Thundering Herd* (1953), *Woody Herman With The Erroll Garner Trio* (1954), *The Third Herd Live In Stockholm Vols 1 & 2* (1954), *Jackpot* (1955), *Road Band* (1955), *Woody Herman With Barney Kessel And His Orchestra* (1957), *Woody Herman And His Orchestra* i (1957), *Woody Herman Live Featuring Bill Harris Vols 1 & 2* (1957), *Live At Peacock Lake, Hollywood* (1958), *The Fourth Herd* (1959), *Woody Herman's New Big Band At The Monterey Jazz Festival* (1959), *1960* (1960), *The Woody Herman Quartet* (1962), *Woody Herman And His Orchestra* ii (1962), *Live At Basin Street West* (1963), *Encore* (1963), *The New World Of Woody Herman* (1963), *Woody Herman At Harrah's Club* (1964), *Woody's Winners* (1965), *Live In Seattle* (1967), *Light My Fire* (1968), *Heavy Exposure* (1969), *Woody* (1970), *Brand New* (1971), *The Raven Speaks* (1972), *Giant Steps* (1973), *Woody Herman And His Orchestra* iii (1974), *Herd At Montreux* (1974), *Woody Herman With Frank Sinatra* (1974), *Children Of Lima* (1974), *King Cobra* (1975), *Woody Herman In Warsaw* (1976), *40th Anniversary: Carnegie Hall Concert* (1976), *Lionel Hampton Presents Woody Herman* (1977), *Road Father* (1978), *Together: Flip & Woody* (1978), *Chick, Donald, Walter & Woodrow* (1978) *Woody Herman And Friends At The Monterey Jazz Festival* (1979), *Woody Herman Presents A Concord Jam Vol. 1* (1980), *Woody Herman Presents Four Others Vol. 2* (1981), *Live At The Concord Jazz Festival* (1981), *Live In Chicago* (1981), *Aurex Jazz Festival '82* (1982), *Woody Herman Presents A Great American Evening* (1983), *50th Anniversary Tour* (1986), *Woody's Gold Star* (1987). Compilations: *The Band That Plays The Blues* (1937-42 recordings), *The V-Disc Years Vol. 1* (1944-45 recordings), *The First Herd* (1945 recordings), *The Best Of Woody Herman* (1945-47 recordings), *Woody Herman At Carnegie Hall* (1946 recordings), *Summer Sequence* (1946-47 recordings), *The Thundering Herds Vols 1-3* (40s recordings), *Early Autumn* (1952-53 recordings), *The V Disc Years 1944 - 46* (Hep Jazz 1993).
Further reading: *Woody Herman*, Steve Voce. *The Woodchopper's Ball*, Woody Herman with Stuart Troup.

Herring, Vincent

b. 19 November, 1964, California, USA. One of the most exciting young players working in the hard bop idiom, he idolizes Cannonball Adderley and was chosen by Cannonball's brother Nat Adderley to play in the Cannonball Adderley Legacy Band. His playing also evokes Jackie McLean in its acrid tone and incisive phraseology. In July 1984, when his band was playing in the Manhattan streets, Herring was approached by record-label proprietor Sam Parkins with the offer of a recording date. Since then he has gigged or recorded with many distinguished figures, including Horace Silver, Cedar Walton, Art Blakey, McCoy Tyner, Larry Coryell, Jack DeJohnette, Beaver Harris, Lionel Hampton, and David Murray. In 1988 in Paris he took part in an alto summit with Phil Woods, Frank Morgan, Bob Mover, C. Sharps and McLean. In 1990 he toured Europe with his own quintet to much acclaim.
Albums: *Scene One* (1989), *American Experience* (S&R 1990),

with Nat Adderley: *Talkin' About You* (1991), with Adderley *We Remember Cannon* (1991), *Evidence* (Landmark 1991), *Dawnbird* (Landmark 1994).

Hession, Paul

b. 19 September 1956, Leeds, England. Although Hession's grandfather had played the drums in a cavalry regiment, his own first musical exposure was to the guitar, a gift from his parents when he was seven years old. About the same time he started singing in a church choir, and credits choir-leader and improvising organist William Isles-Pulford with instilling in him a love of music. He began playing drums himself in 1971, a new departure which involved the usual apprenticeship in Working Men's Club rock bands. Seeing Elvin Jones at Ronnie Scott's Club in 1975 gave him 'food for thought for years'. In 1979 he formed a partnership with alto saxophonist Alan Wilkinson, which has carried on into the 90s. In 1983 they (together with guitarist Paul Buckton and live electronics improviser John McMillan) founded the Leeds Termite Club, both performing free improvised music and promoting players from the UK, Europe and the USA. In 1987 Hession proved his bop credentials by backing west coast bebop tenor saxophonist Teddy Edwards. Word of the quality of the Leeds improvisation scene reached London, and Hession played at Derek Bailey's Company Week in 1988. A partnership with Wuppertal-based tenor Hans-Peter Hiby resulted in *The Real Case* in 1988. In a trio format with Wilkinson and bassist Simon Fell, Hession toured in 1991 under the title 'October Onslaught'. His torrential polyrhythmic style and his ability to raise the stakes in formidable company establish him as a prime mover in the attempt to inject excitement and power back into total improvisation - a return to its roots in free jazz.
Albums: with Hans-Peter Hiby *The Real Case* (1988), with Simon Fell *Compilation 2* (1991).

Hibbler, Al

b. 16 August 1915, Little Rock, Arkansas, USA. After singing for several years in relative obscurity, Hibbler joined Jay McShann in 1942 and the following year was hired by Duke Ellington, proving to be one of the best singers he had ever employed. Hibbler subsequently recorded with several well-known jazz musicians in his backing groups, among them Harry Carney, Billy Kyle, Count Basie and Gerald Wilson. In the 50s his recordings of songs such as 'It Shouldn't Happen To A Dream', which he had recorded with Ellington, 'The Very Thought Of You' and 'Stardust' proved popular, while his version of 'Unchained Melody' was outstanding. A powerful, rich-toned baritone, Hibbler cannot be regarded as a jazz singer but as an exceptionally good singer of 20th-century popular song who happened to work with some of the best jazz musicians.
Selected albums: *Al Hibbler Sings Love Songs* (1952), *Melodies By Al Hibbler* (1954), *After The Lights Go Down Low* (Atlantic 1956), *Monday Every Day* (1961), *Early One Morning* (1964), with Rahsaan Roland Kirk *A Meeting Of The Times* (1972), *For Sentimental Reasons* (1982), *Its Monday Every Day* (Dicovery 1988).

Higginbotham, J.C.

b. 11 May 1906, Social Circle, Georgia, USA, d. 26 May 1973. After playing trombone with J. Neal Montgomery, an Atlanta-based territory bandleader of the early 20s, Higginbotham worked outside music for a number of years. In the middle of the decade he tried his hand at bandleading and then was briefly with the bands of Wingie Carpenter, Chick Webb and Willie Lynch before joining Luis Russell. In 1931 he moved on to Fletcher Henderson's band, worked for Benny Carter, the Mills Blue Rhythm Band, Henderson again and Louis Armstrong, who was then fronting the Russell band. Towards the end of 1940 Higginbotham shifted from big band work to play in a small group led by Red Allen, with whom he remained for about seven years. Thereafter, he played in or led small bands in New York, Boston and Cleveland, recorded extensively, appeared at the 1957 Great South Bay Jazz Festival as a member of the Fletcher Henderson reunion band, and visited Europe. In the 60s Higginbotham continued his established pattern of work, often playing in tandem with trumpeter Joe Thomas. Towards the end of the decade ill-health affected his career and he died in May 1973. A powerful, gutsy player with a solid traditional approach to his instrument overlaid with a keen appreciation of swing era styling, Higginbotham was one of the best trombone soloists in big band jazz.

Albums: with Henderson All Stars *Big Reunion* (1957), *J.C. Higginbotham All Stars* (1966). Compilations: with Fletcher Henderson *A Study In Frustration* (1923-38 recordings), *Higgy Comes Home* (Jazzology 1990).

Higgins, Billy

b. 11 October 1936, Los Angeles, California, USA. Higgins began playing drums at the age of 12 and early in his career played with R&B bands. He was soon involved in jazz, playing with other local musicians, including Dexter Gordon. In 1957 he was in the quartet led by Red Mitchell which also included pianist Lorraine Geller and tenor saxophonist James Clay. This band recorded for Lester Koenig's Contemporary label, on what was Higgins' first record date. In New York in 1959 he appeared with Ornette Coleman at the altoist's controversial Five Spot concerts, in a band which also included Don Cherry and Charlie Haden. Later that year he joined Thelonious Monk and in 1960 was with John Coltrane. Throughout the 60s Higgins was in demand for tours, club dates and a staggering number of recording sessions, many of them for the Blue Note label. Amongst the artists with whom he played were Sonny Rollins, Steve Lacy, Donald Byrd, Gordon, Lee Morgan, Herbie Hancock and Hank Mobley. His activities increased during the 70s and he worked extensively with Cedar Walton and was also on dates with Milt Jackson and Art Pepper. In the 80s his musical companions included Coleman, Pat Metheny and Slide Hampton. Although the musical styles of Higgins' associates have latterly ranged through freeform, jazz-rock and jazz-funk, he has readily established himself as one of the two or three leading exponents of each form of drumming. He brings to his playing a remarkable subtlety and lithe swing akin to that of the best bop drummers, while readily accommodat-

ing the complex needs of the styles in which he plays. Eagerly sought out for clinics, he continues to influence many younger drummers.

Albums: *Presenting Red Mitchell/Red Mitchell Quartet* (1957), *Something Else! The Music Of Ornette Coleman* (1958), with Coleman *The Shape Of Jazz To Come* (1959), with Coleman *Free Jazz* (1960), with Sonny Rollins *Our Man In Jazz* (1962), with Dexter Gordon *Go!* (1962), with Hank Mobley *Dippin'* (1965), *Soweto* (Red 1979), *The Soldier* (Timeless 1980), *Mr Billy Higgins* (Evidence 1985).

Hill, Andrew

b. 30 June 1937, Chicago, Illinois, USA. Port Au Prince, Haiti, is usually given as Hill's birthplace, but he actually hails from Chicago. He studied composition privately with Paul Hindemith and Bill Russo, and played accordion and tap-danced on the streets where Earl Hines heard him. In his teens he was in Paul Williams's R&B band, played with Charlie Parker, Coleman Hawkins, Gene Ammons, Von Freeman, Johnny Griffin, Malachi Favors and John Gilmore, and became virtually Chicago's 'house' pianist for visiting artists. Having spent some months in New York as Dinah Washington's accompanist he relocated there in 1960 whilst working with Johnny Hartman. From 1962-63 he worked in Los Angeles with Rahsaan Roland Kirk and Jimmy Woode among others. In 1963 he returned to New York to work with Joe Henderson. During the 60s he made a number of excellent albums for Blue Note (under his own name and with Bobby Hutcherson and Joe Henderson), probably the best-known being *Black Fire* and the highly-acclaimed *Point Of Departure*, which featured Henderson, Eric Dolphy and Kenny Dorham. Later Blue Note sessions (several of which remain unissued) often show a dense, turbulent music that is both strikingly individual and intensely gripping; *Compulsion* has John Gilmore in ferocious form, while a set recorded with Sam Rivers (and later released under the tenorist's name as one half of the double-set *Involution*) has a moving, almost desperate, sombreness. When the contract ran out in 1970 Hill moved to upstate New York. His career during the 70s is rather a mystery and he has seemed reluctant to clarify it, but he did hold a number of academic posts, including composer-in-residence at Colgate University in New York (where he wrote pieces for string quartet and orchestra) and with the Smithsonian Institute, for whom he toured rural areas of the US, playing hospitals, prisons and introducing jazz to an entirely new audience. In 1977 he moved to Pittsburgh, California (near San Francisco), and from the early 80s his career seemed to take off again, with more record releases (most notably 1986's *Shades*, with Clifford Jordan) and tours, including a season at New York's Knitting Factory, and a Contemporary Music Network tour of Britain with Howard Riley, Joachim Kuhn and Jason Rebello in 1990. Now resigned to the new Blue Note, where he has been paired with the upcoming alto saxophonist Greg Osby, Hill is a highly individual pianist and composer who is often compared with Thelonious Monk and Cecil Taylor, if only by virtue of his uniqueness. This quality has persisted through the brooding power of his 60s music to the more celebratory feel of recent releases. 'I'd say interesting . . . happy . . . warm', is how Hill responded to a 1976 request to describe his style. 'There was an angry period, but you get tired of pounding the piano. It's too good an instrument.'

Albums: *So In Love With The Sound Of Andrew Hill* (1956), *Black Fire* (1964), *Judgement* (1964), *Point Of Departure* (Blue Note 1965), *Smokestack* (1965), *Andrew!* (1966), *Compulsion* (1966), *Grass Roots* (1968), *Lift Every Voice* (1969), *Invitation* (Steeplechase 1975), *Spiral* (Freedom 1975), *Blueblack* (1975), *Homage* (1975), *Live At Montreux* (Freedom 1975), *One For One* (1975, rec 1970, 1965), With Sam Rivers *Involution* (1975, rec 1966), *Divine Revelation* (1976), *Nefertiti* (1976), *From California With Love* (1979), *Dance With Death* (1980, rec 1968), *Strange Serenade* (Soul Note 1980), *Faces Of Hope* (Soul Note 1980), *Solo Piano* (Artists House 1981), *Shades* (Soul Note 1987), *Verona Rag* (Soul Note 1988), *Eternal Spirit* (Blue Note 1989), *Black Fire* (Blue Note 1989), *But Not Farewell* (Blue Note 1991).

Hill, Teddy

b. Theodore Hill, 7 December 1909, Birmingham, Alabama, USA, d. 19 May 1978. After playing drums and trumpet, Hill switched to reed instruments and toured theatre circuits. In 1928 he joined Luis Russell as both sideman and assistant manager. In the early 30s he worked with James P. Johnson and then led his own big band, which survived until 1940. Hill's band held an occasional residency at the Savoy in Harlem and in 1937 toured Europe and the UK. During its existence, the band was home at one time or another to several outstanding jazzmen, including Chu Berry, Dicky Wells and a succession of fine trumpeters, among whom were Roy Eldridge, Bill Coleman, Shad Collins, Frankie Newton and Dizzy Gillespie. In 1940, Hill became manager of Minton's Playhouse and thus presided benevolently over the emergence of bebop, as his former sideman Gillespie joined with other revolutionaries in experimentation. While this might seem far removed from Hill's earlier role in jazz, in fact it reflected his lifelong interest in new developments. After Minton's closed, Hill continued in club management elsewhere.

Compilations: one side only *Teddy Hill And Cab Calloway* (1935-36 recordings), *Uptown Rhapsody* (Hep Jazz 1992).

Hines, Earl 'Fatha'

b. 28 December 1903, Dusquene, Pennsylvania, USA, d. 22 April 1983. An outstanding musician and a major figure in the evolution of jazz piano playing, Hines began his professional career in 1918. By that time he had already played cornet in brass bands in his home town. By 1923, the year in which he moved to Chicago, Hines had played in several bands around Pittsburgh and had been musical director for singer Lois Deppe. He performed in bands in Chicago and also toured theatre circuits based on the city. Among the bands with which he played were those led by Carroll Dickerson and Erskine Tate. In 1927 he teamed up with Louis Armstrong, playing piano, acting as musical director and, briefly, as Armstrong's

partner in a nightclub (the third partner was Zutty Singleton). With Armstrong, Hines made a series of recordings in the late 20s which became and have remained classics: these were principally Hot Five, Hot Seven or Savoy Ballroom Five tracks but also included the acclaimed duet 'Weather Bird', one of the peaks of early jazz. Also in 1927 he was with Jimmy Noone's band and the following year was invited to form a band for a residency at Chicago's Grand Terrace. Although enormously popular at this engagement, the long residency, which lasted throughout the 30s, had an adverse effect upon the band's standing in big band history. Less well-known than the bands that toured the USA during the swing era, it was only through records and occasional radio broadcasts from live venues that the majority of big band fans could hear what Hines was doing. With outstanding arrangers such as Jimmy Mundy and topflight sectionmen including Trummy Young, Darnell Howard and Omer Simeon, the band was in fact advancing musically at a speed which outstripped many of its better-known contemporaries. This was particularly so after 1937 when arranger Budd Johnson arrived, bringing an advanced approach to big band styling which foreshadowed later developments in bebop. The reason why Hines stayed at the Grand Terrace for so long is open to question, but some who were there have suggested that he had little choice: the Grand Terrace was run by mobsters and, as Jo Jones remarked, 'Earl had to play with a knife at his throat and a gun at his back the whole time he was in Chicago'.

In the early 40s Hines hired several musicians who modernized the band's sound still further, including Dizzy Gillespie, Charlie Parker and Wardell Gray, which led to Duke Ellington dubbing the band 'the incubator of bebop'. Hines also hired singers Billy Eckstine and Sarah Vaughan; but he eventually folded the big band in 1947 and the following year joined Louis Armstrong's All Stars, where he remained until 1951. He then led his own small groups, holding a long residency at the Club Hangover in San Francisco. In 1957 he toured Europe as co-leader, with Jack Teagarden, of an all-star band modelled on the Armstrong All Stars. For all this activity, however, Hines's career in the 50s and early 60s was decidedly low-profile and many thought his great days were over. A series of concerts in New York in 1964, organized by writer Stanley Dance, changed all that. A succession of fine recording dates capitalized upon the enormous success of the concerts and from that point until his death Hines toured and recorded extensively.

Despite the heavy schedule he set himself the standard of his performances was seldom less than excellent and was often beyond praise. If, in later years, his accompanying musicians were of a very different calibre to their leader, his own inventiveness and command were at their peak and some of his performances from the 70s rank with his groundbreaking work from half a century before. A brilliant and dynamic player, Hines had an astonishing technique which employed a dramatic tremolo. As indicated, as a soloist his powers of invention were phenomenal. However, he was initially an ensemble player who later developed into a great solo artist, unlike many pianists who began as soloists and had to adapt their style to suit a role within a band. Hines adopted an innovative style for the piano in jazz in which he clearly articulated the melody, used single note lines played in octaves, and employed his distinctive tremolo in a manner that resembled that of a wind player's vibrato. All this helped to land his technique with the potentially misleading term, 'trumpet style'. The number of pianists Hines influenced is impossible to determine: it is not too extravagant to suggest that everyone who played jazz piano after 1927 was in some way following the paths he signposted. Certainly his playing was influential upon Nat 'King' Cole, Mary Lou Williams, Billy Kyle and even the much less flamboyant Teddy Wilson, who were themselves important innovators of the 30s. During this period, perhaps only Art Tatum can be cited as following his own star.

Selected albums: *Earl Hines And His New Sound Orchestra* (1954), *The Earl Hines Trio* i (1954), *Earl Hines At Club Hangover* (1955), *Earl 'Fatha' Hines Plays Fats Waller* (1956), *Earl 'Fatha' Hines And His All Stars Vols 1 & 2* (1956), *After You've Gone* (1956), *Here Is Earl Hines* (1957), *The Earl Hines Trio* ii (1957), *The Earl Hines Trio* iii (1957), *The Jack Teagarden-Earl Hines All Stars In England* (1957), *The Earl Hines Quartet* i (1958), *The Earl Hines Quartet* ii (1960), *A Monday Date* (1961), *Earl Hines And His All Stars* i (1961), *Earl Hines And His All Stars* ii (1961), *Earl Hines With Ralph Carmichael And His Orchestra* (1963), *Spontaneous Explorations* (1964), *The Earl Hines Trio At The Little Theatre, New York* (1964), *Fatha* (1964), *The Earl Hines Quartet* iii (1964), *The Earl Hines Trio* iv (1964), *The Earl Hines Trio With Roy Eldridge And Coleman Hawkins Live At The Village Vanguard* (1965), *Earl Hines & Roy Eldridge At The Village Vanguard* (1965), *Hines '65/Tea For Two* (1965), *Blues In Thirds* (1965), *Paris Session* (1965), *Father's Freeway* (1965), *Once Upon A Time* (1966), *Hines' Tune* (1965), *The Earl Hines Trio* v (1966), *Earl Hines At The Scandiano di Reggio, Emilia* (1966), *Blues So Low (For Fats)* (1966), *Dinah* (1966), *The Earl Hines Trio* vi (1966), *Blues And Things* (1967), *Fatha Blows Best* (1968), *A Night At Johnnie's* (1968), *Master Jazz Piano Vols 1 & 2* (1969), *Earl Hines At Home* (1969), *Boogie Woogie On St Louis Blues* i (1969), *Quintessential Recording Session* (1970), *Fatha And His Flock On Tour* (1970), *Earl Hines And Maxine Sullivan Live At The Overseas Press Club, New York* (1970), *Earl Hines In Paris* (1970), *It Don't Mean A Thing If It Ain't Got That Swing* (1970), *Master Jazz Piano Vols 3 & 4* (1971), with Jaki Byard *Duet* (1972), *Earl Hines* i (1972), *Solo Walk In Tokyo* (1972), *Tour De Force* (1972), *Earl Hines Plays Duke Ellington Vols 1-3* (1972), *My Tribute To Louis* (c.1972-73), *Hines Does Hoagy* (c.1972-73), *Hines Comes In Handy* (c.1972-73), *Back On The Street* (1973), *Live At The New School* (1973), *Quintessential Recording Session Continued* (1973), *An Evening With Earl Hines And His Quartet* (1973), *Earl Hines Plays George Gershwin* (1973), *The Earl Hines Quartet* iv (1973), *Swingin' Away* (1973), *Quintessential 1974* (c.1973-74), *Earl Hines* ii (1974), *One For My Baby* (1974), *Masters Of Jazz Vol. 2* (Storyville 1974), *Earl Hines At The New School Vol. 2* (1974), *West Side Story* (1974), *Live!* (1974), *Fireworks* (1974), *Hines '74* (1974), *At Sundown* (1974), *The Dirty Old Men* (1974), *Jazz Giants In Nice* (1974), *Piano Portraits Of Australia* (1974), *Concert In Argentina* (1974), *Earl Hines In New Orleans With Wallace Davenport And Orange Kellin Vols 1 & 2* (1975), *Earl Hines Plays Duke Ellington Vol. 4* (1975), *Earl Hines At Saralee's* (1976), *Live At Buffalo* (1976), *Jazz Is His Old Lady And My Old Man* (c.1977), *Lionel Hampton Presents Earl 'Fatha' Hines* (1977), *Giants Of Jazz Vol. 2* (Storyville 1977), *Earl Hines In New Orleans* (1977), *Father Of Modern Jazz Piano/Boogie Woogie On St Louis Blues* ii (1977), *East Of The Sun* (1977), *Texas Ruby Red* (1977), *Deep Forest* i (1977), with Harry 'Sweets' Edison *Earl Meets Harry* (1978), with Edison, Eddie 'Lockjaw' Davis *Earl Meets Sweets And Jaws* (1978), *Fatha's Birthday* (1981), *Deep Forest* ii (1982), *Earl Hines Live At The New School* (1983). Compilations: *Louis Armstrong Classics Vol. 3* (1928 recordings), *Swingin' Down* (1932-33 recordings), *Fatha Jumps* (1940-42 recordings), *The Indispensable Earl Hines* (RCA 1983, 1944-66 recordings), *Earl Hines Big Band* (1945-46 recordings), *Father Steps In* (Tring 1993).

Further reading: *The World of Earl Hines*, Stanley Dance.

Hino, Motohiko

b. 3 January 1946, Tokyo, Japan. Hino's father was a musician and dancer and Motohiko was a tap dancer when he was eight before learning the drums when he was 10. He turned professional when he was 17 and from 1972 won, yearly, the *Swing Journal* polls as Japan's top drummer. He moved to New York in 1978. There he worked with Joe Henderson, Chuck Rainey, Jean-Luc Ponty and others before joining Hugh Masekela's band in 1979. Since 1980 he has played in the trio of JoAnne Brackeen, his sharp, dynamic drumming reflecting the playing of his two favourites, Tony Williams and Elvin Jones.

Albums: *First Album* (1970), *Toko: The Motohiko Hino Quartet At Nemu Festival* (1975), *Flash* (1977), *Sailing Stone* (1992).

Hino, Terumasa

b. 25 October 1942, Tokyo, Japan. Following, more or less literally, in the footsteps of his trumpet- playing, tap-dancing father, Hino learned to tap at the age of four, and took up the trumpet when he was nine years old. He taught himself the principles of jazz improvisation by transcribing solos by Miles Davis (from whom, no doubt, he learned his conviction about the importance of space), Louis Armstrong, John Coltrane, Clifford Brown, Lee Morgan and Freddie Hubbard. He began playing publicly in American army clubs in 1955 in Japan, then joined Hiroshi Watanabe and Takao Kusagaya, but his first major job was with the Hideo Shiraki Quintet, where he stayed from 1965-69. During 1964-65 he had led his own group, and left Shiraki at the end of the decade in order to lead his own band full-time. In 1974 he worked with Masabumi Kikuchi, then in June 1975 he went to the USA and worked with Joachim Kuhn (1975), Gil Evans, Jackie McLean and Ken McIntyre (1976), Hal Galper (1977), Carlos Garnett (1977), Sam Jones (1978), Elvin Jones (1982) and Dave Liebman, as well as continuing to lead his own group, the band which John Scofield credits as moving him from fusion to jazz. By then Hino was dividing his time equally between the USA and

Japan. He plays trumpet and flugelhorn with a mellow fire, and his fame in Europe continues to grow almost matching his reputation in Japan and the USA. He toured Europe with Eddie Harris in November 1990.

Albums: *Hi-Nology* (1965), *Vibrations* (Enja 1971), *Taro's Mood* (Enja 1973), *Speak To Loneliness* (1975), *Live In Concert* (1975), *Hogiuta* (1976), *Maiden Dance* (1978), *Terumasa Hino* (Denon 1986), *Bluestruck* (Blue Note 1990), *From The Heart* (Blue Note 1992), *Warsaw Jazz Festival 1991* (Jazzmen 1993).

Hinton, Milt

b. 23 June 1910, Vicksburg, Mississippi, USA. During the 20s Hinton played bass with artists such as Boyd Atkins, Tiny Parham and Jabbo Smith. In the early 30s he established his reputation as one of the most reliable and forward-thinking contemporary bass players during engagements with Eddie South, Erskine Tate, Zutty Singleton and Fate Marable. In 1936 he began a sustained period with Cab Calloway. Not only was he a stalwart of an excellent rhythm section but he was also a featured soloist. He left Calloway in 1951, thereafter working as a freelance session and studio musician, appearing on countless record dates. Many of these recordings were with jazzmen but his skills were such that he was in demand for sessions by pop singers too. Nicknamed 'the Judge', Hinton also toured extensively in the 70s and 80s, including one stint with Bing Crosby, appeared at jazz festivals and clubs around the world and still found time to establish himself as a teacher and jazz photographer. An important transitional figure in jazz bass playing, Hinton's career comfortably spanned the change from swing to bop, whilst his versatility ensured that so long as popular songs were being recorded he could work anywhere.

Albums: *The Milt Hinton Quartet* (1955), *Milt Hinton With Manny Albam's Orchestra* (1955), *Here Swings The Judge* (1964-75), *Basically With Blue* (1976), *The Trio* (1977), *Back To Bassics* (Progressive 1984), *We Three Live In New York* (1985), *Old Man Time* (1989-90). Compilations: *Sixteen Cab Calloway Classics* (1939-41).

Further reading: *Bass Line*, Milt Hinton and David Berger.

Hinze, Chris

b. 30 June 1938, Hilversum, The Netherlands. Hinze's father was a conductor and he learned the piano and flute as a child. He studied flute at the Royal Conservatory in The Hague and then learned arranging at the Berklee College Of Music in the USA. He won a prize for the best soloist at the Montreux Jazz Festival in 1970 and formed his jazz fusion group the Combination the following year. He founded his own record label Keytone and has often worked as a producer for other musicians. He moved to New York in 1976 but in the late 70s toured Europe with Chris Hinze And Friends and then in a duo with guitarist Sigi Schwab. In 1972 he won the Beethoven Award of the City of Bonn for a suite called *Live Music Now*. He continued to write and record symphonic works as well as presenting jazz versions of Baroque composers with his band. He recorded an album of flute solos in the Ellora Caves in India in 1979 and the following year recorded a reggae album with Peter Tosh. He has since included African and Indian musicians in the Combination.

Albums: *Stoned Flute* (1971), *Virgin Sacrifice* (1972), *Mange* (1974), *Variations On Bach* (1976), *Silhouettes* (1977), *Flute And Mantras* (1979), with Peter Tosh *World Sound And Power* (1980), *Chris Hinze/Sigi Schwab Duo* (1980), *Mirror Of Dreams* (1982), *Backstage* (1983), *Saliah* (1985).

Hirt, Al

b. 7 November 1922, New Orleans, Louisiana, USA. After studying classical music, trumpeter Hirt divided his professional career between symphony orchestras and dance bands and still found time to play dixieland jazz in New Orleans clubs. Among the bands with which he played were those led by Tommy Dorsey and Ray McKinley, and a sideman in one of his own first bands was Pete Fountain. In the 60s an important recording contract (which resulted in albums under his own name and as accompanist to some transiently popular singers) a successful residency at his own club and a spectacular technique all helped to turn him into one of the best-known trumpeters in jazz. In the 60s, Hirt had 17 albums in the US jazz charts. As often happens, commercial success brought a measure of condemnation from jazz hardliners but Hirt was unmoved. He continued to perform in clubs and to record throughout the 70s, shrugging off a lip injury, and was still playing his high-spirited, good-humoured jazz in the 80s.

Selected albums: *The Greatest Horn In The World* (1961), *Al (He's The King) Hirt And his Band* (1961), *Bourbon Street* (1962), *Horn-A-Plenty* (1962), *Trumpet And Strings* (1963), *Our Man In New Orleans* (Novus 1963), *Honey In The Horn* (1963), *Beauty And The Band* (1964), *Cotton Candy* (1964), *Sugar Lips* (1964), *Pops Goes The Trumpet* (1964), *That Honey Horn Sound* (1965), *Live At Carnegie Hall* (1965), *They're Playing Our Song* (1966), *The Happy Trumpet* (1966), *Music To Watch Girls Go By* (1967), *Al Hirt Plays Bert Kaempfert* (1968), *Solid Gold Brass* (RCA 1982), *Al Hirt* (Audio Fidelity 1984), *Pops Goes The Trumpet* (1985). Compilation: *The Best Of Al Hirt* (1965).

Hiseman, Jon

b. 21 June 1944, Woolwich, London, England. Hiseman studied violin and piano from an early age, but only applied himself to drums when he was 13 years old. The skiffle craze resulted in Hiseman playing all kinds of blues, jazz and hokum in the early 60s. In 1964 he was a founder member of the New Jazz Orchestra. Between 1966 and 1967 he drummed for the Graham Bond Organisation and then left to join Georgie Fame in the Blue Flames. After six months with John Mayall he formed his own Colosseum in 1968, a celebrated jazz/rock band which included saxophonist Dick Heckstall-Smith and Dave Greenslade on electric piano. Colosseum attracted a lot of attention and was one of the leading jazz/rock combos of all time. Hiseman's drums were much in demand, and he recorded frequently with pianist Mike Taylor, Jack Bruce and John Surman. In 1970 Colosseum released *Daughter Of Time* with Chris Farlowe on vocals, and ambitious lyrics from Hiseman that were typical of the period. Farlowe then left to form Atomic Rooster. After a year of studio work Hiseman formed Tempest, which was not a success. In 1975 he helped to organize the United Jazz & Rock Ensemble, and also formed Colosseum II with Gary Moore of Thin Lizzy. In 1979 he joined his wife, saxophonist Barbara Thompson, in Paraphernalia, which has made sporadic tours and albums ever since. The impact of punk aligned the couple with the musical establishment; they recorded for Andrew Lloyd Webber on *Variations* and on 1982's hit musical, *Cats*. Hiseman now runs a record company, TM Records, a PA hire company and manages Thompson, plays in her band as well as maintaining a busy schedule of production and session work.

Albums: all with Colosseum *Those Who Are About To Die* (1969), *Valentyne Suite* (1969), *The Grass Is Greener* (1970), *Daughter Of Time* (1970), *Colosseum Live* (1971), *Collectors Colosseum* (c.70s), with Colosseum II *Strange New Flesh* (1975), with Colosseum II *Electric Savage* (1976), with Paraphernalia *Live In Concert* (1980).

Hodes, Art

b. 14 November 1904, Nikoliev, Ukraine, d. 4 March 1993. A few months after Hodes was born, his family emigrated from Russia and settled in Chicago, Illinois. He began playing piano and by his late teenage years was working in dance halls and clubs. He played with several local bands, including Wingy Manone's, but also established himself as a solo performer. For the next 10 years he was active in Chicago, but in 1938 moved to New York, where he played with jazzmen including Joe Marsala, Sidney Bechet and Mezz Mezzrow, continuing into the early 40s. During this time he had his first experience as a radio broadcaster, presenting record shows. He also began to write, and for some years was editor of *Jazz Record* magazine. He led his own bands for engagements at many clubs and restaurants in and around New York, but at the end of the 40s decided to move back to Chicago. For the next four decades he led bands, played solo piano, taught, broadcast on radio and television, all in and around Chicago. In the 60s he recorded with Truck Parham and Estelle 'Mama' Yancey. Hodes made occasional tours, including trips to Denmark, Europe and Canada, where he worked with Jim Galloway, one of their concerts being recorded and released as *Live From Toronto*. In the early 80s he appeared again in New York, but he remained true to his adopted hometown. Stylistically, Hodes was strongly rooted in the blues. His knowledge of blues piano and stride, allied to his teaching, writing and demonstration, helped keep the forms alive. In 1977 some of his earlier and perceptive writings for *Jazz Record* were published in book form.

Selected albums: *Mama Yancey Sings, Art Hodes Plays Blues* (1965), *Someone To Watch Over Me* (1981), *Art Hodes: South Side Memories* (1984), *Blues In The Night* (1987), *Joy to The World - Yuletide Piano Solos* (1987), with Wally Fawkes *Midnight Blue* (1987), *Live From Toronto* (1988), *The Music Of Lovie Austin* (1988), *Pagin' Mr Jelly* (Candid 1988), with Volly DeFaut *Up In Volly's Room* (Delmark 1993, rec. 50s), *Sessions At Blue Note* (Dormouse 1991),

Further reading: *Selections From The Gutter: Jazz Portraits From 'The Jazz Record'*, Art Hodes.

Hodges, Johnny

b. 25 July 1907, Cambridge, Massachusetts, USA, d. 11 May 1970. One of the greatest alto saxophonists in jazz, Hodges first tried other instruments before settling upon the one that would best serve his glorious romanticism. Largely self-taught, Hodges played in a number of minor bands in Boston and New York in the early 20s but also spent a little time with Willie 'The Lion' Smith, in whose band he replaced Sidney Bechet - who had given him some of the little instruction he ever took. In 1926 he joined Chick Webb, where his brother-in-law, Don Kirkpatrick, was pianist-arranger. Two years later Hodges began an association with Duke Ellington that would continue virtually uninterrupted for the rest of his life. Apart from playing on hundreds of records with Ellington, soloing magnificently on many, Hodges also originated several tunes which Ellington developed, among them 'Jeep's Blues' and 'The Jeep Is Jumpin'' ('Jeep' was one of Hodges's nicknames; others were 'Rabbit' and 'Squatty Roo'). From 1951-55 Hodges led his own band, which briefly included John Coltrane in its ranks and had a hit record with 'Castle Rock'. In 1958 and again in 1961 he worked outside the Ellington orchestra but always in an Ellingtonian style. Although capable of playing low-down blues, Hodges was in his true element as a balladeer. The lush beauty of his playing was perfectly exhibited on compositions created for his special talents by Ellington and by Billy Strayhorn. Among the many tunes on which he played, and frequently recorded, were 'I Let A Song Go Out Of My Heart', 'Warm Valley', 'Black Butterfly', 'Isfahan' (from the 'Far East Suite') and 'Empty Ballroom Blues'. Hodges recorded several albums for Norman Granz, including a 1952 jam session which teamed him with fellow altoists Benny Carter and Charlie Parker and organist Wild Bill Davis. Despite the excellence of all his other forays, however, it is his work with Ellington for which he will be remembered. The liquid beauty of Hodges's contribution to the sound of the Ellington band, and especially to the manner in which it played ballads, was so crucial that his death in May 1970 marked the end of an era: as Ellington himself observed, 'our band will never sound the same'. Throughout his long career Hodges was indisputably among the finest alto players in jazz. Even if, after the early 40s, Charlie Parker took the alto saxophone in other directions, Hodges remains one of the giants of the instrument.

Selected albums: *Johnny Hodges At Buckminster Square* (1951), with Benny Carter, Charlie Parker *Jam Session Vol. 1* (1952), *The Jeep Is Jumpin'* (1952), *At A Dance Party* (1954), *A Man And His Music* (1955), *Johnny Hodges And His Band* (1955), *Ellingtonia '56* (1956), with Duke Ellington *At Newport* (1956), *Johnny Hodges And His Orchestra* i (1956), *The Big Sound* (1957), *Johnny Hodges And His Orchestra* ii (1958), *Not So Dukish* (1958), *Johnny Hodges And The Stuttgart Light Orchestra* (1958), with Ellington *Back To Back And Side By Side* (1959), *The Smooth One* (1959), with Ellington *The Nutcracker Suite* (1960), *Master Of Jazz* (1960), *The Johnny Hodges*

Quintet (1960), *The Johnny Hodges All Stars/The Johnny Hodges-Harry Carney Sextet* (1961), *Johnny Hodges At The Sportspalast, Berlin* (1961), *Johnny Hodges In Scandinavia* (1961), *Johnny Hodges And Wild Bill Davis* (1961), *Johnny Hodges With Billy Strayhorn And His Orchestra* (1961), *Johnny Hodges With Oliver Nelson's Orchestra* (1962), *Johnny Hodges And Lalo Schifrin* (1963), *Mess Of Blues* (1963), *Johnny Hodges With Claus Ogermann's Orchestra* (1963), *Everybody Knows Johnny Hodges* (Impulse 1964), with Wild Bill Davis *Blue Pyramid* (1965), with Davis *Wings And Things* (1965), *Johnny Hodges With Lawrence Welk's Orchestra* (1965), *Johnny Hodges And His Orchestra* iii (1966), *Johnny Hodges And His Orchestra* iv (1966), with Earl Hines *Stride Right* (1966), *In A Mellotone* (Bluebird 1966), with Ellington *Far East Suite* (1966), *Triple Play* (1967), *Johnny Hodges And His Orchestra* v (1967), *Johnny Hodges And Earl Hines* (1967), *Rippin' And Runnin'* (1968), *3 Shades Of Blue* (1970). Compilations: *The Indispensable Duke Ellington Vols 1/2, 3/4, 5/6* (1928-40), *Love In Swingtime* (1938-39), with Ellington *The Blanton-Webster Band* (1940-42), *The Complete Johnny Hodges Sessions 1951-1955* (1989, 6 album box-set), *Rarities And Private Recordings* (Suisa 1992).

Hodgkinson, Colin

b. 14 October 1945, Peterborough, England. Hodgkinson is a self-taught bass player who turned professional with a jazz trio in 1966. In 1969 he began a long association with Alexis Korner, during which time they played in everything from a duo to a big band. In 1972 Hodgkinson and Ron Aspery (reeds) took time off in Yorkshire to write music. The two were joined by drummer Ron Hicks in the trio Back Door in which Hodgkinson had an opportunity to display his amazing technical facility. The band toured Europe and the USA and played at the Montreux Jazz Festival. In 1978 he began another long association, this time with Jan Hammer. Though he had written a lot for Back Door, with Hammer he writes lyrics more than tunes. In the late 80s he also played with Brian Auger's Blues Reunion.
Albums: with Alexis Korner *New Church* (1970), *Back Door* (1972), with Jan Hammer *Black Sheep* (1979), *Hammer* (1980), *Here To Stay* (1982), *City Slicker* (1986).

Holder, Terrence

b. c.1898. Holder's early background is extremely sketchy, but by the early 20s he was well-established as lead trumpet and principal soloist with Alphonso Trent's important territory band. In the middle of the decade he formed his own band, the Dark Clouds Of Joy, which was based in Dallas, Texas. In 1929, while undergoing financial and domestic strain, Holder resigned and the band was taken over by one of his leading sidemen, Andy Kirk. Although Kirk retained most of the original name, calling the band the Clouds Of Joy, Holder was undeterred and formed a new band with the same name as before. He continued to play into the mid-30s, employing a number of outstanding musicians who used his and other territory bands as training grounds before gaining major success elsewhere. Among the artists who played with Holder at vari-

ous times were Don Byas, Budd Johnson, Herschel Evans, Earl Bostic, Carl 'Tatti' Smith and Buddy Tate. After folding his band in the late 30s Holder drifted in and out of music, never making the breakthrough into national fame. Reputedly a fine player, Holder was still working intermittently into the 60s. It must be assumed that he is now dead, although like his music, his demise has gone unrecorded.

Holdsworth, Allan

b. 6 August 1946, Leeds, England. The professional regard for this Leeds guitarist is illustrated by the range of people with whom he has appeared, starting with Ian Carrs' Nucleus in 1972. The end of Holdsworth's time with Nucleus coincided with a spell in Jon Hiseman's Tempest (in which he also played the violin). In its turn this overlapped with membership of Soft Machine. 1977 brought a brief period with Gong, prior to forming the band UK with Bill Bruford, John Wetton, and Eddie Jobson. When Bruford left to form his own outfit, Holdsworth went with him. Typically Holdsworth soon left them, rejoining Soft Machine prior to going solo in the late 70s. After a fallow period Holdsworth seems to be more active and his work in the late 80s and 90s has shown has shown his former frantic sparkle.
Albums: with Nucleus *Belladonna* (1972), with Tempest *Jon Hiseman's Tempest* (1973), with Soft Machine *Bundles* (1975), with New Lifetime *Believe It* (1976), *Direct Hits* (1976), with Gong *Gazeuse* (1977), with Esther Phillips *Capricorn Princess* (1977), with Jean-Luc Ponty *Enigmatic Ocean* (1977), with John Stevens *Touching On* (1978), *Expresso 2* (1978), with UK *UK* (1978), with Bill Bruford *Feels Good To Me* (1978), *Time Is The Key* (1979), *One Of A Kind* (1979), *Land Of Cockayne* (1981). Solo: *Velvet Darkness* (1977), *Road Games* (1983), *Metal Fatigue* (JMS 1985), *IOU* (1985), *Atavachron* (JMS 1986), *Sand* (JMS 1987), *With A Heart In My Song* (JMS 1989), *Secrets* (Cream 1989), *Wardenclyffe Tower* (Cream 1993), *Hard Hat Era* (Cream 1993).

Holiday, Billie 'Lady Day'

b. Eleanora Harris, 7 April 1915, Philadelphia, Pennsylvania, USA. d. 17 July 1959. Billie Holiday began singing during her early years in Baltimore, Maryland, where she was brought up until moving to New York in 1929. Inaccuracies, myth and exaggeration clouded the picture of her formative years. Not until Stuart Nicholson's immaculately researched book appeared in 1995 was a detailed and reliable account of these years available. Nicholson's research revealed that some of the statements made by the singer in her 1956 autobiography, *Lady Sings The Blues*, were true, despite having been dismissed as exaggeration by other writers. Holiday's teenage parents, Sadie Harris (aka Fagan) and probable father, guitarist Clarence Holiday, never actually lived together and Billie spent much of her childhood with relatives and friends. One result of this was a period in care early in 1925. Holiday quickly learned how to survive extreme poverty, race prejudice and the injustice of black ghetto life. Deserted by Clarence, Sadie took herself and her daughter to New York and a life of continuing poverty, degradation and - amazingly - opportunity. She had already survived rape at age 11 and a further period in care which followed this attack. In New York she endured a brief stint as a prostitute for which she (and her mother) were arrested in 1929. For this she served time on Ryker's Island. Despite these traumatic times, a lack of formal education and music training, her singing developed and she began to appear at New York clubs and speakeasies such as Pods' and Jerry's Log Cabin, the Yeah Man, the Hot-Cha, Alhambra Grill, Dickie Wells's place and the Covan, where singer Monette Moore appeared. She was heard by John Hammond Jnr. when she deputized for Moore who was herself standing in for Ethel Waters on Broadway. Hammond's account of her singing appeared in the press as far away as London and he was also instrumental in setting up a recording date. In the course of three sessions during November and December 1933, two songs were recorded with Benny Goodman in charge of a nine-man studio group most of whom were strangers to the already nervous Holiday. 'Your Mother's Son-in-Law' was the first record she made; 'Riffin' The Scotch', a lightweight novelty concoction, was the second. Neither was wholly successful as a showcase for her - nor, in truth, designed to be - because her role in the proceedings presented Holiday as band vocalist in a setting which stressed the instrumental prowess of Goodman, trombonist Jack Teagarden and other soloists. Nevertheless, even at this early stage in her career, several of the distinctive characteristics of her highly individual vocal style were already in place and can be heard in the film *Symphony In Black*, made with Duke Ellington and released in 1935. Holiday continued her round of club dates and, late in 1934, her career was given a boost when she appeared at the Apollo Theatre, Harlem's most famous and, for up-and-coming artists, formidable entertainment centre. Holiday, then just 20 years old, appeared with pianist Bobbie Henderson and her notices were, at best, mildly critical. Clearly, her relaxed, seemingly lazy, behind-the-beat style did not appeal to the Apollo's often vociferous patrons. Nevertheless, when the entire show was held over for a second week, at which time she appeared with Ralph Cooper's orchestra, her notices improved thanks to her capacity to adapt. By this time, Holiday had settled on the spelling of her name (earlier, her given name, Eleanora, was also subject to variation).

In mid-1935, the singer returned to the recording studio for a session organized by Hammond and directed by Teddy Wilson. Although Wilson would later declare that he never liked her singing style, it is a measure of his consumate professionalism that in him she found the sympathetic partner she needed to reveal the full range of her talents. The four songs picked for this groundbreaking date were above average and the easygoing jam-session atmosphere suited Holiday admirably. She responded to Wilson's masterly accompaniments and solo playing, and to the brilliance of Goodman, Roy Eldridge and Ben Webster. Here was a rising star who could invest ordinary popular songs with the emotional kick of a first-rate blues or ballad composition. Between 1937 and 1938 Holiday sang with the band of Count Basie, where she had an affair with married guitarist Freddie Green. She quit, or more probably

was fired, in February of 1938 and, reservations about the touring life notwithstanding, joined Artie Shaw almost at once and was on the road again, this time with a white band. She ran into trouble with racists, especially in Southern states, and before the end of the year had left Shaw. It was to be her final appearance as a band member; from now on she would be presented as a solo artist. She continued to make records and it seems likely that closest to her heart were those made in association with Wilson, trumpeter Buck Clayton and Lester Young. The inspirational partnership of Holiday and Young led to some of the finest vocal interpretations of her life. Undeniably, these recordings and others made between 1935 and 1942 are among the finest moments in jazz. Early in 1939, Holiday's career took a giant step upwards. Again Hammond proffered a helping hand, as did nightclub owner Barney Josephson. She opened at Café Society with Frankie Newton's band that January, scored at once with the multi-racial audience and had her first taste of stardom at the Café whose slogan read 'The wrong place for the right people'. This engagement and recordings made for Milt Gabler's Commodore label - which included the grimly dramatic 'Strange Fruit' - was a turning point in her career. Unfortunately, during the 40s she responded positively if unwisely to some of the changes in the musical and social climate. Already an eager drinker, smoker of tobacco and marijuana, eater, dresser and shopper, and with a sexual appetite described as 'healthy-plus', she embraced the hard-drug culture of the 40s as to the manner born. She was having troublesome love affairs, nothing new to her, but on 25 August 1941 married Jimmy Monroe. It was a union that did nothing to ease her situation, being an on-off affair which lasted until their divorce in 1957. Nobody now can say when exactly, and by whom, but Holiday was turned on to opium and then heroin. At first the addiction hardly affected her singing, although her behaviour grew increasingly unpredictable, and she gained a reputation for unreliability. At last she was earning real money, as much as $1,000 weekly, it was reported, and about half that sum went to pay for her 'habit'. Nevertheless, she now had the public recognition she craved. In the first *Esquire* magazine poll (1943) the critics voted her best vocalist, with Mildred Bailey and Ella Fitzgerald in second and third places respectively. In spite of drug problems, one accompanist spoke years later of her 'phenomenal musicianship.' At this stage of her life Holiday experienced regular bouts of depression, pain and ill-health. In 1947 she was sentenced to a term in the Federal Reformatory, West Virginia, her arraignment coming, surprisingly, at the behest of her manager, Joe Glaser. From the 50s on, Billie Holiday and trouble seemed often inseparable. As a consequence of her criminal record on drugs, her cabaret card was withdrawn by the New York Police Department. This prevented her appearance at any venue where liquor was on sale, and effectively ruled out New York nightclubs. A side-effect of this was a diminution of her out-of-town earning capacity.

In England during 1954 she spoke with assurance of being able to do things with a song she could never have achieved in girlish days. In 1949 she had been arrested for possession and was again, though not charged, in 1956. She was still making good money but two years on drink and drugs crucially influenced her vocal control. At the end of May 1958 she was taken to hospital suffering from heart and liver disease. Harried still by the police, and placed under arrest in the hospital, she was charged with possession and placed under police guard - the final cruelty the system could inflict upon her. Thus the greatest of jazz singers died in humiliating circumstances at 3.10 am on 17 July 1959. Even at the end squabbles had begun between a lawyer, virtually self-appointed, and her second husband, Louis McKay, whom she had married on 28 March 1957. She did not live to rejoice in the flood of books, biographical features, critical studies, magazine essays, album booklets, discographies, reference-book entries, chapters in innumerable jazz volumes, films and television documentaries which far exceed any form of recognition she experienced in her lifetime. In defiance of her limited vocal range, Billie Holiday's use of tonal variation and vibrato, her skill at jazz phrasing, and her unique approach to the lyrics of popular songs, were but some of the elements in the work of a truly original artist. Her clear diction, methods of manipulating pitch, improvising on a theme, the variety of emotional moods ranging from the joyously optimistic, flirtatious even, to the tough, defiant, proud, disillusioned and buoyantly barrelhouse, were not plucked out of the air, acquired without practice. Holiday paid her dues in a demanding milieu. That she survived at all is incredible; that she should become the greatest jazz singer there has ever been - virtually without predecessor or successor - borders on the miraculous. Today she is revered beyond her wildest imaginings in places which, in her lifetime, greeted her with painfully closed doors. Sadly, she would not have been surprised. As she wrote in her autobiography: 'There's no damn business like show business. You had to smile to keep from throwing up'.

Selected albums: *The Billie Holiday Story* (1973), *Lady And The Legend Vols 1, 2* and *3.* (1984), *Billie Holiday At Monterey 1958* (1986), *The Legendary Masters* (1988), *Quintessential Vols 1-9* (Columbia 1988), *Lady In Autumn* 2-CD (Verve 1991), *Billie Holiday: The Voice Of Jazz* (1992, 8 CD set), *The Complete Recordings 1933-1940* (Charly 1993).

Further reading: *Lady Sings The Blues*, Billie Holiday with William Dufty, *Billie Holiday*, Stuart Nicholson.

Holland, Dave

b. 1 October 1946, Wolverhampton, Staffordshire, England. Holland plays guitar, piano, bass guitar and also composes, but it is as a bassist and cellist that he has made an international reputation. He studied at London's Guildhall School of Music and Drama from 1965-68 and was principal bassist in the college orchestra. On the London scene he worked with John Surman, Kenny Wheeler, Evan Parker, Ronnie Scott and Tubby Hayes and deputized for Johnny Mbizo Dyani with Chris McGregor's group. In 1968 Miles Davis heard him at Ronnie Scott's club and asked him to join his band in New York. Holland did so in September in time to appear on some of the tracks for *Les Filles De Kilimanjaro*. He stayed until autumn 1970, appearing on the seminal *In A Silent Way* and

Bitches Brew, then he and Chick Corea (who had joined Davis at about the same time as Holland had) formed Circle with Anthony Braxton and Barry Altschul. Circle broke up in 1972 when Corea left, but Braxton, Altschul and Sam Rivers played on Holland's *Conference Of The Birds*. Holland also played in Rivers's and Braxton's groups in the 70s, as well as in the occasional trio Gateway (with John Abercrombie and Jack DeJohnette). The 1977 *Emerald Tears* was a solo bass album, and in 1980 Holland played at Derek Bailey's Company Festival, recording *Fables* with Bailey, George Lewis and Evan Parker. Since the early 80s, following recovery from serious illness, he has lead his own much-admired group, which has included Kenny Wheeler, Julian Priester, Marvin 'Smitty' Smith, Kevin Eubanks and Steve Coleman, and in 1984 he began a series of fine records for ECM, perhaps most notably 1990's highly-acclaimed *Extensions*. In 1986 he toured Europe in a remarkable quartet with Albert Mangelsdorff, John Surman and Elvin Jones which, regrettably, did not issue any recordings; and in the late 80s also played with the London Jazz Composers Orchestra, recording on their Zurich Concerts collaboration with his longtime associate Anthony Braxton.

Albums: with Barre Phillips *Music From Two Basses* (1971), *Conference Of The Birds* (ECM 1973), with John Abercrombie, Jack DeJohnette *Gateway* (1975), *Emerald Tears* (1978), with Abercrombie, DeJohnette (1978), with Company *Fables* (1980), *Life Cycle* (ECM 1983), *Jumpin' In* (ECM 1984), *Seeds Of Time* (ECM 1985), *The Razor's Edge* (ECM 1987), *Triplicate* (ECM 1988), *Extensions* (ECM 1990), with Steve Coleman *Phase-Space* (1993).

Holland, Peanuts

b. Herbert Lee Holland, 9 February 1910, Norfolk, Virginia, USA, d. 7 February 1979. Holland was one of several young boys to get his musical start in the Jenkins' Orphanage Band in Charleston, South Carolina, for which he played trumpet. In the late 20s and early 30s he was with Alphonso Trent's famous territory band and also worked with the Jeter-Pillars Orchestra, Willie Bryant and Jimmie Lunceford. By the end of the 30s he was based in New York, where he played in bands led by Coleman Hawkins and Fletcher Henderson and then helped to break racial restraints by becoming one of a succession of black jazzmen hired by Charlie Barnet. In 1946 he joined Don Redman for a European tour and stayed behind, first in Stockholm and later in Paris, to attain great popularity, and played on into the early 70s.

Albums: *Peanuts Holland With Michel Attenoux In Concert At The Salle Pleyal, Paris* (1952), *Peanuts Holland In Paris* (1954), *Peanuts Holland In Finland* (1959). Compilations: with Alphonso Trent, included on *Sweet And Low Blues* (1933), *Charlie Barnet In Discographical Order Vol. 16* (1942-43).

Holley, Major

b. 10 July 1924, Detroit, Michigan, USA, d. 26 October 1990. After starting out on violin and occasionally doubling on tuba, Holley switched to bass while serving in the US Navy. In the 40s he worked with Dexter Gordon, Earl Bostic, Coleman

Hawkins and Charlie Parker and in 1950 recorded with Oscar Peterson. In the 50s he was first resident in the UK, where he worked in the studios of the BBC, then toured with Woody Herman and was a member of a small group co-led by Al Cohn and Zoot Sims. Throughout the 60s he was in great demand as a session player, recording with many leading jazz artists. Late in the decade he also taught at Berklee College Of Music. In the 70s Holley recorded and toured with many jazzmen and became a familiar and popular figure on the international festival circuit. Affectionately known as 'Mule' (a name bestowed by Clark Terry, with whom he worked in navy bands), Holley is one of a small number of bass players to effectively adopt Slam Stewart's habit of singing in unison with his own arco playing. Although strongly identified with the post-war bebop scene, Holley was happy to play in all kinds of company and while in the UK worked with traditionally-orientated musicians such as Mick Mulligan and Chris Barber. He also played classical music with the Westchester Symphony Orchestra.

Albums: *The Good Neighbors Jazz Quartet* (1958), *Woody Herman* (1958), with Coleman Hawkins *Today And Now* (1962), *Mule!* (Black And Blue 1974), *Excuse Me, Ludwig* (1977), *Major Step* (Timeless 1990)

Holloway, Red

b. James W. Holloway, 31 May 1927, Helena, Arkansas, USA. Holloway grew up in a musical family, his father and mother were both musicians, and he started out playing piano. He grew up in Chicago where he attended DuSable High School and the Conservatory of Music. While still at school, where his classmates included Von Freeman and Johnny Griffin, he took up the baritone saxophone, later switching to tenor. He played in and around Chicago, working with Gene Wright's big band for three years before entering the US Army. After his discharge he returned to Chicago, where he became deeply involved in the local jazz scene, playing with such artists as Yusef Lateef and Dexter Gordon. In 1948 he joined Roosevelt Sykes for a US tour. He remained based in Chicago throughout the 50s and early 60s, playing with many leading blues artists. In the early 60s he was resident in New York, then went back to Chicago for a spell. In the mid-60s Holloway toured with Lionel Hampton and 'Brother' Jack McDuff and also led his own small groups. Towards the end of the decade he settled on the west coast. At first he worked in the studios, but eventually secured a lengthy club engagement in Los Angeles. In the earlier part of his career Holloway worked with many bluesmen, including Willie Dixon, Junior Parker, Bobby 'Blue' Bland, Lloyd Price, John Mayall, Muddy Waters, Chuck Berry and B.B. King. His jazz affiliations over the years include leading artists such as Billie Holiday, Ben Webster, Jimmy Rushing, Sonny Rollins, Red Rodney, Lester Young and Wardell Gray. He has worked with big bands, including Juggernaut, but became best known internationally after he teamed up with Sonny Stitt in 1977. During this partnership, Holloway began playing alto saxophone (at Stitt's insistence). After Stitt's death, Holloway resumed touring as a single, but occasionally worked with jazzmen such as Jay McShann and Clark Terry and jazz singer Carmen McRae. A driving player with a rich and bluesy sound, Holloway's late emergence on the international stage has attracted well-deserved attention to a solid and dependable musician.

Selected albums: *The Burner* (1963), *Cookin' Together* (1964), *Sax, Strings & Soul* (1964), *Red Soul* (1965), with Sonny Stitt *Just Friends* (1977), *Red Holloway And Company* (Concord 1986), with Carmen McRae *Fine And Mellow* (1987), with Clark Terry *Locksmith Blues* (Concord 1988), with Knut Riisnaes *The Gemini Twins* (1992).

Holman, Bill

b. 21 May 1927, Olive, California, USA. After studying at Westlake College, California, in the late 40s, tenor saxophonist Holman played in Charlie Barnet's big band for three years, and then for four years with Stan Kenton. During this period Holman was not only playing but also contributing extensively to the Kenton band's book, his charts being amongst the most swinging Kenton ever played. In common with many other Kentonians of the time, Holman was also active in the various small groups experimenting on the west coast. Among the musicians with whom he worked, and sometimes recorded, were Shorty Rogers, Conte Candoli, Art Pepper and Shelly Manne (whose Blackhawk band used a Holman tune, 'A Gem From Tiffany', as their theme). He subsequently wrote for Count Basie, Louie Bellson, Maynard Ferguson, Woody Herman and Gerry Mulligan. His arrangements were also popular with the Boston-based band of Herb Pomeroy. During the late 50s he formed occasional big bands for record dates, but then came a 27-year spell during which Holman was active only in the studios. He still wrote jazz charts, however, notably for the Basie and Buddy Rich bands, and in these intervening years he often arranged for pop musicians too (e.g. 'Aquarius' by Fifth Dimension). It was not until 1975 that he reformed a big band specifically to play his own arrangements and compositions, and another 13 years elapsed before his band was eventually recorded. A sometimes overlooked arranger, Holman's contribution to latterday big band music has nonetheless been considerable.

Albums: *The Bill Holman Octet* (1954), *The Fabulous Bill Holman* (1957), *In A Jazz Orbit* (1958), *Bill Holman's Great Big Band* (Creative World 1960), *World Class Music* (1987), *Bill Holman Band* (Fresh Sounds 1988), *Jive For Five* (VSOP 1988).

Holmes, Richard 'Groove'

b. 2 May 1931, Camden, New Jersey, USA, d. 29 June 1991, St. Louis, Missouri, USA. A self-taught organist, early in his career Holmes worked along the east coast. A 1961 recording session with Les McCann and Ben Webster resulted in widespread interest in his work. He toured and recorded throughout the 60s, achieving widespread acceptance among mainstream and post-bop jazz audiences. Customarily working in a small group format, Holmes developed a solid working relationship with Gene Ammons and their playing exemplified the soul-heavy organ-tenor pairings which proliferated in the early and mid-60s. Displaying his wide-ranging interests, Holmes also played with big bands including that led by Gerald Wilson, with whom he made a fine album, and recorded with singer Dakota Staton. His powerful playing style, with its thrusting swing and booming bass notes lent itself to soul music but his playing had much more than this to offer. Later in his career Holmes's appeal to crossover audiences sometimes led to the unjustified indifference of many jazz fans. Holmes understood the power of a simple riff and like Jimmy Smith and Jimmy McGriff 'he had soul'.

Selected albums: *Groove* (1961), *Groovin' With Jug* (1961), *Tell It Like It Is* (1961), *The Groove Holmes Trio* (1962), *The Groove Holmes Quintet* (1962), *Groove Holmes With Onzy Matthews And His Orchestra* (1964), *Soul Message* (1965), *Living Soul* (1966), *Misty* (1966), *Spicy* (1966), *Super Soul* (1967), *Soul Power* (1967), *Get Up And Get It* (1967), *The Groover* (1968), *That Healin' Feelin'* (1968), *Welcome Home* (1968), *Blues Groove* (Prestige 1968), *Workin' On A Groovy Thing* (1969), with Gerald Wilson *You Better Believe It!* (c.60s), *Dakota Staton* (60s), *X-77* (c.1970), *Night Glider* (c.1973), *Comin' On Home* (c.1974), *Six Million Dollar Man* (1975), *I'm In The Mood For Love* (c.1975), *Slippin' Out* (Muse 1977), *Star Wars-Close Encounters* (1977), *Good Vibrations* (Muse 1977), *Nobody Does It Better* (Manhattan 1980), *Broadway* (Muse 1980), *Swedish Lullaby* (1984), *Hot Tat* (Muse 1989), *Blues All Day Long* (Muse 1992).

Hope, Elmo

b. 27 June 1923, New York City, New York, USA. Influenced by Bud Powell, Hope was regarded by some as a mere imitator. However he did develop his own highly individual piano style. His playing could be just as effective in the context of hard bop with John Coltrane and Hank Mobley on 'All Star Session', or in his trio work with drummer Frank Butler. Other collaborations include Harold Land 'The Fox' and the Curtis Counce Quintet 'Exploring The Future'.

Album: *Meditation* (Original Jazz Classics 1958), *Hope Meets Foster* (Original Jazz Classics 1956), *Homecoming* (Original Jazz Classics 1962).*Elmo Hope Trio with Jimmy Bond And Frank Butler* (Fresh Sounds 1988), *Trio And Quartet* (Blue Note 1991).

Hopkins, Claude

b. 24 August 1903, Alexandria, Virginia, USA, d. 19 February 1984. Hopkins was born into a well-educated, middle-class family, both parents being members of the faculty of Howard University. He studied formally at Howard before starting a career as a dance band pianist. In the mid-20s he visited Europe as leader of a band accompanying Joséphine Baker. Later in the decade and into the early 30s he worked in and around New York, leading bands at many prestigious dancehalls, including the Savoy and Roseland. In 1934 he began a residency at the Cotton Club, sharing headline space with the Jimmie Lunceford band, which lasted until the club closed its Harlem premises in February 1936. In the late 30s and early 40s Hopkins toured extensively but folded the band in 1942.

He regularly employed first-class musicians such as Hilton Jefferson, Edmond Hall, Vic Dickenson and Jabbo Smith. After a spell outside music he returned to the scene, fronting a band in New York in 1948, and continued to appear in the city and other east coast centres, with large and small groups, into the 70s. Among the musicians with whom he performed during these years were Red Allen, Wild Bill Davison and Roy Eldridge. The bands which Hopkins led always had a relaxed, lightly swinging sound, eschewing powerhouse bravura performances.

Selected albums: *Yes, Indeed!* (1960), *Let's Jam* (1961), *Swing Time* (1963), with others *Master Jazz Piano Vol. 1* (1969), with others *The Piano Jazz Masters* (1972), *Crazy Fingers* (1972), *Soliloquy* (1972), *Safari Stomp* (1974), *Sophisticated Swing* (1974). Compilations: *Harlem* (1935), *Claude Hopkins And His Orchestra* (1935), *Singin' In The Rain* (1935), *Claude Hopkins 1932-34* (Original Jazz Classics 1993), *Claude Hopkins 1934-35* (Original Jazz Classics 1993), *Claude Hopkins 1937-40* (Original Jazz Classics 1994).

Hopkins, Fred

b. 11 October 1947, Chicago, Illinois, USA. Hopkins began to play double bass while a student at DuSable High School in Chicago. In the late 60s he became involved in the AACM. In 1970 he played and recorded with Kalaparush Maurice McIntyre. In 1971 he worked in a trio with altoist Henry Threadgill and drummer Steve McCall, which evolved into the group Air and remained active until the mid-80s. Gifted with a springy, propulsive rhythm and blues-drenched tone, Hopkins is the pre-eminent bass player of his generation. His scything, 'out' explorations using the bow combine folk and *avant garde* classical freedoms to devastating effect. He has contributed to the power of Threadgill's later Sextet in no small way and has supplied rhythmic bounce to the work of Oliver Lake, David Murray (recording on the seminal *Flowers For Albert* in 1977), Hamiet Bluiett, Marion Brown, Muhal Richard Abrams, and Craig Harris. In 1988 he toured in a trio with Murray and the founder of free drumming, Sunny Murray, showing that the spirit of leaderless free jazz is still alive.

Albums: with David Murray *Flowers For Albert* (1976), with Henry Threadgill *X-15 Vol I* (1979), with Threadgill *Just The Facts And Pass The Bucket* (1983), with Craig Harris *Black Bone* (1983), with Hamiet Bluiett *Ebu* (1984), with Threadgill *You Know The Number* (1986), with Muhal Richard Abrams *Colors In Thirty Third* (1987).

Horn, Paul

b. 17 March 1930, New York, USA. Horn started to play the piano at the age of four and moved on to the saxophone when he was 12. He studied the flute at Oberlin College Conservatory during 1952 and went on to the Manhattan School of Music the following year. He played with the Sauter-Finnegan Orchestra as tenor soloist before joining Chico Hamilton's Quintet (1956-58). Then he settled to work in Hollywood's film studios. He was the main soloist in Lalo

Schifrin's *Jazz Suite Of Mass Texts* in 1965 and worked with Tony Bennett the following year. During 1967 he went to India where he became a teacher of transcendental meditation. Later he toured China (1979) and the USSR (1983). In 1970 he had settled on an island near Victoria, British Colombia where he formed his own quintet, presented a weekly television show and founded his own record company called Golden Flute (1981). He wrote scores for the Canadian National Film Board and won an award for the score of *Island Eden*. His education and keen travelling encouraged and enabled him to expand his music beyond jazz into what he hoped would be 'universal music'. In 1968 he had recorded an album of solo flute pieces in the Taj Mahal making use of the half minute reverberation time; he later recorded at the Great Pyramid of Cheops near Cairo and even produced a record using the sound of whales as an accompaniment. For Horn, the term jazz merely describes the revival in this century of the art of improvisation and it is this that he continues to do either solo on a variety of flutes including the Chinese ti-tzi, or in a duo with David Friesen on bass.

Albums: *Inside Taj Mahal* (1968), *Inside The Great Pyramid* (Kickuck 1976), with David Friesen *Heart To Heart* (1983), *Traveller* (1985), *China* (Kuckuck 1987), *Inside The Cathedral* (Kuckuck 1987), *Something Blue* (Fresh Sounds 1988), *Peace Album* (Kickuck 1988), *Inside The Taj Mahal* (Kickuck 1989), *Paul Horn* (Cleo 1989), *A Special Edition* (TM 1989), *Altitude Of The Sun* (TM 1989), *The Jazz Years* (Black Sun 1991), *Brazilian Images* (Black Sun 1992).

Horn, Shirley

b. 1 May 1934, Washington, DC, USA. After studying piano formally, Horn continued her musical education at university. She began leading her own group in the mid-50s and made several records, often in company with front-rank bop musicians. For some years Horn spent much of her time in Europe where her cabaret-oriented performances went down especially well. Nevertheless, this absence from the USA tended to conceal her talent, something her return to the recording studios in the 80s has begun to correct. Although her piano playing is of a high order most attention is centred upon her attractive singing. Interpreting the best of the Great American Song Book in a breathily personal manner, Horn continues to perform and record. She is strikingly adept at the especially difficult task of accompanying herself on the piano.

Albums: *Embers And Ashes* (1961), *Live At The Village Vanguard* (1961), *Loads Of Love* (Mercury 1963), *Shirley Horn With Horns* (Mercury 1963), *Shirley Horn* (1965), *Trav'lin Light* (Impulse 1965), *A Lazy Afternoon* (Steeplechase 1978), *All Night Long* (Syeeplechase 1981), *Violets For Your Furs* (Steeplechase 1981), *The Garden Of The Blues* (Steeplechase 1984), *Softly* (Audiophile 1987), *I Thought About You* (Verve 1987), *Close Enough For Love* (Verve 1988), *You Won't Forget Me* (Verve 1990), *Heres To Life* (Verve 1991), *Light Out Of Darkness (A Tribute To Ray Charles)* (1993).

Howard, Kid

b. Avery Howard, 22 April 1908, New Orleans, Louisiana, USA, d. 28 March 1966. Howard played drums in bands in and around his home town for several years. He then switched to trumpet and by the late 20s was leading a popular local band. Although he occasionally played outside the city, New Orleans was where he was at ease and he remained there throughout the next two decades. In the 50s he ventured further afield, even visiting Europe with George Lewis. By the 60s he was back home, where he continued to play despite illness until shortly before his death, in 1966. Highly regarded by his fellow New Orleans musicians, Howard was reputed to have been a powerful player with a rich sound and fierce attack that revealed the influence of players such as Chris Kelly and Louis Armstrong. By the time of his appearances with Lewis, however, his lip was in poor shape and he was capable of only a few flashes of the power displayed on his scarce early recordings.

Selected albums: *George Lewis In Europe Vols. 1* and *2* (1959), *George Lewis In Europe Vol. 3/Pied Piper* (1959), *Kid Howard And La Vida Jazzband* (Jazzology 1990), *Heart And Bowels Of Jazz* (Jazzology 1990), *Lavida* (American Music 1993).

Hubbard, Freddie

b. 7 April 1938, Indianapolis, Indiana, USA. Hubbard began playing trumpet as a child, and in his teens worked locally with Wes and Monk Montgomery. When he was 20 he moved to New York, immediately falling in with the best of contemporary jazzmen. Amongst the musicians with whom he worked in the late 50s were Eric Dolphy (his room-mate for 18 months), Sonny Rollins, J.J. Johnson and Quincy Jones. In 1961 he joined Art Blakey's Jazz Messengers, quickly establishing himself as an important new voice in jazz. He remained with Blakey until 1966, leaving to form his own small groups, which over the next few years featured Kenny Barron and Louis Hayes. Throughout the 60s he also played in bands led by others, including Max Roach and Herbie Hancock and was featured on four classic 60s sessions: Ornette Coleman's *Free Jazz*, Oliver Nelson's *Blues And The Abstract Truth*, Eric Dolphy's *Out To Lunch* and John Coltrane's *Ascension*. Although his early 70s jazz albums *First Light* and *Straight Life* were particularly well received, this period saw Hubbard emulating Herbie Hancock and moving into jazz fusions. However, he sounded much more at ease in the hard bop context of V.S.O.P., the band which retraced an earlier quintet led by Miles Davis and brought together ex-Davis sidemen Hancock, Hayes, Wayne Shorter and Ron Carter, with Hubbard taking the Davis role. In the 80s Hubbard was again leading his own jazz group, attracting very favourable notices for his playing at concerts and festivals in the USA and Europe. He played with Woody Shaw, recording with him in 1985, and two years later recorded *Stardust* with Benny Golson. In 1988 he teamed up once more with Blakey at an engagement in Holland, from which came *Feel The Wind*.

In 1990 he appeared in Japan headlining an American-Japanese concert package which also featured Elvin Jones, Sonny Fortune, pianists George Duke and Benny Green, bassists Carter and Rufus Reid and singer Salena Jones. An exceptionally talented virtuoso performer, Hubbard's rich full tone is never lost, even when he plays dazzlingly fast passages. As one of the greatest of hard bop trumpeters, he contrives to create impassioned blues lines without losing the contemporary context within which he plays. Although his periodic shifts into jazz-rock have widened his audience, he is at his best playing jazz. He continues to mature, gradually leaving behind the spectacular displays of his early years, replacing them with a more deeply committed jazz.

Selected albums: *Open Sesame* (Blue Note 1960), *Minor Mishap* (Blue Note 1961), *Ready For Freddie* (1961), *Hub Cap* (1961), *The Artistry Of Freddie Hubbard* (Impulse 1962), *Hub-Tones* (Blue Note 1962), *Here To Stay* (1963), *Breaking Point* (Blue Note 1966), *The Night Of The Cookers* (Blue Note 1966), *Backlash* (Atlantic 1967), *The Hub Of Hubbard* (1969), *Straight Life* (1970), *First Light* (1972), *Keep Your Soul Together* (CTI 1973), *Sky Dive* (CTI 1973), *High Energy* (1974), *Liquid Love* (1975), *V.S.O.P.* (1976), *Super Blue* (1978), *Mistral* (1980), *At The Northsea Jazz Festival* (1980), *Back To Birdland* (c.1980), *Anthology* (1981), *Outpost* (Enja 1981), *Ride Like The Wind* (1981), *Splash* (1981), *A Little Night Music* (1981), *Born To Be Blue* (Original Jazz Classics 1981), *Face To Face* (Pablo 1982), *Sweet Return* (1983), with Woody Shaw *Double Take* (1985), with Shaw *The Eternal Triangle* (1987), with Benny Golson *Stardust* (1987), with Art Blakey *Feel The Wind* (Timeless 1988), *Minor Mishap* (Black Lion 1989), *Times 'Are Changin'* (Blue Note 1989), *Bolivia* (Limelight 1991), *Live At Fat Tuesday's* (1992), *Live At The Warsaw Jazz Festival* (Jazzmen 1992), *Topsy* (Enja 1993). Compilation: *The Best Of Freddie Hubbard* (Blue Note 1990).

Hubble, Eddie

b. 6 April 1928, Santa Barbara, California, USA. Hubble's father played trombone, composed and arranged for a radio station staff band in Los Angeles. Hubble was thus encouraged to pursue a career in music and at the age of 12 was playing trombone in the LA County Band. In 1944 the family moved to New York, where he continued his schooling in company with Bob Wilber. Heavily influenced by Jack Teagarden and Miff Mole, Hubble's first full-time professional job was with Red McKenzie in 1947 and around this time he also made his first records, substituting for George Brunis on a Doc Evans date. After a brief spell with the Alvino Rey band Hubble joined Buddy Rich, with whom he remained for about three years. Throughout the 50s he worked steadily, sometimes leading his own group, and in 1966 joined the Dukes Of Dixieland. In 1968 he was a member of the newly-formed World's Greatest Jazz Band - led by Bob Haggart and Yank Lawson. In the early 70s Hubble worked with musicians such as Flip Phillips, Pee Wee Erwin and Bernie Privin. A road accident in 1979 interrupted his career, but he was soon back on the bandstand again. He worked with Jim Cullum in Texas and continued to tour into the 80s, playing in a style and with a warmth of tone that mirrors his principal influences on the trombone.

Albums: with World's Greatest Jazz Band *Century Plaza* (1972), *Pee Wee Erwin Memorial* (1981).

Hucko, Peanuts

b. Michael Andrew Hucko, 7 April 1918, Syracuse, New York, USA. Between his arrival in New York in 1939 and his induction into the US Army Air Force in 1942, Hucko had played in several bands, usually on tenor saxophone. They included outfits led by Jack Jenney, Will Bradley, Joe Marsala, Charlie Spivak and Bob Chester. In the army, Hucko switched over to clarinet as the tenor was not an easy instrument to play while marching. He was recommended to Glenn Miller by Ray McKinley and Zeke Zarchy and, after several delays resulting from typical military 'snafus', he finally made the AAF band. Eventually settled in with the band, as lead alto saxophonist doubling on clarinet, Hucko became noted for his version of 'Stealin' Apples', a tune with which he has subsequently remained associated. After the war Hucko worked with Benny Goodman (on tenor) and McKinley, spent time in radio bands, and also played dixieland with Jack Teagarden, Eddie Condon and others. He was a member of the Teagarden-Earl Hines band that toured Europe in 1957 and the following year he joined Louis Armstrong's All Stars. In the 60s he was employed mostly in studio work at CBS, NBC and ABC, where, for 15 years, he played lead clarinet in their light orchestra and second clarinet in the classical orchestra. In between these engagements, he found time to play in jazz clubs with Condon and squeeze in solo tours around the world. In the 70s he played for Lawrence Welk, continued to tour, sometimes as leader of the Glenn Miller Orchestra, and also led his own band, which featured his wife, Louise Tobin, on vocals. In the 80s he was still touring, sometimes as a single, sometimes with his band, the Pied Pipers. Late in 1991 he toured Europe and the UK, leading a small band which included Glenn Zottola and Roy Williams in its Anglo-American ranks.

Selected albums: *Peanuts Hucko And His Orchestra* i (1953), *Peanuts Hucko And His Orchestra* ii (1956), *Peanuts Hucko And His Orchestra* iii (1957), *The Jack Teagarden Earl Hines All Stars In England* (1957), *Peanuts Hucko And His Roman New Orleans Jazz Band* (1959), *Live At Eddie Condon's* (1960-61), with Eddie Condon *Midnight In Moscow* (1962), with Red Norvo *Live In Pasadena* (1970-72), *Peanuts...* (1975), *Peanuts Hucko With His Pied Piper Quintet* (1978), *Peanuts In Everybody's Bag* (c.1980), *Stealin' Apples* (c.1982), *Tribute To Louis Armstrong* (1983), *Tribute To Benny Goodman* (1983). Compilations: with Glenn Miller *Rare Performances* (1943-44), *Jam With Peanuts* (1947-48), *The Sounds Of The Jazz Greats* (Zodiac 1981), *Jam With Peanuts* (Swing House 1984).

Hufstetter, Steve

b. 7 February 1936, Monroe, Michigan, USA. Hufstetter began his musical career as a teenager, playing trumpet in Phoenix, Arizona, where he was raised. In 1959 he moved to Los Angeles, California, where he joined Stan Kenton's orchestra. He remained with Kenton for a year, then in the early 60s played in bands led by Si Zentner, Les Brown and others. In the mid-60s he worked with the band led by Louie Bellson to accompany Pearl Bailey and was also briefly with Ray Charles. He then played in the band led by Preston Love for Motown shows. At the end of the decade he played with Clare Fischer and in the studio band for the Donald O'Connor television show. In 1970 he began a working relationship with Willie Bobo which lasted, on and off, for a decade. Another long-lasting musical relationship began in 1973, when he became an important member of the big band co-led by Toshiko Akiyoshi and Lew Tabackin. Also during the 70s, Hufstetter played with Bob Florence, whom he had first met in the Zentner band, making many concert and record dates. Throughout the 80s Hufstetter worked with Florence, Gordon Brisker, Bellson, Dave Pell, Bill Berry and Poncho Sanchez, all the while being much in demand for studio work. Towards the end of the decade and into the 90s his busy schedule included tours with Akiyoshi, Benny Carter and Supersax, and concert appearances with a Kenton reunion band formed for a 1991 engagement at Newport Beach, sponsored by KLON, which also featured Bill Holman and Shorty Rogers. Although comfortably at home with all kinds and sizes of bands, much of Hufstetter's best work comes when he is with a contemporary big band. Combining fiery, powerful trumpet playing with a warm and intimate ballad style on flügelhorn, Hufstetter is one of the outstanding talents of the day. The facts that much of his work has been concentrated in the Los Angeles area and that many of his recordings have been made as a sideman have tended to keep his name from the wider jazz audience.

Albums: with Stan Kenton *Two Much* (1960), with Kenton *Stan Kenton's Christmas* (1961), with Clare Fischer *Thesaurus* (1969), with Akiyoshi-Tabackin *Road Time* (1976), with A-T *Insights* (1976), with A-T *Live At Newport '77* (1977), with Bob Florence *Live At Concerts By The Sea* (1979), with Florence *Westlake* (1981), with A-T *Tanuki's Night Out* (1981), with Florence *Trash Can City* (1986), with Gordon Brisker *New Beginning* (1987), with Florence *State Of The Art* (1989), *Circles* (c.1990).

Hug, Armand

b. 6 December 1910, New Orleans, Louisiana, USA. d. 19 March 1977. Taught to play piano by his mother, Hug worked for a while as a pianist in silent movie theatres before starting to play in a dance band. Still only in his early teens, he quickly built a solid reputation in his home town. In the mid-30s he recorded with Sharkey Bonano but by the end of the decade had decided upon a career as a soloist. He played several long club residencies in New Orleans culminating, in 1967, in a lifetime contract at a leading Cresent City hotel. In later years, Hug occasionally returned to playing in bands, including those led by Bonano and Johnny Wiggs, but was at his best as a single. His repertoire mixed traditional New Orleans music with the popular songs of his hey-days. Solid, reliable, with a stirring left hand, Hug was a thorough professional and throughout his career ably continued the great tradition of New Orleans jazz pianists.

Selected albums: *Armand Hug Plays Armand Piron* (1953), *Piano Solos* (Nola 1968), *Armand Hug Of New Orleans: 1971* (Swaggie 1971), *Armand Hug Of New Orleans: 1974* (Swaggie 1974), *In New Orleans On Sunday Afternoon* (1974-75), *Armand Hug Plays Jelly Roll Morton* (Swaggie 1976), *New Orleans Piano* (unk. date), *Huggin' The Keys* (Swaggie 1983), with Eddie Miller *New Orleans Dixielanders and Rhythm Pals* (Southland 1988).

Humble, Derek

b. 1931, Livingston, Durham, England, d. 22 February 1971. Humble began playing alto saxophone as a child, becoming a professional musician in his mid-teens. In the early 50s he played in bands led by Vic Lewis, Kathy Stobart and others, working alongside Peter King. In 1953 he joined Ronnie Scott where he remained for the next few years during which he recorded extensively with Vic Feldman, Jimmy Deuchar, Tony Crombie and other leading British modernists. In 1957 he went to Germany where he began a long association with Kurt Edelhagen and, a few years later, with the Clarke-Boland Big Band with whom he made several records. In 1970 he began a stint with Phil Seamen but his health, never good owing to his lifestyle, deteriorated sharply following a mugging. A gifted player with a direct, passionate solo style, Humble was one of the outstanding alto saxophonists of his generation. His long periods in Europe kept him from attracting the international status he warranted and his early death has helped make him one of the forgotten men of UK jazz.

Album: with Clarke-Boland *More Smiles* (1968).

Humes, Helen

b. 23 June 1913, Louisville, Kentucky, USA, d. 13 September 1981. Coming from a happy, close-knit, musical family, Humes learned to play trumpet and piano. As a child she sang with the local Sunday School band, which boasted future jazz stars such as Dicky Wells and Jonah Jones. In 1927 she made her first records, for the OKeh label in St. Louis. Humes then went to New York where she recorded again, this time accompanied by James P. Johnson, and worked for several years with the orchestra led by Vernon Andrade, star of Harlem's Renaissance Ballroom. She also recorded with Harry James. In 1937 she was offered a job by Count Basie but turned it down because the pay was too little. The following year she changed her mind and signed up, replacing Billie Holiday. Her recordings with Basie mixed attractive performances of poor-quality songs and marvellous versions of the better material she was given. She left Basie in 1941 to freelance, and by 1944 was working on the west coast; she had moved into the then popular R&B field. Humes had a big hit with 'Be-Baba-Leba', recorded with Bill Doggett. On a 1947 session in New York, supervised by John Hammond Jnr., she made some excellent mainstream jazz records with Buck Clayton and Teddy Wilson. By the 50s, despite another big hit with 'Million Dollar Secret', her career was in the doldrums as the R&B tag she had acquired proved somewhat limiting. This hiatus continued into the late 60s, at which time she retired to care for ailing members of her family. In 1973 the writer and record producer Stanley Dance persuaded her out of retirement and into an appearance with Basie at the Newport Jazz Festival. This date was a great success and Humes returned to full-time singing. Equally at home with ballads, to which she brought faultless jazz phrasing, blues shouting and R&B rockers, Humes was one of the outstanding singers of her day. Her light, clear voice retained its youthful sound even into her 60s, and late-period recordings were among the best she ever made.

Selected albums: *T'ain't Nobody's Biz-ness If I Do* (Contemporary 1959), *Helen Humes* (1959), *Songs I Like To Sing* (1960), *Swingin' With Humes* (1961), *Helen Comes Back* (1973), *Helen Humes* (1974), *On The Sunny Side Of The Street* (Black Lion 1974), *Sneaking Around* (Black And Blue 1974), *The Incomparable Helen Humes* (1974), *Talk Of The Town* (1975), *Helen Humes And The Muse All Stars* (Muse 1979), *Helen* (Muse 1980), *The New Years Eve* (Le Chant Du Monde 1980), *Live At The Aurex Jazz Festival, Tokyo, '81* (1980), *Let The Good Times Roll* (Black And Blue 1983), *Swing With Helen Humes And Wynton Kelly* (Contemporary 1983), *Helen Humes With The Connie Berry Trio* (Audiophile 1988), *New Million Dollar Secret* (Whiskey Women And Song (1988). Compilation: *Be-Baba-Leba* (Whiskey Women And Song 1991, 1944-52 recordings).

Humphrey, Willie

b. 29 December 1900, New Orleans, Louisiana, USA, d. 7 June 1994. A member of a highly musical family, Humphrey started out on violin before switching to clarinet. His brothers Earl and Percy Humphrey played trombone and trumpet respectively. After playing in local bands and on riverboats, Humphrey moved to Chicago in 1919, playing briefly in bands led by Freddie Keppard and Joe 'King' Oliver. Between 1920 and the early 30s he played in New Orleans and St Louis. After a short spell in Lucky Millinder's big band, Humphrey settled in New Orleans where, war service and an occasional tour apart, he remained. Over the years he played in several bands including those led by Paul Barbarin, Sweet Emma Barrett and De De Pierce. Playing in a forceful manner, deeply rooted in the New Orleans tradition, Humphrey remained a vigorous and enthusiastic performer into his old age.

Albums: *Billie And De De Pierce In Scandanavia* (1967), *New Orleans Clarinet* (1974), *New Orleans Jazz* (GHB 1989), *Two Clarinets On The Porch* (GHB 1992).

Hunt, Fred

b. 21 September 1923, London, England, d. 25 April 1986. A self-taught pianist, Hunt began playing jazz in the 40s. In the next decade he emerged as a significant figure in traditional jazz when, after stints with Mike Daniels and Cy Laurie, he joined Alex Welsh. Throughout the 50s and 60s, Hunt could be heard with Welsh where he was a featured soloist as well as a stalwart member of the robustly swinging rhythm section. His work with Welsh did not prevent him from accompanying visiting Americans, including recording with the four-tenor group, Tenor Of Jazz, featuring Ben Webster and Eddie 'Lockjaw' Davis, which toured in the late 60s. In the mid-70s Hunt left

the UK, residing successively in South Africa, Denmark and Germany. At the end of the decade he returned to the UK but soon afterwards retired through ill health. Although remembered primarily for his long association with Welsh, Hunt's eclectic, strong style made him a sought-after and thoroughly dependable player in both traditional and mainstream settings. Albums: with Alex Welsh *The Melrose Folio* (1958), with Welsh *Echoes Of Chicago* (1962), *Pearls On Velvet* (1968).

Hunt, Pee Wee

b. Walter Hunt, 10 May 1907, Mt. Healthy, Ohio, USA, d. 22 June 1979, Plymouth, Massachusetts, USA. A bandleader since the mid-40s, Pee Wee Hunt came from a musical family, his father being a violinist and his mother a banjoist. Hunt also started playing banjo during his teen years and after graduating from Cincinnati Conservatory of Music and Ohio State University, he began playing with local bands. He played both banjo and trombone before becoming trombonist with Jean Goldkette's Orchestra in 1928. A year later he joined Glen Gray's Orange Blossoms, a Detroit band that eventually became known as the Casa Loma Orchestra, and remained a heavily featured member of that unit for many years, providing not only a solid line in trombone choruses but also a large portion of likeable vocals. Hunt eventually left the Casa Loma in 1943, and became a Hollywood radio disc jockey for a while before spending the closing period of the war as a member of the Merchant Marine. He returned to the west coast music scene again in 1946, forming his own dixieland outfit and playing the Hollywood Palladium, where audience reaction to his pure hokum version of '12th Street Rag' was so enthusiastic that Hunt decided to record the number at one of the band's Capitol sessions. The result was a hit that topped the US charts for eight weeks in 1948. Five years later, Hunt was in the charts again with a cornball version of 'Oh!', an evergreen song from 1919. Like '12th Street Rag' it became a million-seller and charted for nearly six months. This proved to be Hunt's last major record and the trombonist dropped from the limelight, but still continued playing his happy music until his death in June 1979.

Albums: *Plays And Sings Dixie* (1958), *Cole Porter A La Dixie* (1958), *Blues A La Dixie* (1959), *Dixieland Kickoff!* (1959), *Dance Party* (1960), *Saturday Night Dancing Party* (1961). Compilation: *Masters Of Dixieland, Volume Six* (1975).

Hunter, Alberta

b. 1 April 1895, Memphis, Tennessee, USA, d. 17 October 1984. Growing up in Chicago, Hunter began her remarkable career singing at Dago Frank's, one of the city's least salubrious whorehouses. There she sang for the girls, the pimps and the customers, earning both their admiration and good money from tips. Later, she moved on and marginally upwards to a job singing in Hugh Hoskins's saloon. She continued to move through Chicago's saloons and bars, gradually developing a following. She entered the bigtime with an engagement at the Dreamland Cafe, where she sang with Joe 'King' Oliver's band. Amongst the songs she sang was 'Down Hearted Blues', which she composed in collaboration with Lovie Austin and which was recorded in 1923 by Bessie Smith. During the 20s and early 30s Hunter often worked in New York, singing and recording with many leading jazzmen of the day, amongst them Louis Armstrong, Sidney Bechet, Eubie Blake, Fletcher Henderson and Fats Waller. She also appeared in various shows on and off Broadway. A visit to London prompted so much interest that she was offered the role of Queenie in *Show Boat* at the Drury Lane Theatre, playing opposite Paul Robeson. This was in the 1928/9 season and during the 30s she returned frequently to London to appear at hotels and restaurants, including an engagement at the Dorchester Hotel with Jack Jackson's popular band. She also appeared in the UK musical film, *Radio Parade Of 1935*. The 30s saw her in Paris and Copenhagen too, always meeting with enormous success. In the 40s she continued to appear at New York clubs and to make records, notably with Eddie Heywood. Amongst these recordings are two of her own compositions, 'My Castle's Rockin'' and 'The Love I Have For You'. In the war years she toured extensively to perform for US troops. In the early 50s she visited the UK with Snub Mosley and again toured with the USO, this time to Korea. She played a number of club dates but these were increasingly hard times and in 1954 she retired from showbusiness. By then aged 60, she began a new career as a nurse. In 1961 writer and record producer Chris Alberston persuaded her to record two albums, but she remained at her new profession. Then, in 1977, her employers caught onto the fact that diminutive Nurse Hunter was 82 and insisted that she should retire. Having already lived a remarkably full life she could have been forgiven for calling it a day, but she was a tough and spirited lady. She supplied the score for the film, *Remember My Name* (1978) and, invited to sing at Barney Josephson's club, The Cookery in Greenwich Village, New York, she was a smash hit and began her singing career all over again. She made numerous club and concert appearances, made more records and appeared on several television shows. Early in her career she sometimes performed and occasionally recorded under different names, including May Alix and Josephine Beaty. She sang with power and conviction, her contralto voice having a distinct but attractive vibrato. Inimitably interpreting every nuance of lyrics, especially when they were her own, she made many fine recordings. Even late in her career, she controlled her audiences with a delicately iron hand, all the while displaying a sparkling wit and a subtle way with a risqué lyric. It is hard to think of any singer who has improved upon her performances of certain songs, notably 'The Love I Have For You' and 'Someday, Sweetheart'.

Selected albums: *Alberta Hunter With Lovie Austin And Her Blues Serenaders* (1961), *Amtrak Blues* (c.1980), *The Glory Of Alberta Hunter* (c.1980), *Classic Alberta Hunter: The Thirties* (Stash 1981, 1935-40 recordings), *The Legendary* (DRG 1983), *The Glory Of* (CBS 1986).

Husband, Gary

b. 14 June 1960, Leeds, England. A drummer who comes from a musical family (his father played flute and composed, his mother danced), Husband started on piano lessons at the age of seven, then took up drums in 1970. An infant prodigy, he created a stir in the local jazz clubs with his precision and fire. Drawn towards jazz-rock and its older protagonists (punk had made virtuosity unfashionable in rock), he gravitated to London in the late 70s, playing and recording with Gordon Beck, Barbara Thompson and Allan Holdsworth.

Albums: *Allan Holdsworth IOU* (1982), *Metal Fatigue* (1984), with John Themis *Ulysses & the Cyclops* (1984).

Hutcherson, Bobby

b. 27 January 1941, Los Angeles, California, USA. After formal tuition on piano, Hutcherson switched to playing jazz vibraphone when he heard records by Milt Jackson. He worked briefly on the west coast then, in 1961, moved to New York, where he established himself as an inventive, forward-thinking musician. He played with many of the outstanding artists of the 60s, among them Archie Shepp, Eric Dolphy, Herbie Hancock, Andrew Hill and McCoy Tyner. Hutcherson made many records, sometimes as sideman (including the important *Out To Lunch* album with Dolphy), but regularly led his own groups, which often featured tenor saxophonist Harold Land, with whom he co-led a quintet from 1968-71. By now back on the west coast, Hutcherson played with Gerald Wilson and remained in San Francisco through the 70s, though he also toured around the world. In the late 80s, often playing in all-star bebop revival groups, Hutcherson continued to make numerous records, bringing his superb technique to bear upon an eclectic choice of material that demonstrated his awareness of his jazz roots. Despite this late flurry of activity, Hutcherson undeservedly remains one of the lesser-known of contemporary jazzmen.

Selected albums: with Eric Dolphy *Out To Lunch* (Blue Note 1964), *Dialogue* (Blue Note 1965), *Components* (1965), *Happenings* (Blue Note 1966), *Stick Up!* (1966), *Total Eclipse* (Blue Note 1967), *Oblique* (Blue Note 1967), *Bobby Hutcherson* (1968), *Patterns* (1968), *Spiral* (1968), *Now* (1969), *Medina* (1969), *San Francisco* (c.1971), *Head On* (1971), *Natural Illusions* (1972), *Live At Montreux* (1973), *Cirrus* (1974), *Linger Lane* (1974), *Montara* (1975), *Waiting* (1976), *The View From The Inside* (1976), *Knucklebean* (1977), *For Bobby Hutcherson/Blue Note Meets The Los Angeles Philharmonic* (1977), *Highway One* (1978), *Conception: The Gift Of Love* (1979), *Un Poco Loco* (1979), *Bobby Hutcherson Solo/Quartet* (Original Jazz Classics 1982), *Farewell Keystone* (Theresa 1982), *Four Seasons* (Timeless 1984) *Good Bait* (Landmark 1984), *Colour Schemes* (Landmark 1985), *In The Vanguard* (Landmark 1987), *Cruisin' The Bird* (Landmark 1988), *Ambos Mundos: Both Worlds* (Landmark 1989), *Mirage* (Landmark 1992), *Farewell Keystone* (1993), *Components* (Connoisseur 1994), with McCoy Tyner *Moodswings* (Blue Note 1994).

Hyder, Ken

b. 29 June 1946, Dundee, Scotland. Hyder took up the drums at the age of 15 and began playing bebop in Edinburgh and Dundee. He soon switched to free jazz, inspired by the music of John Coltrane and Albert Ayler - and, in particular, by their drummers Elvin Jones and Sunny Murray. At the end of the 60s Hyder moved to London and in 1970 set up his group Talisker to explore and combine his interest in free jazz and Celtic folk musics. He guided Talisker through two decades and various personnel changes (though saxophonists John Rangecroft and Davie Webster play on most of the albums), and has provided a blueprint for the increasing number of European musicians who have been incorporating elements of folk music into their jazz. Hyder's own interest in Scottish and Irish traditional musics had led to collaborations with Dick Gaughan, Irish uillean piper Tomas Lynch and Scottish bagpipes player Dave Brooks. A more recent fascination with shamanic singing has taken him on research trips to Canada and Siberia and brought projects with vocalists Valentina Ponomareva, Sainkho Namchilak and Anatoly Kokov. Back in the 70s, Hyder played with Julian Bahula's Jo'burg Hawk and in the 80s was busy on the UK improvised music scene, co-founding the occasional Orchestra Of Lights, recording *Under The Influence* with his octet, Big Team (which included Chris Biscoe, Elton Dean and Paul Rogers), and the duo Shams with ex-Henry Cow member Tim Hodgkinson. His latest group is the leftfield, 'polytempic' One Time, with members of B-Shops For The Poor and the Honkies.

Albums: with Talisker *Dreaming Of Glenisla* (1975), with Talisker *Land Of Stone* (1977), with Talisker *The Last Battle* (1978), with Talisker *The White Light* (1980), *Under The Influence* (1984), with Dick Gaughan *Fanfare For Tomorrow* (1985), with Talisker *Humanity* (1986), with Tim Hodgkinson *Shams* (1987), with Hodgkinson, Valentina Ponomareva *The Goose* (1992).

Hyman, Dick

b. 8 March 1927, New York City, New York, USA. After studying classical music, Hyman broadened his interests to encompass jazz and many other areas of music. In the late 40s he played piano in and around his home town, working with leading bop musicians, including founding fathers Charlie Parker and Dizzy Gillespie. Early in the 50s he began a long career as a studio musician, playing piano, arranging, composing and leading orchestras. His work in the studios did not keep him from actively participating in jazz dates, many of which he organized. He also became deeply interested in the history of jazz and especially the development of jazz piano. He demonstrated his interest in radio broadcasts and concert performances. His enormously eclectic taste allowed him to range from ragtime to freeform with complete confidence. Through performances and recordings with the New York Jazz Repertory Orchestra, he encouraged interest in the music of Jelly Roll Morton, Fats Waller, James P. Johnson and Louis Armstrong. He also formed a small group, the Perfect Jazz Repertory Quintet. During his freeform period he played electric piano and later added the organ to the instruments at his command, recording *Cincinnati Fats, New School Concert* and other duo albums with Ruby Braff. Later still, he recorded with Braff using, however improbably in a jazz context, a Wurlitzer

organ. Unusual though it might be, *A Pipe Organ Recital Plus One* was a critical and popular success. As a composer Hyman has written for large and small ensembles and composed the score for the film *Scott Joplin* (1976). A master of jazz piano, his performances not only display his extraordinary virtuoso technique but also demonstrate his deep understanding and abiding love for the great traditions of the music. Through his broadcasting and lectures, and by way of his enthusiasm and example, he has helped to expand interest in and appreciation of jazz of all kinds.

Selected albums: *The Electric Eclectics* (c.1969), *The Happy Breed* (1972), *Genius At Play* (1973), *Some Rags, Some Stomps And A Little Blues* (1973), with NYJRO *Satchmo Remembered* (1974), *Scott Joplin: The Complete Works For Piano* (c.1975), *A Waltz Dressed In Blue* (c.1977), *Charleston* (c.1977), *Sliding By* (1977), *Ragtime, Stomp And Stride* (c.1977), with NYJRO *The Music Of Jelly Roll Morton* (1978), *Dick Hyman And His Trio* (Grape Vine 1979), *Dick Hyman Piano Solos* (Monmouth Evergreen 1979), *The Perfect Jazz Repertory Quintet Plays Irving Berlin* (1979), with Ruby Braff *Cincinnati Fats* (1981), with Braff *A Pipe Organ Recital Plus One* (1982), *Live At Michael's Pub* (Jazz Mania 1982), *The New School Concert 1983* (1983), *Kitten On The Keys: The Music Of Zez Confrey* (1983), with Braff *The New School Concert 1983* (1983), *They Got Rhythm* (Jass 1984), *Eubie* (1984), *Manhattan Jazz* (1985), *Gulf Coast Blues The Music Of Clarence Williams* (Stomp Off 1987), *14 Jazz Piano Favourites* (Music And Arts 1989), *Music Of 1937* (1990), *Plays Harold Arlen* (Musicmasters 1990), with Ruby Braff *Manhattan Jazz* (S&R 1990), *Plays Fats Waller* (Reference 1990), with Braff *Younger Than Swingtime* (1990), *Music Of 1937* (Concord 1991), *Stride Piano Summit* (Milestone 1991), *Plays Duke Ellington* (Reference 1991).

Ibrahim, Abdullah

b. Adolph Johannes Brand, 9 October 1934, Cape Town, South Africa. Ibrahim began playing piano as a small child, learning church music and hearing many other forms, including jazz, from radio and records. Known initially by the name Dollar Brand, he began his professional career in the mid-50s playing popular music of the day, but by the end of the decade had formed a band that included Hugh Masakela and which concentrated on jazz. In the early 60s his political activities drew the attention of the authorities and he embarked upon a protracted visit to Europe with singer Sathima Bea Benjamin, whom he married. In Switzerland they attracted the much more benign and welcome attention of Duke Ellington, who helped arrange a recording date and opened other doors which led to appearances in the USA in the mid-60s. Later resident in New York City, Ibrahim played with leading exponents of free-form music, amongst them John Coltrane, Don Cherry and Ornette Coleman. He also continued to develop his involvement in politics and religion and in the late 60s he converted to Islam, subsequently adopting the name by which he has since been known. The banning of the African National Congress made it difficult for Ibrahim to retain close personal ties with his homeland but he returned there occasionally for recording dates. Despite the enforced separation from his roots he continued to explore African music and the manner in which it could be blended with contemporary American jazz. As a consequence, his extensive performing and recording dates, often of his own compositions, are shot through with rare intensity. In the early 80s Ibrahim expanded his musical horizons with the composition of an opera, *Kalahari Liberation*, which was performed throughout Europe to great acclaim. From the mid-80s his seven-piece band, Ekaya, has recorded and performed in concert and at festivals. As a performer, Ibrahim's playing of the piano (he also plays cello, flute and soprano saxophone) is vigorously rhythmic, intriguingly mixing bop with the music of his homeland and overlaid with touches of Ellington and Thelonious Monk. As a composer Ibrahim has ably and convincingly mixed the music of two cultures creating a distinctive style through which his highly motivated political and religious beliefs can be spread to a wide, mixed audience.

Selected albums: *Jazz Epistles: Verse I* (1960), *Duke Ellington Presents The Dollar Brand Trio* (1963), *Anatomy Of A South African Village* (1965), *The Dream* (rec 1965), with Gato Barbieri *Hamba Khale* (rec 1968), *This Is Dollar Brand* (1973, rec. 1965), *African Piano* (1973, rec 1969), *Sangoma* (rec 1973), *African Portraits* (rec. 1973), *Ode To Duke Ellington* (West Wind 1973), *African Sketchbook* (Enja 1974), *African Space Program* (Enja 1974), with Johnny Dyani *Good News From Africa* (1974), *Ancient Africa* (1974), *The Children Of Africa* (Enja 1976), *African Herbs* (1976), *Blues For A Hip King* (1976), *Black Lightning* (1976), *The Journey* (1978), with Max Roach *Streams Of Consciousness* (1978), *Soweto* (Bellaphon 1978), *Africa - Tears And Laughter* (1979), with Dyani *Echoes From Africa* (Enja 1980), *Memories* (1980), *African Market Place* (1980), *At Montreux* (Enja 1980), *Matsidiso* (1981), *South African Sunshine* (1982), *Duke's Memories* (1982), *African Dawn* (Enja 1982), *Mannenberg - Is Where It's Happening* (1983, probably rec. mid-70s), *Zimbabwe* (1983), *The Mountain* (Kaz 1983), *Autobiography* (1983, rec. 1978), *Ekaya* (Blackhawk 1984), with Carlos Ward *Live At Sweet Basil Vol. 1* (Blackhawk 1984), *Water From An Ancient Well* (Tiptoe 1986), *Mindiff* (Enja 1988), *Desert Flowers* (Enja 1993, rec. 1991), *Fats, Duke & Monk* (Sackville 1993, rec. 1973), *S'En Fout La Mort* (1993), *Knysna Blue* (Enja/Tip Toe 1994).

Ind, Peter

b. 20 July 1928, Uxbridge, Middlesex, England. After studying piano and composition formally, Ind began playing bass at the age of 19 and was soon hired to play in a band working on transatlantic liners. In 1951 he settled in New York where over the next few years he played with many noted jazz artists, including Lee Konitz, Warne Marsh and Buddy Rich. He also continued his studies under Lennie Tristano. In the early 60s he relocated to California, then returned to the UK. By performing and recording unaccompanied, Ind has greatly extended acceptance of the bass as a solo instrument. He has also worked in bass duos with Bernie Cash. In addition to his playing, Ind operates his own record company, Wave, and until the mid-90s ran his own London club, The Bass Clef.

Selected albums: with Lennie Tristano *Descent Into The Maelstrom* (1951), with Lee Konitz *Timespan* (1954-76), *Warne Marsh New York* (1959-60), *Looking Out* (Wave 1957-61), *Improvisation* (Wave 1968), with Sal Mosca *At The Den* (1969, recorded 1959), *No Kidding* (1974), *Peter Ind Sextet* (1975), with Bernie Cash *Contrabach* (1975), with Konitz, Marsh *London Concert* (1976), *At The Den* (1979), with Martin Taylor *Triple Libra* (1981), with Taylor *Jazz Bass Baroque* (1987).

Ingham, Keith

b. 5 February 1942, London, England. Ingham is a self-taught jazz pianist who turned professional in 1964. He played with artists including Sandy Brown and Bruce Turner. In 1974 he recorded in London with Bob Wilber and Bud Freeman and recorded two solo albums for EMI. In 1978 he moved to New York where he played with Benny Goodman and the World's Greatest Jazz Band. He became musical director and record producer for Susannah McCorkle as well as recording with Maxine Sullivan. He works with guitarist Marty Grosz in various bands including the Orphan Newsboys in which they perform some of the lesser known music of the 30s and 40s.

Albums: with Bud Freeman *Superbud* (1977), with Dick Sudhalter *Get Out And Get Under The Moon* (1989), with Marty Grosz *Unsaturated Fats* (1990), with the Orphan Newsboys *Laughing At Life* (1990), *Out Of The Past* (Stomp Off 1992).

International Sweethearts Of Rhythm

In 1937, Laurence Clifton Jones, administrator of a school for poor and orphaned children at Piney Woods, Mississippi, USA, decided to form a band. At first his enterprise was only mildly successful, but by the end of the decade it had achieved a high standard of musicianship and was growing in reputation. In 1941 the band came under new management and hired Eddie Durham as arranger and musical director. Soon afterwards, Durham was replaced by Jesse Stone, a noted Kansas City bandleader and arranger. Although mostly using black female musicians, a few white women were hired but, given the existence of segregation, these often had to 'pass' for black. At the end of World War II the Sweethearts toured American bases in Europe, played the Olympia Theatre in Paris, and broadcast on the Armed Forces Radio service. In 1949 the band folded but their leader for many years, Ann Mae

Winburn, formed a new group. By the mid-50s, however, this band too had ceased to exist. All but forgotten, memories of the band were revived largely through the efforts of record producer Rosetta Reitz, who released an album of the Sweethearts' AFRS broadcasts. Reminiscences by former members of the band were recorded in books on women jazz players by Sally Placksin (*Jazz Women*), Linda Dahl (*Stormy Weather*) and others, and in a television documentary which included footage of the band in performance. At its peak, in the early 40s, the Sweethearts were an excellent, swinging band with a style and power similar to that of bands such as Lucky Millinder's. Although the band led by Ina Ray Hutton was more popular with the general public, the Sweethearts were more accomplished musicians; unfortunately they were ignored in certain important areas of show business, like the motion-picture industry, because they were black. Among the long-serving members of the band were several excellent musicians, of whom trumpeter Ray Carter and alto saxophonist Roz Cron are worthy of mention. The band's outstanding players were another trumpeter, Ernestine 'Tiny' Davis, Pauline Braddy and Vi Burnside. Davis was a fine jazz player who also sang; Braddy was a superb, driving drummer whose advisers and admirers included 'Big' Sid Catlett and Jo Jones. The solo playing of Burnside, a tenor saxophonist (one of whose high school classmates was Sonny Rollins) shows her to have been a player who, had she been male, would have been ranked alongside the best of the day. Her breathy sound resembled that of Ben Webster, but there was never any suggestion that she was merely a copyist. Burnside was a major jazz talent and the International Sweethearts Of Rhythm were one of the best big bands of the swing era. The fact that they are so often overlooked is a sad reflection on the male-dominated world in which they strove to make their mark.

Compilations: *The International Sweethearts Of Rhythm* (1945-46), with others *Women In Jazz Vol. 1* (1945-46).

Israels, Chuck

b. Charles H. Israels, 10 October 1936, New York City, New York, USA. After extensive studies in the USA and France, Israels began playing bass with various leading jazzmen in the mid-50s. He recorded with Cecil Taylor, John Coltrane, George Russell and Eric Dolphy. In 1961 he joined the Bill Evans trio, taking over from Scott La Faro. He remained with Evans for five years, concurrently recording with several other artists including Herbie Hancock, Stan Getz and Hampton Hawes. In the early 70s Israels was instrumental in establishing the National Jazz Ensemble, a big band which brought contemporary ideas and techniques to the music of early jazzmen, such as Jelly Roll Morton and Louis Armstrong, while simultaneously developing for big band the creations of Thelonious Monk and other leading bop musicians. After the dissolution of the NJE in 1978 Israels performed less, although he did make occasional record dates in the early 80s.

Albums: with Bill Evans *How My Heart Sings!* (1962), with Evans *The Second Trio* (1962), *National Jazz Ensemble* (1975-76).

Jackson, Chubby

b. Greig Stewart Jackson, 25 October 1918, New York City, New York, USA. As a youth Jackson started out playing clarinet but switched to bass in the mid-30s. In 1937 he began playing professionally, working in a number of minor dance bands. In 1942 he joined the Charlie Barnet band and, the following year, was a member of Woody Herman's First Herd, where he played alongside Ralph Burns, Billy Bauer and Dave Tough in one of the most exciting rhythm sections in the history of big band jazz. After leaving Herman in 1946 Jackson freelanced, playing with various bands for record dates, including those led by Charlie Ventura and Herman. He also led a bop-orientated small group, featuring Conte Candoli, Terry Gibbs, Frank Socolow, Lou Levy, Denzil Best and others, with which he toured Scandinavia. In the late 40s and early 50s Jackson was active in the studios, led his own big band and made numerous record dates with artists including Bill Harris, Zoot Sims and Gerry Mulligan. Jackson was also a member of the Charlie Ventura Big Four with Marty Napoleon and Buddy Rich. In the 60s Jackson worked in television, hosting a programme for children. He intermittently led bands during these years and also freelanced, playing in bands led by Harold Baker and Bill Coleman. To a great extent, however, Jackson was largely forgotten by the jazz world other than through his earlier records. Then, in the late 70s, he reappeared as a member of the all-star band which Lionel Hampton led on a tour of festivals in the USA, UK and Europe. One of the most overtly enthusiastic musicians in jazz, Jackson's forceful, attacking style was particularly suited to the bands of Herman, Ventura and Hampton. His son is Duffy Jackson, drummer with Count Basie and Hampton. In the late 80s Jackson was still around the jazz scene, lending his exhilarating support to a variety of bands.

Albums: with Charlie Ventura *The Big Four* (1951), *Chubby's Back!* (1957), with Lionel Hampton *All Star Band At Newport '78* (1978). Compilations: *The Best Of Woody Herman* (1945-47), with Woody Herman *Carnegie Hall Concert* (1946), *Jam Session* (1947), *Choice Cuts* (Esquire 1986), *The Happy Monster 1944-1947* (Cool 'n' Blue 1993).

Jackson, Cliff

b. 19 July 1902, Culpeper, Virginia, USA, d. 24 May 1970. After studying piano formally Jackson turned to jazz, working in various east coast cities before coming to New York in the early 20s. During the rest of the decade he played in several minor bands, eventually joining one led by Elmer Snowden. Jackson later formed his own small group for club engagements. In the 30s he worked mostly as a soloist but also accompanied singers. In the 40s he was with Sidney Bechet, Eddie Condon and others, appearing regularly throughout this and the following decade at New York's top jazz clubs, including Nick's Cafe Society (Downtown) and Jimmy Ryan's. Also in the 60s he worked with his wife, Maxine Sullivan. He was resident at the RX Room from 1968 until the night before his death in May 1970. His widow later turned their home into a museum, the 'House That Jazz Built'. A vigorous performer, early in his career Jackson was a leading stride pianist, greatly feared in cutting contests where he would happily take on much bigger names.

Albums: *Cliff Jackson's Washboard Wanderers* (1961), *Uptown And Lowdown* (1961), *Carolina Shout!* (Black Lion 1961-62), *Hot Piano* (1965), *Parlor Social Call* (1968), Cliff Jackson And His Crazy Cats (Fountain 1981), *Hot Piano* (Ri-Disc 1988), with Lil Armstrong *B&W Masters* (Storyville 1988).

Jackson, Milt 'Bags'

b. 1 January 1923, Detroit, Michigan, USA. Jackson's first professional engagement, at the age of 16, was in his hometown, playing the vibraphone alongside tenor saxophonist Lucky Thompson (one year his junior). Jackson benefited from the 40s loose attitude towards band personnel, spending six years accompanying visiting musicians, as well as studying at Michigan State University. In 1945 Dizzy Gillespie heard him and invited him to join his band for a west coast tour. Later moving to New York, the brilliant young vibes player found himself much in demand, playing and recording with Howard McGhee and Thelonious Monk (including Monk's classic 1951 session for Blue Note). A spell with Woody Herman (1949-50) and more work with Gillespie established him as the pre-eminent player on his instrument. Jackson's recording debut as a leader was for Gillespie's Dee Gee label in 1951. He also had the depth of experience to play with both Ben Webster and Charlie Parker. In 1954 the Milt Jackson Quartet transformed itself into the Modern Jazz Quartet, with pianist John Lewis becoming musical director. For the next 20 years, Milt Jackson led a Dr Jeckyll and Mr Hyde existence, playing the consummately sophisticated music of the MJQ, all dressed in their famous tuxedoes, and leading his own dates in the swinging company of Coleman Hawkins, Lucky Thompson or Horace Silver. In 1961 Jackson accompanied Ray Charles on *Soul Meeting*, on which the soul singer restricted himself to electric piano and alto saxophone. Sleevenote writers loved to debate how happy Jackson could be with the MJQ's starchy charts. Certainly when he broke up the group in 1974, it was due to what he considered its financial exploitation rather than musical antagonism. Before Jackson, the vibes were an instrument associated with the hot, swinging proto-R&B of big band leaders Lionel Hampton and Johnny Otis. By slowing the vibrato and giving the right-hand mallet sweeping lines like a saxophone, Jackson gave the instrument sensuality and soul. Not until the appearance of Bobby Hutcherson in the mid-60s did anyone come up with an alternative modern approach to playing it. Jackson's harmonic sense was unerringly inventive and he also kept his ears open for new talent. He championed guitarist Wes Montgomery and recorded with him for the Riverside label (*Bags Meets Wes*, 1961). Jackson was a strong force in the reintegration of bebop with swing values and musicians, the very definition of what came to be known as 'mainstream' jazz. His own quintets included players such as Cedar Walton, Jimmy Heath and James Moody. The 70s were a hard period for jazz players, but even in the dated arrangements of Bob James on a record like *Olinga* (recorded in 1974 for CTI) his caressing, ebullient vibes playing shines through. The 80s jazz revival was reflected by the MJQ reforming and appearing at countless jazz festivals. In 1985 Jackson toured Europe under his own name. The Pablo record label continued to document his music into the 90s.

Selected albums: *In The Beginning* (Original Jazz Classics 1947-48 recordings), *Milt Jackson Quartet* (1954), *Opus De Jazz* (Savoy 1955), *Jackson's Ville* (Savoy 1956), *Meet Milt Jackson* (Savoy 1957), *Roll 'Em Bags* (Savoy 1957), *The Jazz Skyline* (Savoy 1957), *Bluesology* (1957), *Plenty Plenty Soul* (1957), *Ballads & Blues* (1958), *Bags' Opus* (Blue Note 1959), with John Coltrane *Bags Meets Trane* (Atlantic 1959), *Bags Meets Wes* (1961), *Invitation* (Original Jazz Classics 1963), *Big Bags* (Original Jazz Classics 1963), with Ray Charles *Soul Meeting* (1964), *Vibrations* (1964), *At The Village Gate* (Original Jazz Classics 1964), *For Someone I Love* (Original Jazz Classics 1964), *Statements* (Impulse 1965), *Olinga* (1974), *Milt Jackson Big 4* (1975), *Montreaux '77* (Original Jazz Classics 1978), *Feelings* (Original Jazz Classics 1978), *Soul Fusion* (Original Jazz Classics 1978), *Milt Jackson + Count Basie + The Big Band Vols 1 and 2* (Original Jazz Classics 1978), *Soul Believer* (Original Jazz Classics 1979), *Night Mist* (1980), *All Too Soon* (Original Jazz Classics 1981), Soul Route (Pablo 1984), *It Don't Mean A Thing If You Can't Tap Your Foot To It* (Original Jazz Classics 1985), *Brother Jim* (Pablo 1986), *A London Bridge* (Pablo 1986), *Milt Jackson* (1987), *Bebop* (1988), *The Harum* (Limelight 1991), *Reverence And Compassion* (Qwest 1993). Compilation: *The Best Of Milt Jackson* (Pablo 1982).

Jackson, Oliver

b. 28 April 1933, Detroit, Michigan, USA, d. 29 May 1994, New York, USA. In the mid-40s drummer Jackson was active among Detroit R&B and bebop musicians, picking up the nickname 'Bops Jnr.' in the process. Among the artists with whom he worked during his formative years were Barry Harris, Donald Byrd and Tommy Flanagan, as well as the equally young and inexperienced John Coltrane. Jackson established a reputation as a sensitive accompanist to pianists and later in the decade played in trios with Flanagan and Dorothy Donegan. Then, in collaboration with fellow drummer Eddie Locke, Jackson formed a tap-dancing duo, Bops And Locke, which met with considerable success. Throughout the 50s he played with a variety of jazzmen, shifting comfortably between exponents of traditional and of modern music such as Red Allen and Yusef Lateef. In the early 60s he worked with Charlie Shavers, Buck Clayton, Benny Goodman and Lionel Hampton and then spent the rest of the decade with Earl Hines. In 1969 he formed the JPJ Quartet (with Budd Johnson, Bill Pemberton and Dill Jones), which played extensively in the

USA. In the 70s and 80s Jackson appeared with Sy Oliver, Hampton again, Oscar Peterson, Doc Cheatham, Vic Dickenson, Buddy Tate, a band he co-led with Haywood Henry, and with his own groups, which featured Irving Stokes, Norris Turney and his bass-playing brother, Ali Jackson (who died in 1987). During this period Oliver became a familiar and popular figure at jazz festivals in the USA and Europe. Jackson's playing ranged over the full spectrum of jazz and he made an important contribution to many excellent concert and recording sessions.

Albums: *The Oliver Jackson-Jack Sels Quartet* (1961), with Buck Clayton *Olympia Concert* (1961), *Coleman Hawkins And The Earl Hines Trio* (1965), with Doc Cheatham *Jive At Five* (1975), with Haywood Henry *Real Jazz Express* (1977), *The Oliver Jackson Trio* (1979), *Oliver Jackson Presents Le Quartet* (1982), *Billie's Bounce* (Black And Blue 1984).

Jackson, Preston

b. 3 January 1902, New Orleans, Louisiana, USA, d. 12 November 1983. From his early teens Jackson lived in Chicago, where he learned the trombone in 1920. He played with several local bands throughout the 20s and in the early 30s was in demand by prominent local bandleaders such as Dave Peyton and Erskine Tate. In 1926 he recorded with Luis Russell and with a band led by clarinettist Arthur Sims; he also fronted his own pick-up group on a 1928 date. In 1931 he joined Louis Armstrong, then worked with Frankie Jaxon, recording with him in 1933, Carroll Dickerson, Jimmie Noone, Zilner Randolph, Walter Barnes and others, mostly touring the mid-western and south-west states by the end of the decade. However, Jackson was musically active only on a part-time basis. During the 40s and 50s he was involved in musicians' union work, but occasionally formed bands for club and record dates and also worked briefly with Richard M. Jones, Johnny Dodds, Lillian Armstrong and others. He continued this sporadic activity into the next decade, towards the end of which he worked with Little Brother Montgomery. In the 70s he toured with Kid Thomas and, resident once more in New Orleans, played with the Preservation Hall Jazz Band. During his playing career Jackson's style moved with the times. Although his occupation began in Chicago, he based his early playing on that of other relocated New Orleans jazzmen. In mid-career he incorporated swing era developments into his repertoire, then late in life returned to his roots but with a sophisticated stylistic patina. Deeply interested in the history of jazz, Jackson wrote extensively for magazines over a 40-year period.

Album: with Kid Thomas *The New Orleans Joymakers* (1973). Compilation: *Louis Armstrong And His Orchestra Vol. 9* (1931).

Jackson, Quentin

b. 13 January 1909, Springfield, Ohio, USA, d. 2 October 1976. As a child Jackson had learned to play piano, organ and violin, but in his late teens he took up the trombone. He received tuition from his brother-in-law, Claude Jones, who played in McKinney's Cotton Pickers; after a couple of years of intensive touring with various territory bands, in 1930 Jackson, too, joined McKinney. Two years later he switched to the band formed by the McKinney band's musical director, Don Redman. During his long stay with Redman he picked up the nickname, 'Butter', and attracted considerable attention from other trombone players and bandleaders. In 1939 he joined Cab Calloway, with whom he remained for eight years, then moved on to the Duke Ellington orchestra for an even longer period, eventually leaving in 1959. In the early 60s Jackson was briefly with Quincy Jones and Count Basie, Ellington again, and recorded important albums with Charles Mingus. Jackson then settled into a combination of studio work and appearances with big bands led by Louie Bellson and Gerald Wilson and in the early 70s was in the Thad Jones-Mel Lewis Jazz Orchestra. A strong and reliable section player, Jackson was also an excellent soloist with a rich, emotional tone.

Albums: *Ellington '55* (1953-54), with Ellington *Such Sweet Thunder* (1957), *Mingus, Mingus, Mingus, Mingus* (1963), with Thad Jones-Mel Lewis *Suite For Pops* (1972).

Jackson, Ronald Shannon

b. 12 January 1940, Fort Worth, Texas, USA. Jackson studied piano at the age of five, taking up clarinet and drums at school. He began professional work when he was 15, gigging regularly in Dallas with James Clay and Leroy Cooper who were then in the Ray Charles's band. He studied history and sociology before gaining a music scholarship in New York, where he worked with artists including Albert Ayler, Charles Tyler, Betty Carter, Charles Mingus and Stanley Turrentine. From 1975-79 Jackson played alongside James 'Blood' Ulmer in the Ornette Coleman Sextet which evolved into Prime Time, and also worked with Cecil Taylor. Jackson joined Ulmer's band until setting up his own innovative and highly acclaimed Decoding Society in 1981. Although continuing to be based in Coleman's theory of harmolodics, the music of the Decoding Society changed its sound and direction with each album during the late 80s, often radically changing its instrumental line-up too. However, the foundation was always Jackson's thunderous, supple percussion. In 1986 he set up Last Exit with Peter Brötzmann, Sonny Sharrock and Bill Laswell, and in 1987 formed the trio Power Tools with Bill Frisell and Melvin Gibbs. In the late 80s and early 90s Jackson was re-united with Ulmer on record and in tours with a blues/funk-based power trio.

Selected albums: *Eye On You* (1981), *Nasty* (1981), *Man Dance* (1982), *Barbecue Dog* (Antilles 1984), *Decode Yourself* (Island 1985), *When Colors Play* (1987), with Power Tools *Strange Meeting* (1987), *When Colours Play* (Caravan Of Dreams 1987), *Live At The Caravan Of Dreams* (1987), *Texas* (1989), *Taboo* (Virgin 1990), *Red Warrior* (Axiom 1991), *Raven Roc* (DIW 1992).

Jacquet, Illinois

b. Jean Baptiste Jacquet, 31 October 1922, Broussard, Louisiana, USA. Raised in Texas, Jacquet started out on drums, later switching to alto and soprano saxophones. He worked in the popular territory band led by Milt Larkins and after stints

with other units ended up on the west coast, where he was invited to join Lionel Hampton's new band. In fact, Hampton had wanted Jacquet's section-mate in the Larkins band, tenor saxophonist Arnett Cobb, but when Cobb refused to leave, Hampton took Jacquet on condition he switch instruments. Jacquet took the plunge and his solo on Hampton's 1942 recording of 'Flying Home' established him as a major figure in jazz. Indeed, his solo was eventually integrated into subsequent performances of the tune. At the end of 1942, when Cobb finally agreed to leave Larkins and join Hampton, Jacquet moved on first to Cab Calloway and then to Count Basie. Also in the early 40s, he was involved with Norman Granz, appearing in the short film, *Jammin The Blues* (1944), and appearing with Granz's Jazz At The Philharmonic. From the mid-40s and on through the 50s Jacquet combined leading his own bands with JATP tours. In the 50s and 60s he became a popular figure at international festivals, leading his own groups, working in all-star ensembles and periodically appearing with Hampton. In the 80s Jacquet continued to record, and late in the decade formed a fine big band for occasional concerts and recording sessions. An important if often overlooked transitional figure in the development of the tenor saxophone, Jacquet has made a significant contribution to the mainstream of jazz while retaining a strong affinity for the blues of his adopted state. This blues feeling, superbly realized on his first recording of 'Flying Home', helped immeasurably in giving rise and substance to the Texas tenor style. His reputation as a wild man of the tenor, based in part upon his time with JATP, is ill-deserved. Indeed, although his high-note playing in the uptempo flagwavers was a demonstration of his incredible technical ability, almost any concert performance or recording date will attest that Jacquet is also a consummate interpreter of ballads.
Selected albums: *Swing's The Thing* (Verve 1957), *Illinois Flies Again* (Argo 1959), *Desert Winds* (1964), *Spectrum* (1966), *Go Power!* (1966), *Bottoms Up* (Original Jazz Classics 1968), *The King* (1968), *The Blues That's Me* (Original Jazz Classics 1969), *The Soul Explosion* (Original Jazz Classics 1970), *Genius At Work* (Black Lion 1971), *The Comeback* (Black Lion 1972), *The Blues For Louisiana* (1973), *Illinois Jacquet And Wild Bill Davis* (Black And Blue 1973), *Jacquet's Street* (1974-76), with Buddy Tate *Texas Tenors* (1976), with Howard McGhee *Here Comes Freddy* (1976), *Jacquet's Street* (Black And Blue 1977), *Midnight Slows Vol. 8* (Black And Blue 1978), *God Bless My Solo* (1978), *Battle Of The Horns* (1980), *Illinois Jacquet With His All Star New York Band* (1980), *Groovin'* (Verve 1981), *Illinois Jacquet And His Big Band* (1988), Selected compilations: with Lionel Hampton *Leapin' With Lionel* (1942-46), *The Black Velvet Band* (Bluebird 1988, 1947-67 recordings), *Flying Home: The Best Of The Verve Years* (Bluebird 1992).

Jamal, Ahmad

b. Fritz Jones, 2 July 1930, Pittsburgh, Pennsylvania, USA. A professional pianist from before his teenage years, Jamal (who changed his name in the early 50s) managed to break through to a wider audience than most jazz artists. His trio work produced many excellent recordings and his accompanists included Israel Crosby. The most influential of his advocates was Miles Davis, who recognized Jamal's interesting rhythmic concepts as being something which he could incorporate into his own work. Jamal worked extensively in the USA throughout the 60s, 70s and 80s, usually in trio format but occasionally with larger backing for record dates, and also appeared with Gary Burton. Jamal is an important figure among mainstream pianists and their post-bop successors, mainly as a result of the indirect influence he has had through Davis. A lyrical, gently swinging musician, Jamal's playing is a constant delight.
Selected albums: *Chamber Music Of The New Jazz* (1955), *The Ahmad Jamal Trio* i (1955), *Count 'Em* (1956), *But Not For Me* (1958), *Ahmad Jamal At The Pershing* (1958), *The Ahmad Jamal Trio* ii (1958), *The Ahmad Jamal Trio* iii (1959), *Happy Moods* (1960), *Listen To The Ahmad Jamal Quartet* (1960), *Ahmad Jamal's Alhambra* (1961), *Ahmad Jamal At The Blackhawk* (1961), *Macanudo* (1962), *Naked City Theme* (1963), *The Roar Of The Greasepaint, The Smell Of The Crowd* (1965), *Extensions* (1965), *Ahmad Jamal With String* (1965), *Heat Wave* (1966), *Cry Young* (1967), *The Bright, The Blue And The Beautiful* (1968), *Tranquillity* (1968), *Jamal At The Top/Poinciana Revisited* (1968), *The Awakening* (1970), *Free Flight Vol. 1* (1971), *Outer Time Inner Space* (1971), *Jamal Plays Jamal* (1974), *Live At Oil Can Harry's* (1976), *Prelude To A Kiss* (1976-8), *Steppin' Out With A Dream* (c.1977), *Genetic Walk* (c.1978), *Intervals* (c.1979), *Ahmad Jamal Live At Bubba's* (Kingdom Jazz 1980), *Night Song* (Motown 1980), *Ahmad Jamal In Concert* (1981), *American Classical Music* (1982), *Digital Works* (Atlantic 1985), *Rossiter Road* (Atlantic 1985), *Live At The Montreaux Jazz Festival* (Atlantic 1986), *Goodbye Mr Ecans* (Black Lion 1988), *Crystal* (WEA 1993), *Chicago Revisited* (Telarc 1993), *Live In Paris 92* (Birdology 1993).

James, Harry

b. 15 March 1916, Albany, Georgia, USA, d. 5 July 1983. James father played trumpet in the band of a touring circus. At first Harry played drums but then he, too, took up the trumpet and at the age of nine was also playing in the circus band. He showed such enormous promise that his father had soon taught him everything he knew. Harry left the circus and played with various bands in Texas before joining Ben Pollack in 1935. Early in 1937 James was hired by Benny Goodman, an engagement which gave him maximum exposure to swing era audiences. Heavily featured with Goodman and, with Ziggy Elman and Chris Griffin, forming part of a powerful and exciting trumpet section, James quickly became a household name. He remained with Goodman a little under two years, leaving to form his own big band. James popularity increased and his public image, aided by his marriage to film star Betty Grable, reached remarkable heights for a musician. The band's popularity was achieved largely through James own solos, but a small part of its success may be attributed to his singers, Louise Tobin, to whom he was briefly married before Grable, Frank Sinatra, who soon left to join Tommy Dorsey, Dick Haymes and Kitty Kallen. James maintained his band throughout the 40s and into the early 50s, establishing a solid reputation thanks to distinguished sidemen such as Willie Smith, Buddy Rich, Corky Corcoran and Juan Tizol. Owing chiefly to the recorded repertoire, much of which featured James playing florid trumpet solos on tunes such as 'The Flight Of The Bumble Bee', 'The Carnival of Venice', 'I Cried For You' and 'You Made Me Love You', his band was at times less than popular with hardcore jazz fans. This view should have altered when, in the mid-50s, after a period of re-evaluation, James formed a band to play charts by Ernie Wilkins and Neal Hefti. One of the outstanding big bands, this particular group is often and very unfairly regarded as a copy of Count Basie's, a point of view which completely disregards chronology. In fact, James band can be seen to have pre-empted the slightly later but much more widely recognized middle-period band led by Basie, which also used Wilkins's and Hefti's charts. James continued leading into the 60s and 70s, dividing his time between extended residencies at major hotel and casino venues, mostly in Las Vegas, Nevada, and touring internationally. Amongst the first-rate musicians James used in these years were Willie Smith again, a succession of fine drummers (including Rich, Sonny Payne and Louie Bellson) and lead trumpeter Nick Buono, who had joined in December 1939 and showed no signs of relinquishing his chair and would, indeed, remain until the end. In his early years James was a brashly exciting player, attacking solos and abetting ensembles with a rich tone and what was at times an overwhelmingly powerful sound. With his own band he exploited his virtuoso technique, performing with great conviction the ballads and trumpet spectaculars that so disconcerted his jazz followers but which delighted the wider audience at whom they were aimed. Over the years James appeared in several movies - with his band in *Private Buckaroo* (1942), *Springtime In The Rockies, Best Foot Forward, Bathing Beauty, Two Girls And A Sailor, Do You Love Me?, If I'm Lucky, Carnegie Hall*, and *I'll Get By* (1950) - and as a solo artist in *Syncopation* (1942) and *The Benny Goodman Story* (1956). He also played trumpet on the soundtrack of *Young Man With A Horn* (1950). Later in his career, James work combined the best of both worlds - jazz and the more flashy style - and shed many of its excesses. He remained popular into the 80s and never lost his enthusiasm, despite suffering from cancer, which eventually claimed him in 1983.

Selected albums: with Benny Goodman *Carnegie Hall Concert* (1938), *The New James* (1958), *Harry's Choice!* (1958), *Harry James And His New Swingin' Bands* (1959), *The Spectacular Sound Of Harry James* (1961), *Harry James Plays Neal Hefti* (1961), *The Solid Trumpet Of Harry James* (1962), *Double Dixie* (1962), *On Tour In '64* (1964), *Harry James Live At The Riverboat* (1966), *Live From Clearwater, Florida Vols 1-3* (1970), *Live In London* (1971), *King James Version* (1976), *Still Happy After All These Years* (1979). Selected compilations: with Goodman *Jazz Concert No. 2* (1937-38), *Texas Chatter* (1938), *The Unheard Harry James* (1939), *The Young Harry James* (1939), *Flash Harry* (1942-44), *Coast To Coast* (1944), *The Uncollected Harry James Vols 1-5* (c.1939-46), *Sounds Familiar* (1946), *Spotlight On Harry James* (1946), *Trumpet Blues* (1949-50), *Big John Special* (1949-50), *The Best Of Harry James , The*

Capitol Years (Capitol 1992), *The Music Maker* (Empress 1993).

Jarman, Joseph

b. 14 September 1937, Pine Bluff, Arkansas, USA. When he was a child Jarman's family moved to Chicago, where he studied drums at high school. While in the army he played saxophone and clarinet; after demobilisation he travelled until settling back in Chicago in 1961. He joined the AACM in 1965, leading various groups and playing in Richard Muhal Abrams's the Experimental Band. During that year he also collaborated with controversial classical composer John Cage on a multimedia event. A poet himself, Jarman's concerts would often include poets or dancers, his taste for the theatrical having been developed when he studied drama at the Second City Theatre School and the Art Institute of Chicago School. In 1969, dispirited by the death of Charles Clark and Chris Gaddy, two of his regular sidemen, he disbanded his own group and joined the Art Ensemble Of Chicago, with whom the bulk of his work has been done since then. Like his partners in the Ensemble (Lester Bowie, Roscoe Mitchell, Malachi Favors and Don Moye) he plays a dazzling number of instruments, the primary ones being sopranino, soprano, alto, tenor and bass saxophones, bassoon, oboe, flutes and clarinets as well as various percussion and 'little instruments'. If Jarman is the dramatist of the Ensemble to Mitchell's purer musician, he has nonetheless written a number of rigorous compositions for large groups. Regrettably, little of his work away from the AEC has been recorded during the 70s and 80s; that which has is mostly in small groups which he co-leads with Moye, though he sometimes guests with other bands - playing, for example, with the Reggie Workman Ensemble in the late 80s.

Albums: *Song For* (Delmark 1966), *As If It Were The Seasons* (1968), *Sunbound* (1976), with Don Moye *Egwu-Anwu* (1978), *The Magic Triangle* (1979), *Black Paladins* (1980), *Earth Passage - Density* (1981).

Jarreau, Al

b. 12 March 1940, Milwaukee, Wisconsin, USA. Although Jarreau sang from childhood, it was many years before he decided to make singing his full-time occupation. Working outside music for most of the 60s, he began to sing in small west coast clubs and eventually achieved enough success to change careers. By the mid-70s he was becoming well known in the USA, and owing to records and a European tour greatly extended his audience. Singing a highly sophisticated form of vocalese (scat singing), Jarreau's style displays many influences. Some of these come from within the world of jazz, notably the work of Jon Hendricks, while others are external. He customarily uses vocal sounds that include the clicks of African song and the plosives common in oriental speech and singing patterns. This range of influences makes him both hard to classify and more accessible to the wider audience for crossover music. More commercially successful than most jazz singers, Jarreau's work in the 70s and 80s consistently appealed to young audiences attuned to fusions in popular music. By the early 90s, when he was entering his 50s, his kinship with youth culture was clearly diminishing; but his reputation was by now firmly established.

Albums: *1965* (1965), *We Got By* (1975), *Glow* (Reprise 1976), *Look To The Rainbow* (WEA 1977), *We Got By* (Reprise 1977), *All Fly Home* (WEA 1978), *This Time* (WEA 1980), *Breakin' Away* (WEA 1981), *Jarreau* (WEA 1983), *Spirits And Feelings* (Happy Bird 1984), *Ain't No Sunshine* (Blue Moon 1984), *High Crime* (WEA 1984), *Al Jarreau Live In London* (WEA 1984), *You* (Platinum 1985), *L As In Lover* (WEA 1986), *Hearts Horizon* (WEA 1988), *Manifesto* (Masters 1988), *Heaven And Earth* (WEA 1992), *Tenderness* (WEA 1994).

Jarrett, Keith

b. 8 May 1945, Allentown, Pennsylvania, USA. Growing up in a highly musical family, Jarrett displayed startling precocity and was playing piano from the age of three. From a very early age he also composed music and long before he entered his teens was touring as a professional musician, playing classical music and his own compositions. He continued with his studies at Berklee College Of Music in the early 60s but was soon leading his own small group. From the mid-60s he was based in New York where he was heard by Art Blakey who invited him to join his band. Jarrett stayed with Blakey for only a few months but it was enough to raise his previously low profile. In 1966 he joined Charles Lloyd's quartet which made his name known internationally, thanks to extensive tours of Europe and visits to the Soviet Union and the Far East. During his childhood Jarrett had also played vibraphone, saxophone, and percussion instruments, and he resumed performing on some of these instruments in the late 60s. In 1969 he joined Miles Davis, playing organ for a while, before turning to electric piano. During his two years with Davis he also found time to record under his own name, enhancing his reputation with a succession of fine albums with Charlie Haden, Dewey Redman and others. After leaving Davis he resumed playing acoustic piano and established a substantial following for his music, which he has described as 'universal folk music'. *Facing You* in 1971 created a considerable response and was an extraordinary demonstration of speed, dynamics and emotion. The now familiar Jarrett characteristic of brilliantly adding styles was first aired on this album. Country, folk, classical, blues and rock were given brief cameos.

Subsequently, Jarrett has become a major figure not only in furthering his own music but in 'showing the way' for contemporary jazz and in particular the growth of ECM Records and the work of Manfred Eicher. He has often worked and recorded with artists including Jan Garbarek, Jack DeJohnette and Gary Peacock, but regularly returns to solo performances on piano and occasionally on pipe organ. It is as an outstanding solo pianist that Jarrett has arguably created a genre. Jarrett's remarkable improvisational skills have led to his ability to present solo concerts during which he might play works of such a length that as few as two pieces will comprise an entire evening's music. His pivotal 1975 solo *The Köln Concert*, recorded during a European tour, received numerous accolades

in the USA and Europe. It remains his biggest selling work and is a must for any discerning music collection. Similarly *Solo Concerts Bremen/Lausanne* and *Sun Bear Concerts* are rich journeys into the improvisational unknown. Jarrett's solo improvised work has not resulted in his turning his back on composing and he has written and recorded music for piano and string orchestra resulting in albums such as *In The Light* and *The Celestial Hawk*. His interest in this form of music has added to his concert repertoire and during the 80s, in addition to solo and small group jazz concerts he also played classical works. Jarrett's continuing association with ECM Records has helped advance his constantly maturing musical persona. Technically flawless, Jarrett's playing style draws upon many sources reaching into all areas of jazz while simultaneously displaying a thorough understanding of and feeling for the western classical form. One of the most dazzling improvising talents the world of music has ever known, Jarrett is also remarkable for having achieved recognition from the musical establishment as well as the jazz audience while also enjoying considerable commercial success.

Selected albums: *Somewhere Before* (Atlantic 1968), *Facing You* (ECM 1971), *Expectations* (ECM 1972), *Fort Yawuh* (Impulse 1973), *In The Light* (1973), *Solo Concerts: Bremen And Lausanne* (ECM 1973), *Belonging* (ECM 1974), *Luminessence* (ECM 1974), *Arbour Zena* (ECM 1975), *The Köln Concert* (ECM 1975), *Sun Bear Concerts* (ECM 1976), *The Survivor's Suite* (1976), *Silence* (Impulse 1976), *My Song* (ECM 1977), *Nude Ants* (ECM 1979), *Personal Mountains* (ECM 1979), *Expectations* (Columbia 1979), *Invocations: The Moth And The Flame* (1980), *The Celestial Hawk* (ECM 1980), *Concerts Bregenz And München* (1981) *Concerts (Bregenz)* (1982), *Bop-Be* (1982), *Standards Vols 1* (ECM 1983), *Changes* (ECM 1983), *Backhand* (1983), *Works* (1983), *Eyes Of The Heart* (ECM 1985), *Spirits* (1985), *Staircase* (1985), *Standards Live* (1985), *Sacred Hymns* (ECM 1985), *Still Live* (ECM 1986), *Book Of Ways* (1986), *Spheres* (ECM 1986), *Dark Intervals* (1988), *Standards Vol 2* (ECM 1988), *Changeless* (1989), *Treasure Island* (Impulse 1989), *The Well Tempered Clavier Book* (1989), *Paris Concert* (ECM 1990), *Tribute* (ECM 1991), *The Cure* (ECM 1992), *Vienna Concert* (ECM 1992), with Jack DeJohnette *Ruta & Daitya* (ECM 1993), *Bye Bye Blackbird* (ECM 1993), with Gary Peacock, Paul Motian *At The Deer Head Inn* (ECM 1994). Compilation: *Works* (ECM 1989).

Jazz At The Philharmonic

In 1944 the tyro jazz impresario Norman Granz began a series of jazz concerts at the Philharmonic Auditorium in Los Angeles, USA. Reputedly, the name by which these concerts became known, JATP, arose from an abbreviation of the foregoing. The form, style and content of the concerts caught the jazz public's imagination and they continued through the rest of the decade and into the 50s, gradually becoming bigger and more spectacular musical packages. Fortunately, Granz had the foresight and acumen to record all his concerts. The release, on the new long-playing records, of these extended jam session performances proved commercially profitable and helped to establish Granz as a leading record producer. From 1957 onwards JATP tours were confined to Europe and in 1967, after a farewell tour of the USA, the concept was largely abandoned, although Granz continued to tour artists under the generic banner. Indeed, in some measure it might be claimed that his concept is mirrored in many latterday festival packages. Although often criticized for their showier aspects, JATP concerts included a wealth of fine playing by a succession of outstanding mainstream and bebop performers. Among the musicians who appeared with JATP over the years have been trumpeters Joe Guy, Howard McGhee, Buck Clayton, Charlie Shavers, Dizzy Gillespie and Roy Eldridge, trombonists J.J. Johnson, Bill Harris and Tommy Turk, saxophonists Charlie Parker, Willie Smith, Benny Carter, Lester Young, Coleman Hawkins, Illinois Jacquet, Flip Phillips and Stan Getz, pianists Oscar Peterson, Nat 'King' Cole, Hank Jones and Kenny Kersey, and drummers Gene Krupa, Buddy Rich, J.C. Heard, Jo Jones and Louie Bellson. Granz also included the entire Count Basie and Duke Ellington orchestras in some of his more ambitious packages, and Ella Fitzgerald too was a mainstay for many years.

Albums: *JATP* (1944), *JATP: Vols 1 & 3* (1944-46), *JATP: Vols 2 & 6/JATP: Bird And Pres* (1946), *JATP: Vol. 14* (1946), *JATP: Vols 4 & 5* (1946), *JATP: Vol. 7* (1946), *JATP: Vol. 8* (1947), *JATP: Vols 9 & 10* (1947), *JATP: Vols 12 & 13* (1949), *JATP: Vol. 15* (1953), *JATP: Live At The Nichigeki Theatre, Tokyo* (1953), *JATP: Hartford, Connecticut* (1954), *JATP: The Exciting Battle, Stockholm '55* (1955), *JATP All Stars At The Opera House, Chicago* (1957), *JATP: In London 1969* (1969), *JATP: At The Montreux Festival* (1975).

Jazz Warriors

Formed in London in the mid-80s, largely through the efforts of Courtney Pine and Gail Thompson, the Jazz Warriors drew musicians from the growing group of young black musicians who were active in the UK during the 80s. Initially the band was around 20 pieces and made extensive use of Afro-Caribbean percussive patterns overlaid with powerhouse brass. Many of the band's early soloists demonstrated their enthusiasm for John Coltrane, but in later years a wider range of influences was evident. The freedom from stylization that the Warriors displayed in their approach to big band music allowed the introduction of disparate musical forms, and proved a heady mixture which attracted many fans from the fringes of jazz. This freedom also extended into the band's public performances, which were sometimes undisciplined and disorganized. At their best, however, and with excellent soloists such as Pine, Phillip Bent, Orphy Robinson and singer Cleveland Watkiss, the Warriors offered an interesting concept of how big band music might evolve. In the late 80s, the Warriors worked with guest American leaders Henry Threadgill and Craig Harris, while another, home-grown, project was a suite in tribute to Joe Harriott. By the early 90s the lack of discipline and commitment displayed by some of its members allowed the band to drift and led to the defection of some elder statesmen,

such as Harry Beckett. Sad though this was, several of the individual members retained a measure of their initial popularity and embarked upon successful solo careers.

Album: *Out Of Many, One People* (Antilles 1987).

Jefferson, Eddie

b. 3 August 1918, Detroit, Michigan, USA, d. 9 May 1979, Detroit, Michigan, USA. Beginning his show business career as a dancer and occasional singer, Jefferson gradually concentrated on his latter talent. After achieving limited success, as a scat singer in the mid- to late 40s, Jefferson was largely responsible for the creation of so-called 'vocalese', devising lyrics to fit solos originally improvised by leading jazz musicians. Among the solos to which Jefferson wrote words was that played on 'Body And Soul' by Coleman Hawkins (with whom he had briefly worked in the early 40s), 'Parker's Mood' by Charlie Parker and James Moody's version of 'I'm In The Mood For Love'. This tune, variously retitled but usually known as 'Moody's Mood For Love' was recorded by King Pleasure, and achieved considerable success, thus opening doors for its adaptor. Jefferson subsequently worked with Moody's small group as both singer and manager, an association which lasted for almost 20 years. He continued to adapt solos by important musicians, including Miles Davis and Horace Silver. In the early 70s Jefferson sang with Richie Cole but on 9 May 1979, during an engagement at the Showcase in Detroit and within days of being filmed in performance there, he was fatally shot in the street outside the club.

Albums: *The Jazz Singer* (Evidence 1962), *Hipper Than Thou* (Zu Zazz, 1959-61 recordings), with James Moody *Letter From Home* (Original Jazz Classics 1962), *Moody's Mood/Moody/Hi-Fi Party* (1962), *Body And Soul* (Original Jazz Classics 1968), *Come Along With Me* (Original Jazz Classics 1969), *Things Are Getting Better* (1974), *Still On The Planet* (1976), *The Live-liest* (1976), *Godfather Of Vocalese* (Muse 1977), *The Main Man* (1977), *There I Go Again* (Prestige 1984).

Jefferson, Hilton

b. 30 July 1903, Danbury, Connecticut, USA, d. 14 November 1968. After playing banjo in various outfits in the north-eastern states, Jefferson switched to alto saxophone and by 1926 had graduated to the Claude Hopkins band in New York. During the next few years he played briefly with ensembles led by King Oliver (recording on 'Shake It And Break It'), Benny Carter, McKinney's Cotton Pickers and Fletcher Henderson ('You Can Take It' and 'Harlem Madness') but was mainly in the Chick Webb and Hopkins bands. After these years of restlessness he joined Cab Calloway, staying as lead alto saxophonist for nine years. With Calloway he was featured only occasionally but used such moments to great advantage, placing on record some of his gorgeously lyrical performances as, for example, on 'Willow Weep For Me'. He left Calloway in 1949, returned in 1951 and then worked with Duke Ellington and Don Redman (accompanying Pearl Bailey). In 1953 Jefferson left music to work as a bank guard, but frequently turned up at club sessions, reunions and on recording dates, including the magnificent *Big Reunion* by former members of the Fletcher Henderson orchestra.

Albums: with Henderson All Stars *The Big Reunion* (1957). Compilations: with Fletcher Henderson *A Study In Frustration* (1923-38), *Cab Calloway's Sixteen Classics* (1939-41).

Jenkins, Freddie

b. 10 October 1906, New York City, New York, USA, d. 1978. A student at Wilberforce University, trumpeter Jenkins played in the band directed by Horace Henderson, that later turned professional. Jenkins's light, airy style, coupled with an outgoing musical personality, attracted the attention of Duke Ellington, who hired him in 1928. Jenkins's health deteriorated, however, and six years later he had to leave the band because of respiratory problems. He continued to play intermittently, recording with his own band and playing in the bands of Luis Russell and Ellington again, but retired from music in 1938.

Album: *The Indispensable Duke Ellington Vols 1/2 & 3/4* (1929-34).

Jenkins, Leroy

b. 11 March 1932, Chicago, Illinois, USA. Jenkins began playing violin as a small child and, although he later tried other instruments, it was as a violinist that he became known in local jazz circles. In the early 60s he taught music in Alabama and back in Chicago, which is where, in 1965, he became involved with Muhal Richard Abrams in the AACM. He joined Anthony Braxton's first group with Leo Smith, and moved to Paris in 1969. The unit added drummer Steve McColl, recorded several albums, became known as the Creative Construction Company, but then broke up and Jenkins returned to the USA. In 1971, the Creative Construction played a reunion concert with guests Abrams and Richard Davis, which was recorded and later released in two parts by Muse Records. In 1971 Jenkins formed the Revolutionary Ensemble, a trio with bassist Sirone and drummer Jerome Cooper. After the Revolutionary Ensemble folded in the late 70s, Jenkins was associated with the New York-based Composer's Forum and also recorded with both upcoming musicians such as Anthony Davis, George Lewis and James Newton and veterans Muhal Richard Abrams and Andrew Cyrille. In his playing style Jenkins ignored the conventions of the European classical violin. Although a jazz predecessor, Stuff Smith, had used the instrument in a manner which also ignored preconceptions, scraping the strings and striking the box to create whatever sounds his imagination demanded, Jenkins went much further. In his hands the violin became many instruments; it could be a richly lyrical singer of ballads, it could be used to deliver harsh and sometimes raucous counterpoint, it could be a means to play driving rhythmic patterns. In freeing the instrument from previous constraints, Jenkins has established himself as a major figure in contemporary music. He has also occasionally recorded on viola. The 80s saw him devoting much of his time to composing, though he also led a blues-inspired band, Sting, which featured a front-line of violins and two guitars.

Albums: with Creative Construction Company *Creative Construction Company, Vols 1 And 2* (1975, 1976, rec 1971), *George Lewis* (Black Saint 1978), *For Players Only* (1975), *Solo Concert* (India Navigation 1977), *The Legend Of Ai Glatson* (Black Saint 1978), *Space Minds, New Worlds, Survival Of America* (Tomato 1979), with Muhal Richard Abrams *Lifelong Ambitions* (Black Saint 1981, rec 1977), *Revolutionary Ensemble* (Enja 1982), *Mixed Quintet* (1983, rec 1979), with Sting *Urban Blues* (Black Saint 1984), *Live!* (Black Saint 1993).

Jenney, Jack

b. 12 May 1910, Mason City, Indiana, USA, d. 16 December 1945. After performing in a band directed by his father, a music teacher, Jenney played trombone in various bands, including one led by Mal Hallett and a junior edition of the high-class Isham Jones band. In the late 30s Jenney became a studio musician but also recorded with Red Norvo and Glenn Miller. Towards the end of the decade he briefly led his own big band, but when this collapsed he joined Artie Shaw. In the early 40s he resumed studio work, then tried leading again and recorded with his wife, singer Kay Thompson; soon afterwards he was inducted into the US Navy. On his discharge he returned to the studios, but died in December 1945 after surgery for appendicitis. A polished stylist, Jenney is highly regarded by musicians for his flawless technique.

Album: *Jack Jenney And His Orchestra* (1938-40).

Jensen, Papa Bue

b. Arne Jensen, c.1928, Denmark. After becoming hugely popular in his own country during the late 50s and early 60s, trombonist Jensen's reputation spread as his band was used to accompany many visiting American jazz artists. Although these performances were usually restricted to Scandinavian countries, recordings with the visitors helped to give the band and its leader a following elsewhere. In more recent years Jensen has capitalized upon this popularity by travelling the international festival circuit. The mostly traditional musicians with whom he has played, sometimes on record, have included Wild Bill Davison, George Lewis, Edmond Hall, Wingy Manone and Albert Nicholas.

Albums: *Papa Bue's Viking Jazz Band: The Anniversary Album* (1956-66), *Papa Bue's Viking Jazz Band* (1958), *George Lewis With Papa Bue's Viking Jazz Band* (1959), *Papa Bue's Viking Jazz Band With Wingy Manone And Edmond Hall* (1966), *Down By The Riverside* (1968), *Wild Bill Davison With Papa Bue's Viking Jazz Band* (1974-75).

Jeter-Pillars Orchestra

When the popular territory band led by Alphonso Trent broke up in 1933, two of the saxophonists decided to form their own small band. These musicians, friends from boyhood, were alto saxophonist James Jeter and tenor saxophonist Hayes Pillars. Taking their example from Trent, they set very high standards of musicianship and owing to careful choice of sidemen and the development of a popular repertoire, they became very successful on the dancehall circuits of the mid and south-western states. Based for many years at the Plantation Club, St. Louis, Missouri, the band played sophisticated danceband charts with considerable elan. Although it was never a jazz orchestra, over the years future jazz stars such as Art Blakey, Jimmy Blanton, Sid Catlett, Charlie Christian, Kenny Clarke, Harry Edison, Jimmy Forrest, Jo Jones and Walter Page were in the ranks. The band played on into the late 40s before disbanding. The Jeter-Pillars Orchestra had only one recording date, cutting four sides in 1937 during a period when none of its future stars was in the band. These records were unexceptional and the band's considerable reputation rests therefore upon the recollections of those who heard it in person or on the air, for the many fine musicians who graced its ranks.

Album: one track incl. on *The Territory Bands* (1937).

Johnson, Budd

b. Albert J. Johnson, 14 December 1910, Kansas City, Missouri, USA, d. 20 October 1984. Before taking up the tenor saxophone Johnson had earlier played piano and drums. In his teens he performed in a number of territory bands in the midwest and in Texas, including those led by Terrence Holder, Jesse Stone and George E. Lee. In the mid-30s he worked in Chicago, playing in several bands, most notably, Louis Armstrong's, but was most often with Earl Hines. In the 40s he played in units led by Hines, Don Redman, Al Sears, Sy Oliver and Dizzy Gillespie. During these years Johnson was also a busy arranger, providing charts for the bands of Georgie Auld, Woody Herman, Buddy Rich and Boyd Raeburn. Johnson was deeply involved in the early days of bebop, writing for numerous small groups and acting as musical director for Billy Eckstine's big band. During the 50s Johnson often led his own small groups for club and record dates, and was also active in music publishing and as a recording company executive. In the late 50s and early 60s he played with Benny Goodman, Count Basie, Quincy Jones, Gerald Wilson, Hines and Jimmy Rushing. In 1969, after yet another stint with Hines, Johnson formed the JPJ Trio with Dill Jones, Bill Pemberton and Oliver Jackson. After the dissolution of JPJ in 1975 Johnson worked with the New York Jazz Repertory Orchestra, appeared at numerous international festivals and managed to fit in time as a teacher. It was as an arranger and contributor to bop that Johnson made his most lasting mark on jazz. Although he never approached the extraordinary improvisational flights of men like Gillespie and Charlie Parker, he was one of the musicians who helped give the new form coherence and structure. In his later playing career Johnson's style - on tenor, alto, soprano and clarinet - had thoroughly absorbed the influences of the beboppers with whom he had worked but he remained strongly identified with the jazz mainstream in which he had spent so much of his life. (NB: this artist should not be confused with Buddy Johnson.)

Albums: *Blues A La Mode* (1958), *Budd Johnson And The Four Brass Giants* (1960), *Let's Swing* (1960), *Ya! Ya!* i (1964), with Earl Hines, Jimmy Rushing *Blues And Things* (1967), *Ya! Ya!* ii (1970), *JPJ Quartet* (1973), *In Memory Of A Very Dear Friend* (1978), *The Old Dude And The Fundance Kid* (1984).

Johnson, Bunk

b. William Geary Johnson, 27 December 1889, New Orleans, Louisiana, USA, d. 7 July 1949. Johnson's early career has only recently been unravelled, and then only partly, thanks to his own, often inaccurate testimony. Until his enforced retirement from music in 1934 Johnson was certainly an active musician, playing in numerous New Orleans-based bands. He claimed to have worked with Buddy Bolden and Jelly Roll Morton; however as has been determined by recent researchers such as Christopher Hillman, these associations were unlikely given Johnson's age (he had, for years, claimed to be 10 years older than he was). He certainly played in some of the best New Orleans brass and marching bands, including the Superior and the Eagle bands. Johnson also claimed to have been an important influence upon and teacher of Louis Armstrong, but this assertion too should be treated with caution. Undoubtedly, Johnson was an important musician in New Orleans during the early years of jazz; yet he was a somewhat wayward character, whose presence in a band was not always a guarantee of musical excellence. Around 1914 Johnson moved to Alexandria, Louisiana and, from then until the late 20s, he played in scores of bands in many towns and cities of the deep south. By the early 30s, however, Johnson's career was in disarray and the loss of his front teeth had made playing difficult to the point of impossibility. In 1938 research by jazz writers Frederic Ramsey Jnr. and Charles Edward Smith located Johnson, who was then living at New Iberia, Louisiana. During correspondence with the writers Johnson insisted that, if he could be given money with which to buy false teeth and a trumpet, he could play again. The money was raised and Johnson duly returned to active performing. His return to the jazz public's consciousness came in 1940 and from that point until his death he made a tremendous impact upon that area of the early jazz scene currently enjoying a resurgence of interest. Johnson toured, playing concerts and making broadcasts, and made several records; all the while enhancing his new-found and self-perpetuated reputation as one of the originators of jazz. The quality of the playing which Johnson demonstrated on the records he made in these years shows him to have been a good player of the blues and suggests that in his hey-day he must have been a better-than-average trumpeter. There are also strong hints that he possessed a measure of musical sophistication which, had his career not foundered when he was approaching his prime, would have made him an important figure in the mainstream. As it was, Johnson's reappearance on the jazz scene, which helped to cement the Revival Movement of the early 40s, tied him firmly to a musical style that, as his biographer Hillman observes, he had probably outgrown. Instead, Johnson, together with his near contemporary George Lewis, was responsible for resurrecting an interest in early jazz that still has remained strong.

Selected albums: *Bunk Johnson And His Superior Jazz Band* (Good Time Jazz, 1942 recordings), *Bunk Johnson In San Francisco* (American Music, 1944 recordings), *Bunk And Lou* (Good Time Jazz, 1944 recordings), *Old New Orleans Jazz* (1942), *Spicy Advice* (1944), *The American Music Recordings*

J.J. Johnson

(1944), *Bunk Johnson & Lu Watters* (Contemporary 1983, 1944 recordings), *The King Of The Blues* (American Music, 1944-45 recordings), *Bunk Johnson: The Last Testament* (1947). Further reading: *Bunk Johnson: His Life And Times*, Christopher Hillman.

Johnson, Gus

b. 15 November 1913, Tyler, Texas, USA. Active in music from about the age of 10, Johnson played piano, bass, drums and sang in a vocal quartet. Choosing drums, he played in a number of territory bands, then in 1938 joined the Jay McShann band in Kansas City. This was the unit that included the young Charlie Parker. Johnson stayed with McShann until entering the US Army in 1943. After the war he played with several bands, including those led by Earl Hines and Cootie Williams, and in 1949 joined Count Basie, with whom he remained until 1954; playing in both the sextet Basie briefly led during hard times and the powerful new-style big band that heralded a change in the leader's fortunes. Later Johnson worked as a freelance, accompanying singers including Lena Horne and Ella Fitzgerald and playing on numerous club dates, concert and recording sessions with Buck Clayton, Jimmy Rushing, Woody Herman and the World's Greatest Jazz Band. An exemplary drummer, Johnson's style combined fluid grace with skilful dynamics and he was just as happy discreetly supporting singers and soloists as explosively driving a big band. By the early 70s he was living in semi-retirement in Denver, Colorado. Albums: with Jay McShann *Early Bird* (1940-43), *Count Basie Octet* (1950), with Count Basie *Sixteen Men Swinging* (1953), with World's Greatest Jazz Band *Century Plaza* (1971).

Johnson, J.J.

b. James Louis Johnson, 22 January 1924, Indianapolis, Indiana, USA. Johnson began playing trombone at the age of 14; by the time he was 18 years old, he had performed professionally with various bands culminating in that led by Benny Carter. Johnson was with Carter for three years during which period he also worked with Jazz At The Philharmonic. In the mid-40s he was briefly with Count Basie and for the rest of the decade was active in small bebop groups in New York. In the early 50s he joined Oscar Pettiford but then was forced to earn a living outside music. In 1954 he returned to the jazz scene and immediately attracted widespread attention through the band he co-led with Kai Winding. This band, Jay And Kai, remained together for two years, by which time Johnson was re-established and now both leading small jazz groups and composing extended works that encompassed jazz and classical forms. In the early 60s he played with Miles Davis and toured with his own groups, and at the end of the decade was also involved in studio work. The 70s saw Johnson writing for films and television but finding time to play too in a variety of settings. In the 80s he began to devote more of his time to playing, demonstrating in the process that his ability had not diminished in the slightest. Tours of Japan with JATP groups led to a brief association on record with another trombone player, Al Grey. A major figure in jazz trombone, Johnson was one of very few players of that instrument to succeed in bebop. In his earlier years, especially when playing in bebop groups with artists such as Charlie Parker, Dizzy Gillespie, Fats Navarro and Max Roach, his extraordinary technique often dominated the content of his solos; however, in later years the content matured and expanded while his technique showed no signs of faltering. Johnson remains one of the major trombonists in modern mainstream jazz.

Selected albums: *Trombone By Three/Looking Back/Early Bones* (1949), *J.J. Johnson Sextet* (1953), with Kai Winding *Jay And Kai* i (Savoy 1954), *Jay And Kai At Birdland* (1954), *Jay Jay Johnson, Kai Winding, Bennie Green* (1954), *The Eminent Jay Jay Johnson Vols 1-3* (Blue Note 1955), *Jay And Kai* ii (1955), *Jay And Kai* iii (1955), *Jay And Kai Trombone Octet* (1956), *Jay And Kai At Newport* (1956), *Jay And Kai* iv (1956), *Jay Jay Johnson Quintet* (Savoy 1956), *Poem For Brass* (1956), with Stan Getz *At The Opera House* (1957), *Live* (1957), *Jay Jay Johnson Quartet* i (1957), *Live At The Cafe Bohemia* (Fresh Sound 1957), *Jay Jay Johnson Sextet* i (1959), *J.J. Johnson With Frank De Vol's Orchestra* (1960), *Jay Jay Johnson Sextet* ii (1960), *The Great Kai And J.J.* (1960), *Jay Jay Johnson Quartet* ii (1960), with André Previn *Mack The Knife* (1961), *J.J.'s Broadway* (1963), *Proof Positive* (1964), *Tribute To Charlie Parker* (1964), *The Dynamic Sound Of J.J. With Big Band* (1964), *J.J.!* (1964), *Goodies* (1965), *J.J. Johnson And His Orchestra* (1965), *J.J. Johnson & Kai Winding* i (1968), *J.J. Johnson & Kai Winding* ii (1968), *J.J. Johnson & Kai Winding* iii (1969), *The Yokohama Concert* (Pablo 1977), *Pinnacles* (Milestone 1979), *Concepts In Blue* (1980), with others *All Star Jam At The Aurex Jazz Festival '82, Tokyo* (1982), with Al Grey *Things Are Getting Better All The Time* (Original Jazz Classics 1983), *Live At The Village Vanguard* (Emarcy 1988), *Standards* (Emarcy 1989), *Vivian* (Concord 1992), *Let's Hang Out* (Emarcy 1993). Selected compilations: *Jay Jay Johnson's Quintets/Mad Be Bop* (Savoy 1985, 1949 recordings), *The Total J.J. Johnson* (RCA 1985), *The Eminent J. J. Johnson Vols 1* and *2* (Blue Note 1989).

Johnson, James P.

b. 1 February 1894, New Brunswick, New Jersey, USA, d. 17 November 1955. Taught piano by his mother, Johnson assimilated a wide range of musical styles. In the years following his family's relocation to New York, he continued his studies and by his late teens was working in clubs in the Hell's Kitchen district. Johnson was adept in ragtime, blues, and all the popular musical forms of the day. He was also a capable performer of classical music. By the early 20s Johnson was a leading light on New Yorks burgeoning jazz scene and was already known for his compositions, including 'Carolina Shout', which demanded virtuoso technical ability. During this period Johnson became the acknowledged master of stride piano. He also attracted the attention of Broadway producers and in 1923 composed the musical *Runnin' Wild*, in which he introduced his composition 'The Charleston'. He also engaged the admiration of emerging pianists; the young Fats Waller was an eager pupil. In the mid-20s and especially during the 30s, Johnson's interest in classical music surfaced in his own work; he composed several long pieces, including 'Yamekraw', a piano rhapsody, 'Harlem Symphony', 'Jassamine', a piano concerto, 'Spirit Of America' a string quartet, and a blues opera, 'De Organizer'. Unfortunately, many of his scores have since been lost. (An album of piano arrangements of some of the surviving pieces, performed by William Albright, was issued in 1983 under the somewhat misleading title, *The Symphonic Jazz Of James P. Johnson*.) Although Johnson continued to play in the 40s, often in small groups with companions such as Eddie Condon, Albert Nicholas and Wild Bill Davison, ill-health damaged his career. A series of strokes culminated in a severe attack in 1951, which left him bedridden and he died in November 1955. As a pianist Johnson was outstanding, not only for his dazzling technique but also for the construction of his solos. However intricate they might be, his solos were logical, non-repetitive and effectively incorporated much of his catholic musical background. Records by Johnson include transcriptions from some early piano rolls and even in this form his music generates excitement. As a composer, the manner in which his work has lasted testifies to its inherent timelessness. Apart from the excitement of 'The Charleston', 'Carolina Shout' and 'Runnin' Wild', there were reflective melodic delights such as 'Old Fashioned Love', 'If I Could Be With You One Hour Tonight' and 'Just Before Daybreak'. Apart from Waller, Johnson influenced most of the pianists working in New York in the 20s and 30s, which means almost everyone of importance. Among the older players were Count Basie, Duke Ellington, Art Tatum and Teddy Wilson, while the younger group included Erroll Garner, Johnny Guarnieri and Thelonious Monk. In the history of jazz piano, Johnson's contribution is of paramount importance.

Selected albums: *James P. Johnson* (1921-26), *James P. Johnson* (1921-39), *The Original James P. Johnson* (1943-45), *Yamekraw* (1962, rec date unk), *A Flat Dream* (1980, rec 1939-45), *From Ragtime To Jazz: The Complete Piano Solos 1921-1939* (1985), with others *The Complete Edmond Hall/James P. Johnson/Sidney De Paris/Vic Dickenson Blue Note Sessions* (1985, rec 1943-44, six album boxed-set), *Ain'cha Got Music* (Pumpkin 1986), *Carolina Shout* (Biograph 1991), *Snowy Morning Blues* (GRP 1991).

Further reading: *James P. Johnson: A Case of Mistaken Identity*, Scott E. Brown.

Johnson, Ken 'Snakehips'

b. Kenrick Reginald Hymans Johnson, 10 September 1914, Georgetown, British Guiana (now known as Guyana), d. 8 March 1941. Son of a Guyanese doctor and Surinamese mother, Johnson played piano and violin as a child. On completing his schooling in England, he began dancing, making an early appearance in the provinces on the variety circuit. Studying with the African-American choreographer Clarence 'Buddy' Bradley, he gained professional confidence and contacts in the USA. These brought him film work in New York and cabaret in Hollywood, and the chance to observe black American practitioners of jazz and dance at firsthand. On the same trip he

made a series of Caribbean appearances; these inspired a host of imitators with the belief that a West Indian could become part of the British showbusiness establishment and were responsible for launching several noteworthy careers. In London he persuaded Jamaican trumpeter Leslie Thompson to form a band for him to front; this, later known as the West Indian Dance Orchestra, was the first regular black band of any size in Britain. It included musicians from the Caribbean, such as clarinettist Carl Barriteau, as well as local instrumentalists of African descent, among them Welsh-born guitar-playing brothers Joe and Frank Deniz, and the latter's wife, pianist Clare Deniz. By the start of the war the 'West Indians' were broadcasting regularly and featured artists such as Barbadian trumpeter/vocalist Dave Wilkins and Welsh-born vocalist Don Johnson, whose father came from Barbuda, became household names. To many listeners, the Johnson band was the first local unit to 'swing' in the American manner, but the prominence of local black musicians ended when the leader was killed in an air-raid while on stage at London's exclusive Café de Paris in 1941.

Albums: with others *And The Bands Played On* (1938), with others *Swing Classics From Europe* (1938), with others *Al Bowlly - The Big Swoon Of The Thirties* (1940).

Johnson, Pete

b. 25 March 1904, Kansas City, Missouri, USA, d. 23 March 1967. After playing drums when a teenager, Johnson switched to piano in 1926 and swiftly became a leading exponent of the blues. He was also an excellent accompanist to blues singers; especially Joe Turner, with whom he established a partnership that lasted for the rest of his life. In 1936 the ubiquitous John Hammond Jnr. brought Johnson and Turner to New York where they played at the Famous Door. Two years later Johnson played at one of Hammond's Spirituals To Swing concerts at Carnegie Hall and later performed and recorded with Albert Ammons and Meade 'Lux' Lewis as the Boogie Woogie Trio. During the 40s, Johnson continued his solo career, interspersed with engagements with Ammons and, often, Joe Turner. In the 50s Johnson toured the USA and Europe and made several records with Turner and with Jimmy Rushing. As a blues and boogie-woogie pianist, Johnson was superb and his thunderous left hand was always a joy to hear. In the recordings he made with Turner he invariably rose above himself, delivering both forceful solos and lifting the singer to some of his best work. Shortly after playing at the Newport Jazz Festival in 1958 Johnson suffered a stroke which incapacitated him. He did venture back to the recording studios in 1960 but did not appear again in public until 1967, when he was helped onstage to receive an ovation from the audience at the Spirituals To Swing 30th Anniversary concert. He took a bow and was being led off when the band swung into his best-known composition, 'Roll 'Em Pete', and his old companion, Joe Turner, prepared to sing. Johnson sat down at the piano alongside Ray Bryant and began picking uncertainly at the keys. Then, gradually, with Bryant laying down a solid left hand, Johnson showed that there was still music inside him. It was a long way from great piano playing but given the circumstances it was a highly emotional moment, made more so when, two months later, Johnson died.

Albums: with others *Spirituals To Swing* (1938-39), *The Essential Jimmy Rushing* (1955), with Joe Turner *The Boss Of The Blues* (1956), with others *Spirituals to Swing 30th Anniversary Concert* (1967). Compilations: *Master Of Blues And Boogie Woogie Vols 1-2* (1939-49), *The Boogie King* (1940-44), *The Rarest Pete Johnson Vols 1, 2* (1947-54), *Classics 1939-41* (Original Jazz Classics 1992), *Central Avenue Boogie* (Delmark 1993, 1947 recordings).

Johnson, Plas

b. 21 July 1931, Donaldsonville, Louisiana, USA. After being taught soprano saxophone by his father, Johnson took up the tenor as well. Resident on the west coast in the 50s he worked in the studios but played jazz dates with artists including Benny Carter. His film and television work increased and his work (though not his name) became known to millions when he was featured playing the main title theme on the soundtrack of *The Pink Panther* (1963). He continued to make infrequent jazz appearances, playing on record dates and at clubs and the occasional festival. Among the musicians with whom he worked in the 70s and 80s were Bill Berry, Herb Ellis, Carl Fontana, Jake Hanna, Dave McKenna and the Capp-Pierce Juggernaut. A highly melodic player with an effortlessly graceful ballad style, Johnson's choice of career has meant that he is often overlooked by jazz audiences.

Albums: *This Must Be Plas* (1959), under pseudonym Johnny Beecher *Sax Fifth Avenue* (1962), with Jake Hanna, Carl Fontana *Live At The Concord Festival* (1975), *The Blues* (Concord 1975), *Positively* (1976), *Rockin' With The Plas* (Capitol 1983), *LA 55* (1983), *Hot Blue And Saxy* (Carell 1989).

Jolly, Pete

b. 5 June 1932, New Haven, Connecticut, USA. As a small child Jolly became adept on both accordion and piano. From the early 50s he was resident in Los Angeles, where he became a much in-demand pianist for many of the recording sessions that helped to establish the so-called west coast school of bebop. Among the dates on which Jolly appeared were those for *The Swinging Mr Rogers* with Shorty Rogers And His Giants in 1955, when he joined Jimmy Giuffre, Curtis Counce and Shelly Manne and played a fine solo on 'Michele's Meditation'. Also in 1955 he recorded with the Cy Touff Quintet and the following year played with the Chet Baker-Art Pepper Sextet on *Playboys*. During the late 50s and most of the 60s Jolly led his own small groups but spent much of his time in film and television studio work. In the 80s he again recorded with Pepper and occasionally deputized with west coast big bands, including that led by Bill Berry. Jolly's playing was always of high quality and he made an important contribution to the west coast jazz of the 50s. Some authorities hold his accordion playing in high regard, although this instrument has yet to make a serious impact in the jazz world.

Albums: *Jolly Jumps In* (1955), *The Pete Jolly Duo, Trio And Quartet* (Fresh Sounds 1955), with Shorty Rogers *The Swinging Mr Rogers* (1955), *Cy Touff, His Octet And Quintet* (1955), with Chet Baker, Art Pepper *Playboys* (1956), *The Pete Jolly Trio* i (1956), with Ralph Pena *The Pete Jolly Duo* (1959), with Pepper *Smack Up!* (1960), *5 O'Clock Shadows* (1962), *Little Bird* (1963), *Sweet September* (1963), *The Sensational Pete Jolly Gasses Everybody* (1963), *Hello, Jolly* (1964), *The Pete Jolly Trio* ii (1965), *Pete Jolly With Marty Paich And His Orchestra* (1968), *Give A Damn* (c.1969), *Sessions, Live* (c.1969), *Strike Up The Band* (1980), *The Five* (Fresh Sounds 1988), *Gems* (1990).

Jones, Carmell

b. 19 July 1936, Kansas City, Kansas, USA. After attracting favourable attention for his trumpet playing in bands in the Kansas City area, Jones moved to Los Angeles in 1961, where he joined Bud Shank for an engagement at the Drift Inn, Malibu. He recorded with this group and later worked with Gerald Wilson and the Red Mitchell-Harold Land Quintet with whom he also recorded. Most of 1965 was spent touring with Horace Silver and by the end of the year Jones had become resident in Germany. He played regularly as a member of radio and studio orchestras, mainly in Berlin, and also worked with his old high-school friend, Nathan Davis. In the music he recorded in the 60s Jones displayed an affinity with Clifford Brown and his return to the US jazz scene in the early 80s showed that in maturity he had developed into an accomplished player, who deserved a wide audience.

Albums: *The Remarkable Carmell Jones* (1961), with Bud Shank *New Groove* (1961), with Red Mitchell, Harold Land *Hear Ye!* (1961), *Brass Bag* (1962), *Business Meetin'* (1962), *Jay Hawk Talk* (1965), *Carmell Jones In Europe* (1965), with Nathan Davis *Happy Girl* (1965), *Carmell Jones Returns* (1982).

Jones, Dill

b. Dillwyn O. Jones, 19 August 1923, Newcastle Emlyn, Wales, England, d. 22 June 1984. After formal studies at London's Trinity College of Music, Jones began associating with the younger jazzmen who were playing bebop. He had already played jazz while serving in the navy and his fluent, inventive style quickly made him a welcome addition to the London scene. In 1948 he performed at the first Nice Jazz Festival and was regularly heard in company with musicians including Humphrey Lyttelton, Ronnie Scott, Joe Harriott and Bruce Turner. Jones visited the USA during the 50s while working on a transatlantic liner, and in the early 60s he settled in New York. During the next few years he played with several noted American jazz stars, including Roy Eldridge and Gene Krupa. In 1969 he became a member of the JPJ Quartet with Budd Johnson, Bill Pemberton and Oliver Jackson. His fine soloing, whether in subtly developed ballads or on roof-raising spectaculars such as his version of 'Little Rock Getaway', showed his wide stylistic range.

Albums: *The Dill Jones Trio* i (1955), *The Dill Jones Trio* ii

(1956), *The Dill Jones Quintet* (1959), *Jones The Jazz* (1961), with others *Jazz Piano Masters* (1972), *Up Jumped You With Love* (1972), *The Music Of Bix Beiderbecke* (c.1972), *The Welsh Connection* (c.1982).

Jones, Elvin

b. 9 September 1927, Pontiac, Michigan, USA. The youngest of the remarkable Jones brothers (see also Thad Jones and Hank Jones), Elvin grew up in a musical atmosphere. He played drums with local bands before and after military service and by the early 50s was playing regularly with Billy Mitchell's small group. In the middle of the decade Jones relocated in New York, rapidly establishing himself as a leading exponent of bop drumming. He worked with several notable musicians including J.J. Johnson, Donald Byrd and Sonny Rollins, and in 1960 became a member of John Coltrane's quartet. He played with Coltrane for five years during which period he grew into one of the outstanding drummers in jazz history. The role he occupied in this period was of considerable importance in the development of post-bop drumming. Jones's career after Coltrane was mainly as a leader of small groups, where he was able to exercise full control over the musical policy (although he was briefly, in 1966, with Duke Ellington). In the late 60s and on through the 70s and 80s Jones toured ceaselessly, playing clubs, concerts and festivals around the world. His sidemen have included Joe Farrell, George Coleman and Wilbur Little.

In 1979 he recorded *Very R.A.R.E.* with Art Pepper and that same year saw the release of a documentary film, *Different Drummer: Elvin Jones.* Jones extended the scope of the work done by proto-bop drummers such as Max Roach and Art Blakey. Although associated with free jazz, in which context his example was an incentive to later occupants of *avant garde* drum chairs, his own playing was always closely linked to what had gone before. Nevertheless, in his expansion of the role of the post-bop jazz drummer, Jones was responsible for a major stylistic shift: he integrated the drums so thoroughly with the improvisations of the front line musicians that the drummer now became their partner on equal terms not merely the accompanist or pulse provider of previous eras. Through his example and his astonishing technical mastery, Jones has become one of the master drummers of jazz and is currently seeing something of a revival in his fortunes with a spate of recently recorded albums.

Selected albums: *Thad Jones-Billy Mitchell Quintet* (1953), with Sonny Rollins *A Night At The Village Vanguard* (Enja 1957), *Together* (1961), *Elvin!* (Original Jazz Classics 1961), with John Coltrane *Live At The Village Vanguard* (1961), with Coltrane *Live At Birdland* (1963), with Coltrane *A Love Supreme* (1964), *Dear John C* (1965), *Midnight Walk* (1966), *Heavy Sounds* (Impulse 1968), *Puttin' It Together* (1968), *Poly-Currents* (1969), *Coalition* (1970), *Genesis* (1971), *Live At The Lighthouse* (1972), *Mr Thunder* (1974), *New Agenda* (1975),

Elvin Jones

Summit Meeting (1976), *Time Capsule* (1977), *Remembrance* (1978), *Very R.A.R.E.* (1979), *Soul Trane* (1980), *Brother John* (1982), *Earth Jones* (1982), *The Elvin Jones Jazz Machine In Europe* (Enja 1992), *Live In Japan* (Konnex 1992), with Takehisa Tanaka *When I Was At Aso-Mountain* (Enja 1993), *Youngblood* (Enja 1993), *Going Home* (Enja 1994).

Jones, Hank

b. Henry Jones, 31 July 1918, Vicksburg, Mississippi, USA. Eldest of three remarkable brothers in jazz (Thad Jones and Elvin Jones), Hank Jones was raised in Pontiac, Michigan and by the beginning of his teenage years played piano professionally in local bands. In 1944 he went to New York where he joined the Oran 'Hot Lips' Page band. Although Jones had previously been in the mainstream of jazz, he was an eager student and fully aware of the changes currently taking place in the music. He incorporated bebop into his repertoire but remained an eclectic player, happily adapting to suit the needs of the artists he accompanied (who ranged from Coleman Hawkins to Charlie Parker). Jones freelanced extensively throughout the 50s, working with Jazz At The Philharmonic, Benny Goodman and Milt Jackson among many, and ended the decade by becoming a staff musician at CBS where he remained until the mid-70s. During this long period of studio activity, Jones accompanied countless performers outside jazz and continued to record with numerous names in jazz. Since the mid-70s he has continued to work in various jazz contexts, as soloist, as duettist with Tommy Flanagan, George Shearing and other pianists, as accompanist to singers and instrumentalists, and as leader of his own small groups. A masterly musician, adept in most aspects of the jazz repertoire, Jones has been an important influence, as much for his professionalism as for the immense sweep of his talent.

Selected albums: *The Jazz Trio Of Hank Jones* (Savoy 1955), *Bluebird* (Savoy 1955), *Have You Met Hank Jones* (1956), *The Hank Jones Quartet* (Savoy 1956), *Relaxin' At Camarillo* (Savoy 1956), *Hank Jones Swings Songs From Gigi* (1958), *The Talented Touch* (1958), *Porgy And Bess: Swinging Impressions By Hank Jones* (1960), *Here's Love* (1963), *The Hank Jones Trio* ii (1964), *Hank Jones With Oliver Nelson And His Orchestra* (1966), *Hanky Panky* (1975), *Satin Doll* (1976), *Love For Sale* (1976), *Hank* (All Art 1976), *Jones-Brown-Smith* (Concord 1976), *Arigato* (1976), *Bop Redux* (Muse 1977), *The Great Jazz Trio At The Village Vanguard Vols 1 & 2* (1977), *Just For Fun* (Original Jazz Classics 1977), *Tiptoe Tapdance* (Original Jazz Classics 1977-78), *I Remember You* (Black And Blue 1977), *Have You Met This Jones?* (1977), *Kindness, Joy, Love And Happiness* (1977), *Direct From L.A.* (1977), *The Trio* (1977), *Groovin' High* (1978), *Milestones* (1978), *Compassion* (1978), *Ain't Misbehavin'* (1978), with Tommy Flanagan *Our Delights* (1978), *Easy To Love* (1979), *Live In Japan* (Jazz Alliance 1979), *Piano Playhouse* (1979), *Bluesette* (Black And Blue 1979), *The Great Jazz Trio* (c.1980), *Chapter II* (1980), *The Incredible Hank Jones* (Stash 1980), *The Great Jazz Trio Revisited At The Village Vanguard Vols 1 & 2* (1980), *The Great Jazz Trio And Friends At The Aurex Jazz Festival, Tokyo '81*

(1981), *Threesome* (1982), *The Club New Yorker* (1983), with Flanagan *I'm All Smiles* (MPS 1983), *Monk's Moods* (1984), with George Shearing *The Spirit Of 176* (1988), *Duo* (Timeless 1988), *Lazy Afternoon* (Concord 1989), *The Oracle* (Emarcy 1990), *Essence* (DMP 1991), *Live At the Maybank Recital Hall, Vol 16* (Concord 1991), *Jazzpar 91 Project* (Storyville 1991), *Handful Of Keys* (Emarcy 1992), *Upon Reflection* (Verve 1993).

Jones, Isham

b. 31 January 1894, Coalton, Ohio, USA, d. 19 October 1956. A multi-instrumentalist, Jones was leading his own band by his late teens. He played mostly in the Chicago area until the early 20s, when he moved to New York. After a brief visit to the UK in 1924, he returned to form a new band, which by the end of the decade he had developed into an outstanding dance orchestra. The band enjoyed enormous popularity with audiences. A 1930 recording of Hoagy Carmichael's 'Stardust', arranged as a ballad, was a huge hit and changed perceptions of how this song might be performed. Arrangements were by Jones, together with Gordon Jenkins and Victor Young, and created a relaxed, melodic style unusual among bands of this type. Fine musicians who played in the band at one time or another included Jack Jenney and Pee Wee Erwin. In 1936, with the swing era freshly launched and big bands fast becoming popular, Jones went against all logic and decided to fold his band. Some of the more jazz-orientated members decided to go ahead with their own outfit under the leadership of one of the saxophone players, Woody Herman. In the late 30s Jones concentrated on composing and arranging, but by the 40s he was working mostly outside music. A possibly apocryphal tale recounts that when his wife bought him a new piano for his 30th birthday, he was so worried at the expense she had incurred, he sat up all night at his birthday gift and by morning had composed three tunes to help restore the family fortunes: 'It Had To Be You', 'Spain' and 'The One I Love Belongs To Somebody Else'.

Albums: *Isham Jones And His Orchestra* (Fountain 1979, 1920-24 recordings), *Isham Jones And His Orchestra* (1929-30), *Isham Jones And His Orchestra Featuring Woody Herman* (1936).

Jones, Jimmy

b. 30 December 1918, Memphis, Tennessee, USA, d. 29 April 1982. Jones started out on guitar while growing up in Chicago but later switched to piano. In the early and mid-40s he played with several prominent jazzmen including Stuff Smith, Don Byas and Coleman Hawkins. Later in the decade he also played on many recording sessions with such Ellingtonians as Ben Webster, Johnny Hodges and Paul Gonsalves. In 1947 he began accompanying Sarah Vaughan with whom he established a great musical rapport. Apart from a two-year break, he remained with Vaughan until 1958. Throughout the 60s Jones was deeply involved with arranging and composing, often working with Duke Ellington although he did tour Europe in 1966 as musical director for Ella Fitzgerald. An adept and elegant accompanist, Jones chose to follow a musical path which frequently led to his working almost anonymously with brighter stars. For all this apparently deliberate avoidance of the spotlight, his solo work, when heard, displays a musician with orderly thoughts and a lightly swinging touch.

Selected albums: *The Jimmy Jones Trio* (1954), with George Wallington *Trios* (1993).

Jones, Jo

b. Jonathan Jones, 7 October 1911, Chicago, Illinois, USA, d. 3 September 1985. While he was still a child Jones became adept on several instruments, including trumpet and piano. In his teens he worked as a singer and dancer, taking up drums along the way. By the late 20s he was drumming in territory bands, eventually settling in Kansas City in the early 30s. It was here that he met Count Basie, at the time still plain Bill Basie, and worked with him on a number of occasions before joining the band full-time in 1936. Here Jones became a member of the magnificent 'All-American Rhythm Section' with Basie, Freddie Green and Walter Page. The flowing, rhythmic pulse of the band was aided enormously by Jones's changes to previous conceptions of jazz drumming. He shifted the dominant role among the instruments at his disposal from the bass drum to the hi-hat cymbal, thus creating an enviable looseness in which he was free to punctuate the ensemble and 'goose' the soloists with accented bass, snare and tom-tom beats. Although Jones always gave credit for such innovations to others, there is no doubt that he popularized and refined this way of playing himself. After his innovations, the way was open for the further changes in the drummer's role that occurred in bebop. The sleek power of the Basie rhythm section, and Jones's part in its success, made him the envy of and model for numerous other drummers, even if swing era audiences tended to prefer more extrovert, busier and showboating percussionists. Jones left the Basie band when he was inducted into the US Army in 1944; after the war he freelanced with numerous major jazz stars, among them Lester Young, Teddy Wilson and Roy Eldridge, worked with Jazz At The Philharmonic and led his own groups on record and for club engagements. In his later years Jones worked the international festival circuits, playing with wit, polish and always that extraordinary subtle swing that had led Don Lamond to describe him as the man who played like the wind. A highly perceptive and articulate man, Jones also grew steadily more and more disillusioned with the jazz life, which occasionally created stars out of musical nonentities and lavished attention upon individuals whose talent was minuscule in comparison to his own. His knowledge and understanding of jazz drumming was extensive and, although he preferred to accompany rather than play solo, in his later years he would sometimes enliven his performances by demonstrating the techniques and idiosyncrasies of fellow drummers, often appearing to play even more like them than they did themselves.

Selected albums: *Jo Jones Special* (1955), with Lester Young, Teddy Wilson *Prez And Teddy* (1956), *The Jo Jones Special* (Vanguard 1956), *Jo Jones Plus Two* (Vanguard 1958), *The Jo Jones Trio* (Fresh Sounds 1959), *The Jo Jones Quintet* (1960), with Milt Hinton *The Jo Jones Duo* (1960), with Willie 'The

Lion' Smith *The Drums* (1973), *Caravan* (1974), *The Main Man* (1976), *Papa Jo And His Friends* (1977), *Our Man, Papa Jo* (1977). Compilations: *Count Basie: Complete Recorded Works In Chronological Order* (1937-39), *Count Basie At The Chatterbox* (1937).

Jones, Jonah

b. Robert Elliott Jones, 31 October, 1909, Louisville, Kentucky, USA. As a youth Jones played trumpet with numerous local and territory bands before joining Horace Henderson in 1928. After drifting through various other minor bands, he joined Jimmie Lunceford and then in Buffalo, in 1932, began a highly profitable musical partnership with Stuff Smith. Although he found time for excursions with Lillian Armstrong and McKinney's Cotton Pickers, he was still with Smith when they took their little band into New York and a residency at the Onyx Club in early 1936. For the next four years the band captivated audiences with their hot music, eccentric appearance and crazy clowning. In 1940 Jones left to work with the big bands of Benny Carter, Fletcher Henderson and then spent a decade with Cab Calloway. He next played with Earl Hines but from the mid-50s led his own small band, which attained great popularity with the fringe jazz audience. Musically, this and the later bands Jones fronted offered a repertoire that was a long way from the rough and ready excitement of the group he had co-led with Smith. Indeed, as the years passed, it was often seen to be unadventurous, predictable and a little bland, concentrating on straightforward arrangements of show tunes and popular songs of the day. It was easy-listening jazz for the masses, although Jones's playing was always skilful and consistently showed that he had not forgotten the roots of his music. He continued playing throughout the 60s, 70s and into the 80s, proving remarkably durable and, latterly, still to be capable of a few surprises.

Selected albums: *Harlem Jump And Swing* (1954), *The Jonah Jones Quartet* i (1956), *The Jonah Jones Quartet* ii (1957), *The Jonah Jones Quartet* iii (1958), *The Jonah Jones Quartet* iv (1958), *The Jonah Jones Quartet* v (1958), *I Dig Chicks* (1958), *Swingin' 'Round The World* (1958-59), *An Evening With Fred Astaire* (1959), *The Jonah Jones Quartet* vi (1960), *The Jonah Jones Quartet* vii (1961), *The Jonah Jones Quartet* viii (1961), *The Jonah Jones Quartet* ix (1962), *A Touch Of Blue* (1962), *Greatest Instrumental Hits Styled By Jonah Jones* (1962), *Jonah Jones With Glen Gray And The Casa Loma Orchestra* (1962), *The Jonah Jones Sextet* (1962), *The Jonah Jones Quartet* x (1963), *The Jonah Jones Quartet* xi (1963), *On The Sunny Side Of The Street* (1965), *The Jonah Jones Quartet* xii (1966), *The Jonah Jones Quartet* xiii (1966), *The Jonah Jones Quartet* xiv (1966), *The Jonah Jones Quartet* xv (1967), *The Jonah Jones Quartet* xvi (1968), *The Jonah Jones Quartet* xvii (c.1969), *Confessin'* (1978). Compilations: *Stuff Smith And His Onyx Club Orchestra* (1936), *Sixteen Classics By Cab Calloway* (1939-41), *Low Down Blues* (1944), *Butterflies In The Rain* (Circle 1987, 1944 recordings), with Hot Lips Page *Swing Street Showcase* (1944-45), *Harlem Jump And Swing* (Affinity 1983).

Jones, Philly Joe

b. Joseph R. Jones, 15 July 1923, Philadelphia, Pennsylvania, USA, d. 30 August 1985. Jones began his drumming career in his home town, later moving to New York where he worked with many leading bebop musicians. Despite this early exposure to Charlie Parker, Dizzy Gillespie and other innovators, Jones was able to adapt to the stylistic needs of any group in which he played. Although proficient in bands led by mainstreamers such as Ben Webster and Lionel Hampton he was happiest in his many fruitful associations with modernists, among whom were Tadd Dameron, John Coltrane and Miles Davis. His tenure with Davis occupied a substantial slice of the 50s; in the following decade he played and recorded with Gil Evans, Bill Evans and led his own groups. In the late 60s he lived briefly in the UK, playing with musicians such as Kenny Wheeler and Pete King and also teaching. (He once advised the Who drummer, Keith Moon, not to bother with lessons just so long as he could make millions playing the way he did.) In the early 80s Jones formed the band Dameronia, with which to play the music of his former associate. Whether subtly encouraging or with sustained power, often working with a minimal, scaled-down drum kit, Jones was able to adjust his playing style to accommodate any group or individual.

Selected albums: with Tadd Dameron *A Study In Dameronia* (1953), with John Coltrane *Blue Train* (1957), with Miles Davis *Milestones* (1958), *Blues For Dracula* (Original Jazz Classics 1958), *Drums Around The World* (Original Jazz Classics 1959), *Showcase* (Original Jazz Classics 1959), *Philly Joe's Beat* (1960), *Trailways Express* (Black Lion 1968), *'Round Midnight* (1969), *Mo' Jo* (Black Lion 1969), *Mean What You Say* (Sonet 1977), *Philly Mignon* (1977), *Drum Song* (Galaxy 1978), *Advance!* (1978), *To Tadd With Love* (1982), *Dameronia* (Uptown 1983), *Look, Stop And Listen* (Uptown 1983), *Filet De Sole* (Marge 1992).

Jones, Quincy

b. 14 March 1933, Chicago, Illinois, USA. Jones began playing trumpet as a child and also developed an early interest in arranging, studying at the Berklee College Of Music. When he joined Lionel Hampton in 1951 it was as both performer and writer. With Hampton he visited Europe in a remarkable group which included rising stars Clifford Brown, Art Farmer, Gigi Gryce and Alan Dawson. Leaving Hampton in 1953, Jones wrote arrangements for many musicians, including some of his former colleagues and Ray Anthony, Count Basie and Tommy Dorsey. Mostly, he worked as a freelance but had a stint in the mid-50s as musical director for Dizzy Gillespie, one result of which was the 1956 album *World Statesman*. Later in the 50s and into the 60s Jones wrote charts and directed the orchestras for concerts and record sessions by several singers, including Frank Sinatra, Billy Eckstine, Brook Benton, Dinah Washington (an association which included the 1956 album *The Swingin' Miss 'D'*), Johnny Mathis and Ray Charles, whom he had known since childhood. He continued to write big band charts, composing and arranging albums for Basie, *One More Time* (1958-59) and *Li'l Ol' Groovemaker...Basie* (1963).

By this time, Jones was fast becoming a major force in American popular music. In addition to playing he was busy writing, arranging and was increasingly active as a record producer. In the late 60s and 70s he composed scores for about 40 feature films and hundreds of television shows. Among the former were *The Pawnbroker* (1965), *In Cold Blood* (1967) and *In The Heat Of The Night* (1967) while the latter included the long-running *Ironside* series and *Roots*. He continued to produce records featuring his own music played by specially assembled orchestras. As a record producer Jones had originally worked for Mercury's Paris-based subsidiary Barclay but later became the first black vice-president of the company's New York division. Later, he spent a dozen years with A&M Records before starting up his own label, Qwest. Despite suffering two brain aneurysms in 1974 he showed no signs of letting up his high level of activity. In the 70s and 80s he produced successful albums for Aretha Franklin, George Benson, Michael Jackson, the Brothers Johnson and other popular artists. With Benson he produced *Give Me The Night*, while for Jackson he helped to create *Off The Wall* and *Thriller*, the latter proving to be the best-selling album of all time. He was also producer of the 1985 number 1 charity single 'We Are The World'. Latterly, Jones has been involved in film and television production, not necessarily in a musical context. As a player, Jones was an unexceptional soloist; as an arranger, his attributes are sometimes overlooked by the jazz audience, perhaps because of the manner in which he has consistently sought to create a smooth and wholly sophisticated entity, even at the expense of eliminating the essential characteristics of the artists concerned (as some of his work for Basie exemplifies). Nevertheless, with considerable subtlety he has fused elements of the blues and its many offshoots into mainstream jazz, and has found ways to bring soul to latterday pop in a manner which adds to the latter without diminishing the former. His example has been followed by many although few have achieved such a level of success. A major film documentary, *Listen Up: The Lives Of Quincy Jones*, was released in 1990.

Selected albums: *Clifford Brown Memorial Album* (1953), *This Is How I Feel About Jazz* (Impulse 1956), *The Birth Of A Band* (1959), *The Great Wide World Of Quincy Jones* (Mercury 1959), *Quincy Jones Live At Newport* (1961), *Quintessence* (MCA 1961), *Strike Up The Band* (Mercury 1961-64 recordings), *Walking In Space* (A&M 1969), *Gula Matari* (1970), *Smackwater Jack* (A&M 1971), *Mellow Madness* (A&M 1972), *The Hot Rock* (1972), *I Heard That!* (1973), *Body Heat* (1973), *Roots* (1977), *Sounds...And Stuff Like That* (A&M 1978), *The Dude* (A&M 1980), *Music In My Life* (Hallmark 1983), *Bossa Nova* (Mercury 1983), *Love And Peace* (Street Life 1988), *Back On The Block* (WEA 1989), with Miles Davis *Live At Montreux* (1993, rec. 1991). Compilation: *The Best* (A&M 1982).

Video: *Miles Davis And Quincy Jones: Live At Montreux* (1993).

Jones, Reunald

b. 22 December 1910, Indianapolis, Indiana, USA, d. 1989. Jones came from a musical family; his father and two brothers were professional musicians and he was a cousin of Roy

Eldridge. Jones played trumpet with various bands around Minneapolis in the late 20s; joined Speed Webb's noted territory band in 1930, and thereafter swung through many leading bands of the 30s and early 40s, notably those of Don Redman, Claude Hopkins, Chick Webb, Jimmie Lunceford and Duke Ellington. In 1952 he joined Count Basie, playing lead trumpet until 1957. He subsequently played with Woody Herman and spent several years working in studio bands, a period which included stints backing Nat 'King' Cole on television and playing with Gene Ammons. A strikingly good lead trumpeter, Jones seldom attracted attention, unless it was as a result of a calculatedly casual habit he adopted while with Basie of playing with one hand in his pocket. His few recorded solos included some with Chick Webb, 'Let's Get Together' and 'When Dreams Come True', and 'Swingin' With The Fat Man' with Redman.

Album: with Count Basie *Sixteen Men Swinging* (1953). Compilation: *The Chronological Chick Webb* (1929-34).

Jones, Thad

b. Thaddeus J. Jones, 28 March 1923, Pontiac, Michigan, USA, d. 20 August 1986. A self-taught trumpet player, Jones began playing with a band led by his older brother, Hank Jones, in his early teens. He developed his technique and advanced his musical knowledge during military service and in several dancebands. In the early 50s he played in a band led by Billy Mitchell, which also included his younger brother, Elvin Jones. In 1954 Thad was with Charles Mingus; the same year he also joined Count Basie, an engagement that lasted until 1963. In the mid-60s Jones formed The Jazz Orchestra, which he co-led with Mel Lewis. During this period he extended his writing activities, composing and arranging the bulk of this remarkable band's outstanding book. In 1979 Jones quit The Jazz Orchestra and emigrated to Denmark, where he wrote for and performed with the Danish Radio Big Band, often playing valve trombone (which he had taken up following a lip injury). He also appeared with the Swedish Radio Big Band and formed a band of his own, Eclipse. In 1985 he took on the leadership of the Count Basie Orchestra, leaving in February the following year, some six months before his death. A lyrical player, especially on the slightly mellower flügelhorn, Jones was a superbly inventive, bebop-influenced soloist with a crisp tone. Despite such gifts, however, Jones's major contribution to jazz was his extensive library of compositions and arrangements for big bands. In these he ranged widely, experimenting with meters not usually adopted by jazz orchestras, and comfortably incorporating various popular fads and fancies into jazz with a skill that ensured their survival long after fashions had changed.

Selected albums: *The Fabulous Thad Jones* (Original Jazz Classics 1954), with Count Basie *April In Paris* (1955-56), *The Magnificent Thad Jones* (1957), *Mad Thad* (Fresh Sounds 1957), *Motor City Scene* (1959), with Pepper Adams *Mean What You Say* (1966), with Mel Lewis *The Jazz Orchestra* (1966), with Lewis *Presenting Joe Williams* (1966), with Lewis *Live At The Village Vanguard* (1967), with Lewis *Featuring Miss Ruth Brown* (1968), with Lewis *Monday Night* (1968), with Lewis *Central Park North* (1969), with Lewis *Paris-1969* (1969), with Lewis *Consummation* (1970), with Lewis *Suite For Pops* (1972), *Thad Jones, Mel Lewis, Manuel De Sica And The Jazz Orchestra* (1973), with Lewis *Live In Tokyo* (1974), with Lewis *Potpourri* (1974), with Swedish Radio Big Band *Greetings And Salutations* (1975), with Lewis *New Life* (1975), *The Thad Jones-Mel Lewis Jazz Orchestra* (1976), with Lewis *Live In Munich* (1976), with Lewis *Thad And Aura Rully* (1977), *Monica Zetterlund And The Thad Jones-Mel Lewis Jazz Orchestra* (1977), *The Thad Jones-Mel Lewis Quartet* (1977), *Thad Jones-Mel Lewis And Umo* (1977), *By Jones, I Think We've Got It* (1978), with Danish Radio Big Band *A Good Time Was Had By All* (1978), *Live At Monmarte* (Storyville 1978), *Eclipse* (Storyville 1979), *Jazzhus Slukefter* (1980), *Three And One* (Steeplechase 1985).

Jordan, Clifford

b. 2 September 1931, Chicago, Illinois, USA, d. 27 March 1993, New York City, New York, USA. Jordan began his professional career playing tenor saxophone in R&B bands in the Chicago area. In 1957 he moved to New York, made the album *Blowin' In From Chicago* with fellow tenor saxophonist John Gilmore and then spent time in groups led by Max Roach and Horace Silver. In the 60s he played with artists including J.J. Johnson, Charles Mingus, Kenny Dorham, Julian Priester and also led his own bands, touring extensively. In 1965 he released a tribute to Leadbelly, *These Are My Roots*, and in the late 60s began to record for the Strata East label: outstanding releases include *In The World* and *Glass Bead Game*. In the 70s he worked with Cedar Walton, often in a quartet context with Sam Jones and Billy Higgins (known as the Magic Triangle), recording some distinctive large ensemble albums for Muse (*Remembering Me-Me*, *Inward Fire*), and he also established a reputation as a teacher. In the 80s Jordan continued to record regularly, both as a guest with leaders such as Slide Hampton (*Roots*) and in various small groups of his own, where his associates have included Walton again (*Half Note*), Barry Harris (*Repetition*) and Junior Cook (*Two Tenor Winner*). With his roots in blues and the bebop mainstream tempered by work with modernists such as Mingus, Eric Dolphy and Don Cherry, Jordan was both an accessible, adventurous player and an impressive, under-rated composer/arranger.

Albums: with John Gilmore *Blowing In From Chicago* (1957), *Clifford Jordan All Stars* (1957), *Cliff Craft* (1957), *Spellbound* (1960), with Sonny Red *A Story Tale* (1961), *Starting Time* (1961), *Bearcat* (1961-62), *These Are My Roots* (1965), *Clifford Jordan And His Orchestra* (1966), *In The World* (1969), *Glass Bead Game* (Strata East 1973), *The Highest Mountain* (Steeplechase 1975), *Night Of The Mark VII* (1975), *On Stage Vols 1-3* (Steeplechase 1975), *Firm Roots* (Steeplechase 1975), *The Highest Mountain* (1975), *Remembering Me-Me* (1976), *Inward Fire* (1977), *The Adventurer* (1978), *Hello Hank Jones* (1978), *Adventurer* (Muse 1981), with Jaki Byard *Dr Chicago* (1984), *Repetition* (Soul Note 1984), with Junior Cook *Two Tenor Winner!* (Criss Cross 1984), *Half Note* (1985), *Royal*

Ballads (Criss Cross 1986), *Masters From Different Worlds* (Mapleshade 1990), *Down Through The Years* (Milestone 1992).

Jordan, Duke

b. Irving Sidney Jordan, 1 April 1922, New York City, New York, USA. After studying classical music, Jordan played piano in a number of swing era bands, including Al Cooper's Savoy Sultans. In the mid-40s, he became involved in bebop, playing with Charlie Parker and others. Later in the decade and in the early 50s Jordan played in bands led by Sonny Stitt and Stan Getz and thereafter led his own units. Also in the early 50s, he married the singer Sheila Jordan, but they later split up. Jordan's career drifted for a while in the late 60s, but from 1972 onwards he was very active, playing in many parts of the world, especially in Scandinavia, and since 1978 he has lived in Denmark, recording extensively for the Copenhagen label Steeplechase. A lyrically inventive player, Jordan has also composed a number of tunes, one of which, 'Jordu', became a bebop classic.

Selected albums: *The Duke Jordan Trio* (Savoy 1954), *Do It Yourself Jazz* (Savoy 1955), *The Street Swingers* (1955), *The Duke Jordan Quintet* (1955), *Flight To Jordan* (1955), *Les Liaisons Dangereuses* (1962), *East And West Of Jazz* (1962), *Brooklyn Brothers* (1973), *The Murray Hill Caper* (1973), *Flight To Denmark* (Steeplechase 1973), *Two Loves* (Steeplechase 1973), *Truth* (1975), *Duke's Delight* (1975), *Misty Thursday* (Steeplechase 1975), *Lover Man* (1975), *The Duke Jordan Trio Live In Japan* (Steeplechase 1976), *Osaka Concert: Vols 1 and 2* (Steeplechase 1976), *Flight To Japan* (1976), *I Remember Bebop* (1977), with others *They All Played Bebop* (1977), *Duke's Artistry* (Steeplechase 1978), *The Great Session* (Steeplechase 1978), *Midnight Moonlight* (1979), *Tivoli One* (Steeplechase 1979), *Wait And See* (Steeplechase 1979), *Solo Masterpieces* (Steeplechase 1979), *Lover Man* (1979), *Change A Pace* (1979), *Thinking Of You* (Steeplechase 1979), *Blue Duke* (RCA 1983), *As Time Goes By* (Steeplechase 1986), *Time On My Hands* (Steeplechase 1986).

Jordan, Louis

b. Louis Thomas Jordan, 8 July 1908, Brinkley, Arkansas, USA, d. 4 February 1975, Los Angeles, California, USA. Saxophonist and singer, Jordan began touring as a teenager with the Rabbit Foot Minstrels, and supported classic blues singers Ma Rainey, Ida Cox and Bessie Smith. In the 30s, after relocating to New York City, he played in the bands of Louis Armstrong, Clarence Williams, Chick Webb and Ella Fitzgerald, appearing with these orchestras on records for RCA Victor, Vocalion and Decca, and making his vocal debut with Webb's band on novelty songs such as 'Gee, But You're Swell' and 'Rusty Hinge'. In 1938 Jordan formed his first combo, the Elks Rendez-Vous Band (after the club at which he had secured a residency), and signed an exclusive deal with Decca. While he had been with Webb, he had often been brought to the front to perform a blues or novelty swing number. These spots had been so well-received that, from the start of his own band,

Jordan had decided to promote himself as a wacky musical comedian with a smart line in humorous jive. In early 1939, in line with this image, he changed the band's name to the Tympany Five and enjoyed steady, if unspectacular, success with recordings of 'T-Bone Blues' (1941), 'Knock Me A Kiss' and 'I'm Gonna Move To The Outskirts Of Town' (1942), 'What's The Use Of Gettin' Sober (When You Gonna Get Drunk Again)' and 'Five Guys Named Moe' (1943). After World War II, the Tympany Five really hit their stride with a string of million-selling records, including 'Is You Is Or Is You Ain't My Baby?' (1944), 'Caldonia (Boogie)' (1945), '(Beware, Brother) Beware!', 'Choo Choo Ch'boogie' (1946) and 'Saturday Night Fish Fry' (1949). Other hits which were not so commercially successful, but which are inextricably linked with Jordan's name nevertheless include 'G.I. Jive', 'Buzz Me', 'Ain't Nobody Here But Us Chickens', 'Let The Good Times Roll', 'Reet, Petite And Gone', 'Open The Door, Richard', 'School Days', and 'Blue Light Boogie'. Jordan remained with Decca until 1954, when he switched briefly to Aladdin (1954), RCA's 'X' subsidiary (1955) and Mercury (1956-57) but, sadly, his reign was coming to an end; the new generation wanted 'fast and loud' not 'smooth and wry', and Jordan, dogged by ill-health, could not compete against rock 'n' roll artists such as Little Richard and Chuck Berry, even though his songs were being recycled by these very performers. Chuck Berry ('Run Joe' and 'Ain't That Just Like A Woman') and B.B. King 'Do You Call That A Buddy?', 'Early In The Morning', 'Just Like A Woman', 'How Blue Can You Get?', 'Buzz Me', 'Let The Good Times Roll' and 'Jordan For President!' in particular, have been successful with Jordan covers. Surprisingly, his performances were taken to the heart of many Chicago blues artists with songs like 'Somebody Done Hoodooed The Hoodoo Man', 'Never Let Your Left Hand Know What Your Right Hand's Doin'' and 'Blue Light Boogie'; even Bill Haley would often admit that his 'revolutionary' musical style was simply a copy of the Tympany Five's shuffles and jumps that had been recorded the previous decade in the same Decca studios.

Owing to his fluctuating health Louis Jordan spent the 60s and 70s working when he could, filling summer season engagements and recording occasionally for small companies owned by old friends including Ray Charles (Tangerine Records), Paul Gayten (Pzazz) and Johnny Otis (Blues Spectrum). His last recordings were as a guest on trumpeter Wallace Davenport's *Sweet Georgia Brown*, after which he suffered eight months of inactivity due to his deteriorating health, and a fatal heart-attack on 4 February 1975. The main factor that set Jordan apart from most of the competition was that he was at once a fine comedian and a superb saxophonist whose novelty value was never allowed to obscure either his musicianship or that of his sidemen, who at one time or another included trumpeters Idrees Sulieman and Freddie Webster (both major influences on boppers like Miles Davis and Dizzy Gillespie), tenor saxophonists Paul Quinichette, Maxwell Davis and Count Hastings, drummer Shadow Wilson, and pianists Wild Bill Davis and Bill Doggett. That Louis Jordan influenced all who came after him, and continues to be a prime source of material for films, theatre, television advertising, R&B bands and bluesmen, 40 or 50 years after his heyday, is a testament to his originality and talent. In 1990 a musical by Clarke Peters entitled *Five Guys Named Moe*, which featured 'music written or originally performed by Louis Jordan', opened in London. Four years later it overtook *Irma La Douce* to become the longest-running musical ever at the Lyric Theatre. After initially lukewarm revues, another production enjoyed a decent run on Broadway.

Selected albums: *Go! Blow Your Horn* (1957, reissued 1982), *Somebody Up There Digs Me* (1957), *Man, We're Wailin'* (1958), Let *The Good Times Roll* (1958), *Hallelujah...Louis Jordan Is Back* (1964), *One Sided Love* (1969), *Louis Jordan's Greatest Hits* (1969), *Louis Jordan* (1971), *Great R&B Oldies* (1972), *I Believe In Music* (1974), *In Memoriam* (1975), *Louis Jordan's Greatest Hits Volume 2* (1975), *The Best Of Louis Jordan* (1975), *Louis Jordan With The Chris Barber Band* (1976), *Three Hot Big Band Sessions In 1951* (1976), *More Stuff* (1976), *Some Other Stuff* (1977), *Louis Jordan And His Tympany Five* i (1977), *Come On...Get It...* (1978), *Prime Cuts* (1978), *Collates* (1979), *Good Times* (1980), *The Best Of Louis Jordan* (1981), with Oran 'Hot Lips' Page *Jumpin' Stuff* (1981), *Louis Jordan And His Tympany Five* ii (1982), *The Last Swinger, The First Rocker* (1982), *Choo Choo Ch'boogie* (1982), *G.I. Jive* (1983), *Cole Slaw* (1983), *Look Out!...It's Louis Jordan And The Tympany Five* (1983), *Louis Jordan And His Tympany Five, 1944-1945* (1983), *Louis Jordan On Film - Reet, Petite And Gone* (1983), *Louis Jordan On Film - Look Out Sister* (1983), *Go! Blow Your Horn - Part 2* (1983), *Jump 'N' Jive With Louis Jordan* (1984), *Louis Jordan And Friends* (1984), *Jivin' With* Jordan (1985), *Hoodoo Man 1938-1940* (1986), *Knock Me Out 1940-1942* (1986), *Somebody Done Hoodooed The Hoodoo Man* (1986), *Louis Jordan And His Tympany Five, More 1944-1945* (1986), *Rock And Roll Call* (1986), *Rockin' And Jivin', Volume 1* (1986), *Rockin' And Jivin', Volume 2* (1986), *Louis Jordan And His Tympany Five* (1986), *Out Of Print* (1988), *Greatest Hits* (1989), *The V-Discs* (1989), *Hits And Rarities* (1989), *More Hits, More Rarities* (1990), *Rock 'N' Roll* (1990), *The Complete Aladdin Sessions* (1991), *The Complete Recordings 1938 - 1941* (1992).

Further reading: *Let The Good Times Roll: A Biography Of Louis Jordan*, John Chilton.

Jordan, Sheila

b. Sheila Jeanette Dawson, 18 November 1928, Detroit, Michigan, USA. Raised in poverty in Pennsylvania's coal-mining country, Jordan began singing as a child and by the time she was in her early teens was working semi-professionally in Detroit clubs. Her first great influence was Charlie Parker and, indeed, most of her influences have been instrumentalists rather than singers. Working chiefly with black musicians, she met with disapproval from the white community but persisted with her career. She was a member of a vocal trio, Skeeter, Mitch And Jean (she was Jean), who sang versions of Parker's solos in a manner akin to that of the later Lambert, Hendricks And Ross. After moving to New York in the early 50s, she mar-

ried Parker's pianist, Duke Jordan, and studied with Charles Mingus and Lennie Tristano, but it was not until the early 60s that she made her first recordings. One of these was under her own name, the other was *The Outer View* with George Russell, which featured a famous 10-minute version of 'You Are My Sunshine'. In the mid-60s her work encompassed jazz liturgies sung in churches and extensive club work, but her appeal was narrow even within the confines of jazz. By the late 70s jazz audiences had begun to understand her uncompromising style a little more and her popularity increased - as did her appearances on record, which included albums with pianist Steve Kuhn, whose quartet she joined, and an album, *Home*, comprising a selection of Robert Creeley's poems set to music and arranged by Steve Swallow. A 1983 duo set with bassist Harvie Swartz, *Old Time Feeling*, comprises several of the standards Jordan regularly features in her live repertoire, while 1990's *Lost And Found* pays tribute to her bebop roots. Both sets display her unique musical trademarks, such as the frequent and unexpected sweeping changes of pitch which still tend to confound an uninitiated audience. Entirely non-derivative, Jordan is one of only a tiny handful of jazz singers who fully deserve the appellation and for whom no other term will do.

Albums: with George Russell *The Outer View* (1962), *Portrait Of Sheila* (Blue Note 1962), *Confirmation* (1975), *Grapevine Discovery* (1976), *Sheila* (Steeplechase 1977), with others *Lennie Tristano Memorial Concert* (1979), *Playground* (1979), with Harvie Swartz *Old Time Feeling* (Palo Alto 1982), *The Crossing* (Blackhawk 1984), *Songs From Within* (MA Recordings 1989), *Lost And Found* (Muse 1990), with Mark Murphy *One For Junior* (Muse 1994).

Jordan, Stanley

b. 31 July 1959, Chicago, Illinois, USA. Having absorbed a certain amount of theory from an early training on the piano, Jordan taught himself the guitar while in his teens, and performed with the numerous pop and soul groups working around Chicago in the mid-70s. However, winning a prize at the 1976 Reno Jazz Festival inspired Jordan to devote some time to a serious study of music. Studying electronic music, theory, and composition at Princeton University, his reputation quickly spread and he soon found himself playing with Dizzy Gillespie and Benny Carter. In 1982 he recorded his first album: *Touch Sensitive* was a relatively uninspiring solo collection which registered poor sales. But three years later, Jordan's second album *Magic Touch* was a huge commercial success. Produced by Al DiMeola, it featured Onaje Allen Gumbs, Charnett Moffett, and Omar Hakim, while retaining some unaccompanied tracks. Since *Magic Touch*, Jordan's band has become a regular feature of the major international jazz festivals. He is commonly known for his development of a complex technique of 'hammering-on' which has enabled him to accompany himself with bass lines and chords.

Albums: *Touch Sensitive* (1982), *Magic Touch* (Blue Note 1985), *Standards* (Blue Note 1986), *Flying Home* (EMI Manhattan 1988), *Cornucopia* (Blue Note 1990), *Stolen Moments* (Blue Note 1991), *Bolero* (Arista 1994).

Jordan, Taft

b. James Jordan, 15 February 1915, Florence, South Carolina, USA, d. 1 December 1981. Jordan began playing trumpet professionally in 1929 and within four years had achieved such a standard that he was hired by Chick Webb. Apart from a few weeks with Willie Bryant, Jordan stayed with the band until Webb's death and then continued until 1941 during the period when the band was nominally led by Ella Fitzgerald. After briefly leading his own outfit he joined Duke Ellington in 1943. From 1947 he worked with various bands, some of which were relatively obscure. In the mid-50s he led his own bands and also played with Benny Goodman. In the 60s he was active in the studios and theatre-land, occasionally playing in clubs. In the 70s he worked with the New York Jazz Repertory Company and played with Earle Warren. Although the influence of Louis Armstrong affected some of his earlier work, both as a trumpeter and a singer, Jordan was a fiery and often inventive player whose solos could ignite a band. He died in December 1981.

Albums: *Taft Jordan* (1960), *Taft Jordan With George Rhodes And His Orchestra* (1960), *Mood Indigo* (1961). Compilations: *Taft Jordan And The Mob* (1935), *The Chronological Chick Webb* (1935-39), *The Indispensable Duke Ellington Vols 11/12* (1944-46).

K

Kahn, Tiny

b. Norman Kahn, c.1923, New York City, New York, USA, d. 19 August 1953. After learning to play drums while in school, Kahn performed with a number of important and progressively-minded big bands of the late 40s - including those of Boyd Raeburn, Georgie Auld and Charlie Barnet. While with these bands Kahn began writing, and his arrangements for Chubby Jackson's band were especially successful. This aspect of his talent was also employed by Elliot Lawrence in the early 50s. Kahn's writing was an influence upon other young arrangers of the period, including Al Cohn and Johnny Mandel. Extremely overweight (his nickname was ironical), Kahn died of cardiac problems in August 1953.

Albums: with Stan Getz *Jazz At Storyville* (1951), *Elliot Lawrence Plays Kahn And Mandel* (1956).

Kaminsky, Max

b. 7 September 1908, Brockton, Massachusetts, USA, d. 6 September 1994, Castle Point, New York, USA. Kaminsky was a trumpet player with a vigorous style, who played briefly with some big bands, including Tommy Dorsey and Artie Shaw, but was mainly associated with white Chicago-style small groups. Kaminsky started out with bands in Boston around 1924. In the late 20s, he played with George Wettling and Bud Freeman in New York, and toured with Red Nichols. During the 30s and early 40s he worked for several bandleaders, including Leo Reisman, Joe Venuti, Pee Wee Russell, Tony Pastor, Tommy Dorsey, Alvino Rey and Joe Marsala. Between 1942 and 1943, he played for Artie Shaw's famous Navy Band. After his discharge, he led his own popular combo in New York and Boston clubs until 1946, when he resumed freelancing with dixieland groups with artists such as Eddie Condon and Art Hodes. In 1957, he toured Europe with a Jack Teagarden-Earl Hines All Star group, and the following year travelled to Asia with Teagarden. From then on, he was generally based in New York, mainly freelancing, but sometimes leading small groups at venues such as the Gaslight Club, and at Jimmy Ryan's, where he was still appearing occasionally until 1983. He appeared on several US television jazz programmes, including a 1973 Timex Special. His few recordings as leader included 'Love Nest', 'Everybody Loves My Baby', 'Dippermouth Blues', 'Someday Sweetheart' plus the albums *Chicago Style, Ambassador Of Jazz* and *Dixieland Horn*. He recorded prolifically with other groups including George Brunis ('I Used To Love You', 'I'm Gonna Sit Right Down And Write Myself A Letter' and 'In The Shade Of The Old Apple Tree'); Bud Freeman ('China Boy' and 'The Eel'), Art Hodes ('Sweet Georgia Brown' and 'Sugar Foot Stomp'), Willie 'The Lion' Smith ('Muskrat Ramble' and 'Bugle Call Rag'), Tommy Dorsey ('Maple Leaf Rag', 'That's A Plenty' and 'Keepin' Out Of Mischief Now').

Albums: *Chicago Style* (unk. date), *Ambassador Of Jazz* (unk. date), *Dixieland Horn* (unk. date), *Jack Teagarden And Max Kaminsky* (1982) with various artists *Art Ford's Jazz Party, 1958* (Jazz Connoisseur 1987).

Further reading: *My Life In Jazz*, Max Kaminsky.

Kamuca, Richie

b. 23 July 1930, Philadelphia, Pennsylvania, USA, d. 22 July 1977. After working in groups in and around his home town, Kamuca joined the Stan Kenton Orchestra on tenor saxophone in 1952. Two years later he was in Woody Herman's band and then settled on the west coast, where he played and recorded with, among others, Shelly Manne and Shorty Rogers. Kamuca was also on the 1955 Cy Touff Octet and Quintet sessions for Pacific Jazz which featured Harry Edison and used charts by Johnny Mandel. The following year Kamuca was again on dates for Pacific, as a member of the Chet Baker-Art Pepper Sextet and also on a Bill Perkins album that included Pepper. In 1959, he again recorded with Pepper and was also featured on the highly successful live recordings made by Manne at the Black Hawk club in San Francisco. In the early 60s, Kamuca moved to New York, where he worked in a small group with Roy Eldridge and became a member of the studio orchestra for the Merv Griffin television show. He was a founder member of Bill Berry's rehearsal band, which comprised mostly musicians from the studio orchestra, and when the Griffin show abruptly moved to Los Angeles, Kamuca went too. There, he worked with Berry in his re-formed big band, recording with him and under his own name for the Concord label. A fine player of ballads, with a warm and impassioned style, Kamuca's indebtedness to Lester Young is apparent, but he never slavishly followed his idol. One of his last recordings was dedicated to Charlie Parker, and throughout his later years he can be heard developing original ideas and gradually changing his style as he matured.

Albums: with Stan Kenton *Sketches On Standards* (1953), with Woody Herman *Road Band* (1955), *Cy Touff, His Octet And Quintet* (1955), with Bill Perkins *Just Friends* (1956), *The Richie Kamuca Quartet* (VSOP 1957), *Jazz Erotica* (Fresh Sound 1958), with Art Pepper *Modern Jazz Classics* (1959), *Shelly Manne And His Men At The Black Hawk* (1959), *West Coast Jazz In Hi-Fi* (Original Jazz Classics 1960), with Roy Eldridge *Comin' Home Baby* (1965-66), with Bill Berry *Hot & Happy* (1974), *Drop Me Off In Harlem* (1977), *Richie* (1977), *Charlie* (1977).

Kay, Connie

b. Conrad Henry Kirnon, 27 April 1927, Tuckahoe, New York, USA, d. 30 November 1994, New York City, New York, USA. A self-taught drummer, in his late teens Kay played with leading bop musicians, including Miles Davis. He gained big band experience with Cat Anderson late in the decade. In the early 50s, he was playing R&B in studio backing bands - but was mostly playing in small modern jazz groups with Lester Young, Stan Getz, Davis, Charlie Parker and others. In 1955, he took over from Kenny Clarke in the Modern Jazz Quartet, remaining with the group for the next 20 years. During these years he also performed with other artists on record dates, amongst them Chet Baker, Paul Desmond, Cannonball Adderley and fellow MJQ member John Lewis. He played on Van Morrison's masterpiece *Astral Weeks*. After the MJQ disbanded in 1974 Kay worked with Lewis and other jazzmen, including Benny Goodman in whose band he played at the Carnegie Hall 40th Anniversary Concert. In the late 70s he was mostly working in New York playing jazz-club dates which included several years in the house band at Eddie Condon's. In 1981, he was again a member of the MJQ when the group re-formed. Despite his wide experience in several areas of jazz, Kay was understandably best known for his highly sophisticated work with the MJQ in which context he played with great subtlety and deftly understated swing.

Albums: with Lester Young *Lester's Here* (1953), with MJQ *Concorde* (1955), with MJQ *Fontessa* (1956), with Chet Baker *Chet* (1959), with John Lewis *Improvised Meditations & Excursions* (1959), with Paul Desmond *Easy Living* (1964), with MJQ *Blues At Carnegie Hall* (1966), with Benny Goodman *40th Anniversary Concert At Carnegie Hall* (1978), with MJQ *Echoes* (1984).

Keane, Ellsworth 'Shake'

b. Ellsworth McGranahan Keane, 30 May 1927, St. Vincent, West Indies. Although taught music by his father as a child,

Keane did not turn to the trumpet as a career until the mid-50s. Originally a teacher in St. Vincent, he came to England in 1952 to study English literature. He was already an accomplished poet - his nickname is short for 'Shakespeare' - with two collections of verse published, but could find no work in London except as a musician. For several years he played as a sideman in nightclubs and on recording sessions, performing calypso and Latin music as well as blues and jazz. One regular employer was calypso king Lord Kitchener, while a selection of tracks Keane originally made for the west African market with Guyanese pianist Mick McKenzie was reissued on the compilation *Caribbean Connections: Black Music In Britain In The Early 50s, Vol. 2*. From 1959-65, Keane was a member of the Joe Harriott Quintet, which pioneered freeform and abstract jazz in the UK. Keane played on all their classic recordings, notably *Free Form*, *Abstract* and *Movement*. When the group disbanded in the mid-60s he moved to Germany, becoming a featured soloist with Kurt Edelhagen's Radio Band. In the 70s he returned to St. Vincent and was Minister of Culture for several years. In the early 80s, he settled in New York, where he occasionally played reggae and soca but spent most of his time writing poetry. In 1989, however, he toured the UK with the Joe Harriott Memorial Quintet, which also included original members Coleridge Goode and Bobby Orr. Equipped with flawless technique and brilliant invention, Keane - equally adept at calypso and bebop, freeform and classical - is recognized as one of the outstanding trumpeters of his generation.

Albums: with Joe Harriott *Free Form* (1960), *In My Condition* (1961), with Harriott *Abstract* (1962), *Shake Keane And The Boss Men* (1962), *The Shake Keane And Michael Garrick Quartet* (1963), with Harriott *Movement* (1963), with Harriott *High Spirits* (1964), *Shake Keane And The Keating Sound* (1965), with Harriott *Indo-Jazz Fusions* (1966), *Shake Keane And His Orchestra* I (1966), *Shake Keane And His Orchestra* II (1968).

Kellaway, Roger

b. 1 November 1939, Waban, Massachusetts, USA. Kellaway was initially attracted to jazz by the piano playing of George Shearing. He switched from piano to double bass and studied at the New England Conservatory (1957-59). He played the bass with Jimmy McPartland before returning to work full-time at the piano. In the mid-60s he played with the bands of Kai Winding, Al Cohn and Zoot Sims, and Clark Terry/Bob Brookmeyer, as well as working in the studios with musicians as varied as Ben Webster, Wes Montgomery and Sonny Rollins. In 1966, he moved to Los Angeles and played with the Don Ellis band. Since the late 60s he has worked as musical director for Bobby Darin (1967-69) and concentrated on studio work with musicians as diverse as Joni Mitchell and Jimmy Knepper. He has written numerous film scores including *The Paper Lion* (1968), *A Star Is Born* (1976) and *Breathless* (1983), as well as writing a ballet *PAMTGG* (1971), commissioned by George Balanchine and *Portraits Of Time* (1983), commissioned by the Los Angeles Philharmonic Orchestra. In 1984, he returned to New York to studio work and a duo with Dick Hyman.

Selected albums: *Portrait Of Roger Kellaway* (Fresh Sound 1963), *Roger Kellaway Trio* (1965), *Spirit Feel* (1967), *Cello Quartet* (1971), *Come To The Meadow* (1974), *Nostalgia Suite* (1978), *Say That Again* (1978), *Fifty-Fifty* (Natasha 1987), with Red Mitchell *Alone Together* (Dragon 1989), *In Japan* (All Art Jazz 1987), with Red Mitchell *Life's A Take* (Concord 1982), *Live At the Maybank Recital Hall Vol 11* (Concord 1991).

Kellin, Orange

b. Örjan Kjellin, 21 July 1944, Ljungby, Sweden. Kellin began playing clarinet at the age of 15 and two years later formed his first band in partnership with pianist Lars Edegran. The band played music in the New Orleans manner. Kellin made his first records in his native Sweden at the age of 17. In 1966, he moved to New Orleans where he became a regular performer at several leading jazz venues including the Preservation Hall. In 1968 he was a founder member of the New Orleans Ragtime Orchestra. He also led his own bands in the city including, in 1970, a band which held a residency at the Maison Bourbon Club. Two years later he formed the New Orleans Joymakers. Kellin recorded with several veteran New Orleans musicians including Josiah 'Cié' Frazier, Preston Jackson, Jim Robinson, Jabbo Smith, Zutty Singleton and Kid Thomas Valentine. In 1978, Kellin played with the NORO for the soundtrack of the film *Pretty Baby*. The following year he appeared in New York with the stage musical *One Mo' Time* for which he was musical director and co-arranger in addition to playing in the onstage band. In the early 80s he appeared with the same show during its long and successful run in London's West End. Kellin has toured extensively with his own bands and with bands formed largely from New Orleans veterans. In 1992 he made his first solo tour of the UK. A gifted and highly musicianly clarinettist, Kellin's dedication to the music of New Orleans has contributed greatly to the preservation of the style. He has an excellent technique and solos with flair and eloquence. As an admirable ensemble player, he lends authority to any group of which he is a member.

Albums: *Orange Kellin In New Orleans* i (1967), *Orange Kellin In New Orleans* ii (1967), *Scandanavians In New Orleans* (c.1971), *New Orleans Ragtime Orchestra* (1971), *Pretty Baby* (1978, film soundtrack).

Kelly, George

b. 31 July 1915, Miami, Florida, USA. Kelly began playing tenor saxophone in childhood and was a bandleader in his home state while still in his teenage years. After playing with several territory bands during the late 30s he joined Al Cooper's Savoy Sultans in New York. After leaving the Sultans, he played in and around New York for the rest of the 40s and on through the 50s. Occasional visits further afield attracted a small amount of attention, but it was not until the late 70s that he made an impact on the jazz world's consciousness. In 1979, David 'Panama' Francis, who had played in Kelly's Florida band, formed a new version of the Savoy Sultans and invited Kelly into the group. Thanks to successful records and hugely popular appearances at festivals around the world, Kelly's qualities were widely recognized. During the 80s and into the early 90s he worked with Francis and led his own bands for tours and record dates, amongst which was a set paying tribute to Don Redman on which Kelly was joined by Glenn Zottola. A fine tenor saxophonist with a relaxed style, Kelly is also an accomplished arranger and entertaining singer.

Albums: *Stealin' Apples* (c.1976), *George Kelly In Cimiez* (1979), with David 'Panama' Francis *Gettin' In The Groove* (1979), *Fine And Dandy* (1982), *Live At The West End Cafe* (1982), *The Cotton Club* (1983), *George Kelly Plays The Music Of Don Redman* (Stash 1984), *Fine And Dandy* (Barron 1988).

Kelly, Wynton

b. 2 December 1931, Jamaica, West Indies, d. 12 April 1971. Raised in New York, Kelly first played piano professionally with various R&B bands, where his musical associates included Eddie 'Lockjaw' Davis. In the early 50s, he played with Dizzy Gillespie, Dinah Washington and Lester Young. In 1954, after military service, he rejoined both Gillespie and Washington for brief stints and later played with many important contemporary musicians, notably Charles Mingus and Miles Davis, with whom he worked from 1959-63. Kelly also led his own trio, using the bass (Paul Chambers) and drums (Jimmy Cobb) from Davis's band, and also recorded successfully with a variety of artists such as Wes Montgomery, Freddie Hubbard and George Coleman. A subtle and inventive player, Kelly's style was his own even if his work denotes his awareness both of his contemporaries and the piano masters of an earlier generation. Throughout his records there is a constant sense of freshness and an expanding maturity of talent, which made his death, in April 1971, following an epileptic fit, all the more tragic.

Selected albums: *New Faces, New Sounds* (1951), *Piano Interpretations By Wynton Kelly* (Blue Note 1951), *The Big Band Sound Of Dizzy Gillespie* (1957), *Wynton Kelly* i (1958), *Autumn Leaves* (1959), *Kelly Blue* (Original Jazz Classics 1959), *Kelly Great!* (1959), *Kelly At Midnight* (1960), *Wynton Kelly* ii (1961), with Miles Davis *Some Day My Prince Will Come* (1961), *Miles Davis At Carnegie Hall* (1961), *The Wynton Kelly Trio With Claus Ogermann And His Orchestra* i (1963), *The Wynton Kelly Trio With Claus Ogermann And His Orchestra* ii (1964), *Undiluted* (1965) with Wes Montgomery *Smokin' At The Half Note* (1965), *Blues On Purpose* (Xanadu 1965), *Wynton Kelly And Wes Montgomery* (1965), *Full View* (1967), *Wynton Kelly And George Coleman In Concert* (1968), *In Concert* (Affinity 1981), *Live In Baltimore* (Affinity 1984), *Wrinkles* (Affinity 1986), *Last Trio Session* (Delmark 1988), *Takin' Charge* (Le Jazz 1993).

Kenton, Stan

b. 15 December 1911, Wichita, Kansas, USA, d. 25 August 1979. After playing piano in various dance bands, including those of Everett Hoagland and Vido Musso, mostly on the west coast, Kenton decided to form his own band in 1941. Although geared partially to the commercial needs of the dancehall circuit of the time, Kenton's band, which he termed the 'Artistry In Rhythm' orchestra, also featured powerful brass section work and imaginative saxophone voicings, unlike those of his more orthodox competitors. The band developed a substantial following among the younger elements of the audience who liked their music brash and loud. During the remainder of the 40s Kenton's popularity increased dramatically, seemingly immune to the declining fortunes that affected other bands. A succession of exciting young jazz musicians came into the band, among them Buddy Childers, Art Pepper, Kai Winding, Shelly Manne, Bob Cooper and Laurindo Almeida, playing arrangements by Kenton, Gene Roland and Pete Rugolo. His singers included Anita O'Day, June Christy and Chris Connor. In the 50s, his enthusiasm undimmed, Kenton introduced a 43-piece band, his 'Innovations In Modern Music' orchestra, again featuring Pepper and Manne as well as newcomers such as Maynard Ferguson and Bud Shank. Complex, quasi-classical arrangements by Bob Graettinger and others proved less appealing, but a 1953 tour of Europe ensured Kenton's international reputation. Reduced to a more manageable 19-piece, his New Concepts In Artistry In Rhythm band continued playing concerts and recording, using arrangements by Roland, Gerry Mulligan and Johnny Richards. Always eager to try new ideas, and to clearly label them, in the 60s Kenton introduced his 'New Era In Modern Music' orchestra, a 23-piece band using mellophoniums, and the 'Neophonic' orchestra, five pieces larger and tempting fate with neo-classical music. In the 70s, he embraced rock rhythms and looked as if he might go on forever. By 1977, however, his health had begun to deteriorate and although he returned from hospitalization to lead his band until August 1978, his bandleading days were almost over. He died in August 1979.

More than most bandleaders, Kenton polarized jazz fans, inspiring either love or hatred and only rarely meeting with indifference. Almost half a century after the event it is hard to understand what all the fuss was about. Certainly the band did not swing with the grace of, say, the Jimmie Lunceford band but it was just as wrong to declare, as did many critics, that Kenton never swung at all. Certainly if some of the arrangements were too monolithic for effective jazz performances, the abilities of some of his key soloists were seldom buried for long. Kenton's band was important for bringing together many excellent musicians and for allowing arrangers free rein to experiment in big band concepts that few other leaders of the period would tolerate. As a leader, Kenton brought to jazz an unbridled enthusiasm that persisted long after he could have retired in comfort to study psychology, the other consuming passion in his life.

Selected albums: *Stan Kenton At The Hollywood Palladium* (1945), *Progressive Jazz* (1946-47), *One Night Stand With Nat 'King' Cole And Stan Kenton* (1947), *One Night Stand At The Commodore* (1947), *Stan Kenton And His Orchestra With June Christy* (c.1949), *Innovations In Modern Music* (1950), *One Night Stand With Stan Kenton* i (1950), *Nineteen Fifty-One* (1951), *One Night Stand With Stan Kenton* ii (1951), *Carnegie* (1951), with Charlie Parker *Kenton And Bird* (1951-54), *Artistry In Tango* (1951-52), *Concert In Miniature* (1952), *Concert In Miniature No 9 And 10* (1952), *Concert In Miniature No 11 And 12* (1952), *Concert In Miniature No 13 And 14* (1952), *New Concepts Of Artistry In Rhythm* (1952), *Concert Encores* (1953), *The Definitive Stan Kenton With Charlie Parker And Dizzy Gillespie* (1953-54), *Stan Kenton In Berlin* (1953), *Europe Fifty Three Part One and Two* (1953), *Paris, 1953* (1953), *Sketches On Standards* (1953-54), *Artistry In Kenton* (1954), *Stan Kenton Festival* (1954), with June Christy *Duet* (1955), *Contemporary Concepts* (1955), *Stan Kenton In Hi-Fi* (1956), *Kenton In Concert* (1956), *Kenton In Stereo* (1956), *In Stockholm* (1956), *Cuban Fire* (1956), *Kenton '56* (1956), *Rendez-vous With Kenton/At The Rendezvous Vol. 1* (1957), *Back To Balboa* (1958), *The Ballad Style Of Stan Kenton* (1958) *Lush Interlude* (1958), *The Stage Door Swings* (1958), *On The Road* (1958), *The Kenton Touch* (1958), *Stan Kenton At The Tropicana* (1959), *In New Jersey* (1959), *At Ukiah* (1959), *Viva Kenton* (1959), *The Road Show Vols 1 & 2* (1959), with Ann Richards *Two Much* (1960), with Christy *Together Again* (1960), *Stan Kenton's Christmas* (1961), *The Romantic Approach* (1961), *Stan Kenton's West Side Story* (1961), *Mellophonium Magic* (1961), *Sophisticated Approach* (1961), *Adventures In Standards* (1961), *Adventures In Blues* (1961), *Adventures In Jazz* (1961), *The Sound Of Sixty-Two* (1962), *Adventures In Time* (1962), *Stan Kenton's Mellophonium Band* (1962), *Artistry In Bossa Nova* (1963), *Artistry In Voices And Brass* (1963), *The Best Of Brant Inn* (1963), *Kenton In England* (1963), *Wagner* (1964), *Stan Kenton Conducts The Los Angeles Neophonic Orchestra* (1965), *Rhapsody In Blue* (1965), *Stan Kenton Conducts The Jazz Compositions Of Dee Barton* (1967), *Live At Redlands University* (Creative World 1970), *Live At Brigham Young University* (Creative World 1971), *Live At Fairfield Hall, Croydon* (1972), *Live At Butler University* (Creative World 1972), *National Anthems Of The World* (1972), *Stan Kenton Today* (1972), *Birthday In Britain* (Creative World 1973), *7.5 On The Richter Scale* (Creative World 1973), *Solo: Stan Kenton Without His Orchestra* (1973), *Stan Kenton Plays Chicago* (Creative World 1974), *Fire, Fury And Fun* (Creative World 1974), *Kenton 1976* (Creative World 1976), *Journey Into Capricorn* (Creative World 1976), *Stan(dard) Kenton: Stan Kenton In Warsaw* (1976), *Stan Kenton In Europe* (1976), *Live At Sunset Ridge Country Club Chicago* (Magic 1977), *Live In Cologne 1976 Vols 1 and 2* (Magic 1977), *Street Of Dreams* (Creative World 1977). Selected compilations: *The Kenton Era (1940-53)* (1955, reissued 1985), *Stan Kenton's Greatest Hits (1943-51)* (1983), *The Christy Years (1945-47)* (1985), *The Fabulous Alumni Of Stan Kenton (1945-56)* (1985), *Collection: 20 Golden Greats* (1986), *Retrospective 1943-1968* (Capitol 1992, 4-CD box set).

Further reading: *Straight Ahead: The Story Of Stan Kenton*, Carol Easton. *Stan Kenton: Artistry In Rhythm*, William F. Lee. *Stan Kenton: The Man And His Music*, Lillian Arganian.

Keppard, Freddie

b. 27 February 1890, New Orleans, Louisiana, USA, d. 15 July 1933. Before choosing to play the cornet, Keppard experimented with various other instruments, none of which was especially suitable for performing jazz. In the years before World War I he played with the Olympia Orchestra in New Orleans and several other parade and concert bands. He was leader of the Original Creole Orchestra which toured California and the east coast, and also worked in Chicago. After the war Keppard settled in Chicago, where he worked with Joe 'King' Oliver, Jimmie Noone and other luminaries of the city's jazz scene. In the early 20s he played in various bands, sometimes leading his own, almost always in or around Chicago. Among the last bands with which he worked were those of Erskine Tate and Charlie Elgar. He seldom played after 1928 and died in July 1933. Keppard's few recordings barely support his status as a leading hornman of early jazz and a direct link to the legendary playing of Buddy Bolden. Nevertheless, there are suggestions of his qualities and it is hard to question the reputation he enjoyed among fellow musicians such as Sidney Bechet and Milt Hinton. Along with Edward 'Kid' Ory, Keppard was important in helping to spread jazz into areas of the west coast not previously familiar with the music.

Selected albums: *Carol Kidd* (1984), *All My Tomorrows* (1985), *Nice Work* (1987), *Night We Called It A Day* (1990), *I'm Glad We Met* (1991). Compilations: *The Legend Of Freddie Keppard (1923-27)* (1973), *Freddie Keppard (1923-28)* (Jazz Treasury 1988), *Complete Freddie Keppard* (King Jazz 1993).

Kessel, Barney

b. 17 October 1923, Muskogee, Oklahoma, USA. After playing in various bands (including one led by Chico, the piano-playing Marx brother), Kessel began to establish a name for himself on the west coast. He appeared in the Norman Granz-produced short film *Jammin' The Blues* (1944), then played in various big bands of the late swing era. From the mid-40s he was in great demand for studio work, jazz record sessions, club and concert dates, and on tours with Jazz At The Philharmonic. Among the artists with whom he performed and recorded over the next 20 years were Charlie Parker, Oscar Peterson, Billie Holiday and Harry Edison. By the mid-60s he was one of the best-known and most-recorded guitarists in jazz. He continued to tour and record in groups and as a solo artist. In the early 70s, he teamed up with Herb Ellis and Charlie Byrd to perform as the group Great Guitars. This project continued to tour into the 80s, which saw Kessel as active as ever. An exceptionally gifted musician with a very wide range, Kessel's versatility has ensured that he is always in demand. In a jazz context he plays in a boppish, post-Charlie Christian style, but has his own distinctive flavour. In the context of Great Guitars, he ably fills the mid-ground between Byrd's latent classicism and Ellis's blues-tinged swing. In person, Kessel has a swift and waspish sense of humour, a characteristic which often appears in his music. Incapacitated by a stroke in 1992, Kessel was making a slow recovery during the following year.

Selected albums: *To Swing Or Not To Swing* (Original Jazz Classics 1955), *Plays Standards* (Original Jazz Classics 1955),

with Billie Holiday *Lady In Autumn* (1955-57), *Easy Like* (1956), *Sessions, Live* (1956), *Let's Cook* (1957), *Music To Listen To Barney Kessel By* (Original Jazz Classics 1957), with Holiday *Body And Soul* (1957), *The Poll Winners* (Original Jazz Classics 1958), *The Poll Winners Ride Again* (Original Jazz Classics 1959), *Some Like It Hot* (Original Jazz Classics 1959), *Plays Carmen* (Original Jazz Classics 1959), *Workin' Out* (1961), *On Fire* (1965), *Swinging Easy* (1968), *Kessel's Kit* (1969), with others *Limehouse Blues* (Black Lion 1969), *Autumn Leaves* (Black Lion 1970), *Just Friends* (Sonet 1973), *Yesterday* (Black Lion 1974), *Two-Way Conversation* (1975), *Three Guitars* (Concord 1975), *Plays Barney Kessel* (Concord 1975), *Soaring* (Concord 1977), *Great Guitars: Straight Tracks* (c.1978), *Live At Sometime* (Storyville 1978), *Great Guitars At The Winery* (Concord 1980), *Jelly Beans* (Concord 1981), *Great Guitars At Charlie's, Georgetown* (Concord 1982), *Solo* (Concord 1983), *Summertime In Montreux* (1985), *Spontaneous Combustion* (JVC 1987), *Kessel Plays Standards* (Contemporary 1989). Compilation: *The Artistry Of Barney Kessel* (Fantasy 1987).

Khan, Steve

b. 28 April 1947, Los Angeles, California, USA. Khan is the son of lyricist Sammy Cahn and learned to play the piano and drums as a child. He was the drummer with the surf group the Chantays (1962-63) and only turned to the guitar when he was 20. After graduating in music from UCLA in 1969, he settled in New York where he became a prolific session musician recording with artists as varied as George Benson, Hubert Laws, Maynard Ferguson, Billy Joel and Steely Dan. In 1977, he worked with Larry Coryell and Randy and Michael Brecker before touring Japan with the CBS All Stars. In 1978, he published a transcription of solos by Wes Montgomery. He has continued to develop his skills as a composer as can be seen in his tribute to pianist Thelonious Monk on *Evidence*. In 1981, he formed Eyewitness with Manolo Badrena, Anthony Jackson and Steve Jordan.

Albums: with Larry Coryell *Two For The Road* (1977), *Tightrope* (1977), *Evidence* (Arista 1980), with Eyewitness *Eyewitness* (Antilles 1981), with Eyewitness *Casa Loco* (1983), *Local Colour* (Denon 1988), *Public Access* (GRP 1990), *Let's Call This* (Polydor 1991), *Headline* (Polydor 1993). Compilation: *Best Of Steve Khan* (CBS 1980).

Kidd, Carol

b. 19 October 1945, Glasgow, Scotland. Kidd began her career singing in and around Glasgow in the early 60s, entering numerous talent shows where one of her regular fellow contestants was Marie McDonald, later to find fame as pop singer Lulu. At the age of 15, Kidd was singing with a traditional jazz band; two years later she married the trombone player and started a family, then spent a further five years with another trad band. By this time she was developing an appreciation of the finer aspects of popular music. Unfortunately, her options were limited, trad and rock being the only commercially viable choices. Frustrated at not being able to sing how and what she wanted, she retired from the music scene for four years, return-

ing only when a Glasgow-based quartet asked her to join them for a Saturday morning session. She stayed for 11 years, the quartet evolving into a trio with which she worked regularly until early 1990. This long relationship proved invaluable in allowing Kidd to develop an extensive and well-honed repertoire that has at its centre a fine selection of standards. Her record albums, appearances at Ronnie Scott's and an annual engagement at the prestigious Edinburgh Festival helped to expand her audience. A series of concert appearances in 1989 and 1990 with Humphrey Lyttelton's band also opened new doors. Midway through 1990, with different accompanists, including the excellent pianist David Newton, and a wholesale change in her repertoire, Kidd re-launched her career. An invitation to open at a Frank Sinatra concert and an appearance at London's Queen Elizabeth Hall, in November 1990, helped to raise her career profile. Although she has still to achieve her ambition to appeal to more than a specialist jazz audience, there seems little chance that her rich talent will go unrecognized in the larger public arena through another decade.
Albums: *Carol Kidd* (Linn 1984), *All My Tomorrows* (Linn 1985), *Nice Work (If You Can Get It)* (Linn 1987), *Night We Called It A Day* (Linn 1990), *I'm Glad We Met* (Linn 1992), *When I Dream* (1992).

King, Peter

b. 11 August 1940, Kingston-upon-Thames, Surrey, England. Self-taught on several reed instruments, by the late 50s King had established himself as an important and exciting alto saxophonist on the UK jazz scene. Over the next few years he worked with John Dankworth, Tubby Hayes, Stan Tracey and other leading British musicians. He also worked with numerous visiting American artists, ranging stylistically from Ray Charles to Red Rodney, from Jimmy Witherspoon to Hampton Hawes. By the 70s King's stature had grown until he was on the verge of becoming a major international figure. During the 80s he consolidated his gains and amply fulfilled his potential. In the early 90s King was one of the world's outstanding hard bop alto saxophonists. Playing with a hard-edged brilliant tone, his remarkable agility and technical virtuosity are at the command of an exceptionally fast mind. Although his remarkable imagination and improvisational ability are best displayed on up-tempo tunes he is also a lyrical balladeer. His latest release, an attempt to reach a wider audience, was co-produced by Everything But The Girl's Ben Watt.
Albums: *My Kind Of Country* (Tank 1977), *New Beginning* (Spotlite 1982), *East 34th Street* (Spotlite 1983), *Hi Fly* (Spotlite 1984), *90% Of 1%* (Spotlite 1985), *Live At The Bull* (1987), *Brother Bernard* (Miles 1988), *Blues For Buddy* (1988), *Crusade* (Blanco Y Negro 1989), *New Years' Morning '89* (1989).

Kinsey, Tony

b. 11 October 1927, Sutton Coldfield, West Midlands, England. Kinsey was a key drummer in the London jazz scene of the 50s, having studied formally in the UK and USA before joining the John Dankworth Seven in 1950. He later formed his own groups, working with many leading jazz musicians, including Joe Harriott, Peter King and a succession of visiting American stars. Kinsey's early musical studies had extended into composition, and he has written many longer works for jazz orchestra and for classical groups. He has also written for films and television, but in the late 80s was still leading his small jazz groups around London clubs. As a skilful technician, Kinsey is comfortable playing in bebop or mainstream settings and is an outstanding jazz drummer.
Albums: *Starboard Bow* (1955), *Jazz At The Flamingo* (1956), *The Tony Kinsey Quartet* (1957), *The Tony Kinsey Quintet* i (1957) *The Tony Kinsey Quintet* ii (1958), *The Tony Kinsey Quintet* iii (1959), *Foursome* (1959), *The Tony Kinsey Quintet* iv (1961), *How To Succeed In Business* (1963), *The Thames Suite* (Spotlite 1976).

Kirby, John

b. 31 December 1908, Baltimore, Maryland, USA, d. 14 June 1952. Kirby's career began in New York but suffered a hiatus when his first instrument, a trombone, was stolen. Replacing this with a tuba, he resumed his musical career, joining Fletcher Henderson in 1930. Soon after this he began using a string bass, at first alternating between the two instruments. He spent about two years with Chick Webb, then rejoined Henderson, but in 1937 decided to form his own band. Securing a residency at New York's Onyx Club, Kirby set about melding his group into a smooth, thoroughly rehearsed and musicianly outfit. Although this was the height of the big band-dominated swing era, he settled on a six-piece band and within a year saw his judgement pay off. The John Kirby Sextet, billed as 'The Biggest Little Band In The Land', became the yardstick by which nearly all sophisticated small jazz groups were measured. For most of the band's four-year existence the personnel was stable; Charlie Shavers, Buster Bailey, Russell Procope, Billy Kyle and drummer O'Neill Spencer. The addition of Kirby's wife, Maxine Sullivan, did the group's popularity no harm at all. The group disbanded with the onset of World War II and, although Kirby re-formed after the war, he never again achieved either the quality or the popularity of his first band. He was planning a comeback when he died in June 1952.
Selected albums: *John Kirby* (Atlantic 1986), *The Biggest Little Band In The Land (1938-41)* (Giants Of Jazz 1987), *John Kirby And His Orchestra, With Maxine Sullivan* (1988), *More* (Circle 1988), *John Kirby And Onyx Club Boys Vol 1-4* (Collectors Classics 1988), *John Kirby And His Orchestra* (Circle 1988), *Biggest Little Band* (Columbia 1993).

Kirk, Andy

b. 28 May 1898, Newport, Kentucky, USA. Raised in Colorado, Kirk dabbled in music as a child, learning to play several instruments. He studied assiduously, one of his tutors being Wilberforce Whiteman, father of Paul Whiteman. Kirk played in several bands in and around Denver, in particular that led by George Morrison which played popular music of the day mixed with a smattering of light classics. It was a solid musical apprenticeship for the young man, but he was cautious about his career and all the while maintained other regular employment. In 1927, he moved to Dallas, Texas, where he joined Terrence Holder's band, the Dark Clouds Of Joy. By this time Kirk was mostly playing tuba, doubling on baritone and bass saxophones. In 1929, Holder, an erratic individual on his own ideas on how to run the band's finances, was persuaded to quit and Kirk took over leadership. The band's name underwent various minor changes but thereafter was mostly known as Andy Kirk And His Clouds Of Joy. At the instigation of George E. Lee, the band auditioned for and obtained an engagement at Kansas City's prestigious Pla-Mor Restaurant. During their stay at the Pla-Mor the band auditioned again, this time for a recording contract. When Marion Jackson, the regular pianist, could not make the date, Kirk brought in Mary Lou Williams. In addition to playing on the date, Williams also supplied several arrangements, some of which were of her own compositions. She so impressed the record company's executives, Jack Kapp and Dick Voynow, that they insisted she appear on all the band's record dates. Soon afterwards, Jackson tired of this implied slur, quit the band. Williams joined the band full-time and quickly became one of its most important and influential members. The band's personnel was relatively stable over the years and included many excellent musicians such as Buddy Tate (tenor saxophone), Edgar Battle (trumpet), Claude Williams (violin), Ben Thigpen (drums), Pha Terrell (vocals) and Mary Lou's husband, John Williams (alto saxophone). A subtly swinging band, epitomizing the best of the more commercial end of the Kansas City Jazz sound, the Clouds Of Joy enjoyed several years of success. There were difficult moments, not least in early 1931 when the band had to take engagements and record dates under the nominal leadership of Blanche Calloway, but they survived into the late 40s. The size of the band, usually ranging between 11-13 pieces, meant that it was smaller than the average swing era big band and this, allied to Mary Lou Williams's skilful charts, gave it an enviable cohesion. Mary Lou Williams left in 1942 to develop her remarkable career. Williams apart, the band's outstanding soloist was tenor saxophonist Dick Wilson. A light-toned player with a sound, if not style, akin to that of Lester Young, he contributed many memorable moments to the band's recorded output. Wilson's death, in 1941 at the age of 30, was a great loss to the band. For all the enormous talents of Williams and Wilson, however, as far as the non-jazz public was concerned, the band's greatest asset for many years was singer Pha Terrell. He had a light tenor voice with little or no jazz feeling but had several hit records, of which the best known was 'Until The Real Thing Comes Along'. One of the few territory bands to gain a national reputation, the Clouds Of Joy folded in 1948. Thereafter, Kirk played occasionally but eventually dropped out of music to take up hotel management. In the 60s, he was occasionally active in music, then dabbled in real estate. In the 80s he took a job with the local New York American Federation of Musicians, where he continued to put in appearances until long after retirement age.

Compilations: *Walking And Swinging (1936-42)* (Affinity 1983), *Andy's Jive (1944-45)* (Swing House 1984), *Cloudy (1929)* (Hep Jazz 1984), *All Out For Hicksville (1931)* (Hep Jazz 1988), with Mary Lou Williams *Mary's Idea* (GRP 1993), *Mellow Bit Of Rhythm* (RCA 1993), *Kansas City Bounce* (Black And Blue 1993, rec 1936-40).

Further reading: *Twenty Years On Wheels*, Andy Kirk as told to Amy Lee.

Kirk, Rahsaan Roland

b. 7 August 1936, Columbus, Ohio, USA, d. 5 December 1977. Originally named 'Ronald', Kirk changed it to 'Roland' and added 'Rahsaan' after a dream visitation by spirits who 'told him to'. Blinded soon after his birth, Kirk became one of the most prodigious multi-instrumentalists to work in jazz, with a career that spanned R&B, bop and the 'New Thing' jazz style. According to Joe Goldberg's sleevenotes for *Kirk's Works* (1961), Kirk took up trumpet at the age of nine after hearing the bugle boy at a summer camp where his parents acted as counsellors. He played trumpet in the school band, but a doctor advised against the strain trumpet-playing imposes on the eyes. At the Ohio State School for the Blind, he took up saxophone and clarinet from 1948. By 1951 he was well-known as a player and was leading his own dance band in the locality. Kirk's ability to play three instruments simultaneously gained him notoriety. Looking through the 'scraps' in the basement of a music store, Kirk found two horns believed to have been put together from different instruments, but which possibly dated from late 19th century Spanish military bands. The manzello was basically an alto sax with a 'large, fat, ungainly' bell. The strich resembled 'a larger, more cumbersome soprano'. He found a method of playing both, plus his tenor, producing a wild, untempered 'ethnic' sound ideal for late-60s radical jazz. He also soloed on all three separately and added flute, siren and clavietta (similar to the melodica used by Augustus Pablo and the Gang Of Four) to his armoury. With all three horns strung around his neck, and sporting dark glasses and a battered top hat, Kirk made quite a spectacle. The real point was that, although he loved to dally with simple R&B and ballads, he could unleash break-neck solos that sounded like a bridge between bebop dexterity and *avant garde* 'outness'. His debut for a properly distributed label - recorded for Cadet Records in Chicago in June 1960 at the behest of Ramsey Lewis - provoked controversy, some deriding the three-horn-trick as a gimmick, others applauding the fire of his playing. In 1961, he joined the Charles Mingus Workshop for four months, toured California and played on *Oh Yeah!*. He also played the Essen Jazz Festival in Germany. In 1963, he began the first of several historic residencies at Ronnie Scott's club in London. Despite later guest recordings with Jaki Byard (who had played on his *Rip Rig & Panic*) and Mingus (at the 1974 Carnegie Hall concert), Kirk's main focus of activity was his own group, the Vibration Society, with whom he toured the world until he suffered his first stroke in November 1975, which paralysed his right side. With characteristic single-mindedness, he taught himself to play with his left hand only and started touring again. A second stroke in 1977 caused his death. Long before the 80s 'consolidation' period for jazz, Kirk presented a music fully cognizant of black American music, from Jelly Roll Morton and Louis Armstrong on through Duke Ellington and John Coltrane; he also paid tribute to the gospel and soul heritage, notably on *Blacknuss*, which featured songs by Marvin Gaye, Smokey Robinson and Bill Withers. Several of his tunes - 'The Inflated Tear', 'Bright Moments', 'Let Me Shake Your Tree', 'No Tonic Pres' - have become jazz standards. His recorded legacy is uneven, but it contains some of the most fiery and exciting music to be heard.

Selected albums: *Rahsaan Roland Kirk* (1956), with Booker Ervin *Soulful Saxes* (Affinity 1957), *Introducing Roland Kirk* (Chess 1960), with Jack McDuff *Kirk's Work* (Original Jazz Classics 1961), *We Free Kings* (Emarcy 1962), *Domino* (1962), *Roland Kirk In Copenhagen* (1963), *Meets the Benny Golson Orchestra* (1963), *Gifts & Messages* (1964), *I Talk To The Spirits* (1964), *Rip Rig & Panic* (Emarcy 1965), *Now Please Don't You Cry, Beautiful Edith* (Verve 1967), *The Inflated Tear* (Affinity 1968), *The Case Of The Three Sided Dream In Audio Colour* (Atlantic 1969), *Volunteered Slavery* (Rhino 1970), *Rahsaan, Rahsaan* (1970), *Roller Coaster* (Bandstand 1971), *Blacknuss* (Rhino 1972), *Bright Moments* (Rhino 1973), *The Return Of The 5000 lb Man* (1975), *Other Folks' Music* (1976), *Boogie-Woogie String Along For Real* (1977), *Prepare To Deal With A Miracle* (Atlantic 1978), *Vibration Society* (Stash 1987), *Paris 1976* (1990). *Soul Station* (Affinity 1993). Compilations: *The Art Of Rahsaan Roland Kirk (1966-71)* (1973), *The Man Who Cried Fire (60s/70s)* (Virgin 1990), *Complete Mercury Recordings* (Mercury 1991), *Rahsaan* (Mercury 1992, 11 CD box set).

Kirkland, Kenny

b. 28 September 1957, New York City, New York, USA. After graduating from the Manhattan School of Music in 1977, Kirkland toured with Michal Urbaniak, and joined Miroslav Vitous in 1979. But it was with Wynton Marsalis (1981-85) that he gained his reputation as a skilful Herbie Hancock-influenced pianist, and he has since been in demand from a host of bandleaders including Branford Marsalis and Chico Freeman. His work with Sting, and the resulting 1985 *Dream Of The Blue Turtles*, helped widen Kirkland's audience.

Selected albums: with Miroslav Vitous *Miroslav Vitous Group* (1980), with Wynton Marsalis *Black Codes From The Underground* (1985), *Kenny Kirkland* (GRP 1991).

Klemmer, John

b. 3 July 1946, Chicago, Illinois, USA. After trying guitar and alto saxophone in early childhood, Klemmer settled on tenor saxophone in his early teens. He studied extensively, playing in school and other youth bands, then played professionally with several name dancebands of the early 60s, including those led by Les Elgart and Ralph Marterie. In the late 60s he made his first records and then joined Don Ellis's formidable big band. During these years he also played in small groups led by Oliver Nelson and Alice Coltrane. During this time he led his own groups, making jazz and jazz-fusion records. He experimented with electronics and fusion and some of his 1969 recordings

slightly pre-date Miles Davis's *Bitches Brew*. Sometimes Klemmer used electronic enhancements to allow him to record complex solo saxophone albums. He continued to develop these electronic concepts throughout the 70s and into the 80s. Playing with a diamond-hard tone, Klemmer's solos are filled with daring lines and imaginative ideas, often tossed out almost casually. On ballads, at which he excels, he introduces a breathy quality which aids the sometimes light and airy feeling he imparts. Many of his recordings feature his own compositions. Musically, his interest in areas on the fringes of jazz has tended to keep him from acceptance by the jazz world at large.

Albums: with Don Ellis *Autumn* (1968), with Oliver Nelson *Black, Brown And Beautiful* (1969), *Eruptions* (1969), *All The Children Cried* (1969), *Blowin' Gold (Eruptions/All The Children Cried)* (Chess 1969), *Constant Throb* (1971), *Solo Saxophone I: Cry* (1975), *Arabesque* (1977), *Nexus For Duo And Trio* (1978), *Nexus One (For Trane)* (1979), *Straight From The Heart* (1979), *Hush* (Elektra 1981), *Finesse* (Elektra 1983), *Solo Saxophone II: Life* (1985), *Barefoot Ballet* (MCA 1987), *Music* (MCA 1989), *Waterfalls* (Impulse 1990).

Klink, Al

b. 28 December 1915, Danbury, Connecticut, USA, d. 8 March 1991. One of the many unsung heroes of the swing era, Klink's career took him through the bands of Benny Goodman and Tommy Dorsey and he was a mainstay of the Glenn Miller Orchestra during its most successful period. Although an excellent soloist on both saxophones and clarinet, Klink was usually overshadowed either by soloing leaders or other more favoured sidemen. After World War II he worked mostly in the studios, recording with Billie Holiday, the Sauter-Finegan Orchestra and Ruby Braff. In the late 70s and early 80s he joined fellow veterans Bob Haggart and Yank Lawson in their World's Greatest Jazz Band and also freelanced with several other jazz groups.

Albums: one side only *The Al Klink Quintet* (1955), *The World's Greatest Jazz Band Of Yank Lawson And Bob Haggart On Tour* (1975).

Kluger, Irving

b. 9 July 1921, New York City, New York, USA. In the early 40s, after studying music at high school and while still at university, Kluger drifted into New York's bebop scene. He played drums in Georgie Auld's modernistic band and also worked with Dizzy Gillespie, appearing with him on a 1945 recording date which produced the hugely popular 'Salt Peanuts' and 'Good Bait'. Kluger then moved on to the adventurous Boyd Raeburn band and also worked with Stan Kenton and Artie Shaw in the late 40s. In the 50s and subsequently, Kluger played in studio, as well as in theatre and casino orchestras, across the country, eventually settling on the west coast. In the early 80s he was an executive of the American Federation of Musicians in Las Vegas and talked of returning to drumming in his 'retirement', and, time permitting, also of writing his memoirs.

Albums: *Boyd Raeburn - On The Air Vol. 2* (1945-47), with

Milt Bernhardt *Modern Brass* (1955). Compilations: with Stan Kenton *The Kenton Era* (1940-55 recordings).

Klugh, Earl

b. 16 September 1953, Detroit, Michigan, USA. Jazz guitarist Klugh has an unorthodox style in that when he sits down he rests the guitar on his right knee instead of the left. After studying piano and nylon string guitar as a child, Klugh settled on the latter instrument. While still in his mid-teens he recorded with Yusef Lateef and George Benson, with whom he also toured. He continued to work with Benson and briefly with Return To Forever and, in the mid-70s, he also led his own groups for a solo career. Influenced by a wide range of guitarists including Benson (jazz), Chet Atkins (country) and folk, Klugh's style contains elements of all, yet is presented with a strong feeling for the great tradition of post-Charlie Christian jazz guitar through which his own personality constantly shines.

Albums: with Yusef Lateef *Suite 16* (1970), with George Benson *White Rabbit* (1971), *Earl Klugh* (1976), *Living Inside Your Love* (Liberty 1976), *Finger Paintings* (Liberty 1977), *Magic In Your Eyes* (United Artists 1978), *Heart String* (United Artists 1979), with Bob James *One On One* (1979), *Dream Come True* (EMI 1980), with Hubert Laws *How To Beat The High Cost Of Living* (1980, film soundtrack), *Late Night Guitar* (United Artists 1980), *Crazy For You* (Liberty 1981), with Bob James *Two Of A Kind* (Capitol 1982), *Low Ride* (Capitol 1983), with Hiroki Miyano *Hotel California* (Mercury 1984), *Wishful Thinking* (Capitol 1984), *Nightsongs* (Capitol 1983), *Soda Fountain Shuffle* (WEA 1985), *Life Stories* (WEA 1986), with Benson *Collaboration* (1987), *A Time For Love* (Capitol 1988), *Solo Guitar* (WEA 1989), *Sounds And Visions* (1993). Compilations: *The Best Of Earl Klugh (1977-84)* (Blue Note 1985), *World Star* (1985), *The Best Of Earl Klugh Vol 2* (Blue Note 1993).

Knepper, Jimmy

b. 22 November 1927, Los Angeles, California, USA. Knepper learned to play trombone as a small child, later studying intensively. In the early 40s he played in local dance bands, playing jazz with various small groups. From the late 40s and into the early 50s he played with numerous name bands, including those led by Freddie Slack, Roy Porter, Charlie Spivak, Charlie Barnet, Woody Herman and Claude Thornhill. Later in the 50s Knepper worked extensively with Charles Mingus and also with Art Pepper and Stan Kenton. During the 60s he was with Mingus again, Benny Goodman and he also began a long-lasting if intermittent association with Gil Evans. Towards the end of the 60s he began another long-term musical relationship, this time with the Thad Jones-Mel Lewis Jazz Orchestra. In the 70s he was a member of the nine-piece band led by Lee Konitz and also worked with Mingus Dynasty. He made several records under his own name, including *Cunningbird* which featured such distinguished jazz musicians as Al Cohn, Roland Hanna and Richard Davis. A virtuoso performer, Knepper's bop-influenced style is technically on a par with that of J.J.

Johnson, one of the few other trombonists to adapt wholly to bop. Nevertheless, Knepper's style is very much his own, with few obvious direct influences. His remarkable technical dexterity allows him to develop solo lines of startling ingenuity and imagination. In the 80s, Knepper was active on both sides of the Atlantic, renewing interest among older fans and finding a new audience for his exceptional skills and talent.

Selected albums: with Charles Mingus *Tijuana Moods* (1957), with Mingus *East Coasting* (1957), *A Swinging Introduction To Jimmy Knepper* (1957), *Pepper And Knepper* (1958), with Mingus *Blues And Roots* (1959), *Mingus Dynasty* (1959), *Cunningbird* (Steeplechase 1976), *JK In LA* (1977), *Just Friends* (1978), *Tell Me...* (1979), *Primrose Path* (1980), with Bobby Wellins *Primrose Path* (Hep Jazz 1982), *Idol Of The Flies* (Affinity 1982), *I Dream Too Much* (Soul Note 1984), *Dream Dancing* (Criss Cross 1987), *Muted Joys* (Affinity 1989).

Koglmann, Franz

b. 22 May 1947, Vienna, Austria. Koglmann took up the trumpet after seeing a Louis Armstrong concert at the age of 13. Despite this epiphany, he studied exclusively classical trumpet at the Vienna Conservatory and his interest in jazz was reawakened only in 1968, this time by an encounter with Miles Davis. Koglmann, trumpeter, flügelhorn player and composer, is serious about 'roots' and the influence of countrymen Schubert, Berg and Krenek is to be discerned in his music, tempering and shaping the nature of the jazz, and giving new credence to the maligned ideas of Third Stream Music. Though *A White Line*, specifically setting out to celebrate the (under-recognized) achievements of white jazz musicians, prompted predictable sermonizing from (white) critics, other Koglmann recordings draw upon the music of Thelonious Monk and Dizzy Gillespie, and the list of distinguished soloists who have played with Koglmann's band includes Bill Dixon and Alan Silva, as well as Paul Bley, Ran Blake and Steve Lacy. Most of Koglmann's music is written for his 10-12 piece band, the Pipetet, launched in 1973. The prevalent mood is one of melancholy, the compositional structures are labyrinthine, the execution is brilliant.

Albums: *Flaps* (1973), *Opium/For Franz* (1976), *Schlaf Schlemmer, Schlaf Magritte* (Hat Art 1984), *Good Night* (1985), *Ich, Franz Koglmann* (Hat Art 1986), *About Yesterday's Ezztheticis* (Hat Art 1987), *Orte Der Geometrie* (Hat Art 1988), *A White Line* (Hat Art 1989), *The Use Of Memory* (Hat Art 1990), *L'Heure Bleue* (Hat Art 1991), *Canto I-IV* (Hat Art 1993), with Paul Bley, Gary Peacock *Annette* (1993).

Komeda, Krzysztof

Long before western Europe enthused over Zbigniew Namyslowski and the Ganelin Trio, pianist and composer Komeda showed that Warsaw Pact countries, especially Poland, were capable of producing fine jazz. He composed the music for Roman Polanski's films *Two Men And A Wardrobe*, *When Angels Fall*, *The Fat And The Lean*, *Knife In The Water*, *Cul-De-Sac*, *Dance Of The Vampires* and *Rosemary's Baby*. The score for *Knife In The Water*, featuring fast and freewheeling themes for saxophone and rhythm, demonstrated that he had kept abreast of modern jazz developments, and his album *Astigmatism*, taking up the directions pointed out by Miles Davis's mid-60s Quintet and featuring Namyslowski, has just been re-issued by the Polish state record label. His last work was on Buzz Kulik's film *Riot* in 1968. In April 1969, he died from an illness resulting from a head injury sustained in November 1968.

Albums: *Knife In The Water* (1962), *Polish Jazz Volume 3* (Polskie Nagrania Muza 1960, 1961, 1965 recordings), *Live In Copenhagen* (Polonia 1965), *Astigmatism* (1967), *Rosemary's Baby* (1968).

Konitz, Lee

b. 13 October 1927, Chicago, Illinois, USA. Konitz began on clarinet, studying in the classical form, later switching to alto saxophone. In the mid-late 40s he played in the bands of Jerry Wald and Claude Thornhill, appeared on jazz dates with Miles Davis and was simultaneously studying with Lennie Tristano, with whom he also recorded. In the early 50s he worked for a while with Stan Kenton and although he left the band before the end of 1953, he had established his name and an international reputation. From the mid-50s onwards Konitz generally led his own bands, recording and playing publicly, and made a brief return visit to work with Tristano. He also became involved in teaching. During the following years Konitz's interest in teaching developed and soon he was running clinics and workshops, giving private tuition and also conducting worldwide correspondence courses. In the mid-70s he recorded several albums with Warne Marsh, all finding immediate critical and commercial popularity. He also formed a nine-piece band modelled upon the one led by Davis in which he had played 30 years earlier. One of very few alto saxophonists of his generation not to have been influenced by Charlie Parker, Konitz managed to avoid being cast in any mould other than that which he created himself. Unlike many of his peers, he has proved to be flexible and capable of continually growing to accommodate new concepts. In performance his sound has changed over the years. Originally he played with a deliberately thin sound but he thickened this during his time with Kenton, a necessity to avoid being drowned by the volume of the band. ('It was not easy playing alto in that band. Next time around, I'd rather be the drummer.') Deeply interested in and committed to jazz education, Konitz encourages his students to respect their material and through his courses strives to teach solo improvisation, something he regards as being just as much a measurable discipline as ensemble playing. His own playing remains exemplary of that strain of contemporary music which emphasizes thoughtfulness rather than instinctive responses.

Selected albums: *Subconscious Lee* (Original Jazz Classics 1949-50 recordings), *Lee Konitz Meets Gerry Mulligan* (Pacific 1953), *Jazz At Storyville* (Black Lion 1954), *Konitz* (Black Lion 1954), *Quintets* (Vogue 1954), *Swingtime* (1956), *Very Cool* (Verve 1957), *Motion* (1961), *Timespan* (Wave 1977, 1954-61 recordings), *Together Again* (Moon 1966), *The Lee Konitz Duets* (Original Jazz Classics 1967), *Spirits* (1971), *Lone-Lee* (Steeplechase 1974), *Oleo* (Sonet 1975), *Jazz A Juan* (Steeplechase 1975), *Chicago 'N' All That Jazz* (LRC 1976), *The Nonet* (1976), *Windows* (Steeplechase 1977), *Pyramid* (Improvising Artists 1977), *Yes, Yes, Nonet* (Steeplechase 1979), *Live At The Berlin Jazz Days* (1980), *Live At Laren* (Soul Note 1980), *Toot Sweet* (Owl 1982), *Dovetail* (1984), *Wild As Springtime* (1984), *Stereokonitz* (RCA 1985), *Ideal Scene* (Soul Note 1986), *Medium Rare* (Label Blue 1986), *Wild As Springtime* (GFM 1987), *Blew* (Philology 1988), *Round And Round* (Limelight 1988), *Shades Of Kenton* (Hep Jazz 1988), *Songs Of The Stars* (1988), *The New York Album* (Soul Note 1988), *Spirits* (Milestone 1988), *12 Gershwin In 12 Keys* (Philology 1989), *Frank-Lee Speaking* (West Wind 1990), *In Rio* (MA Music 1990), *Once Upon A Live* (Musidisc 1991), *Zounds* (Soul Note 1991), *S'Nice* (Nabel 1991), with Peggy Stern *Lunasea* (Soul Note 1992), *From Newport To Nice* (Philology 1992, 1955-80 recordings), *So Many Stars* (Philology 1993), *A Venezia* (Philology 1994).

Kowald, Peter

b. 21 April 1944, Masserberg, Germany. Kowald, who plays bass, tuba and alphorn, is one of the key figures in the development of European improvisation. Before he became a professional musician he was a translator, and his multilingual abilities have stood him in good stead on his travels. Kowald opened up the contacts between the German free-jazzers and their British counterparts, and played with the Spontaneous Music Ensemble in London in 1967. He was responsible for bringing Peter Brötzmann and Dutch drummer Han Bennink together, and that there exists a Greek free-jazz scene at all has much to do with his endeavours. Kowald was also one of the first of his generation of players to journey to the USA and Japan. He was also instrumental in the revival of Globe Unity in 1973 and for five years co-led this free orchestra with Alexander Von Schlippenbach. Globe Unity's *Jahrmarkt/Local Fair* (1977), on which the improvisers encounter a Greek folk group and 25 Wuppertal accordion players, is a typically Utopian Kowald project.

Albums: *Peter Kowald Quintet* (1972), with Michel Pilz, Paul Lovens *Carpathes* (1976), with Barre Phillips *Die Jungen: Random Generators* (1979), with Leo Smith, Günter Sommer *Touch The Earth* (1980), with Smith, Sommer *Break The Shells* (1981), with Barry Guy *Paintings* (1982), with Maarten Altena *Two Making A Triangle* (1982), with Frank Wright, A.R. Penck *Run With The Cowboys* (1987), with Danny Davis, Takehisa Kosugi *Global Village Suite* (1988), *Open Secrets* (1988), *Duos Europa/USA/Japan* (FMP 1992, rec. 1984-90).

Kral, Roy

b. 10 October 1921, Chicago, Illinois, USA. Kral played piano and sang alone and in small groups until, in the mid-40s, he met singer Jackie Cain (b. 22 May 1928, Milwaukee, Wisconsin, USA). Together, Kral and Cain became very popular, working as Jackie And Roy. They joined Charlie Ventura's 'Bop for the People' band for which Kral also played piano and contributed arrangements. In 1949, Kral and Cain quit Ventura, were married, and continued to perform as a duo throughout the 50s. In the 60s Kral was active in the studios but they frequently performed together, recording on into the late 80s. Apart from interesting and duly deferential interpretations of the great standards, Kral and Cain are noted for their vibrant enthusiasm, the sparkling audacity of their bop styling and their use of vocalese. Kral has also performed with his sister, the singer Irene Kral.

Albums: *Jackie Cain And Roy Kral* (1954), *Spring Can Really Hang You Up The Most* (1955), *Free And Easy* (1957), *Like Sing* (1962), *Lovesick* (1966), *Time And Love* (1972), *Concerts By The Sea* (1976), *Star Sounds* (1979), *East Of Suez* (1980), *High Standards* (1982), *A Stephen Sondheim Collection* (1982), *We've Got It: The Music Of Cy Coleman* (1984), *Bogie* (1986), *One More Rose* (1987), *Full Circle* (1988). Compilation: *Jackie & Roy With Charlie Ventura And His Orchestra* (1948).

Kress, Carl

b. 20 October 1907, Newark, New Jersey, USA, d. 10 June 1965. An outstanding and highly-respected guitarist, Kress was active throughout the 20s and 30s, making numerous recordings. Often he worked in company with other guitarists, including Eddie Lang and Dick McDonough, with whom he recorded duets. In the 40s and 50s Kress retained his earlier unusual chordal style and preference for the acoustic instrument, despite changes generated by Charlie Christian and others. He continued to work into the 60s, frequently in partnership with George Barnes, and was performing with him in Reno, Nevada, when he collapsed and died in June 1965.

Albums: *Carl Kress* (1958), with George Barnes *Two Guitars* (Stash 1962), with Barnes *Guitars Anyone?* (1963), with Barnes *Town Hall Concert* (1963).

Kriegel, Volker

b. 24 December 1943, Darmstadt, Germany. Kriegel taught himself guitar at the age of 15 and started his own trio when he was 18. Both he and the trio won awards at the 1963 German Amateur Jazz Festival. While studying social science and psychology at Frankfurt University he met Emil and Albert Mangelsdorff and continued to develop his jazz interests. An offer to join the new band being set up by American expatriate vibes-player Dave Pike led him to give up his studies to become a full-time musician. He stayed with the Dave Pike Set until the leader returned to the USA, at which point Kriegel and Eberhard Weber founded Spectrum. When Weber left in 1976 Kriegel started the Mild Maniac Orchestra. In the meantime, in 1975, he had been a co-founder of the United Jazz And Rock Ensemble. In 1977 he co-founded Mood Records. As well as his musical activities, he is a distinguished cartoonist (both for journals and record sleeves), animator and broadcaster.

Albums: *Spectrum* (1971), *Missing Link* (1972), *Topical Harvest* (1975), *Octember Variations* (1976), *Elastic Menu* (1977), *Houseboat* (MPS 1978), *Long Distance* (MPS 1979), *Missing Link* (MPS 1981), *Journal* (1981), *Star Edition* (MPS 1981), *Schone Aussichten* (1983), *Palazzo Blue* (1987), with the United Jazz And Rock Ensemble: *Live In Schutzenhaus* (1977), *Teamwork* (1978), *The Break Even Point* (1980), *Live In Berlin* (1981), *United Live Opus Sechs* (1984).

Krog, Karin

b. 15 May 1937, Oslo, Norway. Although she had already worked extensively in Scandinavia with players such as Jan Garbarek and Arild Andersen, vocalist Krog's first impact on the international jazz scene came in 1964 with her appearance at the Antibes Jazz Festival. She subsequently toured Europe and the USA, frequently working with some of the more progressive musicians. In the late 60s she performed, and sometimes recorded, with Don Ellis and Clare Fischer and during the following decade she extended her reputation through sessions with Warne Marsh, Dexter Gordon, Archie Shepp, Red Mitchell and Bengt Hallberg. In the 80s and 90s she recorded and toured with John Surman, with whom she had first performed in the early 70s. An effortless singer, with a good vocal range and excellent taste in material, Krog's penchant for more modern music has tended to restrict her popularity to the hardcore jazz audience, although her repertoire does incorporate the sophisticated songs of Dave Frishberg alongside standards and jazz classics. By the mid-80s her repertoire had extended still further to encompass African click rhythms and Indian Alap music, which she performs with absolute confidence and considerable charm. She is also an experienced television producer and has made several programmes on jazz, which have been broadcast in Norway.

Albums: *By Myself* (1964), *Jazz Moments* (1966), *Eleven Around Karin* (1967), with Jan Garbarek, Arild Andersen *Joy* (1968), *Blue Eyes* (1969), with others *Gittin' To Know Y'all* (1969), *Different Days, Different Ways* (1970), with Dexter Gordon *Some Other Spring* (Storyville 1970), *My Workshop Songbook* (1970), *Karin Krog* (1973), *You Must Believe In Spring* (1974), *Jazz Jamboree '75 Vol. 2* (1975), with Archie Shepp *Hi-Fly* (Meantime 1976), *The Malmö Sessions* (1976), with Bengt Hallberg *A Song For You* (Phontastic 1977), with Red Mitchell *Three's A Crowd* (1977), with John Surman *Cloud Line Blue* (1978), *With Malice Toward None* (1980), with Warne Marsh, Mitchell *I Remember You* (Spotlite 1980), *Swingin' Arrival* (1980), with Hallberg *Two Of A Kind* (1982), with Surman *Such Winters Of Memory* (ECM 1983), *Freestyle* (Odin 1985), *Something Borrowed...Something New* (Meantime 1989), *Grog Sings Gershwin* (Meantime 1993).

Krupa, Gene

b. 15 January 1909, Chicago, Illinois, USA, d. 16 October 1973. Krupa began playing drums as a child and after his mother failed to persuade him to become a priest, most of his large family actively encouraged his career in music. He studied formally, his most important teacher being Roy C. Knapp. However, growing up in Chicago in the 20s meant that he was inevitably drawn to jazz. He listened to relocated New Orleans masters such as Baby Dodds, Zutty Singleton and Tubby Hall. In his teens he played in several local dancebands, among them those led by Al Gale, Joe Kayser, Thelma Terry and Mezz Mezzrow and the Benson Orchestra. In 1927, Krupa made his first records in a band nominally fronted by visitor Red McKenzie but actually organized by Eddie Condon whose record debut this also was. This date is reputed to be the first on which a drummer used a bass drum and tom-toms (engineers feared the resonance would cause the needle to lift off the wax). The records were successful and when, in 1929, Krupa and Condon decided to move to New York, their reputation had preceded them. Although highly regarded in the jazz world the new arrivals found the going tough. Mostly, Krupa worked in theatre pit bands, including some directed by Red Nichols, in which he played alongside Benny Goodman and Glenn Miller. In the early 30s, Krupa played in dance bands led by Russ Columbo, Mal Hallett and Buddy Rogers. Late in 1934, he joined Goodman's recently-formed big band. Krupa was the most enthusiastic of sidemen, urging the band along as if it were his own and helping to establish the distinctive sound of the Goodman band. After the band's breakthrough in August 1935 Krupa quickly became a household name. His fame and popularity with the fans built upon his highly visual playing style and film-star good looks, eventually irritated Goodman, although Krupa's frequent alteration of the tempos the leader set did not help their relationship. Soon after the band's Carnegie Hall concert in 1938 Krupa and Goodman had a public quarrel and Krupa quit. He formed his own band, which swiftly became one of the most popular of the swing era. In 1941, after he had hired Roy Eldridge and Anita O'Day, the band also became one of the best. Success was short-lived, however, and in 1943 it folded after Krupa was jailed following a drugs bust in San Francisco. By the time that he was released on bail pending an appeal against his 1-6 years sentence, he believed his career was over. He returned to New York, planning to spend his time studying and writing music, but was persuaded by Goodman to join a band with which he was touring east coast US Army bases. When Goodman prepared to extend the tour across the USA, Krupa opted to stay behind. He was convinced that audiences would react against him and instead joined Tommy Dorsey, believing that the comparative anonymity of working in a band based at a New York movie theatre would be best for him. In fact, his appearance, unannounced, at the Paramount Theatre was greeted with rapturous applause and proved to be a remarkably emotional milestone in his rehabilitation. He went on tour with Dorsey and when the charges against him were deemed to have been improper, he decided to form a new band of his own. He maintained a band throughout the rest of the 40s, adapting to bop by incorporating musicians such as Charlie Ventura, Red Rodney and Don Fagerquist and playing charts by Gerry Mulligan, even though Krupa himself was never able to adapt his own playing style which, since his arrival in New York at the end of the 20s, had been closely modelled upon that of Chick Webb. Krupa managed to keep the band working until 1951 and thereafter continued playing with a small group, usually a quartet, touring with Jazz At The Philharmonic and, for a while, operating a drum school with William 'Cozy' Cole. During the 60s he began to appear at occasional reunions of the Benny Goodman Quartet (with Teddy Wilson and Lionel Hampton). The 60s

also saw his health deteriorate, first with heart trouble and later with leukaemia. By the early 70s, he was limited to working around New York and most public performances, usually now with Goodman, Wilson and Hampton, had to be preceded by a blood transfusion. He died in October 1973.

Stylistically, Krupa was usually a heavier-handed version of Webb, the man he always acknowledged as his greatest influence and for whom he had genuine admiration and respect. There can be little doubt that Krupa was a major contributor to the powerful attack of the pre-1939 Goodman band. Apart from the 1943 stint with Goodman, when he came close to the standards set by Webb, his big band playing never had the subtlety and swing of his mentor or other contemporaries such as Jo Jones. His spectacular visual style, adored by the fans, tended to alienate critics, though another great contemporary, 'Big' Sid Catlett, was even more flamboyant. Krupa's best playing came in his performances with the Goodman trio and quartet. On these recordings, usually playing only with brushes, he performs with subtlety, skill and great verve. Krupa made the jazz drummer into a highly visible and extremely well-paid member of the band. His countless imitators usually supplied the flash and spectacle without the content, but thanks to his example and encouragement many fine swing style drummers continued to play in the decades following his death. Even in the 90s echoes of his work can still be heard.

Selected albums: with Benny Goodman *Carnegie Hall Concert* (1938 recordings), *Drum Boogie* (1952), *The Exciting Gene Krupa* (1953), *The Gene Krupa Sextet/Driving Gene* (1953), *Sing, Sing, Sing* (1953), *The Jazz Rhythms Of Gene Krupa* (1954), *Krupa And Rich* (1955), *The Big Band Sound Of Gene Krupa* (1956), *Hey, Here's Gene Krupa* (1957), *Gene Krupa Plays Gerry Mulligan* (1958), *The Essential Gene Krupa* (1958), *The Gene Krupa Story/Drum Crazy* (1959), *Percussion King* (1961), *Classics In Percussion* (1961), *Gene Krupa Meets Buddy Rich/The Burning Beat* (1962), *Perdido* (1962), with Louie Bellson *The Mighty Two* (1963), with Goodman *Together Again!* (1963), *The Great New Gene Krupa Quartet* (1964), *The Swingin' Gene Krupa Quartet* (1965), with Eddie Condon *Jazz At The New School* (1971). Compilations: *Gene Krupa, Vols. 1-14 (1935-41)* (Ajax 1979), *The Indispensable Benny Goodman Vols 1/2 (1935-36)* (1986), with Goodman *The Complete Small Combinations Vols 1/2 (1935-37)* (1986), *The Indispensable Benny Goodman Vols 3/4 (1936-37)* (1986), *The Gene Krupa Collection - 20 Golden Greats* (1987), *Gene Krupa - On The Air (1944-46)* (1988), *The Drummer* (Flapper 1993).

Further reading: *Gene Krupa: His Life & Times*, Bruce Crowther.

Kuhn, Joachim

b. 15 March 1944, Leipzig, Germany. Between the ages of five to his mid-teens, Kuhn took lessons in classical piano and composing, then became a professional jazz musician. He set up his own trio in 1962, which lasted until 1966, when he established a quartet with his brother, clarinettist Rolf Kuhn. When this band ended in 1969 he led his own group in Paris, until joining the Jean-Luc Ponty Experience in 1971. He left Ponty in

1972 to co-lead a group with Eje Thelin. Since then he has frequently worked solo, but has also been a member of the acclaimed Tony Oxley Quintet. While he has done work which might be categorized as 'new age' in the late 80s, recent concerts have shown that he can still play in tougher fashion.

Albums: *Boldmusic* (1969), *Piano* (1971), *Solos* (Futura 1971), *This Way Out* (1973), with Rolf Kuhn *Connection 74* (1973), with Rolf Kuhn *Transfiguration* (c.70s), *Open Strings* (c.70s), *Spring Fever* (Atlantic 1977), Distance (CMP 1984), *Wandlungen/Transformations* (CMP 1987), *Ambiance* (AMB 1988), *Get Up Early* (AMB 1991),.with Ray Lema *Euro African Suite* (1993).

Kuhn, Steve

b. 24 March 1938, New York, USA. Kuhn began playing the piano when he was five and was studying with Serge Chaloff's mother when he was 12. He first played professionally at the age of 13. He graduated from Harvard in 1959 and worked with Kenny Dorham before spending two months with John Coltrane. He joined Stan Getz in 1961 and stayed right through the bossa nova craze. After two years with trumpeter Art Farmer, he settled in Stockholm, Sweden in 1966, working with his own trio throughout Europe. Since his return to New York in 1971, he has worked extensively in the world of commercial music. He has also performed with his own quartet which includes Sheila Jordan and has become an ECM Records solo artist. Kuhn is an accomplished musician whose playing and compositions have developed from standard post-bop to include increasingly dissonant harmony and unusual time signatures and phrase lengths. Kuhn's favourites range from Fats Waller to Bill Evans.

Albums: *Stan Getz/Bob Brookmeyer* (1961), *Ecstasy* (1974), *Trance* (1974), *Mobility* (1977), *Non Fiction* (1978), *Last Year's Waltz* (ECM 1981), *Life's Magic* (Blackhawk 1986), *The Vanguard Date* (Owl 1986), *Mostly Ballads* (New World 1987), *Raindrops Live In My* (Muse 1988), *Porgy* (Jazz City 1988), *Oceans In The Sky* (Owl 1990), *Looking Back* (Concord 1991), *Live At The Maybank Recital Hall Vol 13* (Concord 1991), *Years Later* (Concord 1993).

Kuryokhin, Sergey

b. 16 June 1954, Murmansk, Russia. Kuryokhin started to play piano at the age of four and when his family settled in Leningrad in 1971 he attended the Leningrad Conservatory and later the Institute of Culture, but was expelled from both for failing to attend classes. After playing in rock groups at school, he was attracted to jazz by McCoy Tyner's playing on the John Coltrane records he heard broadcast on 'Voice Of America' radio programmes. Later piano influences have included Cecil Taylor, Muhal Richard Abrams and Alex Von Schlippenbach, though he has said that his chief inspirations have been contemporary saxophonists such as Anthony Braxton, Evan Parker and, particularly, his compatriots Vladimir Chekasin and Anatoly Vapirov. He first came to notice playing with Vapirov in 1977 and later worked in groups with Chekasin and Boris Grebenshikov (with whom he

co-led the rock group Aquarium) as well as forming his own Crazy Music Orchestra. The tapes of his first record, the solo *The Ways Of Freedom*, were smuggled out of the USSR and released by the London-based Leo Records in 1981. The album established him as a virtuoso technician, but many critics considered there was more style than substance to his music. Later releases on Leo included sessions with Chekasin (*Exercises*), Vapirov (*Sentenced To Silence, Invocations, De Profundis*) and Grebenshchikov (*Subway Culture* and the minimalist organ/guitar duo, *Mad Nightingales In The Russian Forest*) as well as further solos (*Popular Zoological Elements, Some Combinations Of Fingers And Passion*) and concerts with Pop Mechanics, the name he has given to all his ensembles since 1984. Increasingly eclectic in style and anarchic in spirit, Pop Mechanics became a major presence in the Russian musical underground; their one UK appearance, in Liverpool in 1989, featured massed electric guitars, bagpipes, African drummers, gospel singers, the Bootle Concertina Band and the brass section of the Liverpool Philharmonic, as well as theatrical elements such as onstage karate fights, Kuryokhin eating flowers and brief appearances by assorted cows and goats! The same year he toured the USA, playing with a range of musicians from John Zorn to Henry Kaiser to Boz Scaggs and recording for the Nonesuch label. The first international celebrity to emerge from the Russian jazz scene, Kuryokhin is now as much a performance artist as a pianist and is also in demand as a composer, collaborating on recent projects with both Alfred Schnittke and the Kronos String Quartet.

Albums: *The Ways Of Freedom* (Leo 1981), with Anatoly Vapirov *Sentenced To Silence* (1983, rec. 1981), with Boris Grebenshchikov *Subway Culture* (Leo 1986), *Introduction In Pop Mechanics* (Leo 1987), *Popular Zoological Elements* (Leo 1987), *Pop Mechanics No 17 Live In Novosibirsk 1983* (Leo 1988), with Grebenshchikov *Mad Nightingales In The Russian Forest* (Leo 1989), with others *Document* (1990, eight-CD box-set), *Some Combinations Of Fingers And Passion* (Leo 1992).

Kyle, Billy

b. 14 July 1914, Philadelphia, Pennsylvania, USA, d. 23 February 1966. Kyle began playing piano semi-professionally while still at school and in the mid-30s was accompanying the popular singer Bon Bon Tunnell. Later in the decade he played with Tiny Bradshaw and Lucky Millinder and in 1938 joined John Kirby's band, where he remained until drafted for military service in 1942. After the war, Kyle rejoined Kirby for a while, then worked with Sy Oliver and also led his own small groups. Studio and theatre work occupied him for the next few years until, in 1953, he joined Louis Armstrong's All Stars. He remained with the All Stars until his death in February 1966. Although a highly-accomplished technician, Kyle preferred the accompanist's role, content to lend rhythmic support to his front-line colleagues. His delicate touch fitted superbly into the Kirby band and, although somewhat at odds with the flamboyance of the Armstrong band (he succeeded Earl 'Fatha' Hines), there were times when he appeared to be its most musicianly member.

Album: *Louis Armstrong Plays W.C. Handy* (1954). Compilations: with John Kirby *The Greatest Little Band In The Land (1939-42)* (1987), *Finishing Up A Date 1939-46* (Collectors Item 1988).

L

La Faro, Scott

b. 3 April 1936, Newark, New Jersey, USA, d. 6 July 1961. After playing clarinet and saxophones in his early teens, La Faro switched to bass when he was 17 years old. Despite this late start, it was only a couple of years before he was good enough to join the Buddy Morrow band. Alerted to contemporary developments in jazz bass playing by listening to Percy Heath and Paul Chambers on records, La Faro quit Morrow late in 1956 while the band was in Los Angeles. During the next two years he played with several prominent west coast musicians, including Chet Baker, Buddy De Franco, Sonny Rollins and Herb Geller. In 1958, La Faro recorded with Harold Land and Hampton Hawes, and the following year joined Paul Motian and Bill Evans to form the Bill Evans Trio. This group played an important role in reshaping ideas on how the bass should function in a piano/bass/drums line-up. From being merely a supportive instrument which had only briefly enjoyed front-line status, after La Faro's work with Evans the bass became a major instrumental voice in its own right with considerable harmonic freedom. In 1959, La Faro worked with Thelonious Monk and the following year recorded with Ornette Coleman. La Faro's exceptional technique was facilitated by modifications he made to his instrument to accommodate his remarkably fast fingering. La Faro's death, in a road accident, came when he was just turned 25 years of age. His influence on bass playing in jazz was akin to that of Jimmy Blanton who, with sad coincidence, also died in his early twenties.
Selected albums: with Harold Land *For Real!* (1958), with Bill Evans *Portrait In Jazz* (1959), with Ornette Coleman *Free Jazz* (1960), with Evans *Explorations* (1961), with Evans *Waltz For Debby* (1961), *Joe Gordon And Scott La Faro* (1993, reissue), with Joe Gordon *West Coast Days* (Fresh Sounds 1994).

La Roca, Pete

b. Peter Sims, 7 April 1938, New York City, New York, USA. Although classically trained, drummer La Roca's early professional work was with Latin bands (hence his adopted name). Before he was out of his teens he was playing jazz with some of the music's leading exponents, including Sonny Rollins with whom he worked for two years. In the late 50s and early 60s La Roca played with Jackie McLean, Slide Hampton and John Coltrane. Later, he worked with, among others, Art Farmer and Freddie Hubbard, but, disenchanted with the music scene of the mid-60s, he retired in 1968 to practice law. Subsequent returns to music have proved only fleeting. He was a vigorous exponent of the complex free-time school of jazz, a concept that defies all preconceptions of the drummer's role.
Albums: with Sonny Rollins *A Night At The Village Vanguard* (1958), with Rollins *St Thomas* (1959), with Art Farmer *Sing Me Softly Of The Blues* (1965), *Basra* (1965), *Bliss!/Turkish Women At The Baths* (1967).

Lacy, Steve

b. Steven Lackritz, 23 July 1934, New York City, New York, USA. Few modern jazzmen have chosen the soprano saxophone as their main instrument; Steve Lacy is probably unique in choosing it as his only one. Reputed to be the player who inspired John Coltrane to take up the soprano (after which, thousands followed!), he is ultimately responsible for the renaissance and current popularity of the straight horn. He may also be unique for a career that has taken him through virtually every genre of jazz, from dixieland to bebop, free-form and total improvisation. As a child he started piano lessons, then changed to clarinet and finally soprano saxophone. Inspired initially by Sidney Bechet, he began his career playing dixieland (two 1954 dates led by trumpeter Dick Sutton were reissued under Lacy's name as *The Complete Jaguar Sessions* in 1986). Then, in an extraordinary switch, he spent the mid-50s working with *avant garde* pioneer Cecil Taylor (*In Transition*) and by the end of the decade had also played with Gil Evans (*Pacific Standard Time*), Jimmy Giuffre and Sonny Rollins. His own 1957 debut, *Soprano Saxophone*, featured Wynton Kelly and the follow-up, *Steve Lacy Plays The Music Of Thelonious Monk*, marked the beginning of a long, and continuing association with Mal Waldron. Both albums also included several tracks by Thelonious Monk, by whose music Lacy had become increasingly beguiled. In 1960, he persuaded Monk to hire him as a sideman for 16 weeks, and between 1961 and 1965 he and Roswell Rudd co-led a group that played only Monk tunes - 'to find out why they were so beautiful'. (This fascination has remained with him - *School Days*, *Epistrophy*, *Eronel*, *Only Monk* and *More Monk* are all devoted to further exploring, in group and solo context, the great man's compositions.) In 1965, Lacy moved to Europe, where he worked with Carla Bley in the Jazz Realities project and co-led a group with Enrico Rava, with whom he also toured South America in 1966. In this period, influenced in part by earlier collaborations with Don Cherry, Lacy was playing mostly free jazz (*Sortie* and *The Forest And The Zoo*). The focus of his attention would later shift back towards jazz compositions, especially after the mid-60s when he completed his first major piece, 'The Way', a suite based on text from the ancient Chinese *Tao Te Ching*; he has maintained an occasional involvement with total improvisation, most notably on records with Derek Bailey (*Company 4*) and Evan Parker (*Chirps*). In 1966, he revisited New York and played in a quintet with Karl Berger and Paul Motian but, finding work scarce, he returned to Europe in 1967, settling in Rome with his Swiss wife, Irene Aebi, who sings and plays cello and violin on many of his albums. Three years later, he relocated to Paris, which has since been his home base. Leading his own group (usually a sextet), he has in the last two decades built up one of the most impressive and diverse recording catalogues in jazz, hitting a peak in the 80s with a series of albums - *Prospectus, Furturities, The Gleam* and *Momentum* - which show the group honing to perfection the intricate dialogues and seamless blends of invention and discipline so typical of their music. Important group members over the years have included Steve Potts (saxophone), Kent Carter and Jean-Jacques Avenal (both bass), Bobby Few (piano), Oliver Johnson (drums), guest George Lewis (trombone) and - perhaps most crucially - Aebi, for whose severe, lieder-style vocals Lacy created what is virtually a new concept of jazz songwriting. He has often set texts by modern writers - *Sons* is a collaboration with Brion Gysin, *Futurities* a series of poems by Robert Creely - but *Tips* is more unusual still, with Lacy shaping his tunes around extracts from the notebooks of painter Georges Braque. Outside of his regular group (currently one of the most adventurous in jazz), Lacy's recent projects have included duos with Potts, Ran Blake, Mal Waldron and Gil Evans; plus tributes to Monk and Herbie Nichols (*Regenerations, Change Of Season* and *The ICP Orchestra Performs Nichols - Monk*) in the company of Misha Mengelberg and Han Bennink, who also collaborated on the *Dutch Masters* recording. Lacy is also one of today's outstanding practitioners of solo saxophone music. Inspired by hearing the solo work of Anthony Braxton, he began to develop his own soprano saxophone repertoire in the early 70s and has since developed this over a succession of solo concerts and recordings, the latter including such notable examples of the genre as *Hocus Pocus, The Kiss* and *Remains*. Incredibly prolific, Lacy has released over 80 albums under his own name and probably appeared on as many again as a sideman: paradoxically, 1991's *Itinerary* was his first-ever release as leader of a big band. A brilliant composer and improviser, Lacy can be counted one of the most significant jazz figures of the era, his music sure to stand as an enduring treasure. He is, as well, simply an enchanting player. To quote Graham Lock's 1983 comment: 'There are few sounds as distinctive or as lovely as Lacy's soprano, with its comet-trails of bare bones lyricism.'

Albums: *Soprano Saxophone* aka *Soprano Today* (Original Jazz Classics 1957, reissued as *With Wynton Kelly*), *Steve Lacy Plays The Music Of Thelonious Monk* (Original Jazz Classics 1958, reissued as *Reflections*), *The Straight Horn Of Steve Lacy* (Candid 1960), with Don Cherry *Evidence* (Original Jazz Classics 1962), *Disposability* (1965), *Sortie* (1966), *The Forest And The Zoo* (1967), *Epistrophy* (1970, reissued as *Steve Lacy Plays Monk*), *Moon* (1970), *Roba* (1971), *Wordless* (1971), *Lapis* (1971), *Solo* (In Situ 1972), *The Gap* (1972), *Mal Waldron With The Steve Lacy Quarter* (1972), *Estilhaços (Chips) - Live In Lisbon* (1972), *The Crust* (1973), *Flaps* (1973), *Scraps* (1974), *Saxophone Special* (1974), *Flakes* (1974), *School Days* (Hat Art 1975, rec. 1963), *Dreams* (1975), *Lumps* (1975), *Trickles*

(Black Saint 1976), *Solo At Mandara* (1976), *Torments (Solo In Kyoto)* (1976), with Andrea Centazzo *Clangs* (1976), *Stabs* (1976), *Stalks* (1976), *The Wire* (1976), *Distant Voices* (1976), with Michael Smith *Sidelines* (Improvising Artists 1977), with Centazzo, Kent Carter *Trio Live*, (1977), *Threads* (1977), *Raps* (1977), *Straws* (1977), *Clinkers* (1977), with Derek Bailey *Company 4* (Incus 1977), *Axieme 1 & 2* (Red 1978, rec. 1975), *Follies* (1978), *Points* (1978), *Catch* (1978), *Crops/The Woe* (1979 rec. 1973/1976), *Troubles* (Black Saint 1979), *The Owl* (1979), with Maarten Altena *High, Low And Order* (Hat Art 1979), *Stamps* (1979), *Eronel* (1979), *Tao* (1980, rec. 1976), *Shots* (1980), *The Way* (1980), with Walter Zuber Armstrong *Alter Ego* (1980), with Armstrong *Call Notes* (1980), with Steve Potts, Irene Aebi *Tips* (1981 rec. 1979), *NY Capers* (1981), with Brion Gysin *Songs* (Hat Art 1981), *Ballets* (1982), *The Flame* (Soul Note 1982), with Mal Waldron *Snake Out* (1982), with Waldron *Herbe D'Oublie* (1983, rec. 1981), *Prospectus* (1983), with Roswell Rudd, Misha Mengelberg and others *Regeneration* (1983), *Blinks* (1984), *Futurities* (Hat Art 1985), with Evan Parker *Chirps* (1985), with Mengelberg and others *Change Of Season* (1985), *The Complete Jaguar Sessions* (1986, rec. 1954), *Hocus Pocus* (1986), *Morning Joy: Live At Sunset Paris* (Hat Art 1986), with Waldron *Let's Call This* (1986, rec. 1981), *The Condor* (Soul Note 1986), *Outings* (1986), *Only Monk* (Soul Note 1987), with Ulrich Gumpert *Deadline* (Sound Aspects 1987, rec. 1985), *This Kiss* (1987), *Momentum* (1987), with Waldron *Sempre Amore* (Soul Note 1987), *The Gleam* (1987), *One Fell Swoop* (1987), with Potts *Live In Budapest* (West Wind 1988), with Helen Merrill *Music Makes* (1988), with Gil Evans *Paris Blues* (1988), *The Window* (Soul Note 1988), *The Door* (Novus 1989), with Steve Argüelles *Image* (Ah Um 1989), *Morning Joy* (1989, rec. 1986), with Eric Watson *Your Tonight Is My Tomorrow* (1989), *Anthem* (Novus 1990), with Waldron *Hot House* (Novus 1991), *In Situ* (1991, rec. 1985), *Rushes: 10 Songs From Russia* (Nuerva 1990), *More Monk* (Soul Note 1991, rec. 1989), with Potts *Flim-Flam* (Hat Art 1991, rec. 1986), *Itinerary* (Hat Art 1991), with Mengelberg and others *Dutch Masters* (1992, rec. 1987), *Remains* (Hat Art 1992), *Live At Sweet Basil* (1992), *Spirit Of Mingus* (Freelance 1992), *We See* (Hat Art 1993), *Vespers* (Soul Note 1994), *Lets Call This Esteem* (Slam 1994).

Ladnier, Tommy

b. 28 May 1900, Florenceville, Louisiana, USA, d. 4 June 1939. As a child Ladnier played trumpet locally, as well as in nearby Mandeville where he was heard by George Lewis and Bunk Johnson. Later, during Johnson's renaissance, he claimed to have taught Ladnier. In 1917, Ladnier travelled to Chicago where he played in several bands, culminating, in 1924, with the band led by his idol, Joe 'King' Oliver. Early in 1925, Ladnier was hired by Sam Wooding with whom he visited Europe. During the next few years Ladnier played in Germany, Poland, France and other European countries with, among others, Wooding, Benny Peyton, Louis Douglas, Noble Sissle and also played engagements back in the USA, mainly with Fletcher Henderson. In the early 30s, Ladnier teamed up with

Sidney Bechet to co-lead a band they named the New Orleans Feetwarmers. In 1933, Ladnier and Bechet continued their partnership but on a non-musical basis, jointly running a tailors shop in New York. In the mid-30s, Ladnier led his own small groups in comparative obscurity, but in 1938 he played with Bechet on recording dates for the French jazz writer Hugues Panassie. The two musical partners also played at a Carnegie Hall concert, *Spirituals To Swing*, organized by John Hammond Jnr. Ladnier's playing style was a simple and direct exposition of the blues and as an accompanist to blues singers, like Ma Rainey, he displayed considerable empathy.

Compilations: *Ma Rainey's Complete Recordings Vol. 1* (1923-24), with others *Spirituals To Swing Concert* (1938-39), with Sidney Bechet *The Panassie Sessions* (1938-39).

Lafitte, Guy

b. 12 January 1927, St. Gaudens, France. Lafitte took up the tenor saxophone in his early 20s, having earlier played clarinet with gypsy bands in the Toulouse area. He later led his own bands in Paris and worked extensively with visiting American jazz and blues artists, including Big Bill Broonzy, Mezz Mezzrow, Bill Coleman and Buck Clayton. This was in the early 50s and by the end of the decade he had also played with Lionel Hampton and Arnett Cobb, and appeared in the film *Paris Blues* (1961), in which Louis Armstrong and Duke Ellington also featured. Although capable of powerful, earthy playing, Lafitte is at his best as a balladeer where the early influence of Coleman Hawkins gleams through his solos.

Albums: *Club Sessions No. 2* (1954), *Blue And Sentimental* (1954), *Guy Lafitte Et Son Orchestre* (1954), *Guy Lafitte, Son Saxo-ténor Et Son Orchestre* (1954), *Guy Lafitte Et Son Quartette* (1955), *Guy Lafitte Avec Frank Pourcel Et Son Orchestre* (1955), *Les Classiques Du Jazz Vol. 1* (1955), *Do Not Disturb* (1956), *Guy Lafitte Quartet i* (1956), *Guy Lafitte Et Son Grand Orchestre* (1957), *Classiques Du Jazz Vol. 2* (1957), *Guy Lafitte Et Son Grand Orchestre, Sextet Et Quartet* (1959), *Guy Lafitte Quartet ii* (1960), *10 Sax Succes* (1960), *Guy Lafitte* (1961), *Guy Lafitte Jazz Sextet* (1962), *Love In Hi-Fi* (1962), *Jambo!* (1963), *Guy Lafitte Quintet* (1964), *Blues* (1969), *Blues In Summertime* (1970), *Sugar And Spice* (1972), with Bill Coleman *Mainstream At Montreux* (1973), *Guy Lafitte Joue Charles Trenet* (1977-84), *Corps Et Ame* (1978), *Happy!* (1979), *Three Men On A Beat* (1983), with Wild Bill Davis *Lotus Blossom* (Black And Blue 1983), *The Things We Did Last Summer* (Black And Blue 1990).

Lagrene, Bireli

b. 4 September 1966. Saverne, Alsace, France. The son of Fiso Lagrene, a popular guitarist in pre-war France, Lagrene displayed a prodigious talent as a very young child. Born into a gypsy community, his origins and his fleet, inventive playing style inevitably generated comparisons with Django Reinhardt. In 1978, he won a prize at a festival at Strasbourg and subsequently made a big impact during a televised gypsy festival. In his early teenage years Lagrene toured extensively playing concerts and festivals across Europe, often accompanied by distin-

guished jazz artists such as Benny Carter, Benny Goodman, Stéphane Grappelli and Niels-Henning Ørsted Pedersen. He also made his first record *Routes To Django*, which helped to prove that early estimates of his capabilities were not excessive. An outstanding technician, Lagrene has revealed influences other than Reinhardt, happily incorporating bebop phraseology, rock rhythms and Brazilian music into his work. By the late 80s he had moved substantially from his early Reinhardt-style to fully embrace jazz-rock and other electronically-aided fusions, a shift which, while extending his popularity to a wider audience, tended to lower his standing among jazz purists. In mid-summer 1991, he was one of several leading guitarists featured at the International Guitar Festival in Seville, Spain.

Albums: *Routes To Django: Live At The Krokodil* (Jazzpoint 1980), *Bireli Swing '81* (Jazzpoint 1981), with Joseph Bowie Concert *And Space* (Sackville 1981), *15* (Antilles 1982), *Down In Town* (Antilles 1983), *Musique Tzigane/Manouch* (1984), *Erster Tango* (c.1985), *Bireli Lagrene Ensemble Live Featuring Vic Juris* (1985), *Stuttgart Aria* (Jazzpoint 1986), *Special Guests Freitag 2 Mai, Samstag 3 Mai, Mühle Hunziken* (1986), *Foreign Affairs* (c.1986), *Inferno* (Blue Note 1987), with Larry Coryell, Miroslav Vitous *Bireli Lagrene* (1988), *Acoustic Moments* (Blue Note 1990) *Standards* (Blue Note 1992).

Laine, Cleo

b. 28 October 1927, Southall, Middlesex, England. Her earliest performance was as an extra in the film, *The Thief Of Bagdad* (1940). Laine's singing career started with husband John Dankworth's big band in the early 50s working with some of the best modern jazz musicians available. She married Dankworth in 1958 and since then they have become one of the UK's best-known partnerships, although they have clearly developed additional separate careers. Throughout the 60s, Laine began extending her repertoire adding to the usual items like 'Riding High', 'I Got Rhythm' and 'Happiness Is Just A Thing Called Joe', arrangements of lyrics by literary figures like Eliot, Hardy, Auden and Shakespeare (*Word Songs*). Her varied repertoire also includes Kurt Weill and Schoenberg's 'Pierrot Lunaire'. She possesses a quite unique voice which spans a number of octaves from a smokey, husky deep whisper to a shrill but incredibly delicate high register. Her scat-singing matches the all time greats including Ella Fitzgerald and Sarah Vaughan. In 1976, she recorded 'Porgy And Bess' with Ray Charles in a non-classical version, which is in the same vein as the earlier Ella Fitzgerald and Louis Armstrong interpretation. She has recorded, with great success, duets with flautist James Galway and guitarist John Williams. Additionally, Laine is an accomplished actress having appeared in a number of films and stage productions. In addition to her incredible vocal range and technique she has done much, through her numerous television appearances, to broaden the public's acceptance of different styles of music in a jazz setting, and in doing so she has broken many barriers.

Selected albums: *Cleo Laine Live At Carnegie Hall*, (RCA 1973), *Day By Day* (1974), *A Beautiful Thing* (RCA 1974), *Born On A Friday* (1976), with Ray Charles *Porgy And Bess*

(1976), *A Lover And His Lass* (1976), *Feel The Warm* (1976), with John Williams *Best Friends* (RCA 1978), *Cleo* (1978), *Word Songs* (1978), *Return To Carnegie* (RCA 1979), *I Am A Song* (RCA 1979), with James Galway *Sometimes When We Touch* (1980), *The Incomparable Cleo Laine* (1980), *Gonna Get Through* (1980), *This Is Cleo Laine* (1981), *Smilin' Through* (1982), *Let The Music Take You* (1983), *Off The Record* (1984), *Themes* (1985), *That Old Feeling* (Music Collection 1987), *Cleo Sings Sondheim* (1987), *Shakespeare And All That Jazz* (Affinity 1988), *Woman To Woman* (RCA 1989), with Mel Tormé *Nothing Without You* (1993). Compilations: *Platinum Collection* (Cube 1981), *The Essential Collection* (1987), *Cleo's Choice* (1988), *Unforgettable Cleo Laine* (PRT 1988), *Portrait Of A Song Stylist* (Masterpiece 1989), *Blue And Sentimental* (1993).

Further reading: *Cleo*, Cleo Laine.

Lake, Oliver

b. 14 September 1942, Marianna, Arkansas, USA. Lake's family moved to St. Louis, Missouri in 1943. He played in high school, but only applied himself seriously to alto saxophone at the age of 20. Lake worked in R&B and soul bands with Lester Bowie, then formed his own group with Floyd LeFlore (trumpet) and Leonard Smith (drums). In 1968, he received a BA in music education from Lincoln University and taught music in St. Louis schools for three years. During this time he became a founder member of the Black Artists Group (BAG) and co-ordinated exchange concerts with Chicago's AACM. He studied arrangement and composition with Oliver Nelson and bassist Ron Carter. In 1972, he joined other BAG members in Paris, played with Anthony Braxton and explored electronic music. He relocated to New York in September 1973, but returned to Paris to record *Passing Thru*, a solo alto saxophone record with a sax/synthesizer dialogue called 'Whap', in May 1974. Braxton used his position at Arista Records to get Lake a record contract and wrote a sleevenote for *Heavy Spirits* (1975). The album was a masterpiece of chilled modernity, including three tracks of improvised alto against scored strings. Lake subsequently lightened his approach, to mixed results. A band with Michael Gregory Jackson (guitar) and Paul Maddox (drums, later Pheeroan akLaff) played startlingly original music (1976-8), spikey *avant garde* classical sonorities threaded with pliant saxophone. *Prophet*, recorded in 1980 for the Black Saint label, was a tribute to Lake's idol Eric Dolphy, while the next year's *Clevont Fitzhubert*, was classic free-bop. Later signed to Gramavision, Lake attempted to come on as a pop band (*Jump Up*), but despite spirited playing they never seemed to quite get the hang of the reggae rhythms they attempted to use. Lake had played in a saxophone quartet brought together by Braxton for his *New York, Fall 1974* and in 1977, with David Murray replacing Braxton, they called themselves the World Saxophone Quartet. By the mid-80s the group were firm favourites at international jazz festivals. Lake meanwhile led small groups that often included Geri Allen, akLaff and Fred Hopkins, producing shining, incisive music that seemed to bring together all the diverse threads of his career. In the late

80s he was also playing with Reggie Workman in the bassist's own Ensemble and in the collective Trio Transition, and he can also be heard in electrifying form on Marilyn Crispell's live 1991 *Circles*.

Albums: *Passing Thru* (1974), *Heavy Spirits* (1975), *NTU: Point From Which Creation Begins* (1976, rec. 1971), *Holding Together* (Back Saint 1976), *Life Dance Of Is* (1978), *Shine* (1978), *Prophet* (Black Saint 1981), *Clevont Fitzhubert* (Black Saint 1981), *Jump Up* (Gramavision 1982), *Plug It* (Gramavision 1983), *Expandable Language* (1985), *Gallery* (Gramavision 1986), *Impala* (1987), *Otherside* (Gramavision 1988), *Trio Transition With Oliver Lake* (1989), *Again And Again* (Gramavision 1991), *Zaki* (Hat Art 1992), *Prophet* (1993, rec. 1980), with Donai Leonellis Fox *Boston Duets* (Music And Arts 1992), *Virtual Reality (Total Escapism)* (1993). Compilation: *Compilation* (1990, rec. 1982-88).

Lambert, Hendricks And Ross

In the late 50s a group of singers began informal 'vocalese' jam sessions at the New York apartment of Dave Lambert (b. 19 June 1917, Boston, Massachusetts, USA, d. 3 October 1966). At these sessions singers would improvise vocal lines in much the same manner as jazz instrumentalists. Ten years previously, Lambert had worked as arranger and singer in Gene Krupa's band, recording 'What's This?', an early example of a bop vocal. In 1955, Lambert teamed up with Jon Hendricks to record a vocalized version of 'Four Brothers'. In 1958, Lambert and Hendricks added to their duo the highly distinctive singer Annie Ross to record the album, *Sing A Song Of Basie*. The concept of the Lambert, Hendricks And Ross recordings was simple although highly complex in execution. The singers performed wordless vocal lines, matching the brass and reed section parts of the Count Basie band's popular recordings. With this formula they enjoyed great success in the late 50s and early 60s. In 1962, Ross left the trio and was replaced by Yolande Bavan (b. 1 June 1940, Colombo, Ceylon). Two years later Lambert also left and soon thereafter the trio concept was abandoned. Subsequently, Lambert worked briefly as a studio arranger before his death in 1966.

Albums: *Sing A Song Of Basie* (Impulse 1957), *The Swingers* (Affinity 1959), *The Hottest Group In Jazz/Everybody's Boppin'/The Best Of Lambert, Hendricks And Ross* (CBS 1959), *Lambert, Hendricks And Ross Sing Ellington* (1960), *High Flying* (1960), *Lambert, Hendricks And Bavan: Having A Ball At The Village Gate* (RCA 1963).

Lamond, Don

b. 18 August 1920, Oklahoma City, Oklahoma, USA. Lamond's early drumming career was spent in and around Washington, DC, where he was raised, and later in Baltimore, Maryland. In the early 40s he played in Sonny Dunham's dance band and in the forward-looking big band of Boyd Raeburn. In 1945, he joined Woody Herman's First Herd where he had the unenviable task of replacing the excellent if unstable Dave Tough. Lamond stood up well to the test and became an important member of Herman's band, playing in the Second

Herd in the late 40s. Lamond also made records with several small bebop groups of the period, including those led by Charlie Parker and by fellow Herdsman Serge Chaloff. Lamond's abilities are such that he proved a welcome addition to bands covering a wide range of jazz, from bebop to dixieland by way of big and small mainstream groups. Always swinging, he played with Benny Goodman, Zoot Sims, Sonny Stitt, Quincy Jones, Johnny Guarnieri and the Sauter-Finegan Orchestra. In the 60s, Lamond toured extensively, visiting Europe and the following decade began leading an occasional big band formed from eager young musicians in Florida where he had become resident.

Albums: with Quincy Jones *Birth Of A Band!* (1959), with Woody Herman *Road Band (1948)* (1981), as Don Lamond And His Big Band *Extraordinary* (Progressive 1983). Compilations: *The Best Of Woody Herman And His Orchestra (1945-47)* (1988), with Sonny Dunham *Half Past Jumping Time (1945)* (1989).

Land, Harold

b. 18 December 1928, Houston, Texas, USA. Resident in California from early childhood, tenor saxophonist Land practised extensively with Eric Dolphy, holding informal, all-day sessions at Dolphy's home. Arising from the local fame these sessions engendered, Land was hired as replacement for Teddy Edwards in the Max Roach-Clifford Brown Sextet. This was in 1954, and by the time he left the band in November of the following year, Land's name and reputation were thoroughly established. In 1956, he became a member of Curtis Counce's influential group, made numerous important record dates with many leading west coast musicians, led his own groups and also co-led a fine band with Red Mitchell. An exceptionally gifted player, Land developed his own distinctive style early in his career although he later acknowledged John Coltrane by incorporating some of the latter's stylistic patterns into his own highly original work.

Albums: *The Harold Land All Stars* (1949), *Clifford Brown And Max Roach* (1954), *The Curtis Counce Group/Landslide* (1956), *You Get More Bounce With Curtis Counce* (1957), with Curtis Counce *Carl's Blues* (1958), *Harold In The Land Of Jazz* (Original Jazz Classics 1958), *Grooveyard* (Contemporary 1958), *The Fox* (Contemporary 1959), *West Coast Blues!* (1960), *Eastward Ho! Harold Land In New York* (Original Jazz Classics 1960), *Take Aim* (1960), with Red Mitchell *Hear Ye!* (1961), *The Harold Land Quintet* (1963), *The Harold Land-Carmell Jones Quintet* (1963), *The Pace-maker* (1968), *Choma* (c.1971), *Damisi* (1974), with Blue Mitchell *Mapanzi* (Concord 1977), *Live At Junk* (1980), *Xocia's Dance (Sue-sha)* (Muse 1981).

Lang, Eddie

b. Salvatore Massaro, 25 October 1902, Philadelphia, Pennsylvania, USA, d. 26 March 1933. The first truly significant guitarist in jazz, Lang began his career playing violin but was familiar with what was to become his main instrument through his father's work as a guitar maker. As a youth, Lang became acquainted with Joe Venuti, forming a musical partnership of exceptional quality. After working in bands in his home town and Atlantic City he joined the Mound City Blue Blowers, visiting London with the band in 1924. Later, Lang played in a band led by Venuti and then the pair joined Roger Wolfe Kahn, Adrian Rollini, led their own band, then were hired by Paul Whiteman. During their stint with Whiteman, Lang recorded with Bing Crosby and appeared in the films, *King Of Jazz* (1930) and *The Big Broadcast* (1932). After leaving Whiteman, Lang accompanied Crosby, who had a clause in his recording contract stipulating that the guitarist should always be present on his record dates. During this time, Lang continued to record with Venuti. Lang's playing was notable for his single-string solos and his deft accompaniments. Until his emergence the guitar had been thought of as little more than a rhythm instrument, but his work opened the way for it as an effective solo voice. During his brief career he made numerous records including superb duets with Lonnie Johnson and sessions with Crosby and Joe 'King' Oliver, but is best-remembered for those with Venuti which remain classics of their kind. Lang died in March 1933 while undergoing a tonsillectomy.

Compilations: with Venuti *The Golden Days Of Jazz: Stringing The Blues* (1976), *Joe Venuti And Eddie Lang (1926-28)* (1983), *Jazz Guitar Virtuoso* (Yazoo 1988), with Lonnie Johnson, King Oliver *A Handful Of Riffs (1927-29)* (Living Era 1989), *Jazz Guitar Rarities* (Recording Arts 1993).

Lanphere, Don

b. 26 June 1928, Wenatchee, Washington, USA. Lanphere first played tenor saxophone professionally at 13, having already played in public as a guest with visiting bands. At the age of 17 he guested with the Jimmie Lunceford Orchestra when they played a gig in his home town. After studying music at Northwestern University, Illinois, Lanphere recorded in New York under his own name with, among others, Fats Navarro and Max Roach. In 1949, he joined Woody Herman and the following year was with Artie Shaw. In 1951, he was in Sonny Dunham's band which was touring with Bob Hope. It was then that addiction to narcotics interrupted his career but he straightened out and made brief appearances in bands led by Herman, Charlie Barnet, Billy May, Herb Pomeroy and others during the period 1958-61. Further personal problems, with alcohol and drugs, then arose and little was heard of him until the early 80s. Thoroughly straight this time, actively supported by his wife, Midge, and encouraged by UK record producer Alastair Robertson, Lanphere subsequently toured extensively and made many fine records. Originally a Coleman Hawkins disciple, Lanphere later absorbed the work of Lester Young and Charlie Parker, but was able to retain his own strikingly individual approach to jazz. In addition to tenor, Lanphere also plays alto and, since his return, has proved to be an especially adept and interesting player on soprano saxophone and, in turn, exhilaratingly inventive on fast numbers and lyrical on ballads.

Albums: *Don Lanphere Quartet With Fats Navarro* (1949),

Woody Herman's Big New Herd (1959), *Out Of Nowhere* (Hep Jazz 1982), *Into Somewhere* (Hep Jazz 1983), *Stop* (Hep Jazz 1983), *Don Loves Midge* (Hep Jazz 1984), *Go Again* (Hep Jazz 1988), with Larry Coryell *Lanphere/Coryell* (Hep Jazz 1990), *Jazz Worship: A Closer Walk* (1993).

Lateef, Yusef

b. William Evans, 9 October 1920, Chattanooga, Tennessee, USA. Raised in Detroit, Michigan, Lateef began playing tenor saxophone in his late teens. In New York in the mid-40s he played in bands led by Lucky Millinder, Roy Eldridge and other leading jazz musicians of the swing era, but later in the decade, in Chicago, he played with Dizzy Gillespie. Thereafter, his work was consciously modern in style. In the mid-50s he adopted the Muslim faith and took the name by which he is now known. He led several small bands during this period and also began to play flute. At the end of the decade he was again in New York, this time working with leading modernists amongst whom were Charles Mingus and Cannonball Adderley. He also led his own groups for public performance and record dates. In the 70s and 80s Lateef extended the number of instruments upon which he performed, now including the oboe and bassoon and also a wide range of similar Asian and African reeds. He revealed himself as a gifted performer on all these instruments and later recordings showed an increasing interest in various ethnic musical forms, sometimes - not always - fused with jazz. In addition to his performing career in music he has also taught music and has become proficient as writer and painter.

Selected albums: *Jazz And The Sounds Of Nature* (1957), *Jazz Moods* (Savoy 1957), *Prayer To The East* (1957 recordings). *Yusef Lateef At Cranbrook* (1958), *The Dreamer* (1959), *Contemplation* (1960), *Cry! Tender* (Original Jazz Classics 1960), *The Centaur And The Phoenix* (Original Jazz Classics 1961), *Into Something* (1961), *Eastern Sounds* (Original Jazz Classics 1961), *Live At Pep's Music Lounge* (Impulse 1965), *The Golden Flute* (1966), *The Blue Yusef Lateef* (Atlantic 1968), *The Gentle Giant* (Atlantic 1974), *The Doctor Is In...And Out* (1976), *Sax Masters* (Vogue 1976), *In A Temple Garden* (1979), *In Nigeria* (1985), *Yusuf Lateef's Little Symphony* (Atlantic 1988), *Concerto For Yusef Lateef* (Atlantic 1988), *Nocturnes* (Atlantic 1990), *Yusek Lateef's Encounters* (Atlantic 1991), *Heart Vision* (YAL 1992), *Tenors i* (YAL 1992), *Plays Ballads* (YAL 1993), *Tenors ii* (YAL 1994). Compilations: *The Live Session* (1978, rec. 1964).

Further reading: *The Pleasures of Jazz: Leading Performers On Their Lives, Their Music, Their Contemporaries*, Leonard Feather.

Laurence, Chris

b. 6 January 1949, London, England. Laurence was born into a musical family and studied at the Royal Junior College of Music and the Guildhall School of Music. He started playing the bass professionally at the end of the 60s as one of a remarkable wave of new British jazz musicians. He worked with the bands of Mike Westbrook, Mike Pyne, John Surman, John

Taylor and Kenny Wheeler. The breadth of his musicianship has made him one of the most dependable bass players in any rhythm section. During the 80s he played in the Orchestra of the Academy of St. Martins in the Fields and the London Bach Orchestra as well as in trios with Tony Oxley, Alan Skidmore and Tony Coe as well as continuing to appear in the various bands of John Surman.

Albums: with Frank Ricotti *Our Point Of View* (1969), with the London Jazz Composers Orchestra *Ode* (1972), with John Surman *Morning Glory* (1973), with Tony Coe, Tony Oxley *Nutty On Willisau* (1983), *Aspects Of Paragonne* (1985).

Laurie, Cy

b. 20 April 1926, London, England. A leading figure in the post-war traditional jazz boom in the UK, clarinettist Laurie led his own band in the late 40s and early 50s. He also played with the band led by Mike Daniels. Dividing his time between playing and running a popular London jazz club, Laurie became a seemingly immovable fixture on the scene but in 1960 dropped out of music. In the early 70s he was back and by the end of the decade had re-established his following. In the 80s he was a very popular figure on the UK traditional jazz scene, recording and playing concerts with fellow-veterans Ken Colyer and Max Collie. Although rooted in the playing of Johnny Dodds, Laurie's performances display an acute ear for changing musical fashions and there are often hints that his range could be much wider than either he or his fans have ever allowed.

Albums: *Cy Laurie Blows Blue-Hot* (c.1956), *Cy Laurie And Les Jowett* (1957), *Shades Of Cy* (Suntan 1984), with Max Collie, Ken Colyer *New Orleans Mardi Gras* (1985), *That Rhythm Man* (1989), *Delving Back With Cy* (Esquire 1986).

Laws, Ronnie

b. 3 October 1950, Houston, Texas, USA. Laws played the saxophone from the age of 12, growing up with the musicians who were to become the Crusaders - the band with which his brother Hubert played. Ronnie studied flute at the Stephen F. Austin State University and then at Texas Southern University. When he was 21 he moved to Los Angeles, where he worked with Von Ryans Express, Quincy Jones, pianist Walter Bishop and Kenny Burrell. After playing with Earth, Wind And Fire for 18 months, during the period when they recorded *Last Days In Time* (1972), he worked with Hugh Masekela and Ujima. His solo career in the late 70s and early 80s saw him achieve a popularity with a smooth jazz style similar to that of Bob James, Earl Klugh, Lonnie Liston Smith and Grover Washington.

Albums: with Hubert Laws *In The Beginning* (1974), with Pressure *Pressure Sensitive* (EMI 1975), *Fever* (Blue Note 1976), *Friends And Strangers* (EMI 1977), *Flame* (United Artists 1978), *Every Generation* (United Artists 1980), *Solid Ground* (Liberty 1981), *Mr. Nice Guy* (Capitol 1983), *Mirror Town* (CBS 1986), *All Day Rhythm* (CBS 1987), *Identity* (New Note 1992), *Deep Soul* (1993), *True Spirit* (Par 1993), *Brotherhood* (101 South 1993). *Fever* (Blue Note 1993), Compilations:

Ronnie Laws (1987), *Classic Masters* (1988), *The Best Of Ronnie Laws* (Blue Note 1992).

Lawson, Yank

b. John R. Lauson, 3 May 1911, Trenton, Missouri, USA. After playing the trumpet in various local bands, in 1933 Lawson joined Ben Pollack's popular band. When this group developed into the co-operative Bob Crosby band Lawson was one of its dominant musical voices. He later played in the bands of Tommy Dorsey and Benny Goodman and then spent a quarter of a century, on and off, in the studios, making occasional jazz club and record dates. Reunions with other veterans of the Crosby band eventually led to a partnership with Bob Haggart. Their co-led band eventually evolved into the World's Greatest Jazz Band and when this group folded in the late 70s Lawson and Haggart continued to perform together well into the 80s. A striking and aggressive player, Lawson dominated any of the dixieland-oriented jazz bands with which he played and drew admiration from such leading jazz artists as Louis Armstrong, with whom he appeared on record.
Selected albums: *Lawson-Haggart Jazz Band* (1952), with Haggart *South Of The Mason-Dixon Line* (1953), with Louis Armstrong *Satchmo: A Musical Autobiography* (1957), with Crosby *Porgy And Bess* (1958), *The Best Of Broadway* (1959), *Ole Dixie* (1966), with Haggart *The Best Of Dixieland (1952-53)* (1975), *Live At Louisiana Jazz Club* (1979), *Century Plaza* (World Jazz 1979), with Haggart *Best Of Jazz At The Troc* (World Jazz 1981), *Plays Mostly Blues* (Audiophile 1987), *Something Old, Something New, Something Borrowed, Something Blue* (1988), *Easy To Remember* (Flyright 1989), with Bob Haggart *Yank Lawson And Bob Haggart* (Jazzology 1992).

Le Sage, Bill

b. 20 January 1927, London, England. From the mid-40s Le Sage was a popular figure on the London jazz scene, leading his own group and also playing in the John Dankworth Seven. At this point in his career Le Sage played piano, on which he was self-taught. In the early 50s he began playing vibraphone, the instrument he later became associated with. During the 50s and 60s he played with bands led by Tony Kinsey, Ronnie Ross and also led his own groups. In 1970, he formed his Bebop Preservation Society band which remained in existence until midway through the following decade. During this period he also worked with many of the UK's leading contemporary jazz artists including Barbara Thompson and Martin Drew. Alongside his playing career, Le Sage has also written music for a number of television shows.
Albums: *The Bill Le Sage-Ronnie Ross Quartet* (1963), *Directions In Jazz* (1964), *Road To Ellingtonia* (1965), *Martin Drew And His Band* (1977), with John Dankworth *Gone Hitchin'* (1983).

Léandre, Joëlle

b. 12 September 1951, Aix-en-Provence, France. One of Europe's most gifted and versatile young bassists, Léandre is equally at home performing scores by *avant garde* composers

such as Giacinto Scelsi or playing total improvisation with the likes of Maggie Nicols and Irène Schweizer. She studied both double bass and piano as a child; later graduated from the Conservatoire National Superieur de Musique de Paris; played with Pierre Boulez's Ensemble Intercontemporain and studied in the USA with John Cage. Her 1981 debut, *Contrebassiste*, featured mostly her own composed music, but also included vocals, overdubbing and pre-recorded tapes (of taxi-drivers refusing to take her bass in their cabs!) - intimations of the invention and droll humour that have become hallmarks of her improvisations (along with her *bravura* technique). The recording of *Live At The Bastille* in 1982, with Nicols and Lindsay Cooper, was completely improvised and this has been the dominant mode on most of her subsequent recordings (the exceptions being *Contrebasse Et Voix*, which includes pieces by Scelsi and Cage and the recent *All Scelsi*). *Sincerely* was another solo, while other releases feature duos and trios with leading European improvizers, such as Schweizer, Derek Bailey, Barre Phillips, Peter Kowald, the Portuguese violinist Carlos Zingaro, plus US trombonist George Lewis and violinist Jon Rose; the latter of whom she recorded a duo album of 'domestic' noises, including pieces for television set, fridge, bathroom, creaking door and pet dog! In 1983, Léandre joined Schweizer's European Women's Improvising Group and played with her at the 1986 Canaille Festival of Women's Improvised Music in Zurich, as well as appearing on the pianist's *Live At Taktlos* and *The Storming Of The Winter Palace*, and recording the duo *Cordial Gratin* with her. In 1988, Léandre played at Canada's Victoriaville Festival, recording with Anthony Braxton on his *Ensemble (Victoriaville) 1988*: a duo project with Braxton released in late 1992 as is an album by her current Canvas Trio with Zingaro and reedman/accordionist Rüdiger Carl.
Albums: *Contrabassiste* (1983, rec. 1981), with Maggie Nicols, Lindsay Cooper *Live At The Bastille* (1984, rec. 1982), *Les Douze Sons* (Nato 1984), *Sincerely* (1985), with Irène Schweizer *Cordial Gratin* (1987), *Paris Quartet* (1989, rec. 1985), *Contrebasse Et Voix* (1989, rec. 1987), *Urban Bass* (Adda 1990), with Jon Rose *Les Domestiques* (1990, rec. 1987), with Carlos Zingaro *Ecritures* (Adda 1990), with others *Unlike* (1990), with Eric Watson *Palimpeste* (Hat Art 1992), *Canvas Trio* (1992), *All Scelsi* (1992), *L'Histoire De Mme Tasco* (Hat Art 1993), *Blue Goo Park* (FMP 1993), with Giacinto Scelsi *Okanagon* (1993).

Lee, Jeanne

b. 29 January 1939, New York City, New York, USA. Lee studied modern dance at Bard College (1956-60), where she met Ran Blake. They began to work as a duo, with Lee improvising on vocals, recording together in 1961 (*The Newest Sound Around*) and toured Europe in 1963. In 1964, she moved to California and married the sound-poet David Hazelton. Returning to Europe in 1967, she began a long association with Gunter Hampel, recording with him on his Birth label on numerous occasions over the next two decades (*The 9th July 1969*, *Spirits* in 1971, *Journey To The Song Within* in 1974, *Fresh Heat* in 1985), including one entirely improvised session with him and Anthony Braxton in 1972. Although a striking singer in conventional terms, with a strong, husky voice, Lee developed a new, inventive approach to vocals, often improvising wordlessly and using lip, throat and mouth sounds rather than standard pitches. In the 60s and 70s she was a prominent member of the jazz *avant garde*, working with fellow pioneers Archie Shepp (*Blasé*), Marion Brown (*Afternoon Of A Georgia Faun*), Braxton again (*Town Hall 1972*) and Enrico Rava, as well as recording her own *Conspiracy* and, later, in a trio with Andrew Cyrille and Jimmy Lyons. In the 80s and 90s she has worked with the group Vocal Summit (with Bobby McFerrin, Lauren Newton, Urszula Dudziak and Jay Clayton) and with the Reggie Workman Ensemble (*Images*), but has concentrated more on writing her own material. Her works include a five-part suite, *Emergence*, and a ten-act oratorio, *A Prayer For Our Time*. In 1990, she again recorded a duo album with Blake, with whom she has been teaching in the Third Stream department of the New England Conservatory of Music since 1976. Albums: with Ran Blake *The Newest Sound Around* (1961), *The Gunter Hampel Group Und Jeanne Lee* (1969), with Hampel, Anthony Braxton *Familie* (1972), *Conspiracy* (1974), with Andrew Cyrille, Jimmy Lyons *Nuba* (1979), with Vocal Summit *Sorrow Is Not Forever - Love Is* (1983), with Blake *You Stepped Out Of A Cloud* (1990), *Natural Affinities* (Owl 1992).

Leeman, Cliff

b. 10 September 1913, Portland, Maine, USA, d. 26 April 1986. After playing in the percussion section of a local symphony orchestra, Leeman turned to danceband and jazz drumming as a career. In 1936, he joined Artie Shaw, playing an important role in the band's swing era success story. After leaving Shaw, he played in several leading big bands, including those led by Tommy Dorsey, Charlie Barnet and Woody Herman. In the late 40s, as the big bands became fewer, Leeman played in many small groups along New York's 52nd Street, returning briefly to big band work whenever opportunities were offered. In the 50s he worked in the studios but continued to play in jazz groups, usually those with a traditional bent. During this and the following decade he worked with Big Joe Turner, (appearing on the singer's classic *Boss Of The Blues*), Eddie Condon, Ralph Sutton (with whom he recorded a duo album, *I Got Rhythm*), Wild Bill Davison, Yank Lawson and Bob Haggart. In the 70s he toured extensively, including a trip to Japan with Condon and an all-star band that featured Buck Clayton, Pee Wee Russell and Jimmy Rushing. Leeman also recorded with Bobby Hackett, Bud Freeman, Don Ewell, Joe Venuti, Zoot Sims and Lawson and Haggart's group, the World's Greatest Jazz Band. A powerful yet self-effacing big band drummer and a subtly encouraging small group player, Leeman's work was always exemplary. In the dixieland bands, with which he spent many of his later years, he played with zesty enthusiasm. In all of these settings his playing maintained a standard which should have eclipsed many of his better-known contemporaries. Sadly, he was the one who was often overshadowed and he remains one of the unsung heroes of jazz drumming.

Selected albums: *I Got Rhythm* (1953), with Joe Turner *The Boss Of The Blues* (1956), *Eddie Condon In Japan* (1964), with Bobby Hackett *String Of Pearls* (1970), with Hackett *Live At The Roosevelt Grill Vols. 1-4* (1970), with Joe Venuti, Zoot Sims *Joe And Zoot* (1974), with Bud Freeman *The Joy Of Sax* (1974). Compilation: *The Indispensable Artie Shaw Vols. 1/2 (1938-39)* (1986).

Lemer, Pepi

b. 25 May 1944, Ilfracombe, Devon, England. Lemer was born into a musical family and had classical singing lessons from the age of five. She went on to stage school and has worked in cabaret and the theatre both in the UK and abroad. Lemer was able to cover all sorts of singing styles from the most abstract improvisation to popular song and has done session work with Alan Price and Mike Oldfield. In the 60s and early 70s she worked with John Stevens' Spontaneous Music Ensemble, Pete Lemer's E, Keith Tippett's Centipede, Mike Gibbs and Barbara Thompson's Paraphernalia. Then with Jeff Clyne she led the band Turning Point, which undertook an Arts Council UK tour in 1971 with guests Allan Holdsworth and Neil Ardley, who later wrote 'The Harmony Of The Spheres' for a 9-piece ensemble with her voice and that of Norma Winstone. Albums: *Will Power* (1974), with Turning Point *Creatures Of The Night* (1977), with Neil Ardley *The Harmony Of The Spheres* (1978), *Silent Promise* (1979).

Lemon, Brian

b. 11 February 1937, Nottingham, England. After playing piano in and around his home town, Lemon moved to London in the mid-50s where he joined the Freddy Randall band. During the late 50s and early 60s he played with several bands ranging from those of a traditional bent through to the mainstream and into post-bop. Amongst the leaders with whom he has worked are Betty Smith, Al Fairweather, Sandy Brown, Dave Shepherd, Danny Moss, George Chisholm and Alex Welsh. A regular member of the house band at leading London venues such as the Pizza Express and Ronnie Scott's, he has also backed visiting Americans jazz musicians, including Benny Goodman, Ben Webster, Milt Jackson and Buddy Tate. Always displaying considerable flair and switching styles with rare ease, by the 70s Lemon had become a familiar and popular figure on the UK jazz scene, a role he maintained throughout the 80s and into the early 90s. He is also in demand as a session musician on radio, performing and writing music within and beyond the framework of jazz.
Albums: *Our Kind Of Music* (Hep Jazz 1970), *Piano Summit* (1975).

Leonard, Harlan

b. 2 July 1905, Kansas City, Missouri, USA, d. 1983. After working in various bands in and around Kansas City, including that led by George E. Lee, in 1923, saxophonist Leonard joined Bennie Moten for a lengthy stay. In 1931, he co-led a band with Thamon Hayes that they named the Kansas City Skyrockets, which, by 1934, had relocated to Chicago, becom-

Brian Lemon

ing Harlan Leonard And His Rockets. In 1937, the band folded, but Leonard reformed it in 1938, this time keeping the
band together until the mid-40s. Despite some important
engagements at such venues as the Savoy Ballroom in Harlem
and the Hollywood Club in Los Angeles, the Rockets remained
relatively little known among jazz fans. Thanks to the handful
of records they made it is possible to see that the band had
many important qualities. Notably, it was an early testing
ground for arranger Tadd Dameron whose arrangements for 'A
La Bridges' and 'Dameron Stomp', recorded in 1940, were
ahead of their time. There were also some sidemen of merit; in
addition to drummer Jesse Price, tenor saxophonists Jimmy
Keith and Henry Bridges stood out, both composing and soloing on 'A La Bridges'. This same track also features the band's
outstanding soloist, trombonist Fred Beckett, who later joined
Lionel Hampton. In the mid-40s Leonard left music to work
for the US Internal Revenue Service.
Compilation: *Harlan Leonard Vols 1/2* (1939-40 recordings),
Harlan Leonard And His Rockets 1940 (Original Jazz Classics
1992)

Levey, Stan

b. 5 April 1925, Philadelphia, Pennsylvania, USA. After working as a professional heavyweight boxer and part-time drummer in his home town, Levey moved to New York while still in
his teens. Abandoning boxing and concentrating on drumming, he was soon in great demand. He had already gigged

with Dizzy Gillespie in Philadelphia and worked with him
again, also playing in bebop bands such as those led by Oscar
Pettiford, Charlie Parker, Coleman Hawkins and George
Shearing. In 1945, he was a member of the remarkable band
co-led by Gillespie and Parker, of which the other members
were Al Haig and Ray Brown (and sometimes Milt Jackson and
Eli 'Lucky' Thompson), which took the bebop message around
the USA. Perhaps the most notable point on the tour was Billy
Berg's nightclub in Los Angeles, an engagement which proved
to be the catalyst for the creation of the west coast school of
bebop. In the late 40s Levey played in a number of big bands
including those of Georgie Auld and Woody Herman and in
1952 joined Stan Kenton. After leaving Kenton in 1954, Levey
became resident in Los Angeles, working with Howard
Rumsey's Lighthouse All Stars, where he replaced Max Roach,
and recording extensively, often under his own name, with
musicians such as Conte Candoli, Frank Rosolino, Lou Levy,
Richie Kamuca, Art Pepper and Dexter Gordon. In such company, Levey appeared on several of the best albums made by the
west coast beboppers. He also played in the Shorty Rogers big
band assembled for a record date in 1956. Subsequently, Levey
worked in film and television studio bands and appeared on
many recording dates, occasionally playing jazz gigs. One of
the best of the early bebop drummers, Levey's playing was
marked by his clean, precise attack which was at its most striking at fast tempos.
Albums: with Dizzy Gillespie *The Development Of An American*

Artist (1945), *Stan Levey Plays Bill Holman, Jimmy Giuffre* (1954), *This Time The Drum's On Me/Stanley The Steamer* (1955), *Grand Stan* (1956), with Shorty Rogers *Blues Express* (1956), with the Lighthouse All Stars *Double Or Nothin'* (1957), *The Stan Levey Quintet* (VSOP 1957), with Max Roach *Drummin' The Blues* (1957).

Leviev, Milcho

b. 19 December 1937, Plovdiv, Bulgaria. Leviev studied formally at the Bulgarian State Music Academy, and by the early 60s was playing piano and directing orchestras on radio and television. He was also active as a composer, experimenting with music to be played by classical and jazz ensembles. In the early 70s he was in Germany and soon moved to the USA, where he began a fruitful association with Don Ellis. In addition to playing with Ellis he also composed and arranged, finding considerable rapport with Ellis's imaginative use of complex time signatures and incorporation of ethnic concepts. Also in the 70s, Leviev played in small groups led by, amongst others, John Klemmer and Billy Cobham. In the early 80s, Leviev worked with Art Pepper, with whom he appeared at Ronnie Scott's, an occasion recorded on *Blues For The Fisherman* and *True Blues*. He also worked with Al Jarreau and led his own small band, Free Flight. Although Free Flight was a jazz-rock fusion band, Leviev continued to associate with big bands, working with Gerald Wilson and others. In the mid-80s he formed a duo with Charlie Haden and later in the decade was involved in a number of US west coast-based small groups. In addition to the valuable contribution he has made through his writing, Leviev consistently demonstrates his skills as a keyboard player, bringing his classical training to bear upon the complexities of the advanced musical style in which he frequently chooses to work.
Albums: *Jazz Focus 65* (1967), *Piano Lesson* (1977), *Music For Big Band And Symphony Orchestra* (1981), *Blues For The Fisherman* (1981, rec. 1980), *What's New?* (1980), *True Blues* (1982, rec. 1980), *Milcho Leviev Plays The Music Of Irving Berlin* (1983).

Levine, Henry 'Hot Lips'

b. 26 November 1907, London, England. Levine's family emigrated to the USA early in 1908. In 1917, Levine heard Nick La Rocca playing with the Original Dixieland Jazz Band, an event which determined his future career. He learned to play trumpet and turned professional in 1925; by extraordinary coincidence his first job was with the ODJB, by then much-changed from the line-up Levine had seen as a child. Levine played in several studio bands of the mid-20s, recording with Nat Shilkret, Vincent Lopez and others, but in 1927 was hired by British bandleader Bert Ambrose. He opened with Ambrose at the Mayfair Hotel in London in March and in June made records with the band. The following month he recorded under the leadership of Fred Elizalde. Towards the end of the year, he returned to New York where, for the next few years, he played in bands led by Cass Hagan, Rudy Vallee and other popular entertainers of the period. He then returned to studio work,

among other things leading NBC's Chamber Music Society of Lower Basin Street jazz group. After World War II Levine directed radio, television and hotel orchestras in various parts of the USA, settling in Las Vegas in 1961 where he played in numerous hotel and casino bands. He retired in 1982. A fine lead trumpeter and an effective soloist, Levine remains little known among jazz fans despite his long and active career.
Album: *Chamber Music Society Of Lower Basin Street* (1940-41 recordings).

Levitt, Rod

b. 16 September 1929, Portland, Oregon, USA. A regular trombone player in studio orchestras, Levitt first attracted attention in the jazz world through a job with Dizzy Gillespie, with whose big band he played in 1956. Apart from Gillespie, he also recorded with big bands led by Ernie Wilkins, Sy Oliver and Gil Evans. In the early 60s, he recorded with his own octet which included Bill Berry and Rolf Ericson but was most often heard on big band sessions under leaders such as Quincy Jones, Oliver Nelson and the Chuck Israels's National Jazz Ensemble. Apart from his sound playing ability, Levitt is also a gifted arranger.
Albums: *Dynamic Sound Patterns* (1963), *Insight* (1964), *Solid Ground* (1965), *42nd Street* (1966).

Levy, Hank

b. Henry J. Levy, 27 September 1927, Baltimore, Maryland, USA. After an extensive period of formal study, baritone saxophonist Levy joined Stan Kenton in 1953. By the 60s Levy was mostly writing, arranging and, in many instances, composing original material for Kenton, Don Ellis and other bands. Towards the end of the decade Levy entered musical education on a full-time basis. His work with students at Towson State University has generated considerable interest and enthusiasm, and many of his graduates found work in latter-day 'name' bands.
Albums: by Don Ellis *Live At Monterey* (1966), by Ellis *Connection* (1972), by Stan Kenton *Journey To Capricorn* (1976).

Levy, Lou

b. 5 March 1928, Chicago, Illinois, USA. Among Levy's early piano jobs were stints in the late 40s with the big bands of Georgie Auld and Woody Herman. He also accompanied Sarah Vaughan in 1947, the first of many singers with whom he worked over the years. Others included Ella Fitzgerald, Anita O'Day, Nancy Wilson and Peggy Lee, whom he accompanied sporadically for 18 years from 1955. Among the bands with which he has played are those led by Terry Gibbs, Benny Goodman and Stan Getz. He also worked with Supersax, Conte Candoli, Shelly Manne, Zoot Sims and Al Cohn. Influenced by Bud Powell but with his own forthright style and a distinctive soloist and superb accompanist, Levy remains an important if sometimes overlooked jazz pianist.
Albums: *The Lou Levy Trio* (1954), with Conte Candoli *West Coast Wailers* (1955), *Solo Scene* (1956), *Jazz In Four Colors*

(1956), *A Most Musical Fella* (1956), *Award Winner: Stan Getz* (1957), *Piano Playhouse* (1957), *Lou Levy Plays Baby Grand Jazz* (1958), with Ella Fitzgerald *Ella Swings Lightly* (1958), *The Hymn* (1963), with Candoli *Tempus Fugue-It* (1977), with Supersax *Chasin' The Bird* (1977), *Touch Of Class* (c.1978), with Anita O'Day *Mello'Day* (1979), with Getz *The Dolphin* (1982), *The Kid's Got Ears* (1982).

Lewis, George (clarinettist)

b. George Louis Francis Zeno, 13 July 1900, New Orleans, Louisiana, USA, d. 31 December 1968, New Orleans, Louisiana, USA. Lewis began playing clarinet in his early teens and between 1917 and the early 20s had worked alongside many leading New Orleans musicians including Buddy Petit and Edward 'Kid' Ory. Through the 20s and 30s, Lewis chose to play mostly in and around his home town, thus missing the attention paid to many early jazz musicians who visited Chicago, New York and other urban centres outside the south. In the early 40s Lewis benefited from the resurgence of interest in New Orleans jazz and began recording extensively, sometimes in partnership with Bunk Johnson. By the middle of the decade, however, Lewis was back in New Orleans, but the 50s found him touring all over the USA and to Europe. Although he lacked the sophisticated grace of, say, an Edmond Hall, Lewis's playing was marked by an often delightful simplicity and his fans were happy to overlook occasional musical inconsistencies in order to enjoy what they regarded as his authentic style. At his best, especially on some of the records made by William Russell in his American Music series, Lewis played with a charming distinction, which went a long way to deter criticism of his occasionally out-of-tune performances. On those records cited, and others where he was in complete control of the style in which his accompanists played, Lewis's work gives a taste of how some facets of early jazz might well have been and, as such, should be heard by anyone interested in the origins of the music. Plagued by ill-health during the 60s, Lewis continued playing almost to the end of his life.

Selected albums: *George Lewis At Herbert Otto's Party* (1949), *A Very Good Year* (1957), *The Perennial George Lewis* (1959), *George Lewis In Japan, 1 In Osaka* (1963), *George Lewis In Japan, 2 In Tokyo* (1965), *George Lewis In Japan, 3 In Kokura* (1965), *George Lewis And The Moustache Stompers* (1965). Compilations: *The Oxford Series Vol. 1* (1952), *On Parade* (1953), *George Lewis Memorial Album* (1953), *New Orleans Stompers, Vol. 1 & 2* (1974), *Pied Piper, Vols. 1-3 (1959)* (1981), *George Lewis Authentic New Orleans Ragtime Jazz Band* (1981), *Live At The Club Hangover (1953-54)* (1986), *In Japan Vols 1-3* (GHB 1986), *In New Orleans* (Ace 1993).

Further reading: *Call Him George*, Jay Alison Stuart (Dorothy Tait). *George Lewis: A Jazzman from New Orleans*, Tom Bethell.

Lewis, George (trombonist)

b. 14 July 1952, Chicago, Illinois, USA. By chance George Lewis went to school with Ray Anderson, the other leading trombonist to emerge in the late 70s. Lewis took up trombone at the age of nine and taught himself by copying Lester Young's

tenor saxophone solos from records. He studied philosophy at Yale, playing there with pianist Anthony Davis and percussionist Gerry Hemingway. In 1971, he returned to Chicago where the AACM was active: he studied with Muhal Richard Abrams and began a long association with reeds player Douglas Ewart. He developed a virtuoso technique, combining tailgate bluster with bebop agility - something he attributes to listening to saxophonists and practising from Eddie Harris's exercise books. He then studied music at Yale, graduating with a BA in 1974. In 1976, he spent two months with Count Basie. In 1976, he started working with Anthony Braxton, recording duo, quartet and orchestra pieces with him (*Elements Of Surprise, Quartet (Dortmund) 1976, Creative Orchestra Music 1976*); later he became an international figure of the *avant garde*, playing with Richard Teitelbaum of Musica Elettronica Viva and free-improvisers Derek Bailey and Dave Holland. He also played in the Gil Evans Orchestra, with pianist Randy Weston, recorded regularly with Abrams and worked with Steve Lacy (*Prospectus, Futurities* and the Herbie Nichols tribute *Change Of Season*). Lewis appeared in several of Bailey's Company line-ups and with leading European improvisers such as Joëlle Léandre and Irène Schweizer. He also recorded again with Braxton, both on the saxophonist's own *Four Compositions (Quartet)* 1983 and with him on Teitelbaum's extraordinary *Concerto Grosso*. In 1987, he recorded *News For Lulu*, a retrospective of hard bop tunes, with John Zorn and Bill Frisell, showing a stunning combination of bebop chops and free-improvising imagination. From the early 80s Lewis began to develop an interest in electronics, amazing people with improvised duets with programmed computers, and in recent years much of his time has been devoted to this project. From 1980-82 he was also the director of the New York radical theatre and music venue, The Kitchen.

Albums: with Anthony Braxton *Elements Of Surprise* (1976), *Jazz At Ohio Union* (1976), *The George Lewis Solo Trombone Record* (1977), *Shadowgraph 5* (Black Saint 1978), *Chicago Slow Dance* (1979, rec. 1977), *George Lewis - Douglas Ewart* (1979), *Homage To Charles Parker* (Black Saint 1979), with Evan Parker *From Saxophone & Trombone* (1980), with Company *Fables* (1980), with Derek Bailey, John Zorn *Yankees* (1983), with Parker *Hook, Drift & Shuffle* (1985), with various *Change Of Season* (1985), with Zorn, Bill Frisell *News For Lulu* (1987), with Zorn, Frisell *More News For Lulu* (1992), *More News From Lulu* (1992).

Lewis, John

b. 3 May 1920, LaGrange, Illinois, USA. A formally trained pianist from a very early age, Lewis first took an interest in jazz after meeting Kenny Clarke. In 1946, both men joined Dizzy Gillespie's big band with Lewis writing charts in addition to his rhythm section duties. In the late 40s and early 50s, Lewis continued his musical studies and also accompanied numerous important jazz artists including Charlie Parker, Miles Davis and Milt Jackson. His association with Jackson continued with their group taking the name, the Modern Jazz Quartet. The MJQ stayed in existence until 1974 after which Lewis turned to teaching. In the 80s the MJQ reformed and Lewis also worked with his own sextet and as musical director of the American Jazz Orchestra, a group especially dedicated to the performance of big band music and which played and recorded such important pieces as Benny Carter's 'Central City Sketches'. Although he began his jazz career in bebop, a style which is always apparent in his playing, Lewis's classical training and extensive musical studies emerge in many of his compositions, which use 18th and 19th century European musical forms. In the 80s Lewis was also musical director of the Monterey Jazz Festival, a role he gave up as his long-lived playing career continued to blossom.

Selected albums: *Modern Jazz Quartet* (1955), with MJQ *Fontessa* (1956), *2 Degrees East, 3 Degrees West* (1956), *Grand Encounter* (Blue Note 1956), *The John Lewis Piano* (1956), *Afternoon In Paris* (1956), *European Windows* (1958), *Improvised Meditations And Excursions* (1959), *Odds Against Tomorrow* (1959), *The Modern Jazz Quartet And Orchestra* (1960), with MJQ *The Golden Striker* (1960), *The Wonderful World Of Jazz* (Atlantic 1960), *Jazz Abstractions: John Lewis Presents Contemporary Music* (1960), *Original Sin* (1962), *A Milanese Story* (1962), *Essence* (1962), with Svend Asmussen *European Encounter* (1962), *John Lewis-Albert Mangelsdorff* (1962), *John Lewis-Helen Merrill* (1976), *John Lewis Solo/Duo With Hank Jones* (1976), *I Remember Bebop* (1977), *Mirjana* (1978), with Hank Jones *An Evening With Two Grand Pianos* (1979), with Jones *Piano Playhouse* (1979), *Piano, Paris 1979* (1979), *The John Lewis Album With Putte Wickman And Red Mitchell* (1981), *Kansas City Breaks* (DRG 1982), *Slavic Smile* (1982), *J.S. Bach Preludes And Fugues From The Well-Tempered Clavier, Book 1* (1984), *The Bridge Game* (Philips 1984), with the American Jazz Orchestra *Central City Sketches* (1987), *Private Concert* (Emarcy 1991). Compilation: *Dizzy Gillespie (1946-1949)* (1983).

Lewis, Meade 'Lux'

b. 4 September 1905, Chicago, Illinois, USA, d. 7 June 1964. Although he was popular in Chicago bars in the 20s, Lewis was little known elsewhere and made his living running a taxicab firm with fellow-pianist Albert Ammons. A record he made in 1927, 'Honky Tonk Train Blues', but which was not released until 1929, eventually came to the attention of John Hammond Jnr. some half-dozen years later. Encouraged by Hammond and the enormous success of 'Honky Tonk Train Blues', which he re-recorded in 1936 (and later), Lewis became one of the most popular and successful of the pianists to enjoy fleeting fame during the boogie-woogie craze. With Ammons and Pete Johnson, billed as the 'Boogie Woogie Trio', he played at Hammond's Carnegie Hall 'Spirituals to Swing' concert and at many top New York clubs. Later resident in Los Angeles, Lewis continued to record and tour and make records. From the mid-30s onwards, Lewis often played celeste and records such as those he made in the early 40s with Edmond Hall's Celeste Quartet, where the remaining members of the group were Israel Crosby and Charlie Christian, showed him to be much more versatile than his mass audience appeared to assume. Lewis died following a road accident in 1964.

Selected albums: *Yancey's Last Ride* (1954), *Cat House Piano* (1955), *Barrel House Piano* (1956), *The Meade 'Lux' Lewis Trio* (1956), *The Blues Artistry Of Meade 'Lux' Lewis* (Original Jazz Classics 1961), *Boogie Woogie House Party* (1962). Selected compilations: *Honky Tonk Piano* (Classic Jazz Masters 1988), with others *Meade Lux Lewis Vol. 1 (1927-39)* (1988), *Meade Lux Lewis Vol. 2 (1939-54)* (1989), *Tell Your Story* (1989), *Meade Lux Lewis 1927-1939* (Original Jazz Classics 1993).

Lewis, Mel

b. 10 May 1929, Buffalo, New York, USA, d. 3 February 1990. Following in the footsteps of his father, Lewis took up drumming as a child and was playing professionally by his early teens. In 1948, he joined Boyd Raeburn's modern big band, then played in a number of well-known dance bands of the late swing era, including those of Ray Anthony and Tex Beneke. In 1954, he was hired by Stan Kenton and then worked in the west coast film studios, with the big bands of Bill Holman and Woody Herman, later performing with various small jazz groups until the end of the decade. In the 60s, he played with numerous bands, including those led by Gerry Mulligan, Benny Goodman and Dizzy Gillespie. Settling in New York, Lewis established a musical partnership with Thad Jones, which in 1965 resulted in the formation of the Jazz Orchestra, a big band formed from the many fine jazz players living in the city and earning their living in non-jazz work in radio and television orchestras. The Thad Jones-Mel Lewis Jazz Orchestra, with a regular weekly gig at the Village Vanguard and a series of fine recordings, became a byword for the best in contemporary big band music. National and international tours helped spread the word and by the time the Jones-Lewis partnership was dissolved, in 1978, there were few comparable units left in existence. With Jones gone, Lewis decided to continue with the band (as someone was to remark, 'Mel and Thad got divorced, Mel got the kids') and with Bob Brookmeyer providing new arrangements to augment the magnificent library Jones had created, the band was still a big attraction. A skilled and always swinging drummer, equally at home subtly urging a small group or punching along a powerful big band, Lewis was a master of his craft and greatly respected among his peers.

Selected albums: *The Mel Lewis Septet* (1956), with Stan Kenton *Cuban Fire* (1956), *Woody Herman's New Big Band At The Monterey Jazz Festival* (1959), with Gerry Mulligan *A Concert In Jazz* (1961), with Thad Jones And The Jazz Orchestra (TJO) *Live At The Village Vanguard* (Red Baron 1967), with TJO *Central Park North* (1969), with TJO *Paris 1969 Vol. 1* (1969), with TJO *Consummation* (1970), with TJO *Suite For Pops* (1972), *Mel Lewis And Friends* (1976), *Thad Jones-Mel Lewis Quartet* (1977), *The Mel Lewis Quintet Live* (1978), *Naturally* (Telarc 1979), *The New Mel Lewis Quintet Live* (1979), *Live At The Village Vanguard* (1980), *Mel Lewis Plays Herbie Hancock: Live In Montreux* (1980), *Mellofluous* (1982), *Make Me Smile And Other New Works By Bob Brookmeyer* (1982), *Twenty Years At The Village Vanguard* (Atlantic 1985), *The Definitive Thad Jones* (1988), *Soft Lights*

And Hot Music (1988), *Got Cha* (Fresh Sounds 1988), *The Lost Art* (Limelight 1989), *Jazz At The Smithsonian Vol 3* (Parkfield 1990), *Soft Lights Hot Music* (S&R 1990).

Lewis, Vic

b. 29 July 1919, London, England. Lewis began playing a four-string banjo while still a child, later switching to guitar. In his teens he formed his own quartet, having developed an interest in jazz through listening to records. His quartet appeared on a talent show and soon obtained radio work on the BBC and Radio Luxembourg and also in London theatres. In the London jazz clubs Lewis met and played with artists such as Django Reinhardt, Stéphane Grappelli, George Shearing and George Chisholm. In 1938, he visited New York where he played with Joe Marsala, Marty Marsala, Joe Bushkin, Buddy Rich, Pee Wee Russell, Bobby Hackett and other noted jazzmen, even sitting in with Tommy Dorsey, Jack Teagarden and Louis Armstrong. He also made a handful of records during this trip with Hackett, Eddie Condon and Zutty Singleton in the band. He returned to England and with the outbreak of war served in the RAF where he played in a band whenever the opportunity presented itself. After the war, Lewis formed a new unit, teaming up with Jack Parnell to co-lead a small group. When Parnell moved on, Lewis continued to lead the band which proved very popular and broadcast frequently on the BBC. In the late 40s Lewis formed a big band, employing musicians such as Ronnie Chamberlain, Bob Efford and Gordon Langhorn, which emulated the music of Stan Kenton. He also formed an orchestra which backed visiting American artists including Armstrong and Johnny Ray. On occasion, Lewis sat in with Armstrong and Kenton, playing trombone. In the 60s, Lewis switched tracks, becoming a manager and agent, handling tours by Count Basie, whom he had met in New York in 1938, Dudley Moore (his first client), Judy Garland, Carmen McRae, Johnny Mathis, Andy Williams and Nina Simone. Lewis was also deeply involved with NEMS Enterprises, working with Brian Epstein, the Beatles and Cilla Black. Lewis's activities in these areas continued through the 70s when he organized tours for Shirley Bassey and Elton John. He retained his jazz links, however, recording a bossa nova album in 1963, half in the USA with several Kenton alumni and half in London with a band featuring Tubby Hayes and Ronnie Scott. In the early 80s he began to form occasional big bands for jazz dates. He recruited visiting American stars such as Shorty Rogers and Bud Shank to perform on a series of records. As a bandleader and promoter, Lewis has been active for many decades and has brought to the UK jazz scene a great deal of enthusiasm; his activities on the pop scene were also of much value. For all that, as his autobiography hints, he would probably have given away his entire musical career for the chance to play cricket for England, just once.
Selected albums: *Mulligan's Music And At The Royal Festival Hall* (1955), *Vic Lewis And His Bossa Nova All Stars* (1963), *Vic Lewis At The Beaulieu Jazz Festival* (c.1965), *Vic Lewis Plays The Music Of Donovan Leith* (1968), *Vic Lewis With Maynard Ferguson* (1969), *Don't Cry For Me Argentina* (1974), *Vic Lewis*

And R.P.O. (RCA 1977), *Back Again* (1984), *Vic Lewis Big Bands* (1985), *Tea Break* (1985), *Vic Lewis And The West Coast All Stars* (1989), *Know It Today, Know It Tomorrow* (1993), *Shake Down The Stars* (Candid 1993), *Play Bill Holman* (Candid 1994). Selected compilations: *My Life, My Way* (1975, 4 record set), *New York, 1938* (1986), *Vic Lewis Jam Sessions, Vol. 1-6 (1938-49)* (Harlequin 1986), *Vic Lewis Plays Stan Kenton (1948-54)* (Harlequin 1987), *The EMI Years* (EMI 1991).
Further reading: *Music And Maiden Overs: My Show Business Life*, Vic Lewis with Tony Barrow.

Lewis, Willie

b. 10 June 1905, Cleburne, Texas, USA, d. 13 January 1971. Lewis's first important job was as a clarinettist and saxophonist in the band led by Will Marion Cook, one of the leading black musicians in New York in the first quarter of the century. In the mid-20s Lewis joined another popular New York-based bandleader, Sam Wooding, with whom he toured Europe. In 1931, Lewis decided to stay in Europe and formed his own band for a residency at a Parisian nightclub. By the end of the decade, Lewis had built-up a big name for himself and his band, which featured a number of visiting American jazz musicians including Benny Carter and Bill Coleman. In 1941, Lewis was forced to fold the band and left Europe for his homeland. Back in New York, he drifted on the edges of music for a while but then worked outside the business for the rest of his life.
Compilation: *Willie Lewis In Paris* (1925-37) (1988).

Liebman, Dave

b. 4 September 1946, New York City, New York, USA. After studying theory and composition with Lennie Tristano, and saxophone and flute with Charles Lloyd, Liebman's first important job was with Elvin Jones in 1971. When he joined Miles Davis in 1974, he was simultaneously running Lookout Farm, one of many groups that have tried to fuse jazz and Indian music. Touring with Chick Corea and leading a highly successful quintet in the late 70s, featuring Terumass Hino, John Scofield, Ron McLure and Adam Nussbaum. Liebman was already one of the leading saxophonists playing improvised fusion. In the 80s he co-led Quest, and is today very active in jazz education. His recent output has been extraordinary, over a dozen albums so far this decade, including the smooth (by his standards) *Setting The Standard*.
Selected albums: *Doin' It Again* (Timeless 1980), *If They Only Knew* (Timeless 1980), *Pendulum* (Artists House 1981), *Quest* (1981), *Opal Heart* (Enja 1982), *Spirit Renewed* (Owl 1983), *The Loneliness Of The Long Distance Runner* (CMP 1985), *One Of A Kind* (Core 1985), *Double Edge* (Storyville 1985), *Homage To John Coltrane* (Owl 1987), *Quest II* (Storyville 1987), *Trio + One* (Owl 1989), *The Tree* (Soul Note 1990), *Time Line* (Owl 1990), *Chant* (CMP 1990), *Nine Again* (Red 1990), *The Blessing Of The Old Long Sound* (Neuva 1991), *Dedications* (CMP 1991), *First Visit* (West Wind 1991), *West Side Story* (Today) (Owl 1991), *Classic Ballads* (Candid 1992), *Classique* (1992), *Joy* (1993), *Setting The Standard* (Red 1993).

Lightfoot, Terry

b. 21 May 1935, Potters Bar, Middlesex, England. Lightfoot made his first appearance on the UK jazz scene as a clarinettist in the early 50s. After leading his own band throughout the 50s, he maintained a band into the next decade, having established a reputation strong enough to shrug off the decline in popularity of his brand of music. During the trad boom of the early 60s he appeared in the film *It's Trad Dad*. Apart from a brief spell in Kenny Ball's band he continued to lead into the 70s only stepping sideways into hotel management towards the end of the decade. He continued to play however, and by the mid-80s was back in full-time music. Amongst the most polished of British traditional clarinettists, Lightfoot achieved and maintained high standards of performance not only from himself but also from the many fine musicians he employed over the years.

Selected albums: *King Kong* (1961), *Personal Appearance* (1975), *Terry Lightfoot In Concert* (Black Lion 1979), *Clear Round* (Plant Life 1981), *As Time Goes By* (PRT 1986), *At The Jazzband Ball* (Bold Reprive 1988), *Stardust* (Upbeat 1990), *New Orleans Jazzmen* (Hanover 1990), *When The Saints* (See For Miles 1991).

Lightsey, Kirk

b. 15 February 1937, Detroit, Michigan, USA. A gifted modern jazz pianist, and a competent if occasional singer, Lightsey has not yet received the attention his talents deserve, despite a career that has included sessions with some of America's finest modern jazz instrumentalists, and a series of enjoyable recordings under his own name. He began working in jazz in the mid-50s, largely accompanying vocalists, first in New York and then, in the early 60s, on the west coast. He recorded with the great bebop saxophonist Sonny Stitt in 1965, and began an association with the subtle west coast singer/trumpeter Chet Baker, that resulted in five fine album recordings. During the beginning of the 80s, his career received a boost when he joined the popular saxophonist Dexter Gordon's band for four years. He has since worked with individualistic trumpeter Don Cherry, guitarist Jimmy Rainey and brilliant tenor saxophonists Clifford Jordan and James Moody, as well as touring and recording with the Leaders, a daring, Chicago-orientated group featuring trumpeter Lester Bowie and saxophonists Arthur Blythe and Chico Freeman. He has earned a reputation as a fine solo performer, visiting the UK regularly. Recommended recordings include *Isotope*, a lively trio plus percussion date from 1983, and *Everything Happens To Me*, a subtle date under Chet Baker's deft, romantic leadership.

Albums: with Chet Baker *Groovin' With The Chet Baker Quintet* (1965), with Harold Land *Mapanzi* (1977), *Lightsey* (1982), with Dexter Gordon *American Classic* (1982), with Jimmy Raney *The Master* (1983), with Baker *Everything Happens To Me* (1983), *Shorter By Two* (1983), *Isotope* (1983), with Clifford Jordan *Two Tenor Winner* (1984), *Lightsey Live* (1985), *First Affairs* (1986), *Everything Is Changed* (1986), *Kirk'n'Marcus* (1986), with James Moody *Something Special* (1986), with the Leaders *Out Here Like This* (1986/87), with

Ricky Ford *Saxotic Stomp* (1987), with Woody Shaw *Imagination* (1987), with the Leaders Trio *Heaven Dance* (1988), *From Kirk To Nat* (1990).

Lincoln, Abbey

b. Gaby Wooldridge, 6 August 1930, Chicago, Illinois, USA. Lincoln began singing publicly in the early 50s, working in Chicago nightclubs and using a variety of pseudonyms, including Anna Marie and Gaby Lee, as well as her real name. By the middle of the decade she was using the name by which she has since been largely known. She appeared successfully at the Moulin Rouge in Los Angeles and also made her first records, with Benny Carter, but was soon associating with bop musicians including Thelonious Monk, Mal Waldron and Max Roach. Her style changed during these years and following her marriage to Roach in 1962 she also became more politically aware. She wrote some of her own material, much of it stressing the rising tide of black consciousness in the USA. She collaborated with Roach on some important works, including *We Insist!, Freedom Now Suite* and *Straight Ahead.* In the 60s Lincoln had a simultaneous career as an actress, co-starring in the films *Nothing But A Man* (1964) and *For Love Of Ivy* (1968), for both of which she received excellent notices. Following a tour of Africa in the mid-70s, she adopted the name Aminata Moseka (her marriage to Roach had ended in 1970) and subsequent albums have been released, generally, under this name while reissues of early albums still use that of Abbey Lincoln. With a deeply emotional singing voice, she has always made a close connection with her audiences. Her style veers between powerful versions of ballads from her early years and the sometimes bitter polemic of her middle period. By the late 80s her repertoire was once again featuring love songs and more accessible material akin to that of her youth. Nevertheless, it is probable that her politically motivated material will prove to be her most lasting contribution to black American culture.

Albums: *Affair* (EMI 1956), *That's Him!* (Original Jazz Classics 1957), *It's Magic* (Original Jazz Classics 1958), *Abbey Is Blue* (Original Jazz Classics 1959), *Straight Ahead* (Candid 1961), *People In Me* (1973), *Golden Lady* (1980), *Talking To The Sun* (Enja 1983), *Thats Him* (Riverside 1984), *A Tribute To Billie Holiday* (Enja 1987), with Dave Liebman *People In Me* (ITM 1990), *Abbey Sings Billie Vol 2* (Enja 1992), *The World Is Falling Down* (Verve 1991), *Devil's Got Your Tongue* (Verve 1992), with Stan Getz *You Gotta Pay The Band* (Verve 1992), *Painted Lady* (1993), *When There Is Love* (Verve 1993).

Liston, Melba

b. 13 January 1926, Kansas City, Missouri, USA. Although she was born and spent her childhood in Kansas City during its hottest jazz years, Liston's entry into music began in Los Angeles where her family moved when she was 11 years old. At the age of 16, she joined the pit band, playing trombone, at the Lincoln Theatre and the following year, 1943, joined Gerald Wilson's orchestra. With Wilson's guidance and encouragement, she began arranging but remained an active performer,

Abbey Lincoln

appearing on record with an old school friend, Dexter Gordon. When the Wilson band folded while on a tour of the east coast, Liston was hired by Dizzy Gillespie. This was in 1948 and the following year she toured briefly with Wilson who was leading a band accompanying Billie Holiday. The tour was a disaster and the experience led to Liston quitting music for a while. She worked as an educational administrator in California, played occasionally in clubs, and also worked as an extra in films. In 1956, and again in 1957, she returned to Gillespie for his State Department tours of the Middle East, Asia and South America. She then began a musical association with Quincy Jones, writing scores for his band and working on the show *Free And Easy* with which they toured Europe. In the 60s, she wrote extensively for Randy Weston and occasionally for Duke Ellington, Solomon Burke and Tony Bennett. Her arrangements were used on Johnny Griffin's *White Gardenia*. In the 70s she was involved in a number of jazz educational projects, especially in Jamaica where, for almost six years, she ran the pop and jazz division of the country's School of Music. She continued to write charts for the bands of Ellington and Count Basie and singers such as Abbey Lincoln and Diana Ross. At the end of the 70s she was persuaded to return to the USA as the headline attraction at the first Kansas City Women's Jazz Festival. There, she led her own band, with an all-woman line-up, and made a great impact. Her successful return to playing led to a revitalisation of her performing career and although her band later developed into a 'mixed' group, she has continued to play an important role in furthering the role of women in jazz. A sound section player whose ballad solos are particularly effective, Liston is one of the best latter-day arrangers in jazz. Unfortunately, the male domination of so many aspects of the jazz life has resulted in this enormously talented artist remaining little-known, even within the jazz community itself.

Albums: with Dexter Gordon *The Chase* (1947), *Dizzy Gillespie At Newport* (1957), *Melba Liston And Her Orchestra* (1958), with Randy Weston *Uhuru Afrika* (1960), with Weston *Volcano Blues* (1993).

Little, Booker

b. 2 April 1938, Memphis, Tennessee, USA, d. 5 October, 1961. One of the most promising of all trumpeters in the second bebop wave of the 50s, Booker Little was equipped with a superb technique, crystal clarity of intonation and rhythmic originality. His imagination extended beyond the strict harmonic disciplines of bop however, and hinted at the vision of Ornette Coleman or Miles Davis, but an early death from uraemia consigned such promise to the realm of speculation. Little was born into a musical family, and played clarinet before taking up the trumpet at the age of 12. He was involved in Memphis jam sessions with local pianist Phineas Newborn Jnr. in his teens, but moved to Chicago in 1957 to enrol at the city's Conservatory. During this period Little worked with Johnny

Griffin's band, but his most significant engagement of the period was with Max Roach, replacing another gifted trumpeter, Clifford Brown. His recordings with Roach include *Deeds Not Words*, *We Insist!*, *Freedom Now Suite* and *Percussion Bitter Sweet*. Little's originality quickly marked him out, as did his flexibility about non-bop settings, and he collaborated with Eric Dolphy on *Far Cry* and *Live At The Five Spot* (reissued as *The Great Concert Of Eric Dolphy*) and John Coltrane on the *Africa/Brass* recording. Little's own recordings featured some outstanding players, including Roach, Dolphy (*Out Front*), Booker Ervin and the 'legendary quartet' of Scott La Faro, Roy Haynes and both Wynton Kelly and Tommy Flanagan taking turns on piano. He worked too with Donald Byrd (*The Third World*), Abbey Lincoln (*Straight Ahead*) and Frank Strozier. By the time of his death Little was balancing tonality and dissonance with an insight that suggested his influence on jazz directions in general might have been even more substantial.

Albums: *Booker Little 4 And Max Roach* (Blue Note 1959), *Booker Little* (Time 1960), *In New York* (Jazz View 1960), *The Legendary Quartet Album* (1960), *Out Front* (Candid 1961), with Booker Ervin *Sounds Of The Inner City* (1961), *Victory And Sorrow* (Affinity 1961).

Lloyd, Charles

b. 15 March 1939, Memphis, Tennessee. Lloyd was self-taught on tenor saxophone, which he played in his high school band. He gained a Masters Degree at the University of Southern California and became a music teacher at Dorsey High in Los Angeles. In October 1960, he joined the Chico Hamilton Quintet, where he played flute, alto and clarinet as well as tenor, and soon became the band's musical director. In January 1964, he joined the Cannonball Adderley Sextet, where he stayed until forming his own quartet with guitarist Gabor Szabo, bassist Ron Carter and drummer Tony Williams in July 1965. Soon Szabo was replaced by pianist Keith Jarrett and Carter and Williams returned to the Miles Davis group. At the start of 1966 Cecil McBee came in on bass (he was replaced by Ron McClure in 1967), Jack DeJohnette took the drum chair and the stage was set for a jazz phenomenon. Manager George Avakian decided to market the band in the same way he would a rock group, and the tactic paid off. In modern jazz terms the Quartet was hugely successful, playing to massive rock audiences at the Fillmore Stadium in San Francisco and becoming the first American band to appear in a Soviet festival. While the public and musicians such as Miles Davis and Ian Carr admired the band, the critics were predictably cynical, criticizing the musicians' clothes, hair styles and hippy attitudes but ignoring the basic virtues of the music itself, which included rhythmic vitality, a sound foundation in bop and the blues, and Lloyd's surging and emotionally affecting tenor sound. In due course his public looked elsewhere and, eventually, Lloyd left music to pursue his interest in philosophy and meditation, although during this period he did work and record with the Beach Boys (*Surf's Up*) as a result of his friendship with Mike

Charles Lloyd

Love. In the early 80s he edged back onto the jazz scene, notably with a Montreux Festival performance featuring Michel Petrucciani, and he began to tour again with a quartet containing Palle Danielson and Jon Christensen. During his semi-retirement his flute playing had become stronger whilst his tenor took on some of the ethereal quality his flute former-ly had.

Albums: with Chico Hamilton *Passing Thru'* (1963), *Discovery!* (1964), *Of Course Of Course* (1965), *Dream Weaver* (Atlantic 1966), *Live At Antibes* (1966), *Forest Flower* (1966), *Charles Lloyd In Europe* (1966), *Love-In* (1967), *Live In The Soviet Union* (1967), *Journey Within* (1969), *The Flowering Of The Original Charles Lloyd Quartet* (1971), *Moonman* (1971), *Warm Waters* (1971), *Geeta* (1972), *Waves* (1972), *Weavings* (1978), *Big Sur Tapestry* (1979), *Montreux '82* (1982), *A Night In Copenhagen* (Blue Note 1989), *Fish Out Of Water* (ECM 1990), *Notes From Big Sur* (ECM 1992), *The Call* (EMC 1994).

Lloyd, Jon

b. 20 October 1958, Stratford-upon-Avon, Warwickshire, England. Lloyd dabbled with piano at the age of 12, and then taught himself tenor saxophone at 23. His first public appear-ances were with a pop/soul band in the mid-80s and with an ECM-inspired duo, Confluence. His first professional job was with a duo playing standards on the restaurant/wine-bar/pub circuit. Despite his relatively late start on saxophone he has developed an individual style of music that is exhibited to espe-cially good advantage on his first, privately-produced record-ing. His influences include Jan Garbarek, John Surman, Trevor Charles Watts and, 'more for affirmation than emulation', Eric Dolphy, Evan Parker, Jimmy Lyons, Anthony Braxton and Arthur Blythe. He has also been inspired by composers Olivier Messiaen (who has influenced several non-classical figures, notably Mike Ratledge of the Soft Machine and Mike Gibbs) and Benjamin Britten. He has organized several worthy attempts at regular venues for improvised music, including the 'Sun Sessions' in Clapham, south London. Apart from his own trio and quartet he has worked with Dave Fowler and in duos with Evan Shaw Parker and Phil Wachsmann, and organizes Anacrusis, a nine-piece improvising group containing several major names.

Albums: *Pentimento* (1988), *Syzygy* (Leo 1990), with Dave Fowler *As It Was* (1990), *Head* (Leo 1993).

Lockwood, Didier

b. 11 February 1956, Calais, France. Lockwood studied classi-cal violin at the Conservatoire de Musique de Paris, but expo-sure to the blues of Johnny Winter and John Mayall persuaded him to cut short formal study in 1972 and form a jazz-rock group with his brother, Francis. A three-year stint with Magma followed, but Lockwood was more excited by the improvising of Jean-Luc Ponty, whom he heard on Frank Zappa's 'King Kong'. He listened to other jazz violinists, particularly the Pole, Zbigniew Seifert and the veteran Stéphane Grappelli. The lat-ter quickly realised the talent in Lockwood and played with

him whenever possible. During the late 70s Lockwood played and recorded with many major European and American artists including Tony Williams, Gordon Beck, John Etheridge, Daniel Humair and Michal Urbaniak. In 1981, Lockwood recorded *Fusion*, which typified the approach he has followed throughout the 80s: a solid rock-based rhythm with plenty of soloing room for Lockwood's lightning improvisations on the 160-year-old violin he continues to use, emphasizing the long tradition of French jazz violinists of which he is a part and which his love of the music of John Coltrane, and his rock influences have helped to update.

Albums: with Magma *New World* (MPS 1979), *Fusion* (1981), *New World* (1984), *1,2,3,4* (JMS 1987), *Pheonix 90* (1990), *DLG* (JMS 1993), *Martial Solal* (JMS 1993).

Longo, Pat

b. 11 September 1929, Passaic, New Jersey, USA. Adept on several reed instruments, Longo concentrated on alto saxo-phone and clarinet. During military service he played in the band of the 2nd Marine Airwing and following his discharge studied music full-time. Although intent on a career in music, throughout the 60s and into the early 70s Longo found it nec-essary to support himself by working in a bank. However, in 1974 and resident in Los Angeles, he decided the time was right to give up banking and just play music. He joined the Harry James band but had ambitions to lead his own big band. In 1979, he achieved his goal and formed a big band which quickly gained regular bookings in and around LA. In the late 70s and early 80s Longo's Super Big Band successfully blended the more traditional aspects of big band music with currently popular jazz-rock funkiness. His line-ups usually featured many of the best west coast session men and a useful handful of talented jazzmen, including Gordon Brisker, Lanny Morgan, Bob Efford, Buddy Childers, Frank Szabo and Nick Ceroli. Intent on developing other areas of exposure for the band, Longo has recently been involved in the planning of a televi-sion series.

Albums: *Crocodile Tears* (1980), *Billy May For President* (1982), *Chain Reaction* (1983).

Loose Tubes

Appearing on the London scene in 1984 this big (20-piece plus) band appealed to (and reflected) the new, smart young audience jazz was attracting at the time, and seemed likely to prove a considerable 'crossover' success. It was run as a collec-tive, although trombonist Ashley Slater acted as 'frontman' and Django Bates emerged as a main writer for the band. Characterized by clever arrangements, technically slick soloing and an urbane stage-presence, Loose Tubes was acclaimed by many critics and created interest in jazz among sections of the public which had not previously paid the genre any attention. It spawned several other successful units, which indulged in various styles (funk, African, soca, bebop and so on), including Human Chain, Pig Head Son, Lift, the Iain Ballamy Quartet, the Steve Berry Trio, the Tim Whitehead Band, Parker Bates Stubbs and the Julian Argüelles Quartet. By the early 90s the parent group had disbanded - although reunions should never be ruled out.

Albums: *Loose Tubes* (Loose Tubes 1986), *Delightful Precipice* (Loose Tubes 1986), *Open Letter* (Editions EG 1988).

Lorber, Jeff

b. 4 November 1952, Philadelphia, USA. Lorber started playing the piano when he was four and played in local R&B bands while he was still at school. While studying at the Berklee College Of Music in Boston he came under the influence of Herbie Hancock and his contemporaries. When he left Berklee he studied privately with Ran Blake. In 1979, he moved to Portland, Oregon and taught improvisation at Lewis and Clark College. In 1977, he had recorded *Jeff Lorber Fusion* and in 1979 he was able to form a band of the same name. Lorber's compositions are characterized by syncopated, chromatic melody and modal writing which facilitated a funk style. In the early 80s he started singing on record and playing the guitar and his music incorporated increasing pop elements.

Albums: *Jeff Lorber Fusion* (1977), *Soft Space* (1978), *Water Sign* (1978), *Jeff Lorber Fusion* (1979), *Wizard Island* (1979), *Galaxian* (1980), *Its A Fact* (1981), *In The Heat Of The Night* (1983), *Step By Step* (1984), *Worth Waiting For* (1993).

Lovano, Joe

b. 29 December 1952, Cleveland, Ohio, USA. Lovano grew up to the sounds of jazz, thanks to a father who played tenor saxophone professionally and also owned a large record collection. In 1971, he went to the Berklee College Of Music, where he studied with Gary Burton and first met with future collaborators Bill Frisell and John Scofield. Returning to Ohio in the mid-70s, he played tenor saxophone with Lonnie Liston Smith, making his recording debut with him on 1974's *Aphrodisiac For A Groove Merchant*, and later toured with another organist, Brother Jack McDuff. Lovano moved to New York in 1976 and, after work with Albert Dailey and Chet Baker, played with the Woody Herman band until 1979. The following year he joined the Mel Lewis big band (with which he still works on occasion) and a little later met up with Paul Motian, in whose groups he has played and recorded for the last decade, renewing his acquaintance with Frisell in the process. (Motian and Frisell also play on Lovano's own *Worlds*.) In 1987, he toured Europe with Elvin Jones and in the late 80s worked with Charlie Haden's Liberation Music Orchestra (*Dream Keeper*) and recorded a duo album with drummer Aldo Romano. Reuniting with Scofield, he played on the guitarist's highly-acclaimed Blue Note Records debut *Time On My Hands* together with the follow-up *What We Do*, and was signed by the label himself, his *Landmarks* appearing in 1991. Lovano's third album on Blue Note, *Universal Language*, comprised a line-up of Jack DeJohnette, Charlie Haden, Steve Swallow, Tim Hagans, Scott Lee, Kenny Werner and Judi Silverman. An admirer of Hank Mobley, Sonny Stitt, John Coltrane and Sonny Rollins, Lovano's own saxophone playing is distinguished by a lovely tone, fluent line and lucid sense of time - still showcased to best advantage, perhaps, in the company of

Motian and Frisell on recordings such as *One Time Out, On Broadway* and *Bill Evans* (all under the drummer's name). Lovano's output with Blue Note during the early 90s is particularly inspiring especially *From The Soul* and *Rush Hour* (Orchestrated by Gunther Schuller). He now stands in the very top league of tenor players, side by side amongst the finest artists of the century.

Albums: *Tones, Shapes And Colours* (Soul Note 1986), *One Time Out* (Soul Note 1988), *Village Rhythm* (Soul Note 1989), with Aldo Romano *Ten Tales* (Owl 1989), *Worlds* (1990), *Landmarks* (Blue Note 1991), *Sounds Of Joy* (Enja 1991), with Paul Motian, Bill Frisell *Motian In Tokyo* (1992), *From The Soul* (Blue Note 1992), *Universal Language* (Blue Note 1993), *Tenor Legacy* (Blue Note 1994), *Rush Hour* (Blue Note 1995).

Lowe, Frank

b. 24 June 1943, Memphis, Tennessee, USA. Although originally categorized as a 'new thing' (the US 60s free-jazz movement) player, Lowe has grown into one of the most distinctive and thoughtful of contemporary tenor saxophonists. Growing up in Memphis, one of his first jobs was at the Satellite record shop and its offshoot label, Stax. A liking for the records of Gene Ammons developed into a fascination with the newer musics of John Coltrane, Ornette Coleman and the AACM. He attended the University of Kansas, then moved to San Francisco and studied with Rafael Garrett, Sonny Simmons and Bert Wilson. Moving to New York in the mid-60s, he worked with Sun Ra then, after a spell at the San Francisco Conservatory, he settled in New York, playing with numerous musicians from the jazz *avant garde*, including Rashied Ali (*Duo Exchanges*), Alice Coltrane (*World Galaxy*) and Don Cherry (*Relativity Suite, Brown Rice*), while his own debut as leader - *Black Beings* - had Joseph Jarman guesting. In the mid-70s he formed a group with Joe Bowie and Charles 'Bobo' Shaw, recording *Fresh* (which also featured Lester Bowie) and *The Flam* (with Leo Smith). While in San Francisco, he had met Lawrence 'Butch' Morris, who has become one of his most frequent collaborators (*Current Trends In Racism In Modern America*), as has Billy Bang, with whom he plays in the collective quartet Jazz Doctors (*Intensive Case*) and in the violinist's own group (*Valve No 10*). Always open to new ideas, Lowe has played with leftfield rock musicians such as Eugene Chadbourne and seems as comfortable with New York's 80s *avant garde* downtown scene as he does with 60s jazzers such as Cherry and Charles Moffett: indeed, his own recordings feature a diverse array of artists, from John Zorn (*Lowe And Behold*) to Geri Allen and Grachan Moncur III (*Decision In Paradise*). As he told *Cadence* magazine, 'I've always tried to go in *and* out', though adding that even when playing in, he likes to 'experiment with time and colours'.

Albums: *Black Beings* (ESP 1973), *Fresh* (Freedom 1975), *The Flam* (Black Saint 1976), *Lowe And Behold* (1977), *The Other Side* (1977), *Tricks Of The Trade* (1977), *Doctor Too-Much* (1977), *Don't Punk Out* (1977), *Skizoke* (1981), *Exotic Heartbreak* (Soul Note 1982), with the Jazz Doctors *Intensive Care* (1984), *Decision In Paradise* (Soul Note 1985),

Inappropriate Choices (ITM Pacific 1991).

Lowe, Mundell

b. 21 April 1922, Laurel, Mississippi, USA. Guitarist Lowe began playing at the age of six and seven years later, left home and headed for New Orleans, Louisiana. He listened and learned at many of the city's clubs before he was found by his Baptist minister father and taken back home. He soon made another try for an early career in music, this time visiting Nashville where he played in the Pee Wee King band. Taken home again he graduated from school in 1940 and promptly joined the Jan Savitt band. Drafted for military service, Lowe was posted to a camp near New Orleans. At a nearby camp the entertainments officer was John Hammond Jnr. and their meeting helped Lowe establish his career after the war. Hammond introduced him to Ray McKinley who was leading the postwar Glenn Miller band and thereafter the guitarist worked with Benny Goodman, Wardell Gray, Fats Navarro and Red Norvo among many leading jazz musicians. During the late 40s and early 50s, Lowe worked mostly in New York, playing club dates and recording sessions with a remarkable array of top-flight artists, including Lester Young, Buck Clayton, Charlie Parker and Billie Holiday. During the 50s Lowe played in the NBC studio orchestra, was musical director on the *Today* show on television, acted on and off Broadway and continued to play and record with such well-known jazz musicians as Georgie Auld, Ruby Braff, Ben Webster, Carmen McRae and Harold Ashby.

Since 1965, Lowe has been based in Los Angeles, again working in television and radio and also establishing himself as a writer of scores for films and television. He also became active as an educator but despite his busy schedule found time to continue his recording career, accompanying such musically diverse artists as Sammy Davis Jnr., Tony Bennett, Bill Berry, Richie Kamuca and many others. In the early 80s he formed a small band he named TransitWest, in which he was joined by Sam Most, Monty Budwig and Nick Ceroli, which made its first major appearance at the 1983 Monterey Jazz Festival. A quietly elegant player with a cool but surging swing, Lowe's playing style, with its deceptively sparse exploration of the often-overlooked subtleties of many standards from the jazz and popular song repertoires, is in the great tradition of jazz guitar. Nevertheless, his experimentations with 12-tone compositions have also put him in the forefront of jazz-guitar thinking.

Albums: *The Mundell Lowe Quartet* (Original Jazz Classics 1955), *Guitar Moods* (Riverside 1956), *The Mundell Lowe Trio* (1956), *New Music Of Alec Wilder* (1956), *A Grand Night For Swinging* (1957), *Porgy And Bess* (RCA 1958), with Donald Byrd and others *TV Themes* (1959), *The Mundell Lowe All Stars* (1960), *Mundell Lowe And His Orchestra* i (1961), *Mundell Lowe And His Orchestra* ii (1962), *California Guitar* (1974), *Guitar Player* (1976), with Richie Kamuca *Richie* (1977), with Bill Berry *Shortcake* (1978), *TransitWest* (1983), *Souvenirs A Tribute To Nick Carroll* (Jazz Alliance 1992).

Lowther, Henry

b. 11 July 1941, Leicester, England. As a child Lowther learned trumpet from his father and took private violin lessons before going on to study with Manoug Parakian at London's Royal Academy of Music. From the mid-60s on he worked with Mike Westbrook, the New Jazz Orchestra, Keef Hartley, John Mayall, Manfred Mann, Michael Garrick, Norma Winstone (in *Edge Of Time*), John Dankworth, Art Themen, Alan Jackson (in the superb *Kinkade*), Barbara Thompson (*Jubiaba*), John Stevens, Kenny Wheeler, Mike Gibbs, Tony Coe, John Surman, Gordon Beck, Gil Evans, John Taylor, the BBC Symphony Orchestra and the London Brass Virtuosi as well as his own groups, Quarternity and Group Sounds Five. That list is in itself a testimony to his versatility and craftsmanship. As well as playing trumpet, flügelhorn, cornet and violin he has composed for jazz and orchestral groups. Influenced by sources as varied as Indian music, Karlheinz Stockhausen, Joe 'King' Oliver, Weather Report and the Average White Band, Lowther is still playing with as much freshness and directness as ever, touring in the early 90s with Kenny Wheeler and Barry Guy's London Jazz Composers Orchestra.

Selected albums: with Keef Hartley *The Battle Of North West Six* (Deram 1969), *Child Song* (1970).

Lunceford, Jimmie

b. 6 June 1902, Fulton, Mississippi, USA, d. 12 July 1947. At school in Denver, Colorado, Lunceford studied under Wilberforce Whiteman, father of Paul Whiteman. He later read for a degree in music at Fisk University, where his studies included composition, orchestration and musical theory and he also developed his precocious ability as a performer on many instruments although he preferred alto saxophone. After leaving Fisk, he worked briefly in New York in bands led by Elmer Snowden and others before taking up a teaching post at Manassas High School in Memphis, Tennessee. He formed a band at the school which included Moses Allen (bass) and Jimmy Crawford (drums). Later, Willie Smith and pianist Eddie Wilcox were added before Lunceford took the band on tour. They became very popular and after several such tours Lunceford decided in 1929 to make the band his full-time activity. For the next few years, with the same nucleus of musicians, he toured and broadcast throughout the mid-west. In 1933, the band reached New York and quickly established a reputation. More broadcasts, national tours and, eventually, some successful records made Lunceford's one of the most popular black bands of the swing era. The band's arrangers were originally Wilcox and Smith but later additions were Eddie Durham and Sy Oliver. It was the arrival of Oliver that set the seal on Lunceford's greatest period. Thanks to excellent charts, brilliantly performed by a meticulously rehearsed reed section (credit due largely to Smith), biting brass and a powerful rhythm section sparked by Crawford, the band became one of the best of the period. In addition to the band's sound they also looked good on stage. The Lunceford band was chiefly responsible for the showmanship which crept into many subsequent big band performances, but although many copied, none ever equalled the *élan* of Lunceford's band, especially the members of the trumpet section who would toss their horns high into the air, catching them on the beat. Apart from Smith, the band had good soloists in tenor saxophonist Joe Thomas and trombonist Trummy Young who gave the band a hit recording with his own composition, 'Tain't What You Do (It's The Way That You Do It'. Oliver's departure in mid-summer 1939 to join Tommy Dorsey was a blow but the band continued to use his arrangements. How long this state of affairs could have continued is debatable because the band's days were numbered. Lunceford's personal behaviour was distressing many of his long-serving sidemen. Their dismay at the manner in which he spent money (on buying airplanes for example), while refusing to meet what they saw as reasonable pay demands led, in 1942, to a mass walk-out. The band continued with replacements but the flair and excitement had gone. Although recordings over the next few years show a new promise any further improvement was forestalled when Lunceford died suddenly in July 1947. Although often overlooked in surveys of swing era big bands, during its glory days Lunceford's was one of the best in its precision playing of superbly professional arrangements, it had no betters and very few equals.

Selected compilations: *Jimmie Lunceford And Louis Prima 1945* (1979), *The Golden Swing Years* (1981), *Jimmie Lunceford (1935-41)* (1982), *Strictly Lunceford* (Jasmine 1983), *The Complete Jimmie Lunceford (1935-41)* (Jasmine 1986), *Oh Boy* (Happy Days 1987), *Runnin' A Temperature* (Affinity 1986), *Oh Boy!* (1987), *Stomp It Off Vol 1 1934-1935* (Decca 1992), *Jimmie Lunceford And His Orchestra Vol. 1 1934 - 1939* (Black And Blue 1993), *For Dancers Only* (Charly 1993).

Lyons, Jimmy

b. 1 December 1933, Jersey City, New Jersey, USA, d. 19 May 1986. A self-taught alto saxophone player, Lyons was encouraged while still in his early teens by such leading jazzmen as Buster Bailey, Bud Powell and Thelonious Monk. He first worked with Cecil Taylor in 1960 and through this association became known as a leading exponent of free-jazz. In the early 70s he was actively engaged in musical education while simultaneously pursuing his own studies. This period saw him broadening his musical base but he retained his links with Taylor, touring with him in various parts of the world. In the early 80s Lyons formed a quartet with Andrew Cyrille, Joseph Jarman and Don Moye. Soon thereafter his health began to fail and he died of cancer in 1986.

Albums: with Cecil Taylor *Nefertiti, The Beautiful One Has Come* (1962), with Taylor *Conquistador* (1966), *Other Afternoons* (Affinity 1969), *Push Pull* (1978), *Jump Up/What To Do About* (1980), with Taylor *Calling It The 8th* (1981), *Jump It Up* (Hat Art 1981), *Something In Return* (Black Saint 1981), *Wee Sneezawee* (1983), *Give It Up* (Black Saint 1985), with Andrew Cyrille *Burnt Offering* (Black Saint 1991).

Lyttelton, Humphrey

b. 23 May 1921, Eton, Buckinghamshire, England. Raised in an academic atmosphere, his father was a Housemaster at Eton

College, he taught himself to play a variety of instruments including the banjolele. His prodigious talent was spotted early and he was given formal lessons on piano and, a little later, in military band drumming. Eventually, his education took him back to Eton College this time as a pupil. He joined the school orchestra as a timpanist but after a while drifted away from the orchestra and the instrument. At the age of 15 he discovered jazz, thanks to records by trumpeters Nat Gonella and, decisively, Louis Armstrong. By this time Lyttelton had switched to playing the mouth-organ but realizing the instrument's limitations, he acquired a trumpet which he taught himself to play. Forming his own small jazz band at the college, he developed his playing ability and his consuming interest in jazz. With the outbreak of World War II he joined the Grenadier Guards, continuing to play whenever possible. After the war he resumed playing, this time professionally and in 1947 became a member of George Webb's Dixielanders. The following year he formed his own band and quickly became an important figure in the British revivalist movement. In the late 40s and through to the mid-50s Lyttelton's stature in British jazz increased. Significantly, his deep interest in most aspects of jazz meant that he was constantly listening to other musicians, many of whom played different forms of the music. Although he was never to lose his admiration for Armstrong he refused to remain rooted in the revivalist tradition. His acceptance and absorption of music from the jazz mainstream ensured that when the trad boom fizzled out, Lyttelton continued to find an audience. In the mid-50s he added alto saxophonist Bruce Turner to his band, outraging some reactionary elements in British jazz circles, and a few years later added Tony Coe, Joe Temperley and other outstanding and forward-thinking musicians.

In the early 60s Lyttelton's reputation spread far beyond the UK and he also developed another important and long-term admiration for a trumpet player, this time Buck Clayton. By this time, however, Lyttelton's personal style had matured and he was very much his own man. He was also heavily involved in many areas outside the performance of music. In 1954, he had published his first autobiographical volume and in the 60s he began to spread his writing wings as essayist, journalist and critic. He also broadcast on radio and television, sometimes as a performer but also as a speaker and presenter. These multiple activities continued throughout the next two decades, his UK BBC Radio 2 series, *The Best Of Jazz*, running for many years. His writings included further autobiographical work and his ready wit found outlets in such seemingly unlikely settings such as the quizmaster on the long-running radio comedy-panel series, *I'm Sorry I Haven't A Clue*. During this time he continued to lead a band, employing first-rate musicians with whom he toured and made numerous records. Amongst the sidemen of the 70s and 80s were Dave Green, Mick Pyne, John Surman, John Barnes, Roy Williams and Adrian Macintosh. He also toured and recorded with singers Helen Shapiro, Carol Kidd and Lillian Boutté.

Back in the late 40s Lyttelton had recorded with Sidney Bechet and in the 70s and 80s he made occasional albums with other

American jazz stars including Buddy Tate, on *Kansas City Woman*, and Kenny Davern, *Scatterbrains* and *This Old Gang Of Ours*. In the early 80s Lyttelton formed his own recording company, Calligraph, and by the end of the decade numerous new albums were available. In addition to these came others, mostly on the Dormouse label, which reissued his earlier recordings and were eagerly snapped up by fans of all ages. Although he has chosen to spend most of his career in the UK, Lyttelton's reputation elsewhere is extremely high and thoroughly deserved. As a trumpet player and bandleader, and occasional clarinettist, he has ranged from echoing early jazz to near-domination of the British mainstream. For more than 40 years he has succeeded in maintaining the highest musical standards, all the while conducting himself with dignity, charm and good humour. In the early 90s touring with Kathy Stobart, he showed no signs of letting up and barely acknowledged the fact that he had sailed passed his 70th birthday.

Selected albums: *Humph At The Conway* (Calligraph 1954), *I Play As I Please* (1957), *Triple Exposure* (1959), *Back To The 60s* (Philips 1960-63 recordings), *Humphrey Lyttelton And His Band 1960-63* (Philips), *21 Years On* (1969), *South Bank Swing Session* (1973), *Kansas City Woman* (1974), *Spreadin' Joy* (1978), *One Day I Met An African* (Black Lion 1980), *It Seems Like Yesterday* (1983), *Movin' And Groovin'* (1983), *Scatterbrains* (1984), *Humph At The Bull's Head* (Calligraph 1985), *...This Old Gang Of Ours...* (1985) with Helen Shapiro *Echoes Of The Duke* (Calligraph 1985), *Gonna Call My Children Home: The World Of Buddy Bolden* (1986), *Movin' And Groovin'* (Black Lion 1986), *Gigs* (1987), *Doggin Around* (Wam 1987), *The Dazzling Lillian Boutté* (1988), *In Canada* (Sackville 1980), *The Beano Boogie* (Calligraph 1989), with Helen Shapiro *I Can't Get Started* (Calligraph 1990), *Rock Me Gently* (Calligraph 1991), *Hook Line And Sinker* (Angel 1991), *At Sundown* (Calligraph 1992), *Rent Party* (Stomp Off 1992), *Movin' And Groovin'* (1993), *Hear Me Talkin' To Ya* (Calligraph 1994). Compilations: *Delving Back And Forth With Humph* (1948-86 recordings), *Bad Penny Blues: The Best Of Humph* (1949-56 recordings), *Tribute To Humph Vols 1-8* (1949-56 recordings), *The Parlophone Years* (Dormouse 1989, 1949-56 recordings), *Jazz At The Royal Festival Hall & Jazz At The Conway Hall* (1951-54 recordings), *Dixie Gold* (1960-63 recordings).

Further reading: *I Play As I Please*, Humphrey Lyttelton. *Second Chorus*, Humphrey Lyttelton. *Take It From The Top*, Humphrey Lyttelton.

Machito

b. Frank Raul Grillo, 16 February 1912, Tampa, Florida, USA, d. 15 April 1984. Raised in Cuba, Machito became a singer and maracas player, working with many of the best-known bands on the island. After arriving in New York in the late 30s, he became similarly well-known as an accomplished player in various Latin-American dancebands. In 1941 he formed his own unit, the Afro-Cubans, and the following year his brother-in-law, Mario Bauza, until then lead trumpeter with Chick Webb, joined him. Under Bauza's watchful eye, the Afro-Cubans became one of the leading exponents of their particular form of Latin-American music. In the late 40s, and throughout the 50s, Machito's band regularly teamed up with leading jazz musicians, especially beboppers, for recording sessions, some of the earliest of which were produced by Norman Granz. These artists included Charlie Parker, Dizzy Gillespie, Joe 'Flip' Phillips, Buddy Rich and Howard McGhee. His music appealed greatly to Stan Kenton, helping prompt Kenton's long-lasting love affair with Latin rhythms. Machito played percussion instruments on some of Kenton's recordings, including the original version of 'Peanut Vendor'. Machito had a number of successful records during the mambo craze of the 60s, but it was the increasing popularity of salsa which helped keep him in the front rank of popular entertainment until his death in April 1984, which occurred during an engagement in London.

Selected albums: *Afro-Cubop* (1949), *Macho Mambo* (1949), *Machito* i (1952), *Kenya/Latin Soul Plus Jazz* (1957), *With Flute To Boot* (1958), *Machito At The Crescendo* (late 50s), *The World's Greatest Latin Band* (early 60s), *Machito* ii (1967), *Machito* iii (1971), *Fireworks* (early 70s), *Afro-Cuban Jazz Moods* (1975), *Machito And His Salsa Big Band 1982* i (1982), *Live At North Sea '82* (1982) *Machito And His Salsa Big Band* ii (1983), *Cubop City* (1992), *The Original Mambo Kings* (1993), *Tremendo Cumban 1949-52* (1993).

Mainieri, Mike

b. 24 July 1938, the Bronx, New York, USA. Mainieri was playing the vibraphone by the time he was 10 years old and performing publicly at 14. He studied at the Juilliard School and then joined the Paul Whiteman Band before touring with the Buddy Rich Orchestra (1956-62). He left Rich to become a session musician in New York. During the 70s he wrote music for television and films. He played with Jeremy Steig's band Jeremy And The Satyrs at the Cafe A Go Go, formed a 16-piece rock band and led his own quartet with Steve Gadd on drums. He invented the synthi-vibe, which not only allowed him to treat the sound of the vibes electronically but also to be heard in high-volume situations. In 1979, he brought together a group of session musicians to tour Japan. The unit

included Gadd (later replaced by Peter Erskine), Michael Brecker, Don Grolnick (piano), and Eddie Gomez. They were named Steps, later to be Steps Ahead, and were described as 'a contemporary bebop band'.
Albums: *Free Smiles* (1978), *Wanderlust* (NYC 1981), *Steps Ahead* (1983), *Modern Times* (1984), *Magnetic Love* (1986), *Come Together* (NYC 1993).
Video: *Mike Mainieri Quintet* (Kay Jazz 1988).

Makowicz, Adam

b. 18 August 1940, Czechoslovakia. Makowicz's piano teacher mother taught him to play. He studied classical music at the Fryderyck Chopin School in Kracow, but left when he became interested in jazz. His first work was with Tomasz Stanko (trumpet) in one of the first European groups to be influenced by the free style of Ornette Coleman. In 1965, he moved to Warsaw, where he had his own trio and played with Zbigniew Namyslowski (alto) with whom he toured worldwide. Makowicz's interest in composition grew during this period and he became involved with electric keyboards. In 1970, he joined Michal Urbaniak in his new group Constellation and recorded an album with Urbaniak's wife, Urszula Dudziak. Between 1973 and 1976 he played in a group called Unit with Tomasz Stanko and played the piano with the Duke Ellington Orchestra at a concert in Prague (1976). In 1977 he went to the USA as a solo performer, playing in a way which reflected his interest in Art Tatum, Keith Jarrett and romantic piano music. He settled in New York in 1977 and became an American citizen in 1986.
Albums: with Urszula Dudziak *Newborn Light* (1972), with Michel Urbaniak *Michal Urbaniak Fusion* (1975), *Live Embers* (1975), *Winter Flowers* (1978), *From My Window* (1980), *Naughty Baby* (1987), *The Solo Album: Adam In Stockholm* (Verve 1987), with George Mraz *Classic Jazz Duets* (Stash 1987), *Name Is Makowitz* (Sheffield Lab 1988), *Solo* (Sonet 1988), *Live At The Maybank Recital Hall Series, Vol 24* (Concord 1993), *Music Of Jerome Kern* (Concord 1993).

Mance, Junior

b. Julian Clifford Mance, Jnr., 10 October 1928, Chicago, Illinois, USA. Taught piano by his father, a professional jazz musician, Mance was playing professionally long before he entered his teenage. In the late 40s, still in his teens, he joined a band led by Gene Ammons and in 1950 worked with Lester Young. After military service he became a resident at a Chicago jazz club before becoming Dinah Washington's accompanist. In the mid-60s he played with Cannonball and Nat Adderley, whom he had first met in an army band, then joined Dizzy Gillespie. By the early 60s, Mance had decided on a career as leader and from then onwards worked clubs throughout the USA. Although primarily known for his work in bop and post-bop groups, Mance's playing reveals echoes of his father's early instruction which drew heavily upon the blues piano tradition. A gifted player with a fluent technique and subtle touch, Mance's reputation worldwide is somewhat less than his talent deserves.

Albums: *The Soulful Piano Of Junior Mance* (1960), with Eddie 'Lockjaw' Davis, Johnny Griffin *Tough Tenors* (1960), *Junior Mance Trio At The Village Vanguard* (Carrere 1961), *Holy Mama* (1976), *Smokey Blues* (JSP 1980), *Deep* (JSP 1982), with Martin Rivera *For Dancers Only* (1983), with Rivera *The Tender Touch Of* (Niva 1984), *Junior Mance Special* (Sackville 1989), *Play The Music Of Dizzy Gillespie* (Sackville 1993).

Mangelsdorff, Albert

b. 5 September 1928, Frankfurt-Am-Main, Germany. From a musical family, Mangelsdorff and his brother, saxophonist Emil, learned about jazz from secret meetings of the Frankfurt Hot Club, since jazz was banned by the Nazis. He has subsequently become one of the most important and distinctive European jazz players. After playing violin and danceband guitar, he took up the trombone at the age of 20 and extended its range with the use of multiphonics (playing more than one note at a time) through his technique of humming and growling while playing, so that the brass-generated note is augmented by the vocal sound. He won awards in Germany in 1954, and in 1958 gained attention in the USA as a member of the Newport International Band. In 1962 he recorded with John Lewis. In 1964 he toured Asia with his own band and at that time began to move towards free jazz. He also recorded an album with Ravi Shankar. In the late 60s he joined the Globe Unity Orchestra. In 1975, he joined the United Jazz And Rock Ensemble. From 1976-82 Mangelsdorff worked with Michel Portal, and in 1981 he co-founded the French/German Jazz Ensemble with J.F. Jenny-Clark. In the mid-70s he augmented John Surman's The Trio (with Barre Phillips and Stu Martin) to create MUMPS. In 1986 he and Surman joined with Elvin Jones and Dave Holland for a tour of Europe.
Selected albums: with John Lewis *Animal Dance* (Atlantic 1962), *Tension* (1963), *New Jazz Ramwong* (L+R 1964), with Lee Konitz, Attila Zoller *ZO-KO-MA* (1967), *And His Friends* (1967), *Wild Goose* (1969), *Never Let It End* (1970), *Live In Tokyo* (Enja 1971), *Spontaneous* (Enja 1971), *Birds Of Underground* (1972), *Trombirds* (1973), *The Wide Point* (MPS 1975), *Solo Now* (1976), *Tromboneliness* (1976), with Alphonse Mouzon, Jaco Pastorious *Trilogue-Live* (1976), with MUMPS *A Matter Of Taste* (1977), *A Jazz Tune I Hope* (1978), *Albert Live In Montreux* (1980), *Eternal Rhythm* (MPS 1981), *Three Originals* (MPS 1981), *Triple Entente* (1983), with Wolfgang Dauner *Two Is Company* (1983), with Peter Brötzmann, Günter Sommer *Pica Pica* (1983), *Hot Hut* (1985), with Konitz *The Art Of The Duo* (1988, rec 1983), *Internationales Jazzfestival Munster* (Tutu 1989), with John Surman *Room 1220* (Konnek 1993, 1970 recording).

Mangione, Chuck

b. Charles Frank Mangione, 29 November 1940, Rochester, New York, USA. Mangione began playing trumpet as a child, studying formally at the Eastman School of Music. He gained experience accompanying visiting jazzmen, then in 1960 went to New York where he formed a band with his brother, pianist Gap Mangione. The band, the Jazz Brothers, remained in existence for five years, playing hard bop. In 1965, Mangione played in the trumpet sections of the Woody Herman and Maynard Ferguson bands and later that year he joined Art Blakey, with whom he remained until 1967. After leaving Blakey, Mangione taught at his old school and again formed his own small band. He began making albums with which he achieved considerable popular success. He had started to dabble on flügelhorn and eventually abandoned the trumpet altogether in favour of the more mellow-sounding instrument. Throughout the 70s and into the 80s Mangione continued to capitalize upon his successful recordings, appearing widely in concert and making more records which again appealed to a wide audience. To a great extent, Mangione achieved his popular success by offering melodic and uncluttered music, sometimes with interesting hints of Latin influence. Although much of his popular material failed to excite the hardcore jazz audience, there can be little doubt that he helped to introduce the music to many who might otherwise have passed it by. His compositions have appealed to a wide range of musicians, being played by artists as different as Percy Faith and Cannonball Adderley. Perhaps the best known of his compositions is 'Land Of Make Believe', which has frequently been recorded. Additionally, Mangione has written for films, notably *The Children Of Sanchez* (1978).

Selected albums: *The Jazz Brothers* (Milestone 1960), *Hey Baby!* (Original Jazz Classics 1961), *Spring Fever* (Original Jazz Classics 1961), *Recuerdo* (Original Jazz Classics 1963), with Art Blakey *Buttercorn Lady* (1966), *Land Of Make Believe* (1972), *Bellavia* (1975), *Feels So Good* (1977), *Feels So Good* (A&M 1978), *The Children Of Sanchez* (1978), *An Evening Of Magic* (A&M 1979), *Tarentella* (A&M 1981), *Love Notes* (Columbia 1982), *Journey To A Rainbow* (CBS 1983), *Disguise* (1984), *Save Tonight For Me* (CBS 1987), *Eyes Of The Veiled Temptress* (CBS 1988). Compilations: *The Best Of Chuck Mangione* (Mercury 1983), *Compact Jazz* (Mercury 1984).

Mann, Herbie

b. 16 April 1930, New York City, New York, USA. After learning to play the clarinet while still a small child, Mann took up the flute. He developed his musical experience during military service. After leaving the US army, he was active in film and television studios as both performer and composer. He played in several small jazz groups during the late 50s, including his own Afro-Jazz Sextet with which he toured internationally. Early in the 60s, his interest in Brazilian music led to a series of profitable recordings, notably 'Coming Home Baby'. Although rooted in bop and recording with leading jazzmen such as Bill Evans, by the late 60s, Mann's writing and playing had broadened to include musical influences from many lands - especially those of the Middle East. He was also open-minded about rock and by the early 70s was a leading figure in jazz-rock fusion. Indeed, his wide acceptance of areas of popular music outside jazz created some difficulties of categorization, especially when he embraced, however briefly, reggae and disco-pop. He has become one of the widest known flautists in jazz, gaining a considerable measure of credibility for an instrument

which has always had an uncertain status in jazz circles. In addition to his performing and writing, Mann has also been active as a record producer, running his own label, Embryo, under the Atlantic aegis for a decade. Subsequently, he formed his own independent label, Herbie Mann Music.

Selected albums: *Mann In The Morning* (1956), *Salute To The Flute* (1956), *Mann Alone* (1957), *Yardbird Suite* (Savoy 1957), *Flute Souffle* (Original Jazz Classics 1958), *Just Wailin'* (1958), with Bill Evans *Nirvana* (Atlantic 1961-62), *Herbie Mann At The Village Gate* (Atlantic 1962), *Herbie Mann Today* (1965), *Memphis Underground* (Atlantic 1968), *Push* (WEA 1971), *Mississippi Gambler* (Atlantic 1972), *London Underground* (Atlantic 1973), *Reggae* (1973), *Gagaku And Beyond* (1974), *Discotheque* (1974-75), *Surprises* (c.1976), *Brazil - Once Again* (1978), *Astral Island* (1983), *Opalescence* (Kokopelli 1989), *Caminho De Casa* (Chesky 1990), *The Jazz We Heard Last Summer* (Savoy 1993), with Bobby Jaspar *Deep Pocket* (Kokopelli 1994). Compilation: *Best Of Herbie Mann* (WEA 1993).

Manne, Shelly

b. Sheldon Manne, 11 June 1920, New York City, New York, USA, d. 26 September 1984. After switching to drums from saxophone, Manne worked with a number of dance and swing bands of the late 30s and early 40s, including Joe Marsala's big band. He was also active in small groups in New York, accompanying Coleman Hawkins as well as some of the upcoming bebop artists. He first attracted widespread attention in 1946, the year he joined Stan Kenton. On and off, he was with Kenton until 1952, finding time in between stints to work in bands led by George Shearing, Woody Herman and others. From the early 50s, he was resident in Los Angeles, working in the studios by day and gradually becoming one of the most important musicians in the rising west coast school of jazz. In 1951, he had recorded with Shorty Rogers and become a member of the house band at Howard Rumsey's Lighthouse Cafe at Hermosa Beach. During the next few years he took part in many fine record sessions, notably for Contemporary, with Teddy Edwards, Jimmy Giuffre, Art Pepper, Lennie Niehaus, Bud Shank, Bob Cooper, Maynard Ferguson, Hampton Hawes and most of the other west coast stars. Among the most successful of these recordings were those made with Rogers in 1951 and 1955/6, a set he recorded with Russ Freeman and Chet Baker, and an album of tunes from the Broadway Show, *My Fair Lady*, which he recorded with Leroy Vinnegar and André Previn. This set, the first ever complete album of jazz versions of tunes from a single show, was particularly successful. Almost as popular was another album made by the same trio with visiting guest, Sonny Rollins. Although recording with many different musicians, Manne kept a fairly constant personnel together for his regular working band, and towards the end of 1959 was booked into the Blackhawk in San Francisco. The band comprised trumpeter Joe Gordon, Richie Kamuca, Monty Budwig, who had recently taken over from Vinnegar, and Freeman's replacement, Vic Feldman. It was immediately apparent to Manne that the band he had assembled for this two-week engagement was something special, and he persuaded Les Koenig of Contemporary to travel to San Francisco to record them. The resulting four albums became some of the most successful in Contemporary's catalogue and an outstanding example of the west coast's so-called 'cool' sounds at their smokiest. In 1960, Manne opened his own nightclub, Shelly's Manne-Hole, which remained in existence until the middle of the following decade. In the 60s he recorded with Bill Evans and in 1974 was a founder member of the LA Four, with Shank, Ray Brown and Laurindo Almeida. By the late 70s Manne was a familiar figure on the international jazz festival circuit, appearing at the 1980 Aurex festival in Japan with Benny Carter's Gentlemen of Swing. Although deeply rooted in the swinging tradition of drumming, Manne's sensitive, explorative playing made him an ideal accompanist in almost any setting and one of the finest drummers of the post-war period.

Selected albums: with Shorty Rogers *Modern Sounds* (1951), with Rogers *Cool And Crazy* (1953), *The Three And The Two* (1954), with Lennie Niehaus *The Quintet* (1954), *The Shelly Manne-Russ Freeman Duo* (1954), with Rogers *The Swinging Mr Rogers* (1955), *Concerto For Clarinet And Combo* (1955), *The West Coast Sound* (Original Jazz Classics 1955), with Rogers *Martians Come Back!* (1955), with Rogers *Big Band Express/Blues Express* (1956), *Swinging Sounds* (1956), *Quartet: Russ Freeman And Chet Baker* (1956), *Shelly Manne And His Friends* (Original Jazz Classics 1956), *More Swinging Sounds* (Contemporary 1956), *My Fair Lady* (Original Jazz Classics 1957), *The Gambit* (1957), with Sonny Rollins *Way Out West* (1957), *The Bells Are Ringing* (1958), *Shelly Manne And His Men Play Peter Gunn* (1959), *Son Of Gun* (1959), *Shelly Manne And His Men At The Blackhawk Vols 1-4* (Original Jazz Classics 1959), *The Proper Time* (1960), *West Coast Jazz In England* (1960), *Shelly Manne And His Men Live At The Manne-Hole Vols 1 and 2* (Original Jazz Classics 1961), *Checkmate* (1961), *Sounds Unheard Of* (1962), with Bill Evans *Empathy* (1962), *My Son, The Jazz Drummer* (1962), *Shelly Manne And His Orchestra* i (1964), *Shelly Manne And His Orchestra* ii (1965), *Manne - That's Gershwin!* (1965), *Perk Up* (1967), *Shelly Manne And His Orchestra* iii (1967), *Jazz Gun* (Atlantic 1968), *Outside* (1969), *Alive In London* (Original Jazz Classics 1970), *A Night On The Coast* (Moon 1969-1970 recordings), *Mannekind* (Original Master Recordings 1972), *Hot Coles* (1975), *The LA Four Scores!* (1975), *Rex - Shelly Manne Plays Richard Rodgers* (1976), *Essence* (Galaxy 1977), *French Concert* (1977), *Jazz Crystallizations* (1978), *The Manne We Love* (1978), *Interpretations Of Bach And Mozart* (Trend 1980), *In Concert At Carmelo's/Double Piano Jazz Quartet Vol. 1* (Trend 1980), *Double Piano Jazz Quartet Vol. 2* (Trend 1980), with Benny Carter *The Gentlemen Of Swing* (1980), *Hollywood Jam* (1981), *Fingering* (1981), *Remember* (1984), *In Concert At Carmelo's Vols 1 and 2* (Trend 1986).

Manone, Joseph 'Wingy'

b. 13 February 1900, New Orleans, Louisiana, USA, d. 9 July 1982. Manone lost his right arm in a road accident while still a child, but took up trumpet playing, turning professional in his mid-teens. The 20s were hectic times for Manone. He worked with many riverboat and territory bands, visited St. Louis where he made his first records in 1924, moved on to New York in 1929 to record with Benny Goodman, and settled in Chicago. He led his own band at nightclubs, then took it to New York for a string of successful engagements which were enhanced by the popularity of his recording of 'The Isle Of Capri'. By the early 40s he was in California, appearing in films and becoming a regular on Bing Crosby's radio show, visiting New York and other centres for concerts and record dates with, for example, Sidney Bechet. In the mid-50s Manone moved to Las Vegas, playing there for several years but making occasional trips to New York and visiting Europe for festivals and tours of clubs. Manone's vocal style, although popular with audiences, was filled with rather forced humour. Contrastingly, he played trumpet with a forthright, honest style which compounded his love for the playing of Louis Armstrong with the New Orleans tradition he heard in his childhood. His early recordings are solidly entertaining.

Albums: *Wingy Manone And His Band* i (1954), *Wingy Manone And His Band* ii (1957), *Wingy Manone And His Band* iii (1957), *Wingy Manone And His Band* iv (1959-60), *Wingy Manone And His Band* v (1960), with Papa Bue Jensen *A Tribute To Wingy Manone* (1966), *Jazz From Italy* (1975). Compilations: *Wingy Manone Vol. 1* (1928-34), *Wingy Manone Vol. 2* (1934-35), *Wingy Manone/Sidney Bechet - Together at Town Hall, 1947* (1947), *Collection Vols 1-3* (Collectors Classics 1989).

Mantler, Michael

b. 10 August 1943, Vienna, Austria. Mantler took up trumpet at the age of 12, and from 14 worked in dance bands, playing stock arrangements with little opportunity for creative jazz. He found more musical freedom after moving to the USA in 1962. After what he regarded as educationally barren years at the Berklee College Of Music in Boston, he moved to New York in 1964 and immediately became involved with musicians such as Paul Bley, Carla Bley (whom he would later marry) and Cecil Taylor. In 1965-66 he toured Europe with Carla Bley and Steve Lacy in the Jazz Realities quintet. In more recent times, he has toured with Carla Bley's Sextet and Charlie Haden's Liberation Music Orchestra, and has recorded several albums of his own pieces. Although a striking player, he concentrates most of his energy on organizing, producing and composing (often setting the words of Samuel Beckett, Harold Pinter and Edward Gorey to music). He was a co-founder of the Jazz Composers' Guild and the Jazz Composers' Orchestra Association. He also set up two record labels with Carla Bley: Watt, for their own recordings, and JCOA Records, to promote the work of others.

Albums: *Jazz Composers' Orchestra* (1968), *No Answer* (1974), with Carla Bley *13 & 3/4* (1975), *The Hapless Child* (Watt 1976), *Silence* (1977), *Movies* (1978), *More Movies* (1980), *Something There* (ECM 1982), *Alien* (Watt 1985), *Live* (Watt 1987), *Many Have No Speech* (Watt 1988), *Folly Seeing All This* (ECM 1993).

Marcus, Steve

b. 18 September 1939, New York, USA. Marcus studied at the Berklee College Of Music in Boston (1959-61) before joining Stan Kenton's Orchestra in 1963. From 1967-70 he played with the Herbie Mann Group as well as for bands as diverse as those of Woody Herman and the Jazz Composers Orchestra. In the early 70s, he played with Larry Coryell (1971-73) before forming his own Count's Rock Band (1973-75). He joined Buddy Rich in 1975, and played with him regularly over the next 10 years. His tenor playing blends R&B stylings with the influence of John Coltrane in much the way Sal Nistico, another Rich tenor, does: it is a style which can punch its way through the ebullient backings of the big band in full swing.
Albums: *Count's Rock Band* (1974), *Buddy Rich Plays And Plays And Plays* (1975), *Lionel Hampton Presents Buddy Rich* (1977), *201* (Red Baron 1992).

Mariano, Charlie

b. 12 November 1923, Boston, Massachusetts, USA. One of many fine students to emerge from Boston's Berklee College Of Music, Mariano gained most of his early experience in and around his home town. Among the musicians with whom he played in the formative years of the late 40s and early 50s were Herb Pomeroy, Nat Pierce, Gigi Gryce, Quincy Jones and Jackie Byard. In 1953, he joined Stan Kenton for a two-year spell and then worked in Los Angeles with Shelly Manne. By 1958 he was back in Boston, this time teaching at Berklee College Of Music. The following year he was briefly with Kenton again, then met, married and formed a band with Toshiko Akiyoshi. This association lasted into the mid-60s, with part of that time spent in Japan. During the 60s Mariano also played with Charles Mingus, spent more time teaching at Berklee, travelled extensively in the far-east, and led his own jazz-rock group. In the 70s and 80s Mariano lived mostly in Europe, leading bands with Philip Catherine and others, continuing to explore eastern music and playing many kinds of fusion music with, among other groups, the United Jazz And Rock Ensemble and Eberhard Weber's Colours. Throughout his career, Mariano has displayed a striking ability to encompass many diverse musical forms and incorporate them into jazz without losing the emotional intensity of his early bebop-orientated playing style. Through his continued exploration of ethnic musical forms, particularly those of eastern origin, Mariano has established a secure and significant place as a truly international jazz artist.
Selected albums: *Charlie Mariano With His Jazz Group* (1950-51), *The Modern Saxophone Stylings Of Charlie Mariano* (1950-51), *Charlie Mariano* i (1951), *Charlie Mariano Boston All Stars* (Original Jazz Classics 1953), *Charlie Mariano* ii (1953), *Swinging With Mariano* (Affinity 1954), *Charlie Mariano* Plays (Fresh Sound 1954), *Alto Sax For Young Moderns/Johnny One-note* (Affinity 1954), with Stan Kenton *Contemporary Concepts* (1955), *Charlie Mariano* iv (1957), *Toshiko-Mariano Quartet* i (1960), with Charles Mingus *The Black Saint And The Sinner Lady* (1963), *Toshiko-Mariano Quartet* (1963), *A Jazz Portrait Of Charlie Mariano* (1963), *Folk Soul* (1967), with Sadao Watanabe *Iberian Waltz* (1967-68), *Charlie Mariano And His Orchestra* (c.1970), *Cascade* (1974), *Reflektions* (1974), *Jazz Confronto 15/JaC's Group Featuring Charlie Mariano* (1975), *The Door Is Open/Pork Pie* (1975), *Helen 12 Trees* (1976), *October* (1977), with United Jazz And Rock Ensemble *Teamwork* (1978), *Crystal Bells* (1979), *Tea For Four* (1980), *Some Kind Of Changes* (c.1982), *Jyothi* (ECM 1983), *The Charlie Mariano Group* (1985), *Mariano* (Intuition 1987), *Charlie Mariano And The Karnataka College Of Percussion: Live* (1989), *Live* (Verabra 1990), *It's Standard Time* (Fresh Sound 1990), *Innuendo* (Lipstick 1992).

Marmarosa, Dodo

b. Michael Marmarosa, 12 December 1925, Pittsburgh, Pennsylvania, USA. After formal studies and gigging with local bands, Marmarosa played piano with a succession of name big bands of the early and mid-40s, including those of Gene Krupa, Tommy Dorsey and Artie Shaw. In 1946, he settled in Los Angeles, playing and recording with several leading jazz musicians, including Barney Kessel, Lester Young and Charlie Parker. His affinity with bebop made him, briefly, one of the outstanding exponents of the form, but ill-health drove him from the scene around 1948. Marmarosa returned to music in 1961, recording alone and with Gene Ammons. Within a couple of years he was again forced into retirement.
Selected albums: *Dodo's Back!/The Return Of Dodo Marmarosa* (1961), with Gene Ammons *Jug & Dodo* (1962), *The Chicago Sessions* (Affinity 1989, 1961-62). Compilations: with Barney Kessel, others *Central Avenue Breakdown Vols 1 & 2* (1945-46), *The Dial Masters* (1946), *Piano Man* (Phoenix 1981, 1946 recording), with Charlie Parker *The Legendary Dial Masters* (1946-47), *A 'Live Dodo'* (Swing House 1979, 1947 recording), *Experiment In Bop* (Raretone 1989).

Marsala, Joe

b. 4 January 1907, Chicago, Illinois, USA, d. 4 March 1978. After playing locally, Marsala's first name-band job was with Wingy Manone in 1929. In the early 30s he gigged in Chicago and elsewhere, returning several times to Manone, with whom he appeared at a number of leading New York nightspots. In 1935, he played and recorded with Adrian Rollini's Tap Room Gang before yet another spell with Manone, this time at the Hickory House. Taking over the band on Manone's departure in 1936, Marsala became one of the first bandleaders on 52nd Street to regularly front a racially-mixed band which included Red Allen. The Hickory House engagement was another long-running affair, extending into the mid-40s, but interspersed with leading bands on cruise ships he also briefly led a big band which played charts commissioned from Don Redman. In some of these bands, Marsala was joined by his brother, trumpeter Marty Marsala (b. 2 April 1909, d. 27 April 1975). In 1938, Marsala married harpist Adele Girard with whom he recorded and later collaborated on the composition of a number of songs, including such popular hits as 'Little Sir Echo' and 'Don't Cry, Joe'. During the early 40s, the bands Marsala led at the Hickory House included not only swing era veterans but also several younger musicians in transition to bebop and the mainstream, among them Buddy Rich, Charlie Byrd and Shelly Manne. He was also instrumental in giving an early career boost to Frankie Laine. The Hickory House job finally ended in 1947; thereafter, Marsala redirected his career to songwriting and administrative work in music publishing and related businesses. During the 60s, he sometimes played on recording sessions, on one occasion teaming up with Bobby Hackett to accompany Tony Bennett. Although he deliberately ended his full-time playing career while still at his peak, Marsala left some very good recordings featuring his Jimmie Noone-inspired clarinet playing.

Compilations: *Joe Marsala And His Orchestra Featuring Adele Girard* (Aircheck 1979, 1942 recording), *Joe Marsala And His Band* (Jazzology 1986, 1944), *Hickory House Jazz* (Affinity 1991).

Marsalis, Branford

b. 26 August 1960, Breaux Bridge, Louisiana, USA. With their father, Ellis Marsalis, a bop pianist, composer and teacher, it is not surprising that his sons Branford, Delfeayo and Wynton Marsalis all took up music in childhood. Branford Marsalis's first instrument was the alto saxophone, which he played during his formative years and while studying at Berklee College Of Music. In 1981, he played in Art Blakey's Jazz Messengers and the following year began a spell with a small band led by Wynton. During this period Marsalis switched instruments, taking up both soprano and tenor saxophones. He also played on record dates with leading jazzmen such as Miles Davis and Dizzy Gillespie. After three years in his brother's band, he began a period of musical searching. Like many young musicians of his era, Marsalis often played in jazz-rock bands, including that led by Sting. He also formed his own small group with which he toured and recorded. By the late 80s he had established a reputation as a leading post-bop jazz saxophonist, but also enjoyed status in fusion and even classical circles (*Romances For Saxophone*). Like most jazzmen, Marsalis drew early inspiration from the work of other musicians, amongst them John Coltrane, Ben Webster, Wayne Shorter, Ornette Coleman and especially Sonny Rollins. In some of his recordings these influences have surfaced, leading to criticisms that he has failed to build a personal style. Closer attention reveals that these stylistic acknowledgements are merely that and not an integral part of his musical make-up. His 1993 outing with *I Heard You Twice The First Time* showed a strong leaning towards the blues, both John Lee Hooker and B. B. King are featured in addition to his brother. Perhaps of more significance to Marsalis's development as a musician is the fact that his career appears fated to be constantly compared to and contrasted with that of his virtuoso brother Wynton. If this should result in his long-term overshadowing it will be, at least, unfortunate, because by the early 90s Branford Marsalis had proved himself to be an inventive soloist with considerable warmth. His best work contains many moments of powerful emotional commitment.

Albums: *Wynton Marsalis* (1981), *Scenes In The City* (Columbia 1983), with Dizzy Gillespie *New Faces* (1984), with Wynton Marsalis *Black Codes (From The Underground)* (1985), with Sting *Bring On The Night* (c.1986), *Royal Garden Blues* (Columbia 1986), *Random Abstract* (Columbia 1987), *Renaissance* (Columbia 1987), *Trio Jeepy* (Columbia 1988), *Crazy People Music* (Columbia 1990), *The Beautyful Ones Are Not Yet Born* (Columbia 1992), *I Heard You Twice The First Time* (Columbia 1993), *Bloomington* (Columbia 1993), *Spike Lee's Mo Better Blues* (1993).

Video: *Steep* (CMV 1989).

Marsalis, Wynton

b. 18 October 1961, New Orleans, Louisiana, USA. Marsalis took up the trumpet at the age of six, encouraged by his father, Ellis Marsalis, a pianist, composer and teacher. His brothers, Delfeayo and Branford Marsalis are also musicians. Before entering his teenage years he was already studying formally, but had simultaneously developed an interest in jazz. The range of his playing included performing with a New Orleans marching band led by Danny Barker, and playing trumpet concertos with the New Orleans Philharmonic Orchestra. Marsalis later extended his studies at two of the USA's most prestigious musical education establishments, Berkshire Music Center at Tanglewood and the Juilliard School of Music in New York City. By the age of 19, he was already a virtuoso trumpeter, a voracious student of jazz music, history and culture, and clearly destined for great things. It was then that he joined Art Blakey's Jazz Messengers, perhaps the best of all finishing schools for post-bop jazzmen. During the next two years he matured considerably as a player, touring and recording with Blakey and also with other leading jazzmen, including Herbie Hancock and Ron Carter. He also made records under his own name and, encouraged by his success, decided to form his own permanent group. In this he was joined by his brother Branford. During 1983, he again worked with Hancock. The following year he recorded in London with Raymond Leppard and the National Philharmonic Orchestra, playing concertos by Hayden, Hummell and Leopold Mozart - a side-step which led to his becoming the unprecedented recipient of Grammy Awards for both jazz and classical albums. He next toured Japan and Europe, appearing at many festivals, on television and making many recording sessions. By 1991, and still only just turned 30, he had become one of the best- known figures on the international musical stage. Insofar as his classical work is concerned, Marsalis has been spoken of in most glowing terms. In his jazz work his sublime technical ability places him on a plateau he shares with very few others. Nevertheless, despite such extraordinary virtuosity, the emotional content of Marsalis's work often hints only lightly at the possibilities inherent in jazz. Sometimes, the undeniable skill and craftsmanship are displayed at the expense of vitality. If compared to, say, Jon Faddis, eight years his senior, or Clifford Brown, who died at the age of only 26, then there is clearly some distance to go in his development as a player of emotional profundity.

Selected albums: with Art Blakey *Recorded Live At Bubba's* (1980), with Blakey *Straight Ahead* (1981), *Wynton Marsalis*

Wynton Marsalis

(Columbia 1981), *Think Of One* (Columbia 1982), with Branford and Ellis Marsalis *Fathers And Sons* (Columbia 1982), *The Herbie Hancock Quintet* (1982), with Blakey *Keystone 3* (1982), *Hot House Flowers* (Columbia 1984), *Black Codes (From The Underground)* (Columbia 1985), *J Mood* (Columbia 1986), *Marsalis Standard Time, Volumes 1-3* (Columbia 1986), *Live At Blues Alley* (Columbia 1987), *The Majesty Of The Blues* (Columbia 1988), *Crescent City Christmas Card* (1989), *Thick In The South* (Columbia 1991), *Uptown Ruler* (Columbia 1991), *Levee Low Moan* (Columbia 1991), *Tune In Tomorrow* (Columbia 1991), *Blue Interlude* (Columbia 1992), *Citi Movement* (Columbia 1993, 2-CD), *Resolution To Swing* (Columbia 1993), *In This House, On This Morning* (Columbia 1994, 2-CD).

Marsh, Warne

b. 26 October 1927, Los Angeles, California, USA, d. 18 December 1987, Los Angeles, California, USA. Tenor saxophonist Marsh first played professionally in the early 40s with the Hollywood Canteen Kids, later working with Hoagy Carmichael's Teenagers. By the end of the decade, he had spent time in Buddy Rich's band and had also begun an important association as student and sideman of Lennie Tristano. In the late 40s and early 50s, he made a number of milestone recordings with temporary musical partners such as Lee Konitz, among them 'Wow', 'Crosscurrent' and 'Marshmallow'. The 50s and 60s saw Marsh active mainly in teaching and there

were only occasional forays into playing and recording with, among a few others, Art Pepper and Joe Albany. In the 70s he became rather more prominent, working with Supersax, Lew Tabackin and Konitz. He also toured overseas, attracting considerable attention from the more discerning members of his audiences as well as from among his fellow musicians who held him in highest regard. Also in the 70s, he recorded rather more extensively, including material from an especially successful engagement in London with Konitz. A meticulously accurate yet free-flowing improviser, Marsh was comfortable in most bebop-orientated settings. His ballad playing was especially attractive, replete with clean and highly individual phrasing which constantly and consistently demonstrated his total command of instrument and genre. He died on-stage at Donte's, a Los Angeles jazz club, in December 1987.

Selected albums: *Live In Hollywood* (Xanadu 1952), *Lee Konitz With Warne Marsh* (1955), *Jazz Of Two Cities* (1956), with Art Pepper *The Way It Was!* (1956-57), *Warne Marsh Quartet* i (1957), *Warne Marsh Quartet* ii (1958), *The Art Of Improvising Vols 1 & 2* (Revelation 1959), *New York* (1959-60), *Jazz From The East Village* (Wave 1960), *Live At The Montmartre Club* (Storyville 1965), *Ne Plus Ultra* (Hat Art 1969), *Warne Marsh Quintet* (Storyville 1975), *All Music* (Nessa 1976), with Lee Konitz *London Concert* (1976), with Lew Tabackin *Tenor Gladness* (1977), *Warne Out* (1977), *How Deep/How High* (1977-79), *Star Highs* (Criss Cross 1982), *A Ballad Album* (Criss Cross 1983), *In Norway/Sax Of A Kind* (1983),

Posthumous (Interplay 1985), *Back Home* (Criss Cross 1986), *Two Days In The Life Of...* (Storyville 1987), *Music For Prancing* (Criss Cross 1988), *Noteworth* (Discovery 1988), *For The Time Being* (1987), *Newly Warne* (Storyville 1990).

Marshall, John

b. 28 August 1941, London, England. Marshall is one of the most impressive drummers Britain has produced, equally powerful, flexible and reliable in rock, jazz or fusion. He played at school, but became more heavily involved with music while reading psychology at university. He studied drums privately with Allan Ganley and Philly Joe Jones, and worked with Alexis Korner's Blues Incorporated (1964), Graham Collier (1965-70), Nucleus (of which he was a founder member with Ian Carr in 1969, and which he returned to in 1982), Mike Gibbs, Jack Bruce (1971-72), and, in February 1972, he began his long-term membership of Soft Machine. On leaving the band he joined Eberhard Weber's Colours (1977-81). He has been a regular associate of John Surman over many years, and has also worked with Michael Garrick, Keith Tippett, Chris McGregor, John McLaughlin, John Taylor, Graham Bond, Mike Westbrook, Tubby Hayes, Jaspar Van't Hof, Kenny Wheeler, Gil Evans, Alan Skidmore, Ronnie Scott and many others, including those in the contemporary classical field and in session work.

Marshall, Kaiser

b. Joseph Marshall, 11 June 1899, Savannah, Georgia, USA, d. 3 January 1948. While he was still a child Marshall's family moved to Boston, Massachusetts, where he began playing drums, tutored by George L. Stone. In 1923, by now in New York, he joined Fletcher Henderson's band during its rise to fame and prominence but left in 1930 just as Henderson entered his headiest period. In the late 20s, Marshall made some landmark recordings with Louis Armstrong's small studio groups. A solid reliable drummer, in the late 30s and early 40s he found regular work, playing and recording with many leading figures of the jazz world including Duke Ellington, Cab Calloway, Wild Bill Davison, Art Hodes, Sidney Bechet and Bunk Johnson. Marshall's work was thought of sufficiently highly for him to be called upon to deputize for Chick Webb when the more famous drummer was too sick to play all night with his own band.
Compilations: with Fletcher Henderson *A Study In Frustration* (1923-38), *The Louis Armstrong Legend Vols 1-4* (1925-29).

Marshall, Wendell

b. 24 October 1920, St. Louis, Missouri, USA. He took up the bass thanks to the example of his cousin, Jimmy Blanton, who was also his first tutor. Although Wendell played regularly in his younger years, including brief stints with Lionel Hampton, Stuff Smith and others, he did not fully enter the bigtime until the late 40s when he moved to New York. Briefly with Mercer Ellington, he joined Duke Ellington in 1948 where he remained until 1955. During the rest of the 50s he worked with many important jazz artists including Carmen McRae,

Hank Jones and Art Blakey. By the end of the decade, however, he was turning more and more to work in New York theatre pit bands where he remained until his retirement from regular playing in the late 60s. A gifted soloist with a full tone, Marshall's solid rhythmic playing and adaptable style made him a valuable member of any band in which he played.
Albums: with Duke Ellington *Seattle Concert* (1952), *Duke Ellington Plays Duke Ellington* (1953), *Wendell Marshall With The Billy Byers Orchestra* (1955), with Mary Lou Williams *A Keyboard History* (1955), with Carmen McRae *By Special Request* (1955).

Martin, Claire

b. 6 September 1967, Wimbledon, London, England. In 1982, after spending 10 years at stage school, Martin became resident singer at the Savoy Hotel in Bournemouth. In 1987 she sang on cruise liners for Cunard, including the *QE II*. In 1990 she visited the USA where she studied with Marilyn J. Johnson in New York. In 1991 she returned to the UK to form her own band, playing many prestigious London jazz venues including Ronnie Scott's, the 100 Club and the Pizza On The Park, and also toured extensively. In 1992 she played a return engagement at Ronnie Scott's and also appeared at the Glasgow and Sheffield Jazz Festivals. In addition to leading her own band, Martin also works regularly with Mick Hutton's group, Straight Face, which includes Steve Argüelles and Iain Ballamy, with Ray Gelato's Giants Of Jive, and with a free-music band led by John Stevens. She has also recorded with Bobby Wellins. A remarkably versatile singer, Martin's repertoire ranges happily from R&B to free music, incorporating along the way the great standards of which she is an accomplished interpreter. Despite her youth, Martin's work displays exceptional maturity which, allied to her warm, sensual sound, makes her performances a constant delight. Her choice of musical associates (her own group comprises pianist Jonathan Gee, bassist Arnie Somogyi and Clark Tracey) reveals her commitment to jazz. Although still at the beginning of her career, Martin has already made it clear that she is one of the most important new singers to emerge on the jazz scene in recent years.
Albums: *The Waiting Game* (Linn 1991), with Bobby Wellins *Remember Me* (1992), *Devil May Care* (Linn 1993), *Old Boyfriends* (Linn 1994).

Martyn, Barry

b. Barry Martin Godfrey, 23 February 1941, London, England. Martyn began playing drums in his early teens and was soon leading his own band and making records. Playing in the New Orleans tradition, Martyn's musical interest led him to visit New Orleans in the early 60s where he studied with Josiah 'Cié' Frazier. Martyn recorded in New Orleans with many leading local jazzmen and also organized and led international tours by major figures such as George Lewis and Albert Nicholas. Resident in the USA since the early 70s, Martyn has continued to play and record New Orleans jazz to a very high standard with the likes of Barney Bigard and the Eagle Brass Band. In addition to bands under his own name Martyn was

Claire Martin

also leader of the Legends Of Jazz, a group of elderly but still musically active New Orleans jazzmen. Deeply committed to preserving the great tradition of New Orleans jazz, over the years Martyn has done much more than play and record. He formed his own recording company, writes extensively, and, perhaps most importantly, has recorded for archive purposes numerous interviews with New Orleans jazz survivors.
Albums: *Barney Bigard And The Pelican Trio* (1976), with the Eagle Brass Band *Last Of The Line* (1983).

Masso, George

b. 17 November 1926, Cranston, Rhode Island, USA. Coming from a musical background, Masso began on trumpet, then became a competent multi-instrumentalist, playing piano and vibraphone. However, it was hearing a Lou McGarity trombone solo on Benny Goodman's recording of 'Yours' which determined his final choice of instrument. Despite his background, and a two-year stint with Jimmy Dorsey in the late 40s, Masso opted for a career as a teacher of music. In 1973, with his family grown up, he decided to return to playing after persistent needling from Bobby Hackett. He spent a year and a half with Goodman's Sextet, played with the World's Greatest Jazz Band and on some of Buck Clayton's later Jam Sessions. Since then, Masso has toured extensively, usually as a single, sometimes in harness with Scott Hamilton, Warren Vaché, Spike Robinson, Bobby Rosengarden and other mainstream artists, playing clubs and festivals around the world. A fluent and always tasteful musician, Masso in the 80s and 90s is more than making up for his 25-year absence from the scene.
Albums: *Buck Clayton Jam Session* (1975), *Choice NYC 'Bone* (1978), *Dialogue At Condon's* (1979), *A Swinging Case Of Masso-ism* (1980), *Pieces Of Eight* (1982), *No Frills, Just Music* (1983).

Maupin, Bennie

b. 29 August 1940, Detroit, Michigan, USA. Maupin played saxophone in high school before studying music at the Detroit Institute for Music Art. He came to New York, in 1963 making his living from commercial music while playing with saxophonists Marion Brown and Pharoah Sanders. In 1966, he played with Roy Haynes and in 1968 joined the Horace Silver Quintet. By 1969, drummer Jack DeJohnette had introduced him to Miles Davis who made his bass clarinet improvisations an integral part of *Bitches Brew*. He went on to play with pianists Chick Corea and Andrew Hill before joining Herbie Hancock's sextet in 1970. He played with the band which recorded the influential *Headhunters,* and continued with Hancock when the sextet became the funk band. He settled in Los Angeles where he has worked ever since.
Albums: with Miles Davis *Bitches Brew* (1969), with Chick Corea *Sundance* (1969), with Andrew Hill *One For One* (1970), with Herbie Hancock *Mwandishi* (1971), *Crossings* (1972), *Sextant* (1973), *Headhunters* (1973), *The Jewel In The Lotus* (1974), *VSOP* (1976), *Slow Traffic To The Right* (1977).

Mauro, Turk

b. Mauro Turso, 11 June 1944, New York City, New York, USA. Mauro began playing clarinet while still in school and was largely self-taught. By the age of 15, he was sufficiently proficient both on this instrument and the alto saxophone to obtain his union card. In 1960, he joined Red Allen's quartet, playing at clubs in Queens and Harlem. After graduation, Mauro decided to become a professional musician and around this time switched to tenor saxophone. Not surprisingly for a musician of his generation, he was attracted to jazz-rock, though between these gigs he would sit in at the Half Note club with jazzmen such as Zoot Sims, Al Cohn, Nat Pierce and Dave Frishberg. In the late 60s, he played at holiday resorts in upstate New York - originally as a sideman - but later leading a danceband playing Latin American music. Subsequently, he led a small group at the Half Note, then worked with Richie Cole before becoming resident at Sonny's Place, a club on Long Island where he remained for more than a dozen years. He found time, however, for appearances with the bands of Dizzy Gillespie, Buddy Rich and others. Of greater long-term significance were some appearances with Billy Mitchell, for whom he had to play baritone saxophone. Gradually, over the years, Mauro became steadily more proficient on the baritone until it eventually became his principal instrument. In the early 80s, he worked solo in New York and also toured Europe, both as a single performer and with Cole. He appeared in Paris and London and also at various festivals. Back in New York in the mid-80s, he had to take work outside of music to help make ends meet; but, in 1987, he decided to return to Europe and settle in Paris. Although of an age to have come under more modern influences, Mauro's chief musical mentors are great mainstreamers such as tenor saxophonists Ben Webster, Coleman Hawkins, Lester Young, Stan Getz and Dexter Gordon - though he also acknowledges debts to Sims, Cohn, Mitchell, Gene Ammons and others with whom he has worked. As such a list indicates Mauro still thinks of himself as a tenor player. Perhaps this is what has allowed him to develop an interesting and highly distinctive baritone style. Turk Mauro's playing is forceful, fiery and committed, and his occasional vocal excursions show a tough, no-nonsense approach and considerable rhythmic vitality.
Selected albums: *The Underdog* (Storyville 1978), *The Heavyweight* (Phoenix 1980), *Live In Paris* (Bloomdido 1987), *Jazz Party* (Bloomdido 1993), *Plays Love Songs* (Bloomdido 1993).

Maxwell, Jimmy

b. 9 January 1917, Stockton, California, USA. After extensive studies in all aspects of brass playing, Maxwell established himself as a major-league trumpet player. Among his first professional engagements was one in the early 30s with Gil Evans, who was raised in Maxwell's home town. By the end of the decade he had played in the trumpet sections of several leading dance and swing bands, including those of Jimmy Dorsey and Benny Goodman. His stint with Goodman lasted from 1939-43, when he joined CBS. During the 30 years this job lasted he found time to work with Woody Herman, Count Basie, Gerry Mulligan, Duke Ellington, Quincy Jones and others. Among his Ellington engagements was an informal appearance on stage at the famous Newport concert in 1956, when Willie Cook was late returning to the stand. In the 70s he played with the New York Jazz Repertory Company under Dick Hyman, with Lionel Hampton's All-Star Big Band and with Chuck Israels's National Jazz Ensemble. After Ellington's death, he also played in the band which continued for a while under Mercer Ellington. Since the late 70s, Maxwell has employed his early training and subsequent breadth of playing experience to good effect as a teacher. He has also published a trumpet manual.

Albums: with Benny Goodman *Benny And Sid "Roll 'Em"* (1941), with Chuck Israels *National Jazz Ensemble* (1976), *Strong Trumpet* (1977), *Let's Fall In Love* (c.1980).

McBee, Cecil

b. 19 May 1935, Tulsa, Oklahoma, USA. A full-toned bassist who creates rich, singing phrases in a wide range of contemporary jazz contexts, McBee studied clarinet at school, but switched to bass at the age of 17, playing in local nightclubs. He gained a degree in music from Ohio Central State University, then spent two years in the army, conducting the band at Fort Knox. Moving to Detroit in 1962, he worked with Paul Winter (1963-64), then went to New York and played with Jackie McLean (1964), Wayne Shorter (1965-66), Charles Lloyd (1966), Yusef Lateef (1967-69) and Alice Coltrane (1969-72). He established his own group in 1975, but, as one of the most in-demand sidemen in jazz, has continued to work with others, including Chico Freeman, Freddie Hubbard, Grachan Moncur III, Miles Davis, Bobby Hutcherson, Charles Tolliver, Pharoah Sanders, Lonnie Liston Smith, Sonny Rollins, Michael White, JoAnne Brackeen, Horace Tapscott, Anthony Braxton, Abdullah Ibrahim, Buddy Tate and Harry 'Sweets' Edison.

Albums: *Mutima* (Strata East 1975), *Music From The Source* (Enja 1977), *Compassion* (Enja 1977), *Alternate Spaces* (India Navigation 1979), *Flying Out* (India Navigation 1982).

McCall, Mary Ann

b. 4 May 1919, Philadelphia, Pennsylvania, USA, d. 14 December 1994, Los Angeles, California, USA. McCall's early career was spent singing with the bands of Buddy Morrow, Tommy Dorsey, Woody Herman and Charlie Barnet. During this period, which ended in 1940, she was regarded as an average big band singer. Her return to the spotlight, when she rejoined Herman in 1946, saw her maturing and by the time she left the band in 1950, she was an able, original and forthright jazz singer. She recorded with several leading beboppers in the late 40s and early 50s, including Howard McGhee, Dexter Gordon, Charlie Ventura and her then husband, Al Cohn. During the next three decades, McCall worked extensively as a soloist, making occasional records with jazz musicians such as Jake Hanna and Nat Pierce and singing in jazz clubs and at festivals.

Albums: *An Evening With Charlie Ventura And Mary Ann*

McCall (1954), *Easy Living* (1956), *Detour To The Moon* (1958), with Jake Hanna *Kansas City Express* (1976), with Nat Pierce *5400 North* (1978).

McCall, Steve

b. 30 September 1933, Chicago, Illinois, USA, d. 25 May 1989. McCall studied music at conservatory and university, though his first professional gig was with blues singer Lucky Carmichael. In 1964, he recorded with soul/jazz pianist Ramsey Lewis. McCall was not only a founder member of the AACM, but also a member of its predecessor, the legendary Experimental Band. He brought to both years of experience with blues, dance and show bands, having worked with Gene Ammons, Dexter Gordon and Arthur Prysock. His incisive, precise drumming always had the ability to boil up when necessary. In Chicago, he played with Muhal Richard Abrams and Joseph Jarman. Between 1967 and 1970 he lived in Paris, where he played and recorded with Anthony Braxton on his recordings for the BYG label. When the Chicago musicians played in New York in 1971 under the name of Creative Construction Company, McCall again played drums, relating to the established New York bassist Richard Davis with no problems at all. McCall's most visible gig after that was with Henry Threadgill in the trio Air, a group that rapidly became festival favourites. McCall supplied magically sensitive percussion to the group, so important to their collective sound that when he left in 1982 - to be replaced by Pheeroan akLaff - they changed their name to New Air. He worked, too, with Marion Brown, Chico Freeman, Arthur Blythe and David Murray's Octet: McCall's creative drumming, with its irreverent enthusiasm for past styles, was the ideal accompaniment for Murray's great 'jazz consolidation' band of the 80s. He returned to Chicago later in the 80s, giving solo concerts and leading his own sextet.

Albums: with Anthony Braxton *B-X/N-O-1-47A* (1969), with Marion Brown *Geechee Recollections* (1973), with Brown *Sweet Flying Earth* (1974), with Creative Construction Company *CCC* (1975, rec 1970), with CCC *CCC Vol II* (1976, rec 1970), with Muhal Richard Abrams *I-OQA+19* (1979), with David Murray Octet *Ming* (1980), with Murray Octet *Home* (1981), with Murray *Murray's Steps* (1982).

McCandless, Paul

b. 24 March 1947, Indiana, Pennsylvania, USA. The distinctive, curling sound of Paul McCandless on English horn, oboe, saxophones, flute, clarinet, musette (a French bagpipe from the last century) and wind-driven synthesizers has done much to define the fusion music of Oregon. The nucleus of the group, Ralph Towner, Collin Walcott, and McCandless, came together as members of the influential Paul Winter Consort. Just as the part-time nature of Oregon has enabled its members to undertake other projects, so, too, has McCandless taken that opportunity to work with Art Lande and David Samuels; he also re-united with ex-Consort cellist, David Darling in the Gallery project.

Selected albums: with Cyrus *Cyrus* (1971), with Oregon *Music* of Another Present Era (1973), Distant Hills (1974), Winter Light (1974), In Concert (1975), Friends (1975), Together (1977), Violin (1978), Out Of The Woods (1978), Roots In The Sky (1979), In Performance (1980), Oregon (1983), Crossing (1984), Ecotopia (1987), 45th Parallel (1989), Always, Never, And Forever (1991), Premonition (1993).

McClure, Ron

b. 22. November 1941, New Haven, Connecticut, USA. McClure started playing the accordion when he was five years old, and played the piano at high school. He studied the bass at the Julius Hartt Conservatory in Hartford, and when he left in 1963 went on to study composition with Hall Overton and Don Sebesky. By the time he joined Charles Lloyd in 1967, he had played with Buddy Rich, Herbie Mann and Wynton Kelly backing Wes Montgomery. Lloyd's enormously successful group took McClure on worldwide tours before he returned to San Francisco, where he was a founder member of the fusion group Fourth Way. Later on, he played with the group Blood, Sweat And Tears before settling to studio work in New York. McClure played with musicians as diverse as vocalists Tony Bennett, Dionne Warwick and the Pointer Sisters, and instrumentalists Thelonious Monk, Gary Burton and Joe Henderson. In 1985, he joined the group of Al DiMeola and then worked with Michel Petrucciani and George Russell. His firm bass lines are characterized by rhythmic fills on open strings against the fretboard. He has taught at the Berklee College Of Music (1971) and Long Island University (1983-85).
Albums: with Charles Lloyd Love In (1967), Charles Lloyd In The Soviet Union (1967), with Fourth Way Sun And Moon (1969), with Joe Henderson In Pursuit Of Blackness (1971), Descendants (Ken Music 1992), Yesterday's Tomorrow (EMP 1992).

McConnell, Rob

b. 14 February 1935, London, Ontario, Canada. After playing valve trombone in various bands in his homeland during the mid- and late 50s, McConnell joined fellow-Canadian Maynard Ferguson's New York Band in 1964. Despite the attention he attracted there, he returned to Canada to work with the Phil Nimmons band; he also played in studio orchestras and wrote many arrangements. Towards the end of the 60s he formed a band, the Boss Brass, playing his own charts of currently popular music for a 15-piece brass and rhythm group. In the early 70s McConnell added a reed section and, with the band's musical policy slanted strongly towards jazz, he made a series of outstanding albums. Among the musicians in the band were Sam Noto, Guido Basso, Don Thompson and Ed Bickert. Apart from its own albums, the band also made records with Singers Unlimited, the Hi-Lo's, Phil Woods and Mel Tormé. He also made Old Friends/New Music, using a sextet drawn from the big band. Despite the popularity of the Boss Brass and the success of its albums, by the late 80s McConnell decided it was time to make changes. He accepted a teaching post at the Dick Grove Music School in Los Angeles,

where he relocated at the end of 1988. In the early 90s, he was active in the southern California jazz scene, playing with various rehearsal bands and seriously considering the reformation of his own big band. An excellent arranger with a real affection for hard-swinging, contemporary, big band jazz, McConnell has made an outstanding contribution to the development of this area of music. His decision to enter teaching (while stopping, at least temporarily) the flow of outstanding big band albums, should ensure that a future generation of musicians will develop some of the theories he has already put into practice.
Albums: The Rob McConnell-Guido Basso Quintet (1963), Rob McConnell And His Orchestra (1965), The Boss Brass i (1968), The Boss Brass ii (1972), The Best Damn Band In The Land (1974), Satin Sheets (1975), The Jazz Album (1976), Big Band Jazz (1977), Nobody Does It Better (1977-78), The Boss Brass Again (1978), Are Ya Dancin' Disco (1979), Present Perfect (MPS 1979), The Brass Connection (1980), Live In Digital (Sea Breeze 1980), Tribute (1980), All In Good Time (1982), Atras Da Porta (1983), Old Friends, New Music (Unisson 1984), All In Good Time (Innovation 1984), Boss Brass And Woods (1985), Again (Pausa 1985), Big Band Jazz (Pausa 1985), Mel Tormé/Rob McConnell (1986), Boss Of The Boss Brass (1988), The Rob McConnell Jive Five (Concord 1990), The Brass Is Back (Concord 1991), Live At The 1990 Concord Jazz Festival (Concord 1991), Brassy And Sassy (Concord 1992), Our 25th Year (Bellaphon 1993).

McCorkle, Susannah

b. 1 January 1949, Berkeley, California, USA. In the late 60s, McCorkle lived for a while in Paris. It was during this sojourn that she heard Billie Holiday on records and decided to take up singing. Multi-lingual, she lived for a while in Italy, working as a translator and taking any singing jobs she could find. In 1972, she moved to the UK, singing in clubs and pubs and learning about what she had determined would be her future career. She also made two albums which, although well received, enjoyed only limited circulation. In the late 70s, McCorkle returned to the USA and settled in New York, where a five-month engagement at the Cookery in Greenwich Village brought her to wider public attention and elicited rave reviews from critics. She continued to record during the 80s, and her maturing style and the darkening timbre of her voice greatly enhanced her performances. By the early 90s, with the release by Concord Records of No More Blues and Sabia, two enormously successful albums, McCorkle was poised to make her name known to the wider world. Indeed, her linguistic abilities, skills which enabled her to translate lyrics, notably the Brazilian songs on Sabia, make her a likely candidate for international success. In the meantime, she is consolidating her status in jazz with awards, including the 1989 New York Music Award, and is being recorded by the Smithsonian Institute, the youngest singer ever to be included in their popular music series. A graduate of the University of California at Berkeley, McCorkle has also had several short stories published and, in 1991, was working on her first novel.

Albums: *The Music Of Harry Warren* (1976), *There Will Never Be Another You* (Retrospect 1976), *The Quality Of Mercer* (Black Lion 1977), *Over The Rainbow - Songs Of E.Y. Harburg* (1980), *The People That You Never Get To Love* (1982), *How Do You Keep The Music Playing?* (c.1982), *Thanks For The Memory - Songs Of Leo Robin* (1986), *As Time Goes By* (1987), *Dream* (1987), *No More Blues* (Cocord 1989), *Sabia* (Concord 1990), *I'll Take Romance* (Concord 1992), *From Bessie To Brasil* (Cocord 1993).

McEachern, Murray

b. 16 August 1915, Toronto, Canada, d. 28 April 1982. After learning to play a wide range of musical instruments, McEachern began playing in dancebands during the early 30s. In 1936, he joined the Benny Goodman Orchestra, where he played trombone. After Goodman he was with the Casa Loma Orchestra, playing trombone and alto saxophone; following this there was a short spell with Paul Whiteman. By 1942 McEachern was settled on the west coast and for much of the next three decades he was active in film and television studio work. In 1972, he took the lead alto chair when Bill Berry reformed his big band on moving to Los Angeles, but soon afterwards, McEachern went on the road as leader of the reformed Tommy Dorsey band - this time, naturally enough, playing trombone. A remarkably polished player on trombone with a contrastingly strong and gutsy saxophone style, McEachern was one of the outstanding sidemen in the history of big band music.

Compilations: *The Indispensable Benny Goodman Vols. 1/2* (1935-36), *The Indispensable Benny Goodman Vols. 3/4* (1936-37).

McFarland, Gary

b. 23 October 1933, Los Angeles, California, USA, d. 3 November 1971, New York City, New York, USA. McFarland was a vibraphonist, arranger and orchestra leader. He moved to Grants Pass in Oregon when he was 15 years old, and became interested in jazz while studying at the University of Oregon. He began to play the vibes during a stint in the US Army at Fort Sill, Oklahoma, in 1954, and, three years later, joined a group led by Santiago Gonzalez. Encouraged by musicians such as John Lewis, Buddy Montgomery and fellow vibes player Cal Tjader, McFarland won scholarships to the School of Jazz in Lennox and the Berklee College Of Music in Boston (1959). In the early 60s he blossomed into a fine young jazz writer, contributing arrangements and compositions to albums including those of the Modern Jazz Quintet, Gerry Mulligan, and John Lewis. He also wrote all the charts, and conducted the orchestra for Anita O'Day's *All The Sad Young Men* - although, according to O'Day, she sang to pre-recorded tapes, and did not meet McFarland until four or five years after the record had been released! Presumably he did get personally involved when working on albums with Stan Getz, Bill Evans and other leading musicians. In 1961, he recorded his own jazz version of the Frank Loesser-Abe Burrows Broadway Musical, *How To Succeed In Business Without Really Trying*, and subse-

quent releases included *Soft Samba*, *Point Of Departure*, *Profiles*, *Simpatico*, *Tijuana Jazz* and *America the Beautiful* and *Does The Sun Real, Shine On The Moon?* for the Skye Label, of which he was the co-founder. During the mid-60s, McFarland toured with his own quintet, and, in 1966, wrote the score for the Deborah Kerr-David Niven thriller movie, *Eye Of The Devil*. His latest film music was for another 'whodunnit', *Who Killed Mary What'sername?* in 1971. He died in November of that year. The cause of death was given as a heart attack, although it is rumoured that methadone, a synthetic drug similar to morphine, was put in his drink by a 'joker'.

McFerrin, Bobby

b. 11 March 1950, New York City, New York, USA. To call Bobby McFerrin a jazz vocalist is hardly to do him justice, for when McFerrin performs - he usually appears solo in lengthy concerts-he uses his entire body as a sound-box, beating noises out of his slender frame while emitting a constant accompaniment of guttural noises, clicks and popping sounds. To all this he adds a vocal technique that owes a slight debt to the bop vocalist Betty Carter and her daring swoops and scat vocals. McFerrin was brought up in a musical family- both his parents are opera singers, his father performing on the film sound-track of *Porgy And Bess* in 1959 - but his main jazz influence came from the jazz-rock of Miles Davis' *Bitches Brew* album. Training as a pianist at the Juilliard School and later at Sacramento State College, he worked first as an accompanist, then as a pianist and singer during the 70s. He came to public notice in 1979, when he performed in New York with the singer Jon Hendricks, from whom he learnt much, but it was his accompanied appearance at the 1981 Kool Jazz Festival which brought him widespread acclaim. By 1983, he had perfected his solo style of wordless, vocal improvisations. His debut album contained a dramatic reworking of Van Morrison's 'Moondance', while *The Voice* mixed his fondness for pop classics - this time, the Beatles' 'Blackbird' - with more adventurous pieces, notably the self-descriptive 'I'm My Own Walkman'. The 1988 album *Simple Pleasures* shows off his wide range with its mixture of pop classics and self-composed material. The highlight of the album was his idiosyncratic version of Cream's 'Sunshine Of Your Love', complete with a vocal electric guitar.

Albums: *Bobby McFerrin* (Elektra 1982), *The Voice* (Elektra 1984), *Spontaneous Inventions* (Blue Note 1986), *Simple Pleasures* (EMI Manhattan 1988), *Medicine Man* (EMI Manhattan 1990), with Chick Corea *Play* (Blue Note 1992).

McGann, Bernie

b. 22 June 1937, Sydney, New South Wales, Australia. Arguably Australia's premier saxophonist, McGann began on drums, taking lessons from his father, who was a professional musician. He switched to alto saxophone in 1955, initially inspired by Paul Desmond, though later influences were Sonny Rollins and *avant garde* players such as Ornette Coleman and Albert Ayler. In the late 50s, McGann began a long association with drummer John Pochée, and in 1964, joined him in a

Bobby McFerrin

group called the Heads which also featured pianist Dave MacRae. McGann played regularly at Sydney's El Roco club, but when it closed in 1969, he found jazz gigs extremely scarce and for a while worked as a postman. From 1975, he played in Pochée's group, the Last Straw, and also led his own trio into the 80s, recording with Sonny Stitt on the latter's 1981 Australian tour. He has worked with other visiting Americans, notably Dewey Redman and Red Rodney, continues to perform both with the Last Straw and Pochée's big band, Ten Part Invention, and still leads his own small groups, which usually feature Pochée and bassist Lloyd Swanton. Although active since the 50s and a striking soloist, whose lines have the gnarled beauty of a truly original talent, McGann has rarely recorded. *At Long Last,* on the Emanem label, was his first album as leader after 30 years on the scene and remains his best to date - a twisting, eloquent bebop spiced with modernity.
Albums: *With The Ted Vining Trio* (1986, rec 1983), *At Long Last* (1987, rec 1983), *Kindred Spirits* (1987), *The Last Straw* (1991, rec 1987), *Ten Part Invention* (1991, rec 1987), *Ugly Beauty* (1992).

McGarity, Lou

b. 22 July 1917, Athens, Georgia, USA, d. 28 August 1971. After playing in dancebands in and around Atlanta, Georgia, trombonist McGarity moved north. In 1938, he joined Ben Bernie's popular recording unit and, two years later, became a member of the Benny Goodman band. After military service in World War II, McGarity again played with Goodman, then divided his time between west coast studio work and playing in small jazz groups, often those under the nominal leadership of Eddie Condon, Yank Lawson and Bob Haggart. In the 60s, he played with Bob Crosby And The Bobcats and was with Lawson and Haggart in the World's Greatest Jazz Band. His warm sound and sometimes aggressive style made McGarity a welcome member of any dixieland-orientated jazz band. He worked until the day of his death in August 1971.
Albums: with Lawson-Haggart *Jelly Roll's Jazz* (1951), with Eddie Condon *Jammin' At Condon's* (1954), *Blue Lou* (1959), *Jazz Master* (1970), *In Celebration* (IAJRC 1989).

McGhee, Howard

b. 6 March 1918, Tulsa, Oklahoma, USA, d. 17 July 1987. During the late 30s, McGhee played trumpet in several territory bands in the Midwest before moving to Detroit, where he became well known in that city's lively jazz scene. He first enjoyed major success with Lionel Hampton in 1941; however, he quickly moved on, joining Andy Kirk, for whom he wrote arrangements and was featured soloist. Although he was to work in other big bands of the early 40s, including Charlie Barnet's and Georgie Auld's, McGhee soon became most closely associated with bebop. From the mid-40s he could be heard playing in clubs and on records with Charlie Parker, Fats Navarro and others. He was present on the notorious Parker recording date for Dial which produced 'Lover Man' and was, in fact, largely responsible for salvaging the session from potential disaster when Parker broke down. During the 50s, McGhee's career was damaged by drug addiction and his private life was blighted by some of the worst excesses of racism: his marriage to a white woman resulted in his wife being beaten up and he himself was framed on drugs-related charges. However, he survived and, in the early 60s, was making records with Teddy Edwards, George Coleman and others and later returned to regular playing. A big band he formed at this time and a 1969 appearance at the Newport Jazz Festival with Buddy Tate helped to prove that he still had talent to spare. One of the most melodic of bebop trumpeters, McGhee was an important influence on two major figures, Navarro and Clifford Brown, both of whom, ironically, were to die many years before him.

Albums: *The Howard McGhee Sextet With Milt Jackson* (Savoy 1948), *The Howard McGhee All Stars* (1949), *Maggie* (Savoy 1950), *The Howard McGhee Korean All Stars* (1951), *The Howard McGhee Sextet With Gigi Gryce* (1953), *That Bop Thing* (1955), *Howard McGhee And His Orchestra* (1960), *The Howard McGhee Quintet* (1960), *Dusty Blue* (Affinity 1960), with Teddy Edwards *Together Again!* (1961), *The Bop Master* (Affinity 1961), *Maggie's Back In Town* (Original Jazz Classics 1961), *Shades Of Blue/Sharp Edge* (Black Lion 1961), *House Warmin'* (1962), *Cookin' Time* (Hep Jazz 1966), *Here Comes Freddy* (Sonet 1976), with Charlie Rouse *Jazzbrothers* (1977), *Just Be There* (Steeplechase 1977), *Home Run* (1978), *Live At Emerson's* (Zim 1978), with Edwards *Young At Heart* (1979), *Trumpet At Tempo* (Spotlite 1983). Compilations: with Andy Kirk *Walkin' And Swingin'* (1942), with Charlie Parker *The Legendary Dial Masters Vol. 1* (1946-47), *Howard McGhee And His Band* (1945), *Trumpet At Tempo* (1946).

McGregor, Chris

b. 24 December 1936, Somerset West, South Africa, d. 27 May 1990. In his early years in the Transkei, McGregor studied classical piano music, but was more significantly affected by the hymns in his father's Church of Scotland mission and the music of the Xhosa people. At the 1962 Johannesburg Jazz Festival, he selected five of the best players (Mongezi Feza, Dudu Pukwana, Nick Moyake, Johnny Dyani and Louis Moholo) and invited them to join him in a new band. Thus, the legendary Blue Notes were created. Apartheid made it impossible for them, as a mixed-race band, to work legally in South Africa, and so, while touring Europe in 1964, they decided not to return home. After a year in Switzerland, they settled in London, where, evolving into the Chris McGregor Group (with Ronnie Beer replacing Moyake on tenor), they made a huge impact with their exhilarating mixture of free jazz and kwela, the South African Township dance music. During that period McGregor established a big band for gigs at Ronnie Scott's Old Place and, in 1970, he formed a regular big band, the Brotherhood Of Breath. He moved to Aquitaine, France, in 1974, often playing solo gigs, although from time to time he revived the Brotherhood. McGregor was an exciting piano player whose style encompassed the power of Cecil Taylor and the gentleness of African folk melodies, but it was as leader of a series of joyful, powerful bands that he made his main reputation. He once told Valerie Wilmer, 'Real musical freedom is the ability to look inside your own personal experience and select from it at will.' He died of lung cancer in May 1990.

Albums: *The African Sound* (1963), *Very Urgent* (1968), *Brotherhood Of Breath* (1971), *Brotherhood* (1972), *Live At Willisau* (1975), *Blue Notes For Mongezi* (1976), *Piano Song Volumes 1 & 2* (1977), *Procession* (Ogun 1977), *Blue Notes In Concert* (1978), *In His Good Time* (Ogun 1979), *Yes, Please* (1982), *Blue Notes For Johnny* (Ogun 1987), *Country Cooking* (Venture 1990), *Grandmother's Teaching* (ITM 1991).

McGriff, Jimmy

b. James Herrell, 3 April 1936, Philadelphia, Pennsylvania, USA. Encouraged by a musical home environment (both his parents were pianists), by the time he left school, McGriff played not only piano but bass, vibes, drums and saxophone. He played with Archie Shepp, Reggie Workman, Charles Earland and Donald Bailey in his youth, but after two years as an MP in the Korean War he decided to take up law enforcement rather than music as a career. This did not satisfy him in the event, and he began moonlighting as a bassist, backing blues stars like Big Maybelle. He left the police force and studied organ at Combe College, Philadelphia, and New York's Juilliard. He also took private lessons with Jimmy Smith, Richard 'Groove' Holmes and Milt Buckner, as well as from classical organist Sonny Gatewood. His career first took off with the single 'I Got A Woman' in 1962, and he had a string of hits released through the legendary Sue label. During this decade Jimmy was arguably the crown prince of the soul jazz organ movement (the King being Jimmy Smith). His stabbing style and shrill tone was much copied, particularly in the UK with the rise of the beat R&B scene. Georgie Fame and Brian Auger were greatly influenced by McGriff. His memorable 'All About My Girl' remains one of his finest compositions, and has become a minor classic. In the late 80s he experienced a revival in his commercial success, collaborating with Hank Crawford on record and in concert. He tours for most of the year, still concentrating on Hammond organ, but also using synthesizers. A fine, bluesy player, he helped popularize a jazz-flavoured style of R&B which is still gathering adherents and is influential in London clubland's so-called 'acid jazz' circles.

Selected albums: *I've Got A Woman* (1962), *Gospel Time* (c.1963), *Topkapi* (1964), *One Of Mine* (c.60s), *At The Apollo* (c.60s), *At The Organ* (c.60s), *Blues For Mister Jimmy* (Stateside 1965), *The Worm* (1968), *The Last Minute* (1983), *The Countdown* (Milestone 1983), *Skywalk* (1985), *State Of The Art* (Milestone 1986), with Hank Crawford *Soul Survivors* (Milestone 1986), *Fly Dude* (1987), *The Starting Five* (1987), *Jimmy McGriff Featuring Hank Crawford* (LRC 1990), *Georgia On My Mind* (LRC 1990), *Tribute To Basie* (LRC 1991), *Funkiest Little Band In The Land* (LRC 1992), *Electric Funk* (Blue Note 1993). Compilation: *A Toast To Jimmy McGriff's Golden Classics* (Collectable 1989).

McIntyre, 'Kalaparush' Maurice

b. 24 March 1936, Clarksville, Arkansas, USA. McIntyre's family moved to Chicago when he was six weeks old, and he grew up on the city's south side. He began to play drums at the age of seven, and clarinet two years later, but he did not really study music seriously until his mid-teens, when he concentrated on tenor saxophone. After a drugs problems in the early 60s, he worked on the Chicago blues scene - performing with Little Milton, recording with J.B. Hutto - and also joined Muhal Richard Abrams's Experimental Band, becoming one of the first members of the AACM in 1965. He played with Roscoe Mitchell's sextet (*Sound*) and with Abrams (*Levels And Degrees Of Light*) before forming his own group, the Light, and recording his first session as leader in 1969 (*Humility In The Light Of The Creator*). That same year he underwent a form of spiritual conversion and changed his name to Kalaparush (or Kalaparusha) Ahrah Difda (or Defda), though subsequent recordings have usually been credited to Kalaparush(a) Maurice McIntyre. He later spent time in New York, recording there for the *Wildflower* series of compilations (volume 1); but he was mostly based in Chicago throughout the 70s and 80s, during which time he played with a variety of artists, including Abrams again, Julius Hemphill, Jerome Cooper, Warren Smith, Roland Alexander, Sonelius Smith and Wilbur Morris. In 1982, he replaced 'Light' Henry Huff in the Ethnic Heritage Ensemble, recording with them on *Welcome* (but did not play on the later *Ancestral Song*). A robust, inventive tenor saxophonist, McIntyre cites his chief influences as Sonny Rollins, Charlie Parker, John Coltrane and Sam Rivers, but he has evolved a personal, rhythmically assured style, bristling with authority on his own *Ram's Run*, waxing more tenderly on *Welcome*. Regrettably, he is one of several AACM stalwarts who has not been recorded as frequently as their talent deserves.

Albums: *Humility In The Light Of The Creator* (1969), *Forces And Feelings* (1972), *Peace And Blessings* (1979), *Ram's Run* (1982), with the Ethnic Heritage Ensemble *Welcome* (1983).

McIntyre, Ken

b. 7 September 1931, Boston, Massachusetts, USA. McIntyre was born into a musical family (his father played mandolin) and took lessons in classical piano between 1940 and 1945. At the age of 19 he began alto saxophone lessons with Andrew McGhee, Gigi Gryce and Charlie Mariano. In 1954, he attended the Boston Conservatory, and after graduating with an MA in composition, he studied at Brandeis University for two years. He formed his own group in Boston and recorded his debut, *Stone Blues*, for the Prestige label in 1959. In 1960, he moved to New York and met Eric Dolphy, who played on his *Looking Ahead* in June of that year. Discouraged by the poor financial returns of the jazz life, McIntyre decided to make teaching his full-time profession. However, he continued to record, releasing *The Years Of The Iron Sheep* and *Way, Way Out* (the latter featuring his own flute, oboe, bass-clarinet and alto sax plus his arrangements for strings). In 1964, McIntyre recorded with the Bill Dixon Septet, and in 1965, he played with the Jazz Composers Guild Orchestra. He was also in the Cecil Taylor group that recorded *Unit Structures* in 1966, a monumental work of intricate jazz modernism. Having taught in schools in New York, he obtained a post at Wilberforce University in Ohio between 1967 and 1969, and taught at the Wesleyan University for two years after that. Since 1971, he has been director of the African-American Music and Dance Department at Old Westbury. The Danish label Steeplechase documented his playing and compositions on a series of five albums in the 70s, since when he has played with Charlie Haden's Liberation Music Orchestra, but made only one more recording under his own name (taken from a 1990 tribute concert to Dolphy, with French reeds player Thierry Bruneau). Although a less innovative talent than Eric Dolphy or Ornette Coleman, McIntyre's work represents an equally valid extension of the music of Charlie Parker and often includes elements of African-Caribbean musics in recognition of the West Indian cultural heritage.

Albums: *Stone Blues* (Original Jazz Classics 1959), *Looking Ahead* (Original Jazz Classics 1960), *The Years Of The Iron Sheep* (1962), *Way, Way Out* (1963), *Hindsight* (1974), *Home* (1975), *Open Horizon* (1976), *Introducing The Vibrations* (Steeplechase 1977), *Chasing The Sun* (1979), with Thierry Bruneau *Tribute* (Serene 1991).

McKenna, Dave

b. 30 May 1930, Woonsocket, Rhode Island, USA. By his late teens, McKenna was active in and around Boston, playing piano with Boots Mussulli's band. In 1949, he joined Charlie Ventura, then worked with Woody Herman until drafted during the Korean War. From 1953 until well into the 60s he was mostly engaged in small group work, playing with Ventura again and with several major artists, including Gene Krupa, Stan Getz and Zoot Sims. From the late 60s until the end of the 70s, he played long residencies at bars and restaurants in the Boston and Cape Cod areas of Massachusetts. His return to the national and international scene happened on several fronts, with record dates, tours and festival appearances with Bob Wilber, Scott Hamilton, Warren Vaché and many other musicians associated with Concord Records. An exceptionally accomplished pianist whether playing solo, as accompanist or in an ensemble role, McKenna's range is wide - although he is clearly happiest playing ballads to which he brings a delightfully melodic touch.

Albums: *Dave McKenna i* (1955), *The Dave McKenna Trio* (1958), with Hal Overton *Dual Piano Jazz* (1960), *Dave McKenna ii* (1963), *Cookin' At Michael's Pub* (1973), *Solo Piano* (1973), *Both Sides Of Dave McKenna* (c.1973), *The Dave McKenna Quartet Featuring Zoot Sims* (1974), *By Myself* (1976), *Dave 'Fingers' McKenna* (1977), *No Holds Barred* (1977), *McKenna* (1977), with Joe Venuti *Alone At The Palace* (1977), *This Is New* (1977), *One Bass Hit* (Concord 1979), *Giant Strides* (1979), *Oil And Viegar* (Honeydew 1979), *Left Handed Compliment* (Concord 1979), *Piano Mover* (1980), *Dave McKenna Plays The Music Of Harry Warren* (1981), *A Celebration Of Hoagy Carmichael* (Concord 1983), *The Keyman* (1984), *The Key Man* (Concord 1985), *Dancing In*

The Dark And Other Music Of Arthur Schwarz (Concord 1985), *My Friend The Piano* (Concord 1986), *No More Ouzo For Puzo* (Concord 1988), *Live At Maybeck Recital Hall Vol 2* (Concord 1989), *Shadows 'N' Dreams* (Concord 1990), *Hanging Out* (Concord 1992), with Gary Sargeant *Concord Duo Series Vol. 2* (1993).

McKenzie, Red

b. William McKenzie, 14 October 1899, St. Louis, Missouri, USA, d. 7 February 1948. Very much a Jazz Age figure, McKenzie was an ordinary singer and something of a hustler. His principal contribution to jazz lay in his associations with several leading jazzmen of his day for whom he worked tirelessly, promoting record dates and gigs often against reluctance and indifference. In the early 20s, he formed the Mound City Blue Blowers, a group which became enormously popular with the fringe audience. McKenzie's singing and playing of an improvised comb-and-paper instrument, together with other instrumentation such as the kazoo, sometimes militated against a true jazz feel, but among the musicians he hired to augment the band for record dates were some of the best available. The results included two tracks featuring Coleman Hawkins, 'Hello Lola' and 'If I Could Be With You One Hour Tonight', which became classics. A later band, the Rhythm Kings, featured Bunny Berigan. A close associate of McKenzie's was Eddie Condon, for whom he arranged a record date, Condon's first, which helped show the outside world what was happening in the white jazz scene in Chicago. By the early 30s, McKenzie's star had waned, but he returned in the mid-40s, playing at Condon's club and making a handful of records.
Compilations: with the Rhythm Kings *Bunny And Red* (1935-36), with Eddie Condon *Chicagoans* (Jazzology 1988).

McKibbon, Al

b. Alfred Benjamin McKibbon, 1 January 1919, Chicago, Illinois, USA. After playing bass in various mid-west bands in the late 30s and early 40s, McKibbon moved to Nw York where he established a solid reputation with leaders of large and small bands, such as Lucky Millinder and Coleman Hawkins. His musical interests were, however, moving away from such late swing era stylists and from the late 40s he became a prominent member of important bop groups including Dizzy Gillespie's big band and the studio band assembled for the Miles Davis-Gil Evans *Birth Of The Cool* sessions. He also worked with Thelonious Monk but maintained his connection with the mainstream and in 1951 joined George Shearing's quintet for a seven-year stint. Throughout the 60s and succeeding decades, McKibbon played and recorded with leading jazzmen, including Monk, Benny Carter and Gillespie. A meticulous sense of time, allied to a robust style has made McKibbon a much sought-after session musician, able to adapt readily to mainstream and bop demands.
Albums: with Dizzy Gillespie *Salle Pleyel Concert* (1948), with Miles Davis *Classics In Jazz* (1949-50), with George Shearing *Latin Escapade* (1956), with Cal Tjader *In A Latin Bag* (1961), with Thelonious Monk *Something In Blue* (1971), *Carter,*

Gillespie, Inc. (1976).

McKinney's Cotton Pickers

Originally formed shortly after the end of World War I by drummer Bill McKinney (b. 17 September 1895, d. 14 October 1969), the band adopted their name in 1926. By this time McKinney was manager, having hired Cuba Austin to replace himself on the drums. Although geared towards harmless hokum, novelty songs and other aspects of currently popular entertainment, the arrival in 1927 of arranger Don Redman turned the band onto a jazz course. Among the many fine musicians who played in the band in its earlier years were Joe Smith, Doc Cheatham, Claude Jones and Fats Waller. Resident for several years at Detroit's Graystone Ballroom, promoter Jean Goldkette's flagship venue, the unit made a huge impression upon other bands and their arrangers. In 1931, Redman left, forming his own outfit from a nucleus of McKinney musicians. This was a blow from which the band never fully recovered. Even though several important jazzmen played in later editions, among them Benny Carter, who became its musical director, the glory days were over. Indeed, the band made no more records even though it stayed in existence for a few more years. McKinney managed to continue leading a band into the early 40s, but by then it was a shadow of what had gone before. During the four years of its supremacy, the Cotton Pickers established new standards towards which all later big bands would strive. Although history would later credit the period Don Redman spent with the Fletcher Henderson Orchestra as being the start of big band music as it is known today, the arranger's work with this earlier band should not be overlooked. In particular, the lively, skilful manner in which they played Redman's arrangements suggest a band well ahead of its time and place in the story of big band jazz. McKinney himself remained only sporadically active in music for the rest of his life. A year or two after his death in 1969, a number of musicians from Detroit formed the New McKinney's Cotton Pickers, using Redman's and Carter's old scores for successful engagements at jazz festivals in America and Europe.
Compilations: *The Complete McKinney's Cotton Pickers Vols 1/2, 3/4, 5* (RCA 1983, 1928-31 recordings), *The Band Don Redman Built* (Bluebird 1990, 1928-30 recordings), *1928-29* (Original Jazz Classics 1992).
Further reading: *McKinney's Music: A Bio-discography Of McKinney's Cotton Pickers*, John Chilton.

McLaughlin, John

b. 4 January 1942, Yorkshire, England. Born into a musical family - his mother played violin - McLaughlin studied piano from the age of nine. He then took up the guitar because, like so many of his generation, he was inspired by the blues. By the time he was 14 years old, he had developed an interest in flamenco - the technical guitarist's most testing genre - and later started listening to jazz. He moved to London and his first professional gigs were as part of the early 60s blues boom, playing with Alexis Korner, Georgie Fame and Graham Bond. As the

60s progressed, McLaughlin became interested in more abstract forms, working and recording with John Surman and Dave Holland. He also spent some time in Germany playing free jazz with Gunter Hampel. His *Extrapolation*, recorded in 1969, with Surman and drummer Tony Oxley, was a landmark in British music. McLaughlin's clean, razor-sharp delivery wowed a public for whom guitars had become an obsession. The rock music of the Beatles and the Rolling Stones seemed to be adding something to R&B that the Americans had not thought of, so when Tony Williams - the drummer who had played on Eric Dolphy's *Out To Lunch* - formed his own band, Lifetime, it seemed natural to invite the young English guitarist aboard. McLaughlin flew to New York in 1969, but left the band the following year. His own *My Goal's Beyond* (1970) flanked his guitar with the bass of Charlie Haden and the percussion of Airto Moreira. Meanwhile, ever conscious of new directions, Miles Davis had used McLaughlin on *In A Silent Way*, music to a rock beat that loosened rhythmic integration (a nod towards what Dolphy and Ornette Coleman were doing). However, it was McLaughlin's playing on the seminal *Bitches Brew* (1970) that set the jazz world alight: it seemed to be the ideal mixture of jazz chops and rock excitement. Nearly everyone involved went off to form fusion outfits, and McLaughlin was no exception. His Mahavishnu Orchestra broke new boundaries in jazz in terms of volume, brash virtuosity and multi-faceted complexity. The colossal drums of Billy Cobham steered McLaughlin, violinist Jerry Goodman and keyboard player Jan Hammer into an explosive creativity bordering on chaos. The creation of rock superstars had found its equivalent for jazz instrumentalists. McLaughlin sported a custom-built electric guitar with two fretboards. By this time, too, his early interest in Theosophy had developed into a serious fascination with Eastern mysticism: McLaughlin announced his allegiance to guru Snr i Chinmoy and started wearing white clothes. When Cobham and Hammer left to form their own bands, a second Mahavishnu Orchestra formed, with ex-Frank Zappa violinist Jean-Luc Ponty and drummer Michael Walden. This group never quite recaptured the over-the-top glory of the first Orchestra, and compositional coherence proved a problem. In the mid-70s, McLaughlin renounced electricity and formed Shakti with Indian violinist L. Shankar and tabla-player Zakir Hussain. This time McLaughlin's customized guitar had raised frets, allowing him to approximate sitar-like drone sounds. In 1978, McLaughlin made another foray into the world of electricity with the One Truth Band, but punk had made the excesses of jazz-rock seem old-fashioned and the band did not last long. In 1978, he teamed up with Larry Coryell and Paco De Lucia as a virtuosic guitar trio. Guitar experts were astonished, but critics noted a rather dry precision in his acoustic playing: McLaughlin seemed to need electricity and volume to really spark him. After two solo albums (*Belo Horizonte, Music Spoken Here*), he played on Miles Davis's *You're Under Arrest* in 1984. In November 1985, he performed a guitar concerto written for him and the LA Philharmonic by Mike Gibbs. The same year he joined forces with Cobham again to create a violin-less Mahavishnu that featured saxophonist Bill Evans as an alternate solo voice. In 1986, they were joined by keyboardist Jim Beard. Two years later, McLaughlin toured with Trilok Gurtu, a percussionist trained in Indian classical music, and was again playing acoustic guitar; a 1989 trio concert (with Gurtu) at London's Royal Festival Hall was later released on record. McLaughlin was back in the UK in 1990, premiering his *Mediterranean Concerto* with the Scottish National Orchestra at the Glasgow Jazz Festival.

Albums: *When Fortune Smiles* (1967), *Extrapolation* (Polydor 1969), *Devotion* (CBS 1969), *My Goal's Beyond* (CBS 1970), *Birds Of Fire* (CBS 1973), *Shakti With John McLaughlin* (Columbia 1975), *A Handful Of Beauty* (CBS 1976), with Shakti *Natural Elements* (CBS 1977), *Johnny McLaughlin, Electric Guitarist* (Columbia 1978), with Al Di Meola, Paco De Lucia *Friday Night In San Francisco* (1978), *Electric Dreams* (CBS 1979), *Belo Horizonte*, (WEA 1982) *Music Spoken Here*, (WEA 1982), with Al DiMeola and Paco De Lucia *Passion Grace And Fire* (Mercury 1983), *Mahavishnu* (1984), *Inner Worlds* (CBS 1987), *Adventures In Radioland* (Polygram 1987), *Live At The Royal Festival Hall* (JMT 1990), *Que Alegria* (Verve 1992), *Time Remembered: John McLaughlin Plays Bill Evans* (1993), *Tokyo Live* (Verve 1994). Compilations: *The Best Of* (CBS 1981), *Compact Jazz* (Verve 1989), *The Collection* (Castle 1991), *Greatest Hits* (CBS 1991), *Where Fortune Smiles* (Beat Goes On 1993).

McLean, Jackie

b. 17 May 1932, New York City, New York, USA. Coming as he did from a musical background (McLean's father played guitar with the Tiny Bradshaw band), Jackie was encouraged by family friends who included Bud Powell. It was through Powell that alto saxophonist McLean came to the attention of Miles Davis, with whom he played in 1951, having previously gigged with Sonny Rollins. Throughout the 50s McLean performed and recorded with numerous leading jazzmen, among them Charles Mingus and Art Blakey. He also led his own groups, touring internationally, and from the early 70s became active in musical education. In the late 70s, he had a surprising entry in the UK pop charts with his 'Dr Jackyll And Mr Funk', a disco favourite, which reached number 53. Strongly influenced by Charlie Parker and Ornette Coleman, McLean's forceful and highly personal playing style reflects his interest in several schools of modern jazz. McLean's son, Rene, is a jazz saxophonist.

Selected albums: *The Jackie McLean Quintet* (1955), *Lights Out* (Original Jazz Classics 1956), *Jackie McLean 4, 5 & 6* (Original Jazz Classics 1956), *Jackie's Pal* (Original Jazz Classics 1956), *McLean's Scene* (Original Jazz Classics 1956), *Jackie McLean & Co* (Original Jazz Classics 1957), *Alto Madness* (Original Jazz Classics 1957), *Makin' The Changes* (Original Jazz Classics 1957), *A Long Drink Of The Blues* (Original Jazz Classics 1957), *Strange Blues* (Original Jazz Classics 1957), *New Soil* (Blue Note 1959), *Swing, Swang, Swingin'* (Boplicity 1959), *Jackie's Bag* (1959), *Capuchin Swing* (1960), *Bluesnik* (Blue Note 1961), *A Fickle Sonance* (Blue Note 1961), *Let Freedom Ring* (Blue Note 1962), *Tippin' The Scales* (Blue Note 1962),

Jackie McLean

Hipnosis (1962-67), *Vertigo* (1963), *One Step Beyond* (1963), *Destination Out* (1963), *It's Time* (1964), *Action* (1964), *Right Now!* (New Note 1965), *Consequence* (Liberty 1965), *Jacknife* (1965-66), *Dr Jackle* (Steeplechase 1966), with others *Charlie Parker Memorial* (1967), *New And Old Gospel* (1967), *'Bout Soul* (1967), *Demon's Dance* (Blue Note 1967), *Live At Montmartre* (Steeplechase 1972), *Ode To Super* (Steeplechase 1973), *A Ghetto Lullaby* (1973), with Dexter Gordon *The Meeting* (Steeplechase 1974) with Gordon *The Source* (Steeplechase 1974), *New York Calling* (Steeplechase 1975), *Antiquity* (1975), *New Wine, Old Bottles* (1978), *Monuments* (1979), *Contour* (Prestige 1980), with others *One Night With Blue Note* (1985), with Mal Waldron *Left Alone '86* (1986), *Fat Jazz* (Fresh Sounds 1988), *Rites Of Passage* (Triloka 1992, rec 1991), *Dynasty* (Triloka 1992, rec live 1988), *Rhythm Of The Earth* (Birdology 1992), *The Jackie Mac Attack* (Birdology 1993).

McPartland, Jimmy

b. 15 March 1907, Chicago, Illinois, USA, d. 13 March 1991. McPartland began playing cornet while still at Austin High School in Chicago, and became a founding member of both the Austin High School Gang (not all of whom were pupils there) and the Blue Friars. At the age of 17, he replaced Bix Beiderbecke in the Wolverines, and two years later was with Art Kassell's Castles In The Air band. In 1927, he joined Ben Pollack for a two-year stint, then freelanced with numerous bands, small and large, playing on many record dates, until World War II. While still on active service, he married British pianist Marian Turner (see Marian McPartland). After the war he returned to playing in small dixieland-orientated bands, toured many countries, and was still entertaining audiences in the mid-80s with appearances at prestigious events such as the Nice Jazz Festival. A fiery, exuberant player, McPartland was also capable of playing with a wistful elegance that recalled his earliest and greatest influence, Bix Beiderbecke.

Selected albums: *Shades Of Bix* (1953), *Jimmy McPartland's Dixieland* (1957), *Meet Me In Chicago* (1959), with Marian McPartland *The McPartlands Live At The Monticello* (1972). Selected compilations: *The Wolverines Orchestra* (1924-25), *One Night Stand* (Jazzology 1987), *On Stage* (Jazzology 1990).

McPartland, Marian

b. Marian Margaret Turner, 20 March 1920, Windsor, Berkshire, England. Prior to World War II, McPartland played British music halls as a member of a four-piano group led by Billy Mayer. While touring with ENSA (the British equivalent of America's USO), she met and married Jimmy McPartland. At the end of the war she went to the USA with her husband, quickly establishing a reputation in her own right. During the late 40s and throughout the following decade, she worked steadily, usually leading a trio, holding down several long residencies, notably an eight-year spell at the Hickory House. During the 60s and 70s she developed a long-lasting interest in education, established her own recording company, Halcyon Records, performed extensively in clubs and at festivals and also began parallel careers as a writer and broadcaster on jazz. A very gifted pianist, rhythmically near-perfect and with a seemingly endless capacity for intelligent improvising, her long-running radio show, *Piano Jazz*, has helped establish her as one of the best-known jazz artists in America. Although divorced from her husband Jimmy, she has latterly made occasional concert appearances with him. She is also a familiar figure at many important jazz festivals around the world. McPartland has also worked successfully in duos with Joe Venuti, and with fellow pianists Teddy Wilson and George Shearing. In addition to her other many activities, she has also made a successful crossover into classical music, performing such works as the Grieg Piano Concerto, George Gershwin's 'Rhapsody in Blue', and a series of popular songs arranged for piano and orchestra by Robert Farnon. Although relatively little known in the country of her birth, McPartland continues to prove herself to be one of the outstanding pianists in jazz. A collection of her articles on jazz, *All in Good Time*, was published in 1987.

Selected albums: *Jazz At Storyville* (1951), *Moods Vol. 2* (1952), *The Magnificent Marian McPartland At The Piano* (1952), *Great Britons* (1952, one side only), *Lullaby Of Birdland* (1953), *Jazz At The Hickory House* i (Savoy 1953), *Jazz At The Hickory House* ii (Savoy 1954), *The Marian McPartland Trio* i (1955), *The Marian McPartland Trio* ii (1956), *With You In My Mind* (1957), *At The London House* (1958), *The Music Of Leonard Bernstein* (1960), *The Marian McPartland Quintet* (1963), *Marian McPartland And Her Orchestra/Marian McPartland January 6th & 8th 1964* (1964), *The Marian McPartland Trio* iii (1968), *Interplay* (c.1969), *Ambiance* (1970), *A Delicate Balance* (c.1971-72), with Teddy Wilson *Elegant Piano* (1972), with Jimmy McPartland *The McPartlands Live At The Monticello* (1972), *Marian McPartland Plays The Music Of Alec Wilder* (Jazz Alliance 1973), *Marian Remembers Teddi* (1973), *Swingin'* (1973), *Solo Concert At Haverford* (1974), *Concert In Argentina* (1974, one side only), *Joe Venuti & Marian McPartland* (1974), *Send In The Clowns* (1976), *Wanted!* (1977), *Make Magnificent Music* (1977), *Now's The Time* (1977), *From This Moment On* (Concord 1978), *Portrait Of Marian McPartland* (Concord 1979), *At The Festival* (1979), *Live At The Carlyle* (1979), *Alone Together* (1981), *Personal Choice* (Concord 1982), *Willow Creek And Other Ballads* (Concord 1985), *Marian McPartland Plays The Music Of Billy Strayhorn* (Concord 1987), *Marian McPartland Plays The Benny Carter Songbook* (Concord 1990), *Live At Maybeck Recital Hall* (Concord 1991), *Piano Jazz With Guest Dave Brubeck* (Bellaphon 1993), *With Rosemary Clooney* (Jazz Alliance 1993), *In My Life* (Concord 1993).

Further reading: *All In Good Time*, Marian McPartland.

McPherson, Charles

b. 24 July 1939, Joplin, Missouri, USA. Often dismissed as a Charlie Parker copyist, McPherson is in fact more than a simple revivalist. While the style in which he plays, bebop, is now outmoded, it is one with which he grew up, and he plays it with fire and conviction. His family moved to Detroit when he was aged nine, and it was at high school, a few years later, that he started playing trumpet and flügelhorn. McPherson took up alto saxophone in his early teens (although he had wanted to play tenor), but his vocation for alto was confirmed, however, when he heard Parker. While in Detroit he spent some time studying with Barry Harris, and then, after moving to New York, he worked in Greenwich Village with Lonnie Hillyer in the early 60s. Fellow Detroit saxophonist Yusef Lateef suggested to Charles Mingus that he should hear McPherson when he was looking for a replacement for Eric Dolphy, and thus McPherson began the first of his stints with Mingus's band, garnering some critical plaudits for his work with one of the more adventurous bop-based leaders. Almost a forgotten man until the late 80s, he deservedly came back into the limelight as a result of a couple of successful European tours. He also played on part of the soundtrack for Clint Eastwood's bio-pic of Parker, *Bird*.

Albums: *Be-Bop Revisited* (Original Jazz Classics 1964), *Con Alma* (1965), *The Quintet Live!* (Original Jazz Classics 1966), *Live At The Five Spot* (Prestige 1966), *From This Moment On* (1968), *Horizons* (1968), *McPherson's Mood* (1969), *Beautiful* (Xanadu 1975), *Live In Tokyo* (Xanadu 1976), *Siku Ya Bibi* (Mainstream 1976). *New Horizons* (Xanadu 1977), *Free Bop!* (1978), *The Prophet* (Discovery 1983).

McRae, Carmen

b. 8 April 1922, New York City, New York, USA, d. 10 November 1994, Beverly Hills, California, USA. One of the best American jazz singers, McRae was also an accomplished pianist and songwriter. Early in her career she sang with bands led by Benny Carter, Mercer Ellington, Charlie Barnet and Count Basie (sometimes under the name of Carmen Clarke, from her brief marriage to Kenny Clarke). Although a familiar figure on the New York jazz club scene, including a spell in the early 50s as intermission pianist at Minton's Playhouse, her reputation did not spread far outside the jazz community. In the 60s and 70s she toured internationally and continued to record - usually accompanied by a small group - but joined on one occasion by the Clarke-Boland Big Band. By the 80s, she was one of only a tiny handful of major jazz singers whose work had not been diluted by commercial pressures. One of her early songs, 'Dream Of Life', written when she was just 16 years old, was recorded in 1939 by Billie Holiday. Although very much her own woman, McRae occasionally demonstrated the influence of Holiday through her ability to project a lyric with bittersweet intimacy. She also sang with remarkable rhythmic ease and her deft turns-of-phrase helped conceal a relatively limited range, while her ballad singing revealed enormous emotional depths. Her repertoire included many popular items from the Great American Songbook, but her jazz background ensured that she rarely strayed outside the idiom. Relaxed and unpretentious in performance and dedicated to her craft, McRae secured a place in the history of jazz singing.

Albums: *Carmen McRae* i (1954), *By Special Request* (1955),

Torchy (1955), *Blue Moon* (1956), *After Glow* (1957), *Carmen For Cool Ones* (1957), *Mad About The Man* (1957), with Sammy Davis Jnr. *Boy Meets Girl* (1957), *Book Of Ballads* (1958), *Birds Of A Feather* (1958), *Carmen McRae ii* (1958), *When You're Away* (1958), *Something To Swing About* (1959), *Carmen McRae Sings Lover Man And Other Billie Holiday Classics* (1961), *Carmen McRae Live At The Flamingo Club, London* (1961), *Carmen McRae iii* (1962), *In Person* (1963), *Carmen McRae Live At Sugar Hill* (c.1963), *Carmen McRae iv* (1964), *Carmen McRae v* (1964), *Carmen McRae vi* (1964), *Carmen McRae vii* (1964), *Woman Talk: Carmen McRae Live At The Village Gate* (1965), *Carmen McRae viii* (1965), *Live And Doin' It* (c.1965-66), *Carmen McRae ix* (1967), *Portrait Of Carmen* (1967), *Carmen McRae x* (1968), with Kenny Clarke, Francy Boland *November Girl* (1970), *Just A Little Lovin'* (1970), *The Great American Songbook* (1971), *As Time Goes By* (1973), *It Takes A Whole Lot Of Human Feeling* (1973), *Carmen McRae And Zoot Sims* (1973), *I Am Music* (1975), *Can't Hide Love* (1976), *Carmen McRae At The Great American Music Hall* (1976), *Live At The Roxy* (1976), *Ronnie Scott Presents Carmen McRae 'Live'* (1977), *For Carmen McRae* (1977), *I'm Coming Home Again* (1978), *Two For The Road* (1980), *Recorded Live At Bubba's* (1981), *Heat Wave* (1982), *You're Lookin' At Me (A Collection Of Nat 'King' Cole Songs)* (1983), *Any Old Time* (1986), *Fine And Mellow: Live At Birdland West* (1987), *Velvet Soul* (Denon 1988, 1973 recording), *Carmen Sings Monk* (Novus 1989), *Sarah Dedicated To You* (Novus 1991), *Woman Talk* (Mainstream 1991), *Sings Great American Songwriters* (GRP 1994, 1955-59 recordings).

McShann, Jay 'Hootie'

b. 12 January 1909, Muskogee, Oklahoma, USA. After playing in many territory bands in the southwest and midwest, pianist McShann settled in Kansas City in the mid-30s, playing in Buster Smith's band, which also included Charlie Parker, in 1937. The following year, McShann formed his own unit which included Gene Ramey and Gus Johnson as well as Parker. By 1941, with the departure from Kansas City of Harlan Leonard, McShann's became the city's top band, Count Basie having moved on to greater things a few years earlier. The most popular member of the band was singer Walter Brown, who was featured on a handful of hit records, although McShann was himself an above-average blues shouter. In retrospect, the 1941 band is regarded as the most interesting of those McShann led because the saxophone section included the fast-developing and revolutionary talent of Parker. In fact, all McShann's bands had the virtues common to most Kansas City bands, those of lithely swinging, blues-based, exciting jazz. In 1944, McShann folded the band to enter the armed forces, reforming in 1945 on the west coast. Once again he showed himself to have a good ear for singers by hiring Jimmy Witherspoon. During the 50s and 60s, McShann was active, sometimes leading small groups, sometimes working as a solo act, but the jazz world was largely indifferent. By the 70s, however, he had become a popular figure on the international festival circuit, playing piano and singing the blues with flair and

vigour. His recording career was also revitalized, and the 70s and 80s saw a steady stream of fine recordings, many of which were in the authentic tradition of the blues.

Selected albums: *McShann's Piano* (1966), *Confessin' The Blues* (1969), *Live In France* (1969), *Roll 'Em* (1969-77), *With Kansas City In Mind* (Swaggie 1969-72 recordings), *Jumpin' The Blues* (1970), *The Man From Muskogee* (1972), *Going To Kansas City* (1972), *Kansas City Memories* (Black And Blue 1973), *Vine Street Boogie* (1974), *Kansas City Joys* (1976), *Crazy Legs And Friday Strut* (1976), *Live At Istres* (1977), *Kansas City On My Mind* (1977), *After Hours* (1977), *The Last Of The Blue Devils* (1977), *Blues And Boogie* (1978), *Kansas City Hustle* (1978), *A Tribute To Fats Waller* (1978), *The Big Apple Bash* (1978), *Tuxedo Junction* (1980), with Al Casey *Best Of Friends* (JSP 1982), *Swingmatism* (Sackville 1982), *Just A Lucky So And So* (1983), *At The Café Des Copains* (Sackville 1983-89), *Magical Jazz* (1984), *Airmail Special* (Sackville 1985), *A Tribute To Charlie Parker* (S&R 1991), *Some Blues* (Chiaroscuro 1993), *The Missouri Connection* (Reervoir 1993). Selected compilations: *Hootie's KC Blues* (1941-42), *Blues From Kansas City* (MCA 1941-1943 recordings), *The Band That Jumps The Blues* (1947-49).

McVea, Jack

b. 5 November 1914, Los Angeles, California, USA. Starting out on banjo, McVea played in his father's band before he reached his teenage years. In the late 20s, he began playing reed instruments, eventually concentrating on tenor saxophone. In the early 30s, after graduating from high school, he turned professional and worked with a number of bands, including that led by Charlie Echols. In 1936, he was with Eddie Barefield and, after a brief spell leading his own unit, joined Lionel Hampton in 1940. With Hampton he mostly played baritone saxophone. After a short stint with Snub Mosley, he became interested in new developments in jazz and worked with Dizzy Gillespie and Charlie Parker. McVea was also featured at an early Jazz At The Philharmonic concert. Despite his interest in bop, McVea appreciated current popular tastes, and his R&B single, 'Open The Door, Richard', a massive hit in 1946, brought him international attention. This celebrity allowed him to maintain a small R&B band for the next several years, playing clubs, hotels, casinos and concerts in various parts of the USA. In the late 50s he also played in bands led by Benny Carter among others. In the mid-60s McVea led a trio at Disneyland, a gig he retained into the 80s.

Album: *Nothin' But Jazz* (Harlequin 1962). Compilations: *Open The Door, Richard* (Jukebox Lil 1985, 1940s), *Come Blow Your Horn* (Ace 1985), *Two Timin' Baby* (Jukebox Lil 1986), *New Deal* (Jukebox Lil 1989).

Melly, George

b. 17 August 1926, Liverpool, Lancashire, England. Deeply involved in the UK trad scene of the late 40s and 50s, Melly sang with Mick Mulligan's band. In the 60s he switched careers, exploiting his interest in and knowledge of both music and art to become one of the UK's most ubiquitous critics and writers. He also became a popular television personality, and published the first volume in a series of three autobiographical works. In the early 70s Melly returned to music, performing regularly with John Chilton's band. He has continued to sing with Chilton, touring extensively and entertaining audiences with his broadly-based repertoire which encompasses early blues, popular songs of 20s and 30s vaudeville, and a smattering of later material, some of it written especially by Chilton, which suits his highly personal, orotund singing style.

Selected albums: *George Melly With Mick Mulligan's Band* (1957), *George Melly* (1961), *Nuts* (WEA 1971), *Son Of Nuts* (WEA 1972), *At It Again* (1976), *Melly Sings Hoagy* (1978), *Ain't Misbehavin'* (1979), *It's George* (c.1980), *Let's Do It* (PRT 1981), *Like Sherry Wine* (1981), *Makin' Whoopee* (1982), *The Many Moods Of Melly* (1984), *16 Golden Classics* (Unforgettable 1986), *Running Wild/Hometown* (1986), *Anything Goes* (PRT 1988), *George Melly And Mates* (One-Up 1991), *Best Of George Melly* (Kaz 1992), *Frankie And Johnny* (D-Sharp 1992).

Further reading: *Owning Up*, George Melly. *Rum, Bum And Concertina*, George Melly. *Scouse Mouse*, George Melly.

Mengelberg, Misha

b. 5 April, 1935, Kiev, Ukraine. Mengelberg was raised in Holland where, for 30 years, he has personified the Dutch *avant garde*. He characterizes himself as 'a rotten piano player' - if that is the case, wittier use has rarely been made of limitations. Mengelberg has consistently aligned himself with iconoclastic and provocative musicians, from straight music's Zen terrorists David Tudor and John Cage in the early 60s, to Eric Dolphy in 1963, to the members of the Dutch Instant Composers Pool, with whom he still works. Together with his long-standing ICP collaborator Han Bennink, he has been one of the main instigators behind three albums which have paid tribute to pianist Herbie Nichols - two with a small group that also featured Steve Lacy, and one with the ICP Orchestra. As an improviser, Mengelberg holds out for the 'responsibility to be different every day' and is against the jazzman's obsession with personal style and touch. All the same, his compositions reveal an identifiable preoccupation with irony, some pieces, in fact, dripping with sarcasm. The ICP Orchestra is currently the main outlet for his writing, but he also composes for the Berlin Contemporary Jazz Orchestra.

Albums: *Misha Mengelberg Trio* (1960), *Kwartet* (1966), *Driekusman Total Loss* (1966), with John Tchicai, Han Bennink *Instant Composers Pool* (1968), *Groupcomposing* (1970), with Tchicai, Bennink, Derek Bailey *Instant Composers Pool 1970* (1971), *Misha Mengelberg/Han Bennink* (1971), with Bennink *Het Scharrebroekse* (1972), with Bennink *Einepartietischtennis* (1974), with Bennink *Coincidents* (1975), with Bennink *Untitled Album* (1975), *Tenterett* (1977), with Bennink *Midwoud* (1977), *Pech Onderweg* (1978), with Dudu Pukwana, Bennink *Yi Yole* (1978), *ICP Tentet In Berlin* (1978), *Mengelberg-Bennink* (1979), with Paul Rutherford, Mario Schiano, Bennink *A European Proposal* (1979), with Peter Brötzmann, Bennink *Three Points And A Mountain* (1980),

ICP Orchestra Live In Soncino (1980), *Japan Japon* (1982), *Change Of Season* (Soul Note 1984), *Impromptus* (FMP 1986), *Two Programs: ICP Performs Nichols/Monk* (1986), with Pino Minafra *Tropic Of The Mounted Sea Chicken* (1990), with others *Dutch Masters* (Soul Note 1992).

Menza, Don

b. 22 April 1936, Buffalo, New York, USA. In 1960, after military service, during which he had become adept as both an instrumentalist and an arranger, tenor saxophonist Menza joined the Maynard Ferguson band. He was then briefly with Stan Kenton but opted to return to his home town, showing a preference for small-group work. In the mid-60s, he lived and worked in Germany. In 1968, he returned to the USA, playing in the Buddy Rich big band. Resident in Los Angeles throughout the next decade, Menza developed his writing, both as arranger and composer. In particular, he wrote for Louie Bellson, with whom he also played and recorded. In the 80s, he played with several Los Angeles-based big bands, including that led by Bill Berry, and also led his own big bands and small groups. He toured extensively, at home and overseas, usually appearing as a single. His thorough musical background and eclectic tastes - he admires and has studied the work of many classical composers - has also allowed him to work in non-jazz contexts. A fiery, aggressive performer, Menza's writing shows his bebop leanings, which he brings even into his big band work.

Albums: with Stan Kenton *Adventures In Time* (1962), *Menza In Munich* (1965), with Buddy Rich *Mercy, Mercy* (1968), with Rich *Channel One Suite* (1968), with Louie Bellson *150 MPH* (1974), *Horn Of Plenty* (1979), *Burnin'* (1980), *Hip Pocket* (Palo Alto 1981), with Bellson *East Side Suite* (1987), *Ballads* (Fresh Souns 1988), with Bellson *Jazz Giants* (1989).

Merrill, Helen

b. 21 July 1930, New York City, New York, USA. Merrill's early career found her singing in exalted bebop company. Among the major artists with whom she sang in the late 40s were Charlie Parker, Miles Davis and Bud Powell. She spent part of the 50s outside music, but continued to make a few records with notable figures such as Clifford Brown; by the end of the decade, was resident in Italy and a familiar figure at European festivals. In the early 60s, she returned to the USA but had difficulty in attracting the attention of either radio and television networks or the major record companies. She did make a handful of records backed by leading musicians such as Thad Jones, Ron Carter, Richard Davis, Elvin Jones and Jim Hall. By the late 60s, Merrill was again resident outside the USA, this time in Japan, where her talents were much appreciated. Back in the USA in the mid-70s, she was still largely overlooked but was periodically recorded, again with excellent jazz backing from the likes of Teddy Wilson, John Lewis and Pepper Adams. In November 1994, Merrill reappeared on the scene, promoting a new album and planning a UK and European tour for 1995. One of the most musical of singers, Merrill customarily explores the emotional depths of the lyrics of the songs she sings, imbuing them with great passion.

Selected albums: *Helen Merrill Featuring Clifford Brown* (Emarcy 1954), *Helen Merrill With Hal Mooney And His Orchestra* i (1955), *Helen Merrill With Gil Evans And His Orchestra* (1956), *Helen Merrill With Hal Mooney And His Orchestra* ii (1957), *Helen Merrill* i (Philips 1957), *Helen Merrill* ii (1959), *Helen Merrill With Quincy Jones And His Orchestra* (1959), *Helen Merrill In Italy* (Liuto 1959-1962 recording), *Helen Merrill* iii (1964), *Autumn Love* (1967), *A Shade Of Difference* (Spotlite 1968), *Helen Merrill In Tokyo* (1969), with Teddy Wilson *Helen Sings, Teddy Swings* (c.1970), *Sposin'* (1971), *Helen Merrill/John Lewis* (1977), *Chasin' The Bird* (1979), *Case Forte* (1980), *The Rodgers & Hammerstein Album* (DRG 1982), *No Tears...No Goodbyes* (Owl 1984), *Music Makers* (Owl 1986), *Collaboration* (Emarcy 1988), *Just Friends* (Emarcy 1989), *Dream Of You* (Emarcy 1993, 1956 recording), *Clear Out Of This World* (Emarcy 1992), Brownie: *Tribute To Clifford Brown* (Verve 1994). Compilation: *Blossom Of Stars* (1954-1992 recordings).

Metcalf, Louis

b. 28 February 1905, Webster Groves, Missouri, USA, d. 27 October 1981. Metcalf was playing trumpet professionally by his early teenage years and spent some five years with Charlie Creath. The 20s were Metcalf's finest decade. Based in New York, he worked and sometimes recorded with blues singers and a galaxy of important jazz artists, including Sidney Bechet, Duke Ellington, J.C. Higginbotham, James P. Johnson, Albert Nicholas, Luis Russell, Jelly Roll Morton and King Oliver. In the 30s and 40s, Metcalf sometimes moved away from New York, frequently visiting Canada as a bandleader. Although his career profile was now much lower he still played with leading figures, including Lester Young and Billie Holiday. He played on through the 50s and 60s, often working at clubs in New York; but Metcalf's later years were overshadowed by his earlier successes. A gifted, blues-orientated trumpeter, with a precisely-articulated style, Metcalf's was an original talent whose recorded work offers only tantalizing glimpses of a major jazz artist.

Album: *Louis Metcalf At The Ali Baba* (1966). Compilations: *The Indispensable Duke Ellington Vols 1/2* (1927-29).

Metheny, Pat

b. 12 August 1954, Kansas City, Missouri, USA. Although classed as a jazz guitarist, Metheny has bridged the gap between jazz and rock music in the same way that Miles Davis did in the late 60s and early 70s. Additionally, he has played a major part in the growth of jazz with the younger generation of the 80s. His first musical instrument was a French horn, and surprisingly he did not begin with the guitar until he was a teenager. His outstanding virtuosity soon had him teaching the instrument at the University Of Miami and the Berklee College Of Music in Boston. He joined Gary Burton in 1974, and throughout his three-album stay, he contributed some fluid Wes Montgomery-influenced guitar patterns. Manfred Eicher of ECM Records saw the potential and initiated a partnership which lasted for 10 superlative albums. He became, along with Keith Jarrett, ECM's biggest selling artist, and his albums regularly topped the jazz record charts. Metheny is one of the few artists to make regular appearances in the pop album charts; such is the accessibility of his music. Both *Bright Size Life*, featuring the late Jaco Pastorious and *Watercolours*, though excellent albums, still showed a man who was feeling his way. His own individualistic style matured with *Pat Metheny Group* in 1978.

Together with his musical partner (and arguably, his right arm), the brilliant keyboardist Lyle Mays, he initiated a rock group format that produced album after album of melodious jazz/rock. Following a major tour with Joni Mitchell and Pastorious (*Shadows And Light*), Metheny released *New Chautauqua* and demonstrated an amazing dexterity on 12-string guitar and, against the fashion of the times, made the US Top 50. He returned to the electric band format for *American Garage,* which contained his country-influenced '(Cross The) Heartland'. The double set *80/81* featured Michael Brecker, Jack DeJohnette, Charlie Haden and Dewey Redman, and was more of a typical jazz album, featuring in particular the moderately *avant garde* 'Two Folk Songs' The record still climbed the popular charts. During this time, Metheny constantly won jazz and guitarist polls. Mays' keyboards featured prominently in the group structure, and he received co-authorship credit for the suite *As Falls Wichita, So Falls Wichita Falls*. Metheny had by now become fascinated by the musical possibilities of the guitar synthesizer or synclavier. He used this to startling effect on *Offramp,* notably on the wonderfully contagious and arresting 'Are You Going With Me?'. The double set *Travels* showed a band at the peak of its powers, playing some familiar titles with a new freshness. The short piece 'Travels', stands as one of his finest compositions, the low-level recording offers such subtle emotion that it becomes joyously funereal. *Rejoicing* was a modern jazz album demonstrating his sensitive interpretations of music by Horace Silver and Ornette Coleman. *First Circle* maintained the standard and showed a greater leaning towards Latin-based music, still with Metheny's brilliant ear for melody; additionally the track 'If I Could' displayed the same sparse subtlety of *Travels*. In 1985, he composed the film score for *The Falcon And The Snowman* which led to him recording 'This Is Not America' with David Bowie. The resulting Top 40 US hit (number 12 in the UK), brought Metheny many new young admirers. The concert halls found audiences bedecked in striped rugby shirts, in the style of their new hero.

Ironically, at the same time, following a break with ECM, Pat turned his back on possible rock stardom and produced his most perplexing work, *Song X*, with free-jazz exponent Ornette Coleman. Reactions were mixed in reviewing this difficult album - ultimately the general consensus was that it was brilliantly unlistenable. He returned to more familiar ground with *Still Life (Talking)* and *Letter From Home,* although both showed a greater move towards Latin melody and rhythm. In 1990, *Reunion* was released, a superb meeting with his former boss Gary Burton and a few months later together with Dave Holland and Roy Haynes he made *Question And Answer.*

Additionally he was heavily featured, along with Herbie Hancock, on the excellent Jack DeJohnette album, *Parallel Realities*. He continued into the 90s with *Secret Story*, an album of breathtaking beauty. Although the album may have made jazz purists cringe it was a realisation of all Metheny's musical influences. His second live album *The Road To You* did not have the emotion of *Travels* it was something to keep the fans quiet before he unleashed an exciting recording with John Scofield, both guitarists having been sharing the honours at the top of jazz polls for the past few years. *Zero Tolerence For Silence* can only be described as astonishing - for many this wall of sound guitar was a self-indulgent mess. After repeated play the music does not get any easier, but at least we can understand his motives more and appreciate what a bold move this thrash metal outing was. Metheny found himself reviewed in the Heavy Metal press for the first (and last) time. *We Live Here* was a return to familiar ground, and a familiar position at the top of the jazz charts. He has an extraordinary sense of melody and his work neither rambles nor becomes self-indulgent; much credit must also be given to the like-minded Lyle Mays, whose quiet presence at the side of the stage is the backbone for much of Metheny's music.

Albums: *Bright Size Life* (ECM 1976), *Watercolours* (ECM 1977), *Pat Metheny Group* (ECM 1978), *New Chautauqua* (ECM 1979), *American Garage* (ECM 1979), *80/81* (ECM 1980), *As Falls Wichita, So Falls Wichita Falls* (ECM 1981), *Offramp* (ECM 1982), *Travels* (ECM 1983), *Rejoicing* (ECM 1983), *First Circle* (ECM 1984), *The Falcon And The Snowman* (1985, film soundtrack), *Song X* (Geffen 1986), *Still Life (Talking)* (Geffen 1987), *Letter From Home* (Geffen 1989), with Gary Burton *Reunion* (Geffen 1990), *Question And Answer* (Geffen 1990), with Jack DeJohnette *Parallel Realities* (Geffen 1990), *Secret Story* (Geffen 1992), *The Road To You - Recorded Live In Europe* (Geffen 1993), with John Scofield *I Can See Your House From Here* (Blue Note 1994), *Zero Tolerance For Silence* (Geffen 1994), *We Live Here* (Geffen 1995). Compilations: *Works* (ECM 1983), *Works 2* (ECM 1988). Video: *More Travels* (Geffen 1993).

Mezzrow, Mezz

b. Milton Mesirow, 9 November 1899, Chicago, Illinois, USA, d. 5 August 1972. After playing club dates in and around his home town during the 20s, clarinettist Mezzrow moved to New York where he became a popular figure, partly owing to his other career as a supplier of marijuana. In the 30s he recorded with Sidney Bechet and Tommy Ladnier on the famous sessions organized by French critic Hugues Panassie, and in the 40s formed his own King Jazz record label to record Bechet and other important jazz artists. In the 50s, he moved to France, touring from a Paris base with visiting musicians (who included Lionel Hampton, Lee Collins and Zutty Singleton), recording and enjoying a level of adulation he had never achieved in his own country. A vehement anti-segregationist, Mezzrow wholly identified with black music and musicians, even to the extent of occasionally 'passing' for black in order to play with his idols. Much written about, critically by Eddie Condon and hyperbolically by himself, Mezzrow's image suffered and he was often dismissed by jazz commentators. In fact, despite the often outrageous claims he made in his racily extravagant autobiography, Mezzrow did much to foster jazz. In his early years in Chicago he encouraged many young musicians, even if later he claimed to have taught them how to play. He was tireless in setting up record dates and he boldly formed multi-racial bands during a period when such groups were rarely seen or heard. Mezzrow's clarinet style was earthy and at times elementary, but among the records he made are flashes of a genuine feeling for the blues.

Selected albums: with Lionel Hampton *The Hamp In Paris* (1953), with Lee Collins *Clarinet Marmalade* (1955). Selected compilations: with Sidney Bechet *The Panassie Sessions* (1938-39), with Bechet *Out Of The Galleon* (1945), with Bechet *Really The Blues* (1945), with Bechet *King Of Jazz Vols 1-5* (Storyville 1986), *The Chronological Mezz Mezzrow 1928-1936* (Original Jazz Classics).

Michelot, Pierre

b. 3 March 1928, Saint Denis, France. Michelot studied classical bass from the age of 16, but it was the playing of Jimmy Blanton and Oscar Pettiford which attracted him to jazz. He played with Rex Stewart in 1948, toured Europe with Kenny Clarke and recorded with Coleman Hawkins. Although such experience must have sharpened his playing, he only got the chance because he was already an accurate, melodic player who could provide a band with a springy rhythm. Throughout the 50s he worked in Paris clubs with Django Reinhardt, tenor players Lester Young, Don Byas, Dexter Gordon, Zoot Sims and Stan Getz. Among his recordings were sessions with Miles Davis in 1956/7, and pianist Bud Powell in the early 60s. Meanwhile he was writing arrangements for trumpeter Chet Baker, Kenny Clarke and for session work. For 15 years, from 1959, he worked with Jacques Loussier's Play Bach Trio and continued to work in the studios. He took part in the filming of Tavernier's film *Round Midnight* in 1986.

Albums: with Django Reinhardt *Blues For Ike* (1953), with Bud Powell *A Portrait Of Thelonius* (1961), with Dexter Gordon *Our Man In Paris* (1963), *Round About A Bass* (1963).

Micus, Stephan

b. 19 January 1953, Stuttgart, Germany. Micus made his first overseas trip to Morocco at the age of 16. Since then he has travelled all over the world, studying traditional wind and string instruments, including the Japanese shakuhachi and sho, the Indian sitar and dilruba, as well as a range of percussion instruments from China, Korea, Bali, Java, Tibet and Ireland. For *East Of The Night* he designed a new type of 10- and 14-string guitar with resonant strings like that of the sitar. He has given concerts in Europe (including one in Düsseldorf with Oregon), the USA, Japan, Taiwan, Israel and Afghanistan. In 1977, his ballet, *Koan*, received its premiere in Cologne. Further performances included London, Paris and New York. *The Music Of Stones*, his compositions for the resonating stone sculptures of Elmar Daucher, were recorded in the atmospheric ambience of Ulm Cathedral and proved to be among his most inspired work. In the recording studio he has preferred to work as a soloist, making sensitive use of multi-track playback techniques. His compositions, often based on improvisation and always difficult to classify, have been widely acclaimed for their meditative and spiritual qualities. His expressed intention is not to play traditional music, but to search for fresh possibilities by using traditional instruments in unconventional combinations. Of this, the jazz writer Joachim E. Berendt, has said: 'He plays them with a profound internationalization of their tradition and spirituality, uniting their sounds in a musical river which makes the stream of inner consciousness audible'.

Selected albums: *Implosions* (ECM 1977), *Koan* (ECM 1981), *East Of The Night* (ECM 1985), *Ocean* (ECM 1986), *Twilight Fields* (ECM 1987), *Wings Over Water* (ECM 1988), *The Music Of Stones* (ECM 1989), *Darkness And Light* (ECM 1990), *Behind Eleven Deserts* (Verabra 1990), *To The Evening Child* (ECM 1992), *Till The End Of Time* (ECM 1993), *Listen To The Rain* (ECM 1993).

Mikkelborg, Palle

b. 6 March 1941, Copenhagen, Denmark. Mikkelborg is a self-taught trumpeter who studied conducting at the Royal Music Conservatory, Copenhagen. After turning professional in 1960, he joined Danish Radiojazzgruppen (1963), of which he was the leader from 1967-72. He was also a member of Radioens Big Band from 1964-71. For both of these, he would write, arrange and conduct as well as play trumpet. In 1966, he formed a quintet with drummer Alex Riel which won first prize at the Montreux Jazz Festival and played at the Newport Jazz Festival (1968). Then he led an octet called V8 (1970-75) and an outfit called Entrance (1975-85). Mikkelborg has also worked with bandleaders George Russell, Gil Evans, George Gruntz, Mike Gibbs and Maynard Ferguson and a wide variety of musicians, including Jan Garbarek, Terje Rypdal, Don Cherry, Abdullah Ibrahim and Charlie Mariano. His trumpet playing is characterized by a clear, firm sound, a huge range and the successful incorporation of a variety of electronic effects. He has written many pieces for his various bands as well as a series of extended pieces for larger ensembles. In 1984, he wrote and later recorded *Aura*, a tribute to Miles Davis, for big band and soloists, featuring Davis himself.

Albums: *Ashoka Suite* (1970), with Entrance *Entrance* (1977), with Terje Rypdal *Waves* (1977), *Descendre* (1978), *Live As Well* (1978), with Shankar, Jan Garbarek *Visions* (1983), with George Gruntz *Theatre* (1984), *Journey To...* (1985), *Aura* (1985), *Heart To Heart* (Storyville 1986), with Niels-Henning Ørsted Pederson *Once Upon A Time* (1992).

Miles, Butch

b. Charles Thornton, 4 July 1944, Ironton, Ohio, USA. After playing the drums as a small child, Miles later studied music in college. As a teenager, he played with a rock band, but his admiration for Gene Krupa inclined him towards jazz drum-

ming. Resident in Charleston, West Virginia, he began playing with small jazz groups and in 1972 became Mel Tormé's regular drummer. In 1975, he quit Tormé and offered his services to Count Basie. When Basie's drummer, Ray Porello, was injured in a road accident, Miles deputized for a week and stayed for four and a half years. In 1979, he joined Dave Brubeck, and the following year was backing Tony Bennett. In the 80s Miles worked extensively with small groups, sometimes as leader, accompanying such artists as Gerry Mulligan, Al Cohn, Buddy Tate, Bucky Pizzarelli, Glenn Zottola, Scott Hamilton and Bob Wilber. Miles also sings occasionally, proving an engaging if uninspired vocalist with a limited range. As a drummer, he is a gifted performer with an eclectic style that revealed his admiration for such big band drummers as Krupa, Chick Webb and Buddy Rich. In a small group setting he is a self-effacing and supportive player but, stylistically, he seems better suited for big band work, where he ably continues the great tradition set by his idols.

Albums: with Mel Tormé *Live At The Maisonette* (1974), with Count Basie *Montreux '77* (1977), *Basie In Europe* (1977), *Miles And Miles Of Swing* (1977), *Butch's Encore* (1977-78), *Lady Be Good* (1978), with Dave Brubeck *Back Home* (1979), *Butch Miles Salutes Chick Webb* (1979), *Butch Miles Salutes Gene Krupa* (1982), *Hail To The Chief! Butch Miles Salutes Basie* (1982), *More Miles . . . More Standards* (1985), *Jazz Express* (1986).

Miley, Bubber

b. James Wesley Miley, 3 April 1903, Aiken, South Carolina, USA, d. 20 May 1932. By his late teens, trumpeter Miley was working extensively in clubs in Chicago and New York and was on the road with Mamie Smith. In 1923, he became a member of Elmer Snowden's band, staying on when Duke Ellington took over as leader. His heavy drinking made him unreliable and erratic, and he left the band in 1929, touring Europe that year with Noble Sissle. He briefly led his own band but was stricken with tuberculosis and died in May 1932. As a formative member of Ellington's orchestra, Miley's influence remained long after his departure. His dramatic use of the plunger mute, together with growls and other unusual sounds, helped to create many of the so-called 'jungle' effects which became an integral part of Ellington's music.

Compilation: *The Indispensable Duke Ellington Vols 1/2* (1927).

Miller, Eddie

b. Edward Raymond Müller, 23 June 1911, New Orleans, Louisiana, USA, d. 6 April 1991, Los Angeles, California, USA. Miller began playing clarinet as a child and in his early teens played in street bands. Before he was 17 years old he was on his way to New York where he played with several bands, including that led by Julie Wintz which had the unenviable task of playing opposite Fletcher Henderson at the Roseland Ballroom. While on this engagement, Miller met Henderson's star tenor saxophonist, Coleman Hawkins, with whom he formed a lifelong friendship. By this time Miller had also taken up the tenor and in 1930, at the age of 19 joined Ben Pollack's band where he remained until its break-up in 1934. A founder-member of the co-operative group which became known as the Bob Crosby Orchestra, Miller was one of the leading soloists of the band and played an important part in its huge success. He was composer of 'Slow Mood', a hit for the band. In 1943, he briefly led his own unit before entering the US army. On his discharge, following illness, he reformed a band, but by the mid-40s he had become a studio musician in Hollywood where he remained for the next 10 years. Miller appeared in the film *Pete Kelly's Blues* (1955) and its television spin-off series, but by the late 50s was back on the jazz circuit. In the 60s, he played dates across the USA as a single and was also a member of the band led by Pete Fountain as well as that run by his former Crosby soulmates Yank Lawson and Bob Haggart, the World's Greatest Jazz Band. During the 70s and 80s Miller continued his career, touring as a single and working with the WGJB and its later version, the Lawson-Haggart Jazz Band. Amongst his associates in the band was pianist Lou Stein, with whom he recorded a duo album, *Lazy Mood For Two*. He also appeared at several Crosby reunions. He was still active when, while with the Lawson-Haggart band in 1988, he suffered a disabling stroke which ended his playing career. A later stroke was even more damaging and he eventually died in April 1991. A fluid player with a relaxed and smoothly elegant style, Miller was at his best on ballads, although his uptempo excursions with Crosby, especially on the numbers performed by the Bobcats, the band-within-the-band, lent weight to his status as one of the best white tenor players of his generation.

Albums: *Tenor Of Jazz* (1967), *A Portrait Of Eddie* (1971), *Live At Capolinea* (c.1976), with Lou Stein *Lazy Mood For Two* (1978), *It's Miller Time* (1979), *Street Of Dreams* (1983). Compilations: with Bob Crosby *South Rampart Street Parade* (1935-42), with Crosby *Big Noise From Winnetka* (1937-42), *Soft Jive* (1943-44), *Live At Michele's Silver Stope* (Audiophile 1988), *Piano Blues 1929-34* (Blues Document 1989). Further reading: *Stomp Off, Let's Go!: The Story Of Bob Crosby's Bob Cats & Big Band*, John Chilton.

Miller, Ernest 'Punch'

b. Ernest Burden, 10 June 1894, Raceland, Louisiana, USA. d. 2 December 1971. Miller began playing cornet as a child, playing with local dance and early jazz bands. Shortly after World War I he settled in New Orleans for a while before joining the northward migration. Resident in Chicago from the mid-20s, he played with many bands including those led by Freddie Keppard and Jelly Roll Morton. From the mid-40s he was often in New York where he recorded with Jimmy Archey, Ed Hall, Ralph Sutton and others and also appeared on Rudi Blesh's *This Is Jazz* radio show. By the middle of the following decade, however, he had returned to New Orleans. In the early 60s he toured with George Lewis. A technically proficient trumpeter, Miller's playing mingled the New Orleans tradition with a deep feeling for the blues. His solos were often pungent and moving. He sang in a casual yet engaging manner, in this department, at least, displaying the influence of Louis Armstrong. In 1971 he was the subject of an exceptionally fine film documentary, *'Til The Butcher Cuts Him Down*.

Albums: *Punch Miller And His Jazz Band* (1960), *Punch Miller's Hongo Fongo Players* (1961), *Punch Miller's Bunch And George Lewis* (1962), *Punch's Delegates Of Pleasure* (1962), *Preservation Hall* (1962), *The River's In Mourning* (1962), *George Lewis And His New Orleans All Stars In Tokyo* (1963), *Oh! Lady Be Good* (1967). Compilations: *Kid Punch Miller: Jazz Rarities* (1929-30), *The Wild Horns* (1941), *Punch Miller And His All Star Band, New York 1947* (1947), *Delegates Of Pleasure* (Jazzology 1990).

Miller, Harry

b. 21 April 1941, Johannesburg, South Africa, d. 16 December 1983. A highly impressive and emotional bass player, Miller played R&B (with Manfred Mann) in South Africa. He moved to the UK in 1961, and then worked in bands on transatlantic liners, so that he heard New York jazz at first hand. Settling back in London, he made a reputation playing with John Surman, Keith Tippett (Ovary Lodge and Centipede), Dudu Pukwana (Spear), Elton Dean (Ninesense and Just Us), Stan Tracey (Tentacles and the Octet), Alan Skidmore (part of the quintet that won the 1969 Press prize at Montreux), Louis Moholo, Kenneth Terroade, Chris McGregor, Mike Westbrook and Mike Osborne, forming, with Louis Moholo, the superb Mike Osborne Trio for several years. He also worked in a trio with Moholo and Peter Brötzmann. He also led bands of his own, notably the ferocious and all-star Isipingo, and the Quartette A Tête, which he co-founded with Tippet, Radu Malfatti and Paul Lytton. He co-founded the Lambeth New Music Society and Ogun records, both of which showcased many of the best UK-based musicians. He also ran regular gigs through his Grass Roots agency. He died as a result of a road-accident in 1983. His widow, Hazel, continues to make an important contribution to the scene through Ogun, and by the intermittent, tenacious organisation of benefits and other gigs. Selected albums: *Children At Play* (1974), with Isipingo *Family Affair* (1977), *In Conference* (1978), with Radu Malfatti *Bracknell Breakdown* (1978), with Peter Brötzmann, Louis Moholo *The Nearer The Bone The Sweeter The Meat* (1980), with Brötzmann, Moholo *Opened, But Hardly Touched* (1981), with Malfatti *Zwecknagel* (1981).

Miller, Mulgrew

b. 13 April 1955, Greenwood, Massachusetts, USA. Miller learnt the piano while a child and studied music at university, all the while playing in local gospel and R&B groups. After playing with Mercer Ellington's Orchestra in the late 70s, he joined vocalist Betty Carter before moving on to the quintet of Woody Shaw and Art Blakey's Jazz Messengers (1983-86). He has added all the innovations of recent piano playing to this solid background, and fused them with a brilliant technique. In the late 80s he continued with his prolific studio career and played with the quintet of Tony Williams.

Albums: with Art Blakey *Blue Night* (1985), *Keys To The City* (1985), *Live At Sweet Basil's* (1985), *Work!* (1986), with James Spalding *Gotshabe A Better Way* (1988), with Benny Golson

Benny Golson Quartet (1990), with Kenny Garrett *African Exchange Student* (1990), *Time And Again* (1992), *Hand In Hand* (1993).

Millinder, Lucky

b. Lucius Millinder, 8 August 1900, Anniston, Alabama, USA, d. 28 September 1966, New York, USA. Growing up in Chicago, Millinder worked in clubs and theatres in the late 20s as a dancer and master of ceremonies. His engaging personality resulted in his being appointed leader of several bands in Chicago, New York, and on tour. In 1933, he brought a band to Europe, playing as part of an all-black revue. The following year he was appointed leader of the Mills Blue Rhythm Band, fronting it at the Cotton Club in Harlem. Beginning in 1938, he had a few bad years, part of the time leading the Bill Doggett band but mostly suffering acute financial embarrassment. In 1940, he formed a new band of his own, hiring some quality musicians - including, at one time or another in the first few years, trumpeters Dizzy Gillespie, Joe Guy and Freddie Webster, saxophonists Tab Smith, Eddie 'Lockjaw' Davis and Sam 'The Man' Taylor, and in the rhythm section Doggett, Trevor Bacon and David 'Panama' Francis. Millinder also had Sister Rosetta Tharpe in the band for a while. He enjoyed considerable success, playing dance dates, often at the Savoy Ballroom in Harlem, broadcasting and touring, with occasional recording dates for good measure. Despite the changing times, Millinder kept the band afloat throughout the 40s, eventually calling it a day in 1952. Thereafter, he earned his living outside music, but formed occasional bands for special concerts. Although he was not a musician and could not read music, Millinder was an exceptional front man, conducting his bands with flair and showmanship. Given the fact that many of the arrangements used by his bands over the years were complex, he clearly had a good ear and was able to create the effect of leading when in reality he was following the musicians under his baton. Although it might be said with some justification that the Mills Blue Rhythm Band and his own band of the early 40s owed little to him musically, there can be little doubt that they owed him much for the success they enjoyed.
Selected compilations: *Big Bands Uptown!* (1931-43), *Lucky Millinder And His Orchestra 1941-1943* (1941-43), *Apollo Jump* (Affinity 1983), *Let It Roll Again* (Jukebox Lil 1985), *Shorty's Got To Go* (Jukebox Lil 1985), *Lucky Millinder And His Orchestra* (Hindsight 1987), *Ram-Bunk-Shush* (Sing 1988), *Stompin' At The Savoy 1943-44* (Bandstand 1988), *Lucky Millinder 1941-42* (Original Jazz Classics 1993).

Mills Blue Rhythm Band

Late in 1929, a group of New York musicians, under the nominal leadership of drummer Willie Lynch, formed a big band which they named the Blue Rhythm Band. A succession of front men, who included pianist Edgar Hayes and singer Cab Calloway, led the band, but despite high musical standards, it failed to gather a large following. In 1931, Irving Mills took over management of the band and appended his name. The Mills Blue Rhythm Band became third string in Mills's stable,

behind the bands of Duke Ellington and Calloway. Later conducted by Jimmy Ferguson ('Baron Lee') and then Lucky Millinder, the band made many fine records. Subsequently billed as the Instrumental Gentlemen From Harlem, the band eventually folded in 1938. During its existence, several top-flight musicians played in its ranks, among them trumpeters Henry 'Red' Allen, Shelton Hemphill, Charlie Shavers, Harry Edison and Edward Anderson, trombonist J.C. Higginbotham, saxophonists Charlie Holmes, Caster and Ted McCord, and clarinettist Buster Bailey. Especially in its middle and later years, the band was musically outstanding, playing fine arrangements by Tab Smith, Joe Garland and others. Regrettably, the band's lack of a charismatic frontman seemed to carry more weight with the public than its musical excellence, and the Mills Blue Rhythm Band sank into undeserved latterday obscurity. In the late 40s, the band was briefly reformed for record dates.
Selected compilations: *Henry 'Red' Allen And The Mills Blue Rhythm Band* (1934-35), *Big Bands* (1947), *Blue Rhythm* (Hep Jazz 1986 1930-31 recordings), *1937* (CJM 1987), *Rhythms Splash* (Hep Jazz 1987), *Savage Rhythm* (Hep Jazz 1987, 1931-32 recordings), *Rhythm Spasm* (Hep Jazz 1993, 1932-33 recordings).

Mince, Johnny

b. 8 July 1912, Chicago Heights, Illinois, USA. A highly accomplished clarinettist, Mince's early career saw him playing with several of the most sophisticated bands of the early swing era. At the age of 17, he was with Joe Haymes's excellent danceband, and during the 30s, Mince moved on to Ray Noble, Bob Crosby and Tommy Dorsey. During the spell with Noble, Mince played an important part in helping to establish the 'sound' of Glenn Miller's arrangements, a sound which Miller later developed with his own band. After military service, Mince was mostly active in studio work, but he returned occasionally to play jazz dates in clubs and on record. In later years, Mince became a familiar and popular figure at international jazz festivals, touring extensively with a variety of musicians, such as the Kings Of Jazz, and with the bands of dixieland veterans led by Yank Lawson and Bob Haggart and by British trumpeter Keith Smith. On all such forays, Mince attracted the favourable attention of a new generation of fans through his superb technique and distinctive style.
Albums: *Summer Of '79* (1979), *The Master Comes Home* i (c.1980), *I Can't Give You Anything But Love* (1982), with others *Swingin' The Forties With The Great Eight* (1983), *The Master Comes Home* ii (1983). Compilations: with Tommy Dorsey *The Sentimental Gentleman* (1941-42).

Mingus, Charles

b. 22 April 1922, Nogales, Arizona, USA, d. 5 January 1979, Cuernavaca, Mexico. Mingus was never allowed the luxury of the feeling of belonging. Reactions to his mixed ancestry (he had British-born, Chinese, Swedish and African American grandparents) produced strong feelings of anger and confirmed his sense of persecution. However, this alienation, coupled with his own deep sensitivity and tendency to dramatize his experiences, provided substantial fuel for an artistic career of heroic turmoil and brilliance. Formative musical experiences included both the strictures of European classical music and the uninhibited outpourings of the congregation of the local Holiness Church, which he attended with his stepmother. The latter included all manner of bluesy vocal techniques, moaning, audience-preacher responses, wild vibrato and melismatic improvisation, along with the accompaniment of cymbals and trombones - all of it melding into an early gospel precursor of big band that heavily influenced Mingus's mature compositional and performance style. Other influences were hearing Duke Ellington's band, and recordings of Richard Strauss's tone poems and works by Debussy, Ravel, Bach and Beethoven. Thwarted in his early attempts to learn trombone, Mingus switched from cello to double bass at high school.

He studied composition with Lloyd Reese and was encouraged by Red Callender to study bass with Herman Rheimschagen of the New York Philharmonic. He developed a virtuoso bass technique and began to think of the bass finger-board as similar to a piano keyboard. First professional dates as a bassist included gigs with New Orleans players Kid Ory and Barney Bigard, and then stints with the Louis Armstrong Orchestra (1943-1945) and Lionel Hampton (1947), but it was with the Red Norvo Trio (1950) that he first gained national recognition for his virtuosity. Work with other great pioneers of his generation such as Charlie Parker, Miles Davis, Thelonious Monk, Bud Powell, Sonny Stitt, Stan Getz, Lee Konitz, Dizzy Gillespie, Quincy Jones and Teddy Charles continued throughout the 50s. He joined Duke Ellington's band briefly in 1953, but a more artistically profitable association with his hero occurred with the trio album *Money Jungle*, which they made with Max Roach in 1962. Mingus was a pioneer of black management and artist-led record labels, forming Debut in 1953, and the Charles Mingus label in 1964. His early compositions were varying in success, often due to the difficulty of developing and maintaining an ensemble to realize his complex ideas. He contributed works to the Jazz Composers' Workshop from 1953 until the foundation of his own workshop ensemble in 1955. Here, he was able to make sparing use of notation, transmitting his intentions from verbal and musical instructions sketched at the piano or on the bass. Mingus's originality as composer first began to flourish under these circumstances, and with players such as Dannie Richmond, Rahsaan Roland Kirk, Jaki Byard, Jimmy Knepper and Booker Ervin he developed a number of highly evolved works. Crucial amongst his many innovations in jazz was the use of non-standard chorus structures, contrasting sections of quasi-'classical' composed material with passages of freeform and group improvisations, often of varying tempos and modes, in complex pieces knitted together by subtly evolving musical motifs. He developed a 'conversational' mode of interactive improvisation, and pioneered melodic bass playing. Such pieces as *The Black Saint And The Sinner Lady* (1963) show enormous vitality and a great depth of immersion in all jazz styles, from New Orleans and gospel to bebop and free jazz. Another multi-sectional piece, 'Meditations For A Pair Of Wire Cutters', from the album *Portrait* (1964), is one of many that evolved gradually under various titles. Sections from it can be heard on *Mingus Plays Piano* (1963), there called 'Myself When I Am Real'. It was renamed 'Praying With Eric' after the tragic death of Eric Dolphy, who made magnificent contributions to many Mingus compositions, but especially to this intensely moving piece.

In the mid-60s, financial and psychological problems began to take their toll, as poignantly recorded in Thomas Reichman's 1968 film *Mingus*. He toured extensively during this period, presenting a group of ensemble works. In 1971, Mingus was much encouraged by the receipt of a Guggenheim fellowship in composition, and the publication of his astonishing autobiography, *Beneath The Underdog*. The book opens with a session conducted by a psychiatrist, and the work reveals Mingus's self-insight, intelligence, sensitivity and tendency for self-dramatization. Touring continued until the gradual paralysis brought by the incurable disease Amyotrophic Lateral Sclerosis prevented him doing anything more than presiding over recordings. His piece 'Revelations' was performed in 1978 by the New York Philharmonic under the direction of Gunther Schuller, who also resurrected *Epitaph* in 1989. Also in 1978, Mingus was honoured at the White House by Jimmy Carter and an all-star jazz concert. News of his death aged 56 in Mexico was marked by many tributes from artists of all fields. Posthumously, the ensemble Mingus Dynasty continued to perform his works.

Mingus summed up the preoccupations of his time in a way which transcended racial and cultural divisions, whilst simultaneously highlighting racial and social injustices. Introducing the first 1964 performance of *Meditations*, Mingus tells the audience, 'This next composition was written when Eric Dolphy told me there was something similar to the concentration camps down South, [...] where they separated [...] the green from the red, or something like that; and the only difference between the electric barbed wire is that they don't have gas chambers and hot stoves to cook us in yet. So I wrote a piece called *Meditations* as to how to get some wire cutters before someone else gets some guns to us.' Off-mike, he can be heard saying to fellow musicians, 'They're gonna burn us; they'll try.' In the turmoil of his life and artistic achievements, and in his painful demise, Mingus became his own artistic creation. A desperate, passionate icon for the mid-20th century to which all can relate in some way, he articulated the emotional currents of his time in a way superior to that of almost any other contemporary jazz musician.

Selected albums: *Red Norvo Jazz Trio* (1951), with Spaulding Givens *Strings And Keys* (1951), *The Red Norvo - Charles Mingus - Tal Farlow Trio* (1951), *Autobiography In Jazz* (1953), with others *Quintet Of The Year/Jazz At Massey Hall* (1953), *Jazz Composers Workshop* (Savoy 1954), *Jazz Experiments* (1954), *Charles Mingus And Thad Jones* (1955), *Jazz Composers Workshop No 2* (Savoy 1955), *Mingus At The Bohemia* (1955), *Pithecanthropus Erectus* (Atlantic 1956), *The Clown* aka *Reincarnation Of A Lovebird* (1957), with Gunther Schuller, George Russell *Adventures In Sound* (1957), *Jazz Workshop*

Presents: Jimmy Knepper (1957), *East Coasting* (1957), *Dukes Choice* aka *A Modern Jazz Symposium Of Music And Poetry* (1957), with Langston Hughes *Weary Blues* (1958), with Billie Holiday etc *Easy To Remember* (1958), *Wonderland* aka *Jazz Portraits* (1959), *Blues And Roots* (Atlantic 1959), *Mingus Ah-Um* (Columbia 1959), *Nostalgia In Times Square* (1959), *Mingus Dynasty* (1959), *Pre-Bird* aka *Mingus Revisited* (Emarcy 1960), *Mingus At Antibes* (1960), *Charles Mingus Presents Charles Mingus!* (Candid 1960), *Mingus* (1960), *The Jazz Life* (1960), *Newport Rebels* (1960), with Tubby Hayes *All Night Long* (1960), *Oh Yeah!* (Oh Yeah 1961), *Tonight At Noon* (1961), *Hooray For Charles Mingus* (1962), *J-For-Jazz Presents Charles Mingus* (1962), with Duke Ellington, Max Roach *Money Jungle* (1962), *Town Hall Concert* (1962), *The Black Saint And The Sinner Lady* (Impulse 1963), *Mingus Mingus Mingus Mingus Mingus* (Impulse 1963), *Tijuana Moods* (RCA 1964, rec 1957), *Town Hall Concert (Portrait)* (Original Jazz Classics 1964), *Live in Oslo* (rec 1964), *Charles Mingus Sextet Live In Europe Vols 1, 2* and *3* (1964), *The Great Concert Of Charles Mingus* (1964), *Mingus In Europe Vols 1 and 2* (1964), *Charles Mingus In Amsterdam* (1964), *Mingus In Stuttgart* (1964, 2 vols), *Right Now!* (1964), *Charles Mingus In Europe* (Enja 1964), *Mingus At Monterey* (Prestige 1964), *Music Written For Monterey 1965, But Not Heard* (1965), *My Favourite Quintet* (1965), *Statements* (1970), *Charles Mingus In Paris* (DIW 1970), *Pithy Canthropus Erectus* aka *Blue Bird* (1970), *Charles Mingus In Berlin* (1970), *Charles Mingus And The New Herd* (1971), *Let My Children Hear Music* (1971), *Charles Mingus And Friends In Concert* (1972), *Jazz Jamboree* (1972), *Charles Mingus Meets Cat Anderson* (1972), *Mingus Mingus* (1973), *Mingus At Carnegie Hall* (1974), *Cumbria And Jazz Fusion* (Atlantic 1977), *Three Or Four Shades Of Blue* (1977), *Lionel Hampton Presents: The Music Of Charles Mingus* aka *His Final Works* (1977), *Me Myself An Eye* (1978), *Something Like A Bird* (1978), *The Charles Mingus Memorial Album* (1978), with Joni Mitchell *Joni Mitchell - Mingus* (1978). Selected compilations: *The Mingus Connection* (1957, rec 1951-53), *The Debut Recordings* (1951-57), *Vital Savage Horizons* (1952, 1961-62), *The Atlantic Years* (1956-1978), *Better Git It In Your Soul* (1959), *The Complete Candid Recordings Of Charles Mingus* (1960), *Charles Mingus/Cecil Taylor: Rare Broadcast Performances* (1962, 1966), *The Impulse Years* (1963), *Portrait* (1964, 1966), *Re-Evaluation: The Impulse Years* (1973, rec 1963-64), *The Art Of Charles Mingus* (1974), *Passions Of A Man* (1979, rec 1956-61, 1973, 1977), *Nostalgia In Times Square* (1979, rec 1959), *Great Moments With Charles Mingus* (1981, rec 1963-64), *Mingus, The Collection* (1985, rec c.50s), *Charles Mingus - New York Sketchbook* (1986, rec c.50s), *Charles Mingus - Shoes Of The Fisherman's Wife* (1988, rec 1959, 1971), *Abstractions* (1989, rec 1954, 1957), *Charles Mingus - Mysterious Blues* (1989, rec 1960), *Charles Mingus 1955-1957* (1990), *Charles Mingus* (1991), *Charles Mingus - The Complete Debut Recordings* (Debut 1991, 12-CD box set, rec c.50s), *Thirteen Pictures: The Charles Mingus Anthology* (Rhino, 1956-77 recordings), *Meditations On Integration* (1992, rec 1964).

Further reading: *Beneath The Underdog*, Charles Mingus. *Mingus: A Critical Biography*, Brian Priestley.
Video: *Charles Mingus Sextet* (KJazz 1994, rec 1964).

Mitchell, Billy

b. 3 November 1926, Kansas City, Missouri, USA. Mitchell studied in Detroit and worked with Nat Towles's band in the late 40s before moving to New York with Lucky Millender's Orchestra. He spent a couple of months in Woody Herman's Second Herd, and then lead his own bop quintet back in Detroit, which included Thad Jones on trumpet and Elvin Jones on drums (1950-53). In the mid-50s, after a couple of years with Dizzy Gillespie, he recorded with Ray Charles and joined Count Basie's Orchestra. He co-led a sextet with ex-Basie trombonist Al Grey, and worked as musical director for Stevie Wonder in the mid-60s, before rejoining Basie (1966-67). He uses a tough, bluesy tone to construct fluent solo lines. In the 70s Mitchell settled in New York and undertook studio work, as well as teaching and performing with the Xanadu All Stars.
Albums: with Ray Charles *Soul Brothers* (1957), with Count Basie *One More Time* (1958), *Al Grey With Billy Mitchell* (1961), *Little Juicy* (1963), with Xanadu *Xanadu At Montreux* (1978), with Paul Lingle *Vintage Piano Vol 3* (Euphonic 1979), *De Lawd's Blues* (1980), *Faces* (Optimism 1987), *In Focus* (Optimism 1989).

Mitchell, Blue

b. Richard Allen Mitchell, 13 March 1930, Miami, Florida, USA, d. 21 May 1979. Mitchell's early professional career found him playing trumpet in a number of R&B bands, including that led in the mid-50s by Earl Bostic. Later in the decade he worked briefly with Cannonball Adderley in New York, and then joined Horace Silver's band, an engagement which established Mitchell's reputation. When Silver disbanded in 1963, Mitchell formed his own group, employing most of his fellow musicians, with Silver's place being taken by Chick Corea. This band continued until the end of the decade, at which time Mitchell joined the band that was backing Ray Charles. During the early 70s, Mitchell played with a number of artists in fields outside jazz, notably bluesman John Mayall and popular singers such as Tony Bennett and Lena Horne. Resident in Los Angeles from the mid-70s, Mitchell played in both small and big bands, including those led by Harold Land, Louie Bellson and Bill Berry. A gifted, soulful player with a full, rich tone, Mitchell's frequent excursions into areas of music outside jazz never caused him to lower his standards. Indeed, he enhanced every record date, concert or club engagement on which he played with the sincerity of his playing and the beautiful sound he drew from his instrument.
Albums: *Big Six* (Original Jazz Classics 1958), with Horace Silver *Finger Poppin'* (1959), *Out Of The Blue* (Original Jazz Classics 1959), *Blue Soul* (Original Jazz Classics 1959), with Silver *Horace-Scope* (1960), *Blues On My Mind* (Original Jazz Classics 1960), *Blue Moods* (1960), *Smooth As The Wind* (1960), *A Sure Thing* (1962), *The Cup Bearers* (Original Jazz

Classics 1963), *Step Lightly* (1963), *The Thing To Do* (Blue Note 1964), *Down With It* (1965), *Bring It Home To Me* (1966), *Boss Horn* (1966), *Heads Up!* (1967), *Collisons In Black* (1968), *Bantu Village* (1969), *Blue Mitchell* (1971), *Vital Blue* (1971), with John Mayall *Jazz Blues Fusion* (1971), *Blue's Blues* (1972-74), *Graffiti Blues* (Audio Fidelity 1973-74), *Many Shades Of Blue* (1974), with Bill Berry *Hot & Happy* (1974), *Stratosonic Nuances* (c.1975), *Funktion Junction* (1976), with Berry *Hello Rev* (1976), with Dexter Gordon, Al Cohn *True Blue* (1976), with Harold Land *Mapenzi* (1977), with Land *Best Of The West* (1977), *Last Dance* (1977), *African Violet* (1977), *Summer Soft* (1977).

Mitchell, Red

b. Keith Moore Mitchell, 20 September 1927, New York City, New York, USA, d. 8 November 1992. After studying piano and alto saxophone, Mitchell took up the bass while serving in the armed forces. In the late 40s he played in bands led by Jackie Paris, Mundell Lowe, Chubby Jackson (with whom he played piano) and Charlie Ventura. He spent two years with Woody Herman, but was hospitalized with tuberculosis in 1951. In the early 50s he worked with Red Norvo and Gerry Mulligan, opting to stay in California when Mulligan headed back to New York. Resident in Los Angeles from 1954, Mitchell became an important figure on the west coast scene, accompanying and sometimes leading artists such as Chet Baker, Bill Perkins, André Previn, Mel Lewis, Hampton Hawes, Don Cherry, Ornette Coleman and Harold Land. In the late 60s, Mitchell moved to Sweden, remaining in Europe for 10 years, accompanying visiting American musicians and leading his own groups, which included Communication. During the 80s, Mitchell divided his time between Europe and the USA, playing and recording extensively with jazzmen including Lee Konitz, Warne Marsh, Art Pepper and Jimmy Rowles. Mitchell's playing in the 50s was advanced for its time, and in some of his technical developments he opened the way for artists such as Scott La Faro. His clean articulation made his solo work of particular interest and an unaccompanied album, *Home Suite*, clearly revealed his remarkable talent. (His brother Whitey Mitchell, also a bass player, was active in the 50s and 60s, but later left the jazz scene.)

Selected albums: *The Fabulous Gerry Mulligan Quartet* (1954), *The Red Mitchell Sextet* (1955), *Jam For Your Bread* (Affinity 1955), *Hampton Hawes Trio* (1955), with Hawes *All-Night Session* (1956), *Sessions, Live* (1957), *Presenting Red Mitchell* (1957), with André Previn *Pal Joey* (1957), with Previn *West Side Story* (1959), *Red Mitchell At The Renaissance* (1960), with Harold Land *Hear Ye!* (1961), *The Red Mitchell Trio* (1969), *The Red Mitchell Quartet* (1972), with Konitz *I Concentrate On You* (1974), *Communication* (1974), *Red Mitchell Meets Guido Manusardi* (1974), *Blues For A Crushed Soul* (Sonet 1976), *Chocolate Cadillac* (1976), *Red Mitchell And Friends* (1978), *Jim Hall/Red Mitchell* (1978), *Red Mitchell Plays Piano And Sings* (1979), with Art Pepper *Straight Life* (1979), *Empathy* (1980), with Tommy Flanagan *You're Me* (1980), *Home Cookin'* (1980), *Soft And Warm And Swinging* (1982), *When I'm Singing*

(1982), *Holiday For Monica* (1983), *The Jimmy Rowles/Red Mitchell Trio* (1985), *Home Suite* (1985), with Clark Terry *To Duke And Basie* (c.1986), with Terry *Jive At Five* (c.1986), with Kenny Barron *The Red Barron Duo* (1986), with Herb Ellis *Doggin' Around* (1988), with Putte Wickman *The Very Thought Of You* (1988), with Roger Kellaway *Alone Together* (Dragon 1988), *Talking* (1989), *Evolution* (1990).

Mitchell, Roscoe

b. 3 August 1940, Chicago, Illinois, USA. As a child Mitchell enjoyed listening to Nat 'King' Cole, Lester Young and Charlie Parker. He studied clarinet and baritone saxophone in high school, taking up alto saxophone in his senior year and continuing with it while in the army. He went to Europe with an army band, where he heard Albert Ayler, who was also playing in a military band. After demobilization, he played bop in an outfit with Henry Threadgill, but Ayler's music had been a revelation to him. Back in Chicago, he jammed with Threadgill, Malachi Favors, Jack DeJohnette, and Muhal Richard Abrams. Abrams was even more of an influence than Ayler. In 1965 Mitchell, was a charter member of the AACM, having played in the Experimental Band (organised by Abrams, the AACM President, inspirer and prime mover) since 1961. His debut *Sound* was the first and one of the most famous recordings to come out of the AACM, characterizing the Chicagoan's new emphasis on sound-as-texture and the importance of the relationship between sound and silence. On these tracks, wrote critic John Litweiller, 'Music is the tension of sounds in the free space of silence'. For a while Mitchell led his own groups, and it was from one of these (a quartet including Lester Bowie, Favors and Phillip Wilson) that the Art Ensemble Of Chicago grew. He once explained: 'It was my band, but I couldn't afford to pay those guys what they deserved, so everybody was shouldering an equal amount of responsibility. We became a co-operative unit in order to remain committed to one another and in order to survive.' Since co-founding the Art Ensemble in 1969, most of his work has been accomplished with them, but he has continued to lead bands of his own, including Space (a trio with saxophonist Gerald Oshita and vocalist Tom Buckner) and Sound (a quintet with trumpet, guitar, bass and percussion). He has also worked with Byron Austin, Scotty Holt and DeJohnette; and has assembled an impressive body of solo saxophone music. Like his partners in the Art Ensemble, Mitchell plays a dazzling number of instruments, the primary ones being soprano, alto, tenor and bass saxophones, oboe, flute, piccolo and clarinet as well as various percussion and 'little instruments'. He and Joseph Jarman represent the two poles of the Ensemble's art: Jarman brings the bulk of the theatrical impulse, while Mitchell - the one member of the group who does not habitually wear facepaint or costume - is the musical structuralist who, despite the apparent freedom of the Ensemble's music, worries about how true an improviser will be to the composer's intention. As a composer he has been an influence on Anthony Braxton and Leo Smith. There is an ascetic streak to his art, and it is not insignificant that as soon as he was able, he went to live on a 365-acre farm in Wisconsin, dissatisfied with the life-style necessitated by constant touring. Recent projects have included *Songs In The Wind*, which features Steve Sylvester on 'bull roarers and wind wands'; a meeting with the Stockholm-based Brus Trio (*After Fallen Leaves*); and *Four Compositions*, which shows Mitchell evolving into an impressive writer of classical chamber music.

Albums: *Sound* (Delmark 1966), *Solo Saxophone Concerts* (1974), *The Roscoe Mitchell Quartet* (1975), *Old/Quartet* (1975, rec 1967), *Nonaah* (1977), *L-R-G/The Maze/S II Examples* (1978), *Duets With Anthony Braxton* (1978), *Congliptious* (Nessa 1978), *Roscoe Mitchell* (Chief 1979), *Sketches From Bamboo* (1979), *Snurdy McGurdy And Her Dancin' Shoes* (1981), with Tom Buckner, Gerald Oshita *New Music For Woodwinds And Voice* (1981), *3x4 Eye* (1981), *More Cutouts* (Cecma 1981), *Concert Toronto 4/5 October 1975* (Sackville 1981), with Space *An Interesting Breakfast Conversation* (1984), *And The Sound And Space Ensembles* (1984), *Live At The Muhle Hunziken* (1986), *The Flow Of Things* (Black Saint 1987), *Four Compositions* (1987), *Live In Detroit* (1989), *Songs In The Wind* (Victo 1991), with Brus Trio *After Fallen Leaves* (Silkheart 1992, rec. 1989), *Live At The Knitting Factory* (Black Saint 1992, 1987 recording), with Muhal Richard Abrams *Solos And Duets At Merkin Hall* (Black Saint 1992), *This Dance Is For Steve McCall* (Black Saint 1993).

Mobley, Hank

b. Henry Mobley, 7 July 1930, Eastman, Georgia, USA, d. 30 May 1986. Tenor saxophonist Mobley began his professional career with an R&B band in 1950. The following year, he was attracting the attention of such important beboppers as Max Roach and Dizzy Gillespie, and by 1954 his stature was such that he was invited to become a founder member of Horace Silver's Jazz Messengers. When Silver reformed a band under his own name, bequeathing the Messengers to Art Blakey, Mobley went along, too. In the late 50s he was briefly with Blakey, then worked with Dizzy Reece and, in 1961, spent a short but memorable time with Miles Davis. Throughout the 60s, Mobley worked with many distinguished musicians, among them Lee Morgan, Barry Harris and Billy Higgins, often leading the bands, and recording several outstanding sessions for Blue Note. In the 70s, Mobley was dogged by poor health, but he worked sporadically, including a stint as co-leader of a group with Cedar Walton. Mobley played even less frequently in the 80s, but shortly before his death in 1986, he worked with Duke Jordan. The seemingly casual ease with which Mobley performed, comfortably encompassing complex rhythmical innovations, and the long period spent on the sidelines have tended to obscure the fact that his was a remarkable talent. Also militating against widespread appeal was his sometimes detached, dry and intimate sound, which contrasted sharply with the more aggressively robust style adopted by many of his contemporaries.

Selected albums: with Art Blakey *The Jazz Messengers At The Cafe Bohemia* (1955), *The Hank Mobley Quartet* (1955), *The Jazz Message Of Hank Mobley* (Savoy 1956), *Mobley's Message* (1956), *Mobley's Second Message* (Savoy 1956), *The Hank Mobley Sextet* (1956), *Hank Mobley-Lee Morgan: Hank's Shout* (1956), *Hank Mobley And His All Stars* (1957), *The Hank Mobley Quintet* (1957), *Hank* (1957), *Hank Mobley* (1957), *Poppin'* (1957), *Peckin' Time* (Blue Note 1958), *Monday Night At Birdland* (1958), *Soul Station* (Blue Note 1960), *Roll Call* (1960), with Miles Davis *Carnegie Hall 1961* (1961), with Davis *At The Blackhawk* (1961), *Workout* (Blue Note 1961), *Another Workout* (1961), *Straight No Filter* (Blue Note 1963-65), *No Room For Squares* (Blue Note 1963), *The Turnaround* (1965), *Dippin'* (Blue Note 1965), *A Caddy For Daddy* (Blue Note 1965), *A Slice Of The Top* (1966), *Third Season* (1967), *Hi Voltage* (1967), *Far Away Lands* (Blue Note 1967), *Reach Out* (1968), *The Flip* (1969), *Thinking Of Home* (1970).

Modern Jazz Quartet

In 1951, four musicians who had previously played together in the Dizzy Gillespie big band formed a small recording group. Known as the Milt Jackson Quartet, the group consisted of Jackson (vibraphone), John Lewis (piano), Ray Brown (bass), and Kenny Clarke (drums). Brown's place was soon taken by Percy Heath, and by the following year, the group had adopted the name, Modern Jazz Quartet. Although initially only a recording group, they then began playing concert engagements. In 1955, Clarke dropped out to be replaced by Connie Kay. The new line-up of Jackson, Lewis, Heath and Kay continued performing as a full-time ensemble for the next few years, later reducing their collective commitments to several months each year. Seen as both a black response to the intellectualism of the Dave Brubeck quartet and New York's answer to west coast cool jazz, the MJQ were both very popular and very controversial, their detractors claiming that their music was too delicate and too cerebral. Whatever the case, there was certainly no denying that the group brought the dignity and professionalism of a classical quartet to their jazz performances. In 1974, the MJQ was disbanded, but reformed once more in 1981 for a concert tour of Japan. The success of this comeback convinced the members to reunite on a semi-permanent basis, which they did in the following year. Since 1982 they have continued to play concert and festival dates. Among the most sophisticated of all bop ensembles, the MJQ's directing influence has always been Lewis, whose sober performing and composing style was never more apparent than in this context. Lewis's interest in classical music has also been influential in MJQ performances, thus placing the group occasionally, and possibly misleadingly, on the fringes of third-stream jazz. The playing of Heath and Kay in this, as in most other settings in which they work, is distinguished by its subtle swing. Of the four, Jackson is the most musically volatile, and the restraints placed upon him in the MJQ create intriguing formal tensions which are, in jazz terms, one of the most exciting aspects of the group's immaculately played, quietly serious music.

Selected albums: *Django* (1953), *Concorde* (1955), *The Artistry Of* (Prestige 1956), *The MJQ At Music Inn* (1956), *Django* (Original Jazz Classics 1956), *Fontessa* (Atlantic 1956), *Live* (Jazz Anthology 1956), *One Never Knows* (1957), *Third Stream Music* (1957), *MJQ* (Original Jazz Classics 1957), *Concorde*

(Original Jazz Classics 1957), *Live At The Lighthouse* (Atlantic 1957), *Plus* (1957-71), *At Music Inn: Vol 2* (Atlantic 1958), *Odds Against Tomorrow* (1959), *Longing For The Continent* (LRC 1959), *European Concert* (1960), *Pyramid* (Atlantic 1961), *Lonely Woman* (Atlantic 1962), *The Comedy* (Atlantic 1962), *The Sheriff* (Atlantic 1963), *A Quartet Is A Quartet* (Atlantic 1963), *Blues At Carnegie Hall* (1966), *Under The Jasmine Tree* (Apple 1968), *Space* (1969), *Plastic Dreams* (Atlantic 1971), *The Legendary Profile* (Atlantic 1972), *Blues On Bach* (Atlantic 1974), *The Complete Last Concert* (Atlantic 1974), *In Memoriam* (1977), *Together Again!* (Pablo 1982), *Together Again!: Echoes* (Pablo 1984), *The Best Of The MJQ* (1984-85), *Three Windows* (Atlantic 1987), *For Ellington* (East West 1988), *MJQ & Friends* (Atlantic 1994), *A Celebration* (Atlantic 1994). Compilation: *MJQ 40* (Atlantic 4CD box set, 1952-88 recordings).

Moholo, Louis

b. 10 March 1940, Cape Town, South Africa. Moholo is simply one of the great drummers, regardless of genre. In common with Blackwell and Billy Higgins, both alumni of Ornette Coleman's Quartet, he has developed a sharp, clean, agile style, and shares with Higgins a remarkable ability to play with considerable dynamic restraint without losing strength and momentum. He is equally capable of thunderous, breakneck playing, which commands attention as much through its constant inventiveness as through its inexorable power. He grew up in a musical environment (his father a pianist, his mother and sister, singers). At the age of 16 he co-founded the Cordettes big band. In 1962, he won the Best Drummer award at the Johannesburg Jazz Festival and, together with four more of the best players at the Festival, he was invited by Chris McGregor to form a band. Thus the legendary Blue Notes were created. As a mixed-race band it was impossible for them to work under apartheid and so, in 1964, while touring Europe, they decided to stay in Switzerland. After a year there they settled in London, where, ultimately evolving into the Chris McGregor Group, they made a huge impact. As well as playing in the six-piece McGregor Group and the Brotherhood Of Breath big band, Moholo put his stamp on many fine bands, including Elton Dean's Ninesense, the Mike Osborne Trio, and Keith Tippett's extra-big band, Ark. In 1966, he toured South America with Steve Lacy, Enrico Rava and Johnny Dyani. In the 70s and 80s he often worked in Europe, particularly in trios with Irène Schweizer and Rudiger Carl, and Peter Brötzmann and Harry Miller, and recorded a duo concert with Schweizer in 1986. Moholo has also worked in duos with Tippett and Andrew Cyrille, and organized the African Drum Ensemble. He currently leads Viva La Black as well as a trio with Gary Curzon and Paul Rogers (recalling the classic Osborne trio) and plays in a percussion duo with Thebe Lipere.

Albums: with Irène Schweizer, Rudiger Carl *Messer* (1975), *Blue Notes For Mongezi* (1976), with Schweizer, Carl *Tuned Boots* (1977), *Blue Notes In Concert Volume I* (1978), *Spirits Rejoice* (1978), with Peter Brötzmann, Harry Miller *The Nearer The Bone, The Sweeter The Meat* (1980), with Keith Tippett *No Gossip* (1980), with Brötzmann, Miller *Opened, But Hardly Touched* (1981), with Tippett, Larry Stabbins *Tern* (1982), *Irène Schweizer/Louis Moholo* (1987), *Blue Notes For Johnny* (1987), *Viva La Black* (1988), with Cecil Taylor *Remembrance* (1989), *Exile* (Ogun 1991).

Mole, Miff

b. Irving Milfred Mole, 11 March 1898, Roosevelt, Long Island, New York, USA, d. 29 April 1961. A youthful multi-instrumentalist, Mole had settled on the trombone by his mid-teenage years. Gigging extensively in and around New York, he worked with many small early jazz bands, including one led by pianist-turned-comedian Jimmy Durante, and was also a member of the Original Memphis Five, led by Phil Napoleon. In the mid-20s he became a close friend and musical associate of Red Nichols; they made many records together and generally encouraged one another's development. After a stint with Roger Wolfe Kahn's popular society band, Mole began a long period of studio work, and in 1938 joined Paul Whiteman. In the early 40s Mole began teaching, worked briefly with Benny Goodman, and led his own small bands at nightspots in New York and Chicago. Ill-health restricted his career in the 50s. Although subsequently overshadowed by outstanding contemporaries such as Jack Teagarden and Tommy Dorsey, Mole played an important role in the development of jazz trombone. He was a major influence in elevating the instrument from its slightly jokey status as a purveyor of unusual sounds, ably demonstrating that it could be a tasteful, melodic vehicle on which to play effective jazz solos. His exceptional technique also provided a standard by which trombonists could be measured, at least until the arrival on the scene of latterday technical wizards. He died in April 1961.

Selected compilations: *Miff Mole's Molers '1927'* (Swaggie 1983, 1927 recording), *Miff Mole's Molers '1928/30'* (Swaggie 1983, 1928-30 recording), with Bobby Hackett *At Nick's* (1944).

Moncur, Grachan, III

b. 3 June 1937, New York City, New York, USA. An early starter (his father played bass with Al Cooper's Savoy Sultans), Moncur had already mastered several other instruments when, at the age of 11, he turned to the trombone. In his teens, Moncur worked with local bands and also studied music. In the early 60s he was with Ray Charles, and was a member of the Art Farmer-Benny Golson Jazztet. He also worked with Jackie McLean and Sonny Rollins, recorded for Blue Note and, by the late 60s, was a leading figure of the free jazz movement, playing with Archie Shepp in the USA and Europe. In the 70s, Moncur worked with the Jazz Composers' Orchestra, and in the 80s, with Frank Lowe, among others. In the last decade or so, his experience has also been applied to teaching and to several major compositions in musical areas ranging from jazz to ballet. An accomplished performer, Moncur's fluid style has helped to make his playing more readily accessible than that of many other free jazz trombonists. Through his teaching and recording he continues to exercise considerable influence upon the rising generation of musicians.

Albums: *Evolution* (Blue Note 1963), *Some Other Stuff* (1964), *New Africa* (Affinity 1969), with Jazz Composers Orchestra *Echoes Of Prayer* (1974).

Monk, Meredith

b. 20 November 1943, Lima, Peru. In 1964, Monk graduated in performing arts from Sarah Lawrence College where she had been encouraged to mix the arts in a variety of projects. She saw herself as an 'orchestrator of music and image and movement', someone making 'live movies'. She first appeared in New York at Washington Square Gallery and was one of a group of artists, including painter Robert Rauschenberg, creating mixed-media pieces like Duet For Cat's Scream And Locomotive at Judson Church. She presented her theatre piece, *Juice*, at New York's Guggenheim Museum in 1969, and brought her group the House to Liverpool in 1972 to perform *The Vessel*. In the same year, she received a *Village Voice* Award for outstanding achievement in the Off-Broadway Theatre. She also performed solo vocal pieces like 'Raw Recital', from which 'a definite American Indian quality emerged'. She sees herself as performing ethnic music from a culture she has herself created. In 1978, she formed the Vocal Ensemble to perform compositions which consist of simple, often modal melodies or melodic cells which are repeated with small variations and contrasted with different material. These performances are sometimes accompanied by repetitive keyboard parts reminiscent of the minimalist movement, and usually depend on extended vocal techniques. The success of *Dolmen Music* and *Turtle Dreams* has brought the Ensemble to an international audience.

Albums: *Our Lady Of Late* (1973), *Key: An Album Of Invisible Theatre* (Lovely 1977), *Songs From The Hill* (1979), *Dolmen Music* (1980), *Dolmen Music* (ECM 1981), *Turtle Dreams* (ECM 1983), *Do You Be* (ECM 1987), *Book Of Days* (ECM 1990), with Robert Een *Facing North* (1992), *Atlas* (ECM 1993).

Monk, Thelonious

b. 11 October 1917, Rocky Mount, North Carolina, USA, d. 17 February 1982. Monk's family moved to New York when he was five years old. He started playing piano a year later, receiving formal tuition from the age of 11 onwards. At Stuyvesant High School he excelled at physics and maths, and also found time to play organ in church. In the late 30s he toured with a gospel group, then began playing in the clubs and became pianist in Kenny Clarke's house band at Minton's Playhouse between 1941 and 1942. He played with Lucky Millinder's orchestra in 1942, the Coleman Hawkins Sextet between 1943 and 1945, the Dizzy Gillespie Big Band in 1946 and started leading his own outfits from 1947. It was Hawkins who provided him with his recording debut, and enthusiasts noted a fine solo on 'Flyin' Hawk' (October 1944). However, it was the Blue Note sessions of 1947 (subsequently issued on album and CD as *Genius Of Modern Music*) that established him as a major figure. With Art Blakey on drums, these recordings have

operated as capsule lessons in music for subsequent generations of musicians. An infectious groove makes complex harmonic puzzles sound attractive, with Monk's unique dissonances and rhythmic sense adding to their charm. They were actually a distillation of a decade's work. ''Round Midnight' immediately became a popular tune and others - 'Ruby My Dear', 'Well You Needn't', 'In Walked Bud' - have become jazz standards since. In his book, *Bebop*, Leonard Feather recognized Monk's genius at composition, but claimed his playing lacked technique (a slight he later apologised for). Monk certainly played with flat fingers (anathema to academy pianists), but actually his barebones style was the result of a modern sensibility rather than an inability to achieve the torrents of Art Tatum or Oscar Peterson. For Monk, the blues had enough romance without an influx of European romanticism, and enough emotion without the sometimes over-heated blowing of bebop. His own improvisations are at once witty, terse and thought-provoking. A trumped-up charge for possession of drugs deprived Monk of his New York performer's licence in 1951, and a subsequent six-year ban from playing live in the city damaged his career. He played in Paris in June 1954 (recorded by Vogue Records). Riverside Records was supportive, and he found sympathetic musicians with whom to record - both under his own name and guesting with players such as Miles Davis, Sonny Rollins and Clark Terry. *Plays Duke Ellington* (1955) was a fascinating look at Duke Ellington's compositions, with a non-pareil rhythm section in bassist Oscar Pettiford and drummer Clarke. *Brilliant Corners* in 1956 showcased some dazzling new compositions and featured Sonny Rollins on tenor saxophone. Regaining his work permit in 1957, Monk assembled a mighty quintet for a residency at the Five Spot club: Shadow Wilson (drums), Wilbur Ware (bass) and John Coltrane (tenor). Coltrane always spoke of what an education he received during his brief stay with the band - though the group was never recorded live, the studio albums that resulted (*Thelonious Monk With John Coltrane, Monk's Music*) were classics. Monk repaid Coleman Hawkins' earlier compliment, and featured the tenorman on these records: history and the future shook hands over Monk's keyboard. Previously considered too 'way out' for mass consumption, Monk's career finally began to blossom. In 1957, he recorded with Gerry Mulligan, which helped to expose him to a wider audience, and worked with classical composer Hall Overton to present his music orchestrally (*At Town Hall*, 1959). He toured Europe for the first time (1961) and also Japan (1964). He formed a stable quartet in the early 60s with Charlie Rouse on tenor, John Ore (later Butch Warren or Larry Gales) on bass and Frankie Dunlop (later Ben Riley) on drums. Critics tend to prefer his work with other saxophonists, such as Harold Land (1960) or Johnny Griffin (the late 50s), but the point was that Rouse really understood Monk's tunes. He may not have been the greatest soloist, but his raw, angular tone fitted the compositions like a glove.

In the early 70s, Monk played with Pat Patrick (Sun Ra's alto player), using son T.S. Monk on drums. Illness increasingly restricted his activity, but he toured with the Giants Of Jazz (1971-72) and presented a big band at the Newport Festival in

1974. Two albums recorded for the English Black Lion label in 1971 - *Something In Blue* and *The Man I Love* - presented him in a trio context with Al McKibbon on bass and Blakey on drums: these were stunning examples of the empathy between drummer and pianist - two of Monk's best records. When he died from a stroke in 1982, at Englewood, New Jersey, leaving his wife (for whom he had written 'Crepuscule With Nellie') and son, he had not performed in public for six years. Monk's influence, if anything, increased during the 80s. Buell Neidlinger formed a band, String Jazz, to play only Monk and Ellington tunes; Steve Lacy, who in the early 60s had spent a period playing exclusively Monk tunes, recorded two solo discs of his music; and tribute albums by Arthur Blythe (*Light Blue*, 1983), Anthony Braxton (*Six Monk's Compositions*, 1987), Paul Motian (*Monk In Motian*, 1988) and Hal Wilner (*That's The Way I Feel Now*, 1984, in which artists as diverse as the Fowler Brothers, John Zorn, Dr. John, Eugene Chadbourne, and Peter Frampton celebrated his tunes) prove that Monk's compositions are still teaching everyone new tricks. His son, T.S. Monk, is a gifted drummer who continues a tradition by encouraging young musicians through membership of his band. One of the most brilliant and original performers in jazz, Thelonious Monk was also one of the century's outstanding composers. ''Round Midnight' is probably the most recorded jazz song of all time. His unique ability to weld intricate, surprising harmonic shifts and rhythmic quirks into appealing, funky riffs means that something special happens when they are played: his compositions exact more incisive improvising than anybody else's. In terms of jazz, that is the highest praise of all.

Selected albums: *Genius Of Modern Music, Vols One And Two* (Blue Note, rec. 1947-52), *Thelonious Monk Trio* (1953), *And Sonny Rollins* (1954), *Pure Monk* (1954), *Solo 1954* (Vogue 1955), *Plays Duke Ellington* (Original Jazz Classics 1956), *The Unique* (Original Jazz Classics 1956), *Brilliant Corners* (Original Jazz Classics 1957), *Thelonious Himself* (Original Jazz Classics 1957), *With John Coltrane* (Original Jazz Classics 1957), with Gerry Mulligan *Mulligan Meets Monk* (Original Jazz Classics 1957), *Art Blakey/Thelonious Monk* (1958), *Monk's Music* (Original Jazz Classics 1958), *Thelonious In Action* (Original Jazz Classics 1958), *Misterioso* (Original Jazz Classics 1958), *The Thelonious Monk Orchestra At Town Hall* (Original Jazz Classics 1959), *Five By Monk By Five* (Original Jazz Classics 1959), *Thelonious Alone In San Francisco* (Original Jazz Classics 1960), *At The Blackhawk* (Original Jazz Classics 1960), *Two Hours With Thelonious* (1961), *Criss Cross* (Columbia 1963), *Monk's Dream* (Columbia 1963), *Big Band And Quartet In Concert* (1964), with Miles Davis *Miles & Monk At Newport* (1964, rec 1963, 1958), *It's Monk's Time* (Columbia 1964), *Monk* (1964), *Solo Monk* (Columbia 1965), *Straight No Chaser* (Columbia 1966), *Monk's Blues* (Columbia 1968), *Underground* (Columbia 1968), *Epistrophy* (1971), *Something In Blue* (1972), *The Man I Love* (1972), *Sphere* (1979, rec. 1967), *April In Paris/Live* (1981, rec. 1971), *Live At The It Club* (Columbia 1982, rec. 1964), *Live At The Jazz Workshop* (Columbia 1982, rec. 1964), *Tokyo Concerts* (1983,

rec. 1963), *The Great Canadian Concert Of Thelonious Monk* (mid-80s, rec. 1965), *1963 - In Japan* (1984, rec. 1963), *Live In Stockholm 1961* (1987, rec. 1961), *Solo 1954* (1993), *The Nonet Live* (Charly 1993, 1967 recording), Selected compilations: *Always Know* (1979, rec. 1962-68), *Memorial Album* (1982, rec. 1954-60), *The Complete Blue Note Recordings Of Thelonious Monk* (1983, rec. 1947-52, four-album box-set), *The Complete Black Lion And Vogue Recordings Of Thelonious Monk* (1986, rec. 1971, 1954, four-album box-set), *The Composer* (Giants Of Jazz 1987).

Monterose, J.R.

b. Frank Anthony Monterose, 19 January 1927, Detroit, Michigan, USA. After gaining experience playing tenor saxophone in a number of mid-western bands of the 40s, Monterose joined Buddy Rich in the early 50s. Subsequently, he became well known on the New York bebop scene, playing and recording with a wide range of musicians, including Charles Mingus and Kenny Dorham. Although he has worked elsewhere, including a spell of some three years in Belgium, Monterose has chosen to spend much of his career in and around New York and Albany, thus limiting his international reputation. A soft-spoken, introverted individual, Monterose plays with a rich and warm sound and in an intensely melodic style.

Albums: *J. R. Monterose* (1956), *Straight Ahead* (1960), *In Action* (Studio 4 1964), *Live In Albany* (Uptown 1979), *Luan* (1979), with Tommy Flanagan *...And A Little Pleasure* (Uptown 1981), *Bebop Loose And Live* (1981), *The Message* (Fresh Sounds 1993).

Montgomery, Marian

b. 1934, Natchez, Mississippi, USA. Montgomery quit school to sing on television in Atlanta, Georgia. After working in advertising and publishing, performing in plays and singing in strip joints and jazz clubs, she became an established cabaret performer, playing Las Vegas, New York and Los Angeles. She moved to the UK in 1965 to sing at a new London club, the Cool Elephant, with the John Dankworth Band. That same year she married composer and musical director Laurie Holloway. Possessing a voice which has been likened to 'having a long, cool glass of mint julep on a Savannah balcony', she expanded her career with a starring role in the 1969 West End revival of *Anything Goes*, and frequent appearances on radio and television, as well as concerts and cabaret in the UK and abroad. Her one-woman show was televised by the BBC in 1975. Besides her musical association with Holloway, she successfully collaborated with classical composer/pianist Richard Rodney Bennett on several projects, including *Puttin' On The Ritz, Surprise Surprise* and *Town And Country*. With an instantly recognizable, relaxed and intimate style, she has become one of a handful of American artists to take up permanent residence in the UK, a factor which has helped her maintain her high profile.

Selected albums: *Swings For Winners And Losers* (1963), *Let There Be Marian Montgomery* (1963), *Lovin' Is Livin'* (1965),

Marian Montgomery On Stage (1979), with Richard Rodney Bennett *Town And Country* (1978), with Bennett *Surprise Surprise* (1981), with Bennett *Puttin' On The Ritz* (1984), *I Gotta Right To Sing* (1988), *Sometimes In The Night* (1989), *Nice And Easy* (1989).

Montgomery, Wes

b. John Leslie Montgomery, 6 March 1923, Indianapolis, Indiana, USA, d. 15 June 1968. Montgomery was inspired to take up the guitar after hearing records by Charlie Christian. Nearly 20 years old at the time, he taught himself to play by adapting what he heard on records to what he could accomplish himself. Guided in part by Christian's example, but also by the need to find a way of playing which did not alienate his neighbours, he evolved a uniquely quiet style. Using the soft part of his thumb instead of a plectrum or the fingers, and playing the melody line simultaneously in two registers, Montgomery was already a distinctive stylist by the time he began to work with local bands . In 1948 he joined Lionel Hampton, touring and recording. In the early 50s he returned to Indianapolis and began playing with his brothers Buddy and Monk Montgomery in the Montgomery-Johnson Quintet (the other members being Alonzo and Robert Johnson). During an after-hours session at a local club, the visiting Cannonball Adderley asked him if he would like a record date. On Adderley's recommendation, Montgomery was recorded by Riverside in a series of trio albums which featured artists such as Hank Jones and Ron Carter. These albums attracted considerable attention and Montgomery quickly became one of the most talked about and respected guitarists in jazz. In the early 60s he worked with his brothers in Northern California and also played with John Coltrane. Further recordings, this time with a large string orchestra, broadened Montgomery's horizons and appealed to the non-jazz public. However, despite such commercially successful albums as *Movin' Wes*, *Bumpin'*, *Goin' Out Of My Head* and *A Day In The Life*, he continued to play jazz in small groups with his brothers and with Wynton Kelly, Herb Alpert, Harold Mabern and others. In 1965 he visited Europe, playing club and festival dates in England, Spain and elsewhere. His career was at its height when he died suddenly in June 1968. An outstanding guitarist with an enormous influence upon his contemporaries and countless successors, Montgomery's highly personal style was developed deliberately from Christian, and unwittingly shadowed earlier conceptions by musicians such as Django Reinhardt. In Montgomery's case he stumbled upon these methods not with deliberate intent but through what jazz writer Alun Morgan has described as 'a combination of naivety and good neighbourliness'.

Selected albums: *Far Wes* (1958-59), *The Wes Montgomery Trio/A Dynamic New Sound* (Original Jazz Classics 1959), *Movin' Along* (Original Jazz Classics 1960), *The Incredible Jazz Guitar Of Wes Montgomery* (Original Jazz Classics 1960), *So Much Guitar* (Original Jazz Classics 1961), *Far Wes* (Pacific 1961), *Full House* (Original Jazz Classics 1962), *Fusion* (Original Jazz Classics 1963), *Portrait Of Wes* (Original Jazz Classics 1963), *The Alternative Wes Montgomery* (Milestone 1960-63 recordings), *Boss Guitar* (Original Jazz Classics 1964), *Wes Montgomery Plays The Blues* (1964-66), *Goin' Out Of My Head* (1965), *Bumpin'* (1965), *'Round Midnight* (1965), *Straight No Chaser* (1965), *Movin' Wes* (Verve 1965), *Live In Paris* (1965), *Smokin' At The Half Note* (1965), *Tequila* (Verve 1966), *A Day In The Life* (1967), *Road Song* (1968). Compilation: *Verve Jazz Masters Wes Montgomery* (Verve 2-CD set).

Further reading: *Wes Montgomery*, Adrian Ingram.

Montoliu, Tete

b. Vincente Montoliu, 28 March 1933, Barcelona, Spain. Blind from birth, pianist Montoliu studied classical music as a child, but at the start of his teens was already listening to jazz and later played with Don Byas. In the mid-50s he regularly sat in with visiting American artists, including Lionel Hampton. By the end of the decade he had ventured north to play at a number of important European jazz festivals and had also played in Scandinavia. In the late 60s he played in New York, thereafter establishing an international reputation as a gifted soloist with enormous technical gifts which never obstruct his ability to generate a powerful swing. Among the musicians with whom he has worked are Ben Webster, Anthony Braxton, Roland Kirk and Dexter Gordon.

Selected albums: *The Tete Montoliu Trio* (1965), *Blues For Nuria* (1968), *Ben Webster Meets Don Byas In The Black Forest* (1968), *Interpreta A Serrat* (1969), *Ricordando A Line* (c.1971), *Songs For Love* (Enja 1971), *That's All* (Steeplechase 1971), *Body And Soul* (1971), *Lush Life* (Steeplechase 1971), *Temi Latino Americani* (1973), *Temi Brasiliani* (1973), *Music For Perla* (Steeplechase 1974), *Catalonian Fire* (Steeplechase 1974), *Tete* (Steeplechase 1974), *Vampyria* (1974), *Tete A Tete* (Steeplechase 1976), *Tootie's Tempo* (Steeplechase 1976), *Words Of Love* (1976), *Blues For Myself* (1977), *Yellow Dolphin Street* (Timeless 1977), *Secret Love* (1977), *Boleros* (1977), *Catalonian Folksongs* (Timeless 1977), *Al Palau* (1979), *Live At The Keystone Corner* (Timeless 1979), *Lunch In LA* (1980), *Catalonian Nights Vols 1-2* (Steeplechase 1980), *Boston Concert* (Steeplechase 1980), *I Wanna Talk About You* (1980), *Face To Face* (1982), *Carmina* (1984), *The Music I Like To Play Vols 1-2* (Soul Note 1986), with Peter King *New Year's Morning '89* (1989), *Sweet N' Lovely Vols 1-2* (Fresh Sound 1990), *The Man From Barcelona* (Timeless 1991), *A Spanish Treasure* (Concord 1992).

Moody, James

b. 26 February 1925, Savannah, Georgia, USA. Beginning to play saxophones in his mid-teens, Moody developed his abilities as an instrumentalist during a spell in the American armed forces. Discharged in 1946, he joined Dizzy Gillespie's big band (on tenor saxophone), later touring Europe (mostly playing alto saxophone). His 1949 recording of 'I'm In The Mood For Love' became a hit and greatly enhanced his reputation at home and abroad. During the 50s he led a number of small groups, some of which were R&B oriented. In the 50s he also began to play the flute. By the 60s he had become a major figure on the USA club scene and the international festival circuit. An able and melodic soloist on all three of his instruments, Moody is especially effective on ballads.

Selected albums: *Sax Talk* (Vogue 1952), *Hi Fi Party* (Original Jazz Classics 1955), *Wail Moody Wail*(Original Jazz Classics 1955), *Flute'n The Blues* (1956), *Moody's Mood For Blues* (Original Jazz Classics 1956), *Moody's Mood For Love* (1956), *Easy Living* (1956-63), *Last Train From Overbrook* (1958), *James Moody* i (1959), *Hey! It's James Moody* (1959), *Moody With Strings* (1961), *Cookin' The Blues* (1961), *Another Bag* (1962), *Great Day* (1963), *Comin' On Strong* (1963), *Running The Gamut* (1964), *Group Therapy* (1964), *The Blues And Other Colours* (1967), *Don't Look Away Now* (1969), *Heritage Hum* (c.1971), *Lush Life* (1971), *Too Heavy For Words* (1971), *Never Again!* (1972), *Feelin' It Together* (1973), *James Moody* ii (1973), *James Moody* iii (c.1975), *Beyond This World* (1977), *Something Special* (Novus 1987), with Stan Getz *Tenor Contrasts* (Esquire 1988), *Moving Forward* (Novus 1988), *Sweet And Lovely* (Novus 1990), *Honey* (Novus 1991). Compilations: *James Moody And His Modernists* (1948), *Bebop Revisited Vol. 4* (1948-50), *Bebop Enters Sweden* (1949), *The James Moody Story* (1951-53).

Moondoc, Jemeel

b. 5 August 1951, Chicago, Illinois, USA. Despite being a creative musician from Chicago, saxophonist Moondoc never touched base with the AACM - by the time he was looking for people to play with in the late 60s, Anthony Braxton, Leroy Jenkins and the Art Ensemble Of Chicago had left for Paris and New York. Turning down a career as an architect in the early 70s he studied music with Ran Blake in Boston, where he also played in the James Tatum Blues Band, and then followed Cecil Taylor to Wisconsin University and Antioch College, playing alto and soprano saxophones in Taylor's student orchestras. He moved to New York in 1972, where he met and played with *avant garde* luminaries such as bassist William Parker and trumpeter Roy Campbell, and also formed his Ensemble Munta, which lasted for nearly 10 years. In 1981 he toured Poland and recorded *The Intrepid* for the Poljazz label. In 1984 he formed the Jus Grew Orchestra, a wild 15-piece which had a residency at the Neither/Nor club on the Lower East Side. He says 'I try to speak through the horn - it's something I learned from Jimmy Lyons and Ornette Coleman', and he often plays deliberately sharp, like a free version of Jackie McLean. Moondoc's approach, which combines the looseness of bar-room blues with post-Ornette multi-key valency, found a willing accomplice in guitarist Bern Nix from Ornette's harmolodic outfit Prime Time. Their band - with Parker on bass and Dennis Charles on drums - provided a tipsy, dislocated jazz that was excellently captured on *Nostalgia In Times Square*. Moondoc remains a strikingly individual musical mind in a jazz scene too often willing to conform to the standards of the past.

Albums: *First Feeding* (1977), *The Evening Of The Blue Men* (1979), *New York Live* (1981), *Konstanze's Delight* (1981), *The*

Intrepid Live In Poland (1981), *The Athens Concert* (1982), *Judy's Bounce* (1982), *Nostalgia In Times Square* (1985).

Moore, Brew

b. Milton Aubrey Moore, 26 March 1924, Indianola, Mississippi, USA, d. 19 August 1973. After learning to play a range of instruments, Moore concentrated on tenor saxophone and in his teens sought work in various parts of the USA. A melodic player with a liquid ballad style, Moore's roots were in the style of the early Lester Young, and the advent of bebop restricted his progress. Nevertheless, he made many records in the 50s, then in 1961 became resident in Europe where, apart from a three-year return to the USA (1967-70), he remained for the rest of his life. Although his decision to stay away from America for so many years, allied to his refusal to move with the times, kept him out of the spotlight, it is now generally acknowledged that the quality of Moore's ballad playing was of the very highest order. His early death from a fall, attributed to his dependence upon alcohol, silenced a player whose talent, if not his career, was comparable to that of near-contemporaries such as Stan Getz and Zoot Sims.

Selected albums: *Brewer's Brew* (c.1949-50), *Fru And Brew* (1953), *The Brew Moore Quintet* (1955-56), *Danish Brew* (1959), *The Brew Moore Quartet* i (1962), *Svinget 14* (Black Lion 1963), *If I Had You* (1965), *I Should Care* (Speeplechase 1965), *Brew's Stockholm Dew* (1971), *No More Brew* (Storyville 1971). Compilations: *The Brew Moore Quartet* ii (1948 recording), *The Brew Moore Septet* (1949 recording), *Danish Brew* (Jazz Mark 1988).

Moore, Glen

b. 28 October 1941, Portland, Oregon, USA. It was on sets with Tim Hardin and Cyrus that Moore came to public notice. However, upon uniting with Ralph Towner, Paul McCandless, and Collin Walcott within the fluid context of Oregon Moore's bass style was best showcased. Like his co-members he revealed an easy command of classical, folk, Eastern, and jazz overtones. Since Oregon was formed in 1970, Moore's distinctive upright bass sound has distinguished each of their albums, wherein he has also been known to play viola and flute. The intermittent development of Oregon has allowed Moore the freedom to pursue a parallel career in sessions.

Albums: with Tim Hardin *Bird On A Wire* (1970), with Annette Peacock *Bley/Peacock Synthesizer Show* (1971), with Cyrus *Cyrus* (1971), with Peacock *I'm The One* (1972), with Oregon *Music Of Another Present Era* (1973), with Oregon *Distant Hills* (1974), with Oregon *Winter Light* (1974), with Larry Coryell *Restful Mind* (1975), with Oregon *In Concert* (1975), with Ralph Towner *Trios/Solos* (1975), with Oregon *Friends* (1975), with Oregon *Together* (1977), with Oregon *Violin* (1978), with Oregon *Out Of The Woods* (1978), with Oregon *Roots In The Sky* (1979), with Zbigniew Seifert *We'll Remember Zbiggy* (1980), with Oregon *In Performance* (1980), *Oregon* (1983), with Oregon *Crossing* (1984), with Oregon *Ecotopia* (1987), with Oregon *45th Parallel* (1989), with Oregon *Always, Never And Forever* (1991).

Moore, Oscar

b. 25 December 1912, Austin, Texas, USA, d. 8 October 1981.
Moore formed his first band with his brother Johnny (who was
also a guitarist), while still in his mid-teens. In 1937 he became
a founder member of the Nat 'King' Cole Trio, and for the next
several years was an important part of the group's success. In
1947 Moore joined the Three Blazers, a group led by his brother, and also led his own groups for recording sessions. In the
mid-50s he dropped out of music, but returned occasionally to
gig and make record dates as a sideman. An outstanding guitarist in the mould of Charlie Christian, Moore was an exceptionally gifted soloist and an accompanist of rare distinction.
The quicksilver exchanges between him and Cole on their early
records provide eloquent testimony to his talent and make his
long and presumably self-determined absence from the scene a
matter of considerable regret.
Albums: *The Oscar Moore Quartet* (1954), *Tribute To Nat King
Cole* (1965). Compilation: *The Complete Capitol Recordings Of
The Nat 'King' Cole Trio* (1942-61).

Moore, Russell 'Big Chief'

b. 13 August 1912, nr. Sacaton, Arizona, USA, d. 15
December 1983. A native American, of the Pima tribe, Moore
began playing trombone in the Chicago area before settling in
the mid-30s in Southern California, where he played in one of
Lionel Hampton's first bands. By the end of the decade he had
moved to New Orleans, where he became a regular musical
associate of many of the older generation of traditional
jazzmen. In 1944 he joined Louis Armstrong for a three-year
spell, then worked in and around New York with Sidney
Bechet, Eddie Condon, Buck Clayton, Red Allen, Oran 'Hot
Lips' Page, Pee Wee Russell and many others. Occasional trips
to Europe brought him to the attention of a wider range of fans
and a short period with Armstrong's All Stars, beginning in
1964, further enhanced his reputation. He spent part of the
60s in Canada and led his own bands, recording occasionally
on into the 70s. In the early 80s he was again on tour in Europe
but died in December 1983. Moore's style was well-suited to
the ensemble playing of the traditional New Orleans-style
band, but his soloing, especially in the 50s and 60s, had much
to commend it.
Albums: *Russell 'Big Chief' Moore* (1953-74), *Russell 'Big Chief'
Moore's Pow Wow Jazz Band* (1973).

Moreira, Airto

b. 5 August 1941, Itaiopolis, Brazil. Moreira moved to Rio de
Janeiro when he was 16 years old. In the 60s he played in a
quartet with the pianist/flautist Hermeto Pascal, travelling the
length and breadth of Brazil collecting and using over 120 percussion instruments. He moved to Los Angeles in 1968 and
then to New York in 1970. He was a musician who managed
to be in the right place at the right time; jazz was being opened
up to the kind of extra rhythmic subtlety a second percussionist could offer. Moreira describes how 'you look and listen for
your own place in the music - your own space - and then you
start to make sounds . . . music is like a picture; it's not just

sound'. He worked with Miles Davis in 1970 as he sought to
establish the changes announced in *Bitches Brew*. He played
percussion on the Weather Report debut album in 1971 and
then worked with Chick Corea's Return To Forever. Since then
he has worked with tenor saxophonists Stan Getz and Gato
Barbieri to the Grateful Dead's drummer Mickey Hart with
whom he recorded the percussion soundtrack for Francis Ford
Coppola's film *Apocalypse Now*. He worked most regularly with
his wife Flora Purim. In the mid-80s he played with the Al
DiMeola Project, with which he came to Europe.
Albums: with Miles Davis *At Fillmore* (1970), *Black Beauty*
(1970), *Live - Evil* (1970); *Weather Report* (1971), with Chick
Corea *Return To Forever* (1972), *Fingers* (1973), with Stan Getz
Captain Marvel (1975), with Mickey Hart *Rhythm Devils Play
River Music* (1980), with Flora Purim *Colours Of Life* (In &
Out 1988), *Struck By Lightning* (Virgin 1989), *The Other Side
Of This* (Rykodisk 1992), Forth World (Jazz House 1992),
with the Gods Of Jazz *Killer Bees* (B&W 1993).

Morello, Joe

b. 17 July 1928, Springfield, Massachusetts, USA. After studying violin Morello turned to playing drums while still at
school. He played locally, accompanying fellow high school
student Phil Woods among others. In the early 50s he moved
to New York, performing with many bands in a wide variety of
musical settings, including the big band of Stan Kenton. He
was, however, most often to be found playing in small groups,
notably those led by guitarists Johnny Smith, Tal Farlow, Sal
Salvador and Jimmy Raney, pianist Marian McPartland and
singers Jackie Cain and Roy Kral. He first attracted wide attention when he joined the Dave Brubeck Quartet in 1956. He
remained with Brubeck for 12 years and, Paul Desmond apart,
was that band's most accomplished jazzman. Indeed, Morello's
playing with Brubeck was exemplary in its unassertive precision which, allied to a remarkably delicate swing, provided
object lessons during a period when jazz drumming was
notable for its aggression. After leaving Brubeck in 1967
Morello, who was partially-sighted from childhood, was
involved mostly in teaching. He occasionally led small groups
in the 70s and also made a handful of records with Brubeck,
McPartland and Salvador. An outstanding small group drummer, Morello's long stint with Brubeck, while giving him a
highly visible presence, resulted in a considerable loss to the
wider world of jazz.
Albums: with Marian McPartland *Jazz at The Hickory House*
(1953), with Tal Farlow *The Tal Farlow Album* (1954), with
Dave Brubeck *Jazz Impressions Of The USA* (1956), with
Brubeck *Time Out* (1959), *It's About Time* (1961), *The Dave
Brubeck Quartet At Carnegie Hall* (1963), *The Dave Brubeck
Quartet's 25th Anniversary Reunion* (1976), with Sal Salvador
Juicy Lucy (1978).
Further reading: *All In Good Time*, Marian McPartland.

Morgan, Frank

b. 23 December 1933, Minneapolis, Minnesota, USA. The
west coast bebop altoist Frank Morgan's career was obscured for

over 30 years by prison sentences for narcotics offences and it is only in recent times that his talents and imagination have been more widely displayed or discussed. Morgan began playing guitar under the tuition of his guitarist father then, after moving to Los Angeles in 1947, learned alto saxophone at LA's Jefferson High from the same teacher who taught Dexter Gordon, Wardell Gray and Don Cherry. He began on saxophone as a Charlie Parker admirer, then grew closer to the interpretation of his west coast contemporary, Art Pepper, whom he resembles in his sharply accented sounds, fragmented figures and blurted, episodic delivery. Morgan once told the American critic Francis Davis 'for me, prowess isn't as important as rapport' and he has always spaced out his statements with patience, artifice, a wide tonal palette and an avoidance of fireworks. At the age of 15 he won a television talent contest, which eventually led to a place in Lionel Hampton's band. He also recorded as a sideman with Ray Charles, Teddy Charles, Kenny Clarke and others before releasing his debut as leader, *Introducing Frank Morgan*, in 1955. Since 1953 Morgan's drug problems have resulted in several prison sentences.

Although largely absent from the jazz scene he did continue to play (mostly inside prison). Morgan returned to the outside jazz world in the mid-80s to startle audiences with his exhilarating Parker-inspired style. Morgan was over 50 before he made his second record, *Easy Living*, which introduced his sparkling bebop to a new generation of admirers. With further releases and tours to his credit, he is now recognized as one of the premier bebop altoists of the day. Interviewed in 1988 by Stan Woolley for *Jazz Journal International*, Morgan declared that he was 'one of the old purists and proud of it.' New albums and appearances on the international circuit have brought his strikingly inventive playing to the attention of a new and admiring audience. His recovery from the problems which beset him during more than half his lifetime is fortunate and he appears to be well aware of how much he has lost. In the same interview he spoke of the present and future, remarking, 'I just want to take time and absorb everything.'

Albums: *Introducing Frank Morgan* (1955), *Easy Living* (1985), *Lament* (Contemporary 1986), *Double Image* (Contemporary 1987), *Bebop Lives!* (JVC 1987), *Quiet Fire* (Contemporary 1987), *Major Changes* (Contemporary 1987), *Yardbird Suite* (Contemporary 1989), *Reflections* (Contemporary 1989), *Mood Indigo* (Antilles 1989), *A Lovesome Thing* (Antilles 1991), *You Must Believe In Spring* (Antilles 1992), *Listen To The Dawn* (Antilles 1994).

Morgan, Lanny

b. Harold Lansford Morgan, 30 March 1934, Des Moines, Iowa, USA. As a child he played violin before taking up the alto saxophone. When he was 10 his family moved to Los Angeles and he continued his studies. As a young man he played in big bands including those led by Charlie Barnet, Terry Gibbs and Bob Florence, then settled for a while in New York where he worked with Maynard Ferguson. Back on the west coast he played and recorded with several bands including Supersax and that led by Bill Berry. In addition to performing, Morgan also

developed a reputation as a teacher. Since the mid-80s he had played mostly in small groups and has toured Europe and the UK as a single. A hard blowing saxophonist, with a crisply incisive tone, Morgan is a commanding musician and is much respected by his peers.

Albums: *Maynard Ferguson Sextet* (1965), with Bill Berry *Hello Rev* (Concord 1976), with Supersax *Dynamite!* (1978), *It's About Time* (Pausa 1981), with Jeff Hamilton *Indiana* (1982).

Morgan, Lee

b. 10 July 1938, Philadelphia, Pennsylvania, USA, d. 19 February 1972. Prodigiously talented, Morgan played trumpet professionally at the age of 15 and three years later joined Dizzy Gillespie's big band. During this same period he recorded with John Coltrane, Hank Mobley and others. In 1958 the Gillespie band folded and Morgan joined Art Blakey's Jazz Messengers where he made a tremendous impact not only nationally but around the world, thanks to the group's recordings. In the early 60s Morgan returned to his home town, where he played in comparative obscurity, but by 1963 he was back in New York, leading his own groups and also working for a while with Blakey in 1964. Morgan's popularity was enhanced by the success of a recording of his own composition, the irresistibly catchy 'The Sidewinder' which helped to spark a jazz/funk mini-boom and has remained a dance floor favourite ever since. Morgan's trumpet style was marked by his full-blooded vitality aided by the richness of his tone. Playing with the strictly-controlled Blakey band impacted his natural enthusiasm and the resulting tensions created some of the best hard-bop trumpet playing of the period. Indeed, despite the passage of time and the many fine trumpeters to have entered jazz in his wake, only a handful have attained Morgan's remarkable standards of emotional virtuosity. In the late 60s, Morgan's career was damaged for a while by personal problems but a woman friend helped him recover. Unfortunately, this same woman became jealous of a new relationship he had formed and on 19 February 1972 she shot and killed him at the New York nightclub, where his quintet were performing.

Selected albums: *Lee Morgan Indeed* (1956), with Hank Mobley *Hank's Shout* (1956), *City Lights* (1957), with John Coltrane *Blue Train* (1957), *The Cooker* (Blue Note 1957), *Introducing Lee Morgan* (Savoy 1957), *Peckin' Time* (1958), *Candy* (Blue Note 1959), with Thad Jones *Minor Strain* (1960), *Lee-Way* (1960), *Indestructible Lee* (Affinity 1960), with Art Blakey *The Freedom Rider* (1961), *Take Twelve* (Original Jazz Classics 1962), *Delightfulee Morgan* (Blue Note 60s), *Cornbread* (Blue Note 60s), *The Sidewinder* (Blue Note 1964), *Search For The New Land* (Blue Note 1964), *Tom Cat* (Blue Note 1964), *The Rumproller* (Blue Note 1965), *Infinity* (1965), *The Cat* (1965), *Charisma* (1966), *The Rajah* (Blue Note 1966), *The Procrastinator* (1967), with Mobley *Dippin'* (1965), *Caramba* (1968), *Live At The Lighthouse* (Fresh Sound 1970), *Capra Beach* (1971), *We Remember You* (Fresh Sound 1972).

Morris, Lawrence 'Butch'

b. 10 February 1947, Long Beach, California, USA. Playing cornet on the west coast, Morris worked with bop tenor saxophonist J.R. Monterose, bassist George Morrow and *avant garde* players Frank Lowe and Don Moye as well as studying with well-known west coast mentors, Horace Tapscott and Bobby Bradford (which is where he first met his longtime associate David Murray). In 1975 he relocated to New York, playing free jazz in the Loft scene. From 1976-77 he lived in Paris, working with Lowe and bassist Alan Silva. In 1977 he joined Murray's seminal Octet, recording on *Ming*, *Home* and *Murray's Steps*. Morris developed what he called 'conduction', a method of leading improvisers with visual instructions, conducting the David Murray Big Band at Sweet Basil in 1984 (recorded for Black Saint). Meanwhile, Morris had also been recording his own music: *In Touch...But Out Of Reach* was a 1978 live concert with a sextet that included trombonist Grachan Moncur III and drummer Steve McCall; *The New York City Artists' Collective Plays Butch Morris* had him conducting an eight-piece group, which featured vocalist Ellen Christi, through a set of his own pieces. In 1985 he recorded a free-improvisation record with guitarist Bill Horvitz (*Trios*) and 1988 saw the appearance of two albums featuring a trio of Morris, Wayne Horvitz, and Robert Previte, (*Nine Below*, *Todos Santos*), the latter album showcasing the compositions of pianist/singer Robin Halcomb. In 1986 he released *Current Trends In Racism In Modern America*, an innovative music in which he led 10 musicians (including Lowe, John Zorn, harpist Zeena Parkins and drummer Thurman Barker) through poignant, desolate and highly charged 'free-improvisations'. *Homeing* (1987) and *Dust To Dust* (1991) continued his search for a new method of assembling musicians drawn from both the black *avant garde* and white avant-rock circles. In a period where conservatism has become the normal approach, Morris has bravely taken steps to provide a part of the future.
Albums: *In Touch...But Out Of Reach* (1982, rec 1978), *The New York City Artists' Collective Plays Butch Morris* (1984, rec 1982), with Bill Horvitz, J.A. Deane *Trios* (1985), *Current Trends In Racism In Modern America* (Sound Aspects 1986), *Homeing* (Sound Aspect 1988), with Robert Previte, Wayne Horvitz *Nine Below* (1988, rec 1986), with Previte, Wayne Horvitz *Todos Santos* (1988), *Dust To Dust* (New World 1991).

Morrissey, Dick

b. 9 May 1940, Horley, Surrey, England. A self-taught tenor saxophonist who is also adept on clarinet, flute and soprano saxophone, Morrissey became a professional musician at the end of his teens. In 1960 he played in a band led by Harry South and soon afterwards formed his own quartet with South, Phil Bates and Phil Seamen. He maintained a small band throughout the 60s, playing club engagements in the UK, backing visiting American jazzmen (including Jimmy Witherspoon) and making records. In the 70s Morrissey was deeply involved in jazz-rock, co-leading the band highly respected If, working with Herbie Mann, and recording with the Average White Band. The most important of the bands in

this idiom with which he was associated was the Morrissey-Mullen band he co-led with Jim Mullen. The band became one of the UK's best-known jazz-rock bands and remained in existence into the mid-80s, after which Morrissey returned to leading a more mainstream jazz-orientated group.
Selected albums: *It's Morrissey, Man!* (1961), *Have You Heard?* (1963), *Jimmy Witherspoon At The Bull's Head* (1966), *Storm Warning* (1967), *After Dark* (Coda 1983), *Resurrection Ritual* (Miles 1988), *Souliloquy* (Coda 1988). As Morrissey-Mullen *Up* (1977), *Cape Wrath* (1979), *Badness* (1981), *Life On The Wire* (1982), *It's About Time* (1983), *This Must Be The Place* (1985), *Happy Hour* (1988).

Morton, 'Jelly Roll'

b. Ferdinand Morton, 20 October 1890, New Orleans, Louisiana, USA, d. 10 July 1941. A gifted musician, Morton played various instruments before deciding to concentrate on piano. In the early years of the 20th century he was a popular figure on the seamier side of New Orleans nightlife. He played in brothels, hustled pool and generally lived the high-life. His reputation spread extensively, owing to tours and theatrical work in various parts of the Deep South and visits to Kansas City, Chicago, Los Angeles and other important urban centres. He also worked in Canada, Alaska and Mexico. From 1923 he spent five years based in Chicago, touring and recording with various bands, including the New Orleans Rhythm Kings and his own band, the Red Hot Peppers. He later worked with Fate Marable and W.C. Handy, and by the end of the 20s had moved to New York for residencies and more recording sessions. He also formed a big band, with which he toured throughout the east coast states. Various business ventures played a part in his life, often with disastrous financial consequences, but he remained musically active throughout the 30s, even though he was on the margins of the commercial success which many jazzmen enjoyed in that decade. During the 30s Morton moved to Washington, DC, where he made many recordings, also playing and reminiscing for Alan Lomax Snr. of the US Library of Congress. By 1940 his health was failing and he moved to Los Angeles, where he died in July 1941.
One of the major figures in jazz history and a significant musical conceptualist, in particular the role of the arranger, Morton's penchant for self-promotion worked against him and for many years critical perceptions of his true worth were blighted. Many of the recordings which he made during his stay in Chicago have proved to be classics, not least for the construction of those songs he composed and the manner in which they were arranged. Although some thought that carefully arranged music went contrary to the spirit of improvisation that was inherent in jazz, Morton's arrangements, to which he insisted his musicians should strictly adhere, inhibited neither soloists nor the ability of the ensembles to swing mightily. In his arrangements of the mid-20s, Morton foreshadowed many of the musical trends which only emerged fully a decade later as big band jazz became popular. Curiously, Morton failed to grasp the possibilities then open to him and preferred to concentrate on small group work at a time when popular trends

were moving in the opposite direction. His compositions include many jazz standards, among them 'The Pearls', 'Sidewalk Blues', 'King Porter Stomp', 'Dead Man Blues', 'Grandpa's Spells', 'Doctor Jazz', 'Wolverine Blues', 'Black Bottom Stomp' and 'Mister Jelly Lord'. As a pianist, Morton's early work was ragtime-oriented; but unlike many of his contemporaries, he was able to expand the rather rigid concept of ragtime to incorporate emerging jazz ideas and his later playing style shows a vital and often exhilarating grasp of many styles. It was, however, as an arranger that Morton made his greatest contribution and he can be regarded as the first significant arranger in jazz. Morton himself certainly never underestimated his own importance; quite the opposite, in fact, since he billed himself as the Originator of Jazz, Stomps and Blues. Shortly before his death he became involved in a mildly embarrassing public wrangle over the origins of the music, denying (rightly, of course) that W.C. Handy was the 'originator of jazz and the blues' and counter-claiming that he had created jazz in 1902. This outburst of self-aggrandizement was ridiculed and created an atmosphere in which few fans, critics or fellow musicians took his work seriously. By the early 50s, however, some more perceptive individuals began to reassess his contribution to jazz and this reappraisal gradually swelled into a tidal wave of critical acclaim. By the 70s musicians were eager to play Morton's music, and through into the 90s many concerts and recordings in the USA and UK have been dedicated to his achievements.

Selected albums: *The Gennet Piano Solos* (1923-24), *Jelly Roll Morton Vols 1-3* (1926-30), *The Centennial: His Complete Victor Recordings* (RCA 1926-39), *The Complete Jelly Roll Morton Vols 1/2, 3/4, 5/6, 7/8* (RCA, 1926-40 recordings), *Library Of Congress Recordings Vols 1-8* (Swaggie 1938 recordings), *Rarities And Alternatives 1923-1940* (Suisa 1991), *Mr Jelly Lord* (Pickwick 1992).
Further reading: *Mister Jelly Roll: The Fortunes Of Jelly Roll Morton, New Orleans Creole And 'Inventor Of Jazz'*, Alan Lomax.

Morton, Benny

b. 31 January 1907, New York City, New York, USA, d. 28 December 1985. Largely self-taught, Morton played trombone in bands in and around New York during his teenage years and by 1926 was sufficiently advanced to be hired by Fletcher Henderson. He subsequently played in bands led by Chick Webb, Don Redman and Count Basie; in 1940 he became a member of Teddy Wilson's superb sextet. He also made record dates with Billie Holiday. In 1943 he joined Edmond Hall's small group, then led his own band for a few years before becoming active in theatre pit bands in New York. In the 50s and 60s he was also busy in radio and recording studio bands, but occasionally turned up on record dates with artists such as Buck Clayton and Ruby Braff, and by the end of the 60s was mostly back on the jazz scene. He toured widely, playing in various bands including the Saints And Sinners package and outfits led by Wild Bill Davison, Bobby Hackett and Sy Oliver. A smooth and polished player with a relaxed and elegant style,

Morton was one of the unsung heroes of the swing era.
Album: with Buck Clayton, Ruby Braff *Buck Meets Ruby* (1954). Compilation: with Count Basie *Swinging The Blues* (1937-39 recordings).

Mosca, Sal

b. Salvatore Joseph Mosca, 27 April 1927, Mount Vernon, New York, USA. A student, disciple and close friend of Lennie Tristano, pianist Mosca has followed his mentor's example by recording and touring only rarely. In the 50s he did play on several Lee Konitz albums, and some sessions with Peter Ind later appeared on the bassist's Wave label. In the 70s Mosca again worked with Konitz and with Warne Marsh, toured Europe as a solo artist and played at the Lennie Tristano Memorial Concert in 1979. In the 80s he was seldom heard as a performer, but remained active as a teacher. A remarkably subtle player, with the sophisticated harmonic ear characteristic of Tristanoites, Mosca can disguise the chord changes of the best-known standard so cleverly that he makes it virtually unrecognizable, creating an entirely new tune in the process.
Albums: Wirh Peter Ind *At The Den* (1969, rec. 1959), *On Piano* (1969, rec 1955, 1959), *Sal Mosca Music* (1977), *For You* (1979), with others *Lennie Tristano Memorial Concert* (1979), with Warne Marsh *How Deep, How High* (1980, rec. 1977, 1979), *A Concert* (Jazz Records 1990, rec 1979).

Moses, Bob

b. 28 January 1948, New York, USA. Moses grew up surrounded by musicians like Charlie Mingus, for whom his father was press agent. Largely self-taught, he started to play drums when he was 10 years old and also played vibes in local Latin bands in his teens. He appeared with Rahsaan Roland Kirk in the mid-60s and formed Free Spirits with Larry Coryell, one of the first jazz-rock bands. After a short stay with Dave Liebman's Open Sky he joined Gary Burton. In the early 70s he formed Compost with Harold Vick (tenor) and Jack DeJohnette and toured the UK with the Mike Gibbs Orchestra before returning to the groups of Gary Burton and Pat Metheny. At this stage he was also writing for large ensembles and formed his own label - Mozown Records - to release the results. The music was recorded by all-star line-ups of New York musicians and was accorded great critical acclaim. Moses makes personal use of a wide range of influences to create colourful, complex yet swinging music. In the 80s he played with the Steve Kuhn/Sheila Jordan Band (1979-82), George Gruntz Big Band and his own quintet. He is the author of the drum method *Drum Wisdom*.
Albums: with Rahsaan Roland Kirk *I Talk With the Spirits* (1966), with Kirk *Rip, Rig And Panic* (1966), with Gary Burton *Lofty Fake Anagram* (1967), with Compost *Life Is Round* (1971), with Mike Gibbs *The Only Chrome Waterfall Orchestra* (1975), with Pat Metheny *Bright Size Life* (1975), with Steve Swallow *Bittersweet In The Ozone* (1975), with Swallow *Home* (1979), with Swallow *When Elephants Dream Of Music* (1982), with Swallow *Visits With The Great Spirit* (Gramavision 1983), *Wheels Of Coloured Light* (Open Minds

1983), with Gibbs *Big Music* (Virgin 1988), *Story Of Moses* (Gala 1989), with Billy Martin *East Side* (ITM 1989).

Mosley, Snub

b. Lawrence L. Mosley, 29 December 1905, Little Rock, Arkansas, USA, d. 21 July 1981. Starting out on trombone, in the 20s Mosley joined in the popular territory band led by Alphonso Trent. Noted for his aggressive, attacking style, Mosley was dissatisfied with what he saw as the limitations of the trombone and invented his own instrument. This was a slide saxophone, which he thereafter preferred to a more orthodox instrument, although he still continued to play trombone. Leaving Trent in 1933, Mosley worked with some of the best-known bands of the period, including those led by Claude Hopkins, Fats Waller and Louis Armstrong. He also tried his hand at bandleading, but while he worked steadily throughout the 40s and into the 50s, accommodating shifts in musical tastes by playing and singing R&B, he never made the breakthrough to nationwide success. In the late 70s he became a popular figure on the international club and festival scene.
Album: *Snub Mosley Live At The Pizza Express* (1978).

Moss, Danny

b. 16 August 1927, Redhill, Surrey, England. By the late 40s tenor saxophonist Moss had established a reputation as an outstanding musician and was hired by many of the leading UK jazz and dancebands of the day, including those of Ted Heath, Oscar Rabin, Vic Lewis, John Dankworth and Humphrey Lyttelton. From the early 60s Moss led his own small groups, touring the UK and sometimes working with fellow UK musicians such as Sandy Brown and Dave Shepherd. Additionally, he was in great demand as an accompanist and featured soloist with visiting American artists, most notably with a succession of leading singers that included Ella Fitzgerald, Sarah Vaughan and Rosemary Clooney. In 1990 Moss, whose wife is singer Jeannie Lambe, took up residence in Australia. In the summer of the same year he was awarded an MBE in the Queen's Birthday Honours List. A committed jazzman, Moss's distinctive playing style shows him to be at ease whether on uptempo swingers, where his full-bodied sound is a delight, or on soulful ballads to which he brings great emotional depth.
Albums: *Danny Moss Quintet With Strings* (c.1966), *The Good Life* (1968), *Straighten Up And Fly Right* (1979), *Danny Moss Quartet With Geoff Simkins* (1979), *Jeannie Lambe* (1980), with Lambe *Blues And All That Jazz* (c.1982), with Simpkins *Danny Moss And Geoff Simpkins Vol 2* (Flyright 1982), with Lambe *The Midnight Sun* (1984).

Moten, Bennie

b. 13 November 1894, Kansas City, Missouri, USA, d. 2 April 1935. In his youth, Moten gained a substantial reputation in and around his home town as a pianist; by 1920 he had become an established and respected bandleader. His unit, originally a small outfit, gradually expanded until it was a big band ready to take advantage of the upsurge in interest in this kind of ensemble. As a pianist and an accomplished arranger,

Moten deftly blended New Orleans concepts into the freewheeling style popular in the midwest. Beginning its recording career in 1923, the band built a reputation far afield, and residencies in New York followed. Moten attracted many excellent musicians until his was the outstanding band of the region. Some of the best men were poached from Walter Page's Blue Devils, among them Bill (not yet Count) Basie, Oran 'Hot Lips' Page, Eddie Durham and Jimmy Rushing. Eventually, Walter Page went along, too. Later additions to the band included Ben Webster, Herschel Evans, Eddie Barefield and Lester Young. By the mid-30s the band was not merely the finest in the region, but was superior to many of the headline bands in the east and elsewhere. In 1935 the unit visited Chicago to audition for a residency at the Grand Terrace Ballroom. When they headed for home Moten remained behind for a tonsillectomy and died when the surgeon's knife slipped and severed his jugular vein. The band subsequently broke up, but later many of the musicians reformed under the leadership of Buster Smith and Basie, and later still the band became Basie's. As the leader of an outstanding band, Moten occupies an important position in the history of Kansas City jazz, even if he was understandably overshadowed by his musical legatees.
Selected compilation: *The Complete Bennie Moten Vols 1/2, 3/4, 5/6* (RCA, 1923-32 recordings).

Motian, Paul

b. 25 March 1931, Providence, Rhode Island, USA. Motian played guitar in Providence in his teens, then served a term in the US army. On his discharge in 1954 he went to New York to study music at the Manhattan School. By 1956 he was playing drums for George Wallington and Russell Jacquet. Between 1956 and 1958 he worked with Tony Scott, with whom he met the pianist Bill Evans. His work in the Evans trio (1959-64) has since achieved legendary status for delicacy and balance. Motian also played with Oscar Pettiford, Zoot Sims and Lennie Tristano in the late 50s. In the mid-60s he worked with singers Mose Allison and Arlo Guthrie and was part of the Paul Bley trio in 1964. Motian had met Ornette Coleman's bassist Charlie Haden in 1959 and got a chance to work with him in Keith Jarrett's band with Dewey Redman (1967-76); he also joined Haden's Liberation Music Orchestra for its debut recording in 1969 and toured with the re-formed Orchestra in the 80s. In the 70s he was active in the Jazz Composers' Orchestra and played on Carla Bley's *Escalator Over The Hill* in 1972. He emerged as a leader in 1974, since when he has released an impressive series of albums on the ECM, Soul Note and JMT labels that have confirmed his stature as a drummer and composer. *Tribute* (1974) featured Carlos Ward on alto, while *Dance* and *Le Voyage* from the late 70s boast rare appearances by saxophonist Charles Brackeen. In the 80s he began long-term associations with guitarist Bill Frisell, whose arching, tremulous interpretations of Motian's melodies are particularly sympathetic, and the inventive tenorist Joe Lovano. In the late 80s he renewed his acquaintance with Paul Bley on a marvellous album of improvised duets (*Notes*), and joined with Haden and pianist Geri Allen to form one of the most thoughtful of contemporary piano trios; a guest appearance with Marilyn Crispell's trio (*Live In Zurich*, 1991) proved he was also at home in more exploratory modes. Motian's examination of Thelonious Monk (*Monk In Motian*), standards (*Motian On Broadway*) and his piano-less tribute to Bill Evans (1991) show a questing musical mind, still working as keenly as ever.

Albums: *Conception Vessel* (ECM 1974), *Tribute* (ECM 1974), *Dance* (1977), *Le Voyage* (ECM 1979), *Psalm* (ECM 1982), *The Story Of Maryam* (ECM 1984), *It Should've Happened A Long Time Ago* (ECM 1985), *Jack Of Clubs* (ECM 1985), *Misterioso* (Soul Note 1986), with Paul Bley *Notes* (1987), with Geri Allen, Charlie Haden *Etudes* (1988), *Monk In Motian* (JMT 1988), *Paul Motian On Broadway Vol 1* (JMT 1989), with Allen, Haden *In The Year Of The Dragon* (1989), with Allen, Haden *Segments* (1989), *One Time Out* (Soul Note 1990), *Paul Motian On Broadway Vol 2* (JMT 1990), *Motian In Motian* (JMT 1989), *Bill Evans* (JMT 1991), with Allen, Haden *Live At The Village Vanguard* (1991), *Motian In Tokyo* (JMT 1992), *On Broadway Vol. 3* (JMT 1992), *And The Electric Bebop Band* (JMT 1992), with Keith Jarrett, Gary Peacock *At The Deer Head Inn* (ECM 1994), *Trioism* (JMT 1994).

Mouzon, Alphonze

b. 21 November 1948, Charleston, South Carolina, USA. Mouzon started playing when he was four years old and was taught drums at high school. He relocated to New York when he was 17 and in 1969 played in the Broadway musical *Promises, Promises*. He released his first record in the same year, with Gil Evans. He freelanced for a time before playing with Weather Report in 1971, McCoy Tyner (1972-73), Larry Coryell's Eleventh House (1973-75) and in a trio with Albert Mangelsdorff and Jaco Pastorius. After that Mouzon again freelanced until he joined Herbie Hancock in the late 70s. Mouzon tries to bring 'jazz polyrhythms to a rock pulse' and in this he succeeds, with his furiously propulsive drumming which is as welcome in a rock setting as in straight jazz.

Albums: *Gil Evans* (1969), *Weather Report* (1971), with McCoy Tyner *Sahara* (1972), with Larry Coryell *Introducing The Eleventh House* (1973), *Funky Snakefoot* (1973), *Mind Transplant* (RPM 1975), with Albert Mangelsdorff, Jaco Pastorius *Trilogue-Live* (1976), with Herbie Hancock *Mr. Hands* (1980), *In Search Of A Dream* (MPS 1981), *Back To Jazz* (L&R 1986). Compilation: *Best Of Alphonse Mouzon* (Black Sun 1989).

Mraz, George

b. Jírí Mraz, 9 September 1944, Písek, Czechoslovakia. A gifted musician as a child, Mraz studied formally at the music conservatory in Prague. Although skilled on several instruments, he settled eventually on the bass. He worked in his homeland and in Germany, then in 1968 emigrated to the USA. He entered Berklee College Of Music for further studies, after which he played with Dizzy Gillespie, Oscar Peterson and other leading jazzmen. In New York in the mid-70s he became

a member of the Thad Jones-Mel Lewis Jazz Orchestra and also recorded with Stan Getz, Pepper Adams, Zoot Sims, Stéphane Grappelli and in duos with Walter Norris and his fellow Jones-Lewis rhythm section-mate, Roland Hanna. Towards the end of the decade he worked with the New York Jazz Quartet and with John Abercrombie. By the 80s Mraz, who became an American citizen in 1973, was established as a major force among jazz bass players. As his association with Jones-Lewis and Abercrombie reveals, he is able to play in many idioms but he is at his considerable best in small bop and post-bop bands.

Albums: *Stéphane Grappelli Meets The Rhythm Section* (1973), with Roland Hanna *Sir Elf + 1* (1977), with Zoot Sims *Warm Tenor* (1978), with John Abercrombie *M* (1980), with Pepper Adams *Urban Dreams* (1981).

Mseleku, Bheki

b. 1955, Durban, South Africa. Proper recognition of this fine multi-instrumentalist's (pianist/composer/vocalist/saxophonist) jazz talents seemed long overdue, but since 1991 this modest and dignified performer has been very much in the limelight, touring internationally and releasing an album annually. One of a number of supremely talented improvising musicians who have left South Africa and its oppressive apartheid system to take up residence in London, Mseleku made the move relatively recently, touring out of South Africa in the late 70s, moving to Sweden in 1980 and finally settling in London in 1985. A Ronnie Scott's club debut in 1987, with some of the more prominent figures from London's jazz revival, including Courtney Pine and Cleveland Watkiss, did much to bring his talents to the notice of the local scene, and helped pave the way for *Celebration* - a star-studded, major label debut featuring London-based musicians Pine, Steve Williamson, Eddie Parker and Jean Toussaint and a high-power American rhythm section comprising Michael Bowie and Marvin 'Smitty' Smith. A lively and enthusiastic record, it mixed gentle, township-inspired compositions with modal, post-John Coltrane burnouts, and was marked by a hectic touring campaign and a deserved nomination for British Mercury Music Prize for Album Of The Year. After the media furore had died down, Mseleku resumed the solo performances in which he excels, accompanying overtly spiritual and dedicatory vocal-lines with gently rocking, township-inspired piano voicings, and punctuating the whole with sparkling, McCoy Tyner-style runs and one handed riffs on the tenor saxophone. *Meditations*, a live recording from the Bath International Music Festival, captured this absorbing style on two long tracks. Signing to the Verve/Polygram label at the end of 1993, Mseleku's *Timelessness* found him in the company of some top American heavy-weights, including Joe Henderson, Pharoah Sanders, Abbey Lincoln and Elvin Jones, and was accompanied by another media furore.

Albums: *Celebration* (World Circuit 1992), *Meditations* (1993), *Timelessness* (Verve 1994).

Muhammad, Idris

b. Leo Morris, 13 November 1939, New Orleans, Louisiana, USA. Immaculate, imaginative and equally at home on contemporary jazz and more popular funk and soul sessions, Idris Muhammad is one of America's most impressive and swinging drummers. Playing since the age of eight, he began working professionally in the soul scene in the early 60s, accompanying vocalists Jerry Butler, Sam Cooke and the Impressions. The gifted bebop alto saxophonist Lou Donaldson hired Muhammad for his soul-jazz group in 1965, and work with guitarist George Benson followed. In the early 70s, Muhammad became house drummer for the Prestige label, again playing mainly an unadventurous soul/jazz that offered him little room to stretch out and take advantage of his talents. Spells with Roberta Flack followed, but by the end of the 70s, Muhammad was able to put together his own band and started concentrating on modern jazz. Toward the end of the decade he joined hard-bop tenor saxophonist Johnny Griffin, and then began a celebrated spell with fellow tenor saxophonist Pharoah Sanders. He continues to work intermittently with Sanders, and recently toured internationally and recorded with an all-star saxophone-orientated band, that included Chico Freeman, Arthur Blythe, Sam Rivers and pianist Don Pullen. Albums: with Charles Earland *Black Talk!* (1969), with George Coleman *Big George* (1977), with Johnny Griffin *NYC Underground* (1979), with Pharoah Sanders *Journey To The One* (1980), *Kabsha* (1981), with Lou Donaldson *Sweet Poppa Lou* (1981), *Heart Is A Melody* (1982), *Live* (1982), *Manhattan Panorama* (1983), with James Moody *Something Special* (1986), *Africa* (1987), with Tony Coe *Canterbury Song* (1988).

Mullen, Jim

b. 26 November 1945, Glasgow, Scotland. After starting out on guitar while he was still a small child, Mullen switched to bass in his early teens. He played in various dance bands in his home town before forming his own trio and reverting to guitar. At the end of the 60s he relocated to London and moved into R&B. In the early 70s he was frequently associated with jazz-rock and other fusion bands including Paz, the Average White Band, Kokomo (UK) and Herbie Mann's group. He also formed a group with Dick Morrissey, Morrissey-Mullen, which became one of the best known jazz-rock bands in the UK. The band remained in existence until 1985, after which Mullen led his own small bands. Towards the end of the decade he occasionally appeared again with Morrissey, performing at jazz festivals throughout the UK. A dynamic and forceful player, Mullen's years in jazz-rock and his deep affinity with the blues give his music a quality of earthy excitement. Selected albums: *Thumbs Up* (Coda 1984), *Into The 90s* (Castle 1990), *Soundbites* (EFZ 1993). As Morrissey-Mullen *Up* (1977), *Cape Wrath* (1979), *Badness* (1981), *Life On The Wire* (1982), *It's About Time* (1983), *This Must Be The Place* (1985), *Happy Hour* (1988).

Mulligan, Gerry

b. 6 April 1927, New York City, New York, USA. Raised in Philadelphia, Mulligan started out on piano before concentrating on arranging. He also took up the saxophone, first the alto and a few years later the baritone. Among the name bands which used his arrangements were those led by Gene Krupa and Claude Thornhill and he occasionally played in their reed sections. While writing for Thornhill he met and began a musical association with fellow-arranger Gil Evans. In New York in 1948 Mulligan joined Evans and Miles Davis, for whom he wrote and played, by now almost exclusively on baritone. In the early 50s Mulligan led his own groups but continued to arrange on a freelance basis. In this capacity his work was performed by Stan Kenton (these charts also being performed in the UK by Vic Lewis). In 1952 Mulligan began a musical association which not only attracted critical acclaim but also brought him widespread popularity with audiences. This came about through the formation with Chet Baker of a quartet which was unusual for the absence of a piano. When Baker quit in 1953, Mulligan subsequently led other quartets, notably with Bob Brookmeyer in the mid-50s. Although the quartet format dominated Mulligan's work during this part of his career he occasionally formed larger groups and early in the 60s formed his Concert Jazz Band. This band was periodically revived during the decade and beyond. He interspersed this with periods of leading groups of various sizes, working and recording with other leaders, including Dave Brubeck, in frequently rewarding partnership with musicians such as Paul Desmond, Stan Getz, Johnny Hodges, Zoot Sims and Thelonious Monk and writing arrangements on a freelance basis. In the early 70s Mulligan led big bands, some of which used the name Age Of Steam, and small groups for worldwide concert tours, recording sessions and radio and television appearances. The 80s and early 90s saw him following a similar pattern, sometimes expanding the size of the big band, sometimes content to work in the intimate setting of a quartet or quintet. As an arranger, Mulligan was among the first to attempt to adapt the language of bop for big band and achieved a measure of success with both Krupa (who recalled for George T. Simon that Mulligan was 'a kind of temperamental guy who wanted to expound a lot of his ideas'), and Thornhill. For all the variety of his later work, in many ways his music, as writer and performer, retains the colours and effects of his 50s quartets. In these groups Mulligan explored the possibilities of scoring and improvising jazz in a low-key, seemingly subdued manner. In fact, he thoroughly exploited the possibilities of creating interesting and complex lines which always retained a rich melodic approach. His compositions from the 50s, including 'Night At The Turntable', 'Walkin' Shoes', 'Soft Shoe' and 'Jeru', and his arrangements for 'Bernie's Tune', 'Godchild' and others helped establish the sound and style of the so-called 'cool school'. The intimate styling favoured in such settings was retained in his big band work and his concert band recordings from the 60s retain interest not only for their own sake but also for the manner in which they contrast with most other big band writing of the same and other periods. As a player, the lightness of touch Mulligan uses in his writing is uniquely brought to the baritone saxophone, an instrument which in other, not always lesser hands sometimes overpowers the fragility of some areas of jazz. It is hard to see in Mulligan's work, whether as writer or performer, a clearly discernible influence.

Similarly, despite the enormous popularity he has enjoyed over more than four decades, few if any writers or players seem to have adopted him as role model. At the least, this must be something to regret.

Selected albums: with Miles Davis *Birth Of The Cool* (Capitol 1951), *Mulligan Plays Mulligan* (Original Jazz Classics 1951), *Jazz Superstars* (1952), *The Gerry Mulligan Quartet With Chet Baker* (Pacific 1952-53), with Lee Konitz *Konitz Meets Mulligan* (1953), *California Concerts Vols 1 & 2* (1954), *Presenting The Gerry Mulligan Sextet* (1955), *Gerry Mulligan Live In Stockholm* (1955), *Mainstream Of Jazz* (1955), *At Storyville* (1956), *Gerry Mulligan, The Arranger* (1957), *Quartet Live In Stockholm* (Moon 1957), *Gerry Mulligan Meets Stan Getz* (1957), *Desmond Meets Mulligan* (1957), *Blues In Time* (Verve 1957), *Gerry Mulligan Meets The Saxophonists* (1957), with Thelonious Monk *Mulligan Meets Monk* (1957), with Monk *Alternate Takes* (1957), *At Storyville* (Pacific 1957), with Baker *Reunion* (Pacific 1957), *Gerry Mulligan Quartet At Newport* (1958), *I Want To Live* (1958), *What Is There To Say?* (Columbia 1959), with Ben Webster *Gerry Mulligan Meets Ben Webster* (Verve 1959), *Gerry Mulligan And The Concert Band On Tour* (1960), *New York-December1960* (Jazz Anthology 1960), *Gerry Mulligan And The Concert Band* i (1960), *Gerry Mulligan Meets Johnny Hodges* (1960), with Judy Holliday *Holliday With Mulligan* (1961), *Gerry Mulligan Presents A Concert In Jazz* (1961), *The Gerry Mulligan Quartet* (1962), *Jeru* (1962), *Gerry Mulligan And The Concert Band* ii (1962), with Paul Desmond *Two Of A Mind* (1962), *Gerry Mulligan And The Concert Band* iii (1963), *The Shadow Of Your Smile* (1965), *The Gerry Mulligan Quintet* (1965), *Gerry Mulligan Meets Zoot Sims* (1966), *Live In New Orleans* (1968), *The Age Of Steam* (A&M 1971), *Summit* (1974), *Tango Nuevo* (1974), *Carnegie Hall Concert* (1974), *Gerry Mulligan Meets Enrico Intra* (1975), *Idle Gossip* (1976), *Lionel Hampton Presents Gerry Mulligan* (1977), *Mulligan* (LRC 1977), with Benny Carter *Benny Carter/Gerry Mulligan* (LRC 1977), *Walk On The Water* (1980), *LA Menace* (1982), *Little Big Horn* (GRP 1983), with Barry Manilow *2 am Paradise Cafe* (1984), with Scott Hamilton *Soft Lights & Sweet Music* (Concord 1986), *Symphonic Dream* (Sion 1988), *Lonesome Boulevard* (A&M 1990), *Re-Birth Of The Cool* (GRP 1992). Compilations: *Gerry Mulligan And Chet Baker* (1951-65 recordings), *The Best Of The Gerry Mulligan Quartet With Chet Baker* (1952-57 recordings).

Mulligan, Mick

b. 24 January 1928, Harrow, Middlesex, England. Mulligan taught himself to play trumpet during early jazz revival of the 40s. Ignoring the fact that he was practically a raw beginner, he promptly formed his own group which he named the Magnolia Jazz Band. With the enthusiastic support of sidemen such as Bob Dawbarn, Roy Crimmins, Archie Semple, Ian Christie and singer George Melly, the band became very popular. With radio broadcasts, occasional appearances on television and endless one-night stands at clubs, pubs and theatres throughout the UK, the band established itself as a driving force of the British trad boom. Later renamed Mick Mulligan's Jazz Band, the group continued until the early 60s before folding in the face of a new kind of popular music. Mulligan stayed on in music for a short while before retiring. A forceful player, Mulligan has left behind only a few records but his band's often hilarious exploits have been extensively recounted in books by Melly and the band's manager, Jim Godbolt. Although in its early days the Mulligan band was noted more for enthusiasm than skill, towards the end it had become one of the finest examples of UK trad.

Album: *George Melly With Mick Mulligan's Band* (1957).

Further reading: *Owning Up*, George Melly. *All This And Many A Dog*, Jim Godbolt.

Murphy, Mark

b. 14 March 1932, Syracuse, New York, USA. Murphy began singing as a child and in his mid-teens was performing with a band led by his brother. He worked in many parts of the USA, and had built a small reputation for himself in New York when the appearance of several albums in the late 50s announced that the jazz world had a new and important singer in its midst. During the 60s he continued to tour, visiting Europe and making more fine records with Al Cohn (*That's How I Love The Blues*) and a group drawn from the Clarke-Boland Big Band (*Midnight Mood*). In the middle of the decade he decided to settle in Europe and worked extensively on the Continent, with occasional visits to the UK. In the early 70s he returned to the USA, where he recorded with Michael and Randy Brecker on *Bridging A Gap* and the later *Satisfaction Guaranteed*, and continued to attract new audiences. Murphy's repertoire is extensive and draws upon sources as diverse as Big Joe Turner and Jon Hendricks. An accomplished stylist who sings with panache, good humour and great vocal dexterity, Murphy has remained dedicated to jazz. This commitment has been unswayed by the fact that his warm voice and highly personable stage presentation would almost certainly have guaranteed him a successful and much more lucrative career in other areas of popular music. In the early 90s Murphy was still on tour, still pleasing his old audience, and still, remarkably, pulling in newcomers.

Albums: *Meet Mark Murphy* (c.1956), *Let Yourself Go* (c.1956), *Sessions, Live* (c.1958), *Rah!* (Original Jazz Classics 1961), *That's How I Love The Blues* (1962), *Midnight Mood* (1967), *Bridging A Gap* (1972), *Mark II* (1973), *Red Clay: Mark Murphy Sings* (1975), *Mark Murphy Sings Dorothy Fields And Cy Coleman* (1977), *Stolen Moments* (1978), *Satisfaction Guaranteed* (1979), *Bop For Kerouac* (1981), *Mark Murphy Sings The Nat 'King' Cole Songbook, Vols. 1 & 2* (1983), *Beauty And The Beast* (Muse 1986), *Night Mood* (Milestone 1986), *Kerouac Then And Now* (Muse 1987), *September Ballads* (Milestone 1987), *What A Way To Go* (Muse 1991), *Very Early* (1993), with Sheila Jordan *One For Junior* (Muse 1994).

Murphy, Turk

b. Melvin Murphy, 16 December 1915, Palermo, California, USA, d. 30 May 1987. Murphy's early career was as a trombonist in popular dancebands such as that led by Mal Hallett, but in the late 30s he joined the revivalist band led by Lu Watters and remained there for most of the next decade. After leaving Watters he formed his own band, gaining just as much fame and popularity as Watters had, and a similarly high level of critical disdain. Murphy opened his own club, Earthquake McGoon's, in San Francisco and continued to lead his band there and around the world until shortly before his death in 1987. An earthy, sometimes raucous but always entertaining player, Murphy was one of the key figures in retaining public interest in traditional jazz during a period, and in a place (the west coast) that saw most critical attention directed to other styles of music.

Albums: *Turk Murphy's Jazz Band Favourites* (Good Time Jazz, 1949-51 recordings), *The Music Of Jelly Roll Morton* (1953), *Music For Losers* (1957), *Turk Murphy At The Newport Jazz Festival 1957* (1957), *Turk Murphy In Concert Vols 1 & 2* (1972), *Southern Stomps* (1980-86), *San Francisco Memories* (c.1986), *Concert In The Park* (Merry Makers 1986), with Jim Cullum *Turk At Carnegie Hall* (1987). Compilations: *San Francisco Jazz, Vol. 1* (1949-50 recordings), *San Francisco Jazz, Vol. 2* (1950-52 recordings), *Live At Easy Street Vols 1-3* (Dawn Club 1979), *The Best Of Turk Murphy* (Merry Makers 1993).

Murray, David

b. 19 February 1955, Oakland, California, USA. Murray is regarded by many critics as the most important tenor saxophonist of his generation. While he was still an infant his family moved from the Oakland ghetto to integrated Berkeley. He learnt music from his mother, a church pianist, and took up the tenor saxophone at the age of nine years old, learning the fingering from his clarinet-playing older brother. Three years later he was leading R&B bands. On the day that Martin Luther King was assassinated he was asked, as president of the student body at his junior high school, to address his fellow students. He led the soul revue, the Notations Of Soul, in a two-hour session which helped avert violence in response to Dr. King's murder. He continued formal study at Pomona College, Los Angeles, where he was taught by Stanley Crouch and Margaret Kohn. He and Crouch later worked together as part of Black Music Infinity and in Murray's 1975 Trio. It was with this unit that Murray re-located to New York, becoming involved with the loft circuit of experimental musicians. He linked up with three of these (Hamiet Bluiett, Oliver Lake, and Julius Hemphill) to form the World Saxophone Quartet in 1977. In the early 80s he joined the comparable Clarinet Summit, led by John Carter. He also worked with Curtis Clarke, Billy Bang, Fred Hopkins, Phil Wilson, Sunny Murray, Jack DeJohnette (in duo and in the drummer's group Special Edition) and James 'Blood' Ulmer (with whom he also played in Music Revelation Ensemble), and, while still in California, he had played with Bobby Bradford, James Newton, Arthur Blythe and Butch Morris, the latter still supplying him with many of the tunes he records. In 1978 he established a big band, out of which distilled the more economically and logistically viable Octet. Throughout the 80s he led a quartet as well as the octet and,

when feasible, the big band. Each of these units has been highly-praised throughout the world. Murray's bands offer well-crafted, distinctive writing and adventurous, though equally well-crafted, solos. His own playing on tenor, soprano, bass-clarinet and flute welds traces of his R&B and gospel background, the freedom of Albert Ayler (one of his early heroes) and the classic quality of players like Paul Gonsalves into an individualist whole. He told Francis Davis: 'When I first came to New York I was playing more melodically, almost the way I play now. If you listen to my records chronologically you'll hear me gradually laying off the overblown notes, but I still use energy techniques as a kind of capper to my solos.' He is both a polished and a passionate improviser, whose other influences include Coleman Hawkins, Ben Webster and Duke Ellington. To date, the best of his work can be found among the many albums he recorded for Black Saint during the 80s (notably *Ming, Morning Song, Children, The Hill* and *I Want To Talk About You*) together with *Ming's Samba* on the Portrait label, and the set of four 1988 quartet records released by DIW: *Deep River, Lovers, Spirituals* and *Ballads*. His 90s output is (so far) considerable and to a high standard. Highly recommended are *Death Of A Sideman, Fast Life, Real Deal* and *Tenors*. Quite how many more albums he will have put out by the end of the century is mind expanding.

Selected albums: with others *Wild Flowers 4* (1976), *Flowers For Albert* (West Wind 1976), *Low Class Conspiracy* (1976), with Synthesis *Sentiments* (1976), with James Newton *Solomon's Sons* (1977), *And Low Class Conspiracy Volume 1: Penthouse Jazz* (1977), *And Low Class Conspiracy Volume 2: Holy Siege On Intrigue* (1977), *Live At The Lower Manhattan Ocean Club Vols 1 & 2* (India Navigation 1978), *Last Of The Hipmen* (1978), *Let The Music Take You* (1978), *Sur-Real Saxophone* (1978), *Conceptual Saxophone* (1978), *Organic Saxophone* (1978), *Interboogieology* (Black Saint 1978), *The London Concert* (1979), *3D Family* (Hat Art 1979), *Sweet Lovely* (Black Saint 1980), *Solo Live Vols 1 & 2* (1980), with Music Revelation Ensemble *No Wave* (1980), *Ming* (Black Saint 1980), *Home* (Black Saint 1982), *Murray's Steps* (Black Saint 1983), with Wilber Morris *Wilber Force* (1983), *Morning Song* (Black Saint 1984), with Clarinet Summit *Concert At The Public Theater* (1984, rec. 1982), *Live At Sweet Basil Volume 1* (Black Saint 1985), *Children* (Black Saint 1985), with Clarinet Summit *Concert At The Public Theater Volume 2* (1985, rec 1982), *Live At Sweet Basil Volume 2* (Black Saint 1986), *David Murray* (1986), with Jack DeJohnette *In Our Style* (DIW 1986), *New Life* (1987), with Randy Weston *The Healers* (Black Saint 1987), *The Hill* (Black Saint 1988, rec. 1986), with McCoy Tyner and others *Blues For Coltrane* (1988), *Lovers* (1988), with Clarinet Summit *Southern Belles* (1988), *Music Revelation Ensemble* (1988), *The People's Choice* (1988), *I Want To Talk About You* (Black Saint 1989, rec 1986), *Deep River* (DIW 1989), *Ming's Samba* (1989), with Kahil El' Zabar *Golden Sea* (1989), with others *Lucky Four* (Tutu 1990), *Ballads* (DIW 1990, rec. 1988), *Spirituals* (DIW 1990, rec. 1988), with Music Revelation Ensemble *Elec. Jazz* (1990), *Hope Scope* (Black Saint 1991, rec. 1987), *Special Quartet*

(1991), *Live At The Peace Church* (1991, rec. 1976), *Remembrances* (DIW 1992), *Shakill's Warrior* (DIW 1992), *Big Band* (DIW 1992), *A Sanctuary Within* (Black Saint 1992), with Music Revelation Ensemble *After Dark* (1992), with Dave Burrell *In Concert* (1992), *Fast Life* (DIW 1993), with Milford Graves *Real Deal* (DIW 1993, rec. 1991), *Death Of A Sideman* (DIW 1993, rec 1991), *The Jazzpar Prize* (Enja 1993), *Tea For Two* (Fresh Sound 1993, rec 1990), *Black And Red* (Red Baron 1993), *Ballads For Bass Clarinet* (DIW 1993) *Live '93 Acoustic Octfunk* (Sound Hills 1994), *Tenors* (DIW 1994), *Picasso* (DIW 1994), *Body And Soul* (Black Saint 1994), *Saxman* (Red Baron 1994), *Jazzosaurus Rex* (Red Baron 1994).

Murray, Sunny

b. James Marcellus Arthur Murray, 21 September 1937, Idabel, Oklahoma, USA. Murray is probably the most influential and certainly the most controversial drummer to emerge from the 60s new wave. He began to teach himself drums at the age of nine, subsequently flirting briefly with trumpet and trombone. In 1956 he moved to New York and worked with figures as diverse as Henry 'Red' Allen, Willie 'The Lion' Smith, Jackie McLean, Rocky Boyd, Ted Curson and Cecil Taylor. In 1963 he went with Taylor and Jimmy Lyons to Europe, where he joined Albert Ayler in the legendary trio that produced *Ghosts* and *Spiritual Unity*. He later played on several more Ayler albums, including *New York Eye And Ear Control*, *Bells* and *Spirits Rejoice*, while Ayler guested on Murray's debut, *Sunny's Time Now*. He lived in France from 1968-71, then moved to Philadelphia, Pennsylvania, USA, where he worked with an equally influential drummer from the hard bop era, Philly Joe Jones. In the 70s and 80s Murray remained extremely active, co-leading the Untouchable Factor, running a trio (that included tenor tyro David Murray - no relation) and recording with pianists Don Pullen (*Applecores*) and Alex Von Schlippenbach (on the duo *Smoke*) as well as renewing his old association with Cecil Taylor (*It Is In The Brewing Luminous*) and Jimmy Lyons. A player with an abstract and oblique approach to the beat, paying at least as much attention to the cymbals as the drums, Murray nevertheless creates a strong feeling of pulse for the music. He has played with most of the major figures of *avant garde* jazz, including Archie Shepp, Ornette Coleman, Don Cherry, John Coltrane, John Tchicai, Roswell Rudd, and Grachan Moncur III.

Albums: *Sunny's Time Now* (1966), *Sunny Murray Quintet* (1966), *Sunny Murray* (ESP 1969), *Big Chief* (1969), *Homage To Africa* (1969), *Sunshine* (1969), *An Even Break (Never Gives A Sucker)* (Affinity 1970), *New American Music Vol. 1* (1973), with others *Wildflowers Vols. 1 & 5* (1977), with Untouchable Factor *Charred Earth* (1977), *Applecores* (Philly Jazz 1978), *Live At Moers Festival* (Moers Music 1979), *African Magic* (1979), with Jimmy Lyons *Jump Up/What To Do About* (1981), *Indelicacy* (West Wind 1987), with Alex Von Schlippenbach *Smoke* (1990).

Musso, Vido

b. 13 January 1913, Carrini, Sicily, d. 9 January 1982. Musso's family emigrated to the USA in 1920, settling in Detroit, where he began playing clarinet. Relocating to Los Angeles in 1930, he became friendly with Stan Kenton and the two men worked together in various bands, including one led by Musso and one they co-led. In the mid-30s Musso, by now playing tenor saxophone, joined Benny Goodman and thereafter played in the big bands of Gene Krupa, Harry James, Tommy Dorsey and others, rejoining Kenton in 1946. He stayed only a year and then formed another band of his own, continuing to lead jazz-orientated dancebands until the mid-50s. An entirely untutored musician, Musso's powerful, buzzing sound and aggressive solo style inclined him to the more extrovert areas of jazz and big band music. Untouched by the changes which took place in jazz in the 40s, Musso became something of an anachronism and for the rest of his career he played in relatively obscure settings, often in Las Vegas show bands.

Albums: *Vido Musso And His Orchestra* i (1954), *Vido Musso And His Orchestra* ii (c.1955), *One Night Stand With Vido Musso* (Savoy 1982, 1947 recording). Compilations: *The Indispensable Benny Goodman Vols 3/4* (1936-37 recordings), *Stan Kenton's Greatest Hits* (1943-51 recordings), *Vido Musso's All Stars* (1946 recordings), *Loaded* (Savoy 1993).

Myers, Amina Claudine

b. 21 March 1942, Blackwell, Arkansas, USA. As a young woman, Myers played piano and sang in church. In the mid-60s she moved to Chicago, became a member of the AACM and over the next 10 years or so worked frequently with fellow-members such as Kalaparush Maurice McIntyre (*Humility In The Light Of The Creator*), Muhal Richard Abrams, Henry Threadgill and Lester Bowie (*African Children*, *The 5th Power*). In the early 70s she also played with Gene Ammons, Sonny Stitt and Little Milton as well as leading her own trio. She moved to New York in the mid-70s and spent some time in Europe in the early 80s, recording there with Frank Lowe (*Exotic Heartbreak*) and with Martha and Fontella Bass and David Peaston on the highly-praised gospel set, *From The Root To The Source*. Her first recording as leader, for London's Leo Records featured her on piano, organ and vocals, and were powerful, even stark, evocations of her blues and gospel roots. Inexplicably, later recordings - particularly an ill-judged couple of fusion-based albums for Novus - largely failed to capture the outstanding talents that have won her a high standing among her peers. From the mid-80s she has been playing with Charlie Haden's Liberation Music Orchestra, recording with them on *Dream Keeper*.

Albums: *Song For Mother E* (Leo 1980), *Salutes Bessie Smith* (Leo 1980), *Poems For Piano: The Music Of Marion Brown* (1980), with Muhal Richard Abrams *Duet* (1981), *The Circle Of Time* (1983), *Jumping In The Sugar Bowl* (Minor 1984), *Country Girl* (Minor 1986), *Amina* (Novus 1988), *In Touch* (Novus 1989).

N

Namyslowski, Zbigniew

b. 9 September 1939, Warsaw, Poland. Namyslowski's *Lola*, recorded during his visit to the UK in 1964, caused quite a stir, since few people in the West were aware of the state of the jazz art in Soviet bloc countries (formerly). However, it was not simply the surprise of Eastern European musicians playing modern, post-bop jazz at all that impressed: Namyslowski was very good indeed, with a hard, emotional tone and considerable facility on the alto saxophone. He had begun his musical studies on piano at the age of six, switching to the cello at 12. He also plays soprano saxophone, flute and trombone. He studied music theory at the Warsaw High School of Music and began his career playing trombone with a trad band and 'cello with a modern group. Concentrating on alto, he set up his quartet in 1963 and toured Europe, Asia and Australasia as well as the USSR. He plays with the kind of intensely personal passion one associates with Jackie McLean and Mike Osborne, weaving in strong strands of Polish folk music in both his writing and improvising. In the late 70s and early 80s he moved away from the more *avant-garde* side of his style and, without losing his individuality, used rock-fusion elements. There was also an adventurous album, *Zbigniew Namyslowski*, for orchestra and large jazz group. By the late 80s, he was back in the hard-bop mainstream, sounding a little less dangerous than in his early days, but just as sincere and inventive. He has also worked with Krzysztof Komeda and Air Condition, the fine Polish fusion band which he led in the early 80s.
Albums: *Lola* (1965), *Zbigniew Namyslowski Quartet* (1966), with Krzysztof Komeda *Astigmation* (1967), *Winobranie* (1973), *All Stars After Hours* (1974), *Kujaviek Goes Funky* (1975), with Michael J. Smith *Geomusic III* (1975), *Namyslowski* (1977), *Zbigniew Namyslowski* (1980), with Air Condition *Follow Your Kite* (1980), *Air Condition* (Affinity 1982), *Polish Jazz Vol 4:* (Polskie Nagrania, 1966-87 recordings), *Open* (1988), *The Last Concert* (Polonia 1992).

Nance, Ray

b. Willis Nance, 10 December 1913, Chicago, Illinois, USA, d. 28 January 1976. A gifted multi-instrumentalist, Nance studied formally for several years and played in various small bands, mostly in the Chicago area. By the early 30s he was a popular local entertainer, leading his own bands and playing several instruments, including trumpet and violin, as well as singing, dancing and performing engaging comedy routines. The 30s also saw him playing in the Chicago big bands led by Earl 'Fatha' Hines and Horace Henderson. He joined Duke Ellington in 1940 and quickly became an integral, valued and much-loved part of the organization. He left Ellington for a short spell in the mid-40s to lead his own band, but returned at the end of 1945; this time he remained virtually without a

break, until 1963. From 1964 until his death he led his own small bands but returned regularly to guest with the Ellington band. Whether playing trumpet - later cornet - or violin, Nance was a highly distinctive musician and his contributions to the Ellington band's recordings are many and marvellous. His violin playing on 'Moon Mist' and his trumpet solo on the 1941 version of 'Take the 'A' Train' are particularly fine examples of his work. Outside the Ellington band he made some excellent recordings with ex-Ellingtonians Paul Gonsalves and Johnny Hodges, while a 1971 Jimmy Rushing recording includes a moving violin solo on 'When I Grow Too Old To Dream'.
Albums: *Duke Ellington Presents* (1956), with Johnny Hodges *Duke's In Bed* (1956), with Duke Ellington *Black, Brown And Beige* (1958), *Body And Soul* (1969), with Paul Gonsalves *Just A-Sittin' And A-Rockin'* (1970), with Jimmy Rushing *The You And Me That Used To Be* (1971), *Huffin' 'N' Puffin'* (1971), *Ray Nance Quartet And Sextet* (Unique 1986). Compilation: with Ellington *The Blanton-Webster Years (1940-42)* (1987).

Nanton, Joe 'Tricky Sam'

b. Joseph N. Irish, 1 February 1904, New York City, New York, USA, d. 20 July 1946. After playing trombone with a number of small bands in the early and mid-20s, including two stints with Cliff Jackson, Nanton joined Elmer Snowden and by 1926 was in the re-formed band led by Duke Ellington. Along with Bubber Miley, Nanton was a major force in creating the distinctive 'jungle' sound of Ellington's early work. Although occasionally beset by illness, Nanton remained with Ellington until he suffered a stroke in 1945. An inventive soloist capable of producing fascinating excursions within a narrow range, and with a marked penchant for creating sounds which closely resembled the human voice, Nanton helped to establish a role for the trombone in the Ellington band which, thereafter, had to be followed, more or less faithfully, by most of his successors.
Compilations: *The Indispensable Duke Ellington Vols. 1/2, 3/4, 5/6 (1927-40)* (1983), with Duke Ellington *The Blanton-Webster Years (1940-42)* (1986).

Napoleon, Marty

b. 2 June 1921, New York City, New York, USA. A member of a musical family (his father was a professional musician, as were several uncles of whom the most famous is Phil Napoleon), Marty played piano in several second-string big bands of the 40s, including those led by Lee Castle and Joe Venuti. Later, he joined Charlie Barnet and also spent a brief spell with Gene Krupa. In the 50s, Napoleon began playing with his uncle Phil's revived Original Memphis Five and then showed his versatility by becoming a member of Charlie Ventura's Big Four. He next spent periods with Louis Armstrong's All Stars, as well as bands led by his brother Teddy (who was also a professional musician), Coleman Hawkins, Ruby Braff and others. Since the beginning of the 60s he has worked mostly as a solo artist, but has made occasional appearances with small groups, which have included Red Allen, and also played return stints with Armstrong and Krupa. Napoleon's wide stylistic range, which has taken him from dixieland to the edges of bop, has tended to limit appreciation of his talent among those members of the jazz public who like to label musicians.

Albums: *Trio* (1955), with Ruby Braff *Little Big Horn* (1955), with Red Allen *Ride, Red, Ride In Hi-Fi* (1957), with Louis Armstrong *Louis* (1966).

Napoleon, Phil

b. 2 September 1901, Boston, Massachusetts, d. 30 September 1990. A child prodigy, Napoleon came from a very musical family, two of his nephews being Marty and Teddy Napoleon. He played trumpet in public at the age of five and made his first records 10 years later. In 1922 he was a founder-member of the Original Memphis Five, an exceptionally good dixieland band which made numerous records, many of which sold very well. By the end of the 20s, however, Napoleon had folded the band and gone into studio work where he remained for a decade or more. At the end of the 30s, after an unsuccessful attempt to run a big band, he stopped playing for some years. In the early 50s he returned to the music scene, reviving the Memphis Five and thereafter leading a succession of dixieland bands. He continued to play well into the 80s, often at his own club, Napoleon's Retreat, in Miami, Florida. A fiery player with an attacking style, Napoleon was never on a par with such near-contemporaries as Bix Beiderbecke, although he claimed to have been influential on Beiderbecke and Red Nichols. Nevertheless, his many records show him to have been a distinctive and clear-toned trumpeter. These records, together with his remarkably long playing career, made him an important figure in the spread of jazz throughout the world.

Album: *Phil Napoleon And His Memphis Five* (1959). Compilations: with Red Nichols *New York Horns* (1924-29), *Bailey's Lucky Seven* (Queendisc 1983), *Red Nichols And Phil Napoleon* (Zeta 1991).

Napoleon, Teddy

b. 23 June 1914, New York City, New York, USA, d. 5 July 1964. Older brother of Marty Napoleon and nephew of Phil Napoleon, Teddy played piano in a band led by Lee Castle in the early 30s. After touring extensively with minor bands he arrived in New York at the end of that decade. He played in yet more minor dancebands but then, in 1944, joined Gene Krupa. Featured not only in the big band but also in Krupa's band-within-a-band, a trio which was often rounded out by Charlie Ventura, Napoleon continued this association even after Krupa had folded the big band. He toured the world with Krupa's trio in the 50s, making concert, club and festival appearances and several records. He also played and sometimes recorded with Flip Phillips, Bill Harris and his brother Marty.

Albums: with Gene Krupa *The Rocking Mr Krupa* (1953), with Krupa *Krupa Rocks* (1957). Compilation: *Drummin' Man Vol. 2 (1945-49)* (1987).

Nascimento, Milton

b. 26 October 1942, Rio de Janeiro, Brazil. Singer/songwriter Nascimento draws much of his inspiration from Brazil's Portuguese heritage, where even the jolliest tune can be counted on to contain more than a *frisson* of melancholy. His biggest successes, both at home and abroad, came in the 70s with *Milagre Dos Peixes* (1973, re-released in the UK in 1990), and *Milton* (1977), the latter featuring contributions from Herbie Hancock, Wayne Shorter, Airto Moreira, Roberto Silva and Laudir De Oliviera. First teaming with Shorter on his 1975 album *Native Dancer*, Nascimento was widely taken up by the Los Angeles music fraternity over the next few years, most notably guesting on albums by Flora Purim, Deodato and Charlie Rouse.

Selected albums: *Milagre Dos Peixes* (1973), with Flora Purim *500 Miles High* (1976), *Milton* (1977), *Travessia* (Sign 1986), *Meetings And Farewells* (Polydor 1986), *Ship Of Lovers* (Verve 1987), *Yauarete* (CBS 1988), *Txai* (Columbia 1991), *Planeta Blue Estrada Do Sol* (1992), *Noticias Do Brasil* (Tropical 1993), *Angelus* (Warner 1994).

National Youth Jazz Orchestra

In 1965 Bill Ashton, a teacher at a London school, formed the London Schools Jazz Orchestra. This was an organization in which youngsters could pursue musical ambitions in a setting that related to music which interested them, rather than forms imposed upon them by the educational hierarchy. Thanks to Ashton's persistence in the face of establishment hostility the orchestra survived, later becoming known as the London Youth Jazz Orchestra and, eventually, the National Youth Jazz Orchestra. In 1974 NYJO became a fully professional organization and remains the UK's only full-time professional big band playing jazz. Although Ashton's conception was to create an atmosphere in which young musicians could develop their craft, NYJO has long since passed the stage of being either a training ground or even a 'youth' orchestra. The extraordinarily high standard of musicianship demanded by the band means that newcomers to its ranks must have already achieved a very high standard of technical competence before auditioning. Ashton's leadership is a mixture of democracy and benign autocracy. The band's members choose the music, which varies from the brand new to charts originally played by editions of NYJO that were on the road when present members were barely walking, and Ashton organizes the musicians' choices into an entertaining programme. Although the nature of the orchestra means that it is in an almost constant state of flux, NYJO has developed an identifiable sound. Much of the music that is played by the band is original, often written by members, and everything is especially arranged. While many arrangements are 'in-house', others come from outside. Amongst the arrangers are Paul Higgs, David Lindup, Brian Priestley, Chris Smith, Terry Catharine, Bill Charleson, Neil Ardley, Alec Gould and Ashton. Many exceptional talents have passed through NYJO's ranks over the years, including Steve and Julian Argüelles, Chris Hunter, Lance Ellington, Paul Hart, David O'Higgins, Phil Todd, Mark and Andy Nightingale, Stan Sulzmann, Chris Laurence, Richard Symons, Gerard Presencer and Guy Barker. Ashton's interest in songwriting has ensured a succession of good singers with the band, including

Carol Kenyon, Helen Sorrell and Litsa Davies. Over the years NYJO has travelled extensively, appearing in various European countries and also visiting the USA. The band's many albums have proved successful and help spread the sound of a remarkable orchestra which, although effectively the creation of one man, has come to represent the best in big band jazz and consistently denies its name by being both international and fully mature.

Selected albums: *Return Trip* (1975), *Eleven Plus: Live At LWT* (1976), *In Camra* (1977), *The Sherwood Forest Suite* (1977), *To Russia With Jazz* (1978), *Mary Rose* (1979), *Down Under* (1980), *Why Don't They Write Songs Like This Any More?* (1982), *Playing Turkey* (1983), *Born Again* (1983), *Full Score* (1985), *Concrete Cows* (1986), *With An Open Mind* (1986), *Shades Of Blue And Green* (1987), *Big Band Christmas* (1989), *Maltese Cross* (NYJO 1989), *Rememberance* (NYJO 1990), *Cookin' With Gas* (NYJO 1990), *Looking Forward Looking Back* (NYJO 1992), *These Are The Jokes* (1992), *Merry Christmas And A Happy New Year* (NYJO 1993).

Navarro, Fats

b. Theodore Navarro, 24 September 1923, Key West, Florida, USA, d. 7 July 1950. After starting to learn the tenor saxophone and piano, Navarro opted for trumpet and by his mid-teens was playing professionally. In 1943 he joined the Andy Kirk band, working alongside Howard McGhee, and two years later was in the trumpet section of Billy Eckstine's bebop-oriented big band. He later settled in New York, where he played with leading beboppers such as Kenny Clarke, Ernie Henry, Howard McGhee, Tadd Dameron, Bud Powell, Charlie Parker, Leo Parker, Sonny Rollins and Dizzy Gillespie, the last of whom he had replaced in the Eckstine band. Navarro also played with mainstreamers like Coleman Hawkins and Eddie 'Lockjaw' Davis. Most of these musical associations resulted in a legacy of fine recordings, with the Dameron sessions proving to be especially fruitful. During his short life Navarro displayed a precocious talent, his rich full tone contrasting with the thin sound adopted by many of the other young bebop trumpeters of the day. In this respect his sound resembled that of an earlier generation of trumpeters who were a little out of fashion by the late 40s. His last years were dogged by ill-health, exacerbated by an addiction to heroin, and he died in 1950. Despite his brief life, Navarro proved to be one of the most accessible of the early bop trumpeters and was an influence on another similarly short-lived talent, Clifford Brown.

Selected albums: with Billy Eckstine *Together!* (1947), with Charlie Parker *One Night In Birdland* (1950), *The Tadd Dameron Band 1948, Vols. 1 & 2 (1948)* (1976), *The Fabulous Fats Navarro Vols. 1 & 2 (1947-49)* (Blue Note 1983), *Fat Girl - The Savoy Sessions (1947)* (1985), *Memorial* (Savoy 1992).

Neidlinger, Buell

b. 2 March 1936, Westport, Connecticut, USA. After studying piano, trumpet and bass, Neidlinger concentrated on teaching himself the last instrument more extensively. He led bands in high school, then attended Yale for a year, winding up as a disc jockey. In 1955 he relocated to New York, where he gigged with Coleman Hawkins, Tony Scott and Zoot Sims. He made his name with Cecil Taylor, negotiating the pianist's difficult compositions with astonishing aptitude; he was part of Taylor's famous residency at the Five Spot in 1957 and played with him in a 1960 staging of *The Connection*. Always one for a surprising career move, Neidlinger then worked in singer Tony Bennett's band for six months. Subsequent work included stints with Gil Evans and Steve Lacy. He studied music at Buffalo State University (1964-66), played with the Budapest Quartet at Tanglewood in 1965 and gave several recitals of works for solo bass by Sylvano Bussotti and Mauricio Kagel. In the late 60s he became a member of the Boston Symphony Orchestra. In 1970 Neidlinger played bass on Frank Zappa's suite for violinist Jean-Luc Ponty, 'Music For Electric Violin And Low Budget Orchestra', brought in, according to Zappa, 'because he's the only man I could think of who could play the bass part'. In 1971 he became professor of music at the California Institute of the Arts and was also busy in the Hollywood recording studios. Neidlinger's ability to relate to different kinds of music is only equalled by his interest in them: at various times he has played with Willie 'The Lion' Smith, Roy Orbison, Barbra Streisand and Archie Shepp. He has several bands: Buellgrass provides a unique blend of country and jazz: an updated western swing; Thelonious plays Thelonious Monk tunes exclusively; String Jazz interprets Duke Ellington and Monk on saxophone, drums and various string instruments. Most of his releases are on the K2B2 label, which he co-runs with tenor saxophonist Marty Krystall, a playing associate of his for over 20 years. A caustic interviewee, Neidlinger has continually involved himself with the cutting edge of jazz and has an inimitable sound on his instrument.

Albums: with Cecil Taylor *New York City R&B* (1961, reissued as *Cell Walk For Celeste*), *Cecil Taylor All Stars Featuring Buell Neidlinger* (1961, reissued as *Jumpin' Punkins*), *Ready For The 90s* (1980), *Our Night Together* (1981), *Big Day At Ojai* (1982), with Thelonious Monk *Thelonious* (1987), with String Jazz *Locomotive* (Soul Note 1988), *Big Drum* (KB Records 1991). Compilations: *The Complete Candid Recordings Of Cecil Taylor And Buell Neidlinger* (1989, rec. 1960-61, six album box-set), *Rear View Mirror* (KB Records 1991, rec. 1979-86).

Nelson, 'Big Eye' Louis

b. 28 January c.1885, New Orleans, Louisiana, USA, d. 20 August 1949. Nelson settled on playing the clarinet after trying out a wide range of instruments. Throughout his career he rarely played outside his home town, choosing to work in the emerging jazz bands and the traditional New Orleans marching and brass bands. Nelson is reputed to have played in Buddy Bolden's band, on bass, and he also worked with leading New Orleans jazzmen such as John Robichaux, Joe 'King' Oliver and Jelly Roll Morton. Nelson made few records - a handful of tracks with Kid Rena in 1940, and a few more in 1949 with 'Wooden' Joe Nicholas and as leader, using the name Louis DeLisle, under which he sometimes worked. From these recordings it is possible to understand the high regard in which

Nelson was held by musicians such as Baby Dodds and Sidney Bechet, whom Nelson tutored for a while. He played with a full sound and employed a facile technique. His records with Rena provide interesting testimony to the skill and stylistic devices of the earliest New Orleans jazz musicians.

Selected albums: with Wooden Joe Nicholas *Wooden Joe's New Orleans Band* (1945-49), *Louis Delisle's Band* (1949).

Nelson, Louis

b. 17 September 1902, New Orleans, Louisiana, USA, d. 5 April 1990. Nelson grew up in a cultured family; his mother was a graduate of the Boston Conservatory of Music, his father was a physician. After starting out on alto horn, he switched to trombone in the 20s. Working mostly with bands in and around New Orleans, including those led by Oscar 'Papa' Celestin and Kid Rena, he built a sound reputation during the 30s. During this period he also worked often with the popular big band led by Sidney Desvigne. In the early 40s he joined Kid Thomas and in the 50s was a regular member of the band led by George Lewis, with whom he toured extensively. In the 60s Nelson also worked with the New Orleans Joymakers, the Legends Of Jazz, Kid Thomas, Peter Bocage, Sammy Rimington and other leading New Orleans-style musicians. For many years he was a frequent performer at Preservation Hall in his home town. Although best known for his New Orleans playing, Nelson's style incorporated many elements foreign to the form; an attribute that is due, most observers believe, to the time spent with Desvigne. This gave him a somewhat different approach to music than that followed by stalwarts of the tradition, such as Jim Robinson. Indeed, many keen followers of Nelson's work consider his sophisticated trombone playing to be more akin to that of Tommy Dorsey rather than that of the earthier New Orleanians. Nelson could still be heard at Preservation Hall in the late 80s and into early 1990, when, in April, he was the victim of a hit-and-run accident. He continued working for a few days, but one night on the bandstand he complained of feeling unwell and collapsed. He died the following day.

Albums: *Kid Thomas At Moulin Rouge* (c.1955), *George Lewis And His New Orleans All Stars* (1963), *Peter Bocage At San Jacinto Hall* (1964), *Louis Nelson's Big Four Vols 1 & 2* (1964), *Skater's Waltz* (1966), *Louis Nelson's New Orleans Band* (1970), *New Orleans Tradition* (1971), with Kid Thomas *Preservation Of Jazz Vol. 2* (1973), *Everybody's Talkin' Bout The* (GHB 1986), *Louis Nelson All Stars Live In Japan* (1987), *April In New Orleans* (GHB 1989), *New Orleans Portraits Vol 3* (Storyville 1990).

Nelson, Oliver

b. 4 June 1932, St. Louis, Missouri, USA, d. 28 October 1975. After studying piano and alto saxophone, he settled on playing the latter instrument, paying his dues in various territory bands. In the late 40s he was with the popular Jeter-Pillars Orchestra as well as that led by Nat Towles. Early in the 50s he was briefly with Louis Jordan but then resumed his studies at universities in Washington, DC, and Missouri, also taking lessons from the respected composer Elliott Carter. In New York in the late 50s, he worked in bands led by Erskine Hawkins and Louie Bellson, then moved on to the bands of Duke Ellington and Quincy Jones. He was writing extensively at this time, both as arranger and composer, and made several records under his own name, the best-known with a small group that often featured leading jazz soloists such as Eric Dolphy and Freddie Hubbard. He later turned more to big band work, recording with numerous soloists who included Johnny Hodges and Pee Wee Russell. By the mid-60s Nelson was in great demand as a teacher and arranger and he was also called upon to write scores for films and television. His arrangements with Jimmy Smith during this period were particularly fertile, and included orchestrations of *Bashin'* and *The Dymanic Duo* (with Wes Montgomery). He played much less often in these years but did lead a small band from time to time and also formed all-star big bands for festival appearances. Nelson's work ranged widely, covering R&B and modal jazz, and he also composed pieces in the classical form. Much of his writing suggests considerable facility, though at times slipping a little into being merely facile. Nevertheless his recordings as a performer, especially *The Blues And The Abstract Truth*, on which he is joined by Dolphy and Hubbard, are extremely rewarding, while many of those he made as composer-leader such as the excellent *Sound Pieces* are interesting for their unstinting professionalism. He died from a heart attack in 1975.

Selected albums: *Meet Oliver Nelson* (Original Jazz Classics 1959), *Screamin' The Blues* (Original Jazz Classics 1960), *Soul Battle* (Original Jazz Classics 1960), *Nocturne* (Original Jazz Classics 1960), *Straight Ahead* (Original Jazz Classics 1961), *The Blues And The Abstract Truth* (Impulse 1961), *Main Stem* (Original Jazz Classics 1961), *Taking Care Of Business* (Original Jazz Classics 1961), *Afro-American Sketches* (Original Jazz Classics 1962), *Fantabulous* (1964), *More Blues And The Abstract Truth* (Impulse 1965), *Live From Los Angeles* (1967), *Sound Pieces* (Impulse 1967), *Black, Brown And Beautiful* (RCA 1970), *Berlin Dialogue For Orchestra* (1970), *Swiss Suite* (1971), *Oliver Nelson With Oily Rags* (1974), *Stolen Moments* (1975).

Nesbitt, John

b. c.1900, Norfolk, West Virginia, USA, d. 1935. In the early 20s Nesbitt played trumpet with various bands before joining the band led by Bill McKinney, which eventually evolved into McKinney's Cotton Pickers. He stayed with the band for several years, playing and writing arrangements. In the early 30s he was resident in New York, playing in the bands of Fletcher Henderson and Luis Russell, before returning to territory bands, including those of Zack Whyte and Speed Webb. Poor health damaged his career and he died in 1935.

Compilation: *McKinney's Cotton Pickers (1928-29)* (1983).

Further reading: *McKinney's Music: A Bio-discography Of McKinney's Cotton Pickers*, John Chilton.

New Jazz Orchestra

The New Jazz Orchestra was founded in 1963 by Clive Burrows and resurrected and directed by Neil Ardley between 1964 and 1968. It provided the up-and-coming generation of British jazz musicians with the experience of working with a large jazz orchestra, its personnel including Harry Beckett, Henry Lowther and Ian Carr (trumpets), Paul Rutherford and Mike Gibbs (trombones), Don Rendell, Trevor Watts, Dick Heckstall-Smith and Barbara Thompson (saxophones), Michael Garrick (piano), Jack Bruce (bass) and Jon Hiseman (drums). It is not surprising that with such quality musicians *The Times* critic, Miles Kington, would write that the NJO 'makes most big bands sound like trained elephants with two tricks'. It was not the only purpose of the NJO to provide such invaluable big band experience for these musicians; it also fostered a workshop atmosphere to provide its arrangers with a chance to try out scores. Among those who wrote for the orchestra were Ardley, Alan Cohen, Gibbs, Rutherford, Garrick and Mike Taylor. 'I learnt by my mistakes,' Ardley said later and by the time he had become the leader he was producing major scores like 'Shades Of Blue' from the first album and 'Dejeuner Sur L'Herbe' from the second. All the material in the latter is derived from two/four bar motifs in the main theme. There are no repeated chord sequences or scales; rather, the piece grows organically in the manner of classical music. This is not merely a third stream piece but an attempt to write jazz in new way. It was the kind of experiment the NJO was formed to encourage and a score Ardley would have been lucky to get performed anywhere else. The NJO gave some concerts in London and at festivals. They also had a fruitful pairing with Colosseum. Despite what a contemporary described as its 'fiercely swinging rhythm, first class solos and brilliant ensemble' it gained no recognition abroad though in time many of its members have become very well known on the continent.

Albums: *Western Reunion* (1965), *Le Dejeuner Sur L'Herbe* (1969).

New Orleans Rhythm Kings

After the hugely popular Original Dixieland Jazz Band created a storm of interest in Chicago in the early 20s other musicians decided to try their luck at the new jazz music. Amongst them were Georg Brunis, Jack Pettis, Arnold Loyacano, Louis Black, Elmer Schoebel and Frank Snyder. They formed a band they named the New Orleans Rhythm Kings for an engagement at the Friars Inn. With the ODJB safely on their way to international fame in New York and London, the NORK became Chicago's top jazz band. They recorded in 1922 and looked set to become one of the mainstays of the suddenly vital white jazz scene. With a few personnel changes the band was strengthened, but by 1925 they had folded, leaving behind a handful of records and a lasting impression upon the next generation of musicians who would form the basis of Chicago-style jazz.

Compilations: *The New Orleans Rhythm Kings 1922-23* (Swaggie 1988), *The New Orleans Rhythm Kings* 1923 (Swaggie 1988), *The New Orleans Rhythm Kings Vol 1* (King Jazz 1992), *The New Orleans Rhythm Kings Vol 2* (Village Jazz 1992).

Newborn, Phineas, Jnr.

b. 14 December 1931, Whiteville, Tennessee, USA, d. 26 May 1989. In the late 40s and early 50s Newborn, a gifted multi-instrumentalist who had studied extensively, played piano in a number of R&B and blues bands in and around Memphis, Tennessee. He had two brief spells with Lionel Hampton before military service interrupted his career. Subsequently, he led his own small group in New York, played with Charles Mingus, Oscar Pettiford and Kenny Clarke among others, made several records and appeared in the John Cassavetes film *Shadows* (1960). Relocated in Los Angeles in the 60s, he continued to record with artists such as Howard McGhee, Teddy Edwards, Ray Brown and Elvin Jones. His career then faltered, largely through a nervous breakdown and an injury to his hands, but the mid-70s saw his return to public performances. Newborn's early records were marked by displays of his phenomenal technique, while those made later suggested a growing maturity. Unfortunately, the interruptions to his career did not allow his potential full rein, and further illness prevented him from working for most of the 80s. Doctors discovered lung tumour in 1988; he died in 1989. The last years of his life are movingly recounted in a chapter of Stanley Booth's book on Memphis musicians, *Rhythm Oil*.

Albums: *Here Is Phineas* (1956), *Phineas Rainbow* (1956), *Phineas Newborn With Dennis Farnon Orchestra* (1957), *Phineas Newborn And His Orchestra* (1957), *Fabulous Phineas* (1958), *We Three* (1958), *Stockholm Jam Session Vol 1 and 2* (Steeplechase 1958 recording), *Phineas Newborn Plays Again* (1959), *Piano Portraits* (1959), *Newborn Piano* (1959), *A World Of Piano* (Original Jazz Classics 1961), *The Great Jazz Piano Of Phineas Newborn* (Original Jazz Classics 1962), *The Newborn Touch* (Original Jazz Classics 1964), *Please Send Me Someone To Love* (JVC 1969), *Harlem Blues* (Original Jazz Classics 1969), *Solo Piano* (Atlantic 1974), *Solo* (1975), *Look Out...Phineas Is Back* (Pablo 1976), *Phineas Is Genius* (1977).

Newman, David 'Fathead'

b. 24 February 1933, Dallas, Texas, USA. Newman was a tenor/baritone/soprano saxophone player and flautist, whose work contains elements of both jazz and R&B. In the early 50s he toured with Texan blues guitarist 'T-Bone' Walker and recorded the classic 'Reconsider Baby' with Lowell Fulson in 1954. For the next 10 years Newman was part of Ray Charles' orchestra, appearing on landmark recordings such as 'I Got A Woman', 'What'd I Say' and 'Lonely Avenue'. Other tenures have included the saxophone position in Herbie Mann's Family Of Mann (1972-74). He has recorded some two dozen albums as a leader since 1958, most tending towards mainstream and post-bop jazz with a funk edge, and has worked extensively as an accompanist in the blues, rock and jazz fields. He worked on Natalie Cole's best-selling *Unforgettable* (1990), and received much acclaim for his involvement in the *Bluesiana Triangle* benefit projects in aid of the homeless. *Blue Greens And Beans* was a collection of bop standards also featuring another Texan player, Marchel Ivery.

Albums: as leader *Lonely Avenue* (1971), *Mr. Fathead* (1976),

Fire! Live At the Village Vanguard (Atlantic 1989), *Blue Greens And Beans* (Timeless 1991), *Blue Head* (Candid 1991), with Art Blakey, Dr. John *Bluesiana Triangle* (1990), *Return To The Wide Open Spaces* (Meteor 1993). Compilation: *Back To Basics* (1990).

Newman, Joe

b. 7 September 1922, New Orleans, Louisiana, USA, d. 4 July 1992. After playing with and leading a college band, trumpeter Newman joined Lionel Hampton in 1941. Two years later he joined Count Basie at the start of a long association. In the late 40s and early 50s he spent some time in bands led by Illinois Jacquet and J.C. Heard and also led his own bands for club and record dates. By 1952 he was back in the Basie fold and he remained with the band, handling most of the trumpet solos, until 1961. Subsequently, he toured world-wide, usually as a solo act, but occasionally in specially formed bands such as those led by Benny Goodman and Hampton. He also became active in jazz education. This pattern of work continued throughout the 80s and into the early 90s. A powerful player with a wide repertoire, Newman's style acknowledged latterday developments in jazz trumpet while remaining rooted in the concepts of his great idol, Louis Armstrong.

Albums: *Joe Newman And His Band* (1954), *Joe Newman And The Boys In The Band* (1954), *The Joe Newman Sextet* (1954), *All I Wanna Do Is Swing* (1955), *The Count's Men* (Fresh Sound 1955 recording), *I'm Still Swinging* (1955), *I Feel Like A Newman* (Black Lion 1955-56), *Salute To Satch* (1956), *The Joe Newman-Frank Wess Septet* (1956), *Jazz For Playboys* (Savoy 1957), *The Happy Cats* (Jasmine 1957), *The Joe Newman-Zoot Sims Quartet* (1957), *Soft Swingin' Jazz* (1958), *Joe Newman And His Orchestra* (1958), *Joe Newman And Count Basie's All Stars* (1958), *Jive At Five* (Original Jazz Classics 1960), *Good 'N' Groovy* (1961), *Joe's Hap'nin's* (1961), *The Joe Newman-Oliver Nelson Quintet* (1961), *In A Mellow Mood* (1962), *Shiny Stockings* (c.1965), *Way Down Blues* (c.1965), with Lionel Hampton *Newport Uproar!* (1967), *I Love My Baby* (1978), *Joe Newman-Jimmy Rowles Duets* (1979), *Similar Souls* (Vogue 1983), with Joe Wilder *Hangin' Out* (1984).

Newton, David

b. 2 February 1958, Glasgow, Scotland. As a child he took lessons on piano, clarinet and bassoon, but while studying at the Leeds College of Music he decided to concentrate on piano. After playing in various bands as a semi-pro, he secured his first professional engagement leading a trio at a restaurant in Bradford, Yorkshire, in 1978. Around this time he also played in numerous other bands, ranging musically from traditional jazz to funk, from strict-tempo dancebands to classical. In the early 80s he worked extensively in the theatre, especially with Scarborough-based playwright Alan Ayckbourn. Newton then returned to Scotland, and from a base in Edinburgh quickly established himself as a rising star of the jazz world. He played in backing groups for many visiting jazzmen, including Art Farmer, Bud Shank, Shorty Rogers and Nat Adderley. He also recorded with Buddy De Franco. By the late 80s he had settled

in London, recording with Alan Barnes, the Jazz Renegades, Martin Taylor, with whom he toured India, and also playing club dates with Andy Cleyndert, Don Weller, Spike Robinson and others. At the end of the decade he became accompanist and musical director to Carol Kidd, recording with her and making numerous concert appearances. An outstanding talent, Newton's wide-ranging experience has ensured that he is at home in most musical settings. Despite his eclecticism he has developed a distinctive and distinguished personal style. As he matures he appears likely to become one of Europe's leading jazz musicians, well-equipped to take the music into the 21st century.

Albums: with Alan Barnes *Affiliation* (1987), *Given Time* (GFM 1988), *Victim Of Circumstance* (Linn 1991), *Eye Witness* (Linn 1991), *Return Journey* (Linn 1993).

Newton, Frankie

b. 4 January 1906, Emory, Virginia, USA, d. 11 March 1954. In the late 20s and early 30s Newton played trumpet in a number of leading New York bands, including those led by Charlie 'Fess' Johnson, Sam Wooding and Chick Webb. He later joined Charlie Barnet and was briefly with Andy Kirk. The 40s saw him playing in various bands on the verge of the bigtime, including those led by Lucky Millinder and Pete Brown. Apparently without direction, his career drifted and he worked mostly in clubs in New York and Boston, sometimes in company with James P. Johnson, 'Big' Sid Catlett and Edmond Hall. By the 50s he was playing only rarely. A gifted player with a full, burnished sound, Newton was especially attuned to the needs of singers and played on a number of memorable vocal recordings, including Bessie Smith's last date, plus Maxine Sullivan's 'Loch Lomond', and Billie Holiday's 'Strange Fruit' sessions. Newton's briefly shining talent promised much, but his lack of ambition steadfastly countered any chance of popular success. But then, the easy-going life he led was perhaps what he really wanted.

Selected compilations: *At The Onyx Club 1937-1939* (Tax 1987), *Frankie's Jump* (Affinity 1993).

Nicholas, 'Wooden' Joe

b. 23 September 1883, New Orleans, Louisiana, USA, d. 17 November 1957. A well-known figure in his native city, Nicholas started out on clarinet but took up the cornet under the influence of Buddy Bolden and Joe 'King' Oliver. He worked in marching bands, forming his own, the Camelia Band, in 1918. A powerful player with an earthy, basic style, Nicholas embodied the traditions of the music but never managed to achieve the panache of his idols and mentors. His nephew was the distinguished clarinettist Albert Nicholas.

Albums: with others *Echoes From New Orleans (1945)* (1988), *Echoes From New Orleans Vol. 2 (1949-51)* (1988).

Nichols, Herbie

b. 3 December 1919, New York City, New York, USA, d. 12 April 1963. In the late 30s and early 40s Nichols played piano with numerous bands in a wide variety of styles. The bands

David Newton (left) and Alan Barnes

included those of Herman Autrey, Illinois Jacquet, Lucky Thompson, Edgar Sampson and Arnett Cobb, while the styles ranged across small-group swing, dixieland and R&B. A remarkably original and talented musician, Nichols developed a personal music that owed a debt to bebop, particularly to its more idiosyncratic practitioners such as Thelonius Monk, but for much of his life the only gigs he could get were playing Dixieland music, which he came to dislike intensely. In the early 60s, he was able to work occasionally with modern musicians closer to his advanced thinking, among them Roswell Rudd and Archie Shepp, but by then he was terminally ill with leukaemia (though Rudd also blamed 'a broken heart' brought on by 'years of frustration, neglect and disillusionment'). In recent years Nichols's reputation has grown rapidly and there have been several tribute albums that feature his compositions, notably two on the Soul Note label and one by Holland's Instant Composers Pool Orchestra. Nichols's own recorded legacy, though small, is of outstanding quality: two Blue Note trio sessions, reissued as the double album *The Third World*, feature sympathetic support from Art Blakey and Max Roach. A later trio set for Bethlehem has George Duvivier and Dannie Richmond. These records mostly feature his own distinctive and delightful compositions, some of which - '2300 Skiddoo', 'Shuffle Montgomery', 'House Party Starting', 'Hangover Triangle' - look like becoming established standards in the 90s. 'There is charm and interest all around you', Rudd wrote of Nichols's music, 'from bright ripples on down to heavy undercurrents. What a beautiful sense of space! What incredible lyricism! What soulfullness! What grace! What an expansive palette of sonorities!. Wit, taste, discretion, subtleties, nuances . . . and all so personal and individual.'
Selected albums: *The Herbie Nichols Quartet* (1952), *M+N N* (1952), *The Prophetic Herbie Nichols Vol.s 1 & 2/The Third World* (1955), *The Herbie Nichols Trio* (Blue Note 1955), *The Third World* (1955), *Out Of The Shadows* (Affinity 1957), *The Bethlehem Sessions* (Affinity 1957), *Love, Gloom, Cash, Love* (1957).
Further reading: *Four Lives In The Bebop Business*, A.B. Spellman.

Nichols, Keith

b. 13 February 1945, Ilford, Essex, England. Although he was playing the trombone and leading the band at school Nichols also became All-Britain junior accordion champion. He can now play most of the instruments in the bands he leads but excels on piano and trombone. He played with Dick Sudhalter's Anglo-American Alliance (1969) before leading bands of his own like the New Sedalia in the early 70s. He led the Ragtime Orchestra which played scholarly versions of the repertoire, before going to the USA to record with the New Paul Whiteman Orchestra. He wrote arrangements for the New York Jazz Repertory Company, for Dick Hyman and for the Pasadena Roof Orchestra. By 1978 he was well equipped to found the Midnite Follies Orchestra with Alan Cohen. Their aim was to play the music of the 20s and 30s and original pieces in a similar vein. Nichols is an authority on ragtime and

earlier styles of jazz, and he works ceaselessly to keep them being performed. In the mid-80s he played with Harry Gold (bass saxophone) and led the Paramount Theatre Orchestra. He now leads his own Cotton Club Band.
Albums: *Ragtime Rules OK?* (1976), *Hotter Than Hades* (1978), *Jungle Nights In Harlem* (1981), *Shakin' The Blues Away* (Stomp Off 1988), *Doctors Jazz* (Stomp Off 1988), *Chitterlin' Strut* (Stomp Off 1989), *Syncopated Jamboree* (Stomp Off 1992), *Keith Nichols* (Stomp Off 1992), *I Like To Do Things For You* (Stomp Off 1993).

Nichols, Red

b. Ernest Loring Nichols, 8 May 1905, Ogden, Utah, USA, d. 28 June 1965. Taught by his father, cornetist Nichols quickly became a highly accomplished performer. Strongly influenced by early white jazz bands, and in particular by Bix Beiderbecke, he moved to New York in the early 20s and was soon one of the busiest musicians in town. He recorded hundreds of tracks, using a bewildering array of names for his bands, but favouring the Five Pennies, a group which was usually eight pieces or more in size. In these bands Nichols used the cream of the white jazzmen of the day, including one of his closest friends, Miff Mole plus Jimmy Dorsey, Joe Venuti, Eddie Lang, Pee Wee Russell, Benny Goodman and Jack Teagarden. Although his sharp business sense and desire for formality and respect alienated him from hard-living contemporaries such as Eddie Condon, Nichols remained enormously successful, continuing to lead bands and record until the outbreak of World War II. After a brief spell outside music Nichols returned to performing with a short stint with Glen Gray, and then resumed his bandleading career from his new base in California. A sentimental Hollywood bio-pic, *The Five Pennies* (1959), starring Danny Kaye, gave his career a boost and during the last few years of his life he was as busy as he had ever been in the 20s. A polished player with a silvery tone and a bold, attacking style which reflected his admiration for Beiderbecke, Nichols at his best came close to matching his idol. As a bandleader he left an important recorded legacy of the best of 20s' white jazz.
Selected albums: *Syncopated Chamber Music* (1953), *Hot Pennies* (1957), with the Charleston Chasers *Thesaurus Of Classic Jazz, Vol. 3* (1961). Selected compilations: *Class Of '39 - Radio Transcriptions* (1979), with Miff Mole *Red And Miff, 1925-31* (Village 1982), *Rhythm Of The Day* (ASV 1983), *Feelin' No Pain (1920s-30s)* (Affinity 1987), *Great Original Performances 1925-30* (1988), *Red Nichols And Other Radio Transcriptions* (Meritt 1988), *Red Nichols And The Five Pennies Vols 1-5* (Swaggie 1989).

Niehaus, Lennie

b. 11 June 1929, St. Louis, Missouri, USA. After completing his studies at university in California, to where his family had moved when he was seven years old, alto saxophonist Niehaus joined Jerry Wald and then Stan Kenton in 1951. Apart from a spell away in the army, he remained with the Kenton band until 1960. During this period Niehaus also recorded under his own name and played and recorded with other small groups, including that led by Shorty Rogers. From the 60s onwards Niehaus was active in film and television studios, writing scores for a number of films including two, *City Heat* (1984) and *Pale Rider* (1985), which starred Clint Eastwood. When Eastwood came to make his film about Charlie Parker, *Bird* (1988), he invited Niehaus to handle the complex musical problems, which included writing the score and 'engineering' Parker's solos so that they could be re-recorded with new accompaniments. The skill and integrity with which Niehaus accomplished this difficult task represent one of the highlights of the film. A brilliant technician, playing with a hard-edged sound, Niehaus sometimes fails to engage the emotions of his listeners, but for the most part overcomes this failing through his extraordinary rush of exciting ideas.

Albums: *Lennie Niehaus Vol. 1: The Quintet* (1954-56), *Lennie Niehaus Vol. 2: The Octet/Zounds!* (1954-56), *Lennie Niehaus Vol. 3* (1955), *The Lennie Niehaus Quintet With Strings* (1955), *The Lennie Niehaus Sextet* (1956), *Lennie Niehaus* (1957). Compilation: *Patterns* (Fresh Sounds 1990).

Nistico, Sal

b. Salvatore Nistico, 12 April 1940, Syracuse, New York, USA, d. 3 March 1991. Nistico started out on alto saxophone, later switching to tenor and joining an R&B band. In the late 50s he joined the Jazz Brothers, a band led by Gap and Chuck Mangione. In 1962 he became a member of the Woody Herman band, to which he returned frequently during the next two decades. Also in the 60s he spent some time in the band of Count Basie and early in the 70s he was with Don Ellis. In the next few years he worked with Buddy Rich and Slide Hampton, with whom he visited Europe. Eventually he settled in Europe, working there through the 80s. A bristling, aggressive player in the post-bop tradition, Nistico's live and recorded performances are filled with excitement and a vitality that made his sudden death in 1991 all the more tragic.

Albums: with Chuck Mangione *Hey Baby!* (1961), *Heavyweights* (1961), *Comin' On Up* (1962), *Woody Herman, 1963* (1963), *Encore* (1963), with Herman *Woody's Winners* (1965), *The Buddy Rich Septet* (1974), *Just For Fun* (1976), *East Of Isar* (1978), *Neo/Nistico* (1978).

Noone, Jimmie

b. 23 April 1895, Cut Off, Louisiana, USA, d. 19 April 1944. One of numerous students of Lorenzo Tio, Noone turned to the clarinet after first playing guitar. In the years immediately prior to World War I he played in bands led by notable New Orleans musicians such as Freddie Keppard and Buddy Petit. In 1918 he worked with Joe 'King' Oliver in Chicago and two years later was with Doc Cooke, remaining there for five years. In 1926 Noone took his own band into Chicago's Apex Club, thus beginning a remarkable period of sustained creativity during which he became the idol of countless up-and-coming young musicians, black and white, clarinettists and all. During part of its existence, the Apex Club band included Earl 'Fatha' Hines. Noone had made records during his stints with Oliver and Cooke, but now embarked on another series of recordings,

including his theme, 'Sweet Lorraine', which remain classics of their kind. In the early 40s he moved to Los Angeles where he worked with Kid Ory, led his own band and appeared as a member of the New Orleans All Stars on Orson Welles's weekly radio show, as well as playing with the Capitol Jazzmen. Noone appeared well poised to capitalize upon the upsurge of interest in traditional music heralded by the Revival movement, but he died suddenly in April 1944. One of the most important of the New Orleans clarinettists, he had a remarkable technique and exercised full control of his instrument. Playing with a deep appreciation of the blues, his records stand as significant milestones in the history of jazz. His son, Jimmie Noone Jnr. (1938-1991), also played clarinet and from the 80s enjoyed a successful international career.

Selected compilations: *Jimmie Noone And His Apex Club Orchestra Vol. 1* (1979), *Jimmie Noone (1931-40)* (Queendisc 1981), *King Of New Orleans* (Jazz Bird 1982), *With The Apex Club Orchestra 1928* (Swaggie 1992), *Collection Vol 1* (Collectors Classics 1992), *The Complete Recordings Vol 1* (Affinity 1992).

Norvo, Red

b. Kenneth Norville, 31 March 1908, Beardstown, Illinois, USA. After playing in a marimba band, Norvo was hired by Paul Whiteman in the late 20s. With this band he played xylophone and was called upon largely to deliver novelty effects. While with Whiteman he met and married one of the band's singers, Mildred Bailey; in 1933 they went to New York and embarked upon a career which culminated with them being billed as 'Mr and Mrs Swing'. During the 30s Norvo played and recorded with many leading jazz musicians of the day and remained in demand into the mid-40s, at which time he joined Benny Goodman and switched to vibraphone. During the 40s Norvo worked with leading bop musicians such as Dizzy Gillespie and Charlie Parker, and in 1945 became a member of Woody Herman's First Herd. In the early 50s he was resident in California (his marriage to Bailey had ended in 1945), working in a trio he formed with Tal Farlow and Charles Mingus. He continued to play throughout the 60s and on into the mid-70s, when he decided to retire. This decision proved to be only temporary and the 80s saw him engaged in a series of worldwide tours as a solo artist, performing with Benny Carter, and in a reunion with Farlow. Norvo's vibraphone style retains the sound and feel of his earlier xylophone work, a fact which ensures a rhythmic urgency to much of his playing and which might well be the motive behind his long-standing preference for working in groups without a drummer. The assurance with which he incorporated bop phrasing into his work makes him unusual among musicians of his generation and brings an added quality to his work which ensures that it is always interesting and exploratory.

Selected albums: *Time In His Hands* (1945), *Red Norvo's Nine* (1945), *The Red Norvo Septet* i (1947), *The Red Norvo Trio* i (c.1949-50), *The Red Norvo Trio* ii (1950), *The Red Norvo Trio* iii (1953), *The Red Norvo Trio* iv (1953), *The Red Norvo Trio* v (1954), *The Red Norvo Trio* vi (1955), *The Red Norvo Trio* vii

(1955), *The Red Norvo Septet* ii (1956), *The Red Norvo Quartet* (1956), *The Red Norvo Sextet* (1957), *Music To Listen To* (1957), *Norvo - Naturally!* (1957), *The Forward Look* (Reference Recordings 1957), *Red Norvo And His Orchestra* (1958), *Sessions, Live* (1958), *The Red Norvo Septet* iii (1958), *Command Performance* (c.1959), *The Red Norvo Quintet* (1969), *Swing That Music* (Affinity 1969), *Vibes A La Red* (1975), *The Second Time Around* (1975), *Red In New York* (1977), *Live At Rick's Cafe Americain* (1978), with Ross Tompkins *Red & Ross* (1979), with Bucky Pizzarelli *Just Friends* (1983), with others *Swing Reunion* (1985), *Benny Carter All Stars* (1985). Compilations: *Red Norvo And His All Stars* (1933-38), *The Band Goes To Town* (1935), *Small Band Jazz* (1936-44), *Small Band Jazz: Rare Broadcasts* (1943).

Noto, Sam

b. 17 April 1930, Buffalo, New York, USA. After playing trumpet in a number of leading 50s big bands, including that led by Stan Kenton, Noto worked in small groups until joining Count Basie for two spells in the mid- and late 60s. He then returned to small group format, co-leading a band with Joe Romano. After spending part of the 70s in show bands in Las Vegas, Noto moved to Canada where he worked with Rob McConnell, playing and arranging for the latter's big band. During the late 70s and throughout the 80s Noto played on the international festival circuit and also worked in clubs in his home town and in Canada. A fluent improviser, Noto's composing and arranging reveal an exceptional talent although his chosen locations for much of his best work has unwarrentedly kept him hidden from the attention of audiences.
Albums: *Entrance!* (Xanadu 1975), *Act One* (Xanadu 1975), with Rob McConnell *The Jazz Album* (1976), *Notes To You* (Xanadu 1977), *Noto-riety* (Xanadu 1978), *2-4-5* (Unisson 1988).

Nottingham, Jimmy

b. 15 December 1925, New York City, New York, USA. After a brief apprenticeship with Cecil Payne, trumpeter Nottingham served in the US Navy, where he was a member of a band directed by Willie Smith. After World War II, he joined Lionel Hampton and during the late 40s also worked in the big bands led by Lucky Millinder and Charlie Barnet. Then he joined Count Basie's Orchestra, where he remained until 1950. In the 50s he played mostly in small groups and was also with bands specializing in Latin-American dance music. From the mid-50s until the mid-70s he was a staff musician with CBS Records, but continued to play jazz with artists such as Dizzy Gillespie, Edgar Sampson, Quincy Jones and Benny Goodman. From 1966 until the end of the decade, his Monday evenings were spent at the Village Vanguard as a member of the Thad Jones-Mel Lewis band. A powerful lead trumpeter with a searing high register, Nottingham's skill and versatility make him a notable member of any band in which he plays.
Albums: with Edgar Sampson *Swing Softly Sweet Sampson* (1956), with Thad Jones *Mel Lewis Live At The Village Vanguard* (1957), with Lionel Hampton *Newport Uproar!*

(1967), with Jones-Lewis *Central Park North* (1969).

Nucleus

The doyen of British jazz-rock groups, Nucleus was formed in 1969 by trumpeter Ian Carr. He was joined by Chris Spedding (guitar, ex-Battered Ornaments), John Marshall (drums) and Karl Jenkins (keyboards). The quartet was signed to the distinctive progressive outlet, Vertigo, and their debut, *Elastic Rock*, is arguably their exemplary work. The same line-up completed *We'll Talk About It Later*, but Spedding's subsequent departure heralded a bewildering succession of changes which undermined the group's potential. Carr nonetheless remained its driving force, a factor reinforced when *Solar Plexus*, a collection the trumpeter had intended as a solo release, became the unit's third album. In 1972 both Jenkins and Marshall left the group to join fellow fusion act, Soft Machine, and Nucleus became an inadvertent nursery for this 'rival' ensemble. Later members Roy Babbington and Alan Holdsworth also defected, although Carr was able to maintain an individuality despite such damaging interruptions. Subsequent albums, however, lacked the innovatory purpose of those first releases and Nucleus was dissolved during the early 80s. Nucleus took the jazz/rock genre further into jazz territory with skill, melody and a tremendous standard of musicianship. Their first three albums are vital in any comprehensive rock or jazz collection.
Albums: *Elastic Rock* (1970), *We'll Talk About It later* (1970), *Solar Plexus* (1971), *Belladonna* (1972), *Labyrinth* (1973), *Roots* (1973), *Under The Sun* (1974), *Snake Hips Etcetera* (1975), *Direct Hits* (1976), *In Flagrante Delicto* (1978), *Out Of The Long Dark* (1979), *Awakening* (1980), *Live At The Theaterhaus* (1985).

Nunez, Alcide 'Yellow'

b. 17 March 1884, New Orleans, Louisiana, USA, d. 2 September 1934. One of his home town's most noted musicians, Nunez's career was dogged by bad luck and poor timing. After playing clarinet with several famous marching and brass bands, including Papa Laine's, Nunez visited Chicago, where he teamed up with Nick La Rocca and others to form a band. He fell out with La Rocca, however, and quit to work in vaudeville with a music and comedy act. Meanwhile, La Rocca and the band, calling themselves the Original Dixieland Jazz Band, went on to international fame and fortune. After working with obscure bands in Chicago, Nunez returned to New Orleans in 1927 and remained there for the rest of his life. Although an enormously skilled musician, Nunez displayed a penchant for the shrill, jokey, barnyard effects popular with audiences in the early years of this century. As a result, his few records have received attention more for their curiosity value than for their musical content.

Nussbaum, Adam

b. 29 November 1955, New York, USA. Nussbaum had initially learnt to play the piano and alto saxophone, then switched to studying drums with Charlie Persip and majoring in music at the Davis Centre, City College of New York. After freelancing in New York he played through the late 70s and 80s with the bands of John Scofield, Dave Liebman, Stan Getz, Gil Evans, Randy Brecker, George Gruntz and Gary Burton. Nussbaum has attained a wide knowledge of the history of jazz drumming. He has a bright, swinging style which he has been able to adapt to all these differing contexts.

Albums: with Dave Liebman *If Only They Knew* (1980), with John Scofield *Shinola* (1981), *Out Like A Light* (1981), with Bill Evans *Living On The Crest Of A Wave* (1983), with Gil Evans *Live At Sweet Basil* (1984).

O'Day, Anita

b. Anita Colton, 18 October 1919, Kansas City, Missouri, USA. As Anita Colton, in her early teens she scraped a living as a professional Walkathon contestant (marathon dancer). During this period she changed her surname to O'Day. Along with other contestants she was encouraged to sing and during one Walkathon was accompanied by Erskine Tate's orchestra, an event which made her think that singing might be a better route to showbiz fame than dancing. By her late teens she had switched to singing and was told by Gene Krupa, who heard her at a Chicago club, that if he ever had a slot for her he would call. In the meantime she failed an audition with Benny Goodman, who complained that she did not stick to the melody, and upset Raymond Scott, who disliked her scatting (vocalese) - actually, she had momentarily forgotten the words of the song. Eventually Krupa called and O'Day joined the band early in 1941, just a few weeks before Roy Eldridge was also hired. The combination of Krupa, Eldridge and O'Day was potent and the band, already popular, quickly became one of the best of the later swing era. O'Day helped to give the band some of its hit records, notably 'Let Me Off Uptown', (also a feature for Eldridge), 'Alreet', 'Kick It' and 'Bolero At The Savoy'. After Krupa folded in 1943, O'Day went with Stan Kenton, recording hits with 'And Her Tears Flowed Like Wine' and 'The Lady In Red'. In 1945 she was back with the reformed Krupa band for more hit records including, 'Opus No. 1'. In 1946 she went solo and thereafter remained a headliner. She made a number of fine albums in the 50s, including a set with Ralph Burns in 1952, and made a memorable appearance at the 1958 Newport Jazz Festival. This performance, at which she sang 'Tea For Two' and 'Sweet Georgia Brown', resplendent in cartwheel hat, gloves, and stoned out of her mind, was captured on film in *Jazz On A Summer's Day* (1958). Drug addiction severely damaged O'Day's life for

many years, although she continued to turn out excellent albums, including *Cool Heat* with Jimmy Giuffre, *Trav'lin' Light* with Johnny Mandel and Barney Kessel and *Time For Two* with Cal Tjader. Extensive touring, high living and a punishing life style (not to mention a dozen years of heroin addiction) eventually brought collapse, and she almost died in 1966. Eventually clear of drugs, O'Day continued to tour, playing clubs, concerts and festivals around the world. She recorded less frequently, but thanks to forming her own record company, Emily, in the early 70s many of the albums that she did make were entirely under her control. In 1985 she played Carnegie Hall in celebration of 50 years in the business, and towards the end of the decade appeared in the UK at Ronnie Scott's club and at the Leeds Castle Jazz Festival in Kent. O'Day's singing voice is throaty and she sings with great rhythmic drive. Her scat singing and the liberties she takes on songs, especially when singing up-tempo, result in some remarkable vocal creations. In her hey-days her diction was exceptional and even at the fastest tempos she articulated clearly and precisely. On ballads she is assured and distinctive, and although very much her own woman, her phrasing suggests the influence of Billie Holiday. On stage she displays enormous rapport with musicians and audience, factors which make some of her studio recordings rather less rewarding than those made in concert. Late in her career some of her performances were marred by problems of pitch but, live at least, she compensated through sheer force of personality. Her autobiography makes compulsive reading.

Selected albums: *Specials* (1951), *Singing And Swinging* (1953), *Collate* (1953), *Anita O'Day* (1954), *Anita O'Day Sings Jazz* (1955), *An Evening With Anita O'Day* (1956), *Anita* (1956), *Pick Yourself Up* (1956), *The Lady Is A Tramp* (1956), *Anita Sings The Most* (1957), *Anita Sings The Winners* (1958), *Anita O'Day At Mr Kelly's* (1958), *Cool Heat* (1959), *Anita O'Day Swings Cole Porter With Billy May* (1959), *Waiter, Make Mine Blues* (1960), *Incomparable!* (1960), *Anita O'Day And Billy May Swing Rodgers And Hart* (1960), *Trav'lin' Light* (1961), *All The Sad Young Men* (1961), *Time For Two* (1962), *Anita O'Day And The Three Sounds* (1962), *Anita O'Day In Tokyo 1963* (1963), *Once Upon A Summertime* (c.1969), *Live At The Berlin Jazz Festival* (1970), *Anita '75* (1975), *My Ship* (1975), *Live In Tokyo* (1975), *Live At Mingo's* (1976), *Skylark* (1978), *Angel Eyes* (1978), *Mello' Day* (GNP 1979), *Live At The City, Vols 1 & 2* (1979), *Misty* (1981), *A Song For You* (c.1984), *Wave* (Essential 1986), *In A Mellow Tone* (1989), *At Vine St Live* (Disque Suisse 1992), *Rules Of The Road* (Pablo 1994). Compilations: *Anita O'Day Sings With Gene Krupa* (1941-42), *Singin' And Swingin' With Anita O'Day* (1947), *Hi Ho Trailus Boot Whip* (1947), *Anita O'Day 1949-1950* (1949-50), *Tea For Two* (1958-66), *The Big Band Sessions* (1959-61), *1956-62* (1993).

Further reading: *High Times, Hard Times*, Anita O'Day with George Eells.

O'Farrill, Arturo 'Chico'

b. 28 October 1921, Havana, Cuba. After playing trumpet in

several Cuban-based bands throughout the 40s, O'Farrill moved to the USA where he concentrated on arranging. During the 50s his work was played and recorded by Benny Goodman, Stan Kenton, Dizzy Gillespie among others and he also collaborated with Machito on albums featuring such leading American jazzmen as Charlie Parker and Joe 'Flip' Phillips. O'Farrill also toured and recorded with his own band. He spent the early 60s in Mexico, then returned to the USA taking up a staff post with CBS but retained his jazz links by arranging for Count Basie. In the 70s and 80s O'Farrill continued to be active but his jazz work gradually diminished. An outstanding exponent of Latin-American music, O'Farrill's arrangements consistently demonstrate his comprehensive grasp of the music's potential and are often far more imaginative than others who work in this field.

Albums: by Machito *Afro-Cuban Jazz Suite* (1950), *Chico O'Farrill And His Orchestra* i (1951), *Chico O'Farrill And His Orchestra* ii (1952), *Chico O'Farrill And His Orchestra* iii (1952), *Mambo Latin Dances* (c.1953), *Tropical Fever* (mid-50s), *Torrid Zone* (mid-50s), *Chico O'Farrill And His Orchestra* iv (1966), *Chico O'Farrill And His Orchestra* v (1966), with Dizzy Gillespie, Machito *Afro-Cuban Jazz Moods* (1975), *Latin Roots* (1976).

Oliver, Joe 'King'

b. 11 May 1885, Louisiana, USA, d. 10 April 1938. Raised in New Orleans, cornetist Oliver became well-known through appearances with local marching and cabaret bands during the early years of this century. After playing with such notable early jazzmen as Kid Ory and Richard M. Jones in 1918, he left for Chicago and two years later was leading his own band. After a brief trip to California, Oliver returned to Chicago and performed an engagement at the Lincoln Gardens. This was in 1922 and his band then included such outstanding musicians as Johnny and Baby Dodds, Lil Hardin and Honore Dutrey. Not content with being merely the best jazz band in town, Oliver sent word to New Orleans and brought in the fast-rising young cornetist Louis Armstrong. His motives in hiring Armstrong might have been questionable. Hardin, who later married Armstrong, reported that Oliver openly stated that his intention was to ensure that by having the newcomer playing second cornet in his band he need not fear him as a competitor. Whatever the reason, the Oliver band with Armstrong was a sensation. Musicians flocked to hear the band, marvelling at the seemingly telepathic communication between the two men. The band's glory days did not last long; by 1924 the Dodds brothers had gone, dissatisfied with their financial arrangements, and Armstrong had been taken by his new wife on the first stage of his transition to international star. Oliver continued leading a band but he quickly discovered that his example had been followed by many, and that even if his imitators were often musically inferior they had made it harder for him to obtain good jobs. His own judgement was also sometimes at fault; he turned down an offer to lead a band at New York's Cotton Club because the money was not good enough and lived to see Duke Ellington take the job and the radio exposure that went with it. In the early 30s Oliver led a succession of territory bands with a measure of local success but he rarely played. He was suffering from a disease of the gums and playing the cornet was, at best, a painful exercise. By 1936 he had quit the business of which he had once been king and took a job as a janitor in Savannah, Georgia, where he died in 1938. An outstanding exponent of New Orleans-style cornet playing, Oliver was one of the most important musicians in spreading jazz through his 1923-24 recordings, even if these did not gain their internationally-accepted status as classic milestones until after his death. His role in the advance of Armstrong's career is also of significance although, clearly, nothing would have stopped the younger man from achieving his later fame. Stylistically, Oliver's influence on Armstrong was important although here again the pupil quickly outstripped his tutor in technique, imagination and inventiveness. Setting aside the role he played in Armstrong's life, and the corresponding reflected glory Armstrong threw upon him, Oliver can be seen and heard to have been a striking soloist and a massively self-confident ensemble leader. He was also a sensitive accompanist, making several fine records with popular blues singers of the day.

Compilations: *King Oliver And His Creole Jazz Band: The OKeh Sessions* (1923), *King Oliver Vol. 1 1923-1929* (CDS 1923-29 recordings), *Farewell Blues* (1926-27), *King Oliver And His Dixie Syncopators* (1926-28), *King Oliver Vol. 2* (1927-30), *King Oliver And His Orchestra* (1929-30), *New York Sessions* (RCA 1990), *Sweet Like This* (1929-30), *Complete Vocalion/Brunswick Recordings 1926 - 1931* (1992).

Further reading: *King Joe Oliver*, Walter C. Allen and Brian A.L. Rust. *'King' Oliver*, Laurie Wright.

Oliver, Sy

b. Melvin James Oliver, 17 December 1910, Battle Creek, Michigan, USA, d. 28 May 1988. Born into a family in which both parents were music teachers, Oliver played trumpet as a child and at the age of 17 was a member of the popular territory band led by Zack Whyte. During this stint he began arranging, primarily to prove to his older and supposedly wiser fellow sidemen that his theories about harmony were sound. After the Whyte band, Oliver played in another important territory band, led by Alphonso Trent. Then, after some of his arrangements had been accepted by Jimmie Lunceford, Oliver took a job with his band, playing in the trumpet section, singing and arranging. Lunceford had already enjoyed the benefits of good arrangers in Eddie Durham and, especially, Ed Wilcox; but, more than anyone, it was Oliver who shaped the sound of the Lunceford band from 1933 until 1939, the period of its greatest commercial and aesthetic success. Oliver's use of two-beat rhythm, stop-time breaks, intricate saxophone choruses and ear-splitting brass explosions, brilliantly executed by Lunceford's musicians, in particular drummer Jimmy Crawford and lead alto saxophonist Willie Smith, not only sealed Lunceford's success but created a style of big band music which proved widely influential. Oliver's arranging style was especially suitable to the more commercial aspects of the swing era and was taken up and adapted by many of his contemporaries and successors. Although employed by Lunceford, Oliver did arrange for other bands too, including Benny Goodman's, and his reputation in the business was enviable. Tiring of his work with Lunceford, Oliver decided to quit music and study law, but Tommy Dorsey made him an offer he could not refuse: $5,000 a year more than he'd earned with Lunceford. Oliver's arrangements for Dorsey propelled the band into a new era of success, which transcended what had gone before for both arranger and leader. 'Swing High', 'Well, Git It!', 'Sunny Side Of the Street' and 'Opus No. 1' were all massively popular and the records became big sellers. After military service during World War II, Oliver briefly led his own musically excellent but commercially unsuccessful big band and worked as a freelance arranger, his charts being used by Dorsey and by studios for recording orchestras' dates with singers such as Ella Fitzgerald and Frank Sinatra. In the 60s he once again tried bandleading, but as before was not prepared to bow to commercial pressures. In the late 60s and 70s he toured extensively, resumed trumpet playing and undertook several club residencies in New York, a pattern which persisted into the 80s. A major figure in the development of jazz arranging, Oliver was almost single-handedly responsible for the creation of what later became definable as mainstream big band music. His use of attacking brass and clean ensemble passages was picked up and modified, sometimes simplified, but rarely if ever improved.

Selected albums: *Sy Oliver And His Orchestra* i (1954), *Sy Oliver And His Orchestra* ii (1957), *Sy Oliver And His Orchestra* iii (1958), *Sy Oliver And His Orchestra* iv (1958), *Back Stage* (1959), *77 Sunset Strip* (1959), *Just A Minute* (c.1960), *Annie Laurie* (1960), *Four Roses Dance Party* (1961), *Sy Oliver And His Orchestra* v (c.1962), *Sy Oliver And His Orchestra* vi (c.1962), *Easy Walker* (1962), *Take Me Back* (1972), *Yes, Indeed!* (1973), *Sy Oliver And His Orchestra Play The Famous Rainbow Room* (1976). Compilations: *The Indispensable Tommy Dorsey, Vols 7/8* (1939 recordings), *The Complete Jimmie Lunceford* (1939-40 recordings).

Oregon

This inventive and influential progressive jazz chamber group were formed in 1970 from the nucleus of the Paul Winter Consort, an aggregation led by Paul Winter. Oregon comprised Ralph Towner (b. 1 March 1940, Chehalis, Washington, USA; guitar/keyboards), Collin Walcott (b. 24 April 1945, New York City, USA, d. 8 November 1984; percussion/sitar/tabla/clarinet), Glen Moore (bass/violin/piano/flute) and Paul McCandless (b. 24 March 1947, Indiana, Pennsylvania, USA; alto saxophone/oboe/bass clarinet). Walcott's death from a car accident in 1984 seemed a fatal blow to the band, but after a year in mourning they returned. The recruitment of Walcott's friend Trilok Gurtu (b. 30 October 1951, Bombay, India; tabla/drums/percussion) gave them a fresh incentive. Their debut on ECM Records in 1983 was an eclectic, part-electric album. Oregon explore the boundaries of jazz, using uniquely disparate influences of classical, folk, Indian and other ethnic

music. Their chamber-like approach encourages hushed auditoriums and intense concentration, which is required to get maximum benefit from their weaving style. Occasionally they will burst into a song of regular form and pattern, as if to reward a child with a treat. One such number is the evocatively rolling 'Crossing' from the same album. Another outstanding piece from their immense catalogue is 'Leather Cats'. Their refusal to compromise leaves them a lone innovative force and one of the most important jazz-based conglomerations of the past three decades.

Selected albums: *Music Of Another Present Era* (Vanguard 1972), *Distant Hills* (Vanguard 1973), *Winter Light* (Vanguard 1974), *In Concert* (1975), *Oregon/Jones Together* (1976), *Friends* (1977), *Out Of The Woods* (1978), *Violin* (1978), *Roots In The Sky* (1979), *Moon And Mind* (1979), *In Performance* (1980), *Oregon* (ECM 1983), *Crossing* (ECM 1985), *Ectopia* (ECM 1987), *45th Parallel* (Verabra 1989), *Always, Never, And Forever* (Verabra 1991).

Ørsted Pedersen, Neils-Henning

b. 27 May 1946, Osted, Denmark. Ørsted Pedersen first learned to play piano but took up the bass as his friend Ole Kock Hansen was also a pianist and they wanted to play duets together. He achieved an amazing facility on his new instrument while still in his mid-teens, making his first record at the age of 14. Playing regularly at the noted Montmartre Club in Copenhagen from early in 1961, he accompanied and occasionally recorded with visiting and ex-patriot American jazz stars, including Brew Moore, Yusef Lateef, Sonny Rollins, Bud Powell and Bill Evans (with whom he toured in the early 60s having earlier refused an invitation to join Count Basie). He recorded frequently in the 60s, 70s and 80s, happily ranging from mainstream through bop to free jazz with artists such as Don Byas, Ben Webster, Tete Montoliu, Kenny Dorham, Dexter Gordon, Anthony Braxton and Albert Ayler. By the end of the 70s he had sealed his international reputation, thanks in part to a long stint with Oscar Peterson which continued well into the 80s. He has made a number of fine duo albums with Kenny Drew (*Duo*), Joe Pass (*Chops*) and Archie Shepp (*Looking At Bird*). A superbly accomplished technician, his brilliant virtuosity is underpinned with a great sense of time and dynamics. His solos are always interesting and display his awareness of the roots of jazz bass whilst acknowledging the advances made in more recent years.

Selected albums: *Oscar Peterson Big Six At The Montreux Jazz Festival 1975* (1975), *Jay Walkin'* (Steeplechase 1975), *Double Bass* (Steeplechase 1976), with Peterson *The Paris Concert* (1978), with Joe Pass *Chops* (1978), *Dancing On The Tables* (Steeplechase 1979), *Just The Way You Are* (1980), with Archie Shepp *Looking At Bird* (1980), with Count Basie *Kansas City Six* (1981), *The Viking* (1983), with Palle Mikkelborg *Once Upon A Time* (1992).

Ory, Edward 'Kid'

b. 25 December 1886, La Place, Louisiana, USA, d. 23 January 1973. A gifted, hard-blowing trombonist and a competitive musician, Ory came to New Orleans when in his mid-twenties and he quickly established a fearsome reputation. An aggressive music maker and a tireless self-promoter, he was determined to be successful and very soon was. By 1919 he was one of the city's most popular musicians and bandleaders but he left town on medical advice. Taking up residence in California, he became just as popular in Los Angeles and San Francisco as he had been in New Orleans. In 1922 Ory became the first black New Orleans musician to make records and the success of these extended his fame still further. In 1925 he travelled to Chicago, playing and recording with Joe 'King' Oliver, Jelly Roll Morton and Louis Armstrong, with whom he made many classic Hot Five and Hot Seven sides. In 1930 he was back in Los Angeles, joining Mutt Carey, who had taken over leadership of the Ory band. By 1933, however, Ory had tired of the business and the lack of success he was enjoying compared to that of his earlier days and quit music. He returned in the early 40s, sometimes playing alto saxophone or bass. Encouraged by some prestigious radio dates, he was soon bandleading again and playing trombone and was thus well-placed to take advantage of the boom in popularity of traditional jazz which swept the USA. Throughout the 50s and into the early 60s he played successfully in San Francisco and Los Angeles, where he had his own club, touring nationally and overseas. He retired in 1966. A strong soloist and powerful ensemble player, Ory's work, while redolent of New Orleans-style jazz, demonstrated that his was a much richer and more sophisticated ability than that of many early trombonists. His compositions included 'Ory's Creole Trombone' and 'Muskrat Ramble', which became a jazz standard.

Selected albums: *Kid Ory's 'This Is Jazz' Broadcast* (1947), *Live At The Club Hangover Vol. 1* (1953), *Live At The Club Hangover Vol. 2* (1953), *Live At The Club Hangover Vol. 3* (1954), *Live At The Club Hangover Vol. 4* (1954), *Kid Ory's Creole Jazz Band* (1954), *Live In England* (1959). Compilations: *Louis Armstrong Hot Five And Hot Seven* (1925-28), *Edward 'Kid' Ory And His Creole Band* (1948), *This Kid's The Greatest!* (Contemporary 1983, 1953-56 recordings), *The Legendary Kid* (Good Time Jazz 1993), *Creole Jazz Band* (Good Time Jazz 1993), *Kid Ory Favourites* (Fantasy 1993).

Osborne, Mike

b. 28 September 1941, Hereford, England. Osborne played violin in the school orchestra, but when he went to the Guildhall School it was to study clarinet. He could play piano too, but since turning professional his main instrument has always been alto saxophone. His favourite players are Phil Woods, Joe Henderson and Jackie McLean, with whom he shares a sharp-edged, slightly distressed-sounding tone, but he is often compared with Ornette Coleman for the urgency of his sound and his ability to create long, intense, graceful skeins of free melody. He first came to notice with the Mike Westbrook Concert Band when it reformed after Westbrook's move to London from Plymouth. 'Ossie' sat in for a couple of gigs and was asked to join permanently in early 1963, when he was one of only two professional musicians in the orchestra. Over the next few years he was an important constituent of several fine bands, including the Michael Gibbs Band, Chris McGregor's Brotherhood Of Breath, Harry Miller's Isipingo and the group, ranging from a quartet to an octet, which he co-led with John Surman during 1968 and 1969. He also worked with John Warren, Alan Skidmore, Kenneth Terroade, Rik Colbeck, and Humphrey Lyttelton. In 1969 he established his own exceptionally exciting trio with Harry Miller and Louis Moholo, which, apart from many fine public gigs, recorded several superb sessions for BBC Radio's Jazz Club. In the early 70s he began a fruitful association with Stan Tracey in wholly improvised duets, which brought Tracey back from the brink of retirement through disillusion with the music business. In 1973 he co-founded S.O.S., probably the first regular all-saxophone band, with Alan Skidmore and John Surman. He was voted best alto saxophonist in the *Melody Maker* poll every year from 1969-73. During the late 70s he became increasingly ill and has been unable to play since 1980. His relatively small recorded oeuvre does show the range of his playing, from deeply moving but unsentimental ballad interpretations with Westbrook to scorchingly intense free explorations with Isipingo or the trio.

Albums: *Outback* (Future Music 1970), with Stan Tracey *Original* (1972), *Border Crossing* (Ogun 1975), *All Night Long* (Ogun 1975), *SOS* (1975), with Tracey *Tandem* (1976), *Marcel's Muse* (Ogun 1977), *Gold Hearted Girl* (Crosscut 1988), *A Case For The Blues* (Crosscut 1993).

Osby, Greg

b. 1961, St Louis, Missouri, USA. New York-based saxophonist who has attached jazz's cool to a militant hip hop beat. Following his work with the M-Base project (including Steve Coleman and Cassandra Wilson), Osby decided he wanted to record a more free-ranging, one-off hip hop record: 'The purpose for this record was to function as an 'either/or', meaning that it could rest solely as a hardcore hip hop record without any jazz or musicians at all, and that it also would be a strong musical statement without breakbeats or anything. I wanted it to bridge the gap'. Alongside jazz musicians like Geri Allen and Darrell Grant, he enlisted the aid of hip hop producers Ali Shaheed Muhammed (A Tribe Called Quest) and Street Element, and a variety of rappers. Osby had actually begun life as an R&B musician, only discovering jazz when he attended college in 1978. Though setting up M-Base as a street-sussed jazz/hip hop enclave, he had little time for the work of Gang Starr or Digable Planets, who sample from jazz but do not, generally, work with live musicians. That did not stop him from being bracketed alongside those artists however.

Albums: *Greg Osby And Sound Theatre* (Watt 1987), *Mind Games* (JMT 1989), *Season Of Renewal* (JMT 1990), *Man Talk For Moderns Vol X* (Blue Note 1991), *3-D Lifestyles* (Blue Note 1993).

Oxley, Tony

b. 15 June 1938, Sheffield, Yorkshire, England. Oxley began to teach himself piano at the age of eight, and did not pursue the drums seriously until he was 17. During his National Service (1957-60) he studied drums and theory and for the following four years he led his own group in Sheffield. From 1963-67 he worked with Derek Bailey and bassist/composer Gavin Bryars in developing an abstract, freely improvised genre. In 1966 he moved to London, and was for some years in the house band at Ronnie Scott's club, backing many famous visiting musicians. He was also in Scott's octet, the Band, and worked with Howard Riley, Gordon Beck, Alan Skidmore, Mike Pyne and Barry Guy's London Jazz Composers Orchestra (LJCO). In 1970 he co-founded Incus Records with Evan Parker and Bailey and was a founder member of the London Musicians' Co-operative, and from 1973 was an organizing tutor at the Barry Summer School in Wales. In the mid-70s he led his own band, Angular Apron, which included Riley, Guy and Dave Holdsworth. In 1978 he moved to East Germany, then (clandestinely) to West Germany in 1981, but has returned to the UK for concerts. He also plays in the trio SOH (with Skidmore and Ali Havrand), with Didier Levallet and in the Quartet. Since the late 80s he has been a regular associate of Cecil Taylor, playing in the pianist's Feel Trio and recording the *Leaf Palm Hand* duo with him at FMP's special Taylor festival in Berlin in 1988. His Celebration Orchestra comprised four brass players, six strings, piano and five drummers, but he enjoys small group improvising best: witness the excellence of the trio Coe, Oxley & Co. (with Tony Coe and Chris Laurence). Oxley is a highly-skilled and versatile drummer whose fierce dedication to his music has gained him a reputation for being a difficult person to deal with. His playing is, however, that of a responsive and supportive colleague.

Albums: *The Baptised Traveller* (1969), *Four Compositions For Sextet* (1970), *Ichnos* (1971), with Alan Davie *Duo* (1974), *Tony Oxley* (Incus 1975), *February Papers* (1977), *Nutty (On) Willisau* (1984), with Phil Wachsmann *The Glider And The Grinder* (1987), *Tomorrow Is Here* (1988), with Cecil Taylor *Leaf Palm Hand* (1989), *The Tony Oxley Quartet* (Incus 1993).

P

Page, Oran 'Hot Lips'

b. 27 January 1908, Dallas, Texas, USA, d. 5 November 1954. In the 20s Page played trumpet mostly in his home state but also toured in bands accompanying some of the best of the day's blues singers, among them Ma Rainey, Bessie Smith and Ida Cox. Towards the end of the 20s Page joined Walter Page's Blue Devils, a band formed in Oklahoma City out of the remnants of a touring band in which the trumpeter had worked.

With the Blue Devils Page built a reputation as a powerful lead and solo trumpet, an emotional blues player and singer, and an inspirational sideman. In 1931 he was one of several Blue Devils enticed into Bennie Moten's band, where he remained until Moten's death in 1935. The following year he joined Count Basie in Kansas City where he was heard by Louis Armstrong's manager, Joe Glaser, who signed him up. Glaser's motives have been much-speculated upon. At the time Armstrong was suffering lip trouble and Glaser certainly needed a trumpeter/singer. However, the neglect displayed by the manager towards his new signing once Armstrong was back suggests that he might well have seen Page as a competitor to be neutralized. In the late 30s Page led bands large and small, mostly in and around New York and appeared at numerous after-hours sessions and on many record dates, including Ida Cox's comeback date after her retirement. At the start of the 40s he was briefly in Artie Shaw's band, with which he made a superb recording of 'St James Infirmary'. The rest of this decade was spent much as he had spent the late 30s, playing and recording in a succession of bands mostly in the New York area. He also featured on several excellent record dates, including the excellent 1944 V-Disc sides. At the end of the 40s he made another hit record, this time 'Baby, It's Cold Outside' coupled with 'The Hucklebuck' with Pearl Bailey, a record which helped establish her stardom. In the early 50s Page often played in Europe until his death in 1954. Although he was strongly influenced by Armstrong during part of his career, Page was in fact an inventive and exceptionally interesting blues-orientated trumpet player in his own right as well as an excellent singer of the blues. Whatever the reason, Page's career was partially overshadowed by Armstrong and during his lifetime he was rarely granted the critical appraisal his talents deserved. Almost four decades after his death, his re-evaluation remains incomplete.

Selected albums: *Hot Lips Page In Sweden* (1951), *Hot Lips Page* (1952-53), *Hot Lips Page 1951* (Jazz Society 1989). Compilations: *Hot Lips Page 1938-1940* (Official 1989, 1938-40 recordings), *Oran 'Hot Lips' Page Vols 1/2* (1942-53), with others *Midnight At V-Disc* (1944), *Play The Blues In B* (Jazz Archives 1993).

Page, Walter

b. 9 February 1900, Gallatin, Missouri, USA, d. 20 December 1957. Page was one of many pupils of Major N. Clark Smith who gained fame in jazz circles. In the early 20s, Page played bass with Bennie Moten in Kansas City. In 1925 Page was stranded in Oklahoma City when a band he was playing in folded. He decided to form his own group out of the wreckage and this band became the legendary Blue Devils. One of the outstanding territory bands of the southwest and instrumental in helping form the musical concept which eventually became known as Kansas City style, Page gathered many fine musicians into his band. Among them were Oran 'Hot Lips' Page, Jimmy Rushing, Lester Young and Bill Basie (in the days before he was ennobled). After Moten headhunted some of his best sidemen Page kept going for a while but eventually gave up the struggle and he too joined Moten. He later played in Basie's band where he became one fourth of the fabled All American Rhythm Section (with Basie, Freddie Green and Jo Jones). Leaving Basie in 1942 he played with several leading territory bands, including those led by Nat Towles and Jesse Price, and in the middle of the decade was back with Basie. Later, he played in various pick-up groups, often in New York but with occasional tours, a pattern of work which continued into the mid-50s. He died in 1957. A solid player with an impeccable sense of time, Page is generally credited as one of the originators of the 'walking bass', a style of playing in which the bassist plays passing notes, up or down the scale, in addition to the three or four root notes of the chord, thus creating a flowing line.

Compilations: *Kansas City Hot Jazz* (1926-30), incl. on *Sweet And Low Blues*, *Big Bands And Territory Bands Of The 20s* (1929), with Count Basie *Swinging the Blues* (1937-39).

Paich, Marty

b. 23 January 1925, Oakland, California, USA. While still undergoing long and thorough academic training, Paich began writing arrangements. After military service, during which he was able to continue his musical career, he returned to his studies and by the end of the 40s had gained numerous qualifications. In the early 50s he worked with a number of dancebands and also with Shelly Manne and Shorty Rogers, with whom he appeared on the successful and influential album *Cool And Crazy*. Also in the early 50s he was for a while pianist and arranger for Peggy Lee and made arrangements for Mel Tormé. He also wrote charts for another highly successful west coast album, *Art Pepper Plus Eleven*. An inventive and inquiring mind is clearly at work in all Paich's writing, whether as arranger or composer, and he proved particularly adept at creating material for small to medium-sized groups that allows the bands to sound as though they involve many more musicians. His work with such singers as Ella Fitzgerald, Ray Charles, Anita O'Day, Sammy Davis, Lena Horne and Sarah Vaughan, whether as arranger or musical director and conductor, denotes an acute appreciation of the particular needs of interpreters of the Great American Songbook. In recent years Paich has been active writing for films and television but the late 80s saw him back on the road with Tormé and some of his former Dek-tette sidemen, reunions which updated past glories with no hint of repetition and resulted in some remarkable record albums.

Selected albums: *Tenors West* (GNP 1956 recording), *Mel Tormé With The Marty Paich Dek-tette* (1956), *What's New?* (1957), *I Get A Boot Out Of You* (1957), *The Picasso Of Big Band Jazz* (Candid 1958), with Mel Tormé *Reunion* (1988), *Hot Piano* (VSOP 1988), *In Concert Tokyo* (1988), *Moanin'* (1993).

Parenti, Tony

b. 6 August 1900, New Orleans, Louisiana, USA, d. 17 April 1972. By his early teenage years, Parenti was playing clarinet in various local bands which performed an incipient style of jazz. While still in his teens he formed his own band and made some records. In the late 20s he tried his luck in New York, playing with several popular dance bands including those of Meyer Davis, Ben Pollack and Freddie Rich. He worked in the studios for many years in the 30s, but at the end of the decade joined Ted Lewis for a five-year stint. In the late 40s he played at several clubs in New York and Chicago. He spent the early 50s in Florida playing with local bands before returning to New York to lead bands for residencies that extended throughout the 60s at clubs such as Eddie Condon's and Jimmy Ryan's. A fluent player in the dixieland tradition, Parenti deserves rather more attention than he has gained. His neglect results largely from his long periods in New York's clubland and a relatively small recorded output.

Albums: *Jazz, That's All* (1955), *Tony Parenti's Talking Records* (1958).

Parham, Tiny

b. Hartzell S. Parham, 25 February 1900, Winnipeg, Manitoba, Canada, d. 4 April 1943. Raised in Kansas City, pianist and organ player Parham played in a number of lesser-known territory bands in the early 20s. During the later years of the decade he recorded with blues singers and such jazzmen as Johnny Dodds. In the late 20s and early 30s he led his own small and big bands in and around Kansas City but by 1936 abandoned bandleading in favour of a career as a solo organist mostly in Chicago.

Selected compilations: *Tiny Parham And His Musicians* (1928-29), *Tiny Parham 1928-1929* (Swaggie 1988), *Tiny Parham 1929-1930*, (Neovox 1993), *Tiny Parham And His Musician's 1929-1940* (Classic Jazz Masters 1993).

Paris, Jackie

b 20 September 1926, Nutley, New Jersey, USA. From the early 40s Paris was active in New York as singer and guitarist. He worked mostly with bop groups and his singing soon became his primary activity. He achieved a considerable measure of critical acclaim but failed to attract a popular following amongst the jazz audience. During the 50s and 60s he worked steadily but mostly in clubs and resort hotels although he did record with jazzmen such as Donald Byrd, Gigi Gryce and Charles Mingus. Paris sings with an urgent attack, his voice throaty and rhythmically infectious. At his best on up-tempo boppish numbers, he can also bring qualities of understanding and depth to ballads. His wife is singer Anne Marie Moss.

Albums: with Donald Byrd, Gigi Gryce *Modern Jazz Persepctives* (1957), *Jackie Paris* (Audiophile 1988), *Nobody Else But Me* (Audiophile 1988), with Marc Johnson, Carlos Franzetti *Jackie Paris/Marc Johnson/Carlos Franzetti* (Audiophile 1994).

Parker, Charlie 'Bird'

b. 29 August 1920, Kansas City, Kansas, USA, d. 12 March 1955. Although he was born on the Kansas side of the state line, Parker was actually raised across the Kaw River in Kansas City, Missouri. His nickname was originally 'Yardbird' due to his propensity for eating fried chicken - later this was shortened to the more poetic 'Bird'. Musicians talk of first hearing his alto saxophone as if it were a religious conversion. Charles Christopher Parker changed the face of jazz and shaped the course of 20th-century music. Kansas City saxophonists were a competitive bunch. Ben Webster and Herschel Evans both came from Kansas. Before they became national celebrities they would challenge visiting sax stars to 'blowing matches'. It is this artistically fruitful sense of competition that provided Charlie Parker with his aesthetic. Live music could be heard at all hours of the night, a situation resulting from lax application of prohibition laws by the Democrat Tom Pendergast (city boss from 1928-39). While in the Crispus Attucks high school Parker took up the baritone. His mother gave him an alto in 1931. He dropped out of school at the age of 14 and devoted himself to the instrument. A premature appearance at the High Hat Club - when he dried up mid-solo on 'Body & Soul' - led to him abandoning the instrument for three months; the humiliation was repeated in 1937 when veteran drummer Jo Jones threw a cymbal at his feet to indicate he was to leave the stage (this time Parker just went on practising harder). Playing in bands led by Tommy Douglas (1936-7) and Buster Smith (1937-8) gave him necessary experience. A tour with George E. Lee and instructions in harmony from the pianist Carrie Powell were helpful. His first real professional break was with the Jay McShann band in 1938, a sizzling swing unit (with whom Parker made his first recordings in 1941). Parker's solos on 'Sepian Bounce', 'Jumpin' Blues' and 'Lonely Boy Blues' made people sit up and take notice: he was taking hip liberties with the chords. Brief spells in the Earl 'Fatha' Hines (1942-3) and Billy Eckstine (1944) big bands introduced him to Dizzy Gillespie, another young black player with innovative musical ideas and a rebellious stance. Wartime austerities, though, meant that the days of the big bands were numbered.

Parker took his experience of big band saxophone sections with him to Harlem, New York. There he found the equivalent of the Kansas City 'cutting contests' in the clubs of 52nd Street, especially in the 'afterhours' sessions at Minton's Playhouse. Together with Dizzy and drummers Kenny Clarke and Max Roach, and with the essential harmonic contributions of Charlie Christian and Thelonious Monk, he pioneered a new music. Furious tempos and intricate heads played in unison inhibited lesser talents from joining in. Instead of keeping time with bass and snare drums, Clarke and Roach kept up a beat on the cymbal, using bass and snare for accents, whipping up soloists to greater heights. And Parker played *high*: that is, he created his solo lines from the top notes of the underlying chord sequences - ninths, 11ths, 13ths - so extending the previous harmonic language of jazz. Parker made his recording debut as a small combo player in Tiny Grimes's band in September 1944.

In 1945 Savoy Records - and some more obscure labels like Guild, Manor and Comet - began releasing 78s of this music, which the press called 'bebop'. It became a national fad, Dizzy's trademark goatee and beret supplying the visual element. It was a proud declaration of bohemian recklessness from a black community that, due to wartime full employment, was feeling especially confident. Charlie Parker's astonishing alto - so flu-

ent and abrupt, bluesy and joyous - was the definition of everything that was modern and hip. 'Koko', 'Shaw Nuff', 'Now's The Time': the very titles announced the dawning of a new era. A trip to the west coast and a residency at Billy Berg's helped spread the message.

There were problems. Parker's addiction to heroin was causing erratic behaviour and the proprietor was not impressed at the small audiences of hipsters the music attracted (apart from an historic opening night). In January 1946 Norman Granz promoted Charlie Parker at the LA Philharmonic and the same year saw him begin a series of famous recordings for Ross Russell's Dial label, with a variety of players that included Howard McGhee, Lucky Thompson, Wardell Gray and Dodo Marmarosa. However, Parker's heroin-related health problems came to a head following the notorious 'Loverman' session of July 1946 when, after setting his hotel-room on fire, the saxophonist was incarcerated in the psychiatric wing of the LA County Jail and then spent six months in a rehabilitation centre (commemorated in 'Relaxin' At Camarillo', 1947). When he emerged he recorded two superb sessions for Dial, one of them featuring Erroll Garner. On returning to New York he formed a band with Miles Davis and Max Roach and cut some classic sides in November 1947, including 'Scrapple From The Apple' and 'Klact-oveeseds-tene'. Parker toured abroad for the first time in 1949, when he played at a jazz festival in Paris. In November 1950 he visited Scandinavia. He felt that his music would be taken more seriously if he was associated with classical instrumentation. The 'With Strings' albums now sound hopelessly dated, but they were commercially successful at the time. Fans reported that Parker's playing, though consummate, needed the spark of improvisers of his stature to really lift off on the bandstand. A more fruitful direction was suggested by his interest in the music of Edgard Varese, whom he saw on the streets of Manhattan, but Parker's untimely death ruled out any collaborations with the *avant garde* composer.

His health had continued to give him problems: ulcers and cirrhosis of the liver. According to Leonard Feather, his playing at the Town Hall months before his death in March 1955 was 'as great as any period in his career'. His last public appearance was on 4 March 1955, at Birdland, the club named after him: it was a fiasco - Parker and pianist Bud Powell rowed onstage, the latter storming off followed shortly by bassist Charles Mingus. Disillusioned, obese and racked by illness, Parker died eight days later in the hotel suite of Baroness Pannonica de Koenigswarter, a wealthy aristocrat and stalwart bebop fan. His influence was immense. Lennie Tristano said, 'If Charlie wanted to invoke plagiarism laws, he could sue almost everybody who's made a record in the last ten years.' In pursuing his art with such disregard for reward and security, Charlie Parker was black music's first existential hero. After him, jazz could not avoid the trials and tribulations that beset the *avant garde*.

Selected albums: *The Charlie Parker Story* (Savoy 1945 recording), *Bird On 52nd Street* (1948), with Lester Young *Bird & Pres Carnegie Hall 1949* (1949), *Dance Of The Infidels Broadcasts* (1950), *Bird At St Nick's* (1950), *Just Friends* (1950), *Apartment Sessions* (1950), *One Night In Chicago* (1950), *At*

The Pershing Ballroom (1950), *Bird In Sweden* (1950), *The Mingus Connection* (1951), *Norman Granz Jam Session* (1952), *Inglewood Jam* (1952), *Live At Rockland Palace* (1952), *New Bird Vols 1 & 2* (1952-53), *Yardbird* (1953), *Jazz At Massey Hall* (1953, reissued as part of *The Greatest Jazz Concert Ever*), *Birdland All Stars At Carnegie Hall* (1954), *One Night At Birdland* (1977, rec. 1950), *One Night In Washington* (1982, rec. 1953), *Charlie Parker At Storyville* (1985, rec. 1953). Compilations: *Charlie Parker On Dial, Vols. 1-6* (1974, rec. 1945-47), *Bird With Strings* (1977, rec. 1950-52), *Summit Meeting At Birdland* (1977, rec. 1951, 1953), *The Complete Savoy Studio Sessions* (1978, rec. 1944-48, five-album box-set), *The Complete Charlie Parker On Verve* (1989, rec. 1950-54, 10-CD box-set), *The Savoy Master Takes* (1989, rec. 1944-48), *The Legendary Dial Masters, Vols. 1 & 2* (1989, rec. 1946-47), *Bird At The Roost, Vols. 1-4* (1990, rec. 1948-49), *The Complete Dean Benedetti Recordings Of Charlie Parker* (Mosaic 1991, rec. late 40s, seven-CD box-set), *Gold Collection* (1993), *The Complete Dial Sessions* (Spotlight 1993).

Further reading: *Bird Lives!*, Ross Russell. *Bird: The Legend Of Charlie Parker*, Robert Reisner. *Celebrating Bird*, Gary Giddins.

Parker, Evan

b. Evan Shaw Parker, 5 April 1944, Bristol, Avon, England. Soprano and tenor saxophonist Parker has one of the most awesome techniques in any field of music. When playing solo he combines circular breathing, multiphonics and tonguing tricks to build up complex, contrapuntal masses of sound which are credible only to those who have heard him live and can testify that there is no overdubbing involved. (However, with his 1991 album, *Process And Reality*, he has begun to experiment with multi-tracking techniques, but not simply to mimic his solo feats: the overdubbed tracks find him producing more lyrical, though equally complex interweaving lines.) He is also to be heard from time to time in conventional big band contexts (such as Orchestra UK led by Kenny Wheeler at the start of the 90s) and at all points between there and total abstract improvisation. (Not forgetting occasional work in the pop field, with Scott Walker and Annette Peacock, and with contemporary classical composers Michael Nyman and Gavin Bryars.) While he has created a unique style and sound-world, which would seem to exclude other players, he can glory in any type of jam, digging in for the gritty blues with the best of them, sparking off players like Annie Whitehead, Dudu Pukwana, Mark Sanders, Paul Rogers and John Stevens so that he and they play their best. His mother, an amateur pianist, introduced him to jazz in the shape of Fats Waller. He studied saxophone with James Knott from 1958 until 1962 when he went to Birmingham University to study botany. He left to concentrate on music, playing with Howard Riley from time to time and developing his taste for free improvisation. In 1966 he moved to London to play with Stevens's Spontaneous Music Ensemble and with Derek Bailey, with whom he co-founded the Music Improvisation Company in 1968 and the Incus Records label in 1970. As well as some remarkable solo concerts and albums, Parker has gigged or recorded with Chris McGregor, Tony Oxley, Barry Guy, Paul Lytton, George Lewis, the Globe Unity Orchestra, Steve Lacy, Peter Brötzmann, several Company line-ups, electronics expert Walter Prati and, with Paul Lovens, has long been a member of the regular trio led by Alex Von Schlippenbach. He currently leads his own trio too, with Paul Rogers on bass and Mark Sanders on drums, participates in Jon Lloyd's Anacrusis and continues to develop his singular solo saxophone improvisations.

Albums: with Derek Bailey, Han Bennink *The Topography Of The Lungs* (1970), *Music Improvisation Company* (1971), *The Music Improvisation Company 1968-71* (1971), with Paul Lytton *Collective Calls (Urban) (Two Microphones)* (1972), with Lytton *At The Unity Theatre* (1975), with Bailey *The London Concert* (1975), *Saxophone Solos* (1975), with others *Company I* (1976), with Bailey, Anthony Braxton *Company 2* (1976), with Lytton *RA 1+2* (1976), with John Stevens *The Longest Night Vols 1 & 2* (1977), with Alvin Curran, Andrea Centazzo *Real Time* (1977), *Monoceros* (1978), with Greg Goodman *Abracadabra* (1978), *At The Finger Palace* (1978), with others *Four Four Four* (1980), with Company *Fables* (1980), with George Lewis *From Saxophone & Trombone* (1980), *Six Of One* (1980), with Barry Guy *Incision* (1981), *Zanzou* (1982), with Guy, Lytton *Tracks* (1983), with Lewis, Guy, Lytton *Hook Drift & Shuffle* (1983), with Company *Trios* (1983), with Bailey *Compatibles* (1985), with Guy *Tai Kyoku* (1985), with Steve Lacy *Chirps* (1985), *The Snake Decides* (1986), with others *Supersession* (1988, rec. 1985), with others *The Ericle Of Dolphi* (1989, rec. 1985, 1977), with Cecil Taylor, Tristan Honsinger *The Hearth* (1989), with Guy *Duo Improvisations* (1990), with others *Dithyrambisch* (1990), *Atlanta* (Impulse 1990), with Walter Prati *Hall Of Mirrors* (1990), *Hall Of Mirrors* (MMT 1991), *Process And Reality* (FMP 1991), *Conic Sections* (Ah-Um 1993, rec. 1989), *Corner To Corner* (Ogun 1994). Compilation: *Collected Solos* (1989).

Parker, John 'Knocky'

b. 8 August 1918, Palmer, Texas, USA, d. 3 September 1986. During the 30s Parker played piano in several Texas bands, some of which were only on the edges of jazz. In the mid-40s he was working on the west coast with leading traditional jazz musicians such as Albert Nicholas. Parker later went into education, teaching at colleges and universities, but still found time to play with Omer Simeon, Tony Parenti and others during the 50s and 60s. In the early 60s he undertook an extensive recording programme of ragtime music, notably including the works of Scott Joplin and James Scott. A few years later he turned his attention to early jazz piano with a set of music by Jelly Roll Morton. In the early 80s he recorded a fine album with Big Joe Turner.

Selected albums: *The Complete Piano Works Of Scott Joplin* (1960), *The Complete Piano Works Of James Scott* (1962), *Golden Treasury Of Ragtime* (1968), *The Complete Piano Works Of Jelly Roll Morton* (1970), *Big Joe Turner With Knocky Parker And His Houserockers* (1983), *From Cakewalk To Ragtime* (Jazzology 1986), *Texas Swing - And The Blues* (1987), *Texas Swing - Boogie Woogie* (1987), *Texas Swing - The Barrel-House*

(1987), *Knocky Parker And Galvanised Washboard Band* (GHB 1994).

Parker, Leo

b. 18 April 1925, Washington, DC, USA, d. 11 February 1962. Starting out on alto saxophone, an instrument on which he recorded with Coleman Hawkins, Parker switched to baritone in 1944 when he joined the bebop-orientated big band led by Billy Eckstine. For the next year or so was a member of the band's so-called 'unholy four'. Fellow saxophonists in the band included Dexter Gordon, Sonny Stitt and Gene Ammons but it was another Eckstine alumni, his namesake Charlie Parker, who appears to have exercised most musical influence upon him. After leaving Eckstine, Parker played in New York with Dizzy Gillespie and Fats Navarro before joining Illinois Jacquet's popular band. A record date with Sir Charles Thompson featured Parker on a tune entitled 'Mad Lad' and this became his nickname. Despite several other fine record dates with Gordon, and club sessions with Stitt, Ammons, Teddy Edwards, Wardell Gray and others, at all of which he more than held his own, Parker's career proved short-lived. By 1947 drug addiction was severely affecting his health. He played on into the 50s, but only intermittently, making occasional record dates, on some of which he rallied sufficiently to play superbly. One of the major baritone saxophonists in jazz, Parker died in 1962.

Selected albums: *Leo Parker's All Stars* (1947), *Leo Parker's Sextette/Quintette* (1948), *Leo Parker And His Mad Lads* i (1950), *Leo Parker And His Mad Lads* ii (1950), *The Leo Parker Quintet* (1951), *The Leo Parker Quartet* (1953), *Let Me Tell You 'Bout It* (Blue Note 1961), *Rollin' With Leo* (Blue Note 1961).

Parlan, Horace

b. 19 January 1931, Pittsburgh, Pennsylvania, USA. Parlan played piano from an early age, his first professional work being in R&B bands during the early and mid-50s. In 1957 he joined Charles Mingus in New York, later playing with Lou Donaldson, Booker Ervin, Eddie 'Lockjaw' Davis, Johnny Griffin, Roland Kirk and others. In the early 70s he settled in Denmark, playing with local and visiting musicians including Dexter Gordon, Archie Shepp and Michal Urbaniak. As a result of contracting polio as a child, Parlan suffered limitations in the use of his right hand; to compensate, he developed a powerful left hand and evolved a distinctive style in which echoes of bop and the blues blend comfortably and to great effect. Although he is always an interesting soloist, it is in the interplay with other musicians that he displays his talents to the full - a fine example is the set of two duo albums - one of blues, one of spirituals - which he recorded with Shepp.

Albums: *Movin' And Groovin'* (1960), *Headin' South* (1960), *Up And Down* (1961), *Happy Frame Of Mind* (Blue Note 1963), *Back From The Gig* (1963), *Arrival* (Steeplechase 1973), *No Blues* (Steeplechase 1975), *Blue Parlan* (Steeplechase 1975), *Frank-ly Speaking* (1977), with Archie Shepp *Goin' Home* (1977), *Hi-Fly* (1978), *Musically Yours* (Steeplechase 1979), *The Maestro* (1979), with Shepp *Trouble In Mind* (1980),

Pannonica (Enja 1981), *Glad I Found You* (Steeplechase 1984), with Shepp *Reunion* (1987), *Splashes* (1987), *Little Esther* (Soul Note 1987).

Parnell, Jack

b. 6 August 1923, London, England. One of the best-known and most popular of post-World War II British jazzmen, Parnell was at his most prominent during a long stint with Ted Heath's big band. Before then, however, he had already made a mark on the UK jazz scene. While still on military service he became a member of Buddy Featherstonehaugh's Radio Rhythm Club Sextet, playing alongside Vic Lewis and other jazz-minded servicemen. Between 1944 and 1946 Parnell also recorded with Lewis, and the Lewis-Parnell Jazzmen's version of 'Ugly Child' sold extremely well (50,000 78 rpm discs would probably have made it a hit had there been such a thing as a hit parade in those days). The Lewis-Parnell band played in clubs and also made a number of theatrical appearances. Following a minor disagreement over billing, Lewis took over sole leadership of the band while Parnell joined Heath, where he became one of the band's most popular figures. With the band he also sang, displaying an engaging voice and an attractive stage personality. Leaving Heath after seven years, Parnell became musical director of ATV, directing the pit band for the popular show, *Sunday Night At The London Palladium*, throughout the 60s. Among his later television credits, he was musical director for *The Muppet Show*. In the late 70s, after two decades in television, Parnell returned to the UK jazz scene. He has continued to play in clubs and at festivals, sometimes backing visiting American jazzmen, at other times working with leading British stars. During his early days with the Heath band Parnell had an image of gum-chewing showman drummer, an image which in fact concealed a skilful, swinging and often underrated artist. His later work, with the need for an image no longer necessary, reveals his subtle and propulsive playing.

Selected albums: *Big Band Show* (1976), *Plays Music Of The Giants* (1975), *The Portrait Of Charlie Gilbraith* (1977), *Braziliana* (1977), *Big Band Stereo Spectacular* (1981), *50 Big Band Favourites* (1984), *Memories* (Berkeley 1989).

Pass, Joe

b. Joseph Anthony Passalaqua, 13 January 1929, New Brunswick, New Jersey, USA, d. 23 May 1994, Los Angeles, California, USA. In his mid and late teens guitarist Pass worked with a number of name bands, including those led by Tony Pastor and Charlie Barnet. From the early 50s until the beginning of the following decade, Pass dwelt in self-imposed obscurity playing when and where he could in order to sustain a drug habit for which he also served time. The 60s saw his rehabilitation and revealed an astonishing talent. Following his internment at the Synanon Foundation in Santa Monica, a self-help regime which allowed him to break his habit, Pass was returned to the outside world as a reformed character, and a media-worthy example of the powers of Synanon healing (since largely discredited). The new profile brought engagements with artists as diverse as Julie London and Richard 'Groove'

Holmes. Through the patronage of Norman Granz of Pablo he moved on to work with jazz's biggest names, including duos with leading artists such as Oscar Peterson (winning a Grammy for his album with the latter and bassist Niels-Henning Ørsted Pedersen), Jimmy Rowles and Zoot Sims, or in small groups including Count Basie's reformed Kansas City Six. He proved especially gifted as accompanist to singers, particularly Ella Fitzgerald. It was as a solo performer, however, that he most ably displayed his mastery of guitar, but despite the virtuoso standard of his playing his work never degenerated into a mere display of technical accomplishment. His phenomenal technique, coupled as it was with an intense jazz feel, made him welcome in almost any setting.

Selected albums: *The Complete 'Catch Me' Sessions* (1963), *Joe Pass-John Pisano Quartet* (1963), *Joy Spring* (1964), *For Django* (1964), *The Living Legends* (1969, one side only), *Intercontinental* (1970), *Virtuoso* (Pablo 1973), with Ella Fitzgerald *Take Love Easy* (1973), *Portraits Of Duke Ellington* (1974), *Joe Pass At The Montreux Jazz Festival* (1975), with Oscar Peterson *Porgy And Bess* (1976), *Virtuoso No 2* (Pablo 1976), *Guitar Player* (1976), *Quadrant* (1977), *Virtuoso No 3* (Original Jazz Classics 1977), *Live At Montreux '77* (Original Jazz Classics 1977), *Guitar Interludes* (c.1977), *Tudo Bem!* (Original Jazz Classics 1978), *Chops* (Original Jazz Classics 1978), *I Remember Charlie Parker* (Original Jazz Classics 1979), *Northsea Nights* (1979), *Digital III At Montreux* (1979), *Quadrant Toasts Duke Ellington - All Too Soon* (1980), with Jimmy Rowles *Checkmate* (1981), *Ira, George And Joe/Joe Pass Loves Gershwin* (1981), with Zoot Sims *Blues For Two* (1982), *Eximious* (1982), *Live At Long Beach City College* (1984), *We'll Be Together Again* (1985), *Whitestone* (Pablo 1985), *University Of Akron Concert* (Pablo 1985), *Blues For Fred* (Pablo 1988), *One For My Baby* (Pablo 1988), *Summer Nights* (Pablo 1990), *Appassionato* (Pablo 1990), *Vituoso Live!* (Pablo 1991), *My Song* (Telarc 1993).

Pastorius, Jaco

b. John Francis Pastorius, 1 December 1951, Norristown, Pennsylvania, USA, d. 21 September 1987, Fort Lauderdale, Florida, USA. Encouraged by his father, a drummer and vocalist, to pursue a career in music, Pastorius learned to play bass, drums, guitar, piano, and saxophone while in his teens. As a result of a football injury to his arm, his ambitions were mainly orientated towards the drums, but he soon found work playing bass for visiting pop and soul acts. After backing the Temptations and the Supremes, he developed a cult following, and his reputation spread. In 1975, Bobby Colomby, drummer with Blood, Sweat And Tears, was impressed enough to arrange the recording of Pastorius' first album, and a year later Pat Metheny asked him to play bass on his own first album for ECM Records, additionally he worked with Joni Mitchell. But the most important stage in Pastorius' career came in 1976: joining Weather Report to record the highly influential *Heavy Weather*, his astonishing technique on the fretless bass and his flamboyant behaviour on stage consolidated the band's popularity and boosted his own image to star status. He established

his own band, Word Of Mouth, in 1980, and they enjoyed three years of successful tours, while Pastorius himself recorded intermittently with some of the top musicians in jazz. However, Pastorius suffered from alcoholism and manic depression. In 1987, after increasing bouts of inactivity, he suffered fatal injuries in a brawl outside the Midnight Club in his home town of Fort Lauderdale. Pastorius was one of the most influential bass players since Charles Mingus, and extended the possibilities of the electric bass as a melodic instrument in a way which has affected many bassists since.

Selected albums: *Jaco* (DIW 1974 recording), *Jaco Pastorius* (1975), with Weather Report *Heavy Weather* (1976), *Word Of Mouth* (WEA 1980), *Invitation* (1982), *PDB* (DIW 1987), *Honestly* (Jazzpoint 1986), *Heavy N' Jazz* (Jazzppoint 1987), *Jazz Street* (Timeless 1987), *Live In Italy* (Jazzpoint 1991, 1986 recording), *Holiday For Pans* (Sound Hills 1993, 1980-82 recording).

Patitucci, John

b. 22 December 1959, Brooklyn, New York, USA. Patitucci is a technically gifted bassist best known for his work on both the electric and acoustic instruments for fusion keyboard legend Chick Corea. After playing some pop and rock in his brother's band in New York, he moved with his family to America's west coast, the home of a fearsome tradition for jazz/rock fusion virtuosi, in 1972, and was introduced to the jazz tradition by bass teacher Chris Poehler. Studying the acoustic work of Ron Carter, Dave Holland, Charlie Haden and Eddie Gomez, and the electric bass techniques of Larry Graham, Marcus Miller, Stanley Clarke and, particularly, bass hero Jaco Pastorius, he developed quickly, working with pianist Gap Mangione (brother of Chuck Mangione), and veteran British-borne vibesman Victor Feldman. It was with Feldman that Chick Corea came across him, and asked him to join the newly formed Elektric Band. Patitucci stayed with the Elektric Band throughout its life, recording five albums, and played an important part in the Akoustic Band trio. Since the late 80s he has also been working as a leader on GRP and Stretch – Corea's own subsidiary of the GRP label. An incredible technician on both acoustic and six-string electric basses, Patitucci has unfortunately allowed his output to be dominated by material that works primarily as a means to demonstrate his technique. His best record so far is probably *Sketchbook*, featuring drummer Peter Erskine, tenor saxophonist Michael Brecker and guitarist John Scofield.

Albums: with Chick Corea *The Chick Corea Elektric Band* (1986), with Corea *Light Years* (1987), with Corea *Eye Of The Beholder* (1988), *John Patitucci* (1988), *Chick Corea Akoustic Band* (1989), *On The Corner* (1989), *Sketchbook* (1990), with Corea *Inside Out* (1990), *Beneath The Mask* (1992), *Alive* (1992), *Heart Of The Bass* (1992).

Patton, 'Big' John

b. 12 July 1935, Kansas City, Missouri, USA. Unusually for a Hammond organ supremo, Patton does not come from Philadelphia. His mother played piano in church, and Patton

took it up in 1948. He played in the Lloyd Price band from 1954-59, quitting just as Price topped his 1952 hit 'Lawdy Miss Clawdy' with a string of three million-sellers. Patton moved to New York and switched to organ. He was signed to Blue Note Records on the recommendation of Lou Donaldson, debuting with *Along Came John* in 1963, which featured Grant Green on guitar. In the late 60s he worked with tenor saxophonist Clifford Jordon and guitarist James 'Blood' Ulmer, as well as sitting in with Sun Ra's musicians. In the 70s he moved to East Orange, New Jersey. John Zorn's use of him on a track of *The Big Gundown* in 1985 rekindled interest in his career and in 1989 he toured Britain with jazz musicians including tenor saxophonist Jean Toussaint (ex-Jazz Messengers).
Selected albums: *Along Came John* (1963), *The Way I Feel* (1964), *Oh Baby* (1964), *Blue John* (Blue Note 1964), *Got A Good Thing Goin'* (1965), *Let 'Em Roll* (Blue Note 1966), *Soul Connection* (Nilva 1984), *Blue Planet Man* (Paddlewheel 1993). Compilation: *The Organization!: The Best Of Big John Patton* (Blue Note 1994).

Pavageau, Alcide 'Slow Drag'

b. 7 March 1888, New Orleans, Louisiana, USA, d. 19 January 1969. During his early years Pavageau became known as a competent guitarist and an excellent dancer and he was almost 40 years old before he took up the bass. On this instrument he played with a number of leading New Orleans bands of the day, including Buddy Petit's. His fame did not spread, however, until 1943, when he joined George Lewis. He toured and recorded with Lewis throughout the 40s and also worked with Bunk Johnson. His association with Lewis continued through the 50s and on into the early 60s. Despite his late start, Pavageau became one of the best known New Orleans-style bass players and if much of that fame rested on his long-term relationship with Lewis he was certainly an above-average player. Late in life he became a popular figure, leading street parades in his home town. For all that fame, it was on one of the city's streets that he was attacked and robbed, dying soon afterwards on 19 January 1969.
Album: with George Lewis *Jazz At Vespers* (1954). Compilation: *American Music By George Lewis* (1944-45 recordings).

Payne, Cecil

b. 14 December 1922, New York City, New York, USA. After first learning guitar, alto saxophone and clarinet, Payne took up the baritone saxophone. In 1946, a year in which he played and recorded with J.J. Johnson and Roy Eldridge, he joined Dizzy Gillespie's big band for a three-year stint. Leaving Gillespie in 1949 he joined Tadd Dameron's band, following this with appearances with James Moody and Illinois Jacquet. In the mid-50s he played with Randy Weston, John Coltrane and Duke Jordan. During the 60s he was with Machito, Lionel Hampton, Woody Herman, Count Basie and Gillespie again. In the 70s he worked again for Basie and also formed a double-act with his vocalist sister, Cavril. In the 80s he played in a trio with Bill Hardman and led by Richard Wyand. An accomplished player with a special affinity for bebop, Payne's technical command is on a par with that of many better-known players, whose greater charisma has kept them more in the public eye.
Selected albums: with Randy Weston *Jazz A La Bohemia* (1956), with Tadd Dameron *Fontainebleau* (1956), with John Coltrane *Dakar* (1957), *Bird's Night* (1957), *Patterns Of Jazz* (Savoy 1957), *Cool Blues* (1961), *The Connection* (Jazz Reactivation 1962), *Brookfield Andante* (Spotlite 1966), *The Cecil Payne Quintet* (c.1969-70), *Brooklyn Brothers* (1973), *Bird Gets The Worm* (Muse 1976), *Bright Moments* (Spotlite 1979), *Zodiac* (Strata East 1993).

Payne, Sonny

b. Percival Payne, 4 May 1926, New York City, New York, USA, d. 29 January 1979. Payne began studying drums at an early age, encouraged by the fact that his father, Chris Columbus, was a jazz drummer. Payne's first jobs included spells with Oran 'Hot Lips' Page, Earl Bostic and Tiny Grimes. In 1950 he joined the Erskine Hawkins band, where he spent three years, then led his own band for a couple of years before joining Count Basie. He was with Basie for over 10 years, leaving to form his own small group and working as staff drummer for Frank Sinatra. In 1966 he began another long engagement with a big band, this time led by Harry James. In 1973 he was back with Basie, then played with amongst others Illinois Jacquet during the mid-70s. An aggressive, showman-drummer, Payne was an indifferent timekeeper but brought a sense of sustained excitement to any band in which he played. Even the Basie band, accustomed to such immaculate timekeepers as Jo Jones and Gus Johnson, was given a lift by Payne when he was at his best and, even when he was at his worst, audiences loved him.
Albums: all with Count Basie *The Atomic Mr Basie* (1957), *Basie - Chairman Of The Board* (1959), *On My Way And Shoutin' Again* (1962).

Peacock, Annette

b. New York, USA. A highly individual and challenging songwriter with a distinctive voice, Peacock was in the centre of the Milbrook, New York, psychedelic scene in the 60s, having been 'discovered' by Timothy Leary. Her mother was a classical musician, and she was brought up on chamber music. She discovered jazz for herself at an early age but came into contact with the *avant garde* after she eloped to New York City with Gary Peacock, who was then the bass-player with Albert Ayler. Gary then joined the trio of Paul Bley, who began to use her compositions as well as those of Carla Bley. Paul Bley's 1967 *Ballads* used Annette Peacock's tunes exclusively. Her compositions include such beautiful modern classics as 'Open, To Love' and 'Nothing Ever Was, Anyway'. Touring as the Annette And Paul Bley Synthesizer Show at the start of the 70s, they used what was then state-of-the-art hardware: machines the size of a Welsh Dresser, with wiring like a telephone exchange, which took 10 minutes to 'tune' and programme between numbers. Moogs were then intended only for studio use. Certainly on the road the results were primitive and rough by today's standards, but this was real pioneering stuff. Annette used the technology in her own solo, somewhat more rock-inclined, work to process her voice or, often, used her voice to generate electronic sounds through the synthesizer, as on *I'm The One*, an album which led David Bowie to ask her to record and tour with him. (She told him to learn the synthesizer himself.) So pioneering was her work in this field that recently an electronics expert tried to tell her that the processes she was using were impossible given the technology of the time. Her songs are raw and personal, with an unblinking frankness about emotions and human relationships, and as well as keyboards she plays vibes and electric bass. She set up her own label, Ironic, in 1978. She has worked with Bill Bruford over a number of years and has also played with controversial composer Karlheinz Stockhausen.

Albums: as the Annette And Paul Bley Synthesizer Show *Dual Unity* (1970), with the Synthesizer Show *Improvisie* (1970), *Improvisie* (1970), *Revenge* (1970), *I'm The One* (1972), *X-Dreams* (1978), with Bill Bruford *Feels Good To Me* (1978), *Perfect Release* (1979), *Sky Skating* (1982), *Been In The Streets Too Long* (1983, rec. 1975-83), *I Have No Feelings* (1986), *Abstract Contact* (1988).

Peacock, Gary

b. 12 May 1935, Barley, Idaho, USA. Peacock went to Germany in the late 50s playing the piano in a US Army band. During this period he took up the bass and when he left the army he stayed in Germany playing with local musicians including Albert Mangelsdorff and Attila Zoller and visiting Americans like saxophonists Bud Shank and Bob Cooper. In 1958 he moved to California where he played with a wide range of musicians including Shorty Rogers, Paul Horn and Paul Bley. He continued to work with Bley when he moved to New York in 1962 and got involved in the burgeoning *avant garde* scene. He played with Bill Evans, Rahsaan Roland Kirk, George Russell, Roswell Rudd, Steve Lacy and Albert Ayler with whom he worked in Europe (1964). He is technically an excellent musician with a very full tone able to create appropriate lines in many contexts. In the mid-60s he studied Eastern philosophy and medicine. He later had a brief stint with Miles Davis and played again with Paul Bley before he went to study in Japan, returning to Washington University in 1972 to study biology. In the mid-70s he once again worked with Bley and also in a trio with pianist Keith Jarrett and drummer Jack DeJohnette. In the 80s he taught at Cornish Institute of the Allied Arts in Seattle, Washington.

Selected albums: with Bill Evans *Trio '64* (1963), with Albert Ayler *New York Eye And Ear Control* (1964), with Paul Bley *Ballads* (1967), *Tales Of Another* (ECM 1977), *December Poems* (ECM 1979), *Shift In The Wind* (ECM 1980), *Voice From The Past* (ECM 1981), with Keith Jarrett *Standards* i (1983), with Jarrett *Changes* (1984), with Jarrett *Standards* ii (1985), *Guamba* (ECM 1987), *Partners* (Owl 1990), with Paul Bley, Franz Koglmann *Annette* (1993), with Jarrett, Paul Motian *At The Deer Head Inn* (ECM 1994).

Pearson, Duke

b. Columbus C. Pearson, 17 August 1932, Atlanta, Georgia, USA, d. 4 August 1980. After studying piano and trumpet, Pearson opted for the former and played professionally in various parts of the USA before settling in New York at the end of the 50s. Working as both performer and composer, he associated with several leading musicians, including Donald Byrd, Art Farmer, Benny Golson and Pepper Adams. In 1963 he succeeded Ike Quebec as A&R director of Blue Note Records, a post he held until 1971. During the late 60s Pearson formed a strikingly good big band from New York-based session musicians and jazzmen. The band, designed to perform his own music, made some excellent albums, notably *Now Hear This*. In the 70s Pearson divided his time between performing, accompanying singers such as Carmen McRae and Nancy Wilson, directing his big band and fighting against the onset of multiple sclerosis.

Albums: *Profile* (1959), *Dedication* (1961), *Wahoo* (1964), *Sweet Honey Bee* (Blue Note 1966), *The Right Touch* (1967), *Introducing Duke Pearson's Big Band* (1967), *The Phantom* (1968), *Now Hear This* (1968), *How Insensitive* (Blue Note 1969), *Merry Ole Soul* (1969), *It Could Only Happen To You* (1970), *Wahoo* (Blue Note 1989), *Bags Groove* (Black Lion 1991).

Peplowski, Ken

b. 23 May 1959, Cleveland, Ohio, USA. Peplowski took up the clarinet as a child and played his first professional engagement at the age of 10. He studied formally and played both classical music and jazz, appearing on radio and television in and around his home town. In 1978 his quartet played opposite the Tommy Dorsey Orchestra, at the time under the direction of Buddy Morrow, and he was promptly offered a job. Peplowski toured extensively with the band, including a visit to Europe. During this period he met and briefly studied with Sonny Stitt. After two and a half years with the orchestra he decided to settle in New York. He obtained work in many areas of music, playing with a touring company of the show *Annie*, in symphony orchestras, in studio bands for films and records, and with jazz groups which ranged from traditional to the *avant garde*. Among these engagements, the most prestigious was a television date and two albums with Benny Goodman. During the 80s his reputation spread and he appeared at several festivals, making a great impression at the 1990 Nice Jazz Festival. He has also made records with singers such as Mel Tormé, Peggy Lee and Rosemary Clooney and jazzmen Hank Jones, George Shearing, Dan Barrett, Scott Hamilton and Howard Alden. By the late 80s he was a frequent visitor to the UK and continued to appear at festivals, also making club dates and records. A highly gifted clarinettist who plays alto and tenor saxophones too, Peplowski is strongly rooted in the mainstream. The quality of his playing is such that he is one of a small number of musicians who are helping restore the fortunes of the clarinet in jazz.

Albums: *Double Exposure* (Concord 1987), *Sonny Side* (Concord 1989), *Mr Gentle And Mr Cool* (Concord 1990),

Illuminations (Concord 1990), *The Natural Touch* (Concord 1992), with Howard Alden *Concord Duo Series Vol. 3* (1993), *Steppin' With Peps* (Concord 1993).

Pepper, Art

b. 1 September 1925, Gardena, Los Angeles, California, USA, d. 1 June 1982. Pepper started out on clarinet at the age of nine, switching to alto saxophone four years later. After appearing in school groups, he first played professionally with Gus Arnheim's band. During his mid-teens he developed his jazz style sitting in with otherwise all-black bands along Los Angeles's Central Avenue. After leaving Arnheim he worked with Dexter Gordon in Lee Young's band at the Club Alabam. He then joined Benny Carter, playing alongside artists such as Gerald Wilson, Freddie Webster and J.J. Johnson. In 1943 Pepper joined Stan Kenton but soon afterwards was drafted into the US Army, spending most of his war-time service in England. In 1946 he rejoined Kenton, staying with the band until 1951. That year he also recorded with Shorty Rogers, playing a marvellous version of 'Over The Rainbow', a tune he would play often over the years. Later, he appeared on Rogers's *Cool And Crazy* album. Pepper subsequently freelanced around Los Angeles, making many record dates, some under his own name, and usually playing extremely well. Nevertheless, his career in the 50s and 60s was marred by his drug addiction and interrupted by several prison sentences. At the end of the 60s Pepper began a slow, uphill fight against his addiction, a struggle which was eventually successful and heralded his re-emergence in the mid-70s as a major figure on the international jazz scene. In the last years of his life, he produced a rich crop of recordings, including *Winter Moon*, an album with strings (a long-held ambition of Pepper's), the three-album set *Live At The Village Vanguard* (a fourth volume appeared posthumously) and two records recorded live in London under the name of pianist Milcho Leviev, *Blues For The Fisherman* and *True Blues*. Early in his career Pepper played with a light airy tone, through which burned a rare intensity of emotion that reflected his admiration for Charlie Parker and the lessons he learned playing with Carter. After his rehabilitation and a period playing tenor saxophone, on which instrument he showed both the influence of Lester Young and an awareness of John Coltrane, Pepper developed a strong, bop-rooted alto style which retained much of the richly melodic elements of his earlier playing. Pepper's life story was memorably recounted in his candid autobiography and a subsequent film, *Art Pepper: Notes From A Jazz Survivor* (1982), which offered a potent and harshly unsentimental lesson for any young musician contemplating the use of addictive drugs.

Selected albums: *Two Altos* (Savoy 1952-54 recordings), *Art Pepper Quartet* (1954), *Surf Ride* (Savoy 1954), *The Way It Was* (1956), with Chet Baker *The Route* (1956), with Baker *Playboys* (1957), *The Art Pepper Quintet* (1957), *The Artistry Of Pepper* (Pacific 1957), *Modern Art* (Blue Note 1957), *The Art Of Pepper* (Blue Note 1957), *Art Pepper Meets The Rhythm Section* (1957), *Art Pepper + Eleven* (1959), *Gettin' Together* (Original Jazz Classics 1960), *Smack Up!* (1962, rec. 1960), *The Way It Was* (Original Jazz Classics 1961), *Modern Jazz Classics* (Original Jazz Classics 1960), *Intensity* (Original Jazz Classics 1963, rec. 1960), *Live At Donte's Vol. 1* (1968), *The Omega Man* (1974, rec. 1968), *I'll Remember April* (Syoryville 1975), *Living Legend* (Original Jazz Classics 1976), *The Trip* (Original Jazz Classics 1977), *A Night In Tinisia* (Storyville 1977), *No Limit* (Original Jazz Classics 1978), *Among Friends* (1978), *Live In Japan* (1978), *Art Pepper Today* (1978), *Straight Life* (1979), *Landscape* (1980), *Omega Alpha* (1980, rec. 1957), *So Much In Love* (1980), *Live At The Village Vanguard* (1981, rec. 1977), *Winter Moon* (1981), *Besame Mucho* (1981, rec. 1979), *One September Afternoon* (1981), *Darn That Dream* (1982), *Road Game* (1982), *Goin' Home* (Original Jazz Classics 1982), *Art Lives* (1983, rec. 1981), *Art Works* (1984, rec. 1979), *More For Les: Live At The Village Vanguard, Volume 4* (1985, rec. 1977). Selected compilations: with Wayne Marsh *The Way It Was* (1972, rec. 1956-60), *Early Art* (1976, rec. 1956-57), *Artistry In Jazz* (JVC 1987), *The Art Of Pepper, Volumes 1 & 2* (1988), *The Complete Galaxy Recordings* (Galaxy 1989, 16-CD box set), *Memorial Collection Vols 1-4* (Storyville 1990), *The Best Of Art Pepper* (Blue Note 1993).

Further reading: *Straight Life: The Story Of Art Pepper*, Art and Laurie Pepper.

Perez, Manuel

b. 28 December 1871, New Orleans, Louisiana, USA, d. 1946. One of the Crescent City's legendary figures, Perez was a respected cornet player, bandleader and teacher. He rarely played anywhere else, working in dancehalls and leading the Onward Brass Band in street parades. He made few trips outside his home town, playing in Chicago in 1915 and again in 1928. Fellow musicians thought highly of him, suggesting that his technique and command were at least on a par with his better-known contemporaries. By the 40s he was inactive through ill-health and died in 1946.

Perkins, Bill

b. 22 July 1924, San Francisco, California, USA. Having started out on a career as an electrical engineer, tenor saxophonist Perkins was in his mid-20s before he made an appearance in Jerry Wald's band in 1950. The following year he was with Woody Herman's Third Herd and by 1953 was in Stan Kenton's band. The rest of the 50s were spent alternating between Herman and Kenton during which time his reputation as a subtly inventive soloist grew steadily. His playing at this time was derived from Lester Young by way of Stan Getz, although he was also influenced by Richie Kamuca, who was with him in both the Herman and Kenton bands. His light, relaxed style made him a natural for the currently active west coast school of music. In 1956 he recorded with John Lewis, Richie Kamuca, Art Pepper and others and in 1959 was on Pepper's highly successful *Plus Eleven*. In the 60s he chose to turn his back on life on the road, taking a job with Pacific Jazz Records, but was active in the studios and playing occasional jazz gigs, a pattern which continued into the 70s. By the 80s he was touring widely, and appeared in the UK where he showed that he had lost none of his earlier inventiveness. A relaxed style and an elegant, dry-toned sound characterize his playing.

Selected albums: *The Woody Herman Band!* (1954), *Stan Kenton Plays The Music Of Bill Russo And Bill Holman* (1954), *Grand Encounter* (1956), *Bill Perkins At The Music Box Theatre* (1956), *Tenors Head-On* (1956), with John Lewis *2 Degrees East, 3 Degrees West* (1956), with Richie Kamuca, Art Pepper *Just Friends* (1956), *Bill Perkins With Strings* (1963), *Quietly There* (Original Jazz Classics 1967), *Bill Perkins Plays Lester Young* (1978), *Confluence* (1978), with Pepper Adams *Front Line* (Storyville 1979), *Many Ways To Go* (1980), *Journey To The East* (1984), *Remembrance Of Dino's* (Interplay 1986), *The Right Chemistry* (Jazz Mark 1988), *Our Man Woody* (1991), *I Wished On The Moon* (Candid (1991), with Kamucha *Tenors Head On* (Pacific 1992), with Frank Strazzeri *Warm Moods* (Fresh Sounds 1993).

Perkins, Carl

b. 16 August 1928, Indianapolis, Indiana, USA, d. 17 March 1958. Perkins was a self-taught pianist who, after playing in R&B bands, including those led by Tiny Bradshaw and Big Jay McNeely, settled in California in the late 40s. At this time he changed his musical direction, working in the 50s in jazz mainstream with Illinois Jacquet and Oscar Moore and in bebop with Miles Davis. In the mid-50s he became one of the most active figures on the west coast scene, playing and recording extensively with artists such as Wardell Gray, Dexter Gordon, Jim Hall, Pepper Adams, Mel Lewis, Jack Sheldon and Art Pepper. He was also a member, briefly, of the Max Roach-Clifford Brown group and of the Curtis Counce group. Although physically impaired through contracting polio as a child, Perkins developed a strong sound and his style showed him to be an endlessly inventive musician. As a rhythm section member he made a substantial contribution to jazz in the 50s, playing on many classic west coast albums. Unfortunately, his personal life was a mess and narcotics addiction brought about his early death in 1958.

Album: *Introducing Carl Perkins* (Boplicity 1955).

Persip, Charlie

b. 26 July 1929, Morristown, New Jersey, USA. After taking up drums as a child Persip began playing bop, moving to New York where he worked with Tadd Dameron in the early 50s. From 1953 he was associated with Dizzy Gillespie, playing in small groups and big bands. He also recorded with Lee Morgan, Zoot Sims and Dinah Washington. In 1960 he formed his own band with Freddie Hubbard but continued to record with such artists as Gil Evans, Roland Kirk, Don Ellis and Gene Ammons. In the late 60s he began a long association with Billy Eckstine, playing drums and conducting the touring orchestra. In the early 70s Persip teamed up with several other leading jazzmen to work with Jazzmobile in New York City, teaching and performing. In the mid- to late-70s he recorded with Archie Shepp, Kirk and others and also led his own big band. Hard driving and technically assured, Persip is an excellent bop drummer whose skills are best represented by his

superb big band work.

Albums: with Dizzy Gillespie *World Statesman* (1956), with Gil Evans *Out Of The Cool* (1960), with Don Ellis *How Time Passes* (1960), *The Charlie Persip Sextet* (1960), with Ellis *New Ideas* (1961), with Rahsaan Roland Kirk *We Free Kings* (1961), *Charlie Persip and Gary La Furn's 17-Piece Superband* (1980), *In Case You Missed It* (Soul Note 1984), *No Dummies Allowed* (Soul Note 1988).

Peterson, Marvin 'Hannibal'

b. 11 November 1948, Smithville, Texas, USA. One of many fine musicians to graduate from North Texas State University, Peterson settled on trumpet having previously played cornet and drums. After graduation he moved to New York where he played with Rahsaan Roland Kirk, Elvin Jones, Archie Shepp and other leading jazzmen, notably Gil Evans with whom he formed a lasting musical relationship. Throughout the 60s he toured and recorded with these and other musicians, sometimes leading his own band. He continued performing in similar settings through the 70s, working again with Evans and Jones and also with Pharoah Sanders and Roy Haynes. In the 80s he was touring internationally. For a while in the mid-to-late 70s Peterson played free jazz with Roswell Rudd, but his best work comes in bop and post-bop settings. A sparkling virtuoso trumpeter, Peterson's brilliant technique allows him to do pretty much anything he sets his mind upon; as his playing and writing testify, this ranges over the entire spectrum of jazz.

Albums: with Pharoah Sanders *Black Unity* (1971), with Gil Evans *Svengali* (1973), *Children Of Fire* (1974), *Hannibal* (1975), *Hannibal In Berlin* (1976), *Gil Evans Live At New York Public Theater* (1980), *The Angels Of Atlanta* (1981), *Hannibal In Antibes* (Enja 1982), *Poem Song* (Mole 1983), *Kiss On The Bridge* (Ear Rational 1990).

Peterson, Oscar

b. Oscar Emmanuel Peterson, 15 August 1925, Montreal, Canada. Blessed with an attractive stage personality, this behemoth of mainstream jazz's fluid technique was influenced by Art Tatum, Errol Garner and, later, George Shearing. After studying trumpet, illness redirected him to the piano. His enthusiasm resulted in endless hours of practise which helped mould his remarkable technique. In his mid-teens, after winning a local talent contest in 1940, Peterson was heard regularly on radio in Canada and beyond. By 1944, he was the featured pianist with the nationally famous Johnny Holmes Orchestra before leading his own trio. Peterson was unusual in not serving an apprenticeship as an older player's sideman. Although early recordings were disappointing, he received lucrative offers to appear in the USA but these were resisted until a debut at New York's Carnegie Hall with Norman Granz's Jazz At The Philharmonic in September 1949. Louis Armstrong, Billie Holiday, Count Basie, Dizzy Gillespie, Zoot Sims, Ella Fitzgerald and Stan Getz have been among Peterson's collaborators during a career that has encompassed hundreds of studio and concert recordings. With 1963's *Affinity* as his biggest seller, Peterson's output has ranged from albums drawn

Oscar Peterson

from the songbooks of Cole Porter and Duke Ellington; a Verve single of Jimmy Forrest's perennial 'Night Train', and 1964's self-written *Canadiana Suite*. Although he introduced a modicum of Nat 'King' Cole-type vocals into his repertoire in the mid-50s, he has maintained a certain steady consistency of style that has withstood the buffeting of fashion.

Since 1970, he has worked with no fixed group, often performing alone, although at the end of the 70s Peterson had a long stint with bass player Neils-Henning Ørsted Pedersen which continued well into the 80s. The soundtrack to the movie *Play It Again Sam*; the hosting of a television chat show; a 1974 tour of Soviet Russia, and 1981's *A Royal Wedding Suite* (conducted by Russ Garcia) have been more recent commercial high points of a fulfilling and distinguished professional life. While musicians as diverse as Steve Winwood, Dudley Moore and Weather Report's Joe Zawinul absorbed much from Peterson discs, younger admirers have been advantaged by his subsequent publication of primers such as *Jazz Exercises And Pieces* and *Peterson's New Piano Solos*. Peterson's dazzling technique and unflagging swing have helped make him one of the most highly regarded and instantly identifiable pianists in jazz. Although the technical qualities of his work have sometimes cooled the emotional heart of his material, Peterson's commitment to jazz is undeniable. The high standard of his work over the years is testimony to his dedication and to the care which he and his mentor, Granz, have exercised over the pianist's career. Throughout this time, Peterson has displayed through his eclecticism, an acute awareness of the history of jazz piano, ranging from stride to bop, from James P. Johnson to Bill Evans, but always with Art Tatum as an abiding influence. However this influence is one that Peterson has been careful to control. Tatum may colour Peterson's work but he has never shaped it. Thus, for all his influences, Peterson is very much his own man. Yet, for all the admiration he draws from other pianists, there is little evidence that he has many followers. He may well prove to be the end of the line of master musicians in the history of jazz piano.

Selected albums: *In Concert* (1952), *Jazz At The Philharmonic, Hartford 1953* (Pablo 1953 recording), *1953 Live* (Jazz Band Records 1953 recording), *Verve Jazz Masters* (Verve 1953-1962 recordings), *At Zardi's* (Pablo 1955 recording), *The Silver Collection* (Verve 1959-63 recordings), *A Jazz Portrait Of Frank Sinatra* (Verve 1960), *Plays The Cole Porter Songbook* (Verve 1960), *Plays Porgy And Bess* (Verve 1960), *The Trio Live From Chicago* (Verve 1962), *Very Tall* (Verve 1962), *West Side Story* (Verve 1962), *Night Train* (Verve 1963), *Bursting Out With The All Star Big Band!* (1963), *Affinity* (1963), *Exclusively For My Friends* (1964), *Oscar Peterson Trio + One* (1964), *Canadiana Suite* (1964), *We Get Requests* (Verve 1965), *My Favourite Instrument* (1968), *Exclusively For My Friends* (MPS 1963-68 recordings), *The Vienna Concert* (Philology 1969), *Motion's And Emotions* (MPS 1969), *Hello Herbie* (MPS 1969),

Tristeza On Piano (MPS 1970), *Three Originals* (MPS 1970), *Tracks* (1970), *Reunion Blues* (MPS 1972), *Terry's Tune* (1974), *The Trio* (Pablo 1975), *The Good Life* (Original Jazz Classics 1975), with Sonny Stitt *Sittin' In* (1975), with Dizzy Gillespie *Oscar Peterson And Dizzy Gillespie* (Pablo 1975), with Roy Eldridge *Oscar Peterson And Roy Eldridge* (Original Jazz Classics 1975), *At The Montreaux Jazz Festival* 1975 (Pablo 1976), *Again* (1977), *Oscar Peterson Jam* (1977), *The Vocal Styling Of Oscar Peterson* (1977), *Montreaux '77* i (Original Jazz Classics 1978), *Montreaux '77* ii (Original Jazz Classics 1978), *The Silent Partner* (1979), *The Paris Concert* (Pablo 1979), *Skol* (Original Jazz Classics 1980), *The Personal Touch* (Pablo 1981), *A Royal Wedding Suite* (Pablo 1981), *Live At The Northsea Jazz Festival* (Pablo 1981), *Nigerian Marketplace* (Pablo 1982), *Romance* (1982), with Stéphane Grappelli, Joe Pass, Mickey Roker, Neils-Henning Ørsted Pedersen *Skol* (1982), *In Russia* (Pablo 1982), *Oscar Peterson & Harry Edison* (Pablo 1982), *Carioca* (Happy Bird 1983), *A Tribute To My Friends* (Pablo 1984), *Time After Time* (Pablo 1984), *If You Could See Me Now* (Pablo 1984), *The George Gershwin Songbook* (1985), *Live!* (Pablo 1987), *Live At the Blue Note* (Telarc 1991), *Saturday Night At The Blue Note* (Telarc 1991), *Last Call At The Blue Note* (Telarc 1992). Selected compilations: *History Of An Artist* (Pablo 1982), *History Of An Artist, Volume 2* (Pablo 1987), *Compact Jazz: Oscar Peterson And Friends* (Verve 1988), *Compact Jazz: Plays Jazz Standards* (Verve 1988), *Exclusively For My Friends Vols. 1-4* (1992).

Further reading: *Oscar Peterson*, Richard Palmer. *Oscar Peterson: The Will To Swing*, Gene Lees.

Petit, Buddy

b. Joseph Crawford, c.1897, White Castle, Louisiana, USA, d.4 July 1931. By his early teens Petit was well known in New Orleans and by 1916 was co-leading a band with Jimmie Noone. The following year he was in California with Jelly Roll Morton. By 1918, however, he was back in his home state and, apart from another brief trip to California, he lived and worked in New Orleans and its environs for the rest of his life. Petit's reputation rests upon the acclaim of fellow musicians - he never recorded - and if they are to be believed he was an outstanding trumpet player with a reputation second only to that of Louis Armstrong. He died after 'over-indulging' in food and drink at an Independence Day celebration in 1931.

Petrucciani, Michel

b. 28 December 1962, Montpelier, France. After playing with Kenny Clarke and Clark Terry at the age of 15, Petrucciani moved to Paris, recorded his first album, and formed a successful duo with Lee Konitz just two years later. Moving to California in 1982, he joined Charles Lloyd's new quartet. However, it was a solo performance at Carnegie Hall as part of the Kool Jazz Festival that resulted in widespread critical acclaim. With hard-hit notes he echoes *Keith Jarrett*, but it is his delicate Peterson-like frills that make him a romantic giant. No pun is intended, because irrespective of his restricted growth, Petrucciani plays with astonishing confidence and

beauty. In the mid-80s Petrucciani signed a contract with Blue Note Records, and this in turn gave him much greater exposure outside the jazz world. *Michel Plays Petrucciani* features all his own compositions and is an album that sets him free, way beyond the restriction of playing somebody else's material, even in a jazz context. This record brims with flowing music (and some sparkling guitar from John Abercrombie). Another necessary record in his catalogue is the solo piano excursion *Promenade With Duke*. From the dozens of Ellington tributes over the years this record oozes respect for the master, so much so that Petrucciani gained both respect and credibility that is already cast in stone. In addition to his solo career worked with Wayne Shorter in Manhattan Project. He is a melodic, thoughtful pianist and one of the brightest stars of jazz piano in recent years.

Albums: *Michel Petrucciani Trio* (Owl 1982), *Estate* (IRD 19 1983), *Oracles's Destiny* (Owl 1983), 100 Hearts (Concord 1983), *Note'n Notes* (Owl 1985), *Live At The Village Vanguard* (Concord 1985), *Pianism* (Blue Note 1986), *Power Of Three* (Blue Note 1986), *Cold Blues* (Concord 1986), *Michel Plays Petrucciani* (Blue Note 1988), *Music* (Blue Note 1989), *Playground* (Blue Note 1991), *Live* (1991), *Promenade With Duke* (1993), *Marvellous* (Dreyfus 1994).

Pettiford, Oscar

b. 30 September 1922, Okmulgee, Oklahoma, USA, d. 8 September 1960. Coming from a musical background, Pettiford was competent on several instruments, settling for bass in the early 40s. He played with Charlie Barnet, Roy Eldridge, Coleman Hawkins, Ben Webster and others; then in the middle of the decade, was active among the New York beboppers. He briefly co-led a band with Dizzy Gillespie, and later led his own groups. From 1945 he was with Duke Ellington, moving on in 1948 to the Woody Herman band. During the 50s he played in several bands, big and small, often leading his own groups, and was usually in the company of important musicians such as Thelonious Monk, Lucky Thompson and Art Blakey. In 1958 he toured Europe with a jazz concert package, remaining behind to take up residence in Denmark where he died in 1960. A major influence upon bop bass players, Pettiford played with a superb tone and clarity. Nevertheless, he was frequently dissatisfied with his own work and also played cello, an instrument which gave him an opportunity to develop ideas sometimes inhibited by the physical limitations of the bass.

Selected albums: *The Oscar Pettiford Memorial Album* (1954), *Oscar Pettiford Group* (1954), *Basically Duke* (1954), *Bohemia After Dark* (Affinity 1955), *Discoveries* (Savoy 1952-57 recordings), *The Oscar Pettiford Orchestra In Hi-Fi* (Jasmine 1957), *The Legendary Oscar Pettiford* (Black Lion 1959), *Radio Tapes* (Jazzline 1958-1960 recordings), *Blue Brothers* (Black Lion 1960), *Monmartre Blues* (Black Lion 1959-60), Compilation: *Oscar Rides Again* (Affinity 1986).

Phillips, Barre

b. 27 October 1934, San Francisco, California, USA. At the

age of three Barre Phillips was giving solo song recitals. He studied romance languages at Berkeley and then moved to New York where he received double bass lessons from Frederick Zimmermann in the early 60s. In March and April 1963 he played with Eric Dolphy at Carnegie Hall, part of Gunther Schuller's Twentieth-Century Innovations series, and from 1964 he was a member of Jimmy Giuffre's revolutionary drumless trio. He worked with Hungarian guitarist Attila Zoller between 1965 and 1967 and also with Archie Shepp, playing on Shepp's side of the famous *New Thing At Newport* and on one track of his classic *On This Night*. In 1969 he played in an orchestral project led by John Lennon and Yoko Ono; with the improvising band Gong (*Magick Brother*) and with Mike Westbrook. Increasingly involved with the European scene, he played with Rolf and Joachim Kuhn (1969) and with English saxophonist John Surman and fellow-expatriate drummer Stu Martin as the Trio (1969-71). In 1971, in conjunction with Dave Holland, he led a whole band of bass players. In 1976 he began recording for ECM Records (*Mountainscape*), an arrangement that lasted until 1983. In the latter year he played and recorded with the classical ensemble Accroche Note and in 1988 with Derek Bailey and Company. 1989 saw him involved with several of British bassist Barry John Guy's projects. Possessed of an acute rhythmic intelligence, Barre Philips is an important link between the free jazz of 60s America and the European free improvisation scene.

Albums: *Unaccompanied Barre* (1968), with John Surman, Stu Martin *The Trio* (1970), *Alors!!!* (1970), with Dave Holland *Music From Two Basses* (1971), *Mountainscape* (1976), *Three Day Moon* (1978), *Journal Violine II* (1980), *Music By* (1981), *Call Me When You Get There* (1983), with Accroche Note *En Concert* (1983), with the Trio *By Contact* (1987, rec. 1971), with Derek Bailey *Figuring* (1988), with Company *Once* (1988), *Camouflage* (1989), *Naxos* (1990), with Jon Rose *Violin Music For Restaurants* (1991).

Phillips, Joe 'Flip'

b. 26 March 1915, New York City, New York, USA. After playing in small groups in the New York area, Phillips joined Woody Herman's First Herd in 1944. By the time he left the band, Phillips's reputation as a tenor saxophonist was established nationally and on record. He then became a member of Norman Granz's touring package, Jazz At The Philharmonic, a move which raised his international profile. He remained with JATP until the late 50s, toured Europe with Benny Goodman and then opted for working outside music by day and leading a small group by night in Florida. This lifestyle continued for 15 years, then, in 1975, Phillips moved to New York and became more active in jazz, touring Europe into the late 80s. A magnificent ballad player, early in his career Phillips was often obliged to play uptempo rabble-rousers which he did with enormous vitality. In later years, in control of his repertoire, he developed the ballad side of his playing and proved himself to be an outstanding interpreter of great songs.

Selected albums: *Flip* (1949), *Flip Phillips Quintet* i (1951), *Flip Phillips Trio* (1952), with JATP *Live At The Nichigeki*

Theatre Tokyo (1953), *Flip Phillips Quintet* ii (1954), *Your Place Or Mine?* (1963), *Phillips' Head* (1975), *Together* (1978), *Flipenstein* (1981), *Flip Phillips And His Swedish Friends* (1982), *A Melody From The Sky* (Doctor Jazz 1986), *A Real Swinger* (1988), *A Sound Investement* (Concord 1988), *The Claw* (Chiaroscuro 1988), *Try A Little Tenderness* (Chiaroscuro1993).

Phillips, Sid

b. 14 June 1902, London, England, d. 23 May 1973. Deeply immersed in the music business from childhood, Phillips played clarinet in various bands, including one led by his brothers, and also worked in music publishing and for record companies. In the early 30s he was staff arranger for the popular band led by Bert Ambrose and later became a member of the band. He also began leading his own small group in the 30s, but it was the bands he led from 1949 onwards that built his reputation. Broadcasting regularly on the radio, Phillips also recorded and his band became one of the best-known dixieland groups in the UK. Among the many fine musicians he employed at one time or another were George Shearing, Kenny Ball and Tommy Whittle. A gutsy, full-toned clarinettist, Phillips was also a skilful arranger and composed jazz-oriented dance tunes and several classical works. Changes in popular taste meant that from the 60s onwards his music was not in great demand, but he continued working until his death in 1973.

Albums: *Sid Phillips And His Band* i (60s), *Stardust* (60s), *Sid Phillips And His Band* (1962), *Sid Phillips And His Band* iii (1964), *Rhythm Is Our Business* (c.1970), *Sid Phillips And His Great Band Play Stomps, Rags And Blues* (1975), *Sid Phillips Plays Barrelhouse Piano* (1975). Selected compilations: *H'ors D'Ouvres* (1976), *Anthology, Volume 1 - Chicago* (1976), *Anthology, Volume 2 - Lonesome Road* (1977), *Anthology, Volume 3 - Way Down Yonder In New Orleans* (1978), *The Best Of Sid Phillips* (1977), *Goody Goody* (President 1983), *I Got Rhythm* (MFP 1990).

Picou, Alphonse

b. 19 October 1878, New Orleans, Louisiana, USA, d. 4 February 1961. An enormously popular musician in his home town, clarinettist Picou worked in numerous bands, whether playing dance music, jazz or military marches. It was his adaptation of a piccolo descant in a military band piece for use in a performance of a jazz number, 'High Society', that ensured Picou's immortality. That descant became a part of 'High Society' and ever afterwards the skills of New Orleans and dixieland clarinettists were measured by the way they played his variation. Relatively inactive in the 30s, Picou returned to the jazz scene during the Revival Movement, recording with Kid Rena in 1940. He worked on through the 40s and the 50s, dying in 1961. A skilful player, Picou's work suggests that for all his fame he was much less committed to jazz than many of his fellow townsmen. Nevertheless, as long as dixieland jazz is played, clarinettists the world over will have to prove themselves by performing Picou's 'test piece'.

Selected albums: with Kid Rena *Down On The Delta* (1940), *Alphonse Picou And His Paddock Jazz Band* (1953).

Pierce, Nat

b. 16 July 1925, Somerville, Massachusetts, USA, d. 10 June 1992. After studying and playing in local bands in his home state, Pierce worked with a handful of name bands, including Larry Clinton's, then briefly led his own band in 1949-51, instigating what is commonly regarded among fellow musicians as being the birth of the so-called 'rehearsal band' concept. In 1951 he joined Woody Herman, in whose band he played piano, arranged, and acted as straw boss until 1955. Thereafter he arranged for several bands and singers, including Count Basie and Ella Fitzgerald. In great demand as a session musician, he made countless record dates, on which he played with almost everyone who was anyone in the upper echelons of jazz. In 1957 he appeared in the television programme *The Sound Of Jazz*, on which he was responsible for several of the arrangements, including the classic performance of 'Dickie's Dream' which featured Basie, Roy Eldridge, Coleman Hawkins, Ben Webster, Joe Newman, Vic Dickenson and Gerry Mulligan among many others. In the late 50s he led a band which included Buck Clayton and which had the doubtful honour of being the last band to play at Harlem's 'Home of Happy Feet', the Savoy Ballroom, before it closed forever. Also in the late 50s he worked with Pee Wee Russell, Quincy Jones, Fitzgerald, Hawkins and others. In 1960 he returned to Herman for a brief spell as road manager and was back again the following year, this time in his former capacities, remaining until 1966. In the early 70s Pierce relocated to the west coast where he played in several bands, including those led by Louie Bellson and Bill Berry. In 1975 he joined Frank Capp as co-leader of a big band that mostly played his arrangements, many of which were in the Basie/Kansas City tradition. This band, which became known as Juggernaut, continued to play through the 80s and on into the 90s. Pierce also continued to write for other musicians and to appear on record dates. He toured extensively, appearing in the UK and Europe with several Basie-alumni bands and other concert packages. A superb pianist in his own right, Pierce's eclecticism was such that at various times he appeared at the piano as substitute for three of the best-known piano-playing bandleaders in big band history: Basie, Duke Ellington and Stan Kenton. In small groups he proved the lynch-pin of the rhythm section, swinging with unflagging enthusiasm. As an arranger, especially for big bands, Pierce made an invaluable contribution to jazz, effortlessly creating swinging charts which underscored the 60s success stories of both Herman and Basie. Apart from his performing and arranging, Pierce was also a major source of information on many aspects of jazz history; a history which, through his personal dedication and extensive contributions, he helped to create.

Selected albums: *The Nat Pierce-Dick Collins Nonet* (1954), *Nat Pierce And His Band* (1955), *The Nat Pierce Octet* (1955), *Kansas City Memories* (1956), *The Nat Pierce Big Band At The Savoy Ballroom* (1957), with various artists *The Real Sound Of Jazz* (1957, television soundtrack), *The Ballad Of Jazz Street* (1961), *Juggernaut* (1977), *Juggernaut Live At Century Plaza* (1978), *5400 North...In Concert With Mary Ann McCall* (1978), *Juggernaut Strikes Again* (1981), *Boston Bustout* (Hep Jazz 1981), *Juggernaut Live At The Alleycat* (1986).

Pine, Courtney

b. 18 March 1964, London, England. Like many of his generation of young, black, British jazz musicians, Pine came from a reggae and funk background. He had been a member of Dwarf Steps, a hard-bop band consisting of Berklee College Of Music graduates, before joining reggae stars Clint Eastwood and General Saint. His interest in jazz was fostered when he participated in workshops run by John Stevens. In 1986 he depped for Sonny Fortune in Elvin Jones's band, and was involved in setting up the Jazz Warriors. He came to wider public notice as a result of playing with Charlie Watts' Orchestra, George Russell's European touring band and with Art Blakey at the Camden Jazz Festival. Blakey invited him to join the Messengers, but he decided to stay in Britain. In 1987 he played at the Bath Festival with the Orchestre National de Jazz. By that time his reputation had spread far beyond jazz circles, and his first album was a massive seller by jazz standards. He appeared before a huge world-wide audience in the Nelson Mandela 70th Birthday Concert at Wembley, backing dancers IDJ, and was the main subject of a number of television arts programmes about jazz in the late 80s, his smart image and articulate seriousness about his music enabling him to communicate with many people who had never before given jazz a hearing. He became much in demand for film and television, and appeared, for example, on the soundtrack of Alan Parker's *Angel Heart* and over the titles of BBC television's *Juke Box Jury*. His current quartet comprises young American luminaries Kenny Kirkland (piano), Charnett Moffett (bass) and Marvin 'Smitty' Smith (drums). Many of his admirers feel that in some ways his high media profile has hindered his development, but his talent, dedication and level-headedness have ensured that he has never been diverted by the hype, and his most recent work illustrates an emotional depth matching his undoubted technical brilliance. He has also continued to play in reggae and other pop contexts (*Closer To Home*), and is a frequent collaborator with UK soul singer Mica Paris.

Albums: *Journey To The Urge Within* (Island 1986), *Destiny's Song And The Image Of Pursuance* (Island 1988), *The Vision's Tale* (Island 1989), *Within The Realms Of Our Dreams* (Island 1991), *Closer To Home* (Island 1992), *To The Eyes Of Creation* (Island 1992).

Pinski Zoo

Like a more user-friendly Last Exit, the loud and joyful Pinski Zoo has combined the free jazz of the 60s, the funk-fusion beat of the 70s and the technology of the 80s to produce a powerful, accessible brand of harmolodics. Head-keeper Jan Kopinski claims Yma Sumac, Jimi Hendrix and John Coltrane as his seminal influences, though clearly Albert Ayler and Ornette Coleman's Prime Time have also been inspirations. The band, one of the most lively and exhilarating working units around, was born in Nottingham, like Kopinski and fellow-founder member Steve Iliffe. Earlier editions included Tim Bullock (drums), Tim Nolan (bass) and Mick Nolan (percussion/vocals), but by the early 90s the personnel comprised Kopinski (soprano and tenor saxophones), Iliffe (keyboards), Karl Wesley Bingham (electric bass) and Steve Harris (drums). The unit won the best small group title in the 1990 *Wirel Guardian* readers' poll, and their albums *Rare Breeds* and *East Rail* were highly acclaimed by UK jazz critics. Kopinski and Bingham are two of the most exciting and individual talents in contemporary jazz.

Albums: *Introduce Me To The Doctor* (1981), *The Dizzy Dance Record* (1982), *The City Can't Have It Back* (1983), *Speak* (1984), *Live In Warsaw* (1985), *Rare Breeds* (JCR 1988), *East Rail East* (JCR 1990), *De-Icer* (Slam 1994).

Pizzarelli, Bucky

b. 9 January 1926, Paterson, New Jersey, USA. Although a self-taught guitarist, Pizzarelli quickly showed a comprehensive grasp of the guitar's potential. He played in large dancebands and small combos, worked as a studio musician, and as accompanist to singers, and even ventured into the classical field. He became a regular sideman with the later bands formed by Benny Goodman and in the 70s also appeared with Soprano Summit, the fine small band co-led by Bob Wilber and Kenny Davern, sometimes playing banjo. The 70s also saw him working with fellow guitarist George Barnes and with Zoot Sims, Bud Freeman and Stéphane Grappelli. He has also toured as a solo and in the 80s formed a duo with his son, John Pizzarelli, also a gifted guitarist, with whom he recorded the album *Swinging Sevens*. One of the finest of the mainstream guitarists in jazz, Pizzarelli remains rather less well known than many of his fellows, a state of affairs which seems likely to change in the 90s thanks to the continued high standard of his performances. Selected albums: *Midnite Mood* (1960), *Green Guitar Blues* (1972), *Bucky Plays Bix: Bix Beiderbecke Arrangements By Bill Challis* (c.1973), *Nightwings* (1975), *Soprano Summit II* (1977), *Bucky's Bunch* (c.1977), *2 x 7 = Pizzarelli* (1980), *New York, New York/Sounds Of The Apple* (1980), *Love Songs* (1981), *The Cafe Pierre Trio* (1982), with John Pizzarelli *I'm Hip* (1983), with John Pizzarelli *Swinging Sevens* (1984), with John Pizzarelli *Hit That Jive, Jack* (1985), *Solo Flight* (Stash 1986), with John Pizzarelli *My Blue Heaven* (1990), *A Portrait* (1992). Compilation: *The Complete Guitar Duos (The Stash Sessions)* (Stash 1988).

Polcer, Ed

b. 10 February 1937, Paterson, New Jersey, USA. Polcer first displayed his musical talents at the age of six when he played the xylophone. He began playing cornet semi-professionally while studying engineering at university. The band there, Princeton's very own Stan Rubin's Tigertown Five, had the distinction of playing both at Carnegie Hall and at the 1956 wedding of Prince Rainier and Grace Kelly in Monaco. In the 50s Polcer played in New York's clubland, returning there perma-

nently after military service in the early 60s. Although gigging regularly at Jimmy Ryan's, the Metropole and other clubs, he remained a semi-pro, continuing his simultaneous business career. Throughout the 70s and into the mid-80s he was steadily more active in jazz, becoming a full-time musician in 1975 and taking on co-ownership of Eddie Condon's club. Apart from co-leading the house band (with Red Balaban, who was also co-owner of the club), he worked with a number of other bands, including recordings with Dick Wellstood and a spell in 1973 with Benny Goodman. In 1975 he toured the USA and Canada with Bob Greene's *World Of Jelly Roll Morton* show. In 1982 Polcer became president of the New York International Art of Jazz Organization, which promotes community and corporate involvement in jazz education and performance. Latterly, he has toured extensively, playing cornet and occasionally adding vibraphone too.

Albums: with Dick Wellstood, Jane Harvey *You Fats...Me Jane* (1975), with Red Balaban *A Night At The New Eddie Condon's* (1975), *Coast To Coast Swingin' Jazz* (Jazzology 1990).

Pollack, Ben

b. 22 June 1903, Chicago, Illinois, USA, d. 7 June 1971, Palm Springs, California, USA. After playing drums with the New Orleans Rhythm Kings in the early 20s, Pollack formed his own band, which he proceeded to stock with the best of the up-and-coming young white jazz and danceband musicians of the day. Among the future stars who played in Pollack's bands in the late 20s were Benny Goodman, Glenn Miller and Jack Teagarden. Despite this interest in fostering emerging jazz talent, Pollack was primarily concerned with commercial success and this led to a number of disputes that often ended with one or another of the musicians quitting. By the mid-30s, Pollack had largely given up drumming to direct the band and concern himself with business affairs, the drum chair being taken over by Ray Bauduc. In his band at this time were Yank Lawson, Gil Rodin and Eddie Miller; when another argument broke out the bulk of the band left to form a co-operative unit, at the head of which they placed Bob Crosby. Pollack formed a new band, featuring another rising star, Harry James, who quit in 1936 to join another former Pollack sideman, Goodman, who was by now the country's most famous bandleader. The years of accumulated resentments propelled Pollack into suing everyone in sight: Goodman, Crosby, Victor Records, Goodman's sponsors, the Camel Cigarette Co., and a motion picture company. The exact reason for some of this litigation is obscure but was presumably directed at recovering some of the financial benefits that had accrued to his protégés. For a while Pollack stopped performing regularly, although he remained in the music business, spending the 40s running a record company and acting as an agent. He also ran a restaurant and occasionally returned to bandleading, achieving a modest success in all these activities. His depression over what he saw as his rightful heritage going to others never fully lifted however, and he took his own life, by hanging, on 7 June 1971.

Selected compilations: *Ben Pollack And His Orchestra (1933-34)* (1979), *Futuristic Rhythm (1928-29)* (Saville 1983).

Pollock, Marilyn Middleton

b. 25 October 1947, Chicago, Illinois, USA. While still at college and university in Chicago, Pollock began singing with folk groups. In the late 60s she continued to sing folk locally and also performed with rock bands. In the early 70s her career encompassed radio and television commercials, tours of the USA with the rock bands Hurricane, Thunder and others, and continued activity as a folk singer. In the early 80s Pollock visited Ireland where she sang with the Chicago-based folk band, the Irish Ramblers. She continued to mix folk and rock performances in her repertoire then, in 1985, she relocated to Glasgow, Scotland. Her folk album, *Nobody Knows You*, won the British Music Retailers Association Award for Excellence in 1989. That same year she began singing jazz, appearing on *Yonder Come The Blues*. In 1990, she consolidated her acceptance as a jazz singer with an appearance at the Bude Festival and the following year joined the Max Collie band. Since then, although still active as a folk singer, Pollock's career has moved more towards jazz. She has recorded several albums and has appeared at numerous festivals including the Edinburgh International Festival and the Burnley Blues Festival at both of which she performed her one-woman show, *Those Women of the Vaudeville Blues*. In 1992, in addition to recording and touring clubs and festivals, both as a single and with Collie, she produced a new one-woman vaudeville blues show, *Jazz Me Blues*. A powerful and dynamic singer with great style and stage presence, Pollock's deep interest in and knowledge of the folk, blues and vaudeville traditions lend her repertoire considerable depth. Her vibrant voice, ranging through sensitivity to raunchiness, is well suited to the breadth and content of her repertoire and since her move to the UK she has established herself as a major contributor to the international jazz scene. In addition to singing, Pollock has also taught herself to play several instruments including guitar and flute.

Albums: *Nobody Knows You* (Fellside 1988), *Yonder Come The Blues* (1989), *Those Women Of The Blues* (Lake 1990), *Max Collie's Mardi Gras Vol. 2* (1991), *A Doll's House* (Fellside 1992).

Pomeroy, Herb

b. 15 April 1930, Gloucester, Massachusetts, USA. After extensive studies at what later became known as the Berklee College Of Music in Boston, Massachusetts, Pomeroy joined the faculty to become one of the most respected teachers of the trumpet in jazz. His experience as a performer included work with the big bands of Lionel Hampton and Stan Kenton and, although he also played in small groups with Charlie Parker and others, it is in a big band context that he has made his greatest mark. Numerous contemporary jazz stars have graduated from Berklee, many of them paying tribute to Pomeroy's contribution to their musical education. His big bands, usually formed from college students and graduates, maintain an enviably high standard of musicianship. Unlike many of the college and university bands, Pomeroy's are not merely showcases for exceptional musical ability but also display an awareness of the underlying emotional qualities of jazz. The fact that his students demonstrate a greater involvement in the music they play is a tribute to his dedication to pursuing aims that transcend the simple imparting of knowledge. Pomeroy has also taught at the Massachusetts Institute of Technology, the Lenox School of Jazz and was, in 1962, employed by the US State Department to direct the house orchestra at Radio Malaya.

Albums: *Jazz In A Stable* (1955), *Life Is A Many Splendoured Gig* (Fresh Sounds 1957), *Band In Boston* (1958), *Herb Pomeroy And His Orchestra* (1958), *Pramlatta's Hips: Live At The El Morocco* (1980).

Ponty, Jean-Luc

b. 29 September 1940, Avranches, France. Ponty grew up in an intensely musical home environment. His father ran a local music school, teaching violin, and his mother taught piano. He was a proficient pianist and violinist while still very young and at the age of 11 he added clarinet to his instrumental arsenal. After studying classical violin at the Paris Conservatoire, he became a professional musician but also developed an interest in jazz. For a while he divided his musical loyalty between the classical violin and jazz clarinet and tenor saxophone. However, he began to play jazz on violin, making this his chief activity from the mid-60s. He played with numerous European musicians (recording with Stuff Smith), sometimes as leader (in HLP). He visited the USA and UK, recording with Frank Zappa on the jazz-rock album *Hot Rats* ('It Must Be A Camel') and thereafter joined George Duke. Zappa later produced Ponty's *King Kong* in 1970. In the early 70s he experimented with free jazz, played again with Zappa on *Overnite Sensation*, as a member of the Mothers, and with John McLaughlin's Mahavishnu Orchestra, *Visions Of The Emerald Beyond* (1974). Subsequently, he led his own band playing jazz-rock and gaining a substantial international following. In the 80s he also recorded with other artists including Cleo Laine and Stéphane Grappelli. A master technician, Ponty was not the first violinist in jazz to use electronic enhancement but he was the first to integrate electronics fully into his playing style. Rather than settle merely for the greater volume, which had been enough for his predecessors, Ponty used electronics in a complex and advanced way. He uses a fully electric violin, not just an electronically-amplified instrument, and incorporates numerous devices to create effects. By switching from bop to rock to free jazz and back to bop again with bewildering ease, he continues to prove himself a musician of many styles and for all seasons of jazz fashion.

Selected albums: with Stuff Smith *Violin Summit* (1966), *Sunday Walk* (1967), *Electric Connection* (1968), with George Duke *The Jean-Luc Experience* (1969), *King Kong* aka *Cantaloupe Island* (Blue Note 1970), *Astrorama* (1970), *Open Strings* (1972), *Live In Montreux* (1972), *Portrait* (1972), *Upon The Wings Of Music* (1975), *Aurora* (Atlantic 1975), *Imaginary Voyage* (Atlantic 1976), *Enigmatic Ocean* (Atlantic 1977), *Cosmic Messenger* (Atlantic 1978), *A Taste For Passion* (1979), *Jean-Luc Ponty Live* (1979), *Sonata Erotica* (Atmosphere 1979), *Civilized Evil* (1980), *Mystical Adventures* (Atlantic 1981),

Individual Choice (Atlantic 1983), with George Benson, Chick Corea *Open Mind* (Atlantic 1984), *Fables* (Atlantic 1985), *The Gift Of Time* (Columbia 1987), *No Absolute Time* (Fnac 1993).

Porcino, Al

b. 14 May 1925, New York City, New York, USA. While still in his teenage years, Porcino joined the Louis Prima band where his high-note trumpet playing attracted excited attention. In the 40s he played in many of the leading big bands of the day, including those led by Tommy Dorsey, Gene Krupa, Stan Kenton and Woody Herman. In the 50s he again worked with Kenton and Herman among others such as Charlie Parker, Count Basie and Elliot Lawrence before settling in Los Angeles, where he did studio work and also made regular appearances in jazz groups, usually big bands including Terry Gibbs's 'dream bands'. He made many record dates with singers including Frank Sinatra, Sarah Vaughan, Ella Fitzgerald, Judy Garland and Ray Charles. He was co-leader with Med Flory of the Jazz Wave Orchestra. In the 60s he continued to play in big bands, adding Buddy Rich and the Thad Jones-Mel Lewis Jazz Orchestra to his list of credits. He rejoined Herman again and also formed his own band, with which he accompanied Mel Tormé. His career continued along similar lines in the 70s and then, in 1977, he settled in Munich, Germany, where he worked with radio bands and led his own big band. During the 80s he made many concert appearances with his big band, some of which were recorded, often in company with visiting American jazzmen such as Al Cohn. One of the outstanding lead trumpeters in big band history, Porcino set remarkably high standards of performance for himself and for his section mates and any band in which he played was assured of a first-rate trumpet section. His German band of the late 80s clearly benefits from his remarkable leadership.

Albums: with Stan Kenton *Contemporary Concepts* (1955), with Med Flory *The Jazz Wave Orchestra* (1957), with Terry Gibbs *Dream Band* (1959), with Gibbs *Live At The Summit* (1961), with Buddy Rich *Mercy, Mercy* (1968), with Jones-Lewis *Consummation* (1969), with Woody Herman *The Raven Speaks* (1972), with Mel Tormé *Live At The Maisonette* (1974), with Jones-Lewis *New Life* (1975), with Jones-Lewis *Live In Munich* (1976), with Al Cohn *In Oblivion* (Jazz Mark 1986), with Cohn *The Final Performance* (1987).

Potter, Tommy

b. 21 September 1918, Philadelphia, Pennsylvania, USA, d. March 1988. After taking up the bass in his early 20s, having previously mastered piano and guitar, Potter was soon involved in early bebop. He played in the bebop-oriented big band led by Billy Eckstine in the mid-40s, then joined Charlie Parker. He recorded with Parker and many other leading bebop musicians, including Fats Navarro, Max Roach and Bud Powell. In the 50s and early 60s he worked with a broader range of musicians, such as Stan Getz, Sonny Rollins, Miles Davis, Artie Shaw and Harry Edison, before retiring from full-time playing in the mid-60s. One of the leading bass players of bebop, Potter set a high standard of performance with clearly articulated lines and impeccable timekeeping.

Albums: *The Sonny Rollins Quartet* (1954), *The Tommy Potter Sextet In Sweden* (1956). Compilations: with Charlie Parker *The Legendary Dial Masters, Volume 4 (1946-47)* (1983), with Parker *The Complete Savoy Sessions, Volume 3 (1947)* (1985).

Powell, Bud

b. Earl Powell, 27 September 1924, New York City, New York, USA, d. 1 August 1966. After learning to play the piano in the classical tradition while still a child, Powell began working around New York's Coney Island, where he played in a band featuring Valaida Snow around 1940. During the next couple of years he became a regular visitor to Minton's Playhouse, where he heard the first stirrings of bebop. In particular he was influenced by Thelonious Monk's harmonic innovations but quickly developed his own style. Despite his leanings towards the new music, he was hired by Cootie Williams for his big band. During his stay with Williams he was arrested in Philadelphia and reportedly badly beaten by police officers, an event usually cited as the beginning of the mental problems which were to dog him for the rest of his life. He retained his links with events on 52nd Street and was soon one of the most striking of the bebop pianists. By 1945, however, he was displaying the first overt signs of acute mental instability and was hospitalized - the first of many incarcerations in mental hospitals, during some of which he was given electro-convulsive therapy.

Throughout the 50s he worked regularly, appearing with all the leading figures of bebop, including Charlie Parker, Dizzy Gillespie and Max Roach. During this same period his mental instability increased, the sudden death in 1956 of his brother Richie Powell adding to his problems. Additionally, his mental and physical health were being gravely damaged by his growing dependence on narcotics and alcohol. At the end of the decade he left New York for Paris, where he spent three years of popular success but was still plagued by his mental and addiction troubles. Back in New York in 1964, his performances became fewer and were frequently fraught with emotional and technical breakdowns. He died on 1 August 1966. At his performing peak, Powell's playing style displayed a startling brilliance, with remarkable ideas being executed with absolute technical mastery, often at extraordinary speeds. By the late 50s his personal problems were such that he rarely played at his best, although the flow of ideas continued, as can be deduced from some of his compositions from these years. He was a major figure in bebop and an influence, either directly or indirectly, upon most pianists in jazz since the 50s.

Selected albums: *Jazz Giant* (Verve 1950), with Charlie Parker *One Night In Birdland* (1950), with Parker *Jazz At Massey Hall: The Quintet Of The Year* (1953), *Broadcast Performances Vols 1 & 2* (1953), *Inner Fires* (1953), *Ornithology* (1953), *The Bud Powell Trio: The Verve Sessions* (1955), *Bouncing With Bud* (Storyville 1955), *The Lonely One* (1955), *Blues In The Closet* (1956), *Strictly Powell* (1956), *Swinging With Bud* (1957), *The Bud* (1957), *Bud Powell In Paris* i (1960), *Bud Powell In Concert* (1960), *Oscar Pettiford Memorial* (1960), *Bud Powell In Europe*

(1961), *A Portrait Of Thelonious* (CBS 1961), *The Bud Powell Trio At The Golden Circle Vols 1 & 2* (1962), *The Bud Powell Trio In Copenhagen* (1962), *Bud Powell '62* (1962), *At The Golden Circle Vols 1-4* (Steeplechase 1962 recordings), *Budism* (Steeplechase 1962 recordings), *Bud Powell In Paris* ii (1963), *Blues For Bouffemont/The Invisible Cage* (1964), *The Bud Powell Quartet* (1964), *The Bud Powell Trio* (1964), *Salt Peanuts* (Black Lion 1964 recording), *Ups 'N' Downs* (1965), *The Return Of Bud Powell* (1965), *At The Blue Note Cafe, 1961* (1981), *The Complete Essen Jazz Festival Concert* (1988, rec. 1960). Compilations: The Genius Of Bud Powell (Verve 1978, 1950-51 recordings), *The Best Years* (1978), *The Amazing Bud Powell, Volumes 1 & 2 (1949-53)* (Blue Note 1982), *The Amazing Bud Powell, Volume 3 (1949-53)* (Blue Note 1984). Further reading: *The Glass Enclosure: The Life Of Bud Powell,* Alan Groves with Alyn Shipton.

Powell, Mel

b. 12 February 1923, New York City, New York, USA. As a teenager Powell played piano at Nick's in New York City and soon thereafter joined Muggsy Spanier. His exceptional and at the time eclectic gifts attracted the attention of Benny Goodman, whom he joined in 1941. During his stint with Goodman he wrote several interesting charts, sometimes for his own compositions, which included 'The Earl', 'Clarinet A La King' and 'Mission To Moscow'. Powell was then briefly on the staff at CBS before military service threatened to disrupt his career. In fact, his army service had the opposite effect and he was soon a member of Glenn Miller's Army Air Force band, playing in the dance band and in the small jazz group, the Uptown Hall Gang. After the war Powell made a few jazz records in Los Angeles, then in the early 50s recorded again with Ruby Braff and Paul Quinichette; he also appeared with Goodman around this same time, but that was the last the jazz world heard of him until the mid-80s. Powell had turned to classical music, playing largely for his own pleasure, teaching and composing classical music. During this same period Powell's health deteriorated and his movements were severely limited. However, his playing ability was unimpaired and his return to the jazz scene, with appearances on the Caribbean jazz cruise ship, the *SS Norway*, and new recordings showed that he had lost none of his capacity for performing inventive, dexterous solos.
Albums: *Classics In Swing: All Star Groups* (Commodore 1942 recording), *The Mel Powell Septet* (1953), *Mel Powell And His All Stars At Carnegie Hall* (1954), with Ruby Braff *Thingamagig* (Vanguard 1954), with Paul Quinichette *Trio* (1954), *Easy Swing* (Vanguard 1954), *Mel Powell And His Band* (1954), *Out On A Limb* (1955), *Bouquet* (Vogue 1980), *Piano Forte* (1986), *The Return Of Mel Powell* (1987). Compilation: with Joe Bushkin *The World Is Waiting, 1942-46* (1982).

Powell, Richie

b. 5 September 1931, New York City, New York, USA, d. 26 June 1956. After studying at college and with Mary Lou Williams, Powell emulated his older brother, Bud Powell, and embarked on a career in jazz. He played with Jackie McLean, a friend and neighbour, then joined Johnny Hodges. Attracted to bebop, Powell became a member of the Max Roach-Clifford Brown quintet in 1954. This engagement was one which allowed him to begin a potentially interesting development, but before he attained his full musical maturity he was killed in a road accident, with Brown, in 1956.
Albums: *Clifford Brown With Max Roach* (1955), with Clifford Brown, Max Roach *Study In Brown* (1955), *Sonny Rollins Plus Four* (1956). Compilation: *More Of Johnny Hodges* (1951-54).

Powell, Rudy

b. Everard Stephen Powell, 28 October 1907, New York City, New York, USA, d. 30 October 1976. Born and raised in a tough district of New York, Powell was one of a number of young men from the same neighbourhood who turned to music and enjoyed distinguished careers (among others was Benny Carter). Taking up clarinet and alto saxophone, Powell worked extensively in the vibrant New York club scene of the late 20s and early 30s including stints with Cliff Jackson, Rex Stewart, Red Allen and, most notably, Fats Waller. In the late 30s and early 40s, Powell's skilful musicianship meant that he was in demand as a sideman in several big bands including those led by Claude Hopkins, Fletcher Henderson and Don Redman. In the late 40s he was with Cab Calloway and in the 50s and 60s he worked with several small groups and also with singers Jimmy Rushing and Ray Charles. In the mid-60s he played with the Saints And Sinners band and then played around his home town until the end of his life. An exciting, hot clarinet player, Powell's playing made a distinctive contribution to many Waller recordings.
Albums: with Fats Waller *My Very Good Friend The Milkman* (1935), *Saints And Sinners In Europe* (1968).

Powell, Seldon

b. 15 November 1928, Lawrenceville, Virginia, USA. Studying and working mostly in New York, tenor saxophonist Powell played and recorded extensively throughout the 50s. His musical associates were many and varied, including Lucky Millinder, Sy Oliver, Neal Hefti, Johnny Richards, Billy VerPlanck and Benny Goodman. Aided by his early training in classical music and his ability to play other instruments, especially the flute, Powell found work in the studios throughout the 60s and 70s. Nevertheless, he was active in jazz, recording with musicians such as Buddy Rich, Louis Bellson, Richard 'Groove' Holmes, Gato Barbieri, Dizzy Gillespie and Anthony Braxton. Powell's early training has allowed him to develop twin careers but within the framework of largely mainstream jazz he has established a sound reputation. As an improvisatory soloist, his work is perhaps less impressive than when he works within a tightly orchestrated framework where he excels.
Albums: *Seldon Powell Plays* (1955), *Seldon Powell Sextet* (1956), with Billy VerPlanck *Jazz For Play Girls* (1957), with others *We Paid Our Dues* (1961).

Powell, Teddy

b. 1 March 1906, Oakland, California, USA. As a boy Powell studied violin and music theory privately, then attended the San Francisco Conservatory of Music. In 1927 he was playing guitar and banjo with Abe Lyman's band, staying with them until 1935 when he became a radio producer for an advertising agency. He also branched out as a songwriter, with hits such as 'Take Me Back To My Boots And Saddle', 'All I Need Is You', 'Snake Charmer' and 'March Winds And April Showers'. Royalties from these and other songs helped finance a big band in 1939, which included some key personnel from the Tommy Dorsey and Benny Goodman bands and had Ray Conniff contributing some arrangements. At first recording for Decca, some of the band's tracks appeared in the UK on Brunswick (Conniff's 'Feather Merchant's Ball'/'Teddy Bear Boogie' by Powell). After a year Powell moved to the Bluebird label, and Regal-Zonophone issued only four tracks in the UK: 'Straight Eight Boogi'/'Ode To Spring' and 'Sans Culottes'/'In Pinetops' Footsteps', all the work of new arranger Bob Mersey. The band opened at New York's Famous Door club to local acclaim but had less success further afield and, returning to Manhattan, Powell bought the club as a showcase for the group. It was a good, clean-sounding outfit with imaginative scores by Mersey and Conniff, and the leader maintained his policy of using jazzmen in key positions no matter how commercial the band's output. Peggy Mann and Gene Barry were the band's vocalists. After the swing era Powell adopted a more commercial policy for hotel work and eventually left the band business to return to songwriting and publishing.

Pozo, Chano

b. Luciano Pozo y Gonzales, 7 June 1915, Havana, Cuba, d. 2 December 1948, New York, USA. Drummer and vocalist Pozo's first appearance in the USA was at a Carnegie Hall concert in September 1947, at which he played with Dizzy Gillespie. Thereafter he worked regularly with Gillespie, making a number of records which were enormously influential on many jazzmen who responded to the intriguing Latin-American rhythms he used. In December 1948, before the two men could fully exploit what was clearly a potentially exciting musical relationship, Pozo was murdered, shot in a Harlem bar. Selected compilations: all with Dizzy Gillespie *Dizzy Gillespie Big Band* (1947-49 recordings), *Afro Cuban Suite* (1948 recordings), *Melodic Revolution* (1948 recordings), with Arsenio Rodriguez, Machito *Legendary Sessions* (Fresh Sounds 1993).

Previn, André

b. 6 April 1929, Berlin, Germany. After studying music in Berlin and Paris, Previn came to the USA in 1938 when his family emigrated. Resident in Los Angeles, he continued his studies and while still at school worked as a jazz pianist and as an arranger in the film studios. From the mid-40s he made records with some measure of success, but it was in the middle of the following decade that he achieved his greatest renown. The breakthrough came with a series of jazz albums with Shelly

Manne, the first of which featured music from the popular show *My Fair Lady*. Previn recorded with lyricist Dory Langdon, who he later married. The marriage broke-up in 1965 and was controversially chronicled in Dory Previn's later solo recordings. In the 60s Previn continued to divide his time between jazz and studio work but gradually his interest in classical music overtook these other fields. By the 70s he was established as one of the world's leading classical conductors. His term as conductor for the London Symphony Orchestra saw him emerge as a popular personality, which involved him television advertising and making celebrated cameo appearances for light-entertainers such as Morecambe And Wise. He became conductor of the Pittsburg Symphony Orchestra in 1976 and later the London Philharmonic, the Los Angeles Philharmonica. He continues to involve himself in many facets of music throughout the 80s and into the 90s. In 1992, a jazz album with opera singer Dame Kiri Te Kanawa and jazz bass player Ray Brown was released.
Selected albums: *Previn At Sunset* (Black Lion 1945), *André Previn All-Stars* (1946), *André Previn Plays Fats Waller* (1953), *Let's Get Away From It All* (1955), *But Beautiful* (1956), with Shelly Manne *My Fair Lady* i (1956), *André Previn And His Friends: Li'l Abner* (1957), *André And Dory Previn* (1957), *Double Play* (1957), *Pal Joey* (1957), *Gigi* (Original Jazz Classics 1958), *Pal Joey* (Original Jazz Classics 1958), *Sessions, Live* (1958), *André Previn Plays Songs By Vernon Duke* (Original Jazz Classics 1958), *King Size* (1958), *André Previn Plays Songs By Jerome Kern* (Original Jazz Classics 1959), *West Side Story* (Original Jazz Classics 1959), with the David Rose Orchestra *Secret Songs For Young Lovers* (1959), *The Previn Scene* (c.1959), *Composer, Arranger, Conductor, Pianist* (60s), *The Magic Moods Of André Previn* (60s), *Like Love* (1960), *André Previn* (1960), *Give My Regards To Broadway* (1960), *Thinking Of You* (1960), *Music From Camelot* (1960), *André Previn Plays Harold Arlen* (1961), *A Touch Of Elegance* (1961), *André Previn And J.J. Johnson Play Mack The Knife And Bilbao Song* (1961), *André Previn And J.J. Johnson* (c.1962), *Two For The See-saw* (c.1962), *Sittin' On A Rainbow* (1962), *The Light Fantastic: A Tribute To Fred Astaire* (c.1963), *4 To Go!* (1963), *André Previn In Hollywood* (1963), *Soft And Swinging* (1964), *Sound Stage* (1964), *My Fair Lady* ii (1964), *Previn At Sunset* (1975), with Itzhak Perlman *A Different Kind Of Blues* (HMV 1981), with Perlman *It's A Breeze* (c.1981), *After Hours* (Telarc 1989), *Uptown* (Telarc 1990), *Old Friends* (Telarc 1992).
Further reading: *André Previn*, Michael Freedland. *Music Face To Face*, André Previn. *Orchestra*, André Previn. *André Previn's Guide To The Orchestra*, André Previn. *No Minor Chords: My Days In Hollywood*, André Previn.

Prevost, Eddie

b. 22 June 1942, Hitchin, Hertfordshire, England. As a teenager Prevost drummed for various trad and skiffle bands and later played jazz. In 1965 he, along with saxophonist Leslie Gare and guitarist Keith Rowe, formed AMM, an *avant garde*, improvising chamber group which remains as radical, uncompromising and *sui generis* in 1992 as it was at its inception.

AMM has been one of Prevost's major projects for most of the last 30 years. Very active in all kinds of free improvisation, Prevost frequently draws attention to the political resonances of playing free music - he also gives lectures and writes articles. His quartet, with Larry Stabbins (tenor saxophone), Veryan Weston (piano) and Marcio Mattos (bass), performed throughout the 70s and 80s and Prevost has also recorded with the collective groups Supersession, Resoundings and the Free Jazz Quartet, releasing their (and his) albums on his own label, Matchless Records. A 1987 album, *Flayed*, on the Californian Silent label, featured Prevost on one side only playing solo. In 1990, with AMM colleagues Gare and Rowe, Prevost formed The Masters Of Disorientation; in 1991 he undertook a brief UK tour in a duo with pianist Marilyn Crispell. An expert percussionist in every mode of improvisation, Prevost cites Max Roach and Ed Blackwell as the jazz drummers he most admires. Albums: *Now-Here-This-Then* (Spotlite 1977), *Live, Volumes 1 & 2* (Matchless 1979), *Continuum* (Matchless 1985), with Resoundings *Resound* (1986), *Supersession* (Matchless 1988, rec. 1984), with Organum *Flayed* (1987), with the Free Jazz Quartet *Premonitions* (1989).

Price, Jesse

b. 1 May 1909, Memphis, Tennessee, USA, d. 19 April 1974. After playing drums locally, Price toured with blues singers (including Ida Cox) and tent shows until 1934, when he settled in Kansas City. There he worked in several territory bands and helped establish the free-flowing rhythmic pulse which is at the heart of the Kansas City style of jazz. He led his own band, was a familiar figure at after-hours jam sessions and then joined Harlan Leonard's Rockets. In the early 40s he worked briefly with Ella Fitzgerald and with the big bands of Louis Armstrong, Stan Kenton, Count Basie and Benny Carter. Despite his importance in the early development of the style refined and polished by such peers as Jo Jones, Price worked in comparative obscurity during his later years and by the end of the 60s was in semi-retirement. In 1971 he appeared at the Monterey Jazz Festival as part of the 'Kansas City Revisited' set, leading a band which included Harry Edison, Jimmy Forrest and Big Joe Turner.
Compilations: *Harlan Leonard Vol. 2* (1940 recordings), *Stan Kenton's Greatest Hits* (1943-51 recordings).

Price, Sammy

b. 6 October 1908, Honey Grove, Texas, USA, d. May 1992. After studying alto horn and piano at schools in Texas, Price won a dancing contest. Arising from this he was invited to tour with the Alphonso Trent band. Back in Texas he accompanied singers on record dates, playing occasional club gigs. He also formed a band of his own, then toured with a succession of popular entertainers. By 1930 he was becoming known in and around Kansas City, but by 1937 was resident in New York where he became house pianist for Decca, playing on countless record dates, mostly with singers. The 40s saw him working as a solo act, leading his own small band, the Bluesicians, and working with Sidney Bechet. Price also found time for a brief

European tour in 1948. During the 50s he divided his time between Texas and New York, playing clubs and recording with artists such as Henry 'Red' Allen. In the 60s he was active in New York and once again toured Europe, a pattern of work which continued through the following decade and into the 80s, sometimes in company with other veterans like Doc Cheatham. Price was an effective singer and his blues piano playing was of a very high standard.
Selected albums: *Blues And Boogie* (1955), *Sammy Price: Concert In Fontainebleau/The Price Is Right* (1956), *Piano Solo* (1956), *Sidney Bechet With Sammy Price's Bluesicians Live In Paris* (1956), *Sammy Price And Doc Cheatham* (1958), *Rib Joint* (1959), *Sammy Price And His All Stars* (1959), *Sammy Price And His Bluesicians* (Circle 1961), *Midnight Boogie* (1969), *Barrelhouse And Blues* (1969), *Blues On My Mind* (1969), *Texas And Louisiana Piano* (1969, one side only), *Fire* (1975), *Rockin' Boogie* (1975), *Boogie And Jazz Classics* (1975), *The New Sammy Price* (1975), *Sammy Price With Fessor's Big City Band* (1975), with Torben Petersen *The Boogie Woogie Twins* (1975), *Just Right* (1977), *Blues And Boogie-Woogie* (1978), with Cheatham *Black Beauty: A Tribute To Black American Songwriters* (1979), *Sweet Substitute* (1979), *Play It Again, Sam* (Whiskey Women And Song 1983).
Further reading: *What Do They Want?*, Sammy Price.

Priestley, Brian

b. 10 July 1946, Manchester, England. Priestley studied piano as a child, later playing in bands whilst studying at university. In the early 70s he wrote arrangements for the National Youth Jazz Orchestra and played in various small groups. Later he was co-leader with Dave Gelly of Stylus. He worked with Alan Cohen on the music of Duke Ellington, recording 'Black, Brown, And Beige' in 1972 and making a public performance at the 1988 Ellington Convention. In the late 80s and early 90s, he led his own group, the Special Septet, recording both a tribute album to Ellington and a live concert with ex-Ellington musician, Bill Berry. In addition to his playing and arranging, Priestley was for many years a regular broadcaster on BBC Radio London. He has also written several books, including works on Charles Mingus, Charlie Parker and John Coltrane, and has contributed articles to several leading music magazines. With Ian Carr and Digby Fairweather he is co-author of *Jazz: The Essential Companion*.
Albums: with Alan Cohen *Black, Brown, And Beige* (1972), with Bill Berry *Live At The Pizza Express* (1987), *Love You Gladly* (Cadillac 1989), with Berry *Bilberry Jam* (1990).

Prime Time (see Coleman, Ornette)

Privin, Bernie

b. 12 February 1919, New York City, New York, USA. A self-taught musician, by his late teens Privin was playing trumpet professionally in dance bands and quickly graduated to some of the best big bands of the swing era, including those of Bunny Berigan, Tommy Dorsey and Artie Shaw (with whom he was featured soloist). In the early 40s he was with Charlie Barnet and Benny Goodman and during World War II played in Glenn Miller's Army Air Force band. After the war he made a brief return to Goodman but then entered studio work, where he remained until the late 60s. In later years he worked in Europe, seizing many opportunities to show that despite his advancing years he still retained much of the biting tone that had characterized his earlier work.

Selected albums: *Bernie Privin And His Orchestra* (1956), *The Bernie Privin Quintet In Sweden* (1969). Compilation: with Artie Shaw *Deux Grandes Annees - In The Blue Room/In The Cafe Rouge (1938-39)* (1983).

Procope, Russell

b. 11 August 1908, New York City, New York, USA, d. 21 January 1981. A neighbour of Benny Carter, Rudy Powell and Bobby Stark, Procope played clarinet and alto saxophone in New York clubs in his late teens and when he was 20 years old recorded with Jelly Roll Morton. A year later he was a member of Carter's big band, then was successively with Chick Webb, Fletcher Henderson, Tiny Bradshaw, Teddy Hill and Andy Kirk. His apprenticeship well and truly served, Procope had to wait until the end of World War II and his army discharge before entering the post for which he had been unconsciously grooming himself. From 1946 until 1974 he was a member of the Duke Ellington orchestra, with only a brief aside in the Wilbur De Paris band in 1961. After Ellington's death, Procope worked in a number of Ellington-inspired small groups and also in the pit band for the show *Ain't Misbehavin'*. His long spell with Ellington was unspectacular, he was a section man rather than a soloist and as such provided the kind of solid base the Ellington band sometimes lacked when its less reliable members had other things on their minds. When he did solo, on such features as 'Mood Indigo', he revealed a warm and full-toned clarinet style that recalled New Orleans rather than New York.

Selected albums: with Duke Ellington *Masterpieces* (1950), *Russell Procope And His Orchestra* (1956), *Duke Ellington's Seventieth Birthday Concert* (1969). Compilation: *John Kirby And His Orchestra (1941-42)* (1988).

Profit, Clarence

b. 26 June 1912, New York City, New York, USA, d. 22 October 1944. By his late teenage years, Profit had played piano with several bands, small and large, performed with Edgar Sampson, a school friend, and formed his own big band. In 1930 he joined Teddy Bunn, touring and playing residencies in various Caribbean locations, but by the middle of the decade was resident in New York as leader of a trio. It was a format which best suited his powerful stride piano style and the next few years saw him achieve a substantial measure of popularity. Before he could take full advantage of the public's liking for his piano-bass-guitar line-up, he died in 1944.

Selected compilations: *Complete 1939-40* (Meritt 1988), *Solo And Trio Sides* (Memoir 1993).

Pukwana, Dudu

b. Mtutuzel Pukwana, 2 September 1941, Port Elizabeth, South Africa, d. 29 June 1990, London, England. Although for the majority of his career Pukwana specialized in the alto saxophone, playing a wild, passionate style which owed more or less equal measures to South African township mbaqanga and sax jive, Charlie Parker and King Curtis, his first instrument was the piano, which he began learning from his father when he was 10 years old. Moving to Cape Town, and still playing piano, he joined his first band, Tete Mbambisa's Four Yanks, in 1957. It was around this time that he began playing saxophone, learning the rudiments from friend and fellow sideman Nick Moyake, and spending a lot of time listening to imported records by Curtis, Parker, Louis Jordan, Sonny Rollins and Ben Webster. In Cape Town, he became friends with the white jazz pianist and bandleader Chris McGregor, who in 1960 invited Pukwana to join his Blue Notes band as saxophonist. He spent the next three years touring South Africa with the Blue Notes, under increasingly difficult conditions, until apartheid legislation made it practically impossible for a mixed race band to appear in public. The group's opportunity to leave the country came in 1963, when they were invited to appear at the annual jazz festival held in Antibes, France. Once the festival was over, the band spent a few months working in Switzerland, until, with the help of London musician and club owner Ronnie Scott, they were able to acquire work permits and entry visas for the UK.

Pukwana remained with McGregor until 1969 (by which time the Blue Notes had been renamed the Brotherhood Of Breath), when he took up an offer to join Hugh Masekela's fledgling Union Of South Africa in the USA. When that band fell apart in 1970, he returned to London and formed his own band, Spear, shortly afterwards renamed Assegai. Pukwana also gigged and recorded with, inter alia, Keith Tippett's Centipede, Jonas Gwangwa, Traffic, the Incredible String Band, Gwigwi Mrwebi, Sebothane Bahula's Jabula, Harry Miller's Isipingo and the Louis Moholo Unit. He made memorable contributions to John and Beverly Martyn's *Road To Ruin* in 1970, and the same year co-led a sax jive/kwela album, *Kwela*, with fellow South African saxophonist Gwigwi Mrwebi. With Assegai, he recorded two albums - *Assegai* and *Assegai Zimbabwe* - before launching the second Spear in 1972. That year, he was also a featured artist on Masekela's London-recorded album *Home Is Where The Music Is*. The new Spear included in its line-up fellow ex-Blue Notes Mongezi Feza (trumpet) and Louis Moholo (drums), along with South Africans Harry Miller (bass) and Bixo Mngqikana (tenor saxophone). Their first album was the superb *In The Townships*, in 1973, which like its follow-up, *Flute Music,* took the mbaqanga/sax jive/jazz fusion into previously uncharted depths of emotional and creative intensity. In 1978, Pukwana disbanded Spear to form the larger band Zila, a horns and percussion dominated outfit whose album debut was *Diamond Express*. He continued leading Zila, recording the occasional album and working the UK and European jazz club and festival circuit, until his death from liver failure in 1990 deprived the jazz and African music scene of one of its most consistently inventive players.

Albums: *In The Townships* (Earthworks 1973), *Flute Music* (1974), with Assegai *Zimbabwe* (1974), *Blue Notes For Mongezi* (1976), *Diamond Express* (1977), *Blue Notes In Concert* (1978), with Zila *Sounds - Live At The 100 Club* (Jika 1981), with Zila *Live At Bracknell & Willisau* (Jika 1984), *Zila '86* (Jika 1986), with John Stevens *Radebe - They Shoot To Kill* (Affinity 1987), *Blue Notes For Johnny* (1987), with Zila *Cosmics Chapter 90* (Ah-Um 1990).

Pullen, Don

b. 25 December 1941, Roanoke, Virginia, USA. After playing piano in church, accompanying gospel singers, Pullen worked in various R&B bands before turning to jazz. In the early 60s he studied with Muhal Richard Abrams, and Giuseppe Logan, with whom he made his recording debut in 1964. Pullen also continued to work in R&B and related fields, usually as accompanist to singers often playing organ, and in 1970 joined Nina Simone for a year. In the meantime, he led his own small bands and formed a long-standing partnership with Milford Graves, recording with him on the SRP label they ran together. In the early 70s he joined Charles Mingus and played briefly with Art Blakey. Later in the decade he played with Sam Rivers and the Art Ensemble Of Chicago. Towards the end of the 70s he formed a lasting musical partnership with George Adams, with whom he co-led, and also worked with Mingus Dynasty. A vibrant, eclectic and usually exciting pianist, Pullen has the technique to match his questing imagination and his playing, whether as soloist or as accompanist, is always interesting. In particular, his interplay with Adams, with whom he has worked over the years, displays his talents to the full.

Selected albums: with Milford Graves *Live At Yale University* (1966), with Graves *Nommo* (1967), *Solo Piano Album* (1975), *Five To Go* (1976), *Capricorn Rising* (Black Saint 1976), *Healing Force* (1976), *Montreaux Concert* (Atlantic 1978), *Don't Lose Control* (1979), with Mingus Dynasty *Chair In The Sky* (1979), *Warriors* (Black Saint 1979), with George Adams *Don't Lose Control* (1979), *Milano Strut* (Black Saint 1979), with Adams *Life Line* (1981), with Adams *Melodic Excursions* (1982), with Adams *Live At The Village Vanguard, Vols 1 & 2* (1983), *Evidence Of Things Unseen* (Black Saint 1983), with Adams *City Gates* (1983), with Adams *Decisions* (1984), *Plays Monk* (Paddle Wheel 1985), *The Sixth Sense* (Black Saint 1985), with Adams *Breakthrough* (1986), *Life Line* (Timeless 1986), *New Beginnings* (Blue Note 1988), *Random Thoughts* (Blue Note 1990), *Kele Mou Bana* (Blue Note 1992), *Ode To Life* (1993).

Purim, Flora

b. 6 March 1942, Rio de Janeiro, Brazil. Purim was raised in a musical atmosphere (her parents were classical musicians) and she played several instruments before settling on a career as a singer. While studying percussion she met and later married Airto Moreira. After moving to the USA in the late 60s she worked with musicians including Stan Getz, Duke Pearson, Gil Evans and George Duke before becoming a member of Chick Corea's Return To Forever unit which also included Moreira. In the early and mid-70s Purim and Moreira had their own band; the singer also made several solo albums, which broadened her appeal into more popular areas of music. In the late 70s and early 80s Purim recorded with David Sanborn and a few years later was again working with Moreira. Purim scats interestingly, and frequently vocalizes wordlessly, her light captivating voice floating over the improvisations of the accompanying musicians. Her sister, Yana Purim, is also a singer.

Albums: *Milestone Memories* (70s), *Butterfly Dreams* (Original Jazz Classics 1973), *Stories To Tell* (1974), *Open Your Eyes You Can Fly* (1976), *500 Miles High At Montreux* (1976, rec. 1974), *Nothing Will Be As It Was...Tomorrow* (1977), *Encounter* (1977), *That's What She Said* (1977), *Everyday, Everynight* (1978), *Humble People* (1985), *The Magicians* (Crossover 1986), *Love Reborn* (Fantasy 1986), with Airto Moreira *The Colours Of Life* (1987), *The Midnight Sun* Venture (1988), *The Sun Is Out* (Crossover 1989).

Purnell, Alton

b. 16 April 1911, New Orleans, Louisiana, USA, d. 14 January 1987. Starting out as a singer, Purnell took up piano in his youth and became a professional musician in his mid-teens. He worked with a number of well-known bands in his home town including those led by Alphonse Picou and Big Eye Louis Nelson before moving to New York in the mid-40s. He played in various bands, including those led by Bunk Johnson and George Lewis. In the mid-50s he moved out to the west coast where he played with many leading New Orleans and Dixieland jazzmen including Kid Ory, Teddy Buckner, Ben Pollack and Barney Bigard. From the mid-60s onwards, Purnell toured extensively, sometimes in bands such as the Legends of Jazz, the Young Men Of New Orleans and Kid Thomas's band. He also toured as a soloist. A strong player who ably blended the traditional New Orleans style of piano playing with elements of Harlem stride, Purnell proved very popular in the later years of his career. His singing was always engaging and entertaining.

Albums: with George Lewis *New Orleans Stompers* (1955), *Alton Purnell Quartet* (1958), *Live With Keith Smith's Climax Jazz Band* (1965), *Tribute To Louis* (1971), *Kid Thomas* (1975), *In Japan* (GHB 1977), *Alton Purnell Meets Houlind* (Nathan 1988), *Alton Purnell Live* (CSA 1989).

Pyne, Chris

b. 14 February 1939, Bridlington, Yorkshire, England. Pyne is a self-taught trombonist whose initial band experience was with a Royal Air Force band during his National Service (1960-1961). He later appeared in a succession of bands throughout the 60s, which included John Cox's band, Alexis Korner's Blues Incorporated, Humphrey Lyttelton, John Dankworth, Ronnie Scott, Tubby Hayes and Maynard Ferguson. Pyne is a consummately professional studio musician who has recorded with Ella Fitzgerald and Tony Bennett and has played on many of Frank Sinatra's UK tours. Pyne has a polished, accurate playing style which reflects an early liking for J.J. Johnson. During the

70s and 80s he worked with, among others: John Taylor, Mike Gibbs, Kenny Wheeler, Gordon Beck and John Surman. Pyne's brother, Mike Pyne, is a jazz pianist.

Selected albums: with Alexis Korner *Blues Incorporated* (1967), with John Dankworth *Million Dollar Collection* (1967), with John Stevens' SME *The Source* (1970), with John Taylor *Pause And Think Again* (1971) with Pete Hurt *Lost For Words* (1984), with Kenny Wheeler *Music For Large And Small Ensembles* (1990).

Pyne, Mike

b. 2 September 1940, Thornton-le-Dale, Yorkshire, England. Pyne's father was a pianist and he encouraged him to play from the age of three. He came to London in 1961 and played piano regularly in a succession of bands - with drummer Tony Kinsey, Alexis Korner's Blues Incorporated, Tubby Hayes and Humphrey Lyttelton. Pyne sometimes gets the chance to play his second instrument, the trumpet, but more regularly contributes his strong solo lines or accompaniments on piano. He has worked with Philly Joe Jones, saxophonists Stan Getz, Rahsaan Roland Kirk, Dexter Gordon and Ronnie Scott, with the Mike Gibbs Orchestra and the Cecil Payne Quintet. In the 80s he also played with Georgie Fame's Stardust Road show and Keith Smith's Hefty Jazz. Pyne's brother, Chris Pyne, is a jazz trombonist.

Albums: with Philly Joe Jones *Trailways Express* (1968), with John Stevens' SME *The Source* (1970), with Humphrey Lyttelton *21 Years On* (1969), with Lyttelton *Once In A While* (Black Lion 1976), with Lyttelton *Alone Together* (Spotlite 1977), with Jon Eardley *Two Of A Kind* (1977), with Tubby Hayes *Mexican Green* (1981), with Lyttelton *Humph At The Bull's Head* (1984), with Tommy Whittle *Straight Eight* (1985), *A Little Blue* (Miles Music 1988).

Quebec, Ike

b. 17 August 1918, Newark, New Jersey, USA, d. 16 January 1963. Quebec played piano at first, then took up the tenor saxophone in 1940. He worked in several well-known bands, including outfits led by Benny Carter, Coleman Hawkins, Roy Eldridge and, later, Cab Calloway, with whom he stayed from 1944-51. He also led his own small groups in the 40s, recording several sessions for Blue Note, the first of which produced the hit 'Blue Harlem'. A close friend of the label's co-founder, Alfred Lion, Quebec advised Blue Note on the bebop scene, recommending that they record both Thelonious Monk and

Bud Powell. For much of the 50s, Quebec struggled against heroin addiction and worked various day jobs, including a stint as a taxi driver. He returned to the music business in 1959, becoming an A&R man for Blue Note and also recording for them again - first making several jukebox singles, then a series of albums that showcased his expertise at slow blues and soulful ballads. He also guested on albums by Sonny Clark, Grant Green, Jimmy Smith and vocalist Dodo Green. In January 1963, he died of lung cancer; and, for many years, appeared to be one of the forgotten men of jazz. Then, in the 80s, Blue Note issued some previously unreleased sessions while Mosaic Records produced lavishly-packaged compilations both of his 40s Blue Note recordings and the later jukebox singles. The appearance of this material sparked a new interest in, and welcome re-evaluation of, Quebec's shapely, affecting, big-toned tenor playing.

Selected albums: *Heavy Soul* (1961), *Blue And Sentimental* (Blue Note 1961), *It Might As Well Be Spring* (1962), *Soul Samba* (1962), *With A Song In My Heart* (1980, rec. 1962), *Congo Lament* (1981, rec. 1962), *Easy Living* (Blue Note 1987, rec. 1962). Compilations: *The Complete Blue Note Forties Recordings Of Ike Quebec And John Hardee* (1987, rec. 40s, four-album box-set), *The Complete Blue Note 45 Sessions Of Ike Quebec* (1987, rec. 1959-62, three-album box-set).

Quinichette, Paul

b. 17 May 1916, Denver, Colorado, USA, d. 25 May 1983. After formally studying clarinet and alto saxophone, Quinichette switched to tenor saxophone. He played in a number of local and territory bands, notably that led by Nat Towles. Amongst the outfits with which he played in the early 40s were those led by Jay McShann, Benny Carter and Johnny Otis. Later in the decade he was active in New York, playing and recording with Louis Jordan, Dinah Washington, Lucky Millinder and others and in the early 50s he worked with Count Basie. Included in his recordings of this period are concert performances with Washington released as *The Jazz Sides* (1954-58). In the mid-50s Quinichette played briefly with Benny Goodman, John Coltrane and Nat Pierce but then drifted out of music for several years. In the 70s he was back on the jazz scene but, plagued by poor health, he made little impact. During the late 40s and early 50s Quinichette attracted attention because of similarities in tone and style to Lester Young, even picking up the nickname 'Vice-Pres'. The resemblance was deliberate and when he was at his best was more than merely superficial. Nevertheless, such comparisons were damaging to Quinichette's career and he rarely overcame the link for long enough to establish a strong personal identity. In retrospect he can be seen as a fine, lyrical and always swinging player; had he not suffered a hiatus in his career, he might well have been able to overcome the disadvantage of following so closely upon Young's unique path.

Albums: *A Look At Yesterday* (Mainstream 1950), *The Vice Pres* (1952-53), *Six Classics Tenors* (EPM 1953), *The Kid From Denver* (Fresh Sounds 1956), *Paul Quinichette's New Stars* (1957), *On The Sunny Side* (RCA 1957), with Charlie Rouse

The Chase Is On (1957), *Cattin' With John Coltrane And Paul Quinichette* (1957), *For Basie* (1957), *Basie Reunion* (1958), *Like Who?* (1959), *Paul Quinichette/Paul Gonsalves* (1974), with Buddy Tate, Jay McShann *Kansas City Joys* (1976). Compilation: with McShann *Early Bird* (1940-43).

R

Raeburn, Boyd

b. 27 October 1913, Faith, South Dakota, USA, d. 2 August 1966, Layfayette, Indiana, USA. Raeburn attended the University of Chicago, where he led a campus band before becoming a professional musician leading a small, light music band, but in the 30s turned his attention to swing. In 1944 he formed a high class band that featured some fine young musicians including Dizzy Gillespie, Sonny Berman (trumpets), Earl Swope, Tommy Pederson (trombones), Al Cohn, Johnny Bothwell (saxophones), while older stars such as Roy Eldridge and Trummy Young played with the band that recorded for the V Disc label. Raeburn was unlucky - a fire at New Jersey's Palisades Amusement Park destroyed the band's library together with many of its instruments. Undeterred, Raeburn put together an astonishing outfit that seemed, in 1945, years ahead of its time. It played numbers like 'Dalvatore Sally', 'Yerxa' and 'Boyd Meets Stravinsky', and the music was as impressionistic as the titles suggest. Vocalists David Allyn and Raeburn's wife Ginny Powell found their songs placed in Debussy-like settings and although the critics loved it all, the public did not take to a band that played non-danceable music. In 1947, although signed to the up and coming Atlantic Records, Boyd broke up the band. The man who fronted the band holding an ungainly bass saxophone had become disenchanted with the scene, and moved on to part ownership of a Fifth Avenue shop, later moving to Nassau in the Bahamas for more business interests. He died of a heart attack in 1966, having outlived his wife Ginny by seven years.
Selected albums: *Teen Rock* (1957), *Boyd Raeburn And His Musicians (1943-48)* (1977), *Rhythms By Raeburn* (Aircheck 1978), *Boyd Raeburn 1945* (1979), *Boyd Raeburn Orchestra - On The Air, Volume One* (1981), *Memphis In June* (1981), *Boyd Raeburn Orchestra - On The Air, Volume Two* (1981), *Jewels* (1985), *Airshots 1944-1946* (IAJRC 1990), *Boyd Meets Stravinsky* (Savoy 1992), *Transcription Performances 1946* (Hep 1993).

Ramey, Gene

b. 4 April 1913, Austin, Texas, USA, d. 8 December 1984. A student of Walter Page, bass player Ramey briefly led his own band in Kansas City before joining Jay McShann. This was in 1938 and he remained with McShann until the band broke up in 1943. During the rest of the 40s Ramey became a regular at numerous club and recording dates in New York, playing with a wide range of top-flight swing and bop stars including Charlie Parker, Coleman Hawkins and Lester Young. In the 50s he freelanced with mainstreamers and beboppers, comfortably fitting in with the musical concepts of Buck Clayton and Art Blakey while also making the transition to dixieland with Muggsy Spanier. Ramey's skills were highly regarded and his musical range meant that he was in demand throughout his musical career and appeared on countless albums with musicians as diverse as Thelonious Monk, Teddy Wilson, Horace Silver, Lennie Tristano, Count Basie and Stan Getz. In the 60s he retired to become a bank security guard but later returned to the jazz scene to play at international festivals with his old comrade McShann. He retired in 1975, moving to Texas to run a smallholding.
Album: *The Count Basie Sextet* (1952).

Ramirez, Roger 'Ram'

b. 15 September 1913, Puerto Rico, d. 11 January 1994, New York, USA. Raised in New York City, Ramirez displayed a prodigious talent as a pianist and at the age of 13 became a member of the American Federation of Musicians. During the mid- and late 30s he worked with various artists, including Monette Moore, the Spirits Of Rhythm, Putney Dandridge, Stew Pletcher and Willie Bryant. He recorded with Dandridge and Bryant in 1936. Mostly working in the New York area, he occasionally led small groups in the early 40s, but was also with Ella Fitzgerald in 1940, in the band she took over after the death of Chick Webb. He next played in bands led by Frankie Newton and Ike Quebec, appearing with the latter on some early Blue Note records. In the mid-40s he was with John Kirby, playing and recording with his reformed sextet. Ramirez also recorded under his own name in 1946, leading a trio with guitarist Jimmy Shirley and bassist Al Hall. In 1944 Billie Holiday recorded Ramirez's composition, 'Lover Man', a song which subsequently became a jazz standard. In the late 40s and early 50s he continued to play in and around New York, and towards the end of this period began to play organ. In the 60s he worked with 'T-Bone' Walker, and the following decade was with the Harlem Blues And Jazz Band. He continued to make appearances with this group into the early 80s. A blues-orientated pianist and organist, Ramirez is perhaps less well known than his skills warrant. Although he visited Europe in 1937 and toured with the Harlem Blues And Jazz band, his decision to spend much of his career in a small geographical area has meant that his international reputation rests largely upon numerous recordings of his most famous composition.
Albums: *Lover Man* (1966-67), *Rampant Ram* (1973-74), *Harlem Blues And Jazz Band, 1973-80* (1973-80).

Randall, Freddy

b. 6 May 1921, London, England. Randall began playing

trumpet in the late 30s and led his own small band in 1939. By the mid-40s he was one of the most respected dixieland trumpeters in the UK, appearing on radio and at clubs and concerts. He was therefore well placed to take advantage of the trad boom which swept the UK from the late 40s and on through the 50s. Randall's band became one of the most popular of the era and he also toured the USA. Ill health forced his retirement in the late 50s but he was back, part-time, in 1963, and thereafter continued to make occasional and usually unscheduled appearances at London clubs and pubs. These gigs found him playing as well as ever and delighting an army of fans which seemed to grow stronger and more numerous as the years passed. A band he formed in the early 70s in collaboration with Dave Shepherd played at international festivals to great acclaim. Reissues of his earlier records confirmed that his qualities were not the result of nostalgic glow. Randall played hard-driving Chicago-style jazz with verve and great skill, and the many fine musicians who played in his band at one time or another responded to his enthusiastic lead.

Albums: *His Great Sixteen* (1951-56), *Something Borrowed, Something Blue* (Alamo 1978, c.50s recordings), *Wild Bill Davison With Freddy Randall's Band* (1965), *Freddy Randall-Dave Shepherd All Stars* (1972), *Freddy Randall-Dave Shepherd All Stars 'Live' At Montreux Jazz Festival* (1973), *Freddie Randall And His Band* (Dormouse 1986).

Raney, Jimmy

b. 20 August 1927, Louisville, Kentucky, USA. After working in the New York and Chicago areas, in bands led by Jerry Wald and Lou Levy, guitarist Raney joined Woody Herman in 1948. Thereafter he played and recorded with a number of leading swing era veterans and up-and-coming stars including Artie Shaw, Stan Getz, Terry Gibbs and Red Norvo. Throughout the 60s he worked in studios, making occasional jazz club appearances. This pattern continued into the 70s with the bias gradually swinging towards jazz work. A relaxed and highly proficient technician, Raney's solo work displays a cool, lambent style which is much admired, although his attraction is often cerebral rather than emotional. His son, Doug, also plays guitar.

Albums: *The Jimmy Raney Quintet* i (1953), *The Jimmy Raney Quartet* ii (1954), *Jimmy Raney Visits Paris* (1954), *Too Marvellous For Words* (1954), *A* (Original Jazz Classics 1955), *Jimmy Raney In Three Attitudes* (1956), *Strings And Swings* (1957-69), *Two Jims And Zoot* (Original Master Recordings 1964), *Momentum* (1974), *The Influence* (1975), *Live In Tokyo* (1976), *The Complete Jimmy Raney In Tokyo* (Xanadu 1977), with Doug Raney *Stolen Moments* (Steeplechase 1979), with Doug Raney *Duets* (Steeplechase 1979), *Here's That Raney Day* (Black And Blue 1980), with Doug Raney *Raney '81* (1981), *The Date* (1981), *The Master* (Criss Cross 1983), with Doug Raney *Nardis* (1983), *Visits Paris* (Fresh Sounds 1988), *Wisteria* (Criss Cross 1985-90), *But Beautiful* (Criss Cross 1993).

Raney, Sue

b. Raelene Claire Claussen, 18 June 1940, McPherson, Kansas, USA. Raised in New Mexico, as a small child Raney was trained by her mother, a professional singer and music teacher. Raney began singing at the age of four and a age eight was singing professionally. Four years on, she had regular radio and television spots including appearances with country singer Glen Campbell. Her early singing idols were in the popular field, although some were jazz-inflected, but by her mid-teens had begun to direct her style more firmly into jazz. She gained some valuable early experience working with the Ray Anthony band. In the early 60s she sang with Nelson Riddle in the UK and made several albums that were critically successful but failed to find a wide audience. She continued to perform, her career remaining regrettably low-key although musical partnerships with Stan Kenton, Michel Legrand, Henry Mancini and others continued to attract critical favour. Further fine albums in the mid-80s and an outstanding 1990 release, *In Good Company*, on which she was backed by jazzmen such as Conte Candoli, Bob Cooper, Bill Watrous and Alan Broadbent, attracted wider attention. Raney is also an accomplished songwriter, contributing lyrics to several songs including 'Statue Of Snow'. Singing with a finely-textured voice, beautifully pitched, always displaying impeccable timing and taste, and with effortless swing, Raney is an exceptionally gifted performer. She is one of the finest living interpreters of the great standards and is an excellent jazz singer. Sadly, even following her most recent albums, she remains relatively little known outside a small circle of justifiably devoted admirers. Her husband is flügelhorn player Carmen Falzone.

Albums: *Sue Raney Sings The Music Of Johnny Mandel* (Discovery 1982), with Bob Florence *Ridin' High* (Discovery 1984), *Flight Of Fancy* (Discovery 1985), with Florence *Quietly There* (Discovery 1988), *In Good Company* (Discovery 1990).

Rank, Bill

b. 8 June 1904, Lafayette, Indiana, USA, d. 20 May 1979. During the mid-20s trombonist and arranger Rank played with Jean Goldkette alongside Bix Beiderbecke. In 1928 he was one of several former Goldkette sidemen who joined Paul Whiteman where he led the trombone section and was for a while featured soloist. Respected by fellow musicians, Rank's career was frequently overshadowed by other trombone luminaries such as Jack Teagarden, with whom he played in the Whiteman band and who took over solo duties. In the late 30s he began working in film studios and thereafter divided his time between playing, mostly in Cincinnati where he led his own band, and non-musical activities.

Album: *Bix Beiderbecke And His Gang* (1927-28).

Rebello, Jason

b. 1969, London, England; of mixed Indian/Portuguese and English ancestry. In 1988, pianist Rebello was one of the most talked-about young musicians on the London jazz scene, having just won the Pat Smythe Award for the most promising young player of that year. Unlike a purely bebop-based performer, Rebello's technique was as strong in either hand, and he was as liable to play snatches of boogie and stride as in a fast, linear improvising style. Rebello's interests as a piano student lay equally in classical music and jazz, but the earliest music he heard was by Jimi Hendrix and the Beatles, and in his mid-teens, exposure to Herbie Hancock's pop-funk Rockit band turned him on to dance music with a strong improvisational flavour. Through Hancock's antecedents, Rebello discovered the jazz piano tradition, went to London's Guildhall School of Music to pursue it, and was soon working with younger UK jazz celebrities such as Courtney Pine, Jean Toussaint, Steve Williamson and Cleveland Watkiss. In the late 80s he was a member of Tommy Smith's group and in 1990 he released his first album as leader, with Wayne Shorter producing.

Album: *A Clearer View* (Novus 1990), *Permanent Love* (1993), *Keeping Time* (Novus 1993), *Make It Real* (RCA 1994).

Redd, Vi

b. Elvira Redd, 10 September 1928, Los Angeles, California, USA. As a child, Redd took up the saxophone and was directed into jazz through the influence of her father, professional jazz drummer Alton Redd. Concentrating on the alto but also playing soprano and singing, Redd's career moved slowly at first but she blossomed in the 60s, appearing nationally and internationally with Earl 'Fatha' Hines, Max Roach, Dizzy Gillespie and other distinguished jazz stars. At the end of the decade she turned to teaching but throughout the 70s and 80s continued to make occasional appearances as a performer. Like most alto saxophonists of her generation, she was deeply influenced by Charlie Parker and, like her idol, her playing is redolent with a strong feeling for the blues, as is her singing.

Albums: *Bird Call* (1962), with Al Grey *Shades Of Grey* (1965), with Gene Ammons, Dexter Gordon *The Chase!* (1973), with Marian McPartland *Now's The Time!* (1977).

Redman, Dewey

b. 17 May 1931, Fort Worth, Texas, USA. After first playing clarinet at school, where one of his musical companions was Ornette Coleman, Redman turned to alto saxophone and later still took up the tenor. One of many well-versed students at North Texas State University, Redman became a professional musician on graduation. In the late 60s and through into the mid-70s he played and recorded with Coleman, Charlie Haden, Roswell Rudd, Keith Jarrett and Carla Bley. In 1976 he formed Old and New Dreams, a quartet completed by Don Cherry, Ed Blackwell and Haden, touring and recording into the mid-80s. An eclectic musician, seamlessly linking the blues with freeform music over a hard bop base, Redman's playing style constantly demonstrates his technical mastery of his instruments which sometimes include the Arabian musette. He also composes and arranges much of the material he performs and records, drawing inspiration from eastern music as well as that of his own heritage.

Albums: *Look For The Black Star* (1966), with Ornette Coleman *New York Is Now* (1968), *Ear Of The Behearer* (1973), *Coincide* (1974), *Old And New Dreams* i (1976), *Soundsigns* (1978), *Old And New Dreams* ii (1979), *Redman And Blackwell In Willisau* (Black Saint 1980), *The Struggle Continues* (ECM 1982), *Living On The Edge* (Black Saint 1989), *Choices* (Enja 1992).

Redman, Don

b. 29 July 1900, Piedmont, West Virginia, USA, d. 30 November 1964. A gifted child, alto saxophonist Redman studied extensively and by his graduation had mastered most of the wind instruments and was also adept at arranging. He then joined a territory band based in Pittsburgh, Pennsylvania, with whom he visited New York. This was in 1923 and by the following year he had begun a musical relationship with Fletcher Henderson that was to alter perceptions of big band jazz. In 1927 he took over leadership of McKinney's Cotton Pickers, continuing to develop the arranging style with which he had experimented while with Henderson. In 1931 Redman formed his own band which remained in existence for almost a decade. During this period Redman wrote charts for numerous other big bands and after his own unit folded he pursued this aspect of his career, writing for Jimmy Dorsey, Count Basic, Jimmie Lunceford, Harry James and many others. In 1946 he formed a new band, taking it to Europe and subsequently worked in radio and television. For several years he was musical director for Pearl Bailey, occasionally recording and dedicating what time he could spare to composing. Originally inspired by the creative genius of Louis Armstrong who joined the Henderson band while he was arranger, Redman went on to lay many of the ground rules for much of what is today regarded as 'big band music'. In his work for Henderson, the Cotton Pickers and his own band he consistently demonstrated his confident grasp of all arranging techniques in use up to his time, extending them to prove that an arranged format need not lose the spontaneity of an improvised performance and, indeed, could enhance the work of a good jazz soloist. In particular, his writing for the reed and brass sections, in which he set up call-and-response passages, while polished to perfection by such successors as Sy Oliver, has rarely been improved upon.

Selected albums: *For Europeans Only* (1946), *Don Redman's Park Avenue Patters* (1957), *July 22nd And 26th, 1957* (1957), *Don Redman And The Knights Of The Round Table* (1959), *Shakin' The African* (Hep Jazz 1986). Selected compilations: *Don Redman And His Orchestra 1931-1933* (1931-33), *Doin' The New Low Down* (Hep Jazz 1984, 1932-33 recordings), *Redman's Red Book* (1932-36), *Smoke Rings* (Nostalgia 1988), *Don Redman* (1932-37), *1936-1939* (Classics 1991), *Doin' What I Please* (1993).

Redman, Joshua

b. 1 February 1969, Berkeley, California, USA. The latest in a long line of intensively marketed young jazz musicians, Joshua Redman saw his star rise dramatically in 1991, when he burst suddenly into the international arena in his (very) early 20s with all the right credentials (a hard-bop influenced style, good looks, a Harvard education, a famous saxophone playing father [see Dewey Redman] and a compelling fluency and originality

that captured the imagination of the older generation of jazz musicians). Despite the inevitable media tag lines, Redman was influenced less by his famous father, whom he saw infrequently, than by his mother, who always encouraged an awareness of music, and enrolled him at Berkeley's Centre For World Music at the age of five, to study Indian and Indonesian music. Whilst his flair for music was obvious, his flair for practise was less clear, and although he played in the jazz big band and combo while at school, he displayed little genuine commitment. Concentrating, instead, on a glittering academic career, he won a place at Harvard to study social sciences. It was there that he began to listen to jazz in earnest, studying records by the post-war master saxophonists, and spending summer breaks in Boston with the Berklee College Of Music jazz students. Graduating in 1991 (with highly distinguished grades), he accepted a place at Yale Law School, but took a year off to dabble in the New York music scene. He began attending jam sessions and playing the odd sideman gig, and then, in the Autumn of 1991, won the Thelonious Monk International Saxophone Competition. This prestigious award threw Redman into the limelight, and he soon found himself working with a host of jazz legends, including Elvin Jones, Jack DeJohnette, Red Rodney, Paul Motian, Roy Hargrove and John Hicks, and winning *Jazz Times* readers' poll Best New Jazz Artist in 1992, *Rolling Stone*'s Hot Jazz Artist Of 1993 and *Down Beat*'s critics' poll's Number 1 Tenor Saxophonist Deserving Of Wider Recognition (1993). Signed to Warners, his eponymous debut album was released in March 1993 to widespread critical acclaim, but never reached the UK. *Wish*, his all-star second featuring Pat Metheny, Charlie Haden and Billy Higgins, helped spread the word to the UK, and serves as a good introduction to his warm and swinging style. In 1994 he joined older saxophone star Joe Lovano on a lively and extrovert two tenor date for the Blue Note label.
Albums: *Joshua Redman* (Warners 1993), *Wish* (Warners 1993), with Joe Lovano *Tenor Legacy* (Blue Note 1994), *Mood Swings* (Warners 1994).

Reece, Dizzy

b. Alphonso Reece, 5 January 1931, Kingston, Jamaica. After playing in Jamaica as a young teenager, trumpeter Reece moved to the UK in 1948. During the next few years he established a reputation in the UK and throughout Europe, working mostly with bop musicians like Kenny Graham, Victor Feldman and Tubby Hayes. Reece also occasionally played with such leading swing era figures as Don Byas. At the end of the 50s, an especially active period of creative work, Reece settled in the USA. There he played with Duke Jordan, Philly Joe Jones and others, and made occasional and usually well-spaced return trips to Europe with bands such as that led by Dizzy Gillespie and the Paris Reunion Band. A technically-gifted player with an eclectic yet distinctive playing style, Reece has not been recorded as often or as well as his talent deserves.
Albums: *Progress Report* (Jasmine 1956), *Victor Feldman In London* (1956), *Blues In Trinity* (1958), *Star Bright* (1959), *Soundin' Off* (1960), with Duke Jordan *Flight To Jordan*

(1960), *Asia Minor* (Original Jazz Classics 1962), with Philly Joe Jones *'Round Midnite* (1966), *From In To Out* (1970), *Possession, Exorcism, Peace* (Honeydew 1972), *Manhattan Project* (Beehive 1978), *Moose The Mooche* (Discovery 1978), *Blowin' Away* (Interplay 1979).

Reich, Steve

b. 3 October 1936, New York City, USA. Reich studied philosophy at Cornell University and composition at Juilliard School of Music and, moving to California, at Mills College with *avant garde* composers Luciano Berio and Darius Milhaud. He supported himself while at college by working as a drummer, but declined to follow an academic career and became a taxi-driver in 1963. In 1966 he formed a group, Steve Reich And Musicians, to play his compositions. In the 70s he studied African drumming in Ghana and gamelan music and Hebrew cantillation in the USA. One of the founders of the Minimalist/Systems/Process/Repetitive (choose your own label) school, his music is deeply rooted in African, Balinese and Baroque music, having less overt connections with (and less influence on) rock and new age than, say, Terry Riley, Louis Andriessen or Philip Glass. However, his astonishing early tape works, *My Name Is*, *Come Out* and *It's Gonna Rain*, anticipated techniques now in common use in scratch and hip-hop by a good 15 years, as well as using them in ways which rock has never caught up with. His work has ranged from the most minimalist (*Clapping Music*, which is just that, two people clapping, working through a pre-determined rhythmic process, and *Pendulum Music*, for microphones which are set swinging over amplifiers until the feedback pulses resolve into a continuous tone) to *The Four Sections*, a concerto for orchestra, and *The Desert Music* for orchestra and choir, which examines the premise that humankind has only survived because it has been unable to realise its ambitions: now that it is able to do so it must change its ambitions or perish. Desert Music characterized Reich's move towards a fuller, more conventional orchestration, a development which had the consequence that performances of his music would have to involve resources beyond those of his own ensemble. (In fact, Reich had never restricted the use of his scores in the way that Philip Glass had done.) However, he still composed for small forces as well, and in 1988 he wrote *Electric Counterpoint* for jazz guitarist Pat Metheny. This was coupled on record with *Different Trains*, a remarkable work reflecting on the Holocaust and devised for live string quartet, pre-recorded string quartet and sampled voices. He is currently nearing completion of a music theatre piece about the prophet Abraham, important to Judaism, Christianity and Islam, called *The Cave*, which will incorporate a video film by his wife, Beryl Corot.
Selected albums: *Drumming* (1970), *Music For 18 Musicians* (1978), *Octet - Music For A Large Ensemble - Violin Phase* (1980), *Tehillim* (1982), *Eight Lines -Vermont Counterpoint* (1985), *The Desert Music* (1986), *Early Works* (1987), *Different Trains - Electric Counterpoint* (1989), *The Four Sections* (1990).

Reinhardt, Django

b. Jean Baptiste Reinhardt, 23 January 1910, Liberchies, near Luttre, Belgium, d. 16 May 1953. Reinhardt first played violin but later took up the guitar. Living a nomadic life with his gypsy family, he played in a touring show before he was in his teens. Following serious injuries which he suffered in a caravan fire in 1928 he lost the use of two fingers on his left hand. To overcome this handicap, he devised a unique method of fingering and soon embarked on a solo career in Parisian clubs. He was hired as accompanist to the popular French singing star, Jean Sablon, and in 1934 teamed up with Stéphane Grappelli to form a band they named the Quintette Du Hot Club De France. Reinhardt was a popular sitter-in with visiting American jazzmen, recording with Eddie South, Benny Carter, Coleman Hawkins and others. It was, however, the recordings by the Quintet that made him an international name. His remarkable playing caused a sensation and it is not an exaggeration to state that he was the first non-American to make an impact upon jazz and become an important influence upon the development of the music. His distinctive, flowing lines were filled with inventive ideas and couched in a deeply romantic yet intensely rhythmic style. Above all, Reinhardt's was an original talent, revealing few if any precedents but becoming a major influence upon other jazz guitarists of the 30s.

With the outbreak of war in 1939, the Quintet folded and Reinhardt returned to his nomadic life, playing in various parts of Europe and ensuring that he kept well clear of the German army. At the end of the war, (by which time he had switched from acoustic to electric guitar) Reinhardt was invited by Duke Ellington to visit the USA and duly turned up in New York. The visit was less than successful and some of the blame might well be laid at Reinhardt's door as he approached the tour with a measure of arrogance out of place with his status as a guest instrumentalist. Some reports of the time suggest that he was eager to pursue the new concepts of jazz created by the bebop revolution: musically, however, the guitarist's gloriously romantic style fitted uneasily into the new music and his efforts in this field were overshadowed by those of another guitarist, the late Charlie Christian. Back in Europe he led his own small band and was occasionally reunited with Grappelli in a reformed Quintet. He continued to tour and record during the late 40s and early 50s, simultaneously pursuing a career as a composer. Reinhardt remains one of the outstanding figures in jazz, and although Christian ultimately became the more profound influence, echoes of Reinhardt's style can be heard today in many musicians, some of whom were born after his death. His brother, Joseph, was also a guitarist and his two sons, Lousson and Babik, are also gifted players of the instrument. In the early 90s Babik Reinhardt was featured at an international jazz and gypsy guitar festival in France.
Selected albums: *Rare Django* (1928-38), *50th Anniversary* (1934-35), *Django Reinhardt And Stéphane Grappelli With The Quintet Of The Hot Club Of France* (1938-46), *The Story* (1947-51), *Rome 1949-50 Vols 1 & 2* (1949-50), *Django Reinhardt Et Ses Rhythmes* (1953), *The Chronological Django* *Reinhardt 1934-1935* (Classics, c.80s), *Djangology Vols 1-20* (EMI 1983), *Swing In Paris 1936-1940* (Affinity 1991), *Rare Recordings* (1993), *Jazz Portraits* (Jazz Portraits 1993).
Further reading: *Django Reinhardt*, Charles Delauney. *La Tristesse De Saint Louis: Swing Under The Nazis*, Mike Zwerin.

Remler, Emily

b. 18 September 1957, New York City, New York, USA, d. 4 May 1990. Emily Remler began playing guitar as a small child and her early preference for rock was superseded by jazz while studying at Berklee College Of Music. After leaving Berklee in 1976 she began performing professionally, playing club, concert and festival engagements across the USA. A residency in New Orleans attracted attention when she was called upon to accompany important visiting instrumentalists and singers. She was heard by Herb Ellis, who actively encouraged her career, helping her to obtain her first recording date, for Concord, and an appearance at the Concord Jazz Festival. She continued to tour, particularly with Astrud Gilberto, and made a fine duo album, *Together*, with Larry Coryell. Other guitarists with whom she worked were Barney Kessel and Charlie Byrd. A strikingly gifted performer with eclectic musical tastes, she played with flair and her dazzling technique was built upon a deep knowledge and understanding of all forms of jazz. Appealing alike to audiences, critics and her fellow musicians, she rapidly gained respect and admiration for her dedication enthusiasm and remarkable skills. That someone as gifted as this should have died so young (though she was addicted to heroin) and so unexpectedly was a major loss to the jazz world. Her death, at the age of 32, came while she was on tour in Australia. Remler had played on David Benoit's *Waiting For Spring* and he wrote the beautiful 'Six String Poet' in her memory on his *Inner Motion*.
Albums: *The Firefly* (Concord 1981), *Take Two* (Concord 1982), *Transitions* (Concord 1983), *Catwalk* (Concord 1985), *Together* (1985) *East To West* (Concord 1988). Compilations: *Retrospective Vols 1 & 2* (Concord 80s), various artists *Just Friends: A Gathering In Tribute To Emily Remler Vol. 2* (1992), *This Is Me* (Justice 1992).

Rena, Kid

b. Henry René, 30 August 1898, New Orleans, Louisiana, USA, d. 25 April 1949. Like Louis Armstrong, trumpeter Rena was a 'graduate' of Joseph Jones's Colored Waifs' Home band. In 1919 he succeeded Armstrong in the Kid Ory band, quitting in 1921 to form his own group. Thereafter, he mostly led his own bands but also played in a number of marching bands. He made his first and only records in 1940 but was unable to participate fully in the Revival Movement because ill health sent him into early retirement. According to the testimony of other musicians, in his prime Rena was a forceful player with a remarkably wide range and melodious style. Unfortunately, his recordings display only the vestiges of his talent, affected as they are by his fast-deteriorating physical condition.
Album: with Bunk Johnson *Down On The Delta* (1940).

Rendell, Don

b. 4 March 1926, Plymouth, Devon, England. Rendell began playing alto saxophone as a child but later switched to tenor. He played in a number of dance bands during the late 40s, and in 1950 became a member of John Dankworth's septet. After leaving Dankworth in 1953 he formed his own small group but also worked with bands led by Tony Crombie, Ted Heath and others. In 1956 he joined Stan Kenton for a European tour, appearing on *Live At The Albert Hall*. In the late 50s he played with Woody Herman. During the 60s Rendell was again leading his own bands, featuring musicians such as Graham Bond, Michael Garrick and Ian Carr, with whom he was co-leader of a successful band. Rendell has also recorded with Stan Tracey, (*The Latin American Caper*), and Neil Ardley (*Greek Variations*). A fluent improviser, with hints of post-bop styling overlaying a deep admiration for the earlier work of Lester Young, Rendell has long been one of the most admired of British jazz artists. For many years he has been tireless in the promotion of jazz through his activities as a sought-after teacher.

Albums: *Meet Don Rendell* (1955), *Recontre A Paris* (1955), *Playtime* (1958), *Roarin'* (1961), *Shades Of Blue* (1964), *Phase III* (1967), *Don Rendell Live* (1968), *Change Is* (1969), *Spacewalk* (1971), with Joe Palin *Live At The Avgarde Gallery, Manchester* (1973), with Barbara Thompson *Just Music* (Spotlite 1974), *Earth Music* (Spotlite 1979), *Set Two* (Spotlite 1979), *Time Presence* (DR 1986), *If I Should Lose You* (Spotlite 1991).

Rich, Buddy

b. Bernard Rich, 30 September 1917, New York City, New York, USA, d. 2 April 1987. In showbusiness from the age of two, Rich achieved considerable fame as a drummer and tap dancer, performing on Broadway when he was four-years-old as a member of his parents' act. Two years later he was touring as a solo artist, playing the USA vaudeville circuit and also visiting Australia. At the age of 11 he formed his own band and within a few more years was attracting attention sitting in with bands in New York clubs. In 1937 he was hired by Joe Marsala and soon thereafter began to rise in critical estimation and public popularity. In quick succession he played in several important bands of the swing era including those of Bunny Berigan, Harry James, Artie Shaw and Tommy Dorsey. After military service he again played with Dorsey, then formed his own big band which survived for a few years in the late 40s. He next worked with Les Brown and also became a regular with Jazz At The Philharmonic. In the early 50s he led his own briefly reformed big band and also became a member of the Big Four, led by Charlie Ventura. He also recorded extensively for Norman Granz, not only with the impresario's JATP but also with Art Tatum, Lionel Hampton, Ray Brown, Oscar Peterson, Flip Phillips, Dizzy Gillespie, Roy Eldridge, Louis Armstrong, Lester Young, Gene Krupa and many others.

Return stints with James and Dorsey followed, but by the late 50s, despite a heart attack, he was appearing as a singer and leading his own small bands. He continued to make records with, amongst others, Max Roach. In the early 60s, Rich was once more with James, but by 1966 had decided to try again with his own big band. He continued to lead a big band for the next dozen years, spent a while leading a small group, then reformed a big band in the 80s, continuing to lead this band for the rest of his life. His later bands frequently featured young, recently-graduated musicians, towards whom he displayed an attitude which resembled that of a feudal lord. Nevertheless, whether through awareness of these musicians' interests or the demands of audiences, the repertoire of many of Rich's 60s and 70s bands contained elements of rock without ever becoming a true fusion band. Rich's playing was characterized by his phenomenal speed and astonishing technical dexterity. His precision and clarity were legendary even if, at times, the band's charts were specifically designed to better display his remarkable skills. During his bandleading years, Rich continued to make records in many settings, in these he would usually revert to the drummer's traditional role of supporting player. In such contexts Rich was a subtle accompanist, adept with brushes but always swinging and propulsive. Early in his career Rich was notorious for his short temper, and during his stint with Dorsey frequently clashed with the band's singer, Frank Sinatra, a similarly short-fused artist. A caustically witty man, later in his life Rich became popular on television chat shows, where his put-downs of ill-equipped pop singers often bordered upon the slanderous. Rich came back frequently from illness and accident (once playing one-handed when his other arm was in a sling, without any noticeable diminution of his ability) but was finally diagnosed as having a brain tumour. Even during his final illness, his wit did not desert him. When a nurse preparing him for surgery asked if there was anything to which he was allergic he told her, 'Only country music.'

Selected albums: with Nat 'King' Cole *Anatomy Of A Jam Session* (1945), *The Lionel Hampton-Art Tatum-Buddy Rich Trio* (1955), *The Monster* (1955), *Gene Krupa Meets Buddy Rich* (1955), with Harry Edison *Buddy And Sweets* (1955), *Buddy Rich Sings Johnny Mercer* (1956), *Big Band Shout* (1956), *Buddy Just Sings* (1957), *The Buddy Rich Quartet In Miami* (1957), *Buddy Rich Versus Max Roach* (1959), *Richcraft* (1959), *The Voice Of Buddy Rich* (1959), *The Driver* (1960), *The Electric Sticks Of Buddy Rich* (1960), *Playmates* (1960), *Blues/Caravan* (1962), *Krupa And Rich/The Burning Beat* (1962), *Swingin' New Big Band* (1966), *Big Swing Face* (1967), *The New One!* (1967), *Rich A La Rakha* (1968), *Mercy, Mercy* (1968), *Buddy And Soul* (1969), *Keep The Customer Satisfied* (1970), incl. on *Jazz Monterey 1958-1980* (1970), *A Different Drummer* (1971), *Buddy Rich-Louie Bellson-Kenny Clare With The Bobby Lamb-Ray Premru Orchestra* (1971), *Very Alive At Ronnie Scott's* (1971), *Time Being* (1971-72), *Stick It* (1972), *The Roar Of '74* (1973), *Ease On Down The Road* (1973-74), *The Last Blues Album Vol. 1* (1974), *Speak No Evil* (1976), *Buddy Rich Plays And Plays* (1977), *Killing Me Forcefully* (1977), *Jam Session* (1977), *Giants Of Jazz Vol. 1* (1977), *Class Of '78* (1977), *Lionel Hampton Presents Buddy Rich* (Kingdom Gate 1977), *The Man From Planet Jazz* (1980), *Rich And Famous* (c.1980), *The Legendary Buddy Rich* (c.1982), *The Magic Of Buddy Rich*

(1984), *Tuff Dude* (LRC 1984), *Live On King Street* (c.1985), *The Cinch* (1985). Compilations: *A Man And His Drums* (1945), *Riot* (1946), *Great Moments* (1946), *Buddy Rich And His Greatest Band* (1946), *Buddy Rich '47-'48* (1947-48), *No Jive* (Novus 1992).

Further reading: *Improvising*, Whitney Balliett.

Richardson, Jerome

b. 15 November 1920, Sealy, Texas, USA. Raised in California, Richardson began playing alto saxophone in local bands in his early teens. In 1941 he was briefly with the Jimmie Lunceford band, then, after military service during World War II he played in bands led by Marshal Royal, Lionel Hampton and Earl 'Fatha' Hines. In 1953 he relocated in New York City, working at Minton's Playhouse with his own group. Later in the decade he worked with such leading swing and bop musicians as Lucky Millinder, Kenny Burrell, Gerry Mulligan and Oscar Pettiford. In 1959 he began an association with Quincy Jones and also accompanied several leading song stylists. In 1965 he was a founder member of the Thad Jones-Mel Lewis big band at New York's Village Vanguard. In 1971 he settled in Los Angeles, working mostly in film studios but also appearing with Quincy Jones, Art Pepper, Bill Berry and others. In the 80s he continued to combine studio work with jazz gigs, the former paying the rent while the latter consistently demonstrated his great versatility and talent as both soloist and section musician.

Albums: *The Oscar Pettiford Orchestra In Hi-Fi* (1956), *The Jerome Richardson Sextet* (1958), *The Great Wide World Of Quincy Jones* (1959), *Roamin' With Jerome Richardson* (1959), *Going To The Movies* (1962), *Midnight Oil* (Original Jazz Classics 1963), *Groove Merchant* (1967), with Thad Jones-Mel Lewis *Central Park North* (1969).

Richman, Boomie

b. Abraham S. Richards, 2 April 1921, Brockton, Massachusetts, USA. In the early and mid-40s Richman played tenor saxophone in bands led by Jerry Wald, Muggsy Spanier and Tommy Dorsey. This last engagement lasted five years and was followed by a long spell of studio work during which he also played and recorded with Benny Goodman, Neal Hefti, Ruby Braff, the Sauter-Finegan Orchestra, Red Allen and Cootie Williams. By the 60s his studio work considerably outweighed his jazz appearances, a fact which did not alter during succeeding decades. As the quality of his musical leaders indicates, Richman is a sound player with considerable versatility and a great sense of swing.

Albums: with Benny Goodman *B. G. In Hi-fi* (1954), *Muggsy Spanier* (1954).

Richmond, Dannie

b. 15 December 1935, New York City, New York, USA, d. 16 March 1988. After starting out as an R&B tenor saxophonist, Richmond switched to drums and direction in the early 50s. His success was such that by 1956 he was a member of Charles Mingus's band, a role he maintained until 1970. After a spell working in rock bands, backing Joe Cocker and Elton John, Richmond returned to Mingus. After Mingus's death in 1979 he became a founder member of the Mingus Dynasty. He also worked in small groups with George Adams and Don Pullen. A powerful drummer with a playing style that allowed him to range widely in music, from jazz to jazz-rock fusion and straight rock, Richmond's long service with Mingus led to his appearing on many seminal recording dates.

Selected albums: with Charles Mingus *Mingus Ah Um* (1958), with Mingus *Town Hall Concert* (1962), *The Great Concert Of Charles Mingus* (1964), with Don Pullen *Jazz A Confronto 21* (1975), with Mingus *Three Or Four Shades Of Blue* (1977), with Pullen *Don't Lose Control* (1979), *Ode To Mingus* (1979), *Dannie Richmond Plays Charles Mingus* (Timeless 1980), *Three Or Four Shades Of* (Tutu 1992).

Ricotti, Frank

b. 31 January 1949, London, England. Ricotti was born into a musical family and followed in his drummer-father's footsteps by taking up percussion. Educational facilities were limited but fortunately Ricotti came to the attention of Bill Ashton, then a teacher in London. With Aston's encouragement, Ricotti was able to extend his studies (and, inspired by Ricotti, Ashton embarked on a project which eventually became the National Youth Jazz Orchestra). Although adept on most percussion instruments, Ricotti concentrated upon the vibraphone and also developed his talents as a composer and arranger. In the late 60s and early 70s Ricotti played and recorded with Neil Ardley, Dave Gelly, Graham Collier, Mike Gibbs, Stan Tracey and Gordon Beck. By the late 70s Ricotti had become established as a studio musician; during the following decade he was deeply involved in the soundtrack music for a succession of popular British television series by Alan Plater, including *The Beiderbecke Affair*. Also in the 80s he was co-leader, with Chris Laurence and John Taylor, of Paragonne.

Albums: *Aspects Of Paragonne* (1985), *The Beiderbecke Collection* (1986-88).

Riley, Howard

b. John Howard Riley, 16 February 1943, Huddersfield, Yorkshire, England. Riley began playing piano at the age of six, although it was another 10 years before he began to play jazz. At university he studied under Bernard Rands at Bangor, North Wales (1961-66) gaining BA and MA degrees, then with David Baker at Indiana, adding M.Mus to his name in 1967. From 1967-70 he studied for his Ph.D at York University under Wilfred Mellers, who wrote a piece (Yeibichai) for symphony orchestra, scat singer and jazz trio which was performed by the BBC Symphony Orchestra, Frank Holder and Riley's trio at the 1969 Proms. Riley had led a trio, at Bangor, then joined Evan Parker's quartet. On his return from Indiana he formed a trio with Barry Guy (or sometimes Ron Rubin) and Jon Hiseman (or Tony Oxley or, later, Alan Jackson) and began writing for bands like the Spontaneous Music Ensemble and the Don Rendell-Ian Carr Quintet. At this time he also began to have his chamber and orchestral pieces performed in concert, and was a founder member of the Musicians' Co-Operative. He has composed for Barry Guy's London Jazz Composers' Orchestra and the New Jazz Orchestra and played with Keith Tippett, John McLaughlin (who had also occasionally sat in with the late 60s trio), Jaki Byard, Elton Dean, the LJCO (being the featured soloist on their *Double Trouble*), Barbara Thompson, Tony Oxley and many others. He has also taught at the Guildhall and Goldsmith's schools of music in London and at the Center Of The Creative And Performing Arts in Buffalo. In the late 80s he began to release both old and new recordings on his own cassette label, Falcon Tapes; and in 1990 he and Elton Dean co-lead a quartet of improvisers on a set of jazz standards, *All The Tradition*.

Selected albums: *Discussions* (1967), *Angle* (1969), *The Day Will Come* (1970), *Flight* (1971), *Synopsis* (1976), *Singleness* (1976), *Interwine* (1977), *Shaped* (Mosaic 1977), *Toronto Concert* (1979, rec 1976), *Facets* (Impetus 1981, rec 1979-81, three album box-set), *Duality* (1982), *The Other Side* (1983), *For Four On Two Two* (Affinity 1984), with Keith Tippett *In Focus* (Affinity 1985), with Jaki Byard *Live At The Royal Festival Hall* (1987, rec 1984), with Elton Dean *All The Tradition* (1990), *Procession* (Wondrous 1991), *The Heat Of Moments* (Wondrous 1993), with Tippett *The Bern Concert* (Future Music 1994), *Beyond Category* (Wondrous 1993).

Rimington, Sammy

b. 29 April 1942, London, England. Rimington began playing clarinet and alto saxophone professionally in his mid-teens as a member of Barry Martyn's band and by 1960 was with Ken Colyer where he remained for four years. In 1965 he visited the USA, playing in New Orleans with several leading veterans including George Lewis and Zutty Singleton. In the late 60s he was back in the UK working with Martyn and touring Americans, such as Kid Thomas and John Handy, but was also experimenting with jazz rock. He was, however, most at home in New Orleans-style music and since the mid-70s has played with many leading exponents of traditional jazz including George Webb, Keith Smith and Chris Barber. On clarinet, Rimington is an exceptionally fine performer in the tradition originating in the style of Lewis whom he clearly admires and he has great flair on this instrument. Like Barber, Rimington has constantly sought to expand the boundaries of his chosen area of jazz and this is most apparent when he plays alto saxophone. On this instrument he plays with great emotional depth, creating fascinating and highly rhythmic solos using a quirky distinctive style that faintly echoes the sound of Pete Brown. Despite his comparative youthfulness, Rimington is one of the outstanding exponents of New Orleans jazz playing today, and thanks to his broad-based musical outlook he can appeal to a much wider audience than this might at first suggest.

Albums: with Kid Thomas *The December Band* (1965), with Zutty Singleton *Zutty And The Clarinet Kings* (1967), with Keith Smith *Way Down Yonder In New Orleans, Then And Now* (1977), *And Red Beans* (1977), *Sammy Rimington And His New Orleans Quartet* (1977), *Reed All About It* (Hefty Jazz 1978),

The Sammy Rimington Band (1980), *Exciting Sax* (Progressive 1986-91), *In Town With Sam Lee* (GHB 1988), *A New Orleans Session With* (GHB 1989), *One Swiss Night* (Music Mecca 1993).

Ritenour, Lee

b. 1 November 1953, Los Angeles, California, USA. The prolific Ritenour has established himself as one of the world's leading jazz fusion guitarists with a series of accessible albums over the past two decades. Known as 'Captain Fingers' Ritenour became a sought-after session player in the mid-70s and like Larry Carlton (both regularly play a Gibson 335) has developed his own solo career. Although heavily influenced in his early days by the relaxed styles of Wes Montgomery, Joe Pass and Barney Kessel he now has his own distinctive sound and fluid style. His list of session work is awesome, but some of his notable performances were with Herbie Hancock, Steely Dan and Stanley Clarke. Since the mid-80s Ritenour has been strongly influenced by Brazilian music. He joined GRP Records around this time, having worked with stablemate Don Grusin in the band Friendship. He recorded the magnificent *Harlequin* with GRP co-owner Dave Grusin in 1985. In the early 90s Ritenour teamed up with Bob James, Harvey Mason and bassist Nathan East under the name of Fourplay, and released two soul/jazz/funk fusion albums, *Fourplay* and *Between The Sheets*, for Warner Brothers. In 1993 Ritenour topped the *Billboard* jazz chart with his accomplished tribute to Wes Montgomery, *Wes Bound*.

Albums: *First Course* (c.1974), *Guitar Player* (c.1975), *Captain Fingers* (1975), *The Captain's Journey* (Elektra 1978), *Gentle Thoughts* (JVC 1978), with Kazume Watanbe *Sugarloaf Express* (Elite 1978), *Feel The Night* (1979), *Friendship* (JVC 1979), *Rit* (Asylum 1981), *Rio* (GRP 1982), *Rit 2* (GRP 1983), *Banded Together* (1983), *On The Line* (1984), with Dave Grusin *Harlequin* (GRP 1985), *American Flyers* (1986), *Earth Run* (GRP 1986), *Portrait* (1987), *Festival* (GRP 1988), *Wes Bound* (GRP 1993).

Rivers, Sam

b. 25 September 1930, El Reno, Oklahoma, USA. Alto, soprano and tenor saxophones, flute, piano and composer. After extensive studies, Rivers began playing in and around Boston, Massachusetts in the late 40s. (His first professional engagement had been with Jimmy Witherspoon during his military service.) During the next few years he played mostly in the Boston area with Jaki Byard, Nat Pierce, Herb Pomeroy and the very young Tony Williams. He also worked in Florida in a band led by Don Wilkerson. It was not until 1964 that he achieved prominence when he joined Miles Davis thanks to the recommendation of Williams, then a member of Davis's band. In the mid-60s he worked in New York, recording for Blue Note with Williams, Byard, Ron Carter and others. In the late 60s he continued recording with such artists as Donald Byrd, Bobby Hutcherson and Julian Priester. Around this time he also began teaching and established a five-year association with Cecil Taylor with whom he visited Europe. Since that time he has continued to teach, compose and perform with a wide variety of musical groups including the San Francisco Symphony Orchestra, his own small groups and has had a lasting relationship with Dave Holland. A highly acclaimed musician, Rivers' concentration on teaching and on developing original musical concepts has tended to make him less accessible to the wider audience. Those who have persevered with his music have found it rewarding in its imaginative blending of many jazz styles, ranging from blues to the *avant garde*. Rivers is particularly effective on flute and soprano, instruments on which he displays a light, dancing style. Whether as performer or composer, it is the remarkably sustained inventiveness which most characterizes his work.

Selected albums: *Fuchsia Swing Song* (Blue Note 1964), with Miles Davis *Miles In Tokyo* (1964), *Streams* (MCA 1973), *Sam Rivers/Dave Holland* (Improvising Artists 1976), *The Tuba Trio Vols 1-3* (1976), *Waves* (Tomato 1978), *Colours* (Black Saint 1983), *Lazuli* (Timeless 1990).

Roach, Max

b. 10 January 1924, New Land, North Carolina, USA. Beginning to play drums in his pre-teen years, Roach later studied in New York and by 1942 was active in the bebop revolution. As a member of the house rhythm section at Monroe's Uptown House and a regular at Minton's Playhouse, he backed all the leading practitioners of the new art. Along with Kenny Clarke he established a new drummers' vocabulary, and his work with Charlie Parker and Dizzy Gillespie from this period demonstrates his inventiveness and masterly technique. In addition to playing bebop, the 40s also found him working in small and big bands led by such swing era veterans as Coleman Hawkins and Benny Carter. Towards the end of the decade, however, he abandoned the older style and was henceforth one of bebop's major voices. He was with Miles Davis for two years from 1948, participating in the seminal *Birth Of The Cool* recording dates. In 1954 Roach formed a quintet with Clifford Brown, a band which was one of the most musically inventive of the period. Brown's accidental death in 1956 was a devastating loss to Roach and it took many years for him to fully shake off the traumatic effect it had upon him. From the late 50s Roach began to take a political stance and was active in many black cultural projects. Inevitably, his work of this period took on elements of his commitment to Civil Rights issues. His compositions included the *We Insist! Freedom Now Suite*. He also experimented with unusual line-ups, sometimes abandoning conventional time structures. In these respects he was in line with concurrent developments in free jazz, but was never a true part of that movement. His own small groups saw an impressive array of talented musical partners including Freddie Hubbard, Sonny Rollins, George Coleman and Stanley Turrentine. He also worked with a variety of singers and vocal groups, including performances with his wife Abbey Lincoln. In the 70s, although he was by then becoming an elder statesman of jazz, Roach continued to associate with musicians of the *avant garde*, recording duo albums with Abdullah Ibrahim, Archie Shepp, Cecil Taylor and Anthony Braxton. One of few

drummers to perform and record extended solo works, Roach achieved a remarkably high standard of performance and overcame the customary negative critical response to such works. Throughout the 80s and into the early 90s, Roach continued to perform and compose, finding time to teach and to maintain his activism in black politics. One of the most technically-gifted musicians in jazz, Roach has long been a major figure in the development of the music and his consistently high standard of performance has never faltered. As a drummer, he is a master of all aspects of his work, a mastery which he demonstrated during his 1990 UK tour by playing as an encore a thoroughly absorbing ten-minute solo using only the hi-hat cymbal. If there is another jazz drummer capable of such feats he has yet to appear in public.

Selected albums: with Miles Davis *The Complete Birth Of The Cool* (1949-50), *The Max Roach-Clifford Brown Quintet* (1954-6), *Study In Brown* (1955), *At Basin Street* (1956), *Max Roach Plus Four* (1956), *Jazz In 3/4 Time* (1957), *Drummin' The Blues* (1957), *Max Plays Charlie Parker* (1957-58), *Max* (1958), *Max Roach Plus Four, Newport 1958 Jazz Festival* (1958), *Deeds, Not Words* (1958), *Sessions, Live* (1958), *The Many Sides Of Max Roach* (1959), *Award-Winning Drummer* (1959), *Quiet As It's Kept* (1960), *Drum Conversation/Long As You're Living* (1960), *Parisian Sketches* (1960), *Again* (1960), *We Insist! Freedom Now Suite* (1960), *Moon-Faced And Starry-Eyed* (1960), *Percussion Bitter Suite* (1961), *It's Time* (1961-62), *Speak, Brother, Speak* (1962), *Paris Concert* (1962-63), *The Legendary Hasaan* (1964), *Members Don't Get Weary* (1968), *Lift Every Voice And Sing* (1971), *Force-Sweet Mao-Suid Afrika '76* (1976), *Max Roach Quartet Live In Tokyo Vols 1 & 2* (1977), *The Loadstar* (1977), *Live In Amsterdam* (1977), *Solos* (1977), *Confirmation* (1978), *Birth And Rebirth* (Black Saint 1978), with Archie Shepp *The Long March* (1979), *One In Two-Two In One* (Hat Art 1979), *Pictures In A Frame* (Soul Note 1979), *Historic Concerts* (1979), *Chattahoochee Red* (1981), *Swish* (1982), *In The Light* (Soul Note 1982), *Live At Vielharmonie, Munich* (Soul Note 1983), *Scott Free* (Soul Note 1984), *Survivors* (Soul Note 1984), *Easy Winners* (Soul Note 1985), *Bright Moments* (Soul Note 1987), *To The Max!* (Enja 1992). Compilation: *The Max Roach Quintet* (1949).

Roberts, Hank

b. 1954, Terre Haute, Indiana, USA. Cellist - and until recently, professional chef - Roberts has become one of the busiest musicians in New York's 'downtown' scene. His music is wide-open experimental and heedless of idiomatic boundaries. It acknowledges his hillbilly roots with a comic barn dance or two, but moves out towards sleek rock, free sound exploration, anything and everything. First heard amongst the massed strings of Michael Mantler's Orchestra on *13* (1975), Roberts began to attract rave notices for his work with guitarist Bill Frisell. The cellist leads his own group Birds Of Prey and co-leads two others: Miniature (with Tim Berne and Joey Baron), and Arcado, a string trio with Mark Dresser and Mark Feldman. Roberts is also a distinctive singer, his vocals having an ethereal quality that has prompted critics to make comparisons with Milton Nascimento and Robert Wyatt. Often doctoring his voice with echo and tape-delay, Roberts uses it to expand the sound of his cello, 'to make the chords bigger'.

Albums: *Black Pastels* (JMT 1988), *Miniature* (1988), *Arcado* (1989), *Hank Robert & Birds Of Prey* (JMT 1990), with Arcado *Behind The Myth* (1990), with Miniature *I Can't Put My Finger On It* (1991), with Arcado *For Three Strings And Orchestra* (1992), *Little Motor People* (JMT 1993).

Roberts, Luckey

b. Charles Luckyeth, 7 August 1887, Philadelphia, Pennsylvania, USA, d. 5 February 1968. After working in vaudeville as a child, Roberts moved to New York where he established a minor reputation as a composer and a major one as a performer of rags and, later, stride piano. In the years between the wars, Roberts's composing talents were recognized more and several of his musical shows were produced. During the 40s and early 50s he owned and regularly played at a Harlem bar. Roberts made few records and most of these were early piano rolls while his later records were made after he had suffered strokes and injuries in a road accident. Nevertheless, it is possible to understand the awe felt by such pianists as Fats Waller, James P. Johnson and Willie 'The Lion' Smith at his astonishing technique, a technique which was greatly facilitated by his remarkably large hands.

Album: *Harlem Piano Solos* (1958).

Roberts, Marcus

b. 7 August 1963, Jacksonville, Florida, USA. If Thelonious Monk frequently pursued improvisation through harmonic as well as (or sometimes instead of) melodic routes, Roberts is an appropriate inheritor of the method. Like Wynton Marsalis, later to be his employer, Roberts is a dedicated respecter of earlier jazz traditions, and his technique comfortably encompasses stride, many variations of blues, and bebop. He took up the instrument early, exposed to a mixture of classical and gospel music, and studied piano at Florida State, winning competitions on the instrument by the mid-80s. Roberts's vitality, knowledge, technique and admiration for his keyboard predecessors brought him a place in the Wynton Marsalis group by 1985 and - as with Marsalis - a series of albums as leader took him further back into the archives, albeit with a continuing grace and swing. 1990's *Alone With Three Giants* demonstrated Roberts's singleminded determination to subjugate self-expression to interpretation of classic works, including pieces by Jelly Roll Morton and Monk.

Albums: *The Truth Is Spoken Here* (Novus 1989), *Deep In The Shed* (Novus 1990), *Alone With Three Giants* (Novus 1990), *Prayer For Peace* (Novus 1991), *As Serenity Approaches* (Novus 1992), *If I Could Be With You* (Novus 1993).

Robertson, Zue

b. C. Alvin Robertson, 7 March 1891, New Orleans, Louisiana, USA, d. 1943. After learning to play piano, Robertson switched to trombone and first played professionally in his early teenage. He worked with such leading New Orleans musicians as Manuel Perez, John Robichaux and Richard M. Jones. He was also a member of the band accompanying a touring wild west show which featured frontiersman Kit Carson. Dividing his time between New Orleans and Chicago, Robertson became a proficient performer and by the early 20s had recorded with Jelly Roll Morton and King Oliver. After spending most of the 20s on the road he settled in New York where he reverted to piano and also played organ, giving up the trombone entirely. He played on through the 30s, relocating in California, and took up yet another instrument, the bass.

Robichaux, John

b. 16 January 1886, Thibodaux, Louisiana, USA, d. 1939. Resident in New Orleans from the last years of the 19th century, violinist and drummer Robichaux formed a dance orchestra in 1893 and thereafter continuously led a band until his death. He worked with many noted New Orleans musicians including Lorenzo Tio and Manuel Perez. Although he was active during the birth and early development of jazz, Robichaux mostly, apart from this musical trend, concentrated instead on providing dance music for the wider audiences of the day. His nephews include Joseph Robichaux and John Robichaux, a drummer, who worked on into the 70s.

Robichaux, Joseph

b. 8 March 1900, New Orleans, Louisiana, USA, d 17 January 1965. A nephew of John Robichaux, he played piano in New Orleans and Chicago in the years immediately after World War I. In the early 20s he was a member of the Black Eagle Band and also worked with the Davey Jones-Lee Collins Astoria Hot Eight. In the early 30s he played with Kid Rena and also formed his own band, the New Orleans Rhythm Boys which stayed in existence until 1939. During the 40s Robichaux worked as a soloist in New York. In the 50s he was accompanist to Lizzie Miles and then joined the George Lewis band, touring internationally and recording. He remained with Lewis until 1964, then returned to New Orleans where he died in 1965. He was a solid ensemble pianist with a lively solo style.

Albums: *Joe Robichaux And His New Orleans Boys* (1933), with George Lewis *The Perennial George Lewis* (1958), *The Perennial George Lewis* (1958). Compilations: *Joe Robichaux And His New Orleans Boys* (1933), *1933* (Classic Jazz Masters 1986), *The Complete* (Blu-Disc 1988).

Robinson, Jim

b. 25 December 1890, Deer Range, Louisiana, USA, d. 4 May 1976. After playing guitar for a number of years, Robinson took up the trombone while serving in the US Army during World War I. In the immediate post-war years he played regularly in New Orleans, and was good enough to be hired by such leading New Orleans musicians as Kid Rena and Sam Morgan. He later played in the bands of John Handy and Kid Howard but, like many other New Orleans jazzmen, he retained his 'day job'. In his case he worked as a longshoreman well into the 30s. The Revival Movement persuaded him that he could make his living playing jazz and in the 40s he played with Bunk Johnson and in the 50s was a regular member of George Lewis's band. He toured extensively in the 60s, with Billie and De De Pierce, Percy Humphrey and the Preservation Hall Jazz Band. An outstanding ensemble player, Robinson played with great attack and brought drive and enthusiasm to any band of which he was a member.

Albums: *George Lewis At The San Jacinto Hall* (1964), *Robinson's Jacinto Ballroom Orchestra* (1964), with Percy Humphrey *Climax Rag* (1965), *Economy Hall Breakdown* (1965), *Jim Robinson And Tony Fougerat* (1967), *Living New Orleans Jazz* (1976). Compilations: *Bunk Johnson With George Lewis* (1944), *Jim Robinson And His New Orleans Band* (Center 1992), *Classic New Orleans Jazz Vol 2* (Biograph 1993).

Robinson, Spike

b. Henry Berthold Robinson, 16 January 1930, Kenosha, Wisconsin, USA. Beginning on alto saxophone in his early teenage years, Robinson soon discovered that it was hard to make a living playing the kind of music he wanted to play. So, in 1948 he joined the US Navy as a musician and by 1950 was based in the UK. He was soon regularly jamming at London's Club Eleven, Downbeat Club and Studio 51 with leading UK beboppers, including Tommy Pollard and Victor Feldman. He made a few records for Carlo Krahmer's Esquire label but eventually was transferred home and demobilized. Unhappy with the music scene in the Chicago area, he took advantage of the GI Bill to study electronic engineering at university. For most of the next 30 years he lived and worked in Colorado, eventually taking up music again, this time playing tenor saxophone and working nights at local clubs. A constant musical companion of these times was Dave Grusin. In 1981 Robinson recorded for the first time since his London sessions, in a band led by Feldman. Encouraged to visit the UK by a British fan, in 1984 Robinson began a series of tours which were so successful that he took early retirement from his engineering job to turn to a full-time career in music. Throughout the rest of the 80s and into the early 90s, he has played at clubs and festivals throughout the UK, Europe and in various parts of the USA, making his New York debut at Christmas 1990. A succession of superb record albums, most as leader but some with artists such as Louis Stewart, Harry Edison, Al Cohn, Roy Williams and Claude Tissendier, have attracted high critical and public praise. Despite his bebop beginnings, the mature musician who emerged in the 80s from self-imposed exile is a consummate ballad player who eagerly explores the endless archives of the Great American Song Book. His rhapsodic, breathy style is instantly identifiable and the effortless loping swing of everything he plays has helped to make Robinson into one of the outstanding tenor saxophonists of his generation. In the early 90s Robinson was touring extensively from a UK base, recording many albums and headlining at clubs and festivals in Europe and the USA.

Selected albums: *The Guv'nor* (1951), with Victor Feldman *The Music Of Harry Warren* (1981), *Spike Robinson At Chesters Vols 1 & 2* (Hep 1984), *London Reprise* (1984), with Roy Williams *It's A Wonderful World* (1985), *The Gershwin Collection* (1987), with Al Cohn *Henry B. Meets Alvin G.* (1987), with Elaine Delmar *In Town* (Hep 1987), *The Odd Couple* (Capri 1988), with Louis Stewart *Three For The Road* (Hep 1989), with Harry Edison *Jusa Bit O' Blues Vols 1 & 2* (Capri 1989), with Claude Tissendier *Saxomania Presenting Spike Robinson* (1989), *Stairway To The Stars* (Hep 1990), *One Man In His Time* (1991), *Spike Robinson And George Masso Play Arlen* (Hep 1992), *Reminiscin'* (Capri 1993).

Roché, Betty

b. 9 January 1920, Wilmington, Delaware, USA. After winning an amateur talent contest in the early 40s, Roché sang with Al Cooper's Savoy Sultans. Joining Duke Ellington in 1943 she appeared at Carnegie Hall, then, after a brief spell with the Earl Hines band, she drifted out of the big time. In 1952 she was back with Ellington, appearing at clubs and concerts and also broadcasting with the band. A further period out of the spotlight followed although she made several albums under her own name in the late 50s and early 60s. After this she again returned to obscurity. An attractive song stylist, Roche was one of the best to work for Ellington, who, after Ivie Anderson, was notoriously casual with his choice of vocalists.

Albums: with Duke Ellington *Carnegie Hall Concert: January 1943* (1943), with Ellington *The Duke Is On The Air* (1952), *Take The 'A' Train* (1956), *Singing' And Swingin'* (Original Jazz Classics 1961), *Lightly And Politely* (Original Jazz Classics 1961).

Rodin, Gil

b. Gilbert A. Rodin, 9 December 1909, Russia, d. 17 June 1974. Raised in Chicago, Rodin played clarinet and saxophones in a number of local dance bands before moving to California. In 1927 he became a member of the Ben Pollack band. He quickly became a key figure in the band as both player and administrator. He also wrote a number of arrangements. In 1935, following disagreements with Pollack, Rodin was one of the founders of a new co-operative band which was eventually fronted by Bob Crosby. Once again, Rodin assumed multiple roles, one of which was as president of the Crosby corporation, and was the mastermind of the band's huge popularity. After World War II he worked with another ex-Crosby sideman, Ray Bauduc and in a reconstituted Crosby band. At the end of the 40s he moved out of music and into radio and television where he worked as a programme producer.

Album: with Bob Crosby *South Rampart Street Parade* (1935-42).

Rodney, Red

b. Robert Chudnick, 27 September 1927, Philadelphia, Pennsylvania, USA, d. 27 May 1994, Boynton Beach, Florida, USA. Within a few years of taking up the trumpet (first presented to him by a great aunt at his Bar Mitzvah) Rodney was hired by dance band leader Jerry Wald. While still in his teens he also played with Jimmy Dorsey, Elliot Lawrence and Benny Goodman. By 1946, when he joined Gene Krupa, Rodney was a highly experienced big band trumpeter but was already experimenting with bebop. These inclinations were encouraged by Krupa, Claude Thornhill and Woody Herman with whom he also played in the late 40s. In 1949, with his reputation as a rising bop star fast gaining ground, he joined the Charlie Parker quintet (via an introduction from Dizzy Gillespie). For the next two years he was acclaimed as one of the best bebop trumpeters around and was certainly among the first white players to gain credibility and acceptance in the field (he would go on to help record the soundtrack to Clint Eastwood's film tribute to Parker, *Bird*. Among the anecdotes to emerge from this time was the tale of Parker telling his agent that Rodney was in fact an albino, in order to ensure he wasn't barred from a tour of the South). Ill health and drug addiction nevertheless damaged his career and the 50s and 60s were bleak periods - despite arranging an elaborate fraud whereby he impersonated the similar-looking General Arnold T. MacIntyre in order to obtain money by deception. During the early 70s Rodney returned to the centre of the jazz stage, playing better than ever and displaying inventiveness and thorough mastery of his instrument in all bop and post-bop settings. He continued to be in demand playing in festivals, concerts and clubs around the world until his death, from lung cancer, in 1994.

Selected albums: *Georgie Auld/Red Rodney On The Air* (1947), with Charlie Parker *Live At Carnegie Hall* (1949), *The New Sounds* (1951), *Modern Music From Chicago* (1955), *Red Arrow* (1957), *The Red Rodney Quintet* (1958), *Fiery* (Savoy 1958), *Bird Lives!* (Muse 1973), *Superbop* (Muse 1974), *Red Rodney With The Bebop Preservation Society* (1975), *Red Rodney With The Danish Jazz Army* (1975), *The Red Tornado* (Muse 1975), *Yard's Pad* (Sonet 1976), *Red, White And Blues* (Muse 1976), *Home Free* (Muse 1977), *The Three Rs* (1979), *Hi Jinx At The Village Vanguard* (Muse 1980), *Live At The Village Vanguard* (1980), *Spirit Within* (1981), *Night And Day* (1981), *Sprint* (1982), *Red Giant* (Steeplechase 1988), *No Turn On Red* (Denon 1988), *One For Bird* (Steeplechase 1988), *Red Snapper* (Steeplechase 1988), *Then And Now* (Chesky 1992). Compilation: with Gene Krupa *Drummin' Man* (1945-49).

Rogers, Paul

b. 1956, Luton, Bedfordshire, England. Bassist Rogers moved to London in 1974. A versatile player, he has worked with Paul Rutherford, Art Themen, Keith Tippett, John Stevens, Elton Dean, Mike Osborne, Stan Tracey, Louis Moholo, Alan Skidmore's Tenor Tonic, and 7 RPM (with Tony Marsh and Simon Picard). Among European musicians, those he worked with include Alexander Von Schlippenbach and Joachim Kuhn. In 1981 he played on the British debut recording of Brazilian saxophonist Andres Boiarsky (*Plays South Of The Border*). He took part in two notable foreign tours by British musicians: Harry Beckett (touring the Middle East in 1984) and Evan Parker (Rumania, Yugoslavia and Greece in 1985). Since the late 80s he has been working frequently with drummer Mark Sanders, and together they have provided a powerful and flexible engine for Atlas (with pianist John Law), Parker, Dennis Gonzalez, and the Elton Dean/Howard Riley

Quartet (*All The Tradition*). Recently he has also been a member of Tippett's intense quartet Mujician and the Louis Moholo trio. An Arts Council grant led to the composition of a suite (Anglo American Sketches) for three saxophonists, flute, bass and drums, which was well received when it was toured nationally in 1990. In the same year Rogers also toured in a trio with Andrew Cyrille.

Album: with Atlas *Trio Improvisations* (1989).

Rogers, Shorty

b. 14 April 1924, Great Barrington, Massachusetts, USA, d. 7 November 1994, Los Angeles, California, USA. After studying in New York, Rogers played trumpet in the bands of Will Bradley, where he first met Shelly Manne, and Red Norvo. Military service interrupted his career, but in 1945 he joined Woody Herman for a spell during which he also wrote a number of bop-flavoured big band charts. After Herman, he played with and arranged for the Stan Kenton band, thus increasing his public exposure still more. While with Kenton he also composed a number of features for fellow sidemen such as Art Pepper and Maynard Ferguson. During the 50s Rogers worked mostly in California, still writing hard-swinging charts for Kenton but trying to get work locally. He worked in films, appearing on-screen and on the soundtrack of *The Man With The Golden Arm* (1955). He also recorded with his own big band, effectively 'borrowing' most of the current Kenton band, but he was most often in a succession of important small groups. Rogers's involvement in the west coast scene was intense and he, more than any other single musician, is most readily identifiable as a prime mover in the movement's success. The first small group record date Rogers organized was in October 1951 and resulted in the influential *Modern Sounds*, on which he was joined by Manne, Pepper, Jimmy Giuffre, Hampton Hawes and others. He also appeared on the *Lighthouse All Stars*, then led his own groups through a succession of fine recordings including the big band *Cool And Crazy*, on which he used Kenton's men.

On these and his many other albums of the 50s, including *The Swinging Mr Rogers* and *Martians Come Back*, Rogers ably demonstrates his arranging gifts and magnificently showcases the musicians hired for the occasion. This use of several young veterans of the swing era tradition to play music that drew heavily upon the newer vocabularies of bebop created a perfect blending of all that was best of both forms. There was little or no evidence of the cliches which were, by then, adversely affecting the performances of many of the surviving big bands. While the Rogers brand of west coast jazz did not have the aggressive urgency of its east coast counterpart, it always swung lithely. Rogers was constantly on the lookout for new and unusual sounds and styles and was an early jazz experimenter with 12-tone writing. He continued playing and writing throughout the 60s, 70s and 80s, touring extensively and always eager to work with young musicians in the USA or UK and with old friends like Bud Shank and Vic Lewis. In the early 90s he most frequently played flügelhorn, the warmer, denser sound admirably suiting his expressive playing style.

Selected albums: *Modern Sounds* (Affinity 1951), *Popo* (1951), *Cool And Crazy* (1953), *Short Snort* (1953), *Blues Express* (RCA 1953-56), *Shorty Rogers Courts The Count* (1953), *Shorty Rogers And His Giants* (1954), *The Swinging Mr Rogers/Martians Stay Home* (Atlantic 1955), *Martians Come Back/Way Up There* (1955), *Clickin' With Clax* (Atlantic 1956), *Wherever The Five Winds Blow* (1956), *Shorty Rogers Plays Richard Rodgers* (1957), *Portrait Of Shorty* (1957), *Gigi In Jazz* (1958), *Afro-Cuban Jazz Inc.* (1958), *Chances Are, It Swings* (1958), *Wizard Of Oz* (1959), *Shorty Rogers Meets Tarzan* (1959), *The Swinging Nutcracker* (1960), *Fourth Dimension* (1961), *Bossa Nova* (1962), *Jazz Waltz* (Discovery 1962), *Gospel Mission* (1963), *West Coast Jazz* (Atlantic 1976), *Re-entry* (1983), *Yesterday, Today And Forever* (Concord 1983), *Shorty Rogers And The West Coast Giants* (1983), with Vic Lewis, Bud Shank *Back Again* (Concept 1984), *Shorty Rogers And Bud Shank Live At The Concorde Club, Southampton* (1984), *California Concert* (1985), with Shank *America The Beautiful* (Candid 1991), *Eight Brothers* (Candid 1992).

Roker, Mickey

b. 3 September 1932, Miami, Florida, USA. Raised in Philadelphia, Pennsylvania, Roker played drums with R&B bands but was attracted to jazz. He worked briefly with such visiting and local jazzmen as Jimmy Heath, Lee Morgan and McCoy Tyner and it was not until the end of the 50s that he went to New York. During the next few years he played in bands led by Gigi Gryce, Ray Bryant, Duke Pearson, Art Farmer, Sonny Rollins, Milt Jackson, Clifford Jordan and Morgan. He was for a while in the house band at Blue Note Records and played on many dates. In 1971 he began a long association with Dizzy Gillespie which lasted through the rest of the decade. Freelancing in the 80s has brought him into groups led by Oscar Peterson, Ray Bryant, Zoot Sims, Jackson and Ray Brown. A forceful, dynamic drummer, Roker's style is rooted in swing but has the urgent attack of the best of the beboppers.
Albums: with Gigi Gryce *Rat Race Blues* (1960), with Duke Pearson *Wahoo!* (1964), with Lee Morgan *Live at The Lighthouse* (1970), *Dizzy Gillespie's Big 4* (1974), with Gillespie *Dizzy's Party* (1976), with Ray Bryant *Potpourri* (1980).

Roland, Gene

b. 15 September 1921, New York City, New York, USA, d. 11 August 1982. In the early 40s many of Roland's arrangements played an important part in establishing the success of the Stan Kenton band. Among his arrangements was the June Christy hit, 'Tampico'. During this period he sometimes played trumpet in the band, later switching to trombone. Generally credited with Jimmy Giuffre as co-creator of the 'Four Brothers' sound of the Woody Herman band, Roland arranged for and played piano with Stan Getz, Giuffre (with whom he had studied at North Texas State Teachers' College, forerunner of NTSU), Herbie Steward and Zoot Sims in a small group which was heard by Herman in 1947. Later in the 40s Roland played in the bands of Georgie Auld, Count Basie, Charlie Barnet and

Lucky Millinder, sometimes on trumpet, other times on trombone. He tried his hand at bandleading in 1950 with an adventurous but ill-fated bebop big band which featured Charlie Parker, Don Fagerquist, Red Rodney, Jimmy Knepper, Sims and Al Cohn. In the 50s he again wrote for Kenton and Herman, helping create the former's 'mellophonium band'. During the 60s Roland worked in Scandinavia, writing and directing a radio orchestra, and in the 70s, back in the USA, he continued to write challenging big band charts and to play on a variety of instruments.
Albums: *The Band That Never Was* (1950), *A Swinging Introduction To Jimmy Knepper* (1957), *The Gene Roland Sextette* (1957), with Stan Kenton *Adventures In Blues* (1961), *Swinging Friends* (1963).

Rollins, Sonny

b. Theodore Walter Rollins, 7 September 1929, New York, USA. Although an older brother played violin and, at the age of nine, he took piano lessons, Rollins was destined for the saxophone. In 1944 he played alto saxophone in high school and when he left in 1947 he began gigging round New York on tenor. His first inspiration was Coleman Hawkins, but he was well aware of the beboppers, many of whom lived in his neighbourhood. His first recording date was with scat-singer Babs Gonzalez for Capitol Records in 1948. Soon he was recording with Bud Powell, Fats Navarro and J.J. Johnson, who recorded his first composition, 'Audubon'. Rollins's assured version of Charlie Parker on tenor was embraced by the top jazz artists: in 1949 he played with Art Blakey, in 1950 with Tadd Dameron, in 1951 with Miles Davis and in 1953 with Thelonious Monk. In 1954 Davis recorded with Rollins, including in the set three important Rollins compositions: 'Airegin' (Nigeria backwards - a salute to the newly independent African state), 'Oleo' and 'Doxy'. However, Rollins left for Chicago and Davis chose John Coltrane when he formed his new quintet. In January 1956, when the Clifford Brown/Max Roach quintet lost its tenor (Harold Land) in Chicago, Rollins stepped in, and played with them for 18 months. After that, Rollins began leading his own groups. In May 1956 he recorded *Tenor Madness* for Prestige, with the Paul Chambers/Philly Joe Jones rhythm team from Coltrane's group. The title track consisted of a mighty 'tenor battle' with Coltrane himself, Rollins's melodious expansion contrasting with Coltrane's pressure-cooker angularity.
In April 1956 Rollins recorded *Saxophone Colossus*, generally regarded as his first masterpiece. However, the advent of Ornette Coleman caused a deal of self-reflection and he retired for two years (1959-1960), amidst rumours that he was practising on Williamsburg Bridge. In 1961 he re-emerged to work with Jim Hall and then with two musicians associated with Ornette: trumpeter Don Cherry and drummer Billy Higgins. *Our Man In Jazz* shows him taking on the new freedoms with confidence and passion: the 20-minute 'Oleo' was a *tour de force*. He then toured as a soloist, using local rhythm sections (European tours in 1965, 1966 and 1967). In 1966 he recorded *East Broadway Rundown* with the Jimmy Garrison/Elvin

Jones rhythm section from Coltrane's classic quartet. The music, with its blistering title track and tremulous version of 'We Kiss In A Shadow' was superb, but it was indicative of Rollins's problems that it was a one-off group. Rollins found it difficult to deal with the possibilities opened up by the assaults on form of the *avant garde*. He again took a two-year sabbatical (1968-71), this time studying in India and Japan.

In 1973 he recorded *Horn Culture* using electric accompaniment. On electric bass Bob Cranshaw lacked the fire he had shown on *Our Man In Jazz* and despite Rollins's self-overdubs and characteristically ambitious solos, he seemed to be mired in pedestrian jazz-rock. *The Cutting Edge* (1974) had a bravura *a cappella* rendition of 'To A Wild Rose' but a similarly subdued band. In 1978 he toured with the Milestone All Stars. Here, a band of the stature of McCoy Tyner, Ron Carter and Al Foster could not fail to spark him, but these musicians were all leaders in their own right and could not work with him regularly. At this point Rollins refused all further nightclub performances and resolved to play festivals and concert halls exclusively. In 1985 Rollins attempted to do without rhythm sections altogether in *The Solo Album* and then toured Europe with a band featuring ex-Weather Report bassist Victor Bailey and drummer Tommy Campbell. In 1986 his *Concerto For Saxophone And Orchestra* was premiered in Japan. 1988 saw him linking up with some of the new names of the jazz revival: Marvin 'Smitty' Smith provided him with ferociously good drumming at live appearances. However, a rather tight and commercial sound made *Dancing In The Dark* unsatisfactory. Rollins is a soloist *par excellence*. His indecision about the form of his music - whether it is to be free/electric/acoustic - reflects the general quandary of jazz in the 80s. He is still capable of the solo flights that caused Davis to vote for him as 'greatest tenor ever' in a poll conducted by Leonard Feather at the end of the 60s.

Selected albums: *First Recordings* (1951), *Sonny And The Stars* (1953), *Movin' Out* (Original Jazz Classics 1954), *Worktime* (1956), *With The Modern Jazz Quartet* (Original Jazz Classics 1956), *Plus Four* (Original Jazz Classics 1956), *Tenor Madness* (Original Jazz Classics 1956), *Work Time* (Original Jazz Classics 1956), *Saxophone Colossus* (Original Jazz Classics 1956), *Sonny Rollins Vol 1* (Blue Note 1956), *Plays For Bird* (Original Jazz Classics 1957), *Tour De Force* (Original Jazz Classics 1957), *Sonny Rollins, Volume Two* (Blue Note 1957), *Newk's Time* (Blue Note 1957), *A Night At The Village Vanguard Vol 1* (Blue Note 1957), *The Sound Of Sonny* (Original Jazz Classics 1957), *Way Out West* (Blue Note 1957), *A Night At The Village Vanguard Vol 1* (1958), *A Night At The Village Vanguard Vol 2* (Blue Note 1958), *Meets The Big Brass* (1958), *Brass/Trio* (1958), *And The Contemporary Leaders* (1959), *The Bridge* (RCA 1962), *What's New* (1962), *Our Man In Jazz* (1962), *Sonny Meets Hawk* (1963), *Now's The Time!* (1964), *The Standard Sonny Rollins* (1965), *On Impulse* (Impulse 1965), *Plays Alfie* (Impulse 1966), *East Broadway Rundown* (Impulse 1966), *There Will Never Be Another You* (1967), *Next Album* (Original Jazz Classics 1972), *Horn Culture* (Original Jazz Classics 1973), *In Japan* (1974), *The Cutting Edge* (Original Jazz Classics 1974), *Nucleus* (Original Jazz Classics 1975), *More From The Vanguard* (1975, rec 1957), *The Way I Feel* (Original Jazz Classics 1976), *Easy Living* (1977), *Don't Stop The Carnival* (Milestone 1978), with others *Milestone Jazz Stars* (Milestone 1978), *Don't Ask* (1979), *Love At First Sight* (1980), *The Alternative Rollins* (1981, rec 1964), *No Problem* (1982), *Reel Life* (1982), *St Thomas: In Stockholm 1959* (1984, rec 1959), *Sunny Days, Starry Nights* (Milestone 1984), *In Paris* (1984, rec early 60s), *The Solo Album* (Milestone 1985), *Alternate Takes* (1986, rec 1957-58), *Plays G-Man* (Milestone 1986), *Dancing In The Dark* (Milestone 1988), *Falling In Love With Jazz* (Milestone 1990), *Here's To The People* (Milestone 1991), *What's New* (1993), *Old Flames* (Milestone 1994).

Romano, Joe

b. 17 April 1932, Rochester, New York, USA. After playing alto and tenor saxophones with various bands in the northeastern states, Romano joined Woody Herman in 1956. Subsequently, he worked with Chuck Mangione, Gus Mancuso, Sam Noto and others, returning frequently to Herman. In the late 60s and early 70s he played in bands led by Buddy Rich and Les Brown. In the mid-70s he was a member of Chuck Israel's National Jazz Ensemble and in 1978 joined the Louie Bellson band which played in the USA and UK. He has also played with the Thad Jones-Mel Lewis band and has recorded with Bill Watrous and Don Menza. An aggressive, bebop-influenced player, Romano's career has rarely been settled for long periods, making it difficult to form an accurate assessment of his status in the jazz world. Nevertheless, the regularity with which important leaders have called upon his services is an indicator of his standing among fellow musicians. The power and dynamism of his section work is particularly impressive and his solos display fiery urgency and an impressive flow of ideas.

Albums: with Sam Noto *Act One* (1975), with Noto *Notes To You* (1977), with Bill Watrous *Watrous In Hollywood* (1978), with Louie Bellson *Matterhorn* (1978), *Louie Bellson's Big Band Explosion Live At Ronnie Scott's* (1979), with Bellson *London Scene* (1980), with Don Menza *Burnin'* (1980), *And Finally Romano* (Fresh Sounds 1988).

Roney, Wallace

b. 25 May 1960, Philadelphia, Pennsylvania, USA. Roney is one of the most interesting of all the younger trumpeters to have emerged under the worldwide umbrella of Miles Davis (though he also cites Clifford Brown as a great favourite). Rather than simply copying the phrasing, he has often captured the edited essence of earlier Davis in his tight, muted sound and distinctive phrasing, using space and delay both to enrich solos and galvanize rhythm sections too. Roney's early successes were recording opportunities with Chico Freeman (the 1982 *Tradition in Transition*) and Ricky Ford (1983's *Interpretations*) and 1986 brought a stretch with Art Blakey's Jazz Messengers, and then employment by drummer Tony Williams, for whom Roney still works. Roney has also been hired for recordings by drummer Marvin 'Smitty' Smith (*Keeper Of The Drums* and *The Road Less Travelled*) and saxophonists Christopher Hollyday and Kenny Garrett. Roney's devotion to Davis, and yet his independence in expressing it, were acknowledged in the trumpeter's role as support to Davis in the re-creation of some of the Gil Evans scores of the 50s and 60s at the Montreux Jazz Festival of 1991.

Albums: *Verses* (Muse 1987), *Intuition* (Muse 1988), *The Standard Bearer* (Muse 1990), *Obsession* (Muse 1991), *Seth Air* (Muse 1992), with Wayne Shorter, Ron Carter, Herbie Hancock, Tony Williams *A Tribute To Miles* (QWest/Reprise 1994).

Roppolo, Leon

b. 16 March 1902, Lutcher, Louisiana, USA, d. 14 October 1943. After being taught clarinet by his father, Roppolo began playing in bands in and around New Orleans including those led by George Brunis and Santo Pecora. After playing on riverboats he made his way to Chicago where, in 1921, he became a member of the Friars' Inn Society Orchestra. This band, led by Paul Mares and which included Brunis, later evolved into the New Orleans Rhythm Kings. In 1923 Roppolo and Mares quit and went to New York and the following year Roppolo was in Texas playing with Peck Kelley's Bad Boys. In 1925 he was back in New Orleans and was once again teamed with Mares in a reformed NORK. By this time Roppolo's bad habits, he was a heavy drinker and used marijuana, allied to ill-health had begun to take their toll. That same year he suffered a severe mental breakdown and was committed to a state asylum. Apparently he continued to play while in the institution, taking up the tenor saxophone. He was released in 1940 and died in 1943. Roppolo played clarinet with a full, rich tone and was always experimenting with technique and phrasing. His imaginative work influenced many of his contemporaries and the younger musicians who heard him.

Album: with NORK incl. on *Jazz Sounds Of The Twenties* (1922-25).

Rosengarden, Bobby

b. 23 April 1924, Elgin, Illinois, USA. After starting to play drums while still a child, Rosengarden studied at university and played in military bands during his army service. In 1945 he played in a New York dance band with Henry Busse and during the next two decades played drums and percussion with many bands in a wide range of styles including jazz with Miles Davis and Benny Goodman, television studio bands, and symphony orchestras. In the 70s he was with the World's Greatest Jazz Band and the Bob Wilber-Kenny Davern group, Soprano Summit. With Davern and Dick Wellstood he formed the Blue Three and he also played with Dick Hyman's New York Jazz Repertory Orchestra and at Dick Gibson's Colorado Jazz Parties. He has also played with Gerry Mulligan and led his own bands. A driving, enthusiastic drummer, Rosengarden's broad-based technique allows him to feel at home in most settings especially those with a traditional to mainstream bias. His deep interest in Brazilian music also makes its presence felt in his work.

Albums: *Colorado Jazz Party* (1971), *Soprano Summit* (1973), with Dick Hyman *Satchmo Remembered* (1974), *The World's Greatest Jazz Band Of Yank Lawson And Bob Haggart On Tour* (1975), *The Blue Three Live At Hanratty's* (1981), *By Request* (Statiras 1987).

Rosewoman, Michele

b. 19 March 1953, Oakland, California, USA. Rosewoman comes from a musical family: her parents ran a record shop and her elder brother is a musician, so she was exposed to jazz and world music at an early age. She began playing piano at the age of six and when she was 17 years old she met pianist Edwin Kelly, who introduced her to hard bop and the music of Thelonious Monk and John Coltrane and gave her lessons. She also studied Cuban percussion with Orlando 'Puntilla' Rios and Shona (Zimbabwean) and Yoruba (Nigerian) traditional music. San Francisco's Keystone Korner was a centre for jazz, where she heard Cecil Taylor. She met trumpeter Baikida Carrol and altoist Oliver Lake from BAG (Black Artists Group) in St. Louis and also members of the AACM. In 1978 she relocated to New York - her first appearance was with Lake at Carnegie Hall. Since then she has performed regularly as sidewoman and leader. In 1981 she played on Billy Bang's *Rainbow Gladiator*. She also worked with a number of Cuban groups, notably Los Kimy, with whom she recorded. Her interest in Afro-Cuban music led her to form the 15-piece New Yor-Uba: in December 1983 she premiered 'New Yor-Uba, A Musical Celebration Of Cuba In America' at the Public Theatre in New York to great acclaim. She made her recording debut as a leader in 1985 with *The Source* for Soul Note. In 1986 she formed a quintet, Quintessence, which has released *Quintessence* and *Contrast High*. In Summer 1991 she toured with Carlos Ward. 1991's *Occasion To Rise* was a trio recording with Rufus Reid on bass and Ralph Peterson Jnr. on drums. Michele Rosewoman's broad musical vision, welcome in a period of jazz neo-conservatism, is matched by the strength of her compositions and the energy of her playing.

Albums: *The Source* (1985), *Quintessence* (Enja 1987), *Contrast High* (Enja 1989), *Occasion To Rise* (1991), *Harvest* (Enja 1993).

Rosolino, Frank

b. 20 August 1926, Detroit, Michigan, USA, d. 26 November 1978. After dabbling with guitar, Rosolino took up the trombone while in his teens. After military service during World War II he played in a succession of big bands, including those of Bob Chester and Glen Gray. In 1948 he was one of several bebop-influenced musicians playing in Gene Krupa's big band (contributing the scat vocalizing on the band's hit record of 'Lemon Drop'). After playing in several other dance bands he briefly led his own group before joining Stan Kenton in 1952. Two years later he left the band and settled in California, where he divided his time between studio and jazz work. He recorded with Dexter Gordon, Stan Levey, Conte Candoli and many of the musicians who frequented the Lighthouse. In the mid-

70s Rosolino again worked with Candoli, visiting Europe, and he also played several times with Benny Carter, who was one of the trombonist's greatest admirers. Also in the 70s he played in Med Flory's band, Supersax, and with Quincy Jones. A brilliant technician with a precisely articulated attacking style, Rosolino was one of the finest trombonists of his time and one of few practitioners on the instrument to fully adapt to bebop. His later work showed him to be a consummate section player whether in big bands or small groups. He died in 1978 in acutely tragic circumstances, shooting both of his children (one of whom survived) before shooting himself.

Albums: with Stan Kenton *New Concepts Of Artistry In Rhythm* (1952), one side only *The Trombone Album/Swing Not Spring* (1952), *Stan Kenton Presents: Frank Rosolino Sextet* (1954), *Frankly Speaking* (1955), with Stan Levey *This Time The Drum's On Me* (1955), with Levey *Grand Stan* (1956), *I Play Trombone* (1956), with Lighthouse All Stars *Double Or Nothin'* (1957), *The Most Happy Fella* (1957), with Benny Carter *Aspects* (1958-59), *Turn Me Loose!* (1961), *Conversations* (1975), *Just Friends* (1975), *Thinking About You* (1976), *In Denmark* (1978).

Ross, Annie

b. Annabelle Short Lynch, 25 July 1930, Mitcham, Surrey, England. After working as a child actress in Hollywood, she then toured internationally as a singer. She sang with both Tony Crombie and Jack Parnell during the 50s. Ross had recorded successful wordless jazz vocals before becoming a member of the famous scat (vocalese) trio, Lambert, Hendricks And Ross from 1958-62. Her song 'Twisted', written with Wardell Gray, was expertly covered by Joni Mitchell, among others. In the mid-60s Ross operated Annie's Room, a jazz club in London, and in later years worked in films and television as both actress and singer, at one point being briefly reunited with Jon Hendricks. Personal problems affected the continuity of Ross's career but despite the resulting irregularity of her public performances she maintained an enviably high standard of singing. Her scat singing was some of the finest ever heard. In the early 80s she found a compatible musical partner in Georgie Fame with whom she toured and recorded.

Selected albums: *Annie Ross Sings* (Original Jazz Classics 1953), *Annie By Candlelight* (1956), with Gerry Mulligan *Annie Ross Sings A Song With Mulligan* (EMI Manhattan 1958), *Gypsy* (1958-59), with Zoot Sims *A Gasser* (Pacific Jazz 1959), *You And Me Baby* (c.1964), *Annie Ross And Pony Poindexter With The Berlin All Stars* (1966), with Georgie Fame *In Hoagland '81* (Bald Eagle 1981), *Sings A Handful Of Songs* (Fresh Sounds 1988).

Ross, Ronnie

b. 2 October 1933, Calcutta, India, d. 12 December 1991. Ross came to England in his early teens where he first took up the tenor saxophone. In the mid-50s he joined Don Rendell who persuaded him to change to baritone. Thereafter, Ross built a reputation as an outstanding player of the instrument, working in bands led by Ted Heath, Marshall Brown and Woody Herman. He was also co-leader with Allan Ganley of the Jazzmakers. In the early 60s he was leader of his own small band and also participated in numerous recording sessions, including some with John Dankworth. The 60s also saw him spending time in Europe where he played with the Clarke-Boland Big Band. Ross continued leading his own groups and recording under various leaders during the 70s and into the 80s, including an appearance on rock singer Lou Reed's hit single 'A Walk On The Wild Side'. A forceful player, Ross's baritone has long been one of the treasures of the British jazz scene although he seldom achieved the recognition his talent deserves.

Albums: *The Ronnie Ross Quintet* (1958), *Swinging Sounds Of The Jazz Makers* (1959), *Beatle Music By The Session Men* (1967), *Cleopatra's Needle* (1968).

Rouse, Charlie

b. 6 April 1924, Washington, DC, USA, d. 30 November 1988. After learning to play clarinet, Rouse took up the tenor saxophone; by the end of his teens he was proficient enough to be hired by Billy Eckstine for his bebop-orientated big band. Thereafter, Rouse played with Dizzy Gillespie, Tadd Dameron and Fats Navarro. At the end of the 40s he worked in an R&B band but also subbed with Duke Ellington and Count Basie. In the early 50s he played and recorded with a number of important small groups, including those led by Clifford Brown, Art Farmer, Paul Quinichette and Oscar Pettiford. In the second half of the decade he led his own small bands, was briefly with Buddy Rich and the Gerry Mulligan Concert Band and then, at the end of 1958, began a long and fruitful relationship with Thelonious Monk which lasted until 1970. During this period he made records with others, including Donald Byrd and Benny Carter, appearing on the latter's fine *Further Definitions*. Throughout the 70s and 80s he freelanced, sometimes leading bands, including Sphere, touring as a single or playing as accompanist. A distinctively quirky player, Rouse's long musical partnership with Monk had the advantage of bringing his work to a very wide audience and the disadvantages of linking him with an often overpowering personality, and enclosing him in a very specific fairly limited area of bop.

Albums: with Thelonious Monk *5 By Monk By 5* (1959), *Takin' Care Of Business* (Original Jazz Classics 1960), with Benny Carter *Further Definitions* (1961), *Unsung Hero* (Columbia 1962), *Bossa 'N' Bacchanal* (1962) with Monk *Misterioso* (1963-65), *Two Is One* (Strata East 1974), *Cinnamon Flower* (Rykodisk 1976), *Moment's Notice* (1977), *The Upper Manhattan Jazz Society* (Enja 1981), *Flight Path* (1983), with Paul Quinchette *Chase Is On* (Affinity 1986), with Stan Tracey *Playin' In The Yard* (Steam 1987), *Epistrophy* (Landmark 1988).

Rowles, Jimmy

b. 19 August 1918, Spokane, Washington, USA. A self-taught pianist, Rowles first attracted wide attention in Southern California in the early 40s as a member of small groups led by Slim Gaillard, Lester Young and others. Later in the decade he was with big bands led by Woody Herman, Tommy Dorsey,

Les Brown and Benny Goodman, and was also in great demand as accompanist to singers. His reputation in this last respect was enhanced by his work with Peggy Lee, Billie Holiday, Sarah Vaughan, Carmen McRae and Ella Fitzgerald. His long years as a studio musician in Los Angeles, and later in New York, failed to dampen either his own talent or the regard in which he was held by musicians. He has recorded with George Mraz, Al Cohn, Zoot Sims, Stan Getz, Dexter Gordon, Herbie Harper, Pepper Adams and Mel Lewis among many others. A highly gifted player, his deft touch and a seemingly endless store of ideas, which he imparts with wit and skill, combine to make Rowles one of the best mainstream pianists in jazz. As an accompanist to singers he has few, if any, superiors. His many record albums are ample testimony to his talent yet he remains one of the least known of jazz players. His daughter Stacy (b. 11 September 1955) is an accomplished jazz trumpeter, and the Rowleses worked together in Los Angeles during the early 80s, later recording *Tell It Like It Is* in 1984.

Selected albums: *Rare - But Well Done* (1954), with Billie Holiday *Music For Torching* (1955), with Pepper Adams, Mel Lewis *Critics' Choice* (1957), *The Upper Classmen* (1957), *The Jimmy Rowles Sextet* (1958), *The Jimmy Rowles Quartet* i (1960), *The Jimmy Rowles Quintet* (1962), *Some Other Spring* (c.1970), with Carmen McRae *The Great American Songbook* (1971), *Sarah Vaughan And The Jimmy Rowles Quintet* (1972), *Jazz Is A Fleeting Moment* (1974), *The Special Magic Of Jimmy Rowles* (1974), *Zoot Sims Party* (1974), *Music's The Only Thing That's On My Mind* (1976), *Grand Paws* (1976), *Paws That Refresh* (1976), with Stan Getz *The Peacocks* (Columbia 1977), *If I'm Lucky* (1977), *I Remember Bebop* (1977), *Heavy Love* (1977), *Isfahan* (Sonet 1978), *Scarab* (1978), *As Good As It Gets* (1978), *We Could Make Such Beautiful Music Together* (Xanadu 1978), *Nature Boy* (1978), with Red Mitchell *Red 'N' Me* (1978), *My Mother's Love* (1979), *Jimmy Rowles At The Philharmonic, Warsaw* (1979), *Jimmy Rowles Plays Duke Ellington And Billy Strayhorn* (1981), *In Paris* (Columbia 1981), *Profile* (Columbia 1982), with Stacy Rowles *Tell It Like It Is* (1984), *The Jimmy Rowles Quartet* ii (1985), *Looking Back* (Delos 1989), *Remember When* (Mastermix 1989), *Trio* (Capril 1991).

Royal, Marshal

b. 12 May 1912, Sapulpa, Oklahoma, USA. Royal learned several instruments as a child, finally concentrating on alto saxophone in his teenage years. In the 30s he moved to Los Angeles and played there in several bands, including a long spell with Les Hite. Among his fellow musicians in this band, were his brother, Ernie Royal, and Lionel Hampton. When Hampton formed his own band in 1940 Royal joined and became the band's straw boss, ruthlessly drilling the younger musicians. One of them, Dexter Gordon, later paid tribute to Royal as being largely responsible for teaching him to breathe and phrase correctly. After military service in World War II, he played briefly in New York before returning to Los Angeles and work in the studios. In 1951 he joined Count Basie's small group and when Basie reformed his big band Royal took on

similar duties to those he had carried out for Hampton. Under his watchful eye, the Basie band became a crisp and efficient outfit. He remained in the band for 20 years, touring the world several times but then, while absent due to ill-health, was quietly replaced. Resident once more in Los Angeles, Royal became lead alto with the big bands of Bill Berry and Frank Capp-Nat Pierce. He also played many club and festival dates, recording with Dave Frishberg, Snooky Young and others. In 1989 he returned to Europe to play club and festival dates, sometimes alone, at other times with Berry and Buster Cooper. Also in 1989, Royal visited Japan with the Basie-style big band co-led by Frank Wess and Harry Edison, receiving a rapturous welcome from audiences who revelled in his soaring romanticism. Although Royal's main contribution to jazz may well be his important if relatively anonymous work as lead alto in a succession of fine bands, for the fans it is the rich flowing solos, especially on romantic ballads, that have made him universally popular.

Albums: with Count Basie *Basie* (1957), *Marshal Royal With Gordon Jenkins And His Orchestra* (1960), *Back To Basie* (1962), with Bill Berry *Hot & Happy* (1974), with Berry *Hello Rev* (1976), with Frank Capp-Nat Pierce *Juggernaut* (1976), with Dave Frishberg *Getting Some Fun Out Of Life* (1977), with Snooky Young *Snooky And Marshal's Album* (1978), with Berry *Shortcake* (1978), *First Chair* (1978), *Royal Blue* (1980), with Capp-Pierce *Juggernaut Strikes Again!* (1981), with Frank Wess-Harry Edison *Dear Mr Basie* (1989).

Rucker, Ellyn

b. 29 July 1937, Des Moines, Iowa, USA. Coming from a very musical family, Rucker first took an interest in piano when she was eight years old. Later, she studied classical piano but by the age of 13 her brother had persuaded her to listen to jazz. She began playing clubs and hotels in her hometown area, but it was 1979 before she became a full-time professional musician. By this stage in her career, she had also begun to sing occasionally to her own accompaniment. She spent several years working in Denver, Colorado, where she was heard by Mark Murphy who advised her to try for the 'big time'. Although essentially a solo player, sometimes working with a rhythm section, she has occasionally worked with visiting jazzmen, including Roy Eldridge, James Moody, Clark Terry, Richie Cole and Buddy Tate. In 1986 she played at the Northsea Jazz Festival in Holland and in subsequent years toured Europe and the UK. Latterly, Rucker has continued to concentrate on solo tours but has also worked with Spike Robinson on a number of occasions. Her accompanists on records have included Robinson, Pete Christlieb and John Clayton. An eclectic pianist, with a wide-ranging repertoire, Rucker is gradually becoming accepted as an inventive and skilled jazz musician. Her playing style can be elegantly poised or dynamically forceful depending upon the material or the mood that she is in. Her singing, although less strongly promoted than her piano playing, is easy and natural.

Albums: with Spike Robinson *Nice Work* (Capri 1985), *Ellyn* (Capri 1987), *This Heart Of Mine* (Capri 1988).

Rudd, Roswell

b. 17 November 1935, Sharon, Connecticut, USA. Rudd studied singing and French horn at college and theory at Harvard (1954-58). Like several other members of the 60s *avant garde* he began his jazz career playing dixieland, a fact which points up the line of evolution between the New Orleans roots and the New Thing, and his big, fulsome trombone sound strongly recalls the early 'tailgate' players, even when he is working in the most abstract surroundings. Rudd moved to New York in 1954 and played in various traditional bands. He began to work in a modern context with Herbie Nichols (1960-62) and in 1961 he joined Steve Lacy (who also started out playing traditional jazz). His conversion to free-form jazz began as a result of meeting Bill Dixon. In 1964 he formed the New York Art Quartet with John Tchicai, to whom he had been introduced by Dixon (*Mohawk, New York Art Quartet*). When the Quartet disbanded in 1965 he became a member of Archie Shepp's highly-influential group until 1967 (*Four For Tranc, Mama Too Tight*). In 1968 he formed the Primordial Quintet (which ended up as a nine-piece band) with Lee Konitz. During the late 70s and 80s he toured extensively with his own groups, and in 1982 was reunited with Lacy in the Monk Project with Misha Mengelberg. He has also worked with Cecil Taylor, Jazz Composers Orchestra (who, in 1973, commissioned the *Numatik Swing Band* from him), Albert Ayler, Karl Berger, Enrico Rava, Perry Robinson, Gato Barbieri, Robin Kenyatta and Charlie Haden's Liberation Music Orchestra, and in 1961 he appeared in the film *The Hustler*. He has also worked with the distinguished ethno-musicologist Alan Lomax, and became professor of Music Ethnology at the University of Maine. He has tried to show the connections between jazz, so-called ethnic music and the European classical tradition in his compositions. In the early 90s he was reportedly playing dixieland again in upstate New York.

Albums: *Roswell Rudd Quartet* (1965), *Everywhere* (1966), *Numatik Swing Band* (1973), *Flexible Flyer* (1974), with Steve Lacy *School Days* (1975, rec 1963), *Blown-bone* (1976), *Inside Job* (Freedom 1976), *Maxine* (1976), with Giorgio Gaslini *Sharing* (1978), *The Definitive Roswell Rudd* (1979), with Misha Mengelberg and others *Regeneration* (Soul Note 1982).

Rugolo, Pete

b. 25 December 1915, San Piero, Sicily. After studying composing and arranging under classicist Darius Milhaud, Rugolo began writing arrangements for Stan Kenton. Many of Kenton's most successful recordings of the late 40s were Rugolo charts and of these a high proportion were also his compositions. After his full-time collaboration with Kenton ended in 1949, Rugolo produced a number of recording sessions for Capitol Records including some with Miles Davis, Mel Tormé, Peggy Lee and Nat 'King' Cole. He also recorded with a studio band under his own name. The period with Capitol also saw him writing additional material for Kenton and his Innovations in Modern Music Orchestra, and he was arranger and musical director for June Christy's *Something Cool* album. In the 50s he joined Columbia Records and in the late 50s was

with Mercury Records, writing for Sarah Vaughan, Billy Eckstine and others. From the 60s into the early 80s he worked in film and television studios, eventually retiring in 1985. Heavily influenced by Kenton, Rugolo's arrangements demonstrate his interest in developing ideas for the modern orchestra often as displays of technical virtuosity and as such sometimes leaving the jazz content behind.

Albums: *Music For Hi-Fi Bugs* (1956), *Out On A Limb* (1956), *Pete Rugolo And His Orchestra* i (1956), *Pete Rugolo And His Orchestra* ii (1958), *Pete Rugolo And His Orchestra* iii (1958), *The Music From Richard Diamond* (1959), *Pete Rugolo And His Orchestra* iv (1959), *The Thriller* (c.1960), *Pete Rugolo And His Orchestra* v (1960), *Ten Trumpets And Two Guitars* (1961), *Pete Rugolo And His Orchestra* vi (1961), *The Diamonds Meet Pete Rugolo* (c.1961), *TV Themes* (1962). Compilations: by Stan Kenton *The Kenton Era* (1940-53), *Rugolomania* (Fresh Sounds 1988).

Ruiz, Hilton

b. 29 May 1952, New York City, New York, USA. Ruiz studied piano from an early age, performing public recitals as a small child. In the mid- to late 60s he worked as a professional musician in bands playing Latin American music. In the early 70s he turned to jazz, studying with Mary Lou Williams. Later in the decade he played on numerous club, concert and recording dates with Joe Newman, Freddie Hubbard, Clark Terry, Charles Mingus, Rahsaan Roland Kirk (with whom he recorded *Return Of The 5000lb Man*), Chico Freeman, (on *Beyond The Rain*), Betty Carter and Archie Shepp. He continued an active career in the 80s, appearing with Terry's all-star big band at festivals and on television and making records, including some as a member of Marion Brown's group. A strikingly inventive pianist, Ruiz's jazz style incorporates many elements from his continuing interest in Latin music.

Albums: *Piano Man* (Steeplechase 1975), *Excitation* (1977), *New York Hilton* (1977), *Fantasia* (1978), *The Hilton Ruiz Trio* (1978), *Cross Currents* (1984), *Vibration Society: The Music Of Rahsaan Roland Kirk* (1986), *El Camino* (1987), *Strut* (Novus 1988), *Cross Currents* (Stash 1987, 1984-86 recordings), *Doin' It Right* (Novus 1989), *A Moment's Notice* (Novus 1991), *Live At Birdland* (Candid 1993).

Rumsey, Howard

b. 7 November 1917, Brawley, California, USA. After briefly playing piano and drums, Rumsey took up the bass while still at school. In the late 30s he played in the Vido Musso band alongside Stan Kenton and went with the pianist when he formed his own band in 1941. From 1943 he mostly freelanced but played in the bands of Freddy Slack and Charlie Barnet. At the end of the decade he was directly responsible for establishing a jazz club at the Lighthouse Cafe at Hermosa Beach. He was himself a member of the house band at the Lighthouse, a venue which became the focus of the west coast jazz scene. Throughout the 50s Rumsey played at the Lighthouse, eventually taking over the running of the Café. During this period he played and recorded with many of the outstanding musicians of the day, among them Teddy Edwards, Sonny Criss, Hampton Hawes, Shorty Rogers, Jimmy Giuffre, Conte Candoli, Rolf Ericson, Frank Rosolino, Bob Cooper, Art Pepper and Shelly Manne. He continued his activities into the 60s but eventually ceased playing and severed his connection with the Lighthouse. In the early 70s he returned to the scene by opening another club, Concerts By the Sea. A solid player with a good ear for the best in musical talent, Rumsey's greatest achievement in jazz remains the fact that he provided a setting and format that gave great encouragement to one of the most important areas of jazz in the 50s.

Selected albums: *At Last! Miles Davis And The Lighthouse All Stars* (1953), *Sunday Jazz A La Lighthouse* (Original Jazz Classics 1953), *Howard Rumsey And The Lighthouse All Stars* i (1954), *Howard Rumsey And The Lighthouse All Stars* ii (1955), *In The Solo Spotlight* (Original Jazz Classics 1954-57), *Music For Lighthouse-Keeping* (1956), *Jazz Rolls Royce* (Fresh Sounds 1957), with Max Roach *Drummin' The Blues* (1957), *Volume 6* (Original Jazz Classics 1957), *Lighthouse At Laguna* (Original jazz Classics 1958).

Rushing, Jimmy

b. 26 August 1902, Oklahoma City, Oklahoma, USA, d. 8 June 1972. He began singing while still studying music at school in his home town. By 1923 he was a full-time professional singer, working in California with, among others, Jelly Roll Morton and Paul Howard. Back home in the mid-20s he teamed up with Walter Page and then joined Bennie Moten and by 1935 was a member of the Count Basie band. He remained with Basie until 1948 and then worked as a solo, sometimes leading a small band. During these later years he regularly worked with leading jazz artists including Benny Goodman, Buck Clayton, Basie, and, during tours of the UK, with Humphrey Lyttelton.

Rushing's voice was a slightly nasal high tenor which carried comfortably over the sound of a big band in full cry. The fact that he sang at a somewhat higher pitch than most other male blues singers gave his performances a keening, plaintive quality. In fact, his singing style and repertoire made him far more than merely a blues singer and he was comfortably at ease with romantic ballads. Nevertheless, he tinged everything he sang, from love songs to up-tempo swingers, with the qualities of the blues. Despite his extensive repertoire, in later years he favoured certain songs, including 'Going To Chicago', 'Every Day I Have The Blues' and 'Exactly Like You', but even repeated performances at clubs, concerts and record dates were infused with such infectious enthusiasm that he never palled. Known because of his build as 'Mr Five By Five', Rushing was at his best in front of a big band or a Kansas City-style small group but even when he stepped out of character, as on his final formal record date, he could enchant listeners. By the early 70s, and his last date, his voice was showing signs of decades of wear and tear but he retained his unflagging swing and brought to unusual material, such as 'When I Grow Too Old To Dream' and 'I Surrender Dear', great emotional depths and a sharp awareness of the needs of both music and lyrics. An exception-

ally gifted artist, Rushing was always unmistakable and never imitated. He was original and unique and one of the greatest singers jazz has ever known. He died in 1972.

Selected albums: *Goin' To Chicago* (1954), *The Essential Jimmy Rushing* (1954-57), *The Jazz Odyssey Of James Rushing Esq* (1956), *If This Ain't The Blues* (1957), with Buck Clayton *Copenhagen Concert* (1959), *Little Jimmy Rushing And The Big Brass* (1958), *Rushing Lullabies* (1959), *The Smith Girls* (1960), *Gee, Baby, Ain't I Good To You* (1967), *Who Was It Sang That Song* (1967), *Every Day I Have The Blues* (1968), *The You And Me That Used To Be* (Bluebird 1971). Compilations: with Count Basie *Good Mornin' Blues* (1937-39 recordings), with Basie *Do You Wanna Jump...?* (1938 recordings), with Basie *The Jubilee Alternatives* (1943-44 recordings), *His Complete Vangaurd Recordings* (Vanguard 1954-57 recordings), *The Essential Jimmy Rushing* (Vogue 1983).

Russell, George

b. 23 June 1923, Cincinnati, Ohio, USA. One of modern jazz's leading composers, Russell started out as a drummer with Benny Carter, but first came to prominence in the mid-40s writing for Dizzy Gillespie, notably 'Cubano Be, Cubano Bop'. He also wrote for Artie Shaw and Claude Thornhill and his 'A Bird In Igor's Yard', combining elements of Charlie Parker and Stravinsky, was recorded by the Buddy De Franco big band in 1949. Periods of hospitalization for tuberculosis led to him developing his theoretical *The Lydian Chromatic Concept Of Tonal Organization*, first published in 1953 and a crucial influence on the later modal jazz of Miles Davis and John Coltrane. In the 50s Russell wrote 'All About Rosie' on a commission from Brandeis University and taught both privately and at the School of Jazz in Lennox, Massachusetts: his students, then and later, included Carla Bley, Rahsaan Roland Kirk, Don Ellis and Steve Swallow (the later pair also recording with him). In the early 60s he led a sextet and made several celebrated recordings, often featuring *avant garde* artists such as Sheila Jordan ('You Are My Sunshine'), Eric Dolphy (*Ezz-Thetics*) and Don Cherry (*At Beethoven Hall*). In the mid- to late 60s, Russell was based in Sweden, where he experimented with electronic music and worked with upcoming players, such as Jan Garbarek, Terje Rypdal and Palle Mikkelborg. In 1969 he returned to the USA to teach at the New England Conservatory, but still continued to record in Sweden. (Many of the recordings he made in Scandinavia in the 60s and 70s have since reappeared on the Soul Note label in the 80s.) From the late 70s he began playing and recording regularly in the USA, often working with a big band. He was one of the first artists signed up by the reactivated Blue Note label, and in the mid- to late 80s he toured the UK with bands that included several well-known British players, for example, Chris Biscoe, Ian Carr, Andy Sheppard and Kenny Wheeler. Russell has continued with his theoretical work, completing a second volume of his *Lydian Chromatic Concept* in 1978. This stands as one of the central texts of modern jazz theory. A complex work, its basic premise is that traditional jazz structures, such as chord sequences, can be overlaid with scales or modes that introduce a degree of pan-tonality

and so allow the player more choices for improvising.
Selected albums: *The Jazz Workshop* (Bluebird 1956), *New York, NY* (1959), *Jazz In The Space Age* (1960), *At The Five Spot* (1960), *In Kansas City* (1960), *Stratosphunk* (1960), *Ezzthetic* (Original Jazz Classics 1961), *The Outer View* (Original Jazz Classics 1962), *At The Beethoven Hall Vols. 1 & 2* (1965), with Bill Evans *Living Time* (1972), *Electronic Sonata For Souls Loved By Nature 1980* (Soul Note 1980), with Jan Garbarek *Othello Ballet Suite* (Soul Note 1981, rec 1967), with Garbarek *Trip To Prillarguri* (Soul Note 1982, rec 1970), *New York Big Band* (Soul Note 1982, rec 1978), *Listen To The Silence* (1983, rec 1972), *The Essence Of George Russell* (1983, rec 1966-70), *Live In An American Time Spiral* (Soul Note 1983), *The African Game* (1985, rec 1983), *So What* (Blue Note 1986), *Time Space* (Polygram 1988), *The London Concert Vols 1-2* (Stash 1990).
Further reading: *The Lydian Chromatic Concept Of Tonal Organization*, George Russell.

Russell, Hal

b. Harold Russell Luttenbacher, 28 August 1926, Detroit, Michigan, USA, d. 5 September 1992. Russell grew up in Chicago and first became involved in music by playing drums. He attended the University of Illinois, receiving both bachelor and masters degrees in musical education. Although he had learned the trumpet as part of his degree course, he abandoned it for 30 years while he worked in jazz groups as a drummer and vibraphonist. In 1950 he played with Miles Davis and later in the decade performed with many leading jazz artists, such as Sonny Rollins, Duke Ellington, Billie Holiday, Erroll Garner and Sarah Vaughan. From 1961 he played drums in the Joe Daley Trio, one of Chicago's first free jazz groups, then in the late 60s, inspired by the high-energy music of *avant gardists*, such as Albert Ayler and Sunny Murray, he began to lead his own groups. From the late 70s Russell headed a quintet and a trio in what he called NRG Ensembles, and was perhaps most creative in the freedom granted him by the latter format. The incompetence of the group's original saxophonist led Russell to take up saxophone himself - at the age of 50 - and he became an enthusiastic performer on tenor and soprano. 'I thought God, what a fool I am! I should have been playing saxophone all along! I shouldn't have played drums at all!' In 1990 he released *Hal On Earth*, with an unusual quintet consisting of two saxophones, two basses and drums - with three members of the ensemble doubling on didjeridoo! Russell stated: 'I find that the more popular you become the less you like the music you are playing. This makes you search for new forms and ways of musical expression'. In 1991 ECM Records recognized what had previously been underground success by releasing the live *Finnish-Swiss Tour* by an NRG Ensemble that comprised Russell and longtime associates Mars Williams (best-known for his work with the Psychedelic Furs), Steve Hunt, Brian Sandstrom and Kent Kessler. In the summer of 1992 Russell became ill and was rushed into hospital for heart bypass surgery. The operation was considered a success, but he died three weeks later.
Albums: *The Hal Russell NRG Ensemble* (1981), with Mars

Williams *EFT Soons* (1981), with Charles Tyler *Generation* (Chief 1982), *Conserving NRG* (Principally Jazz 1984), *Hal On Earth* (1990), *The Finnish-Swiss Tour* (ECM 1991), *Hal's Bells* (ECM 1992), *The Hal Russell Story* (ECM 1993).

Russell, Luis

b. 6 August 1902, Careening Clay, Bocas Del Toro, Panama, d. 11 December 1963. After playing various instruments in his homeland, Russell moved to New Orleans in 1919 and thereafter played piano in local saloons and clubs. In the early 20s he played with Albert Nicholas among others, and also led bands. He played with King Oliver in Chicago in 1925 and in 1927 became leader of a band in New York. For the next few years he led his band in the city and on tours, often backing Louis Armstrong. In 1935 the band became known as Armstrong's but Russell stayed on until the early 40s, when he formed a new band for touring. From the late 40s he ran a business outside music but continued to lead small bands for club dates. Russell's bands never had the impact on the jazz public achieved by many of his contemporaries. Nevertheless, he was a dedicated musician and made serious attempts to integrate some of the fundamental concepts of the New Orleans style into big band music. He died in 1963.
Albums: with others *Gut Bucket Blues And Stomps - Chicago* (1926-28), *New York Jazz* (1928-33), *1930-1934* (VJM 1986), *Luis Russell And His Orchestra 1929-30* (Swaggie 1988), *Savoy Shout* (JSP 1989).

Russell, Pee Wee

b. Charles Ellsworth Russell, 27 March 1906, Maple Wood, Missouri, USA, d. 15 February 1969. Russell began playing clarinet in the early 20s and by 1927, the year he came to New York, had already worked with luminaries such as Jack Teagarden, Frank Trumbauer and Bix Beiderbecke. In the late 20s and throughout the 30s and 40s, Russell played with numerous jazzmen working in the traditional sphere, among them Bobby Hackett, Wild Bill Davison, Louis Prima, Billy Butterfield, Muggsy Spanier, George Wettling and Art Hodes. He also enjoyed a long association with Eddie Condon, although enjoyed is perhaps an inappropriate term for what Russell later described as a time of sadness - because thanks to his hangdog expression and idiosyncratic style of playing, he was often treated as a clown. In the 50s Russell's health was suspect, he suffered from alcoholism, but by the 60s he was back playing at clubs, concerts and festivals around the world. One of the most endearing eccentrics in jazz, Russell's playing style was unique and at first and sometimes even second hearing might be thought primitive. Nevertheless, the sometimes grating sounds he produced on his instrument and the seemingly indecisive placing of notes during solo and ensemble passages had a cumulative effect which demonstrated the existence of an inquiring and adventurous musical mind. This became more overtly apparent when he blended easily with such diverse musical associates as Thelonious Monk, Henry 'Red' Allen and Coleman Hawkins. In the 60s he played in a pianoless quartet with Marshall Brown and on a big band album with Oliver

Nelson, as well as working again in more traditional contexts. A totally original and often brilliant clarinettist, he inspired writer George Frazier to enthuse about 'the bliss and the sadness and the compassion and the humility that are there in the notes he plays'. Finally, the liver condition that had almost killed him in the 50s returned to finish the job, and he died in February 1969.

Selected albums: *The Definitive Pee Wee Russell* (1958), *The Pee Wee Russell Quintet* i (1958), *Portrait Of Pee Wee Russell* (1958), *A Salute To Newport* (1959), *Swinging With Pee Wee* (1960), with Coleman Hawkins *Jazz Reunion* (Candid 1961), *Pee Wee Russell-Coleman Hawkins All Stars* (1961), *The Pee Wee Russell Quintet* ii (1962-63), *Thelonious Monk At Newport* (1963), *Hot Licorice* (c.1964), *Gumbo* (c.1964), *Ask Me Now* (1965), *The College Concert* (1966), with Oliver Nelson *The Spirit Of '67* (1967). Compilations: *The Great Soloists - Pee Wee Russell* (1932-35), *The Pied Piper Of Jazz* (1941-44), *Muggsy And Pee Wee* (1941-57), *The Individualism Of* (Savoy 1985), *Portrait Of Pee Wee* (Fresh Sounds 1991).

Further reading: *Pee Wee Russell: The Life Of A Jazzman*, Robert Hilbert.

Russo, Bill

b. 25 June 1928, Chicago, Illinois, USA. After extensive studies in arranging, Russo wrote for Lennie Tristano and also occasionally played trombone. One of the earliest musicians to lead a rehearsal band, his experimental style came to the attention of Stan Kenton in the early 50s. In the mid-50s he concentrated on performing with a small group but by the end of the decade was again deeply involved in writing for larger jazz ensembles. He was also active as a teacher and this combination of work continued on throughout the 60s and early 70s. After spending some time in film and television work he returned to teaching in the 80s. He remains one of the more interesting of writers for the large modern jazz orchestra.

Albums: *Bill Russo And His Orchestra* i (1951), by Stan Kenton *New Concepts Of Artistry In Rhythm* (1952), by Kenton *Portraits On Standards* (1953-54), *The Wall Of Alcina* (1955), *Bill Russo Plus The Hans Koller Ensemble* (1955), *Bill Russo And The New Jazz Group, Hanover* (1955), *Bill Russo And His Orchestra* ii (1960), *The Seven Deadly Sins* (1960), *Suite No. 1 Opus 5 & Suite No. 2 Opus 8* (1962), *Bill Russo On The Air In London* (1963), *Bill Russo And The London Jazz Orchestra* (1964).

Rypdal, Terje

b. 23 August 1947, Oslo, Norway. The son of a nationally famous conductor, Rypdal had piano lessons as a child, but taught himself the electric guitar. Studying composition at Oslo University, he also studied George Russell's theories of improvisation with Russell himself, and then played in his big band and sextet. In the late 60s he began to collaborate with Jan Garbarek, and played on Garbarek's first two albums for ECM Records; but he received more exposure in the 1969 German Free Jazz Festival, playing with musicians from the burgeoning Chicago free jazz scene in a band led by Lester

Bowie. Forming Odyssey in the 70s, Rypdal, now recording, also began touring, which he has continued strenuously ever since. Odyssey made a highly successful tour which included the USA, and since then he has made annual appearances at the major European jazz festivals, leading a trio in the mid-80s with Bjorn Kjellemyr and Audun Kleive, and performing with Palle Mikkelborg in Norway. Rypdal has made an important contribution to the European genre. Writing for orchestra as well as jazz ensemble, he is noted for his system of bowing the guitar in the manner of violin.

Albums: *What Comes After* (ECM 1974), with Jan Garbarek *Afric Pepperbird* (ECM 1974), *Odyssey* (ECM 1975), *Whenever I Seem To Be Far Away* (ECM 1975), *After The Rain* (ECM 1976), *Waves* (ECM 1978), *To Be Continued* (ECM 1981), *Eos* (ECM 1984), *Chaser* (ECM 1985), *Sunrise* (1985), *Terje Rypdal/Miroslav Vitous/Jack DeJohnette* (ECM 1985), *Descendre* (ECM 1986), *Blue* (ECM 1987), *The Singles Collection* (ECM 1989), *Undisonus* (1990), *Q.E.D.* (1993). Compilation: *Works* (ECM 1989).

Safranski, Eddie

b. 25 December 1918, Pittsburgh, Pennsylvania, USA, d. 10 January, 1974. Safranski first played bass in high school but was in his early 20s before he joined a name band, that led by Hal McIntyre, with whom he played for four years, departing in 1945 to join a small group led by Miff Mole. Later that year he joined Stan Kenton and, from 1948, spent about a year with Charlie Barnet. From then onwards, a handful of jazz engagements apart, Safranski was mostly engaged in studio work in New York, teaching and working for a company which manufactured musical instruments. A powerful player with a good sense of the swing style, his bass playing with Kenton's band was exemplary.

Albums: with Stan Kenton *The Kenton Era (1940-53)* (1955), *Stan Kenton's Greatest Hits (1943-51)* (1983), *Loaded* (1946).

Salvador, Sal

b. 21 November 1925, Monson, Massachusetts, USA. Like so many other guitarists, Salvador was inspired by Charlie Christian and, by the late 40s, was making an impact on the New York scene. Briefly working with Stan Kenton in the early 50s, Salvador then worked mostly in small groups but formed a big band of his own late in the decade. After spending many years working in studios and teaching, with only occasional recording dates, Salvador returned to the jazz scene in the late

70s, making records with artists such as Billy Taylor, Mel Lewis and Eddie Bert and leading his own band.

Selected albums: *The Sal Salvador Quartet/Quintet* (1953), *Boo Boo Be Doop* (1954), *The Sal Salvador Quartet* (1956), *A Tribute To The Greats* (1957), *Colors In Sound* (1958), *Sal Salvador And His Orchestra* (1960), *The Sal Salvador Quartet* ii (1963), *Starfingers* (1978), *Parallelogram* (c.1978), *Juicy Lucy* (1978), *In Your Own Sweet Way* (1982), *The World's Greatest Jazz Standards* (1983), *Sal Salvador Plays Gerry Mulligan/Bernie's Tune* (1984), *Sal Salvador And Crystal Image* (c.1989).

Sample, Joe

b. 1 February 1939, Houston, Texas, USA. While still at high school, Sample co-founded a group that would dominate his working life. Known from 1960 as the Jazz Crusaders, the band, with its core of Sample on piano, Wayne Henderson, Wilton Felder and Nesbert 'Stix' Hooper, produced a series of popular albums that helped define the term soul jazz. A change of name, to the Crusaders, led to a change of direction in 1972, with increasing emphasis on a soul and funk repertoire. Sample stayed with the group throughout the 70s and, in a number of reformations, into the 80s, but throughout these periods, Sample, and the other group members, have maintained solo careers. Sample worked as an accompanist with the Bobby Hutcherson/Harold Land quintet in 1967 and during the late 60s became a regular Motown session musicians working with artists such as Diana Ross and the Jackson Five. Further session work in Hollywood studio bands followed until, in the early 70s, Sample joined Tom Scott's group LA Express, an experience that led to more session work for many pop and folk musicians, notably Joni Mitchell. Recent interest in jazz funk of the early 70s has introduced the Crusaders to a new audience, and Sample continues to produce solo works.

Selected albums: as the Joe Sample Trio *Try Us* (1969), with Bobby Hutcherson *San Francisco* (1971), with Blue Mitchell *Blue's Blues* (1974), with Mitchell *Graffiti Blues* (1974), *Rainbow Seeker* (MCA 1978), *Carmel* (MCA 1979), *Fancy Dance* (Sonet 1979), *Voices In The Rain* (MCA 1981), with David T Walker *Swing Street Cafe* (MCA 1982), *The Hunter* (MCA 1983), *Oasis* (MCA 1985), *Spellbound* (WEA 1989), with Miles Davis *Amandla* (1989), *Ashes To Ashes* (WEA 1990), *Roles* (MCA 1992), *Invitation* (1993). Compilation: *Joe Sample Collection* (GRP 1991).

Sampson, Edgar

b. 31 August 1907, New York City, New York, USA, d. 16 January 1973. One of the outstanding arrangers in big band jazz, Sampson played alto saxophone and violin in a number of bands during the 20s and 30s, including those led by Duke Ellington, Rex Stewart and Fletcher Henderson, but his most notable period was a two-year spell with Chick Webb that began in 1934. Apart from writing many excellent arrangements of popular songs for the Webb band he also composed several tunes which became jazz standards, among them 'Stompin' At The Savoy', 'Don't Be That Way' (later adopted by Benny Goodman as his theme tune), 'If Dreams Come

True' and 'Blue Lou'. After leaving Webb he continued to write for him and several other bandleaders, including Goodman, Artie Shaw and Teddy Wilson. He also resumed playing occasionally, sometimes on alto and also on tenor and baritone saxophones. He briefly led his own big band in the late 40s and early 50s, forming small groups thereafter. Although often overlooked in accounts of the development of big band arranging, Sampson's work was always of the very highest standard and bears favourable comparison with that of the better-known arrangers of the period. In the 50s and early 60s he showed his versatility by writing for Tito Puente and several other currently popular Latin bands.

Album: *Swing Softly Sweet Sampson* (Jasmine 1956).

Sanborn, David

b. 30 July 1945, Tampa, Florida, USA. Sanborn's virtuosity has now spanned four decades, taking him from being a band member (with the seminal Paul Butterfield) to a leading session player for artists such as David Bowie, James Taylor and Stevie Wonder. His alto saxophone solo on Bowie's 'Young Americans' is regarded by some as a classic piece. He grew up in St Louis and played with some of the finest Chicago school bluesmen, including Albert King. Nowadays, under his own name, Sanborn records and performs regularly. His blistering alto saxophone style competes somewhere between Junior Walker and Dick Heckstall-Smith. and is all the more remarkable because for many years as a child he suffered from polio and had breathing difficulties. Sanborn does not flirt with his instrument, he blows it hard. His solo debut was in 1975 with *Takin' Off*. Over the next decade he produced a series of albums that were all successful, and won a Grammy for *Voyeur*. In 1985, *A Change Of Heart* proved to be a big hit in the jazz charts, although much of it was in the rock style, notably the unrelenting and powerful 'Tintin' along with the pure funk of 'High Roller'. *Close Up* featured a sensitive (though raucous) reading of the Diana Ross and Marvin Gaye hit 'You Are Everything'. In 1991 Sanborn made his first ever 'pure jazz album' and achieved the esteem of the jazz reviewers. *Another Hand* was a critical success and lifts Sanborn to the peak of his already lengthy career.

Albums: *Taking Off* (Warners 1975), *Sanborn* (1976), *David Sanborn Band* (1977), *Heart To Heart* (Warners 1978), *Hideaway* (1980), *Voyeur* (Warners 1981), *As We Speak* (Warners 1982), *Backstreet* (Warners 1983), *Let It Speak* (1984), *Love And Happiness* (1984), *Straight To The Heart* (Warners 1985), *A Change Of Heart* (Warners 1987), *Close Up* (Reprise 1988), *Another Hand* (Elektra 1991), *Upfront* (Elektra 1992), *Hearsay* (Elektra 1993).

Sanders, Mark

b. 31 August 1960, Beckenham, Kent, England. A self-taught drummer who combines power with agility and precision, Sanders began his career playing with a disco band at UK American Air Force bases. He turned to jazz in 1984, studying with Will Evans who, along with Elvin Jones and Tony Oxley, was a major influence. His first jazz engagements were with

Lyn Dobson, Stu Brown, Pete Nu and Elton Dean. In 1987 he joined Mervyn Afrika's Kaap Finale and formed a duo with Phil Durrant. Since 1988 he has played in duos and trios with Evan Parker, and has often worked with bassist Paul Rogers. He and Rogers have provided an intense and versatile rhythm section for Atlas (with John Law on piano), Parker, Dennis Gonzalez and the Elton Dean Trio. He has recently been working with Jon Lloyd and Spirit Level, and was part of the Paul Rogers Sextet which toured Britain in 1990 with the Arts Council-commissioned Anglo American Sketches. He has also played with Dreamtime (with Nick Evans), Dick Heckstall-Smith's DHSS, and in a quartet with Peter Cusack, Clive Bell and Dean Broderick.

Albums: with Atlas *Trio Improvisations* (1989), with Spirit Level *New Year* (1990), with Elton Dean/Howard Riley Quartet *All The Tradition* (1991), with Jon Lloyd *Syzygy* (1991).

Sanders, Pharoah

b. 13 October 1940, Little Rock, Arkansas, USA. By the time he left high school Sanders was proficient on several instruments, but eventually chose the tenor saxophone. After working in R&B bands he settled in New York in the early 60s where he became a frequent musical associate of Don Cherry, Albert Ayler and others active in the 'free jazz' movement and worked for a while in the Sun Ra Arkestra. For a couple of years beginning in 1965, he worked frequently with John Coltrane, playing on several influential recording dates during the period when Coltrane was extending the boundaries he had previously breached with his music. Sanders's playing with Coltrane was marked by a ferocious tone which sometimes growled, sometimes screeched and, within a limited range, he shaped intriguing and often adventurous phrases. In 1968, he played with the Jazz Composers' Orchestra led by Mike Mantler and Carla Bley. In his mid-career Sanders rarely extended the format of his earlier popular success and many of his 70s and 80s records were curious and unsuccessful mixtures of jazz, fusion, strings and vocals that offered fairly banal paeans to peace and love. In the late 80s, he reverted to a more purely instrumental jazz and later was a familiar figure at international festivals, playing in a style which displayed a clear understanding of bebop and which hinted only occasionally at his earlier espousal of the sometimes less accessible aspects of the freedom principle.

Selected albums: *Pharoah's First* (ESP 1965), *Tauhid* (Impulse 1967), *The Jazz Composers' Orchestra* (1968), *Karma* (1969), *Thembi* (1971), *Love Will Find A Way* (1977), *Rejoice* (Evidence 1981), *Pharoah Sanders Live* (1982), *Heart Is A Melody* (Evidence 1982), *Black Unity* (Impulse 1985), *Africa* (Timeless 1987), *A Prayer Before Dawn* (Evidence 1989), *Moon Child* (Timeless 1989), *Welcome To Love* (Timeless 1990), *Shukuru* (Evidence 1992), *Izipho Zam* (1993, rec. 1969), *Tauhid* (1993), *Oh Lord Let Me Do No Wrong* (Dillion 1992), *Ed Kelly & Pharoah Sanders* (1993).

Sauter, Eddie

b. 2 December 1914, New York City, New York, USA, d. 21 April 1981. After studying arranging and composition at the Juilliard School of Music, Sauter became staff arranger for Red Norvo. In 1939, after four years with Norvo, he freelanced, writing charts for several prominent big bands, including Artie Shaw, Woody Herman and Tommy Dorsey. He made his greatest impact with Benny Goodman, for whom he wrote 'Clarinet A La King' in the early 40s. He later worked for Ray McKinley where, unusually for an arranger at that time (or any other), he was given prominent billing. While hospitalized with tuberculosis Sauter began corresponding with Bill Finegan and in 1952 the two arrangers formed their own orchestra. The resulting 21-piece band was conceived as a studio band but its records, which included the joyous 'The Doodletown Fifers' and the irresistible 'Midnight Sleigh Ride', were so popular that they took it on the road. In 1957, Sauter became musical director of the South-West German Radio Big Band in Baden-Baden. He later worked with Stan Getz, the New York Saxophone Quartet and in films and television.

Selected albums: *The Sauter-Finegan Orchestra* (1952), *Historic Donanschingen Jazz Concert 1957* (1957), by Stan Getz *Focus* (1961), *The New York Saxophone Quartet* (1980). Compilations: *Eddie Sauter In Germany (1975-58)* (1980), *The Return Of The Doodletown Fifers* (Capitol 1985), *Directions In Music* (RCA 1989).

Savoy Sultans

The Savoy Sultans were a highly accomplished US small band (usually nine pieces) led by alto saxophonist/clarinettist Al Cooper. They were formed originally out of a band in which Cooper and trumpeter Pat Jenkins had played at New York's 101 Club and New Jersey's Harlem-on-the-Hudson. The band was heard by John Hammond and Willie Bryant who recommended them to Charles Buchanan, manager of the Savoy Ballroom in New York's Harlem. The band opened at the Savoy on Labor Day, 1937, and was an instant success with Savoy's hyper-critical dancers.

The Sultans had excellent soloists in Sam Massenberg (trumpet), George Kelly (tenor saxophone) and Rudy Williams (alto saxophone), and had a fine rhythm section in pianist Cyril Haynes (piano), Grachan Moncur (bass, also Cooper's half-brother and father of trombonist Grachan Moncur III) and Razz Mitchell (drums). Despite its relatively small size and its occasionally rather rudimentary arrangements, the Sultans swung mightily and maintained their popularity, and a remarkably stable personnel, until they broke up in 1946. Stylistically, the Sultans' brand of swinging dance music was slightly aside from that offered by most big bands of the day and had greater affinity with the small jump bands of the same period. In 1974, David 'Panama' Francis, who had played drums with the Lucky Millinder band in the early 40s, formed a small band modelled on the original Sultans. From the late 70s and on into the 90s, Panama Francis And His Savoy Sultans, which regularly included Kelly in its ranks, revived the spirit of the original band while offering its own exciting brand of swinging jazz music.

Sbarbaro, Tony

b. 27 June 1897, New Orleans, Louisiana, USA, d. 30 October 1969. After playing drums in several local bands in his home town, Sbarbaro moved to Chicago where, in 1916, he became a member of the Original Dixieland Jazz Band. In 1925 he took over leadership of the band and was involved in various ODJB recreations and reformations for much of the next three decades, often playing kazoo as well as drums. Although he did not have the polished jazz technique of his black counterparts from New Orleans, or indeed of some of the better white dixieland drummers, Sbarbaro (who frequently used the name Tony Spargo) was a lively drummer who brought great enthusiasm to his performances.

Album: *The Original Dixieland Jazz Band (1918-36)* (1979).

Schoof, Manfred

b. 6 April 1936, Madgeburg, Germany. This innovative jazz trumpet and flügelhorn player wrote his first arrangements for his school band. From 1955-58 he studied at the Musikakademie at Kassel and from 1958-63 at the Cologne Musikhochschule where he took a course in jazz run by the West German bandleader Kurt Edelhagen. After writing arrangements for Edelhagen's Radio Big Band and touring with Gunter Hampel, he led his own pioneering free jazz quintet in 1965, which included Alex Von Schlippenbach and Gerd Dudek. The quintet later formed the nucleus of the Manfred Schoof Orchestra in 1969, which brought together some of the leading exponents of European improvised music, such as Evan Parker, Derek Bailey, Peter Brötzmann, Irène Schweizer and Han Bennink. Schoof was also a member of George Russell's orchestra from 1969-71. During the 70s and 80s he toured throughout Europe, recording with the New Jazz Trio, the Globe Unity Orchestra, Jasper Van't Hof, Albert Mangelsdorff and others. In 1987, he performed and recorded with the George Gruntz Concert Jazz band in Fort Worth, Texas. Schoof has also composed in a contemporary classical vein, most notably for the Berlin Philharmonic.

Albums: *The Early Quintet* (1966), *European Echoes* (1969), with New Jazz Trio *Alternate Takes* (1970), with the Globe Unity Orchestra *Pearls* (1975), *Scales* (1977), *Light Lines* (1977), with Peter Brötzmann a.o. *In A State Of Undress* (1989), *Shadows And Smiles* (Wergo 1989).

Schuller, Gunther

b. 22 November 1925, New York City, New York, USA. After studying several instruments together with arranging and composition and music theory, Schuller played in several symphony orchestras before turning to jazz. He recorded with Miles Davis in the late 40s and early 50s and subsequently was a prime mover in what he termed 'third stream' music, a form which sought to blend jazz with appropriate aspects of western classical music. Schuller continued to combine his interests in classical music and jazz in his playing, composing and teaching career. Among the jazz musicians for whom he has written special pieces, and in some cases has recorded with, are Ornette Coleman, Eric Dolphy, Bill Evans and John Lewis. His teaching has included spells at the Lennox School of Jazz, of which he was a co-founder, and the New England Conservatory. He has also been active in music publishing and recording, forming his own companies in both fields. He has also written extensively on jazz and, apart from numerous magazine articles, he is the author of an important trilogy of which the first two volumes are *Early Jazz: Its Roots And Musical Development* (1968) and *The Swing Era: The Development Of Jazz, 1930-1945* (1989).

Selected albums: *Three Little Feelings* (1956), *The Gunther Schuller Orchestra* i (1957), with Miles Davis *Porgy And Bess* (1958), *Jazz Abstractions* (1960), *The Gunther Schuller Orchestra* ii (c.1966), *Ellington's Symphony In Black* (1980), *Vintage Dolphy* (1986).

Further reading: *Early Jazz: Its Roots And Musical Development*, Gunther Schuller. *The Swing Era: The Development Of Jazz 1930-1945*, Gunther Schuller.

Schutt, Arthur

b. 21 November 1902, Reading, Pennsylvania, USA, d. 28 January 1965. After playing piano in silent-movie theatres, Schutt joined a band led by Paul Specht. During the 20s Schutt played piano in several of the more popular society bands, including those of Specht, Roger Wolfe Kahn and Freddy Rich. Towards the end of the decade he was involved in recording sessions with several of the leading white jazzmen of the day, notably Bix Beiderbecke, Red Nichols, Frank Trumbauer and Benny Goodman. Throughout the 30s and early 40s he was mostly active in the studios but found time for occasional club dates in New York. Later in the 40s and on through the 50s he continued with studio work but was now based in Hollywood, where he played clubs only rarely.

Schweizer, Irène

b. 2 June 1941, Schaffhausen, Switzerland. Her interest in music sparked by the dance bands who played in her parents' restaurant, Schweizer began to play folk songs on the accordion at the age of eight and took up the piano four years later. By her late teens she was playing hard bop in a student band, but a brief stay in England in the early 60s alerted her to the more modern approaches of Joe Harriott and Tubby Hayes. Settling in Zurich she formed a trio, whose recordings show her music was still relatively conservative - Junior Mance and Bill Evans were early heroes - but by the time she recorded with Pierre Favre's groups in the late 60s (*Santana, This Is Free Jazz*) she was investigating the freer music that has since remained her chief focus of interest (and was partly inspired by hearing Cecil Taylor in the mid-60s). One of the first members of Berlin's FMP organization, Schweizer released most of her recordings on their label for the next 15 years, many featuring her in partnership with saxophonist Rüdiger Carl, though other associates included Manfred Schoof, John Martin Tchicai and Louis Moholo, plus a guest appearance with the group, Henry Cow (*Western Culture*). In 1978, Lindsay Cooper invited her to join the newly-formed Feminist Improvising Group (FIG) and in 1983 Schweizer set up the European Women's Improvising

Group (EWIG); she has remained a committed advocate for women's music, helping to organize the Canaille Festival of Women's Improvised Music in Zurich in 1986. In the mid-80s, with FMP in financial crisis, she was instrumental in setting up Switzerland's annual, three-city Taktlos Festival of improvised music plus its associated label, Intakt, on which many of her own recent releases have appeared. Prominent among these have been two CD releases of solo music and a series of duets - with drummers Moholo, Günter Sommer and Andrew Cyrille (Schweizer herself is a capable drummer), plus bassist Joëlle Léandre (a frequent collaborator) and pianist Marilyn Crispell. One of Europe's premier improvisers, Schweizer can play the entire gamut of piano, from dynamic, percussive attack to delicate and humorous interplay. Her latest UK tour was in 1991 with the London Jazz Composers' Orchestra, whose leader Barry Guy wrote 'Theoria' for her, a 'kind of piano concerto' to celebrate her 50th birthday.

Selected albums: *Jubilation* (rec. 1962), *Brandy* (rec. 1964), *Willem's Fun Feast* (1973), *Ramifications* (1975, rec. 1973), with Rüdiger Carl *Goose Pannee* (1975), with Carl, Louis Moholo *Messer* (1976), with John Tchicai *Willi The Pig* (1976), *Wilde Señoritas* (1976), *Hohe Ufer Konzerte* (1977), *Early Tapes* (1978, rec. 1967), *Hexensabbat* (1978), with Carl, Moholo *Tuned Boots* (1978), with Carl *The Very Centre Of Middle Europe* (1979), with Carl *Die V-Mann Suite* (1981), *Live At Taktlos* (1986, rec. 1984), with Joëlle Léandre *Cordial Gratin* (1987), *Irène Schweizer - Louis Moholo* (1987), with others *Canaille* (1988, rec. 1986), *The Storming Of The Winter Palace* (1988), *Irène Schweizer - Günter Sommer* (1988), *Irène Schweizer - Andrew Cyrille* (1989), *Piano Solo Volume One* (Intakt 1991), *Irene Schweizer And Pierre Favre* (Intakt 1990), *Piano Solo Volume Two* (Intakt 1991), with Marilyn Crispell *Overlapping Hands: Eight Segments* (1991).

Sclavis, Louis

b. 2 February 1953, Lyon, France. Louis Sclavis specializes in soprano saxophone, clarinet and bass clarinet; when he plays the clarinets, in particular, he does so with an authority very few modern jazz players can even approximate. Sclavis first came to attention with the group Workshop de Lyon, with whom he recorded five albums between 1975 and 1985. In 1976, he was a founder member of the Association à la Récherce d'un Folklore Imaginaire which proposed (amongst other things) that rather than be constrained by musical 'roots', a group of musicians should be free to dream up their own culture. Correspondingly, Sclavis's own recordings cover a wide and colourful terrain. Still much in demand as a sideman, Sclavis has played with Anthony Braxton, Cecil Taylor, Chris McGregor's Brotherhood Of Breath and others. On *Alms/Tiergarten (Spree)* by the Cecil Taylor European Orchestra, Sclavis emerges as one of the most powerful voices in a power-packed band.

Albums: with Jean Bolcato *Champ De Frigg* (1975), *Ad Augusta Per Angustia* (Nato 1981), *Rencontres* (Nato 1985), *Clarinettes* (IDA 1985), *Chine* (IDA 1987), *Chamber Music* (IDA 1989), with André Ricros *Le Partage Des Eaux* (1989), with Evan Parker, Hans Koch, Wolfgang Fuchs *Duets (Dithyrambische)* (1990), *Rouge* (ECM 1992), *Ellington On The Air* (Ida 1993), *Acoustic Quartet* ECM 1993).

Scobey, Bob

b. 9 December 1916, Tucumcari, New Mexico, USA, d. 12 June 1963. In the 30s Scobey played trumpet in several dance bands, mostly in California where he grew up. In 1938, he began a long-lasting musical association with Lu Watters, which brought him to the forefront of the jazz revival movement. During the 50s, he led his own traditional band, which attained a level of popularity similar to those of Watters and Turk Murphy, another companion in the west coast dixieland revival. In the 60s Scobey ran his own club in Chicago and remained a popular figure at festivals of traditional jazz. A sound, if unspectacular, trumpet player, Scobey's great enthusiasm for his music rubbed off on the sideman in any band of which he was a member.

Selected albums: *Bob Scobey's Alexander's Jazz Band* (Dawn Club 1986, 1946-47 recordings), *Bob Scobey's Frisco Band Vol. 1* (1950-51), *Vol. 2* (1952-53), *Direct From San Francisco* (Good Time 1993).

Scofield, John

b. 26 December 1951, Ohio, USA. From an early background of playing with local R&B groups, guitarist Scofield attended the renowned Berklee College Of Music in Boston during the early 70s. He recorded with Gerry Mulligan and Chet Baker and eventually received an invitation to join Billy Cobham as replacement for John Abercrombie. Following a two-year stint he played with Charles Mingus, Gary Burton, and Dave Liebman. His early solo work built slowly and steadily into a style that is uniquely his. *Shinola* was recorded live and is a mellow album, bordering on the lethargic, and features the bass playing of Scofield's acknowledged mentor Steve Swallow. Between 1983 and 1985 Scofield was an integral part of Miles Davis' band, playing on a number of recordings including *Decoy* and *You're Under Arrest*. Following this exposure, Scofield had accumulated a considerable following. During the mid-80s he played with McCoy Tyner, Marc Johnson and the French National Orchestra. *Electric Outlet* showed that Scofield had now created his own uniquely rich and creamy sound, and *Still Warm* capitalized on this burst of creativity and became the first of a series of outstanding albums on Gramavision. Great excitement preceded its release, following a giveaway record in *Guitar Player* magazine. The album became a big seller and was a flawless work. He continued in a similar funky, though less jazzier, vein for *Blue Matter* and *Loud Jazz*, the former featuring some impressive drum work from Dennis Chambers. *Flat Out* featured diverse and interesting arrangements of standards like Sammy Fain/Paul Francis Webster's 'Secret Love' and Jerome Kern/Oscar Hammerstein II's 'All The Things You Are'. A live offering, *Pick Hits*, brilliantly encapsulated the best of Scofield's recent work, and demonstrated his growing importance as a class player. *Time On My Hands* was a critics' favourite and another strong seller. For many, it was the jazz album of 1990. Scofield's playing had now reached a point where he was regarded as one of the world's top guitarists. His compositional skills continued to blossom; his interplay with Charlie Haden and Jack DeJohnette was imaginative and uplifting. Maintaining an extraordinarily prolific musical peak, he delivered another exciting record in the shape of *Meant To Be* and toured with the Mike Gibbs Orchestra during 1991, where his accessible and rich jazz guitar blended harmoniously with Gibbs' innovative compositions. *Grace Under Pressure* and *What We Do* continued his run of first-rate and highly popular albums, still showing Scofield full of fresh ideas. *Hand Jive* was his return to funk and soul/jazz with some excellent contributions from the saxophone of Eddie Harris. Jim Ferguson, writing in *Guitar Player*, perceptively stated that Scofield's solos are 'like the chase scene in *The French Connection* - incredibly exciting, intense and constantly flirting with disaster, but rarely out of control'. Scofield is one of the most original and talented guitarists currently playing.

Albums: *John Scofield Live* (Enja 1977), *Rough House* (Enja 1978), *Who's Who* (Novus 1979), *Bar Talk* (Enja 1980), *Shinola* (Enja 1981), *Out Like A Light* (Enja 1981), *John Scofield - John Abercrombie* (c.80s), *More Sightings* (c.80s), *Electric Outlet* (Gramavision 1984), *Still Warm* (Gramavision 1987), *Blue Matter* (Gramavision 1987), *Loud Jazz* (Gramavision 1987), *Flat Out* (Gramavision 1989), *Pick Hits Live* (Gramavision 1989), *Time On My Hands* (Blue Note 1990), *Slo Sco* (Gramavision 1990) *Meant To Be* (Blue Note 1991), *Grace Under Pressure* (Blue Note 1992), *What We Do* (Blue Note 1993), with Pat Metheny *I Can See Your House From Here* (Blue Note 1994), *Hand Jive* (Blue Note 1994).

Scott, Cecil

b. 22 November 1905, Springfield, Ohio, USA, d. 5 January 1964. Scott began playing clarinet and saxophones as a child and had his own band while still a teenager. His bandleading career lasted throughout the 20s and by the end of that decade he was resident in New York, where he made a big impression on audiences and rival bands. His sidemen included his brother, drummer Lloyd Scott, plus Dicky Wells, Johnny Hodges, Chu Berry and a succession of distinguished trumpeters, such as Bill Coleman, Joe Thomas, Frankie Newton and Roy Eldridge. Scott continued to lead a band until the early 30s, when a bad leg injury interrupted his career. From the mid-30s into the early 40s he played with various small groups, mostly in the New York and Chicago areas. In 1942, he returned to leading a big band and subsequently a series of small groups, activities which continued throughout the 50s and into the early 60s. During this late period he worked with Willie 'The Lion' Smith and was recorded with the encouragement of Chris Barber. A driving, gutsy player on clarinet and tenor saxophone, Scott was a forceful leader who demanded and received enthusiastic support from his sidemen. At its peak his band was one of the best of the New York-based black bands and had it not been for his enforced layoff just as the swing era was getting under way he might have achieved greater recognition.

Selected album: *Chris Barber Presents Harlem Washboard: Cecil Scott And His Washboard Band* (1959).

Scott, Ronnie

b. 28 January 1927, London, England. Scott began playing on the soprano saxophone but switched to tenor in his early teens. After playing informally in clubs he joined the Johnny Claes band in 1944, before spells with Ted Heath, Bert Ambrose and other popular British dance bands. Scott also played on transatlantic liners in order to visit the USA and hear bebop at first hand. By the late 40s he was a key figure in the London bop scene, playing at the Club Eleven, of which he was a co-founder. During the 50s he led his own band and was also co-leader with Tubby Hayes of the Jazz Couriers. In 1959, he opened his own club in Gerrard Street, London, later transferring to Frith Street. During the 60s he divided his time between leading his own small group and running the club, but also found time to play with the Clarke-Boland Big Band. In the 70s and 80s he continued to lead small bands, usually a quartet, occasionally touring but most often playing as the interval band between sessions by the modern American jazz musicians he brought to the club. As a player, Scott comfortably straddles the mainstream and modern aspects of jazz. His big tone lends itself to a slightly aggressive approach, although in his ballad playing he displays the warmth which characterized the work of Zoot Sims and late-period Stan Getz, musicians he admires, but does not imitate. Although a gifted player, Scott's greatest contribution to jazz lies in his tireless promotion of fine British musicians and in his establishment of his club, a venue which has become renowned throughout the world for the excellence of its setting and the artists on display. In 1981, Scott was awarded an OBE in recognition of his services to music.

Albums: *Battle Royal* (Esquire 1951), *The Ronnie Scott Jazz Group* i (1952), *Live At The Jazz Club* (1953), *The Ronnie Scott Jazz Group* ii (1954), *The Jazz Couriers In Concert* (1958), *The Last Word* (1959), *The Night Is Scott And You're So Swingable* (1965), *Live At Ronnie's* (1968), *Scott At Ronnie's* (1973), *Serious Gold* (1977), *Great Scott* (1979), with various artists *Ronnie Scott's 20th Anniversary Album* (1979), *Never Pat A Burning Dog* (Jazz House 1990).

Further reading: *Let's Join Hands And Contact The Living*, John Fordham.

Scott, Shirley

b. 14 March 1934, Philadelphia, Pennsylvania, USA. Although she had studied both piano and trumpet as a child, Scott's breakthrough occurred when she switched to organ in the mid-50s. Mostly working in small groups with a saxophone leader and a drummer, she became very popular. Her musical associates have included such outstanding jazzmen as Eddie 'Lockjaw' Davis, Stanley Turrentine (to whom she was married for a while), Jimmy Forrest and Dexter Gordon. A gifted player with an eclectic style that encompasses the blues and bebop, Scott is one of only a handful of organists to satisfactorily fit a potentially unsuitable instrument into a jazz setting. Her career received a boost in the 90s when the Hammond organ became fashionable once more.

Albums: *Shirley's Sounds* (1958), *The Eddie Lockjaw Davis Cookbook* (1958), *Great Scott!* (1958), *Scottie* (1958), *Shirley Scott Plays Duke* (1959), *Soul Searching* (1959), *The Shirley Scott Trio* i (1960), *Soul Sisters* (1960), *Mucho Mucho* (1960), *Like Cozy* (1960), *Satin Doll* (1961), *Stompin'* (1961), *Hip Soul* (1961), *Blue Seven* (1961), *Shirley Scott Plays Horace Silver* (1961), *Hip Twist* (1961), with Stanley Turrentine *Dearly Beloved* (1961), *Happy Talk* (1962), *The Soul Is Willing* (1963), *Drag 'Em Out* (1963), *Soul Shoutin'* (1963), *Travellin' Light* (1964), *Blue Flames* (Original Jazz Classics 1964), *Shirley Scott And Her Orchestra* i (1964), *The Great Live Sessions* (1964), *The Shirley Scott Sextet* (1965), *Queen Of The Organ* (Impulse 1965), *The Shirley Scott Trio* ii (1966), *The Shirley Scott Trio* iii (1966), *Shirley Scott And Her Orchestra* ii (1966), *The Shirley Scott Quintet* (1972), *One For Me* (1974), *Oasis* (Muse 1990), *Blues Everywhere* (Candid 1993).

Scott, Tony

b. Anthony Sciacca, 17 June 1921, Morristown, New Jersey, USA. Scott learned to play clarinet as a child, later studying formally at the Juilliard School in Manhattan. During the late 40s and beyond, he made his living playing in big bands and as a sideman in mainstream groups, sometimes playing tenor saxophone. Fascinated by the new jazz sounds emerging from Minton's Playhouse and other New York venues, he became a strongly committed bop musician. Unfortunately for the development of his career, bop and the clarinet were uneasy bedfellows, although Scott was one of the tiny number of clarinettists to achieve some recognition, building a reputation through the 50s as one of the best new players on his instrument. He was also active as an arranger and musical director for several singers, including Harry Belafonte, Billie Holiday and Sarah Vaughan. In 1959 he recorded the remarkably forward-looking *Sung Heroes*, with Bill Evans, Scott La Faro and Paul Motian, but the same year left America, tired of music business racism and despairing of the fact that so many of his close friends - Oran 'Hot Lips' Page, Charlie Parker, Art Tatum, Sid Catlett, Lester Young, Billie Holiday - had recently died. Scott spent six years travelling, both in Europe and (mostly) the Far East, and began to incorporate into his repertoire elements of ethnic music, especially from India and the Orient, creating a personal precedent for world music long before the genre was acknowledged. The records he made in the mid-60s as aids to meditation proved to be popular and consistent sellers - 'a godsend' he said of them in 1988, claiming that their royalties were still his main source of income. In the early 70s Scott settled in Italy, playing at festivals and touring, often to the far east, making occasional records and as often as not anticipating trends and fashions in music - even if, as so often happens with pioneers, his work has been overshadowed by that of other less-talented musicians. His latest project to date has been a double album consisting entirely of different versions of Billy Strayhorn's standard, 'Lush Life'. 'No one has sung it right yet', Scott told *Wire* in 1988, 'including Nat 'King' Cole, Sarah

Vaughan, everybody - they all goof it'.

Albums: *A Touch Of Tony Scott* (1956), *Scott's Fling* (1957), *The Modern Art Of Jazz* (1957), *A Day In New York* (Fresh Sound 1958), *South Pacific Jazz* (1958), *52nd Street Scene* (1958), *Golden Moments* (1959), *Sung Heroes* (1959), *Dedications* (Core 1957-59 recordings), *Music For Zen Meditation* (Verve 1964), *Music For Yoga Meditation And Other Joys* (c.1967), *Tony Scott* (c.1969), *Prism* (1977), *Boomerang* (1977), *African Bird: Come Back! Mother Africa* (Soul Note 1984), *Lush Life Vols 1 and 2* (Core 1989), *Astral Meditation: Voyage Into A Black Hole 1-3* (Core 1989), *The Clarinet Album* (Philology 1993).

Seamen, Phil

b. 28 August 1928, Burton-on-Trent, Staffordshire, England, d. 13 October 1972. Seamen first attracted attention when he played drums with post-war British dance bands, including those led by Nat Gonella and Joe Loss. By the early 50s he was a key figure in the nascent London bop scene, working with Ronnie Scott, Tubby Hayes, Joe Harriott and other leading musicians. Later in the decade he recorded with Stan Tracey, on *Little Klunk* (1959) and the following year with Harriott, on the saxophonist's *Free Form*. In the early 60s Seamen tried his hand in blues bands, including those of Georgie Fame and Alexis Korner. In the late 60s he was back with Scott but also played in rock bands, including Air Force which was led by one of his students, Ginger Baker. The range of Seamen's musical interests is apparent from the company he kept, and he brought to everything he did enormous enthusiasm and vitality. His dynamic playing enhanced countless club and pub sessions in and around London, a handful being captured on record. Sadly, for all his skills, Seamen's career and ultimately his life were blighted by drug addiction. Seamen's virtuosity was remarkable: his work with Harriott was noteworthy for the manner in which he adapted to free jazz, and he coped admirably with the very different demands required by his performances in rock and blues bands. Despite such performances, however, it is a bop drummer that he made his most notable mark on the British jazz scene.

Albums: *Third Festival Of British Jazz* (1956), *Now!...Live!* (1968), *Phil On Drums! A Jam Session At The Hideaway* (1971), *Phil Talks And Plays/The Phil Seamen Story* (1972).

Sears, Al

b. 21 February 1910, Macomb, Illinois, USA, d. 23 March 1990. After playing alto and baritone saxophones in various bands in the north-eastern states, Sears switched to tenor saxophone and moved to New York, where he was soon in demand. In the late 20s he was with Chick Webb and Zack Whyte, then briefly played with Elmer Snowden before forming his own band. In 1941 he folded his band and joined Andy Kirk, then Lionel Hampton, and, in 1944, succeeded Ben Webster in the Duke Ellington band. Sears remained with Ellington until 1949 and soon thereafter joined Johnny Hodges's band, which had a successful record with Sears's composition 'Castle Rock'. Sears subsequently ran his own music publishing business in partnership with Budd Johnson, playing occasionally in R&B

bands and using the name Big Al Sears. A forceful player with enormous drive and energy, Sears needed only a slight coarsening of his naturally rasping tone to adapt readily into the R&B fold. Despite such later manifestations, however, his recorded solos with Ellington indicate a musician of considerable sophistication, and his recordings, which include 'Hiawatha' from Ellington's 'The Beautiful Indians', frequently offer fine examples of his craft.

Selected albums: *Duke Ellington At Carnegie Hall* (1946), *Duke Ellington And His Orchestra 1946* (1946), with Ellington *Liberian Suite* (1947), with Johnny Hodges *Rabbit On Verve Vol. 1* (1951), *Al Sears And His Orchestra* (1960), *Swing's The Thing* (1960), *Sear-iously* (Bear Family 1992).

Sedric, Gene

b. 17 June 1907, St. Louis, Missouri, USA, d. 3 April 1963. Sedric began playing clarinet in local bands, later taking up the tenor saxophone, as well. His first important jobs were with Charlie Creath, Fate Marable and other bandleaders playing in the region and on the riverboats. In the early 20s he arrived in New York with a touring band and there joined Sam Wooding, with whom he visited Europe. In 1934, he became a member of Fats Waller's small group, remaining there until the leader's death in 1943. Subsequently he led his own small bands, also playing and recording with other leaders. In the early 50s he again visited Europe, playing with Mezz Mezzrow, Buck Clayton and others. In 1953 he joined a band led by Conrad Janis and at the end of the decade freelanced until ill-health forced him into retirement. Although he was not an exceptional performer on either instrument, Sedric fitted well into the cheerful music that Waller's accompanists offered. Thanks to this association he enjoyed a long and successful career.

Compilation: *Fats Waller And His Rhythm 1934-36 (Classic Years In Digital Stereo)* (1988).

Seifert, Zbigniew

b. 6 June 1946, Cracow, Poland, d. 15 February 1979, Munich, Germany. Seifert studied violin from the age of six and took up the alto saxophone in his teens. He studied music at the Chopin School of Music in Cracow and graduated from the Higher School of Music in 1970. In 1965 he had started his own quartet modelled on the style of John Coltrane's classic quartet. By the time he played with Tomasz Stanko's band (1969-73) he was playing a freer form of jazz, gradually incorporating more violin and dropping the alto altogether in 1971. The free style was well served by his passionate, tough and technically adept playing which measured up to his desire to 'play as Coltrane would if he played the violin'. He moved to Germany in 1973 and worked with Hans Koller's Free Sound (1974-75) and appeared at the Montreux Jazz Festival with John Lewis in 1976. Hamburg Radio commissioned a large scale piece from him and he played and recorded with Oregon. He died from cancer at the age of 32.

Albums: with Tomasz Stanko *Purple Sun* (1973), *Man Of The Light* (1976), with Oregon *Violin* (1977), with Charlie Mariano *Helen 12 Trees* (1977), *Passion* (1978).

Semple, Archie

b. 1 March 1928, Edinburgh, Scotland, d. 26 January 1974. After first playing clarinet in bands in his homeland, Semple moved to London in the early 50s. There he became an important voice in the burgeoning traditional jazz scene, playing with the bands of Mick Mulligan, Freddy Randall and Alex Welsh, with whom he remained until the early 60s. During that decade he played with various bands, led his own small groups and made many records, despite the fast-encroaching effects of a severe drinking problem. A very distinctive player with a rich and quirky musical imagination, Semple was one of the most strikingly individualistic musicians to emerge from the sometimes predictable British trad scene. His presence in the already formidable Welsh band helped create much memorable music.

Albums: *The Clarinet Of Archie Semple* (1957-58), with Welsh *It's Right Here For You* (1960), *The Archie Semple Trio* (1960), *Archie Semple And His Orchestra* (1962), *The Archie Semple Quartet* (1963).

Shank, Bud

b. Clifford Everett Jnr., 27 May 1926, Dayton, Ohio, USA. After studying and gigging on most of the reed instruments, Shank concentrated on alto saxophone, later doubling on flute and baritone saxophone. From 1947 he was resident on the west coast, playing in the big bands of Charlie Barnet, Alvino Rey, Art Mooney and Stan Kenton but making his greatest impact in small groups. With Shorty Rogers, Milt Bernhardt, Bob Cooper, Art Pepper and Shelly Manne, he was one of the tightly-knit group of Los Angeles-based musicians who formed the nucleus of the white west coast jazz scene of the 50s. As a member of the Lighthouse All-Stars and groups recording under the names of one or another of the leaders of the movement, Shank built a substantial reputation. He also recorded with Laurindo Almeida, beginning an association which was renewed several years later with the formation of the LA Four. Although active in the film and television studios during the 50s and 60s, Shank continued to make jazz dates, and with increasing frequency. In 1974 he was a founder-member of the LA Four. In the early 80s, by then wholly engaged in jazz, he toured as a single and also with Rogers, appearing in the UK with the Vic Lewis big band and recording with the Royal Philharmonic Orchestra. Shank's extensive recorded output over four decades allows an interesting examination of his development as a musician. His early alto playing was derivative of Charlie Parker and Art Pepper, while his flute playing, taken up during his stint with Kenton, was highly original and greatly advanced the use of the instrument in bebop settings. In later years his alto style became highly personalized and no longer showed influences outside of his own creative impulse. Indeed, by the mid-80s he had reputedly abandoned his other instruments in order to concentrate fully on alto.

Selected albums: with Shorty Rogers *Cool And Crazy* (1953), with Shelly Manne *The West Coast Sound* (1953), *The Bud Shank Quintet* i (1953), *The Bud Shank-Laurindo Almeida Quartet: Brazilliance Vol. 1* (1953), *The Bud Shank-Shorty Rogers Quintet* (1954), *Bud Shank And Three Trombones*

(1954), *Bud Shank And Strings* (1955), *The Bud Shank-Bill Perkins Quintet* (1955), *The Bud Shank-Bob Cooper Quartet* (1956), *Live At The Haig* (1956), *The Bud Shank Quartet* i (1956), *The Bud Shank-Russ Freeman Quartet* (1956), *The Bud Shank Quartet* ii (1956), *Sessions, Live* (1956), *The Bud Shank-Bob Cooper Quintet* (1956), *The Bud Shank Quartet* iii (1957), *The Bud Shank-Laurindo Almeida Quartet: Brazilliance Vol. 2* (1958), *I'll Take Romance* (1958), *Misty Eyes* (West Wind 1958), *The Bud Shank Quartet* iv (1958), *The Bud Shank Quartet* v (1959), *The Bud Shank Quintet* ii (1961), *The Bud Shank Sextet* ii (1961), *New Groove* (1961), *The Bud Shank Septet* i (1962), *The Bud Shank Septet* ii (1963), *The Bud Shank Quartet* vi (1963), *Bud Shank And His Brazilian Friends* (c.1965), *Brazil '65* (1965), *Bud Shank-Chet Baker* i (1966), *Bud Shank-Chet Baker* ii (1966), *Bud Shank And His Orchestra* i (1966), *Bud Shank And His Orchestra* ii (1966), *Bud Shank And His Orchestra* iii (1967), *Bud Shank And His Orchestra* iv (1967), *Bud Shank-Chet Baker* iii (1968), *The Windmills Of Your Mind* (1969), *Bud Shank And The Bob Alcivar Singers* (1969-70), *The LA Four Scores!* (1975), *Sunshine Express* (Concord 1976), *Heritage* (1977), with LA Four *Watch What Happens* (1978), *Crystal Moments* (1979), *Explorations 1980* (Concord 1979), *Shades Of Dring* (1981), with Rogers *Yesterday, Today, And Forever* (1983), with Rogers, Vic Lewis *Back Again* (1984), *This Bud's For You* (1984), *California Concert* (1985), *Concert For Alto Saxophone And Symphony Orchestra* (c.1987), *Serious Swingers* (Contemporary 1987), *Tomorrow's Rainbow* (Contemporary c.1987), *At Jazz Alley* (JVC 1987), *Tales Of The Pilot* (1989), *Lost In The Stars* (Fresh Sound 1991), *The Doctor Is In* (1992), with Laurindo Almeida *Baa-Too-Kee* (1993), *I Told You So* (Candid 1994).

Sharon, Ralph

b. 17 September 1923, London, England. Sharon came to prominence as pianist with the Ted Heath band in the years immediately after World War II. He also played, and sometimes recorded, with British bop musicians of the late 40s, including Ronnie Scott and Victor Feldman. In the early 50s he moved to the USA, became an American citizen, and continued to play piano in a variety of settings, frequently in distinguished company. He also established a reputation as a sympathetic accompanist to singers, notably Tony Bennett and Chris Connor. On one of his albums with Bennett, Sharon wrote arrangements for the Count Basie band, playing piano on most tracks, while on another album, three decades later, he arranged songs by Irving Berlin for his own small group, with added guests who included George Benson, Dexter Gordon and Dizzy Gillespie. Sharon's habitual diffidence has kept him hidden from the spotlight he clearly deserves. Among his early American recordings were some with his wife, the singer Sue Ryan.
Selected albums: *The Ralph Sharon Sextet* i (1955), *The Ralph Sharon Trio* i (1956), *Mr & Mrs Jazz* (Fresh Sounds 1956), *The Ralph Sharon Sextet* ii (1957), *The Ralph Sharon Quartet* (1958), with Tony Bennett *Bennett/Basie* (1959), *Ralph Sharon With The Rolena Carter Chorale* (c.1962), *The Ralph Sharon Trio* ii (c.1965), with Bennett *Bennett/Berlin* (1987), *The Magic Of George Gershwin* (Horatio Nelson 1988), *The Magic Of Irving Berlin* (Horatio Nelson 1989), *The Magic Of Cole Porter* (Horatio Nelson 1989).

Sharrock, Sonny

b. Warren Hardin Sharrock, 27 August 1940, Ossining, New York, USA, d. 26 May 1994, Ossining, New York, USA. Now regarded as one of the most remarkable guitarists in contemporary jazz, Sharrock was a late starter, teaching himself the instrument at the age of 20. Before that he sang in a doo-wop group, the Echoes. He recorded with them for Alan Freed but the tracks were never released. When he was 21 he spent a few months studying formally at Berklee College Of Music. Starting in 1965 he worked with a succession of major names in the *avant garde* (including Pharoah Sanders, Don Cherry, Sunny Murray and Olatunji, John Gilmore and Byard Lancaster) then from 1967-73 provided the 'outside' element in Herbie Mann's band. In 1970 he contributed to 'Yesternow', the second part of Miles Davis's *Jack Johnson*. In 1973 he formed a band with his then wife, Linda Sharrock (Chambers), and made his solo debut in 1986 with *Last Exit*. At the time of its release he was playing with Peter Brötzmann, Bill Laswell, and Ronald Shannon Jackson. After a fascinating and innovative solo album, *Guitar*, he established a more conventional band which toured successfully with packages organized by New York's Knitting Factory club. In 1991 he released *Ask The Ages*, with an all-star quartet containing Sanders, Charnett Moffett and Elvin Jones. Sharrock died of a heart attack in May 1994.
Selected albums: with Pharoah Sanders *Tauhid* (1967), with Herbie Mann *Memphis Underground* (1968), with Wayne Shorter *Super Nova* (1969), *Black Woman* (1970), with Miles Davis *Jack Johnson* (1970), *Monkie Pockie Boo* (Affinity 1974), *Paradise* (1974), with Material *Memory Serves* (1981), *Guitar* (Enemy 1986), with Last Exit *Last Exit* (1986), *The Noise Of Trouble, Cassette Tapes* (1987), *Seize The Rainbow* (Enemy 1987), *Live In New York* (Enemy 1990), *Iron Path, The Cologne Tapes* (1990), *Ask The Ages* (1991), *Highlife* (Highlife 1991), with Nicky Skopelitis *Faith Moves* (1991), *Ask The Ages* (Axiom 1991).

Shavers, Charlie

b. 3 August 1917, New York City, New York, USA, d. 8 July 1971. Shavers took up trumpet in his teens and played with various minor bands before joining Tiny Bradshaw in 1937. In the same year he played with Lucky Millinder, Jimmie Noone and John Kirby. The Kirby sextet proved an ideal setting for him, both as trumpeter and arranger, and he stayed for seven years. Among his compositions written while with Kirby are 'Pastel Blue', which with lyrics added became 'Why Begin Again', and 'Undecided', which became a jazz standard in its own right and with added lyrics a hit for Ella Fitzgerald. In 1944 he left Kirby for the Tommy Dorsey orchestra, where for a decade he was featured soloist. He made records throughout these years with various leaders, including a session under the nominal guidance of Herbie Haymer that featured Nat 'King' Cole and Buddy Rich. This set was issued, fluffs, retakes, off-microphone comments and all, under the title *Anatomy Of A Jam Session*. Another admirable date from this period was a Gene Norman concert at Pasadena, California, issued under Lionel Hampton's name. In the 50s and 60s Shavers played mostly in small groups, often as leader, touring extensively as a single and with Jazz At The Philharmonic. A masterly musician, Shavers was capable of adapting to almost any mainstream setting. In the right company he would produce emotionally powerful playing; with Kirby he played with the elegance and finesse this group demanded, and in his later years with JATP he would deliver wildly exciting bravura solos, all with remarkable ease and overt good humour.

Selected albums: with Nat 'King' Cole and Buddy Rich *Anatomy Of A Jam Session* (1945), with Lionel Hampton *Stardust* (1945), *Jazz At The Philharmonic: Hartford 1953* (1953), *The Charlie Shavers Sextet* (1954), *The Most Intimate Charlie Shavers* (1955), *Gershwin, Shavers And Strings* (1955), *We Dig Cole!* (1958), *Art Ford's Jazz Party* (1958), *The Charlie Shavers Quartet* i (1958-59), *The Charlie Shavers Quartet* ii (1959), *Memorial* (1959), *The Charlie Shavers Quartet* iii (1960), *The Charlie Shavers Quartet* iv (1961), *Swing Along* (1961) *Swinging With Charlie* (1961), *The Charlie Shavers-Wild Bill Davis Combo* (1961), *A Man And His Music* (c.1962), *Live At The London House* (1962), *Live From Chicago* (1962), *Charlie Shavers And His Orchestra* (1963), *Charlie Shavers At Le Crazy Horse Saloon In Paris* (c.1964), *The Last Session* (1970), *Live!* (Black And Blue 1970). Compilations: *November 1961 & March 1962* (1980), *Trumpet Man (1944-58)* (1981).

Shaw, Artie

b. Arthur Jacob Arshawsky, 23 May 1910, New York City, New York, USA. Shaw took up the alto saxophone at the age of 12 and a few years later was playing in a Connecticut dance band. In 1926, he switched to clarinet and spent the next three years working in Cleveland, Ohio, as arranger and musical director for Austin Wylie. He also played in Irving Aaronson's popular band, doubling on tenor saxophone. In New York from the end of 1929, Shaw became a regular at after-hours sessions, sitting in with leading jazzmen and establishing a reputation as a technically brilliant clarinettist. He made numerous record dates with dance bands and jazz musicians including Teddy Wilson, with whom he appeared on some of Billie Holiday's sessions. In 1936, Shaw formed a band which included strings for a concert and, with the addition of regular dance band instruments, secured a recording contract. The band did not last long and in April 1937 he formed a conventional big band that was an immediate success, thanks in part to melodic arrangements by Jerry Gray. The band made several records including 'Begin The Beguine', which was a huge popular success. Musically, Shaw's band was one of the best of the period and, during the first couple of years of its existence, included Johnny Best, Cliff Leeman, Les Robinson, Georgie Auld, Tony Pastor and Buddy Rich. During 1938 Shaw briefly had Holiday as the band's singer; but racial discrimination in New York hotels and on the band's radio shows led to a succession of disagreeable confrontations which eventually compelled the singer to quit. Other singers Shaw used were Kitty Kallen and Helen Forrest. Always uneasy with publicity and the demands of the public, Shaw abruptly folded the band late in 1939, but a featured role in the 1940 Fred Astaire-Paulette Goddard film, *Second Chorus*, brought another hit, 'Frenesi', and he quickly reformed a band. The new band included a string section and a band-within-a-band, the Gramercy Five. The big band included Billy Butterfield, Jack Jenney, Nick Fatool and Johnny Guarnieri. In the small group, Guarnieri switched from piano to harpsichord to create a highly distinctive sound. More successful records followed, including 'Concert For Clarinet', 'Summit Ridge Drive' and 'Special Delivery Stomp'. Shaw's dislike of celebrity caused him to disband once again, but he soon reformed only to be forced to fold when the USA entered the war. In 1942 he headed a band in the US Navy which included several leading jazzmen. After the war he formed a new band that featured Roy Eldridge, Dodo Marmarosa, Barney Kessel, Chuck Gentry, Stan Fishelson and other top musicians. This band, like all the others, was short-lived and during the rest of the 40s Shaw periodically formed bands only to break them up again within a few months. At the same time he also studied classical guitar and began to develop a secondary career as a writer. By the mid-50s he had retired from music and spent much of his time writing. He lived for a number of years in Spain but in the late 60s returned to the USA, where he continued to expand his writing career. In the 80s he reformed a band, under the direction of Dick Johnson, and performed at special concerts. In 1985 a film documentary, *Time Is All You've Got*, traced his career in detail. In June 1992 he appeared in London at a concert performance where Bob Wilber recreated some of his music.

During the late 30s and early 40s Shaw was set up as a rival to Benny Goodman, but the antagonism was a creation of publicists; in reality the two men were amicable towards one another. Nevertheless, fans of the pair were divided, heatedly arguing the respective merits of their idol. Stylistically, Shaw's playing was perhaps slightly cooler than Goodman's, although his jazz sense was no less refined. Like Goodman, Shaw was a technical marvel, playing with remarkable precision yet always swinging. His erratic bandleading career, allied as it was to a full private life - amongst his eight wives were some of Hollywood's most glamorous stars - militated against his ever achieving the same level of success as Goodman or many other bandleading contemporaries. Nevertheless, his bands were always musicianly and his frequent hiring of black musicians, including Holiday, Eldridge and Oran 'Hot Lips' Page, helped to break down racial barriers in music.

Selected compilations: *Artie Shaw Recreates His Great '38 Band* (1963), *The 1938 Band In Hi-Fi (1938)* (1979), *Swinging Big Bands, 1938-45, Volume 1* (1981), *Melody And Madness Vols. 1-5 (1938-39)* (1982), *This Is Artie Shaw* (1983), *Traffic Jam* (1985), *The Indispensable Artie Shaw Vols 1/2 (1938-39)* (1986), *The Indispensable Artie Shaw Vols 3/4 (1940-42)* (1986), *The Rhythmakers Vols 1-3 (1937-38)* (1987), *Thou*

Swell (1936-37) (1988), *Gloomy Sunday* (Pickwick 1992), *Frenesi* (Bluebird 1992), *The Last Recordings, Rare And Unreleased* (S&R 1992), *Let's Go For Shaw* (1993), *Lets Go For Shaw* (Avid 1993).

Further reading: *The Trouble With Cinderella: An Outline Of Identity*, Artie Shaw.

Shaw, Arvell

b. 15 September 1923, St. Louis, Missouri, USA. Although he had previously studied other instruments, Shaw began playing bass while working with the Fate Marable band in the early 40s. Shortly after this, military service interrupted his career but soon after World War II ended he joined Louis Armstrong, a job which, on and off, lasted for a quarter of a century. First, he was with Armstrong's big band; he rejoined when the All Stars were formed in 1945, staying until 1953 (with a short break to study in Switzerland). In the mid-to-late 50s and in the 60s he made frequent return visits to Armstrong but found time for appearances with Benny Goodman, Teddy Wilson and others. After Armstrong's death in 1971, Shaw worked with a number of mainstream jazz artists, including Buddy Tate, Dorothy Donegan and Earl Hines, freelanced in the USA and Europe and then, in the 80s, re-entered the Armstrong fold by joining Keith Smith's *Wonderful World Of Louis Armstrong* concert package. A solid and thoroughly dependable member of the rhythm section, Shaw is also an energetic and accomplished soloist whose playing always commands attention.
Albums: with Louis Armstrong *Satchmo At Symphony Hall* (1947), *Louis Armstrong Plays W. C. Handy* (1954), *Louis Armstrong At The Crescendo* (1955), *The Many Faces Of Dorothy Donegan* (1975).

Shaw, Charles 'Bobo'

b. 15 September 1947, Pope, Mississippi, USA. Shaw studied with a string of drummers and also learned bass and trombone with Frank Mokuss. He played drums in R&B bands, backing soul saxophonist Oliver Sain, singers Ike And Tina Turner and bluesman Albert King. He moved to St. Louis, Missouri, and was a founder of BAG (Black Artists Group). There he met and played with altoist Oliver Lake as well as playing in the St. Louis Symphony Orchestra. In the early 70s he moved with other BAG members to Europe, where he played with Anthony Braxton, Steve Lacy, Frank Wright and Alan Silva. He calls his bands the Human Arts Ensemble or (more recently) the Red, Black & Green Solidarity Unit. In 1972 the Human Arts Ensemble made its debut recording with *Whisper Of Dharma*, followed a year later by *Under The Sun*, which featured Lake and Lester Bowie as guest artists. In 1974 Shaw moved to New York, and in the next few years recorded with Frank Lowe (*Fresh, The Flam*), Bowie (*Fast Last, Rope-A-Dope*) and Lake (*Heavy Spirits*). In 1977 he recorded a duo album with Bowie (*Bugle Boy Bop*), although this was not released until 1983. He also teamed up with Bowie's trombonist brother, Joseph Bowie, in a new line-up of the Human Arts Ensemble and in the next two years released *P'nk J'zz, Trio Performances Vol 1*, which featured guitarist James Emery (from String Trio Of New York);

Vol 2, which featured Luther Thomas on alto and John Lindberg (also from STONY) on bass; and *Junk Trap*, which combined all five players. Shaw also played on two Human Arts Ensemble dates led by Thomas (*Funky Donkey Vol 1*, *Poem Of Gratitude*) and as a member of the St Louis Creative Ensemble, which played Europe in 1979 and recorded *I Can't Figure Out*. Since this burst of activity little has been heard from him, apart from appearances with Marion Brown and Bowie's punk-funk group Defunkt.
Albums: with the Human Arts Ensemble *Whisper Of Dharma* (1973), *Streets Of St Louis* (1974), with HAE *Under The Sun* (1975, rec. 1973), with Luther Thomas/HAE *Poem Of Gratitude* (70s), with Luther Thomas/HAE *Funky Donkey Vol 1* (1977), with HAE *P'nk J'zz* (1977), with HAE *Trio Performances Vols 1* and *2* (1978), with HAE *Junk Trap* (1978), with St Louis Creative Ensemble *I Can't Figure Out* (1979), with Lester Bowie *Bugle Boy Bop* (1983, rec. 1977).

Shaw, Woody

b. Herman Shaw II, 24 December 1944, Laurinburg, North Carolina, USA, d. 11 May 1989. Shaw was raised in Newark, New Jersey, where his father sang in a gospel group. Taking up the trumpet at the age of 11, he quickly attained a level of proficiency which allowed him to sit in with visiting jazzmen. He left school when he was 16 years old to work in New York with Willie Bobo in whose band he played alongside Chick Corea and Joe Farrell. He also met Eric Dolphy, recording with him on 1963's *Iron Man*. The following year Dolphy invited Shaw to join his European tour, but died before the trumpeter had arrived. Shaw decided to go to Europe anyway, and stayed for a while in France, playing with Kenny Clarke, Bud Powell and others. Back in the USA in the mid-60s he joined Horace Silver, recording *The Cape Verdean Blues* (1965) and *The Jody Grind* (1966) and also worked with McCoy Tyner and Art Blakey. In the late 60s and early 70s he was busy as a studio musician and to some extent his jazz reputation suffered through his absence from the scene. He began recording for the Muse label in 1974 and this heralded a revival of interest in his work. He again played with Corea and Blakey and his group backed Dexter Gordon on his return to the USA, recording *The Homecoming* (1976). In the early 80s Shaw's band was in constant flux and amongst the musicians he used were Teri Lyne Carrington and Larry Willis. In 1984 he was featured with the Paris Reunion Band, appearing on two fine albums, *French Cooking* and *For Klook*. Shaw suffered periods of severe illness, mostly induced through problems of drug addiction. He was going blind when, early in 1989, he visited the Village Vanguard to hear Max Roach. On the way home, he appeared to stumble down the steps at a New York subway station and fell under an approaching train, which severed an arm. Though rushed to hospital, he remained in a coma and died three months later. Shaw's playing was filled with the crackling brilliance of a post-Dizzy Gillespie trumpeter and yet he had the warmth which characterized musicians such as Clifford Brown and Freddie Hubbard, in whose shadow he laboured. Given a slight shift in time, and a major change in his personal habits,

Shaw could well have been one of the great names of contemporary jazz.

Selected albums: *Blackstone Legacy* (1971), *Cassandranite* (Muse 1972), *Song Of Songs* (1973), *The Moontrane* (1974), *Love Dance* (1976), *At The Berliner Jazztage* (1977), *Little Red's Fantasy* (1978), *Stepping Stones* (1978), *Rosewood* (1978), *Woody III* (1979), *The Iron Men* (1981, rec. 1977), *United* (1981), *Lotus Flower* (1982), *Master Of The Art* (1982), *Time Is Right* (Red 1983), *Setting Standards* (1985), *Woody Shaw With The Tone Jansa Quartet* (Timelss 1986), *Imagination* (Muse 1987), *Solid* (Muse 1987), *The Eternal Triangle* (1987), *In My Own Sweet Way* (In And Out1989).

Shearing, George

b. 13 August 1919, London, England. Shearing was born blind but started to learn piano at the age of three. After limited training and extensive listening to recorded jazz, he began playing at hotels, clubs and pubs in the London area, sometimes as a single, occasionally with dance bands. In 1940 he joined Harry Parry's popular band and also played with Stéphane Grappelli. Shortly after visiting the USA in 1946, Shearing decided to settle there. Although at this time in his career he was influenced by bop pianists, notably Bud Powell, it was a complete break with this style that launched his career as a major star. Developing the locked-hands technique of playing block-chords, and accompanied by a discreet rhythm section of guitar, bass, drums and vibraphone, he had a succession of hugely popular records including 'September In The Rain' and his own composition, 'Lullaby Of Birdland'. With shifting personnel, which over the years included Cal Tjader, Margie Hyams, Denzil Best, Israel Crosby, Joe Pass and Gary Burton, the Shearing quintet remained popular until 1967. Later, Shearing played with a trio, as a solo and increasingly in duo. Amongst his collaborations have been sets with the Montgomery Brothers, Marian McPartland, Brian Torff, Jim Hall, Hank Jones and Kenny Davern (on a rather polite dixieland selection). Over the years he has worked fruitfully with singers, including Peggy Lee, Ernestine Anderson, Carmen McRae, and, especially, Mel Tormé, with whom he performed frequently in the late 80s and early 90s at festivals, on radio and record dates. Shearing's interest in classical music resulted in some performances with concert orchestras in the 50s and 60s, and his solos frequently touch upon the musical patterns of Claude Debussy and, particularly, Erik Satie. Indeed, Shearing's delicate touch and whimsical nature should make him an ideal interpreter of Satie's work. As a jazz player Shearing has sometimes been the victim of critical indifference and even hostility. Mostly, reactions such as these centre upon the long period when he led his quintet. It might well be that the quality of the music was often rather lightweight but a second factor was the inability of some commentators on the jazz scene to accept an artist who had achieved wide public acceptance and financial success. That critical disregard should follow Shearing into his post-quintet years is inexplicable and unforgivable. Many of his late performances, especially his solo albums and those with Torff, bassist Neil Swainson, and

Tormé, are superb examples of a pianist at the height of his powers. Inventive and melodic, his improvisations are unblushingly romantic but there is usually a hint of whimsy which happily reflects the warmth and offbeat humour of the man himself.

Selected albums: *Great Britain's* (Savoy 1947 recordings), *Latin Escapade* (1956), *Velvet Carpet* (1956), *Black Satin* (1957), *Burnished Brass* (1958), with Peggy Lee *Americana Hotel* (1959), *Shearing On Stage* (1959-63), *White Satin* (1960), *San Francisco Scene* (1960), *The Shearing Touch* (1960), with the Montgomery Brothers *Love Walked In* (1961), *Satin Affair* (1961), *Nat 'King Cole' Sings/George Shearing Plays* (1962), *Jazz Concert* (1963), *My Ship* (1974), *Light, Airy And Swinging* (1974), *The Way We Are* (1974), *Continental Experience* (1975), with Stéphane Grappelli *The Reunion* (1976), *The Many Facets Of George Shearing* (1976), *500 Miles High* (MPS 1977), *Windows* (1977), *On Target* (1979), with Brian Torff *Blues Alley Jazz* (Concord 1979), *Getting In The Swing Of Things* (1979), *On A Clear Day* (1980), with Carmen McRae *Two For The Road* (Concord 1980), with Marian McPartland *Alone Together* (Concord 1981), with Jim Hall *First Edition* (Concord 1981), *An Evening With Mel Tormé And George Shearing* (1982), with Mel Tormé *Top Drawer* (1983), *Bright Dimensions* (1984), *Live At The Cafe Carlyle* (Concord 1984), *Grand Piano* (Concord 1985), with Tormé *An Elegant Evening* (1985), *George Shearing And Barry Treadwell Play The Music Of Cole Porter* (Concord 1986), *More Grand Piano* (Concord 1986), *Breakin' Out* (Concord 1987), *Dexterity* (Concord 1987), *A Vintage Year* (1987), with Ernestine Anderson *A Perfect Match* (Concord 1988), with Hank Jones *The Spirit Of '76* (Concord 1988), *Piano* (Concord 1989), *George Shearing In Dixieland* (Concord 1989), with Tormé *Mel And George 'Do' World War II* (1990), *I Hear A Rhapsody* (Telarc 1992). Compilations: *The Young George Shearing (1939-44)* (1983), *The Best Of George Shearing* (MFP 1983), *White Satin - Black Satin* (Capitol 1991), *The Capitol Years* (Capitol 1991).

Sheldon, Jack

b. 30 November 1931, Jacksonville, Florida, USA. After studying trumpet as a child, Sheldon played professionally while still in his early teens. In the late 40s, now relocated in the Los Angeles area, he played with many leading west coast musicians, including Art Pepper, Dexter Gordon and Wardell Gray. He was also closely associated with comedian Lenny Bruce. In 1955 he was one of the first of the west coast school to record for the Pacific Jazz label. In the mid-50s he recorded with the Curtis Counce group, which included Harold Land, and later in the decade with Dave Pell and Pepper. He also toured with Gray, Stan Kenton and Benny Goodman. In the 60s Sheldon's natural wit brought him work as a stand-up comedian and he also took up acting, playing the lead in a US television series, *What Makes Sammy Run?* In the 70s he worked with various bands, big and small, including Goodman's, Woody Herman's and Bill Berry's and also led his own small bands for club and record dates. Sheldon's trumpet playing is deeply rooted in bebop but he ably adapts it to the mainstream settings in which he often works. His live appearances always include examples of his engaging singing style and his sparkling, frequently abrasive wit. Much less well-known internationally than his talent deserves, Sheldon has survived many problems, including drug addiction and alcoholism, which would have ended the careers of less durable men.

Albums: *The Jack Sheldon Quartet* (1954), *The Jack Sheldon Quintet* (1956), *The Curtis Counce Group* (1956), *You Get More Bounce With Curtis Counce* (1957), *Jack Sheldon And His Orchestra* i (1957), *Jack's Groove* (1957-59), *Art Pepper Plus Eleven* (1959), with Pepper *Smack Up* (1960), *Jack Sheldon And His Orchestra* ii (1962), *Jack Sheldon With Orchestra Conducted By Don Sebesky* (1968) with Bill Berry *Hello Rev* (1976), *Singular* (1980), *Angel Wings* (1980), *Playin' It Straight* (1980), *Stand By For The Jack Sheldon Quartet* (Concord 1983), *Blues In The Night* (Phontastic 1984), *Hollywood Heroes* (Concord 1988), with Ross Tomkins *On My Own* (Concord 1992).

Video: *In New Orleans* (Hendring 1990).

Shepherd, Dave

b. 7 February 1929, London, England. In the years following World War II, Shepherd took up the clarinet and quickly developed into one of the UK's most respected and admired musicians. An eclectic performer, ranging from Dixieland through most aspects of the mainstream to the fringes of bop, he has played with many British and American musicians. These include artists as diverse as Freddy Randall and Billie Holiday. Despite a short spell in the USA in the mid-50s and appearances at international festivals, Shepherd's career has centred on the UK and he works regularly with the Pizza Express All Stars, with Digby Fairweather, Roy Williams, Len Skeat and others. A superbly professional musician, Shepherd's ability to recreate the immaculate styling of Benny Goodman has led to an unfair tendency to narrow the focus of critical attention. In fact, when allowed free rein to his talent, he consistently demonstrates unfailing swing and a quality of musical elegance conspicuously absent in many better-known players.

Albums: *Shepherd's Delight* (1969), *Freddy Randall/Dave Shepherd Live At Montreux* (1973), *Benny Goodman Classics* (1975), *Dixieland Classics* (1976), *Airmal Special* (Chevron 1984), *Tribute To Benny Goodman* (Music Masters 1992).

Shepp, Archie

b. 24 May 1937, Fort Lauderdale, Florida, USA. Shepp was raised in Philadelphia. While studying dramatic literature at college he began playing on various instruments including the alto saxophone. His first professional engagement was on clarinet and he later played tenor saxophone with R&B bands. Settling in New York he tried to find work as an actor but was obliged to make a living in music, playing in Latin bands. He also played jazz with Cecil Taylor, Bill Dixon, Don Cherry, John Tchicai and others during the early 60s. With Cherry and Tchicai he was co-leader of the New York Contemporary Five. Shepp's musically questing nature drew him into the orbit of John Coltrane, with whom he established a fruitful musical relationship. Through Coltrane, Shepp was introduced to Bob Thiele of Impulse! Records and began recording under his own name for the label. Shepp's collaborations with Coltrane included an appearance at the 1965 *Down Beat* Festival in Chicago. That same year he appeared at the Newport Festival and had a play staged in New York. Although closely associated with the free jazz movement of the 60s, Shepp's music always included elements that were identifiably rooted in earlier forms of jazz and blues and he was very conscious of the importance of the music's roots. In an article in *Down Beat*, he wrote of the *avant garde*, 'It is not a movement, but a state of mind. It is a thorough denial of technological precision and a reaffirmation of *das Volk*.' With his name and reputation established by 1965, Shepp embarked upon a period of successful tours and recordings. He was busily writing music and occasionally stage plays, many of which carried evidence of his political convictions and concern over civil rights issues. At the end of the 60s he played at the Pan African Festival in Algiers, recorded several albums during a brief stop-over in Paris, then returned to the USA, where he became deeply involved in education, teaching music and literature, and was eventually appointed an associate professor at the University of Massachusetts. Over the next decade Shepp expanded his repertoire, incorporating aspects of jazz far-removed from his earlier freeform preferences, amongst them R&B, rock, blues and bop. Some of his recordings from the late 70s and early 80s give an indication of his range: they include improvised duo albums with Max Roach, sets of spirituals and blues with Horace Parlan and tribute albums to Charlie Parker and Sidney Bechet. In the 80s Shepp had matured into an all-round jazz player, impossible to pigeon-hole but capable of appealing to a wide audience through the heart and the mind. Although he has added the soprano saxophone to his instrumental arsenal, Shepp still concentrates on tenor, playing with a richly passionate tone and developing commanding solos shot through with vigorous declamatory phrases that emphasize his dramatic approach.

Selected albums: *Archie Shepp-Bill Dixon Quartet* (1962), *Archie Shepp And The New York Contemporary Five* (1963), *Four For Trane* (1964), *Fire Music* (Impulse 1965), *On This Night* (1965), *New Thing At Newport* (Impulse 1965), *Archie Shepp Live In San Francisco* (1966), *Mama Too Tight* (1966), *Freedom* (JMY 1968), *The Way Ahead* (1968), *Yasmina & Poem For Malcolm* (Affinity 1969), *Blase* (Charly 1970), *Attica Blues* (1972), *Montreux One/Two* (1975), *There's A Trumpet In My Soul* (Freedom 1975), *A Sea Of Faces* (1975), *Steam* (Enja 1976), *Montreaux One* (Freedom 1976), *Hi Fly* (1976), *Ballads For Trane* (Denon 1977), *On Green Dolphin Street* (Denon 1977), *Goin' Home* (1977), *Day Dream* (Denon 1978), with Abdullah Ibrahim *Duet* (Denon 1978), *Perfect Passions* (West Wind 1978), with Max Roach *The Long March* (1979), with Roach *Sweet Mao* (c.1979), *Lady Bird* (Denon 1979), *Bird Fire* (West Wind 1979), *The Long March Part 1* (Hat Art 1980), *Trouble In Mind* (1980), *Tray Of Silver* (Denon 1980), *I Know About The Life* (1981), *My Man* (1981), *Looking At Bird* (Steeplechase 1981), *Soul Song* (Enja 1982), *Mama Rose* (Steeplechase 1982), *African Moods* (1984), *I Know About the*

Life (Sackville 1984), *Down Home In New York* (Soul Note 1984), *Live On Broadway* (Soul Note 1985), *The Fifth Of May* (1987), *Reunion* (L&R 1988), with Chet Baker *In Memory Of* (1988), *First Set* (52 Rue Est 1988), *Second Set* (52 Rue Est 1988), *Splashes* (L&R 1988), *Lover Man* (Timeless 1988), *In Memory Of First And Last Meeting 1988* (L&R 1989), *Art Of The Duo* (Enja 1990), *I Didn't Know About You* (Timelss 1991), *Black Ballad* (Timelss 1993).

Sheppard, Andy

b. 20 January 1957, Bristol, Avon, England. Sheppard attempted to learn saxophone at school, but was told he would have to take up clarinet first. In disgust he bought a guitar instead, but began on tenor saxophone after hearing John Coltrane. He also played the flute and sang solo in the choir while at school. He later discovered that he had perfect pitch, and only learned to read music in his late 20s. He took up the soprano under the influences of Steve Lacy and alcohol, having sold his tenor to a friend when drunk. Before moving to London Sheppard played with Sphere (not to be confused with the US band of the same name). He also played in Klaunstance, then spent two years in Paris working with Laurent Cugny's big band, Lumiere, and Urban Sax. Returning to the UK he played with Paul Dunmall and Keith Tippett. In early 1987 Sheppard formed his own small band, recording two acclaimed albums and undertaking several successful tours. He also became a regular performer in bands led by Carla Bley, Gil Evans and George Russell. In 1990 he set up the Soft On The Inside big band, which produced an album and a video, and he also recorded an acclaimed set of duo improvisations with Tippett. Since early 1991 Sheppard has run an electric small group, In Co-Motion (featuring the fine trumpeter Claude Deppa), alongside the big band, and he recently composed a piece for ice-dancers Torville and Dean. He also played in an occasional trio with Bley and Steve Swallow (producer on most of his albums). Sheppard is one of the most assured and versatile (and least flashy) saxophonists on the scene today.

Albums: *Andy Sheppard* (Antilles 1987), with Sphere *Sphere* (1988), *Present Tense* (1988), *Introductions In The Dark* (Antilles 1989), *Soft On The Inside* (Antilles 1990), with Keith Tippett *66 Shades Of Lipstick* (1990), *In Co-Motion* (Antilles 1991), *Rhythm Method* (Blue Note 1993), *Delivery Suite* (Blue Note 1994).

Shew, Bobby

b. 4 March 1941, Albuquerque, New Mexico, USA. Shew taught himself to play trumpet and was playing semi-professionally as he entered his teens. During military service he decided to make music his career and soon in 1964, after his discharge became a member of the Tommy Dorsey Orchestra. The following year he moved on to Woody Herman, then Buddy Rich, and thereafter took a succession of jobs with bands in hotels and casinos in Las Vegas. In the early 70s he settled in Los Angeles, playing in the studios but also working jazz gigs, including a sustained period with the Toshiko Akiyoshi-Lew Tabackin big band. His spell with the band produced

many fine albums, notably *Kogun* (1974), *Tales Of A Courtesan* (1975) and *Insights* (1976). Also during the 70s he played in many Los Angeles-based rehearsal bands, including Don Menza's and Juggernaut. He played, too, in small groups, as well as teaching privately and directing clinics and workshops. In the late 70s he toured Europe and the UK with Louie Bellson's big band, appearing on some of the live recordings: *Dynamite!* (1979) and *London Scene* (1980). During these tours he expanded his teaching activities wherever he went. In the 80s Shew's playing was mostly in small groups, as both sideman and leader, but he made occasional appearances with youth bands including the UK's Wigan Youth Jazz Orchestra, with whom he recorded *Aim For The Heart* in 1987. In the late 80s and early 90s Shew's teaching role developed still further and he remains in great demand around the world. In performance he rarely uses his spectacularly wide range simply for its own sake. The soft, warm sound he creates from his instrument is especially suitable for ballads and lends a distinctive quality to any trumpet section in which he appears. An important influence through his teaching activities, Shew is ensuring that in a period when dazzling technical proficiency is becoming almost commonplace the emotional qualities of jazz are not forgotten. Albums: *Telepathy* (1978), *Outstanding In His Field* (1978-79), *Class Reunion* (1980), *Parallel 37* (1980), *Play Song* (1981), *Trumpets No End* (Delos 1983), *Breakfast Wine* (1984), with Wigan Youth Jazz Orchestra *Aim For The Heart* (1987).

Shihab, Sahib

b. Edmund Gregory, 23 June 1925, Savannah, Georgia, USA, d. 24 October 1989. After learning to play several reed instruments, Shihab concentrated on alto saxophone and played professionally while still in his early teens. At the age of 19 he was lead alto with Fletcher Henderson and also played in Roy Eldridge's big band. After 1947, the year in which he adopted the Muslim faith and changed his name, Shihab played with several of the leading bop musicians, including Thelonious Monk, with whom he made the first recording of ''Round Midnight', Tadd Dameron, Art Blakey (playing in the first of the drummer's Jazz Messengers groups to record), Dizzy Gillespie and John Coltrane, the last performing on the tenorman's first recording date as leader. In the 50s Shihab began to play baritone saxophone and at the end of the decade travelled to Europe with Quincy Jones. He remained on the Continent for several years, playing with the Clarke-Boland Big Band for almost a decade. During this period he added soprano saxophone and flute to his instrumental armoury, and in 1965 composed a jazz ballet based on Hans Christian Andersen's *The Red Shoes*. In the early 70s Shihab returned to the USA to work in film studios, but was frequently back in Europe during the remaining part of the decade and into the early 80s. He finally settled in the USA in 1986, which is where he died in 1989. Over the years, Shihab's inventiveness when playing flute and soprano surpassed his earlier work on alto. It was, however, on baritone that he made his most distinctive contribution, weaving thoughtfully agile solos with a remarkably light sound. Selected albums: with Thelonious Monk *Genius Of Modern*

Music Vol. 1 (1947), *Jazz Sahib* (Savoy 1957 recordings), *The Jazz We Heard Last Summer* (1957), *Jazz-Sahib* (1957), *Companionship* (1964-65), *Sahib Shihab And The Danish Radio Jazz Group* (1965), *Seeds* (1968), *Sentiments* (1971), *Sahib Shihab And The Jef Gilson Unit* (1972), with others *Flute Summit* (1973), *Conversations* (1992).

Shorter, Wayne

b. 25 August 1933, Newark, New Jersey, USA. Shorter first played clarinet, taking up the tenor saxophone during his late teens. He studied music at New York University during the mid-50s before serving in the US army for two years. During his student days he had played with various bands, including that led by Horace Silver, and on his discharge encountered John Coltrane, with whom he developed many theoretical views on music. He was also briefly with Maynard Ferguson. In 1959 he became a member of Art Blakey's Jazz Messengers, remaining with the band until 1963. The following year he joined Miles Davis, staying until 1970. Late that year he teamed up with Joe Zawinul, whom he had first met in the Ferguson band, to form Weather Report. During his stints with Blakey and Davis Shorter had written extensively and his compositions had also formed the basis of several increasingly experimental record sessions under his own name for the Blue Note label. He continued to write for the new band and also for further dates under his own name and with V.S.O.P., with whom he worked in the mid- and late 70s. In the mid-80s he was leading his own band and also recording and touring with other musicians, thus reducing his activities with Weather Report.

As a player, Shorter developed through his period with Blakey into a leading proponent of hard bop. His fiery, tough-toned and dramatically angular playing was well-suited to the aggressive nature of the Blakey band. During his time with Davis another side to his musical personality emerged, in which a more tender approach greatly enhanced his playing. This side had made its appearance earlier, on *Wayning Moments*, but was given greater scope with Davis. On Davis's *Bitches Brew*, Shorter also played soprano saxophone: two weeks later he employed this instrument throughout on his own *Super Nova*, playing with exotic enthusiasm. The years with Zawinul broadened his range still further, highlighting his appreciation of freer forms and giving rein to his delight in musical exotica. Although laying ground rules for many later fusion bands, Weather Report's distinction lay in the way the group allowed the two principals to retain their powerful musical personalities. Later, as the band began to sound more like other fusion bands, Shorter's exploratory nature found greater scope in the bands he formed away from Weather Report. As a composer, Shorter was responsible for some of the best work of the Blakey band of his era and also for many of Davis's stronger pieces of the late 60s. A major innovator and influence on hard boppers and fusionists alike, Shorter remains one of the most imaginative musicians in jazz, constantly seeking new horizons but - thanks to his broad musical knowledge - retaining identifiable links with the past.

Selected albums: *The Vee Jay Years* (Affinity 1959), *Wayne Shorter* (1959-62), *Wayning Moments* (Affinity 1961-62), *Night Dreamer* (1964), *Juju* (1964), *Speak No Evil* (Blue Note 1964), *Night Dreamer* (Blue Note 1964), *The Best Of Wayne Shorter* (1964-67), with Miles Davis *Live At The Plugged Nickel* (1965), *The Soothsayer* (1965), *The All-Seeing Eye* (1965), *Etcetera* (1965), *Adam's Apple* (Blue Note 1966), *Schizophrenia* (1967), *Super Nova* (Blue Note 1969), *Odyssey Of Iska* (1970), *Moto Grosso Feio* (c.1971), *Native Dancer* (Columbia 1974), *Atlantis* (CBS 1985), *Endangered Species* (1985), *Phantom Navigator* (CBS 1986-87), *Joy Ryder* (CBS 1987), *Second Genesis* (Affinity 1993), with Herbie Hancock, Ron Carter, Wallace Roney, Tony Williams *A Tribute To Miles* (QWest/Reprise 1994), *All Seeing Eye* (Connoisseur 1994).

Sidran, Ben

b. 14 August 1943, Chicago, Illinois, U.S.A. A Ph.D. in musicology and philosophy, Sidran became embroiled in rock music upon joining the Ardells, a popular attraction at the University of Wisconsin which also featured Steve Miller and Boz Scaggs. Sidran later travelled to London to complete a doctoral thesis on the development of black music in America. This was published as *Black Talk* in 1971. Here he became reacquainted with Miller during the recording of the latter's *Brave New World*, an album marked by Sidran's memorable piano work and compositional skills. He remained an associate member of Miller's band, contributing to *Your Saving Grace* and *Number 5* before making numerous session appearances. The artist's solo career began in 1971 with the release of *Feel Your Groove*; he has since pursued an idiosyncratic, jazz-based path, eschewing commercially-minded motives in favour of a relaxed, almost casual, approach. His best work, captured on *Puttin' In Time On Planet Earth* (1973) and *The Doctor Is In* (1977), reveals a laconic wit redolent of Mose Allison, but elsewhere Sidran's under-achievements suggest lethargy rather than control. He nonetheless remains a highly-respected musician and is best-known in the UK as host to *On The Live Side*, a perennial favourite of late-night television. In 1991 he released *Cool Paradise* to favourable reviews and helped re-launch the career of Georgie Fame, now a stable-mate on the new jazz label Go Jazz.

Albums: *Feel Your Groove* (1971), *I Lead A Life* (1972), *Puttin' In Time On Planet Earth* (1973), *Don't Let Go* (1974), *Free In America* (1976), *The Doctor Is In* (1977), *A Little Kiss In The Night* (1978), *The Cat And The Hat* (1979), *Live At Montreaux* (1979), *Old Songs For The New Depression* (Antilles 1982), *Bop City* (1984), *On The Live Side* (Windham Hill 1987), *Too Hot To Touch* (Windham Hill 1988), *Cool Paradise* (Go Jazz 1991), *Enivre D'Amour* (Go Jazz 1992), *Heat Wave* (Go Jazz 1992), *A Good Travel Agent* (Go Jazz 1992), *Life's A Lesson* (Go Jazz 1993). Compilation: *That's Life I Guess* (1988).

Signorelli, Frank

b. 24 May 1901, New York City, USA, d. 9 December 1975. Playing piano from childhood, Signorelli became a founder-member of the Original Memphis Five while still a teenager.

He also played with the Original Dixieland Jazz Band and during the 20s was ceaselessly active. During this decade he worked with Joe Venuti, Eddie Lang, Adrian Rollini, Bix Beiderbecke and a host of leading white jazzmen of the day. He also played with Paul Whiteman, but he remained most closely associated with Phil Napoleon, a friend and musical companion from his youth. During the 30s he resumed his connection with the ODJB and in the 50s with the OMF, recording with them and with Connee Boswell. A sound if unexceptional pianist, Signorelli also composed a number of tunes that became standards, amongst which are 'I'll Never Be The Same' and 'Stairway To The Stars'.

Album: *Connee Boswell And The Original Memphis Five In Hi-Fi* (1956).

Silver, Horace

b. 2 September 1928, Norwalk, Connecticut, USA. Silver studied piano and tenor saxophone at school, settling on the former instrument for his professional career. Early influences included Portuguese folk music (from his father), blues and bop. He formed a trio for local gigs which included backing visiting musicians. One such visitor, Stan Getz, was sufficiently impressed to take the trio on the road with him in 1950. The following year Silver settled in New York, playing regularly at Birdland and other leading venues. In 1952 he began a long-lasting association with Blue Note, recording under his own name and with other leaders. In 1953 he formed a band named the Jazz Messengers with Art Blakey, who would later adopt the name for all his own groups. By 1956 Silver was leading his own quintet, exploring the reaches of bop and becoming a founding father of the hard bop movement. Silver's line-up - trumpet, tenor saxophone, piano, bass and drums - was subject to many changes over the years, but the calibre of musicians he hired was always very high. Amongst his sidemen were Donald Byrd, Art Farmer, Michael and Randy Brecker, Woody Shaw, Blue Mitchell, Hank Mobley and Joe Henderson. He continued to lead fine bands, touring and recording extensively during the following decades, and in the late 80s and early 90s could still be heard at concerts around the world performing to an impressively high standard. As a pianist Silver is a powerful, thrusting player with an urgent rhythmic pulse. As a composer, his early musical interests have constantly reappeared in his work and his incorporation into hard bop of elements of gospel and R&B have ensured that for all the overall complexities of sound his music remains highly accessible. Several of his pieces have become modern standards, amongst them 'Opus de Funk', 'Doodlin'', 'Nica's Dream' and 'The Preacher'. The introduction on Steely Dan's 'Ricki Don't Lose That Number' was strongly influenced by Silver's memorable 'Song For My Father'. During the 70s Silver experimented with compositions and recordings which set his piano playing and the standard quintet against larger orchestral backing, often achieving far

Horace Silver

more success than others who have written and performed in this way.

Selected albums: *Horace Silver Trio* (Blue Note 1954), *Horace Silver And The Jazz Messengers* i (Blue Note 1954), *Horace Silver Quintet Vols 1 & 2* (1955), *Horace Silver And The Jazz Messengers* ii (1955), *Six Pieces Of Silver* (1956), *Silver's Blue* (1956), *The Stylings Of Silver* (1957), *Finger Poppin'* (1959), *Blowin' The Blues Away* (Blue Note 1959), *Horace-Scope* (Blue Note 1960), *The Tokyo Blues* (1962), *Song For My Father* (Blue Note 1964), *Live 1964* (1964), *Cape Verdean Blues* (Blue Note 1965), *The Jody Grind* (Blue Note 1967), *Serenade To A Soul Sister* (1968), *You Gotta Take A Little Love* (1969), *That Healin' Feelin' (The United States Of Mind, Phase I)* (1970), *Total Response (Phase II)* (c.1971), *All (Phase III)* (c.1973), *Silver 'N' Brass* (1975), *Silver 'N' Wood* (1976), *Silver 'N' Voices* (1976), *Silver 'N' Percussion* (1977), *Silver 'N' Strings Play The Music Of The Spheres* (1978), *Guides To Growing Up* (1981), *Spiritualizing The Senses* (1983), *There's No Need To Struggle* (1983), *It's Got To Be Funky* (Columbia 1993), *Pencil Packin' Papa* (1994). Compilation: *The Best Of Horace Silver - The Blue Note Years* (Blue Note 1988).

Simeon, Omer

b. 21 July 1902, New Orleans, Louisiana, USA, d. 17 September 1959. Although taught clarinet by fellow New Orleanian Lorenzo Tio, Simeon's musical education took place in Chicago where he lived from 1914. After playing in various bands he joined Charlie Elgar's popular Chicago-based danceband, where he remained for several years. During his stint with Elgar he appeared on a number of record dates with Jelly Roll Morton and also left the band for a short engagement with Joe 'King' Oliver. In the late 20s he played with Luis Russell in New York and then resumed his association with Morton. Back in Chicago in 1928 he spent a couple of years with Erskine Tate and then joined Earl 'Fatha' Hines for a six-year spell at the Royal Gardens. In the 40s he played with various bands, including Jimmie Lunceford's, and he spent most of the 50s with Wilbur De Paris in New York. A bold and imaginative clarinettist, Simeon's long periods in big bands afforded him only limited opportunities to solo, although his recordings with small groups give frequent if tantalizing hints of a gifted musician.

Album: with Wilbur De Paris *Rampart Street Ramblers* (1952). Compilations: *The Complete Jelly Roll Morton Vols 1/2 (1926-27)* (1983), *Omer Simeon 1926-29* (Hot n' Sweet 1993).

Simmons, John

b. 14 June 1918, Haskell, Oklahoma, USA, d. 19 September 1979. While living in California Simmons took up the bass when a sporting injury affected his trumpet playing. He advanced quickly on his new instrument and worked with Nat 'King' Cole and Teddy Wilson in the mid-to-late 30s. In the early 40s he moved to Chicago, playing with Roy Eldridge, Benny Goodman, Louis Armstrong and other leading jazzmen. In the remaining years of the decade he appeared on countless small group recording dates, backing distinguished artists such

as Hot Lips Page, Ben Webster, Billie Holiday, Erroll Garner, Coleman Hawkins, Benny Carter and Ella Fitzgerald. Although essentially a mainstream musician with a robust sound and unflagging swing, Simmons also coped comfortably with the demands of playing with beboppers, who included Thelonious Monk. In the 50s he toured and recorded with Harry Edison, Tadd Dameron, Phineas Newborn Jnr. and others but these and his later years were dogged by poor health. He died in 1979.

Album: with Phineas Newborn *I Love A Piano* (1959).

Sims, Zoot

b. John Haley Sims, 29 October 1925, Inglewood, California, USA, d. 23 March 1985. Sims played clarinet in grade school but took up the tenor saxophone to work with singer Kenny Baker in 1941. He played with Bobby Sherwood from 1942-43, Sonny Durham in 1943 and the Benny Goodman big band in 1944. His recording debut was with Joe Bushkin's small group in 1944. The years 1944-46 were spent in the army. On discharge Sims rejoined Goodman, playing alongside his brother Ray until 1947 when he joined Woody Herman, becoming famous as one of the 'Four Brothers' (the other saxophonists were Stan Getz, Herbie Steward and Serge Chaloff). He left to play with Artie Shaw from 1949-50, then toured Europe with Goodman at regular intervals (1950, 1958, 1972 and 1976) and also toured with Stan Kenton and Gerry Mulligan. In the early 70s Sims started playing soprano saxophone as well as tenor, and later in the decade embarked on a prolific period of recording for Norman Granz's Pablo label, making approximately 15 albums between 1975-84. In 1972 and 1978 he took part in re-union concerts with Herman. He also liked to freelance, especially in company with tenor saxophonist Al Cohn, with whom he had first worked in the early 50s. Sims was the first American to play a residency at Ronnie Scott's following the lifting of the embargo on visiting musicians in 1961, and he returned there many times, his last visit being in 1982. He toured Scandinavia in 1984, but the doctors had diagnosed terminal cancer, of which he died in 1985. Zoot Sims was a redoubtable exponent of the tenor style developed by Lester Young and contributed swinging, lithe solos to countless big band arrangements.

Selected albums: *Zoot Swings The Blues* (1950), *Tenorly* (Vogue c.1954), with Gerry Mulligan *The Concert Jazz Band Live* (1955), *Zoot!* (Original Jazz Classics 1956), *Tonite's Music Today* (Black Lion 1956), *Morning Fun* (Black Lion 1957), *Zoot Sims In Paris* (EMI/Pathe 1957), *Al And Zoot* (1957), *Down Home* (1960), *Jive At Five* (1960), *Either Way* (Evidence 1962), *Suitably Zoot* (1965), with Joe Venuti *Joe & Zoot* (1968), with Count Basie *Basie And Zoot* (1975), *Hawthorne Nights* (1976), *Zoot Sims And The Gershwin Brothers* (Original Jazz Classics (1976), *Soprano Sax* (1976), *If I'm Lucky* (Original Jazz Classics 1978), *Warm Tenor* (Pablo 1979), *Just Friends* (Original Jazz Classics 1979), *Passion Flower* (1980), with Joe Pass *Blues For Two* (Original Jazz Classics 1982), *I Wish I Were Twins* (1983), *Suddenly Its Spring* (Original Jazz Classics 1984), *Quietly There* (Original Jazz Classics 1984), *In A Sentimental*

Mood (1984), *I Hear A Rhapsody* (1992), *A Summer Thing* (1993). Compilations: *The Best Of Zoot Sims* (Pablo 1982).

Singleton, Zutty

b. Arthur James Singleton, 14 May 1898, Bunkie, Louisiana, USA, d. 14 July 1975. Playing drums from his early childhood, Singleton first worked professionally in 1915. After military service in World War I he played in several leading New Orleans bands, including those of Oscar 'Papa' Celestin and Louis Nelson, then worked the riverboats with Fate Marable in the early 20s. After spending time in New Orleans and St Louis, where he played with Charlie Creath (whose sister he married), Singleton moved to Chicago where he played in bands led by Dave Peyton and Jimmie Noone, then teamed up with Louis Armstrong and Earl 'Fatha' Hines for record dates and a brief spell as co-owners of a club. As a member of the Carroll Dickerson band he went to New York, where he subsequently played with many leading jazzmen of the day. He also led his own band, securing residencies at several clubs and recording extensively throughout the 30s with musicians such as Roy Eldridge, Mezz Mezzrow and Sidney Bechet. In the 40s he worked in bands that played in a startlingly wide range of styles, accompanying musicians as diverse as T-Bone Walker and Charlie Parker, Wingy Manone and Dizzy Gillespie. In the 50s he toured Europe, teaming up with Bill Coleman, Oran 'Hot Lips' Page, Mezzrow again and also leading his own bands. He recorded extensively in this period and throughout the 60s. A stroke in 1970 effectively ended his playing career, but he remained a father-figure in the jazz community, especially in New York where he and his wife made their home. Although Singleton had all the fundamental skills displayed by Baby Dodds, generally regarded as the master of New Orleans drummers, he was far more flexible, as the range of his musical companions demonstrates. His joyously springy playing style enhanced numerous recording sessions and his solo excursions managed the usually impossible task of being highly musical, even melodious, while being compellingly rhythmic. He appeared in several films, including *Stormy Weather* (1943) and *L'Aventure Du Jazz* (1969).
Albums: *Zutty And The Clarinet Kings* (1967), *L'Aventure Du Jazz* (1969, film soundtrack). Compilations: *Louis Armstrong Classics Vol. 3* (1928), with Mezz Mezzrow *Clarinet Marmalade* (1951), with Bill Coleman *Rarities* (1952).

Skidmore, Alan

b. Alan Richard James Skidmore, 21 April 1942, Kingston-on-Thames, London, England. 'Skid' plays soprano and tenor saxophones, flutes and drums. He is the son of Jimmy Skidmore, who gave him a discarded tenor which Alan ignored until he was about 15. At that time he decided to teach himself to play. A muscular and versatile player himself, the musicians he particularly admires include Sonny Rollins, Dexter Gordon, Michael Brecker, Ronnie Scott, Andy Sheppard and, above all, John Coltrane. Skid began playing professionally in 1958, and did various commercial engagements, including tours with comedian Tony Hancock and singer Matt Monro and five

years in the house band at London's Talk Of The Town night club. In 1961 he made the first of many appearances on BBC radio's *Jazz Club*, and also met his idol, Coltrane. In the following years Skidmore worked with numerous important and/or successful bands, including Eric Delaney where he replaced his father when Jimmy decided to leave (in 1963), Alexis Korner (1964), John Mayall's Blues Breakers (1964), Ronnie Scott (1965), Georgie Fame And The Blue Flames (1970), Mike Westbrook (1970-71), Michael Gibbs (1970-71), and Chris McGregor's Brotherhood Of Breath (1971). In 1969 he had formed his own quintet, with which he won the best soloist and best band awards at the Montreux Jazz Festival and gained a scholarship to Berklee, though he did not take this up. In 1973 he co-founded S.O.S., probably the first all-saxophone band, with Mike Osborne and John Surman. He has subsequently had various small groups of his own, including El Skid (co-led with Elton Dean), SOH, and Tenor Tonic, and has worked with the George Gruntz Concert Band, the Elvin Jones Jazz Machine, the Charlie Watts Orchestra, Stan Tracey, Van Morrison, Georgie Fame again, and with the West German Radio Band as featured soloist from 1981-84. In April 1991 he was reunited with Surman when they played as a duo at a benefit for Osborne.
Selected albums: *Once Upon A Time* (1969), with Mike Westbrook *Marching Song* (1969), *TCB* (1970), with Michael Gibbs *Michael Gibbs* (1970), *Tanglewood 63* (1971), with Chris McGregor *Brotherhood Of Breath* (1971), *S.O.S.*(1975), *El Skid* (1977), *SOH* (Ego 1979), *SOH Live* (1981), with Charlie Watts *Live At Fulham Town Hall* (1986), *Tribute To Trane* (Miles Music 1988), with Peter King *Brother Bernard* (1988), *From East To West* (Miles Music 1993). Compilations: *Jazz In Britain 68-69* (1971), *Alexis Korner And... 1961-72* (1986).

Slingsby, Xero

b. Matthew Coe, 23 November 1957, Skipton, Yorkshire, England, d. 16 August 1988. Coe's name change came in the mid-70s when punk rock made colourful stage-names *de rigueur*. He grew up in Bradford, where an accident at the age of 10 damaged his left hand: he took up the bass guitar as an alternative to therapeutic rubber-ball squeezing. He fell in with a motorbike crowd and played electric bass in numerous heavy rock bands. Sick of endless guitar indulgence, Ornette Coleman's *New York Is Now!* was a revelation to him. He sold his Fender and Marshall amps and bought a double bass. He also acquired an alto saxophone. After spells as a grave-digger and a tractor-driver for Bradford Council, he attended a two-year course at Harrogate Music School, supplemented by gigs with tenor player Richard Ward. In 1979 Xero played in Ghent, the first of many visits to the more receptive European audiences. After a long apprenticeship playing Monk standards and free jazz, he formed a band called Xero Slingsby And The Works with bassist Louis Colan and drummer Gene Velocette. The idea was to present free jazz with punk-type brevity and was remarkably successful: the Works became part of the 'punkjazz' flowering in England that included Blurt, Rip, Rig

And Panic and Pigbag. Baritone saxophonist Alan Wilkinson and drummer Paul Hession readily acknowledge their debt to Xero's inspirational belief in musical communication. After fighting brain cancer for three years - probably caused by his childhood accident - he died in 1988. The obituary in *The Wire* concluded: 'As jazz at the end of the 80s faces the twin temptations of purist pessimism or commercial betrayal, Xero's scorched alto sound, his booting lines and clamorous compositions, as well as his understanding of music as event and spectacle, could well become the crucial lessons.'
Albums: *Shove It* (1985), *Up Down* (1986).

Smith, Betty

b. 6 July 1929, Sileby, Lincolnshire, England. After studying piano and tenor saxophone as a child, Smith concentrated on the latter instrument at the start of her professional career. In the early 50s she played in Freddy Randall's popular traditional band, but her real forte was in the mainstream. From the late 50s she regularly led her own small group and also played and sang with the Ted Heath band. Her solo career continued through the next two decades and in the 70s she was one of the highlights of the touring package, 'The Best Of British Jazz'. In the 80s she was still active and playing as well as ever. An outstanding performer, Smith is one of only a few women of her generation to successfully overcome the offensive yet seemingly immovable prejudice against women instrumentalists in jazz. The quality of her playing and the high standards she has set herself reveal the absurdity of such prejudices.
Albums: with others *The Best Of British Jazz* (1981), with others *The Very Best Of British Jazz* (1984).

Smith, Buster

b. Henry Smith, 24 August 1904, Aldorf, Texas, USA. Smith first taught himself to play clarinet, working professionally in Texas in the early 20s. He then added alto saxophone and in 1925 joined Walter Page's Blue Devils in Oklahoma City. Smith was one of several Blue Devils who left *en masse* to join Bennie Moten in Kansas City and briefly led this band after Moten's sudden death. He then co-led a band with Count Basie, but bowed out when the band left the familiar surroundings of Kansas City. Whatever the motive behind his decision to stay in Kansas City, when the band he had helped form went on to greatness, his career thereafter achieved less than earlier potential had promised. Forming a new band in 1937, Smith employed Jay McShann, the excellent if almost forgotten trombonist Fred Beckett, and a teenage saxophonist named Charlie Parker. During his career Smith had also written many arrangements for the bands in which he worked and also for other leaders. In the late 30s and early 40s his bandleading activities suffered when his attempts to break into the New York scene failed, a circumstance which diverted him more and more to arranging. In the early 40s he returned to his home state, settling in Dallas and leading small bands there for the greater part of the next four decades. Generally credited as being a major influence on Parker, Smith's own playing career has thus been overshadowed and his few recordings do little to

confirm his legendary status.
Album: *The Legendary Buster Smith* (1959). Compilations: with others *Kansas City 1926 To 1930* (1926-30), with others *Original Boogie Woogie Piano Giants* (1938-41), with others *Kansas City Jazz* (1940-41).

Smith, Carrie

b. 25 August 1941, Fort Gaines, Georgia, USA. Smith appeared at the 1957 Newport Jazz Festival as a member of a New Jersey church choir, but her solo professional career did not take off until the early 70s. An appearance with Dick Hyman and the New York Jazz Repertory Orchestra at Carnegie Hall in 1974 should have alerted audiences to her exceptional qualities, but for the rest of the decade she was much better received in Europe than in the USA. Her tours of festivals and concert halls were sometimes as a single, but also in company with NYJRO, Tyree Glenn, the World's Greatest Jazz Band and others. Smith's style is rooted in the blues and gospel but her repertoire is wide, encompassing many areas of 20th-century popular music. Her voice is deep and powerful and she is especially effective in live performances. Although her reputation has grown throughout the 80s, she still remains far less well-known than her considerable talent warrants.
Albums: with Dick Hyman *Satchmo Remembered* (1974), *Do Your Duty* (1976), *When You're Down And Out* (1977), *Carrie Smith* (1978), with others *Highlights In Jazz Anniversary Concert* (1985).

Smith, Clarence 'Pine Top'

b. 11 January 1904, Troy, Alabama, USA, d. 15 March 1929, Chicago, Illinois, USA. Often considered to be the founder of the boogie woogie style of piano playing, 'Pine Top' Smith was actually a vaudeville performer. From his mid-teens, Smith toured tent shows and theatres as a pianist and dancer. He gradually concentrated on piano and, encouraged by Charles 'Cow Cow' Davenport, made a handful of records. Smith's style was largely in the mould of humorous songs backed up by vigorous two-handed playing. His small list of recordings also included blues but his fame rests, more than anything, on his recording of 'Pine Top's Boogie Woogie' (1928). This song represents, possibly, the first documented use of the term. His work on the circuits took him all over the south in the company of such artists as Butterbeans And Susie, and Ma Rainey but it was in Chicago that his promising career was cut short when he was accidentally shot by a man named David Bell during a skirmish in a dance hall. He was 25 and left a wife and two children. He has been recorded by many artists over the years, 'Pine Top's boogie woogie' remains as satisfying today as it was when it made its initial impact in 1928.
Selected albums: *Compilation 1928-29-30* (Oldie Blues 1986), *Pine Top Smith And Romeo Nelson* (1987), *Compilation 1929-30* (Oldie Blues 1988).

Smith, Derek

b. 17 August 1931, London, England, England. After starting to play piano as a tiny child, Smith quickly developed until he was playing professionally at the age of 14. He began playing jazz and in the early 50s, working with Kenny Graham, John Dankworth, Kenny Baker and other leading British bands. In the mid-50s he moved to New York where he was soon in demand as a session musician, playing in studio orchestras and on record dates. However, he also played jazz with Benny Goodman, Connie Kay and others. During the 60s, Smith's career followed similar lines, mixing studio work with jazz, and towards the end of the decade he became a long-serving member of the *Tonight* show orchestra. In the 70s he again played with Goodman, touring overseas, and also worked with Scott Hamilton and in bands led by Nick Brignola, Arnett Cobb and others. As the 80s progressed Smith became steadily more active on the international jazz festival circuit, sometimes as soloist, other times in a trio with Milt Hinton and Bobby Rosengarden. A stylish player with a wide-ranging repertoire and a gift for elegantly presenting a constant fund of ideas, Smith is very much a musician's musician but by the early 90s was deservedly becoming better known to audiences.

Albums: *Love For Sale* (Progressive 1978), *The Man I Love* (Progressive 1978), *Plays The Music Of Jerome Kern* (Progressive 1981), *Dark Eyes* (East Wind 1985), *Plays Passionate Piano* (Hindsight 1992).

Smith, Jabbo

b. Cladys Smith, 24 December 1908, Pembroke, Georgia, USA, d. 16 January 1991. Smith was taught trumpet and trombone while still a small child and later toured with a youth band. At the age of 16 he was working professionally as a trumpeter (although he would periodically play trombone in later years). In New York from about 1925 he played with Charlie Johnson, Duke Ellington, James P. Johnson and others. Stranded in Chicago when a show in which he was playing folded, he worked in bands led by Carroll Dickerson, Earl 'Fatha' Hines, Erskine Tate and Charlie Elgar. During the 30s he played with Fess Williams, Dickerson, led his own band, then returned to New York with Claude Hopkins and also played with Sidney Bechet. By the mid-40s, reputedly exhausted through high-living, he was leading his own band in the comparative musical backwater of Milwaukee and for the next dozen years mostly played in that city. He also worked outside music, for a car rental company, into the late 50s. Thereafter, he played less and less until he was brought to New York in 1975 to receive an award at Carnegie Hall. This event prompted him to begin practising again and he was soon touring internationally, playing and singing with Sammy Rimington, Orange Kellin and others. In the early 80s he suffered a series of heart attacks but kept on playing, often working in harness with seemingly unlikely musical companions such as Don Cherry. In these later years he increasingly turned to composing, writing music for the Mel Lewis orchestra, often in collaboration with Keith Ingham. Despite his remarkable durability and longevity, Smith remains a little-known figure in jazz and, given the extremely high regard in which he is held by fellow musicians, he is also very much under-recorded. In his youth he was often considered to be a potential rival to Louis Armstrong and although he has none of Armstrong's creative genius, his recordings display many flashes of spectacular brilliance.

Selected albums: *Jabbo Smith Vols 1 & 2* (1927-29), *Jabbo Smith Vols 1 & 2* (1928-38), *The Ace Of Rhythm* (1929), *Jabbo Smith And The Hot Antic Band* (1982), *Sweet 'N' Lowdown* (Affinity 1986, 1927-29 recordings), *Jabbo Smith Vol 1 1928-29* (Retrieval 1990), *Complete 1928-38 Sessions* (Jazz Archives 1993).

Smith, Jimmy

b. James Oscar Smith, 8 December 1925, Norristown, Pennsylvania, USA. The sound of the Hammond Organ in jazz was popularized by Smith, often using the prefix monicker 'the incredible' or 'the amazing'. Smith has become the most famous jazz organist ever and arguably the most influential. Brought up by musical parents he was formally trained on piano and bass and combined the two skills with the Hammond while leading his own trio. He was heavily influenced by Wild Bill Davis. By the mid-50s Smith had refined his own brand of smoky soul jazz which epitomized laid-back 'late night' blues-based music. His vast output for the 'soul jazz' era of Blue Note Records led the genre and resulted in a number of other Hammond B3 maestro's appearing, notably, Jimmy McGriff, 'Brother' Jack McDuff, 'Big' John Patten, Richard 'Groove' Holmes and 'Baby Face' Willette. Smith was superbly complemented by outstanding musicians. Although Art Blakey played with Smith, Donald Bailey remains the definitive Smith drummer, while Smith tackled the bass notes on the Hammond. The guitar was featured prominently throughout the Blue Note years and Smith used the talents of Eddie McFadden, Quentin Warren and Kenny Burrell. Further immaculate playing came from Stanley Turrentine (tenor saxophone), Lee Morgan (trumpet) and Lou Donaldson (alto saxophone). Two classic albums from the late 50s were *The Sermon* and *Houseparty*. On the title track of the former, Smith and his musicians stretch out with majestic 'cool' over 20 minutes, allowing each soloist ample time. In 1962 Jimmy moved to Verve Records where he became the undisputed king, regularly crossing over into the pop best-sellers and the singles charts with memorable titles such as 'Walk On The Wild Side', 'Hobo Flats' and 'Who's Afraid Of Virginia Woolf'. These hits were notable for their superb orchestral arrangements by Oliver Nelson, although they tended to bury Smith's sound. However, the public continued putting him in the charts with 'The Cat', 'The Organ Grinder's Swing' and, with Smith on growling vocals 'Got My Mojo Working'.

His albums at this time also made the best-sellers and between 1963 and 1966 Smith was virtually ever present in the album charts with a total of 12 albums, many making the US Top 20. Smith's popularity had much to do with the R&B boom in Britain during the early 60s. His strong influence was found in the early work of Steve Winwood, Georgie Fame, Zoot Money, Graham Bond and John Mayall. Smith's two albums with Wes Montgomery were also well received; both allowed each other creative space with no ego involved. As the 60s ended Smith's music became more MOR and he pursued a soul/funk path during the 70s, using a synthesizer on occasion. Organ jazz was in the doldrums for many years and although Smith remained its leading exponent, he was leader of an unfashionable style. During the 80s after a series of low-key and largely unremarkable recordings Smith delivered the underrated *Off The Top* in 1982. Later in the decade the Hammond organ began to come back in favour in the UK with the James Taylor Quartet and the Tommy Chase Band and in Germany with Barbara Dennerlein. Much of Smith's seminal work has been re-mastered and reissued on compact disc since the end of the 80s almost as vindication for a genre which went so far out of fashion, it disappeared. A reunion with Kenny Burrell produced a fine live album *The Master* featuring re-workings of classic trio tracks.

Selected albums: *The Champ* (Blue Note 1956), *Plays Pretty Just For You* (1957), *The Sermon* (Blue Note 1958), *House Party* (Blue Note 1958), *Cool Blues* (Blue Note 1958), *Home Cookin'* (1958), *Crazy Baby* (Blue Note 1960), *Midnight Special* (Blue Note 1960), *Open House* (Blue Note 1960), *Back At The Chicken Shack* (Blue Note 1960), *Peter And The Wolf* (1960), *Plays Fats Waller* (1962), *Bashin'* (Verve 1962), *Hobo Flats* (1963), *I'm Movin' On* (1963), *Any Number Can Win* (1963), *Rockin' The Boat* (1963), with Kenny Burrell *Blue Bash!* (1963), *Prayer Meetin'* (Liberty 1964), *Who's Afraid Of Virginia Woolf* (Verve 1964), *The Cat* (Verve 1964), *Organ Grinder's Swing* (Verve 1965), *Monster* (1965), *'Bucket'!* (1966), *Get My Mojo Workin'* (Verve 1966), *Christmas Cookin'* (Verve 1966), *Hoochie Coochie Man* (1966), with Wes Montgomery, *Jimmy & Wes The Dynamic Duo* (Verve 1966), with Montgomery *Further Adventures Of Jimmy And Wes* (1966), *Respect* (1967), *Livin' It Up* (1968), featuring George Benson *The Boss* (1969), *Groove Drops* (1970), *Mr Jim* (Manhattan 1981), *Off The Top* (Elektra 1982), *Keep On Comin'* (1983), *Go For Whatcha Know* (Blue Note 1986), *Jimmy Smith At The Organ* (1988), *The Cat Strikes Again* (Laserlight 1989), *Prime Time* (Milestone 1991), *Fourmost* (Milestone 1991), *Sum Serious Blues* (Milestone 1993), *The Master* (Blue Note 1994). Selected compilations: *Compact Jazz: The Best Of Jimmy Smith* (Verve 1968), *Jimmy Smith's Greatest Hits* (1968), *Compact Jazz: Jimmy Smith Plays the Blues* (Verve 1988).

Smith, Keith

b. 19 March 1940, London, England. Taking up the trumpet in his youth, Smith originally favoured New Orleans style and established a considerable reputation in this field. In the late 50s and through to the mid-60s he played with several bands, leading his own in Europe and the USA, where he performed and recorded with George Lewis and 'Captain' John Handy. Smith was also a member of the New Orleans All Stars, a package of mostly American musicians who toured Europe in the 60s. After a spell in Denmark with Papa Bue Jensen's band in the early 70s, he again formed his own band in the UK. He named the band Hefty Jazz, a name he also gave to his own record company and booking agency, and established a practice of touring with well-conceived thematic package shows.

Among these were 'The Wonderful World Of Louis Armstrong', for which he hired such ex-Louis Armstrong sidemen as Arvell Shaw and Barrett Deems, '100 Years Of Dixieland Jazz' and 'The Stardust Road', a tribute to the music of Hoagy Carmichael, which was headlined by Georgie Fame. A dedicated musician who also combines effective business and entrepreneurial skills, Smith remains at the forefront of the UK's traditional jazz scene in the 90s.

Albums: *Keith Smith's American All Stars In Europe* (1966), *Way Down Yonder In New Orleans, Then And Now* (1977), *Ball Of Fire* (Hefty Jazz 1978), *Up Jumped The Blues* (Hefty Jazz 1978), *Keith Smith's Hefty Jazz* (Jazzology 1988).

Smith, Leo

b. 18 December 1941, Leland, Mississippi, USA. Smith's stepfather was blues guitarist Alex 'Little Bill' Wallace and in his early teens Smith led his own blues band. He was already proficient on trumpet, which he later studied in college and continued to play in various army bands. In 1967 he moved to Chicago, where he joined the AACM, recording with Muhal Richard Abrams and 'Kalaparusha' Maurice McIntyre and becoming a member of Anthony Braxton's trio. In 1969, the group moved to Paris, but broke up a year later. Smith returned to the USA and settled in Connecticut. He recorded again with Abrams and Braxton in the Creative Construction Company and also worked with Marion Brown in the Creative Improvisation Ensemble and in a duo format. Smith continued to play occasionally with AACM colleagues such as Braxton and Roscoe Mitchell ('L-R-G') during the 70s, but his chief focus of interest now was his own music. He set up a label, Kabell, formed a group, New Dalta Ahkri, and also began to develop his solo music in a series of concerts and records (*Creative Music-1*, *Solo Music/Ahkreanvention*). New Dalta Ahkri, whose members included Anthony Davis, Oliver Lake and Wes Brown, made a handful of albums renowned for their spacious, abstract beauty, as did Smith's trio (with Bobby Naughton and Dwight Andrews). *Divine Love* also featured guest artists Lester Bowie, Charlie Haden and Kenny Wheeler, while *Spirit Catcher* had one track ('The Burning Of Stones') on which Smith played with a trio of harpists. Smith's trumpet style blended the terseness of Miles Davis with the lyricism of Booker Little (his two chief influences), while his music was based on the innovatory concepts of 'ahkreanvention' and 'rhythm units', alternative methods of structuring improvisation which he had been refining since the late 60s. A writer too, his *Notes (8 Pieces)* set out his views on African-American music history and included scathing attacks on jazz journalism and the mainstream music business. The late 70s found him making several trips to Europe, playing at Derek Bailey's Company Week (*Company 5, 6, 7*) and in 1979 recording both the big band *Budding Of A Rose* and the first of two trio discs with Peter Kowald and drummer Gunter Sommer.

In 1983 he recorded *Procession Of The Great Ancestry*, with Naughton and Kahil El'Zabar among the players ('a music of ritual and blues, of space and light,' enthused *Wire*). The same year he visited Canada to record *Rastafari* with the Bill Smith trio, the title signalling a conversion to Rastafarianism that led him, on later albums, to explore more popular forms, including reggae (*Jah Music, Human Rights* - though the latter also has one side of free improvisation with Kowald and Sommer from 1982). At the end of the 80s Smith was still playing in the New York area, but was also working as a teacher and had released no new recordings for several years. Hailed by Braxton as 'a genius' and by Anthony Davis as 'one of the unsung heroes of American music', the belated appearance of his *Procession Of The Great Ancestry* in 1990 prompted many to lament his long absence from the recording studio: as writer Graham Lock put it, 'such a silence hurts us all'.

Albums: *Creative Music-1* (1972), *Reflectativity* (1975), with Marion Brown *Duets* (1975, rec. 1970), with Anthony Braxton *Trio And Duet* (1975), with Creative Construction Company *CCC* (1975, rec 1970), with CCC *CCC-2* (1976, rec 1970), *Song Of Humanity* (1977), *The Mass On The World* (1978), *Divine Love* (ECM 1979), *Solo Music/Ahkreanvention* (1979), *Spirit Catcher* (Nessa 1979), *Budding Of A Rose* (1980), with Peter Kowald, Gunter Sommer *Touch The Earth* (1980), *Go In Numbers* (Black Saint 1982, rec 1980), with Kowald, Sommer *Break The Shells* (1982), with Bill Smith Trio *Rastafari* (1983), *Jah Music* (1986, rec. 1984), *Human Rights* (Gramm 1986, rec 1982-85), *Procession Of The Great Ancestry* (Chief 1990, rec. 1983), *Kulture Jazz* (ECM 1993).

Further reading: *Notes (8 Pieces)*, Leo Smith.

Smith, Russell

b. 1890, Ripley, Ohio, USA, d. 27 March 1966, Los Angeles, California, USA. The Smiths were a musical family though the two trumpeters Joe and Russell could scarcely have been less similar. Russell was a sober, ordered man who long outlived his more volatile brother. Russell became a professional musician in 1906 and moved to New York in 1910. He first played in Army Bands and then in reviews. He joined Fletcher Henderson's band in 1925 and stayed for 15 years. He was very much the straight musician willing to leave the jazz to others and perfectly suited to playing lead in a big band. After Henderson he played with Cab Calloway (1941-46) and then with Noble Sissle (1946-50) before retiring to California in the 50s.

Album: with Fletcher Henderson *A Study In Frustration* (1923-38).

Smith, Stuff

b. Hezekiah Leroy Gordon Smith, 14 August 1909, Portsmouth, Ohio, USA, d. 25 September 1967. Smith began playing violin as a child; he had some formal tuition but left home at the age of 15 to make his way as a professional musician. In 1926 he became a member of the popular Alphonso Trent band, where he remained, with side trips to other bands, for four years. In 1930 he settled in Buffalo, where he formed his own group, and in 1936 he took to New York for a long and highly successful residency at the Onyx Club. This band, which included Jonah Jones and Cozy Cole, established Smith's reputation as forceful, hard-swinging jazzman with an anarchic

sense of humour (he performed wearing a battered top hat and with a stuffed parrot on his shoulder). Off-stage he was an aggressive and disorganized individual, and in the late 30s he was forced to disband because of trouble with his sidemen, bookers, club owners and the union. Following Fats Waller's death in 1943, Smith took over the band but this too was a short-lived affair. By the late 40s his career was in decline, but a series of recordings for Norman Granz in the late 50s, in which he was teamed, improbably but successfully, with Dizzy Gillespie, brought him back in to the spotlight. He began to tour, especially in Europe where he was extremely popular, settled in Denmark and continued to record. Perhaps the most exciting and dynamic of all the jazz fiddlers, Smith concentrated on swinging, attacking his instrument with wild fervour and producing a rough-edged, almost violent sound. His performance of 'Bugle Call Rag' at a New York Town Hall concert in 1945 vividly demonstrates his all-stops-out approach to jazz and is a remarkable bravura display. Despite his swing era roots, Smith's recordings with Gillespie are filled with interesting explorations and he never seems ill-at-ease. A hard-drinker, Smith's later years were beset by hospitalizations, during which parts of his stomach and liver were removed. A visit to a Paris hospital resulted in his being declared a 'medical museum' and he was placed on the critical list, but within a few days he was back on the concert platform. He died in September 1967.

Selected albums: *Swingin' Stuff* (Storyville 1956), *Have Violin, Will Swing* (1957), *Soft Winds* (1957), *Dizzy Gillespie With Stuff Smith* (1957), *Violins No End* (1957), *Sessions, Live* (1958), *Stuff Smith* (1959), *Cat On A Hot Fiddle* (1959), *Blues In G* (1965), with Stéphane Grappelli *Stuff And Steff* (1965), *Live In Paris* (Frances Concert 1965 recording), with Grappelli, Jean-Luc Ponty *Violin Summit* (1966), *Black Violin* (1967), *Hot Violins* (Storyville 1965-67 recordings), *Live At Monmartre* (Storyville 1990). Compilations: *Stuff Smith And His Onyx Club Orchestra* (1936), *The Varsity Sessions* (1938-40), with others Town Hall Concert Vol. 2 (1945).

Further reading: *Stuff Smith: Pure At Heart*, Anthony Barnett and Evan Logager.

Smith, Tab

b. Talmadge Smith, 11 January 1909, Kinston, North Carolina, USA, d. 17 August 1971. After learning to play piano and C melody saxophone, Smith settled on alto and soprano saxophones. It was on alto that he made his name, working in bands led by Fate Marable, Lucky Millinder and Frankie Newton during the 30s. He also played in Teddy Wilson's ill-fated big band, at this time often playing tenor. In 1939 and into the early 40s he was in great demand, recording with Billie Holiday, Earl Hines, Charlie Shavers, Coleman Hawkins, playing with Count Basie and Millinder again, and also leading his own band. In the late 40s and early 50s he played only part time but, after making some popular R&B recordings, he was soon back leading a band, which he continued to do throughout most of the 50s. Late in the decade he again dropped out of full-time music, ending his career playing organ in a St. Louis restaurant. Smith was a forceful player on both alto and soprano, his solos having an attractively restless urgency. His sound was burred and possessed a surging intensity that helped him make the transition into R&B. Underrecorded in his lifetime and largely overlooked since his death, Smith's contribution to jazz was inevitably if unjustly overshadowed by better-known contemporaries such as Benny Carter, Willie Smith and, perhaps his closest musical counterpart, Pete Brown.

Selected albums: *Tab Smith* i (1959), *Tab Smith* ii (1960). Selected compilations: *Lucky Millinder And His Orchestra 1941-1943* (1941-43), with Coleman Hawkins *Swing* (1944), with Charlie Shavers incl. on *Hawkins And Hines* (1944), *Because Of You* (1951-55), *I Don't Want To Play In Your Kitchen* (Saxophonograph 1987), *Jump Time 1951-52* (Delmark 1987), *Joy At The Savoy* (Saxophonograph 1987), *Because Of You* (Delmark 1989), *Worlds Greatest Altoist - These Foolish Things* (Saxophonograph 1989), *Aces High* (Delmark 1992).

Smith, Tommy

b. 27 April 1967, Luton, England. Smith grew up in Edinburgh and started playing saxophone at the age of 12. He wowed the jazz clubs with his precocious brilliance and appeared on television in 1982, backed by pianist Gordon Beck and bassist Niels-Henning Ørsted Pedersen. The next year, aged only 16, he recorded *Giant Strides* for Glasgow's GFM Records. It was an astonishing debut. The young tenor made mistakes, but the stark recording honed in on his major assets: a full, burnished tone and a firm idea of the overall shape of his solos. It shone out of the British jazz of the time like a beacon, a herald of the 'jazz revival' among younger players. In 1983 he played the Leverkusen Jazz Festival in Germany. The Scottish jazz scene helped to raise the money to send him to Berklee College Of Music, where he enrolled in January 1984. Jaco Pastorius invited him to join his group for club dates, as did vibist Gary Burton. In 1985 Smith formed Forward Motion, with Laszlo Gardonyi (piano), Terje Gewelt (bass) and Ian Froman (drums), and began international tours, playing a spacious, reflective jazz. It was no surprise when ECM producer Manfred Eicher asked him to play on Burton's *Whiz Kids* in 1986, as Smith was sounding more and more like the label's established saxophone maestro, Jan Garbarek. In 1988 he toured under his own name with Froman from Forward Motion, pianist John Taylor and bassist Chris Laurence. In 1989 he introduced a series of 10 jazz television broadcasts and in 1990 worked with pop band Hue And Cry. In May 1990 he premiered a concerto for saxophone and string ensemble commissioned by the Scottish Ensemble. Signed to Blue Note in the late 80s, he has so far released three albums on the label. Albums: *Giant Strides* (GFM 1983), with Forward Motion *Progressions* (1985), with Forward Motion *The Berklee Tapes* (1985), *Step By Step* (Step By Step 1989), *Peeping Tom* (Blue Note 1990), *Standards* (Blue Note 1991), *Paris* (Blue Note 1992), *Reminiscence* (Linn 1994).

Smith, Willie

b. 25 November 1910, Charleston, South Carolina, USA, d. 7 March 1967. Smith began playing clarinet while still at school, performing professionally in his mid-teens. While at Fisk University he met Jimmie Lunceford, joining him in an orchestra there which eventually became a full-time professional organization. By now playing alto saxophone, Smith became a key member of the Lunceford band, meticulously drilling the saxophone section into perfection. He was with Lunceford until 1942, shortly before entering the US Navy where he directed a band. After the war he joined Harry James, bringing with him a level of commitment and dedication similar to that he had brought to Lunceford's band. He was with James until 1951, then played briefly with Duke Ellington and Billy May, then joined Jazz At The Philharmonic, touring internationally. During the remainder of the 50s he was with the ill-fated Benny Goodman/Louis Armstrong all-star package, followed by James and May again, then he did film studio work while combating a drink problem. In the early 60s Smith worked in various minor show bands in Los Angeles, Las Vegas and, briefly, led his own band in New York. Before the arrival of Charlie Parker, Smith, along with Benny Carter and Johnny Hodges, was one of the three major alto saxophonists in jazz. As a section leader he was outstanding, as almost any record by the Lunceford band will testify. As a soloist he had a sinuously beautiful tone, marked by a definitive hard edge that prevented him from ever slipping into sentimentality.

Selected albums: *Jazz At The Philharmonic* (1944-46), *Jazz At The Philharmonic 1946 Vol. 2* (1946), *Jazz History Vol. 12: Harry James* (1959-62), *Alto Saxophonist Supreme* (1965). Compilation: *The Complete Jimmie Lunceford* (1939-40).

Smith, Willie 'The Lion'

b. 25 November 1897, Goshen, New York, USA, d. 18 April 1973. Smith began playing piano at the age of six, encouraged by his mother. He continued with his informal musical education and by his mid-teenage years, he had established a formidable reputation in New York as a ragtime pianist. During World War I Smith acquired his nickname, apparently through acts of great heroism. In the post-war years he quickly developed into one of Harlem's best-known and feared stride pianists. Despite his popularity in Harlem and the respect of his fellows, including Fats Waller, James P. Johnson and Duke Ellington, he made few records and remained virtually unknown outside the New York area. In the 40s he travelled a little further afield, and during the 50s and 60s gradually extended his audience, playing and reminiscing at the keyboard, and recording numerous albums which demonstrated his commanding style.

Selected albums: *The Lion Roars* (1957), *Music On My Mind* (1966), *Pork And Beans* (Black Lion 1966), *The Memoirs* (1967), *Live At Blues Alley* (1970), *The Lion's In Town* (Vogue 1993, 1959 recording). Selected compilations: *The Original 14 Plus Two* (1938-39), *Tea For Two* (Jazz Live 1981), *Memoirs Of Willie The Lion* (RCA 1983), *Memorial* (Vogue 1988, 1949-50 recordings) *Reminiscing The Piano Greats* (1950).

Further reading: *Music On My Mind*, Willie 'The Lion' Smith and George Hoefer (ed.)

Smythe, Pat

b. 2. May 1923, Edinburgh, Scotland, d. 6. May 1983, London, England. Smythe practised as a lawyer in Edinburgh before moving to London in the late 50s. He played with trumpeter Dizzy Reece before joining Joe Harriott's Quintet (1960-64). Harriott was developing the beginnings of a European free jazz quite unlike Ornette Coleman's American form. Smythe was able to help both as pianist in the band and with suggestions to organize the new ideas. He stayed on with Harriott in the Indo Jazz Fusions which again organized improvization along new lines. Throughout the 70s he worked in a variety of contexts with Kenny Wheeler. He was a skilled accompanist especially of singers like Anita O'Day, Blossom Dearie, Tony Bennett, Annie Ross, Elaine Delmar and Mark Murphy. So respected a musician was he that after his death the Pat Smythe Memorial Trust and Award was established in his memory.

Albums: with Joe Harriott *Free Form* (1960), *Abstract* (1961-62), *Movement* (1963), *High Spirits* (1964), *Indo Jazz Suite* (1966), *Indo Jazz Fusions* (1966), *Personal Portrait* (1967), *Sandra King In A Concert Of Vernon Duke* (1982).

Soft Machine

Founded in 1966, the original line-up was Robert Wyatt, Kevin Ayers, Daevid Allen, Mike Ratledge and, very briefly, guitarist Larry Nolan. By autumn 1967 the classic line-up of the Softs' art-rock period (Ayers, Wyatt and Ratledge) had settled in. They toured with Jimi Hendrix, who, along with his producer, ex-Animals member Chas Chandler, encouraged them and facilitated the recording of their first album. (There had been earlier demos for Giorgio Gomelsky's Marmalade label, but these were not issued until later, and then kept reappearing in different configurations under various titles.) From the end of 1968, when Ayers left, until February 1970, the personnel was in a state of flux (Lyn Dobson, Marc Charig and Nick Evans were members for a while), and the music was evolving into a distinctive brand jazz-rock. Arguably, *Volume Two* and *Third* contain their most intriguing and exciting performances. Highlighted by Wyatt's very English spoken/sung vocals, the group had still managed to inject some humour into their work. The finest example is Wyatt's mercurial 'Moon In June'. By mid-1970 the second definitive line-up (Ratledge, Wyatt, Hugh Hopper and Elton Dean) was finally in place. It was this band that Tim Souster showcased when he was allowed a free hand to organise a late-night Promenade Concert in August 1970. In autumn 1971, Wyatt left to form Matching Mole (a clever pun on the French translation of Soft Machine; Machine Molle), and Phil Howard came in on drums until John Marshall became the permanent drummer. For the next few years, through a number of personnel changes (farewell Dean and Hopper, welcome Roy Babbington, Karl Jenkins) the Soft Machine were, for many listeners, the standard against which all jazz-rock fusions, including most of the big American names, had to be measured. However, with Ratledge's departure in January 1976 the group began to sound like a legion of other guitar-led fusion bands, competent and craftsmanlike, but, despite the virtuosity of Allan Holdsworth

and John Etheridge, without the edge of earlier incarnations, and certainly without the dadaist elements of Wyatt's time. In 1984, Jenkins and Marshall brought together a new edition of the band (featuring Dave Macrae, Ray Warleigh and a number of new Jenkins compositions) for a season at Ronnie Scott's club. It is their first three albums which contain the best of their work which clearly shows they were one of the most adventurous and important progressive bands of the late 60s and one that gently led their followers to understand and appreciate jazz.

Albums: *Soft Machine* (1968), *Soft Machine Volume Two* (1969), *Third* (1970), *Fourth* (1971), *Fifth* (1972), *Six* (1973), *Seven* (1973), *Bundles* (1975), *Softs* (1976), *Triple Echo* (1977, a 3-album set, mainly a compilation but including some previously unissued material), *Live At The Proms 1970* (1988), *The Peel Sessions* (1990), *The Untouchable* (1990), *As If . . .*(1991).

Soloff, Lew

b. Lewis Michael Soloff, 20 January 1944, New York City, New York, USA. After studying piano, trumpet and music theory at several colleges of music, Soloff played jazz trumpet with several leaders, notably Maynard Ferguson and Gil Evans and the Latin groups of Machito, Tito Puente, and Chuck Mangione. In the late 60s he moved into jazz/rock, joining Blood, Sweat and Tears with whom he remained for five years. During this same period he also played jazz, recording with the Thad Jones-Mel Lewis band and Clark Terry's big band. Throughout the 70s and early 80s, Soloff continued to mix pop and jazz work, playing and recording with musicians as diverse as Evans, Sonny Stitt, George Russell, Jon Faddis and with Spyro Gyra. He also demonstrated his versatility by playing classical music. A fiery, gutsy player, Soloff's broad repertoire has caused some jazz fans to overlook his work. He is, nevertheless, a musician of considerable depth, integrity and flair.

Albums: with Clark Terry *Live On 57th Street* (1970), with Sonny Stitt *Stomp Off, Let's Go* (1976), with Gil Evans *Parabola* (1978), *Yesterdays* (Paddle Wheel 1986), *Gil Evans And The Monday Night Orchestra Live At The Sweet Basil vols 1+2* (1988), *But Beautiful* (Paddle Wheel 1988), *My Romance* (Paddle Wheel 1989), *Little Wing* (Sweet Basil 1992).

South, Eddie

b. 27 November 1904, Louisiana, Missouri, USA, d. 25 April 1962. Taught violin as a child, South was educated for a career as a classical musician. Sadly, this goal proved overly optimistic; in the USA in the 20s there was no place on concert stages for black performers. Inevitably, therefore, he became a danceband musician, mainly in Chicago, at first working with artists such as Jimmy Wade, Charlie Elgar and Erskine Tate. In the late 20s he teamed up with Mike McKendrick and then led his own band, the Alabamanians, recording with both. In 1928 he visited Europe, proving extremely popular, and during a visit to Budapest he resumed his studies and also established an interest in eastern-European gypsy music which remained with him for the rest of his life. In the early 30s he was again leading a band in Chicago, but did not enjoy the popular success of many of his contemporaries. In 1937 he returned to Europe to play at the International Exhibition in Paris. During this visit he recorded some outstanding sides with Django Reinhardt. From 1938 onwards he worked in the USA, mostly in a small group context but briefly led a big band. He played clubs and radio dates throughout the 40s and 50s, usually as leader but also with artists such as Earl 'Fatha' Hines. He had his own radio show for a while and also appeared on television. The most stylish and melodic of all the jazz violinists, South's classical training is evident on all his recorded work. Nevertheless, he played with a powerful swing and the neglect shown by record companies in the years since his death is regrettable.

Album: *The Dark Angel Of The Fiddle* (1958). Selected compilations: *No More Blues* (1927-33), *Django Reinhardt And His American Friends* (1937-38), *Earl 'Fatha' Hines* (1947), *Eddie South 1923-37* (Original Jazz Classics 1993), *Eddie South In Paris 1929 & 1937* (DRG 1993).

Spanier, Muggsy

b. Francis Joseph Spanier, 9 November 1906, Chicago, Illinois, USA, d. 12 February 1967. Spanier began playing cornet while barely in his teens and within a couple of years was a professional musician. His first job was with Elmer Schoebel. By the end of the 20s he had established a reputation mostly in and around Chicago and had been hired by Ted Lewis for his popular band. He remained with Lewis until the mid-30s, then joined Ben Pollack. After a short period of serious illness he formed his own band, the Ragtimers, for a hotel residency in 1938 and also recorded with the band the following year. Although short-lived, the Ragtimers made an enormous impact on the public. During the 40s Spanier mingled leading his own bands with working for other artists such as Bob Crosby, Pee Wee Russell, Art Hodes and Miff Mole. In the 50s he worked frequently with Earl Hines, playing at numerous hotels, clubs and festivals all across the USA. Highly regarded by his fellow musicians, as much for his personal qualities as for his playing, Spanier's style was simple and direct, akin in these respects to that of earlier jazzmen. In spirit, however, he was very much a product of his home town. The 16 tracks recorded by Spanier's Ragtimers in 1939 are classics of a kind of jazz which retains its popularity, even if his successors rarely achieve their quality. Spanier's last years were dogged by poor health; he was forced to retire in 1964 and died in February 1967.

Albums: *Hot Horn* (1957), *Spanier In Chicago* (VJM 1958). Selected compilations: *Francis Joseph Muggsy Spanier* (1926-29), *The Great Sixteen* (1939), with Pee Wee Russell *Muggsy And Pee Wee* (1941-57), *Muggsy Spanier On V-Disc* (Everybody's 1987, 1944-45 recordings), *One Of A Kind* (Glendale 1987), *Mugsy Spanier Collection* (Deja Vu 1987), *Mugsy Spanier 1939-44* (Giants Of Jazz 1987), *Mugsy Spanier Vol 1 1924-27* (King Jazz 1993), *Mugsy Spanier Vol 2 1928-29* (King Jazz 1993).

Spontaneous Music Ensemble

Formed in 1965 by drummer John Stevens, SME was a group dedicated to free interplay between musicians. Early members included Trevor Watts, Kenny Wheeler, Dave Holland, and Derek Bailey, with guest appearances from artists such as Paul Rutherford (*Challenge*), Evan Parker (*Karyobin*), Johnny Dyani (*Oliv*) and Bobby Bradford. Rather like Company with Bailey, SME became a name for any improvised music project that John Stevens became involved in (though, unlike Bailey, Stevens also had other group names for 'less spontaneous' music: the Septet, Splinters, Away, Freebop etc). In 1970 Stevens formed the Spontaneous Music Orchestra to explore improvisation in larger groups, and SME became a core quartet of Stevens, Watts, singer Julie Tippetts and bassist Ron Herman (*Birds Of A Feather, 1, 2, Albert Ayler*). The *SME For CND* album featured Stevens and Watts with a workshop group, while *Bobby Bradford Plus SME* initiated a long association between Stevens and the west coast trumpeter. *Face To Face* was a particularly successful duo encounter between Stevens's drums and the soprano saxophone of Watts. As his interest turned to more structured musics, Stevens's SME projects became less frequent but the group was still playing on an occasional basis into the early 90s. Stevens seems to have little time for the 'no leader' aspect of many freely improvised encounters: unlike Company, whatever the line-up of SME, the instigator is well in charge.

Albums: *Challenge* (1966), *Karyobin* (Chronoscope 1968), *Oliv* (1969), *The Source* (Tangent 1971), *SME For CND For Peace And You To Share* (1971), *Birds Of A Feather* (1971), *So What Do You Think?* (Tangent 1971), *Bobby Bradford Plus SME* (1971), *Face To Face* (1975), with SMO "+=" (1975), *Biosystem* (Incus 1977), *Live - Big Band And Quartet* (1979, rec. 1977), *1,2, Albert Ayler* (1982, rec. 1971), *85 Minutes, Parts 1 & 2* (Emanem 1986, rec. 1974), *Live At Notre Dame Hall* (Sweet Folk All 1987).

Spyro Gyra

Formed in 1975 by saxophonist Jay Beckenstein and pianist Jeremy Wall, the original Spyro Gyra comprised Chet Catallo (electric guitar), David Wolford (electric bass), Eli Konikoff (drums), and Gerardo Velez (percussion). After a modest start in Buffalo, New York, and an album on a small independent label, Beckenstein's hard work and commitment through countless changes of personnel resulted in appearances at major international jazz festivals in the 80s, and several gold albums. In addition to having four hits in the USA the band found considerable success in the UK with the infectious 'Morning Dance'. The band's mainstream treatment of a mixture of funk, Latin, and jazz remains popular today.

Albums: *Spyro Gyra* (Infinity 1978), *Morning Dance* (Infinity 1979), *Catching The Sun* (MCA 1980), *Carnival* (MCA 1980), *Freetime* (MCA 1981), *Incognito* (MCA 1982), *City Kids* (MCA 1983), *Access All Areas* (MCA 1984), *Breakout* (MCA 1986), *Stories Without Words* (MCA 1987), *Point Of View* (MCA 1989), *Fast Forward* (GRP 1990), *Alternating Currents* (GRP 1992), *Three Wishes* (GRP 1992), *Rites Of Summer* (GRP 1992), *Dreams Beyond Control* (GRP 1993). Compilation: *The Collection* (GRP 1991). Video: *Graffiti* (GRP 1992).

St. Cyr, Johnny

b. 17 April 1890, New Orleans, Louisiana, USA, d. 17 June 1966. After teaching himself to play guitar on a home-made instrument, St. Cyr began leading his own little band in New Orleans while still in his early teenage years. He subsequently played guitar and banjo with many of the biggest names in New Orleans, including Freddie Keppard, Oscar 'Papa' Celestin, Joe 'King' Oliver and Manuel Perez. In 1923 he went to Chicago, playing and sometimes recording there with Oliver, Jimmie Noone, Louis Armstrong, Jelly Roll Morton and others. In the 30s and 40s he played only part time but continued into the 50s and early 60s with compatible spirits such as Alphonse Picou and Paul Barbarin. For a substantial part of his career St. Cyr played an instrument he devised himself, which incorporated elements of a six-string guitar and a banjo head, thus creating an unusual sound that greatly enhanced his many record dates.

Album: *Johnny St. Cyr And His Hot Five* (1954). Compilations: *Louis Armstrong Hot Five And Hot Seven* (1925-28), *The Complete Jelly Roll Morton Vols 1/2* (1926-27).

Stacy, Jess

b. 11 August 1904, Bird's Point, Missouri, USA, d. 1 January 1995, Los Angeles, California, USA. After teaching himself to play piano, Stacy worked the riverboats for a number of years, arriving in Chicago in the mid-20s. There, he played with numerous bands, including that of Paul Mares, on through into the early 30s. In 1935, John Hammond Jnr. brought him to the attention of Benny Goodman and for the next four years Stacy was a member of the latter's band, playing at the 1938 Carnegie Hall concert during which he contributed a remarkable if out-of-context solo in the middle of the gallery-pleasing excesses of 'Sing Sing Sing'. He was with Bob Crosby from 1939-42, then returned to Goodman for a couple of years. He recorded with Lee Wiley, to whom he was married for a while, and directed her accompanying orchestra for a number of years. By the late 40s he was playing in west coast bars. Although he made a few return appearances with Goodman, he drifted towards the edges of the music business and by 1963 had abandoned playing altogether. In 1974, he performed again, this time at the Newport Jazz Festival, where he was rapturously received by audiences and critics. Thereafter, he resumed his playing career for a while, giving his last public performance on 20 September 1975. Even at this late stage he continued to delight audiences. In 1992 he was presented with the Benny Carter Award by the American Federation of Jazz Societies. A distinctive and accomplished pianist, Stacy was capable of playing fearsome, two-fisted stride piano and contrastingly delicate solos, all marked by striking inventiveness.

Selected albums: with Benny Goodman *Carnegie Hall Concert* (1938), one side only *Stacy 'N' Sutton* (Affinity 1953), *Tribute To Benny Goodman* (1955), *The Return Of Jess Stacy* (c.1962), *Stacy Still Swings* (Chiaroscuro 1974), *Blue Notion* (Jazzology 1988). Selected compilations: *Jess Stacy And Friends* (1944), *On The Air* (Aircheck 1986).

Stamm, Marvin

b. 23 May 1939, Memphis, Tennessee, USA. After studying trumpet at school and later at North Texas State University, Stamm joined the Stan Kenton Mellophonium Orchestra. In the mid-60s he was with Woody Herman, then became a studio player based in New York. During the next few years he also played many jazz dates, including work with the Thad Jones-Mel Lewis Jazz Orchestra, Frank Foster, Chick Corea and with Duke Pearson's rehearsal band. In the 70s and on into the 80s he continued mixing studio work with jazz, playing with Benny Goodman, leading his own small groups and working with the American Jazz Orchestra and with George Gruntz. Stamm's decision to spend a substantial part of his career to date working in the studios has limited the number of opportunities for the jazz audience to hear him. When those occasions have arisen he has proved to be an interesting and enthusiastic player whose best work is always precise and controlled.

Albums: with Stan Kenton *Adventures In Time* (1962), with Woody Herman *Jazz Hoot* (1966), *Machinations* (1968), *Stammpede* (1982), with Benny Carter *Central City Sketches* (1987).

Stanko, Tomasz

b. 11 July 1942, Rzeszow, Poland. Stanko learnt the violin and piano at school and studied trumpet at the music high school in Cracow (1969). He has a wide range and formidable technique. He formed the group Jazz Darings (1962) with Adam Makowicz and played with various other local musicians. In the early 70s he played with the Globe Unity Orchestra and the European Free Jazz Orchestra at Donaueschingen. He then formed a quintet which included Zbigniew Seifert who switched from alto saxophone to violin while he was with the band. Later on he formed the Unit again with Makowicz and this band earned widespread praise being described as a 'white Ornette Coleman'. In fact the band was more traditionally based, though there was an element of free playing in the music. He has since also played as an unaccompanied soloist at the Taj Mahal and Karla Caves Temple as well as performing with Chico Freeman, James Spaulding, Jack DeJohnette, Gary Peacock and the Cecil Taylor Big Band.

Albums: *Music For K* (1970), *We'll Remember Komeda* (1973), *Balladyna* (ECM 1975), *Music From The Taj Mahal And Karla Caves* (1980), with Gary Peacock *A Voice From The Past* (1981), with Cecil Taylor *Winged Serpent* (1985), *The Montreaux Performance* (ITM 1988), *Tales For A Girl 12/A Shakey Chica* (Jam 1992), *Bluish* (Power Bros 1992), *Bosanossa And Other Ballads* (GOWI 1994).

Stegmeyer, Bill

b. 8 October 1916, Detroit, Michigan, USA, d. 19 August 1968. Stegmeyer began playing clarinet and saxophones while still at school, then joined the Austin Wylie band. A colleague there was Billy Butterfield, a friend from his university days. While with the Wylie band Stegmeyer also arranged and worked on local radio. In 1938 he joined Glenn Miller and the following year played in Bob Crosby's band. His interest in arranging gradually superseded his playing and in later decades he worked extensively in radio in Detroit and New York. From time to time he made appearances with jazz groups, among them the band co-led by Yank Lawson and Bob Haggart. Very highly regarded by fellow musicians, the direction taken by Stegmeyer in his career resulted in his being little known by fans. He died in August 1968.

Album: *The Best Of Dixieland: The Legendary Lawson-Haggart Jazz Band 1952-3* (1975).

Stern, Mike

b. 1954, Boston, Massachusetts, USA. Whilst always a rock-orientated electric guitarist, Stern's forays into contemporary jazz have never lacked edge or excitement. A student of Pat Metheny whilst at Berklee College Of Music, his first break came in 1976, when he joined Blood, Sweat And Tears. He worked with seminal fusion drummer Billy Cobham towards the end of the 70s, before being hired by legendary trumpeter Miles Davis. Following Davis' band, Stern worked with bass virtuoso Jaco Pastorius' Word Of Mouth, and began touring and recording as a leader in the early 80s. Some of his most exciting recent work has been with extraordinary tenor saxophonist Michael Brecker, in Brecker's own band or with the fast-fingered fusion group Steps Ahead. Recommended recordings include *Time In Place*, which features some of the New

York fusion/studio virtuosi with whom Stern has become associated, including Michael Brecker and Bob Berg on tenor saxophones, keyboardist Don Grolnick, fusion drummer Peter Erskine and sought after percussionist Don Alias. He plays some subtle guitar on Michael Brecker's *Don't Try This At Home*, amongst a line-up that includes pianist Herbie Hancock, drummer Jack DeJohnette and bassist Charlie Haden.

Albums: with Miles Davis *The Man With The Horn* (1981), with Davis *We Want Miles* (1981), with Billy Cobham *Stratus* (1981), with Davis *Star People* (1983), *Upside Downside* (1985), with Harvie Swartz *Urban Earth* (1985), with Swartz *Smart Moves* (1986), with Lew Soloff *Yesterdays* (1986), *Time In Place* (1987), with Michael Brecker *Don't Try This At Home* (1988), *Jigsaw* (1989), with Bob Berg *Cycles* (1989), with Berg *In The Shadows* (1990), with Berg *Back Roads* (1991), with Berg *Short Stories* (1992).

Stevens, John

b. 10 June 1940, Brentford, Middlesex, England, d. 13 September 1994, London, England. Stevens, whose father was a tap dancer, studied at Ealing Junior Art School and Ealing College of Higher Education. In 1958 he joined the Air Force, where he played drums in various bands after studying at the RAF's Music School. He spent three and a half years in Cologne, where he was able to see concerts by modern players

Mike Stern

such as John Coltrane and Eric Dolphy; there he also played with future German *avant gardists*, Manfred Schoof and Alex Von Schlippenbach. The late 50s skiffle boom had awakened his interest in blues and jazz - both New Orleans and modern - and back in England he played with Joe Harriott, Ellsworth 'Shake' Keane and Tubby Hayes. By 1964 he was centrally involved with modern jazz in London, playing with Ronnie Scott and Stan Tracey, then joining a quartet that comprised Jeff Clyne, Ian Carr and Trevor Watts, whom he had met in the RAF in 1958 and who would become one of his most frequent collaborators over the next 10 years. In 1965 he formed a septet that included Kenny Wheeler, Alan Skidmore and Ron Mathewson and, together with Watts and Paul Rutherford (another ex-RAF colleague), he also initiated the Spontaneous Music Ensemble, a launchpad for many free improvising musicians. In 1966, Stevens began organizing concerts at the Little Theatre Club, which rapidly became the epicentre of the new British jazz. Stevens moved back into more mainstream areas with the group Splinters in 1971, which he co-led with fellow-drummer Phil Seamen. In 1971, he formed the John Stevens Dance Orchestra and, in 1974, Away, his jazz-rock group. During this time he recorded and toured with John Martyn. In 1982, he formed Freebop and Folkus (their musical inclinations can be read from their names). In 1985, he published a book of workshop techniques, something he had been involved with since the mid-60s, winning the 1972 Thames Television award for community work. From 1983 he directed the UK Jazz Centre Society's Outreach Community Project, nurturing the talents of prominent figures in the mid-80s jazz revival, including Courtney Pine. In 1988, *Live Tracks* brought together many of his collaborators, including Pine, USA trumpeter Bobby Bradford, UK saxophonists Pete King and Evan Parker and trombonist Annie Whitehead, in a celebration of the joys of untrammelled bop-based improvisation.

Albums: *Springboard* (1967), with Evan Parker *The Longest Night Vols 1 & 2* (1976), *Somewhere In Between* (1976), *Application, Interaction And...* (Spotlite 1979), with Folkus *The Life Of Riley* (Affinity 1983), *Freebop* (Affinity 1983), with Dudu Pukwana *Radebe - They Shoot To Kill* (1987), with Free Bop *Live Tracks* (1988).

Steward, Herbie

b. 7 May 1926, Los Angeles, California, USA. Steward took up clarinet and alto and tenor saxophones while still a youth, but later concentrated on tenor. In the early and mid-40s he gigged in the Los Angeles area, playing with Barney Kessel and then signing on with a succession of big bands, including those of Artie Shaw, Alvino Rey and Butch Stone. In the latter band he played alongside Stan Getz, Shorty Rogers and Don Lamond. In 1947 he played in the Gene Rowland rehearsal band, in which the leader experimented with unusual saxophone voicings using the talents of Steward, Getz, Zoot Sims and Jimmy Giuffre. When the entire section was hired by Woody Herman, Steward became one of the original 'Four Brothers' saxophone team but stayed only three months before moving on. Later in the 40s and in the early 50s he played with more big bands.

including those led by Tommy Dorsey, Harry James and Claude Thornhill. During the remainder of the 50s and on through the 60s he worked in show and studio bands, by now usually preferring the alto to the tenor. In these decades and in the 70s he made occasional returns to the jazz scene for record dates. From the early 70s he was resident in San Francisco and could still be heard playing with rehearsal bands. In 1987, he returned to centre stage with appearances on the international festival circuit, playing alto, tenor and soprano saxophones. A highly-regarded player, Steward's coolly elegant tone fitted well into the Four Brothers concept and the more introspective small groups. His early work showed few signs of major influences and although his later work displays his awareness of musical developments in jazz, everything is filtered through his highly personal and eminently tasteful style.

Albums: *Passport To Pimlico* (1950), with Zoot Sims, Serge Chaloff, Al Cohn *Four Brothers Together Again* (1957), *So Pretty* (1962), *Herbie Steward With Orchestra Directed By Dick Hazard* (1962), *Barney Plays Kessel* (1975), *The Three Horns Of Herbie Steward* (1981). Compilation: *The Best Of Woody Herman* (1945-47).

Stewart, Louis

b. 5 January 1944, Waterford, Eire. After playing guitar in a succession of show bands, Stewart began playing jazz in the early 60s. By the end of the decade he had achieved a substantial reputation and had worked with such leading jazzmen as Tubby Hayes and Benny Goodman. Throughout the 70s he continued to enhance his standing in both the UK and the USA, recording with Peter Ind and others. He also toured Europe, attracting considerable attention everywhere he played. In the 80s his reputation grew apace, despite his preference for spending a substantial part of his time in his homeland, and he made well-received albums with Martin Taylor, Brian Dunning, Spike Robinson and others. A brilliant sound allied to a crystal-clear tone has helped make Stewart one of the outstanding guitarists in jazz. A virtuoso technique allows him to realize fully his endless inventiveness.

Albums: *Louis Stewart In Dublin* (1975), with Peter Ind *Baubles, Bangles And Beads* (1975), *Out On His Own* (Livia 1976-77), *Milesian Source* (1977), with Brian Dunning *Alone Together* (Livia 1979), *I Thought About You* (Lee Lambert 1979), with Martin Taylor *Acoustic Guitar Duets* (1985), *Good News* (Villa 1986), with Spike Robinson *Three For The Road* (1989).

Stewart, Rex

b. 22 February 1907, Philadelphia, Pennsylvania, USA, d. 7 September 1967. Stewart began playing cornet in his early teens, having previously tried several other instruments. By 1921 he was in New York where he played in a succession of bands over the next three or four years. A spell with Elmer Snowden in the mid-20s was followed by a job with Fletcher Henderson. Over the next few years he played in a number of bands, frequently returning to Henderson, and then, in 1934, joined Duke Ellington. He remained with Ellington until

1945, with spells out of the band for engagements with Benny Carter and others. In the late 40s and 50s he led his own bands in the USA and Europe and was the driving force behind the reformed Henderson All Stars band at the South Bay Jazz Festival in 1957. In the 60s Stewart developed a parallel career as broadcaster and writer. One of the most distinctive cornetists in jazz, Stewart developed the half-valve style of playing into an art form. His featured numbers with Ellington, especially 'Boy Meets Horn', have been frequently imitated but never surpassed. The biting, electrifying solos he played on numerous record dates, notably with the Henderson All Stars reunion band, have enormous energy and constantly display a strikingly original mind.

Selected albums: *Boston 1953* (1953), *The Irrepressible Rex Stewart* (c.1954), *The Big Challenge* (1957), with Henderson All Stars *The Big Reunion* (1957), *Rendezvous With Rex* (1958), *Porgy And Bess Revisited* (1958), *Rex Stewart-Dickie Wells* (1959), *The Rex Stewart Quintet* (1959), *The Rex Stewart Sextet* i (1960), *The Happy Jazz Of Rex Stewart* (1960), *The Rex Stewart Sextet* ii (1960), *Rex Stewart Meets Henri Chaix* (1966), *Rex Stewart Memorial* (1966). Compilations: with Fletcher Henderson *Swing's The Thing Vol. 2* (1931-34), *The Indispensable Duke Ellington Vols 5/6* (1940), with Duke Ellington *The Blanton-Webster Band* (1940-42), *Rex Stewart's Big Eight* (1940), *Hollywood Jam* (1945), *Finesse* (Affinity 1992), An *Introduction To Rex Stewart* (Best Of Jazz 1993)

Further reading: *Jazz Masters of the Thirties*, Rex Stewart with Stanley Dance.

Stewart, Slam

b. Leroy Stewart, 21 September 1914, Englewood, New Jersey, USA, d. 10 December 1987. He studied bass at Boston Conservatory, having earlier played violin. Almost from the start of his career Stewart was experimenting with his distinctive style in which he bowed the bass while humming in unison, an octave higher. John Chilton suggests that the concept was originally violinist Ray Perry's but certainly Stewart developed this technique into a fine art. In New York in 1937, Stewart met Slim Gaillard and together they became hugely popular on radio and records, their 'Flat Foot Floogie' being an enormous hit. During the late 30s and through the 40s he worked mostly in small groups, accompanying Gaillard, Art Tatum, Lester Young, Benny Goodman and others. In the 50s he played with Tatum, Roy Eldridge and also became a regular accompanist to singer Rose Murphy. In the 60s he added classical music to his repertoire. He continued to tour extensively in the 70s and 80s, playing with a wide range of artists, mostly in the mainstream of jazz. Stewart consistently displayed a comprehensive technique yet always played in an intensely rhythmic manner which he was never afraid to temper with wit.

Albums: *Slam Stewart* (Black And Blue 1971), *Slamboree* (1975), *Slam Stewart/Georges Delerue* (1975), *Fish Scales* (Black And Blue 1975), *Two Big Mice* (Black And Blue 1977), with Bucky Pizzarelli *Dialogue* (1978), with Major Holley *Shut Yo' Mouth* (1981). *New York New York* (Stash 1981). Compilation:

with Slim Gaillard *Original 1938 Recordings, Volume 1* (1989).

Stiles, Danny

b. USA. Stiles played trumpet and flügelhorn in New York in the late 60s and early 70s, in a studio band for the Merv Griffin and Dick Cavett shows. On the former, he met Bill Watrous, with whom he began an important musical relationship. He also played lead trumpet in Watrous's Manhattan Wildlife Refuge big band.

Album: with Watrous *Manhattan Wildlife Refuge* (1974).

Stitt, Sonny

b. Edward Stitt, 2 February 1924, Boston, Massachusetts, USA, d. 22 July 1982. Starting out on alto saxophone, Stitt gained his early experience playing in the big bands led by Tiny Bradshaw and Billy Eckstine. Influenced by Charlie Parker and by the many fine young beboppers he encountered on the Eckstine band, Stitt quickly developed into a formidable player. He played with Dizzy Gillespie, Kenny Clarke and others but by the late 40s was concerned that he should develop a more personal style. In pursuit of this he switched to tenor saxophone and formed the first of many bands he was to lead and co-lead over the years. Amongst his early collaborators was Gene Ammons, whom he had met during the Eckstine stint. In the late 50s he was with Jazz At The Philharmonic and in 1960 was briefly with Miles Davis. Throughout the 60s and 70s Stitt maintained a high level of performances at home and abroad, despite periodic bouts of ill-health generated by his drug addictions. In the early 60s he recorded with Paul Gonsalves, *Salt And Pepper*, and in the early 70s toured with Gillespie as a member of the Giants Of Jazz, continuing to make many fine record albums. His early 80s albums included *Sonny, Sweets And Jaws*, with Harry Edison and Eddie 'Lockjaw' Davis, and a fine set made just weeks before his death. Although his early career was overshadowed by Parker, Stitt was never a copyist. Indeed, his was a highly original musical mind, as became apparent after he switched to tenor and forged a new and appreciative audience for his work. In later years he played alto saxophone as often as he played tenor, by which time it was plain to see that the likening to Parker was largely a result of critical pigeon-holing.

Selected albums: *Sonny Stitt/Bud Powell/J. J. Johnson* (1949), *A Very Special Concert* (1950), *Symphony Hall Swing* (1952-56), *Super Stitt! Vols 1 & 2* (1954), *Tenor Battles* (1954), *Sonny Stitt With The New Yorkers* (1957), *Only The Blues* (1957), *Sonny Stitt* (c.1957-58), *Newport* (1958), *Burnin'* (1958), *The Hard Swing* (1959), *Sonny Stitt Sits In With The Oscar Peterson Trio* (1959), *Sonny Stitt At The D.J. Lounge* (1961), *Low Flame* (1962), *Autumn In New York* (1962-67), with Jack McDuff *Sonny Stitt Meets Brother Jack* (Original Jazz Classics 1962), *Sonny Stitt Plays Bird* (1963), *Salt And Pepper* (1963), *My Main Man* (1964), *Interaction* (1965), *Sonny* (1966), *Stardust* (1966), *What's New!!! Sonny Stitt Plays The Varitone* (1966), *Night Work* (1967), *Autumn In New York* (Black Lion 1968), *Night Letter* (1969), *Black Vibrations* (c.1971), *So Doggone Good* (1972), *Constellation* (Muse 1972), *Tune Up!* (Muse 1972), *The Champ*

(Muse 1973), *Satan* (1974), *In Walked Sonny* (1975), *I Remember Bird* (1976), *Moonlight In Vermont* (1977), *Back To My Old Home Town* (Black And Blue 1979), *Groovin' High* (1980), *Sonny, Sweets And Jaws* (1981), *At Last* (1982), *The Last Stitt Sessions* (Muse 1982).

Stobart, Kathy

b. 1 April 1925, South Shields, Co. Durham, England. Stobart in her long career as a leading jazz saxophonist has recorded and played with countless top musicians, yet her own recorded output is comparatively sparse. From her professional debut at the age of 14 she eventually moved to London where work was more plentiful, playing with Art Pepper (then a serviceman) while posted in the UK during the war. Following a spell with the Vic Lewis Big Band during the late 40s Stobart married trumpeter Bert Courtley and formed her own band in the early 50s. Her work over many years with Humphrey Lyttelton has produced some of her finest playing and Lyttelton rightly regards her as a world-class musician. Her other credits include work with Johnnie Griffin, Al Haig, Earl 'Fatha' Hines, Buddy Tate, Zoot Sims, Harry Beckett and Dick Hyman. Stobart topped the bill at the first British women's jazz festival in 1982 and was a member of Gail Force 17 (the women's big band) during the mid-80s. Additionally she has made a reputation as a music teacher. Still refusing to retire from the road, she was on tour with Lyttelton again in 1992.
Albums: *Arderia* (1983), *Saxploitation* (1983).

Stockhausen, Markus

b. 1957, Cologne, Germany. Son of the composer Karlheinz Stockhausen, Markus studied piano and trumpet at the Cologne Musikhochschule. He also plays flügelhorn and synthesizer. In 1981 he won the German Music Competition. Since 1974 he has worked regularly with his father, who has written a number of works for him, including 'Sirius'. In particular, the solo trumpet parts in Stockhausen perés massive opera cycle, Licht, were created for Markus. Outside of the contemporary 'classical' field he has played free improvised music with various groups, and currently has a band, Aparis, with his brother Simon on saxophones and keyboards.
Albums: with Gary Peacock: *Cosi Lotano...Quasi Dentro* (ECM 1989), *Aparis* (ECM 1990), *Tagtraum* (New Note 1992), *Despite The Fire Fighters' Efforts* (ECM 1993.

Stoller, Alvin

b. 7 October 1925, New York City, USA, d. 19 October 1992. Taking up the drums as a child, Stoller's dues were paid while he was still a teenager with stints in bands led by Raymond Scott, Teddy Powell, Benny Goodman and Charlie Spivak. In 1945 he followed Buddy Rich into the drum chair with the Tommy Dorsey band, bringing with him much of his predecessor's enthusiasm - and not a little of his fiery temperament. Through the late 40s and 50s, Stoller's career found him playing in name bands such as those led by Georgie Auld, Harry James, Billy May, Charlie Barnet, Claude Thornhill and Bob Crosby. This same period saw him in constant demand as a studio musician, especially for Norman Granz, backing artists such as Erroll Garner, Billie Holiday, Ben Webster, Ella Fitzgerald and Benny Carter, with whom he appeared on *Additions To Further Definitions*. Tastefully discreet when backing singers or in a small group setting and powerfully propulsive when driving a big band, Stoller was one of the best late swing era drummers even if he was sometimes overlooked thanks to his long service in film and television studios in late years.
Albums: with Harry Edison *Sweets At The Haig* (1953), *The Art Tatum-Roy Eldridge-Alvin Stoller-John Simmons Quartet* (1955), *Around The Horn With Maynard Ferguson* (1955-56), *The Genius Of Coleman Hawkins* (1957), with Benny Carter *Additions To Further Definitions* (1966).

Stone, Jesse

b. 1901, Atchison, Kansas, USA. As a young man, pianist Stone worked extensively in the southwest playing in numerous bands. During the greater part of the 20s he led his own territory band but at the end of the decade became arranger and musical director for other leading territory bands including those of Terrence Holder, George E. Lee and Thamon Hayes. He returned to bandleading in the mid-30s, continuing in this capacity throughout the next decade before becoming an A&R man. Stone, who made very few recordings, was one of the lesser, but still important, figures in the development of Kansas City Jazz. His arrangements and expertise as leader and director helped fashion the propulsive swing which marked the style.

Strange, Pete

b. 19 December 1938, London, England. Strange is a self-taught trombonist who started his career with Eric Silk's Southern Jazz Band. He played with a variety of bands before joining Bruce Turner's Jump Band. When that folded he played semi-professionally for a number of years before joining Keith Nichols' Midnite Follies Orchestra in the late 70s. He wrote arrangements for, and played with the band of trumpeter Digby Fairweather. Strange also organized his own unusual five trombone band Five-A-Slide and played with Alan Elsdon's band. In 1983 he moved on to Humphrey Lyttelton's band for which he has written many fine arrangements as well as providing stylish trombone playing derived principally from Lawrence Brown and Dicky Wells.
Albums: with Bruce Turner *Going Places* (1963), with Humphrey Lyttelton *It Seems Like Yesterday* (1983), *Echoes Of The Duke* (1984), *Humph At The Bull's Head* (1985).

Strayhorn, Billy

b. 29 November 1915, Dayton, Ohio, USA, d. 31 May 1967. After studying music at school and privately, Strayhorn began writing music and late in 1938 submitted material to Duke Ellington. Early the following year Ellington recorded the first of these works, and Strayhorn was soon involved in writing original material and arrangements for the Ellington band. The association with Ellington largely excluded all other musical activity during the rest of Strayhorn's life. When he did write arrangements for and play piano with other artists, they were usually present or former Ellingtonians. Although he played piano on record dates with various Ellingtonians and on piano duets with Ellington himself, Strayhorn's greatest contribution to jazz must be the many superb compositions immortalized by the Ellington orchestra. The best known of these might well be the Ellington theme, 'Take The "A" Train', but his other masterpieces are almost all sumptuous ballads and include 'Day Dream', 'Passion Flower', 'Lotus Blossom', 'Raincheck', 'Chelsea Bridge' and 'Lush Life'. This last piece was written in 1938 but Strayhorn withheld publication for many years, preferring to wait until a singer emerged capable of interpreting the song as he imagined it. The first recording was by Nat 'King' Cole in 1949 but, good as this was, Strayhorn later remarked that he had still to hear the song sung right. The intertwining of Strayhorn's writing with that of Ellington complicates a thorough understanding of his importance, and Brian Priestley is one of several musicians/writers who have indicated the value of intensive research in this area. When Strayhorn was hospitalized in 1967, he continued working almost to the end on his final composition, 'Blood Count'. A few months after his death in May 1967, Ellington recorded a tribute album of Strayhorn compositions, *And His Mother Called Him Bill.*

Selected albums: *Ellington-Strayhorn Duets* (1950), by Duke Ellington *Historically Speaking, The Duke* (1956), by Ellington *Such Sweet Thunder* (1956-57), *Cue For Saxophones* (Affinity 1958), *Billy Strayhorn And The Paris String Quartet* (1961), by Ellington *Far East Suite* (1966), *The Billy Strayhorn Project* (Stash 1991), *Lush Life* (Red Baron 1992). Compilation: by Ellington *The Blanton-Webster Band* (1940-42).

Studer, Fredy

b. 16 June 1948, Lucerne, Switzerland. Studer is a self-taught musician who started playing drums when he was 16 years old and appeared in a wide range of bands from rock through jazz to experimental. In 1970, he moved to Rome with a rock trio. He became a consultant for the development of Paiste cymbals. Throughout the 70s he was with the jazz/rock band Om and then played in the rock band Hand In Hand. Studer formed a trio with Rainer Bruninghaus and Markus Stockhausen between 1981 and 1984 and then played in the Charlie Mariano/Jasper Van't Hof band. He also performed in the percussion group Singing Drums with Pierre Favre, Paul Motian and Nana Vanconcelos. Studer has toured extensively including trips to the USA, Central and South America, the Carribbean, North Africa and Japan.

Albums: with George Gruntz *Percussion Profiles* (1977), *Om With Dom Um Romao* (1977), *Continuum* (1983), with Singing Drums *Singing Drums* (1985), as Doran, Studer, Minton, Bates, Ali *Play The Music Of Jimi Hendrix* (Call It Anything 1994).

Sudhalter, Dick

b. 28 December 1928, Boston, Massachusetts, USA. Sudhalter played as an amateur while engaged in a career in journalism. Playing cornet in various parts of the USA and UK, he established a quiet reputation mostly amongst musicians. As he expanded his career in music, Sudhalter's virtues as a player and a tireless organizer became more widely apparent. He was involved in the creation of the New Paul Whiteman Orchestra and also worked with Bobby Hackett, Keith Nichols, the New York Jazz Repertory Orchestra and others in faithful but undogmatic re-creations of early jazz, in particular the music of Bix Beiderbecke. His interest in the life and career of Beiderbecke led him to write the biography, *Bix: Man And Legend* and his other writings have extended into the *New York Post*. His late 80s and early 90s playing ventures include performances with Dick Wellstood and Marty Grosz in the band known as the Classic Jazz Quartet, and with Loren Schoenberg and singers Barbara Lea and Daryl Sherman in the group named Mr Tram Associates.

Albums: *Friends With Pleasure* (Audiophile 1981), with Mr Tram Associates *Getting Some Fun Out Of Life* (1988), *Get Out And Get Under The Moon* (1989), *Dick Sudhalter And Connie Jones* (Stomp Off 1992).

Sulieman, Idrees

b. Leonard Graham, 7 August 1923, St. Petersburg, Florida, USA. After playing trumpet for a number of years with territory bands, in 1943 Sulieman joined Earl 'Fatha' Hines. After some more dues-paying in minor bands, he came to New York where he played with Thelonious Monk and then began a tour through an impressive succession of big bands, including those led by Cab Calloway, Count Basie and Lionel Hampton. He also played in small groups led by Mal Waldron, Randy Weston and others. In the 60s he moved to Sweden, then settled in Denmark where he has remained. From the mid-60s he played with the Clarke-Boland Big Band and also took up alto saxophone. In the 70s he continued to work in Denmark, mostly with radio big bands, but made occasional record dates as leader and with musicians such as Horace Parlan. Despite being one of the first jazz musicians to play bop, Sulieman's long residency away from the international spotlight has meant that he has had little influence upon others.

Albums: with Mal Waldron *Mal 1* (1956), with Horace Parlan *Arrival* (1973), *Now Is The Time* (1976).

Sullivan, Ira

b. 1 May 1931, Washington, USA. Sullivan is that rare thing, a true multi-instrumentalist, capable of improvising statements of worth on all his instruments. He was taught trumpet by his father, saxophone by his mother and played both in 50s' Chicago with such seminal figures as Charlie Parker, Lester Young, Wardell Gray and Roy Eldridge, garnering a reputation as a fearsome bebop soloist. After playing briefly with Art Blakey (1956), and mastering alto and baritone saxophone, Sullivan moved south to Florida and out of the spotlight in the early 60s. His reluctance to travel limited his opportunities to play with musicians of the first rank, but Sullivan continued to play in the Miami area, often in schools and churches. Contact with local younger players, notably Jaco Pastorius and Pat Metheny lead to teaching and to a broadening of his own musical roots to include the lessons of John Coltrane's music and elements of jazz rock. With the addition of flute and soprano saxophone to his armoury, Sullivan moved to New York and in 1980 formed a quintet with legendary bop trumpeter Red Rodney. Resisting the temptation to follow current trends and play the music of their youth, Sullivan and Rodney worked on new material and fostered young talent to produce some of the freshest and most stimulating music of the decade.

Albums: *Nicky's Tune* (Delmark 1958), *Ira Sullivan Quartet* (Delmark 1974), *Ira Sullivan* (Flying Fish 1976), *Peace* (1978), with Red Rodney *Live At The Village Vanguard* (1980), Bird Lives (Affinity 1981), *Horizons* (Discovery 1983), *Does It All* (Muse 1988), *Tough Town* (Delmark 1992).

Sullivan, Joe

b. 4 November 1906, Chicago, Illinois, USA, d. 13 October 1971. After studying piano formally, Sullivan began working in theatres and clubs in and around Chicago while still a teenager. Throughout the 20s he was one of the busiest musicians in Chicago, playing at clubs and on numerous record dates with leading jazzmen, mostly in small groups. He also worked as accompanist to Bing Crosby during the early 30s. At various times in that decade he played in several larger ensembles, among them bands led by Roger Wolfe Kahn and Bob Crosby. Ill health drove him from the Crosby band just as it hit the big-time. In the 40s he played with Bobby Hackett and Eddie Condon and also frequently worked as a single. He continued playing alone, not from choice, and in small jazz groups through the 50s. From the early 60s onwards his career was dogged by both poor health and critical disregard. An eclectic pianist, Sullivan's robust style displayed elements of stride but he was at his propulsive best playing in a lively Chicago-style band. Among his compositions are 'Gin Mill Blues' and 'Little Rock Getaway'.

Albums: *Fats Waller First Editions* (1952), *New Solos By An Old Master* (1953), *Mr Piano Man* (1955), *Gin Mill* (Pumpkin 1963). Selected compilations: *Joe Sullivan And The All Stars (1950)* (Shoestring 1981), *At The Piano* (Shoestring 1981), *Piano Man (1935-40)* (1988).

Sullivan, Maxine

b. Marietta Williams, 13 May 1911, Homestead, Pennsylvania, USA, d. 7 April 1987. Sullivan began singing in and around Pittsburgh, Pennsylvania, before travelling to New York in 1937. She joined the Claude Thornhill band and made a hugely successful record of 'Loch Lomond'. The popularity of this recording led to her making several more jazzed-up folk songs, including 'Annie Laurie', which, for all their frequent banality, she sang with effortless charm. In the late 30s and early 40s she made several feature films and also worked and recorded with her husband John Kirby. After a brief retirement she began appearing again in New York and also travelled to Europe. In the mid-50s she quit singing to take up nursing but returned in 1958. In addition to singing she also played flügelhorn,

valve-trombone and pocket trumpet. She continued to work through the 60s, often with Cliff Jackson, who had become her second husband, and with Bob Wilber. Her career blossomed in the late 70s and throughout most of the 80s, thanks to performances with the World's Greatest Jazz Band and Scott Hamilton. In her later years she devoted some of her considerable energy to running the 'House that Jazz Built', a museum she created at her home and dedicated to Jackson's memory. The hallmarks of her singing were charm and delicacy, qualities which were often out of favour and probably accounted for the ups and downs of her career. Her later work, especially the recordings with Wilber, proved that her talent was far greater than public taste had allowed.

Albums: with others *Seven Ages Of Jazz* (1958), *Maxine Sullivan* i (1969), *Close As Pages In A Book* (1969), *Queen Of Song* (1970), *Maxine Sullivan* ii (1971), *Maxine* (1975), *Harlem Butterfly* (1975-77), *We Just Couldn't Say Goodbye* (1978), *Maxine Sullivan And Ike Isaacs* (1978), *Sullivan, Shakespeare, Hyman* (Audiophile 1979), *Maxine Sullivan And Her Swedish Jazz All Stars* (1981), *It Was Great Fun!* (1983), *Good Morning, Life* (1983), *The Queen; Something To Remember Her By* (Kenneth 1985), *The Great Songs From The Cotton Club By Harold Arlen And Ted Koehler* (Mobile Fidelity 1985), *Uptown* (Concord 1985), *The Lady's In Love With You* (1985), *I Love To Be In Love* (c.1986), *Maxine Sullivan And Scott Hamilton* (1986), *Songs Of Burton Lane* (1986), *Together: Maxine Sullivan Sings Julie Styne* (c.1986), *Swingin' Street* (Concord 1987), *Spring Isn't Everything* (Audiophile 1987). Compilations: *It's Wonderful* (1992), *1944 To 1948* (1993).

Sulzmann, Stan

b. 30 November 1948, London, England. From his mid-teens Sulzmann was playing saxophones on the blues circuit, but in 1964 he joined the first edition of Bill Ashton's National Youth Jazz Orchestra. Following this he worked on the Queen Mary crossing to New York and then returned to London to study at the Royal Academy of Music. Subsequently, as well as winning the *Melody Maker* New Star award, he played with Mike Gibbs, Graham Collier, John Dankworth, John Taylor (with whom he also established a quartet in 1970), John Warren, Clark Terry, Brian Cooper, Alan Cohen, the Clarke-Boland Big Band, Kenny Wheeler, Gordon Beck's Gyroscope and Gil Evans' early 80s London band. Equally adept on soprano, alto and tenor saxophones and flutes and clarinet, Sulzmann was one of the earliest of several distinguished graduates from the NYJO, and his influences range from Frank Zappa, through to Kenny Wheeler (whose compositions he showcased on *Everybody's Song But My Own*) and Miles Davis to Debussy and Delius.

Selected albums: with Michael Gibbs *Tanglewood '63* (1971), *On Loan With Gratitude* (1977), *Krark* (1979), with John Taylor *Everybody's Song But My Own* (1987), with Tony Hymas *Flying Fortress* (1991), *Feudal Rabbits* (Ah-Um 1991), with Marc Copland *Never At All* (Future 1993).

Sun Ra

b. Herman P. Blount, 22 May 1914, Birmingham, Alabama,

USA, d. 30 May 1993, Birmingham, Alabama, USA. One of the most extraordinary figures in 20th century music, Sun Ra claims to have arrived here from the planet Saturn on a date that can't be revealed because of its astrological significance! More down-to-earth researchers have suggested the birthdate above, although this remains unconfirmed. There is a similar uncertainty about his original name: while he sometimes went under the name of Herman 'Sonny' Blount in the 30s and 40s, he also used the name Sonny Lee and has claimed that his parents' name was Arman. However, for approximately 40 years he was known as Sun Ra - or, as he's announced to countless concert audiences, 'Some call me Mr Ra, some call me Mr Re. You can call me Mr Mystery.' His first musical memories are of hearing classic blues singers such as Bessie Smith and Ethel Waters and he grew up a fan of the swing bands, especially those led by Fletcher Henderson. His early work experience as pianist, arranger and composer included stints with Fess Wheatley and Oliver Bibb in the Chicago area in the mid-30s, but this period of his life remains largely undocumented. In 1946 he was at Chicago's Club DeLisa, playing behind visiting jazz and blues artists such as Joe Williams and LaVern Baker and writing arrangements for his idol, Henderson, who had a 15-month residency at the club. Ra then worked with bassist Eugene Wright's Dukes Of Swing in 1948 and also played with Coleman Hawkins and Stuff Smith. In the early 50s he began to lead his own small groups, which soon featured Pat Patrick and John Gilmore, and by the middle of the decade he had assembled a 10-piece big band, the Arkestra, who recorded their debut, *Sun Song*, in 1956. Originally playing an idiosyncratic bebop, with arrangements that also showed the influence of Duke Ellington and Tadd Dameron, the Arkestra had developed by the early 60s into possibly the era's most advanced and experimental group. Ra was one of the first jazz leaders to use two basses, to employ the electric bass, to play electronic keyboards, to use extensive percussion and polyrhythms, to explore modal music and to pioneer solo and group freeform improvisations.

In addition, he made his mark in the wider cultural context: he proclaimed the African origins of jazz, reaffirmed pride in black history and reasserted the spiritual and mystical dimensions of music (all important factors in the black cultural/political renaissance of the 60s). In the late 50s Ra set up his own label, Saturn Records (aka Thoth), one of the first musician-owned labels, and most of his 100-plus recordings have been released on Saturn, although many have been issued or reissued on other labels (notably Impulse! in the 60s and 70s). Nearly all Saturn albums have been limited-edition pressings that appear in plain white or hand-drawn sleeves and are now valued collector's items. (The facts that they are extremely rare, that they often contain no recording details, that they are sometimes reissued under different titles and that some 'new' releases actually comprise a side each from two older albums, all mean that a complete and accurate Sun Ra discography is almost impossible to compile.)

Despite years of severe poverty and relocations from Chicago to New York (1961) and then to Philadelphia (1968), Sun Ra kept the Arkestra in existence for over three decades, though they played under a different name almost every year: examples include the Astro-Infinity Arkestra, the Blue Universe Arkestra, the Cosmo Jet Set Arkestra and the Year 2000 Myth Science Arkestra. The list of illustrious band members over the years takes in Ahmed Abdullah, Marion Brown, Richard Davis, Robin Eubanks, Craig Harris, Billy Higgins, Frank Lowe, Julian Priester, Pharoah Sanders and James Spaulding, (there are dozens more), while occasional guest performers have included Lester Bowie, Don Cherry and Archie Shepp. Many players returned for further stints, though the financial rewards were never great, and a handful remained virtually without a break since the very beginning - notably Gilmore and Marshall Allen. Several core band members lived together in a communal house where Ra reportedly imposed strict discipline: he allowed no drugs, no alcohol and was fond of waking everyone up in the middle of the night for extra rehearsals: music was everything. (He was also credited as the person who persuaded John Coltrane to give up drugs: and Coltrane took saxophone lessons from Gilmore.) Almost from the outset the band wore exotic costumes, usually with Ancient Egyptian or outer space motifs, and used elements of spectacle in their stage act: light shows, dance, mime and an endearing habit of winding through the audience chanting about their exploits on other planets ('we travel the spaceways, from planet to planet'). In the 70s Ra began to expand their repertoire to include more traditional material, especially big band numbers by the likes of Ellington, Henderson, Jimmie Lunceford and Jelly Roll Morton. At the same time he kept abreast of jazz-funk and also continued to perform his ear-splitting, freeform synthesizer solos; so any live concert by the Arkestra was likely to span the entire gamut of black creative music. Their recordings proved more erratic (and often very low-fi) but over the years they had accumulated a set of indisputable masterpieces, with apparent creative peaks coming in the early/mid-60s (*Jazz In Silhouette, Rocket Number Nine Take Off For The Planet Venus, The Heliocentric Worlds Of Sun Ra, Volumes 1 & 2, Nothing Is, The Magic City*) and the late 70s (*Media Dreams, Disco 3000, Omniverse, Sleeping Beauty, Strange Celestial Road, Sunrise In Different Dimensions*). The Arkestra made occasional guest appearances (for example, they played on three tracks of Phil Alvin's *Unsung Stories* and contributed 'Pink Elephants' to Hal Willner's Disney tribute, *Stay Awake* - an episode that led to them playing entire sets of Disney tunes in the late 80s) and selected members have occasionally made small-group recordings with Ra: for instance, both *New Steps* and *Other Voices, Other Blues* feature Ra, Gilmore, Michael Ray (trumpet) and Luqman Ali (percussion). Sun Ra himself released a handful of solo piano albums - *Monorails & Satellites, Vols 1 & 2, Aurora Borealis, St Louis Blues Solo Piano* - and the duo *Visions* with Walt Dickerson: his piano style ranged across a variety of influences, including blues, Count Basie's bounce, Thelonious Monk's dissonance and a degree of European impressionism.

A stroke in 1990 left Ra with impaired movement, but the Arkestra's 1991 London concerts proved there had been no diminution of musical quality. His influence has been enormous and has seeped through into every nook and cranny of modern music, from Funkadelic to Karlheinz Stockhausen to the Art Ensemble Of Chicago. 'Musically,' said drummer Roger Blank, 'Sun Ra is one of the unacknowledged legislators of the world.' A poet and philosopher too, Ra published several volumes of writings. In fact, while a few critics have seized on items such as the Arkestra's glitzy costumes and space chants to dismiss them as a circus and Ra himself as a freak or charlatan, most of his ideas and proclamations made perfect sense when viewed in the context of African-American culture. Taking a new name, for instance, is a venerable blues tradition (think of Muddy Waters, Howlin' Wolf, Leadbelly) and Ra's emphasis on Ancient Egypt was just one of the means he used to focus attention on black history and black achievement. More detailed expositions can be found in the chapters on his music and thought in Chris Cutler's *File Under Popular*, John Litweiler's *The Freedom Principle*, Graham Lock's *Forces In Motion* and Valerie Wilmer's *As Serious As Your Life*. A documentary film, *Sun Ra: A Joyful Noise* directed by Robert Muge, was released in 1980. Sun Ra was one of the great modern visionaries: he not only had a dream, but lived it to the full for the last 40 years. He showed that, with imagination, commitment and a love of beauty, you can create your own future and make the impossible real. Sun Ra left planet Earth in May 1993.

Albums: *Sun Song* (1957), *Super-Sonic Jazz* (Evidence 1957), *Angels And Demons At Play* (Evidence 1958), *Sun Ra & His Solar Arkestra Visit Planet Earth* (1958), *We Travel The Space Ways* (1960), *Jazz In Silhouette* (1960), *Fate In A Pleasant Mood* (1961), *The Nubians Of Plutonia* aka *The Lady With The Golden Stockings* (1962), *Rocket Number Nine Take Off For The Planet Venus* aka *Interstellar Low Ways* (1962), *Bad & Beautiful* (1963), *The Futuristic Sounds Of Sun Ra* aka *We Are In The Future* (1963), *Art Forms Of Dimensions Tomorrow* (Evidence 1964), *Secrets Of The Sun* (1965), *When Angels Speak Of Love* (1965), *The Heliocentric Worlds Of Sun Ra, Vol 1* (ESP 1965), *Cosmic Tones For Mental Therapy* (Evidence 1966), *The Heliocentric Worlds Of Sun Ra, Vol 2* (ESP 1966), *The Magic City* (Evidence 1966), *Nothing Is* (ESP 1967), *Other Planes Of There* (1967), *Sound Of Joy* (1968, rec. 1957), *Holiday For Soul Dance* (Evidence 1968), *Atlantis* (Evidence 1968), *When Sun Comes Out* (1969), *Sound Sun Pleasure* (1969), *My Brother The Wind* (1970), *The Night Of The Purple Moon* (1970), *Continuation* (1970), *Pictures Of Infinity* (1971, rec. 1967), *Nuits De La Fondation Maeght, Vols 1 & 2* (1971), *The Solar Myth Approach, Vols 1 & 2* (Affinity 1971), *It's After The End Of The World* (1971), *Song Of The Stargazers* (1971), *Strange Strings* (1972, rec. 1968), *To Nature's God* aka *Sun Ra In Egypt* (1972), *Horizon* (1972), *Nidhamu* (1972), *Monorails & Satellites, Vol. 1* (1973, rec. 1967), *Astro Black* (1973), *Space Is The Place* (Evidence 1973), *Monorails & Satellites, Vol. 2* (1974, rec. 1967), *Discipline 27 - 11* (1974), *Pathways To Unknown Worlds* (1974), *Dreams Come True* (1975, rec. 50s-60s), *My Brother The Wind, Vol. 2* (1975), *The Antique Blacks* (1975), *Cosmo Earth Fantasy* aka *Temple U* aka *Sub-Underground* (1975), *Taking A Chance On Chances* (1975), *The Invisible Shield* (1976, rec. 50s-70s), *Featuring Pharoah Sanders And Black Harold* (1976, rec. 1964), *Live In Paris* aka *Live At The Gibus* (1976), *Outer Spaceways Incorporated* (Black Lion 1977), *Primitone* (1977), *Universe In Blue* (1977), *Discipline 99* aka *Out Beyond The Kingdom Of* (1977), *What's New* (1977), *Over The Rainbow* (1977), *Celebrations For Dial Tunes* (1978), *Cosmos* (1978), *Live At Montreux* (1978), *Solo Piano* (1978), *Unity* (1978), *New Steps* (1978), *Other Voices, Other Blues* (1978), *Media Dreams* (1978), *Sound Mirror* (1978), *Disco 3000* (1978), *Lanquidity* (1978), *St Louis Blues* (1979), *The Soul Vibrations Of Man* aka *Soul Vibrations* (1979), *The Other Side Of The Sun* (1980), *Blithe Spirit Dance* (1980), *Omniverse* (1980), *Seductive Fantasy* (1980), *Of Mythic Worlds* (1980), *Strange Celestial Road* (1980), *Sleeping Beauty* (1980), *Dance Of Innocent Passion* (1980), *Rose Hued Mansions Of The Sun* aka *Voice Of The Eternal Tomorrow* (1981), *Sunrise In Different Dimensions* (1981), *Aurora Borealis* (1981), *I Pharoah* (1981), *Some Blues But Not The Kind That's Blue* aka *My Favourite Things* (1981), *Beyond The Purple Star Zone* (1981), *Journey Stars Beyond* (1981), *Otherness Blue* aka *Just Friends* (1983, rec. 50s-80s), *Hiroshima* (1984), *Sun Ra Meets Salah Ragab In Egypt* (1984), *Ra To The Rescue* (1984), *Live At Praxis '84, Vols 1 - 3* (1984), *A Fireside Chat With Lucifer* (1985), *Cosmo Sun Connection* (1985), *Celestial Love* (1985), *Children Of The Sun* (1986), *Stars That Shine Darkly* (1986), *A Night In East Berlin* (1987), *Reflections In Blue* (1987), *Love In Outer Space* (1988, rec. 1983), *Live At Pit-Inn, Tokyo* (1988), *Blue Delight* (A&M 1989), *Hours After* (1989), *Cosmo Omnibus Imaginable Illusion* (DIW 1989), *Out There A Minute* (1989, rec. 60s), *John Cage Meets Sun Ra* (1989), *Purple Night* (A&M 1990), *Sun Ra & His Year 2000 Myth Science Arkestra - Live In London 1990* (1990), *Mayan Temples* (Black Saint 1992), *Destination Unknown* (Leo 1992), *Friendly Galaxy* (Leo 1993), *Pleiades* (Leo 1993). Further reading: *The Immeasurable Equation*, Sun Ra.

Sunshine, Monty

b. 8 April 1928, London, England. After teaching himself to play clarinet, Sunshine became involved in the UK trad jazz scene of the late 40s. He was a founder member of the Crane River Jazz Band and later teamed up with Chris Barber to form a co-operative group. For a while this band was under the nominal leadership of Ken Colyer, but later reverted to its original democratic status. Sunshine was featured on several records, notably 'Petite Fleur', and helped the band to establish a reputation as one of the best of the UK trad outfits. In 1960 he left Barber to form his own band which, while retaining a high level of popularity for a number of years, never achieved the success of the Barber/Sunshine band. However, Sunshine established a name in Europe, especially in Germany. In the 70s he had occasional reunions with the reformed Crane River Jazz Band and with Barber. Although a proponent of New Orleans jazz, Sunshine's playing style has always favoured the full, romantic sound of musicians such as Sidney Bechet and Barney Bigard. In the 80s he was often on tour as a single, still popular with the audience he had known from his earliest days in the business.

Selected albums: *A Taste Of Sunshine* (1976), *Magic Is The Moonlight* (1978), *Sunshine In London* (Black Lion 1979), *On Sunday* (1987). Compilations: *Monty Sunshine And The Crane River Jazz Band, 1950-53* (1988), *Gotta Travel On* (Timeless 1992).

Surman, John

b. John Douglas Surman, 30 August 1944, Tavistock, Devon, England. Surman, a remarkable player on soprano and baritone saxophones, bass clarinet, bamboo flutes and sometimes tenor saxophone and synthesizers. He was a member of the Jazz Workshop at Plymouth Arts Centre with Mike Westbrook whilst still at school, and came to London with Westbrook's band in 1962. He studied at London College of Music (1962-65) and London University Institute of Education (1966). By the time he ceased to be a regular member of Westbrook's band in 1968 he was also working in Ronnie Scott's nine-piece outfit (the Band) with Humphrey Lyttelton and had twice been voted the world's best baritone saxophone player by *Melody Maker* readers as well as top instrumentalist at the 1968 Montreux International Jazz Festival. Since then various of his albums have collected awards from all over the world. From 1968-69 he led a group, varying from a quartet to an octet, centring round Mike Osborne, Harry Miller and Alan Jackson. During the 60s and 70s he also played with Alexis Korner's New Church, Mike Gibbs, Graham Collier, Chris McGregor, Dave Holland, John McLaughlin (on the guitarist's acclaimed *Extrapolation*), John Warren and Harry Beckett. Owing to lack of work in the UK, he emigrated to Europe where he formed the Trio with Barre Phillips and Stu Martin. Surman next worked with Terje Rypdal (*Morning Glory*), before the Trio briefly reformed, augmented by Albert Mangelsdorff to become MUMPS. At this time he first met Jack DeJohnette with whom he was to work regularly in the 80s and 90s. In 1973 he formed another highly impressive and influential trio, S.O.S., with Osborne and Alan Skidmore. He began experimenting with electronics during this period, a facet of his work explored in depth on his albums of the late 70s and 80s. He formed duos with Stan Tracey and Karin Krog, in 1978 (the latter becoming a regular musical associate), and from 1979-82 worked with Miroslav Vitous. In 1981, Surman formed the Brass Project, and during the 80s he was a member of Gil Evans' British band and later of his New York band. He also worked with Paul Bley and Bill Frisell and, in 1986, toured with Elvin Jones, Holland and Mangelsdorff. A powerful and resourceful improviser, Surman also composes for all sizes of jazz groups, as well as writing pieces for choirs and for dance companies, notably the Carolyn Carlson Dance Theatre at the Paris Opera, with whom he worked from 1974-79.

Albums: with Mike Westbrook *Celebration* (1967), *Release* (1968), *John Surman* (1968), *How Many Clouds Can You See* (1969), with John McLaughlin *Extrapolation* (1969), *Marching Song* (1969), *Where Fortune Smiles* (1970), *The Trio* (1970), with Mike Gibbs *Michael Gibbs* (1970), with Gibbs *Tanglewood '63* (1971), with Chris McGregor *Brotherhood Of Breath* (1971), *Conflagration* (1971), with John Warren *Tales Of The Algonquin* (1971), *Westering Home* (1972), *Morning Glory* (1973), *S.O.S.* (1975), *Live At Woodstock Town Hall* (1975), *Live At Moers Festival* (1975), *Citadel/Room 315* (1975), with Stan Tracey *Sonatinas* (1978), *Surman For All Saints* (1979), *Upon Reflection* (ECM 1979), *The Amazing Adventures Of Simon Simon* (ECM 1981), with Karin Krog *Such Winters Of Memory* (ECM 1983), with Barry Altschul *Irina* (1983), *Withholding Pattern* (ECM 1985), with Paul Bley *Fragments* (1986), with Alexis Korner *Alexis Korner And... 1961-72* (1986), with the Trio *By Contact* (1987, rec. 1971), *Private City* (ECM 1988), *The Paul Bley Quartet* (1988), *The Road To St. Ives* (ECM 1990), with John Taylor *Ambleside Days* (1992), *Adventure Playground* (ECM 1992), with Albert Mangelsdorff *Room 1220* (1993), with Warren *The Brass Project* (ECM 1993), with John Abercrombie, Marc Johnson, Peter Erskine *November* (1994), *Stranger Than Fiction* (ECM 1994).

Sutton, Ralph

b. 4 November 1922, Hamburg, Missouri, USA. After playing piano locally for several years, Sutton joined Jack Teagarden in 1941. During the 40s he attracted widespread attention, thanks to his participation in a series of radio shows hosted by jazz writer Rudi Blesh. From the late 40s through to the mid-50s he played regularly at Eddie Condon's club in New York. In the 60s he worked mostly as a single, but also played in a number of traditional bands and towards the end of the decade was a founder-member of the World's Greatest Jazz Band. Thereafter, Sutton's star rose and remained in the ascendancy with a series of record albums and world tours, solo and in a variety of settings. His musical partners in these ventures included Ruby Braff, Jay McShann, Kenny Davern and Peanuts Hucko.

He continues to perform with great panache and a seemingly undiminished level of invention into the early 90s. An outstanding pianist in the great tradition of stride giants such as James P. Johnson and Fats Waller, Sutton's style is both forceful and lightly dancing, as the needs of his repertoire demand. Although drawing from the century-old tradition of jazz piano, from ragtime through the blues to Harlem stride, Sutton brings to his playing such inventive enthusiasm that everything he does seems freshly-minted.

Selected albums: *Ralph Sutton Plays The Music Of Fats Waller* (1951), *Ralph Sutton At The Piano* (1952), one side only *Stacy 'N' Sutton* (1953), with Lee Collins *The Hangover All Stars Live 1953* (1953), *Ralph Sutton's Jazzola Six* (1953), *Ralph Sutton And The All Stars* (1954), *The Ralph Sutton Quartet* i (1959), *Ragtime USA* (1962-63), *The Ralph Sutton Trio* (1966), with Ruby Braff *On Sunnie's Side Of The Street* (1968), *The Night They Raided Sunnie's* (1969), with Yank Lawson and Bob Wilber *The Ralph Sutton Trio And Guests* (1969), *Piano Moods* (1975), *Off The Cuff* (1975), *Suttonly It Jumped* (1975), *Live!* (1975), *Changes* (1976), *Jazz At The Forum* (1976), *Live At Haywards Heath* (Flyright 1976), *The Ralph Sutton Quartet* ii (1977) with Wild Bill Davison *Together Again* (1977), *Stomp Off, Let's Go* (1977), *The Other Side Of Ralph Sutton* (1980), with Braff *Quartet* (1980), *Ralph Sutton & Ruby Braff: Duets* (1980), with Jay McShann *The Last Of The Whorehouse Piano Players Vols 1 & 2* (Chiaroscuro 1980), *Ralph Sutton & Kenny Davern Trio Vols 1 & 2* (1980), *Ralph Sutton And The Jazz Band* (1981), with Eddie Miller *We've Got Rhythm* (1981), *Ralph Sutton & Jack Lesberg* (1981), *The Big Noise From Wayzata* (1981), *Great Piano Solos And Duets* (1982), *Live At Hanratty's* (1982), *Blowin' Bubbles* (1982), *Partners In Crime* (Sackville 1983), *At Cafe Des Copains* (Sackville 1987), Bix Beiderbecke Suite (Commodore Class 1987), with the Sackville All Stars *A Tribute To Louis Armstrong* (1988), *Alligator Crawl* (Jazzology 1989), *Eye Opener* (J&M 1990), *Maybeck Recital Hall Series Vol 30* (Concord 1993). Selected compilations: *Piano Solos In The Classic Jazz Tradition* (1949-52), *Piano Solos/Beiderbecke Suite* (1950), *The Ralph Sutton Trio* (1950).

Swallow, Steve

b. 4 October 1940, New York City, New York, USA. Swallow started out on trumpet, then took up the double bass at the age of 18. At college he played bebop with Ian Underwood (later saxophonist with Frank Zappa). In 1960, he joined the Paul Bley Trio, later working with Jimmy Giuffre, Art Farmer and George Russell and winning the *Downbeat* critics' poll as new star in 1964. In June 1965 he joined the Stan Getz Quartet, with which he played until 1967. Between 1967 and 1970, he was in Gary Burton's quartet and between 1970 and 1973 he played in San Francisco with pianists Art Lande and Mike Nock before returning to work with Burton. Since the early 70s he has played intermittently with Mike Gibbs, but has worked most regularly with Carla Bley (his current partner), playing in her various groups of the late 70s and 80s. In 1980 he set music to poems by Robert Creeley for the album *Home*. By the mid-70s he was playing nothing but electric bass, using a pick, and producing a sound that was popular with the current arrangers. He is also a prolific composer, with credits on Gibbs, Burton and Chick Corea albums for titles such as 'Arise Her Eyes', 'Chelsea Bells', 'Como En Vietnam' and 'Hotel Hello'. John Scofield, who has recorded and played with Swallow over many years, regards him as his mentor. In the late 80s Swallow recorded a set of duos with Bley and also began to work with UK saxophonist Andy Sheppard, producing his first three albums as a leader and playing with him in 1991 in a trio that also featured Bley. Swallow remains a hugely underrated and highly talented figure in recent jazz.
Selected albums: with Gary Burton *Hotel Hello* (1973), *Home* (ECM 1980), with Carla Bley *Carla* (Xtrawatt 1988), with Carla Bley *Duets* (1989), *Swallow* (Xtrawatt 1991), with Bley *Go Together* (1993), *Real Book* (Xtrawatt 1994).

Szabo, Gabor

b. 1936, Budapest, Hungary, d. 26 February 1982. Guitarist Azabo emigrated to the USA in 1956 to study at the Berklee College Of Music. He came to notice playing with Chico Hamilton and Charles Lloyd. In the late 60s he began to explore a fusion of jazz with the kind of rock which was super-ficially influenced by Indian music. He introduced a number of Eastern styles into his playing. Although his Hungarian roots probably pre-disposed him to an empathy with these elements they were often seen as mere gimmicks, and he was generally dismissed by the critics. The eclectic albums made under his own name were very much of their time, and he was not an important figure, but in his work with Lloyd and Hamilton, he showed himself capable of being a warm-toned and subtle player.
Albums: with Charles Lloyd *Of Course Of Course* (1965), *Spellbinder* (1967), *The Sorcerer* (1967), *Bacchanal* (1968), *Gabor Szabo 1969* (1969), with Lena Horne *Lena & Gabor* (1970), *Nightflight* (1976), *Rambler, Wind, Sky And Diamonds* (1977), *Macho* (1978), *Mizra* (1978), *Belsta River,* (Four Leaf Clover 1988), with Bobby Womack *High Contrast* (Affinity 1988), *Small World* (Four Leaf Clover 1988). Compilation: *His Greatest Hits* (1977).

Tabackin, Lew

b. 26 March 1940, Philadelphia, Pennsylvania, USA. Tabackin studied music extensively - at high school, the Philadelphia Conservatory and privately - before beginning his playing career in 1965. He played tenor saxophone and flute with various bands in and around New York, including those led by Tal Farlow, Maynard Ferguson, Clark Terry, Cab Calloway, the band led by Larry and Les Elgart, the Thad Jones-Mel Lewis Jazz Orchestra and the rehearsal bands of Duke Pearson and Chuck Israels. He also led his own small group and was also active in the east coast television studios. In the late 60s he was briefly in Europe, playing and teaching in Germany and Denmark. In 1970 he began a musical, and eventually personal relationship with Toshiko Akiyoshi. After their marriage he was principal soloist with their orchestra, which was based in Los Angeles during the 70s and in New York from the early 80s. In the late 80s and early 90s he was frequently on tour around the world, usually as a single. A superb technician on tenor saxophone, Tabackin's powerful playing style contains echoes of several of his influences, most strikingly Sonny Rollins. He is, however, a distinctive and accomplished performer in his own right. His solos, often dazzling and lengthy unaccompanied cadenzas interpolated into Akiyoshi's frequently complex charts, are filled with extraordinarily fluent and brilliantly executed ideas. In contrast Tabackin's flute playing gleams with softly executed yet vivid concepts. In addition to his albums with the Akiyoshi-Tabackin band, he has also recorded with Bill Berry (who was instrumental in introducing Tabackin and Akiyoshi to one another), with Louie Bellson, fellow tenorist Warne Marsh, Toshiyuki Miyama and his New Herd on *Vintage Tenor*, and with his own small groups.

Albums: *Tabackin* (1974), *Dual Nature* (1976), *Trackin'* (1976), *Tenor Gladness* (1976), *Rites Of Pan* (1977), *Vintage Tenor* (1978), *Black And Tan Fantasy* (1979), *Lew Tabackin Quartet* (1983), *Angelica* (1984), *Desert Lady* (Concord 1989), *I'll Be Seeing You* (Concord 1992).

Tana, Akira

b. 14 March 1952, San Jose, California, USA. A self-taught drummer, Tana played semi-professionally while still at college. He attended Harvard University where he gained a degree in East Asian Studies/Sociology. He then studied at the New England Conservatory of Music, also taking private tuition from percussionists with the Boston Symphony and Boston Pops Orchestras and from jazz drummer Alan Dawson. During his studies he had the opportunity of working with Helen Humes, Milt Jackson, Sonny Rollins, George Russell, Sonny Stitt and other leading jazz musicians. He also played with the Boston Symphony Orchestra and several of the classical music ensembles at the New England Conservatory. In the early 80s he continued to accompany major artists such as Al Cohn, Art Farmer, Benny Golson, Jim Hall, Jimmy Rowles, Zoot Sims and Cedar Walton. He also performed with artists outside the jazz world, including Charles Aznavour and Lena Horne. Tana recorded extensively during these years and in addition to albums with some of the foregoing also appeared with Ran Blake, Chris Connor, Carl Fontana, Jimmy Heath, Tete Montoliu, Spike Robinson, Warne Marsh and many others. In the early 90s Tana worked with James Moody, Dizzy Gillespie, Frank Wess, Ray Bryant and J.J. Johnson. With Rufus Reid he formed the band TanaReid and, with Reid and Kei Akagi, the Asian American Jazz Trio. A technically accomplished drummer, Tana's wide range is hinted at by the musicians with whom he has worked. Comfortably at home accompanying singers and instrumental ballads, Tana is equally in his element playing hard bop. In the bands he co-leads with Reid he generates an excitingly propulsive rhythmic drive. In addition to playing, Tana has also produced and co-produced several albums including those by TanaReid, the Asian American Jazz trio and Project G-7. He regularly conducts workshops and clinics at colleges and universities, including Berklee College Of Music, and is an adjunct professor at two colleges.

Albums: with Zoot Sims *I Wish I Were Twins* (1983), with TanaReid *Yours And Mine* (1990), with Sumi Tonooka *Taking Time* (1990), with Asian American Jazz Trio *Sound Circle* (1991), with Project G-7 *A Tribute To Wes Montgomery Vol. 1* (1991), with TanaReid *Passing Thoughts* (1992).

Tania Maria

b. 9 May 1948, São Luis, Maranhao, Brazil. A good pianist, powerful singer and excellent live performer, Tania Maria combines in her staccato vocal style the rhythmic virtues of bebop and Latin dance, with a strong commitment to spontaneity.

She learned classical piano at first, discovered the work of Nat 'King' Cole and Oscar Peterson, and moved to Paris in 1974. Maria's vitality won her a contract at a Paris nightclub for a three-month residency, and she stayed in the city for the next seven years, recording several albums that emphasized her Brazilian roots. She played the 1975 Newport Jazz Festival opposite Sarah Vaughan, was encouraged by the guitarist Charlie Byrd, and in 1981 she recorded *Piquant* for the USA label Concord, moved to the USA and began to develop a successful recording career there. Live recordings have captured her essence best (1984's *Wild!* is one of her most impressive), and recent commercial funk outings have obscured her originality and vividness, but her concert performances still reveal an artist of energy, musicality and originality.

Albums: *Brazil With My Soul* (1978), *Live* (1978), *Tania Maria Et Niels-Henning Ørsted Pedersen* (1979), *Piquant* (1981), *Taurus* (1982), *Come With Me* (1983), *Love Explosion* (1984), *Wild!* (1985), *Made In New York* (1985), *The Lady From Brazil* (1987), *Outrageous* (1993).

Tapscott, Horace

b. 6 April 1934, Houston, Texas, USA. Tapscott moved to Los Angeles at the age of nine and, although taught piano by his mother (an accomplished stride player), he decided to concentrate on trombone. Helped by bandleader Gerald Wilson, Tapscott began to play professionally, but after army service in Korea, switched back to piano, jamming on LA's Central Avenue scene with musicians such as Sonny Criss, Eric Dolphy, Red Callender, Charles Lloyd and Buddy Collette. For 18 months he was accompanist to singer Lorez Alexandria, then toured briefly with Lionel Hampton before deciding to remain in Los Angeles where, in 1961, he co-founded the UGMA (the Underground Musicians Association) as a community self-help organization based in the Watts area. The UGMA later became the UGMAA (the Union of God's Musicians and Artists Ascension) but has otherwise survived intact for 30 years, providing a testing ground for generations of upcoming west coast musicians (alumni include Arthur Blythe, David Murray, Roberto Miranda) as has its offshoot big band, the Pan-Afrikan Peoples Arkestra (motto: 'Our music is contributive rather than competitive'). Although (or perhaps because) Tapscott and the UGMAA served the black community and celebrated the black cultural heritage in much the same way as Muhal Richard Abrams and the AACM would do in Chicago, they found themselves neglected by the media and the mainstream record industry. Until a cluster of albums suddenly appeared in the late 70s, Tapscott had only two appearances on record to show for nearly 20 years of making music. The first, in 1968, was on alto saxophonist Criss's *Sonny's Dream: The Birth Of The New Cool*, for which Tapscott wrote and arranged all the tunes and conducted the 10-piece ensemble; the second was his own *The Giant Is Awakened*, a fiercely exciting quintet session that also marked Arthur Blythe's recording debut. (Long a collector's item, it was reissued in 1991 as part of the Novus Series '70 CD, *West Coast Hot*.) The record's evident Black Power sympathies - the 'Giant' of the title was, said Tapscott, 'the New Black

Nation' - perhaps helps to explain why it was almost a decade before Tapscott was able to record again; a sudden flurry of activity producing some small-group albums and, notably, a trio of releases with the Pan-Afrikan Peoples Arkestra (*Flight 17, The Call, Live At The IUCC*) on the small, independent Nimbus label, which also initiated a series of solo piano records (*The Tapscott Sessions*) in the 80s. A dramatic, lyrical pianist - he cites Art Tatum, Thelonious Monk, Andrew Hill, his mother and Vladimir Horowitz as major influences - Tapscott's compositions are, he says, inspired by 'the experience of black people in America'. His tunes celebrate their history, their community, their culture; filled with blues, dance, struggle, dream, they are - as the title of his first solo album declares - the songs of the unsung. By devoting himself to their cause, Tapscott has remained largely unsung himself.

Albums: *The Giant Is Awakened* (1969), *West Coast Hot* (Novus 1970), *Songs Of The Unsung* (1978), *Flight 17* (1978), *The Call* (1978), *In New York* (1979), *Live At The IUCC* (1979), with Everett Brown Jnr. *At The Crossroads* (1980), *Dial 'B' For Barbra* (1981), *Live At Lobero* (1982), *Live At Lobero Vol II* (1982), *The Tapscott Sessions Vols 1-8* (1985-91, rec. 1982-84), *The Dark Tree Vol 1* (Hat Art 1991, rec. 1989), *The Dark Tree Vol 2* (Hat Art 1991, rec. 1989).

Tate, Buddy

b. George Holmes Tate, 22 February 1915, Sherman, Texas, USA. One of the outstanding tenor saxophonists of his generation, Tate paid his dues in a succession of territory bands between 1927 and 1939. Having started out on alto, he quickly developed into a formidable tenor player, lending presence and distinction to the bands of Troy Floyd, Terrence Holder, Andy Kirk and Nat Towles, the latter always regarded by Tate as one of the best in which he ever worked. In 1939 he joined the Count Basie band, having briefly worked with Basie five years earlier. He stayed until the end of the 40s, then played with Lucky Millinder, Oran 'Hot Lips' Page and others, before taking his own band into a residency at the Celebrity Club in Harlem in 1953. He remained there until the mid-70s, taking time out to tour and record extensively with such artists such as Jimmy Rushing and Buck Clayton. In 1975 he briefly co-led a band with Paul Quinichette, but from then onwards worked mostly as a solo, occasionally teaming up with mainstream comrades such as Illinois Jacquet, Al Grey, Scott Hamilton and Bobby Rosengarden. Tate was seriously injured in 1981, scalded in a hotel shower, but returned to the fray only to be stricken with serious illness in the late 80s. The early 90s saw him return tentatively to playing again. His full-toned sound, robust 'Texas Tenor' styling and unflagging swing have earned him a significant place in the history of mainstream jazz. A thoroughly delightful individual, charming, sophisticated and thoughtful, he is a true gentleman of jazz and one of the music's most distinguished ambassadors.

Selected albums: *Buddy Tate's Celebrity Club Orchestra Vol. 1* (1954), *Swinging Like Tate* (Affinity 1958), *Tate's Date* (1959), *Tate A Tate* (1960), *Groovin' With Tate* (1961), *The Buddy Tate-Milt Buckner Trio* (1967), *Buddy Tate's Celebrity Club Orchestra* *Vol. 2* (1968), *Unbroken* (1970), *Buddy Tate And Wild Bill Davis: Midnight Slows Vol. 2* (1972), *Broadway* (Black And Blue 1973), *The Count's Men* (1973), *Buddy Tate And His Buddies* (1973), *Midnight Slows Vols 4 & 5* (Black And Blue 1974), *Kansas City Woman* (Black Lion 1974), *The Texas Twister* (New World 1975), *Swinging Scorpio* (Black Lion 1975), *A Jazz Meeting* (1975), *Jive At Five* (Storyville 1975), *After Midnight* (1975-76), *A Soft Summer Night* (1976), *Buddy Tate Meets Dollar Brand* (1977), *Sherman Shuffle* (Sackville 1978), *The Buddy Tate Quartet* (Sackville 1978), *Buddy Tate And The Muse All Stars Live At Sandy's* (1978), *Hard Blowin': Live At Sandy's* (1978), *The Ballad Artistry Of Buddy Tate* (Sackville 1981), *The Great Buddy Tate* (1981), *Swingin' The Forties With The Great Eight* (1983), *Buddy Tate Meets Torsten Zwingenberger* (1983), *Just Jazz* (Reservoir 1984), *Long Tall Tenor* (1986), with Tete Montollu *Tate A Tete At La Fontain* (Storyville 1988), Selected compilations: with Count Basie *The Jubilee Alternatives* (1943-44), *Jumpin' On The West Coast* (Black Lion 1988, 1947 recordings).

Tate, Grady

b. 14 January 1932, Durham, North Carolina, USA. A self-taught drummer, Tate began playing while still a small child. During his military service he turned to jazz and subsequently worked with Wild Bill Davis. In the early 60s he played in the Quincy Jones big band and then spent time with Count Basie, Duke Ellington and a string of small groups, including those led by Rahsaan Roland Kirk, Oscar Peterson, Zoot Sims, Red Rodney and Ray Brown. He also made some albums as a singer. Tate's interest in singing made him especially sympathetic to vocalists' needs and he has recorded with Ella Fitzgerald, Sarah Vaughan, Lena Horne, as well as Ray Charles among many. Tate's drumming is suited to many areas of jazz and he invariably brings a lithe swing to any band of which he is a member. In recent years he appears to show a preference for singing, not in the jazz idiom but angled towards the popular field.

Albums: as singer *Feeling Life* (1969), as singer *Master Grady Tate* (1977), with Roland Kirk *Now Please Don't You Cry Beautiful Edith* (1967), with Pee Wee Russell, Oliver Nelson *The Spirit Of '67* (1967), with Quincy Jones *Walking In Space* (1969) with Oscar Peterson *Silent Partner* (1979), with Red Rodney *The 3 Rs* (1979), with Ray Brown *Don't Forget The Blues* (1985), *TNT: Grady Tate Sings* (1993).

Tatum, Art

b. 13 October 1909, Toledo, Ohio, USA, d. 5 November 1956. Born into a musical family, Tatum was handicapped from birth by impaired sight. Blind in one eye and only partially sighted in the other, he nevertheless studied piano formally and learned to read music. By his mid-teens he was playing professionally in Toledo. He played briefly in the Speed Webb band, but was mostly active as a soloist or in small groups working in clubs and playing on radio. He was heard by singer Adelaide Hall, who took him on the road as her accompanist. With Hall he travelled to New York in 1932 and the following year made his first recordings. He spent the next few years playing clubs in Cleveland and Chicago but in 1937 was back in New York, where his playing in clubs, on radio and on record established his reputation as a major figure in jazz circles. He toured the USA and also played in the UK. In the early 40s he formed a trio with bassist Slam Stewart and guitarist Tiny Grimes which became extremely popular. For the next decade Tatum toured extensively, performing throughout North America. In the early 50s he was signed by Norman Granz who recorded him in a series of remarkable performances, both as soloist (*The Solo Masterpieces*) and in a small group context with Benny Carter, Buddy De Franco, Roy Eldridge, Lionel Hampton, Ben Webster and others (*The Group Masterpieces*). A matchless virtuoso performer, Tatum's impact on the New York jazz scene in the early 30s had extensive repercussions. Even Fats Waller, an acknowledged master and someone Tatum had listened to on record in his own formative years, was aware of the phenomenal talent of the newcomer, reputedly declaring onstage - when he spotted Tatum in the audience - 'God is in the house tonight'.

Tatum's dazzling extemporizations on themes from jazz and the classics but mostly from the popular song book, became bywords and set standards few of his successors matched and none surpassed. Capable of breathtaking runs, interspersed with striking single notes and sometimes unexpected chords, he developed a unique solo style. His powerful left-hand figures tipped a hat in the direction of stride whilst he simultaneously explored the limits of an orthodox keyboard like no other pianist in jazz (and few elsewhere). A playful habit of quoting from other melodies, a technique which in unskilled hands can be merely irritating, was developed into a singular stylistic device. Unlike some virtuoso performers, Tatum never sacrificed feeling and swing for effect. Although he continued to develop throughout his career, it is hard to discover any recorded evidence that he was never poised and polished. His prodigious talent allowed him to achieve extraordinary recording successes: his solo sessions for Granz were mostly completed in two days - 69 tracks, all but three needing only one take. Ray Spencer, whose studies of the artist are extensive, has commented that Tatum achieved such a remarkable work rate through constant 'refining and honing down after each performance until an ideal version remained needing no further adjustments'. While this is clearly so, Tatum's performances never suggest a man merely going through the motions. Everything he did was fresh and vital, as if minted especially for the occasion in hand. Although he remains a major figure in jazz piano, Tatum is often overlooked in the cataloguing of those who affected the course of the music. He appears to stand to one side of the developing thrust of jazz, yet his creativity and the manner in which he explored harmonic complexities and unusual chord sequences influenced many musicians, including Bud Powell and Herbie Hancock, and especially non-pianists, amongst whom can be listed Charlie Parker and John Coltrane. The word genius is often used carelessly but, in assessing Tatum and the manner in which he transformed ideas and the imagined limitations of the piano in jazz, it is hard to think of a word that is more appropriate.

Selected compilations: *The Chronological Art Tatum* (1932-34), *The Chronological Art Tatum* (1934-40), *Pure Genius* (1934-45), *The Standard Sessions* (1935-43), *Get Happy!* (1938-39), *Pieces Of Eight* (1939-55), with Les Paul *Together* (early 40s), *The Complete Trio Sessions With Tiny Grimes And Slam Stewart Vols 1 & 2* (1944), *Moods* (1944-55), *Pieces Of Eight* (1945-55), *Art Tatum* (1949), *The Complete Capitol Recordings* (1949-52), *Art Tatum At The Piano Vols 1 & 2* (50s), *Art Tatum Piano Discoveries* (1950-55), *Piano Solo* (1952), *Piano Solo Private Sessions* (1952), *The Complete Pablo Solo Masterpieces* (Pablo 1953-56), with Roy Eldridge, Ben Webster and others *The Tatum Group Masterpieces* (1954-56), *Lasting Impressions* (1955-56), *Presenting The Art Tatum Trio* (1956), *Art Tatum On The Air* (Aircheck 1978), *Tatum Group Masterpices Vols 1-9* (Pablo 1978), *Tatum Solo Masterpieces Vols 1-12* (Pablo 1978), *The V Discs* (Black Lion 1979, 1944-46 recordings), *20th Century Piano Genius* (Emarcy 1987), *Complete Art Tatum Vols 1* and *2* (Capitol 1990), *Complete Brunswick And Decca Sessions 1932-41* (Affinity 1993).

Further reading: *Art Tatum: A Guide To His Recorded Music*, Arnold Laubich and Ray Spencer.

Taylor, Art

b. 6 April 1929, New York City, New York, USA, d. 1995. As a teenager Taylor played drums with Sonny Rollins, Howard McGhee and other young bop musicians in New York. In the early 50s he was also to be heard in mainstream groups, playing with Coleman Hawkins and Buddy De Franco. He continued to play with leading beboppers, including Bud Powell, and later in the decade was with Miles Davis and John Coltrane. From time to time he led his own bands, and toured the USA and Europe with several groups. He became resident in Europe in the early 60s, playing with visiting fellow Americans including Dexter Gordon and Johnny Griffin. During this period, Taylor began recording interviews with musicians, the results of which, often acutely angled towards the racial and political circumstances surrounding jazz, were first published in 1977 under the title *Notes And Tones*. In the mid-80s Taylor returned to the USA and hosted a radio show. Albums: *Taylor's Wailers* (Original Jazz Classics 1957), with Gene Ammons *Groove Blues* (1958), with John Coltrane *Soultrane* (1958), *Taylor's Tenors* (1959), with Coltrane *Giant Steps* (1959), *A.T.'s Delight* (Blue Note 1960), with Dexter Gordon *A Day In Copenhagen* (1969), *Mr A. T.* (Enja 1992), *Wailin' At The Vanguard* (Verve 1993).

Further reading: *Notes And Tones*, Arthur Taylor.

Taylor, Billy

b. 21 July 1921, Greenville, North Carolina, USA. After extensive formal studies, Taylor began playing piano with numerous leading jazzmen of the late swing era/early bebop period. These included Ben Webster, Dizzy Gillespie, Stuff Smith and Charlie Parker. By the early 50s Taylor's high reputation led to his being hired as house pianist at Birdland. His main contribution to jazz in the 50s was as leader of a trio, usually in New

York, which continued more or less non-stop for the next three decades. He also appeared regularly on radio and television both as a performer and a presenter of programmes. During recent years he has developed an abiding interest in jazz education, writing piano tutors and forming Jazzmobile, the Harlem-based concert group. Taylor has frequently played and composed music which fuses jazz with the classical form. Among these works are his 'Suite For Jazz Piano And Orchestra', composed in 1973, and 'Homage', a chamber music piece first performed by the Billy Taylor Trio and the Juilliard String Quartet in 1990. An inventive and technically facile player, Taylor's dedication to the development of interest in jazz in the community has sometimes led the wider audience to overlook his undoubted skills. (This artist should not be confused with either Billy Taylor Snr. or Billy Taylor Jnr., father and son bass players.)

Selected albums: *Piano Panorama* (1951), *The Billy Taylor Sextet* (1952), *Jazz At Storyville* (1952), *The Billy Taylor Trio* i (1952), *The Billy Taylor Trio* ii (1953), *The Billy Taylor Trio* iii (1954), *The Billy Taylor Trio With Candido* (Original Jazz Classics 1954), *Cross-Section* (Original Jazz Classics 1954), *Billy Taylor At Town Hall* (1954), *A Touch Of Taylor* (1955), *Billy Taylor* i (1956), *Billy Taylor* ii (1956), *The Billy Taylor Quartet* i (1956), *Billy Taylor At The London House* (1956), *My Fair Lady Loves Jazz* (1957), *Taylor Made Jazz* (1957), *The Billy Taylor Trio* iv (1957), *One For Fun* (1959), *Billy Taylor And Four Flutes* (Original Jazz Classics 1959), *Billy Uptown* (1960), *Warming Up* (1960), *Interlude* (1961), *Billy Taylor With Jimmy Jones And His Orchestra* (1961), *The Billy Taylor Quartet* ii (1962), *The Billy Taylor Septet* (1963), *Billy Taylor With Oliver Nelson's Orchestra* i (1963), *Billy Taylor With Oliver Nelson's Orchestra* ii (1963), *Billy Taylor And His Orchestra* i (1964), *Billy Taylor Today/A Sleeping Bee* (1969), *Billy Taylor And His Orchestra* ii (c.1970), *Live At Storyville* (1977), *Where've You Been?* (1980), *You Tempt Me* (Taylor Made 1985), *White Night And Jazz In Leningrad* (Taylor Made 1988), *Solo* (Taylor Made 1989), *Billy Taylor And The Jazzmobile All Stars* (Taylor Made 1989), *Dr T* (GRP 1993).

Taylor, Cecil

b. 15 March 1929, New York City, New York, USA. A towering figure in post-war *avant garde* jazz, Taylor has been hailed as the greatest piano virtuoso of the 20th century because of the phenomenal power, speed and intensity of his playing. 'We in black music think of the piano as a percussive instrument,' he told writer John Litweiler: 'we beat the keyboard, we get inside the instrument. . . the physical force going into the making of black music - if that is misunderstood, it leads to screaming. . .' Taylor grew up in Long Island, studying piano from the age of five and percussion (with a classical tutor) soon afterwards. He attended the New York College of Music and the New England Conservatory in Boston, though he later claimed he had learned more by listening to Duke Ellington records. Despite an early interest in European classical composers, especially Stravinsky, Taylor's major influences come from the jazz tradition, notably big band leaders such as Ellington, drum-

mers Sonny Greer and Chick Webb and a lineage of pianists that runs through Fats Waller, Erroll Garner, Thelonious Monk and Horace Silver. Although his first gigs were with swing era veterans Hot Lips Page, Johnny Hodges and Lawrence Brown, by the mid-50s Taylor was leading his own small groups and laying the basis for a musical revolution that is still in progress. His early associates included Buell Neidlinger, Dennis Charles, Steve Lacy and Archie Shepp (plus a fairly disastrous one-off encounter with John Coltrane) and his first recordings still bore a discernible, if carefully distanced, relationship to the jazz mainstream. By the early 60s, working with Sunny Murray, Alan Silva and his longest-serving colleague, Jimmy Lyons, Taylor's music had shed all direct reference to tonality and regular time-keeping and sounded almost purely abstract. However, the arrival of Ornette Coleman in New York in 1959, playing his own version of 'free jazz', rather overshadowed all other innovators and Taylor's more radical and complex music was largely ignored by the press and public, although a handful of fellow pioneers - the best-known of whom was Albert Ayler - embraced it enthusiastically. (Another admirer was Gil Evans, whose *Into The Hot* actually comprised one side of music by Taylor and one side by Johnny Carisi: Evans himself is not on the album!) Taylor lived in poverty for much of the 60s, even working as a dishwasher on occasion; but gradually his influence began to permeate the scene, particularly after Blue Note Records released two outstanding 1966 sessions. Both featured his regular partners Lyons, Silva, Andrew Cyrille and Henry Grimes: in addition, *Unit Structures* had Ken McIntyre and trumpeter Eddie Gale Stevens and *Conquistador!* had Bill Dixon (with whom Taylor had worked in the Jazz Composers' Guild). In 1968 Taylor made an album with the Jazz Composers' Orchestra and a 1969 concert with a new group of Lyons, Cyrille and Sam Rivers was released on the French label Shandar; but recording opportunities remained scarce. In the early 70s he became involved in education, teaching at Wisconsin University and colleges in Ohio and New Jersey; in 1973 he briefly ran his own label, Unit Core, releasing *Indents (Mysteries)* and *Spring Of Two Blue-Js*. Finally, the trickle of other releases - on Trio in Japan, on Arista's Freedom label in the USA, on Enja in Europe - began to gather momentum and by the early 80s Taylor was recording regularly for the European Soul Note and Hat Hut labels, while later in the decade Leo Records and FMP also championed his work. During this period his ensembles included Lyons (always), Cyrille (often), Silva (occasionally) plus players such as Sirone, Ronald Shannon Jackson, violinist Ramsey Ameer, trumpeter Raphé Malik, Jerome Cooper, William Parker and percussionist Rashid Bakr: their characteristic sound was a torrential flood of full-tilt, densely-textured, swirling, churning, flying improvisation that could and usually did last for two to three hours without pause.

Taylor also recorded a series of stunning solo albums, notably *Fly! Fly! Fly! Fly! Fly!* and the live double-set *Garden,* which showed he was one of the most dazzling, dynamic pianists in jazz history, and released two memorable duo albums - *Embraced,* with Mary Lou Williams; *Historic Concerts,* with

Max Roach - that further enhanced his reputation. In 1985 the first recording of Taylor's big band music, *Winged Serpent (Sliding Quadrants)*, was released by Soul Note. In 1986 Jimmy Lyons died of lung cancer; Taylor lost both a close friend and his most dedicated musical collaborator. In 1987 he toured with a new Unit (Parker, Carlos Ward, Leroy Jenkins, Thurman Barker: three of their concerts were released by Leo the following year) but since then has worked mostly in a trio format, usually with Parker and Tony Oxley (sometimes calling themselves the Feel Trio). In 1988, FMP brought 20 European improvisers to Berlin for a month-long festival of concerts and workshops that featured Taylor. Several of these were later released in the lavishly-packaged, 11-CD box-set *Cecil Taylor In Berlin '88,* which comprised two discs of Taylor's big band music, one of a big band workshop, one solo concert, one trio set with Tristan Honsinger and Evan Parker, a duo with Derek Bailey and five discs of duos with drummers - Oxley, Günter Sommer, Paul Lovens, Han Bennink and Louis Moholo. The set was released to worldwide acclaim in the music press and sealed Taylor's standing as one of the four or five leading inno-vators in post-bebop jazz. Although he has few direct imitators, he has proved an inspiration to free players everywhere and in particular to many jazz pianists, from Alex Von Schlippenbach to Marilyn Crispell.

The tremendous energy and sweep of his music has fooled many listeners into believing it has no structural underpinning, but Ekkehard Jost, both in his book *Free Jazz* and in one of the several essays in the booklet that accompanies the FMP box-set, has identified certain formal elements that recur in Taylor's work. (There are also useful chapters on his music in John Litweiler's *The Freedom Principle* and Valerie Wilmer's *As Serious As Your Life,* plus a detailed account of his early career in A.B. Spellman's *Four Lives In The Bebop Business.* Taylor himself has always stressed the spiritual and mystical nature of African American music: 'It's about magic and capturing spir-its.') A devotee of dance from Baby Lawrence to contemporary ballet (he once remarked 'I try to imitate on the piano the leaps in space a dancer makes'), Taylor has worked extensively in this field, for example on projects with choreographers/dancers Dianne McIntyre and Mikhail Baryshnikov. A poet too, whose writings often adorn his album sleeves, Taylor's *Chinampus* had him half-reciting, half-chanting a selection of sound-poetry and accompanying himself on various percussion instruments. For many years he has been working on a book about 'method-ological concepts of black music', to be entitled *Mysteries.*

Albums: *Jazz Advance* (Blue Note 1956), with others *At Newport* (1957), *Hard Driving Jazz* (1958, reissued as John Coltrane *Coltrane Time*), *Looking Ahead!* (Original Jazz Classics 1959), *Love For Sale* (1959), *The World Of Cecil Taylor* (1960, reissued as *Air*), with Buell Neidlinger *New York City R&B* (1961, reissued as *Cell Walk For Celeste*), *Cecil Taylor All Stars Featuring Buell Neidlinger* (1961, reissued as *Jumpin' Punkins*), by Gil Evans *Into The Hot* (1961), *The Early Unit 1962* (1962), *Live At The Café Montmartre* (1963, reissued as *Innovations*), *Nefertiti The Beautiful One Has Come* (1963, reissued as *What's New*), *Charles Mingus/Cecil Taylor* (1965), *Unit Structures*

(1966) *Conquistador!* (1967), *Cecil Taylor* (1967, reissued as *Student Studies*), *Soundtrack Ferrari* (1967), *The Jazz Composers' Orchestra* (1968), *Nuits De La Foundation Maeght, Vols 1-3* (1969, reissued as *The Great Concert Of Cecil Taylor*), *Cecil Taylor Quartet In Europe* (1970), *J For Jazz Broadcasts Present Cecil Taylor* (1971), *Indent (Mysteries)* (Arista 1973, reissued as *Indent*), *Akisakila* (Konnex 1973), *Cecil Taylor Solo* (1973), *Spring Of Two Blue-Js* (1974), *Silent Tongues* (Arista 1975), *Dark To Themselves* (1976), *Air Above Mountains (Buildings Within)* (1977), with Mary Lou Williams *Embraced* (1978), *Cecil Taylor Unit* (New World 1978), *3 Phasis* (New World 1979), *Live In The Black Forest* (1979), *One Too Many Salty Swift And Not Goodbye* (Hat Art 1980, rec. 1978), *Spots Circles And Fantasy* (FMP 1979), *It Is In The Brewing Luminous* (Hat Art 1981), *Fly! Fly! Fly! Fly! Fly!* (1981), *Garden Part One* (Hat Art 1982), *Garden Part Two* (Hat Art 1982), *Praxis* (1982, rec. 1968), *Live In Willisau '83* (1983), *Calling It The 8th* (1983, rec. 1981), with Max Roach *Historic Concerts* (1984, rec. 1979), *Winged Serpent (Sliding Quadrants)* (Soul Note 1985), *The Eighth* (1986, rec. 1981), *For Olim* (Soul Note 1987), *Live In Bologna* (Leo 1988), *Live In Vienna* (Leo 1988), *Chinampus* (Leo 1988), *Tzotzil Mummers Tzotzil* (1989), *Cecil Taylor In Berlin '88* (1989, 11-CD box-set, most discs also available singly), *Erzulie Maketh Scent* (FMP 1989), *Pleistozaen Mit Wasser* (FMP 1989), *Leaf Palm Hand* (FMP 1989), *Regalia* (FMP 1989), *Remembrance* (FMP 1989), *Riobec* (FMP 1989), *The Hearth* (FMP 1989), *Legba Crossing* (FMP 1989), *Alms/Tiergarten* (FMP 1989), with Günter Sommer *In East Berlin* (1989), *Looking (The Feel Trio),* (FMP 1990), *In Florescence* (1990), with William Parker, Tony Oxley *Looking (Berlin Version) The Feel Trio* (1990), *Looking (Berlin Version) Corona* (1991), *Looking (Berlin Version) Solo* (1991), *Celebrated Blazons* (FMP 1991), *Double Holy House* (FMP 1991), with Art Ensemble Of Chicago *Thelonious Sphere Monk* (1991), *Olu Iwa* (Soul Note 1994, 1986 recording). Selected compilations: *In Transition* (1975, rec. 1955, 1959), with others *Masters Of The Modern Piano* (1976, rec. 1957), *The Complete Candid Recordings Of Cecil Taylor And Buell Neidlinger* (1989, rec. 1960-61, six-album box-set).

Further reading: *Black Music: Four Lives*, A.B. Spellman. *The Freedom Principle: Jazz After 1958*, John Litweiler.

Taylor, John

b. 25 September 1942, Manchester, England. A self-taught pianist, Taylor had established himself as one of the most respected British jazz pianists by the end of the 60s and has continued to consolidate his reputation ever since. He began his musical career with a dance band until 1964, when he moved to London, and began playing with other young lions of the time, such as John Surman, Alan Skidmore and Norma Winstone, whom he would later marry. He also worked with established stars like Marian Montgomery, Cleo Laine and John Dankworth. In the late 60s he began to lead his own trio and sextet with Kenny Wheeler, Chris Pyne, Stan Sulzmann, Chris Laurence and Tony Levin. He also played in Sulzmann's quartet, with Winstone in Edge Of Time and with Mike

Gibbs. He was a member of Surman's outstanding but short-lived Morning Glory with Terje Rypdal. His collaboration with Surman, which produced some of the most inventive and original jazz-based music of the 70s and 80s, has continued to the present. In the mid-70s he spent some time with the Ronnie Scott quintet. In 1977, with Wheeler and Winstone, he formed Azimuth (not to be confused with Azymuth), for which he writes most of the music. At the end of the decade he played with Jan Garbarek, Arild Andersen and Miroslav Vitous. He has also worked with Lee Konitz, John Warren, Graham Collier, and Harry Beckett. His rich, fluid playing, inspired in part by Bill Evans, is especially distinctive on ballads. He is also an accomplished composer, and credits Gibbs with being a fundamental influence on his writing. In the 90s Taylor continues to work with Azimuth, to play in a regular duo with Winstone and to lead his own trio, with Mick Hutton and Steve Argüelles.

Albums: *Pause And Think Again* (1971), with Michael Gibbs *Michael Gibbs* (1971), with John Surman *Morning Glory* (1973), *Fragment* (1974), with Azimuth *Azimuth* (ECM 1977), with Azimuth *Touchstone* (1979), with Azimuth *Depart* (1980), with Miroslav Vitous *Journey's End* (1982), with Kenny Wheeler *Double Double You* (1983), *Azimuth '85* (1985), with Stan Sulzmann *Everybody's Song But My Own* (1987), with Lee Konitz *Songs Of The Stars* (1988), *Blue Glass* (Jazz House 1992), with Surman *Ambleside Days* (Ah Um 1992).

Taylor, Martin

b. 1956, England. Repeatedly referred to as 'the guitarists' guitarist', Taylor shows an extraordinary flair and natural feel for his instrument, that has enabled him to make subtle and profound contributions in a number of different musical styles, and has resulted in a keen and loyal international audience that makes its presence felt on each Taylor tour. An early starter at the age of four, he was playing his first professional performance (in a Harlow, Hertfordshire, music shop) at eight, and displaying his genuinely prodigious talent in trad and mainstream bands led by Sonny Dee and Lenny Hastings by 1968. Turning professional at the first opportunity three years later, Taylor spent much of the 70s honing his talents in swing bands and cafe residencies, and enjoying the occasional opportunity to sit in with and impress visiting Americans, including Count Basie (whom he met on a cruise ship) and Barney Kessel. His first album, a duo with bassist Peter Ind, was released on Ind's Wave label in 1978, and a year later he established his celebrated and continuing relationship with the legendary swing violinist Stéphane Grappelli, touring internationally, recording with Grappelli and classical violin virtuoso Yehudi Menuhin and broadcasting live on the BBC with Grappelli and popular composer Julian Lloyd Webber. Touring with Grappelli, whose previous guitar partners had included the brilliant Django Reinhardt and Joe Pass, helped introduce Taylor's talents to a wider audience, and appearances during 1981 at Carnegie Hall, the Hollywood Bowl, the Royal Opera House and on

Martin Taylor

Johnny Carson's *Tonight Show* marked the beginning of a busy decade – as Taylor concurrently worked at perfecting his solo style while in the UK, and continued to steadily build a solid reputation amongst America's jazz musicians, touring with guitarist Emily Remler, and recording with Toots Thielemans, Buddy De Franco (their album *Groovin'* was voted Jazz Album of the Year by the British Music Retailers Association), Paulinho De Costa and John Patitucci, Chet Atkins, and finally replacing Herb Ellis in the Great Guitars trio with Charlie Byrd and Barney Kessel. Since 1990, Taylor has been touring increasingly under his own name, playing sell-out dates and televised concerts in Australia, Hong Kong and Israel, and enjoying greater recognition in the UK, partly as a result of a fruitful relationship with Linn Records. His 1993 *Artistry* was the culmination of years spent developing a 'complete' solo style. Performing on a custom-made 'stereo guitar' that separates the bass and treble strings into different channels, Taylor accompanies his own swinging improvisations with chords and walking bass lines, providing a record of the kind of performance that has left so many guitarists stunned in recent years. Selected albums: *Taylor Made* (Wave 1978), with Stéphane Grappelli *At The Winery* (1980), with Grappelli, Yehudi Menuhin *Strictly For The Birds* (1980), with Grappelli, Menuhin *Top Hat* (1981), *Skye Boat* (Concord 1981), with Grappelli *Vintage '81* (1981), with Grappelli *Live In San Francisco* (1982), *A Tribute To Art Tatum* (1984), with Buddy De Franco *Groovin'* (1985), *Innovations* (1985), *Sarabanda* (Gala 1986), with Vassar Clements *Together At Last* (1987), *Don't Fret* (Linn 1990), *Matter Of Time* (1991), *Change Of Heart* (Linn 1991), *Artistry* (Linn 1993), with Grappelli *Reunion* (1993), *Spirit Of Django* (Linn 1994).

Tchicai, John Martin

b. 28 April 1936, Copenhagen, Denmark. Tchicai, the son of a Danish mother and Congolese father, was the only major non-American figure in the free jazz movement of the early 60s. He had studied violin at first, but then took up alto saxophone and clarinet. Since 1983 he has switched primarily to tenor saxophone. He spent three years at the Aarhus Academy of Music and then moved to the Copenhagen Academy. In 1962 he met Albert Ayler during Ayler's stay in Copenhagen, led his own band at the World Youth Jazz Festival in Helsinki, and worked with Jorgen Leth's quintet at the Warsaw Jazz Festival. As a result of his meeting in Helsinki with Archie Shepp and Bill Dixon he moved to New York in 1963 and joined the New York Contemporary Five, which included Shepp, Dixon (later replaced by Don Cherry for a tour of Europe), Don Moore and J.C. Moses. On his return to New York he founded the New York Art Quartet with Roswell Rudd, Milford Graves and Lewis Worrell (or sometimes Steve Swallow or Eddie Gomez) on bass. He also joined the Jazz Composers' Guild and worked with the Jazz Composers' Orchestra and Carla Bley. In 1965 he took part in John Coltrane's controversial and epoch-making *Ascension*. On returning to Europe in 1966 he played with Gunter Hampel and Cherry as well as leading groups of his own, including

Cadentia Nova Danica. CND was an extremely impressive nine-piece band which grew, reaching 26 pieces for its second recording, and finally split, some of its members forming the rock band Burning Red Ivanhoe. In the 70s he worked often with Johnny Dyani, who had emigrated to Denmark, and with the Strange Brothers (1976- 81), the Instant Composers Pool, George Gruntz and Irène Schweizer. In the early 80s he played with Pierre Dørge, the New Jungle Orchestra, Chris McGregor's Brotherhood Of Breath (*Yes, Please*), De Zes Winden (an all-saxophone group) and, again, Dyani, with whom he was touring at the time of the bassist's death. An impressive and personal improviser, he was a lyrical altoist with a rich tone, and his sound is equally distinctive since moving over to tenor. He also plays soprano sax and bass clarinet and has essayed occasional vocals and synthesizer programming on some recent sessions.

Selected albums: with Archie Shepp *Rufus* (1964), with the New York Contemporary Five *Consequences* (1964), *New York Eye And Ear Control* (1964), *New York Contemporary Five Vols. 1 & 2* (1964), with Shepp *Four For Trane* (1964), *New York Art Quartet* (1965), with the New York Art Quartet *Mohawk* (1965), with John Coltrane *Ascension* (1965), *John Tchicai And Cadentia Nova Danica* (Freedom 1969), with CND *Afrodisiaca* (1970), with Irène Schweizer *Willi The Pig* (1976), *Real Tchicai* (1977), with Strange Brothers *Darktown Highlights* (Storyville 1977), *Solo* (1977), *John Tchicai And Strange Brothers* (1978), with Andre Goudbeck *Duets* (1978), with Goudbeck *Barefoot Dance* (1979), with Hartmut Geerken *Continent* (Praxis 1981), *Live In Athens* (Praxis 1981), with Strange Brothers *Merlin Vibrations* (1983), *Put Up The Fight* (Storyville 1987), *Timo's Message* (Black Saint 1987, rec. 1984), *Clinch* (1991), with Vitold Rek *Satisfaction* (Enja 1992).

Teagarden, Charlie

b. 19 July 1913, Vernon, Texas, USA, d. 10 December 1984. A trumpet-playing member of the prodigious Teagarden family, Charlie played in several territory bands during the 20s. At the end of the decade he was in Ben Pollack's band and during the 30s played in bands led by Red Nichols, Paul Whiteman and others. In the 40s he was with Harry James and, most fruitfully, Jimmy Dorsey. Throughout these years he regularly played and recorded with his brother Jack Teagarden. In the 50s he mingled studio work in Hollywood with appearances in the Bob Crosby band and eventually settled in Las Vegas, playing in casino and hotel bands. A rich-toned trumpeter, with a joyous ring to everything he played, Little T's career was inevitably, if rather unfairly, overshadowed by that of his famous brother. He died in 1984.

Albums: with Jimmy Dorsey *Dorseyland Band* (1950), *Big Horn* (1962).

Teagarden, Jack

b. Weldon L. Teagarden, 29 August 1905, Vernon, Texas, USA, d. 15 January 1964. One of the giants of jazz, Teagarden began playing trombone and singing in and around his home town, encouraged by his mother, Helen Teagarden, a pianist.

From his early teens he was playing professionally, touring with various bands, notably that led by Peck Kelley. He continued to gain experience with a number of bands, his reputation spreading ahead of him until, by the time he reached New York City in the late 20s, he was ready for the big time. He joined Ben Pollack in 1928 and through his work with this band, and numerous record dates, he frightened just about every other trombone player in the country into either changing their approach or contemplating premature retirement. He recorded extensively with small bands and with Paul Whiteman, and appeared frequently on radio, sometimes forming his own small groups. An attempt at leading a big band was doomed to failure, due in part to Teagarden's casual and unbusinesslike manner and also to his fondness for drink. In 1946 he became a member of Louis Armstrong's All Stars, touring extensively and reaching audiences who had long idolized him through his recordings. In 1951 he left Armstrong to form his own band. During the remainder of his life he led small groups, some of which included his brother and sister, Charlie and Norma Teagarden. He was also co-leader with Earl Hines of an all-star band, which included Peanuts Hucko, Cozy Cole and Max Kaminsky. The ceaseless touring and drinking weakened him and he died suddenly on 15 January 1964.

Teagarden's trombone playing was smooth and stylish and quite unlike any player before him. Although his consummate skill affected the playing of numerous other trombone players, Teagarden's style was not really developed by his successors. When he played the blues he was much closer to the work of black musicians than any other white musician of his generation. His relaxed sound concealed a thorough command of his instrument and in retrospect it is easy to understand the fear he inspired in musicians like Glenn Miller and Bill Rank. A pointer to the awe with which he was regarded in the profession is the fact that even Tommy Dorsey, himself one of the most technically distinguished trombonists in jazz, refused to play a solo when he found himself on a record date with Teagarden. Heavily influenced by the black blues singers he heard as a child in Texas, Teagarden was also a remarkable singer. He sang in a sleepy drawl and formed a significant bridge in popular music, linking the blues to the white crooning style of Bing Crosby. Despite the success of his blues singing, his later performances with Armstrong inclined more towards the humour and easy-going charm which reflected his personality. Thanks to a succession of definitive recordings, on which he ably demonstrated his superlative trombone technique and lazy vocal charm, Teagarden made many songs his own. These include 'I'm Coming Virginia', 'If I Could Be With You One Hour Tonight', 'Aunt Hagar's Blues', 'The Sheik Of Araby' and, especially, 'Stars Fell On Alabama' and 'Basin Street Blues'.

Selected albums: with Louis Armstrong *Town Hall Concert Plus* (1947), with Armstrong *Satchmo At Symphony Hall* (1949), *Jack Teagarden In San Francisco* (1953), *Meet Me Where They Play The Blues* (1954), *Hangover Club, San Francisco, 1954* (1954), *Jack Teagarden And His Sextet* i (1954), *Jack Teagarden With Herb Geller's Orchestra* (1956), *Jack Teagarden With Van Alexander's Orchestra* (1956), *Jack Teagarden And His Sextet* ii (1957), *The Jack Teagarden-Earl Hines All Stars In England* (1957), *The Jack Teagarden-Earl Hines All Stars At The Olympia Theatre, Paris* (1957), *Jack Teagarden* i (1958), *Jack Teagarden* ii (1958), *Jack Teagarden And His Dixieland Band* (1958), *Jack Teagarden And His Sextet* iii (1959), *Jack Teagarden And His Orchestra* i (1961), *Jack Teagarden And His Orchestra* ii (1961), *Jack Teagarden With Russ Case And Bob Brookmeyer's Orchestra* (1962), *Jack Teagarden On Okinawa* (1959), *Jack Teagarden!!!* (1962), *The Jack Teagarden Sextet In Person* (1963), *Hollywood Bowl Concert* (1963). Compilations: *King Of The Blues Trombone* (1928-40), *I Gotta Right To Sing The Blues* (Queendisc 1981, 1929-34 recordings), *T 'N' T* (1933-34), *Jack Teagarden On The Air* (1936-38), *Jack Teagarden And His Orchestra* iii (1939), *Jack Teagarden's Big Eight* (1940), *Big Band Gems* (1940-41), *Big T And The Condon Gang* (1944), with Armstrong *Satchmo Meets Big Tea* (1944-58), *Jack Teagarden And His Sextet* iv (1947), *Big T's Jazz* (1947-55), *The Swingin' Gate* (1960-63), *Varsity Sides* (RCA 1987), *A Hundred Years From Today* (Happy Days 1989, 1931-34 recordings), *That's A Serious Thing* (RCA 1990).

Further reading: *Jack Teagarden: A Jazz Maverick*, Jay D. Smith and Len Guttridge.

Temperley, Joe

b. 20 September 1929, Cowdenbeath, Scotland. After taking a few lessons on alto saxophone, Temperley began gigging at clubs in Glasgow. When he was 20 he joined the Tommy Sampson band, returning with them to London. He then worked with Harry Parry, Joe Loss, Jack Parnell, Tony Crombie and others, and during this period began playing tenor saxophone. A mid-50s stint with Tommy Whittle brought a further change of instrument, this time onto baritone saxophone. He then joined Humphrey Lyttelton, in whose band he remained for seven years. It was while he was with Lyttelton that he made his first big impression on the international jazz scene and in 1965 he settled in the USA, playing in the bands of Woody Herman, Buddy Rich, Buck Clayton, Duke Pearson and the Thad Jones-Mel Lewis Jazz Orchestra. During the 70s he played in Clark Terry's band and in the Duke Ellington orchestra, which was continuing under the direction of Mercer Ellington. From the late-70s onwards he freelanced, mainly in New York City, but also finding time for touring and recording with several musicians, including Jimmy Knepper, Kathy Stobart and Scott Hamilton. A major saxophonist and one of the outstanding baritone players in jazz, Temperley plays with an enviable sonority, bringing wit and imagination to his solos. The fluidity of his playing shows that in skilled hands this most demanding of instruments is capable not only of power and drive but also of warmth and moving tenderness.

Albums: with Humphrey Lyttelton *Humph Plays Standards* (1960), *Le Vrai Buck Clayton* (1964), with Clark Terry *Live On 57th Street* (1970), with Mercer Ellington *Continuum* (1974-5), with Jimmy Knepper *Just Friends* (Hep 1978), *Nightingale* (Hep 1993).

Art Themen

Terry, Clark

b. 14 December 1920, St. Louis, Missouri, USA. Terry gained invaluable experience playing trumpet in local bands, but developed his remarkable technique while in the US Navy. As he recalled for jazz writer Steve Voce, he practised using a clarinet book, preferring the more fluid sound this generated in his playing. After his military service he joined Charlie Barnet, then became a mainstay of the Count Basie band for three years until 1951, when he joined Duke Ellington for an eight-year stint. At the end of the 50s he went into studio work in New York City, becoming one of the first black musicians to be regularly employed in this way. For a dozen years he was featured in the Doc Severinson band, which played on the Johnny Carson television show. During this time he continued to play in jazz groups for club and record dates, working with Bob Brookmeyer, J.J. Johnson and others, and also leading his own 'Big B-A-D Band', which featured many leading New York session men. During the 70s Terry began playing flügelhorn, eventually making this his principal instrument. The 70s and 80s found him touring extensively, playing concerts, clubs and festivals around the world, usually as leader but ably blending in with almost any background from late swing style to post-bop. Terry's remarkable technical accomplishment has never overwhelmed the depth of emotion which imbues his playing, and neither of these characteristics has ever dampened his infectious humour. This quality is most readily apparent on his singing of 'Mumbles', for which he created a unique variation on scat. His duets with himself, during which he plays flügelhorn and trumpet, are remarkable displays of his astonishing skills yet never degenerate into mere bravura exercises. Terry remains a major figure in the history of jazz trumpet and is one of the music's most respected and widely-admired ambassadors.

Selected albums: *Introducing Clark Terry* (1955), *Swahili* (1955), with Duke Ellington *A Drum Is A Woman* (1956), *Serenade To A Bus Seat* (Original Jazz Classics 1957), *Duke With A Difference* (Original Jazz Classics 1957), *Out On A Limb* (1957), *In Orbit* (Original Jazz Classics 1958), *Top And Bottom Brass* (1959), *Clark Terry* (1960), *Color Changes* (Candid 1960), *Everything's Mellow* (1961), *The Night Life* (1962), *Three In Jazz* (1963), *Tread Ye Lightly* (1963), *What Makes Sammy Swing* (1963), *More* (1963), with Bob Brookmeyer *Tonight* (1964), *The Happy Horns Of Clark Terry* (1964), *Mumbles* (1965), *The Power Of Positive Swinging* (1965), *Gingerbread Men* (1966), *Spanish Rice* (1966), *It's What's Happenin'* (1967), *Clark Terry At The Montreux Jazz Festival* (1969), *Big B.A.D. Band Live On 57th Street* (1970), *Big B.A.D. Band Live at The Wichita Jazz Festival* (Vanguard 1974), *Clark Terry And His Jolly Giants* (1975), *Professor Jive* (1976), *Wham! Live At The Lighthouse* (1976), *Big B. A. D. Band Live At Buddy's Place* (Vanguard 1976), *Clark After Dark* (1977), *The Globetrotter* (1977), *Funk Dumplin's* (1978), *Clark Terry's Big Band In Warsaw* (1978), *Out Of Nowhere* (1978), *Brahms Lullaby* (1978), *Mother...! Mother...!* (1979), *Ain't Misbehavin'* (Pablo 1979), *Clark Terry At Buffalo State* (1979), *Memories Of Duke* (Original Jazz Classics 1980), *'Yes, The Blues'*

(1981), with Red Mitchell *To Duke And Basie* (1986), *Take Double* (1986), with Mitchell *Jive At Five* (Enja 1988), *Portraits* (Chesky 1988), *The Clark Terry Spacemen* (1989), with Oliver Jones *Just Friends* (1989), *Live At The Village Gate* (Chesky 1990), *Having Fun* (Delos 1991).

Teschemacher, Frank

b. 13 March 1906, Kansas City, Missouri, USA, d. 1 March 1932. Raised in Chicago, Teschemacher first took up violin then played various other instruments before settling on alto saxophone. He played with many of the young emergent Chicagoans, including Jimmy McPartland, making many jazz records while playing in dance bands for a living. In 1925 he began playing clarinet, the instrument on which he made his greatest mark. In the late 20s he played in the bands of Ben Pollack, Ted Lewis and Red Nichols, but continued to work in numerous minor groups. At the end of the 20s he resumed playing alto and violin and also occasionally played cornet. Although he appeared on many fine jazz recordings with Red McKenzie, Eddie Condon and others, usually on clarinet, his contributions here rarely support the enormously high regard in which he was held by his fellow musicians. Shortly after he joined a new band formed by Wild Bill Davison he was killed in a road accident in March 1932, just a few days short of his 26th birthday.

Compilation: with various leaders *Chicago Jazz Vol. 1* (1928-30).

Themen, Art

b. 26 November 1939, Manchester, England. A self-taught musician, Themen played tenor saxophone with a university jazz band while studying medicine at Cambridge. After qualifying as a doctor, he moved to London and in the early 60s played in several blues and R&B bands and also worked in the backing groups for numerous pop sessions. During this period he worked with Alexis Korner, Phil Seamen, Dick Heckstall-Smith, Rod Stewart, Joe Cocker and Long John Baldry. In the late 60s and early 70s his musical direction shifted towards jazz and he played with Barbara Thompson, Michael Garrick, Henry Lowther and Graham Collier. In 1974 he began a long and particularly fruitful association with Stan Tracey, which has continued into the 90s. He has also accompanied numerous visiting US jazzmen, including Al Haig, Red Rodney, George Coleman and Nat Adderley. A highly individual playing style marks Themen's performances and had he chosen to adopt music as a full-time career he would have doubtless been an international artist of considerable stature. That he has achieved his present high standing in the jazz world while at the same time pursuing his medical career as a consultant surgeon, is testimony to his remarkable gifts.

Albums: with Stan Tracey *Under Milk Wood* (1976), with Al Haig *Expressly Ellington* (1978), with Tracey *Spectrum* (1982), *Stan Tracey's Hexad Live At Ronnie Scott's* (1985).

Thielemans, Toots

b. Jean Baptiste Thielemans, 29 April 1922, Brussels, Belgium.

Toots Thielemans

A child prodigy, Thielemans played the accordion at the age of three (a home-made version; a real one would have considerably outweighed him), switching to harmonica in his mid-teens. A few years later he added the guitar to his instrumental roll-call and also became an accomplished whistler. The guitar apart, Thielemans's chosen instruments were not especially suited to jazz, but he displayed enough invention and assurance to be hired by Benny Goodman for a European tour in 1950 and by George Shearing in 1953 for a spell which lasted over five years. In the 60s his popularity increased with a successful recording of his own composition 'Bluesette', and he worked frequently in clubs in Europe and the USA and at international festivals. His activity continued throughout the following two decades and he played with leading artists such as Oscar Peterson and Dizzy Gillespie. He has also played on the soundtracks of many films. Most distinctive on harmonica, Thielemans has gone far to correcting the prejudice felt by many jazz fans towards this instrument. A momentary shift in the late 80s into jazz-rock fusion was less than wholly successful; he remains happiest in a bop setting, while displaying a fine command of ballads on his many recordings. Whilst the harmonica has only limited appeal in a jazz setting, Thielemans has made the genre his own.

Selected albums: *Man Bites Harmonica* (Original Jazz Classics 1957), with George Shearing *On Stage!* (1958), *Toots Thielemans And His Orchestra* (1958), *The Toots Thielemans Quartet* i (1959), *Toots Thielemans With Kurt Edelhagen And His Orchestra* (1960), *The Toots Thielemans Quartet* ii (1960), *The Toots Thielemans Quartet* iii (1961), *The Toots Thielemans Trio* (1961), *Toots Thielemans And Arne Domnerus* (1961), *Toots Thielemans And Dick Hyman* (1962), *Toots Thielemans* i (1965), *Contrasts* (c.1967), *Toots Thielemans With Herbie Hancock* (1968), *Toots Thielemans With Orchestra* (1969, overdubbed), *A Taste Of Toots* (1970), *Toots Thielemans* ii (1972), *Live* (1974), *Toots Thielemans And Friends* (1974), *Toots Thielemans Captured Alive* (Polydor 1974), *The Oscar Peterson Big Six At Montreux* (1975), *Live Two* (1975), *Old Friends* (1976), *Live Three* (1976), *Toots Thielemans* iii (1978), *Slow Motion* (c.1979), *Apple Dimple* (Denon 1979), *Live In The Netherlands* (1980), *Dizzy Gillespie At Montreux* (1980), *Jean 'Toots' Thielemans Live!* (1981), *Nice To Meet You* (c.1981), *Your Precious Love* (1985), *Just Friends* (Jazzline 1986), *Do Not Leave Me* (Stash 1986), *Only Trust Your Heart* (Concord 1988), *Footprints* (Emarcy 1989), *For My Lady* (Emarcy 1992), *The Brasil Project* (1992). Compilation: *The Silver Collection* (Polydor 1985).

Thigpen, Ed

b. 28 December 1930, Chicago, Illinois, USA. Following in the footsteps of his father Ben (who played drums with Andy Kirk for almost two decades), Thigpen began playing drums as a child. His first big-name engagement came in 1951 when he joined the Cootie Williams band. Later in the 50s he played with Johnny Hodges, Lennie Tristano, John Coltrane, Bud

Powell and most often with Billy Taylor. In the 60s he followed his Taylor stint with another long spell accompanying a noted pianist, this time Oscar Peterson. His sensitive playing style endeared him to singers and he accompanied Dinah Washington in the early 50s and Ella Fitzgerald in the late 60s and early 70s. In 1972 he settled in Scandinavia, playing with visitors such as Johnny Griffin and Art Farmer, and teaching in Copenhagen and Malmo. Thigpen's neat and contained style is ideally suited to a small group setting while his inquiring mind has caused him to introduce many unusual effects into his performances, drawing on Eastern musical traditions. He has written several manuals on drumming techniques and is a tireless educator.

Albums: with John Coltrane *Cattin'* (1957), *The Oscar Peterson Trio: Live From Chicago* (1961), *Out Of The Storm* (1966), with Johnny Griffin *Blues For Harvey* (1973), *Ed Thigpen's Action-Re-Action* (Sonet 1974), with Art Farmer *Manhattan* (1980), *Young Men And Olds* (Timeless 1989), *Easy Flight* (Reckless 1990), *Mr. Taste* (Justin Time 1992).

Thomas, Joe (saxophone)

b. Joseph Vankert Thomas, 19 June 1909, Uniontown, Pennsylvania, USA, d. 3 August 1986. After starting out on alto saxophone, on which instrument he played with Horace Henderson and others, Thomas switched to tenor saxophone. On this instrument he played with Stuff Smith in 1932 and then joined Jimmie Lunceford for a 14-year-long stay. Heavily featured as an instrumentalist and also as an occasional singer, he was one of several key figures in the band. On Lunceford's death Thomas co-led the band for a while but then formed his own small group. In the early 50s he dropped out of full-time music, but made sporadic appearances at festivals and on recording sessions into the late 70s. A forceful soloist, Thomas's playing steadily improved during his spell with Lunceford where the stern discipline exerted by section leader Willie Smith dramatically affected his work. NB. This musician should not be confused with several others of the same name in jazz, at least two of whom also play tenor saxophone: Joe Thomas (b. 23 December 1908), the brother of Walter 'Foots' Thomas, and Joe Thomas (b. 16 June 1933).

Album: *Raw Meat* (1979). Compilation: *The Complete Jimmie Lunceford* (1939-40).

Thomas, Joe (trumpet)

b. Joseph Lewis Thomas, 24 July 1909, Webster Groves, Missouri, USA, d. 6 August 1984. After playing trumpet in several obscure territory bands during the late 20s and early 30s, Thomas settled in New York City in 1933. There he played with the bands of Fletcher Henderson, Fats Waller, Willie Bryant and Benny Carter. At the start of the 40s he briefly led his own band, then worked with numerous other leaders, including James P. Johnson, Teddy Wilson, Barney Bigard, Roy Eldridge, Don Byas, Cozy Cole and Bud Freeman. He continued to play through succeeding decades, his appearances including a stint in the Fletcher Henderson Reunion band and engagements at Eddie Condon's club and with

Claude Hopkins and J.C. Higginbotham. He played into the 70s before ill-health prompted his retirement. A warm, full tone characterized Thomas's playing and the many small group recordings made during his career show a gifted instrumentalist with an inventive solo capacity.

Albums: with Henderson All Stars *Big Reunion* (1957), one side only *Mainstream* (1958). Selected compilations: *The Indispensable Fletcher Henderson* (1927-36 recordings), with Roy Eldridge *The Jazz Greats - Brass* (1944 recordings), *Don Byas - 1945* (1945 recordings), *Blowin' In From KC* (Uptown 1983, *Raw Meat* (Uptown 1983), *Jumping With Joe* (1987).

Thomas, Walter 'Foots'

b. 10 February 1907, Muskogee, Oklahoma, USA, d. 26 August 1981. Accomplished on most of the saxophone family, as well as clarinet and flute, Thomas played professionally while still at high school. In the late 20s he played with several important New York-based musicians, including Jelly Roll Morton and Luis Russell. At the end of the 20s he joined the Missourians, the band later fronted by Cab Calloway. During several years with Calloway he also wrote many of the band's most popular arrangements. In the early 40s he played with Don Redman and led his own bands, but by the end of the decade had stopped playing to concentrate on other aspects of the music business. He died in August 1981. His brother, Joe Thomas (b. 23 December 1908), was also a saxophonist.

Compilations: *The Most Important Recordings Of Cab Calloway* (1930-49 recordings), one side only *The Walter 'Foots' Thomas All Stars* (1944-45 recordings).

Thompson, 'Lucky'

b. Eli Thompson, 16 June 1924, Columbia, South Carolina, USA. Thompson's professional career began in the early 40s as a sideman in territory bands. After moving to New York in 1943 he played in the bands of Lionel Hampton, Don Redman, Billy Eckstine, Lucky Millinder and in 1944 joined Count Basie. On the west coast he recorded with Dizzy Gillespie and Charlie Parker, being hired by Gillespie for the famous engagement at Billy Berg's to help make up the numbers when Parker failed to turn up or was late. Indeed, Parker failed to show up for a record date with Ross Russell's Dial label and Thompson sat in. When Parker eventually made a date for Russell, this time with Miles Davis, Thompson was again present. Thompson played briefly with Boyd Raeburn and was also active in the studios. In 1946 he was a member of the Stars Of Swing, a co-operative band masterminded by Charles Mingus and Buddy Collette and which also featured Britt Woodman and John Anderson. This band lasted less than two months and unfortunately was never recorded. Back in New York at the end of the 40s, Thompson formed his own band and in the early 50s headlined at the Savoy Ballroom. After dabbling briefly in R&B he made several jazz albums with Oscar Pettiford, Milt Jackson and, notably, with Miles Davis on the famous Prestige session for which Davis hired Thompson, J.J. Johnson, Horace Silver, Percy Heath and Art Blakey and which resulted in superb performances of 'Walkin'' and 'Blue 'N' Boogie'. In 1956 he visited Europe, recording prodigiously in France under his own name and also touring with Stan Kenton. Thompson took a liking to Europe and resided there for several years in the late 50s/early 60s and again at the end of the 60s.

Between these two sojourns he played little, preferring life on a small farm in Michigan, and after his latest return from Europe in 1973 he taught for a while before retiring from music. Thompson's playing on tenor and soprano saxophone ably straddles the main strands favoured by musicians of his generation. Although identifiably influenced by Coleman Hawkins and Don Byas he had absorbed the stylistic departures of Lester Young and Charlie Parker. However, he possessed a fertile imagination and the characteristics of his playing were very much his own; indeed Thompson proved to be one of the most original and inventive saxophonists working in the post-bebop mainstream and his early retirement was a grievous loss to jazz. His departure from music was prompted by his growing dissatisfaction with the way in which musicians were treated by record companies, club owners, promoters and others in the business. He was especially dismayed by discriminatory practices he encountered from bigoted whites who were in positions of power and could control the careers of black musicians and his own relatively small legacy of recordings is probably not unconnected with the fact that he was never afraid to speak out when he felt injustice was being done.

Selected albums: *Lucky Thompson Featuring Oscar Pettiford* (1956), *Lucky Thompson & Gerard Pochonet Et Son Quartette* (1956), *Lucky Standards* (1956), *Lucky Thompson* (1963), *Lucky Thompson Plays Jerome Kern And No More* (1963), *Lucky Strikes* (Original Jazz Classics 1965), *Happy Days Are Here Again* (1965), *Lucky Thompson In Switzerland* (1969) *A Lucky Songbook In Europe* (1969), *I Offer You* (1973), *Brown Rose* (1985, rec. 1956). Compilations: *Dancing Sunbeam* (1975, rec. 1956), *Body And Soul* (1978, rec. 1970), *Paris 1956 Volume One* (1985, rec. 1956), *Illuminations* (1974), *Lucky Sessions* (Vogue 1993).

Thompson, Barbara

b. 27 July 1944, Oxford, England. Classically trained at the Royal College of Music in London, where she studied flute, clarinet, piano and composition between 1965 and 1968, Thompson had private tuition on the saxophone before joining Neil Ardley's New Jazz Orchestra in 1965, her first professional jazz gig. She performed and recorded intermittently with the National Jazz Orchestra until 1978, and met her future husband, drummer Jon Hiseman, while both were members of the band. From 1969, Thompson lead various groups of her own, working with musicians including John Dankworth, Don Rendell and Manfred Mann. In 1975 she formed the jazz-rock group Paraphernalia, which has been the main outlet for her compositional and performing skills. Mixing a range of musics as diverse as Sri Lankan folk tunes, English country music and modern jazz, Paraphernalia has toured extensively throughout Europe and performed at many of the continent's major jazz festivals. Away from Paraphernalia, Thompson has been a member of the United Rock And Jazz Ensemble since 1975, and an active session musician - performing on the albums of Andrew Lloyd Webber's *Variations*, *Cats* and *Requiem* - and from 1973-80 led a Latin-jazz outfit called Jubiaba. In 1988, her *Concert For Saxophone And Orchestra* was premiered in Germany; she has also written three long works for a 20-piece jazz orchestra. With Hiseman, she tours, she runs Temple Music, a music publishing company, and maintains a 24-track studio at their house in Surrey. Paraphernalia re-groups and tours occasionally, always to find a receptive following, especially in Germany where she is rightly appreciated.

Albums: *Barbara Thompson's Paraphernalia* (1978), *Jubiaba* (MCA 1978), *Wilde Tales* (MCA 1979), *Live In Concert* (1980), *Mother Earth* (Verabra 1983), *Ghosts* (1983), *Pure Fantasy* (TM 1984), *Shadowshow* (1984), *Heavenly Bodies* (Verabra 1986), *Lady Saxophone* (1986), *Special Edition* (Verabra 1987), *A Cry From The Heart* (Verabra 1987), *Breathless* (Verabra 1991), *Songs From The Center Of The Earth* (Black Sun 1991), *Everlasing Flame* (Verabra 1993).

Thompson, Butch

b.28 November 1943, Marine, Minnesota, USA. Thompson began playing piano as a child and in his late teens became a member of a popular New Orleans-style band in Minneapolis. The band regularly accompanied such leading New Orleans jazzmen as George Lewis, Kid Thomas and Pops Foster. Thompson also formed his own small group which worked extensively on radio, achieving considerable popularity. During the 70s Thompson began to tour internationally. He also worked with the New Orleans Ragtime Orchestra and his own band dedicated to the music of King Oliver. Thompson's dedication to a tradition that was vintage long before he was born, has ensured that an important strand of jazz piano history remains extant. A sparkling player in the idiom of New Orleans, Thompson regularly revives the music of Jelly Roll Morton, Oliver and other past masters. In recent years he has often worked with several unsung musicians with similarly dedicated concepts, including cornetist Charles DeVore and drummer Hal Smith.

Selected albums: *Kid Thomas At San Jacinto Hall* (1965), *A'Solas* (1981), *Echoes from Storyville* (1984), *Live From The Shattuck Hotel* (1985), *King Oliver's Centennial Band* (1988), *New Orleans Joys* (1989), *Chicago Breakdown* (1989), *Good Old New York* (1989), *Plays Favorites* (Solo Art 1993), *Minnesota Wonder* (Daring 1993).

Thompson, Charles, Sir

b. 12 March 1918, Springfield, Ohio, USA. After starting out on violin Thompson switched to piano and was playing professionally by his mid-teenage years. During the mid- to late 30s he played with several notable territory bands in the southwest, including that led by Nat Towles. In 1940 he was briefly with Lionel Hampton's big band but preferred small group work, although he regularly wrote arrangements for musicians including Count Basie and Jimmy Dorsey. During the 40s and 50s he worked with leading jazzmen such as Lester Young (who bestowed upon him the title by which he was subsequently known), Coleman Hawkins, Illinois Jacquet, Jimmy Rushing and Buck Clayton, the last an especially important musical associate. Through the 60s he continued playing with Roy Eldridge, Clayton and other major artists, and also led his own groups, often switching to organ. Poor health slowed his career in the 70s but by the 80s he was back on the scene again, playing at numerous venues around the world. A particularly effective ensemble player, Thompson's work in the Clayton bands of the mid-50s ably demonstrated his understated skills. His solos display a calm assurance, a largely unused affinity for the blues and a delicate touch on ballads. 'Robbins' Nest', a jazz standard, is his composition.

Albums: *Bop This* (1953), *Buck Clayton Jam Sessions* (1953-54), *The Sir Charles Thompson Quartet/For The Ears* (1954-55), *Sir Charles Thompson With Coleman Hawkins* (1954), *The Sir Charles Thompson Trio* (1955), *The Sir Charles Thompson Quintet* (1960), with Buck Clayton *Kansas City Nights* (1960-61), *Rockin' Rhythm* (1961), with Roy Eldridge *Trumpet Summit* (1967), *Hey, There!* (1974), *Sweet And Lovely* (1977), *Portrait Of A Piano* (1984), *Robbins' Nest* (1993).

Thompson, Eddie

b. 31 May 1925, London, England, d. 6 November 1986. Born blind, Thompson learned to play piano as a child. In the late 40s he was active in London clubs, playing with Carlo Krahmer, Vic Feldman and others. In the 50s he played on radio, in studio bands, made records under his own name and with Tony Crombie, Tommy Whittle, Freddy Randall and others and by the end of the decade was house pianist at Ronnie Scott's club. In the early 60s he went to the USA to live, playing regularly at the Hickory House in New York. Back in the UK in the early 70s, he led a trio which toured extensively and frequently backed visiting American jazzmen, including Buddy Tate, Ruby Braff and Spike Robinson. A dazzlingly inventive player in his early days, Thompson sometimes delivered bravura performances at the expense of feeling but in his maturity he made many memorable appearances at concerts around the UK. He had an enormous repertoire and when in musical sympathy with a guest he could be the best of accompanists. His solo playing was long overlooked by record companies but Alastair Robertson of Hep Records compensated for this with some excellent sessions in the early 80s. Thompson's death at the age of 61 came when he was at the height of his powers.

Selected albums: *I Hear Music* (Dormouse 1956), *By Myself* (77 1970), *Some Strings, Some Skins And A Bunch Of Keys* (c.1975), *Dutch Treat* (1976), *Ain't She Sweet* (1978), *When Lights Are Low* (1980), *Memories Of You* (1983), with Roy Williams *When The Lights Are Low* (Hep Jazz 1988).

Thornhill, Claude

b. 10 August 1909, Terra Haute, Indiana, USA, d. 1 July 1965. Thornhill studied piano formally, playing jazz with a friend, Danny Polo. In the early 30s he was resident in New York City, playing with Hal Kemp, Don Voorhees, Paul Whiteman, Benny Goodman and many other leaders. In the mid-30s he worked with Ray Noble and Andre Kostelanetz. Later in the decade he was busily writing arrangements for several bands and singers, and one song recorded by Maxine Sullivan ('Loch Lomond') was a huge hit. His successes for others led him to form his own band, hiring emerging talents such as Lee Konitz, Red Rodney and Gerry Mulligan, while his arranging staff included Gil Evans, who would later frequently assert how much his time with Thornhill had influenced his writing. In his 1940 band Thornhill sought perfect intonation from his musicians and balance between the sections. He urged his sidemen to eliminate vibrato, aiding this effect by adding French horns, themselves essentially vibratoless instruments. The resulting pastel-shaded musical patterns and sustained chords, against which Thornhill made delicate solo statements on piano, was in striking contrast to the sound of other big bands of the period. Ill health forced him to disband in 1948, but he returned to playing in the 50s and continued on an occasional basis until his sudden death in July 1965. Lasting testimony to Thornhill lies in the arranging styles of both Evans and Mulligan, both of whom long afterwards pursued concepts and sounds rooted in Thornhill's band of the early 40s.

Selected albums: *One Night Stand With Claude Thornhill* (1950), *Claude Thornhill And His Orchestra* i (1953), *Claude Thornhill And His Orchestra* ii (1956), *Claude On A Cloud* (1958), *Claude Thornhill And His Orchestra* iii (1959), *Claude Thornhill And His Orchestra* iv (1963). Compilations: *The Real Birth Of The Cool* (1942-47), *Claude Thornhill* (1947), *The Uncollected Claude Thornhill* (1947), *The Song Is You* (Hep Jazz 1981, 1948-49 recordings), *Tapestries* (Charly 1987, 1937-47 recordings), *Snowfall* (Fresh Sounds 1988).

Threadgill, Henry

b. 15 February 1944, Chicago, Illinois, USA. At college Threadgill shared a saxophone teacher with Anthony Braxton. In the early 60s he played with Roscoe Mitchell and Muhal Richard Abrams in the Experimental Band, the precursor of the AACM. He missed the AACM's beginnings as he spent several years touring America with an Evangelist Camp, contributing saxophone to the gospel services. Two years in the army had him playing everything from marches to classical music to jazz. In the late 60s he returned to Chicago and his AACM colleagues, playing with Amina Claudine Myers and Abrams and also in the house band of a Chicago blues club. In 1971 he formed Air, a trio with Fred Hopkins (bass) and Steve McCall (percussion) though it was only after 1975 that the group became widely active. Adept on alto, tenor and baritone saxophones as well as clarinet, flute and bass flute, Threadgill's playing was characterized by a pliancy and exceptional freshness. In the late 70s he formed X-75, a nonet of strings and winds, which recorded *Volume One* for Arista/Novus. The unusual line-up bewildered promoters and there was no volume two. In 1977 he recorded on Braxton's *For Trio* and later played in David Murray's Octet (1980-2). His X-75 ensemble evolved into his longstanding 'Sextet' (although it has seven members there are only *six parts*), with an interesting deployment of Fred Hopkins on bass, Deidre Murray on cello and two percussionists.

This group became the vehicle for some of the great jazz records of the 80s: *Just The Facts And Pass The Bucket* (1983), *You Know The Number* (1986) and *Rag, Bush And All* (1988). In December 1987 his composition for strings, percussion and voices, *Run Silent, Run Deep, Run Loud, Run High* (based on the laws of particle physics) was premiered at the Brooklyn Academy of Music. By the end of the 80s he had formed a 19-piece band that played dance tunes, a marching band and a septet, Very Very Circus, with an unusual line-up of two tubas, two electric guitars, trombone, drums plus the leader's alto saxophone and flute. In 1991, Very Very Circus released their debut recording, *Spirit Of Nuff...Nuff*, and in 1992 they toured the UK. Together with his AACM colleagues Abrams, Braxton and Mitchell, Threadgill remains on the cutting edge of musical exploration: he is a thrilling improviser and a boldly original composer.

Albums: with X-75 *Volume One* (1979), *When Was That* (1982), *Just The Facts And Pass The Bucket* (1983), *Subject To Change* (1985), *You Know The Number* (RCA 1986), *Easily Slip Into Another World* (RCA 1987), *Rag, Bush And All* (RCA 1988), with Very Very Circus *Spirit Of Nuff...Nuff* (Black Saint 1991), *Live At Koncepts* (Taylor Made 1992), *Too Much Sugar For A Dime* (1993), *Song Out Of My Trees* (Black Saint 1994).

Tiberi, Frank

b. 4 December 1928, Camden, New Jersey, USA. A self-taught tenor saxophonist, Tiberi's early career took him through the bands of Bob Chester, Benny Goodman, Urbie Green and Dizzy Gillespie. A period as a studio musician followed, but in 1969 he was back on the road as Woody Herman's leading saxophone soloist. He remained with the band for the rest of the leader's life, sometimes taking over when ill-health affected Herman. A notable section player and an effective soloist, Tiberi was one of the most dominant figures in the later Herds. Albums: all with Woody Herman *The Thundering Herd* (1974), *50th Anniversary Tour* (1986), *Woody's Gold Star* (1987).

Timmons, Bobby

b. 19 December 1935, Philadelphia, Pennsylvania, USA, d. 1 March 1974. Timmons studied with an uncle who was a musician, and then attended the Philadelphia Academy for a year. After playing piano around his home town he joined Kenny Dorham's Jazz Prophets in February 1956. He next played with Chet Baker (April 1956 to January 1957), Sonny Stitt (February to August 1957), Maynard Ferguson (August 1957 to March 1958) and Art Blakey's Jazz Messengers (July 1958 to September 1959). Although this last stint was no longer than the others, it was with the Messengers that he made his name. He replaced Sam Dockery to become part of a classic line-up, with Wayne Shorter on tenor and Lee Morgan on trumpet, and recorded *Like Someone In Love*. His composition 'Moanin'' became a signature for the Messengers, and has remained a definitive example of gospel-inflected hard bop ever since. In October 1959 he joined Cannonball Adderley, for whom he

wrote 'This Here' and 'Dat Dere'. He rejoined Blakey briefly in 1961, touring Japan in January (a broadcast was subsequently released as *A Day With Art Blakey* by Eastwind) and recording on some of *Roots & Herbs*. From the early 60s Timmons led his own trios and appeared regularly in Washington DC. In Spring 1966 he had a residency at the Village Gate in New York and played throughout Greenwich Village in the early 70s. He died of cirrhosis of the liver in 1974. Timmons was a seminal figure in the soul-jazz movement, which did so much to instil jazz with the vitality of gospel. Although best known as a pianist and composer, he also played vibes during the last years of his life.

Selected albums: *This Here Is Bobby Timmons* (Original Jazz Classics 1956), with John Jenkins, Clifford Jordan *Jenkins, Jordan & Timmons* (1957), *Soul Time* (1960), *Easy Does It* (Original jazz Classics 1961), *The Bobby Timmons Trio In Person At The Village Vanguard* (Original Jazz Classics 1961), *Sweet And Soulful Sounds* (1962), *Born To Be Blue* (1963), *From The Bottom* (1964), *Workin' Out* (1964), *Holiday Soul* (1964), *Chun-king* (1964), *Little Barefoot Soul* (1964), *Chicken And Dumplin's* (1965), *Soul Food* (1966), *The Soul Man* (1966), *Got To Get It* (c.1967), *Do You Know The Way* (1968), *Live At The Connecticut Jazz Party* (1981), *This Here* (Riverside 1984). Compilation: *Moanin'* (c.1963).

Tippett, Keith

b. Keith Tippetts, 25 August 1947, Bristol, Avon, England. As a child Tippett studied piano and church organ privately, and cornet and tenor horn with the Bristol Youth Band. In 1967 he won a scholarship to the Barry Summer School in Wales. Here he met Elton Dean and Nick Evans and invited them to become members of his band. In 1968 the Keith Tippett Sextet was the first beneficiary of the London Jazz Centre Society's scheme to give six-week residencies to new bands at its Monday sessions at London's 100 Club. Following these exciting and exhilarating gigs the reputation of the band and its individual members (Marc Charig, Evans, Dean, Tippett, Gill Lyons and Alan Jackson) spread rapidly. Tippett recorded with King Crimson and appeared on their hit single 'Cat Food.' In 1970 he formed the enormous 50-piece Centipede to play his composition *Septober Energy*, and in 1972 founded Ovary Lodge, a free band, with his wife Julie Tippetts (née Driscoll - she decided to retain the 's'). For the rest of the decade he worked with various bands, including those of Dean (Just Us and Ninesense), Charig, Harry Miller (Isipingo), Louis Moholo and John Stevens (Dance Orchestra) and Trevor Watts (Amalgam, with whom he appeared in a revival of Jack Gelber's play *The Connection* in London in autumn 1974). He also formed the duo TNT with Stan Tracey. In 1975 he resuscitated Centipede and in 1978 he was back with a big band, Ark. During the 80s through to the present he has worked with a septet, a duo with Julie, the powerful quartet Mujician (named for a 1981 solo record) and in a duo with Andy Sheppard. After the acclaim of the 60s and early 70s Tippett seems to have been out of favour with the critics and public in recent years, but he remains one of Britain's most original and provocative talents.

Albums: *You Are Here I Am There* (1969), *Dedicated To You But You Weren't Listening* (1970), *Septober Energy* (1971), *Blueprint* (1972), with Stan Tracey *TNT* (1974), *Ovary Lodge* (1975), *Warm Spirits, Cool Spirits* (1977), *Frames* (1977), with Marc Charig *Pipedream* (1978), with Louis Moholo *No Gossip* (1980), *Mujician* (1982), with Larry Stabbins *Tern* (1983), duet with Howard Riley *In Focus* (1984), *Live - Keith Tippett* (1986), *Mercy Dash* (1986), *Mujician II* (1987), *A Loose Kite In A Gentle Wind...*(1988), duet with Julie Tippetts *Couple In Spirit* (Editions EG 1988), with Tippetts, Maggie Nicols *Mr Invisible And The Drunken Sheilas* (1989, rec. 1987), *Mujician III (August Air)* (FMP 1989, rec. 1987), duet with Andy Sheppard *66 Shades Of Lipstick* (E.G. 1990), *The Dartington Concert* (Editions EG 1992), with Riley *The Bern Concert* (Future Music 1994).

Tissendier, Claude

b. France. While studying classical clarinet and alto saxophone at Toulouse Conservatory, Tissendier began playing jazz. His interests followed a chronological path, starting with New Orleans music, passing through the mainstream into bop. In 1977 he joined the big band led by Claude Bolling and also worked with Gerard Badini and others. In the early 80s he taught at the Paris School of Jazz and in 1983 formed a sextet especially to recreate the music of John Kirby. In demand for club and festival dates, the band won many awards for both live performances and records. In 1987 Tissendier formed Saxomania, a seven-piece band featuring two alto saxophones, two tenors and three rhythm. Once again he won honours and gained invaluable experience and exposure accompanying visiting American jazzmen including Benny Carter, Buddy Tate, Jimmy Witherspoon and Spike Robinson, with some of whom he also recorded. Tissendier's alto playing is striking for its intensity and driving swing and the high musical standards displayed by the Saxomania band ably demonstrate that he is a major talent.

Albums: *Tribute To John Kirby* (1986), *Saxomania Featuring Benny Carter* (1988), *Saxomania Presenting Spike Robinson* (Ida 1989), *Saxomania Out Of The Woods* (1993).

Tizol, Juan

b. 22 January 1900, San Juan, Puerto Rico, d. 23 April 1984. After playing in concert orchestras in his homeland, Tizol came to the USA in 1920. He played valve trombone in a theatre orchestra in Washington, DC, where he met Duke Ellington. He joined Ellington's band in 1929, immediately becoming a major and unique voice in that ensemble. Tizol's formal training gave him an important musical edge and several of his compositions, most of which had a Latin touch, became standards for the band, among them 'Conga Brava', 'Bakiff', and two jazz immortals, 'Perdido' and 'Caravan'. In 1944 he quit Ellington for the Harry James band, where he remained until 1951, then returned to Ellington for two years before another seven-year spell with James. He made some outside record dates, among them one with Nat 'King' Cole, and then, after a couple more brief stays with Ellington, retired in 1961. He subsequently appeared on a few live record dates, including a session with Louie Bellson, but appeared happy to live out his life off the bandstand.

Album: with Nat 'King' Cole *After Hours* (1956). Compilation: *Duke Ellington And His Orchestra* (1941).

Tjader, Cal

b. Callen R. Tjader, 16 July 1925, St. Louis, Missouri, USA, d. 5 May 1982. After studying formally, Tjader played drums with various bands on the west coast before joining Dave Brubeck in 1949. In the early 50s he played with Alvino Rey and also led his own small bands. By 1953, the year he joined George Shearing, he had added vibraphone and various other percussion instruments to his roster. In 1954 he again formed a band of his own, concentrating on Latin American music and making numerous records on the Fantasy and Verve labels. He hired his sidemen with care, employing over the years distinguished musicians such as Lalo Schifrin, Willie Bobo, Donald Byrd and Kenny Burrell, while later musical associates included Hank Jones and Scott Hamilton. For all his undoubted skills as an instrumentalist, much of Tjader's recorded output lacks urgency and vitality, often slipping gently into well-played but undemanding background music.

Selected albums: *Cal Tjader Plays Mucho* (1954), *The Cal Tjader Sextet* (1954), *Cal Tjader Plays Jazz* (1954), *Los Ritmos Caliente* (Fantasy 1954-57 recordings), *Mambo With Tjader* (Original Jazz Classics (Original Jazz Classics 1955), *Tjader Plays Mambo* (Original Jazz Classics 1955), *Latin Kick* (Original Jazz Classics 1956), *The Cal Tjader Quartet* i (1956), *The Cal Tjader Quintet* i (1956), *Sessions, Live* i (1957), *Jazz At The Blackhawk* (1957), *Mas Ritmo Caliente* (1957), *The Cal Tjader-Stan Getz Sextet* (1958), *Sessions, Live* ii (1958), *Latin Concert* (1958), *Latin For Lovers With Strings* (1958), *San Francisco Moods* (1958), *Cal Tjader Goes Latin* (1959), *Concert By The Sea* (1959), *A Night At The Blackhawk* (Original Jazz Classics 1959), *Demasiado Caliente* (1960), *Concert On The Campus* (1960), *West Side Story* (1960), *The Harold Arlen Songbook* (1961), *In A Latin Bag* (1961), *The Cal Tjader Quartet* ii (1961), *Live And Direct* (1961), *The Cal Tjader Quartet* iii (1962), *CT Plays The Contemporary Music Of Mexico And Brasil* (1962), *The Cal Tjader Quartet* iv (1963), *Breeze from The East* (1963), *Several Shades Of Jade* (1963), *Soul Sauce* (1964), *Warm Wave* (c.1964), *Soul Bird* (1965), *Soul Burst* (1966), *El Sonido Nuevo* (Verve 1967), *Hip Vibrations* (1967), *Along Comes Cal* (1967), *Solar Heat* (Rhapsody 1968), *Cal Tjader Sounds Out Burt Bacharach* (1968), *The Cal Tjader Quintet* ii (c.1969), *The Cal Tjader Quintet* iii (1970), *Primo* (c.1971), *Mambo With Tjader* (c.1971), *Concert At Hermosa Beach* (1973), *The Cal Tjader Quintet With Strings* (1973), *Amazonas* (1975), *Cal Tjader At Grace Cathedral* (1976), *Guarabe* (1976), *Breathe Easy* (1977), *Here* (1977), *Huracan* (Crystal Clear 1978), *La Onda Va Bien* (Concord 1979), *Gozame! Peroya* (Concord 1980), *The Shining Sea* (Concord 1981), *A Fuego Vivo* (Concord 1981), with Carmen McRae *Heat Wave* (1982), *Good Vibes* (Concord 1984).

Tomkins, Trevor

b. 12 May 1941, London, England. As a young teenager Tomkins first took up the trombone before switching to the drums on which he made his first professional appearance. Although he studied extensively, mostly in the classical vein, he was deeply interested in jazz and in the early 60s moved permanently into this field, working often with the small group co-led by Ian Carr and Don Rendell. He spent some time in the USA but from the 70s onwards became one of the most sought after jazz drummers in the UK where he has played with Michael Garrick, Barbara Thompson, Mike Westbrook and others. He is also in demand as accompanist to American jazzmen visiting the UK, amongst them Lee Konitz. A gifted mainstream and bop drummer, Tomkins' studies, which encompassed harmony and music theory, allied to a wealth of experience, have given him enviable command. His technical accomplishment is complemented by a subtle sense of swing and the ability to anticipate and fulfil the demands of the musicians he accompanies. He is also a much respected teacher.
Albums: with Don Rendell-Ian Carr *Shades Of Blue* (1964), with Rendell-Carr *Dusk Fire* (1965), with Tony Coe *Zeitgeist* (1977), with Pat Crumly *Third World Sketches* (1984), with Christian Josi *I Walks With My Feet Off The Ground* (1994).

Tompkins, Ross

b. 13 May 1938, Detroit, Michigan, USA. After formal studies Tompkins began playing piano in various small groups in New York City. Although most often in company with mainstream musicians such as Wes Montgomery, Bob Brookmeyer, Al Cohn, Zoot Sims and Clark Terry, he was also at ease with the more adventurous Eric Dolphy. He spent time working in radio and television studios in New York, later resuming this activity in Los Angeles. He continued to record extensively, appeared at festivals and clubs dates with musicians such as Marshal Royal, Herb Ellis, Louie Bellson, Joe Venuti, Ray Brown, Conte Candoli and Scott Hamilton. A solid ensemble player and accompanist, Tompkins is also an inventive soloist, developing long flowing lines of deceptive simplicity.
Albums: with Herb Ellis *A Pair To Draw To* (1975), *Scrimshaw* (1976), with Louie Bellson *Prime Time* (1977), *Live At Concord '77* (1977), *Lost In The Stars* (1977), *Ross Tompkins And Good Friends* (1978), *Festival Time* (1979), *Street Of Dreams* (1982), *Symphony* (1984), *LA After Dark* (1985), with Jack Sheldon *On My Own* (1992), *Aka The Phantom* (Progressive 1993).

Torn, David

b. 26 May 1953, Amityville, New York, USA. A guitar practitioner of what he describes as 'arrogant ambient music', Torn enjoys the conflict between sounds that are hypnotic and sounds that are 'like giant mosquitoes from hell, attacking.' He says, 'If I play something that's too pretty I feel compelled to go after it with razorblades.' Jazz educated, inspired by the minimalism of Terry Riley, a veteran of half a dozen rock and jazz-rock groups, former leader of the Everyman Band, film-music composer and guitarist, Torn is a gifted player still in search of the optimum context. He contributed usefully to Jan Garbarek's and David Sylvian's touring bands; his own records have found him playing idiosyncratic neo-fusion (*Cloud About Mercury*) and, rather ill-advisedly, singing Jimi Hendrix's 'Voodoo Chile' (*Door X*). In 1991, he launched a new 'improvising rock' group with Steve Jansen, Richard Barbieri, and Mick Karn, all ex-members of Japan and Rain Tree Crow. Torn also freelances as a record producer, with albums by Bill Bruford, Mick Karn and others to his credit. *Tripping Over God* in 1995 was a pure solo outing in his words it was 'my public meditation on the insanely unspeakable beauty inherent in the harshness of our mortality, a meditation on limitations: no, I take that back, hand me a beer would you?'
Albums: *Best Laid Plans* (1985), *Cloud About Mercury* (1986), *Door X* (1990), with Mick Karn, Terry Bozzio *Polytown* (CMP 1994), *Tripping Over God* (CMP 1995).

Tough, Dave

b. 26 April 1907, Oak Park, Illinois, USA, d. 9 December 1948. Tough began playing drums as a child and while still at school was a member of the 'Austin High School Gang'. This loosely assembled group of musicians effectively formulated the Chicago style of jazz which became popular in the 20s. Tough, a swinging drummer with a fine sense of musical quality, was a significant member of the group. He travelled to Europe in the 20s and also spent time in New York City making records with Eddie Condon, Red Nichols and others. In 1932 he was forced into temporary inactivity through illness, returning to the scene in 1935. Although his work up to the time of his illness had been primarily in small groups, he now slotted into the big band scene as if made for it. He played first with Tommy Dorsey and later with Red Norvo, Bunny Berigan, Benny Goodman and Dorsey again. Tough then joined Jimmy Dorsey, Bud Freeman, Jack Teagarden, Artie Shaw and others. His employers were a who's who of the best of the white big bands of the swing era. There were a number of reasons for his restlessness, among them his insistence on musical perfection, irritation with the blandness of many of the more commercial arrangements the bands had to play, and his own occasionally unstable personality which was aggravated by his drinking.
During World War II he was briefly in the US Navy (where he played with Shaw) but was discharged on medical grounds. On his discharge he joined Woody Herman, with whom he had played briefly before the war. The records of Herman's First Herd demonstrated to fans worldwide that the physically frail and tiny Tough was a powerful giant among drummers. Despite his broad-based style, Tough believed himself unsuited to bop and for much of his career he sought to develop a career as a writer. Sadly, his drinking became uncontrollable and his disaffection with the changing jazz scene accelerated his physical and mental deterioration, leading to fits. Although helped by many people who knew him, among them writers Leonard Feather and John Hammond Jnr., his lifestyle had numbered his days. Walking home one night, he fell, fractured his skull and died from the injury on 9 December 1948. His body lay

unrecognized in the morgue for three days. Whether playing in small Chicago-style groups or in any of the big bands of which he was a member, Tough consistently demonstrated his subtle, driving swing. It was with Herman, however, that he excelled, urging along one of the finest of the period's jazz orchestras with sizzling enthusiasm.

Compilations: with Bud Freeman *Chicagoans In New York* (1935-40), with Woody Herman *The V-Disc Years 1944-45, Vol. 1* (1944-45), *The Best Of Woody Herman* (1945-47).

Towner, Ralph

b. 1 March 1940, Chehalis, Washington, USA. Towner is primarily known as a highly regarded acoustic guitarist, an instrument he did not even take up until he was 23. Towner was born into a musical family and as a child he played trumpet and taught himself piano. He later studied composition at the University of Oregon, but after graduation in 1963 began to play guitar seriously, studying classical technique in Vienna. Back in the USA from 1968, he worked in New York with a number of jazz groups, mainly playing piano, and first came to public notice in 1971 with a fine 12-string guitar solo on Weather Report's *I Sing The Body Electric*. Since 1970, Towner has mainly pursued a solo career, releasing a series of fine albums for ECM Records, some in company with fellow guitarist John Abercrombie or vibraphonist Gary Burton. In 1971 Towner co-formed Oregon. He is a prolific composer, and many of his composition have been performed by orchestras around the world. All are distinguished by their evocative moods and resonant harmonies.

Selected albums: *Trios/Solos* (ECM 1972), *Diary* (ECM 1973), with Gary Burton *Matchbook* (ECM 1975), *Solstice* (ECM 1975), with John Abercrombie *Sargasso Sea* (ECM 1976), *Sounds And Shadows* (ECM 1977), *Batik* (ECM 1978), *Solo Concert* (ECM 1979), *Old Friends, New Friends* (ECM 1979), with Abercrombie *Five Years Later* (1982), *Blue Sun* (ECM 1983), *Works* (1983), with Burton *Slide Show* (ECM 1986), *City Of Eyes* (ECM 1990), *Open Letter* (ECM 1992), with Arild Andersen, Nana Vasconcelos *If You Look Far Enough* (1993). Compilation: *Works* (ECM 1983).

Tracey, Clark

b. 5 February 1961, London, England. Tracey began playing drums at an early age, often working with his father, Stan Tracey. At the start of his professional career, however, Tracey's drumming was rock-oriented and sat uneasily with the jazz groups with which he often associated. By the early 80s, however, in his playing style it was clear that Tracey had absorbed much from the experience of playing with jazz artists such as Red Rodney, Charlie Rouse and James Moody. With visiting Americans, with bands led by contemporaries and by his father, and also as leader of his own groups, Tracey grew with every appearance. By the early 90s he was a major figure among the new and vital group of young British jazz stars. He is married to singer Tina May.

Albums: *Suddenly Last Tuesday* (Cadillac 1986), *Stiperstones* (Steam 1987), *We've Been Expecting You* (Charly 1992).

Tracey, Stan

b. 30 December 1926, London, England. Tracey taught himself to play piano and by his early teens was performing professionally. In the 50s he was deeply involved in the British modern jazz scene, working with musicians such as Tony Crombie and Ronnie Scott. For most of the 60s he was resident at Scott's club, backing numerous visiting jazzmen. In the middle of the decade he formed a regular band, which included in its personnel at one time or another Bobby Wellins, Peter King and for many years Art Themen. Tracey made numerous albums, many of them on his own label, Steam Records, run with the help of his wife Jackie. Some of his recordings are with a quartet, others have him in duo, with the sextet Hexad, as leader of an octet, and with a powerful big band. Amongst his collaborators on concert and record dates have been Don Weller, Keith Tippett, Tony Coe, John Surman and Mike Osborne, whose 1972 encounter with Tracey helped to revive the pianist's flagging faith in music as a career. For the past few years Tracey's regular quartet has included his son, Clark Tracey, Themen and bassist Roy Babbington. He has also taught for several years, including periods at the Guildhall School of Music. A leading jazz composer, Tracey's work includes *Under Milk Wood*, a suite inspired by Dylan Thomas's play for voices. He is also an accomplished arranger and has employed this talent to great effect, notably when acknowledging his admiration for Duke Ellington on *We Love You Madly* and other albums. As a player, his early work showed the influence of Thelonious Monk but over the years he has consistently displayed a distinctive, sometimes quirkily personal, touch. Tracey is one of the outstanding figures Britain has given to the world of jazz.

Selected albums: *Under Milk Wood* i (Blue Note 1965), *Alice In Jazz Land* (1966), *Stan Tracey...In Person* (1966), *With Love From Jazz* (1967), *The Latin American Caper* (1968), *We Love You Madly* (1968), *Seven Ages Of Man* (1969), with Mike Osborne *Original* (1972), *Alone At Wigmore Hall* (Cadillac 1974), with Keith Tippett *TNT* (1974), *Captain Adventure* (Steam 1975), *Under Milk Wood* ii (1976), *The Bracknell Connection* (Steam 1976), *Salisbury Suite* (1977), with John Surman *Sonatinas* (1978), *'Hello Old Adversary!'* (Steam 1979), *Spectrum/Tribute To Monk* (c.1979), *South East Assignment* (Steam c.1980), *The Crompton Suite* (1981), *Stan Tracey Now* (1983), *The Poet's Suite* (1984), *Stan Tracey Plays Duke Ellington* (Mole 1986), *Live At Ronnie Scott's* (Steam 1986), with Charlie Rouse *Playin' In The Yard* (1987), *Genesis* (Steam 1987), *We Still Love You Madly* (Mole 1988), *Stan Tracey And Don Weller Play Duke, Monk And Bird* (Emanem 1988), *Stan Tracey Now* (Steam 1988), *Portraits Plus* (Blue Note 1993), *Duets* (Blue Note 1993), *Live At The QEH* (Blue Note 1994).

Trent, Alphonso

b. 24 August 1905, Fort Smith, Arkansas, USA, d. 14 October 1959. Born into a middle-class family, Trent learned piano at an early age and by his teens was playing regularly in local dance bands. He formed his own band while in his late teens, then worked briefly for another local leader before taking over his small band and securing a long residency at a hotel in

Dallas, Texas. For this engagement he expanded the band to 10 pieces; and among the excellent musicians he hired were Snub Mosley, James Jeter, Hayes Pillars (who later teamed up to form the Jeter-Pillars Orchestra), drummer A. G. Godley, generally acclaimed as the father of Kansas City style drumming, Stuff Smith, Peanuts Holland and Sy Oliver. Thanks to regular broadcasts from the hotel, Trent's popularity spread throughout the southwestern states. He paid high wages and offered his sidemen exceptionally good conditions which included smart uniforms and personal limousines. The line-up of the band remained remarkably constant and the musicians enthusiastic, well aware that they were envied by less-fortunate members of other territory bands. This consistency, allied to ample rehearsal time and excellent arrangements (apart from Oliver, the band's arrangers included Gus Wilson, brother of Teddy Wilson), helped to build the orchestra into the outstanding territory band of the pre-swing era. Although the band occasionally played in the east, including an appearance at New York's Savoy Ballroom, Trent preferred to remain in the southwest. This parochial attitude, coupled with the fact that the band made only a tiny handful of records, prevented it from making an impact upon the national jazz scene. Worse still, the band's management was inept and in 1933, on the eve of the explosion of interest in big band jazz, Trent was obliged to fold. For the rest of the 30s he continued to play with small groups, for one of which he unearthed the unknown Charlie Christian, but by the early part of the following decade music was only a part-time interest. He died in October 1959. During its existence the Trent band displayed standards of musicianship on a par with those of more famous bands, such as Fletcher Henderson's and Jimmie Lunceford's, but his few records give only a tantalizing glimpse of its qualities.

Compilation: with others *Sweet And Low Blues: Big Bands And Territory Bands Of The 20s* (1928-33).

Tristano, Lennie

b. 19 March 1919, Chicago, Illinois, USA, d. 18 November 1978. Encouraged by his mother, Tristano learned piano and various reed instruments while still a very small child, despite steadily deteriorating eyesight (he was born during a measles epidemic). By the age of 11 he was completely blind but, overcoming this handicap, he studied formally at the American Conservatory in Chicago, graduating in 1943. Before graduation he had already established a reputation as a session musician and teacher, including among his pupils outstanding talents such as Lee Konitz and Bill Russo. He also made a handful of records with Earl Swope. Based in New York from 1946, he worked with Charlie Parker and other leading bop musicians and attracted considerable attention within the jazz community, even if his work was little known outside (his first recordings were not released until many years later). In New York Tristano continued to teach; Warne Marsh was one of his important pupils from this period. The extent of his teaching increased so much that by the early 50s he had founded the first important jazz school in New York, a development which kept him still further away from the wider public. By the mid-

50s he had returned to private teaching and although he made a few recordings and some public appearances, including a mid-60s tour of Europe, he lived out the remaining years of his life in undeserved, but presumably intentional obscurity. An exceptionally original thinker, Tristano's work follows a path which, while related to the development of bop, traces different concepts. He was an early experimenter in playing jazz free from traditional notions of time signatures, but the results were very different from the later free jazz movement developed by Ornette Coleman and others. Among the lessons Tristano imparted to his pupils were those of strict precision in ensemble playing, complete command of the instrument and the ability to play complex shifts of time signature within a piece. He also laid particular significant stress upon listening - 'ear training'. In his own playing he preferred a pure sound and line, devoid of emotional content, and persuaded his pupils to follow this example so that, in Brian Priestley's words, their performances would 'stand or fall on the quality of their construction and not on emotional coloration'. Despite this almost puritanical attitude towards jazz, Tristano's teaching encouraged detailed study of solos by emotional players such as Louis Armstrong, Roy Eldridge and Charlie Parker. Clearly, Tristano was a powerful influence upon the many musicians he taught and through them upon countless more, especially through the work of such pupils as Peter Ind and Konitz, himself an important teacher.

Selected albums: *Live In Toronto* (Jazz Records 1952), *Lines* (1955), *Lennie Tristano* (Atlantic 1955), *New York Improvisations* (1956), *The New Tristano* (Rhino 1962), *Manhattan Studio* (Elektra 1983), Selected compilations: *Live At Birdland 1949* (Jazz Records 1945-49), *The Lost Session* (1946), *The Rarest Trio/Quartet Sessions 1946/7* (1946-47), *Cool In Jam* (1947), *Crosscurrents* (1949), *Wow* (Jazz Records 1950 recording), *Descent Into The Maelstrom* (1951-66).

Trumbauer, Frank

b. 30 May 1901, Carbondale, Illinois, USA, d. 11 June 1956. As a teenager Trumbauer played various instruments, including piano and trombone, before concentrating on the 'C' melody saxophone. He began leading a band while still in his teens and after military service in World War I played with several midwestern dance bands. In the mid-20s he joined the Jean Goldkette organization, leading a band which included Bix Beiderbecke. Trumbauer and Beiderbecke made a number of fine small group recordings during this association, which continued until 1927 when they both joined a big band formed by Adrian Rollini. They then moved on together to the Paul Whiteman band, where Trumbauer remained until the early 30s. He briefly led his own band and was co-leader with Jack and Charlie Teagarden of the Three T's band. By the end of the decade he was working on the west coast. He quit music in 1939, taking up work in the aviation industry. He briefly led a band in 1940 and then, during World War II, he became a test pilot. After the war he played in a number of bands, mostly in the studios, sometimes playing alto saxophone, but by 1947 was back working in aviation. He made occasional appearances at jazz dates, including a special tribute to Beiderbecke held in 1952. He died in June 1956. The precision and control displayed by Trumbauer was greatly admired by other saxophonists, including Benny Carter and Buddy Tate. As a soloist his work was somewhat less relaxed and swinging than his contemporaries but the association with Beiderbecke resulted in several recordings which remain among the classics of 20s jazz. Selected albums: with Jean Goldkette, Paul Whiteman, Bix Beiderbecke *Bixology Vols 2,3,6,7,8* (1924-28), with Beiderbecke *The Studio Groups - Late 1927* (1927), *Bix And Tram* (1927), *The Essential Frank Trumbauer Vol. 4* (1929-30), with Jack Teagarden *T'N'T* (1933-36), *Frankie Trumbauer 1937-38* (IAJRC 1991).

Turner, 'Big' Joe

b. Joseph Vernon Turner, 18 May 1911, Kansas City, Missouri, USA, d. 24 November 1985, Los Angeles, California, USA. 'Big' Joe Turner (aka Big Vernon) began singing in the local KC clubs in his early teens upon the death of his father, and at the age of 15 teamed up with pianist Pete Johnson. Their professional relationship lasted on and off for over 40 years. During the late 20s and early 30s Turner toured with several of Kansas City's best black bands, including those led by George E. Lee, Bennie Moten, Andy Kirk and Count Basie. However, it was not until 1936 that he left his home ground and journeyed to New York City. Making little impression on his debut in New York, Turner, with Johnson, returned in 1938 to appear in John Hammond Jnr.'s *From Spirituals To Swing* concerts and on Benny Goodman's *Camel Caravan* CBS radio show and this time they were well-received. Johnson teamed up with Albert Ammons and Meade Lux Lewis as the Boogie Woogie Boys and sparked the boogie-woogie craze that subsequently swept the nation and the world. Turner's early recordings depicted him as both a fine jazz singer and, perhaps more importantly, a hugely influential blues-shouter. He appeared on top recording sessions by Benny Carter, Coleman Hawkins and Joe Sullivan as well as his own extensive recording for Vocalion (1938-40) and Decca (1940-44), which featured accompaniment by artists such as Willie 'The Lion' Smith, Art Tatum, Freddie Slack or Sammy Price, when Johnson, Ammons or Lewis were unavailable. After World War II, Turner continued to make excellent records in the jazz-blues/jump-blues styles for the burgeoning independent labels - National (1945-47), Aladdin (1947, which including a unique *Battle Of The Blues* session with Turner's chief rival, Wynonie 'Mr Blues' Harris), Stag and RPM (1947), Down Beat/Swing Time and Coast/DooTone (1948), Excelsior and Rouge (1949), Freedom (1949-50), and Imperial/Ba'you (1950), as well as a west coast stint in 1948-49 with new major MGM Records.

As the 40s wore on these recordings, often accompanied by the bands of Wild Bill Moore, Maxwell Davis, Joe Houston and Dave Bartholomew, took on more of an R&B style which began to appeal to a young white audience by the early 50s. In 1951 'Big' Joe started the first of 13 years with the fledgling Atlantic Records, where he became one of the very few jazz/blues singers of his generation who managed to regain

healthy record sales in the teenage rock 'n' roll market during the mid-to-late 50s. His early Atlantic hits were largely blues ballads like 'Chains Of Love' and 'Sweet Sixteen', but 1954 witnessed the release of Turner's 'Shake Rattle And Roll' which, covered by artists such as Bill Haley and Elvis Presley, brought the 43-year-old blues shouter some belated teenage adoration. This was maintained with such irresistible (and influential) classics as 'Hide And Seek' (1954), 'Flip, Flop And Fly', 'The Chicken And The Hawk' (1955), 'Feelin' Happy' (1956) and 'Teenage Letter' (1957). At the height of the rock 'n' roll fever, Atlantic had the excellent taste to produce a retrospective album of Turner singing his old Kansas City jazz and blues with a peerless band featuring his old partner Pete Johnson. The album, *The Boss Of The Blues*, has since achieved classic status.

In the late 50s, Atlantic's pioneering rock 'n' roll gave way to over-production, vocal choirs and symphonic string sections. In 1962 Turner left this fast-expanding independent company and underwent a decade of relative obscurity in the clubs of Los Angeles, broken by the occasional film appearance or sporadic single releases on Coral and Kent. The enterprising Bluesway label reintroduced 'Big' Joe to the general public. In 1971 he was signed to Pablo Records, surrounded by old colleagues like Count Basie, Eddie Vinson, Pee Wee Crayton, Jay McShann, Lloyd Glenn and Jimmy Witherspoon. He emerged irregularly to produce fine one-off albums for Blues Spectrum and Muse, and stole the show in Bruce Ricker's essential jazz film *The Last Of The Blue Devils*. Turner's death in 1985 was as a result of 74 years of hard-living, hard-singing and hard-drinking, but he was admired and respected by the musical community and his funeral included musical tributes by Etta James and Barbara Morrison.

Selected albums: *The Boss Of The Blues* (1956, reissued 1976), *Big Joe Rides Again* (1959, reissued 1988), *Big Joe Singing The Blues* (1967), *Texas Style* (1971), with Count Basie *The Bosses* (1975), *The Things That I Used To Do* (1975), with Pee Wee Crayton *Every Day I Have The Blues* (1976), *Midnight Special* (1976), with Basie, Eddie Vinson *Kansas City Shout* (1978), *Jumpin' The Blues* (1981), *Great R&B Oldies* (1981), with Jimmy Witherspoon *Nobody In Mind* (1982), *In The Evening* (1982), *Best Of Joe Turner* (1982), *The Trumpet Kings Meet Joe Turner* (1982), *Boogie Woogie Jubilee* (1982), *Have No Fear, Joe Turner Is Here* (1982), *Big Joe Turner & Roomful Of Blues* (1983), *Life Ain't Easy* (1983), *Kansas City, Here I Come* (1984), *Jumpin' With Joe* (1984), *Rock This Joint* (1984), *Jumpin' Tonight* (1985), *Blues Train* (1986), with Witherspoon *Patcha Patcha* (1986), *I Don't Dig It* (1986), *Greatest Hits* (1987), *Big Joe Turner Memorial Album* (1987), *Honey Hush* (1988), *Steppin' Out* (1988), *Big Joe Turner* (1989), with 'T-Bone' Walker *Bosses Of The Blues* (1989), *The Complete 1940-1944 Recordings* (1990), *I've Been To Kansas City* (1991), *Every Day In The Week* (1993), *Shouting The Blues* (1993), *Jumpin' With Joe - The Complete Aladdin And Imperial Recordings* (EMI 1994).

Turner, Bruce

b. 5 July 1922, Saltburn, Yorkshire, England, d. 28 November 1993, Newport Pagnall, Buckinghamshire, England. A self-taught clarinettist, Turner took up alto saxophone during military service in World War II. In the immediate post-war years, Turner showed himself to be a thoroughly eclectic and accommodating musician, playing both bebop and dixieland with equal aplomb and ability. Significantly, he also played these diverse forms of jazz with considerable integrity. At the start of the 50s he joined a current trend among British musicians and played aboard transatlantic liners in order to visit New York. While there he studied with Lee Konitz (this at a time when Konitz was himself studying with Lennie Tristano). Despite this exposure to contemporary thought in jazz, on his return to the UK Turner joined Freddy Randall, with whom he had played in the late 40s, and then began a long association with Humphrey Lyttelton. His tenure with Lyttelton was marked at its outset by one of the more extreme examples of the division in loyalties among UK jazz audiences of the era; a banner bearing the words 'Go home, dirty bopper' was waved at a concert and the phrase entered the vocabulary even if, subsequently, it was not always used with defamatory intent.

In 1957 Turner formed his own 'jump' band, a move which appears to have given him the most suitable setting for his quirky, driving playing style, which reflects the work of predecessors such as Pete Brown while remaining distinctively personal. With this band, Turner toured extensively, often accompanying visiting American jazzmen such as Ben Webster, Ray Nance, Bill Coleman and Don Byas. Some of these tours brought personality clashes and led to Turner's decision to fold the jump band. In the mid-60s Turner then returned to a more traditional setting with Acker Bilk. In the early 70s his relationship with Lyttelton was resumed, although Turner continued to lead his own small bands and to work in a richly varied selection of bands, from the traditional, with Keith Smith, to the modern, with Dave Green (notably in the group Fingers). Late in his career Turner also took up soprano saxophone, displaying an effective command of the instrument. One of the outstanding British musicians of his generation, Turner's eclecticism might well have limited the spread of his reputation. Certainly, this enormously talented and well-liked figure deserved to be better represented on records and on the international festival and club circuits.

Albums: with Humphrey Lyttelton *Live At The Royal Festival Hall* (1954), *Accent On Swing* i (1959), *Jumping At The NFT* (1961), *Accent On Swing* ii (1962), *Going Places* (1962), *Bruce Turner-John Barnes: Jazz Masters* (1975), with Keith Smith *Up Jumped The Blues* (1978), with Dave Green *Fingers Remembers Mingus* (1979), *The Dirty Bopper* (Calligraph 1985), *New Orleans* (Metronome 1990), EP *Fishmouth* (Decca 1991), *Shiek Of Araby* (Decca 1991).

Further reading: *Hot Air, Cool Music*, Bruce Turner.

Turner, Joe

b. 3 November 1907, Baltimore, Maryland, USA, d. 21 July 1990. Taught piano by his mother Turner began playing pro-

fessionally in his late teens. Mostly based in New York City, he worked with many leading jazz artists of the 20s, including Hilton Jefferson, June Clark, Louis Armstrong and Benny Carter. He was instrumental in introducing Art Tatum to Adelaide Hall and was himself for many years accompanist to the singer. In 1931 he visited Europe, returning there later in the decade for tours and residencies. He visited France, Turkey and Hungary, where he married a local girl. After military service in World War II, Turner played with Rex Stewart, but before the 40s were over he was back in Europe to be reunited with his wife and daughter. He visited various countries, eventually settling in France, where he remained for the rest of his life. From 1962 he was resident at the Calvados club in Paris, playing Harlem stride piano, singing, and leavening his repertoire with music for the tourists. He made occasional visits to the USA, playing at the Newport Jazz Festival in 1973 and at The Cookery in New York City.

Selected albums: *Stridin' In Paris* (1952), *Sweet And Lovely* (RCA Vogue 1952), *Joe Turner* i (1955), *Joe Turner* ii (1959), *Stride By Stride* (Solo Art 1960), *Smashing Thirds* (1961), *The Joe Turner Trio* (1971), *Joe's Back In Town* (1974), *Harlem Strut* (1974), *King Of Stride* (1975), *Another Epoch: Stride Piano Vols 1 & 2* (1975-76), *Homage A Hugues Panassié* (1976), *Effervescent* (1976), *Joe Turner* iii (1976), *I Understand* (Black And Blue 1979), *Jazz In Tagi '82* (1982), *Walking Through Heaven* (1983).

Turney, Norris

b. 8 September 1921, Wilmington, Ohio, USA. Turney began playing alto saxophone as a child, emulating the sound of Johnny Hodges and nurturing a dream of one day playing in the Duke Ellington orchestra. In the late 30s and early 40s he played in Fate Marable's riverboat band and several territory bands, including the popular Jeter-Pillars Orchestra. In 1945 he was briefly with Tiny Bradshaw and Billy Eckstine. Through the late 40s and much of the following decade he was content to work outside the main centres. Late in the 60s he appeared in the band accompanying Ray Charles on a tour of the Far East and Australia. At the end of the 60s he finally achieved his lifelong ambition and stepped into the Ellington band when Hodges was sick; later, when his idol died, Turney took the altoist's seat permanently. After Ellington's death Turney worked mostly in New York, playing occasional jazz dates but more often in pit bands along Broadway. In the 80s he became a member of the accomplished band assembled by David 'Panama' Francis under the name the Savoy Sultans. He also played a number of festivals as a member of the George Wein Newport Festival All Stars. Turney, who also plays flute and clarinet, is a marvellous ballad player and his liquid sound on alto saxophone amply demonstrates his love for the playing style of Hodges, although he has his own stylistic leanings. Among his compositions is 'Chequered Hat', a song dedicated to Hodges.

Albums: with Duke Ellington *Seventieth Birthday Concert* (1969), with Ellington *Toga Brava Suite* (1971), one side only *The Boys From Dayton* (1975), *I Let A Song* (1979), with

Panama Francis *Gettin' In The Groove* (1979), with George Wein *The Newport Festival All Stars* (1984).

Turrentine, Stanley

b. 5 April 1934, Pittsburgh, Pennsylvania, USA. After playing cello Turrentine took up the tenor saxophone before reaching his teenage years. Born into a musical family (his father, Thomas Turrentine, played tenor with Al Cooper's Savoy Sultans), Turrentine quickly became proficient enough to turn professional. He began playing with blues and R&B bands including those led by Lowell Fulson and Earl Bostic, but in the early 50s he played in a band led by Tadd Dameron. In the late 50s he worked with Max Roach and also began leading his own bands, quickly establishing a reputation for live and recorded performances. For some years he was married to Shirley Scott, with whom he also made records. He also recorded with Jimmy Smith and in such organ/saxophone soul-jazz settings he has achieved considerable commercial success. His series of albums for Blue Note Records during the 60s produced some of the finest ever soul-jazz. Although his early professional experience has left a considerable mark on his playing, evident in his strong affinity for the blues, Turrentine has been able to adapt his style to appeal to the crossover audience for jazz-inflected popular dance music of the late 80s. Some of his albums, such as *Wonderland* with tunes by Stevie Wonder, are tailored for this market, while others are aimed at the hardcore jazz audience.

Selected albums: *Stan 'The Man' Turrentine* (c.1959-60), *Look Out!* (Blue Note 1960), *Blue Hour* (Blue Note 1960), *Jubilee Shouts* (1961), *Up At Minton's* (Blue Note 1961), *Dearly Beloved* (1961), *That's Where It's At* (1962), *Z.T.'s Blues* (Blue Note 1962), *Never Let Me Go* (Blue Note 1963), *A Chip Off The Old Block* (1963), *Mr Natural* (1964), with Shirley Scott *Blue Flames* (1964), *Joyride* (Blue Note 1965), *Let It Go* (Impulse 1966), *Rough And Tumble* (1966), *New Time Shuffle* (1967), *Always Something There* (1968), *Sugar* (1970), *Salt Song* (1971), *Yester Me, Yester You/Another Fine Mess* (1974), *Pieces Of Dreams* (1974), *Everybody Come On Out* (1976), *West Side Highway* (1977), *Soothsayer* (1979), *Inflation* (1980), *Tender Togetherness* (Elektra 1981), *Home Again* (Elektra 1982), *Straight Ahead* (1984), *Wonderland* (Blue Note 1986), *Comin' Your Way* (Blue Note 1988), *La Place* (Blue Note 1989), *If I Could* (Limelight 1994). Compilation: *Best Of Stanley Turrentine The Blue Note Years* (Blue Note 1990).

Twardzik, Dick

b. 30 April 1931, Boston, Massachusetts, USA, d. 1955. Twardzik was an original pianist and composer whose promising career was cut short by his untimely death. His meagre discography suggests that, had he survived, he would have flourished in the young *avant garde* movement of the late 50s. Twardzik started playing when he was nine years old. He pursued an education in classical music at the Longy School of Music in Cambridge, Massachusetts, and the New England Conservatory, but from the age of 14 he played professionally with many of the great names of swing and bop, including

Charlie Parker, Lionel Hampton, Chet Baker and Serge Chaloff. He recorded with Chaloff and Baker in 1954/5, contributing compositions to the former, and in no small way ensuring the classic status of both discs. Twardzik recorded only once under his own name, a trio session including the composition 'Albuquerque Social Swim' which in its extraordinary percussive attack and bizarre creativity emphasizes the pianist's originality. Twardzik summed up his approach: 'Development is not my primary consideration. The ability to project ever-changing emotions or moods, plus rhythmic freedom, is far more important to me'.

Albums: with Chaloff *The Fable of Mable* (1954), *The Last Set* (1954), with Baker *Chet Baker In Paris, Vol. 1* (1955), *Pacific Jazz* (Pacific Jazz 1990).

Tyner, McCoy

b. 11 December 1938, Philadelphia, Pennsylvania, USA. Beginning in his early teens, Tyner studied piano formally for several years before joining the jazztet led by Benny Golson and Art Farmer in 1959. The following year he joined John Coltrane, with whom he had previously gigged in Philadelphia. He remained with Coltrane until 1965 in what became known as the tenorman's 'classic quartet', touring internationally and recording numerous albums, including celebrated works such as *Impressions* (1963) and *A Love Supreme* (1965). In the late 60s he led his own trio, backed many artists of jazz and popular music, and began to record under his own name. Throughout the 70s Tyner toured and recorded, usually with a quartet or quintet. Several of his albums achieved considerable critical and popular success, some winning awards. He continued touring and recording through the 80s, most often as leader but he also played with Sonny Rollins in the Milestone Jazzstars. Early in his career Tyner was influenced by Bud Powell, Thelonious Monk and Art Tatum, but during his years with Coltrane he developed his own distinctive style. Tyner was not content simply to 'comp' with his left hand, but played in a vigorous two-handed manner that echoed the vibrancy and rhythmic excitement of his influences. His playing and, especially, his composing also displayed an advanced harmonic awareness. In some of his later work Tyner has adopted stylistic devices from other fields of music, incorporating African and Asian ethnic music and elements of the European classical tradition.

Selected albums: *Inception* (Impulse 1962), *The Real McCoy* (Blue Note 1967), *Tender Moments* (Blue Note 1967), *Time For Tyner* (Blue Note 1968), *Sahara* (Original Jazz Classics 1972), *Song For My Lady* (Original Jazz Classics 1973), *Echoes Of A Friend* (Original Jazz Classics 1973), *Enlightenment* (1973), *Song Of The New World* (Original Jazz Classics 1974), *Enlightenment* (Milestone 1974), *Reflections* (1975), *Atlantis* (Milestone 1975), *Trident* (Original Jazz Classics 1976), *Fly With The Wind* (Original Jazz Classics 1976), *Focal Point* (1977), *Supertrios* (Milestone 1977), *The Greeting* (1978), *Passion Dance* (1980), *4 x 4* (Milestone 1980), *La Leyenda De La Hora* (1981), *Night Of Ballads And Blues* (Impulse 1982, 1962-63 recordings), *McCoy Tyner Plays Ellington* (Impulse

1982, 1964 recording), with Jackie McLean *It's About Time* (1985), *Double Trios* (Denon 1986), *Revelations* (Blue Note 1988), *Bon Voyage* (Timeless 1988), *Uptown/Downtown* (Milestone 1988), with others *A Tribute To John Coltrane: Blues For Coltrane* (1988), *Live At Sweet Basil, Vols. 1 & 2* (Paddle Wheel 1989), *Things Ain't What They Used To Be* (Blue Note 1989), *New York Reunion* (Chesky 1991), *Remembering John* (Enja 1991), *Blue Bossa* (1991), *Solar* (1992), *Warsaw Concert 1991* (1992), *Soliloquy* (Blue Note 1992), *What's New?* (1993), *The Turning Point* (Birdology 1993), *44th Street Suite* (Red Baron 1994), with Bobby Hutcherson *Moodswings* (Blue Note 1994), *Journey* (Birdology 1994). Compilations: *Great Moments* (1981, rec. 1962-64), *Reflections* (1972-75).

U

Ulmer, James 'Blood'

b. 2 February 1942, St. Matthews, South Carolina, USA. Although taking up guitar in childhood, between the ages of seven and 13 Ulmer's primary musical activity was as a singer in a gospel group, the Southern Sons. In 1959 he moved to Pittsburgh, then to Detroit in 1967, and then to New York in 1971, where he played in the house band at the famous bebop venue, Minton's Playhouse, for nine months. In the 70s he worked or recorded with Art Blakey, 'Big' John Patton, Larry Young, Joe Henderson and Paul Bley. He studied and played with Ornette Coleman from 1974 and in 1977 was a member of Coleman's controversial sextet which later became Prime Time. He was also a member of the Music Revelation Ensemble with David Murray, Amin Ali and Ronald Shannon Jackson. He sings like Jimi Hendrix, but his guitar playing is quite different: choppy, rhythmic, harmonically inventive, with a cutting, ringing tone that slices through the harmolodic contexts in which he frequently works. Over the last few years he has toured with a power blues trio (comprising permutations of Jamaaladeen Tacuma or Amin Ali on electric bass and Grant Calvin Weston or Ronald Shannon Jackson on drums), capable of producing fiercely visceral and danceable music or, as on its spring 1991 visit to London, relatively mainstream funk-fusion. Most of the time he creates an intense, brooding momentum which is irresistible.
Albums: *Revealing* (In + Out 1977), *Tales Of Captain Black* (1978), with Arthur Blythe *Lenox Avenue Breakdown* (1979), *Illusions* (1980), with the Music Revelation Ensemble *No Wave* (1980), *Are You Glad To Be In America?* (1980), *Freelancing* (1981), *Black Rock* (1982), *Odyssey* (1984), *Part Time* (1984),

with Murray *Children* (1985), *Got Something Good For You* (Moers 1985), *Live At The Caravan Of Dreams* (1987), *America Do You Remember The Love?* (1987), *Original Phalanx* (DIW 1988), *In Touch* (DIW 1988), with Grant Calvin Weston *Dance Romance* (1988), *Blues Allnight* (In + Out 1990), *Black And Blues* (DIW 1991), *Blues Preacher* (1993).

Urbaniak, Michal

b. 22 January 1943, Warsaw, Poland. Urbaniak learnt the violin from the age of six and took up the alto saxophone in his teens. He studied at the Academy of Music in Warsaw and although he started playing with dixieland style jazz bands, he quickly moved on to bop. He played with various bands including that of alto saxophonist Zbigniew Namyslowski while he continued to perform classical violin. In 1965 he moved to Scandinavia with a band which included vocalist Urzsula Dudziak whom he later married. In 1971 he won a scholarship to the Berklee College Of Music in Boston, Massachusetts. He later led a band called Constellation In Warsaw before moving to New York in 1974. There, Urbaniak had a band called Fusion the music of which is enlivened by melodies and irregular rhythms derived from Polish folk music. He plays a personalized 5-string violin and violin synthesizer and also the lyricon, a saxophone like electronic instrument which triggers a synthesizer.
Selected albums: *Super Constellation* (1973), *Polish Jazz Volume 9 - Michel Urbaniak* (Polskie Nagrania 1973 recording), *Constellation In Concert* (1973), *Atma* (1974), *Fusion III* (1975), *Urbaniak* (1977), *Future Talk* (1979), *Music For Violin And Jazz Quartet* (1980), *The Larry Coryell/Michal Urbaniak Duo* (1982), *Take Good Care Of My Heart* (Steeplechase 1984), with Scott Cossu *Islands* (1984), *Songbird* (Steeplechase 1991), *Live In New York* (L And R 1991), *Manhattan Man* (1992).

V

Vaché, Warren, Jnr.

b. 21 February 1951, Rahway, New Jersey, USA. Vaché grew up in New Jersey, hearing jazz, thanks to his bass-playing father who led a dixieland band. Vaché took up the cornet and studied formally with, amongst others, Pee Wee Erwin. He played in his father's band, but from the mid-70s was attracting critical acclaim elsewhere. He played with the New York Jazz Repertory Orchestra and with the house band at Eddie Condon's club and was on regular call whenever Benny Goodman formed a band for special engagements. During this period Vaché met and began working with Scott Hamilton; the two men gained the reverent attention of audiences who thought that the mainstream had dried up. In the late 70s and throughout the 80s Vaché worked as a single, in harness with Hamilton, in bands such as George Wein's Newport Jazz Festival All-Stars and the Concord Super Band. Touring extensively across the USA, Europe and Japan, Vaché continued to enhance his reputation as a major jazz talent. Stylistically, he echoes the post-Louis Armstrong tradition, playing with eloquent charm and ably developing the fruitful ground tilled by melodic players such as Bobby Hackett and Ruby Braff. Vaché's style has allowed him to blend comfortably in seemingly disparate company, as witnessed by his *Warm Evenings* album with the Beaux-Arts String Quartet. His brother, Alan Vaché, plays clarinet with the Jim Cullum Jazz Band.

Albums: *Jersey Jazz At Midnight* (1975), *First Time Out* (1976), *Blues Walk* (1977), *Jillian* (1978), with Scott Hamilton *In New York City* (1978), with Hamilton *Skyscrapers* (1979), *Polished Brass* (1979), *Iridescence* (1981), *Swingin' And Singin'* (Jazzology 1990), *Midtown Jazz* (1992).

Valentine, Kid Thomas

b. 3 February 1896, Reserve, Louisiana, USA, d. 16 June 1987. His father, Fernand 'Pete' Valentine, was talented player of most brass instruments and was bandmaster of the Pickwick Brass Band. Kid Thomas began playing trumpet at an early age and when he was in his twenties moved to Algiers, across the river from New Orleans, where he joined the Elton Theodore Band. He quickly became the band's star attraction and in 1926 took over as leader. Valentine chose to stay in Algiers, content to be the town's leading player in jazz. Perhaps as a result of this small but important distancing from New Orleans, Valentine also remained largely independent of the developing trends in jazz trumpet playing, and was one of a small number who displayed little influence of Louis Armstrong, His band, the Algiers Stompers, played on through the decades, often resident at the town's Moulin Rouge. Despite his comparative isolation from the centres of jazz, he was swept up by the second wave of revivalism and in the 60s and made many overseas visits to Europe and Japan. He continued to play, often back in Algiers, into the 80s. A confident, assertive player with incisive attack, his many recordings offer an intriguing insight into the sometimes overlooked variety of styles within the early jazz tradition.

Selected albums: *At Hope Ball* (1951), *At The Moulin Rouge* (Center 1954), *At San Jacinto Hall* (1965), *Red Wing* (1966), *Kid Thomas At Moose Hall* (GHB 1967), *At Kohlman's Tavern* (GHB 1968), *At London's 100 Club* (1968), *Same Old Soupbone* (Jazz Crusade 1969), *Kid Thomas In California* (GHB 1970), *In Scandinavia* (Rarities 1974), *Featuring Alton Purnell* (1975), *His New Orleans Jazz Bird* (Arhoolie 1975), *Kid Thomas Valentine's Creole Jazz Band* (77 1979), *In England* (1981), *In Lugano* (1983), *Kid Thomas And Chester Vardis Visit The Maryland* (1983), *At The Old Grist Mill* (GHB 1986), *And The New Black Eagle Jazz Band* (GHB 1986), *Love Songs Of The Nile* (GHB 1987), *With Sammy Rivington 1981* (Black Label 1988), *On Stage* (GHB 1988), *Kid Thomas* (American

Music 1993), *Dance Hall Years* (American Music 1994). Selected compilations: *The 1957 Lost Sessions Vol 1* (1990), *Portrait Of Kid Thomas Valentine* (Storyville 1990).

Van Eps, George

b. 7 August 1913, Plainfield, New Jersey, USA. Self-taught on banjo, although his father was also a banjo player, Van Eps had played professionally before he was a teenager. At the age of 13 he heard Eddie Lang, decided to switch to guitar and within a couple of years was earning a reputation as a teacher. In the late 20s and early 30s he worked with a number of bands, including those of Benny Goodman and Ray Noble, and also played with his idol, Lang, in the Smith Ballew band. During the late 30s and for much of the following two decades he did studio work in Hollywood, radio dates, wrote a textbook on guitar, appeared in various bands (including Noble's) and made infrequent records with artists such as Matty Matlock, Wild Bill Davison, Jess Stacy and Ralph Sutton. In the 60s and 70s his playing activities were restricted through poor health but in the 80s he made a return to the jazz scene, playing at festivals in the USA and Europe. A marvellously gifted technician with an inventive mind, Van Eps is very much a musician's musician. In contrast, his popularity with audiences has been limited, due in part to the comparative obscurity in which he has chosen to spend the greater part of his working life.

Albums: with Jess Stacy, Ralph Sutton *Stacy 'N' Sutton* (1953), with Matty Matlock *Pete Kelly's Blues* (1955), *Mellow Guitar* (1956), *Wild Bill Davison Plays The Greatest Of The Greats* (1958), *My Guitar* (1966), *George Van Eps' Seven-String Guitar* (1967), *Soliloquy* (c.1968), *Mellow Guitar* (Corinthian 1988), with Howard Alden *13 Strings* (1991).

Van't Hof, Jasper

b. 30 June 1947, Enschede, Netherlands. Both Van't Hof's parents were musicians and he had six years of classical piano lessons. He was a founder member of Association PC (1970-72) before starting his own band Pork Pie with Charlie Mariano and Philip Catherine in the mid-70s. He has continued playing with Mariano right through the 80s as well as with, among others: Archie Shepp, Jean-Luc Ponty and Alphonze Mouzon. He led the band Eyeball including Didier Lockwood and then Pili Pili which included African percussion and computers. Van't Hof is a pianist of great technical facility who has enthusiastically incorporated synthesizers and the possibilities of electronic music of all kinds into his music.

Albums: *Selfkicker* (1974), with Pork Pie *The Door Is Open* (1975), with Mariano/Catherine *Sleep My Love* (1979), *My World Of Music* (1981), with Archie Shepp *Mama Rose* (1982), *Balloons* (1982), *Pili Pili* (1984), *Eyeball* (CMP 1991).

Vasconcelos, Nana

b. Juvenal de Hollanda Vasconcelos, 2 August 1944, Recife, Brazil. Vasconcelos began playing bongos and maracas with his guitarist father's group at the age of 12. He later joined a bossa nova band on the drums. His big break came in the mid-60s when he was offered a place in singer Milton Nascimento's band and he moved to Rio De Janeiro. He learned the berim-bau, a traditional Brazilian instrument with a single wire that is repeatedly buzzed and a gourd resonator that is tapped. In 1971 Gato Barbieri brought him to New York and then to Europe. At the end of the tour he stayed on in Europe for two years, recording and playing and also working with handicapped children. During this period he met jazz trumpeter Don Cherry, who was then living in Sweden and exploring all aspects of world folk music. Vasconcelos also recorded with Egberto Gismonti for ECM Records. In 1976 he relocated to New York and since then has become much in demand as a percussionist, appearing on albums by Pat Metheny, Talking Heads, Keith Jarrett and B.B. King. He played in the trio Codona with Cherry and Collin Walcott before the latter's death, recording three albums with them, and later toured as part of Cherry's Nu in 1988. His own group, Bush Dance, included Cyro Baptista, a Brazilian percussionist who has recorded with Derek Bailey. In the late 80s Vasconcelos was a member of the Jan Garbarek group; in the early 90s he has played with Andy Sheppard and recorded on Paul Simon's *Rhythm Of The Saints*. Vasconcelos has also contributed to the film soundtracks of Susan Seidelman and Jim Jarmusch, notably the latter's *Down By Law*.

Selected albums: *Africa Deus* (1972), *Amazonas* (70s), with Egberto Gismonti *Danca Das Cabaces* (1976), with Perry Robinson, Badal Roy *Kundalini* (1978), *Saudades* (ECM 1980), *Zumbi* (1983), with Gismonti *Duas Vozes* (1985), *Lester* (Soul Note 1986), *Bush Dance* (Antilles 1989), *Rain Dance* (Antilles 1989), with Arild Andersen, Ralph Towner *If You Look Far Enough* (1993).

Vaughan, Sarah

b. Sarah Lois Vaughan, 27 March 1924, Newark, New Jersey, USA, d. 3 April 1990. Although she was not born into an especially musical home environment (her father was a carpenter and her mother worked in a laundry), the young Sarah Vaughan had plenty of contact with music-making. As well as taking piano lessons for nearly 10 years, she sang in her church choir and became the organist at the age of 12. Her obvious talent for singing won her an amateur contest at Harlem's Apollo Theater in 1942, and opportunities for a musical career quickly appeared. Spotted by Billy Eckstine, who was at the time singing in Earl 'Fatha' Hines' big band, she was invited to join Hines' band as a female vocalist and second pianist in 1943. Eckstine had been sufficiently impressed by Vaughan to give her a place in his own band, formed a year later. It was here that she met fellow band members and pioneers of modern jazz Charlie Parker and Dizzy Gillespie. Recording with Eckstine's band in 1945, full as it was of modern stylists, gave her a fundamental understanding of the new music that characterized her entire career.

After leaving Eckstine, she spent a very short time with John Kirby's band, and then decided to perform under her own name. In 1947 she married trumpeter George Treadwell, whom she had met at the Cafe Society. Recognizing his wife's huge potential, Treadwell became her manager, as she began a decade of prolific recording and worldwide tours. She began by recording with Miles Davis in 1950, and then produced a torrent of albums in either a popular vein for Mercury Records, or more jazz-oriented material for their subsidiary label EmArcy. On the EmArcy recordings she appeared with Clifford Brown, Cannonball Adderley and members of the Count Basie band; these remain some of her most satisfying work. By the 60s, as Vaughan rose to stardom, her jazz activity decreased slightly, and the emphasis remained on commercial, orchestra-backed recordings. It was not until the 70s that she began to perform and record with jazz musicians again on a regular basis. Vaughan performed at the 1974 Monterey Jazz Festival and made an album in 1978 with a quartet consisting of Oscar Peterson, Joe Pass, Ray Brown, and Louie Bellson. The following year she recorded her *Duke Ellington Song Book One*, on which a large number of top jazz players appeared, including Zoot Sims, Frank Foster, Frank Wess, J.J. Johnson, and Joe Pass.

In 1980 she appeared in a much-heralded concert at Carnegie Hall, and returned to the Apollo where her career had begun, to sing with Eckstine who had encouraged her at that early stage. They worked the Apollo Theater in a show recorded and broadcast by NBC-TV. She recorded an album of Latin tunes in 1987, and around this time appeared in another televised concert, billed as *Sass And Brass*. With a rhythm section featuring Herbie Hancock, Ron Carter, and Billy Higgins, as well as a collection of trumpeters including Dizzy Gillespie, Don Cherry, Maynard Ferguson, and Chuck Mangione, she proved herself still a musical force to be reckoned with. Sarah Vaughan won the *Esquire* New Star poll in 1945, the *Downbeat* poll (1947-52) and the *Metronome* poll (1948-52). She also sang at the White House as early as 1965; Vaughan's name has been synonymous with jazz singing for two generations. Gifted with an extraordinary range and perfect intonation, she would also subtly control the quality of her voice to aid the interpretation of a song, juxtaposing phrases sung in a soft and warm tone with others in a harsh, nasal vibrato or throaty growl. Her knowledge of bebop, gained during her time with Eckstine's band, enabled her to incorporate modern passing tones into her sung lines, advancing the harmonic side of her work beyond that of her contemporaries. Her recordings will continue to influence vocalists for many years to come.

Selected albums: *Sarah Vaughan* (1954), *Lullaby Of Birdland* (1954), *Sarah Vaughan With Clifford Brown* (Emarcy 1954), *My Kinda Love* (1955), *Sarah Vaughan In The Land Of Hi Fi* (Emarcy 1955), *After Hours With Sarah Vaughan* (1955), *Vaughan And Violins* (1955), *Great Songs From Hit Shows* (1955), *Sarah Vaughan Sings George Gershwin* (1955), *Great Songs From Hit Shows, Volume 2* (1956), *Sarah Vaughan At The Blue Note* (1956), *The Magic Of Sarah Vaughan* (1956), *Linger Awhile* (1956), *Sassy* (1956), *Swinging Easy* (Emarcy 1957), *The Rodgers And Hart Songbook* (Emarcy 1957), *Wonderful Sarah* (1957), *In A Romantic Mood* (1957), *Close To You* (1957), *Sarah Vaughan And Billy Eckstine Sing The Best Of Irving Berlin* (1957), *Sarah Vaughan At Mr. Kelly's* (Emarcy 1958), *After Hours At The London House* (1958), *No Count*

Sarah (1958), *Misty* (Emarcy 1959), *Songs Of Broadway* (1959), *Dreamy* (1960), *Divine One* (1960), *Count Basie/Sarah Vaughan* (1960), *My Heart Sings* (1961), *You're Mine, You* (1962), *Snowbound* (1962), *The Explosive Side Of Sarah* (1962), *Star Eyes* (1963), *Sassy Swings The Tivoli* (Mercury 1963), *Vaughan With Voices* (1964), *Viva Vaughan* (1964), with Dinah Washington, Joe Williams *We Three* (1964), *The Lonely Hours* (1964), *The World Of Sarah Vaughan* (1964), *Sweet 'N' Sassy* (1964), *Sarah Sings Soulfully* (1965), *Sarah Plus Two* (1965), *Mancini Songbook* (1965), *The Pop Artistry Of Sarah Vaughan* (1966), *New Scene* (1966), *Sassy Swings Again* (Emarcy 1967), *I'm Through With Love* (1970), *Sarah Vaughan/Michel Legrand* (1972), *Live In Japan* (1973), *Feelin' Good* (1973), *The Summer Knows* (1973), *A Time In My Life* (1974), *Sarah Vaughan And The Jimmy Rowles Quintet* (1975), with Oscar Peterson, Joe Pass, Ray Brown, Louie Bellson *How Long Has This Been Going On?* (Pablo 1978), *Live At Ronnie Scott's* (1978), *Send In The Clowns* (Pablo 1978), *Duke Ellington Songbook One* (Pablo 1979), *I Love Brazil* (1979), *Songs Of The Beatles* (1981), with Barney Kessel, Joe Comfort *The Two Sounds Of Sarah* (1981), *Copacabana* (Pablo 1981), *Crazy And Mixed Up* (Pablo 1982), *O, Some Brasileiro De* (1984). Selected compilations: with Billy Eckstine *Passing Strangers* (1981, coupled with a Dinah Washington and Brook Benton collection), *Spotlight On Sarah Vaughan* (1984), *The Sarah Vaughan Collection* (Deja Vu 1985), *The Best Of Sarah Vaughan - Walkman Series* (1987), *Compact Jazz; Sarah Vaughan Live* (Mercury 1988), *16 Greatest Hits* (1993), *The Divine One* (Vogue 1993).

Further reading: *Sassy - The Life Of Sarah Vaughan*, Leslie Gourse.

Ventura, Charlie

b. 2 December 1916, Philadelphia, Pennsylvania, USA, d. 17 January 1992, Pleasantville, New Jersey, USA. After playing C melody and alto saxophones during his childhood, Ventura settled on tenor saxophone and in 1942 joined the Gene Krupa band. He was briefly with Teddy Powell during Krupa's enforced disbandment before rejoining his old boss, where he was featured with the big band and as a member of the band-within-the-band, the trio. In 1946 he formed his own big band, cut back to a small group, then increased in size again, this time playing a commercially-oriented form of bebop under the banner of 'Bop For The People'. During this period he also began playing baritone saxophone, but the group eventually disbanded in 1951. He then formed the Big Four with Marty Napoleon, Chubby Jackson and Buddy Rich. For most of the following two decades he alternated between running his own nightclub, the Open House in Philadelphia (which closed in 1954), reunions with Krupa, leading big and small bands at Las Vegas hotels and battles with poor health. Although usually thought of as an exuberant, sometimes exhibitionistic soloist, mainly as a result of his time with Krupa, Ventura was fundamentally a straightahead, swinging soloist whose coarser side was encouraged for commercial reasons. Similarly in conflict with his natural playing instincts was his apparent predilection

for the complexities of bop. Indeed, in his Bop For The People band, which at one time or another included Conte Candoli, Kai Winding, Bennie Green, Boots Mussulli and the singers Jackie Cain and Roy Kral, Ventura's swing-styled playing was something of an exception to the prevailing musical atmosphere. He continued playing throughout the 70s and into the early 80s, delighting small but approving audiences with his stomping big-toned performances. He later died of lung cancer in 1992.

Selected compilations: *The Crazy Rhythms* (Savoy 1945 recordings), *Memorable Concerts: Charlie Ventura And His Band* (1949), *Gene Norman Presents A Charlie Ventura Concert* (MCA 1949 recording), *Charlie Ventura With Special Guest Star Charlie Parker* (1949), *Bop For The People* (1949-53), *The Big Four* (1951), *Charlie Ventura And His Quintet* i (1951), *The Charlie Ventura Quartet* i (1952), *The Charlie Ventura Quartet* ii (1953), *The Charlie Ventura Quartet* iii (1954), *The Charlie Ventura Quartet With Mary Ann McCall* (1954), *Charlie Ventura And His Orchestra* (1954-55), *Charlie Ventura And His Quintet* ii (1956), *Charlie Ventura And His Quintet* iii (c.1956), *Adventures With Charlie* (1957), *Chazz* (1977). Compilations: with Gene Krupa *Drummin' Man* (1938-49), *Charlie Boy* (Pheonix 1981, 1946 recording), *In Chicago 1947* (Zim 1981, 1947 recording), *Euphoria* (Savoy 1985), *Jackie And Roy* (Savoy 1993).

Venuti, Joe

b. 16 September 1903, Philadelphia, Pennsylvania, USA, d. 14 August 1978. According to legend, Venuti took up violin when he and a friend, Eddie Lang, tossed a coin to see who would play which of two instruments they had bought from a Philadelphia pawn shop. Lang got the guitar. Similarly legendary are tales of Venuti's birth and early career. The former has been placed in both Italy and Philadelphia, with a favourite in-between location on board a ship filled with Italian immigrants as it sailed into New York harbour. The date varies too, with a range of anything up to five years either way. More prosaically, Venuti spent his early life working in bands in and around Philadelphia, often in company with Lang, before joining Bert Estlow's band in Atlantic City. By 1924 he had graduated to leading one of Jean Goldkette's bands. Later in the 20s, often still with Lang, he played in the bands of Roger Wolfe Kahn and Adrian Rollini and made many records, including the classic Venuti-Lang Blue Four sides. In 1929 he joined Paul Whiteman shortly before the making of the film *The King Of Jazz* (1930). During a rehearsal for the film he surreptitiously emptied a bag of flour into the bell of a tuba so that when the unfortunate musician eventually managed to puff out a note the entire band disappeared under a drifting white cloud.

While with Whiteman he survived a serious car crash and also befriended Bix Beiderbecke, whom he once tipped, drunk and unconscious, into a bath of purple Jell-O. During the early 30s Venuti appeared on numerous recording sessions with artists such as Red McKenzie, Jack Teagarden, Tommy and Jimmy Dorsey, Frank Trumbauer, Bing Crosby, Lee Wiley and the

Boswell Sisters. Depressed by the sudden death of his friend Lang in 1933, Venuti drifted for a while, visiting Europe and recording in the UK, alternating on violin and guitar. Back in the USA he formed a big band in 1935 but enjoyed only limited success, refusing to take seriously the duties of a bandleader. He folded the big band in 1943 and for a while he played in film and radio studios, becoming a regular on Crosby's show. Throughout the 50s he appeared at clubs and made records, but by the 60s was struggling against alcoholism. In 1967 he was invited to attend a Dick Gibson Colorado Jazz Party; this sparked a revival of interest in his work. He began recording again as leader and in duo with jazzmen such as Earl 'Fatha' Hines; the following year he appeared at the Newport Jazz Festival and the year after that was in England for the Jazz Expo. In 1970 he discovered he had cancer but fought back; during these traumatic years he made some superb recordings with George Barnes, Ross Tompkins, Dave McKenna, Zoot Sims, Marian McPartland, Scott Hamilton and others, defying age, ill-health and a lifetime of hard-living. Throughout his career Venuti played with sparkling invention and enormous vitality, bringing to his playing a sense of urgency and excitement which, on his chosen instrument, was only matched by Stuff Smith. Venuti's was a massive talent, and although his private life was often disastrous - he was often racist and had a propensity for cruel practical jokes - he was still an outstanding musician. Had he chosen to play a more popular instrument, he might have been judged a giant of jazz.

Selected albums: *Joe Venuti Plays Gershwin And Kern* (early 50s), *The Mad Fiddler From Phillie* (Shoestring 1953), *Never Before...Never Again* (1954), *The Joe Venuti Quintet* i (1955), *Joe Venuti* (1956), *Joe Venuti And His Blue Five* (1957), *The Joe Venuti Quintet* ii (early 60s), *Quartet* (1969), *Once More With Feeling* (1969), *The Daddy Of The Violin* (1971), *Violinology* (1971), *The Joe Venuti Quartet* (1971), *Joe Venuti In Milan* (1971), with Marian McPartland *The Maestro And Friend* (1974), with Zoot Sims *Joe And Zoot* (1974), *Blue Fours* (1974), *Joe Venuti And Joe Albany* (1974), *Welcome Joe* (1974), *Fine And Dandy* (1974), *Nightwings* (mid-70s), with Earl Hines *Hot Sonatas* (1975), *Swing Violin Scene* (1975), with George Barnes *Gems* (1975), with Zoot Sims *Joe Venuti-Zoot Sims* (Chiaroscuro 1975), *Joe Venuti-George Barnes Live At The Concord Summer Festival* (1976), with Dave McKenna *Alone At The Palace* (Chiaroscuro 1977), *Ross Tompkins And Joe Venuti Live At Concord '77* (1977), *Sliding By* (Sonet 1977), *In Chicago 1978* (1978), *Electric Joe* (Jump 1988), with Stéphane Grappelli *Venupelli Blues* (1993). Selected compilations: *'S Wonderful Giants Of Swing* (1979), *Joe Venuti And Eddie Lang (1926-28)* (JSP 1983), *The Big Bands Of Joe Venuti (1928-30)* (1987), *The Incredible Joe Venuti* (1987).

VerPlanck, Marlene

b. Marlene Pampinella, Newark, New Jersey, USA. VerPlanck began singing at the age of 19, having previously considered a career in journalism. Her first important engagement was with the big band of Tex Beneke. She later joined Charlie Spivak, where she met trombonist-arranger Billy VerPlanck. Later, the couple met again, this time in the Tommy Dorsey band, and shortly afterwards were married. In the early 60s the VerPlancks worked in radio in New York. During this period VerPlanck sang with many major artists, including Frank Sinatra, but throughout the decade and into the 70s the bulk of her work consisted of singing jingles for countless commercials. She also began to sing in some of New York's best-known jazz clubs. As her reputation spread she appeared at Carnegie Hall and the Kool Jazz Festival, among numerous prestigious venues and events, and attracted the attention of composers such as Loonis McGlohon and Alec Wilder. An outstanding interpreter of ballads, VerPlanck has recorded about a dozen albums, all of which have proved enormously popular and which have drawn lavish praise from critics. She sings with great wit, imagination, flawless diction, understanding and sparkling technique. Her huge repertoire includes the songs of Jerome Kern, Alan J. Lerner, Burt Bacharach, Harry Warren, Johnny Mercer, Benny Carter, Wilder, McGlohon and countless others. Although not strictly a jazz singer, she fits easily into a jazz setting, usually working with piano, bass and drums, but also happily blending with jazz musicians such as Spike Robinson, Sonny Costanzo and Bill Berry. By the early 90s VerPlanck was beginning to be heard internationally and proving conclusively that she is one of the finest living interpreters of the Great American Songbook.

Selected albums: *I Think Of You With Every Breath I Take* (Savoy 1955), *You'd Better Love Me* (Audiophile 1976), *Marlene VerPlanck Loves Johnny Mercer* (Audiophile c.1978), *A New York Singer* (Audiophile c.1979), *A Warmer Place* (Audiophile 1982), *I Like To Sing!* (1983), *Marlene VerPlanck Sings Alec Wilder* (Audiophile 1986), *I Like To Sing* (Audiophile 1986), *Pure And Natural* (Audiophile 1987), *A Quiet Storm* (Audiophile 1989), *A Breath Of Fresh Air* (Audiophile 1993), *Live In London* (Audiophile 1994).

Verrell, Ronnie

b. 21 February 1926, Rochester, Kent, England. While playing in a boy's club band Verrell heard a professional drummer and immediately decided this was what he wanted to do. Seeing and hearing Gene Krupa in a film confirmed his ambition. In 1939 he took one lesson from Max Abrams, the noted British drummer and teacher, but was too impatient to take further lessons. Thereafter, he taught himself and was given his first chance to play in public in Wales, where he had been evacuated when the bombing of London began. On his return to Kent he joined the Claude Giddings band in Gillingham. The outfit was well known for the quality of its young musicians, who included Tommy Whittle and pianist Arthur Greenslade who later worked with Vic Lewis and Shirley Bassey. Verrell also played with Carl Barriteau and the Londonaires band which was briefly popular in Germany. In 1948 Verrell auditioned for the Ted Heath band when Jack Parnell was considering moving on.

He failed the audition but was hired instead by Cyril Stapleton. Three years later Parnell finally left Heath and was replaced briefly by Basil Kirchin before Verrell took over the drum chair.

This was the time when the Heath band reached its peak and as cracks appeared in the UK Musicians Union ban on visiting Americans, Heath was one of the first to tour the USA (on a reciprocal arrangement which brought Stan Kenton to the UK). The Heath band was part of a package which included June Christy, the Four Freshmen and Nat 'King' Cole and which culminated in a concert at Carnegie Hall. The band was a huge success and many of the individual musicians, Verrell among them, attracted favourable attention from critics and fans alike. Apart from the USA tour, Verrell was with the Heath band on its Australasian tour. During his stint with the band Verrell was partly responsible for at least two of their chart successes in the UK. His solo feature on 'Skin Deep' helped the record reach number 9 in 1954, and his lithely swinging backing assisted 'Swingin' Shepherd Blues' to its number 3 spot in 1958.

The band also had a Top 20 album success in 1962 with *Big Band Percussion*. After leaving Heath, Verrell worked extensively in television studio bands, among them the house band at ATV which was directed by Parnell. Subsequently, Verrell played in the Syd Lawrence band but continued to be active on television where he gained a kind of anonymous fame as 'Animal', the drummer on *The Muppet Show*. In the late 80s Verrell began playing occasionally with the Pizza Express All Stars in London and made infrequent appearances backing visiting American jazzmen, including Buddy Tate and Clark Terry. He also played in the re-created Ted Heath band led by Don Lusher. In the 90s he continued to divide his time between studio and jazz work. A solid danceband drummer and excellent timekeeper, Verrell was also explosive when it mattered and his work with the Heath band remains a high spot in the story of big band drumming in the UK.

Selected albums: *Ted Heath At Carnegie Hall* (1956), with Heath *Big Band Percussion* (1962).

Vesala, Edward

b. Martti Vesala, 15 February 1945, Eastern Finland. Easily the most influential Finnish jazz musician of his generation, drummer-composer Vesala did not begin to play until he was 20 years old. Growing up in the middle of the Finnish forest, his only access to music was in the dance halls of neighbouring villages where Nordic tango was available. After a season of playing for country dances he advanced rapidly through psychedelic rock and free jazz, then checked into Helsinki's Sibelius Academy for courses in orchestration, only to drop out impatiently after a year. He roamed through Asia in the early 70s, collecting instruments and soaking up local music in India, Bali and Java. In 1972 he formed a short-lived co-operative trio with Jan Garbarek and Arild Andersen (*Triptykon*), and in 1975 a more compatible quartet co-led with Tomasz Stanko. By this point, Vesala's compositional direction was established. Melody and emotional expression are of prime importance in his work, and his melodies and emotions are complex. He formed Sound And Fury from one of his workshop groups in 1985 and it has come to be one of the outstanding European ensembles, its disciplined young musicians totally committed to Vesala's visions. Although several of his albums have appeared on ECM Records, Vesala also runs his own record label, Leo (not to be confused with the London-based Leo Records), which has released many of his sessions with various European and - notably on *Heavy Life* - American guest musicians.

Albums: *Soulset* (1969), *Edward Vesala Jazz Band* (1969), *Nana* (1970), *I'm Here* (1973), with Peter Brötzmann *Hot Lotta* (1974), *Nan Madol* (ECM 1975), with Jasper Van't Hof, Toto Blanke *Electric Circus* (1976), with Tomasz Stanko *Live At Remont* (1977), with Stanko *Twet* (1977), *Rodina* (1977), *Satu* (1977), *Neitsytmatka* (1980), *Heavy Life* (1980), with Charlie Mariano, Arild Andersen, Van't Hof *Tea For Four* (1982), *Mau-Mau* (1982), *Bad Luck, Good Luck* (1984), *Kullervo* (1985), *Lumi* (ECM 1987), *Afrikan Tähoet* (1989), *Ode To The Death Of Jazz* (ECM 1990), *Invisible Storm* (ECM 1992), *Sound And Fury* (1993).

Vinnegar, Leroy

b. 13 July 1928, Indianapolis, Indiana, USA. After teaching himself to play bass, Vinnegar worked in clubs in the Chicago area, accompanying jazz musicians such as Charlie Parker, before moving to the west coast in 1954. He immediately made an impact on the local music scene, then in the middle of the 'cool jazz' boom. He played and recorded with just about everyone; a short list might include Jack Sheldon, Stan Levey, Shorty Rogers, Dexter Gordon, Cy Touff, Russ Freeman, Elmo Hope, Stan Getz, Harold Land, Carl Perkins (with whom he had gone to school), Art Pepper and Teddy Edwards. He was also a member of the Shelly Manne trio (the third man being André Previn) which recorded *My Fair Lady*. Vinnegar continued to work with a variety of bands, sometimes as leader, at home in large and small groups. He sometimes appeared in non-jazz contexts and his eclecticism allowed him to play comfortably alongside musicians as diverse as Howard McGhee and Les McCann, or Serge Chaloff and film actor George Segal's jazz group. An outstanding exponent of the 'walking bass' technique, Vinnegar always plays with a wonderful plangency, bringing a zestful swing to any performance.

Albums: *Leroy Walks!* (Original Jazz Classics 1957), *Leroy Walks Again!* (Original Jazz Classics 1962), *Walker* (1964), *Glass Of Water* (1975), *The Kid* (1976), with Jessica Williams *Encounters* (1994).

Vinson, Eddie 'Cleanhead'

b. 18 December 1917, Houston, Texas, USA, d. 2 July 1988, Los Angeles, California, USA. Taking up the alto saxophone as a child, his proficiency at the instrument attracted local bandleaders even while young Vinson was still at school, and he began touring with Chester Boone's territory band during school holidays. Upon his graduation in 1935, Vinson joined the band full-time, remaining when the outfit was taken over by Milton Larkin the following year. During his five year tenure with the legendary Larkin band he met T-Bone Walker, Arnett Cobb, and Illinois Jacquet, who all played with Larkin in the late 30s. More importantly the band's touring schedule brought Vinson into contact with Big Bill Broonzy, who taught him how to shout the blues, and Jay 'Hootie' McShann's Orchestra whose innovative young alto player, Charlie Parker, was 'kidnapped' by Vinson for several days in 1941 in order to study his technique. After being discovered by Cootie Williams in late 1941, Vinson joined the Duke Ellington trumpeter's new orchestra in New York City and made his recording debut for the OKeh label in April 1942, singing a solid blues vocal on 'When My Baby Left Me'.

With Williams' Orchestra, Vinson also recorded for Hit Records (1944), Capitol Records (1945) and appeared in a short film, *Film Vodvil*, before leaving to form his own big band in late 1945 and recording for Mercury Records. At Mercury he recorded small group bop and blasting band instrumentals, but his main output was the fine body of suggestive jump-blues sung in his unique wheezy Texas style. Hits such as 'Juice Head Baby', 'Kidney Stew Blues' and 'Old Maid Boogie' were the exceptions, however, as most of Vinson's no-holds-barred songs, including 'Some Women Do', 'Oil Man Blues' and 'Ever-Ready Blues', were simply too raunchy for airplay. After the 1948 union ban, Vinson began recording for King Records in a largely unchanged style ('I'm Gonna Wind Your Clock', 'I'm Weak But Willing', 'Somebody Done Stole My Cherry Red'), often with all-star jazz units. However, his records were not promoted as well as King's biggest R&B stars, like Wynonie Harris and Roy Brown, and he left to return to Mercury in the early 50s, rejoining Cootie Williams' small band briefly in the mid-50s. In 1957 he toured with Count Basie's Orchestra and made some recordings with a small Basie unit for King's jazz subsidiary, Bethlehem Records, after which he retired to Houston. In 1961 he was rediscovered by fellow alto saxophonist, Cannonball Adderley, and a fine album resulted on Riverside Records with the Adderley brothers' small band. From then until his death in 1988, Vinson found full-time employment at worldwide jazz and blues festivals, a steady international touring schedule and dozens of credible albums on such jazz and blues labels as Black & Blue, Bluesway, Pablo, Muse and JSP.

Selected albums: *Cleanhead's Back In Town* (1957), *Back Door Blues* (1961), *Cherry Red* (1967), *Wee Baby Blues* (1969), *Kidney Stew* (1969), *Live!* (1969), *The Original Cleanhead* (1969), *You Can't Make Love Alone* (1971), *Jammin' The Blues* (1974), *Eddie 'Cleanhead' Vinson In Holland* (1976), *Cherry Red Blues* (Bellaphon 1976), *Live In Blue Note, Göttingen* (1976), *Great Rhythm & Blues Volume 2* (1977), *The Clean Machine* (Muse 1978), *Hold It Right There!* (1978), *Live At Sandy's* (1978), *Fun In London* (JSP 1980), *I Want A Little Girl* (1981), with Count Basie, Big Joe Turner *Kansas City Shout* (1982), *Eddie 'Cleanhead' Vinson And A Roomful Of Blues* (1982), *Mr Cleanhead's Back In Town* (Mole 1982), *Kidney Stew* (1984), *Mr Cleanhead Steps Out* (Saxophonograph 1985), *Cleanhead And A Roomful Of Blues* (Muse 1986), *Sings The Blues* (Muse 1987), with Etta James *Blues In The Night: The Early Show* (1988), with Cannonball Adderley *Cleanhead & Cannonball* (Landmark 1988), *The Real 'Mr Cleanhead'* (1989), *Meat's Too High* (1989), *Midnight Creeper* (1989), with

James *Blues In The Night: The Late Show* (1989).

Vitous, Miroslav

b. 6 December 1947, Prague, Czechoslovakia. After studying bass at the Prague Conservatory and then the Berklee College Of Music in Boston, Massachusetts, Vitous had played or recorded with an astonishing list of major jazz artists by 1970, including Freddie Hubbard, Miles Davis, Chick Corea and Wayne Shorter. A founder-member of the influential Weather Report, with Shorter and Joe Zawinul, he left in 1973 to study a custom-made instrument combining electric bass and guitar. Forming a brilliant new group in 1979, with John Surman (saxophone), Kenny Kirkland or John Taylor (piano), and Jon Christenson (drums), Vitous' melodic, folk-influenced bass was important in the creation of the European style recorded by ECM Records.

Selected albums: with Roy Haynes, Chick Corea *Now He Sings, Now He Sobs* (1968), *Mountain In The Clouds* (Atlantic 1977), *First Meeting* (ECM 1979), *Miroslav Vitous Group* (ECM 1981), *Journey's End* (ECM 1983), *Emergence* (ECM 1986), with Haynes, Corea *Trio Music: Live In Europe* (1987), *Miroslav* (Freedom 1988), *Guardian Angels* (Evidence 1990), with Jan Garbarek, Peter Erskine *Star* (1991), *Return* (FNAC 1992), with Garbarek *Atmos* (ECM 1993).

Von Ohlen, John

b. 13 May 1941, Indianapolis, Indiana, USA. Taking up the drums in his teens, Von Ohlen's first major job was with Billy Maxted's Manhattan Jazz Band which he joined in 1967. The following year he played with Woody Herman and then joined Stan Kenton. He was with the Kenton band for two years before settling in Cincinnati, Ohio, where he formed a big band to play at the Blue Wisp club. The band included several highly talented young musicians, such as pianist Steve Schmidt and trumpeters Al Kiger and Tim Hagans. Extensively recorded by Helen Y. Morr of the Cincinnati-based MoPro Records, the Blue Wisp Big Band is an exceptionally fine example of an American rehearsal band. Although Von Ohlen's international reputation rests largely upon his former association with Kenton, his playing with his own big band and with small groups assembled especially for record dates or to accompany such visiting jazzmen as Cal Collins and Bill Berry, shows him to be a versatile drummer capable of great sensitivity and unflagging swing.

Albums: *WKRC-TV & The Blue Wisp Jazz Club Presents The Blue Wisp Big Band Of Cincinnati* (1981), *The John Von Ohlen-Steve Allen Big Band* (1982), with the Blue Wisp Big Band *Butterfly* (1982), with Blue Wisp *The Smooth One* (1983), with Cal Collins *Crack'd Rib* (1984), with Blue Wisp *Live At Carmelo's* (1984), with Blue Wisp *Rollin' With Von Ohlen* (1985).

Von Schlippenbach, Alex

b. Alexander von Schlippenbach, 7 March 1938, Berlin, Germany. Schlippenbach studied piano and composition at school, and his early jazz-related interests were in boogie-woogie and blues piano. After a period influenced by musicians such as Oscar Peterson, Bud Powell and Thelonious Monk, he began playing free jazz in the 60s. He worked with Gunter Hampel in 1963 and Manfred Schoof (1964-67) and in 1966 set up the Globe Unity Orchestra to play his composition *Globe Unity* at the Berlin Jazz Festival. The orchestra's impact enabled him to resuscitate it the following year and on frequent occasions since; over the 70s and 80s, the Orchestra has established itself as the world's leading free jazz big band, its ranks including many outstanding European players (Schoof, Kenny Wheeler, Peter Brötzmann, Albert Mangelsdorff, Peter Kowald) as well as occasional US guests, such as Steve Lacy and Anthony Braxton. In 1970, Schlippenbach formed a quartet with Evan Parker, with whom he has since produced much challenging music both in and out of the Globe Unity Orchestra and in a regular trio (with Paul Lovens). He has also worked frequently in a duo with drummer Sven Ake Johansson. In 1988 Schlippenbach formed the Berlin Jazz Composers' Orchestra and in 1990 recorded the remarkable duo *Smoke* with Sunny Murray. A tireless organizer and electrifying improviser - whose speed and power of execution recall Cecil Taylor - Schlippenbach has long been one of the major figures of the European free jazz scene.

Albums: *Globe Unity* (1966), *The Living Music* (1969), *Payan* (1972), *Pakistani Pomade* (1972), with Globe Unity Orchestra *Live In Wuppertal* (1973), with GUO *Hamburg '74* (1974), *Three Nails Left* (1975), with GUO *Evidence* (1975), with GUO *Into The Valley* (1975), with GUO *Local Fair* (1976), with Sven Ake Johansson *Live At The Quartier Latin* (1976), with GUO *Pearls* (1977), *The Hidden Peak* (1977), with GUO *Improvisations* (1977), *Piano Solo* (1977), with Johansson *Kung Bore* (1978), with GUO *Compositions* (1979), with Johansson *Drive* (1980), with RAI Big Band *Jelly Roll* (1981), with Johansson *Kalfactor A. Falke Und Andere Lieder* (1982), *Detto Fra Di Noi* (1982), *Anticlockwise* (1983), with GUO *Intergalactic Blow* (1983), with Martin Theurer *Rondo Brillante* (1983), with Paul Lovens *Stranger Than Love* (1985), *Berlin Jazz Composers' Orchestra* (1990), with Sunny Murray *Smoke* (FMP 1990), *Elf Bagatellen* (FMP 1991), *Physics* (FMP 1992), *The Morlocks* (FMP 1994).

Wachsmann, Phil

b. 5 August 1944, Kampala, Uganda. Violinist Wachsmann was born into a musical family: his mother sang and his father studied Ugandan traditional music and played violin. After studying music at Durham University, he won a scholarship to Bloomington University, Indiana. In 1968 he studied for a year in Paris with Nadia Boulanger. Between 1969 and 1970 he lectured on music at Durham University and also set up an improvisation workshop. In the early 70s he worked with Yggdrasil, a group that played compositions by John Cage and Morton Feldman, and led his own group Chamberpot. Since then he has involved himself in the UK free-jazz scene, playing with Tony Oxley, Derek Bailey and Barry John Guy. He started his own record label, Bead, which documented free improvisations at the outer limits. He cites Joe Venuti and classical

violinist Itzhak Perlman as influences on his playing, although traces of Gustav Mahler and the Second Viennese School are also apparent: Wachsmann is interested in electronics and in the possibilities of strict 12-tone improvisation (rather than simply 'atonal' playing). In 1989 he formed an especially productive duo with singer Vanessa Mackness.

Albums: with Ian Brighton *Marsh Gas* (1975), *Chamberpot* (1976), *Sparks Of The Desire Magneto* (1977), with Tony Oxley *February Papers* (1977), with Harry de Wit *For Harm* (1979), *Was Macht Ihr Denn* (1982), *Writing In Water* (1985).

W

Walcott, Collin

b. 24 April 1945, New York City, USA, d. 8 November 1984. He played the violin at school and later studied percussion at Indiana University. In 1967 he studied the sitar with the famous Indian sitarist Ravi Shankar and the tabla with Alla Rakha. He began a lifelong association with Oregon in 1971, playing sitar and tabla. In the mid-70s he recorded two albums under his own name with jazz musicians such as John Abercrombie, Dave Holland, Jack DeJohnette and the influential trumpet player Don Cherry. In the late 70s he formed Codona with Cherry and the virtuoso Brazilian berimbau player and percussionist Nana Vasconcelos. The trio toured widely and recorded three albums for ECM Records. Walcott's luminous compositions, which defy easy classification, are among the subtlest and most significant attempts to explore the interconnectedness of various world musical traditions. Walcott died in a car crash in Magdeburg, Germany, in 1984 while on tour with Oregon.

Albums: *Cloud Dance* (ECM 1975), *Grazing Dreams* (ECM1977). Compilation: *Works* (ECM 1989). Selected sessions: with Richie Havens *Richard P. Havens 1983* (Verve 1969), with Tim Hardin *Bird On A Wire* (Verve 1970), with Cyrus *Cyrus* (1971), with the Paul Winter Consort *Icarus* (1972), with David Liebman *Drum Ode* (1975), with Larry Coryell *Restful Mind* (1975), with Meredith Monk *Key* (1977), with Steven Eliovson *Who's To Know, Dawn Dance* (1981).

Waldron, Mal

b. Malcolm Earl Waldron, 16 August 1926, New York City, New York, USA. After studying piano and composition formally, Waldron began playing professionally with a succession of R&B bands. He also recorded with Ike Quebec and from 1954 was a regular associate of Charles Mingus. Waldron's own mid-50s band enjoyed a measure of success in live performances and on record, and he also led the house-band for the Prestige label, playing and arranging on sessions for artists such as John Coltrane and Art Farmer. Late in the decade Waldron became Billie Holiday's regular accompanist remaining with her for nearly two-and-a-half years. After Holiday's death in 1959 he accompanied Abbey Lincoln, but was mainly active in studio work. In the early 60s he played with leading jazz musicians such as Eric Dolphy, Booker Little and Max Roach, but suffered a serious illness which set back his career. From the late 60s Waldron was resident in Europe, finally settling in Munich, where he helped to launch both the ECM and Enja labels by recording their debut releases. Although originally a bop pianist in the mould of Thelonious Monk, Waldron has proved adept at free jazz, most notably in various group sessions that feature soprano saxophonist Steve Lacy, with whom he has also recorded an outstanding series of duos. He has written for films, is the composer of a number of pieces for the ballet and for many years enjoyed the distinction of being the best-selling jazz album artist in Japan, where he has recorded with many local musicians.

Selected albums: with Charles Mingus *Moods Of Mingus* (1955), *Mal 1* (Original Jazz Classics 1956), with Mingus *Pithecanthropus Erectus* (1956), *Mal 2* (Original Jazz Classics 1957), *Mal 3 Sounds* (Original Jazz Classics 1958), with Billie Holiday *Lady In Satin* (1958), *Mal 4* (1959), with Steve Lacy *Reflections* (1959), *Impressions* (Original Jazz Classics 1959), *Left Alone* (1960), *The Quest* (1961), with Eric Dolphy *Eric Dolphy Live At The Five Spot* (1961), *Les Nuits De La Negritude* (1964), *All Alone* (1966), *Trio* (1966), *Sweet Love, Bitter* (1967), *Ursula* (1969), *Set Me Free* (1970), *Free At Last* (ECM 1970), *Tokyo Reverie* (1970), *Tokyo Bound* (1970), *Blood And Guts* (1970), *Spanish Bitch* (1971), *Number Nineteen* (1971), *The Opening* (1971), *The Call* (1971), *Live: 4 To 1* (1971), with Gary Peacock *First Encounter* (1971) *Black Glory* (1971), *Signals* (1971), with Kimiko Kasai *One For Lady* (1971) *Blues For Lady Day* (Black Lion 1972), *A Little Bit Of Miles* (1972), *Journey With End* (1972), *With The Steve Lacy Quintet* (1972), *A Touch Of The Blues* (1972), *Mal Waldron On Steinway* (1972), *Hard Talk* (1974), with Jackie McLean *Like Old Times* (1976), *One Upmanship* (1977), *Moods* (Enja 1978), *Mingus Lives* (1979), *Mal 81* (1981), *What It Is* (1981), *One Entrance, Many Exits* (1982), *Snake Out* (1982), *In Retrospect* (1982), *Breaking New Ground* (1983), *Herbe De L'Oublie* (1983), *Plays Erik Satie* (1984), *You And The Night And The Music* (1984), with David Friesen *Encounters* (1984), with Marion Brown *Songs Of Love And Regret* (Freelance 1985), *Dedication* (Soul Note 1986), *Update* (Soul Note 1986), with Sumiko Yoseyama *Duo* (1986), *Space* (Vent Du Sud 1986), *Sempre Amore* (Soul Note 1986), *Let's Call This...* (1986, rec. 1981), *Eric Dolphy And Booker Little Remembered* (1987), *Left Alone* (1987), *The Git Go* (Soul Note 1987), with Jim Pepper *Art Of The Duo* (Tutu 1988), *Seagulls Of Kristiansund* (Soul Note 1988), *Both Sides Now* (1988), *Our Collines's A Tresure* (Soul Note 1988), *Live At Sweet Basil* (Paddle Wheel 1988), *Much More!* (Freelance 1988), *The Super Quartet Of Mal Waldron* (1988), *Mal, Dance And Soul* (Tutu 1988), *Quadrologue At Utopia, Vol.*

1 (Tutu, 1990), *The Git-Go At Utopia Vol 2* (Tutu 1990), *Hot House* (1991), *Crowd Scene* (Soul Note 1992), with Chico Freeman *Up And Down* (1992).

Wallace, Bennie

b. 18 November 1946, Chatanooga, Tennessee, USA. In his teens Wallace played jazz saxophone and sat in with local country and R&B bands. He studied clarinet at Tennessee University, then moved to New York in the early 70s, working with West Indian-born pianist Monty Alexander and singer Sheila Jordan. Wallace's affinity to Ornette Coleman's new jazz language is shown by his later neglect of the piano: he prefers to work in trios, unconfined by the piano's tempered scales. Mostly playing tenor saxophone, his first trio consisted of Glen Moore (bass) and Eddie Moore (drums), who were replaced in 1978 by Eddie Gomez and Dannie Richmond. His debut with this trio - *The Fourteen Bar Blues*, recorded for Enja in 1978 - was a revelation. Playing with a loose bravado usually heard from musicians with gospel backgrounds, he had found a way to translate Ornette's concept to tenor, on the way picking up echoes of Eric Dolphy and Albert Ayler. The album won the Deutscher Schallenplattenpreis and he was invited to play at the 1979 Berlin Jazz festival with the George Gruntz band. In 1981, at the festival, Wallace fronted the North German Radio Band. *Live At The Public Theatre* (1978) gave him more room to stretch out and confirmed his stature. In 1982 he recorded with Dave Holland and Elvin Jones (*Big Jim's Tango*) and in 1984 reaffirmed his southern roots with a magnificent gospel track featuring the Wings Of Song vocalists (*Sweeping Through the City*). His Blue Note Records debut, *Twilight Time*, explored his southern background even more extensively, and featured guest appearances by Dr. John and Stevie Ray Vaughan. Garrulous, inventive and full of the blues, without a trace of the ubiquitous, studied John Coltrane-influenced sound, Wallace may be just the thing the tenor saxophone needs for its rejuvenation in the 90s.

Selected albums: *The Fourteen Bar Blues* (Enja 1978), *Live At The Public Theatre* (Enja 1978), *Plays Monk* (Enja 1981), *Big Jim's Tango* (1982), *Free Will* (Enja 1982), *Sweeping Through The City* (Enja 1984), *Twilight Time* (1985), *Art Of The Saxophone* (Denon 1988), with Yosuke Yamashita *Brilliant Corners* (Denon 1988), *Border Town* (Blue Note 1989), *Twilight Time* (Blue Note 1989), *The Wings Of Song* (Enja 1991), *The Talk Of The Town* (Enja 1993).

Waller, Fats

b. Thomas Wright Waller, 21 May 1904, Waverley, New York, USA, d. 15 December 1943, Kansas City, Missouri, USA. Influenced by his grandfather, a violinist, and his mother Waller was playing piano at students' concerts, and organ in his father's church by the time he was 10 years old. In 1918, while still in high school, he was asked to fill in for the regular organist at the Lincoln Theatre, and subsequently gained a permanent seat at the Wurlitzer Grand. A year later, he won a talent contest, playing ragtime pianist James P. Johnson's, 'Carolina Shout'. While a protege of Johnson's, Waller adopted the

Harlem stride style of piano playing, 'the swinging left hand', emphasizing tenths on the bass, to which Waller added his own distinctive touch. In 1919, while on tour as a vaudeville pianist, he composed 'Boston Blues' which, when the title was later changed to 'Squeeze Me', with a lyric by Clarence Williams, became one his best known songs. In the early 20s, with the USA on the brink of the 'jazz age', and Prohibition in force, Waller's piano playing was in demand at rent-parties, bootleg joints, in cabaret and vaudeville. Inevitably, he mixed with gangsters, and it is said that his first $100 bill was given to him by Al Capone, who fortunately enjoyed his piano playing. Around this time Waller made his first records as accompanist to one of the leading blues singers, Sara Martin. He also recorded with the legendary Bessie Smith, and toured with her in 1926. His first solo piano recording was reputedly 'Muscle Shoal Blues'.

From 1926-29 he made a series of pipe organ recordings, in a disused church in Camden, New Jersey. Having studied composition from an early age with various teachers including Leopold Godowski and Carl Bohm, Waller collaborated with James P. Johnson and Clarence Todd on the music for the Broadway revue, *Keep Shufflin'* (1928). This was a follow-up to Noble Sissle and Eubie Blake's smash hit, *Shuffle Along* (1921), which starred Joséphine Baker, and was the show which is credited with making black music acceptable to Broadway audiences. Although not on stage in *Keep Shufflin'*, Waller made a considerable impression with his exuberant piano playing from the show's orchestra pit at Daly's Theatre. Andy Razaf, who wrote most of the show's lyrics, including the outstanding number, 'Willow Tree', would become Waller's most regular collaborator, and his closest friend. Just over a year later, in June 1929, Waller again combined with Razaf for *Hot Chocolates*, another Negro revue, revised for Broadway. In the orchestra pit this time, was trumpeter, Louis Armstrong, whose role was expanded during the show's run. The score for *Hot Chocolates* also contained the plaintive ('What Did I Do To Be So) Black, And Blue?'; and one of the team's most enduring standards, 'Ain't Misbehavin'', an instrumental version of which became Waller's first hit and years later, was selected for inclusion in the NARAS Hall of Fame. Both *Keep Shufflin'* and *Hot Chocolates* were first staged at Connie's Inn, in Harlem, one of the biggest black communities in the world. Waller lived in the middle of Harlem, until he hit the really big time and moved to St. Albans, Long Island, where he installed a built-in Hammond organ.

In the late 20s and early 30s, he was still on the brink of that success. Although he endured some bleak times during the Depression he was writing some of his most effective songs, such as 'Honeysuckle Rose', 'Blue, Turning Grey Over You', and 'Keepin' Out Of Mischief Now' (all with Razaf); 'I've Got A Feeling I'm Falling' (with Billy Rose and Harry Link); and 'I'm Crazy 'Bout My Baby' (with Alexander Hill). In 1932 he toured Europe in the company of fellow composer, Spencer Williams, and played prestige venues such as London's Kit Kat Club and the Moulin Rouge in Paris. Worldwide fame followed with the formation of Fats Waller And His Rhythm in

1934. The all-star group featured musicians such as Al Casey (guitar), Herman Autrey (trumpet), Gene Sedric (reeds), Billy Taylor or Charles Turner (string bass), drummers Harry Dial (b. 17 February 1907, Birmingham, Alabama, USA) or Yank Porter (b. c.1895, Norfolk, Virginia, USA, d. 22 March 1944, New York, USA) and Rudy Powell (clarinet). Signed for Victor, the ensemble made over 150 78 rpm records between May 1934 and January 1943, in addition to Waller's output of piano and organ solos, and some big band tracks. The Rhythm records were a revelation. High-class musicianship accompanied Waller's exuberant vocals, sometimes spiced with sly, irreverent asides on popular titles such as 'Don't Let It Bother You', 'Sweetie Pie', 'Lulu's Back In Town', 'Truckin'', 'A Little Bit Independent', 'It's A Sin To Tell A Lie', 'You're Not That Kind', 'Until The Real Thing Comes Along', 'The Curse Of An Aching Heart', 'Dinah', 'S'posin', 'Smarty', 'The Sheik Of Araby', 'Hold Tight' and 'I Love To Whistle'.

Waller had massive hits with specialities such as 'I'm Gonna Sit Right Down And Write Myself A Letter', 'When Somebody Thinks You're Wonderful', 'My Very Good Friend The Milkman' and 'Your Feet's Too Big'. He recorded ballads like 'Two Sleepy People' and 'Then I'll Be Tired Of You', and several of his own compositions, including 'Honeysuckle Rose' and 'The Joint Is Jumpin'' (written with Razaf and J.C. Johnson). In 1935, Waller appeared in the first of his three feature films, *Hooray For Love* which also featured Bill 'Bojangles' Robinson. In the following year he received excellent reviews for his rendering of 'I've Got My Fingers Crossed' in *King Of Burlesque*. In 1938, he toured Europe again for several months, this time as a big star. Besides performing concerts in several cities, including a performance at the London Palladium, he appeared in an early television broadcast from Alexandra Palace, and became the first, and probably the only jazz musician, to play the organ of the Notre Dame de Paris. He returned to England and Scotland the following year. Back in the USA, Waller toured with a combo for a while, and during the early 40s performed with his own big band, before again working as a solo artist. In 1942 he tried to play serious jazz in concert at Carnegie Hall - but was poorly received. In 1943, he returned to Broadway to write the score, with George Marion, for the bawdy musical *Early To Bed*. The comedy high-spot proved to be 'The Ladies Who Sing With The Band'.

Waller teamed with 'Bojangles' Robinson again, in 1943, for the film of *Stormy Weather*, which included a version of 'Ain't Misbehavin''. He stayed in California for an engagement at the Zanzibar Club in Los Angeles. On his way back to New York on the Santa Fe Chief railway express, he died of pneumonia as it was pulling into Kansas City. His life had been one of excess. Enormous amounts of food and liquor meant that his weight varied between 285 and 310 lbs - 'a girthful of blues'. Days of carousing were followed by equal amounts of sleeping, not necessarily alone. Jazz continually influenced his work, even when he was cajoled into recording inferior material. He worked and recorded with leading artists such as Fletcher Henderson, Ted Lewis, Alberta Hunter, Jack Teagarden, Gene Austin and Lee Wiley. Waller felt strongly that he did not receive his fair share

473

of the songwriting royalties. He was known to visit the Brill Building, which housed New York's prominent music publishers, and obtained advances from several publishers for the same tune. Each, however, had a different lyric. He sold many numbers outright, and never received credit for them. Two which are rumoured to be his, but always attributed to Jimmy McHugh, 'I Can't Give You Anything But Love' and 'On The Sunny Side Of The Street', were included in the 1978 Broadway show *Ain't Misbehavin'*. Most of the numbers were genuine Waller, with a few others like 'Mean To Me', 'It's A Sin To Tell A Lie', 'Fat And Greasy' and 'Cash For Your Trash' which, in performance, he had made his own. The majority of his recordings have been reissued and appear on a variety of labels such as RCA, Saville, Halcyon, Living Era, President, Swaggie (Australia) and Vogue (France).

Selected albums: *Ain't Misbehavin'* (1980, released on CD in 1989), *Fats At The Organ* (1981, released on CD in 1988), *20 Golden Pieces* (1982), *Piano Solos (1929-41)* (1983), *African Ripples* (1984), *Live At The Yacht Club* (1984), *Fats Waller In London* (1985), *My Very Good Friend The Milkman* (1986), *Armful O'Sweetness* (1987), *Dust Off That Old Pianna* (1987), *Complete Early Band Works 1927-9* (1987), *Take It Easy* (1988), *Fats Waller And His Rhythm 1934-36 (Classic Years In Digital Stereo)* (1988), *Spreadin' Rhythm Around* (1989), *The Last Years 1940-1943* (Bluebird 1989), *Ragtime Piano Entertainer* (1989), *Loungin' At The Waldorf* (1990), *Audio Archive* (IMD 1992), *1939/40 - Private Acetates And Film Soundtracks* (1993). Further reading: *The Music Of Fats Waller*, John R.T. Davies. *Fats Waller*, Charles Fox. *Fats Waller*, Maurice Waller and Anthony Calabrese. *Ain't Misbehavin': The Story Of Fats Waller*, E.W Kirkeby, D.P. Schiedt and S. Traill. *Stride: The Music Of Fats Waller*, P. Machlin. *Fats Waller: His Life And Times*, Alyn Shipton.

Wallington, George

b. Giacinto Figlia, 27 October 1924, Palermo, Sicily, Italy, d. 13 February 1993. His family emigrated in 1925 and so Wallington was brought up in the USA. In the 40s he worked with Dizzy Gillespie on Manhattan's 42nd Street and went on to play piano for many other leaders. Although the flowing lines of his playing were reminiscent of Bud Powell, his style was developed independently and as well as being an accomplished pianist he was an interesting composer. He wrote 'Lemon Drop' which was a best-seller for Gene Krupa and 'Godchild' which was recorded by the Miles Davis Nonet. In 1953 he travelled to Europe with Lionel Hampton and then led a series of groups of his own including musicians such as Jackie McLean, Phil Woods and Donald Byrd. Wallington withdrew from the music business in 1960, but made something of a comeback in the 80s when he played at the Kool Festival (1985) and recorded several albums.

Selected albums: *George Wallington Trio* i (1951), *George Wallington Trio* ii (1952), *The Workshop Of The George Wallington Trio* (1954), *Jazz For The Carriage Trade* (Fantasy 1956), *Knight Music* (1956), *The New York Scene* (Original Jazz Classics 1958), *Jazz At Hotchkiss* (Savoy 1958), *Virtuoso*

(1984), *The Pleasure Of A Jazz Inspiration* (VSOP 1986), *Symphony Of A Jazz Piano* (Denon 1988), *Virtuoso* (Denon 1988), *Live At The Cafe Bohemia* (Progressive 1993), with Jimmy Jones *Trios* (Vogue 1993).

Wallis, Bob

b. 3 June 1934, Bridlington, Yorkshire, England. Wallis started his first band in Bridlington in 1950 and that lasted right through to 1957. Later he joined Papa Bue's Viking Band (1956), Diz Disley's Jazz Band (1957) and briefly Acker Bilk's Band (1958). From 1958 he had his own Storyville Jazzmen who were very popular throughout the 'trad' boom of the late 50s. His own trumpet playing and singing forcefully reflected the influence of Henry 'Red' Allen. He had two minor UK hits with 'I'm Shy Mary Ellen I'm Shy' (1961, number 44) and 'Come Along Please' (1962, number 33). Change in popular taste brought the demise of the Storyville Jazzmen but Wallis played with a variety of bands including Monty Sunshine's. He then moved to Switzerland where he played throughout the 80s.

Selected albums: *Everybody Loves Saturday Night* (Top Rank 1960), *Bob Wallis's Storyville Jazzmen* (1973), *Live* (Storyville 1975), *Jazz Doctor* (1975), *Doctor Jazz* (Storyville 1988).

Walrath, Jack

b. Jack Arthur Walrath, 5 May 1946, Stuart, Florida, USA. A hugely underrated modern jazz trumpeter, Walrath was one of the most talented instrumentalists to work with bassist Charles Mingus during the later part of the great bandleader's career. Like so many major figures in contemporary jazz, he is a graduate of Boston's Berklee College Of Music, which he attended in the early 60s. After graduating, he crossed from east to west and sunnier, Californian climes, and began to earn a reputation for his big tone and sure technique, touring with Ray Charles (for whom he did a certain amount of arranging) and working locally with bassist Gary Peacock. Moving back to New York in the early 70s, he worked commercially backing singers in soul and R&B bands, before he was discovered by Mingus, who helped revive the Jazz Workshop with Walrath's charismatic musical presence in 1974. Mingus allowed him more opportunity to stretch his composition and arrangement skills – many of Mingus' last recordings carry credits for Walrath's arrangements and direction. After Mingus' death in 1979, Walrath continued to work with Jazz Workshop drummer Dannie Richmond, co-leading a the last Mingus band formation featuring saxophonist Ricky Ford, pianist Bob Neloms and Cameron Brown taking over the bass chair, as well as touring and recording under his name (with his band: the Masters Of Suspense). Walrath is a gifted, confident bop improviser with an infectious sense of humour. Recommended recordings must include the recent *Serious Hang*, a lively quintet performance featuring fellow ex-Mingus man Don Pullen on Hammond, guitarist David Fluczysnki, bassist Michael Formanek and drummer Cecil Brooks III.

Albums: with Charles Mingus *Changes One* (1975), with Mingus *Three Or Four Shades Of Blue* (1977), with Mingus

Cumbia And Jazz Fusion (1976/77), with Dannie Richmond *Plays Charles Mingus* (1980), *Revenge Of The Fat People* (1981), *In Europe* (1982), *Wholly Trinity* (1986), *Killer Bunnies* (1986), *Master Of Suspense* (1986), *Neohippus* (1986/88), with Muhal Richard Abrams *The Hearinga Suite* (1989), with Abrams *Blu Blu Blu* (1990), *Serious Hang* (1994).

Walton, Cedar

b. 17 January 1934, Dallas, Texas, USA. After being taught piano by his mother, Walton studied music formally. In the mid-50s his early career was interrupted by military service, but he was fortunate in that this allowed him to meet and play with several emerging jazz musicians, including Don Ellis. After leaving the armed forces, he played in and around New York with important bop artists such as Kenny Dorham, J.J. Johnson and Art Blakey. He proved an adept accompanist to singers as well as to instrumentalists and in the mid-60s was frequently performing with Abbey Lincoln. Later in the decade he worked with artists such as Lee Morgan, Hank Mobley and George Coleman. In the 70s he worked briefly with Blakey again, and played frequently with Clifford Jordan, but was mostly active as co-leader of groups such as Eastern Rebellion and Soundscapes. A gifted soloist and able accompanist, at home mainly in bop and post-bop settings, Walton's reputation with the public still lags behind the high regard with which he is held by his fellow artists.

Selected albums: *Cedar* (Timeless 1967), *Spectrum* (1968), *Soul Cycle* (1969), *The Electric Boogaloo Song* (1969), *A Night At Boomer's* (Muse 1973), *Firm Roots* (1974), *Pit Inn* (1974), *Mobius* (1975), *Eastern Rebellion* (Timeless 1975), *The Pentagon* (1976), *First Set* (1977), *Second Set* (Steeplechase 1977), *Third Set* (1977), *Animation* (CBS 1977), *Soundscapes* (1979), *The Maestro* (Muse 1980), *Piano Solos* (1981), with Hank Mobley *Breakthrough* (Muse 1981), *Firm Roots* (Muse 1981), *Among Friends* (Theresa 1982), *Bluesville Time* (Criss Cross 1985), *Cedar's Blues* (1985), *Cedar* (1985), *Love* (Red 1987), *Cedar Walton Plays The Music Of Billy Strayhorn* (1988), *Maybeck Recital Hall Series, Vol. 25* (1993), with Steve Grossman *A Small Hotel* (1993), *As Long As There's Music* (Muse 1993).

Ward, Carlos

b. 1 May 1940, Ancon, Panama. Ward moved to Seattle at the age of 13 and started playing clarinet, switching to alto saxophone in 1955. While in the US Army he attended the Navy School of Music in Washington, DC and played in military bands in Germany, also sitting in with *avant garde* outfits led by Albert Mangelsdorff and Karl Berger and hearing Eric Dolphy (a revelation) in Frankfurt. On returning to Seattle he sat in with John Coltrane, who invited him to join his octet. He moved to New York to do so (unfortunately this group was never recorded). In 1969 he toured and recorded with the funk band B.T. Express. Other engagements included work with Sam Rivers, Sunny Murray, Rashied Ali and a two-year stint in the late 70s with Carla Bley (*Social Studies*). He had met Abdullah Ibrahim and Don Cherry in Copenhagen in 1964:

both encounters led to musical associations. In the 70s and early 80s he played with Ibrahim in a variety of ensembles - from duos to big bands to the pianist's group, Ekaya - and in 1985 he formed the co-operative Nu with Cherry, Ed Blackwell, Mark Helias (bass) and Nana Vasconcelos, lending astringent bebop lines to the world-music mix. In 1986 he replaced Jimmy Lyons in the Cecil Taylor Unit (*Live In Bologna*, *Live In Vienna* and *Tzotzil Mummers Tzotzil*). In 1987 he formed a quartet with Ronnie Burrage on drums; *Lito* is a live album that features a guest appearance by Woody Shaw, on what proved to be one of the trumpeter's final recordings.

Selected albums: With Abdullah Ibrahim *Live At Sweet Basil Vol I* (1986, rec. 1983), *Lito* (Leo 1988), *Live At Northsea Festival* (1988 (Leo 1989).

Ware, Wilbur

b. 8 September 1923, Chicago, Illinois, USA, d. 9 September 1979. When Ware's multi-instrumentalist foster-father organized church music he became interested, and eventually learned to play the banjo and then the double bass. He played in amateur string groups in Chicago and recorded with Big Bill Broonzy in 1936. In the 40s he was playing with Stuff Smith (violin), Roy Eldridge (trumpet) and Sonny Stitt (alto saxophone) in the mid-west. He started leading his own groups in 1953 at the Bee Hive Club and the Flame Lounge in Chicago, and also gigged with Thelonious Monk and Johnny Griffin. Between 1954-55 he toured with the bebop-altoist-cum-R&B-singer Eddie 'Cleanhead' Vinson and with the Jazz Messengers in the summer of 1956. He and Art Blakey formed the rhythm section of the renowned Monk group that included both Coleman Hawkins and John Coltrane (1957). He also played with Buddy De Franco that year and recorded with Sonny Rollins. In 1959 he returned to Chicago and was inactive for a while. In the late 60s he went back to New York, playing with Monk (1970) and recording with longtime associate, tenor saxophonist Clifford Jordan in 1969 and 1976. Wilbur Ware participated in some of the crucial music of his time - well documented by Riverside Records - and developed the bass as a force both in solo and ensemble work.

Selected albums: *Presenting Ernie Henry* (1956), *Thelonious Monk And John Coltrane* (1957), *Monk's Music* (1957), with Sonny Rollins *A Night At The Village Vanguard* (1957), with Clifford Jordan *Jenkins, Jordan & Timmons* (1957), *The Chicago Sound* (Original Jazz Classics 1958), with Jordan *Starting Time* (1961), with Jordan *In The World* (1969), with Jordan *Remembering Me-Me* (1977).

Warren, Earle

b. Earle Ronald Warren, 1 July 1914, Springfield, Ohio, USA, d. 4 June 1994, Springfield, Ohio, USA. As a child Warren played a number of instruments in a family band, but by his teens had settled on the alto saxophone. From 1930 he played in numerous territory bands until, in 1937, he joined Count Basie. Playing lead alto and nicknamed 'Smiley', he stayed with Basie until 1945 and thereafter returned several times in between leading his own band for short engagements.

Throughout the 50s he played in various all-star bands, often teamed with other former Basie musicians, among them Buck Clayton, Jimmy Rushing and Dicky Wells. He only left Basie's side for good when his wife became ill, and went on to join vocal group the Platters (on baritone sax). He also managed Johnny Otis' show band. In the 70s and on through the 80s Warren continued to perform, sometimes as a soloist, sometimes in packages featuring other swing era veterans. A striking player with a rich tone, Warren's many years as section leader with Basie have sometimes obscured his importance. Although he was often subordinated in this setting to the solo voices of artists such as Lester Young and Buddy Tate, his solos were always worthy of attention and displayed both an inventive mind and great musical skill. After living in Switzerland for nearly a decade he returned to his home town of Springfield in 1992 for the last two years of his life.

Selected albums: With Buck Clayton *Copenhagen Concert* (1959), *Jazz From A Swinging Era* (1967), *Buck Clayton Jam Session* (1974-76), *Earle Warren And The Anglo-American All Stars* (1974), *Earle Warren* (1974). Compilations: With Count Basie: *Swingin' The Blues (1937-45)* (1983), *Earle Warren & The Counts Men* (Muse 1992).

Washington, Dinah

b. Ruth Jones, 29 August 1924, Tuscaloosa, Alabama, USA, d. 14 December 1963. Raised in Chicago, Dinah Washington first sang in church choirs for which she also played piano. She then worked in local clubs, where she was heard by Lionel Hampton, who promptly hired her. She was with Hampton from 1943-46, recording hits with 'Evil Gal Blues', written by Leonard Feather, and 'Salty Papa Blues'. After leaving Hampton she sang R&B, again achieving record success, this time with 'Blow Top Blues' and 'I Told You Yes I Do'. In the following years Washington continued to sing R&B, but also sang jazz, blues, popular songs of the day, standards, and was a major voice of the burgeoning, but as yet untitled, soul movement. However, her erratic lifestyle caught up with her and she died suddenly at the age of 39. Almost from the start of her career, Washington successfully blended the sacred music of her childhood with the sometimes earthily salacious secularity of the blues. This combination was a potent brew and audiences idolized her, thus helping her towards riches rarely achieved by black artists of her generation. She thoroughly enjoyed her success, spending money indiscriminately on jewellery, cars, furs, drink, drugs and men. Physically, she appeared to thrive on her excesses, as can be seen from her performance in the film of the 1958 Newport Jazz Festival, *Jazz On A Summer's Day*. She was settling down happily with her seventh husband when she took a lethal combination of pills, probably by accident after having too much to drink. Washington's voice was rich and she filled everything she sang with heartfelt emotion. Even when the material was not of the highest quality, she could make the tritest of lyrics appear deeply moving. Amongst her popular successes were 'What A Diff'rence A Day Makes', her biggest hit, which reached number 8 in the USA in 1959, and 'September In The Rain', which made number 35 in the

UK in 1961. Washington usually sang alone but in the late 50s she recorded some duets with her then husband, Eddie Chamblee. These records enjoyed a measure of success and were followed in 1960 with songs with Brook Benton, notably 'Baby (You Got What It Takes)' and 'A Rockin' Good Way (To Mess Around And Fall In Love)', which proved to be enormously popular, achieving numbers 5 and 7 respectively in the US charts. Washington left a wealth of recorded material, ranging from *The Jazz Sides*, which feature Clark Terry, Jimmy Cleveland, Blue Mitchell and others, to albums of songs by or associated with Fats Waller and Bessie Smith. On these albums, as on almost everything she recorded, Washington lays claim to being one of the major jazz voices and probably the most versatile of all the singers to have worked in jazz.

Selected albums: *Dinah Washington Sings* (1950), *Dynamic Dinah* (1951), *Blazing Ballads* (1951), *Music For Late Hours* (early 50s), *Dinah Washington Sings Fats Waller* (early 50s), *After Hours With Miss D* (1954), *Dinah Jams* (1954), *For Those In Love* (Emacry 1955), *Dinah* (Emacry 1956), *In The Land Of Hi Fi* (Emacry 1956), *The Swingin' Miss D* (Emacry 1956), *Dinah Washington Sings Bessie Smith* (Emacry 1958), *What A Difference A Day Makes!* (Emacry 1960), *Unforgettable* (Mercury 1961), *I Concentrate On You* (1961), *For Lonely Lovers* (1961), *September In The Rain* (1961), *Tears And Laughter* (1962), with the Quincy Jones Orchestra *I Wanna Be Loved* (1962), *The Good Old Days* (1963), with Sarah Williams and Joe Williams *We Three* (1964), *Dinah '62* (1962), *In Love* (1962), *Drinking Again* (1962), *Back To The Blues* (1963), *Dinah '63* (1963), *A Stranger On Earth* (1964). Compilations: *This Is My Story, Volume One* (1963), *This Is My Story, Volume Two* (1963), *In Tribute* (1963), *The Best Of Dinah Washington* (1965), with Brook Benton *The Two Of Us* (1978, coupled with a Sarah Vaughan and Billy Eckstine collection), *Spotlight On Dinah Washington* (1980), *The Best Of Dinah Washington* (1987), *The Complete Dinah Washington Vols. 1-14 (1943-55)* (Official 1990), *The Best Of Dinah Washington, The Roulette Years* (Roulette 1992), *50 Greatest Hits* (Double Platinum 1993).

Further reading: *Queen Of The Blues: A Biography Of Dinah Washington*, James Haskins.

Washington, Grover, Jnr.

b. 11 November 1943, Buffalo, New York, USA. Growing up in a musical family, Washington was playing tenor saxophone before he was a teenager. He studied formally and also paid his dues gigging locally on tenor and other instruments in the early 60s. After military service in the late 60s he returned to his career, recording a succession of albums under the aegis of producer Creed Taylor which effectively crossed over into the new market for jazz fusion. By the mid-70s, Washington's popular success had begun to direct the course of his music-making and he moved further away from jazz. Commercially, this brought continuing successes, amongst them 'The Two Of Us', with vocals by Bill Withers, reached number 2 in the US pop charts in 1981, and the popular album *The Best Is Yet To Come* with Patti Labelle. Over the years Washington has had five gold

Grover Washington Jnr.

albums. *Winelight* sold over a million copies, this achieving platinum status, and gained two Grammy awards. Washington's playing displays great technical mastery and early in his career his often blues-derived saxophone styling sometimes gave his playing greater depths than the quality of the material warranted. The fact that much of his recorded output proved to be popular in the somewhat anonymous setting of discos tended to smooth out his playing as the years passed, depleting the characteristics that had attracted so much attention at the start of his career. By the late 80s Washington was still enjoying a degree of popular success, although not at the same high level as a few years before, and had largely lost his jazz following.

Albums: *Inner City Blues* (Motown 1971), *All The King's Horses* (Motown 1972), *Soul Box* (1973), *Mister Magic* (Mister Magic 1975), *Feels So Good* (Motown 1975), *A Secret Place* (Motown 1976), *Live At The Bijou* (Motown 1977), with Locksmith *Reed Seed* (Motown 1978), *Paradise* (Elektra 1979), *Skylarkin'* (Motown 1980), *Winelight* (Elektra 1980), *Come Morning* (Elektra 1981), *The Best Is Yet To Come* (Elektra 1982), *Inside Moves* (Elektra 1984), *Playboy Jazz Festival* (Elektra 1984), *Strawberry Moon* (CBS 1987), *Then And Now* (CBS 1988), *Time Out Of Mind* (Columbia 1989), *Next Exit* (Columbia 1992). Compilations: *Baddest* (1980), *Anthology* (Motown 1981), *Greatest Performances* (1983), *At His Best* (Motown 1985), *Anthology* (Elektra 1985).

Watanabe, Sadao

b. 1 December 1933, Tochigi, Japan. His father was a professional music teacher and Watanabe took up the clarinet to play in the school band before moving on to the alto saxophone. He moved to Tokyo in 1951 and took flute lessons with a member of the Tokyo Philharmonic. He joined the quartet of Toshiko Akiyoshi and became its leader when she left in 1956. He went to study at the Berklee College Of Music in the early 60s and worked with musicians including Gabor Szabo, Chico Hamilton and Gary McFarland. He returned to Tokyo in 1965 where he became director of the Yamaha Institute for Popular Music which was modelled on the Berklee College. He has led his own band since and has toured widely. He once revealed that two trips to Africa in 1971 and 1974 were particularly influential on his music. In the 70s his music moved towards pop, or at least to a fusion sound which brought him enormous popularity, of which *Fill Up The Night*, a number 1 jazz album in the USA and Japan, is a good example. In 1977 he became the first jazz musician to receive a National Award in Japan. He plays with a round, polished tone incorporating vocal effects to heighten the emotional intensity. He has recorded more than 60 albums both with his own bands and with other musicians including, McFarland, Hamilton and Chick Corea.

Selected albums: with Chico Hamilton *El Chico* (1965), with Chick Corea *Round Trip* (1970), *Plays Ballads* (Denon 1970), *Bossa Nova Concert* (Denon 1970), *Dedicated To Charlie Parker* (Denon 1970), *Pastoral* (1970), *Round Trip* (Vanguard 1974), *Pamoja* (1975), *I'm Old Fashioned* (1976), *My Dear Life* (1977), *Bird Of Paradise* (1977), *California Shower* (Miracle 1978),

Morning Island (1979), *Live At The Budokan* (1980), *Orange Express* (CBS 1981), *Fill Up The Night* (1983), *Rendezvous* (1983), *Maisha* (WEA 1985), *Parker's Mood* (Elektra 1986), *Tokyo Dating* (Elektra 1986), *Good Time For Love* (Elektra 1987), *Birds Of Passage* (Elektra 1987), *Modern Jazz Album* (Denon 1988), *Elis* (Elektra 1988), *Made In Coracao* (Elektra 1989), *Selected* (Elektra 1989), *Sweet Deal* (East West 1991), *Earth Step* (Verve Forecast 1993).

Waters, Benny

b. 23 January 1902, Brighton, Maryland, USA. A talented multi-instrumentalist, by his mid-teenage years Waters was adept on most of the saxophone family and also played piano and sang. During the 20s he played in various bands, studied formally and taught, numbering Harry Carney among his pupils. In these early years he played with Joe 'King' Oliver, Charlie 'Fess' Johnson and Clarence Williams, and in the following decade worked in the bands of Fletcher Henderson, Johnson again, and Oran 'Hot Lips' Page. In the 40s he worked with artists such as Jimmie Lunceford and Claude Hopkins. He led his own band for a while and also worked with some R&B bands. In the early 50s, while touring Europe in Jimmy Archey's traditional band, he decided to settle in France. He continued to tour from this base throughout the 60s and 70s and became a favourite at many UK clubs and festivals, where he appeared frequently into the 80s and 90s. In the early summer of 1991 he was featured at London's Barbican Centre in concert with fellow octogenarian Doc Cheatham, the pair making nonsense of their ages. A spirited soloist, favouring tenor among the several saxophones he plays, Waters possesses a dazzling technique underscored by a fervent feeling for the blues. His enthusiasm, skill and intensity would be creditable in a jazzman of any age; coming from a musician entering his 90s they are little short of miraculous.

Selected albums: *Night Sessions In Swing And Dixieland* (1960), *Benny Waters And The Latin Jazz Band I* (1960), *Benny Waters And The Latin Jazz Band II* (1960), *Together On Records For 25 Years* (1961), *Benny Waters In Paris* (1967), *Zigging And Zagging* (1968), *The Many Faces Of Benny Waters* (1969), *The Benny Waters Quartet* (1972), *Benny Waters Et Le Jazz De Pique* (1974), *Jazz Sur Le RTF* (1974), *Benny Waters And His Swedish Band I* (1974), *Swinging Along With Benny Waters* (1974), *Benny Waters And His Swedish Band II* (1975), *The Two Sides Of Benny Waters* (1976), *Lady Be Good* (1976), *Bouncing Benny* (1979), *When You're Smiling* (1980), *On The Sunny Side Of The Street* (JSP 1981), *Live At The Esplanade With Cy Laurie And The Eggy Ley Hot Quintet* (1981), *Live At The Edinburgh Festival* (1982), *Mature* (1983), *Hearing Is Convincing* (1987), *Memories Of The Twenties* (1988), *Small's To Shanri-La* (Muse 1992).

Watkins, Doug

b. Douglas Watkins, 2 March 1934, Detroit, Michigan, USA, d. 5 February 1962. Watkins has the rare distinction of having played bass on a Charles Mingus record, *Mingus Oh Yeah*, on which the volatile leader switched to piano. Watkins never achieved the same critical status as his brother-in-law Paul Chambers, although he too was a very fine player, contributing a solid foundation for one of the most important modern jazz albums, Sonny Rollins' *Saxophone Colossus*. He left Detroit to tour with James Moody in 1953, then, after moving to New York, worked with Kenny Dorham and participated in the Horace Silver recording date, which led to the formation of Art Blakey's Jazz Messengers. He rejoined Silver from 1956-7 and then worked with Kenny Dorham again, and with Rollins, Jackie McLean, Lee Morgan, Donald Byrd, and Hank Mobley. He was relocating to San Francisco when he was killed in a car crash.

Selected albums: with Jackie McLean *4, 5 And 6* (1956), with Sonny Rollins *Saxophone Colossus* (1956), with Gene Ammons *Funky* (1957), with the Prestige All-Stars *Two Guitars* (1957), with Donald Byrd *Two Trumpets* (1957), with Art Farmer, Donald Byrd Sextet *Trumpets All Out* (1957), *Fuego* (1959), *Bluesnik* (1961), with Charles Mingus *Mingus Oh Yeah* (1961).

Watkins, Julius

b. 10 October 1921, Detroit, Michigan, USA, d. 4 April 1977. Watkins started playing French horn in grammar school at the age of nine. Between 1943 and 1946 he worked with Ernie Fields, lived in Colorado for a year and then returned to Detroit to form his own band. He studied with Francis Hellstein of the Detroit Symphony Orchestra and Robert Schultze of the New York Philharmonic Orchestra and spent three years at the Manhattan School of Music. In 1949, he worked with Milt Buckner. Watkins recorded with Kenny Clarke and Babs Gonzales and gigged with bassist Oscar Pettiford, then in 1954 toured with the Pete Rugolo Orchestra and recorded with Thelonious Monk. In early 1956, he had formed Les Modes with Charlie Rouse, which lasted for three years, and he also performed on Miles Davis's *Porgy And Bess*. In August 1959, he joined George Shearing's big band and played in the Charles Mingus Workshop in 1965 and 1971. He also recorded with the Jazz Composers' Orchestra in 1968. The French horn came to symbolize the classical aspirations of 'cool' jazz, but Watkins' playing always had the power and edge of a top jazz improviser.

Selected albums: with Thelonious Monk *Quintet* (1954), with Miles Davis *Porgy And Bess* (1958).

Watkiss, Cleveland

b. October 1959, London, England. The Watkiss family arrived in England from Jamaica in 1955 and he grew up with the sounds of bluebeat, ska and reggae at home and sang pop and soul at school talent competitions where he started to play guitar and take classical piano lessons. In his early 20s he was affected by the Bob Marley explosion of Rastafarian reggae, and followed the Fatman Hi-Fi Sound System. A chance encounter with a tape of Charlie Parker playing 'Night In Tunisia' in 1980 led to a conversion to jazz, confirmed by witnessing Charlie Rouse at Ronnie Scott's Club in 1982. His group, Alumni, featuring brother Trevor Watkiss (piano) and Alan Weekes (guitar), played in London's Covent Garden wine bars and Watkiss also sang with Simon Purcell's Jazz Train, but it was the formation of the Jazz Warriors by Courtney Pine that made his name. Watkiss is an excellent frontman and his skilled, imaginative scatting added a special fire to their turbulent sound (*Out Of Many, One People*). His interest in Thelonious Monk bore fruit with his debut as leader, *Green Chimneys*, where he added delightful words to Monk's tune. Since then, Watkiss has toured with the Who (1989) and mimicked Bob Marley for the Malibu drinks commercial. 'Spend Some Time', produced by Coldcut, was a hilarious compendium of his singing styles, though it failed to reach the sales expected of it. In 1991 he released *Blessing In Disguise*, a dazzling survey of jazz, pop and carnival music. Watkiss has a facility that may be his own worst enemy, but there is no denying the infectious joyousness of his singing.

Albums: *Green Chimneys* (Polydor 1989), *Spend Some Time* (Urban 1989), *Blessing In Disguise* (Polydor 1991).

Watrous, Bill

b. 8 June 1939, Middletown, Connecticut, USA. Although Watrous took some formal musical tuition and also learned trombone from his father, he was largely self-taught. After playing in semi-professional bands, he studied with Herbie Nichols before turning full-time in the early 60s. He played in bands led by artists such as Billy Butterfield, Kai Winding, Maynard Ferguson and Woody Herman. In the late 60s and early 70s he was a studio musician in New York, but kept his jazz career alive playing in several bands for club and record dates. He also formed his own big band, colourfully named Manhattan Wildlife Refuge Big Band, which included Wayne Andre (trombone), Danny Stiles (trumpet), Dick Hyman (piano) and Ed Soph (drums). Relocated in Los Angeles from the mid-70s onwards, he continued to work in studios but made records with Stiles and others. He also toured Europe, performing and teaching. In 1980 he teamed up with trombonists Winding and Albert Mangelsdorff to form Trombone Summit. A dazzling technician with an endless supply of intriguing ideas and concepts, Watrous is one of the most formidable of all contemporary trombonists. His feeling for jazz runs deep and he has never allowed his work to be tainted by the use of technique for its own sake.

Albums: *Bone Straight Ahead* (1972), with Danny Stiles *In Tandem* (1973), *Bill Watrous Manhattan Wildlife Refuge* (1974), with Stiles *One More Time* (c.1974), *The Tiger Of San Pedro* (1975), *Watrous In Hollywood* (1978), *Funk'n Fun* (1979), *I'll Play For You* (1980), *Coronary Trombossa* (1980), *La Zorra* (1980), *Bill Watrous In London: Live At The Pizza Express* (Mole Jazz 1982), *Roaring Back To New York, New York* (1982), *Someplace To Be* (1986), *Reflections* (1987), *Bone-Ified* (GNP 1992). Compilation: *The Best Of Bill Watrous* (1980).

Watson, Bobby

b. 23 August 1953, Lawrence, Kansas, USA. Watson comes from a musical family; his father played tenor saxophone, as well as working at tuning saxophones and repairing instruments. He played piano from the age of 10, and took up clarinet when he was 12-years-old. In his teens he was playing sax-ophone in R&B bands, then studied music theory at the University of Miami between 1972 and 1975. In 1976 he relo-cated to New York and joined Art Blakey's Jazz Messengers the following year, later becoming the group's musical director. By the time Watson left in 1981, he had produced some of the best late-period Messengers music. A number he wrote then, 'ETA (Estimated Time Of Arrival)', became a theme tune for him. Watson's intense, crystalline alto saxophone sound was much in demand and he played with George Coleman (1981 onwards) and Charlie Persip (1982 onwards). In 1983 he co-founded the 29th Street Saxophone Quartet (with Ed Jackson, Jim Hartog and Rich Rothenburg), which has enjoyed world-wide success ever since. In 1984 he worked with Max Roach on the music for playwright Sam Shepard's *Shepard's Sets*. In 1985 he toured with a band, Young Lions, which had Englishman Guy Barker on trumpet, and in 1987 formed the nine-piece High Court Of Swing for a record dedicated to Johnny Hodges, *The Year Of The Rabbit*. After recording several records for the Italian Red label, including the outstanding *Love Remains*, Watson signed to Blue Note Records and formed the group Horizon with drummer Victor Lewis, bringing a rhythmic punch and sense of humour to the music that fully justified the title of their 1991 album, *Post-Motown Bop*.

Albums: *Estimated Time Of Arrival* (1977), *All Because Of You* (1981), *Live In Sweden* (1981), *Straight Ahead* (1981), *Jewel* (1983), *Perpetual Groove* (1984), *Appointment In Milano* (mid-80s), *Round Trip* (mid-80s), *Gumbo* (1984), with Curtis Lundy *Beatitudes* (1985), *Love Remains* (Red 1987), *No Question About It* (Blue Note 1988), *The Year Of The Rabbit* (1988), *The Inventor* (Blue Note 1989), *Post-Motown Bop* (Blue Note 1991), *Tailor Made* (1993), *This Little Light Of Mine* (Red 1993).

Watters, Lu

b. Lucious Watters, 19 December 1911, Santa Cruz, California, USA, d. 5 November 1989. After playing trumpet with several bands, Watters began leading his own combos in the mid-20s and thereafter was rarely out of work. Although his early bands were orientated towards swing and dance music, by the end of the 30s he was more and more dedicated to traditional jazz styles. Inspired by the music of New Orleans, he formed his Yerba Buena Jazz Band with like-minded fellows such as Turk Murphy, Clancy Hayes and Bob Scobey. Watters' band proved to be enormously successful; he played to capaci-ty audiences at clubs, concerts and festivals and made numer-ous albums which sold extremely well. Briefly interrupted by military service, Watters' career continued into the early 50s, despite the loss of Murphy and Scobey, who formed their own popular bands. From the 50s onwards Watters chose to follow a career outside music, making only an occasional recording date thereafter. Although little of Watters' music was original, the devotion with which he recreated the earlier seminal works of jazz musicians, such as Joe 'King' Oliver, Jelly Roll Morton, Louis Armstrong was of great importance in reviving interest in New Orleans jazz. His example was followed by many others

and he proved a key figure in the revival movement of the 40s. Selected albums: *50s Recordings, Volume 1* and *2* (Dawn Club 1979), *Air Shots From The Dawn Club - Lu Watters' Yerba Buena Jazz Band (1941)* (Homespun 1988), *Lu Watters' Yerba Buena Jazz Band Vols 1-6 (1949-64)* (Homespun 1988).

Watts, Trevor

b. 26 February 1939, York, England. A child of jazz-loving par-ents, Watts was largely self-taught, but he did spend one year in the RAF School of Music. He took up the cornet at the age of 12 and the alto saxophone at 18. From 1958-63 he played in the RAF band. At the end of his National Service, he moved to London to join the New Jazz Orchestra and in 1965 was a founder member of the Spontaneous Music Ensemble (SME). In 1967 he founded the SME's sister band, Amalgam. In 1972 he formed Splinters with Stan Tracey and John Stevens, work-ing with Stevens again in the Dance Orchestra. He also played with Pierre Favre and Bobby Lee Bradford in 1972-73, with Stan Tracey (1973-74), the London Jazz Composers' Orchestra (1972-75), Open Circle and Tentacles (both with Tracey in 1975) and the Universal Music Group in 1978. He formed the Trevor Watts String Ensemble in 1976 and Moire Music and the Moire Music Drum Orchestra in 1978. He won the Thames Television Award for schools teaching in 1972. He plays with a sharp, clear, singing tone and has been one of the most significant figures in the British post-Ornette Coleman school.

Albums: *Springboard* (1966), with the SME *Challenge* (1966), *Prayer For Peace* (1969), *Amalgam Play Blackwell And Higgins* (1973), with Bobby Lee Bradford *Love's Dream* (1973), with John Stevens *Face To Face* (1973), *Cynosure* (Ogun 1976), *Endgame* (1978), *Application Interaction And* (1979), with Amalgam *Over The Rainbow* (1979), *Closer To You* (Ogun 1979), *Moire Music* (Arc 1985), *Moire Music Sextet* (Cadillac 1988), with Barry Guy and the London Jazz Composers' Orchestra *Harmos* (1989), *Double Trouble* (1990), with the Moire Music Drum Orchestra *Live In Latin America Volume 1* (1991), with the MMDO *A Wider Embrace* (ECM 1994).

Weather Report

Founded by Joe Zawinul (keyboards) and Wayne Shorter (reeds). The highly accomplished Weather Report was one of the groups credited with inventing jazz-rock fusion music in the 70s. The two founders had worked together as members of Miles Davis's band in 1969-71, playing on *Bitches' Brew*. The first line-up of Weather Report included Airto Moreira (per-cussion) and Miroslav Vitous (bass). Signing to CBS Records, the group's first album included compositions by Shorter and Zawinul and the line-up was strengthened by Eric Gravatt (drums) and Um Romao (percussion) on the best-selling *I Sing The Body Electric*. Among the tracks was Zawinul's ambitious 'Unknown Soldier', evoking the experience of war. During the mid-70s, the group adopted more elements of rock rhythms and electronic technology, a process which reached its peak on *Black Market* where Zawinul played synthesizer and the bril-liant electric bassist Jaco Pastorius made his first appearance with the group. Pastorius left the group in 1980.

Weather Report's popularity was at its peak in the late 70s and early 80s, when the group was a four-piece, with drummer Pete Erskine joining Pastorius and the two founder members. He was replaced by Omar Hakim from George Benson's band in 1982, and for the first time Weather Report included vocals on *Procession*. The singer was Janis Siegel from Manhattan Transfer. During the mid-80s, Zawinul and Shorter made solo albums before dissolving Weather Report in 1986. Shorter led his own small group while Zawinul formed Weather Update with guitarist Steve Khan and Erskine. Hakim went on to become a touring drummer, highly acclaimed for his work with Sting and Eric Clapton.

Albums: *Weather Report* i (CBS 1971), *I Sing The Body Electric* (CBS 1972), *Sweetnighter* (1973), *Mysterious Traveller* (CBS 1974), *Tail Spinnin'* (1975), *Black Market* (CBS 1976), *Heavy Weather* (CBS 1977), *Mr. Gone* (CBS 1978), *8:30* (CBS 1979), *Night Passages* (CBS 1980), *Weather Report* ii (Columbia 1982), *Procession* (CBS 1983), *Domino Theory* (CBS 1984), *Sportin' Life* (CBS 1985), *This Is This* (CBS 1986), *New Album* (CBS 1988). Compilations: *Heavy Weather: The Collection* (CBS 1990), *The Weather Report Selection* (Columbia 1992, 3-CD box set).

Weatherford, Teddy

b. 11 October 1903, Pocahontas, Virginia, USA, d. 25 April 1945. While Weatherford was still a child his family moved to New Orleans where he began playing piano as a teenager. He was still in his teens when he joined the great northward migration, ending up in Chicago in 1922. During the next few years he was in much demand in the city but itchy feet took him abroad, travelling to the Far East in 1926 first as a sideman but later as a bandleader. He played in Malaya, the Philippines and China from where he returned in the mid-30s just long enough to persuade Buck Clayton to take a band to Shanghai. From China, Weatherford moved to India, France, Sweden, back to India and Ceylon and then finally to India yet again where he played, mainly in Calcutta, until his death from cholera. A solid, rhythmically intense player, with a deep-rooted instinct for the blues, Weatherford's peripatetic career makes an accurate assessment of his work difficult to determine. Reputedly, Weatherford's time in Chicago saw him as a rival to Earl 'Fatha' Hines and claims are made that Hines learned from him. However, his relatively few and mostly pre-electric recordings, good as they show him to be, make it hard to justify such assertions.

Compilations: with Louis Armstrong *Young Louis The Sideman* (1924-27), included on *Piano And Swing* 1935-38).

Webb, Chick

b. William Webb, 10 February 1909, Baltimore, Maryland, USA, d. 19 June 1939. Although crippled soon after his birth, Webb's determination to be a drummer overcame his physical infirmities. After playing in local bands, he travelled to New York while still a teenager and soon formed his own band there. By 1927 he had played at the Savoy Ballroom and other pres-

tigious dance halls. In 1931 he began a residency at the Savoy and quickly became this famous venue's favourite act. He hired fine musicians, among them Johnny Hodges (whom he generously encouraged to take up an offer from Duke Ellington), Benny Carter, Jimmy Harrison, Mario Bauza, Wayman Carver, Taft Jordan, Louis Jordan and Bobby Stark. He also employed a succession of excellent arrangers, including Charlie Dixon, Carter and the outstandingly talented Edgar Sampson. Webb's popularity at the Savoy and through records and radio broadcasts was further enhanced when, in 1935, he hired the recently-discovered Ella Fitzgerald. From this point until Webb's untimely death four years later, the band remained at a musical and commercial peak. Throughout his career Webb's physical condition had given cause for concern; he underwent several spinal operations at Johns Hopkins Hospital in Baltimore, but died there on 19 June 1939. (Reputedly, his last words were, 'I'm sorry, I gotta go now.') One of the outstanding big band drummers, Webb's technical skills and driving yet uplifting beat were essential components of his band's success with audiences, especially the hard-to-please dancers at the Savoy who loved him. Although Jo Jones was concurrently changing perceptions of how big band drummers should play, Webb continued to exert influence and his most enthusiastic successor was Gene Krupa, who altered his style completely after first hearing Webb. As he, in turn, influenced countless thousands of drummers around the world, the Webb style even spread among musicians who perhaps had never heard of him.

Selected albums: *Midnite In Harlem (1934-39)* (1962), *A Legend (1929-36)* (1974), *King Of The Savoy (1937-39)* (1974), *Spinning The Webb* (1974), with Ella Fitzgerald *Silver Swing* (1976), *In The Groove* (Affinity 1983), *Rhythm Man 1931-1934* (Hep Jazz 1988), *Stomping At The Savoy* (1988), *For Radio Only Recordings (1939)* (Tax 1989).

Webb, George

b. 8 October 1917, London, England. After playing piano in and around London, Webb was attracted by the revival movement and in 1942 formed his own traditional band. The band proved to be highly popular with British fans, including over the next few years leading lights of the UK jazz scene such as Wally Fawkes, Eddie Harvey, Owen Bryce and Humphrey Lyttelton. In 1948 Webb folded the band, several of the members forming the nucleus of Lyttelton's first band, and thereafter he made only occasional appearances as a performer. Among these was a brief return to the scene as a member of Lyttelton's band, but for the most part he concentrated on his activities as agent, manager and promoter. In the 70s he was again performing, leading a band which included Sammy Rimington.

Compilation: *George Webb's Dixielanders* (Jazzology 1988).

Weber, Eberhard

b. 22 January 1940, Stuttgart, Germany. Weber's father taught him the cello from the age of six and he only turned to the bass in 1956. He liked the sound of Bill Haley's records, saw an old stand-up bass hanging on the wall in the school gym and tried t out. He played jazz in his spare time from making television commercials and working as a theatre director and only turned professional in 1972. With Wolfgang Dauner (keyboards) he had played in a trio inspired by the Bill Evans Trio and in Dauner's psychedelic jazz-rock band, Etcetera. He worked with the Dave Pike Set and then joined Volker Kriegel's Spectrum, but did not share Kriegel's fascination with rock rhythms and left in 1974. Weber had already recorded *The Colours Of Chloë* for ECM Records and had developed the 5-string bass, which gives him his individual sound, from an old Italian bass with a long neck and a small rectangular soundbox he had seen in an antique shop. His composition style seemed to owe something to minimalist writing but had developed when he realised that he only liked bits and pieces of other people's music and he had concluded 'that when I came to compose I would only use chords and phrases I really liked - and use them over and over'. *The Colours Of Chloë* brought him international recognition and he then worked with guitarist Ralph Towner (1974) and Gary Burton (1974-76). Meanwhile he formed his own band Colours with Rainer Bruninghaus, Charlie Mariano and first Jon Christensen and then John Marshall. He wanted a band that played in an absolutely European way with understated rhythm, spacey, impressionistic keyboard sounds and flowing melody. This European tradition provides 'the feeling for group empathy that I am drawn to' while the jazz tradition gives 'the whole feeling for improvisation . . . knowing when to stretch out or lay out'. He disbanded Colours when he could no longer hold these two traditions in balance and has since played with the United Jazz And Rock Ensemble and as a regular member of saxophonist Jan Garbarek's bands. Since 1985 he has also performed solo bass concerts, where his prodigious technique is evident. He is able to conjure from his electric instrument and a limited array of equipment, some glorious sounds.

Albums: *The Colours Of Chloë* (ECM 1974), *Yellow Fields* (ECM 1975), *The Following Morning* (ECM 1976), *Silent Feet* (ECM 1977), *Fluid Rustle* (ECM 1979) *Little Movements* (1980), *Later That Evening* (ECM 1982), *Chorus* (ECM 1984), *Orchestra* (ECM 1988), *Pendulum* (ECM 1994). Compilation: *Works* (ECM 1989).

Webster, Ben

b. 27 March 1909, Kansas City, Missouri, USA, d. 20 September 1973, Amsterdam, Netherlands. After studying violin and piano, and beginning his professional career on the latter instrument, Webster took up the tenor saxophone around 1930. He quickly became adept on this instrument; within a year he was playing with Bennie Moten and later worked with Andy Kirk and Fletcher Henderson. In the mid-30s he also played briefly with numerous bands mostly in and around New York, including spells with Duke Ellington. In 1940 he became a permanent member of the Ellington band, where he soon became one of its most popular and imitated soloists. Although he was with the band for only three years, he had enormous influence upon it, both through his presence, which galvanized his section-mates, and by his legacy. Thereafter, any new tenor saxophonist felt obliged to play like Webster until they were

established enough to exert their own personalities. After leaving Ellington, he led a small group for club and record dates and also played with several small groups led by artists such as Stuff Smith and Red Allen. In the late 40s he rejoined Ellington for a short stay, then played with Jazz At The Philharmonic. From the 50s and on throughout the rest of his life, he worked mostly as a single, touring extensively, especially to Europe and Scandinavia where he attained great popularity. He was briefly resident in Holland before moving to Denmark, where he lived for the rest of his life.

He recorded prolifically during his sojourn in Europe, sometimes with just a local rhythm section, occasionally with other leading American jazz musicians, among them Bill Coleman and Don Byas. Like so many tenor players of his generation, Webster's early style bore some of the hallmarks of Coleman Hawkins; but by the time of his arrival in the Ellington band in 1940, and his first important recording with them, 'Cottontail', he was very much his own man. His distinctive playing style, characterized by a breathy sound and emotional vibrato, became in its turn the measure of many of his successors. A consummate performer at any tempo, Webster's fast blues were powerful and exciting displays of the extrovert side of his nature, yet he was at his best with slow, languorous ballads, which he played with deeply introspective feeling and an often astonishing sensuality. This dichotomy in his playing style was reflected in his personality, which those who worked with him have described as veering between a Dr Jekyll-like warmth and a Mr Hyde-ish ferocity. One of the acknowledged masters of the tenor saxophone, Webster made innumerable records, few of them below the highest of standards. As the years passed, he favoured ballads over the flagwavers that had marked his younger days. From his early work with Ellington, through the small group sides of the 40s, a remarkable set of ballad duets with Hawkins, to his late work in Europe, Webster's recorded legacy is irrefutable evidence that he was a true giant of jazz.

Selected albums: *The Consummate Artistry Of Ben Webster* (1953), *King Of The Tenors* (1953), *Sophisticated Lady* (1954), *Ballads* (1955), *Coleman Hawkins Encounters Ben Webster/Blue Saxophones* (1957), *Soulville* (Verve 1957), *The Soul Of Ben Webster* (1958), *At The Nuway Club* (1958), with Oscar Peterson *Ben Webster Meets Oscar Peterson* (Verve 1959), *The Warm Moods Of Ben Webster* (1960), *Ben Webster At The Renaissance* (Original Jazz Classics 1960), with Richard 'Groove' Holmes *Groove* (1961), *Ben Webster And Associates* (Verve 1961), with Harry 'Sweets' Edison *Ben And Sweets* (Columbia 1962), *Ben Webster And The MJQ: Live* (1962), *Soulmates* (Original Jazz Classics 1963), *Live At Pio's* (Enja 1963), *Layin' Back With Ben* (1964), *See You At The Fair* (1964), *Live At The Montmartre* (1965), *Saturday Night At The Montmartre* (1965), *Midnight At The Montmartre* (1965), *Sunday Morning At The Montmartre* (1965), *Stormy Weather* (Black Lion 1965), *The Jeep Is Jumping* (Black Lion 1965), *Gone With The Wind* (Black Lion 1965), *Duke's In Bed* (1965), *Atmosphere For Lovers And Thieves* (1965), *There Is No Greater Love* (Black Lion 1967), *Remember* (1967), *Tenor Of Jazz In*

London (1967), with Bill Coleman *Bill Coleman/Ben Webster Live In London* (Black Lion 1967), *Swingin' In London* (1967), *Ben Webster Meets Don Byas In The Black Forest* (1968), *Ben Webster In Copenhagen* (1968-70), *At Ease* (1969), *Quiet Days In Clichy* (1969), *Blow, Ben, Blow* (1969), *For The Guv'nor* (1969), *Ben Op Zijn Best* (1970), *No Fool, No Fun* (1970), *Live At The Haarlemse Jazz Club* (1972), *Ben Webster In Hot House* (1972), *Messenger* (1972), *Live In Paris* (1972), *Makin' Whoopee* (1972), *Autumn Leaves* (1972), *Gentle Ben* (1972), *Ben Webster In Europe* (1972-73), *My Man* (Steeplechase 1973), *Last Concert* (1973), *Ben Webster And Joe Zawinul* (1980), *Live In Amsterdam* (1989, rec. 1969). Compilations: *Scandinavian Days (1965-69)* (1981), *The Horn (1944)* (1986), *Ben Webster Plays Duke Ellington (1967-71)* (1989), *The Verve Years* (Verve 1989), *King Of The Tenors* (Verve 1994).

Weckl, Dave

b. 1960, St Louis, Missouri, USA. A technically advanced fusion drummer who specialises in applying jazz's rhythmic complexity to the aggressive sound of the rock kit, Weckl rose to prominence as Chick Corea's fearless drummer, hidden behind a huge, towering kit in the popular Elektric Band. The son of an amateur pianist, Weckl was turned onto the drums by (strangely) jazz big band drummer Buddy Rich, eventually studying jazz at the University of Bridgeport Connecticut. His first gigging experience was with the successful fusion outfit Nitesprite, and he soon dropped out of college to take advantage of the opportunities to gig and tour abroad. He impressed leading fusion drummer Peter Erskine, who helped spread the young musician's name further, and Weckl soon found himself busy in the fusion scene and in the studio, recording lucrative dates for Diana Ross, George Benson, Madonna and Robert Plant. He joined keyboardist Chick Corea in the mid-80s, forming a third of the fast-moving, virtuoso rhythm section with bassist John Patitucci that in its seven years came to represent Corea's 80s style. Since the group's disbandment, Weckl has concentrated on his own career, recording as a leader on the GRP label, and powering the All-Star GRP Big Band live and on record.

Albums: with Chick Corea *The Chick Corea Elektric Band* (1986), with Corea *Light Years* (1987), with Corea *Eye Of The Beholder* (1988), *Chick Corea Akoustic Band* (1989), with Corea *Inside Out* (1990), *Master Plan* (1990), with Corea *Alive* (1991), *Heads Up* (1992), with Corea *Beneath The Mask* (1992), *Hard-Wired* (1994), with GRP All-Star Big Band *All Blues* (1995).

Wein, George

b. 3 October 1925, Boston, Massachusetts, USA. After studying formally, Wein began playing piano professionally in his early teenage years. He led his own band in and around his home town for a period, frequently accompanying visiting jazz musicians. In the early 50s he opened his own club in Boston, the Storyville, formed his own record label (which had the same name) and was thus launched on his second career as a jazz impresario. In 1954 he was invited to organize the first

Newport Jazz Festival and subsequently played an important part in establishing other major international festivals, including the annual Grande Parade du Jazz at Nice in the south of France. In addition to his work on festivals around the world, he has also actively promoted such organizations as the New York Jazz Repertory Orchestra, and taught jazz in Boston. Although his work in promotion has been enormously time-consuming, Wein has never lost his desire to play piano and regularly appears with all-star bands on festival programmes and record dates. While his career as a pianist might perhaps be overlooked, his importance to jazz through his non-playing activities has been of great significance. Together with Norman Granz, he has been a major force in maintaining the highest standards of presentation and performance, and in ensuring that his artists are given the respect that is their due.

Albums: *George Wein And The Newport All-Stars* (1962), *The Newport Jazz Festival All-Stars* (1984), *Magic Horn* (RCA 1993).

Weller, Don

b. 19 December 1947, Croydon, Surrey, England. After studying classical clarinet Weller switched to tenor saxophone, playing jazz with Kathy Stobart. By the late 60s he had become an important figure on the UK jazz scene, working extensively with Stan Tracey, Art Themen and others. During the 70s Weller continued to play with Tracey, also led his own jazz-rock group, Major Surgery, and regularly played straight jazz gigs with his quartet. In the 80s he still led his quartet and also worked with Bryan Spring and Bobby Wellins, appearing at London clubs and festivals at venues throughout the UK. A powerful player with a robust sound which reflects his burly physical appearance, Weller is one of the best post-bop tenor saxophonists to emerge in the UK. Although well-known and respected by visiting American jazz musicians, he has yet to make an appreciable impact upon international audiences.

Selected albums: with Stan Tracey *The Bracknell Connection* (1976), *Don Weller* (Affinity 1979), *Commit No Nuisance* (Affinity 1981), *Stan Tracey And Don Weller Play Duke, Monk And Bird* (1988).

Wellins, Bobby

b. 24 January 1936, Glasgow, Scotland. Wellins studied alto saxophone with his father; his mother had been a singer in the Sammy Miller Show Band. (His parents later performed on stage as a double act.) Wellins also studied formally, learning piano and clarinet. In the mid-50s he was active in London, by now settled on tenor saxophone. He played in bands led by Buddy Featherstonhaugh, Tony Crombie and Vic Lewis, with whom he visited the USA, then joined Stan Tracey, having first met him in Crombie's Jazz Incorporated band. He was with Tracey for some years in the early 60s, as a member of the New Departures Quartet which also featured Jeff Clyne and Laurie Morgan. The group made a number of important albums, moving British jazz forward into areas previously considered, at least by critics and audiences, to be the preserve of Americans. For Wellins, the next few years were disastrous. The late 60s and early 70s vanished under a haze of various personal problems but by the late 70s he was again active, as leader and co-leader with Don Weller of a number of fine hard bop groups. The albums from these years were amongst the best of their genre recorded in the UK. Since his return to jazz, Wellins has been busy as a teacher. A distinctive player, with an intensely emotional sound which reflects his passionate approach to music, by the late 80s Wellins had become a respected figure on the British jazz scene. Amongst his compositions is the suite 'Endangered Species' recorded under the title, 'Birds Of Brazil'. Selected albums: with Stan Tracey *Under Milk Wood* (1965), *Jubilation* (1978), *Dreams Are Free* (1979), *Birds Of Brazil* (Sungai 1989), *Nomad* (Hot House 1994).

Wells, Dicky

b. 10 June 1907, Centerville, Tennessee, USA, d. 12 November 1985. After starting out on other instruments, Wells took up the trombone in his mid-teens and a year later was playing in New York City with the band led by brothers Lloyd and Cecil Scott. He later worked with the bands of Elmer Snowden, Benny Carter, Charlie 'Fess' Johnson, Fletcher Henderson and Chick Webb, then toured Europe with Teddy Hill before joining Count Basie in the summer of 1938. He remained with Basie until 1950, taking some months off to play with Sy Oliver's ill-fated big band in 1946/7. During the 50s Wells worked with several bands, often in Europe, and usually in good company: Jimmy Rushing, Earl Hines, Buck Clayton and Bill Coleman. In the early 60s he spent long spells with Ray Charles and Reuben Phillips, but by the middle of the decade was back on the road again, touring extensively and continuing to record. Unfortunately, this period also saw the onset of personal problems as a result of alcoholism which prompted his premature retirement from music. In 1973, however, his autobiography, *The Night People* (co-written with Stanley Dance), was published and this revealing, warm and witty book helped to encourage him back onto the scene. His reappearance was well-received and, although he suffered ill-health and was mugged twice (one attack putting him into a coma for several weeks), he continued to perform into the early 80s. In his playing, Wells chose to adopt a seemingly casual approach, liberally peppering his inventive solos with musical witticisms and deliberately jokey effects. In lesser hands, his style could have mirrored the comic excesses of an earlier generation of trombone players in jazz and popular music. Fortunately, his stylishness and wit, coupled with exemplary technique, allowed him to establish a reputation as one of the finest and most distinctive trombone soloists in jazz.
Selected albums: *Lonesome Road* (Uptown 1982), *Trombone Four-In-Hand (1958-59)* (Affinity 1986), *Bones For The King (1958)* (Affinity 1986), *In Paris* (Affinity 1992), *Swingin' In Paris* (Le Jazz 1993).
Further reading: *The Night People*, Dicky Wells with Stanley Dance.

Wellstood, Dick

b. 25 November 1927, Greenwich, Connecticut, USA, d. 24 July 1987. After learning to play piano in his home town, Wellstood came to New York City in 1946 and was soon working with able musicians such as newcomer Bob Wilber and veteran Sidney Bechet. In the early 50s he visited Europe with Jimmy Archey's band, but divided his time between music and law studies. After qualifying as a lawyer he returned to full-time music, working mostly solo, but also in small groups with artists such as Roy Eldridge, Henry 'Red' Allen, Coleman Hawkins and Gene Krupa. In the 70s his solo career expanded, but he also played in the World's Greatest Jazz Band. Throughout his career Wellstood recorded extensively, displaying a remarkable command of his instrument and a wide taste in jazz, although his clear preference was for the older traditions. He was an accomplished exponent of stride piano. In the 80s he continued to work as a single but also played in a trio, the Blue Three, with Kenny Davern and Bobby Rosengarden, and briefly practised law.
Selected albums: with Roy Eldridge *Swing Goes Dixie* (1956), *Alone* (1971), *From Ragtime On* (1971), *From Dixie To Swing* (1972), with Joe Venuti, Zoot Sims *Joe And Zoot* (1974), *Walkin' With Wellstood* (1974), *This Is The One* (1975), *At The Cookery* (1975), *Stride Piano* (1977), *Some Hefty Cats!* (1977), with Kenny Davern, Bob Rosengarden *Live At Hanratty's* (Chaz Jazz 1981), with Davern, Chuck Riggs *Dick Wellstood And His Famous Orchestra Featuring Kenny Davern* (Chiaruscuro 1981), *Live Hot Jazz* (1984), *Bob Wilber/Dick Wellstood: Duet* (1984), *Live At The Cafe Des Copains* (1985), with Dick Hyman *Stride Monster* (1986).

Welsh, Alex

b. 9 July 1929, Edinburgh, Scotland, d. 25 June 1982. Welsh began his musical career in Scotland playing cornet, later trumpet, in trad jazz bands. In the early 50s he moved to London and formed a band which quickly became one of the most proficient of its kind. With every chair filled by musicians of great skill and enthusiasm, the Welsh band was a major force in the British trad jazz movement. Eschewing the fancy dress eccentricities and pop music escapades of many of his rivals (although 'Tansy' did reach the UK Top 50 in 1961), Welsh concentrated on creating exciting music that echoed the vitality of the best of Chicago-style dixieland jazz. Amongst Welsh's sidemen over the years were Archie Semple, Fred Hunt, Roy Crimmins, Roy Williams, John Barnes, Lennie Hastings and Al Gay. During the 60s and early 70s Welsh toured the UK and Europe, building up a rapturous following, and also made occasional successful sorties to the USA. In common with Chris Barber, Welsh saw the need to maintain a wide repertoire, drawing (as jazz always has), from the best of popular music and thus creating a band which effectively swam in the mainstream. By the mid-70s Welsh's health was poor, but he continued to play for as long as he could. Throughout his career Welsh blew with great exuberance, sometimes sang too and always encouraged his sidemen by his example. Not only popular with audiences, he was also respected and admired by his fellow musicians.
Selected albums: *Music Of The Mauve Decade* (1957), *The*

Melrose Folio (1958), *Alex Welsh In Concert* (1961), *Echoes Of Chicago* (1962), *Strike One* (1966), *At Home With Alex Welsh* (Dormouse 1967), *Vintage '69* (1969), *Classic Concert* (Black Lion 1971), *If I Had A Talking Picture Of You* (1975), *In A Party Mood* (One-Up 1977), *Dixieland To Duke* (Dormouse 1986), *Live At The Royal Festival Hall (1954-55)* (Lake 1988), *Doggin' Around* (Black Lion 1993, 1973 recordings).

Wess, Frank

b. 4 January 1922, Kansas City, Missouri, USA. Wess started out on alto saxophone, playing in bands in and around Washington, DC, where he was raised. Later, he switched to tenor saxophone and worked briefly in the band led by Blanche Calloway. He developed his musical abilities while on military service and, following his discharge at the end of World War II, he played in the bands of artists such as Billy Eckstine and Lucky Millinder. During this period he began to play the flute. In 1953 he joined the Count Basie band, mostly playing tenor and flute, and becoming a featured attraction with the band both as soloist and as duettist with fellow sideman Frank Foster. In the late 50s Wess reverted to alto saxophone but continued to feature his flute playing, becoming the first major jazz soloist to popularize this instrument and proving in the process that it could be used in a gimmick-free fashion. He left Basie in 1964, thereafter working in studios, leading his own small groups, making records and working in groups such as the New York Jazz Quartet and Dameronia, the band led by Philly Joe Jones. Wess also wrote numerous arrangements, for his own groups and for other bands. In the mid-80s he was briefly with Woody Herman and also continued to lead his own small group and to co-lead a quintet with Foster. In the late 80s and early 90s he was leading a splendid Basie-style big band, which included in its ranks Harry 'Sweets' Edison, Joe Newman, Snooky Young, Al Grey, Benny Powell, Marshal Royal and Billy Mitchell, and which made highly successful appearances in Japan. Albums by this band, *Dear Mr Basie* and *Entre Nous*, showed that Wess had ably assumed the role of big band leader and arranger in the Basie tradition. As a soloist (whichever instrument he uses), Wess plays with uncluttered swing, fashioning his phrases with care. His playing satisfactorily updates the stylistic traditions of the swing era and is always polished and highly sophisticated.

Selected albums: *Frank Wess Quintet* (1954), *Wess Of The Moon* (Commodore 1954), *North, South, East...Wess* (Savoy 1956), *Opus In Swing* (Savoy 1956), *I Hear Ya Talkin'* (Savoy 1959), *Opus De Blues* (Savoy 1960), *Frank Wess Quartet* (1960), *Yo Ho!* (1963), with Coleman Hawkins *Commodore Years* (1973), *Flute Juice* (Progressive 1982), with Frank Foster *Two For The Blues* (1983), *Frankly Speaking* (1984), *Dear Mr Basie* (Concord 1989), *Entre Nous* (Concord 1990), *Trombones And Flute* (Savoy 1992), *Jazz For Playboys* (Savoy 1992).

Westbrook, Mike

b. 21 March 1936, High Wycombe, Buckinghamshire, England. The UK's premier jazz composer, Westbrook grew up in Torquay and tried accountancy, National Service and art

school before realizing that music was his first love. He formed his first band in Plymouth in 1958, soon recruiting the teenage John Surman on baritone saxophone, and in 1962 moved to London, where he led numerous groups and played regularly at the Old Place and the Little Theatre Club while working in the day as an art teacher. His first three records - *Celebration*, *Release* and *Marching Song* - were large-scale, big band works that showed Westbrook rapidly expanding his modern jazz base to include blues, rock 'n' roll, brass band marches, 'The Girl From Ipanema' and Lionel Hampton's 'Flying Home' riff in glorious profusion. His composerly skills in blending all of these together was matched by outbursts of brilliant improvisation from soloists such as Surman, Mike Osborne, Malcolm Griffiths and Paul Rutherford. Two unrecorded pieces, 'Earthrise' and the seven-hour 'Copan/Backing Track', were early examples of his continuing interest in multi-media projects, with Cosmic Circus (1970-72). Another early 70s Westbrook group, Solid Gold Cadillac, explored facets of jazz-rock. Reverting to the big band format, he recorded *Citadel Room 315* in 1975 (again featuring Surman), which is considered his first real masterpiece. Orchestral projects have remained a major focus of interest - the subsequent *The Cortege*, *Westbrook-Rossini* (based on themes from Rossini operas), *On Duke's Birthday* (Duke Ellington tribute taken from a larger work, 'After Smith's Hotel') have all been hailed as outstanding examples of jazz composition. In 1973 Westbrook also formed his Brass Band, featuring old friend and vocalist Phil Minton and his future wife Kate Westbrook (née Bernard), and they toured the UK playing at factories, schools, hospitals and street-theatre festivals. The group later developed into one of Westbrook's most impressive line-ups notably on *Bright As Fire*, a tribute to the poet William Blake, based on music that he had earlier written (and recorded) for the Adrian Mitchell play, *Tyger*. In 1983 Westbrook started a trio with Kate and regular associate Chris Biscoe, which explored the Westbrooks' interest in European cabaret music (*A Little Westbrook Music*). Much of his music is inspired by literary or theatrical sources: for instance, *The Cortege*, widely considered his finest work to date, comprises a series of songs based on texts by poets such as Rimbaud, Hesse, Lorca, Blake and John Clare. More recent albums have included the ambitious, brilliant in parts *London Bridge Is Broken Down* (for voice, jazz orchestra and chamber orchestra) and the Beatles tribute *Off Abbey Road*. Though awarded the OBE in 1988, Westbrook, like many UK jazz musicians, works chiefly on the continent, where he is offered many more opportunities to play and record than he is at home. Proficient on piano and tuba, he is less an instrumentalist than a virtuoso composer, the scope and scale of whose work places him firmly in the lineage of his heroes Ellington, Charles Mingus and Kurt Weill.

Selected albums: *Celebration* (1967), *Release* (1968), *Marching Song, Vols. 1 & 2* (1969), *Love Songs* (1970), *Metropolis* (1971), *Tyger* (1971), *Solid Gold Cadillac* (1972), *Mike Westbrook Live* (1972), *Citadel Room 315* (Novus 1975), *Plays 'For The Record'* (Transatlantic 1976), *Love/Dreams And Variations* (Transatlantic 1976), *Mike Westbrook - Piano* (1978), *Goose*

Mike Westbrook

Sauce (Original 1978), *Mama Chicago* (1979), *Bright As Fire - The Westbrook Blake* (Impetus 1980), *Piano* (1980), *This Is Their Time - Oh Yes* (1981, rec. 1969), *The Paris Album* (1981), *The Cortege* (Enja 1982, three album set), *A Little Westbrook Music* (1983), *Love For Sale* (Hat Art 1986), *Pier Rides* (1986), *Westbrook-Rossini* (Hat Art 1987), *London Bridge Is Broken Down* (Venture 1988, three album box-set), *On Duke's Birthday* (Hat Art 1988, rec. 1984), *Pierides, The Dance Band* (Line 1989), *Off Abbey Road* (Tip Toe 1990).

Weston, Randy

b. Randolph Weston, 6 April 1926, New York City, New York, USA. Weston grew up in Brooklyn and in the late 40s ran a restaurant that was frequented by many of the city's leading bebop musicians. Deciding to pursue a musical career himself, he played piano with various R&B bands (including a record date with the Clovers) and also worked with Eddie 'Cleanhead' Vinson, Kenny Dorham and Cecil Payne. One of the first artists signed to the Riverside label, his debut session, in April 1954, comprised a set of Cole Porter tunes. Later Riverside dates included a solo album and a trio recording with Art Blakey on drums. Long fascinated by all things African, Weston recorded *Uhuru Afrika* in 1960 - a big band suite with lyrics by Langston Hughes and arrangements by Melba Liston: players included Freddie Hubbard, Yusef Lateef, Max Roach and Babatunde Olatunji. In 1961 he travelled to Nigeria with other USA artists to appear at an arts festival in Lagos, and returned again for a lecture tour in 1963. In the early 60s he led a group that featured Booker Ervin and (later) Ed Blackwell, releasing *Highlife* and *African Cookbook*. He also recorded the solo/trio *Berkshire Blues* for Duke Ellington's projected label, but this never materialized and the sessions finally appeared on the Freedom label some 13 years later. Weston started his own label, Bakton, but it quickly folded and, discouraged by the music scene, he left the USA. After a 14-country tour of North and West Africa, he settled in Tangier in 1968, where he ran the African Rhythms Club for several years. Returning to the USA in the early 70s, he released two big band albums, the jazz-funk *Blue Moses* and *Tanjah*, but subsequent releases have concentrated almost exclusively on solo piano and have included tributes to Ellington and Thelonious Monk, his major piano mentors. Notable exceptions are a duo album with David Murray and his recent *The Spirits Of Our Ancestors*, which again has arrangements by Liston and features guest artists Dizzy Gillespie, Dewey Redman and Pharoah Sanders. A powerful player (he is over six-and-a-half feet tall!), Weston is adept at using the piano percussively, although he is also a talented melodist who has written several well-known tunes, such as 'Hi Fly' and 'Little Niles', the latter a 1952 waltz named after his son Azadeen, now a skilled percussionist.

Selected albums: *Cole Porter In A Modern Mood* (1954), *The Randy Weston Trio* (1955), *With These Hands* (1956), *Jazz A La Bohemia* (Original Jazz Classics 1957), *Trio And Solo* (1957), *Little Niles* (1958), *Uhuru Afrika* (1961), *Randy!* (1964),

Highlife (1964), *African Cookbook* (1965), *Monterey '66* (Verve 1967), *Blues* (1967), *Blues Moses* (1972), *Tanjah* (1973), *Informal Solo Piano* (1974), *African Rhythms* (1975), *Blues To Africa* (1975), *Carnival* (Freedom 1975), *African Nite* (Owl 1976), *Randy Weston* (1977), *Perspective* (Denon 1977), *Berkshire Blues* (1978, rec. 1965), *Nuits Americaine* (1982), *Blue* (1984), *The Healers* (1987), *How High The Moon* (1989), *Portraits Of Duke Ellington* (Verve 1990), *Portraits Of Thelonious Monk* (Verve 1990), *Self Portraits* (Verve 1990), *The Spirits Of Our Ancestors* (Verve 1992), with Melba Liston *Volcano Blues* (Verve 1993), *Marrakech In The Cool Of The Evening* (Verve 1993). Compilation: *Zulu* (1977, rec 1955-56).

Wettling, George

b. 28 November 1907, Topeka, Kansas, USA, d. 6 June 1968. Resident in Chicago from his early teenage years, Wettling studied drums under various teachers, including the celebrated Roy C. Knapp (who also taught Gene Krupa). While still in his teens Wettling became a professional musician and worked with numerous bands, mostly based in Chicago and all playing dance and popular music of the day. In the mid-30s he worked with Paul Mares and was a member of Jack Hylton's American band. Later in the decade he moved to New York City and was hired by Artie Shaw for his first big band. He later played in the big band led by Bunny Berigan and was also with Red Norvo and Paul Whiteman. His musical inclinations lay in other areas, however, and during this period he made many records with small dixieland-Chicago-style groups. Gradually, he moved into this field of music, although he did spend time in big bands led by Abe Lyman and Benny Goodman during the early 40s. From the mid-40s onwards he was closely associated with Eddie Condon, playing at Condon's club, touring and recording with Wild Bill Davison, Bud Freeman, Pee Wee Russell, Sidney Bechet and many others. A propulsive and energetic drummer, Wettling played with dash and verve, inspiring his musical companions to give of their best. In addition to his musical career, Wettling was an accomplished painter and his abstract work was exhibited in New York City and has been reproduced in magazines.

Selected albums: *George Wettling's Jazz Band* (JSP 1951), *George Wettling's High Fidelity Rhythms* (1954), with Eddie Condon *Tiger Rag And All That Jazz* (1958), *Is George Really George?* (1962).

Wheeler, Kenny

b. 14 January 1930, Toronto, Canada. Sometimes known as Weeny Keller, this outstanding jazz composer, trumpet, cornet and flügelhorn player is one of the shyest and most self-effacing artists imaginable. Buddy Rich once said 'show me a humble man and I'll show you a nonentity' which must make Wheeler the world's most respected and influential musical nonentity. Major figures from jazz and improvised music, such as John Surman and Evan Parker, have queued up to work with him since the 60s and continue to do so; witness the line-ups he assembled for Orchestra UK and the Kenny Wheeler Big Band at the start of the 90s. He learned cornet at the age of 12

and studied trumpet and harmony at Toronto Conservatory. He moved to London in 1952, mainly working in big bands such as Roy Fox and Vic Lewis. From 1959-65 he was in the John Dankworth band, but also played with the groups of Tubby Hayes and Joe Harriott. In the 60s he studied for a while with Richard Rodney Bennett and Bill Russo, and came into contact with free music at the Little Theatre Club where he worked with Tony Oxley, John Stevens and the Spontaneous Music Ensemble. He guested with the brilliant John Surman-Mike Osborne Quartet in the late 60s and was so lacking in self-confidence that at one gig he played from behind a stack of equipment, producing thrilling and challenging music nonetheless. His CV demonstrates his versatility and status among his peers: he has played with John Taylor, Mike Pyne, Jan Garbarek, Michael Gibbs, the Clarke-Boland Big Band, John Warren, the Globe Unity Orchestra, Graham Collier, Ronnie Scott, Alan Skidmore (in a quintet which was a high-light of Jazz Expo 69), the United Jazz And Rock Ensemble, Dave Holland and Anthony Braxton and has led, apart from Orchestra UK, several starry bands of his own, including Azimuth (which he co-founded in 1977 with John Taylor and Norma Winstone, and which is not to be confused with Azymuth), Coe (Tony Coe) Wheeler & Co, and the superb Freedom For A Change. In the early 90s he toured with the new Michael Gibbs Band featuring John Scofield.

Albums: with Paul Gonsalves *Humming Bird* (1968), *Windmill Tilter* (1968), with Philly Joe Jones *Trailways Express* (1968), with Michael Gibbs *Michael Gibbs* (1970), *Tanglewood '63* (1971), with Globe Unity *Live In Wuppertal* (1973), *Song For Someone* (Incus 1974), *Will Power* (1974), *Gnu High* (ECM 1976), *Deer Wan* (ECM 1978), *Improvisations* (1978), *Around Six* (1980), *Double, Double You* (ECM 1984), with Dave Holland *Seeds Of Time* (1985), *Welcome* (Soul Note 1987), *The Razor's Edge* (1987), *Flutter By Butterfly* (Soul Note 1988), *Music For Large And Small Ensembles* (ECM 1990), *The Widow in The Window* (ECM 1991), *California Daydream* (Musidisc 1991), *Kayak* (Ah Um 1993).

Whigham, Jiggs

b. Haydn Whigham, 20 August 1943, Cleveland, Ohio, USA. Whigham studied extensively as a young man, learning trombone, harmony and composing. In the early 60s he joined the Glenn Miller band led by Ray McKinley, remaining until the middle of the decade. He was then briefly with Stan Kenton before joining Kurt Edelhagen in Germany. Whigham decided to stay on in Germany, freelancing and teaching throughout the 70s and into the early 80s, eventually becoming a member of the faculty of the Cologne Music School. He also recorded *The Third Stone* with Bill Holman and the West German Radio big band. In the mid- to late 80s Whigham occasionally toured as a single, visiting the UK and recording with Vic Lewis. He also made some appearances in duo with Mundell Lowe. Technically faultless, Whigham exudes power tempered with finesse and is greatly respected by his fellow musicians.

Albums: *Hope* (Mons 1976), *The Third Stone* (1982), *The Jiggs Up* (Capri 1989).

White, Andrew

. 6 September 1942, Washington, DC, USA. White's uncle played saxophone, flute and guitar. He studied saxophone himself with John Reed in Nashville (1954-60) and music theory with Brenton Banks (1958-60), then attended Howard University, Washington (1960-64), playing with the University Band and Symphonietta. Early work experience was gained with pianist Don Pullen in the late 50s, by which time White was playing alto and tenor saxophones and double bass. During 1964/5 he played tenor saxophone with Kenny Clarke in Paris. In 1965 he led the New Jazz Trio in Buffalo. Next came stints playing electric bass with Stanley Turrentine and tenor saxophone with the Cyclones and Otis Redding (1967). Between 1968 and 1970 White played electric bass with Stevie Wonder and was the principal oboist and English horn player for New York's American Ballet Theatre Orchestra. He played bass in the popular singing group Fifth Dimension from 1971-76, and in a production of *Hair* in 1971. The following year he guested on Weather Report's *I Sing The Body Electric*, and in 1973 played electric bass and English horn on their historic *Sweetnighter*.

In September 1973 he completed a catalogue of 209 transcribed John Coltrane solos, for which he had set up (in 1971) his own publishing imprint, Andrew's Music. In 1977 he published a further series of 212 transcribed Coltrane solos. Peter Ochiogrosso described White's work as 'doing for 'Trane what Kirschel did for Mozart'. Albums of Coltrane solos, trio work with the artists including Buell Neidlinger, and orchestral works - *Concerto* and *Concertino* - have been produced since, along with books, articles and further transcriptions (including Eric Dolphy and Charlie Parker solos). In 1991 White's catalogue of products for sale totalled 1600 items. In 1984 he stunned the jazz world by producing *Andrew's X-Rated Band Stories*, the first in a series of four X-rated comedy books. In the 80s White played with the Elvin Jones Jazz Machine (1980-81), the Beaver Harris All-Stars (1983) and, since 1987, has worked with Julius Hemphill on several saxophone-based projects. His 1981 classical record, *Petite Suite Francaise*, was, he claims, the 'first-ever feature album recorded by a black oboist', but since the mid-80s he has released no new albums, preferring to concentrate on his voluminous activities as writer, teacher, transcriber and live performer - not to mention single-handedly running Andrew's Music and continuing his unstaunchable dedication to the music of John Coltrane.

Albums: *Andrew Nathaniel White III* (1971), *Live At The New Thing In Washington DC* (1973), *Live In Bucharest* (1973), *Who Got De Funk?* (1973), *Passion Flower* (1974), *Sings For A French Lady* (1974), *Theme* (1974), *Live At The Foolery, Vols 1-6* (1975), *Collage* (1975), *Marathon '75, Vols 1-9* (1976), *Spotts, Maxine And Brown* (1977), *Countdown* (1977), *Red Top* (1977), *Trinkle, Trinkle* (1977), *Ebony Glaze* (1977), *Miss Ann* (1977), *Seven Giant Steps For John Coltrane* (1977), *Live In New York At The Ladies Fort* (1977), *Live In New York, Volumes 1 & 2* (1977), *Bionic Saxophone* (1978), *The Coltrane Interviews, Volumes One and Two* (1979), *Saxophonitis* (1979), *Funk Update* (1979), *I Love Japan* (1979), *Have Band, Will Travel* (1979), *Petite Suite Francaise: Andrew White Plays The Oboe* (1981), *Seven More Giant Steps For John Coltrane* (1983), *Profile* (1984).

White, Michael

b. 24 May 1933, Houston, Texas, USA. White was raised in California and took up the violin when he was nine years old. He first came to public attention when he played with the John Handy Quintet at the Monterey Jazz Festival in 1965. He has a formidable technique regularly including passages of double-stopping in his solos. He has been able to incorporate into his playing influences and techniques from classical and eastern music. In the late 60s he moved in a new direction joining one of the first jazz rock groups, Fourth Way. In the early 70s he returned to *avant garde* jazz working with artists such as tenor saxophone players Pharoah Sanders and Joe Henderson and pianist McCoy Tyner as well as leading his own bands.

Albums: with John Handy *Live At Monterey* (1965), with Fourth Way *The Sun And The Moon Have Come Together* (1969), *Werewolf* (1970), *The Fourth Way* (1970), with Pharoah Sanders *Thembi* (1970), with McCoy Tyner *Song For My Lady* (1972), as leader *The Land Of Spirit And Light* (1973), *Father Music, Mother Dance* (1974), *Spirit Dance* (1975), *The X Factor* (Elektra 1978), *Shake It Break It* (504 1981), *Michael White* (Atlantic 1987), *How Strong We Believe* (King 1991), *Michael White's New Orleans Music* (Nola 1992), *No Rules* (King 1992).

Whitehead, Annie

b. Lena Annie Whitehead, 16 July 1955, Oldham, Lancashire, England. Whitehead joined her school's brass band wanting to play tuba, but - an indication of the patronising attitudes she continues to suffer from as an adult, professional musician - was not allowed to, because it was felt a girl could not cope with the large instrument. She was therefore forced to choose cornet, but after a year took up the euphonium and baritone sax as well. Finally, she was allowed to switch to trombone, on which she has since proved her skill and versatility with rock, reggae and jazz groups. Leaving school at the age of 16, she joined Ivy Benson's all-woman big band to tour Germany where, to Ivy's disapproval, she would sneak off to jam with local musicians. She stayed with Benson for two years, then moved to Jersey, giving up playing almost completely for six years as she was disillusioned with music as a job. In 1979, she formed her own ska band, and two years later moved to London to work as a session musician, re-kindling her interest in jazz at jam sessions in a Finsbury Park, north London pub. In 1983 she toured Africa with Chris McGregor's Brotherhood Of Breath and the USA with Fun Boy Three. In the mid-80s she ran her own band including Louise Elliott, a fine saxophonist with bands like Zubop, and pianist Laka Daisical, and was one of the Sisterhood Of Spit: at the end of the decade she was again the only sister in the Brotherhood Of Breath. She has also worked with John Stevens (duelling memorably with Evan Parker), Charlie Watts Orchestra, Guest Stars, Working Week, Jah Wobble, Lydia D'Ustbyn's Swing Orchestra, Native

Hipsters, District Six, and Smiley Culture. At the end of the 80s she set up a new band, Dance.

Selected albums: with John Stevens' Folkus *The Life Of Riley* (1984), *Mix-Up* (Paladin 1985), with Charlie Watts *Live At Fulham Town Hall* (1986).

Whittle, Tommy

b. 13 October 1926, Grangemouth, Scotland. Whittle began playing tenor saxophone while in his early teens and, in 1942, moved to Chatham, England, where he joined a dance band led by Claude Giddings. Also in the band was Ronnie Verrell and Whittle soon found himself playing with guest artists such as Ralph Sharon and Stéphane Grappelli. He also played with Johnny Claes, Carl Barriteau and, in 1946, joined the Ted Heath band. He remained with Heath for six years before moving on to play in Tony Kinsey's small group. Throughout the 50s he played with several small bands, sometimes leading or co-leading, and his associates included Dill Jones, Kenny Wheeler and Joe Temperley. From the 60s on through to the early 90s, Whittle has remained a prominent figure on the UK jazz scene, playing club and festival dates, and making records with a wide range of jazzmen from the UK and USA, including Benny Goodman. A quiet and introspective individual off-stage, Whittle's playing reflects these personal characteristics and his warm, caressing sound is particularly well-suited to ballads. His many records include several with his wife, the singer Barbara Jay.

Albums: *New Horizons* (1959), *Jigsaw* (1977), *Why Not* (Jam 1979), *The Nearness Of You* (1982), *Straight Eight* (Miles Music 1986), *The Warm Glow* (Teejay 1992). Compilations: *Waxing With Whittle (1953-54)* (Esquire 1979), *More Waxing With Whittle (1954-55)* (Esquire 1987).

Wiggins, Gerry

b. 12 May 1922, New York City, New York, USA. One of Wiggins's first professional jobs was playing piano for the club act of film actor-comedian Stepin Fetchit (Lincoln Perry). After hearing Art Tatum he turned to jazz and, following a spell with Les Hite, worked with Louis Armstrong and Benny Carter. In the mid-40s Wiggins settled in Los Angeles and established a reputation as a reliable accompanist for singers. During the 50s and 60s he worked for Lena Horne, Kay Starr, Nat 'King' Cole, Lou Rawls and Eartha Kitt. Also in the 60s he was active in film and television soundtrack work but he played with several jazz groups too, including Gerald Wilson's big band. In the mid-70s he toured Europe with Helen Humes, then in the 80s worked with Red Callender and also appeared on the international festival circuit. He continued to serve singers well, playing with Linda Hopkins. He also regularly returned to work with Wilson and occasionally led his own small groups. A solid, dependable pianist with eclectic tastes, Wiggins remains relatively unknown despite his many qualities.

Selected albums: *The Gerry Wiggins Trio* i (1950), *The Gerry Wiggins Trio* ii (1956), *The Gerry Wiggins Trio* iii (1956), *The Gerry Wiggins Trio* iv (1957), *Gerry Wiggins* (1958), *The Gerry Wiggins Trio* v (1960), with Helen Humes *Sneakin' Around*

(1974), *Wig Is Here* (Black And Blue 1975), with Red Callender *Night Mist Blues* (1983), *King And I* (Fresh Sounds 1988), *Live At Maybeck Recital Hall* (Concord 1990).

Wilber, Bob

b. 15 March 1928, New York City, New York, USA. After studying clarinet as a child, Wilber began leading his own band and while still a teenager became a student of Sidney Bechet. He recorded with Bechet, grew adept on the soprano saxophone, and was clearly at home in a traditional jazz setting. Nevertheless, Wilber's avid desire to expand his knowledge and expertise led him to further studies under Lennie Tristano. A mid-50s band Wilber led blended traditional with modern concepts in jazz and, perhaps predictably, fell between the two audiences for such music. During the late 50s and on through the 60s, Wilber played and recorded with distinguished leaders, such as Bobby Hackett, Benny Goodman, Bechet, Jack Teagarden and Eddie Condon. At the close of the 60s (at this time also playing alto saxophone), he became one of the original members of the World's Greatest Jazz Band. In the early 70s, he teamed up with Kenny Davern to form Soprano Summit, a band which brought him to the attention of new audiences around the world. This group stayed in existence until 1979 and soon afterwards he formed the Bechet Legacy band, recording extensively, often on his own record label, Bodeswell.

Active in jazz education, Wilber has also been musical director of the Smithsonian Jazz Repertory Ensemble, the house band for some of the Duke Ellington conventions, and has written for films, most notably the recreation of Ellington's music for *The Cotton Club* (1984). He continued leading his Bechet Legacy band throughout the 80s, making records (including a fine set which set out to recapture the essence of the King Oliver band), and accompanying his wife, singer Joanne 'Pug' Horton. He also recreated a Benny Goodman band for anniversary performances of the 1938 Carnegie Hall concert and published his autobiography, *Music Was Not Enough* (in collaboration with Derek Webster). In the early 90s Wilber was reunited with Davern for concert appearances and was still keenly exploring new ways of presenting older musical styles to a contemporary audience.

Selected albums: *Bob Wilber And His Jazz Band* i (1950), *Spreadin' Joy* (1957), *Bob Wilber And His All Star Band* i (1959), *Bob Wilber And His All Star Band* ii (1959), *New Clarinet In Town* (1960), *Evolution Of The Blues* (1960), *Blowin' The Blues Away* (1960), *The Music Of Hoagy Carmichael* (1969), with Kenny Davern *Soprano Summit* (1973), with Davern *Soprano Summit II* (1976), with Davern *Chalumeau Blue* (1976), *Vital Wilber* (1977), *Bob Wilber And The Scott Hamilton Quartet* (c.1977), *Soprano Summit In Concert* (Concord 1977), *At Thatchers* (J&M 1977), *Rapturous Reeds* (Phontastic 1978), *The Many Faces Of Bob Wilber And Pug Horton* (1978), *Groovin' At The Grunewald* (Phontastic 1978), *Original Wilber* (1978), *In The Mood For Swing* (1979), *The Music Of Fats Waller And James P. Johnson* (1979), *Swingin' For The King* (Phontastic 1979), *Dizzy Fingers* (Bodeswell

Bob Wilber

1980), *The Music Of King Oliver's Creole Jazz Band* (1981), *On The Road* (Jazzology 1981), with Joanne 'Pug' Horton *Don't Go Away* (1981), *Bob Wilber And The Bechet Legacy* (1982), *Ode To Bechet* (1982), *Reflections* (1983), *Bob Wilber/Dick Wellstood: Duet* (1984), *The Cotton Club* (1985), with Davern *Summit Reunion* (Chiaroscuro 1990), *Dancing On A Rainbow* (Circle 1990), *Moments Like This* (Phontastic 1992). Compilations: *Bob Wilber And His Wildcats* i (1947), *Bob Wilber And His Wildcats* ii (1947), *Bob Wilber And His Jazz Band* ii (1949), *Sidney Bechet 1949* (1949).

Further reading: *Music Was Not Enough*, Bob Wilber with Derek Webster.

Wilder, Joe

b. 22 February 1922, Colwyn, Pennsylvania, USA. After studying music in his home town, Wilder joined the trumpet section of the Les Hite band in his late teens. From Hite he graduated to the Lionel Hampton band and, before the 40s were over, had played with leaders such as Dizzy Gillespie, Jimmie Lunceford, Lucky Millinder and Sam Donahue. In the 50s he mostly worked in theatre bands but spent several months with Count Basie, and by the end of the decade had embarked upon a long stint as a staff musician in US radio and television studios. During this period, which extended into the early 70s, he found time to play with Benny Goodman on a tour of the Soviet Union. Later in the 70s and throughout the 80s he continued to play in studio orchestras, making occasional recordings, including a fine set with Benny Carter. A top-rank lead trumpeter, Wilder's technical command has ensured his successful career in the studios but that, in turn, has necessarily overshadowed his jazz playing.

Albums: with Count Basie *Dance Session* (1953), *Wilder 'N' Wilder* (Savoy 1956), with Benny Carter *A Gentleman And His Music* (1985), *Alone With Just My Dreams* (Evening Star 1992).

Wiley, Lee

b. 9 October c.1910, Fort Gibson, Oklahoma, USA, d. 11 December 1975. While still in her early teens, Wiley left home to begin a career singing with the Leo Reisman band. Her career was interrupted when, following a fall while horse-riding, she suffered temporary blindness. She recovered her sight and at the age of 19 was back with Reisman again. She also sang with Paul Whiteman and later, the Casa Loma Band. A collaboration with composer Victor Young resulted in several songs for which Wiley wrote the lyrics, including 'Got The South In My Soul' and 'Anytime, Anyday, Anywhere', the latter becoming an R&B hit in the 50s. In the early 40s Wiley began a long succession of fine recording dates, singing many classic songs, usually with backing from small jazz groups, which included musicians such as Bud Freeman, Max Kaminsky, Fats Waller, Billy Butterfield, Bobby Hackett, Eddie Condon, and Jess Stacy, the latter to whom she was married for a while. In 1943 she sang with Stacy's big band and subsequently continued to perform with small groups, notably with Condon-directed jazzmen, and pursued her prolific recording career.

Although she had only a small voice, she possessed a wistful and charming sound and delivered lyrics with a low-key sensuality. The warmth and intimacy she projected resulted in many of her performances becoming definitive versions of the songs. 'I've Got A Crush On You', from 1939 with Waller and Freeman in support, 'How Long Has This Been Going On?', 'Baby's Awake Now' and 'You Took Advantage Of Me', all from 1939 and 1940, and 'I've Got The World On A String', from 1945, with Condon and Ernie Caceres, are all excellent examples of her distinctively delicate singing style. She made fewer appearances and records in the 50s and 60s, although a 1963 television film, *Something About Lee Wiley*, which told a version of her life story, boosted interest in her work. One of her final appearances came in 1972 at the New York Jazz Festival, where she was rapturously received by audiences who were beginning to appreciate what her fellow musicians had known all along: that she was one of the best jazz singers the music had known even if, by this time, her always fragile-sounding voice was no longer at its best.

Selected albums: *Night In Manhattan* (1950), *Lee Wiley Sings Vincent Youmans* (1951), *Lee Wiley Sings Irving Berlin* (1951), *Lee Wiley Sings Rodgers And Hart* (1954), *Duologue* (1954), *West Of The Moon* (1957), *A Touch Of The Blues* (1957), *One And Only Lee Wiley* (1965), *Back Home Again* (Monmouth Evergreen 1971), *I Got The World On A String* (1972). Compilations: *Lee Wiley On The Air, Volume 1 (1932-36)* (Totem 1988), *Lee Wiley On The Air, Volume 2 (1944-45)* (Totem 1989), *Rarites* (Jass 1989), *I Got A Right To Sing The Blues* (Jass 1990), *As Time Goes By* (Bluebird 1991), *Lee Wiley 1931-37* (Original Jazz Classics 1991).

Wilkins, Ernie

b. 20 July 1922, St. Louis, Missouri, USA. Wilkins studied formally, learning piano and violin before taking up the saxophone. He played locally before military service and in the post-war years played in the Jeter-Pillars Orchestra and that led by Earl 'Fatha' Hines. He then freelanced as player, composer and arranger until in 1952 he joined Count Basie, remaining with the band until 1955, playing alto and tenor saxophones. He returned to freelancing, concentrating on writing arrangements for many bands, including those of Basie, Tommy Dorsey, Dizzy Gillespie and Harry James. Wilkins's charts for the James band were outstanding and helped to create one of the best bands the trumpeter led. In many respects these arrangements, loosely swinging and with tight section work, closely resembled similar work that Wilkins did for Basie and which was partly responsible for boosting the Basie band into its second period of greatness. Whether James or Basie was the first to play in this manner remains a matter of some contention. In the 60s Wilkins's career stalled due to addiction problems but he still wrote for several big bands, including that led by Clark Terry. In the early 70s he was A&R director for Mainstream Records and later in the decade worked again with Terry before settling in Denmark. In the 80s he formed his own Almost Big Band. As a big band arranger, Wilkins belongs firmly in the post-Sy Oliver tradition and has consistently adhered to the characteristics of a style which concentrates upon presenting an uncluttered ensemble sound that effectively frames the soloists.

Selected albums: *Ernie Wilkins /Kenny Clarke Septet* (Savoy 1956), *The Trumpet Album* (1957), *Here Comes The Swinging Mr Wilkins* (1960), *The Big New Band Of The 60s* (1960), *A Time For The Blues* (1973), *Ernie Wilkins And The Almost Big Band* (1980), *Ernie Wilkins' Almost Big Band Live* (Matrix 1981), *Ernie Wilkins And The Almost Big Band - Level* (1982), *Montreux* (1983), *K.a.l.e.i.d.o.d.u.k.e.* (Birdology 1991).

Williams, Buster

b. Charles Anthony Williams, 17 April 1942, Camden, New Jersey, USA. Williams was taught to play bass by his father and later studied formally in Philadelphia. In the early 60s he played and recorded with Jimmy Heath, Sonny Stitt and others, and was also in demand for sessions with singers, notably Betty Carter, Sarah Vaughan and Nancy Wilson. Towards the end of the 60s he settled briefly in Los Angeles, where he played with Miles Davis, Bobby Hutcherson and others, but by the end of the decade he had moved to New York and joined Herbie Hancock. In the early and mid-70s he toured and recorded with Hancock and also worked with Mary Lou Williams and fellow bassist Ron Carter. In the late 70s and through the 80s Williams was in constant demand as a session musician, recording with Kenny Barron, Sathima Bea Benjamin, Sphere and the Timeless All Stars. Apart from his exemplary work as an accompanist, Williams is also an accomplished soloist.

Selected albums: *Crystal Reflections* (1976), *Heartbeat* (Muse 1978), *Toku Do* (Denon 1978), *Dreams Come True* (1981), *Pinnacle* (Muse 1981), with Sphere *Four In One* (1982), with Sphere *Sphere On Tour* (1985), with Sphere *Four For All* (1987), *Something More* (In And Out 1989).

Williams, Clarence

b. 8 October 1893, Plaquemine, Louisiana, USA, d. 6 November 1965. Although Williams first made his mark as a pianist, singer and dancer, it was as a composer, record producer, music publisher and entrepreneur that he made a lasting impact on jazz. Before he was in his teens he had decided upon a career in showbusiness and had run away from home to work with a travelling minstrel show. By the time he was 21 he had started composing, formed his first publishing company and was married to blues singer Eva Taylor. His early associates, as performers and/or in business, included Armand Piron and W.C. Handy. First in New Orleans, then Chicago and finally in New York City, Williams established himself as a successful publisher, an energetic record producer and a tireless accompanist to some of the finest jazz and blues artists of the day. Among Williams's most notable recording sessions are those on which he was joined by Louis Armstrong and Sidney Bechet while his sensitive accompaniment enhanced many record dates with singers such as Bessie Smith, Beulah 'Sippie' Wallace and his wife. He was a dedicated promoter of the music of such leading pianist-composers as James P. Johnson and Fats Waller,

his name often appearing as co-composer on works to which he may have contributed little that was creative but a great deal of enthusiastic effort in their promotion. By the late 30s he had decided to concentrate upon composing and, for a while, ran a business outside music. Even an accident which robbed him of his sight did not deter him and he worked steadily until his death in 1965. Williams's legacy to jazz includes many songs which bear his name as composer or co-composer and which became standards, among them 'Baby, Won't You Please Come Home', "Tain't Nobody's Biz-ness If I Do', 'Everybody Loves My Baby', 'Royal Garden Blues', 'West End Blues' and 'I Ain't Gonna Give Nobody None Of This Jelly Roll'.

Selected compilations: *Clarence Williams Jazz Kings (1927-29)* (1979), *Clarence Williams And His Washboard Band, Volume 1 (1933-35)* (1983), *Clarence Williams And His Orchestra (1929-31)* (1986), *WNYC Jazz Festival* (1986), *Clarence Williams (1927-34)* (1988), *The Washboard Bands* (1988), *Jazz Classics In Digital Stereo* (1989), *Clarence Williams 1926-27* (Original Jazz Classics 1993).

Williams, Cootie

b. Charles Melvin Williams, 10 July 1911, Mobile, Alabama, USA, d. 15 September 1985. A self-taught trumpeter, Williams first played professionally in the mid-20s, when he was barely into his teens, appearing in the band run by the family of Lester Young. He later played in several New York bands, including those led by Chick Webb and Fletcher Henderson. In 1929 he replaced Bubber Miley in Duke Ellington's orchestra, remaining there for 11 years. During this stint he made a number of records with other leaders, notably Lionel Hampton and Teddy Wilson (on some of whose sessions he accompanied Billie Holiday). He also led the Rug Cutters, one of the many small groups drawn from within the Ellington band. In 1940 Williams left Ellington and was briefly with Benny Goodman before forming his own big band. In later years, asked about his drinking habits, Williams remarked that he had not been a drinker until he had his own band. Given that his band included unpredictable musicians such as Bud Powell and Charlie Parker it is easy to understand why he turned to the bottle. For all the undoubted qualities of the band, which also featured Eddie 'Lockjaw' Davis and Eddie 'Cleanhead' Vinson, and the high standard of his own playing, by the late 40s Williams was forced to cut the band down in size.

In the early 50s he moved into the currently popular R&B field. For the next few years he continued playing R&B, leading small bands and making record dates - notably, a 1957 session, on which he was co-leader with Rex Stewart, by a band which boasted Coleman Hawkins, Bud Freeman, Lawrence Brown and Hank Jones within its ranks. In 1962 he rejoined Ellington, remaining in the band after the leader's death and during its brief, post-Ducal life, under Mercer Ellington. Although Williams was brought into the 1929 Ellington band to take over the so-called 'jungle effects' originally created by Miley, he quickly became an outstanding soloist in his own right. His full, rich tone and powerful style was showcased by Ellington on 'Concerto For Cootie' ('Do Nothing Till You

Hear From Me'), recorded in 1940. Throughout his years with Ellington, and on many occasions under his own name, Williams readily displayed the command and vigour of his distinctive playing.

Albums: *The Big Challenge* (Fresh Sound 1957), *The Solid Trumpet Of Cootie Williams* (1962), *Salute To Duke Ellington* (1976). Compilations: *Cootie Williams And The Boys From Harlem, 1937-40* (1974), *Cootie Williams And His Rug Cutters, 1937-40* (1974), *Big Band Bounce* (1974), *Cootie Williams And Oran 'Hot Lips' Page* (1974), *New York 1944 - Sextet And Big Band* (1977), *Sextet And Orchestra* (1981), *Echoes From Harlem* (Affinity 1986), *Typhoon* (Swingtime 1986), *Memorial* (RCA 1986), *From Films, 1944-46* (Harlequin 1988).

Williams, Jessica

b. 17 March 1948, Baltimore, Maryland, USA. Learning to play piano as a child and studying classical music at the Peabody Conservatory of Music, Williams turned to jazz and was playing professionally at the age of 14. In Philadelphia, she was a member of the Philly Joe Jones Quartet and also worked with Joe Morello and singer Ethel Ennis. In 1977 she relocated to the west coast which remained her base into the 90s. Her reputation grew in San Francisco, Sacramento and other centres but despite playing in bands led by Stan Getz, Tony Williams, Bobby Hutcherson, Charlie Rouse, Airto Moreira, John Abercrombie and others, and some early recordings, the wider world of jazz remained largely unaware of her existence. All this began to change from the mid-80s when a succession of fine recordings began to appear. Received ecstatically by the jazz press in the USA and UK, awards followed and frequent overseas tours and appearances at international festivals helped consolidate her burgeoning reputation. By the early 90s she was widely accepted as one of the best pianists currently playing jazz and high on the list of all-time greats. In 1994 she had the distinction of seeing two albums appear in the top eight of *Jazz Journal International's* critics poll for the best records of the year. That same year she was awarded a Guggenhein Fellowship for composition. A brilliantly incisive player, with a deft and sure touch, Williams command of her instrument is outstanding. But she is far from merely a superb technician. Her intelligent, strikingly original improvisations are built upon a sure knowledge of the meaning of jazz and the role of the solo piano in the music's development. Her playing reveals not only her admiration for the likes of Thelonious Monk and Bud Powell but also the genius of earlier giants such as Earl 'Fatha' Hines and Art Tatum. Nevertheless, such admiration for her talent was widespread and the long years of anonymity were finally behind her.

Albums: *Jessica Williams* (1976), *The Portal Of Antrim* (Adelphi 1978), *Rivers Of Memory* (Clean Cuts 1979), *Portraits* (Adelphi 1981), *Orgonomic Music* (Clean Cuts 1981), *Nothin' But The Truth* (Blackhawk 1986), with Charlie Rouse *Epistrophy/The Charlie Rouse Memorial Concert* (Landmark 1989), *The Golden Light* (Quanta 1989), *Heartland* (Ear-Art 1990), *And Then, There's This* (Timeless 1991), *In The Pocket* (Hep 1993), *Live At Maybeck: Recital Hall* (Concord 1992),

The Next Step (Hep 1992), *Arrival* (Jazz Focus 1993), *Momentum* (Jazz Focus 1993), *Encounters* (Jazz Focus 1994).

Williams, Joe

b. 12 December 1918, Cordele, Georgia, USA. Williams began his musical career singing in a gospel group in Chicago and by the late 30s was performing regularly as a solo singer. He had short-lived jobs with bands led by Jimmie Noone and others, was encouraged by Lionel Hampton, who employed him briefly in the early 40s, and in 1950 was with Count Basie for a short spell. In 1951 he had a record success with 'Every Day I Have The Blues', but he did not make his breakthrough into the big time until he rejoined Basie in 1954. For the next few years, records by the band with Williams in powerful voice were hugely successful and, coming at a period when Basie's band was at a low commercial ebb, it is hard to say with any certainty who needed whom the most. By the time Williams moved on, in 1961, both the band and the singer had reached new heights of popularity, and they continued to make occasional concert appearances together during the following decades. In the 60s Williams worked mostly as a single, often accompanied by top-flight jazzmen, including Harry Edison, Clark Terry, George Shearing and Cannonball Adderley. He toured and recorded throughout the 70s and 80s, his stature growing as he matured and his voice seemingly growing stronger and more mellow with age. A highly sophisticated artist, whose blues singing has a burnished glow which can contrast vividly with the harsh edge of the lyrics he sings, Williams has built a substantial and devoted audience. His later appearances, with bands such as the Capp-Pierce Juggernaut, frequently contain popular songs which he performs with more than a tinge of blues feeling. He also favours material which allows him to display the good humour which is a characteristic of the man himself. (This artist should not be confused with the singer-pianist Big Joe Williams.)

Selected albums: *Count Basie Swings, Joe Williams Sings* (Savoy 1955), *Joe Williams Sings About You* (1959), *That Kind Of Woman* (1959), *Have A Good Time* (1961), *Together* (1961), *A Swinging Night At Birdland* (Roulette 1962), *One Is A Lonesome Number* (1962), *Me And The Blues* (1963), *Joe Williams At Newport* (1963), *The Song Is YOU* (1964), *Then And Now* (1965), *Mister Excitement* (1965), *Presenting Joe Williams And The Thad Jones-Mel Lewis Jazz Orchestra* (1966), *Something Old, New And Blue* (1968), *Having The Blues Under European Skies* (c.1971), *Joe Williams Live* (1973), with Juggernaut *Live At The Century Plaza* (1977), with Dave Pell *Prez & Joe* (1979), *Nothin' But The Blues* (1983), *Then And Now* (1983), *I Just Want To Sing* (1985), *Ballad And Blues Master* (Verve 1987), *Live At Vine Street* (Verve 1987), *Every Night* (1987), *In Good Company* (Verve 1989), *A Man Ain't Supposed To Cry* (1989), *That Holiday Feelin'* (Verve 1990), with Count Basie Orchestra *Live At Orchestra Hall* (Telarc 1993), *Jump For Joy* (Bluebird 1993). Compilations: *Joe Williams Sings Every Day* (1950-51), *The Overwhelming Joe Williams* (Bluebird 1989).

Williams, Mary Lou

b. Mary Elfrieda Scruggs, 8 May 1910, Atlanta, Georgia, USA, d. 28 May 1981. A child prodigy, Williams played in public at the age of six and by the time she reached her teenage years was already a seasoned professional piano player. At the age of 16 she married saxophonist John Williams, playing in his band throughout the mid-west. When her husband left to join Terrence Holder's band, Mary Lou took over the leadership of the band before eventually she too joined Holder. After this band had metamorphosed into Andy Kirk and his Clouds Of Joy, Williams assumed additional responsibilities as the group's chief arranger. During the 30s, while still with Kirk, her arrangements were also used by Earl 'Fatha' Hines, Tommy Dorsey, Louis Armstrong and Benny Goodman, who had a hit with her composition 'Roll 'Em'. After her marriage to John Williams ended, she married Shorty Baker and co-led a band with him before he joined Duke Ellington. She continued to lead the band but also contributed some arrangements to Ellington.

Throughout the 40s and early 50s she played at clubs in the USA and Europe, sometimes as a solo artist, at other times leading a small group. For a few years in the mid-50s she worked outside music, but returned to the scene in the autumn of 1957 and thereafter played clubs, concerts and festivals for the rest of her life. As an arranger, Williams's greatest contribution to jazz was her work with the Kirk band. Her charts were exemplary, providing this fine group with a distinctive voice and ably employing the individual talents of the band's members. Although her arrangements for other groups were necessarily somewhat impersonal, they were invariably first-class examples of straightforward swinging big band music. Many of her arrangements were of her own compositions and the breadth of her work in this area was such that, in the mid-40s, a classical piece, 'Zodiac Suite', was performed by the New York Philharmonic Orchestra. During this same period, she extended her writing into bop, providing charts for the Dizzy Gillespie big band.

Her deep religious beliefs, which had led to her leaving music for a few years in the 50s, surfaced in some of her longer compositions, which included cantatas and masses. As a pianist, her range was similarly wide, encompassing stride and boogie-woogie, swing and early bop; she even recorded a duo concert with *avant gardist* Cecil Taylor, though this was not an unqualified success. Throughout the later years of her career, Williams extended her repertoire still further, offering performances which, interpreted through the piano, told the story of jazz from its origins to the present day. Williams was a highly articulate and intellectually gifted individual. In interviews she displays a complex and decidedly ambivalent attitude towards life and music, perhaps fostered by the racial antagonism she encountered early in her career and dissatisfaction with the manner in which the entertainment industry demonstrated that it cared more for money than for music. Williams's importance to the fabric of jazz was recognised towards the end of her life and she was honoured by several universities.

Selected albums: *Mary Lou Williams In London* (1953), *On Vogue* (Vogue 1954), *The First Lady Of The Piano* (1955), *Black Christ Of The Andes* (1963), *Mary Lou's Mass* (1977) *From The Heart* (1970), *Zoning* (1974), *The History Of Jazz* (1975), *Free Spirits* (Steeplechase 1975), *Live At The Cookery* (Chiaroscuro 1975), with Cecil Taylor *Embraced* (1977), *My Mama Pinned A Rose On Me* (1977), *Solo Recital At Montreux* (1978), *First Lady Of Piano* (Giants Of Jazz 1987), with Andy Kirk *Mary's Idea* (1993). Compilation: *The Best Of Mary Lou Williams* (Pablo 1982).

Williams, Roy

b. 7 March 1937, Bolton, Lancashire, England. Williams first played trombone with a Manchester-based traditional jazz band. After moving to London he became a well-known figure during the trad jazz boom of the late 50s and early 60s. He played and recorded with Monty Sunshine and other leading lights of the era, earning praise from the many visiting American jazz stars whom he accompanied. In 1965, he joined the Alex Welsh band where he remained for more than a dozen years. After leaving Welsh he joined Humphrey Lyttelton, staying with the band until the early 80s when he began freelancing. As a member of the Pizza Express All Stars, Five-A-Slide and other mainstream bands, touring with various visitors, recording with Spike Robinson and others, and broadcasting, he became one of the most familiar figures on the UK jazz scene. The respect he earned travelled well and in the 80s he was invited to play at one of Dick Gibson's famous Colorado Jazz Parties and he also worked in New York. Superb technical accomplishment, allied to impeccable phrasing, fluid swing and innate good taste, have combined to make Williams one of the best mainstream jazz trombonists in the world.

Selected albums: with various artists *The Melody Maker Tribute To Louis Armstrong* (1970), *Something Wonderful* (Hep Jazz 1981), with Benny Waters *When You're Smiling* (Hep Jazz 1981), *Royal Trombone* (Phontastic 1983), *Again! Roy Williams In Sweden* (1983), with Spike Robinson *It's A Wonderful World* (1985), *A Jazz Concert With Roy Williams* (c.1985).

Williams, Tony

b. 12 December 1945, Chicago, Illinois, USA. Williams was raised in Boston, Massachusetts, where his father, an amateur musician, encouraged him to take up drums. Williams studied with Alan Dawson and was sitting in at local clubs before he entered his teens. At the age of 15, he was freelancing in and around Boston and had already earned the admiration of leading drummers, including Max Roach. In the early 60s he went to New York, where he played with Jackie McLean and in 1963 joined Miles Davis. With Davis, Williams's rhythm section colleagues were Herbie Hancock and Ron Carter and together they made a formidable team which is still widely admired and often cited as Davis' greatest unit. During this period, both with Davis and on his many Blue Note recordings as leader, and sideman, Williams began reshaping modern jazz drumming, developing concepts created by some of his immediate predecessors such as Elvin Jones. Notably, Williams advanced the manner in which drummers could play freely yet retain a

Tony Williams

recognizable pulse. With Williams in a band, free jazz improvisers could dispense with time but were not entirely cut off from a basic rhythmic impulse. At the end of the 60s Williams left Davis to form a jazz-rock band with John McLaughlin. The band, named Lifetime, set the standards to which most subsequent bands in the genre aspired but, insofar as the drumming was concerned, few achieved their aim. After McLaughlin moved on, Williams continued to lead jazz-rock bands but gradually moved back into jazz circles. In the late 70s he was with Hancock again in the V.S.O.P. quintet and also recorded with Gil Evans and Wynton Marsalis. In the late 80s Williams was leading a band with a stable personnel that included saxophonist Billy Pierce and Mulgrew Miller.

Selected albums: *Lifetime* (1964), *Spring* (Blue Note 1965), with Miles Davis *Miles In The Sky* (1968), *Emergency* (Polydor 1969), *Joy Of Flying* (CBS 1979), *Foreign Intrigue* (Blue Note 1986), *Civilization* (1986), *Angel Street* (Blue Note 1988), *Native Heart* (Blue Note 1989), *The Story Of Neptune* (Blue Note 1992), *New Lifetime Collection* (1993), with Wayne Shorter, Ron Carter, Wallace Roney, Herbie Hancock *A Tribute To Miles* (QWest/Reprise 1994).

Williamson, Claude

b. 18 November 1926, Brattleboro, Texas, USA. After studying piano formally at the New England Conservatory in Boston, Massachusetts, Williamson turned to playing jazz in the late 40s. He first worked with Charlie Barnet, where he was featured on 'Claude Reigns', then with Red Norvo and also briefly led his own small group. In the early 50s he toured with Bud Shank before settling in Los Angeles, where he led a trio for many years. He played too with Tal Farlow, appeared in the second edition of the Lighthouse All-Stars with Shank, Rolf Ericson, Bob Cooper and Max Roach, and recorded with Art Pepper. Amongst Williamson's better-known compositions is 'Aquarium', recorded by the All-Stars in 1954. His trio work kept him busy but musically static for several years. However, in the late 70s and early 80s he toured Japan and the records he made there spurred his career. Although he began as mainstream player, Williamson later adapted to bop and most of his subsequent work reflects this interest. Although little known on the international scene, Japan apart, his work bears much closer attention than it has usually enjoyed.

Selected albums: *The Lighthouse All Stars Vol. 3* (1953), *The Lighthouse All Stars Vol. 4: Flute And Oboe* (1954), with Art Pepper *Discoveries* (1954), *Salute To Bud* (Affinity 1954), *Keys West* (Affinity 1955), *The Claude Williamson Trio* (1956), *'Round Midnight* (1957), *Claude Williamson In Italy* (1958), *The Claude Williamson Quintet* i (c.1958), *The Claude Williamson Quintet* ii (1961), *New Departure* (1978), *Holography* (Interplay 1979), *La Fiesta* (Interplay 1979), *Tribute To Bud* (1981), *Theatre Party* (Fresh Sounds 1988), *Mulls The Mulligan Scene* (Fresh Sounds 1988).

Williamson, Steve

b. 1964, London, England. This tenor saxophonist has never received the media attention that near-contemporary colleague Courtney Pine has had and, as a very shy person, has never sought it. This may well have been to Williamson's advantage, since it meant he could develop at his own pace and on his own terms. It also meant, on the minus side, that he did not issue an album under his own name until 1990, but when the opportunity came he was in a position to make demands, such as that the album should be cut in New York - Steve Coleman produced the album and Abbey Lincoln was guest vocalist on the title track. Williamson is a mature and versatile player who convinces whether playing turbo-charged hard bop (such as at the Wembley Nelson Mandela 70th birthday concert where, accompanying dancers IDJ, he and Pine reached their biggest-ever audience), in a free jam, locking horns with the likes of Evan Parker in Joe Gallivan's New Soldiers Of The Road, or contributing to the glorious exuberance of Louis Moholo's *Viva La Black*. He played for a week with Art Blakey at Ronnie Scott's club, and produced some of his finest work on a 1989 four track demo disc with Wayne Batchelor's Quartet which, sadly, is currently not publicly available. His first saxophone was an alto, but he switched to tenor after hearing John Coltrane. On occasions he also plays soprano. Of the many talented young black musicians to emerge from the London jazz scene in the late 80s, Williamson looks set to prove one of the most original and durable.

Albums: with Louis Moholo *Viva La Black* (1988), *A Waltz For Grace* (Polydor 1990), *Rhyme Time* (Polydor 1991).

Wilson, Cassandra

b. 4 December 1955, Jackson, Mississippi, USA. Wilson started piano and guitar lessons at the age of nine. In 1975 she began singing professionally, primarily folk and blues, working in various R&B and Top 20 cover version bands. She emerged as a jazz singer while studying with drummer Alvin Fielder and singing with the Black Arts Music Society in her hometown. In 1981 she moved to New Orleans and studied with saxophonist Earl Turbinton. In 1982 she relocated to New York at the suggestion of trumpeter Woody Shaw and began working with David Holland and Abbey Lincoln. In 1985 she guested on Steve Coleman's *Motherland Pulse* and was asked by the JMT label to record her own album: her debut was *Point Of View*, which featured Coleman and guitarist Jean-Paul Bourelly. New York's finest wanted to work with her. She sang with New Air, Henry Threadgill's trio, and he returned the compliment by helping with arrangements on her second, more powerful album, *Days Aweigh*. Her mix of smoky, knowing vocals and expansive, lush music that travelled between psychedelia and swing was transfixing. The more conservative American audience was won over by her record of standards, *Blue Skies* (1988), which was named jazz album of the year by *Billboard*

Cassandra Wilson

magazine. The follow-up, the innovative sci-fi epic *Jumpworld* (1990), showed that Cassandra Wilson was not to be categorised: it included raps and funk as well as jazz and blues. This stylistic diversity was maintained on 1991's *She Who Weeps*. In the meantime, Wilson has continued to record on Steve Coleman's albums and has also made guest appearances with other musicians associated with Coleman's M-Base organisation, such as Greg Osby and Robin Eubanks.

Albums: *Point Of View* (JMT 1986), with Jim DeAngelis, Tony Signa *Straight From The Top* (1987), *Days Aweigh* (JMT 1987), *Blue Skies* (JMT 1988), *Jumpworld* (JMT 1990), *She Who Weeps* (JMT 1991), *Live* (JMT 1991), *Dance To The Drums Again* (DIW 1992), *After The Beginning Again* (JMT 1993), *Blue Light 'Til Dawn* (Blue Note 1993).

Wilson, Garland

b. 13 June 1909, Martinsburg, West Virginia, USA, d. 31 May 1954. Wilson began playing piano as a child and, when he was 20, moved to New York City, where he enjoyed some success playing in Harlem clubs. His records were very well received and in 1932 he became accompanist to the popular entertainer Nina Mae McKinney, with whom he toured Europe. He stayed in Europe, playing long residencies in Paris and also appearing in London with Jack Payne and his band. With the outbreak of war he returned to the USA, finding work in clubs in New York and Los Angeles, but in 1951 he was back in Europe, travelling between London and Paris, where he later died in 1954.

Compilations: *The Way I Feel (1932-51)* (Collectors Items 1986), *Piano Solos* (Neovox 1990).

Wilson, Gerald

b. 4 September 1918, Shelby, Mississippi, USA. After starting out on piano, Wilson switched to trumpet while at Manassa high school. He studied formally at Cass Tech, Detroit, before joining Jimmie Lunceford in 1939, where he had the unenviable job of replacing Sy Oliver. Like Oliver, Wilson's duties in the Lunceford band not only required him to play trumpet but also to write arrangements. He composed original material for the band, including 'Hi Spook' and 'Yard Dog Mazurka'. After leaving Lunceford in 1942 he settled in Los Angeles, served in the US Navy, where he played in the band directed by Willie Smith (and which included Clark Terry), and also played briefly in bands led by Les Hite and Benny Carter. He formed his first band in 1945, recording and touring with a measure of success. The band included trombonist-arranger Melba Liston, whom Wilson married. He folded the band in 1947 and resumed his studies, this time in composition. During the 50s he was active as an arranger, for Dizzy Gillespie, Count Basie and Duke Ellington among others, and also wrote for films and television. In 1961 he formed a new big band which recorded and played concerts and festivals, including Monterey in 1963 where the band included Teddy Edwards, Joe Pass and Harold Land. In 1969, he began teaching and also presented a radio series on jazz which lasted for six years. During this period he also worked extensively with singers, arranging for and accompanying Ella Fitzgerald, Carmen McRae, Sarah Vaughan, Ray Charles and others.

In 1972 he composed a classical piece, which was performed by the Los Angeles Philharmonic Orchestra under Zubin Mehta, and in later years continued to work in this field. In 1976 he directed the all-star festival band at Monterey in a programme of music that recalled the Lunceford band of the 30s and early 40s. In 1977 he continued his association with Monterey when he directed the Airmen Of Note, the US Air Force's jazz orchestra, in the premiere of his suite, 'The Happy Birthday Monterey Suite', commissioned for the festival. His orchestras have continued to present his own music, compositions and arrangements, and feature top class musicians, both veterans and newcomers, in well-rehearsed, effective performances. A sound, if little-known trumpet player in his earlier years, Wilson's contribution to jazz lies in the many fine bands he has led, in the example he has set by his undiminished enthusiasm and impeccably high standards of musicianship and, perhaps most important of all, in his distinctive writing. His son, Anthony Wilson, is an accomplished guitarist.

Albums: *You Better Believe It!* (1961), *Moment Of Truth* (1962), *Portraits* (1963), *On Stage* (1965), *Feelin' Kinda Blue* (1965), *The Golden Sword* (Discovery 1966), *Everywhere* (1967), *Live And Swinging* (1967), *California Soul* (1968), *Eternal Equinox* (1969), *Lomelin* (Discovery 1981), *Groovin' High* (Hep Jazz 1981), *Jessica* (Trend 1982), *Calafia* (Trend 1984), *Love You Madly* (Discovery 1988), *Jenna* (1989), *Moment Of Truth* (Pacific Jazz 1990), *Portraits* (Pacific Jazz 1992).

Wilson, Phil

b. Phillip Sanford Wilson, 8 September 1941, St. Louis, Missouri, USA, d. 25 March 1992, New York City, New York, USA. A strong drummer who also studied violin, Wilson was a professional from the age of 16 and worked with soul singers such as Solomon Burke and Jackie Wilson as well as with trumpeter Lester Bowie and saxophonists Julius Hemphill and David Sanborn. In 1965 he went to Chicago, where he worked with Otis Rush and played alongside Sanborn again in the Paul Butterfield Blues Band, a mixed-race outfit which featured often frantic versions of blues classics. During this period he became a member of the AACM and joined Roscoe Mitchell's group. He was one of the early, transient occupants of the drum stool in the Art Ensemble Of Chicago (AEC), which grew out of Mitchell's quartet, and Wilson was reunited with Bowie in both of these bands. In 1972 he moved to New York and worked with Anthony Braxton, another AACM alumnus and his association with colleagues from the AACM continued through the 70s and 80s. In 1978 he joined a quintet led by Lester Bowie and until the early 90s (when replaced by Don Moye, his successor in the AEC) he was the one non-brass-playing member of Bowie's Brass Fantasy, where he provided a solid but flexible backbone for the group's rich and witty mixture of doo-wop, blues, marching band pastiches and straight ahead jazz. He also played in the gospel group, From The Root To The Scource (with Fontella Bass and David Peaston) and led his own groups, including a quartet with Frank Lowe and

Olu Dara that recorded at the Moers Festival. Wilson was killed in a shooting incident in 1992.

Selected albums: with Paul Butterfield *The Resurrection Of Pigboy Crabshaw* (1967), *Fruits* (1977), with Lester Bowie *Duet* (1978).

Wilson, Teddy

b. 24 November 1912, Austin, Texas, USA, d. 31 July 1986, New Britain, Connecticut, USA. Born into a middle-class family, Wilson grew up in Tuskegee where his parents moved to take up teaching posts at the university. He studied violin and piano at Tuskegee and later extended his studies at college in Alabama. In 1929, by now concentrating on piano, he became a professional musician in Detroit. He played in bands led by Speed Webb and others in the mid-west until he settled in Chicago, where he worked with Erskine Tate, Eddie Mallory, Louis Armstrong and Jimmie Noone. In the early 30s he played with Art Tatum, holding his own in duets, a feat of considerable distinction. In 1933 he was heard by John Hammond, who encouraged him to move to New York to play in Benny Carter's band, and he also played with Willie Bryant. During this period in his career Wilson made a succession of outstanding records, with Carter in the Chocolate Dandies, leading small bands for which he hired the best available sidemen, and accompanying Billie Holiday on sessions which produced numerous masterpieces of jazz. Back in Chicago he guested with Benny Goodman, made records with Goodman and Gene Krupa and, in April 1936, became a member of the Goodman entourage, where he was featured as a member of the Benny Goodman Trio.

He remained with Goodman until 1939, usually playing as a member of the trio and later the quartet, before leaving to form his own big band. Wilson set high standards of musicianship, which militated against the band's commercial success, and it survived for barely a year. He then formed a sextet, for which he adopted similarly high standards, but fortunately this group attained a measure of success with long residencies and some excellent recordings. After a brief return visit to Goodman, Wilson worked in the studios, taught, toured and recorded over the next dozen years. By the 60s he had become a deserved elder statesman of jazz, a role which he maintained throughout the rest of his life, touring internationally as either a single or in small groups such as the Gentlemen Of Swing, in which he was joined by Harry Edison and Benny Carter.

Although the playing style Wilson adopted early in his career owed much to the influence of Earl 'Fatha' Hines, by the mid-30s he was a highly distinctive performer in his own right. A naturally restrained musician, Wilson's fleet playing and the elegant poise of his solos (the latter a facet which was reflected in his personal demeanour), combined to make him an influential figure in the development of jazz piano. His influence is most directly noticeable in the work of Nat 'King' Cole. His accompaniments to many of Billie Holiday's classic performances were an important factor in the singer's success. The quality of the setting he provided, especially on some of the earlier sessions when Holiday's talent was still unpolished, are object lessons in their deceptive simplicity. The excellence of the arrangements, which aid the instrumental soloists as much as the singer, display his prowess, while his seemingly effortless obbligato and solo contributions add to the quality of these timeless recordings. His performances with the Goodman trio and quartet are scarcely less important, providing a brilliantly intuitive counterpoint to the leader's playing. A noted stickler for quality, Goodman never failed to praise Wilson in a manner that contrasted strikingly with his often dismissive attitude towards other important musicians. Wilson's big band was another musical landmark, although the band's failure to attain commercial success was something which still clearly rankled with its leader four decades after it had folded. The sextet of the early 40s, which included at times artists such as Benny Morton, Jimmy Hamilton, 'Big' Sid Catlett, Bill Coleman, Emmett Berry, Slam Stewart and Edmond Hall, was yet another demonstration of his subtle and understated musicianship. Among important recording dates in later years were sessions with Lester Young and Roy Eldridge in 1956, with Carter in Japan in 1980, and several outstanding solo albums. Although a shy and retiring man, Wilson had no illusions about his musical stature. Late in his life, when an interviewer asked who was his favourite pianist, he answered, with only a hint of a disarming grin, 'I am.'

Selected albums: *The Didactic Mr Wilson* (1953), *Intimate Listening* (1954), *The Creative Mr Wilson* (1955), *I Got Rhythm* (1956), *The Teddy Wilson Trio* i (1956), with Lester Young *Pres And Teddy* (1956), *The Impeccable Mr Wilson* (1957), *These Tunes Remind Me Of You* (1957), *The Teddy Wilson Trio At Newport* (1957), *The Touch Of Teddy Wilson* (1957), *Mr Wilson And Mr Gershwin* (1959), *On Tour With Teddy Wilson* (c.1959), *The Teddy Wilson Trio* ii (1959), *The Teddy Wilson Trio* iii (1959), *Stompin' At The Savoy* (1967), *Air Mail Special* (1968), *The Teddy Wilson Trio In Europe* (1968), *The Noble Art Of Teddy Wilson* (1968), *Swedish Jazz My Way* (1970), *Elegant Piano* (1970), *Teddy Wilson-Eiji Kitamura* i (1970), *Teddy Wilson In Tokyo* (1971), *Teddy Wilson-Eiji Kitamura* ii (1971), *With Billie In Mind* (1972), *Runnin' Wild* (1973), *Teddy Wilson-Eiji Kitamura* iii (1973), *Piano Solos* (1974), *Concert In Argentina* (1974), *Striding After Fats* (1974), *Teddy Wilson And His All Stars* (1976), *Three Little Words* (1976), *Teddy's Choice* (1976), *The Teddy Wilson Trio In Milan* (1976), *Teddy Wilson Revamps Rodgers And Hart* (1977), *Cole Porter Classics* (1977), *Lionel Hampton Presents Teddy Wilson* (1977), *Teddy Wilson Revisits The Goodman Years* (1980), with Benny Carter *Gentlemen Of Swing* (1980), *Swingin' The Forties With The Great Eight* (1983), *Traces* (1983). Selected compilations: *The Teddy Wilson Big Band (1939-40)* (1974), one side only *I Love A Piano* (1979, rec. 1952), *Too Hot For Words (1935)* (1986), with Edmond Hall *Two Of A Kind (1944)* (1987), *Teddy Wilson Collection - 20 Golden Greats* (1987), *Teddy Wilson With Billie Holiday (1935-37)* (1988), *America Dances Broadcasts (1939)* (1988), with Benny Goodman *The Complete Small Combinations Vol. 1/2 (1935-37)* (1989), *Complete All Star And V-Disc Sessions* (Victorious 1991), *How High The Moon* (1992), *Complete Piano Solos* (1993).

Windhurst, Johnny

b. 5 November 1926, New York City, New York, USA, d. November 1981. After teaching himself to play trumpet, Windhurst first played in public, at Nick's in New York, while still in his early teens. Before he was out of his teenage years, he was playing professionally with Sidney Bechet, Art Hodes and James P. Johnson. In the late 40s he played in bands led by Edmond Hall, Hilton 'Nappy' Lamare and Louis Armstrong. He also led his own bands, but in these ventures chose to stay out of the main east coast centres. In the early 50s he worked with Eddie Condon, Ruby Braff and, later in the decade, with Jack Teagarden. He also accompanied a number of singers who found his unassuming nature, as reflected in his discreet playing, an ideal accompaniment. During the 60s and 70s he played mostly in obscure, out-of-the-way corners of the USA, seemingly content to hide his considerable talent from the big-time spotlight. Very much a musician's musician, highly regarded by all who heard him, Windhurst's chosen lifestyle might have robbed jazz of an important figure but, at least, he lived the life he wanted.

Album: *The Imaginative Johnny Windhurst* (1956).

Winding, Kai

b. Kai Chresten Winding, 18 May 1922, Arhus, Denmark, d. 7 May 1983, Spain. Winding's family emigrated to the USA in 1934, and soon thereafter he began teaching himself to play trombone. In the late 30s and early 40s he was with a number of big bands including those of Sonny Dunham and Alvino Rey. After serving in the US Coast Guard during the war, he began frequenting New York clubs, including Minton's Playhouse, and eagerly assimilating bop. He played in Benny Goodman's mid-40s bebop-inclined band, and then he joined Stan Kenton in 1946. Although he moved on the following year, his impact was substantial and he was now both a name to be reckoned with and popular with audiences. He next played with Charlie Ventura, Charlie Parker and Miles Davis, appearing on the *Birth Of The Cool* album. He also developed a penchant for working with other trombonists, starting with J.J. Johnson, with whom he formed a successful quintet in 1954. Later in the 50s he toured with his own bands, including a four-trombone and rhythm line-up, and in the 60s was musical director of the Playboy Club in New York. In the 70s he was leader, co-leader or sideman of various groups, including the Giants Of Jazz with Dizzy Gillespie, Giant Bones with Curtis Fuller, and the Lionel Hampton All-Star Big Band. One of the first trombone players to fully assimilate bop, Winding was an accomplished musician who could readily blend into most musical styles. His playing, in such diverse settings as Kenton's brassy powerhouse band and Davis's coolly restrained group, was always appropriate. His duets with Johnson were exquisitely formed and displayed his total command of the instrument. Towards the end of his life Winding played only when he chose to do so, spending time in semi-retirement in Spain where he died in 1983.

Selected albums: (NB: J.J. Johnson also indicated by 'J.J.' and 'Jay') *Jay And Kay: December 3, 1954* (1954), *Jay And Kai At Birdland* (1954), *Jay Jay Johnson, Kai Winding, Bennie Green* (1954), with Johnson, Frank Rosolino *Trombomania* (1955), *Jay And Kai* i (1955), *Jay And Kai* ii (1955), *Jay And Kai Trombone Octet* (1956), *The Kai Winding Septet* (1956), *Trombone Panorama* (1956), one side only - with the Dave Brubeck Quartet *Jay And Kai At Newport* (1956), *Jay And Kai* iii (1956), *The Axidentals With The Kai Winding Trombones* (1958), *The Swingin' States* (1959), *Dance To The City Beat* (1959), *The Incredible Kai Winding Trombones* (1960), *Great Kai And J.J.* (1960), *Kai Winding And His Orchestra* i (1961), *Kai Winding And His Orchestra* ii (1962), *The Kai Winding Trombones* i (1963), with Kenny Burrell *More!!!* aka *Soul Surfin'* (1963), *January 31st And February 15th 1963* (1963), *The Kai Winding Quartet* (1963), *The Kai Winding Trombones* ii (1963), *The Kai Winding Trombones* iii (1964), *The Kai Winding Trombones* iv (1964), *The Kai Winding Trombones* v (1965), *The Kai Winding Trombones* vi (1965), *The Kai Winding Trombones* vii (1966), *J.J. Johnson & Kai Winding* i (1968), *J.J. Johnson & Kai Winding* ii (1968), *J. J. Johnson & Kai Winding* iii (1969), *Giants Of Jazz* (1971), *Kai Winding's Caravan* (1974), *Danish Blue* (1977), *Showcase* (1977), *Lionel Hampton Presents Kai Winding* (1977), *Duo Bones* (1978), *Giant Bones* (1979), *Trombone Summit* (1980), *Giant Bones At Nice* (1980), *Giant Bones 90* (Sonet 1980). Compilations: *Kai's Krazy Kats* (1945), *Kai Winding* (1989).

Winstone, Norma

b. 23 September 1941, London, England. Although she studied formally as a pianist, Winstone decided to sing as a career and by her mid-teens was a professional vocalist. Although her earliest work was in the mainstream of jazz and jazz-influenced popular song, she was soon orientated towards the modern end of the jazz spectrum. In the 60s she became known for her musical associations with Michael Garrick, her singing developing into a frequently wordless instrumental style. In the late 60s, 70s and early 80s her reputation spread and she was a member of the trio, Azimuth, with Kenny Wheeler and her husband John Taylor. She continued to work with leading contemporary musicians, including Ralph Towner, Mike Westbrook and Eberhard Weber. In the late 80s and early 90s Winstone's repertoire underwent a slight shift and she was again performing many classic songs of earlier decades, often accompanied by Tony Coe. Although her new repertoire is rather more orthodox, Winstone brought to her material overtones of the free form work of her middle period, thus creating intriguing musical blends. In 1994 she was heard in the varied settings of London's Barbican, performing her own English lyrics to *The Songs of the Auvergne*, and as the singing voice for actress Geraldine James and in Alan Plater's BBC Television play, *Doggin' Around*. In this same year she also recorded *Well Kept Secret* with veteran pianist Jimmy Rowles. In February 1995 she launched her band New Friends in a concert at Ronnie Scott's. An exceptionally gifted and highly original singer, Winstone's chosen path has sometimes restricted her acceptance by the wider jazz audience, but those who have followed her work have been rewarded by the consistently high standards and indubitable integrity of her performances.

Albums: with Mike Westbrook *Love Songs* (1970), with Michael Garrick *The Heart Is A Lotus* (1970), *Edge Of Time* (1972), *Azimuth* (1977), *The Touchstone* (1978), *Azimuth '85* (1985), *Somewhere Called Home* (ECM 1987), *In Concert* (Enodoc 1988), *Azimuth '95* (1994), *Well Kept Secret* (1994).

Winter, Paul

b. 31 August 1939, Altoona, Pennsylvania, USA. While Winter was at Northwestern University, Chicago, he played the alto saxophone and the sextet he led won the Intercollegiate Jazz Festival of 1961. John Hammond Jnr. signed the group to CBS Records. The group toured Latin America in 1962 and became the first jazz group to play at the White House. The tour 'absolutely exploded our conception of what the world was' and the music Winter had heard led to the gradual change of the Sextet into the Consort. This was a band with a wholly new instrumentation - classical guitar, English horn, cello, ethnic percussion. The combination of jazz, classical and ethnic instruments has remained constant through numerous personnel changes over the following 20 years. It was difficult at the time for Winter to explain just what it was he was trying to produce and record companies found it hard to categorize. Winter now sees it as 'celebrating the convergence of both roots of American music - European and African'. He has had a series of talented musicians pass through the Consort - Collin Walcott, Paul McCandless, David Darling and Ralph Towner among them. *Icarus* was produced by George Martin and described by him as 'the finest album I have made'. Through the 70s Winter showed an increasing concern with conservation and became an active supporter of Greenpeace. He has recorded music accompanied by the sounds of whales off the Canadian coast and wolves in the mountains of California and Minnesota.

Albums: *Jazz Premiers: Washington* (1962), *Jazz Meets The Bossa Nova* (1962), *New Jazz On Campus* (1963), *Something In The Wind* (1969), *Icarus* (1971), *Earthdance* (1977), *Callings* (1980), *Missa Gaia/Earth Mass* (1982), *Concert For The Earth* (1985), *Canyon* (1985), *Whales Alive* (1987), *Earthbeat* (Living Music 1988).

Wood, Booty

b. Mitchell Wood, 27 December 1919, Dayton, Ohio, USA, d. June 1987. Wood took up the trombone in his teens, beginning his professional career towards the end of the 30s. In the early 40s he was a member of the bands of Tiny Bradshaw and Lionel Hampton. While serving in the US Navy during World War II he played in the band that included Willie Smith and Clark Terry. After the war Wood returned briefly to Hampton, then worked in bands led by Arnett Cobb, Erskine Hawkins and Count Basie. After a spell outside music he returned to the scene in 1959, joining Duke Ellington with whom he played intermittently during the next dozen years. He also appeared with Earl 'Fatha' Hines and in the late 70s and early 80s was with Basie again. A forceful player with a rich open tone, Wood's spell with Ellington ensured that he also became adept at using the mute, performing with colourful effect on many of the band's standards.

Selected albums: with Duke Ellington *Blues In Orbit* (1959), with Ellington *Nutcracker Suite* (1960), *The Booty Wood All Stars* (1960).

Woodard, Rickey

b. 5 August 1950, Nashville, Tennessee, USA. After studying saxophones under Bill Green and majoring in music at Tennessee State University, Woodard worked extensively with a wide range of performers. He worked with jazz artists such as Jimmy Smith, Billy Higgins, Frank Capp and Al Grey and also backed singers from the jazz and pop worlds including Ella Fitzgerald, Ernestine Anderson, Barbara McNair and Prince. He also recorded with Capp and with the big band co-led by Jeff Clayton and Jeff Hamilton. Mostly playing tenor saxophone, he established a solid if localized reputation in the USA before venturing onto the international jazz festival circuit. By the early 90s Woodard was fast becoming a popular visitor to Europe and the UK. Playing alto and soprano saxophones in addition to tenor (he also plays clarinet, flute and guitar), Woodard is a vibrant and forceful soloist, his tenor saxophone styling hinting at an affection for the work of Wardell Grey, Dexter Gordon and, especially, Hank Mobley. For all such stylistic mentors, however, Woodard is very much his own man and this, allied to his playing skills and an engaging personality, assures him of a continuing welcome at jazz venues at home and abroad.

Albums: *The Frank Capp Trio Presents Rickey Woodard* (Concord 1991), *California Cookin'!* (Candid 1991), *Night Mist* (1992), *The Tokyo Express* (Candid 1993).

Woode, Jimmy

b. 23 September 1928, Philadelphia, Pennsylvania, USA. After extensive studies on both piano and bass, Woode settled on the latter instrument. Military service delayed the start of his professional career, but in 1946 he formed his own band which worked in the Boston area. Among his early musical associates were Nat Pierce, Joe 'Flip' Phillips and Zoot Sims, and he was also accompanist to Ella Fitzgerald and Sarah Vaughan. In the early 50s he was a member of the house band at George Wein's Storyville Club in Boston, where he played with numerous visiting jazz stars. By 1955 his reputation was such that he was invited to join Duke Ellington, a job he held for five years. After leaving Ellington he settled in Europe, becoming a member of the Clarke-Boland Big Band throughout most of its existence. The 60s and 70s were busy years for Woode; in addition to playing with various bands on a regular basis, he gigged with visiting Americans, including Don Byas and Johnny Griffin, ran his own music publishing company, and worked in radio, television and recording studios. This pattern continued throughout the 80s, with appearances in the Paris Reunion Band, led by Nathan Davis, and at Ellington reunions, including *Ellington '88* at Oldham, England, where he was reunited with former Ellington rhythm-section partner Sam Woodyard. A solid section player, Woode continues to draw the respect of his fellow musicians.

Selected albums: with Duke Ellington *Such Sweet Thunder* (1957), *The Colorful Strings Of Jimmy Woode* (1957).

Woodman, Britt

b. 4 June 1920, Los Angeles, California, USA. Following in the footsteps of his trombone-playing father, Woodman took up the instrument in childhood to play in his father's band. In the late 30s he worked mostly on the west coast, usually in lesser-known bands, although he ended the decade with Les Hite. After military service in World War II he played in Boyd Raeburn's musically adventurous band and was then with Lionel Hampton. At the end of the 40s he formalized his musical education, studying at Westlake College in Los Angeles, and then joined the Duke Ellington orchestra as lead trombonist. In the mid-50s he found time for record dates with Charles Mingus, a friend from childhood, and Miles Davis. His tenure with Ellington ended in 1960 and thereafter he worked in studio and theatre bands in Los Angeles and New York City. He has continued with his film and television work, but has appeared on record leading his own small band and with small groups led by Bill Berry and Benny Carter. He has also played in the big bands of Berry, Toshiko Akiyoshi and the Capp-Pierce Juggernaut. Woodman's playing style reflects his career-long immersion in big band music, but is shot through with intriguing glimpses of his interest in bop.

Selected albums: with Duke Ellington *Seattle Concert* (1952), with Ellington *Such Sweet Thunder* (1957), with Charles Mingus *Mingus!* (1960), with Bill Berry *For Duke* (1977), *Britt Woodman In LA* (1977).

Woods, Phil

b. 2 November 1931, Springfield, Massachusetts, USA. Woods began playing alto saxophone as a child, studied later at the Juilliard School of Music in New York and by his early 20s had already made a significant mark on jazz. Playing hard bop and acknowledging Charlie Parker but never slavishly so, Woods became a vital force in jazz in the late 50s. He led his own small groups, co-led a band with Gene Quill, played in bands led by artists such as Buddy Rich, Cecil Payne, Thelonious Monk, Quincy Jones and Benny Goodman, and worked as a studio musician and recorded extensively, including appearing on Benny Carter's 1961 *Further Definitions*. During the 60s he was also active as a teacher and towards the end of the decade became resident in France, where he formed the European Rhythm Machine. Woods led this band until his return to the USA in the early 70s where, in 1973, he formed a new quartet which met with great critical and commercial acclaim. This group stayed in operation for the next few years and Woods's stature continued to grow. He also made a dynamic if somewhat anonymous impact on the pop music scene with his solo on Billy Joel's hit single, 'I Love You Just The Way You Are'. In the early 80s Woods was active in the USA, touring internationally, and continuing to record albums of exceptional quality. His quartet had expanded with the addition of Tom Harrell. He also recorded with Dizzy Gillespie, Rob

McConnell and Budd Johnson Although identified with the post-Parker school of alto saxophone playing, Woods has always had his own style. Early records, such as *Bird Calls*, reveal a highly sophisticated performer belying his age with the maturity of his improvisations. He plays with a rich, full sound, avoiding the harshness favoured by some of his contemporaries. By the late 80s Woods was firmly established as a major jazz musician and one of the most successful alto saxophonists the music had known. At the start of the 90s his standards of performance remained outstanding. Although this decade saw him entering his 60s the depth of his imagination was unimpaired and his playing was still filled with the enthusiasm and vitality of his youth.

Selected albums: *Bird's Eyes* (Philology 1947 recordings), *Wood Lore* (Original Jazz Classics 1955), *The Young Bloods* (Original Jazz Classics 1956), *Pairing Off* (Original Jazz Classics 1956), *Warm Woods* (1957), *Four Altos* (Original Jazz Classics 1957), *Phil And Quill* (Original Jazz Classics 1957), *Bird Calls, Volume 1* (1957), *Early Quintets* (1959), *Rights Of Swing* (Candid 1961), *Greek Cooking* (1967), *Alive And Well In Paris* (1968), *The Birth Of The European Rhythm Machine* (1968), *Stolen Moments* (JMY 1969), *Round Trip* (1969), *1968 Jazz* (EMI 1969), *Phil Woods And His European Rhythm Machine At The Montreux Jazz Festival* (1970), *Phil Woods And His European Rhythm Machine At The Frankfurt Jazz Festival* (1970), *Chromatic Banana* (1970), *Musique De Bois* (1974), *Images* (1975), *Live From The Showboat* (1976), *Songs For Sisyphus* (1977), *I Remember...* (1978), *Quartet* (1979), *Crazy Horse* (1979), *European Tour, Live* (1980), *The Macerata Concert* (1980), *Birds Of A Feather* (1981), *Three For All* (1981), *At The Vanguard* (1982), with Rob McConnell *Rob McConnell And The Boss Brass Featuring Phil Woods* (1982), *Piper At The Gates Of Dawn* (1984), *Integrity* (Red 1984), with Budd Johnson *The Old Dude And The Fundance Kid* (1984), *More Mistletoe Magic* (1985), *Gratitude* (Denon 1986), *Dizzy Gillespie Meets The Phil Woods Quintet* (1986), *Bouquet* (Concord 1987), *Bop Stew* (Concord 1987), *Evolution* (Concord 1988), *Here's To My Lady* (Chesky 1988), *Phil's Mood* (Philology 1988), *Flash* (Concord 1989), *Phil On Etna* (Philology 1989), *Embraceable You* (Philology 1989), *Real Life* (Chesky 1990), *All Bird's Children* (Concord 1990), *Flowers For Hodges* (Concord 1992), *Elsa* (Philology 1992), *Full House* (1992), *Live At The Corridonia Jazz Festival* (Philology 1992).

Woodyard, Sam

b. 7 January 1925, Elizabeth, New Jersey, USA, d. 20 September 1988, Paris, France. A self-taught drummer, Woodyard played in several small bands in his home state in the 40s and early 50s. In 1952 he joined Roy Eldridge and the following year played with Milt Buckner. In 1955 he joined Duke Ellington, a job he retained with occasional lay-offs through ill-health and personal waywardness, until the late 60s. He subsequently worked with Ella Fitzgerald and as an extra percussionist with Ellington and Buddy Rich. Occasional gigs with Bill Berry helped his sagging career, but by 1975 he had decided to relocate to Europe. Based in Paris, he played and recorded with local musicians such as Guy Lafitte, other expatriates including Buckner, and visitors like Teddy Wilson, Buddy Tate and Slam Stewart. By the 80s Woodyard's earlier years of hard drinking and wild living had begun to take their toll. The theft of his drum kit added to his decline, but in the mid-summer of 1988 he was a welcome guest at the Ellington '88 convention held at Oldham, England. Although his health was clearly at a very low ebb, he was rejuvenated by the renewal of contact with other ex-Ellingtonians, Berry, Buster Cooper and Jimmy Woode, and by the gift from the assembled delegates of a new drum kit. His playing at the convention was inevitably more tentative than of old, but he enjoyed himself and performed such crowd-pleasing favourites as 'Limbo Jazz' with his eccentric vocal. A short while later, on 20 September 1988, he died in Paris. A vigorous and skilful drummer, Woodyard's erratic temperament sometimes showed itself in his playing and he occasionally slipped into musical extravagances. At his best, however, whether in subtle accompaniments to Ellington's piano solos, or driving the big band along in thunderous performances such as the classic 1956 Newport concert, behind Paul Gonsalves's legendary solo on 'Diminuedo And Crescendo In Blue', or the 1971 UK tour recording of 'La Plus Belle Africaine', he was unmatched.

Selected albums: *Ellington At Newport* (1956), *Duke Ellington Plays Mary Poppins* (1964), with Ellington *Soul Call* (1966), *Duke Ellington - The Pianist* (1966), with Ellington *Togo Brava Suite* (1971), *Sam Woodyard In Paris* (1975).

Workman, Reggie

b. 26 June 1937, Philadelphia, Pennsylvania, USA. One of the premier bassists in post-war jazz, Workman's first involvement in music was 'singing doo-wop at a YMCA'. Piano lessons failed to interest him, but a cousin introduced him to the bass and he was hooked - though his high school's lack of an instrument meant he had to play bass lines on tuba and euphonium for a while. By the time he left school, he was working as a professional bassist playing R&B and jazz standards. At the end of the 50s he moved to New York and played with Gigi Gryce, Eric Dolphy and his mentor, John Coltrane, with whom he'd previously been in contact. Workman toured and recorded with Coltrane in 1961, then joined the leading hard bop group of the time, Art Blakey's Jazz Messengers, remaining for two years and also recording with both the group's tenor saxophonist Wayne Shorter, on his own Blue Note dates such as *Night Dreamer*, *Juju* and *Adam's Apple*, and the group's trumpeter Freddie Hubbard. Workman next played with the radical New York Art Quartet and later worked with a variety of leaders, including Yusef Lateef and Thelonious Monk. Increasingly involved in education, in the 70s he led the Collective Black Arts organization in New York - a community self-help project that for a while published its own newspaper, *Expansions*. He also worked with Max Roach, Marion Brown, Archie Shepp and Charles Tolliver. In the 80s Workman recorded with David Murray, Steve Lacy and Mal Waldron, toured with Alice Coltrane and Rashied Ali in the Coltrane Legacy band, was a founder member of both the all-string Black Swan Quartet and

Trio Transition and became a regular member of pianist Marilyn Crispell's groups, playing on her *Gaia*, *Circles* and *Live In Zurich*. He has also recorded a solo album, *The Works Of Workman*, and since the mid-80s led his own ensemble, whose members over the years have included Crispell, singer Jeanne Lee, drummers Andrew Cyrille or Gerry Hemingway and saxophonists Joseph Jarman, Oliver Lake or, most recently, Don Byron: their two albums are *Images* and *Synthesis*. One of the most versatile and adventurous of bass players, Workman is married to the well-known choreographer and poet Maya Milenovic.

Albums: *Conversation* (1977), *The Works Of Workman* (Denon 1979), *Synthesis* (Leo 1986), *Black Swan Quartet* (1986), *Trio Transition* (1988), *Trio Transition With Oliver Lake* (1989), *Images* (Music And Arts 1990), *Altered Spaces* (Leo 1993).

World Saxophone Quartet

In 1974, Anthony Braxton recorded a composition for a saxophone quartet on his *New York Fall 1974*. The other three players involved - Julius Hemphill, Oliver Lake and Hamiet Bluiett - must have liked the format as in 1977 they and David Murray formed the World Saxophone Quartet. The proud name was no idle boast: these really were four pre-eminent saxophone voices. All the players are multi-instrumentalists, but in general Hemphill and Lake played alto, Murray tenor and Bluiett baritone saxophone. Wearing tuxedos as a reference to the era of big band sophistication, they became sure-fire festival favourites, starting regular European tours in 1978. They all contributed compositions, though perhaps Hemphill and Bluiett have shown most interest in the quartet's possibilities, producing thoughtful arrangements that examine ballads, bop and blues with understanding and affection. Originally located on the jazz *avant garde*, their recent albums have looked back at aspects of the black music tradition (*Plays Duke Ellington*, *Rhythm And Blues*), while the new *Metamorphosis* introduced African drums into the musical mix. In 1991, Hemphill left the group and was replaced by altoist Arthur Blythe, who marked his debut on *Metamorphosis*.

Albums: *Point Of No Return* (Moers 1977), *Steppin' With* (Black Saint 1979), *WSQ* (Black Saint 1981), *Revue* (Black Saint 1982), *Live In Zurich* (Black Saint 1984), *Live At Brooklyn Academy Of Music* (1986), *Plays Duke Ellington* (Elektra 1986), *Dances And Ballads* (Elektra 1987), *Rhythm And Blues* (Elektra 1989), *Metamorphosis* (Elektra 1991), *Breath Of Life* (Elektra 1994), *Moving Right Along* (Black Saint 1994).

Wyands, Richard

b. 2 July 1928, Oakland, California, USA. In mid-teenage, he was playing piano in San Francisco jazz clubs, accompanying local musicians and visitors. In the late 50s he moved to New York where he worked with many jazz artists in both bop and mainstream. By the mid-60s he had settled into a long spell with Kenny Burrell with whom he toured extensively. In 1974 he left Burrell to join JPJ Trio, replacing co-founder Dill Jones. In the late 70s and through the 80s, he continued to play a discreet supporting role with a wide range of jazzmen. Despite such diffidence, however, Wyands is an accomplished and inventive soloist with a light touch and a subtly engaging sense of swing as can be heard on *There Here And Now*, a rare instance of Wyands as leader.

Albums: *Roamin' With Jerome Richardson* (1959), with Elvin Jones *Don't Go To Strangers* (1960), with Kenny Burrell *The Tender Gender* (1966), *Then Here And Now* (Storyville 1978), with Cecil Payne *Casbah* (1985), *The Arrival* (DIW 1992).

Yamashita, Yosuke

b. 26 February 1942, Tokyo, Japan. Although he had played professionally at the age of 17, Yamashita went on to study at the Kunitachi College of Music (1962-67). He established himself playing in the quartets of Masahiko Togashi and Sadao Watanabe. The earliest influence of Bill Evans soon gave way to the influence of Cecil Taylor. When Yamashita formed his own trio with Akira Sakata (alto saxophone) and Takeo Moriyama (drums) and toured Europe (1974) the music was so wild the group was known as the Kamikaze Trio. For inspiration Yamashita looked back to 'the beginning of jazz - Europe had the system but Africa had all the feeling. All the material I use belongs to the system, but as long as I can stand on the outside and approach things from the outside, I will never be suffocated'. He kept a trio going throughout the 70s and continued to play as a sideman with the bands of Kazumi Takeda (tenor saxophone) and Seuchi Nakamura (tenor saxophone). From 1974 he made regular trips to Europe with the trio in Germany as well as playing with Manfred Schoof (1975), then as a soloist and in 1977 in a duo with bassist Adellard Roidinger. He disbanded the trio in 1983 when he felt that he had achieved as much as he could in that format. Yamashita formed a big band with an eclectic style and performed in many varied situations including solo performances of his own versions of classical pieces, playing with Kodo, a Japanese drum choir, and having pieces performed by the Ozaka Philharmonic Orchestra. In the early 90s he was again playing with a trio and touring Europe.

Albums: *Clay* (Unja 1974), *Distant Thunder* (1975), *Banslikana* (Enja 1976), *Ghosts By Albert Ayler* (West Wind 1977), *A Tribute To Mal Waldron* (1980), *In Europe* (1983), *It Don't Mean A Thing* (DIW 1984), *Breath With Hozan Tagoshi* (1984), *Sentimental* (1985), *Asian Games* (Verve 1988), *Kurdish Dance* (Verve 1993), *Dazzling Days* (Verve 1994).

Yancey, Jimmy

b. 20 February 1898, Chicago, Illinois, USA, d. 17 September 1951. While still a small child Yancey appeared in vaudeville as a tap dancer and singer. After touring the USA and Europe he abandoned this career and, just turned 20, settled in Chicago where he taught himself to play piano. He began to appear at rent parties and informal club sessions, gradually building a reputation. Nevertheless, in 1925, he decided that music was an uncertain way to earn a living and took a job as groundsman with the city's White Sox baseball team. He continued to play piano and was one of the prime movers in establishing the brief popularity of boogie-woogie. He made many records and played clubs and concerts, often accompanying his wife, singer Estella 'Mama' Yancey, but retained his job as groundsman until shortly before his death in 1951. Although Yancey's playing style was elementary, he played with verve and dash, and if he fell behind such contemporaries as Albert Ammons and Pete Johnson in technique, he made up most of the deficiencies through sheer enthusiasm.

Selected compilations: *Piano Solos* (1939), *The Immortal Jimmy Yancey* (Oldie Blues 1977, 1940-43 recordings), *Jimmy Yancy Vol 1 1939-40* (Oldie Blues 1988), *In The Beginning* (Jazzology 1990), *Jimmy Yancy Vol 2 1943-50* (Document 1992).

Yellowjackets

Over 12 years, the Yellowjackets have achieved a formidable reputation for their live performances and critical and commercial success with their recordings of electric pop jazz. The members of the band are accomplished musicians in their own right and perhaps this accounts for the Yellowjackets' two Grammys and six nominations. The band includes: Robben Ford, Russell Ford (keyboards), Bob Mintzer (saxophone), Michael Franks (vocals), Ricky Lawson (drums). Their recording career began in 1980 with *The Inside Story*, when Ford heard Jimmy Haslip (bass) playing with veterans Airto and Flora Purim and decided to use them on him on his solo project. By the time of 1982's *Mirage à Trois*, Ford's presence was declining. New saxophonist, Marc Russo featured prominently on *Samurai Samba* (1983) and *Shades* in 1986 rewarded the band's steady touring with a Grammy and six-figure sales. William Kennedy was the next addition to the line-up and this prompted the band to explore some new territory. *Politics* (1988) was another Grammy winner and the band took another radical change of direction. Their next project, *The Spin* was recorded in Oslo, Norway with well-known engineer, Jan Erik Konshaug, and was a more acoustic, resolutely jazz album. *Live Wires*, the band's 1992 release successfully demonstrated the multi-faceted approach the Yellowjackets like to adopt. Indeed, the simplicity of the band's sound belies the diversity of their influences: 'We spend hours experimenting, studying and listening to music from all over the world. You can't be afraid to take chances. That's what it takes to continue to grow!'.

Albums: *The Inside Story* (1980), *Yellowjackets* (1981), *Mirage á Trois* (WEA 1982), *Samurai Samba* (WEA 1983), *Shades* (MCA 1986), *Four Corners* (MCA 1987), *Politics* (MCA 1988), *The Spin* (MCA 1990), *Greenhouse* (1991), *Live Wires*

(GRP 1992), *Like A River* (GRP 1992), *Run For Your Life* (GRP 1994).

Young, Larry

b. 7 October 1940, Newark, New Jersey, USA, d. 30 March 1978. His father was an organ player but at first Young played piano instead. In 1957 he joined an R&B group in Elizabeth, New Jersey and, switching to Hammond organ, recorded with tenor saxophonist Jimmy Forrest in 1961. In 1962 he made his vinyl debut as leader with *Groove Street*. He procured the services of top guitarist Grant Green and, signed to Blue Note, made classic records with artists such as Joe Henderson, Woody Shaw, Donald Byrd and Lee Morgan. In 1964 he visited Europe, playing piano on Nathan Davis's *Happy Girl*. Affected by John Coltrane's expansion of hard bop, he recorded with Coltrane and inducted drummer Elvin Jones into his band, recording *Unity* with him in 1965. He played electric piano on Miles Davis's *Bitches Brew* in 1970, the album which launched the jazz rock genre, worked briefly with John McLaughlin in 1970 and then played in Lifetime, the band run by drummer Anthony Williams. His own *Lawrence Of Newark* featured James 'Blood' Ulmer, making one of his earlier appearances on record. In 1977 Young co-led a group with drummer Joe Chambers, recording *Double Exposure*. Young also worked under his Islamic name of Khalid Yasin. His death at the age of 38 deprived the world of an innovative and passionate player.
Selected albums: *Testifying* (Original Jazz Classics 1961), *Young Blues* (Original jazz Classics 1961), *Groove Street* (1962), *Into Somethin'*, (1965), *Contrasts* (c.60s), *Unity* (Blue Note 1966), *Lawrence Of Newark* (1973), *Spaceball* (1975), with Joe Chambers *Double Exposure* (1977). Compilation: *The Art Of Larry Young* (Blue Note 1990).

Young, Lee

b. 7 March 1917, New Orleans, Louisiana, USA. Before settling on drums Young studied piano and various reed and brass instruments. As a child he played in the family band led by his father and which also included his brother Lester Young. In the early 30s he moved to Los Angeles, playing in a variety of musical settings with bands led by Mutt Carey, Buck Clayton, Fats Waller and others. He was one of the first black musicians to be hired on a regular basis for film studio work but continued to appear in jazz groups in the early 40s, including those led by Lionel Hampton and Nat 'King' Cole. Young also led his own small groups, one of which featured his brother, and he backed many leading artists including Dinah Washington. He was a regular with Norman Granz's Jazz At The Philharmonic in the mid-40s and later in the decade he was with Benny Goodman. In the 50s, still working in the studios, he belatedly rejoined Cole. In the 60s he was active in record production, mostly as producer and administrator with VeeJay Records, and in the late 70s was briefly with Motown Records. A solid player with a good sense of time, Young's career outside jazz, as both studio musician and record company executive, occupied the best of his years.
Albums: *Jazz At The Philhamonic 1944-1946* (1944-46), *Jazz At The Philharmonic 1946* (1946).

Young, Lester

b. 27 August 1909, Woodville, Mississippi, USA, d. 15 March 1959. Born into a musical family, Young was taught several instruments by his father. As a child he played drums in the family's band, but around 1928 he quit the group and switched to tenor saxophone. His first engagements on this instrument were with Art Bronson, in Phoenix, Arizona. He stayed with Bronson until 1930, with a brief side trip to play again with the family, then worked in and around Minneapolis, Minnesota, with various bands. In the spring of 1932 he joined the Original Blue Devils, under the leadership of Walter Page, and was one of several members of the band who joined Bennie Moten in Kansas City towards the end of 1933. During the next few years Young played in the bands of Moten, George E. Lee, King Oliver, Count Basie, Fletcher Henderson, Andy Kirk and others. In 1936 he rejoined Basie, with whom he remained for the next four years, touring, broadcasting and recording. He also recorded in small groups directed by Teddy Wilson and others and appeared on several classic record dates, backing Billie Holiday, with whom he forged a special and lasting relationship. (She nicknamed him 'Pres' or 'Prez', for president, while he bestowed on her the name 'Lady Day'.) In the early 40s he played in, and sometimes led, small groups in the Los Angeles area alongside his brother, Lee Young, and musicians such as Red Callender, Nat 'King' Cole and Al Sears. During this period he returned briefly to the Basie band, making some excellent recordings, and also worked with Dizzy Gillespie. Late in 1944 he was conscripted into the US Army but was discharged in mid-summer the following year, having spent part of his military service in hospital and part in an army prison. In the mid-40s he was filmed by Gjon Mili in the classic jazz short, *Jammin' The Blues*, a venture which was co-produced by Norman Granz. At this time he also joined Granz's Jazz At The Philharmonic package, remaining with the organization for a number of years. He also led small groups for club and record dates, toured the USA and visited Europe. From the mid-40s onwards Young's health was poor and in the late 50s his physical decline became swift. He continued to record and make concert and festival appearances and was featured on television's *The Sound Of Jazz* in 1957. In these final years his deteriorating health was exacerbated by a drinking problem, and some close observers suggest that towards the end he lost the will to live. He died on 15 March 1959.
One of the seminal figures in jazz history and a major influence in creating the musical atmosphere in which bop could flourish, Young's early and late career was beset by critical bewilderment. Only his middle period appears to have earned unreserved critical acclaim. In recent years, however, thanks in part to a more enlightened body of critical opinion, allied to perceptive biographies (by Dave Gelly and Lewis Porter), few observers now have anything other than praise for this remarkable artist's entire output. In the early 30s, when Young appeared on the wider jazz scene, the tenor saxophone was regarded as a forceful, barrel-toned, potentially dominating

instrument. In the early years of jazz none of the saxophone family had met with favour and only the clarinet among the reed instruments maintained a front-line position. This position had been challenged, almost single-handedly, by Coleman Hawkins, who changed perceptions of the instrument and its role in jazz. Despite his authority, Hawkins failed to oust the trumpet from its dominating role. Nevertheless, his example spawned many imitators who attempted to replicate his rich and resonant sound. When Young appeared, favouring a light, acerbic, dry tone, he was in striking contrast to the majestic Hawkins, and many people, both musicians and audiences, disliked what they heard. Only the more perceptive listeners of the time, and especially younger musicians, heard in Young's floating melodic style a distinctive and revolutionary approach to jazz.

The solos he recorded with the Basie band included many which, for all their brevity - some no more than eight bars long - display an astonishing talent in full and magnificent flight. On his first record date, on 9 October 1936, made by a small group drawn from the Basie band under the name of Jones-Smith Inc., he plays with what appears at first hearing to be startling simplicity. Despite this impression, the performances, especially of 'Shoe Shine Swing' and 'Lady Be Good', are undisputed masterpieces seldom equalled, let alone bettered (perhaps not even by Young himself). He recorded many outstanding solos - with the full Basie band on 'Honeysuckle Rose', 'Taxi War Dance' and 'Every Tub'; with the small group, the Kansas City Seven, on 'Dickie's Dream' and 'Lester Leaps In'. On all of these recordings, Young's solos clearly indicate that, for all their emotional depths, a massive intellectual talent is at work. In 1940 he made some excellent records with a small band assembled under the nominal leadership of Benny Goodman which featured Basie, Buck Clayton and Charlie Christian and was clearly at ease in such illustrious company. His sessions with Billie Holiday belong to a higher level again. The empathy displayed by these two frequently-troubled people is always remarkable and at times magical. Almost any of their recordings would serve as an example, with 'Me, Myself And I', 'Mean To Me', 'When You're Smiling', 'Foolin' Myself' and 'This Year's Kisses' being particularly rewarding examples of their joint and separate artistry. Even late in their lives, after they had seen little of one another for several years (theirs was an extremely close although almost certainly platonic relationship), their appearance on the television show The Sound Of Jazz produced a moment of astonishing emotional impact. In a performance of 'Fine And Mellow', just after Holiday has sung, Young plays a brief solo of achingly fragile tenderness that is packed with more emotion than a million words could convey.

After Young left the army his playing style was demonstrably different, a fact which led many to declare that his suffering at the hands of the military had broken his artistic will. While Young's time in the army was clearly unpleasant, and the life was something for which he was physically and psychologically unsuited, it seems unlikely that the changes in his playing were directly attributable to his army service. On numerous record dates he demonstrated that his talent was not damaged by his spell in the stockade. His playing had changed but the differences were almost certainly a result of changes in the man himself. He had matured, moved on, and his music had too. Those critics who like their musicians to be trapped in amber were unprepared for the new Lester Young. Adding to the confusion was the fact that, apart from the faithful Hawkins-style devotees, most other tenor players in jazz were imitating the earlier Lester. His first recordings after leaving the army, which include 'DB Blues' and 'These Foolish Things', are not the work of a spent spirit but have all the elegance and style of a consummate master, comfortably at one with his world. A 1956 session with Teddy Wilson, on which Young is joined by Roy Eldridge and an old comrade from his Basie days, Jo Jones, is another striking example of a major figure who is still in full command of all his earlier powers; and a long-overlooked set of records made at about the same time with the Bill Potts Trio, a backing group that accompanied him during an engagement in a bar in Washington, DC, show him to be as musically alert and inventive as ever.

A withdrawn, moody figure with a dry and slightly anarchic sense of humour, Young perpetuated his own mythology during his lifetime, partly through a personal use of words which he developed into a language of his own (among other things he coined the use of 'bread' to denote money). His stoicism and a marked preference for his own company - or, at best, for a favoured few who shared his mistrustful view of life - set him apart even from the jazz musicians who admired and sometimes revered him. It is impossible to overstate Young's importance in the development of jazz. From the standpoint of the 90s, when the tenor saxophone is the dominant instrument in jazz, it is easy to imagine that this is the way it always was. That the tenor has come to hold the place it does is largely a result of Young's influence, which inspired so many young musicians to adopt the instrument or to turn those who already played it into new directions. Most of the developments in bop and post-bop owe their fundamentals to Young's concern for melody and the smooth, flowing lines with which he transposed his complex musical thoughts into beautiful, articulate sounds. Although other important tenor saxophonists have come, and in some cases gone, during the three decades since Lester Young died, few have had the impact of this unusual, introspective, sensitive and musically profound genius of jazz.

Selected albums: *Lester Young And The Piano Giants* (Verve 1950-56), *Lester Young With The Oscar Peterson Trio* (1952), *Lester Young With The Oscar Peterson Quintet Vols 1 & 2* (1953), *The President Plays* (Verve 1953), *It Don't Mean A Thing* (1954), with Harry Edison *Pres And Sweets* (1955), *The Jazz Giants '56* (1956), *Lester Meets Miles, MJQ And The Jack Teagarden All Stars* (1956), *Pres In Europe* (1956), *Lester Young In Washington DC Vols 1-4* (1956), with Teddy Wilson *Pres And Teddy* (Verve 1956), *Pres Vols 1-4* (1956), with others *The Sound Of Jazz* (1957), *The Real Sound Of Jazz* (1957, TV soundtrack), *Laughin' To Keep From Cryin'* (1958), *Lester Young In Paris* (1959), *In Memoriam* (1959). Selected compilations: *Lester-Amadeus* (1936-38), with Count Basie, Billie Holiday

The Lester Young Story Vols 1-9 (1936-39), *The Alternative Lester* (1936-39), *Prized Pres!* (1936-57), *Count Basie And His Orchestra, 1938* (1938), with Benny Goodman *Together Again* (1940-41), *Pres At His Very Best* (1944), *Jammin' With Lester* (1944-46), *The Genius Of Lester Young* (1945-52), *Live At The Royal Roost* (1948), *Lester Young* (1948-53), *The Lester Young Story* (1949-56), *Lester Swings* (1950), *Jammin' With Lester Vol. 2* (1950), *Pres Is Blue* (c.1950), *Lester Swings Again* (1951), *Lester Young On The Air* (1952), *Savoy Recordings* (RCA 1986), *Prez's Hat Vols 1-4* (Philology 1988).

Further reading: *Lester Young*, Dave Gelly. *Lester Young*, Lewis Porter. *You Got To Be Original, Man: The Music Of Lester Young*, Frank Büchmann-Moller. *You Just Fight For Your Life: The Story Of Lester Young*, Frank Büchmann-Moller.

Young, Snooky

b. Eugene Howard Young, 3 February 1919. Young began playing trumpet while still a small child and by his early teens was working in territory bands. He was heard by Gerald Wilson, who was then playing in the Jimmie Lunceford band, and on his recommendation Young was hired. Young stayed with the Lunceford band until 1942 and in that year played with Count Basie, Lionel Hampton, Les Hite and Benny Carter. In the following year, after a brief return visit to Basie, he joined Wilson's big band in California. In the late 40s he was again with Hampton and Basie, and he was back yet again in the Basie band in the late 50s and early 60s. From the early 60s he worked in television studios in New York City, and was a member of the Thad Jones-Mel Lewis Jazz Orchestra from its inception. Subsequently, Young continued to play in the studios, mostly in Los Angeles, and also appeared at jazz festivals, with occasional return visits to Basie in the late 70s and early 80s. He also made a handful of records as sideman with Ray Bryant, and as either leader or co-leader (with Marshal Royal). A strong lead trumpeter, his solo gifts were frequently underused by his employers. Content to work in the studios for more than a quarter of a century, Young's infrequent jazz excursions in the past three decades have shown him to be an interesting soloist, whether on open horn or with the plunger mute.

Selected albums: with Count Basie *Chairman Of The Board* (1959), one side only *The Boys From Dayton* (1971), with Marshal Royal *Snooky And Marshal's Album* (Concord 1978), *Horn Of Plenty* (1979).

Young, Trummy

b. James Osborne Young, 12 January 1912, Savannah, Georgia, USA, d. 10 September 1984. As a child Young played trumpet and drums but by his teens was concentrating on trombone. Resident in Washington, DC, he played in local bands before relocating to Chicago and working with Earl 'Fatha' Hines. He remained with Hines for four years, making occasional visits to other bands. In 1937 he began a five-year stint with Jimmie Lunceford, becoming an important member of the band as both trombone soloist and singer. He also had a number of hit records with the band, among them 'Margie' and his own composition, 'Tain't What You Do, It's The Way That You Do It'.

In the 40s he worked with bands covering a wide stylistic range, including those led by Boyd Raeburn and Roy Eldridge. He also played with Jazz At The Philharmonic before settling for a while in Hawaii. In 1952 he became a member of Louis Armstrong's All Stars, a job he held for 12 years. After leaving Armstrong he returned to Hawaii, leading his own bands, playing with visiting musicians, and making occasional visits to the mainland for concert and festival appearances. A superbly gifted trombonist, Young's early playing style showed him to be a completely rounded soloist with an approach to his instrument that was, in many respects, very advanced for a 30s big band musician. His playing style changed after he joined Armstrong, with whom he used a deceptively simple approach. The change was highly appropriate for Armstrong's band and Young was in many ways a more suitable partner than his predecessor, the sublime Jack Teagarden, had been. His blistering solos and delightfully melodic ensemble lines, allied to his engagingly casual singing, helped to give the band a strength of character that it lacked after he departed.

Selected albums: *Louis Armstrong Plays W.C. Handy* (1954), *Satch Plays Fats* (1955), *Trummy Young And His Fifty-Fifty Band* (1955), *A Man And His Horn* (c.1975), *Yours Truly: Trummy Young And Friends* (c.1975), *Struttin' With Some Barbecue* (1979). Compilation: *The Complete Jimmie Lunceford 1939-40* (1939-40).

Z

Zardis, Chester

b. 27 May 1900, New Orleans, Louisiana, USA, d. 1990. Zardis began playing double bass in 1916, going against the prevailing preference for brass instruments to play bass lines. In the 20s he performed with many of the leading New Orleans jazzmen, including Chris Kelly and Kid Rena. Throughout the 30s he played in his hometown and on Mississippi riverboats, also recording with Kid Howard. In 1942 he took part in recording dates with the rediscovered Bunk Johnson and the following year recorded with George Lewis. In the late 40s and early 50s he played in New Orleans and after a spell away from music returned to the local scene to become a member of the Preservation Hall Jazz Band. He visited Europe with this band in the mid-60s. Zardis spent the 70s in New Orleans but found time for another trip to Europe, this time with the New Orleans Joymakers in 1972. In the following decade he was still playing regularly, visiting Europe again with Kid Thomas Valentine. A firm player with a lovely tone, Zardis maintained a steady yet fluid beat. One of the best of the New Orleans bass players.

Album: with Eugene Wendell *West Indies Blues* (1978). Compilation: with Kid Howard *Dance New Orleans Style* (1937-41).

Zawinul, Joe

b. Josef Erich Zawinul, 7 July 1932, Vienna, Austria. After studying music at the Vienna Conservatory Zawinul's musical ambitions soon outgrew the limited opportunities for a jazz musician in Austria shortly after the war. But financial necessity meant that he spent the 50s almost exclusively involved in local session work. Playing piano in dance and radio orchestras, and working as the house pianist for Polydor Records, he played only briefly with the talented saxophonist Hans Koller in 1952. However his fortunes improved suddenly in 1959, when he won a scholarship to Berklee College Of Music in Boston. Emigrating to the USA, he immediately received a huge amount of attention, and decided to spend the rest of 1959 touring with Maynard Ferguson. Two years with Dinah Washington followed this, and then in 1961 he began a musical collaboration with Cannonball Adderley (*Mercy, Mercy, Mercy* 1966) which was to last nine years. Although he recorded with other musicians during this period - most notably Miles Davis (*In A Silent Way* 1969, *Bitches Brew* 1969), it was his work with Adderley which spread his reputation as an inventive improviser and talented writer. His composition 'Mercy, Mercy, Mercy' won a Grammy Award for the group. At the end of 1970 he joined Wayne Shorter to form the highly influential Weather Report, the band with which he will always be primarily associated. When the group disbanded in 1985, after 15 years of phenomenal success, Zawinul began touring Europe and the USA again as a soloist. More recently forming Weather Update and Zawinul Syndicate, his dark and ominous chord voicings and electric piano sound will remain a distinctive part of fusion for many years to come.

Albums: *Zawinul* (Atlantic 1970), *Dialects* (CBS 1986), *The Beginning* (Fresh Sounds 1990, 1959 recording), *The Immigrants* (CBS 1988), *Black Water* (CBS 1989).

Zeitlin, Denny

b. 10 April 1938, Chicago, USA. Zeitlin had a classical music training before studying medicine at Johns Hopkins University and then Columbia. In 1963 he successfully auditioned for the record producer John Hammond Jnr. but then moved to San Francisco where he studied psychiatry and played the piano. In 1965 he was involved in a trio with bassist Charlie Haden. His interest in the use of the prepared piano (in which the sound of the piano is changed by attaching nuts, bolts and screws to the strings) encouraged him to experiment with sounds available from synthesizers as these became more readily available in the late 60s. Along with his keyboard playing, he has written instrumental scores, including a film score for Philip Kaufman's *Invasion Of The Bodysnatchers* in 1978.

Selected albums: *Sounding* (1978), *Tidal Wave* (Palo Alto 1981), with Charlie Haden *Time Remembers One Time Once*

(ECM 1983), *Homecoming* (1986), with David Friesen *In Concert* (TM Pacific 1992), *In The Moment* (Windham Hill Jazz 1992), *Trio* (Windham Hill Jazz 1992), *Live At the Maybank Recital Hall Vol 27* (Concord 1993).

Zoller, Attila

b. 13 June 1927, Visegard, Hungary. Zoller learnt to play the violin and trumpet as a child and only turned to the guitar when he chose to make a career in music. He played in a variety of bands in Budapest after the war before political unrest at home sent him to Austria and then, in the mid-50s, to Germany. There he played with Hans Koller and accompanied visiting Americans like Oscar Pettiford. In 1959 he won a scholarship to the Lennox School of Jazz and went to the USA. He is a technically skilful guitarist who performs in a restrained style with a keen harmonic sense which sometimes reveals his east European background. He joined Chico Hamilton's Quintet in 1960 and then played with Herbie Mann until 1965. He performed in a group specializing in modal jazz with Dave Friedman before playing with Red Norvo and then Benny Goodman. In 1968 he was a co-leader in a trio with Albert Mangelsdorff and Lee Konitz. In the early 80s he played with Jimmy Raney. In 1971 he had patented a bi-directional pick-up for the guitar and later developed a magnetic pick-up which could be used with a vibraphone.

Albums: with Albert Mangelsdorff, Lee Konitz *Z0 Ko So* (MPS 1967), *The Horizon Beyond* (Act 1967), *Gypsy Cry* (1971), *The K & K In New York* (L+R 1980), *Memories Of Pannonia* (1987), *Common Cause* (1992), *Live Highlights '92* (Bhakti 1992).

Zorn, John

b. 2 September 1953, New York City, New York, USA. Zorn trained in classical composition, initial inspirations being the American composer-inventors Charles Ives, John Cage and Harry Partch. He developed an interest in jazz when he attended a concert given by trumpeter Jacques Coursil, who was teaching him French at the time. His later jazz idols have included Anthony Braxton, Ornette Coleman, Jimmy Giuffre and Roscoe Mitchell. Since 1974 he has been active on New York's Lower East Side, a leading representative of the 'downtown' *avant garde*, applying 'game theory' to structure-free improvisation, a parallel technique to Butch Morris's 'conduction'. Zorn's keen study of bebop and his razor-sharp alto saxophone technique gained him respect from the jazz players: in 1977 he and guitarist Eugene Chadbourne were included in an 11-piece ensemble playing Frank Lowe's compositions (*Lowe & Behold*). A record collector, Zorn was inspired by Derek Bailey's Incus releases, and in 1983 recorded *Yankees* with him and trombonist George Lewis. The same year he wrote some music for Hal Willner's tribute-to-Thelonious Monk album, *That's The Way I Feel Now*. In 1985 he contributed to Willner's Kurt Weill album *Lost In The Stars* and made a commercial breakthrough with *The Big Gundown*, which interpreted Ennio Morricone's themes by deploying all kinds of unlikely musicians (including Big John Patton and Toots Thielemans). *News For Lulu* (1987), with Lewis and Bill Frisell, presented classic hard bop tunes from the 60s with Zorn's customary steely elegance: it was his second bebop venture, following *Voodoo* by the Sonny Clark Memorial Quartet (Zorn, Wayne Horvitz, Ray Drummond, Bobby Previte). Declaring that hardcore rock music had the same intensity as 60s free jazz, he championed Nottingham's Napalm Death and recorded hardcore versions of Ornette Coleman's tunes on the provocative *Spy Vs Spy* (1989). Naked City (Frisell - guitar, Fred Frith - bass, Joey Baron - bass) became his vehicle for skipping between sleaze-jazz, surf rock and hardcore: they made an impressive debut for Elektra/Nonesuch in 1990. In 1991 he formed Pain Killer with bassist/producer Bill Laswell and Mick Harris (the drummer from Napalm Death) and released *Guts Of A Virgin* on Earache, the Nottingham hardcore label. He played at Company Week 1991, proving by his commitment and enthusiasm that (relative) commercial success has not made him turn his back on free improvisation. Zorn's genre transgression seems set to become the commonsense of creative music in the 90s.

Albums: *School* (1978), *Pool* (1980), *Archery* (1981), *The Classic Guide To Strategy Volume One* (1983), *Locus Solus* (1983), with Derek Bailey, George Lewis *Yankees* (1983), with Jim Staley *OTB* (1984), with Michihiro Sato *Ganryu Island* (1985), *The Big Gundown* (Elektra 1985), *The Classic Guide To Strategy Volume Two* (1986), with the Sonny Clark Memorial Quartet *Voodoo* (1986), *Cobra* (Hat Art 1987, rec 1985-86), *News For Lulu* (Hat Art 1987), *Spillane* (Elektra 1988), *Spy Vs Spy: The Music Of Ornette Coleman* (Elektra 1989), with Naked City *Naked City* (1990), with Naked City *Torture Garden* (Earache 1990), with Pain Killer *Guts Of A Virgin* (1991), with Naked City *Heretic - Jeux Des Dames Cruelles* (1992), *More News For Lulu* (Hat Art 1992), *Filmworks 1986-1990* (Elektra 1992), with Naked City *Grand Guignol* (1993).

Zottola, Glenn

b. 28 April 1947, Port Chester, New York, USA. Zottola first played trumpet at the age of three, his early start explained by the fact that his father not only played trumpet but was also a manufacturer of trumpet mouthpieces. (His brother, Bob Zottola, played with the bands of Charlie Barnet, Maynard Ferguson and Billy May). At the age of nine Glenn was playing in public, and within three years was performing regularly on television and had made an appearance at the Atlantic City Jazz Festival. In the early 60s he played a leading role in a documentary film, *Come Back*. In 1967 he joined the Glenn Miller Orchestra, then under the direction of Buddy De Franco. In 1970 Zottola was briefly with Lionel Hampton and then began a fruitful decade which saw him backing a wide range of artists including Bob Hope, Al Martino, Patti Page, Tony Martin, Robert Merrill and Mel Tormé. Towards the end of the 70s Zottola played lead trumpet in the orchestra accompanying the touring version of *Chicago*. In 1979 he joined Tex Beneke and that same year became a member of the Benny Goodman Sextet for a national tour. Zottola began the 80s in fine style, playing, singing and acting in *Swing*, a musical presented at the Kennedy Center in Washington, DC, before playing in the pit

bands of several Broadway shows including *Evita*, *Annie* and *Barnum*, and also for the Stratford, Connecticut, revival of *Anything Goes*, which starred Ginger Rogers. In the early 80s he joined Bob Wilber's Bechet Legacy band, playing on record dates and international tours. Zottola has also recorded with Butch Miles, George Masso, Keith Ingham and Maxine Sullivan. In the mid-80s, in addition to his regular appearances with Wilber, Zottola led his own big band at the Rainbow Room in New York City and then joined forces with Bobby Rosengarden to co-lead a big band at the Hyatt Regency Hotel in Greenwich, Connecticut. He toured overseas, playing jazz festivals in Ireland, Holland and Finland, while his USA festival appearances have included St. Louis, Sacramento and the Kool Jazz Festival in New York. In 1988 he was featured soloist in Wilber's recreation of Benny Goodman's 1938 Carnegie Hall concert. In 1990 Zottola was headlining at the Clearwater Jazz Festival in Florida and late in 1991 toured the UK and Europe with a band led by Peanuts Hucko. Unusually among brass players, Zottola is also an accomplished saxophonist, playing alto with flair. Although rooted in the mainstream of jazz and with a marked kinship for the swing era, his playing shows flashes of a deep awareness of bop and postbop developments in the music. The exceptional talent he displayed as a child has not been dissipated but has been nurtured into an impressive all-round ability.

Albums: *Live At Eddie Condon's* (1980), *Secret Love* (1981), with Bob Wilber *Ode To Bechet* (1982), with George Masso *Pieces Of Eight* (1982), *Butch Miles Salutes Gene Krupa* (1982), *Stardust* (1983), with Maxine Sullivan *The Lady's In Love With You* (1985), *Christmas In Jazztime* (Dreamstreet 1986).

Zurke, Bob

b. 17 January 1912, Detroit, Michigan, USA, d. 17 February 1944. Learning piano as a child, Zurke displayed a remarkable talent and by his teenage years was playing semi-professionally. He worked regularly in and around Philadelphia in the late 20s and 30s, playing in numerous small bands and also as a single. In 1937 he joined the Bob Crosby band, achieving great success that was due in part to his ability to play convincingly sophisticated boogie-woogie during the brief craze for that style. The band's recording of 'Honky Tonk Train Blues', a feature for Zurke, was a hit. He left Crosby in 1939 to form his own band but this proved unsuccessful and he returned to solo work, playing clubs in Detroit, Chicago, Los Angeles and elsewhere. Although noted particularly for his boogie-woogie playing, Zurke had a much wider range and was an important, if erratic, factor in the Crosby band's success.

Compilations: with Bob Crosby *South Rampart Street Parade* (1935-42), with Crosby *Big Noise From Winnetka* (1937-42), *Bob Zurke And His Delta Rhythm Band* (Meritt 1988, 1939-40 recordings).

Zwerin, Mike

b. 18 May 1930, New York, USA. Zwerin was educated at the High School of Music and Art before going to the University of Miami. During one holiday he played trombone on club dates at the Royal Roost with the Miles Davis nonet which later produced *Birth Of The Cool*. Zwerin moved to Paris in the early 50s but returned to New York in 1958 and worked with the big bands of Claude Thornhill, Maynard Ferguson and Bill Russo. Later he played with Eric Dolphy and John Lewis as well as in Orchestra USA (1962-65) and in the sextet drawn from its ranks. He toured the USSR with Earl Hines's band in 1966. During the early 60s Zwerin was president of his father's steel fabrication company and afterwards became the jazz critic for the *Village Voice* (1964-66) and was subsequently appointed its European Editor. Since then he has been music correspondent for the *International Herald Tribune*. He settled in Paris where he promotes jazz concerts for the American Centre, writes books and contributes articles to music magazines.

Albums: radio broadcast with Miles Davis *Pre-Birth Of The Cool* (1948), *Jazz Versions Of The Berlin Theatre Songs Of Kurt Weill* (1964), with Celestial Communication Orchestra *Desert Mirage* (1982), *Not Much Noise* (Spotlite 1983).

Zwingenberger, Axel

b. 7 May 1955, Hamburg, Germany. After studying classical piano for more than a decade, Zwingenberger began playing boogie-woogie in 1973. Although this was more than 30 years after the style had enjoyed its brief period of popular success, Zwingenberger's technical prowess brought him immediate public recognition in Germany. He released a successful album and was invited to tour and record in the USA, appearing with Joe Turner. By the end of the 70s he had established a reputation throughout Europe and was featured at concerts and festivals, sometimes as a single and also with visiting jazz luminaries such as Lionel Hampton. In the 80s he continued his touring and recording, working with Sippie Wallace, Mama Yancey, Joe Newman and others. Although rightly praised for his remarkable technique, Zwingenberger has shown himself to be a sensitive accompanist to the blues singers with whom he has performed: this, allied to his mastery of his instrument, suggests that he has even more to offer the jazz world.

Albums: *Boogie Woogie Breakdown* (Vagabond 1977), with Joe Turner *Let's Boogie All Night Long* (Vagabond 1978), with Turner, Joe Newman *Between Hamburg And Hollywood* (1978-85), *Powerhouse Boogie* (Vagabond 1979), *Boogie Woogie Live* (Vagabond c.1979), *Boogie Woogie Jubilee* (Vagabond 1981), *Axel Zwingenberger And The Friends Of Boogie Woogie Vols 1 & 2* (Vagabond 1982), *Lionel Hampton Introduces Axel Zwingenberger: The Boogie Woogie Album* (Vagabond 1982), *Axel Zwingenberger With Sippie Wallace And The Friends Of Boogie Woogie* (1983), *An Evening With Sippie Wallace* (1984), *Axel Zwingenberger And Sippie Wallace 'Live'* (Vagabond 1986), *Axel Zwingenberger 'Live'* (1986), *Axel Zwingenberger And The Blues Of Mama Yancey* (Vagabond 1988), *Axel Zwingenberger And The Friends Of Boogie Woogie: Vol 6* (Vagabond 1988), *Boogie Woogie Bros* (Vagabond 1989), *Axel Zwingenberger And The Friends Of Boogie Woogie Volume 7 - Champion Jack Dupree Sings Blues Classics* (Vagabond 1991).